This book is for the San Juan Mountains

and

for John Davis and for Julien Puzey who keep asking the real questions.

SACRED LAND SACRED SEX

RAPTURE OF THE DEEP

CONCERNING DEEP ECOLOGY
AND CELEBRATING LIFE

DOLORES LaCHAPELLE

"Man is not the supreme triumph of nature but rather an element in a supreme activity called life."
R. Murray Schafer

Kivakí

#2B108575

Kivakí Press
585 East 31st Street
Durango, CO 81301

Publisher's Cataloging in Publication

LaChapelle, Dolores, 1926-
    Sacred land, sacred sex: rapture of the deep: concerning deep ecology and celebrating life / Dolores LaChapelle.
    p. cm.
    Reprint of work first published in 1987.
    Includes bibliographical references and index.
    ISBN 1-882308-11-5

    1. Nature—Religious aspects. 2. Human ecology—Religious aspects. 3. Spiritual life. I. Title.

    BL435.L33 1992   291.1′78362
                                      QBI92-1837

First Edition
Second Printing, 1992

Printed in the United States of America

    2   3   4   —   96   95   94   93

Permissions and Acknowledgments

In defining Deep Ecology—a new discipline that not only crosses all normal academic boundaries but the artificial boundary between humans and the rest of life as well—it has proved necessary to quote from the work of authorities in many different fields. While I have made an effort to stay within the usual guidelines on word limits for scholarly works, occasionally, in order to clarify a complex matter, I have had to quote at greater length than that normally allotted for scholarly works. Where I have exceeded such limits, I list the permissions below.

I gratefully acknowledge permission to include quotations and/or poems from the following works: "Origins of Agriculture: Discussion and Some Conclusions," by Charles A. Reed. In *Origins of Agriculture*, ed. by Charles A. Reed, Copyright © 1977 Mouton de Gruyter, A Division of Walter DeGruyter and Co. by permission of the publisher; four poems by Saigyo from Saigyo, *Mirror for the Moon*, Copyright © 1977, 1978 by William R. LaFleur. Reprinted by permission of New Directions Publishing Corporation; "The Temporal and Atemporal Dimensions of Reality in Confucian Metaphysics," by Toshihiko Izutsu, *Eranos Jahrbruch* v. 43

(1974). Reprinted by permission of E. J. Brill, Leiden, The Netherlands; the poem, "Escape," by D.H. Lawrence, from *The Complete Poems of D.H. Lawrence*, edited by Vivian de Sola Pinto and F. Warren Roberts. © 1964, 1971 by Angelo Ravagli and C.M. Weekley, Executors of the Estate of Frieda Lawrence Ravagli. All rights reserved. Reprinted by permission of Viking Penguin, Inc.; "Pan in America" and "The Flying Fish," by D.H. Lawrence. From *Phoenix: The Posthumous Papers of D. H Lawrence*, edited by Edward D. McDonald. Copyright © 1936 by Frieda Lawrence, renewed © 1964 by the Estate of Frieda Lawrence Ravagli. All rights reserved. Reprinted by permission of Viking Penguin, Inc. (Lawrence Pollinger, Ltd., English publisher); From *Taoism: The Road to Immortality* by John Blofeld. © 1978. Reprinted by arrangement with Shambhala Publications, Inc., 300 Massachusetts Ave., Boston, MA 02115; *Apalache*, by Paul Metcalf. © 1976. Permission by Turtle Island Foundation; "Now, Farewell and Hail," by P.L. Travers. Parabola 10:2. By permission

(continued on p. 383)

Now Farewell and Hail
P. L. Travers
(the wisest of women)

Beginning

All things were possible in this world of Now. Near and far were alike to it. Huge, spherical and all-containing, it yet was so local and neighborly that it seemed as though I could put out my arms and take it to my breast.

The Lesson of the White Mist (Taoist)
as retold by John Blofeld

If anyone, in those early years, had asked me where I lived, I would not have been able to answer. For me, my homeland was Here and Now—not a place, not a time, a condition rather, or domain, enormous and yet intimate, close to the stars and the grasses. By night you went about cautiously lest the Pleiades catch in your hair; and by day lest you trod on a passing beetle that might well be a prince in disguise.

All was present and immediate, everything whole and complete, not a thing was missing. No road ever went on and on; it returned to its beginnings. The rainbow was not a mere semi-circle—it continued its course underneath the world, the two ends joined at the horizon. And there the pot of gold would be if you had the luck to find it.

The Sleeping Beauty awaited her moment within our crowding forest; the Argonauts sallied forth in their long-oared ships in search of the Golden Fleece, and the waves of the sea, if not seen by the eye, resounded when you put a shell to your ear. Tilly Saville, carrying the daily pail of milk, scattered the farmyard cockerels that forever crowed three times for Peter who somewhere, behind a shed, would be weeping; angels squatted on the roof top, ready to take your soul if you died; if there was an oak tree anywhere Bonnie Prince Charlie would be sitting in it; the Three Grey sisters, from whom Perseus had to steal an eye and a tooth, were in reality my two great-aunts and one of their aged friends; Lord Nelson, behind my bedroom door, nightly scraped the wall with a pencil in spite of the grown-up assurances that the sound was merely the creaking of wood as the house stretched itself luxuriously after the heat of the day; there were serpents, any one of whom slithering by would be coming direct from the Garden of Eden; the sound of a shot would tell us that Nimrod was away hunting on the thither side of our mountain; tigers burned brightly in the nearby bush and God ubiquitously worked among us, forever unespied—playing the organ in church on Sundays, his feet bare on the pedals; unfolding the flower buds at the dead of night; peering through windows, listening at keyholes—how else could He know everything?—giving Halley's comet a push to speed it on its way to the stars; gossiping with the gossiping trees that no matter how hard you listened for it could never be caught in the act. Once He looked at me through the gap in a fence with the face of a golden sunflower, awesome, quizzical, resolute. I put up my hand and picked Him. This deed was reported to my parents who mildly—after all, it was only a flower!—expostulated with me. But when, in extenuation, I expained to them Who it was, they rose up on their high horses. No one, they said, could pick God and if they could, they would not. It was socially, if not ethically, unacceptable and not the kind of thing people did. I held my peace, knowing that this was not the case. Acceptable or not, *somebody* had done it. And, given the chance, would certainly do it again.

In the reign of the Emperor Shen Tsung (1573-1620), a scholar surnamed Fan, who was a native of I Ping, so distinguished himself in the public examinations that he received a succession of high appointments in various parts of the Empire. No matter where he went, his duties brought him into contact with the evils of society—greed, avarice, lust, vanity, cruelty and oppression. Having taken leave of absence in order to spend the period of mourning for his deceased father in his native town, he decided not to return to official life but to retire to the solitude of the mountains and cultivate the Way. In the vicinity of Mount Omei he acquired a small hut where, during inclement weather, he shut himself up with his books and devoted hours a day to meditation. A nearby stream trickling amidst moss-encrusted rocks and clumps of fern provided him with clear, sweet water; for food he had brought a few sacks of rice and one or two jars of oil, to which slender resources he added the bounty of the forest—silver tree fungus, bamboo shoots and all sorts of delicious, nourishing plants. In fine weather, he rose early to enjoy the panorama of floating clouds richly tinged with coral, pink or crimson and edged with gold, then wandered amidst peaks and valleys searching for medicinal herbs and titbits for his table, often sleeping out beneath the stars. Within three years, his heart had become attuned to the more ordinary mysteries of nature; yet the Tao eluded him. 'I see it is there. I behold its transformations, its giving and its taking; but, shadowy and elusive, how it is to be grasped?' Though known to his few neighbours as a skillful healer and accomplished immortal, to himself he was a wanderer who had left the world of dust in vain.

One day he had a visitor who, though dressed coarsely like a peasant, had the sage yet youthful aspect of a true immortal. Broaching a jar of good wine he had left untouched since the day of his arrival, Fan listened to his guest with veneration. Said the visitor: 'I have the honour to be your nearest neighbour, being the genie of the stream running behind your distinguished dwelling. May I venture to inquire how it happens that a scholar of such high attainment as your good self has failed to find the starting-point of the Way, especially as it lies right in front of your nose?' Then, pitying Fan's confusion and wishing to put him at his ease, the genie added:

STORIES

'It is a sign, sir, of your lofty intelligence. There are recluses in plenty who persuade themselves they have found the Way, but who would be hard put to it to substantiate that claim. Look for it not in the radiant clouds of dawn and sunset, nor in the brilliance pouring down from cloudless skies during early autumn. Seek it in the mists that shroud the valleys at which, hitherto, you have scarcely condescended to glance.' With these words, the genie made him a handsome bow and departed.

Thenceforward our scholar spent his mornings seated upon a knoll gazing down at the white mist swirling in the lower valleys. No spiritual illumination followed, but he persevered. Another three years went by. The woodsmen round about, seeing him sit for hours as still as the rock beneath him, blessed heaven's benignity in sending an immortal to dwell among them. Timely weather was attributed to his virtue; untimely weather was presumed to have been at least mitigated thereby; Fan himself knew otherwise. Then came a day when he hastened joyfully to where the stream bubbled out from an underground cavern and called upon the genie, who straightway appeared clad in a summer robe of brocaded gauze worn over garments of fine silk.

'No need to tell me!' boomed the genie in a voice like muted thunder. 'You have found the Way! May I venture to inquire how you did so?'

'Ha-ha-ha!' laughed Fan. 'Why did you not tell me sooner? I did not *find* but suddenly realized that I had never lost the Way. Those crimson dawn clouds, that shining noonday light, the procession of the seasons, the waxing and waning of the moon—these are not majestic functions or auspicious symbols of what lies behind. They *are* the Tao. To be born, to breathe, to eat, to drink, to walk, to sit, to wake, to sleep, to live, to die—to do this *is* to tread the Way. When you know how to take what comes along, not bothering with thoughts of joy and sorrow, wearing a quilted or unlined robe not because it is the fashion but because nature prompts the change, gathering pine seeds or mushrooms not for the taste but because hunger must be stayed, never stirring hand or foot to do more than passing need requires, letting yourself be borne along without a thought of wishing something to be other than it is—*then* you are one with the valley mists, the floating clouds. You have attained the Way, taking birth as an immortal. Wasting years on seeking what was never lost really is a joke.'

The cavern before which they were standing now echoed and re-echoed with their laughter. Then the genie composed his features. The skirts of his brocaded robe and the ribbons of his silk gauze hat streaming in the breeze, he bowed his head to the earth nine times, as to an emperor, crying joyfully: 'At last, at last, I have met my master!'

BATESON'S "DOG IN THE LAB" STORY
a conversation between Gregory Bateson
and Stewart Brand on the theme of
"The Madness of the Laboratory"
as narrated by Stewart Brand

"No experimenter links up, say, the phenomena of schizophrenia with the phenomena of humor... The two of them *are* closely related, and closely related, both of them, to arts and poetry and religion. So you've got a whole spectrum of phenomena the investigation of none of which is very susceptible to the experimental method."

"Because of non-isolatability?" I think I'm ahead of him this time.

"Because the experiment always puts a label on the context in which you are. You can't really experiment with people, not in the lab you can't. It's doubtful you can do it with dogs. You cannot induce a Pavlovian nervous breakdown—what do they call it, 'experimental neurosis'—in an animal out in the field."

"I didn't know that!" I'm gleeful.

More of the Bateson chortle. "You've got to have a lab."

"Why?"

"Because the smell of the lab, the feel of the harness in which the animal stands, and all that, are context markers which say what sort of thing is going on in this situation; that you're supposed to be right or wrong, for example.

What you do to induce these neuroses is, you train the animal to believe that the smell of the lab and similar things is a message which tells him he's got to discriminate between an ellipse and a circle, say. Right. He learns to discriminate. Then you make the discrimination a little more difficult, and he learns again, and you have underlined the message. Then you make the discrimination impossible.

At this point discrimination is not the appropriate form of behavior. Guesswork is. But the animal cannot stop feeling that he ought to discriminate, and then you get the symptomatology coming on. The one whose discrimination broke down was the experimenter, who failed to discriminate between a context for discrimination and a context for gambling."

"So," says I, "it's the *experimenter's* neurosis that..."

"...Has now become the experimental neurosis of the animal."

"In the field what happens?"

"None of this happens. For one thing, the stimuli don't count. Those electric shocks they use are about as powerful as what the animal would get if he pricked his leg on a bramble, pushing through.

Suppose you've got an animal whose job in life is to turn over stones and eat the beetles under them. All right, one stone in ten is going to have a beetle under it. He cannot go into a nervous breakdown because the other nine stones don't have beetles under them. But the lab can make him do that you see."

"Do you think we're all in a lab of our own making, in which we drive each other crazy?"

"You said it, not I, brother," chuckling. "Of course."

> To change ideas about what the land is for, is to change ideas about what anything is for.
>
> Aldo Leopold

That's why this book doesn't fit into any of the usual categories: it's neither psychology nor philosophy, neither history nor anthropology—not even social anthropology. It's most certainly not "eco-feminist," "new age" or "futurist." Yet, it takes all this in and much more. At the end of his last book, *Mind and Nature*, Gregory Bateson said his next book would have to be called *Where Angels Fear to Tread* because he was "making the same question bigger." While working on the manuscript for this work, I was shocked when I discovered that what Bateson was referring to, is what I am trying to do in this work. Obviously, the task is too much for one person, but at least it's a beginning and others can carry on from here.

How did I get into something so difficult and deep? Why me? The answer to the latter question is easy, because I don't have to worry about tenure, or about being fired or about getting popular recognition. I live and work in the mountains that I love; therefore, many of the usual considerations don't even enter into it. But the first question remains, how did I get myself into this? I knew the writing of this book would be perilous, full of technical problems and that I would be trespassing on "entrenched positions of professional prejudice." I didn't fully realize, however, just how scary it would be to "revalue all values"; but that's precisely, what I found myself trying to do as I got into the nature of "sacred land."

In previous books I've tried to keep my personal self out of it as much as possible, but I've found that at the lectures I give at colleges and the workshops I give at Centers throughout the west, that many of the questions have to do with how did I find all this out. To answer those questions I'll have to start with some personal history.

Let me begin with a quote from *Dreamtime: Concerning the Boundary Between Wilderness and Civilization*, one of the books which helped me as I was completing the manuscript for this work:

[K]nowledge represents *results*. These results only have meaning if we are informed of the manner by which they were gained, so that we can comprehend, we can follow the process towards cognition ourselves.

This work is a manual on deep ecology in the fullest sense; therefore I feel that you, the reader, should be given as much information as possible on how my understanding came about so you can discern the path I took in my long search. This might help you in your own search for how to live validly on this earth of ours.

The origins of this book go back over forty years to when I was in the eighth grade. That's when I began trying to find "the answers," because at that time I happened to check out from my Catholic grade school library, a book titled *Sergeant Lamb's America*. In those days no authority figure ever bothered to censor the books given to a grade school library and stuffed away on the dusty shelves. The book was the diary of a British soldier, fighting for England in the American revolutionary war. What I discovered changed my life because, from then on, I never believed anything they told me in school. For example, instead of being the traitor they told us he was, Benedict Arnold was undoubtedly the best leader we had at that time. But he had to flee to Canada to escape his enemies in the American ruling class.

Hence began my search to find out what really caused the mess we are in. Every movement that begins by taking real human nature into consideration is almost immediately co-opted into something anti-human and anti-nature. Why? These thoughts were going through my head just before the Second World War began, but even then I knew something was very, very wrong. It never bothered me personally because I was able to lead a totally split life with no effort. I was a docile, top of the class student as long as they let me read all the books I wanted to during class to keep from being bored; yet I never took anything I heard in school seriously.

I can remember in the fifth grade, when bored I would try to memorize all the 14,000 ft. peaks in the state of Colorado. Yet I had no idea I would ever be allowed to climb—only the wealthy did that long ago in Colorado. So, although very good at the academic game, my real life was always with the mountains. I could see the peaks of the Front Range from the trees I climbed in front of my house in north Denver. While still in high school, I saw a little notice in the Denver Post about a Mountain Club trip with a phone number, I called it and my life was saved and given direction.

Six years ago I gave a workshop at Notre Dame Continuing Education for a Jungian group and then went on up to the University of Wisconsin at Green Bay for a series of lectures that Jack Frisch had arranged for me. I was gone a total of two weeks. As my plane flew into Denver, tears inadvertently came to my eyes when I saw the peaks of the Front Range and suddenly I realized that's the longest in my life I had ever been out of sight of mountains! I've lived, briefly, in Europe and in Japan and in Washington state, but always in mountains or within sight of mountains. The mountains not only saved me from Eurocentric delusions; they taught me things that our dominant culture lost long ago.

Back to my search for answers. In college, I majored in history but found none of them. I graduated Phi Beta Kappa and continued reading avidly in history of all kinds. Took me a long time to find out that history was the beginning of the problem not the answer. During all my research I kept coming up against a major point. Heidegger and many other authorities admitted that the pre-Socratics of Greece were on the right track, but that ended with Plato. No one seemed to have an answer for what happened just at that time to change it all. I knew that no one man, alone, could have been responsible for such a major change.

Out of college I went to Aspen to teach school so I could live in mountains. This was so long ago that I was the first public school teacher who skied. It was a marvelous culture then, before skiing became something for the masses; thus a way to make money. That long ago you could leave your skis on top of the car forever, anywhere in this state and no one took them. They were of no use except to other skiers and no skier would steal skis. After I was married I moved away from Aspen but still lived in mountains.

I continued reading avidly. Then, in 1956 I found volume two of Joseph Needham's *Science and Civilization in China.* In that book, I saw a brief reference to a modern Chinese philosopher, who said:

> While European philosophy tended to find reality in *substance*, Chinese philosophy tended to find it in *relation*.

That was the beginning of my answers. The next important step—the one that solved the Plato problem for me did not come until 1981. That year I was in the Toronto Canada area for a short time and thus had access to a good library for the first time in my life. No university in Colorado has a good library because the legislature doesn't fund libraries—just buildings. Having just read Heidegger's *The Question Concerning Technology* I was very interested in the subject of technology. So, browsing in technology periodicals, I found

Technology and Culture: The International Quarterly of the Society of the History of Technology and an article by Barrington Nevitt: "Pipeline or Grapevine: The Changing Communications Environment," which finally gave me the answer I was searching for. Nevitt labels it the "Greek language problem," which set it up for Plato to "create intellectuals" and thus begin the long "substance" road to disaster, culminating in the present massive environmental destruction. (See chapter one for more on this.)

Since I had been hunting for this answer for so long I immediately wrote Nevitt, sending him a copy of my *Earth Wisdom.* In his reply he enclosed his resume. His career in communications began in 1920 as a Canadian bush pilot, working with radio transmitters and receivers. He went on to be a communications consultant for every major country in the world including Russia. He was connected with Marshall McLuhan because of their joint interest in the pre-Socratics. Nevitt's most recent book, *The Communication Ecology,* 1982 contains still more information on the Plato/Greek language problem.

Meanwhile my WAY OF THE MOUNTAIN CENTER held our first conference: "Heidegger in the Mountains," with George Sessions, Michael Zimmerman and Bill Devall among others. Excited by my new find, I showed it to the group. Michael, with his Heidegger background, recognized the importance and said, "This is dynamite."

I've provided all the personal history, above, just to explain how this book began. At workshops and lectures I'm often asked questions which would take days to answer. As I started working on this manuscript, I tried to answer those questions and it got deeper and deeper as it went along.

Although I can't possibly list all the people here who have contributed to my understanding through the years I've worked on these problems, I do want particularly to thank the students at the various universities who asked the necessary questions. Also I want to thank the numerous people on my mailing list for the Way of the Mountain annual newsletter. Not only have their orders for books and essays helped me remain financially able to do this kind of "independent scholar" research, their letters and comments continually keep me aware of events in this rapidly expanding field of deep ecology.

Last of all, I especially want to thank Flo Krall of the Educational Studies Department at the University of Utah, who, through the years that she has had me speak to her classes, has been a never-ending source of encouragement. Our annual meetings have become a true "feast of knowledge." All the others that I am indebted to for particular learnings, are mentioned during the course of this work.

Dolores LaChapelle,
WAY OF THE MOUNTAIN CENTER
Silverton, in the San Juan Mountains

INTRODUCTION

...Does it serve the people for seven generations?
...Is it for the children yet to come?...
(The basic criterion of native peoples)

The end of this "temporary anomaly," the present Industrial Growth Society, with its pursuit of "substance" (in this case, money) does not mean the end of human life. Rather it means the return to real living—living in responsible "relationship" to all the beings of your place—both human and non-human and this includes a responsible "relationship" to those yet to come.

Twenty years ago, only a few of us clearly saw that the exploitation of the entire earth to feed the ever-growing industrial system could not last once the World Bank, controlled by our "developed" world, began lending money to third world countries for "development"; but actually, to suck them into the system. It's now obvious this money can never be repaid; hence those third world countries pay interest forever and in their efforts to keep up the payments, destroy the rain forests and increase the deserts throughout the world. But is it possible for our children, seven generations from now, to live with no oxygen to breathe and no food to eat?

Today, however, it's becoming obvious to everyone that this industrial growth system cannot continue, but the way out is not more of the same kind of tactics. The only way out of this spiral of destruction is to relearn or sometimes, just to remember those techniques, which made us human in the first place and which successfully governed humankind in its relations with the earth for at least the past 50,000 years. If these techniques hadn't been successful we wouldn't be here! It's that simple.

In the main part of this book I've tried to provide some insight into these "old ways" so that you can begin gradually incorporating them into your life. It's easier to do it now than later, when the entire industrial system collapses.

This introduction consists of two parts: the first concerns deep ecology; the second is a general introduction to this work.

PART A: DEEP ECOLOGY

This entire book is about deep ecology and yet it manages to give only some of the facets of the relationships between nature, deep within us, humans and the rest of nature in the natural world, outside of us. Although the Norwegian philosopher, Arne Naess was the first one who said the words, deep ecology; once he articulated it, response welled up out of the depths of countless people around the world.

What I will attempt to do here is give as briefly as possible an account of the beginnings and early growth in this country of what is called deep ecology. This is difficult for me, because I know most of the people concerned. However, since I am the only one who knows the story of how *both* books in this country titled, *Deep Ecology*, began, I feel I should do it. Furthermore, since I have been trained as an historian, I fully understand how important it is for someone to make this attempt early on in the history of any movement. Needless to say I'm not going to do it in the usual narrowly academic manner; instead I will also include some insight into the relationships involved. My precedent for this is the best piece of modern historical writing I've ever seen: " 'For God's Sake, Margaret': Conversation with Gregory Bateson and Margaret Mead," about the "famous Macy Conferences (1947-53) that invented cybernetics."

I want to begin by saying what deep ecology is not—it is not a philosophy in the narrow Greek sense. Philosophy, meaning, "love of wisdom," has the connotation of wisdom out of the human head alone. It is not a political movement—politics also being a rather late development in the long span of humanity and fairly unworkable from the beginning. The word comes from the Greek, of course—*politika*. The first of the dictionary definitions for it is: "the art or science of government: a science dealing with the regulation and control of men living in society." Another definition: "competition between competing interest groups or individuals for power and leadership, etc." Writing this in 1987, with all the media propaganda about the U.S. Constitution, I want to point out that although our founding fathers borrowed some of the Iroquois structures for the Constitution, they forgot to include the rituals—which, of course, is how real governing worked for most of human history.

If deep ecology is neither philosophy nor politics—what is it? I think you can begin to see why many academics and intellectuals have such a difficult time with it—if it can't be defined within the narrow Eurocentric tradition then it simply doesn't exist. What they fail to realize is that it is not limited by being trapped within the entire Greek, Christian, humanistic tradition. It's a much bigger concept—based on the essential nature of human beings for at least the last 50,000 years; not the distortions humanity has imposed on itself within the last short span of 2000 years.

Since the remainder of this work, after the Introduction, is devoted to the beginnings of an answer to the question of "what is deep ecology?"; here I will concentrate on how it began.

Arne Naess and the beginnings of deep ecology

Naess first differentiated "deep ecology" from the more prevalent "shallow ecology" at the Third World Futures conference in Bucharest in 1972. In that particular context he clearly defined "shallow ecology as a fight against pollution and resource depletion: Central objective: health of the people in developed countries"; while deep ecology was "rejection of man-in-environment image in favor of the relational, total-field image." Among the more important objectives: "Every form of life has the equal right to live and blossom; diversity and symbiosis; and local autonomy and decentralization."

I first met Arne in 1977 in Claremont, California. Paul Shepard and Joe Meeker had written to me after they read my first book, *Earth Festivals*. As a result of that I drove down to California to take part in the organizing meetings, set up to form the New Natural Philosophy program for International College.

I met Naess at Meeker's house, just after Meeker picked him up at the airport. Naess had flown in from Copenhagen, where he had just received the prestigious Sonningen award for his work on Semantics and Spinoza. The Sonningen award is the highest award in Europe for a contribution to culture. Because I knew Arne was a mountain climber, sometime during the ensuing conversation between the three of us, I told him that I didn't find the L.A. area as bad as I thought I would, because in 20 minutes we could be up on Mt. Baldy.

The next morning, after giving a rigorous philosophy lecture to Paul Shepard's class at Pitzer, he rushed into the room and said, "Let's go." I asked, "Where?" He said up to Baldy. Picking up John Rodman, who had long wanted to meet Arne, I drove up there. We started up the trail in mid-afternoon. As long as we didn't talk we could just barely keep up with Arne. When we stopped to look at a lightning blasted tree, Arne took off like a mountain goat up to the ridge. We continued leisurely walking up to a picnic site. I did Tai Chi there while John Rodman worried.

As it got later in the afternoon, he finally spoke aloud of his fears. I told him that Arne was a Himalayan climber and if he died it was because he wanted to; so don't worry. We started back down the trail in order to reach the car before

dark. Arne had seen us turn around from high up on the ridge so he ran down, passing us on the trail—only stopping long enough to say that because he only had shorts on he didn't want to get cold and would run on. He added: "If you aren't at the car, when I get there, I'll run on down the road to keep warm." Of course we got to the car well after he did, so I drove down the road some distance and picked him up. Naess was 64 years old then. The night before he had been to a big banquet in Copenhagen for the award ceremony and then flown over from Europe. That morning he had given his philosophy lecture to Shepard's class. On top of that most people would have had jet lag, by then. Arne just quietly explained to us that he had hoped to see the desert from that high ridge.

Arne and I talked at length about the underlying changes necessary in our culture. Later, he sent me a poorly-translated, English copy of his book, *Ecology, Community and Lifestyle*, published around 1975 in Norwegian and later translated into Swedish. He hoped that I would be able to find a Norwegian to help me and re-translate it, but this never happened. This book, properly translated is now currently in press in England.

I first heard of Arne long before I met him, when I was told of his connection with the wealthy Naess ship building family in Norway and how he had given up that wealth to devote his efforts to saving the environment. As mentioned above, he is a Himalayan mountain climber and a world-famous expert on both Spinoza and Gandhi. He has given lectures in India on Gandhi's work; and furthermore, uses Gandhi type tactics in his non-violent "actions" to save waterfalls and to help the Lapps prevent roads from splitting their reindeer herds.

The entire eco-philosophy movement, which had an influence on Arne's thinking, began in 1969. Sigmund Kvaloy explains, "if you vividly feel that the roof may cave in any moment, it's just not possible to sit still at an institute of philosophy, analysing some Greek concepts...So, in 1969 on the 24th of June, a group of friends met and founded what we later called the Ecopolitical Ring of Cooperative Action— the RING, for short." Their "first action came in 1970...it had been under preparation for one year. Our aim was to stop the hydro-electrocution of the Mardola Water Fall—the third highest in the world." They used tactics from Gandhi along with Arne Naess' famous cliff exploit, which I recount in *Earth Wisdom*. "We came out as different people," Kvaloy states...we lost the waterfall but started a movement." Kvaloy says:

Much of the thinking of the Norwegian Ecophilosophy group has been formed through posing two basically different sorts of social organization against each other. We have called them *Industrial Growth Society* (IGS) and *Life Necessities Society* (LNS), the first one being based on steady or accelerated growth in the production of industrial articles and the use of industrial methods. The second one is based on producing life necessities and always giving priority to that. There is only one historical example of the first kind of society, our own, which is tending to become global. Most other human societies have been of the second kind.

IGS is an abnormal kind of society, which can exist only for a historical second. Judging from various indications spanning 1-2 million years, the LNS is the human kind of society, and it will remain so. (For this entire essay, see **Back of the Book** section.)

From its beginning in 1969 they called it *eco-philosophy*. When I met Arne in California he had begun using the term, *ecosophy*, a combination of the Greek words, oikos and sophia, meaning wisdom of the household—"earth household," as Gary Snyder calls it. Naess was not using the term, deep ecology, much at that time. In his paper, which he gave Meeker to include in the never-published New Natural Philosophy anthology, he wrote: "I thought until recently that the name 'the deep ecological movement' would adequately suggest the most important components of the trend. The term 'deep' is defined in terms of ultimate arguments, causes, motives and goals." He adds: "But we need something that perhaps is still more comprehensive." However Arne quickly realized that the term, *ecosophy*, was too abstract for most people and he recognized that "deep ecology" was, after all, the best way to say it.

The New Natural Philosophy movement was dropped when International College dropped their press. My *Earth Wisdom* and Joe Meeker's *Comedy of Survival*, first published by them, became technically out of print, and I took over distributing both books.

Origins of the deep ecology movement in the United States

INTRODUCTORY OPENING

Three moons shining
Scattered light
Bound together by no human hands.
          Kenneth Maly, Philosophy Dept. Univ. of Wis.-La Crosse

Last April, I gave a talk for the Phenomenology Conference at the University of Wisconsin. While driving back from the university to his home, Ken Maley asked me an important question that could not be answered, except by telling him the complete story of the publication of the two books on Deep Ecology. After telling this whole story for the first time, I told him that I would have to eventually write it up in the introduction to my new book, but I was dreading the task.

The next morning as I came out of my room, I found him busily writing at the kitchen table. When he finished, he handed it to me. It had come to him in this haiku form in the middle of the night. It has helped me, considerably, in writing this difficult introduction, because even though George Sessions, Bill Devall and I know how much nature has taught us, we still find ourselves caught in the narrow, "merely human" trap and begin thinking we've done it and that's when trouble comes. This haiku shows me what I had already recognized—that deep ecology surfaces from the depths of people. (See the newspaper interview, below). So truly, we three only reflect "scattered light" from the depths of both nature and people.

EARLY BEGINNINGS IN CALIFORNIA

With that introduction, I can now plunge into the complete story of the beginnings of deep ecology here in this country. George Sessions had become interested in environmental conservation, first from fishing and backpacking with his father in the Sierra and later, from climbing in Yosemite. Graduate school at the University of Chicago involved analytic philosophy and the philosophy of science.

His first teaching job (1968-69) was at Humboldt State University, in California, where Devall was also beginning

his first year as a sociology teacher. Lynn White's famous paper, "Historical Roots of Our Ecologic Crisis," came out in 1967 in the Sierra Club Bulletin and from reading that, Sessions "immediately instituted a section in [his] introductory philosophy courses on 'Science and Human Values', using White's and Ehrlich's articles." He and Devall, who "was doing research on his doctorate on the Sierra Club," became friends at that time.

Sessions went on to Sierra College in 1969, "thinking seriously about the philosophical foundations of environmental crisis." He began to teach the history of philosophy and "was thinking about the anthropocentricity running through the Greeks and modern philosophy from Descartes as well as Lynn White's paper." Eventually, this "resulted in about a 60 page paper, called 'The Metaphysics of Ecology', which was completed about 1973—never published although most of it later became 'Anthropocentrism and the Environmental Crisis', published by Bill [Devall] in the Humboldt Journal in 1974." Sessions met Joe Meeker in 1973, and through him, wrote to Naess and "a long correspondence ensued." 1977 was the tercentenary of Spinoza's birth and Arne invited Sessions to the Scandinavian Spinoza Symposium. Although he could not get away for the Symposium, he did contribute his paper on Spinoza and Jeffers to the journal, *Inquiry*, at Naess' urging. Sessions notes that his "Panpsychism paper, given at the 'Rights of Non-Human Nature' conference, was a critique of Moral Extensionism. I was a critic of anthropocentrism from 1968 on, so it was easy to move to deep ecology."

The "Rights of Non-Human Nature" conference, sponsored by John Rodman, a political philosopher, "proved to be a major stimulus for the development of ecophilosophy in this country." The conference included Garrett Hardin, William Leiss, John Lilly, Paul Shepard, John Livingston, Roderick Nash, Vine Deloria Jr., Anthony Storr, John Cobb, Charles Hartshorne, Gary Snyder and Joseph Meeker, as well as Sessions.

Sessions first met Naess in the spring of 1978 when Naess was teaching at UC Santa Cruz and called together a group to discuss Spinoza. About 1975 Sessions began teaching a course called "Rationality, Mysticism, and Ecology," which, as he states "was essentially deep ecology." He has taught this course ever since. He met Michael Zimmerman in 1975 at an American Philosophical Association meeting where Zimmerman read his paper on "Heidegger and the End of Philosophy." They have influenced one another's work ever since.

In the mid-seventies Bill Devall read Naess' article "The Shallow and the Deep, Long-Range Ecology Movements" in *Inquiry* and he wrote a short article, mentioning deep ecology for ECONEWS, a newsletter of the Northcoast Environmental Center in 1977. Sessions urged Devall to turn it into a longer, more in-depth piece and helped him work on it as it slowly grew. "By this time we were both getting excited about it," Sessions remarks. The article eventually became "Streams of Environmentalism" and was finished in 1979. About this time the Natural Resources Journal asked Bill to do an article and he sent "Streams...," which they rejected as being too long. Sessions explains, "Bill was very upset." Sessions helped him through the crisis and Bill rewrote it, submitting it as "The Deep Ecology Movement," which was published in 1980.

As a result of all this, Sessions began to work on the Ecophilosophy II issue of his newsletter (1979), which was a 40 page futher elaboration of the shallow/deep positions. On the basis of that newsletter, which had a wide international circulation to about 150 scholars, Donald Hughes invited Sessions to write the bibliograhical essay on deep ecology for the Earthday X Colloquium at the University of Denver. (April 1980) Sessions writes: "At this conference, I met Hughes, LaChapelle and the rest."

WIDER GROWTH OF DEEP ECOLOGY

During the fall before this conference I had received the call for papers from D.U. and had submitted an abstract. Of the 74 abstracts submitted from all around the country, mine was one of the 20 chosen to complete the papers for the conference. While working on this paper, I got a huge bundle from George Sessions containing all the issues of his Ecophilosophy newsletter. This was very helpful for me at the time—to know I had a colleague out there—in the midst of all my research among the mainline, anthropocentric, Christian environmentalists, whose books I had been consulting for this paper. Later, I got a letter from George in which he wrote: "Do you realize that we are the only two radicals" to be chosen to give papers. My immediate thought was, "what is he worried about he's a tenured professor, I'm the one who should worry."

With both Sessions and I giving papers on deep ecology and Bill Devall in attendance as well, the academics from all around the country could no longer ignore this "new idea" and there was a lot of talk about it. Very suddenly, deep ecology became widely known.

Devall had sent Zimmerman my *Earth Wisdom*, while Zimmerman was in England, in charge of Tulane's year abroad for students. Zimmerman wrote, congratulating me on the good job I'd done with Heidegger, which was very useful for me. During the ensuing correspondence, he eventually wrote: "You know things I don't, it would be great if I could have a look at your files." I wrote back suggesting that if he did come to Silverton, I'd invite Sessions and Devall and we'd have a "Heidegger in the Mountains" conference. That was the origin of our first Way of the Mountain conference, here at my center.

Meanwhile, I had discovered that the words, "deep ecology" had an electrifying effect on people outside the academic field. As an example, in February, I was asked to give a workshop to a group in Salt Lake. The woman in charge had arranged for me to be interviewed by both major newspapers. The Salt Lake Tribune woman showed polite interest as she asked me the usual interview questions, but when I mentioned deep ecology, she suddenly sat up with great interest and wanted to know all about it. I found this same intense interest in the words, deep ecology, in many other people.

I began to realize that the words themselves held some deep appeal, having nothing to do with Arne's original thinking on it. After a talk I gave at Evergreen State College in Washington, there was a dinner for some of those who wanted to meet me. After dinner I brought up the subject of the deep effect these words had on people. Some of them had already noticed that same effect. The ensuing talk ranged from the pornographic movie, "Deep Throat" to fraternity initiations, where one must chug-a-lug beer and if you open your throat you are ok; if you fight it, you may well die, and covered other esoteric matters as well. Out of the great range of this conversation, we all came to the conclusion that the words, deep ecology, did hit at some deep unconscious level.

I began my Way of the Mountain annual newsletter in 1982, when Sessions sent me an interview with Arne Naess in *Ten Directions*, from the Zen Center in Los Angeles. The interview came out of a conference on deep ecology, which included Sessions, Devall, Roshi Aitkin and other Buddhist scholars. Gary Snyder was supposed to be there but was snowed in up at his home in the Sierras and couldn't make it. Snyder, for years had been using deep ecological principles in his poetry—long before Naess defined such a movement. In this *Ten Directions* interview, Naess had pinpointed the essential aspect of living deep ecology:

> But in deep ecology we ask whether the present society fulfills basic human needs like love and security and access to nature. We ask which society, which education is beneficial for all life on the planet as a whole, and then we ask further what we need to do in order to make the necessary changes.

Each year since then, I've covered the most important books or essays for making these necessary changes in my annual newsletter.

VOICES OF DEEP ECOLOGY

Bill Devall wrote me, asking for something to put in his projected anthology, "Voices of Deep Ecology." I sent him a paper on ritual, because no one else works in this area. Then, when he sent me a list of the titles of papers he was planning to use and I saw D. H. Lawrence's great piece on the ponderosa pine, "Pan in America" listed, I wrote back explaining that it would be necessary to have an introduction on Lawrence for that piece to have its proper impact. He asked me to do it and I sent it in.

The next word I heard on the book was this. A man in Salt Lake, who had been at my workshop, called me to say that Bill Devall and Dave Foreman of Earth First had agreed that Earth First would sponsor a book on deep ecology. Marc Brown of Dream Garden Press was raising money for publication by putting on a big event including music, Gary Snyder reading his poems etc. He hoped I could give a presentation there. I was already committed elsewhere. Later, when I went over to Salt Lake in February of 1984 to give my annual lecture at the University of Utah, Marc Brown brought over to me a great pile of miscellaneous papers, which he had received from Devall. Since there was little organization to it, he hoped I could help him sort it out. This was what Devall had turned into him. He and I, together, went through it. Marc had no background on deep ecology and Devall had not enough editing to clarify the project. I promised to provide further help, if needed and returned to Colorado.

PUBLICATION OF DEEP ECOLOGY

Meanwhile, Devall had grown impatient with Dream Garden's efforts to sort it out and had gone up to Gibbs Smith in Layton, Utah. Sessions had been trying for several years to get a Sessions/Devall co-authored collection of their papers on deep ecology published by various East Coast publishers, to no avail. Devall apparently, at this time, set aside his "Voices" anthology and proposed the earlier Sessions/Devall collection to Gibbs Smith. The upshot, as George Sessions explains was that, "Smith agreed to do an edited version of our papers in February of 1984, but after this was presented to him in June, he changed his mind, and wanted a totally written book in *two weeks*." Gibbs Smith was now trying to get a book out ahead of the projected Tobias book on Deep Ecology. Devall, who fervently wanted to get a book out on deep ecology, drove immediately to Utah. Because he was still teaching, Sessions couldn't go; furthermore he was begining to have serious doubts about the project. Devall, together with Smith and his editors, rewrote the original articles and essays into an "original" work to meet Smith's demands.

Shortly thereafter Devall had to leave for Australia to attend a conference, which had been planned for some time, and to work with deep ecologists there, such as John Seed, for the next three months. This left the untidy manuscript, complete with "creative" additions and inappropriate language added by the editors, for Sessions to try to "clean up" before the pending publication date.

Reviewers have written such comments as "its organization leaves me competely baffled." Kirkpatrick Sale in his review, wrote, "It is very peculiarly put together." As well it should be, considering the pressure Devall had to work under. Sessions had devoted years to painstaking, scholarly work in his newsletter on the subject of deep ecology. It was unfortunate that the book had been thrown together in this manner and the whole thing resulted in some very hard feelings between Sessions and Devall.

In retrospect Sessions has said: "It's not the kind of book that I would like to see as representing the ideas of deep ecology to the public at large. It is poorly organized, seriously underargued and has a dogmatic tone to it which is not representative of the overall deep ecology movement. Some ideas such as the concept of the 'minority tradition' and certain views on hunting and fishing, were imposed upon the book by the editors. There was far too much editorial interference as a whole. But overall, Arne Naess thinks the book is doing more good than harm, and a sympathetic reader can perhaps overlook the obvious faults and discover the underlying key deep ecological orientation."

Deep Ecology, EDITED BY MICHAEL TOBIAS

With the other book, we have another whole story, far simpler. It begins in the mountains. Michael Tobias is also a mountain climber and I first met him right up here in my own San Juan Mountains on Red Mountain Pass, which is nearly 11,000 ft. high. Here's how it began. Arne Naess had bought many copies of my book, *Earth Wisdom*, and given them to people back in Norway. One of these was Nils Faarlund, connected with the Norwegian Nature Life movement, called *Friluftsliv*, for young people. When they decided to begin classes for young people in this country, Nils and the others came to Red Mountain Pass, because my Way of the Mountain

Center was here in Silverton. They rented an old log house from Chris George, who runs a cross country ski place up there. One of the young women, studying with them in Norway, knew Tobias from when she had him as a professor in an environmental studies course at a university in this country. Because she thought a lot of his work, they had Tobias come from California and me come up from Silverton. We all met together in the old log house way up on the mountain. As long as Tobias was in the cabin he seemed an honest, sincere environmentalist. But once outside, when only the two of us were talking, was a different story.

Michael Tobias is actually a charming young man—some call him charismatic; others, a superb manipulator. As we stood there talking, with the mountains that I deeply love spread out before us, he said: "Now that I've climbed all the mountains I want, I'm going to become rich and famous." This shocked me far more when stated there in the mountains, than it would have, had I been down in the city and I asked him, "How?" He said, "Write books." And that's just about what he's done. Unfortunately, I had mentioned to him, sarcastically, that the only way to do that was to write a pornographic, occult climbing novel. And he did just that in his first book, *Deva*. To find out some background he needed for that book he called me. At the meeting with the Norwegians I mentioned that I had recently met a 130 year old man. He called to find out more about him, because his hero in that book is a very old, but active man, hidden way up in a mountain in the Himalayas. On the phone, during the ensuing conversation, Tobias asked me what I was working on and wondered if I could contribute something to his next book. Since I had been working on a book on D. H. Lawrence, which was never published because International College's Press was dropped, I figured I would use some of what I learned from writing that ms. and told him that I could send him something. This essay titled, *Sacred Land, Sacred Sex*, was published in his *Deep Ecology*.

The original title of Tobias' book was *Humanity and Radical Will*—the title of his own lead essay. Some of us said that the title should be changed because "radical human will" is the cause of the problem, not the solution. His publisher circulated a form letter to all of us, asking what we thought the title should be. Not trusting him for a moment, I suggested a phrase from a Robinson Jeffers poem. Others were not so cautious. Of course, he had heard of Arne Naess when we were talking with the Norwegians up at Red Mountain Pass. He got a short piece from Arne and called the book, *Deep Ecology*. Of course only four out of the twenty one writers in the book, could in any way be considered deep ecologists: Paul Shepard, George Sessions, Arne Naess and I. And Paul Shepard had to threaten to sue them if they reprint the book with the erroneous title they gave to his essay. None of the reviewers have ever read the entire book. My essay was mentioned often, simply because I began it with a Lawrence quote, but the best thing in the entire book has never been mentioned and that's Alan Grapard's "Nature and Culture in Japan."

What I want to make clear here is that very little of the book is about deep ecology; yet, people are still trying to take the book, seriously, as a statement of deep ecology and then wasting their time and that of their readers, trying to demolish deep ecology through this book's treatment of it. Without the accidental naming of Tobias' book, *Deep Ecology*, thus creating a race in publication dates; the whole subject might have been introduced in a much clearer form.

"But," as George Sessions writes "the deep ecology movement, as a wider public phenomenon under that title, was launched." Bill is now doing very worthwhile work for the environment in his position with the Earth First Foundation and George is continuing his work, with a new book in prospect, titled, *The New Ecology: Readings in Deep Ecology, Ecofeminism, Bioregionalism, and Green Politics.*

Before ending this section on the beginnings of deep ecology, I want to add that deep ecology is a flourishing movement in many other parts of the world. In Canada, Alan Drengson's journal, *The Trumpeter*, provides the central communication in the movement. In Australia there are many facets including Warwick Fox's important scholarly work; John Martin's newsletter, *The Deep Ecologist*; and the work of men such as John Seed, in his efforts to save the rain forests. (See **Reference Notes**)

Important aspects of deep ecology

I trust that the long explanation, above, will help clear up some of the confusion about deep ecology resulting from these two books coming out so close together and thus help answer some of the questions I've been asked at workshops and lectures in the past few years.

In a short paper that Arne Naess wrote for the projected New Natural Philosophy anthology, he called "Essentials of a new Philosophy of Nature" (circa 1979), he writes: "Certain kinds of systems-thinking or gestalt-thinking is a necessary tool to understand the holistic character of Nature" and refers to Konrad Lorenz as "a central figure in the attempt to train scientists as gestalt finders." Further on he writes: "What is needed is a 'deep' conception and plan of action going down

to the roots, societal, political, economic of the present impasse." That is the approach I am using in this work.

As a brief summation of the most important aspects of deep ecology, rather than try to shorten Naess and Sessions' careful, rigorous, language (as given in "Basic Principles of Deep Ecology," April 1984, p. 70 in *Deep Ecology*), I am going to quote a piece from the projected book, *Wisdom and the Open Air*, by a young American who has been working with Arne Naess for some time in Norway, David Rothenberg:

THE BASIC POINTS OF THE PLATFORM OF DEEP ECOLOGY

	THE BASIC POINTS OF THE PLATFORM OF DEEP ECOLOGY
LIFE!	I. There is intrinsic value in all life.
NATURE!	II. Diversity, symbiosis, and thus complexity explain the life of nature itself.
MAN IN/AND NATURE!	III. Humanity is a part of nature, but our potential of power means that our responsibility towards the Earth is greater than that of any other species.
NO FALSE DISTANCE!	IV. We feel estranged from the Earth because we have imposed complication upon the complexity of nature.
OUTSIDE CHANGE!	V. On the outside, we should change the basic structures of our society and the policies which guide them.
INSIDE CHANGE!	VI. On the inside, we should seek quality of life rather than higher standard of living, self-realization rather than material wealth.
SPREAD OF IDEAS!	VII. New kinds of communication should be found that encourage greater identification with nature. Only then will we see our part in it again.

CONCLUSION: ACTION! Those who accept the above points have an obligation to try to implement the necessary changes.

In closing, we have to find a way to draw on those same depths, which gave us the words, deep ecology (which the inner depths of people respond to so readily) and that means ritual, which is the reason for my subtitle, "concerning deep ecology and celebrating life."

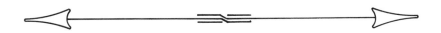

PART B: GENERAL INTRODUCTION

About the title

The title of this work was not just dreamed up out of my head to be outrageous; instead it grew slowly over the years as I worked on this manuscript.

Sacred land, sacred sex. During the last few years there have been a great deal more references to the concept of sacred land. That's quite a change from the previous 2000 years of Christian thought where, at best the land was something to be subdued for the use of humanity and, if the land wasn't subdued, it became "wasteland," the abode of the devil. In

most of the rest of the world however, in the primitive—or what I am calling "traditional"—cultures, religion developed out of their relationship to the land.

The words, "sacred land," first came to me when I was working on the manuscript for a projected book on D.H. Lawrence. I read his novel, *St. Mawr* in 1977, but he wrote it way back in 1925. That long ago, he had his heroine, Lou, say of her place in the American Southwest: "This place is sacred." When I was working on my essay for Tobias' book, *Deep Ecology,* I soon discovered that without the concept of "sacred sex," a human society soon overpopulated its land; hence my title, "Sacred Land, Sacred Sex."

Of course, I've had some negative comments from

people about writing a book with "sacred sex" in the title, with the problem of AIDS so common in the news. When I began this work, two years ago, I was fairly sure that AIDS should really be classified within the new Environmental Illness category. Even less controversial manifestations of Environmental Illness than AIDS, "can be a catastrophic experience. Many sufferers, in fact, end by taking their own lives." Writing about one such case, Dickson says: "The abundance of chemicals and synthetic substances in the environment had taxed her adaptive mechanisms to their limit." Although AIDS can be sexually transmitted, it is essentially a failure of the "immune system." In the last few months new data has appeared, usually in nutrition related magazines. The September issue of the regular nutrition related magazine I get from my local Bible and Health Food Store down in Durango carried an article titled, "Vitamin C: A Clue for AIDS Treatment," referring to the work of Dr. Cathcart and Dr. Rivici. A little booklet put out by the Theosophical Society contained information about a new book, "Healing AIDS Naturally," by Lawrence Badgley M.D. Both these sources mention nutrition to build up the immune system. Another article in "The Mountain Ark Trader," from Arkansas, a source for bulk natural foods, is even more specific. It mentions that "back in 1982, macrobiotic educator Michio Kushi began to see people suffering from AIDS who had been given up on by orthodox medicine." Out of his work, the Dept. of Nutrition at Boston University Hospital began a program. Of the original group, four have survived for more than 3 years and two for more than five years. The normal life expectancy from AIDS is two years after diagnosis. So there is more going on here than is apparent with media hype concerning this matter. Kushi saw AIDS as having to do with processed foods which rob the body of minerals and weaken the immune response. "Add to this a promiscuous lifestyle, in which the immune system is dealing with semen from multiple sex partners and you have a formula for disaster," Kushi points out. **Reference Notes** provides further bibliography for reading on the nutritional aspect of AIDS.

What I want to make explicit here is that AIDS is *another* symptom of the deadly pollution we now have on this earth. There is a possible breakdown of the immune system of every human in trying to cope with the deadly toxins in our water and air. The earth, itself, may also be approaching the breaking point. For example, trees are an essential component of the earth's immune system; yet they are being destroyed all over the globe! Yes, AIDS is deadly, but the environmental destruction we are causing throughout the entire earth may be just as deadly to us and the earth.

Returning to my original discussion, "sacred land, sacred sex" in the title of this work refers to the reciprocal relationship between humans and land as recognized by most humans until recent times. (See chapter fifteen.)

Rapture of the deep. I spent some months trying to figure out a word for "finding ourselves where we've always been until we threw ourselves out." Of course there is no such verb in any European language. I needed this concept in the title because there are so many books coming out these days with titles which refer to "reweaving the sacred web," "healing the

earth," etc.— all implying that we humans can accomplish the necessary work by still more human planning and ideas. But it's not the earth that threw us out; we threw ourselves out and rational, human planning is part of the problem, not part of the solution.

Finally, one of my colleagues in Utah, Julien Puzey came up with the phrase, "rapture of the deep;" which, of course, is the term given in deep sea diving when there is such a high concentration of nitrogen in the body that the diver feels euphoric; but the result can be death.

Rapture of the Deep, however, in my title refers first of all to deep ecology with its connections between nature, deep within us and all of nature, outside of us. It also refers to "reinhabitation of place." If one stays in their own deeply loved place on earth for a long time, everything gets deeper and deeper; until even a single flower or the sunlight through autumn grasses gives one "rapture." The quickest insight into this "rapture" comes from the nature haiku of Japan. The great Japanese Buddhist poet, Saigyō, often uses the words *fukaku irete* ("deeply entered into"). Saigyō immersed himself deeply into the phenomenon of nature and there found "the sacred" and identified with it. I go into his work extensively in chapter thirteen.

In our European heritage, before the Greek language problem and Plato, we can find this concept of the "deep" within the pre-Socratic thinkers. Heraclitus wrote:

> You could not discover the limits of the soul (*psyche*)
> even if you traveled every road so deep is its measure (*logos*).

After Plato, the concept of the soul as the cognitive or rational element came into being, while, as Kahn points out, in the earlier view of the psyche it was "essentially biological, emotional, or non-rational." Going deeply into this "biological soul" of the human being, one contacts all of life.

A similar concept appears in a very ancient Chinese document, the *Huai Nan Tzu:* "The Tao of Heaven operates mysteriously and secretly; it has no fixed shape; it follows no definite rules; it is so great that you can never come to the end of it, it is so deep that you can never fathom it."

The philosopher, Merleau-Ponty provides still another aspect of the word, "deep," when he states: "We mean that carnal being, as a being of depths, of several leaves or several faces, is a prototype of Being of which our body, the sensible sentient, is a very remarkable variant..." In another place he writes: "The world is universal flesh."

The psychologist, Abraham Maslow wrote of "the great frontal attack upon an overconfident and isolated rationalism, verbalism, and scientism that is gathering force...These have been conceived as controllers of the dark, dangerous, and evil human depths. But now as we learn steadily that these depths are not only the wellsprings of neuroses, but also of health, joy, and creativeness, we begin to speak of the healthy unconscious, of healthy regressions, healthy instincts, healthy nonrationality, and healthy intuition."

In the first volume of his work on Nietzsche, Heidegger writes: "Rapture [*rausch*] is feeling, an embodying attunement, an embodied being that is contained in attunement, attunement woven into embodiment." This "rapture" allows deeper relationships with the other beings on this earth.

The best insight I've found concerning what the word, rapture, refers to in my title, comes from Southeast Asia, where there is a type of sacred (yet including all else) poetics called the "sounding of the text." Each poem begins with "an invocation, which sets forth the poet's understanding of the relationship between himself, his text, and the world." Zoetmulder, an expert on old Javanese explains, "The god concerned is always the god who is present in everything that can be described as *langö,* the god of beauty in its widest sense. He is found in the beauty of the mountains and sea, in the pleasure-garden with its charms of trees and flowers and in the month when they are in full bloom…in the description of nature, in the feeling that beauty arouses in the heart of the lover and of the poet." He continues, "Alangö means both 'enraptured' and 'enrapturing.' It can be said of a beautiful view as well as of the person affected by its beauty. It has what we might call a 'subjective' and an 'objective' aspect, for there is a common element…which makes them connatural and fit to become one…" Lansing, commenting on the above, writes about the "way langö knits the essence of man and nature together, harmonizing the 'Small' and 'Great Worlds'. " He continues, "Sounding the text dispels the illusions of ordinary consciousness and brings to light the underlying structures that bind man and nature, past and present, inner and outer." Such is the nature of "enraptured" and "enrapturing" in old Javanese poetics.

From all the above and more, which I go further into during the course of this work, I can say here that "rapture of the deep" is life—lived to its fullest. This is what triggers all the hormones and brain chemicals, which current scientific research is continually discovering and remarking, in effect, "now that we clever humans have found this out, we can program ourselves better than nature does." But we got all these hormones and brain chemicals from hundreds of thousands of years of living in intimate relationship with all of nature, not from "merely human," scientific research.

This same kind of narrow, rational research and planning mentality leads to certain "deadly delusions," or traps, which the European mentality keeps falling into. These not only prevent us from living fully but also lead to destruction of the earth itself; yet, we continue to think we can solve the present environmental problems by simply more of these same tactics. Throughout this work I'll be going into why these "delusions" are harmful not only to human life but to all life. Below, I've arbitrarily placed them into seven main categories.

THE SEVEN DEADLY DELUSIONS

1) Ideas and ideal—dating back to Plato.

2) The false dichotomy of spirit vs nature.

3) Eurocentrism—that Europeans discovered everything first and know how to run the world better than any other culture.

4) Noosphere—that humans create the mind/wisdom of the earth.

5) Anthropocentrism—that man is the most significant entity in the universe; therefore the entire earth is for human "use."

6) Perfectionism.

7) Tragic heroism.

The structure of this book

BEFORE THE MAIN TEXT

The **Beginning Stories** present the core of this work.

In each chapter, you will find first, an opening series of quotations to provide some insight into the range of what will be covered within. This is followed by a **Personal Introduction**, connecting particular events in my life, outside in nature, with the contents of the chapter. Next comes **Preview**—a quick oversight into what will be covered in that particular chapter—followed by the main text of the chapter.

You will occasionally find certain facts or particular stories repeated in this work in order to show how various aspects of a particularly complex discussion fit together.

MAIN TEXT

> But in deep ecology we ask whether the present society fulfills basic human needs like love and security and access to nature. We ask which society, which education is beneficial for all life on the planet as a whole, and then we ask further what we need to do in order to make the necessary changes.
>
> Arne Naess

The main text is divided into three parts, more or less along the lines of this quotation.

Part I—Uprooting

Each of the three chapters in Part I investigates the progressive "uprooting" from the earth, which took place in our European heritage. I want to clarify the fact that when I attack the European mentality throughout this book, I am not attacking the original, tribal groups within what later became Europe. Each of these had their own local, valid culture based on the needs of their own land. But they were subjected to wave after wave of so-called superior civilizations: Greek, Roman, and Christian, each progressively killing off more of their local gods thus separating them still further from their local earth.

Chapter two explains the real origins of agriculture throughout the world versus the narrow, "human centered" approach in Europe. The quickest insight into the importance of this differentation comes from Lathrap where he states:

> All I wish to do is overturn most of the current thinking about agricultural origins…and about the kind of patterned human behavior involved in the very beginning of agriculture.

Essentially, it was the gourd that taught most humans about agriculture. The gourd is introduced in chapter two and it provides the main unifying symbol throughout the remainder of the book.

Part I ends with chapter three, concerning capitalism, which at the present time means essentially, the multi-national corporations operating worldwide and destroying the earth in each local place for the private profit of a few individuals. I want to take the space here to point out that the "corporation" is not something ordained by a god in the sky, instead it was created by humans, very recently in time. To quote Ralph Borsodi:

> Many of the ills that bedevil mankind and the planet today, you know, stem from a statute passed by the New York State Legislature in 1811. That law, for the first time, authorized the formation of corporations for *private* profit. Up until then you could only organize a corporation for public, or quasi-public, purposes: The construction of a toll road or a bridge or something of that nature.
>
> In 1811, however, the New York statute granted corporations the status of artificial persons…with special privileges denied to natural people. And that was the start of the tremendous corporate exploitation from which we now suffer.

To make the problem even clearer I want to quote Gregory Bateson, where he explains: "In biological fact these entities are precisely *not* persons and are not even aggregates of whole persons. They are aggregates of *parts* of persons. When Mr. Smith enters the board room of his company…[he] is expected to act as a pure, uncorrected consciousness—a dehumanized creature."

Part II—Our Roots in the "Old Ways"

It is important to keep in mind how recently we humans arrived on the scene. It's often been pointed out that if we consider the entire history of the earth as taking place within 24 hours, starting with midnight on Sunday; then organic life began only at 5 PM, Monday afternoon; mammals come on the scene at 11:30 PM that night; and we, humans developed out of the mammals only a few seconds before midnight.

We, "recently arrived" humans, still have all of this heritage from our evolutionary past deep within us. As John Livingston says: "I will be here, in myriad forms, for as long as there are forms of life on Earth. I have always been here, and with a certain effort of will, I can sometimes remember." These are the "old ways" in us.

In Part II I go into these "old ways" in detail, beginning with what we learned from the animals. Then I go into the "archetypes," which are "the psychological aspects of the biological facts, the patterns of behavior by which we live and are lived."

This is followed by what we learned from primitive cultures. For instance, primitives discovered all "our major drug plants" and all the plants used for food. "[I]n the five thousand years of recorded history man has not added a single major crop to his list of domesticates."

The following chapter is on Taoism, because essentially, Taoism is the result of intellectuals, just like us, who, when the Warring States period began in China, were wise enough to go out into nature herself to learn. Due to the geography of China there were still fully-functioning primitive societies up in the mountains between the "civilized" river valleys, thus allowing these Taoists to learn how "original" human cultures worked. Furthermore, due to early writing in China, all these matters were written down; thus we have direct access to their findings.

The last chapter in Part II is concerned with how we actually see; not how our culture programs us to see.

Part III—Following the "Root-traces": The Return

> Heaven and earth and the natural seasons 'move' according to a prescribed order, and according to this 'movement,' new phenomena or…'root-traces' are born.
>
> Anshō Togawa

This statement is the heart of the Shugendō, (Mountain Buddhism), spring "opening of the peak" Festival. Two of their most powerful men remain in the mountain all winter to learn from the earth itself what was needed so that their own, human culture could continue to flourish within all of nature.

Part III, these "root traces" deep within us, show us the way to continue to learn how to live, using the same methods that made us human in the first place. This method is through rituals and festivals. Anthropologist, Roy Rappaport tells us that ritual can give access to information that can be secured in no other way.

"Without festival all the arts are homeless." In most traditional human cultures the festival combined all the factors that we now go to specialists for: social services, physiotherapy, psychotherapy, religion, doctors, entertainment etc. etc. This was accomplished all at the same time, by all the people, together with their land, during the great Festivals. Celebration of these festivals links us to the true source of all our knowledge, the "old ways."

In Part III I do not presume to tell you how to do it, I merely explain how to set up structures so that nature herself, in your own place, can once again begin to teach you. In this kind of learning, there is no knowledge, in the usual sense, to process and convey; there is instead a deepening of attention to the pattern of all life around you so that you begin to live your life according to that pattern.

AFTER THE MAIN TEXT

After the main text there is an appendix, **Skillful Strategies,** which gives practical steps in beginning to live nature's patterns in your life.

The **Back of the Book** section has the complete text of some of the more important essays that I quote from in the book.

Resources has a list of names and addresses for going deeper into matters covered in the book. This is followed by detailed **Reference Notes** for every point covered in the main text. In **Definitions,** I list words or terms, which might be unfamiliar to the general reader. For the most important words, I provide the definitions of people from various fields.

Academic Introduction

This section is addressed to anyone using this text for college classes or other academic purposes. Although this work is primarily for the general reader, the **Reference Notes** provide all necessary background for scholarly use of the text.

First of all I want to make it very clear that this book does not fall into the "substance" trap, so common in Western history since Plato. It is quite definitely not "objective." For further explanation here, I will tell the story about the well-known psychologist, Alfred Adler. When he began a talk, Adler would spit into a glass and then set it down on the table. From time to time he might spit into it again. At the end of the talk, he would pick up the glass and drink its contents, which aroused considerable disgust among his audience. He then explained, "One cannot re-incorporate the objective, it becomes objectionable."

This work contains no isolated "substances," separated off from everything else, as in the European view of reality; instead the entire book is an attempt to show many levels of relationship, as in the Chinese view of reality. This, of course, makes it difficult to separate out the various levels for academic purposes, but I trust the **Reference Notes** will help.

Another problem, which requires extensive referencing, is that in this book I've crossed all the academic boundaries as well as a few, never even considered by a university. I draw on and try to integrate approaches from the disciplines of archeology, ethnology, folklore, history, philosophy etc. and, as Jack Goody puts it so well, "I know too that I have trespassed on the well-cultivated gardens of other scholars, classicists, orientalists, psychologists, linguists, and others, without having the comprehensive understanding of their subjects which they would expect of one another." I have to cross these boundaries, so carefully set up in our Western culture, to provide a way to consider all of life, not just human life in our decisions.

In my underlying philosophic approach, I am indebted to the work of Heidegger, Merleau-Ponty, and the philosophers connected with recent Continental Philosophy, especially Deleuze. While, in general, these names seldom appear in the main text, I give credit, when useful, in the **Reference Notes**. In addition, a great deal of underlying background is derived from ancient Taoist concepts in China.

What I've tried to do in the **Reference Notes** is to give you quick access to any point you may wish to check in the main text, as well as access to the source of all quotations. In many cases I do not give the author within the main text; chiefly because I do not want to confuse the average reader, who may not care who said it.

PART I
UPROOTING

"The last three thousand years of mankind have been an excursion into ideals, bodilessness, and tragedy and now the excursion is over... We have to go back, a long way, before the idealist conceptions began, before Plato, before the tragic idea of life arose, to get onto our feet again. For the gospel of salvation through the Ideals and escape from the body coincided with the tragic conception of human life. Salvation and tragedy are the same thing, and they are now both beside the point."

D.H. Lawrence

"[T]here were (at least) two ways to advance from primitive participative thought, one (the way taken by the Greeks) to refine the concepts of causation in such a manner as to lead to the Democritean account of natural phenomena [eventually, becoming the 'substance' approach]; the other, to systemize the universe of things and events into a pattern or structure, by which all the mutual influences of its parts were conditioned. On one world-view, if a particle of matter occupied a particular point in space-time, it was because another particle had pushed it there; on the other, it was because it was taking up its place in a field of force alongside other particles similarly responsive."

Joseph Needham

Concerning Chinese characters—"But this concrete <u>verb</u> quality, both in nature and in the Chinese signs, becomes far more striking and poetic when we pass from such simple, original pictures to compounds. In this process of compounding, two things added together do not produce a third thing but suggest some fundamental relation between them. For example, the ideograph 'messmate' is a man and a fire...

In the second definition [as in the West] of the sentence, as 'uniting a subject and a predicate,' the grammarian falls back on pure subjectivity. <u>We</u> do it all; it is a little private juggling between our right and left hands. The subject is that about which <u>I</u> am going to talk; the predicate is that which <u>I</u> am going to say about it. The sentence according to this definition is not an attribute of nature but an accident of man as a conversational animal."

Ernest Fenollosa

"The greatest recent event—that 'God is dead' that the belief in the Christian god has become unbelievable—is already beginning to cast its first shadows over Europe."

Friedrich Nietzsche

CHAPTER ONE

"[In the West] the idea of substance is absolutely necessary in thought, in the same way as the subject is absolutely necessary in language. This is the reason why in the history of Western philosophy, no matter how different the arguments may be, pro or con, about the idea of substance, it is the idea of substance which itself constitutes the central problem."
Chang Tung-Sun

Concerning Chinese poetry—"Here is poetry, clear, concise, etched sharply on the clear minds of the people and written in characters that more than any alphabet conspire to make the word read the same as the thing seen, the emotion experienced, the thought made luminous."
Robert Payne

"[Francis Bacon] speaks of his concern with Greek philosophy as a pollution. What did he mean by this? What did he mean when he said about Plato and Aristotle that no denunciation could be adequate for their monstrous guilt?...What, then, precisely, was the nature of the sin which had rendered Aristotelianism and so much else of Greek philosophy fruitless for good? It was the sin of <u>intellectual pride</u>, manifested in the presumptuous endeavour <u>to conjure the knowledge of the nature of things out of one's own head, instead of seeking it patiently in the Book of Nature."</u>
    B. Farrington, discussing Bacon's (1561-1626) "extreme hostility to all the Greeks except Democritus and some of the other pre-Socratics." Bacon is generally acknowledged as the forerunner of modern European science.

Heidegger explains: "[T]he terms 'God' and 'Christian god' in Nietzsche's thinking are used to designate the suprasensory world in general. God is the name for the realm of Ideas and ideals. This realm of the suprasensory has been considered since Plato...to be the true and genuinely real world. In contrast to it the sensory world is only the world down here...The pronouncement 'God is dead' means: The suprasensory world is without effective power. It bestows no life. Metaphysics, i.e., for Nietzsche Western philosophy understood as Platonism, is at an end."

The Greek Language Problem and Plato

Preview

Contrary to generally accepted opinions, it was neither Christianity nor the development of agriculture alone which created the split between humans and the rest of nature in our European tradition. Other peoples on earth have managed to survive monotheism or agriculture and yet retained their place within the whole of nature. The crucial event, unique in Europe, which led to this split has been labelled "the Greek language problem." It's not reading and writing as such that caused the difficulty but the particular events surrounding the development of the Greek *written* language. Because all other European languages developed out of the Greek, this "problem" left us speechless, literally, when it came to recognizing the unity between nature and ourselves.

The second half of this chapter is concerned with Plato, who by using certain structures built into the Greek written language, succeeded in formulating the philosophy which further alienated humanity from nature.

Contrasting the Greek with other Written Languages

First of all, Greek was the only written language in the history of the world which did not develop directly out of the spoken language. On the surface, this may not seem that important but let me quote from world communications expert, Barrington Nevitt:

> The very process of reading and writing Greek...transformed the tribal dream into the private psyche of ego-trips unlimited; it had divorced thinking from doing; it had...replaced myth replaying universal human experience, with history recounting particular events about individual people; and it had substituted abstract Nature for chaotic existence as the basis, not only for science and philosophy, but for all thought and action that constitute Western civilization.

Because it did not develop out of their spoken language, in the Greek written language neither the individual letter nor the syllable had any meaning in itself. This seems so normal to us that we cannot conceive of any other possibility; but in other written languages such is not the case. For instance, each of the letters, J or H or V means nothing to us. But the meaning of *each* of these letters to the ancient Jews was so powerful that to put them all together into the word, JHVH (Jehovah) was blasphemous. The complete word was too powerful for human beings to utter. Near Eastern written languages developed directly out of the spoken language so that the meaning remained present to them in the sound of each letter—in other words, orally.

In China, the meaning is visual. It lies in the individual ideographs of the Chinese written word. Their written script grew directly out of the drawings of actual physical things in the environment, which had been scratched on the ancient oracle bones. Thus, even today, the written character for each word has some strokes which have to do with the human being, some with nature, and quite often some with the gods. For example, if we analyze the Chinese character which means "abundant, rich, fertile, prosperity, plenty" we find that the origin goes back to the pictograph of a sacrificial vessel with a bunch of green plants in it. In this one written character we have some of the lines showing the sacrificial vessel, other lines showing the vessel made by humans, which was to serve the gods and still other lines showing the bounty

of nature contained within it. Thus the underlying meaning of prosperity must include all three aspects—nature, man and gods—of their world. There is no possibility of the "arrogance of humanism" here. Everything connects with everything else in the Chinese organic philosophy of life.

The poet, Ezra Pound, explains that Ernest Fenollosa "got to the root of the matter, to the root of the difference between what is valid in Chinese thinking and invalid or misleading in a great deal of European thinking and language." Fenollosa pointed out that if you ask an educated European to define something, the definition begins with the familiar things which both of you know and then moves away toward increasing levels of abstraction. To paraphrase Fenollosa's example, if you ask what "red" is, he will say it is a "color." If you then ask what a "color" is, he will explain that it is a division of the "spectrum" or a vibration of the "ether" and so on, until his explanation finally becomes so abstract that neither you nor he knows what you are talking about. On the contrary, if you ask an educated Chinese to define red, he will put together a character with abbreviated pictorial forms of the rose, the cherry, iron rust, and the flamingo. The Chinese manifest the meaning of red by simultaneous juxtaposition of examples that both you and he can understand. He makes the meaning clear by putting the necessary information together in a relationship within the written character itself. As Barrington Nevitt remarks: "Any language written in this way simply has to stay poetic, just as every word is a pun that reverberates across the entire culture." Thus in the Chinese language, the human cannot get himself out of the total picture—nature and human are always interconnected.

In the West we keep moving to levels of greater abstraction because we try to get at the ultimate substance of what "red" is. Actually "red" is not a substance at all—it is a relationship between the human eye and brain, certain wavelengths of light refracting from an object, other surrounding colors, the distance of the "red" object, and, sometimes, the movements of the human being. This example clearly indicates the difference between the Chinese view of ultimate reality as "relationship" and the Western view of ultimate reality as "substance."

The Beginnings of the Greek Written Language

Now with some understanding of the difference between "meaning in each syllable or individual line" as in Near Eastern and the Chinese language and the "meaninglessness" of syllables in Greek written language, it is possible to return to the account of how the Greek written language got that way. Phoenician traders, travelling throughout the Mediterranean, used a Semitic script to keep track of how many boxes of figs they delivered to a Greek port or how many barrels of olive oil they loaded on from that port. Greeks began using the same script to keep their records and, gradually, for other matters. Thus the North Semitic alphabet of some 22 letters was gradually spread among the Greeks. When the Greeks began using this Semitic alphabet, they took over the Semitic names of the letters. "These names in the original Semitic were names of common objects like 'house' and 'camel' and so on." But, for the Greeks who did not speak that language, they had no meaning at all.

By 403 BC the Ionic alphabet was officially adopted at Athens and later it was adopted by other Greek city states. This alphabet became the common Greek alphabet of 24 letters, spread not only by traders but by the far-reaching influence of the Delphic oracle.

Comparison with the Hopi Language

In order to make this matter of the Greek written language still plainer, I need to refer to one more language—the Hopi spoken language. It belongs to the Shoshonean branch of the Uto-Aztecan language stock; ours belongs to the Indo-European stock. The grammar of our own language determines not only the way we build sentences but also the way we view nature. We cut up and organize events because that's the way our language forces us to do it, "not because nature itself is segmented in exactly that way." Whorf points out that English terms such as "hill" and "swamp," "persuade us to regard some elusive aspect of nature's endless variety as a distinct *thing*, almost like a table or a chair." In our language, each of these things can exist in its own right—as a noun. Further, our sentences must have a subject, that which does the action, the verb (what is done) and the object (that which it is done to). Whorf explains, "We are constantly reading into nature fictional acting—entities, simply because our verbs must have substantives in front of them. We have to say, "It flashed," setting up something that does the flashing. So we say, "it" or "lightning" performs what we call an action—"to flash." The Hopi language reports the flash with a simple verb, *ri pi*—"flash" (occurred). There is no "it" that does the action. One could say that it's a relationship between the build up of electrical charges in the clouds—the result of which—reaches our eyes and later, our ears. In describing this entire relationship, we say: "It's lightning." But, of course, there is no single "it" doing the lightning. Whorf further points out that the Hopi verb forms establish a general contrast between two types of experience: the "particle" and

the "field of vibrations." Whorf writes that modern physics deals with similar situations but that the Hopi "language is better equipped to deal with it than our latest scientific terminology." The reason being that the Hopi *live* in that world because of their language; while, European science—until recently—was part of the separated-out-world of Newtonian space, time and matter. Newton, of course, developed these concepts, using our European language.

In all European languages, locked as they are into the Greek grammar, we have a subject, (that which does the action), the verb (what is done), and the object (that which it is done to). Since, for the newly literate Greek, there was no longer any implicit meaning in each letter or syllable of the sentence, he, himself, the writer or reader, *gave* the meaning. For example, as Havelock explains: "In phonetic reading, these counterparts are elements of sound <u>usually meaningless in themselves, though the brain of him</u> who is visually scanning athe script..." etc. (My underlining for emphasis.) Thus we see how the writer or reader must of necessity *give* the meaning. From this it is only a short step to the illusion that man gives meaning to the rest of the world. Without the knower, (the reader or writer), the rest of the world has no meaning.

Plato

Plato, living "in the midst of this first Western Communication revolution," as Barrington Nevitt puts it, "became its prophet and champion." Plato's work, the *Republic*, opens and closes with an attack on the bards and poetry. Plato had to destroy the bards. They were the ones who painlessly taught all that was needed for living in Greek society. They were the teachers, scholars and jurists of the culture. Only much later did they become mere entertainers.

The original Greek spoken language could not "frame words to express the conviction that 'I' am one thing and all the rest of the world is another; that 'I' can stand apart from the rest of the world and examine it." All this began to change by the time the 4th century was under way due to the growing influence of writing on the Greek language; thus setting the stage for Plato's "philosophy." In the *Republic*, Plato wrote, "poetry ... we then dismissed from our republic ... for *reason* obliged us." Plato characterized the effect of poetry as "a crippling of the mind." It's like a disease for which one has to acquire an antidote. The antidote consists of a knowledge of "what things really are."

But, due to the changes in the Greek language, since writing came in, this knowledge could only henceforth come from the human brain (actually, only the rational part of the neo-cortex). Plato and others of the Academy invented Nature with a capital N by abstracting it from the chaos of total existence. They labelled it *physis* and converted it into a cosmos of visual order. Since that day Western scientists have continued to study this abstract Nature instead of trying to deal with the "buzzing confusion" of all of nature. For Plato, reality is rational, scientific and logical or it is nothing. In Book Four of the *Republic*, the person becomes symbolized as the power to think, to calculate, to cogitate, and to know, in total distinction from the capacity to see, to hear, and to feel. This is the person as subject. "Pure subjectivity" completely ignores the "existence of the things and events that go to constitute an objective world standing opposed to the subject." But this is not the way the world works. Actually, "we must ... recognize that the subject at every instant of its existence is encountered by an ... order of things which is not at the free disposal of the subject, which opposes the subject as something independent of it and which, more positively, acts upon the subject, arouses it, and stimulates it to action in the concrete field of human existence, both social and individual."

This new Platonic "philosophy" is not for "the masses" as Plato clearly pointed out when he said, "the majority can never be intellectuals." "This 'object' which the newly self-conscious 'subject' has to think about has been literally 'torn out' of the epic context [and must be] in isolation from any contamination with anything else." Explaining further, Havelock Ellis states that this is a "mental act which quite literally corresponds to the Latin term 'abstraction'."

A person looking at the written signs could review, rearrange and take a second look at it, "torn out" from its natural context. Hence intellectuals were created. This was the goal of early Platonism—the autonomous thinking subject—working on the wholly abstract "object." This is what Platonic ideas are all about. Plato felt that they should not be real in any way or else the people were in danger of falling back into the bardic world where everything was connected to everything else. These "ideas" had to be in the mind alone—of the new "intellectual." Because we are still caught in the trap of "ideas" and "ideals" it is necessary here to go further into the matter of Platonic "ideas."

Plato used a Greek term *eidos*, generally translated as shape or form. *Eidos* might have referred to that "outline" as used in archaic art where only the outline of the object is shown. When translated as "form" this connection is retained but when translated as "idea," the usual connection is lost. Quoting Havelock here: "If he [Plato] therefore sought to populate the universe and the mind of man with a whole family of Forms which had emerged from God knows where, this was in a sense a necessity for him ... They announced the arrival of a completely new level of discourse which as it became perfected was to create a new kind of experience in the world—the reflective, the scientific, the technological, the theological, the analytic ... The new mental era required its own banner to march under and found it in Platonic Forms." Havelock, being a scholar thinks all this is great, of course. But the scientific, the technological, the analytic *require* that the "object" of research be "torn out" of context in living nature, or the data won't be replicable. Here you can see the beginnings of the split between the human and the natural world.

Conclusion

Gregory Bateson points out the deeper implications of this matter of the object being "torn out" of context in living nature, first, in his remark: "If Lake Erie is driven insane, its insanity is incorporated in the larger system of your thought and experience" and secondly, in his story about the laboratory experiment on dogs. Bateson says: "You cannot induce a Pavlovian nervous breakdown...in an animal out in the field." He continues, "You've got to have a lab ... Because the smell of the lab, the feel of the harness... and all that, are context markers, which say what sort of thing is going on in this situation; that you're supposed to be right or wrong, for example." In the field, this can't happen. If an animal, "whose job in life is to turn over stones and eat the beetles under them," only finds a beetle under one stone in ten, he's not going to go into a nervous breakdown. "But the lab can make him do that, you see." Stewart Brand asks, "Do you think we're all in a lab of our own making, in which we drive each other crazy?" Bateson answers "You said it, not I, brother." Then chuckling, he continues, "Of course."

But only a few, such as Bateson, see this problem clearly. Too many are still pursuing "ideas" and "ideals," blissfully unaware that, that in itself is part of the problem. Beginning with Plato, *physis*, [nature]—"that which was beyond all order and which was holding everything in order—itself became merely matter exposed to the ordering principle, ideas; it became that which can be ordered." So, in the realm of nature itself, humans decided they could organize nature according to what the rational neo-cortex thought it should be. Furthermore, the human psyche itself became "identified as the cognitive or rational element in human beings." But this false understanding "was a new one, and only after Plato did it come to dominate the earlier view of the psyche as essentially biological, emotional, or non-rational." Thus you can see how we became estranged from both our true nature inside and all of nature outside.

As mentioned in the Preview to this chapter, agriculture and Christianity are two other facets in the European split from nature. The next chapter deals with agriculture while Christianity comes under Part III. My approach to agriculture will have two different aspects: first, from the point of view of the true origin of agriculture, which has just recently been recognized thanks to the efforts of Sol Tax in giving us access to academic papers done by Third World men not just Euro-centric scholars. The second aspect concerns how the plants themselves, especially the gourd [not mere human "ideas"] taught us how to feed ourselves without undue damage to the earth.

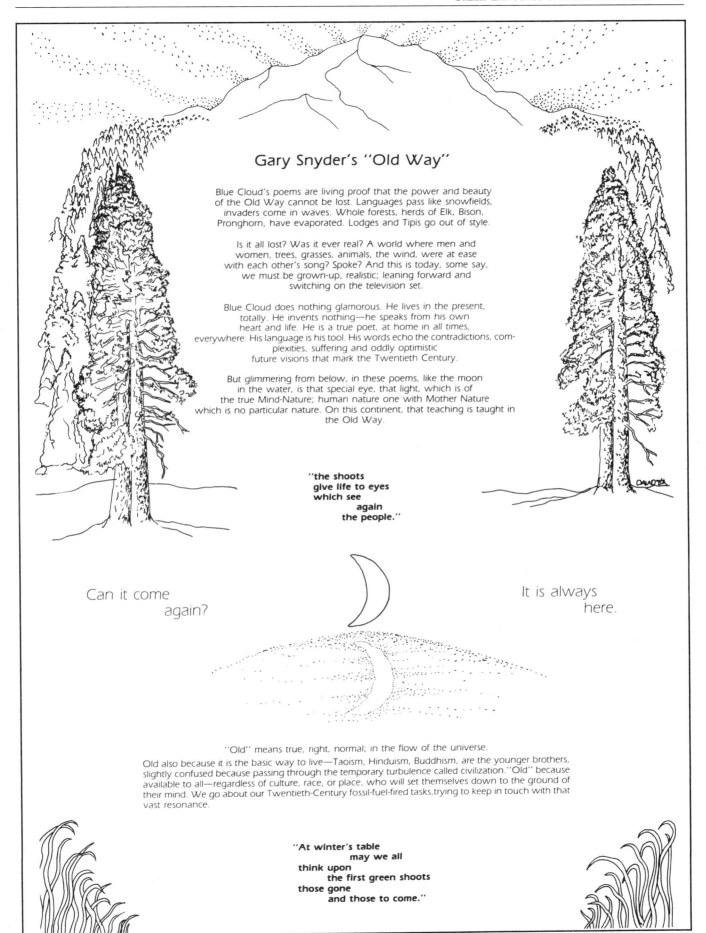

Gary Snyder's "Old Way"

Blue Cloud's poems are living proof that the power and beauty
of the Old Way cannot be lost. Languages pass like snowfields,
invaders come in waves. Whole forests, herds of Elk, Bison,
Pronghorn, have evaporated. Lodges and Tipis go out of style.

Is it all lost? Was it ever real? A world where men and
women, trees, grasses, animals, the wind, were at ease
with each other's song? Spoke? And this is today, some say,
we must be grown-up, realistic; leaning forward and
switching on the television set.

Blue Cloud does nothing glamorous. He lives in the present,
totally. He invents nothing—he speaks from his own
heart and life. He is a true poet, at home in all times,
everywhere. His language is his tool. His words echo the contradictions, complexities, suffering and oddly optimistic
future visions that mark the Twentieth Century.

But glimmering from below, in these poems, like the moon
in the water, is that special eye, that light, which is of
the true Mind-Nature; human nature one with Mother Nature
which is no particular nature. On this continent, that teaching is taught in
the Old Way.

"the shoots
give life to eyes
which see
again
the people."

Can it come
again?

It is always
here.

"Old" means true, right, normal; in the flow of the universe.
Old also because it is the basic way to live—Taoism, Hinduism, Buddhism, are the younger brothers,
slightly confused because passing through the temporary turbulence called civilization. "Old" because
available to all—regardless of culture, race, or place, who will set themselves down to the ground of
their mind. We go about our Twentieth-Century fossil-fuel-fired tasks, trying to keep in touch with that
vast resonance.

"At winter's table
may we all
think upon
the first green shoots
those gone
and those to come."

"Agriculture is not easier than hunting and gathering and does not provide a higher quality, more palatable, or more secure food base. Agriculture has in fact only one advantage over hunting and gathering: that of providing more calories per unit of land per unit of time and thus of supporting denser populations: it will thus be practiced only when necessitated by population pressure."

Mark Nathan Cohen

"A number of authors (notably Sauer, 1952) have suggested that cultivation techniques may have been applied first to plants whose value was magical, medicinal, or utilitarian rather than primarily dietary... agricultural techniques were known and used long before they were brought to bear on the food supply."

Mark Nathan Cohen

"Soil and slope are in genetic relationship. Neither is static. Both naturally are changing very slowly. In the majority of cases the slope gradually grows less and the soil on it weathers more deeply because it forms a bit more rapidly than it is removed at the surface...Soils develop slowly by weathering. The mechanically comminuted rock flour of our glacial lands has acquired approximately optimum characteristics in the course of about 25,000 years. This does not involve weathering that starts from solid rock but from the crushed materials of the glacial mill."

Carl Sauer

 **AGRICULTURE**

Preview

In the previous chapter I showed how the "Greek language problem" began the process of uprooting Europeans from nature. It "substituted abstract Nature for chaotic existence" as Barrington Nevitt observes. In the next step, Plato carried the process further by "creating" intellectuals.

In this chapter I will show how the European approach to agriculture continued this process of uprooting humans from nature. But first, I will give some insight into how agriculture developed in "the rest of the world"—including the pre-European peoples in the territory, which later came to be called Europe. To show just how far-reaching these new insights are, I want to quote Donald W. Lathrap:

> All I wish to do is overturn most of the current thinking about agricultural origins...and about the kind of patterned human behavior involved in the very beginnings of agriculture.

Early Humans and the Gourd

When our ancestors climbed down out of the trees and began walking on their hind legs, it, supposedly, freed the hands for further development; resulting, eventually, in tool using and increasing sophistication of brain power. But have you ever tried to carry four or five different objects in your hands? Very frustrating, isn't it? One or the other of the objects is continually slipping through your fingers, dropping on the ground and, as you lean over to get it, something else slips away.

Fortunately, as these early ancestors of ours were foraging along, possibly on the way to get water at the river, they stumbled onto the gourd—probably an old one—broken open. Here was the answer! Put all those different objects in this "shallow safe container" and proceed along your way. Here was something that could not only hold all the nuts; but also something to dip into the water and hold it so it could be carried back to the young, in hiding back in the bush. Hence began the use of the gourd. Humans and gourds developed together.

It wasn't long before it was noticed that unbroken gourds floated along on the water without sinking, perhaps entangled in riverside vines, carrying them along with whatever happened to be trapped in the mass—small animals or fish. Using this natural example, someone tied vines onto a gourd and threw it into the water to catch a whole bunch of fish; instead of one or two at a time. Thus the net began. In beating the vines with a rock and soaking them in the water at a streamside pool in order to rot away the softer parts to free the essential, strong vine for more efficient lines; they noticed that the fish were stunned so that they could merely pick them out of the water. Thus began the use of fish poisons—the easiest way of all to fish. Carl Sauer points out that some primitive fiber plants are still in use to this day as fish poisons in various parts of the world.

But back to the gourd. It turns out that the gourd was used by almost every early culture as: cups, bowls, water bottles, plates, dippers and spoons. (Here is what was used for millenia before plastic came on the scene—with its destruction of life and the ozone layer.) Gourds were used in medicine and surgery, as floats and rafts, pipes and snuffboxes, cricket cages and bird houses, masks, games, charms, offerings, penis sheaths, and carved decorations of all kinds. The first musical instruments were gourds. These included rattles (also used for religious purposes), as resonators for the African "thumb piano," marimbas in South America, gourd whistles, and trumpets. They are used as resonators in string instruments such as zithers, lyres, the vina, tambura and sitar in India.

The gourd was cultivated as early as 40,000 years ago in Africa, 9000 years ago in Thailand, and 13,000 years ago in the Sierra Madre at Tamaulipas in South America. It figures in religious myths of so many cultures throughout Southeast Asia, the Pacific Islands and other parts of the world that Girardot states:

> The gourd, besides magically yielding grain, appears in many ways. Mankind emerges from a gourd; men escape from the deluge by drifting in a gourd; the gourd's vine serves as a sky-rope ascending to heaven...The gourd lived in human consciousness as the 'mother' of both natural and cultural life.

Lathrap goes even further when he explains: "We may conclude that metaphorically the gourd is a womb, that it is the whole universe, or, stated more simply, the universal womb."

Considering all the data from South America, Melanesia and Africa, Lathrap says:

> The bottle gourd as a cultivated plant furnished the womb in which all more elaborate agricultural systems, developed. Stated more precisely: the artificial propagation of the bottle gourd (and the related cotton and fish poisons) imposed particular disciplines on man and in the context of these behavioral patterns all the other nutritionally significant agricultural systems arose.

The single species, *Lagenaria siceraria* (the bottle gourd) is distributed across the Americas, Africa, Asia and the Nesias (Indo, mela-Micro- and Poly-). Furthermore, the gourd did this world tavelling on its own. It's origin is in Africa but it crossed the Atlantic to the bulge of Brazil long before humans existed on this earth. It can float in sea water for at least a year and still have viable seeds. A single plant can set seeds because there are male and female flowers on the same plant. This, of course, futher enhances its survival. Considering all the above aspects, it becomes obvious that it was the gourd and not the much vaunted human intelligence, alone, that taught us how to grow plants.

At first, humans picked the gourds off the plant wherever one was found, carried the gourds to their settlement and broke them open to clean out the inside, throwing the refuse on their "dump heap." But it wasn't long before there, as if by magic, were new gourd plants. They no longer needed to go off hunting for the plant. The gourd plant came to them. No wonder most cultures have myths concerning the god or goddess dividing up his or her own body to give food for the people. This sudden appearance of the needed plant on the "dump heap" is what Edgar Anderson calls the "dump heap" theory of agriculture.

Edgar Anderson

Right here I must stop to explain a bit about Edgar Anderson. Back in the complacent early fifties, when only a few of us were asking such deep questions, Anderson's and Carl Sauer's books came as lifesaving glimpses of the bigger realities. They opened up level upon level of insight; but trying to follow up on their work was impossible, then. Few were even thinking of these problems, much less groping toward solutions as these two men were. The real push for this kind of thinking did not come until the insights from the drug culture of the sixties had begun to percolate through our culture; thus, beginning to free us from the Platonic trap of merely human "ideas" and allowing us once again to learn directly from the relationships which we find in nature.

Anderson's main book, *Plants, Man and Life*, was republished by University of California Press in 1967. In the preface for that edition, Anderson tells of his battles with the first publisher in the early fifties—they wanted an "interesting digest" of botany. "I presented them instead with a detailed exposition of what even the authorities did not know." Fortunately, the firm went through a "violent crisis having nothing to do with me personally. Far graver problems took nearly all my sponsor's attention." And the real book managed to come out: "a set of related detective stories" is the way Anderson puts it.

Now that we've gone through the mind-opening era of the sixties and the sobering insights of the seventies, into such things as permaculture and sustainable agriculture, his findings don't seem quite as wild and startling. But it is important to remember that Anderson's and Saur's research into the way "primitives" grow their food underlies most of what we are beginning to put to work, now, as far as growing food in a sustainable way is concerned; furthermore, since the underlying principles are still being misunderstood it is necessary, here, to go more deeply into Anderson's work.

Way back in the 1940s when he first started writing *Plants, Man and Life*, he remarked that when he first went to live in Mexico, doing research work, he thought that his Mexican neighbors had "nothing but dump heaps and a few trees in the yards behind their homes." He began to realize, living there, that more was going on than he thought; so that, a year later, when he was supposed to be studying a corn field in Guatemala, "I played hooky and spent an afternoon looking at the gardens." Then he went back home and pondered over what he had learned for a few more years. On his next visit to Guatemala he photographed, plotted and studied one such garden, located on a little height of land between Antigua and Guatemala City. This garden, again, looked like nothing but a pile of useless, overgrown, deserted plants. (Nothing at all like the neat, orderly, human-controlled agriculture which Europeans had been painfully developing for so long.) But Anderson discovered that there was no plant that was not useful to the owner, no noxious weeds, returns per hour of work were very high, and he, personally, learned more about growing vegetables than from anywhere he had ever been. Anderson pointed out that we don't have the right word for such a place. "It's not an orchard, not a pasture...If we don't have the right word to use in writing or talking or thinking, might it not be best to turn our attention first to what people are actually doing with the plants immediately about them?"

Through his studies on this Guatemalan garden, he found that it was a vegetable garden, an orchard, a medicinal garden, a dump heap, a compost heap, and a beeyard—all at once and in all parts of it. It was at the top of a steep hill but there was no erosion because the ground was covered most of the year in one way or another; humidity was kept up almost automatically during the dry season; vegetable pests and diseases could not spread rapidly as similar plants were separated and waste from the house and mature plants was being buried in between the rows when their usefulness was over.

This doesn't sound quite as radical now as it did back in the 1940s when the "victory gardens" were models of linear thinking—straight lines of vegetables with spotlessly clean rows of dirt between them and all "weeds" vigorously rooted out immediately. But, now decades after Anderson's pioneering work in the field, we find that "dump heap" agriculture is characteristic of wide areas of the New World, Asia, and Africa. In fact, long ago "dump heap" agriculture was practiced practically everywhere except Europe and European dominated areas of the New World.

Let's look deeper into the "magical" gift of just the very plants, which the early humans needed. As Anderson explains, it's very difficult for a different type of plant to find a place in a stabilized ecosystem— say a mountain top or a meadow. Everything there is in its own niche in a complex inter-related system. There's no room for something "different." But patches of more or less eroded soil and dump heaps is another matter. These two areas always appear wherever humans are or wherever they move. For centuries these dump heaps bred new plants so that when man first took to growing plants purposefully they were already there for him. Actually, such dump heap gardens pre-date humans, "non-human primates regularly accumulate gardens of their favored product grown from seeds or vegetable parts dropped in the course of eating or in feces."

My Mother, the Gourd

With this necessary background concerning "dump heap" agriculture, we can now return to the gourd, itself, in the New World. The gourd could not really compete with tropical forest as it needs some sun. Furthermore, it needs to be protected from the mass of low dense vegetation which would immediately invade a cleared area which was left for some time. For both these reasons, early humans would keep the important gourd near their houses and occasionally clear the vegetation away so it would grow better. According to Lathrap, the patterns which humans developed in their relationship to the gourd, "were inherently expandable to include other potential and actual cultigens and that in their working out through time these patterns had a built in push toward further cultural elaboration." Such patterns would be easiest to keep up near the house and this became what Lathrap calls a "house garden." Such a garden "would have contained at least the bottle gourd, cotton...and leguminous fish poisons of the genera *Lonchocarpus* and *Tephrosia* ...such patterns must have been extant on the coast of Brazil near the mouth of the Amazon 16,000 B.P. [before present]" Lathrap's description continues:

In the controlled environment around the house, too much sun may have been as undesirable as too little. Certain trees would intentionally have been left or replanted within the modified zone around the house. *Ceiba* is the classic tree to give a light to moderate shade in the areas utilized by man, and it is, typically, left as the rest of the jungle is cleared. Its role as a sacred tree in Africa, as the 'world tree' of the Maya, and as a sacred tree throughout South America probably stems from this function. Certain other trees would be left or transplanted because they provided industrial materials such as thatch, high quality hardwood, and most particularly because they supplied edible fruit available at various times during the year. There should have been little lapse of time, on a scale calibrated to millenia rather than decades, between the instigation of practices necessary to maintain some plants crucial to efficient fishing and the achievement of that remarkable artifact, the house garden.

The gardens of today, which Lathrap studied, may have as many as 50 to 100 discrete botanical entities. He points out that, in addition to food items: "A wide range of grasses and herbs is grown as a source of perfumes. Medicinal plants and plants used to increase specific skills and sensory acuities will run to twenty or thirty items in most gardens."

House garden plants, such as the bottle gourd and seed crops in general are gifts of the "Great Cayman of the Sky"; while root crops, cultivated by cuttings such as manioc, grown in the *chacra* (or communal) field are gifts of the "Great Cayman of the Water." This same "Great Cayman" is the most important god of the Chavin culture high up in the Andes. How does a tropical crocodile god become chief god of the high altitude people living in the mountains? Although I can't go into the whole fascinating story here, I will summarize the parts concerned with the origin of agriculture.

My Father the Cayman

Let's start back at the mouth of the Amazon River with our early human group and their house gardens. When a group gets too big for the sacred ceremonies to hold them together, part of them move off and start another settlement. Let's say we have the normal human group of about 50 people living in the fishing/house garden village about 16,000 years ago. When the group grew to about 80 or so, one part would move off up the river (or along the coast) carrying along the plants for the new house garden, and start their own settlement. Such a splitting off process "would proceed rapidly across the Amazon basin bringing groups with their progressively more elaborate and more productive house gardens to the eastern foot of the Andes within a millenium or so." (The date—about 13,000 years ago) Progressive colonization would be moving up the other major river valleys as well. Gorman has explained in detail the condition at the end of the Pleistocene when there was a general rise in sea level of several hundred feet causing a tremendous reduction of alluvial lowlands in Southeast Asia. The entire huge Sunda Shelf was buried under water thus vastly increasing the population on the remaining land there. This same rise in sea level also affected the South American river valleys. As Lathrap puts it the people were literally "flushed upstream by the rising ocean" and growing concentrations of people appeared on the upper Amazon and its tributaries, reaching the eastern slope of the Andes by about 13,000 BP.

This on-going process put the Giant Crocodile god up in the high Andes. On the famous Tello Obelisk, this deity is celebrated as the giver of manioc and the bottle gourd, both originally crops of the tropical Amazonian area. In fact, the

Giant Crocodile has a gourd coming out of his mouth. Maize (corn) is not even shown. This Sky Cayman (crocodile) of the Chavin religion is the same deity as Itzamn, of the Maya and the same type of god as in Olmec art. The design on a vessel found in the earliest "Formative" culture of the Valley of Oaxaca (Mexico) is the head of the Great Cayman of the Sky adorned with his crest of the harpy eagle. Quetzalcoatl, the famous "plumed serpent" is a further ramification of this Great Cayman of the Sky. In summarizing, Lathrap is of the opinion that "this complex and stratified art mirrors just such a society"; thus there must have been an advance culture in northern South America by the third millenium B.C.

Some New Insights Into Agriculture

As the discussion above indicates, for primitive societies both in Asia and in South America there was no sharp dividing line between gathering and planting. The two activities went right along together, becoming increasingly sophisticated as the humans learned from their plants what was needed. Contrary to the generally accepted opinion concerning the so-called "Neolithic agricultural revolution"—that the brilliant human mind suddenly figured out how to grow food; actually, it was the gourd, which began the process. From that beginning the plants and humans together over a long period of time developed what was later termed agriculture. Lathrap states the case even more clearly:

> We tend to think that by this time man has fully domesticated the cultigen; but, as usual, it is later than we think. What has really happened by this time, is that the cultigen has fully domesticated man. The tyranny of the overbred cultigen over its human protector cannot be too much stressed, and is nowhere more obvious than in central Illinois today, where the farmer is in bondage to the insatiable appetite and immense vulnerability of his monstrous hybrid corn.

Just in the last few years, it has been recognized that "agriculture provides neither better diet, nor greater dietary reliability, nor greater ease, but conversely appears to provide a poorer diet, less reliably, with greater labor costs [and, of course much more destruction of the land], why does anyone become a farmer?" The answer, of course, is overpopulation. Only a decade ago this was considered totally heretical. Even today you won't find this mentioned in most general textbooks at the high school or college level. Of course, neither will you find mention of the other matters I discuss above. The turning point, where this wholly different way of looking at agriculture began, was the major conference on The Origins of Agriculture, which in turn, was "occasioned by an unusual congress which brought together scholars from every continent." No longer was it merely Eurocentric concepts; but "the input of scholars from areas which have until recently been no more than subject matter for anthropology [which, of course, is a product of the European tradition]." For the first time, "perspectives of very different cultural, social, and historical traditions" were recognized at a top level.

This ground-breaking congress was the IXth International Congress of Anthropological and Ethnological Sciences and the man, mainly responsible for it is Sol Tax.

Sol Tax

I must take a moment to tell about Sol Tax. Outside of Gregory Bateson (and most of you have at least heard his name), Sol Tax turns out to be the man who has done the most to expand our horizons out of the narrow Eurocentric approach and begin to see what it is to be a human being within nature. Yet, unless you are a perceptive anthropologist you probably never even heard his name. I had not heard it until my research for this book. But once I realized his importance as the instigator of this Congress, his name kept turning up again and again in my research. To begin with, it turns out that the major breakthrough on the importance of the primitive—the famous Man the Hunter Conference in 1966—occurred because of him. The book, *Man the Hunter* (ed. by Lee and DeVore), has influenced my work for decades as well as the work of Paul Shepard, Gary Snyder and many others; but I never read the Preface until just now. It begins: "In November, 1965, Sol Tax asked us to organize a symposium on current research among the hunting and gathering peoples of the world." This, incidentally was the conference which made it well-known that the Kalahari (and others) work only a few days a week and have enormous leisure time.

Then, I found out that Sol Tax was instrumental in getting the American Indian Chicago Conference going in 1961. "For the first time Indian people of many different tribes from all over the country and representing many different points of view came together..." From the meetings with one another at this conference, came all the current cross-tribal Indian groups in the country.

Next, in my search to find out more about him, I read a book put together by some of his outstanding students: "Essays in Honor of Sol Tax." In that book I found that these students, using his methods of "action anthropology" had uncovered the real reason that the Forest Service was started as well as the Bureau of Land Management (originally, called the Grazing Service). It has little to do with preserving the land; but a lot to do with being sure the cattle ranchers had uncontested rights to graze cattle. The Forest Service came first, to insure their rights in California and the BLM, which came later, to insure their rights in other states. So historically speaking, it's not strange at all that neither agency is protecting the land to the extent that many of us feel is necessary at this time.

In short, I found that Sol Tax is the unsung hero who set up the preliminary structures which will eventually further the development of "reinhabitation of place," show us the way out of Eurocentrism, and into devolution. For further information on him, see Reference Notes.

To bring this praise of Sol Tax back to the subject of this chapter, he wrote the "General Editor's Preface" to the book, *Origins of Agriculture*, published in the Netherlands, which contains the papers from the conference mentioned above. In his Preface he is very clear about the extent of the breakthroughs occasioned by the conference, when he writes about the "changes...in store for anthropology as scholars from the developing countries join in studying the species of which we are all a part." He further states that many who attended the Congress "were convinced that anthropology would not be the same in the future."

Development of Agriculture in the Near East and Europe

Until recently, it was generally held that agriculture originated in the Near East. It did begin there—for us Europeans—but, as we have seen above, not for the rest of the world. Here again, though, we find that it was not human ingenuity, alone (as we have been taught to believe) but a complex process of inter-related events. "After thousands and even tens of thousands of years of hunting and gathering, with slowly differentiating cultural patterns amidst relatively stable Pleistocene environments, a great change occurred in nature—the end of the ice age—and this set in motion a series of events that triggered a cultural change in the one area in which organisms were most easily adapted to human manipulation—the Near East." Herbert Wright continues, in his "Environmental Change and the Origin of Agriculture in the Old and New Worlds," by telling us that the entire Northern Mediterranean region had a cool, dry *Artemisia** steppe climate from at least 35,000 years ago to about 11,000 years ago. Pollen studies in Iran, Syria, Greece, Italy and Spain all show this trend. The prevailing plant was sagebrush (*Artemisia*) throughout this entire region. About 11,000 years ago, with the end of the Pleistocene the sagebrush steppes withdrew to southern Asia. Wright reports that, "The wild cereal grains, which are adapted to a dry summer climate immigrated at this time to the hill-lands and plateaus northeast of the Mediterranean, setting the stage for their domestication."

The wild plants involved with the beginnings of agriculture in this region were einkorn wheat, emmer wheat and barley. Moving up into these hilly areas allowed them to mix with other grasses that were common there during the Pleistocene. The environmental stress caused by this dramatic change at the end of the Pleistocene would have encouraged hybridization and thus set the stage for domestication. To avoid the competition from shrubs and trees, these wild cereal plants would have to grow in poor, thin soil among rocks or in gravelly areas. Hawkes calls them "opportunists"; because they needed to germinate and grow quickly when the rains came in the spring.

They had to complete a full growing cycle and mature their seeds before the ground dried out in the summer. Through the summer, the seeds lay dormant until the following spring rain. In order to survive the long, hot summer the seeds would have to be large to provide enough food reserves to resist the drying out and yet grow quickly when the rains came again. Just such large seeds were what primitive humans preferred to gather; because they were both easier to gather and contained more food value.

Furthermore these wild cereal seeds needed open soil to push down their roots and begin growing. The bare ground of the dump heaps, surrounding human habitation provided an excellent place for them. Accidentally dropped seeds covered the dump heaps with large headed grains. Hawkes continues,

---

Artemisia is sage. See Part III for more on the link between humans and sage from the very beginnings of human life on earth.

"To primitive man it must have seemed little short of miraculous to find the plants needed for food sprang up by his very huts and paths. Perhaps it is not too far-fetched to suggest that this situation might have been the basis for so many folk-legends which attributed the beginnings of agriculture and the introduction of useful plants to gods or supernatural beings." Here we have another reference to "gifts of the gods" as already mentioned above by Lathrap.

Actually, of course, it was the relationship of both human and non-human events which resulted in what we now call agriculture, or, as Wright explains: "The propitious combination of climatic, geologic, geomorphic, vegetational, and human factors at that point in time may have made the whole thing work." Even more credit to the non-human factor is given by the plant specialist, Vavilov, who stresses that "the primitive ancestral forms of cultivated plants possessed tendencies which induced man to cultivate them, that man took what was offered to him and that for many plants the process of their introduction into cultivation took place almost independently of his will." Incredibly enough, this can still happen in today's world in spite of all human efforts to "control" and the story is well worth telling.

Triticale and the "promiscuous, venturesome, stray wheat pollen"

After decades of human effort—with multinational research and millions of dollars invsted—in the push to develop high protein triticale (a cross between rye and wheat), the biggest stumbling block was still problems related to infertility and shriveled seed. In their work on these problems, the scientists kept the plots rigidly segregated and totally controlled, or course. But how these problems were eventually solved is such an amazing story that it's worth quoting Norman E. Borlaug, head of the Mexican triticale project, who, in 1970 received a Nobel peace prize for his outstanding research on high-yielding wheat varieties:

> I must tell you that the largest and most important step toward making the breakthrough in triticale improvement was executed by capricious mother nature herself, one early dawn March morning in 1967 in Ciudad Obregon, Sonora, while scientific man was still in bed. One promiscuous, venturesome, stray wheat pollen grain with a potent and valuable 'genetic load' from the nearby wheat breeding plots floated across the road under cover of darkness and fertilized a sad but permissive tall, sterile, degenerate, triticale plant.
>
> A year later (two generations), scientific man identified several unusually promising plants in a segregating population. The genetic makeup of those plants clearly indicated the value of the illicit stray wheat pollen grain. Its triticale progeny indicated that in the act of fertilization it had dwarfed, introduced partial photoperiodic insensitivity and completely overcome the sterility barrier, which had inhibited progress in triticale improvement for decades. This seems to be nature's way of telling scientists not to become too arrogant.

Borlaug's remarks, praising "mother nature" were printed in the prestigious, *Scientific American*. But then, the article turned right around in the conclusion and stated: "After years of research it now seems certain that triticale will become the first man-made cereal grain to compete successfully with the traditional cereals." How about that for "the arrogance of humanism," still claiming that we humans did it when one of the main researchers had just explained that "nature" herself overcame the main problem?

Conclusion

Returning to our unfolding story of the beginnings of agriculture in the Near East, it turns out that since rainfall is so erratic there, the early dry-farming was very unstable with some lean years and some years where there was so much surplus they could store it. But storage of large amounts of food would increase the tendency toward sedentary living because they would not want to leave it unguarded. Early, primitive kinds of irrigation came in fairly soon and further modified this pattern; it also "aggravated environmental destruction to the point where the return to a wild resource economy would have been nearly impossible. It also set the stage for dramatic population increases in the lowlands and 'ranked' or stratified societies in which a hereditary elite controlled the small percentage of the landscape on which the bulk of the food was produced." Thus early empires, such as the Sumerian and Hittite, eventually developed in these areas.

In the final few pages of the concluding chapter of *Origins of Agriculture*, Reed sums up the most important points, covered in the one thousand page book. Here, I will list only those few points directly concerned with the on-going discussion of my book. (I am using Reed's numbering system here).

> 3. The important cultivated food plants, both cereal grasses and root crops, were part of the earth's environment and were being used as food by many animals, including hominids, for millions of years before they were taken in hand and cultivated...
> 7. Several recent studies of hunters/gatherers have shown that such people expend less energy per individual per unit of time at successful food-getting than do most agriculturists...[this] WAS a successful type of life for millions of years. [Bushmen in the Kalahari get 2100 calories a day with less than three day's worth of foraging per week...Presumably hunter-gatherers in lusher environments in prehistoric time did even better.—information from *Man the Hunter*, ed. by Lee and DeVore]
> 11. Where local resources were and are adequate, settled villages can develop, and have done so, without agriculture. Three such examples are the Natufian culture of the eastern Mediterranean, the coastal peoples of northern Peru, and the peoples of the northwest coast of North America. Of these, the Natufians evolved an agriculture, the coastal Peruvians finally adopted agriculture about which they had known but which they had been avoiding for 1000 years or longer (Cohen, this volume), and the people of the northwest coast retained their traditional life (until it was destroyed by European invaders) without recourse to agriculture.
> 17. Once a population had become so dependent upon its food crops, plant and/or animal, that it could not survive without them it was trapped into continuing the annual agricultural cycle or suffering major losses in population. Only marginal agriculturalists, such as the people of the Fremont culture of western North America (Carr, this volume) could abandon agriculture and return successfully to full-time hunting/gathering.

Reed's 21st and last point: "Many unsolved problems remain."

Afterword

I've shown above that the most recent research into the origins of agriculture agree that it was a relationship between humans and the plants and other natural factors; it was in no way a "triumph" of human planning, alone. Vavilov, even went so far as to say that "for many plants the process of their introduction into cultivation took place almost independently of his will." How, then, did we in the West come to believe for so long that humans, themselves took the giant step "forward" into agriculture? The rest of the world still to this day revere their legends of the god or goddess dismembering himself or herself to give the people the plants for their food.

The latest aspect of this Eurocentrism is that we have "discovered" the right way at last—permaculture and Fukuda's "one-straw revolution," etc. when, each of these methods actually come out of the age-old, valid way to do cultivation of plants—by listening to the plants themselves and their needs and what you learn from them. I am not saying that Mollison or Fukuda are making these claims; but the "new age thinkers" in this country are making such claims about the "new" agriculture, just discovered by us modern humans.

What we have here is the same old "substance" trap, which we inherited from the "Greek language problem" and Plato. If we continue to think that man's ingenuity is responsible for feeding himself we are still caught in the "substance" trap and will, of necessity, keep destroying the earth—its soil, its animals, its forests etc. If we acknowledge that plants taught man and co-evolved, then we can accept man's proper role as subordinate in the hierarchy of nature, we can relax our frantic effort. The latest frantic step, or course, is genetic engineering of plants and animals—utter folly when we couldn't even get the triticale to be fertile without a wild "stray wheat pollen" When we get the entire world genetically engineered what will be left to teach us humans?

In an earlier part of the book, *Origins of Agriculture*, it is stated that "for most" of the ancient period of agriculture, "the only possible domestic crop is the gourd." It taught humans how to grow food. In the early part of this chapter I covered all the other things that the gourd has done for us humans. Obviously, the way for us to get out of the "substance" trap, which we inherited from the Greeks is to follow the "way of the gourd." Why? Because, to repeat what Nevitt said, "The very process of reading and writing Greek...substituted abstract Nature for chaotic existence as the basis, not only for science and philosophy, but for all thought and action that constitute Western civilization." And, the gourd is chaos or Lord Hun-Tun of the Taoists. So who better can show us Westerners the way out of abstract Nature and back into the chaotic existence of real nature. Thus the gourd can best teach us the way out of the "substance" trap. I will go further into this in the remainder of the book, culminating in Part III.

But for the last chapter in Part I, concerning our "uprooting," I will consider capitalism and the New World ripoff; because this vast wealth which we ripped off during the colonial period, came as the final step which trapped us completely within the "substance" mentality.

"The doctrine of a passing frontier of nature replaced by a permanently and sufficiently expanding frontier of technology is a contemporary and characteristic expression of occidental culture—itself an historical geographic product. This 'frontier' attitude has the recklessness of an optimism that has become habitual, but which is residual from the brave days when the north European freebooters overran the world and put it under tribute. We have not yet learned the difference between yield and loot. We do not like to be economic realists."

Carl Sauer (1938)

"The Wasichus did not kill them to eat; they killed them for the metal that makes them crazy, and they took only the hides to sell. Sometimes they did not even take the hides, only the tongues; and I have heard that fire-boats came down the Missouri River loaded with dried bison tongues...And when there was nothing left but heaps of bones, the Wasichus came and gathered up even the bones and sold them."

(wasichu—"he who takes the fat" is the Sioux word for white man)

Black Elk

CHAPTER THREE

*"So also in the American Revolution, the forces of the left found their expression in men such as Daniel Shay, but the resulting synthesis was the rule of the gentry, leading to capitalism, which, under the **exceptional conditions** of abundant natural resources in the North American continent, has ruled America...until today."*
Joseph Needham, considered the greatest scholar of the twentieth century

"[T]he annual, per person consumption of sugar in the United States is about 125 pounds."
Better Nutrition

"Harold Innis' later works provide a vast amount of detail regarding the development and the effects of mass communications on the western world. Such detail furthers his thesis that...the secular 'religious' truths of national politics and capitalism, have been imposed on the mind of western man in a manner and to an extent never before possible.

He described modern states, even democratic ones, as totalitarian. It was this powerful monopoly of knowledge which he feared. Much of his later work consists of an effort to expose these modern truths as in no way absolute, but rather as effects of communication, and to emphasize the importance of oral communication in undermining all truths in the pursuit of truth...Culture is an effect of oral communication...

Modern spatial truths of national politics and commerce are simply too dangerous not to be constantly questioned."
Ronald Keast on Harold Innis, the inspiration for Marshall McLuhan's work.

 ADDICTION, CAPITALISM AND THE NEW WORLD RIPOFF

Personal Introduction

I've been trying to figure this one out since I was in the eighth grade—that's roughly forty years ago. I was an avid reader, going for anything I could find. I happened to come across a book, *Sergeant Lamb's America*, a true account by a British sergeant of his experiences fighting in America during the Revolutionary War. What I learned there was in direct opposition to everything I was learning in school. I discovered that liberty wasn't involved; instead, it was commercial rivalry with England. Furthermore, instead of being the greatest traitor we had, Benedict Arnold was probably the most responsible leader we had; which is why he had to escape to Canada. From the author's explanations it seemed quite clear to me that such was, indeed the case. I read a lot more in this line through high school but got no real answers. In college I was required to take one quarter of economics to complete my history major. What I heard and read there stunned me! Neither, at any time during the entire quarter, nor from any book did I ever hear a word about the natural resources of a country being the source of wealth. Obviously, at that time no one said a word about the destruction to the earth itself from these "economic" activities.

Although this bothered me, being young, I put it aside and continued taking history classes to find answers to the questions, which first came to me from the same book about the Revolutionary War. I never found any of those answers either, of course. Years went by while I gathered bits and pieces concerning these economic issues.

In 1984, a young friend of mine was working on her Ph.D. in economics at the University of Utah. In talking with her I discovered that she had never heard of the fact that the cheap resources of the New World had anything to do with the origin of the capitalist system. No one had ever mentioned such a thing in any of her classes! This galvanized me into the search for a book which could explain it to her—as well as answer some of my long-standing questions. Fortunately, I found a good one; I refer to it often below.

I readily admit I do not know enough to encompass all the information mandatory to present these facts to you. But, one thing I do know is, the right questions to ask—having been asking them for all these years; so I recognize the answers when I find them. My main effort below is to highlight only the most important aspects of the development of capitalism in connection with the New World rip-off, since this is subsidiary to the main purpose of this book. So I must be brief. Of necessity I will be skipping large chunks of material; see Reference Notes for further information.

Preview

Both ecology and economics come from the same Greek root—*ec* or *eco*, having to do with *oikos*, meaning household. The management of the household is economics and the whole household concerns the earth we live on—the source of all life. But economics has come to mean "a social science concerned with descriptions and analysis of the production, distribution and consumption of goods and services." (definition from the dictionary). Not a word about the earth as being the source of all goods.

Other societies have a much clearer understanding. The Congo Pygmies say: "When the forest dies, we shall die." It's really that simple. Why, then is it made so complex in our Eurocentric world? The answer lies in the fact that in what we label capitalism we have the full horrors of the "substance" approach to life pushed to its ultimate conclusion. What I will try to do in this chapter is give some idea why not only the "religion of capitalism" but also it's heresies, communism and socialism, are destructive of human beings and the earth—always, by their very nature. I will begin with the following quote, concerning the incredible loot of only one of the many English pirates, who skimmed the cream off the Spanish loot from the New World, by preying on the Spanish ships on their way back to Spain. The quote is from *A Treatise on Money*, by John Maynard Keynes (1930). We are still largely operating under Keynesian economics today.

> Indeed, the booty brought back by Drake in the Golden Hind may fairly be considered the fountain and origin of British Foreign Investment. Elizabeth paid off out of the proceeds the whole of her foreign debt and invested a part of the balance (about £42,000) in the Levant Company; largely out of the profits of the Levant Company there was formed the East India Company, the profits of which during the seventeenth and eighteenth centuries were the main foundation of England's foreign connections; and so on...this is quite sufficient to illustrate our argument...that the greater part of the fruits of the economic and capital accumulation of the Elizabethan and Jacobean age accrued to the profiteer rather than to the wage-earner...Never in the annals of the modern world has there existed so prolonged and so rich an opportunity for the businessman, the speculator and the profiteer. In those golden years modern capitalism was born.

Gold Addiction

In the same fateful year of 1492 the Spanish finally managed to drive both the Moors and the Jews out and, because of the marriage of Ferdinand and Isabella, the kingdoms of Aragon and Castile were joined; thus setting up the country of Spain.

Having driven out both sources of wealth for the country, the Jews and the Moors, Ferdinand and Isabella were desperately in need of money for their new country. When Columbus arrived seeking backing for his voyage he found it much more readily than in his native Italy. So it was that in 1492 Columbus discovered the New World for Spain while the Portuguese rounded the Cape of Good Hope in Africa to open up the way to India.

Chistopher Columbus himself said, "the best thing in the world is gold. It can even send souls to heaven." Cortez, the Spanish conqueror of Mexico explained to his new subjects: "We Spaniards suffer from a disease of the heart, the specific remedy for which is gold." This "addiction" of the Spaniards for gold eventually resulted in far more damage to the conquered people than that caused by any previous victors in the history of the world.

Previously, such conquests as that of the Aztec or Inca empires in the New World or the Moghul conquest in India had not caused a total overthrow of the previous ways of production to meet the demands for tribute. The new rulers merely skimmed off the top for themselves but allowed the usual ways of producing food and other things to continue.

This permitted the conquered people's culture to continue, relatively undisturbed, as long as they met their tribute payments. But with the Spanish conquest of the New World we have a wholly different situation. To find the reasons for this difference will necessitate a brief excursion into Spanish history.

Brief Summary of Spanish History

The land we now call Spain had numerous other names. The Greek geographer, Strabo wrote of it as Iberia, which derives from a Celtic word meaning river. The early center of Iberian culture was the green valley of the Ebro River. The Greeks referred to it as Hesperia, from Hesperus, meaning west. The Carthaginians called it Spania, "land of rabbits." The early Iberians were small but sturdy, broad shouldered and olive skinned. They are believed to have come from Africa over an existing land bridge. It's only eight and one-half miles between Africa and Spain. The other main ethnic group consisted of Celts, who originally came from the Danube basin. Phoenicians from the Near East traded there early and brought bull-baiting (developed later into the traditional bull-fights of Spain.)

The Spanish earth was very rich in minerals. This was the underlying cause of much of their later history. Exploitation of this mineral wealth enriched the ancient centers of Tyre and Carthage, in North Africa. Carthaginians were descended from the Phoenicians, who very early secured tin and copper (to make bronze) from Spain. When Rome began its conquests Carthage suffered in the first Punic War. In 236 B.C. the Carthaginians, led by Hamilcar and his son, Hannibal (then nine years old) moved a disciplined army and many elephants into Spain. The plan was to make use of the extensive iron mines there to forge swords and then attack Rome. Hamilcar was killed before this transpired, but Hannibal, then 26 years old, led the attack over the Alps into Italy. But eventually, Carthage lost the 2nd Punic War and Spain and its mineral wealth went to Rome. This was the most costly of ancient wars and southern Italy has never quite recovered to this day. With these riches from Spain—including gold, silver, copper, tin, iron and lead, Rome proceeded to conquer the known world.

"Silver and lead flowed in a steady stream from the mines of Almeria and Cartagena," and a contemporary Roman historian stated that 40,000 slaves worked the mines at Cartagena. Mostly these were locals, of course. Thus began the long history of Spanish peoples slaving away in mines for their conquerors. Iberian bred Arabian horses supplied Roman armies and spears, knives and swords from Toledo gave them their arms. Romans called Spain, Hispania. Some famous Romans were born in Spain, of Roman families—for example Seneca and the Roman emperor, Theodosius.

When Rome fell, Visigoths overran Spain but never conquered it. But in 711 the Moslems crossed the channel from North Africa at Jebel-al-Tarik, meaning Mt. of Tarik, (The Straits of Gibraltar) and took over Spain. They stayed there until the last of them were forced out in 1492. Spain, under the Moorish Caliphate "was the richest, most powerful state in all Europe." Through their scholars there was a rebirth of Greek learning in Europe—especially the works of Aristotle. For 800 years, the local Spanish peoples were ruled by a sophisticated, intelligent, artistic *dark-skinned*, people.

This is the crux of the matter for later Spanish behavior in the New World. The local Spanish were slaves in the mines or underlings to the ruling class of dark-skinned peoples; thus, naturally, they never had a chance to learn how to govern themselves. Then, suddenly in 1492, the Moors are thrown out and the Spanish states of Aragon and Castile are united by the marriage of Ferdinand and Isabella. The Spanish might have begun to learn how to govern but at the same time, the entire wealth of the New world was suddenly thrown open to them by Columbus' discoveries. They had no governing experience and a persistent, deep hate of dark-skinned people. Add to this their crusading zeal in baptizing souls for God in Heaven and you have the whole scenario of the destruction they caused in the New World—and the repercussions of this problem continue right down to this day in South America and Mexico.

I must go a bit deeper into the Christian aspect. During the long struggle against the Moslem invaders, "Spain served as an advance post for Christianity, a religious frontier." In short, a constant crusade against the infidel and for Christ. When the Catholic sovereigns, as they called themselves, unified Spain in 1492, the Inquisition was revived. The primary targets were Jewish converts, who by their skill and commercial acumen had amassed considerable fortunes and converted Moslems who were still suspect. At least a quarter of a million Jews survived the Inquisition; those who did not convert were exiled in 1492. When Spain began conquering the New World, this zeal to garner souls for Christ continued unabated as the priests marched right along with the armies. One Spanish chronicler notes that, although they had killed thousands in a particular battle, it was no loss because they had baptized many before they died—thus more souls were saved for God. Conquering of land thus became a religious crusade for the "greater glory of God."

Europe just before Columbus' Discovery of the New World

Before returning to Spanish gold addiction I must add a brief summary of the state of Europe just before Columbus' discovery of the New World. First, there is the matter of the Black Death and secondly, the Christian crusades against local culture. The Black Death destroyed up to half Europe's population between 1348 and 1350. This horrible plague had lasting consequences on the Eurpean mind. In the fifteenth century, the cult of death flourished at its most morbid... a mocking, beckoning, gleeful death led the parade of the Dance Macabre on frescoe walls and in plays and pantomimes. There was a fear of living and a longing for salvation and everlasting life in heaven. Furthermore, in the 1300s there was abnormal cold and much more snow than usual in northern countries, causing poor crops and failed harvests. Alpine glaciers pushed down valleys well beyond where they were in Roman times.

To turn to the on-going "crusades" which the church encouraged against local cultures. For example, the Hussite wars concerned with growing Czech nationalism. In 1420 the

Czechs defeated the forces sent against them, led by Sigismund in a 'crusade' to re-establish orthdoxy. "At the Council of Basle, however, they were strong enough to compel the Church for the first time to conclude a treaty of peace with heretics." But this kind of action was typical in Europe for centuries, crusading against a local culture in the name of God. In a way, attachment to place was made a heresy. Often the only way out was to give into the Christian sovereign of the larger nations.

The Hundred Years war between France and Britain (essentially to do with trade) started in 1337 and finally ended in 1492 with the Treaty of Etaples, thus freeing France and Britain for New World conquests.

With the combined effect of the Black Death, the famine and crop losses due to a colder climate, the suffering of the Hundred Years War and the on-going persecution of any local culture in the name of Christianity, Europe was in a sorry plight. Something needed to be done. But Europe was saved from making any major change in underlying thinking by the fortunate timing of the discovery of the New World. With the cheap resources of the New World they could continue going right along on the same path for hundreds of more years. But, now with these resources finally running out we have reached another impasse, with far greater consequences; because we have now succeeded in pulling the rest of the world into these Eurocentric problems along with us.

Gold and Silver Addiction

Fortunately, for Spain, Columbus found placer gold in the Antilles Islands of the Caribbean in 1492. The amount of gold the Spanish ripped out of the New World is beyond belief. See Reference Notes for further accounts of the enormous quantities involved.

This early placer mining, and later the deep pit mining of silver in previously uninhabited mountain regions caused the death of many Indians. Even more deaths were caused by mining mercury (which was used to refine the silver). New shipments of Indian workers were continuously conscripted from the Spanish colonies to replace the dead workers; thus the native population was decimated in order to meet the insatiable demand of the Spanish for precious metals. Within little more than a century the Indian population declined by 95% in Mexico, Peru and certain other regions. Mining settlements in these fragile high altitude areas caused such masssive deforestation and erosion of soils that such areas remain depressed to this day. Devastation of the native peoples and the land itself was the price paid for the production of precious metals, the "principle contribution of the New World regions to the expansion of trade in the world, the accumulation of capital in the European metropolis and the development of capitalism."

The story of the famous silver mountain, Potosi, in Peru shows the full horror of death and destruction among the native peoples combined with the useless luxury of the Europeans in the mountain town—and all of it inextricably linked with the politics of distant Europe. This "hill of silver," high in the Andes, was discovered by a Bolivian Indian in 1545. "Not long after, it was to have consumed the lives of an estimated eight million of his brothers," Andre Frank tells us. He continues:

> The Spanish king and emperor of the Hapsburgs, Charles V, designated the town that mushroomed there an imperial city. He inscribed on its shield: 'I am rich Potosi, treasure of the world, the king of mountains, envy of kings.' By 1573 the census recorded 120,000 inhabitants, the same number as London and more than Madrid, Paris or Rome. By 1650 the number had risen to 600,000. In the meantime the privileged among these residents enjoyed thirty-six highly ornamental churches, another thirty-six gambling casinos, fourteen academies of dance, and all the world's luxuries imported from Flanders, Venice, Arabia, India, Ceylon, China and of course metropolitan Spain.

Mexican production of silver declined about 1610 and Peruvian silver production about 1630. At the same time the prices, as measured in silver, of food and other agricultural products, "rose astronomically" so that mining became less profitable compared to large-scale agriculture. The resulting need for farm workers brought about the hacienda with its debt-tied peon labor and the inevitable destruction of the soil.

Sugar Addiction

Sugar was the next major addiction developed in world capital accumulation. The Italian city-states had learned about sugar cane and sugar production from the Arabs. Throughout the fifteenth century the Italian city-states, especially Venice, Florence, Milan and Genoa accumulated wealth because they were the connecting link for the spice trade between the Moslems in the East and the Northern Europeans in the West. Some of these city-states established sugar plantations, based on local and imported slave labor, in Palestine and the Mediterranean islands of Cyprus and Crete. Meanwhile the Spanish, too, had established their own plantations in the Canary Islands and the Portuguese in the Madiera Islands of the Atlantic. Some of this sugar production was transported overland to be sold in Northern Europe. Slaves were connected to European sugar production from the beginning but only toward the end of the sixteenth century, with the vastly increased New World demand for them, did the capturing and selling of slaves, in itself, turn into a major business; thus further enriching Europe and "vastly accelerating the process of capital accumulation."

In the New World, when the Portuguese began sugar production in Northeastern Brazil, they first used Indian slaves. These were captured by Portuguese pioneers in the back country and sold to the plantations. By the end of the sixteenth century the price of sugar had risen to six times its 1506 level and continued rising until the French and British got into the lucrative sugar production with their own plantations in the Antilles. This brought sugar prices back down somewhat and Brazil's first "boom and bust" cycle was over. The vastly increased scale of production, investment in slave labor, capital equipment, and transportation facilities had increased so much that the whole enterprise became a totally new and much more destructive mode of production—the plantation system.

The Seventeenth Century Depression and the Origin of the Industrial Growth Society

It was not only the New World peoples and land which suffered during this century of the "first long, sustained, concentrated capital accumulation." In Europe itself, peasants, along with their land, and town workers as well were affected but not at such devastating levels as in the New World. For instance, in Britain in order to get a year's supply of bread in 1495 one had to work for ten weeks; while in 1593 it took 40 weeks of work. Real wages fell more than 50% during this century. Most of Eastern Europe became a supplier of grain, wood and other raw materials to meet the demands of Western Europe's increasing production which, as noted above, was ultimately financed by New World resources. The Eastern European peasants became serfs due to the resulting concentration of land ownership; while the land itself suffered from the inevitable deforestation and soil erosion which always occurs when an area takes on the role of supplying "resources" for a "developing" country. The political consequences led to the Peasant Wars in Germany and to the Protestant Reformation of Martin Luther.

Because the Oriental spice trade now followed the newly discovered ocean routes, it bypassed the previously flourishing Italian city-states and their wealth and power declined.

The seventeenth century depression developed out of all the factors listed above and, as Andre Frank notes, "It was precisely the seventeenth-century *depression*, rather than simply a long term trend of development, which critically accelerated the changes in the division of labor, both domestically in England and elsewhere as well as internationally. These changes in turn permitted the development of capitalism to continue and then to 'take off' propelled by factory and uniform interchangeable parts production."

European pressure on Asia ceased for awhile both because of the "depression" and the drying up of the flow of Spanish American silver which had financed much of the East-West trade. The decline in silver production also ended the Spanish Manila Galleon trade, because Manila had been the exchange point for Chinese silk and other luxuries in return for Mexican silver. Spanish production of gold from the New World fell from 36 million pesos to only 3 million during the decade after 1650. While the Spanish fleet had once been up to 20,000 tons it was down to only 9000 tons by the middle of the seventeenth century.

Dried fish from the North Atlantic fisheries, transported south to feed the slaves on the Caribbean sugar plantations and the growing fur trade were the two most profitable European economic enterprises at this time. Because settlement by European colonists interfered with the trapping of animals, the French left the trapping to the Hurons while the Dutch used the Iroquois Indians. In the newly growing fishery trade, New England was much better off than the French in Canada because the warmer climate allowed two trips per winter to the West Indies while the French could make but one trip. This climatic advantage set the stage for the later triangular trade that eventually developed between England, New England and the Caribbean.

Increased religious persecution in Europe occurred precisely during the very same decades as the most acute economic crises: the Inquisition in Spain; the persecution and emigration of the Huguenots in France; the "religious" rivalry of the princes in the German wars; and the increased persecution of religious dissenters in England, which brought the first big waves of English migrants to North America. These troubled times were mirrored in the classic, *Paradise Lost*. In 1655 Milton retired from politics to devote his life to writing this epic tragedy.

"SUBSTANCE" PUSHED TO ITS LIMITS BY HOBBES AND LOCKE THE BASIS OF MODERN TECHNOLOGICAL CIVILIZATION

In 1651 the English philosopher, Thomas Hobbes produced his *Leviathan*. He took the old Greek idea of "natural law" and shifted it so that it became the "natural rights" of individuals; thus Hobbes became the "founder" of modern political thought. Hobbes thought he was showing the nature of man in his primitive state but, actually, we now know he was showing the nature of man in the civilized state of seventeenth century England. Hobbes summarized this so-called "natural state of man" as consisting of "no arts; no letters; no society; and which is worst of all, continual fear, and danger of violent death; and the life of man, solitary, poor, nasty, brutish, and short." (See Part II of this volume for a more correct account of natural or primitive man.) In Hobbes' natural right of individuals we have the European doctrine of "substance" pushed to its extreme in human life. Until modern European thinking, no human lived as "substance." Real human life is lived in a continuum of relationships, just as most other mammals live.

Another English philosopher, John Locke finished his masterpiece, *An Essay Concerning Human Understanding*, in 1690. Locke's idea was that the proper study of humanity is not political but economic and "economic man" is the end result. Between the two of them, Lockian liberalism, as based on the philosophical foundations already laid out by Hobbes, we have the basis of modern "technological civilization." This civilization is based on the subjugation and negation of nature by labor and industry, which builds the society of acquisitive "economic man." As far as nature goes, Locke's most infamous statement was: "Land that is left wholly to Nature, that hath no improvement of Pasturage, Tillage, or Planting, is called, as indeed it is wast [waste]; and we shall find the benefit of it amount to little more than nothing." Remember, that just at this time there was the combination of great wealth coming to the few exploiters of the vast newly found resources of the New World combined with the increasing poverty and suffering of the dislocated rural peoples of Europe, who were being forced into the cities.

SCIENCE AND TECHNOLOGY FUNDED BY EXPLOITATION OF NEW WORLD RESOURCES

The same factors, as outlined above, contributed to the explosion of scientific and technological inventions, which took place roughly during the same hundred year period: Kepler (1571-1630), Galileo (1564-1642), Bacon (1560-1625), and Descartes (1596-1650). In the second half of the seventeenth century there was Boyle (1627-1691), Leibnitz (1642-1727), and

Newton (1646-1716), who published his main work, *Principia* in 1679. The connection with the temporary economic decline and the hoped for exploitation of New World resources is shown by the following examples, as given by Frank:

> Bacon's concern for the empirically grounded 'mechanical arts,' which yielded 'substance or profit,' as distinct from speculative scientific thought, which in his opinion did not; by Descartes' agreement with Bacon and his interest in constructing telescopes; by Galileo's specific concern to use his research as a basis for constructing a more accurate clock for determining longitude in ocean voyages; by the creation of scientific societies after 1650; and by the employment of mathematicians and scientists by various governments in the seventeenth century to solve pressing problems of navigation and military technology.

It's no accident that the infamous Cartesian split between mind and matter occurred just here in the middle of the seventeenth century—when Europe was shifting into high gear for full-scale exploitation of the New World resources. On the one hand we have the plunder of India and the slave/sugar plantations of the New World and on the other hand the so-called "progress" of the European "enlightened rationalism, scientific research, mechanical invention, and, after the profit rate began to look up, innovation—in short, the Industrial Revolution."

Although we now tend to downplay the exploitation aspects such as slavery; we still look upon the other aspects as outstanding progress for humanity. In reality, these two aspects are just two different ways of looking at the same system, leading to exactly the same end—more "production," using up more of the earth itself for the profit of the few, resulting in the degradation of both the human beings and the land itself in each exploited region. Each of these movements: "enlightened rationalism," "scientific research," and "mechanical invention" in its basic essence consists of the same process: the human being, the self-conscious "subject," taking an "object"—which is literally "torn out" of context, (to quote Ellis' explanation of Plato)—and working on it. In "enlightened rationalism," the object is a human being; in "mechanical invention," the object is a material thing. But in essence it's all the same process—tearing out a single item from a related natural system, tinkering with it either in thought or, as far as technology and invention, physically manipulating it and coming up with another "useful" entity—but in reality useful only for what has recently come to be called the "Industrial Growth System." (See S. Kvaloy's paper in the Back of the Book Section in this volume.) The end result proves, eventually to be destructive in some way, both to the integrity of the natural ecosystem and the integrity of any human beings thus manipulated. It is important to remember that it can't be helpful for the *whole* because it's been torn out of its relationship to the whole *in order* to manipulate it.

COMPARISON OF EUROPE AND CHINA IN SCIENTIFIC ENDEAVORS

To make this matter clearer it will be useful to explore the differences between the sudden surge of Western science, very late in the world's history and Chinese science, which dates from thousands of years ago. Until Joseph Needham's research it was not realized that in almost every field, the Chinese were centuries ahead of the west in their discoveries. In fact so far ahead that at the time of the Western surge of science no one knew where they had come from. Let me quote what Frances Bacon wrote in 1620:

> It is well to observe the force and virtue and consequences of discoveries. These are to be seen nowhere more conspicuously than in those three which were unknown to the ancients, and of which the origin, though recent, is obscure and inglorious; namely, printing, gun powder, and the magnet. for these three have changed the whole face and state of things throughout the world, the first in literature, the second in warfare, the third in navigation; whence have followed innumerable changes; insomuch that no empire, no sect, no star, seems to have exerted greater power and influence in human affairs than these mechanical discoveries.

We now know that all three of these inventions were first discovered by the Chinese centuries before they reached Europe. Printing was discovered by the Chinese in the 8th century, 700 years before it reached Europe; gun powder was discovered in the 9th century, 300 years before it reached Europe, and the magnet, as used in the first compass, in the 4th century B.C., 1500 years before it was known in Europe. In fact practically all the useful arts were first discovered in China, centuries before they reached the West—for example, cast iron was known to the Chinese 1700 years before the West. Important advances in medicine, which we've just begun to grasp, such as the circadian rhythms in the human body, (the latest thing in the 1960s) was known by the Chinese in the 2nd century B.C., 2150 years before we found out about it. Immunization was used by them in the 10th century, some 800 years before we began using it. Over one hundred other basic inventions or processes were first discovered by the Chinese, from 200 years to 2500 years before that particular invention reached Europe.

In fact, as Needham points out: "The only really important mechanical elements which had been missing from Chinese culture were a) the screw...b) the double-force pump for liquids...c) the crankshaft...and d) clockwork." All of these were brought to the Chinese by the Jesuit missionaries in the 17th century.

A very recent book, *The Genius of China*, by Robert Temple (1986) with an introduction by Needham, has drawn together much of Needham's work, formerly available only in the fifteen volumes of Needham's original work. In Temple's opening remarks he states: "It is just as much a surprise for the Chinese as for Westerners to realize that modern agriculture, modern shipping, the modern oil-industry, modern astonomical observatories...decimal mathematics, paper money, umbrellas, fishing reels, wheelbarrows, multi-stage rockets, guns...hot-air balloons, manned flight, brandy, whiskey, printing and even the essential design of the steam engine, all came from China." He states that without China's contribution of ships' rudders, the compass and multiple masts, the European voyages of discovery in the New World could not have taken place; furthermore, "Columbus would not have sailed to America, and Europeans would never have established colonial empires."

I've got into this at such length to answer those critics

who say where would we be without the great European inventions of the seventeenth century. As you can see we'd be doing just fine. The real question here, of course, is why didn't the Chinese use their skill to exploit the rest of the world as we Europeans did? While I can't give any final answers—even Needham doesn't claim any final answers, I will go into this briefly.

To begin with, most of the Chinese discoveries came out of actual conditions in their work and life. They were not done by abstract experimentation. Thus, they fitted in with the situation in that place. It did not occur to anyone to exploit their use by controlling other situations in other places. Further, as Needham explains in volume 1, "there was little or no private profit to be gained from any of these things in Chinese society..." They were the "creations of many centuries of slow growth"; not "the creations of enterprising merchant-venturers with big profits in sight." Thus, any new invention's use spread gradually and thus kept more in harmony with the over-all life of the people in the land.

Needham points out that the beginnings of "modern science" in the seventeenth century in Europe occurred along with the "Renaissance, the Reformation, and the rise of mercantile capitalism followed by industrial manufacture...The reduction of all quality to quantities, the affirmation of a mathematical reality behind all appearances, the proclaiming of a space and time uniform throughout all the universe; was it not analogous to the merchant's standard of value?" Here, we have a very important point. What he is talking about, essentially, is "substance." The single item, "torn out" of context; with no relationship to anything else. Needham provides some further insight into this matter when he writes about the Chheng brothers' conviction that "concentration on one thing or on one small group of things was not the way to natural knowledge..." He quotes Taoist, Chheng I-Chhuan's answer, when he was asked whether one could not just investigate a single thing: "No, indeed, for in that case how could there be comprehensive inter-relation? Even a Yen Tzu [favorite pupil of Confucius and thus a sarcastic remark] would not attempt to understand the patterns of all things by the investigation of only one thing. What is necessary is to investigate one thing after another day after day. Then after long accumulation of experience (the things) will suddenly reveal themselves in a state of inter-relatedness...The scholar should try to observe and understand all Nature—at one extreme the height of the heavens and the thickness of earth—at the other, why a single (tiny) thing is as it is." In another work, Needham states that the Chinese did not "develop anything resembling the Laws of Nature. With their appreciation of relativism and the subtlety and immensity of the universe, they were groping after an Einstein world-picture..." without having gone through the Newtonian stage of science at all. Furthermore, in China: "Wealth as such was not valued. It had no spiritual power."

In Needham's "Introduction" to *The Genius of China*, he writes: "One can only hope that the shortcomings of the distinctively European tradition in other matters will not debauch the non-European civilizations. For example, the sciences of China and of Islam never dreamed of divorcing science from ethics, but when at the Scientific Revolution the final cause of Aristotle was done away with, and ethics chased out of science, things became very different, and more menacing. ...Science needs to be lived alongside religion, philosophy, history and aesthetic experience; alone it can lead to great harm." And he refers to the modern powers of atomic weapons and hopes that "maniacs will not release upon mankind powers that could extinguish not only mankind but all life on earth." This is Needham at the age of 86, clearly seeing the dangers of modern science.

The very heart of European science since the seventeenth century is the experimental method. One must isolate the one item one is studying. All other factors involved in the normal life or situation of that one item must not be considered in the experiment. That, of course, is "substance" at its ultimate. But this is not the way the world works. This, the Chinese understood. While Europeans tended to find "reality in substance"; the Chinese tended to "find it in relation." This "substance" viewpoint of Western science is why it almost inevitably led to the horrors of "atomic weapons" and other destructive aspects of modern science. It's inherent in our kind of science by nature of the kind of experiments we do.

It turns out that the kind of thinking we pride ourselves on in the West, Formal Operational Thinking (Piaget's name for it), which is scientific thinking is not the highest form of thinking. In a very important, but unrecognized paper, H. Koplowitz has defined, using Piaget's own system, Unitary Operational Thinking as a still higher level of human thinking. Unitary Operational Thinking is more in line with Chinese relational thinking. Since Einstein, modern science is moving more in this direction as shown in the work of such men as Pribram, Bohm, and Prigogine. Perhaps we will finally get out of the "substance" trap we've been caught in since Plato. For truly Unitary Operational Thinking, place is a necessity. In "place" one stays there long enough to see how it works—at deeper and still deeper levels—nature shows you the way it works. More on this in Part III.

DESCARTES AND THE UPROOTING OF HUMANS FROM NATURE

Descartes was the man who set it up so that the "substance" approach to reality became the model for all further development of European and American culture. Building on Plato, Descartes ushered in the "modern" world; or, as I prefer to call it, using Kvaloy's terms, the Industrial Growth Society.

René Descartes, a French nobleman, mathematician, philosopher and sometime soldier, went off to Holland in 1629 to try to work out some ideas that had come to him ten years earlier; and, as the philosopher, William Barrett succinctly explains: "What was to emerge from that solitary room in the Dutch inn was nothing less than an intellectual outline of the modern age to come."

Descartes was trying to find a way out of all the confusions of his time so he began by following the "way of doubting." He examined his senses, the parts of his body, and his beliefs and rejected each of these in turn; until he realized that he must at least be conscious in order to be deceived. And this certainty of self-consciousness led to his famous statement: "Cogito ergo sum" (I think; therefore I am).

He next asked, *what* he was:

What then did I formerly think I was? A man. But what is a man? shall I say 'a rational animal'? No, in that case I should have to go on to ask what an animal is, and what 'rational' is and so from a single question I should fall into several of greater difficulty. (Descartes)

"He concluded that he *himself* was simply a thinking being, not an animal at all. His body, though attached in some way to this soul or self, was no part of it, but a distinct physical mechanism. But all the physical processes occurring in an animal belonged to the body. Animals, then, since they did not properly speaking *think*, had no souls."

Essentially, Descartes figured out that he was a soul that can think, and the external world, including his own body (which he called material) is less real than his self—which is spiritual. "Radical subjectivism" is the label for this type of thinking: I, the human being is the one who knows, does, puts it all together. There's no other being on earth who can do this. This way of thinking, of course goes clear back to the nature of the Greek language and Plato. Since the only being that has a soul is the human being, all the rest of the earth is for his use as he goes through life on this earth journeying toward his true home, heaven. As long as the human being sees himself as distinct from nature whether for religious, philosophical or technical reasons, he feels that he is self-contained; his human nature is not influenced by anything around him. Whatever happens to the rest of the world is totally unimportant to him.

The Australian philosopher, William Grey (formerly known as Godfrey-Smith) is well-known for his philosophical writings concerning nature. He provides further insight into the effect of Descartes' thinking on our approach to nature when he explains that:

Descartes divided the world into conscious thinking substances—minds—and extended, mechanically arranged subtances—the rest of nature...An important result of Descartes' sharp ontological division of the world into active mental subtances and inert material substances, has been the alienation of man from the natural world...Descartes' mechanistic conception of nature naturally leads to the view that it is possible in principle to obtain complete mastery and technical control of the natural world. It is significant to recall that for Descartes the paradigm instance of a natural object was a lump of wax, the perfect exemplification of malleability. This conception of natural objects as wholly pliable and passive is clearly one which leaves no room for anything like a network of obligations...[Further], the Cartesian method of inqury is a natural correlate of Cartesian metaphysics, and is a **leitmotif** of our science-based technology.

What is most important for my on-going discussion of the Greek/European "substance" vs Chinese "relational" view of reality is this statement of Grey's: "In rejecting the Cartesian conception, the following related shifts in attitudes can...be discerned." He lists five points but the most important here is number three: "An appreciation of the fact that in modifying biological systems we do not simply modify the properties of a <u>substance</u>, but alter a network of <u>relations</u>."

Ultimately, Cartesian dualism consists in the view that the world is sharply divided. Human, fully rational subjects are on the one side and all the rest of the world is merely "objects," for us, humans to manipulate. I will return to William Barrett for further comment on this Cartesian dualism: He asks: "What, then, is the whole strategy of Descartes' thought?" He answers: *The will in its freedom chooses to go against nature and natural impulses in order to conquer nature and its secrets.* Here is the first step toward the metaphysics of power that will dominate the modern age." (The italics are Barrett's) He continues in a different—refreshing and down to earth—vein:

I wonder about Descartes in that room at the inn in Holland. A few touches, like the bed and the stove, he has made forever memorable to our imagination. But these details are skimpy; the room is no more than the incidental setting to his meditation. He is a bird in passage; he has not lived in that place long enough to stain it with the marks of his own existence. Otherwise he might have found it more difficult to feign the nonexistence of his surroundings. I turn to look around now at this garrett of a study in which I am writing. How much of my life has transpired here, and how many of these objects face me with the accumulated density of a history that has been theirs and mine! Could I possibly pretend now, just for a little moment, and feign a doubt like Descartes? I have an uneasy feeling that this room and its objects would laugh at me: Whom are you trying to kid? And last night my old dog, now incontinent, crawled up here and left her mess. Poor dear beast, what shall I do with her? Bracket her existence? I would have to cancel all that part of my history and the history of the room with which hers is entwined. Cleaning up after her, I was not able for one moment to pretend that what I had to dispose of did not exist. Try it some time, gentle Cartesian!

Further on in this book I will go more deeply into this important matter of "sense of place." But for now, returning to Descartes, it is useful to remember that the "substance"—that which he felt made us human—is, thinking; therefore, the rational mind. In the context of Descartes in the middle of the seventeenth century's exploitation of colonial wealth, I want to quote the English philosopher, Mary Midgley again, as she writes of the individual human psyche: "I want to get away from the essentially *colonial* picture in which an imported governor, named Reason, imposes order on a chaotic, alien tribe of Passions or Instincts. The colonial picture, which is Plato's, was handed down through the Stoics, Descartes, and Spinoza..."

Descartes, of course, believed that this human psyche or soul, where "reason" ruled was created in the image of God, by God himself, who was safely up in heaven. The full consequences of this Cartesian dualism were never fully realized until recently when Gregory Bateson wrote:

If you put God outside and set him vis-a-vis his creation and if you have the idea that you are created in his image, you will logically and naturally see yourself as outside and against the things around you. And as you arrogate all mind to yourself, you will see the world around you as mindless and therefore not entitled to moral or ethical consideration. The environment will seem to be yours to exploit. Your survival unit will be you and your folks or con-specifics against the environment of other social units, other races and the brutes and vegetables.

If this is your estimate of your relation to nature *and you have an advanced technology*, your likelihood of survival will be that of a snowball in hell. You will die either of the toxic by-products of your own hate, or, simply, of over-population and overgrazing. The raw materials of this world are finite...

[T]he ideas which dominate our civilization at the present time date in their most virulent form from the Industrial Revolution. They may be summarized as:

a) It's us *against* the environment.
b) It's us *against* other men.
c) It's the individual (or the individual company, or the individual nation) that matters.
d) We *can* have unilateral control over the environment and must strive for that control.
e) We live within an infinitely expanding "frontier."
f) Economic determinism is common sense.
g) Technology will do it for us.

We submit that these ideas are simply proved false by the great but ultimately destructive achievements of our technology in the last 150 years. Likewise they appear to be false under modern ecological theory. *The creature that wins against its environment destroys itself.*

Sugar and Gold Addiction

Underlying each of the events of the seventeenth century was SUGAR. By the end of the century Britain had by-passed all other rivals and was leading in sugar production with France just behind. The Dutch were out of the race because the Anglo-Dutch Wars had turned out to be of great commercial benefit to Britain. Furthermore, the need for political protection against Spain and France during the hostilities forced Portugal into the hands of the British. In 1703 Portugal and Britain signed the Treaty of Methuen, which gave Britain important privileges in the Portuguese New World trade expansion. This expansion had occurred because of the recent discovery of gold in the Portuguese colony of Brazil. The Treaty of Utrecht in 1713, "transferred from France to Britain the privilege of the sale of specified amounts of slaves to the Spanish possessions in America...and stimulated what would become the lifeline of the eighteenth-century development: the slave trade." Up to that time the Spanish colonial ports had been legally closed to the British.

War gave the English the opportunity to cripple French sugar production. English pamphleteers made this fact very plain. For instance, in 1745 one wrote: "By a well-managed descent upon their sugar islands we should at once ruin them, and promote the welfare of our own for many years. This might be done by only destroying their sugar works and carrying off their slaves."

Gold! The new discovery of gold in 1697 in Minas Gerais, in Portuguese Brazil—so much gold that ultimately it proved to be nearly half of the total output of gold in the rest of the world during the sixteenth, seventeenth and eighteenth centuries. This new gold field production, along with increased, silver production provided the capital for renewed expansion after the "depression" of the seventeenth century. Portugal soon became Britain's third largest customer—paying in Minas Gerais gold. Britain went off the silver standard and established the gold standard. Britain's increased production, both as a result of the influx of gold and the generally optimistic economic climate "prepared that country for 'take-off' at the end of the seventeenth century, into what has since been called the Industrial Revolution."

Sugar, by no means, lost its importance. Sugar plantations continued to grow—eventually dominating the Northeast of Brazil, most of the Caribbean, and other scattered areas of the New World. The plantation system combined three elements: slave trade, capital from European merchants and direction from the planter on the site itself. "It is significant that three of the characteristics developed in manufacture by the Industrial Revolution—commercialism, capitalism and specialization—attained in Southern agriculture as early as the first half of the seventeenth century through the establishment of the plantation system." Here we find out that today's monoculture agri-business is not new! It actually predated the Industrial Revolution. The only real difference, today, is that we exploit only the soil—not slaves—because we use machines as workers.

The "useful" life of the slaves was seven years or less. When sugar prices were highest the most pressure was exerted on the slave; thus the shorter their lives. When prices were lower the planter eased up the intense pressure and life was somewhat better.

Considerable confusion surrounds African involvement in the slave trade. But, as Bohannon and Curtin explain: "A large-scale slave trade would have been impossible if Africa had been truly primitive...But Africa was not primitive." It turns out that, as another historian, Davidson, points out: "Those Africans who were involved in the trade were seldom helpless victims of a commerce they did not understand; on the contrary, they understood it as well as their European partners. They responded to its challenge. They exploited its opportunities."

The problem which faced African leaders was that Europe wanted slaves—no other merchandise; while to defend themselves from other African powers, they had to have guns. The only way to buy firearms was to sell slaves. Davidson explains, "No single state could safely or even possibly withstand this combination of guns and captives." Dahomey, Oyo and other African kingdoms were trapped in the slave trade's chain of cause and effect. And this entire mechanism of horrors was fueled by sugar profits.

"Money! Money! and no time be lost"

Europe had long imported luxury items from India such as cotton and silk textiles; paying for them with the bullion from the New World. All this changed very suddenly after the British victory at Plassey. India had been feudalistic for more than 2000 years; but its form of feudalism did not demand forced labor as in European serfdom; instead, it involved tributes to the lord. The conflicts in Indian history were concerned with the claims of different lords on payments from the peasants not with actual seizure of the peasant's land by the lord. Furthermore, it was to the advantage of all concerned to keep the lands productive. The beginning of the decline of this system of Moghul power in India came in 1707 with the death of Aurangzeb, the last of the great Moghul rulers. Thereafter, in the distintegration of local power, England and France became rivals in India; eventually, England began to get the upper hand with Clive's historical victory over the Bengalis at the Battle of Plassey in 1757. France lost out completely with the destruction of their Fort at Pondicherry during the Seven Years War in 1761, leaving Britain free to systematically take over all of India.

"Money! Money! and no time be lost," was the policy

of Clive, Hastings and the East India Company. Clive, who left England a poor man, amassed a fortune; while he reported, that "fortunes of £100,000 have been obtained in two years" by others in the Company. In only fifty five years (1757-1812), "British colonialists derived a direct income exceeding £100,000,000." As Digby succinctly explains: "The connection between the beginning of the drain of Indian wealth to England and the swift uprising of British industries was not casual; it was causal." He proceeds to quote Brook Adams' opinion that "possibly, since the world began, no investment has ever yielded the profit reaped from the Indian plunder." Using India as a base, the British moved into the next stage of capital accumulation and, once again, it was based on addiction.

Opium Addiction

When King George III of England sent his ambassador to China to "open" China for greater trade—especially in tea—the Chinese Emperor Ch'ien Lung, wrote to the King:

> As your Ambassador can see for himself, we possess all things. I set no value on objects strange or ingenious, and have no use for your country's manufactures...there was therefore no need to import the manufactures of outside barbarians in exchange for our own produce.

The Chinese, however, did need raw cotton; it was their biggest import from India. After the British took over India, their traders offered the cotton in return for Chinese tea. But there was never enough cotton to meet the British demand for tea so the difference was made up in silver. According to Narendra Krishna Sinha, economic historian from India:

> The practice of sending silver from Bengal to China commenced as early as 1757 [the date of the battle of Plassey]... So long as clandestine opium trade with China could not be fully organized bullion poured into China from Bengal..."

But once the British got opium growing sufficiently organized in India, they stopped the silver drain by creating an ever growing demand for opium in China. Commenting laconically, Sinha states: "In the 1790s it became perhaps unnecessary to send bullion for the purchase of tea in China."

According to the famous American scholar on China, John Fairbank:

> This [opium trade] grew into a tide which could not be checked...the most obvious economic reasons for its importation...namely, the constant pressure to balance the Canton tea trade...the production of opium in India became a great vested interest on which the government had come to rely for revenue...Silver inevitably moved out [of China] as opium moved in."

The shipment of Indian opium into China increased from 800 chests in 1770 to 7800 chests in 1795. "Although the tide of opium trading would not sweep over China, causing and benefiting from the Opium Wars, until the mid-nineteenth century, the requirements of British merchants in India and China thus already initiated the flow of opium in the period [of the eighteenth century]" Frank continues by pondering the question of why the Chinese didn't develop capitalism. Earlier on in his book, *World Accumulation*, he states:

> The Chinese had expanded their influence into Southeast Asia and had maintained overland contacts with the West through their Mongol conquerors long before the Portuguese arrived in Canton by sea in 1514. In the early fifteenth century, China had dominated ocean trade with Africa, sending out 28,000 men in fleets of 60 ships, some of them nearly four times as long and seven times as wide as the flagship of Columbus. Yet the people of China...failed to develop their overseas trade, which came to a halt after 1433.

He asks, "Why didn't they?" and goes even further by asking: "Why didn't they colonize us?" He does not make any attempt to find an answer to these questions. As noted above, I have discussed a few aspects of this complex matter earlier in this chapter but I will go deeper into the matter in Part II of this work.

Turning from the English in India to affairs back in England, we find that in England itself the land based rural people were broken by the Acts of Enclosure—taking common land, belonging to all and giving it to the great landowners. The Enclosure Acts began in the decade, 1720 to 1730, with 33 separate Acts of Enclosure but during the following years the rate escalated rapidly so that by the decade, 1800 to 1810 there were 906 separate Acts. This is the "legal" way in which the rural British, who had been nurtured by a culture based on the land, were turned into rootless laborers.

One of the main reasons for the Enclosure Acts was to graze sheep for wool to make textiles. But in addition to that, by taking away the land from the people, essentially the Enclosure Acts created a vast cheap labor market, which, in turn, made it possible for the factory system to develop. As Marx explained the system: "[O]nly the destruction of rural domestic industry can give the internal market of a country that extension and consistence which the capitalism mode of production requires."

The Connection between the Depressions of 1762 & 1789 and the American and French Revolutions—Further Insights into Sugar Addiction

Sugar/Rum/Slaves—the famous "Triangular Trade" of the New England ship captains, laid the foundations for the fortunes of the future leaders of the United States. The ship left New England, loaded mostly with rum. In Africa the rum was exchanged for as many slaves as it would buy (often at the rate of 200 gallons per slave). Loaded with slaves, the ship set sail for the West Indies where the slaves were sold to the sugar plantations and part of the profit invested in molasses. "On the final leg of the voyage," Mannix and Cowley report, "the vessel would carry the molasses back to New England, to be distilled into more rum, to buy more slaves." How much is a human being worth? Two hundred gallons of rum. Here we have another succinct statement of the basic European doctrine of "substance." On one side, a substance—the human being; on the other side, a "substance"—two hundred gallons of rum: absolutely equal for the purposes of trade. What makes it so simple is that both are abstracted out from relationships with anything else—other humans or the land itself. The damage to human society in Africa and the Caribbean as well as soil destruction on the sugar plantations was never taken into account as an expense. This is the heart of capitalism!

In addition to the profits from the basic "Triangular Trade," the American colonies supplied food staples for feeding the slaves on the sugar planatations. For instance, in 1770 the colonies exported to the Caribbean one third of their dried fish, almost all of their pickled fish, most of their oats, corn, peas and beans as well as half their flour and all their butter and cheese.

The importance of the lucrative profits from the "Triangular Trade" led directly to the American Revolution and the War for Independence. As children in school we were told that the war was fought for liberty and the phrase: "taxation without representation is tyranny" summed it all up for us. But, as the economic historian, Guy Callender asks, "Why, did...insignificant taxes, stir up such fierce opposition? Why were the Americans willing to endure the horrors of a long and costly war for what seems now so small a cause?" The answer is: first of all, commerce was the chief source of private fortunes in the colonies and "almost every prominent man was connected to it" and, second, there had been an economic depression for ten years preceding the war both in England and the colonies.

Events leading up to the famous Boston Tea Party actually began in India where the British East India Company's ruinous administration of its newly conquered Indian territories in order to produce private fortunes, had brought on both the severe famine of 1770-1772 in Bengal and the near bankruptcy of the company. This resulted in replacing Clive by Warren Hastings, who represented Parliament. "In Britain the parliament was persuaded to safeguard the national interest and that of the company's stockholders by finding a suitable profitable market for the stock of otherwise unsaleable tea on hand. The result was the Tea Act of 1773, which sought to dump the tea under what amounted to monopoly privileges for the company on the market of the Americans. The Americans reacted by dumping it in Boston Harbor."

The combination of recession in England, the vast war debt left over from the Seven Years War with France and the elimination of the French threat in North America led the British to put increased new taxes on the Americans. The Sugar Act hurt the traders, the small group of rum manufacturers and threatened to lower the market prices for exports to the West Indies, thus lowering the profits on the rum/slave/sugar traffic. The Stamp Act would cut the profits of two other powerful groups in the colonies: the lawyers and the publishers. The third English ruling hurt both the average person in the colonies as well as the leading men. This was the Royal Proclamation which forbade land grants or settlements beyond a "proclamation line" running along the crest of the Allegheny-Appalachian Mountains. The French had lost this vast country in the war; thus, opening it up to the British fur traders but permitting people to settle there would interfere with that lucrative trade. Events escalated into the War for Independence.

Not only was sugar an important factor in the events leading up to the American Revolution but back in England there was a direct connection between the lucrative sugar profits from the West Indies sugar plantations and the technological innova-tions which resulted in the Industrial Revolution. The economic historian, Eric Hobsbawm, has pointed out that: "Whatever the British advance was due to, it was not scientific and technological superiority." For instance, "it was the capital accumulated in the West Indian trade that financed James Watt and the steam engine." Watt received advances from the firm of Lowe, Vere, Williams and Jennings. At one time Boulton wrote Watt that "Lowe, Vere and Company may yet be saved, if ye West Indian fleet arrives safe from ye French fleet...as many of their securities depend on it." (Of course, all the essentials of the steam engine had been developed by the Chinese in the fifth century AD, some 1200 years before Watt came along.)

A further note here, in his fifteen volume work, Needham notes from time to time specific influences on European inventions from letters to European friends, sent by Jesuit missionaries in China. In the case of the steam engine, "these European designs [including Watts] were all derived, through various intermediaries such as Agostino Ramelli (1588), from those of China." The Jesuits had been in China as early as the 1500s and were translating Chinese classics into Latin by 1600.

Just about the same time as Watt's "invention" of the steam engine, there occurred Hargreaves' spinning jenny (1764), Cartwright's power loom (1785), leading to the industrialization of cotton textiles in England, and in 1793, Eli Whitney's cotton gin. New World capital was behind all of these. Hobsbawm pulls it all together when he states that "the advantage of Britain over her potential competitors is quite evident. Unlike some of them (such as France) she was prepared to subordinate *all* foreign policy to economic ends." The result of this century of intermittent warfare—involving England, France and Holland— "was the greatest triumph ever achieved by any state," England secured "the virtual monopoly among European powers of overseas colonies."

Not counted in the expense columns of capital accumulation was the toll of those humans "used" to garner such enormous profits. In his summary Andre Frank includes: "The seven 'useful' years of a slave's life in many parts of the New World, the decline in Indian population in Mexico from 25 million to 1.5 million in little more than a century after the Conquest, not to mention the total decimation of the indigenous population of the Caribbean in half a century, the increased incidence and depth of famine in Bengal after its rape by the British...all testify to the superexploitive character of these processes of accumulation in its preindustrial stage." Even more basic to this accumulation was the destruction of the overflowing abundance of the resources of the New World— not only gold, silver and other ores that were extracted but productive top soil, animals (for furs) and fish were destroyed. Many regions have not yet recovered from this exploitation.

It's very difficult for us, now, to visualize the over-flowing abundance of this land when the whites first invaded North America; therefore, I will give you some excerpts from Paul Metcalf's hauntingly beautiful compilation of original documents written by men who were not poets—just ordinary human beings — giving us an eyewitness account of the eastern coastline of the United States about the middle of the 1600s:

it happens that the land is smelt before it is seen
The fragrance drifts seaward/we smelled the land a hundred
leagues, and farther when they burned the cedars/before we
came in sight of it thirty leagues, we smell a sweet
savour...there came a smell off the shore like the smell of
a garden/the air smelt as sweet and strong/richly scented with
the fragrance of the pines/the wind brought to us the finest
effluvia/the odorous smell and beawtie...which, for a long
distance, exhale the sweetest odors/a marvelous sweet smell

— — —

we viewed the land about vs, being...very sandie and low
towards the waters side, but so full of grapes, as the very beating
and surge of the sea ouerflowed them, of which we found such
plentie, as well as in all places else...the soiles there upon
the seacoaste, and all along the tracte of the greate broad mightie
ryvers, all alonge many hundreth miles into the inland, are
infinitely full fraughte with swete wooddes

— — —

wild Vines runne naturally/the ground doth naturally bring
foorth vines/the wild vines cover all the hills along the
rivers...Vines in many parts on the Sea Shore, bearing
multitude of Grapes, where one would wonder they should
get Nourishment/in suche abdundance, as where soever a man
treads, they are ready to embrace his foote/Grapes so pro-
digiously large/Vines, in bigness of a man's thigh...the Grapes
faire and great/of such greatnes, yet wild/grapes exceeding
good and sweett of to Sorts...a marvellous deepe red...they
bee fatte, and the iuse thicke/black Bunch-Grapes which yield
a Crimson juice ... well knit in Clusters

— — —

The vesture of the earth in most places doth manifestly proue
the nature of the soile to be lusty and very rich exceeding fat
and fertill...excellent black earth a fast fat earth fat and lustie
strong and lustie of its own nature...we stood a while like
men ravished at the beautie and delicacie of this sweet soile
All the spring-time the earth sendeth forth naturally

Summary of Capitalism and Addiction

As shown above, the entire development of capitalism consists
in making a group of people addicted to some "substance"
and selling it to them. Capitalism "worked" as long as we
had an enormous source of cheap natural resources. But there
are no more cheap resources. Continuing its history of
"addiction," capitalism is now relying more and more on
addictive drugs to fuel its growth.

When capitalist entrepeneur, John DeLorean was accused
of selling cocaine to raise the money to produce his "$29,000,
stainless steel, gull-winged, gas-guzzling sports car," many
people were shocked. Raising money for a gigantic capitalist
venture, in which the British government had already promised
$160 million, by selling cocaine to addicts! But, considering
the long history of gold addiction, silver addiction, sugar
addiction and all the other addictions which helped to develop
capitalism, De Lorean's little venture should not have come

as a surprise. That's the way capitalism has been working for a long, long time, since it came out of the European "substance" approach to reality.

For example, Europeans turned the Indians' sacred tobacco into just another substance—unrelated to anything else. And then produced it on plantations and sold it to a world, gradually growing more addicted to it—until now it's one of the leading causes of death. Formerly tobacco was life-enhancing, because smoking the ceremonial pipe strengthened the relationships among all the humans present as well as put the humans into relationship with the "powers" of the sky and of the earth and all the beings on the earth.

Cocaine is another example. Up in the high Andes, where the natives have chewed coca leaves for centuries, modern scientists now find that, indeed it does help the natives live and work at high altitude; in addition to alleviating hunger, fatigue, pain, and cold. In fact, it prevents chronic high altitude sickness and possible death. (See Reference Notes for more on this). Used in their sacred ceremonies it, too, enhances their relationship with the "powers." But "substance" oriented capitalism takes it now and refines it into a fine white powder and people snort it, because this "substance" gives them such a rush of euphoric excitement that they become addicted—which often leads to serious illness and sometimes death. Thus coca leaves, in their native place are life-enhancing but, as modern Europeans use it, death-dealing. In fact drug abuse has now become "America's No. 1 health problem."

Let's take a quick look at the actual money involved in this new source of capital. "Like any successful 'multinational' (estimated 1984 gross U.S. revenues of $110 billion, $20 billion more than Exxon's worldwide sales), the drug networks are reacting to market forces." One Columbian entrepeneur in the drug world is worth at least $2 billion—in short "Latin American drug dealers are the model of the modern corporation." They hire American lawyers and financial advisors, use Miami banks, and hire American pilots to fly their precious cargoes. Bolivian Anti-narcotic agency chief, Rafael Otazo remarks "the narcotic traffic is now stronger than the state." South America has marijuana and poppy plantations as well. Recent figures from Europe show the drug problem is growing just as fast there as in the United States.

I want to make it very plain that addiction continues as a major source of capital and, as we run out of natural resources, this will only grow worse. For example—take the new popular drug, "crack." It turns out that people who've been using marijuana for years can no longer find it from their usual sources; they can only buy "crack." Crack actually inhibits the production of endorphins. In four seconds it goes straight to the brain, gives a quick hit but immediately leaves the person with no way to produce endorphins in the brain. Totally addictive—a wonderful "consumer" product. It makes it necessary to buy it again immediately.

INSIGHTS INTO THE NEUROPHYSIOLOGY OF ADDICTION

For the beginning background here, I am using a very illuminating article which told about the work of Dr. Margaret Patterson, from Scotland, who began working on information she received from a colleague, Dr. Wen, when she was head of surgery at Hong Kong's Tung Wah Hospital, a large charity institute for poor clientele. Dr. Wen, a neurosurgeon had just returned from the People's Republic of China, where he had learned the technique of electroacupuncture—acupuncture,using very low currents of electricity. Some of Dr. Wen's patients began telling him that the electroacupuncture he was using on them, for a variety of ills, was actually stopping their withdrawal symptoms, as well. "I felt as if I'd just had a shot of heroin," one said. Some alcoholics and cigarette smokers had also been freed from their craving.

Beginning from this base, Dr. Patterson continued her work on what was eventually called NeuroElectric Therapy (NET). "In sharp contrast, to most cured addicts, NET patients are said to emerge from treatment feeling healthy, energetic, even cheerful." NET apparently deals with the endorphins in the brain; and Dr. Patterson had an excellent background on this subject because some of her early studies were with Dr. Kosterlitz. "While working with Dr. John Hughes at the University of Aberdeen in 1975, Dr. Kosterlitz identified an endorphin, a natural brain chemical, with a molecular structure very similar to the opiates." Hughes and Kosterlitz received the Lasker Award, America's equivalent to the Nobel Prize in Medicine. Their findings "triggered an explosion in the understanding of the biochemical basis of behavior." Opium, heroin, morphine and other related drugs: "owe their potency" to what A. Goldstein calls "one of nature's most bizarre coincidences—their uncanny resemblance to the endorphins." Since that time, researchers have uncovered enough evidence to show that "almost every mind-altering substance... has an analogue in the brain."

The success of Patterson's NET comes from the fact that in the first stages of narcotic use, it is assumed that the individual has normal levels of endorphins in the brain. "Injecting heroin causes a sudden and drastic elevation of opiates, which is subjectively interpreted as ecstasy." But through repeated use, the brain is regularly flooded with opiates so it begins cutting back on the production of opiates. This is probably the well-known condition of tolerance. When that happens, the addict increases his dosage and the brain compensates by stopping all production. Thus when the drug supply is cut off, the natural opiates are no longer being made inside the brain and withdrawal symptoms result.

After further research Patterson discovered that "low-frequency currents can indeed cause as much as a threefold elevation of endorphin levels." In fact, the "ten-hertz signal speeds up the production and turnover rate of serotonin (a neurotransmitter that acts as a stimulant to the central nervous system)." Summing up these findings, Patterson states: "that drugs—for the very reason that they are foreign—upset the brain's chemistry. NET, on the other hand, simply coaxes the brain to restore its own chemical balance. The body heals itself."

The pioneering work of Hughes and Kosterlitz began a "major conceptual shift in neuroscience." It is now realized that brain function is modulated by numerous chemicals in addition to the classical neurotransmitters. "Many of these informational substances are neuropeptides...their number exceeds 50 and most, if not all, alter behavior and mood states…Neuropeptides and their receptors thus join the brain, glands, and immune system in a network of communication between brain and body, probably representing the biochemical substrate of emotion."

PLANTS, ANIMALS, HUMANS AND DRUGS

Returning now, to Goldstein's remark above, referring to "one of nature's bizarre coincidences"—that addictive drugs have an "uncanny resemblance to the endorphins." Of course, there's no "bizarre coincidence" here. Each of those endorphins is in the brain as the result of millions of years of evolution. Each of them is there for a reason, conducive to the on-going life of the human being or they would not still be there. During the course of real living, as humans did it for millenia on this earth, daily circumstances of life create the conditions necessary to produce each of these endorphins in the brain. Furthermore, during the long course of evolution, humans discovered some of the plants themselves and still other plants they learned about from animals, such as the bear and the chimps. If you understand that humans are within nature; not apart from it; it's no surprise at all that plants, animals and humans—all have the same chemicals.

Yes, animals do use drugs. Ducks eat a variety of narcotic plants, elephants get drunk on fermented fruit, pigs like marijuana. I've seen a whole treeful of starlings, drunk on fermented mountain ash tree berries. Ronald Siegel reports that in his research into animal use of drugs, he discovered a shard from an ancient ceramic bowl in the Peruvian Andes. A painting on it showed two llamas chewing on a branch of coca leaves. "Several Indians were pointing at the llamas and reaching for the leaves with open hands and mouths." He later found a legend, dating back to A.D. 900, telling of an Abyssinian herder who found that his "animals became energized after eating the bright red fruit of a tree that was later named coffee." Of course, animals use drugs and alcohol but, outside of the laboratory they do not become addicts. Being mammals, relationship is the most important thing to them; not "getting high." But in the artificial surroundings of a lab they, too, just like us in our artificial surroundings of civilization easily become addicts.

Every single traditional human culture used either alcohol or a drug. The Eskimos are the only exception and that's because there are not many plants growing that far north. But there was seldom addiction to these drugs before the modern era because they weren't used as a "substance" but rather as a gift of the gods which enhanced their "relationship" to all other beings: human, natural and sacred.

But today in our world, where life itself has been made so boring and monotonous because we humans have been turned into another substance to be managed by multinational corporations; the normal life, which produced these endorphins, automatically, in us is no longer possible. Addiction in some form is the natural result. Over-eating is another form of this addiction. Eating, not because one is hungry but because one is starved for real living. "Western man is the first human being in the history of the world to totally inhabit a commodity-culture…the human being has been now reified into a commodity." Novelist and critic Sylvia Wynter, from Jamaica, continues: "Because of this the difference between Western and non-Western cultures is not the difference between civilized and primitive. That is an ideological reading. *The difference is that between the first commodity-culture in the history of human existence and all other cultures. A mutation has occured.*" And, as the expanding multi-national corporations continue we are drawing the entire world into this Eurocentric "commodity-culture."

But we can begin to move back toward real living—living as relationship; rather than as substance—by clearly recognizing some essential facts. As documented above, the nation-state began as a way to facilitate trade. Each of these nation-states centralized their power by wiping out small, particular, land-based cultures. There followed a period of patriotism, where the national state appealed to the lingering nostalgia for their lost culture, which remained in the conquered people, in order to gain acceptance of the new nation. But that's all over now. We no longer have any nation-states for trading; we now have only multi-national corporations. Most of the world has become part of the Industrial Growth Society (the IGS).

Industrial Growth Society (IGS)

In defining the IGS, the Norwegian ecophilosopher, Sigmund Kvaloy states that it is "based on steady or accelerated growth in the production of industrial articles and the use of industrial methods." And the whole of the earth is merely "substance" to be "used" by humanity for this production. The alternative to the IGS is Life Necessities Society (LNS), "based on producing life necessities and always giving priority to that. There is only one historical example of the first kind of society, our own, which is tending to become global. Most other human societies have been of the second kind. IGS is an abnormal kind of society, which can exist only for a historical second. Judging from various indications spanning 1-2 million years, the LNS is the human kind of society and it will remain so."

The IGS turns everything into substance to be used by us humans because; after all, during our entire Western culture, since Greek writing began, it's been considered that humans are the only beings on the earth who can know. All other beings are merely objects, "torn out" of context for us to know about. If everything else is merely an "object" we can "use" it with impunity. Here's where the European tendency to find reality in substance and the subject/object dichotomy we inherited from the Greek language structure come together. But the IGS, exemplifying the supreme "substance" approach just might be the turn-around point.

Conclusion

Since we no longer have nation-states, merely the IGS, there's no longer any possibility of patriotism. You certainly can't feel much patriotism for the Industrial Growth Society. This leaves us free at last to begin to "devolute"—not revolution, but devolution. It means staying right where you are and paying attention to that immediate place in all its aspects and not leaking off energy by using any of the mass media. It's important to remember that during World War II, while Hitler's radio propaganda had great success in Europe, it had no effect whatsoever on primitive people, living their own local culture. (Television is proving much more pernicious, however. All the more reason to dismiss it from your life.)

Clearly labelling the entire "substance" oriented multi-national corporate system (and that includes communism and socialism and any other economic "ism," as well) is the first step in this turn-around. Each of these is simply a part of the Industrial Growth Society. The only way out of the multi-national, "one world," Industrial Growth Society is a local cuture where it is possible to begin to live in *relationship* with all the other natural beings in that place. Again, this is "devolution"; not revolution. The difference is important. Gregory Bateson makes this very clear when he states: "By a process of addiction, the innovator becomes hooked into the business of trying to hold constant some rate of change. The social addiction to armaments races is not fundamentally different from individual addiction to drugs. Common sense urges the addict always to get another fix." In essence it's "substance" again.

Bateson says that what we need is a civilization which will "consume unreplaceable natural resources *only* as a means to facilitate necessary change (as a chrysalis in metamorphosis must live on its fat). For the rest, the metabolism of the civilization must depend upon the energy income which...Earth derives from the sun." Gary Snyder says much the same thing, when he talks about his own "place" in the foothills of the Sierra, but in a more poetic way, "We're going to stay right here for the next three thousand years and learn how to do it right."

The rest of this book is about learning how to do it right.This first section, Part I has been about "Uprooting": how we got into this present state of thinking we are separate from the rest of life on earth. The next section, Part II concerns our "Roots" in all of life. The last section is Part III, "Following the Root-Traces: The Return."

PART II
OUR ROOTS IN THE "OLD WAYS"

"You cannot go back. You cannot turn the clock back. You cannot become primitive people—that's all behind us. We have to face the modern world in its own terms—existentialism and all that—angst and all that Western philosophy has given us. But, that's only true if we're talking about culture—culture which is always created. It cannot be true if an organism is involved. If we are talking about human needs, rather than needs generated by a particular ideological view, then you can't go _back_, because you haven't left. You aren't going back to something primitive. You are recovering an essential process which should take place within the person...at sixteen years or whatever [stage of the life cycle]."

Paul Shepard

"Civilization is thus an artifact and not a biological phenomenon. The _only_ physiological result it has had in man is the emergence of psychosomatic disorders. It has produced no new organs and no new functions…Man's cultural evolution is brought about by the ever better training of the cortical ability to learn. He is the only living creature that has brought its natural evolution to an end. man has ceased to adjust his body to his environment; he now adjusts his environment to his body."

A.T.W. Simeons. M.D.

"As far as one can now foresee the only enemy that seriously threatens man's continued existence is his own brain, with which he has so far been unable to come to biological terms."

A.T.W. Simeons, M.D.

"[Evans, in writing, warned that] it should not be forgotten that society is older than man, is inherited from prehuman ancestors, and is not a human invention."

Dr. E. Estyn Evans

CHAPTER FOUR

"The human body evolved on this planet in close contact with the earth. Breaking these bonds with the earth leads to peculiar types of insanities found in cities. Breaking the bonds with the earth causes 'the paper reality' of civilization to encroach upon one's consciousness to a point where one believes that the paper reality is real, rather than a convenient construction of man."

John Lilly

"[M]ere purposive rationality unaided by such phenomena as art, religion, dream, and the like is necessarily pathogenic and destructive of life."

Gregory Bateson

"The symbols of the self arise in the depths of the body and they express its materiality every bit as much as the structure of the perceiving consciousness...The deeper 'layers' of the psyche lose their individual uniqueness as they retreat farther and farther into darkness. 'Lower down,' that is to say as they approach the autonomous functional systems, they become increasingly collective until they are universalized and extinguished in the body's materiality, i.e., in chemical substances. **The body's carbon is simply carbon. Hence 'at bottom' the psyche is simply 'world'**... The more archaic and 'deeper,' that is the more _physiological_, the symbol is, the more collective and universal, the more 'material' it is."

C.G. Jung

 ETHOLOGY: THE ROOTS OF HUMAN NATURE

Personal Introduction

How do I *know* that I'm not only a mammal but a close relative of the higher primates? Mount Snowden, 13,077 ft. high, taught me this important lesson. The story begins many years before the climb. It goes back to the time when I was caught in a bigger avalanche than usual while skiing powder snow in Alta Utah. If one is aware, most avalanches give you a bit of a warning and you can slam your skis back down onto the snow and get out of the path. This one didn't allow that maneuver because it threw me into the air immediately. When I woke up in the hospital the next morning, I was in a body cast. Both bones of the left leg broken off clean and the right hip dislocated. From photographs taken of the slide path, it turned out that I had hit the top of a large tree as I flew by in the air. It broke me and I broke it.

Being greedy, I walked much too soon after the cast was off and lost a good inch off the left leg. Having a strong Irish back, it held the pelvis level for roughly 10 years. Then, during a difficult emotional time (impending divorce), the hip finally dropped with ensuing complications. A few years later I began Rolfing treatments with Tom Wing in Boulder. The first spring he began the process and the following spring finished the work. As I departed from the last session, he told me that I would have a lot of pain in the groin while the back began pulling the pelvis up to its normal horizontal position. His last remark was, "But don't worry it will happen by next spring."

So I returned to my home in Silverton and yes, I had a lot of pain in the groin but not unbearable. The more I walked, the better it felt. But it still hurt most of the time. Early September arrived. An old climbing friend, George, and I met on the street and exchanged our ritual greeting at change of seasons. "Well, we didn't get anything climbed this summer, let's go on a ski trip this winter." George's answer this time was "It's not too late, Dolores. Let's climb Snowden tomorrow."

The next morning George arrived with all his hardware. I had thought we would just be walking up the easier side of the mountain because neither of us had been climbing real stuff because of other commitments. George is a good thirty years younger than I but we used to climb together fairly often because he is the only experienced mountaineer in town. Most of the men who climb are really rock climbers, not mountaineers. But George had been very busy building up a new business for several years so it gave him no time to climb.

We start up the trail with me leading because George likes my "Swiss guide pace." We arrive at the rock and just keep on moving. It's steep but not technical. Plenty of holds. As we get higher we move very carefully because it's been a good four years since either of us had done high-angle rock. But it goes just fine. Eventually we rope up for the 5.8 sections. But it goes very well. The mountain just keeps opening up for us. I keep thinking: "Just ahead it's going to very difficult." And then the mountain once again opens up for us to pass through easily. A fine clear fall day with ice green gentians blooming on the rock. One never sees them except in very late summer or early fall and then only in the highest, least travelled areas. We get to the top, which is an absolutely flat space (old peneplain), about as big as a football field. So for an hour we lie in the sun, argue about which mountain is which.

We haven't yet climbed even 1/10th of those close up. We eat and glory in it all.

When we begin the descent, we go down the next buttress over, with George checking me out, often, in the first few moments to see how it's going. But it's going fine. So he merely remarks from time to time: "Don't forget it's a long fall." We both realize we needn't rope up again. This is fourth class rock but it's going well.

Then, the bliss takes over. It's extremely difficult to explain this to non-climbers. It's a state of total relaxation, total joy, and incredible thankfulness that the mountain is allowing you to do this—to proceed so gracefully, beautifully down the vertical rock, always giving you something to hold onto in passing. It's being "at home" totally, completely "at home" like nowhere else. Some friends tell me "Oh yeah! You're just addicted to adrenalin. That's why you feel so good." But that's exactly the point. There's no adrenalin when you feel so safe, so good, so flowing. It's total relaxation.

After we were off the rock, we raced down the trail to the car and were back into town well before sundown. Only after that did I realize there was no pain in the groin and hadn't been for most of the day. I don't even know when it left me. But it was gone for good from that time on. So I puzzled over this. How come a vertical rock climb could accomplish in one day, what was supposed to take nine more months? It didn't take long to figure it out. The only thing that we adults do in our modern life that exactly mimics what we did in the trees for at least 100,000 years is rock climbing. So that's why all the parts of the body for once can feel totally "at home" when climbing steep rock. For once in this modern life everything in the body doing what it was designed to do by millenia of evolution. No wonder there's bliss. And because of the total relaxation of doing just what every part really wants to do my back was able to pull the pelvis up and thus no more pain. I realized that I could no longer ignore ethology because that's who we are—animals.

The next time I was near a big library was in February when I give my annual lectures in Salt Lake. Entering the University of Utah library, I confidently went over to the main subject card catalog and found there was not even a listing for "ethology." This was a shock but then, I knew ethology was a "bad" word. Next spring in Boulder I looked in the University of Colorado catalog and found only four listings. But I began getting books through inter-library loan and learning more and more.

Why is ethology a bad word? Let me quote Paul Layhausen, a cat (*Felidae*) specialist, writing about when he first met his teacher, Konrad Lorenz.

> I was a student of twenty-four and the Institute of Comparative Psychology of the University of Koenigsberg...had just been founded. When I somewhat diffidently told the newly appointed Professor of Psychology, Konrad Lorenz, that I would appreciate his advice as I was interested in animal psychology, his abrupt answer, 'There is only one psychology!' shocked me profoundly. For I had been brought up in the traditional idea that man was something quite apart and that any direct comparison with animals practically bordered on sacrilege.

As long as you safely limit ethology to one aspect—the study of animal behavior—all is well. But if you dare to agree with Konrad Lorenz, the founder of ethology that "there is only one behavior"—not animal behavior and human behavior—then you are in trouble. And, in trouble from all sides of the fence—newagers, psychologists, Christians etc. etc. But at this crucial time when all of life is threatened—not only human but countless other species—we'd better begin to pay attention to who we are. Unless we realize the glory of being both animal and human we will keep trying to destroy the earth in trying to save it with new "ideas."

This chapter is about who we are... and if you read it with an open mind you will say: "Yes, indeed, that's who I am."

Preview

You're at a friend's house for a party. Where is everyone? Not sitting down in the living room where it's comfortable and snacks have been laid out invitingly on tables. Everyone is jammed into the kitchen or else clogging up the hallway to the kitchen. Everyone has to stand—the only real sitting area is the living room. It's difficult to move about—even to get food or drink. The hostess repeatedly urges people to go into the living room and "be comfortable" while she finishes getting things ready and she will join them there. Sometimes, in desperation, she leads a group out of the kitchen but soon they are back, joining those who never left. Why is everyone standing in the kitchen? Because we are mammals and mammals communicate best when they are freely moving one among the other. Communication is through movement in *all* mammals. Few people know this intellectually, but the body *always* knows it and when permitted to do so will act on this knowledge. When coerced into remaining in one place, real communication drops immediately. Such places include a conference table, where everyone is seated (usually in a rigidly hierarchical manner) along the length of a table or a formal lecture, where everyone is sitting with their back to the row behind them, facing one human being standing up there telling them what he wants them to know. There's a saying in ethology "You have to ambulate to communicate. You can't do it just sitting there."

Why do you see colors and your dog doesn't? But even deeper than this first question, how come we humans have binocular vision? Our binocular vision developed in trees where our primate ancestors jumped from limb to limb. They had to know exactly where the next limb was. Thus, in binocular vision all objects at greater or lesser distance from the single point of fixation are out of focus. So the limb is clear; all the rest is a jumble of subliminal double images. Of course, we greedy humans demand to see everything in focus all the time—the result of this nonsense is that we end up wearing glasses (as I do) because we have destroyed the fine-focusing tiny muscles by forcing that tiny fixation point to try to take everything in clearly and all at once.

For a monkey in the tree it's very helpful to be able to see if the fruits hanging in the next tree are ripe or not. Ripe fruit is most often some color along the spectrum from yellow to orange to purplish or red. These colors definitely stand out against a green background. We are still attracted to yellow to red spectrum colors. These colors make us feel happier. Blues and greens tend to give a more withdrawn atmosphere.

Advertising, which provides us with one of the most direct learning experiences for ethological lessons—makes much use of the "warmer" colors.

"The sea eye was first connected to a fishy brain and body." When taken onto land by the first land creatures, this eye continued to see only the spectrum of light transmitted by water—The coolness of the blue depths and the "warmth" of the reddish, sunlit surface. Later, in evoutionary times, the bush apes, beginning to move down out of the trees onto open country, were exposed to the harsh glare of bright sunlight with no dappling. Today we still have an uncomfortable feeling of vulnerability connected with harsh, open glare.

We feel best—just as the higher apes and the early humans felt best—on the edge of trees, where we can look out over a broad place but are relatively protected. Other feelings from our tree borne, primate past are explained by Paul Shepard when he writes:

> An affinity for shade, trees, the nebulous glimmering of the forest interior, the tracery of branches against homogeneous surfaces, climbing, the dizzy childlike joy of looking down from a height, looking through windows and into holes, hiding, the mystery of the obscure, the bright reward of discovered fruits are all part of the woody past. Restfulness to the eyes and temperament, unspoken mythological and psychical attachments, remain part of the forest's contribution to the human personality.

I think it's easier now, to begin to see why the findings of ethology are useful to us; but ethology is also under fire because it is not "scientific" enough, meaning it cannot replicate its findings easily. It's beginning to find acceptance as the study of animal behavior but, in general, it is still thought that human behavior is something entirely different.

In a brief space I can only give a few accounts of what we can learn by paying attention to the research of ethologists. Part of the problem is that such research cannot be restricted to a few experiments, which are concluded within a limited time. The only way to do ethology is by observing the animal or human in the full context of life—not in a laboratory. As we've seen from Bateson's "dog in the lab" story in the opening pages of this volume—that's not life—that's just an experiment in the laboratory.

Konrad Lorenz

Lorenz is the acknowledged founder of ethology. As a child he lived in a large rambling house, surrounded by open country along the Danube. His parents allowed him to follow his own interests. Thus he was able to keep pets both inside the house and outside. His earliest pet was a duckling, acquired when he was six years old. His childhood friend (who later became his wife, Gretl) got the other duckling—both acquired from a neighbor when newly hatched. The marsh, extending along the Danube was their playground. In this marsh, among the dense thickets of willow and scrub brush, Konrad and Gretl played at being ducks. And the newly hatched ducklings followed them about just as if they were ducks. Of course, the ducklings became "imprinted" on them. (At that time there was no such word; Konrad later assigned the word to such activities.) "What we didn't notice," Lorenz remarked much later at the age of seventy, "is that I got imprinted on ducks in the process. I still am, you know. And I contend that in many cases a lifelong endeavour is fixed by one decisive experience in early youth. And that, after all, is the essence of imprinting."

He was ten when he happened to read a book titled, *The Days of the Creation*, by a popular writer, which told of the evolutionary theory of Darwin. Konrad devoured the book with intense excitement and it gave him a glimpse into the order underlying living nature. Later, telling of his new discovery to his father as they walked in the woods, he discovered that his father had known it all along. The deep resentment this stirred in him, that something so important seemed to have been kept from him, remained clearly in his memory—even when he was very old. This conversation in the woods led to young boy's decision to study evolution and become a palaeontologist; Gretl and his play turned toward dinosaurs.

Konrad's father wanted him to become a doctor so, eventually, he joined the anatomy department of Vienna University. While still a student there he met his first jackdaw in a pet shop. The dark bird, cowering in his cage aroused his pity. He bought it and took it home with him, intending to release it. But when he did so; the bird chose instead to stay with him. Thus began the many years of jackdaw living which Konrad shared. The detailed daily journal of his jackdaws, later became his first scientific article, "Observations on Jackdaws," published in 1927 in the Journal of Ornithology in Leipzig.

Oskar Heinroth, a zoologist, was sufficiently impressed by the observations in this paper to work with Lorenz. Heinroth's original paper which he had written in 1910, concerning the comparative methods used in the study of animal forms, had already been extended to behavior by Heinroth himself. So Heinroth's work confirmed for Lorenz what he was already beginning to understand. By 1928 Lorenz had his jackdaw colony well established and his real studies began. In 1936, at a symposium in Leiden, Lorenz met Nikolas Tinbergen, who had been studying a colony of herring gulls near the University of Leiden in Holland. From March to June of 1937 they worked together and, as Lorenz later said: "I would be nowhere without Tinbergen." The productive years of research continued until 1940 when the war intervened.

Because of the controversy surrounding Lorenz' work, even though his work underlies much of the modern research in such widely varying fields as neurophysiology and behavioral psychology, I must take the space here to clear up the origins of this doubt. Much of the criticism of Lorenz has to do with a mistranslation in one of his papers, "Disorders caused by the domestication of species-specific behaviour," published in March of 1940 in the German, *Journal of Applied Psychology and Character Study*. It had to do with the fact that in breeding domestic animals, humans select for traits not necessarily helpful for the animal in the wild. He then went on to show that the civilization of man "has involved processes that are comparable to the domestication of animals," and he calls the process "self-domestication." These changes, of course, may not be really good for humanity. The real attacks on this paper came much later, April 14, 1972, in a speech later published in the American journal, *Science*. Eisenberg of Harvard

Medical School had mistranslated a phrase of Lorenz from this paper. The key phrase in Lorenz' original paper, was "people of the other sex"; but was translated by Eisenberg as "men of the other race." Thus, inferring that Lorenz was a Nazi. When his biographer, Nisbett, asked Lorenz in 1974 whether he thought that the effects of man's self-domestication would ever be studied to his satisfaction, Lorenz answer was: "The 1940 paper tried to tell the Nazis that domestication was much more dangerous than any alleged mixture of races. I still believe that domestication threatens humanity; it is a very great danger. And if I can atone for the (retrospectively) incredible stupidity of having tried to tell the Nazis about this, it is by telling the same obvious truth to quite another sort of society which likes it still less, that same truth!"

Nisbett points out that today, Wilson (and his colleagues) associated with Sociobiology are attacked "at exactly the same point in his argument: the extrapolation to man of what is seen as a politically suspect biological determinism."

Oversimplifying for the sake of brevity, the underlying problem here is that, although it is generally admitted that human bodily structures and internal organs developed out of similar structures in animals, when it comes to the concept that human behavior also has a long evolutionary history and can no more be changed overnight than we can change the basic structure of a leg overnight, there is controversy. Many special interest groups ranging from Christians to "new age" thinkers to Skinnerian psychologists find this untenable. But essentially biological determinism for us humans has to do with fundamental needs of all warm blooded animals—the need for food, sex, interaction with the group (bonding), and, in the northern hemisphere, warmth from the sun. Since we are warm blooded animals, we have the same basic needs and much of our pathology comes from being denied these basic needs in modern civilization. Going even deeper, this refusal to recognize that we truly do come out of nature and have the same basic needs as our animal relatives, contributes to our destruction of nature. I will be going more into these matters throughout Part II of this volume.

What we can learn from cats—the work of Paul Leyhausen

To show how these biological factors work, I will turn to the work of Paul Leyhausen. Furthermore his work also provides us with the simplest account of the sophisticated procedures used by our mammal relatives to limit aggression, that I have found anywhere in my reading of the literature. Of course, these methods have been forgotten by our modern Industrial Growth Society (IGS).

No account of ethology findings can be easily summarized or shortened because the process of discovery depends on day-by-day accounts of the animal's interactions with others and the environment. So I will go into one account in some detail rather than just list the final results. Leyhausen points out some reasons why so few studies have been done on the higher mammals (which are most directly connected to our actions, of course). He says that the higher mammals are not only larger but have "a significantly longer developmental cycle than the small birds, fishes, and insects ethologists prefer. Observing them—or, even more so, keeping and breeding them in large numbers—requires a disproportionately large expenditure in terms of time, money, and space, and results take so much longer to come." Leyhausen studies *Felidae* (cats), which he says are a relatively small group containing only some forty species. His book contains papers on many different aspects of the subject but the one I am referring to here is titled, "Social Organization and Density Tolerance in Mammals."

He begins by stating that methods by which birds, insects, fish etc. space their populations out have been intensively studied, but the methods by which such populations of individuals retain contact with each other have rarely been studied. All the territorial dispersal tactics—fights, displays etc. are much easier to see in the field than any possible "centripetal tendencies." To study the latter would require "uninterrupted, continuous day-and-night records." He and his collaborator, R. Wolff, were the only ones to try—and that on a population of free-ranging domestic cats. They chose an isolated farmhouse in a clearing. The farmhouse had two resident cats and another cat living in a farm only 600 yards away. But the study proved so complex that they could only get a complete record of the activities of one cat. To follow all three would have taken three "well-trained, physically fit, and inexhaustible observers." When they finished the study and published the paper they felt they hadn't accomplished much; but later, after they had compared it with their separate extensive observations through the years on city cats, they discovered they did have much valuable data.

Bateson's "lab-dog" story is relevant here. You can see, now, why people prefer to study animals (or people) in the lab—it so much simpler. Of course, the fact that it has little to do with the real life of the animal is not considered important.

To get gack to the cats. By the time they did this study, Wolff had studied cats in two suburbs of Hamburg and Leyhausen had studied them in the gardens facing his parent's home in Bonn, some cats in Wales, and a small population in a garden area in Zurich for two and a half years. What they discovered is of considerable interest to all of us but especially to those trying to preserve any tiny part of the natural environment.

The individual domestic cat owns a territory which consists of a "first-order home, usually a room or even a special corner in a room of the house where it lives, and a home range which consists of a varying number of more or less regularly visited localities connected by an elaborate network of pathways." Right around the first-order home is the house and garden and the resident cat uses practically every part of this. And beyond that are the paths to places for hunting, courting, contests and fighting etc.

The pathway-networks of neighboring cats overlap. All the cats in the area commonly use the same pathways and also, sometimes, hunting grounds and lookout posts—and especially, in northern cities, the sunbathing spots. This is not simultaneous use, of course, and the animals avoid direct encounters. According to Hediger, many species of animals prevent direct encounter "by following a rather definite timetable, scheduled like a railway timetable so as to make collisions unlikely."

Over a period of time, neighboring cats will work out a rather strict schedule for the good sunbathing spots—especially in winter. However if one cat approaches the sunbathing spot while the other cat is still there, instead of a direct confrontation, the approaching cat sits down and begins cleaning its face—a "displacement activity." Similar responses in humans can be seen—combing back the hair with the hand, smoothing the mustache, tucking in locks of hair, rubbing the nose etc. These are procedures which are not really needed but occur automatically, without thinking, in approaching another person when the relationship is unsure.

Because cats regulate their traffic by visual contact, when the cat sitting in the sun sees the other one approaching, it begins to get ready to move away, gracefully. If two animals, still relatively new to one another, unexpectedly encounter one another then a clash results until a ranking order is established. Even with a lower order cat, a dominant cat does not automatically get its turn at important spots like sun bathing spots. At such spots, the dominant cat will be seen to wait its turn.

At twilight, there occurs the complex cat "paseo"—very similar to the famous paseo as done by humans in the village square in most Spanish speaking countries until the advent of cars. As Leyhausen explains, both male and female cats come to a common meeting place and "just sit around—not far apart—two to five yards or even less—some individuals in actual contact, sometimes licking or grooming each other. There is very little sound, the faces are friendly and only occasionally an ear flattens or a small hiss or growl is heard when an animal closes in too much on a shy member of the gathering." Just as in a human paseo where one smiles at friends, snubs an enemy or conciliates a new rival. And just as in the human paseo, the only threat display seen among cats is a tomcat "parading a little just for fun." In the Paris population of cats, Leyhausen reports that the social gathering would go on for hours, but, usually, around midnight the cats returned to their own sleeping places. During this gathering all were on the same social level—even though at other times particular cats could be seen chasing each other or furiously fighting.

Only females with young regularly and fiercely defend the home territory. When adult tomcats first meet, they fight fiercely but within a short time it has been decided "which is the stronger or the more tenacious, courageous fighter of the two." After that they settle their difficulties by display and there is no more serious fighting. Contrary to general opinion there is not one single dominating tyrant tomcat in the group, excluding all others from mating, mainly because ultimately the female cat has the choice of her partner.

But the more crowded it gets, in the *Felidae* species as in other species, the less relative hierarchy there is. For instance, in a crowded laboratory or a zoo cage, "Eventually a despot emerges, 'pariahs' appear, driven to frenzy and all kinds of neurotic behavior by continuous and pitiless attack by all the others; the community turns into a spiteful mob. They all seldom relax, they never look at ease, and there is ontinuous hissing, growling and even fighting. Play stops altogether and locomotion and exercise are reduced to a minimum."

General Background of Ethology

Tinbergen has given the best overview of ethology, which I will summarize before going further. He defines ethology as "the biological study of behavior and therefore involves four classes of questions, which concern respectively the causation, ontogeny, survival value, and evolution of behavior." The word, survival, here does not primarily refer to the survival of the individual, but of the species. Today, when man threatens the earth itself, we can extend this concept to include the survival of the natural environment.

Tinbergen points out that Darwin was the actual forerunner of ethology. He can't be termed the founder because he had no immediate followers. Darwin realized that if he were trying to explain evolution of animal species by means of natural selection it had to be applied to everything to do with the animal—both structural and functional. Animal behavior could not be ignored even though it was much easier to study the functional items such as how the many toes on the foot of the ancient horse developed into the hoof of the modern horse. Darwin felt that "behavior patterns" should be treated as "organs" too. The reason why there was such a long time lag before anyone else took up this line of research is that the whole idea of evolution was so new that biologists, after Darwin. concentrated on "phylogeny," the course evolution had taken as in the example of the horse's hoof above. So the concentration was on comparative anatomy. Another aspect of the problem was that religious belief hampered the study of animals, which were human-like such as the primates, so the safest thing to study were those further away—fish, insects and birds. A third factor was that observing behavior is extremely complex—so complex that it's not even possible to describe it except by pages and pages devoted to one simple action. Experiential analysis of the entire behavior sequence would take far more pages.

In 1914, Huxley in Britain and in 1911, Heinroth in Germany began to study the behavior of birds. Huxley started with male displays such as the peacock's tail as a signal to attract females. He showed that both the male's action of displaying the tail and the female's reaction were parts of a single action which he called a "signalling system." Work with birds was much safer because generally people do not identify with birds as much as they do with monkeys.

Huxley called Lorenz, "the father of modern ethology." Lorenz' work concentrated on "innate" behavior—how a particular behavior develops within the individual animal over the time of that animal's particular life—and on a learning process which he called "imprinting." He also worked on the integration of both innate and learned behavior in the adult animal. Because most of the early papers on ethology were in German, interest in this new field was, at first, concentrated in Germany and Holland.

General interest in ethology went through three stages: at first, this new approach was mostly ignored; then, as it became apparent it would have wider influence than first thought, it was attacked; and most recently, it's findings have become so self-evident that people tend to forget that they weren't always known.

Instead of saying that animal and human behavior are the same, which is somewhat of an oversimplification, modern ethologists now claim that they have developed methods of study which could and should be applied to human behavior.

Tinbergen explains that any thinking to do with biology—and this includes ethology—is essentially concerned with two problems: "that of causation and that of function in the sense of survival value." In other words, "what makes this happen?" and "how do the effects of what happens influence survival including reproduction?" As increasing research goes on, "the distinction between the fields of ethological, psychological, and physiological research is beginning to fade."

One of the aspects of ethology most useful to the study of human behavior is the problem of innate and acquired behavior. Of particular interest here are the ways in which the non-learned component of complex behavior chains are further programmed and integrated by interactions with the environment. Tinbergen's example concerns squirrels and hazel nuts. Squirrels are able to crack hazel nuts very efficiently by first getting them into a position so that they can "gnaw selectively along the pre-formed groove where the shell is thin; then quickly weakening this groove, and finally cracking the shell along this weakened line." Squirrels raised alone, without the influence of older squirrels and without nuts, do develop ways of manipulating items in their paws and ways of gnawing and biting (all innate), but it's all very irregular. They gnaw all over the nut's surface so that it takes a long time to get the shell weak enough to crack it. It takes them much longer and a great deal of practice to develop a skill that comes quickly to a young squirrel when there are older ones around that it can watch.

This kind of research is useful in understanding human behavior, but we cannot deliberately interfere with children's long-term development in order to do such research directly on humans. Tinbergen sums up the situation: "At the moment, it is neither scientific to claim actual knowledge of our innate behavioural equipment nor that we are infinitely mouldable—that, say, our aggression can be eliminated entirely by educational measures." Studies so far show "how beautifully and intricately the behaviour of each species is adapted to its needs." But this kind of research is very time-consuming and expensive. According to Tinbergen, there are several reasons "why the power of natural selection on moulding behaviour is still much underrated. First, few biologists are engaged in this type of research; the successes of the physical sciences having drawn much of the available talent to physiology, biochemistry, and biophysics. Second, our knowledge of the many pressures that the natural environment exerts on each species is still extremely poor. Third, the analytical method forces us to select for study one behaviour characteristic and one environmental pressure at a time, and one of the very natural reactions after one such study is to think that an animal could perform a particular task much better than it does." Here, again, we see the problem of the "substance" approach characteristic of our European culture.

Tinbergen gives a good example of the complexity of such matters in real life—that of young birds, which are camouflaged as a protection against certain predators. Camouflaged color patterns are useful only when the bird is motionless. But they have to eat and thus move so their behavior has to be a compromise. For instance, the young bird feeds normally, but "freezes" when the parent spots a predator and gives the alarm. "While they could feed more efficiently if they never had to freeze, and would be better protected against predators if they never had to move, they can do neither, and selection, rewarding overall success rather than any isolated characteristics, has produced compromises." This "compromise" in real life, of course takes into consideration all the relationships involved in that species' life.

Tinbergen's final conclusion here is: "Animal behaviourists agree that the conception of Man as an infinitely adjustable species, of which each individual can in its lifetime be modified behaviourally by educational measures to any desired extent, is not necessarily correct; in fact it is *highly unlikely to be true.*" (My italics, for emphasis) Even if it were true, he states that "it would still be abundantly clear that, in our ignorance of the natural control of behaviour ontogeny, we have not yet found the best ways of guiding the development of young individuals." This is why it is necessary for us to allow our young children to play freely. This is the only way that their innate behaviour, as programmed by thousands of years of natural development, can be allowed to develop. See Part III of this volume for more on play in all its dimensions.

Human Emotions

The evolution of human behavior, of course, is more difficult to study than the evolution and use of bodily parts such as arms, legs, teeth etc. Two factors contribute to this—human society is exceedingly complex and the human life span is much longer than other animals. The key to understanding here lies in studying behavior that has gone wrong in the human; just as Freud and Jung began their studies by trying to figure out bizarre psychological behaviors. Konrad Lorenz remarked that when his friend, Bernhard Hellman, saw something odd or weird in the behavior of a captive animal, he asked: "Is this how the constructor meant it?" Lorenz explains, "The 'constructor' being, of course, the factors of evolution which cause structures and functions to achieve survival value." Lorenz feels that a good clue to "the normal" consists in the question "was it meant thus by the constructor." An example, coming out of physiology concerns the Swiss surgeon Kocher, the man who first suspected that the thyroid gland had something to do with Basedow's disease. Kocher removed the thyroid from a number of patients, finding eventually that the disease was not due to any basic change in the function of the thyroid but "to a simple excess of it."

Going still deeper, Lorenz writes: "My late friend Ronald Hargreaves, whom I consider to have been one of the most inspired psychiatrists, once wrote to me that he had disciplined himself to ask whenever he was confronted by some unexplained mental trouble, two simultaneous questions: a) what is the primal survival value of the function here miscarrying? and b) is the malfunction due to an excess or to a deficiency?" The answers to this double question have proved so useful that it seems to "indicate that the sensory-neural system underlying

human behavior, and the innumerable independent motivations it produces, act very much like endocrine glands." In addition there seems to be a necessary self-regulating balance between what Lorenz calls "antagonistic factors." Although recent research in neurophysiology has gone much deeper into these matters, it is caught in the usual "substance" trap and forgotten the "self-regulating balance" aspect.

EMOTIONS

The overall system of human society is so complex that it seems hopeless to figure out where to begin, but, fortunately, human languages throughout the world have labelled the same types of behaviors. Of course the words used are different in each language but the behaviors are the same. As Lorenz points out these behaviors are "labelled by such words as love, friendship, hate, jealousy, envy, lust, fear and rage—but still their number is *finite...*" He continues by explaining that the "question whether any of these motivations be 'good' or 'bad' is quite as much beside the point as to ask whether the thyroid gland be good or bad...On the other hand, it does make sense to ask, in respect to any disturbance of social behavior, whether there is an excess or a deficiency of one of these motivations." Lorenz' concludes that, "Nobody in his right senses can doubt that humanity is a system which at present is thoroughly out of balance, in fact, threatened with destruction...re-establishment of the lost equilibrium is only possible on the base of causal insight into the mechanisms of the normal regulative functions, as well as into the nature of their disturbance." In still another one of his papers, Lorenz is even more emphatic:

> Ronald Hargreaves' double question ought to make everybody realize how inane it is to attribute the adjectives 'good' or 'bad' to any mechanism of behavior, such as love, aggression...and so on. Like any endocrine gland, every one of these mechanisms is indispensable and, again like a gland, every one, by its excess function, can lead to a destructive disequilibration. There is no human vice which is anything else than the excess of a function which, in itself, is indispensable for the survival of the species.

I might add here that to label one emotion such as anger, "bad," and another emotion such as love, "good" is just as stupid as saying that the heart is good and the lungs bad. We can't live without either of them—they are both necessary. And the findings of ethology do show us, just as definitely, that *all* the emotions are necessary for real living.

INNATE BEHAVIOR

How do we know that behaviors are built into our genetic programming? In the case of something like a hand—it's easy to explain. The entire evolutionary history of the hand is well known. The matter of behavior is more complex but just as obvious. Startling evidence comes from the films that Eibl-Eibesfeldt made of small children who had been born deaf and blind. These films show that "they smile and laugh as we do when happy and emit the correct sounds when they do so...they weep as we do, stamp their feet, clench their fists and frown when something annoys them."

These children later lose many of these outward manifestations of behavior for lack of reinforcement, but the point is that they are born with these expressions. They cannot have learned them because they have never seen another human being doing these actions. In essence, we inherit such displays from our animal ancestors. For instance, the smile developed from the nervous pulling back of the lips to show the teeth when confronting an unknown con-specific. You can check on this by realizing how automatically a nervous smile comes to your lips in threatening situations. Laughter has developed out of the higher primates "play face," which they display when "playing" at fighting.

Flirting turns out to be practically identical in every human group. Eibl-Eibesfeldt has filmed such behavior all over the world. He explains: "We found agreement in the smallest detail in the flirting behavior of girls from Samoa, Papua, France, Japan, Africa and South American Indians. The flirting girl at first smiles at the person to whom it is directed and lifts her eyebrows with a quick, jerky movement upward so that the eye slit is briefly enlarged. Flirting men show the same movement of the eyebrow, which can also be observed during a friendly greeting between members of the same sex. After this initial, obvious turning toward the person, in the flirt there follows a turning away. The head is turned to the side, sometimes bent toward the ground, the gaze is lowered, and the eyelids are dropped...Frequently, but not always, the girl may cover her face with a hand and she may laugh or smile in embarrassment. She continues to look at the partner out of the corners of her eyes."

In the mating foreplay of many mammals, the flight of the female is ritualized with the "coy behavior" really being an invitation to pursue her. The reason for the similarity in all these preliminary sexual overtures, is that mating behavior is important to the continuance of the species so the signals must be clear and unambiguous. Humans, of course, often confuse the issue by saying one thing when their body language clearly indicates the opposite.

The behavior of the adult in caring for the young is the foundation for all future behavior and socialization, especially in the sexual sphere. In all mammals the young ones send out specific signals that cause or "release" (the term in ethology) cherishing behavior in the adults. These signals can be by means of the sense of smell, sight or hearing. For instance, young baboons have black coats up to their sixth month. Even old males will help the black coated young one. The dark brown langur has an almost golden yellow coat when an infant. While it is golden, all females will care for it automatically. In humans, the small infant has a big head in relation to its body, a high forehead, chubby cheeks and large eyes. It also has short rounded arms and legs. These "cute" attributes bring out a protective feeling in adults.

In birds there is a very close tie between courtship and care of the young as well. Offering of nesting material often begins the courtship. This has turned into a ritualized signal between male and female. The seizing of the beak of the adult bird by the young one comes out of the fledgling begging for food and then being fed. Adult ravens also seize one another's beaks during courtship.

In higher species, kissing is related to the care of the young. Chimpanzees chew up food and then pass it to the young, mouth to mouth as do many other animals. Adult chimpanzees feed one another mouth to mouth as a friendly gesture. Eibl-Eibesfeldt remarks that until quite recently country women in Austria fed their babies in this manner. In modern advertisements, often lovers are shown passing food from mouth to mouth; for instance each holding the same cracker between their teeth or each biting opposite sides of the fruit at the same time.

Concerning Child Development

Nature has provided a built-in program for the newly born so that it can survive. Among animals this program unfolds without any interference from the adults; while among humans this is not always the case. Growing childhood autism is an indication of what can happen when adults (by intention or well-meaning stupidity) short circuit the built-in programming of emotional development. Although you might think that this is important only to the damaged children and their parents; Tinbergen, on the contrary, recognizes that autism is an indication of the failure of real socialization in our culture. He felt this matter was so important that he spoke out about it in the speech he gave when he received the Nobel Prize (along with Konrad Lorenz and K. von Frisch).

He begins by remarking on "the unconventional decision of the Nobel Foundation to award this year's prize...to three men who had until recently been regarded as 'mere animal watchers'." He points out that finally their work is "being acknowledged as an integral part of the eminently practical field of medicine." Concerning autism, he begins by explaining that Leo Kanner first described it in 1943 and that it is definitely on the increase in Westernized societies. He lists its effects: "In various degrees of severity, it involves, among other things, a total withdrawal from the environment; a failure to acquire, or a regression of, overt speech; a serious lagging behind in the acquisition of numerous other skills, obsessive preoccupation with a limited number of objects; the performance of seemingly senseless and stereotyped movements; and an EEG pattern that indicates high overall arousal." Some recover but others end up in mental hospitals, often diagnosed as schizophrenics.

He and his wife became interested in autism when they realized that normal children at times can show these behaviors. He says that many psychiatrists do not heed the warning that "it is not informative to study variations of behaviour unless we know beforehand the norm from which the variants depart." And, since many autists would not speak, they realized that a better insight into their illness would have to be based on their nonverbal behavior. "And it is just in this sphere that we could apply some of the methods that had already proved their value in studies of animal behavior." They turned their attention to the normal child's behavior, which at times, can include "such things as the child's keeping its distance from a strange person or situation, details of its facial expressions, its bodily stance and its consistent avoidance of making eye contact—an extremely rich set of expressions that are all correlated with overt avoidance."

Long before they began studying austistic children, Tinbergen and his wife had worked out ways of meeting children without causing any of this "conflict." He says that when visiting a family that has young children, after a "very brief, friendly glance, ignore the children completely," at the same time talking with parents but watching the child out of the corner of your eyes. Once in a while, look directly at the child, very briefly. If the child averts its glance, look away. Eventually, the child will stop studying the adult and approach "gingerly" and "reveal its strong bonding tendency by touching one." Such a gesture might be putting a hand tentatively on your knee. This is the "crucial moment." One must not respond by looking at the child as that will set things back; instead respond by "cautiously touching the child's hand." If this seems alright then a game begins by touching and withdrawing between you and the child. Eventually eye contact becomes possible—maybe a game like "peek-a-boo" or "where's Mike," using the child's name. "Once established, the bond can be maintained by surprisingly slight signals." Vocal contact can work too. Bird's calls are basically, "I am here, where are you?" Many children develop an individual contact call, to which one has merely to answer in the same language.

Tinbergen points out that many autistic children are first born children of parents who are "very serious people, people who are themselves under some sort of strain [they are] overefficient and intrusive."

The proven cure is quite basic. The original "defective affiliation with the mother" must be restored and mother and child helped toward proper socialization, which is the heart of the cure.

In one such case, involving three boys, who had all been professionally diagnosed as severely autistic, and who, at the ages of nine to eleven are now being gently integrated into a normal primary school with "results little short of spectacular." Tinbergen reports that a specialist on autistic children, who visited the school told him: "Had the records not shown that these three children were still severely autistic a couple of years ago, I would not now believe it." Tinbergen continues: "This type of evidence, together with that provided by a number of already published case histories has by now convinced us that many autists can attain a full recovery, if only we act on the assumption that they have been traumatized rather than genetically or organically damaged...and our work on normal children has convinced us not only that this type of stress disease is actually on the increase in Western and Westernized countries, but also that very many children must be regarded as semi-autistic, and even more are being seriously at risk."

What Tinbergen's work with autistic children shows us is that modern, well-meaning people are guilty of so far ignoring both their own and their child's basic inbuilt behavior that they are unable to allow their own children to become fully human when all the necessary behaviors are innate and programmed by a hundred thousand years of successful evolutionary development. Play is the one thing necessary for the child in order to allow nature's programs to develop, yet overanxious parents are unwilling to admit this. The famous educator, Jerome Bruner states that play's role during immaturity "appears to be more and more central as one moves up the living primate series from Old World monkeys through Great Apes, to Man—suggesting that in the evolution of primates, marked by an increase in the number of years of immaturity, the selection of a capacity for play during those years may have been crucial." In fact, as Bruner explains "primatologists [are] pondering it's possible centrality in evolution!" See Part III of this work for more on play during childhood and its further development in ritual.

"The appreciation of the separate realities enjoyed by other organisms is not only no threat to our own reality, but the root of a fundamental joy. I learned from River that I was a human being and that he was a wolf and that we were different. I valued him as a creature, but he did not have to be what I imagined he was. It is with this freedom from dogma, I think, that the meaning of the words 'the celebration of life' becomes clear."

Barry Lopez

"The brain as an organ of thought is available for our use only because it was formed and developed before our time. Our organ of thought may be superior, and we play it better, but it is surely vain to believe that other possessors of similar instruments leave them quite untouched."

Donald Griffin

"[A]n archetype...has the divine quality, and that is <u>always based upon the animal</u>. Therefore the gods are symbolized as animals; even the holy ghost is a bird, all the antique gods and the exotic gods are animals at the same time...<u>naturally in possession of the wisdom of nature</u>, like any animal or plant, <u>but the wisdom is represented by a being that is not conscious of itself,</u> and therefore cannot be called wisdom."

C.G. Jung

CHAPTER FIVE

"We are not just rather like animals; we <u>are</u> animals."

Mary Midgley

"We patronize them for their incompleteness, for their tragic fate of having taken form so far below ourselves. And therein we err, and greatly err. For the animal shall not be measured by man. In a world older and more complete than ours they move finished and complete, gifted with extensions of the senses we have lost or never attained, living by voices we shall never hear. They are not brethren, they are not underlings; they are other nations, caught with ourselves in the net of life and time, fellow &beingsé of the splendour and travail of the earth."
Harry Beston

"[According to Erikson] the numinous emotion has its ontogenetic basis in the relationship of the preverbal infant to its mother…[This] mother-child relationship among humans is but a variant of the primate or even mammalian pattern, it may be that the basis of the numinous is archaic, antedating humanity, and it may further be that religion came into being when the emerging, discursive, conventional sacred [of the early human] was lashed to the primordial, non-discursive, mammalian emotional processes that in their later form we call 'numinous.'"
Roy Rappaport

"It is not the case that man, as the being possessed of the highest intellect, stands alone in the universe. His mind is also the mind of birds and beasts, of grass and trees."
Chu Hsi (1130-1200 A.D.)

 RELATIONSHIPS BETWEEN ANIMAL AND HUMAN

Personal Introduction

Of the many encounters I have had with animals in the wild, the one which is most important here concerns the marmot, sunbathing on top of 14,000 ft. Crestone Peak in Colorado; because during this hour-long experience we, humans and the marmot were in a continuous, on-going relationship.

As mentioned elsewhere in this volume, each summer Rick Medrick and I do a program called BREAKING THROUGH. Toward the end of the seven days, we lead our clients up Crestone Peak. Two years ago, as we neared the summit ridge, we met three climbers who had just completed the technical Ellingwood Arete and were on their way down. We exchanged greetings because we had seen them start up the Arete very early that morning. Then we continued onto the small summit itself. When we first climbed over onto the summit block I noticed a perfectly relaxed marmot, sitting in the sun on the far side of the area, with his back to us. Then, as he heard the rattle of loose rock, he turned and looked over his shoulder. Seeing us, he tensed up in a defensive posture, with his head sunk down between his shoulders. Obviously, he was just disgusted that here were more humans interrupting his siesta in the sun when he had just got rid of the first bunch. He turned back to face the sun, not moving from his original position. Our people always show considerable respect for wild life. Some took photos but none bothered him directly. So, after a few more glances back, he relaxed and lay there just as we lay there in the glorious mountain sun. Then, somewhat later as our people had rested and eaten, they began to wander about the small area. Seeing this, the marmot got to his feet and then circled entirely around us to the place where we had first come up onto the ridge. Here he put his arms (forepaws) around a standing rock and leaned up against it—still basking in the sun but on his feet.

When it came time to begin the descent and all of us started stuffing things in packs, the marmot turned and climbed down among some rocks, seemingly heading back to his original spot. Then, as we began filing by on our way off the summit area, he climbed up a narrow crack, put his two hands, (forepaws) on either side of the crack and lifted himself out (in a perfect climbing maneuver) and looked directly at us with a smug expression. We all cracked up with laughter. A marmot does not have to climb such a crack in that fashion. Normally, he just uses his feet and claws to go directly up any rough surface and arrives on top on all fours. It seemed like he was showing us he could climb our way—just as well as we could. Now, of course he probably was not consciously doing that—but who knows? What all of us did know was that for over an hour we and the marmot had taken part in a continuous interchange of messages while we all sat in the high mountain sun, which to both him and us was the main factor, around which all of us mammals were organizing our behavior. Relaxation in the sun was the main activity—not competition or aggression or annoying one another. We respected his prior rights and he acknowledged this by no fear and staying right there on top where the sun was shining; instead of having to go down into the shadows below. On the way down we began joking about our "marmot guru," sitting wisely up there on the mountain top. Marmots do not ordinarily sit on summits because they

don't live up there. In fact that's the first time I ever found one up on top of the mountain. They are usually found sunning themselves down among the rocks where they live.

In this marmot experience we and the marmot shared body language in response to the importance of the sun's warmth on high mountains thus there was no need for spoken words to communicate.

The other outstanding animal experience I've had was also on a mountain—just below the summit of Golden Horn, a 12,900 ft. peak near Silverton. I climb it often, not only because it is a beautiful mountain but to do Tai Chi on the flat platform, the glacier had carved out for us, just below the summit. This particular time, a friend and I had climbed to the top and then come back down to do Tai Chi on this platform which is about 12,500 ft. high. As we finished, birds were chirping out on every side. This is most unusual at such an altitude, and, for a moment we were thinking they had come around in response to the energy of Tai Chi. (Domestic cats always do this and sit in the midst of it; dogs will lie quietly nearby and never disturb you while it's going on.) Then, we both felt something over our shoulder. Turning we looked directly into the eyes of a pine martin, with its glorious tail waving above it, in the wind. He was not the least afraid of us and seemed to be just wondering what was going on; because for at least several more minutes he just looked at us. Then, I assume, because he no longer felt any more of that Tai Chi energy, he turned and disappeared among the rocks on his way down. Then we realized why the birds had been so noisy. He'd climbed up the buttress from tree line, robbing nests on the way and those were alarm calls. Pine martins don't live that high.

I've lived in areas where there are pine martins for years and never seen one before. They are not prone to be near humans at all. Few people ever see them. This one deliberately came to see what we were doing, because he "felt" something different than the usual energy that human beings put out. There's no other reason for a pine martin to be sitting there watching you until you turn around and even then, still standing there, looking at you. Again, no words need be spoken, we exchanged information by means of our common mammalian body language.

Preview

Animals were the teachers of the first humans—showing them what to eat for food; plants to eat for medicine and how to live and even how to die. Animals continue to teach us if we give them a chance. We can learn far more from watching an animal in the wild (when it is involved with its mammalian relationships with all around it) than from cutting it up into pieces in a laboratory to study how a chemical works inside it (substance) and thereby killing it. Below I will go more into what we modern people can learn from animals in the wild.

Animals also continue to teach us through our own older brains—the limbic (midbrain) and so-called reptile brain, (brain stem). Jung suggested that animals in dreams represent activity in these regions and that the "lower" the animal on the phylogenetic scale, the more primitive the region of the brain which is showing activity. The serpent, since the time of Hippolytus has been identified with the spinal cord and the brain stem itself. Snake dreams occur when these oldest brain centers within us are registering activity.

Fear of snakes seems to correlate with our fear of these oldest levels within us, not with actual experience of snakes. Americans have the least experience with snakes and are the most fearful. Peter Steinhart in an essay, "Fear of Snakes" points out that "In India there are 200,000 snakebites and 9,000 fatalities a year. But Hindus are said to tolerate cobras in their houses. In Africa, there are 100,000 bites and 10,000 fatalities. But, [quoting Drewes, who wrote] 'I have never seen the kind of advanced phobias you have here'...In America, there are 8000 snakebites a year, a third of which, are visited upon zoo-keepers and others who handle snakes regularly...Only a dozen people die in the United States each year from snakebite."

Our general fear of wild animals, which is connected with our fear of the animal in us, results in a complete disregard for animal suffering. The claim here is that "they don't feel it." Long ago, in France, Voltaire asked the vivisector: "You discover in it all the same organs of feeling that are in yourself. Answer me, mechanist, has nature arranged all the means of feeling in this animal so that it may not feel?" And Jeremy Bentham explained: "The question is not, Can they *reason*? nor Can they *talk*? but Can they *suffer?*"

Below, because of lack of space, I can only go into detail concerning three of the animals that humans have learned from:

the bear, the wolf-wild dog-coyote type, and the salmon. I will not be discussing what we owe to our immediate ancestors, the higher primates because that is fairly well known. Next I will go into "totemism," leaving my main discussion on the fact that the first gods in cultures all over the world were animals for Part III of this volume.

Acknowledging that animals are our teachers, brings about a real change in our thinking. To show the depth of this change, I want to quote from the anonymous author of the Bear Claw Press calendar for 1977:

> The earliest cultures followed the paths of animals: hunters from the Siberian taiga tracked bears and caribou into North America...It utterly reverses the European view, not only by reconnecting the human destiny with its habitat and fellow-creatures, but by recovering the natural history of Northern peoples and animals, moving together across the land masses.

Paul Shepard goes on from there and remarks that "In tracing the circumpolar traditions of the bear ceremonies, we transcend the usual opposition of European and Native American origins, and that of Asian versus European, because the metaphysical bear legends are a shared heritage, perhaps part of the oldest traditions of mankind. This modification of our history reflects also our new sense of the bear as more than an external being—as part of the deep reality of the human self."

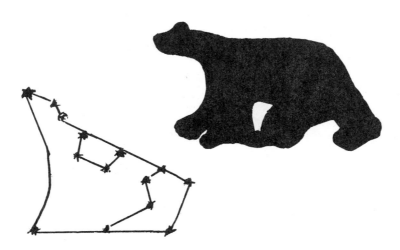

The Bear

> The boundary of Dawn and Evening is the Bear; and opposite the Bear, the Watchman of luminous Zeus.

Heraclitus, the early Greek philosopher thus paid tribute to the importance of the Great Bear in the Sky. Here Dawn stands for the east and Evening for the west. The Bear in the sky is the constellation, Ursus Major. The watchman, *ouros*, opposite the Bear (arktos) must be the important star, Arcturus (Arkt-ouros), whose risings and settings commonly serve to mark the seasons. Here in this fragment from Heraclitus we can see that in the very beginnings of European culture,

for the ancient Greeks, before the time of Plato, the Bear served to mark the limits of the Greek world—both in space and in time. Just as the Great Bear in the sky marked the year for the Skidi Pawnee and other primitive societies as well as for the Chinese, Siberian, and other northern hemisphere cultures.

Since the Big Dipper constellation is much more familiar to most people, in order to find the Bear in the sky, think of the Dipper as a kind of saddle on the back of the Great Bear. As Paul Shepard explains: "At night, the Great Bear comes up, crosses the northern sky, makes a great arc around the North Star, and in doing so sweeps the whole half of the sky and brings the dawn." This is the great hunt in the sky.

In some cultures the Bear is the hunted and in others, the hunter. "The 'pursuit' was like a great gear on an invisible axis, driving the whole stellar panorama through the night, bringing the rising sun, whose brightness was therefore also the bear's doing."

The bear lives on earth but goes underground each year (dies) and is reborn the next spring. Not only that, but she brings back new life (cubs); thus teaching early humans about everlasting life. The oldest burials are associated with Bear bones and bear skulls in niches of the rock wall as in the Drachenloch cave in Switzerland, dating back to Neanderthal times, roughly 50,000 years ago. Emil Bachler, who discovered the cave declared that the cave "supplies the first evidence in man of an already awakened higher spiritual life."

The dictionary shows more than forty-four meanings for the verb "to bear"—in three different categories: navigation, transportation and transformation. We take our "bearings" on the stars in the sky or landmarks; we "bear" burdens and females "bear" children. What all these words show us is that "at some stage, the bear provided the most compelling example or even the concrete reality around which a concept was shaped in human thought." Even today when "the bear no longer seems to be a transcendent being, we can nonetheless see that, deep in our unconscious, where language 'means' in multiple ways, the bear's sacredness is still part of our lives."

When the bear goes underground to hibernate in the fall, it eats various indigestible things such as bark, which form a plug. The bear eats nothing all winter but neither does anything go out. There is no defecation. So, in the spring the bear must eat the proper plants to start the whole process of digestion and elimination. Since the bear (*Ursus*) has been on earth some two and a half million years, it has had time to learn a lot about plants that heal us. Shepard lists some 35 herbs which have the word, "bear" in their common name—such as bear clover, bear grass, bear tongue etc. These are only a few of the hundreds of "bear" herbs, used by cultures throughout the world.

Finally, I will mention a few random aspects concerning how deeply the bear lies within our consciousness. The classical Greek goddesses, Artemis and Demeter were bear goddesses before they became humanized. A young mother I know, Pam Johnson, after hearing Paul Shepard's bear lecture went home and took a look at the children's books she had in the house. Out of her total of forty five books; only twelve of them did not have a picture of a bear! Of course everyone knows how important "teddy bears" have been to children for generations. And finally, C. G. Jung recounts many dreams his patients have of "bear-goddesses" who are "maternally protective." Often, in dreams the bear symbolizes the deeper unconscious layers of the person's psyche.

Wolves-dogs-coyotes

To begin with, early human social organization was probably learned from the Cape hunting dogs. In their paper, "The Relevance of Carnivore Behavior to the Study of Early Hominids," George Schaller and Gordon Lowther suggest just this. The earliest proto-human's meat diet was limited to particular birds and reptiles and the slowest of mammals— possibly the young. But, when humans became organized hunters it was a wholly different matter, and they undoubtedly learned hunting techniques from watching the Cape hunting dogs, the most efficient hunters in the world. Some of the hunting dog's habits would be imitated by the proto-humans. For instance, apes do not bring food back for the young; but these dogs always do, regurgitating it for the pups and going out for more. Also dogs had homes in the ground—holes or caves—which have to be kept clean. Apes, however, live in trees where waste matter automatically falls down to the ground. Everyone knows how easy it is to "housebreak" a dog and how impossible it is to ever housebreak a monkey. Some authorities suggest that it was the dog who "housebroke" us humans. Livingston sums this up when he writes: "Early man was undoubtedly a carnivore who preyed on large mammals; hence the social organization and behavior of the wolf is of theoretical relevance to the reconstruction of early hominid behavior.

The wolf, *Canis lupus* was "probably parent to the domestic dog, *Canis familiaris*, the first large creature who would live with men. Today the wolf's closest relatives are the domestic dog, the dingo, the coyote, and the jackal. Of them all, the wolf is perhaps the most socially evolved and intelligent," according to Barry Lopez in his book, *Of Wolves and Men*. In this book Lopez explains how human hunters have relied on the wolf to find the caribou for them at times when hunting is difficult.

Wolves and human hunters use similar techniques in particular areas. Pueblo Indians and wolves in the Southwest ran deer to exhaustion. In the prairie grass of Wyoming, both the wolf and the Shoshoni Indian lay flat on the ground—the wolf slowly waving its tail; the Indian waving a strip of hide to attract the curious antelope so that it gets close enough to kill.

Conscious identification with the wolf was a mystical experience, not merely practical. The wolf appears in many Indian legends as a messenger or guide for anyone seeking the spirit world. Blind Bull, a Cheyenne shaman learned about things he needed to know from the "comings and goings of wolves, from listening to their howls." Summing up the Indian relationship to the wolf, Lopez writes: "At a *tribal* level, the attraction to the wolf was strong because the wolf lived in a way that made the tribe strong; he provided food that all, even the sick and old could eat; he saw to the education of his children; he defended his territory against other wolves. At a *personal* level, those for whom the wolf was a medicine animal or personal totem understood the qualities that made the wolf stand out as an individual; for example, his stamina and ability to track well and go without food for long periods." "The coyote survives where the wolf is almost extinct throughout the West because, as I've been told, he took no poison bait," Gary Snyder says. At any rate coyote is still with us in spite of all humans do to kill him off. He taught the Indians along the Columbia River how to catch salmon and he's taught many different tribes which plants were edible; "but," as Snyder remarks, "most of the time he's just into mischief."

Coyote figures in myths and stories in tribes throughout the Western part of the American continent. He is a teacher, a culture-hero and as Jung wrote, he is, "god, man & animal at once...both sub-human and super-human...an expression of the polaristic structure of the psyche..."

Recently, his popularity has increased dramatically— partly through Gary Snyder's work; partly through Jaime de Angulo's influence and that of others. But chiefly, because coyote is still with us—no matter what we try to do to him— and still outwitting us.

Dick Dorworth, in "Coyote Song," gives a detailed account of coyote at his best. Dorworth was staying up in a cabin along the Snake River in Wyoming one summer. One early morning he woke up suddenly, hearing a coyote but something was "deeply and terribly wrong with that call...It was a yell of such pathos and pain and nearness that I became both afraid and angry...afraid for the animal itself and afraid, since he undoubtedly was one of the coyotes who had serenaded us in the night for several weeks." Dorworth was furiously angry because it probably meant the coyote had been caught in a trap or poisoned. He crawled out of his sleeping bag, grabbed an axe, and crept down to the edge of a farmer's hay field. There he saw "the most pitiful, wretched coyote ever seen on planet earth. He was pulling himself along mostly with the power of his forepaws." Every so often he would crawl up on a bale of hay and "give out that terrible, caricatured howl that had awakened me." The farmer's dogs, chained near his house, were in a frenzy. Finally, when the farmer finished loading his pickup with tools, he called his dogs into the back of the truck and drove off to the field.

When the truck came near to where the coyote was howl- ing, the dogs leaped off at full speed, the farmer continuing on to the other end of the field to work. The dogs raced along toward the poor crippled coyote, Dorworth fuming about the impending "ugly death" for the coyote. Suddenly, "not fifty feet from the coyote, I saw a second coyote crouched down behind a bale; and even from my perspective I could see the grin upon his face and the life within his eyes. He waited until the hounds were about 70—80 feet from his partner before he broke cover. At that instant the crippled coyote, like Lazarus springing from the grave, blossomed into full-stature coyote and turned on the hounds. One of the grand sights of my life was seeing a couple of full-grown mongrel hounds exhanging ass-holes for noses while involved in a full stride known only to the heat of the hunt, and get that stride headed in the opposite direction." They got turned around and right behind them, now doing the chasing, came the "greatest actor I have ever seen...with coyote's own magnificent tail laid flat out behind, floating like a flag of coyote wildness in the wind of the newly directioned chase."

What more can one say about coyote after that? Only, quoting, Dorworth again, his final thoughts on how important coyote is to him: "Coyote, as every Indian and all spiritual gypsies of the cosmos know, is hunter, trickster, teacher, fool, creator, protector and wife-stealer."

Salmon

Salmon taught wisdom to the ancient Irish culture hero, Finn. For the Ainu, the primitive of Japan, Salmon was the god who connected the ocean with the mountains as he swam through their rivers. Salmon is the totem for the Northwest Indians in our country. Here we see how salmon links the cold water, northern ocean areas throughout the world. To give you some idea of the depth of this connection I can do no better than quote from Freeman House, who is presently restoring the watershed of the Mattole River in California and thus the spawning habitat for wild salmon. He explains the importance of salmon for us:

> Salmon is the totem animal of the North Pacific Range. Only salmon, as a species, informs us humans, as a species, of the vastness & unity of the North Pacific Ocean and its rim. The buried memories of our ancient human migrations, the weak abstractions of our geographies, our struggles toward a science of biology do nothing to inform us of the power and benevolence of our place. Totemism is a method of perceiving power, goodness, & mutuliaty in *locale* through the recogni- tion of & respect for the vitality, spirit & interdependence of other species. In the case of the North Pacific Rim, no other species in- forms us so well as the salmon, whose migrations define the boun- daries of the range which supports us all.

And here is Tom Jay, who lives in Western Washington on the shores of the Pacific Ocean. Sitting by Admiralty Inlet, talking about salmon, his friend said: "The salmon is the soul in the body of the world." Developing this concept further, Tom wrote:

> Indeed the salmon is at least the soul of this biome, this green house. He is the tutelary spirit that swims in and around us, secret silver mystery, salmon of the heart, tree-born soul of our world...The salmon is a kind of current between forest and sea. One study shows that salmon may accumulate rare trace minerals (boron?) that, passed on through the forest food chain, provide chemical materials for green plants that are unavailable to them through local geologic and hydrologic processes. In other words, the trees nurture salmon and salmon nurture trees (alchemical salmon turning sea into soil, salmon eyes in the treetops). The salmon is the archetypal resource—meaningful energy directed by unseen powers. It is the *incarnation* of the forest-sea connection, silver needles sewing the ties that bind, religious fish...The salmon travels in our heart as well, swims in our blood, feeds and eats the dreaming tree of truth. The deep resonance between the salmon of the heart and the salmon of the world is the *note* of our dwelling here.

Totemism

The word "totemism" dates back to 1791 when a merchant by the name of Long published his account of travelling among the Ojibway. It was not until much later, in 1866 that MacLennan's work on totemism led to academic interest in the subject. Still later, Frazer and Robertson Smith wrote about it. Alice Fletcher, in her study on the Omaha, concluded that the totem of the social group must have come into existence in the same manner as the personal guardian spirit, and must have represented an ancestor's vision. The well-known anthropologist, Boas and his followers were greatly interested in the subject. New viewpoints on totemism, coming out of Australian field work, influenced both Durkheim and Freud, who felt that totemism was the beginning of religion. Lévi- Strauss, in the *Savage Mind*, stated that the totemic view looks at social differences among men as similar to species dif- ferences and was the usual way of viewing the world until modern industrial times when the caste system came in—with the idea that some are better than others.

But totemism is much more important than all that. Essentially, it is "the world's most ancient system of thought," as Paul Shepard explains. He continues by telling how in the young person, entering adulthood, "the language brain of the left hemisphere of the cerebrum [must be] brought together with the artistic function of the right hemisphere in order for him to be initiated into cosmic taxonomy and its social extensions. The initiate's new family is the clan, which cuts across other kinds of social relationships and yet takes account of them. The classification of plants and animals provides a model for precisely delineating individual, kin, and tribal society. Nature is the model for culture because the mind has been nourished and weaned on it. Applying classificatory thought from the natural to the cultural is totemism."

The psychological aspects of totemism, are very important for us today if we are ever to find our way back into nature. "Only when animal nature has been befriended, recognized as important, and brought into accord with ego and superego does it lend its power to the total personality. After we have thus achieved an integrated personality, we can accomplish what seem like miracles," according to Bruno Bettelheim. Hans Duerr, discussing shamanism gives us some further insight when he writes: "What actually takes place is not that the shaman *turns into* an animal, but rather that he has now experienced his 'wild,' his 'animal aspect'... For he cannot know his human side until he also becomes aware of what it is *not*. To put it differently, he needs to become estranged from it, to have *seen* it, that is, to have seen it from the *outside*."

THE PERSONAL TOTEM POLE

Steve Gallegos, a psychotherapist, has developed a modern method to achieve some of the powerful integration of our inner nature with nature outside, which traditional totemism provided. Essentially, in this method, by using Jung's techniques of visualization and guided imagery, each chakra center within the body is allowed to represent itself as an animal. Some of the original inspiration for his "personal totem pole" came from Suzuki's statement: "Haiku is the apprehension of the thing by the realization of our own original essential unity with it. The word, realization having the literal meaning here of 'making real in ourselves'." Gallegos writes, that in this therapy, I "always insist that the individual move toward a respect for the animals. It is no more than asking that the individual begin to respect his/her self. Anything else perpetuates dis-integration and lack of wholeness." This doesn't mean that the person need obey each individual animal, which might be counter-productive when that particular animal has been feared and hated and hence has become destructive to the whole of the person. This is a "further reason why the individual needs to get in touch with the council [of animals] as soon as possible so that detractors from unity can be immediately spotted in relation to the whole and worked on." From his written account of this process, it is amazing how each one of these animals, once recognized and honored, becomes transformed into its true wild self with all its power.

I feel that the "personal totem pole" has enormous potential for helping us humans to reconnect with the animal self deep within us and thereby begin to relate to wild animals

once more and thus stop the destruction of the remaining species on earth. Gallegos is working with a publisher at this time and hopes to have a book out on it soon. (See Notes for more on this.)

Here in this limited space I can only give a few details of this process. Gallegos always begins with the "Grounding animal" and moves up toward the "Crown animal." The first chakra is located at the base of the spine and this is called the "grounding animal" because "its psychological function involves one's relationship with the earth and also one's sense of security, the ground on which one *stands*." The second chakra is the gut or belly, centered below the navel, involving emotions or passions; the third, the solar plexus, the power to act clearly and effectively; the fourth, the heart, love, compassion, community; fifth, the throat, communication; and sixth, forehead, intellect and intuition. Located at the very top of the head is the Crown animal. Gallegos, at first did not work with this animal because he had not yet found his own Crown animal. When he eventually discovered it he found that "it was not an animal but a shaft of golden sunlight." I interpret this to indicate his deep longing to return to the sun of his native place, New Mexico from the grey Western coast of Oregon where he was living at that time. He has since moved back to New Mexico.

After contact has been made with an animal in any one of the chakras the rest is easier because that one animal can help contact the others. The Crown animal generally "sets the scene for forming the Council." This Council allows all the animals to come together to work out difficulties. Gallegos notes that, "when bringing the animals together in the healing... it is always fascinating to watch the animals spontaneously take charge of the healing, knowing exactly where and how the healing needs to occur."

Here, today, in the "personal totem pole" we can see bear and coyote still at work within us as healers, just as they healed when called upon in primitive ceremonies.

TAOIST "ANIMAL FROLICS"

Modern Taoists have a form called "Animal Frolics," dating back to primitive times in which the exercises are modelled after animals. These exercises came out of the long hours which Taoists spent standing in animal postures or imitating their methods of movement and self-defense. Ko Hung (A.D. 280-340) in his classic, *Pao P'u Tzu* writes of "writhing like the dragon, stretching like the tiger, waddling like the bear, swallowing like the tortoise, flying like the swallow, twisting like the snake." According to Ken Cohen, modern teacher of the Animal Frolics in this country, "Each animal is considered to have a unique spirit and lesson to teach. Other animals of importance include the monkey for its lightness, agility and cleverness; the eagle for its sharpness of vision; the deer for its elegance; cranes for their deep breathing and contemplative spirit; caterpillars for their ability to metamorphose; and spiders because they can sip the morning dew." I learned the bear posture from Ken and find that it grounds me, immediately, when I've been too involved in mental work. It also prevents insomnia, another aspect, very helpful for a writer. Ken says that the bear is considered the chief of the twelve animals of the Chinese zodiac. "As early as 3000 B.C. there were festivals performed before the new year in which twelve animal-masked individuals led by a bear-masked shaman would dance through a town expelling the pestilences. The bear has remained equally important in Taoism. The main ritual dance performed in Taoist temples, called *Yu Pu*, is modeled after the step of a lame bear."

Conclusion

Totemism does not involve some special magical plant or animal, in other words a "substance"; but, in its essence deals with the relationships of humans both to nature, deep inside our own brain/body and outside of us, in nature itself. It's all the same nature; the boundary we insist on drawing between our human self and the rest of nature is something we inflict on the whole by means of our narrow "merely human" part of the brain. No wonder we seem to have no communication with animals. The German anthropologist, Hans Duerr, says: "Snowy owls do not talk the way they do in fairy-tales, either in English or in German. But it is possible for us to communicate with snowy owls provided that, possibly with the aid of hallucinogens, we *dissolve* the boundaries to our own 'animal nature', separating us from the snowy owls."

Sometimes, it is through silence that one can best dissolve the boundaries and so begin to communicate at a deep level with animals and the rest of nature. The Canadian, deep ecologist, Alan Drengson, who teaches philosophy at the University of Victoria, retells an East Indian story which helps us understand this "silence." Very briefly it concerns a wealthy father who sends his son off to study under an enlightened Master. After several years, the son, Svetaketu, returns walking very proudly. The father is worried and that night quietly asks his son: "Has the Master taught you that which cannot be taught?" The son was puzzled but his father said, "Go back to the Master and ask him to teach you that which cannot be taught." The Master told Svetaketu to take 400 of his animals far into the forest where there were no humans and stay there with the animals until there were 1000 of them and then return. At first the son tried to lecture the animals about all the things he knew and recited things to them. But they paid no attention so he soon stopped doing all that. He began to see differently and to walk differently and he lost all track of time. When the animals became restive he realized that there were now 1000 of them and so he brought them back. "He began dancing as he went to the Master's door. The Master saw him coming and went to greet him. The Master said, 'I see you now have learned that which cannot be taught.'"

Alan Drengson adds: "In this story it is being with the animals in their silence that brings the son to the realization of the larger world of full consciousness: a consciousness undivided by conflicts; a consciousness undivided by opposites and judgments; a consciousness unimpeded by conditioning and the past, undefiled by desire; a consciousness open to all sources of knowing, even those sources that are totally non-verbal and non-conceptual. The son had become a full human, had flowered into a total person; through his silence with the animals he had opened to the whole world."

In Sleep: *"Every night...the heroic ego consigns itself to the deep to hold communion with the ancestral spirits that reside there and, gathering their wisdom and guidance, prepares for the miraculous birth of another day."*

Anthony Stevens

"The archetype—let us never forget this—is a psychic organ present in all of us...hence the 'explanation' should always be such that the functional significance of the archetype remains unimpaired, so that an adequate and meaningful connection between the conscious mind and the archetype is assured. For the archetype is...a vital and necessary component in our psychic economy. It represents or personifies certain instinctive data of the dark, primitive psyche, **the real but invisible roots of consciousness."**

C.G. Jung

[archetypes] "They are essentially the chthonic portion of the mind...that portion through which the mind is liked to nature, or in which, at least, its relatedness to the earth and the universe is most comprehensible. In these primordial images, the effect of the earth and its laws upon the mind is clearest to us."

C.G. Jung

CHAPTER SIX

"...the 2 million year-old man that is in all of us. In the last analysis, most of our difficulties come from losing contact with our instincts; with the age-old unforgotten wisdom stored up in us. And where do we make contact with this old man in us? In our dreams.

C.G. Jung

"The archetypes are as it were the hidden foundation of the conscious mind, or the roots which the psyche has sunk not only in the earth in the narrower sense but in the world in general."

C.G. Jung

The opening part of this quotation was used in the previous chapter; I repeat it here and continue. *"[A]n archetype...has the divine quality, and that is <u>always based upon the animal</u>. Therefore the gods are symbolized as animals; even the holy ghost is a bird, all the antique gods and the exotic gods are animals at the same time...<u>naturally in possession of the wisdom of nature</u>, like any animal or plant, <u>but the wisdom is represented by a being that is not conscious of itself</u>, and therefore cannot be called wisdom. For instance, the glow-worm represents the secret of making light without warmth; man doesn't know how to produce 98% of light with no loss of warmth but the glow-worm has the secret.*

If the glow-worm could be transformed into a being who knew that he possessed the secret of making light without warmth, that would be a man with an insight and knowledge much greater than we have reached; he would be a great scientist perhaps or a great inventor, who would transform our present technique. So the old wise man is the consciousness of the wisdom of ape; it is the wisdom of nature and that is nature itself and if nature were conscious of itself, it would be a superior being of extraordinary knowledge and understanding."

C.G. Jung

"Archetypes are about relationship not substance...Archetypes point toward relationship; while ideas kill reality."

Julien Puzey

 ARCHETYPES: "THE ROOTS OF CONSCIOUSNESS"

Personal Introduction

Several years ago, I got a letter from the Jungian analyst, Louise Mahdi. Written on her plane flight from Zurich to the United States, she urgently requested an appointment with me while she was in this country. Later, she travelled all the way out west to see me here in Silverton. Having read *Earth Wisdom*, she felt that I was the one she needed to give a talk for the Jungian group, connected with continuing education at Notre Dame. What she wanted me to do, was to ground these Jungians by helping them understand the underlying importance of nature both in Jung's life and in his work.

While I had studied Jung before, in connection with my first two books I had not delved very deeply into the matter; however, knowing the importance of mountains in Jung's life, I felt that his work was necessarily grounded in nature, even though most of his humanistic and spiritualistic followers were loathe to admit it.

MOUNTAINS AND ROCK IN JUNG'S LIFE

"This was the best and most precious gift my father had ever given me." Jung wrote, concerning his trip on the cogwheel railway up to the top of Mt. Rigi in Switzerland. When the railway reached the top, he stood in the clear, high mountain air, looking out at the vast distance. He was transported: "Yes, I thought, this is it, my world, the real world, the secret, where there are no teachers, no schools, no unanswerable questions, where one can be without having to ask anything." And that's why it was "the best and most precious gift." Later, after decades of work, Jung wrote that in the unconscious, "The mountain stands for the goal of pilgrimage and ascent, hence it often has the psychological meaning of the Self."

Near the end of his life, in his 85th year, "he suddenly expressed a wish to see the mountains and the old familiar passes at close quarters again. It was far too dangerous an undertaking for an old man with a weak heart, but Ruth Bailey [his long-time housekeeper] took the risk, packed brandy and medicaments in the car and set off to follow his old beloved tracks once more. High up in the mountains...with snowy peaks stretching away above and nothing but the sky marking the horizon, he climbed slowly out of the car and sniffed the mountain air. Later to an old friend he said, 'I think that's the last time I shall meet the mountains.' There were tears in his eyes."

On his study wall, hung a painting of Siva on top of Mount Kailas, which is considered the most sacred mountain in the world. It is my feeling that Jung's experience when he was fourteen years old on top of Mt. Rigi gave him a taste of the bliss of "wholeness"—what it feels like to be whole and connected both inside and outside with nature. He spent the rest of his life trying to help others realize this connectedness between nature, within and without.

Another aspect of his connectedness with nature concerns his life-long fascination with rock. As a small child, sitting on a rock, part of the garden wall at his home, he played a game where he thought: "I am sitting on top of this stone and it is underneath." But the stone could also say "I" and think: "I am lying here on this slope and he is sitting on top of me." The final question was, "Am I the one who is sitting on the stone, or am I the stone on which he is sitting." Later during a time of turmoil in his life he began building his rock tower at Bollingen, which he worked on from time to time for the rest of his life. Just as this rock experience was important to him as a small child, rock came again into his life in his last days.

In a letter to Mr. Serrano, written on June 16, 1961, Ruth Bailey recounted Jung's last days. Near the end of his life—the last time the two of them sat out on the terrace—he told her of the "wonderful" dream he just had. Then he said, "Now I know the truth but there is still a small piece not filled in and when I know that, I shall be dead." Ruth Bailey goes on to tell of this final dream, which came a short time later. "He saw a huge round block of stone sitting on a high plateau and at the foot of the stone was engraved these words: 'And this shall be a sign unto you of wholeness and Oneness.' [she continues] I should have known from this that his life was complete."

FURTHER DISCOVERIES IN MY JUNGIAN RESEARCH

During the research for my lecture I had no difficulty finding material in Jung's writings which proved his deep tie with nature and his amazingly early [before modern ethology] understanding of the archetypes as the animal and the earth itself within us. Needless to say my talk caused considerable controversy. Most of those present could not accept the deep implications and hotly defended the usual "spiritual" approach; but, for a few, this talk changed their lives.

Since then I have had to answer many questions concerning this matter of the archetypes and nature. Fortunately, in my reading after my experience on Mt. Snowden, I discovered Anthony Stevens' book, *Archetypes: A Natural History of the Self*, which has proved invaluable because Stevens is a Jungian analyst and therefore quoting him proves very helpful with Jungians and other psychologists still caught in the anthropocentric (narrowly human) trap.

Before ending this introduction I want to say one more thing about mountains. I've found—in more than thirty years of leading people up mountains that the ones who are most fearful of heights are those who are most fearful of looking at nature within themselves. Interestingly enough, when such a person does begin to work on understanding the self, he or she loses their fear of heights.

Preview

Intellectuals think that we live in a world of ideas which we invent—a domesticated world where we create new hybrids of grains, new breeds of cattle and new ideas—it's all the same — they come out of our ideas. But deep inside us is a wilderness. We call it the unconscious because we can't control it fully so we can't will to create what we want from it. The collective unconscious is a great wild region where we can get in touch with the sources of life.

This quote from C. G. Jung forms the basis of what I will be doing in this chapter. Jung faced enough battles in his life, trying to rescue the "unconscious" from Freud's defining it as the place to throw away repressed desires—a sort of trash barrel. It is obvious now, with the findings of ethology to help us, that Jung understood far more about the true unconscious than he dared to state openly. It is important to realize the problems he faced in order to understand why he had to write in such a veiled and cautious manner. In a conversation with Dr. Carleton Smith, in 1957, Jung referred to some of these difficulties. He said that the European mentality has a "panic fear of the discoveries that might be made in the realm of the unconscious." These fears troubled Freud as well, who, Jung said, "confessed to me that it was necessary to make a dogma of his sexual theory because this was the sole bulwark of reason against a possible 'outburst of the black flood of occultism'." Jung continues: "It is this fear of the unconcious psyche which not only impedes self-knowledge but is the gravest obstacle to a wider understanding and knowledge of psychology. Often the fear is so great that one dares not admit it even to oneself...We are living in what the Greeks called the time for a 'metamorphosis of the gods.' i.e. of the fundamental principles and symbols."

Jung's work is important for all those attempting to heal the split beween human and nature because he is the one who worked for more than fifty years trying to understand this connection. He provided us with great insight but before we can make use of it we must clear away all the accumulated debris of his followers, who want to safely enclose his discoveries within the labels of "spiritual truths" or "humanistic ideals."

Jung himself wrote: "The conscious mind allows itself to be trained like a parrot, but the unconscious does not." Further, concerning that so-called great achievement of humans, ego consciousness, unlike Freud, Jung conceived the essence of ego consciousness as *limitation*: "even though it reaches to the farthest nebulae among the stars. All consciousness separates; but in dreams we put on the likeness of that more universal, truer, more eternal man dwelling in the darkness of primordial night. There he is still whole, and the whole is in him, indistinguishable from nature and bare of all egohood."

Below I will first tell how the English psychiatrist, Anthony Stevens discovered the connection between ethology and Jung's concepts and then go into archetypes at some length, because they are the key to the power of the human unconscious to keep us in connection with nature as a whole. In my chapter on ethology, I indicated some of the aberrations in both physical and mental health caused by ignoring our basic mammalian roots. Stevens gives further examples of such aberrations and explains how they come about by thwarting the built-in archetypes. He also goes into the matter of the underlying prejudice, which continues even today, against the findings of ethology among psychologists and others who work with people.

For the purposes of this work, I am devoting this chapter particularly to Jung's concept of archetypes, rather than attempting an overall view of his research, because archetypes provide one of the clearest methods for modern intellectuals to experience the validity of the "old ways" within us.

Anthony Stevens' work on the Roots of our Humanity

His search began in 1966 when he went to Greece to study "attachment bonds in infancy." The Metera Babin Centre in Athens was dedicated to preventing problems caused by the usual institutional approach with young children where the deprivation of sufficient love and attention often causes severe withdrawal and even death.

The basic idea of the Metera was to insure that the child would be cared for by a number of nurse-mothers and theoretically would form bonds with several of them—such as would occur normally in a Greek village, where the child bonds with mother, aunts, and grandmothers. When Stevens was at the Metera there were 100 infants with 36 qualified and 60 student nurses. The structure involved twelve children to each pavilion, consisting of four compartments, with three children in each compartment. A graduate mother nurse was supposed to be in charge of each of these groups of three children.

According to the current "attachment" theories at that time, these multi-mothered children would form multiple attachments. "Moreover, the nurses to whom a child attached himself would necessarily be arranged in a hierarchy of preference, the nurses at the top of the hierarchy being those who fed him the most."

What Stevens discovered was that despite all the rules and the scrupulous supervision of the matron, the system only worked when she was checking on her rounds. As soon as she was gone "her neat theoretical arrangement" fell apart; but this enabled Stevens to further understand Bowlby's "attachment" theory.

The accepted psychological theory when Stevens was at the Metera was that "the primary reward for eliciting infant attachment behavior was food"; it had gone unquestioned for decades. But at the Metera he found that attachment had little to do with food. The English psychiatrist, Dr. John Bowlby's famous paper attacking the "cupboard love theory," changed the old theory. He said that children become attached to their mothers without any need to learn to love because they were innately programmed to do so from birth; the "mother-infant attachment bond was in us a genetic heritage of our species." But, as Steven remarks, "fury would be closer to the mark" to describe the reaction to Bowlby's work by academic psychologists. His unforgivable sin was that he had drawn parallels between human attachment behavior and that among animals and birds. But more than that, they were angry at Bowlby's applying concepts from the relatively new science of ethology. At first Stevens thought this anger was due to "sour grapes," especially when it came to psychologists; because after many years of research they "were being brilliantly surpassed by an upstart group of zoologists." But he found out that their resistance was really *doctrinal*." It was just like nineteenth century theologians in the face of a religious heresy. "Alone among contemporary scientists, psychologists still argued as if they believed in the 'special creation' of our species."

Stevens found that three quarters of the children became specifically attached to a single nurse, among the twelve or more they saw daily in their "pavilion." The reasons for this pairing off between the child and one particular nurse was not so much due to routine feeding but with play, physical contact and social interaction—more like "falling in love." Bowlby saw the growth of attachment as being due to response patterns in the child—staring, smiling, crying, babbling, laughing—which all release parental feelings in the mother. Each of these is due to innate programming within the child and do not have to be learned. As Stevens remarks, Bowlby's attachment theory provides "simple and more consistent explanations of the data of human attachment formation than the psychoanalytic and learning theories which preceded it." He credits it for being important in "drawing developmental psychology into the mainstream of biology, where it rightly belongs."

When Stevens returned to London in 1967 to complete his training as a psychiatrist, he began to write up the results of his research at Metera, but he felt that he needed a more comprehensive theory to bring all aspects of the attachment phenomena together. He needed something covering both the behavioral manifestation of attachment and the "inner psychic manifestation occurring in consciousness in the form of symbols, images, intuitions, feelings, words, etc." Then, remembering what he'd heard of Jung, he felt that Jung's theory of "archetypes" operating through the collective unconscious might cover what he needed. Furthermore, Jung had been working on this for more than fifty years. But Stevens admits that when he went to the hospital library and began reading in Jung's *Collective Works*, "I began to suffer from the same confusion that I had experienced on other occasions when I tried to read Jung." Browsing through all the volumes he still could not see whether "Jung's ideas were compatible with a biological view of human nature." So, knowing he needed advice from someone more familiar with Jung he went to see Irene Champernowne, who had been his analyst for five years when he was a student. She had trained with Jung and Toni Wolff in Zurich and before that had been teaching biology at a college in London.

This discussion clarified matters for Stephens. Briefly summing up. what he learned was that Jung had deliberately chosen the name, *collective* unconscious, to make it clear that it was different from the *personal* unconscious of Freudian psychoanalysis. Jung felt that all the essential psychic characteristics that distinguish us as human beings are determined by genetics and are in us from the time we are born; these are the "archetypes." Furthermore, Jung felt that the personal experience in the individual human's life was "to develop what is already there."

Irene reassured him that there was nothing "unbiological" about Jung's theories; in fact, that's why she had become a Jungian rather than a Freudian. "Archetypes," she declared, "are biological entities. They are present, in related forms, throughout the animal kingdom…*archetypes evolved through natural selection*." Stevens relates that, to him, "this was a tremendous statement…Once one conceives of archetypes as the neuropsychic centres responsible for co-ordinating the behavioral and psychic repertoires of our species in response to whatever environmental circumstances we may encounter, they become directly comparable to the the 'innate releasing mechanisms' responsible for Lorenz's 'species-specific patterns of behaviour' and Bowlby's 'goal-corrected behavioural systems'." Stevens began to realize that he had been using Jungian concepts in treating patients and ethological concepts

in his research. Combining the two brought such outstanding results in his treatment of difficult patients, that he wrote of what he had learned in his book, *Archetypes: a Natural History of the Self*. (More on this later in the chapter.)

Jung's Efforts to Understand the Archetypes

Jung tells the of the power of the archetypes in his life since he was a small child in his biography, *Memories, Dreams, Reflections*; but he had no words for these concepts until much later in his life. The beginnings of his discoveries in this area occurred in 1909, on a trip to the United States with Freud, where they were together every day for seven weeks and analyzed one another's dreams. A particular dream was most important to Jung and, in fact, led him to the concept of the "collective unconscious." He was in a house where there were fine paintings on the wall on the second floor. He was pleased that this was "his house," but then realized he knew nothing of the lower stories. He went down the stairs to the ground floor where things were much older—medieval and sort of dark. Deciding to "explore the whole house," he found a heavy door and beyond it discovered a stone stairway leading down to the cellar. Going still lower he found walls which he felt were from Roman times. In the floor was a stone slab with a ring in it. Pulling on this, he found stairs going even deeper. He found himself in a low cave cut in the rock. Thick dust was everywhere, covering scattered bones and pieces of pottery and two skulls.

What interested Freud most about this dream, when Jung recounted it to him, was the two skulls. Freud at once decided that the dream was a secret death wish. Jung writes: "I had to name someone whose death was worth the wishing!" But Jung himself grasped that the house was a "kind of image of the psyche" and the cave was the remnants of a primitive culture, "the world of the primitive man within myself." This primitive psyche borders on the life of the animals, just as the early man often lived in caves, where animals had first lived.

Eventually, of course Jung and Freud had a parting of the ways, which left Jung very troubled for some years, as he went through the fearful process of exploring the unconscious all by himself. He was finally rescued from this in 1928 when Richard Wilhelm sent him his translation of an ancient Chinese document, later published under the title, *The Secret of the Golden Flower* and he found that the Taoists had been there before him in this perilous search. This event freed him to continue his work unhampered by further doubts.

This lowest cellar of the house, the "collective unconscious" consists of the archetypes. Jung explained:

> I have chosen the term 'collective' because this part of the unconscious is not individual but universal; in contrast to the personal psyche, it has contents and modes of behaviour that are more or less the same everywhere and in all individuals. It is, in other words, identical in all men and thus constitutes a common psychic substrate of a superpersonal nature which is present in every one of us.

Jung felt, contrary to many of his followers, that there was no split between the biological regions of the human body and man's "spiritual" nature. In fact, his sudden realization of this fact was the impetus that led him to his life work.

Brief Account of Jung's Discoveries

When Jung began his university career his main interest was in evolutionary theory and comparative anatomy. In 1898 he was trying to figure out how he could make a living and still manage to stay with what really interested him. The choice seemed to lie between surgery and internal medicine. But events during the summer completely changed his direction. Certain "poltergeist" phenomena in his parent's home, a heavy walnut table splitting and a knife breaking, led him to join some relatives who met with a medium from time to time as he felt such activities might have some connection with these strange events in his home. As Jung wrote in his biography, this was the "one great experience which…made it possible for me to achieve a psychological point of view."

He was still preparing for a career in medicine, but studying for the state examinations required that he read a book by the psychiatrist, Krafft-Ebing. He was not expecting much from it, but in the preface the author called psychoses "diseases of the personality." Jung says "My heart suddenly began to pound. I had to stand up and draw a deep breath. My excitement was intense, for it had become clear to me, in a flash of illumination, that for me the only possible goal was psychiatry. Here alone the two currents of my interest could flow together. Here was the empirical field common to biological and spiritual facts, which I had everywhere sought and nowhere found. Here at last was the place where the collision of nature and spirit became a reality."

I have recounted this event at some length because it is important to remember that from the beginning Jung was involved in investigating the *biological* nature of the human psyche. In other words, the connection between human nature and nature itself was what interested him. Stevens explains that, "the Jungian archetype is no mere abstract idea but a biological entity, a 'living organism, endowed with a generative force' existing as a 'centre' in the central nervous system, acting…in a manner very similar to the innate releasing mechanism much later postulated by the ethologist, Niko Tinbergen."

Jung's first use of the word, archetype came in 1919. The original Greek word, which Jung adapted, meant "prime imprinter," referring to an original manuscript, from which later copies were made. Analyzing the word, Jacobi explains:

> The first element 'arch' signifies 'beginning, origin, cause, primal source, principle,' but it also signifies 'position of a leader, supreme rule and government'…the second element 'type' means 'blow and what is produced by a blow, the imprint of a coin…form, image, prototype, model, order, and norm,'…in the figurative, modern sense, 'pattern underlying form, primordial form' (the form, for example, 'underlying' a number of similar human, animal or vegetable specimens).

Over a period of years Jung found that in the dreams of normal people and in pathological cases as well there were certain recurring motifs. "Because of their typical nature," Jung wrote, "we can call them 'primordial images,' types or—as I have named them—*archetypes*." An archetype "represents or personifies certain instinctive data of the dark, primitive psyche, the real but invisible roots of consciousness." Jung points out that primitive "magic" deals with these archetypes and goes on to say: "This original form of *religio* ('linking back') is the essence, the working basis of all religious life even today." In another work, Jung goes further into this concept of the "roots of consciousness," when he wrote: "…the roots which the psyche has sunk not only in the earth in the narrower sense but the world in general. The archetypes are thus that portion through which the psyche is attached to nature, or in which its link with the earth and the world appears at its most tangible." The way in which archetypes communicate with the conscious mind is through symbols.

Jung's most definitive statement about the depth of the archetypes comes from *Essays on a Science of Mythology* where he writes:

> The symbols of the self arise in the depths of the body and they express its materiality every bit as much as the structure of the perceiving consciousness…The deeper 'layers' of the psyche lose their individual uniqueness as they retreat further and further into darkness. 'Lower down,' that is to say as they approach the autonomous functional systems, they become increasingly collective until they are universalized and extinguished in the body's materiality, i.e., in chemical subtances. The body's carbon is simply carbon. Hence 'at bottom' the psyche is simply 'world.' In this sense I hold Kerenyi to be absolutely right when he says that in the symbol the *world itself* is speaking. The more archaic and 'deeper,' that is the more physiological, the symbol is, the more collective and universal, the more 'material' it is.

There is "no 'rational' substitute for the archetype anymore than there is for the cerebellum or the kidneys," according to Jung. The archetype is not an idea at all but "an inherited mode of psychic functioning, corresponding to that inborn *way* according to which the chick emerges from the egg; the bird builds its nest…In other words, it is a 'pattern of behavior'." All those aspects just mentioned have to do with the biological aspect of behavior but from within, the person, himself or herself feels that the archetype is "numinous" (holy)…an "experience of fundamental importance."

Contrasting the conscious mind with the unconscious, Jung explains that the nature of the conscious mind is "to concentrate on relatively few contents and to raise them to the highest pitch of clarity." This, of course, means excluding all other potentials, which might be there. In modern civilized man, "the more he trains his will, the more the danger of getting lost in one-sidedness, and deviating further and further from the laws and roots of his being." Primitive man, "being closer to his instincts" knows the dangers and has a "fear of novelty and adherence to tradition." Civilized modern man thinks that the primitive is "painfully backward, whereas we exalt progress." But this progress, which quite often seems to give us immediate benefits, brings with it, in Jung's terms, a "gigantic Promethean debt which has to be paid off from time to time in the form of hideous catastrophes."

Jung explains that the conscious mind "knows nothing

beyond the opposites and, as a result, has no knowledge of the thing that unites them," the unconsious. Furthermore, according to Lawrence Gelb, "In the unconscious mind both opposites are reunited since the function of consciousness created them in the first place."

Some of the archetypes, which Jung named are the "shadow," (all those characteristics we want to conceal from ourselves and the world), the anima (the female part of the male), the animus (the male part of the female), the Old Wise Man, and the Magna Mater or image of the Great Mother. Archetypal symbols include the rock (for wholeness), trees, animals etc. But as Jung points out, "No archetype can be reduced to a simple formula. It is a vessel which we can never empty and never fill...It persists throughout the ages and requires interpreting ever anew...It is a well-nigh hopeless undertaking to tear a single archetype out of the living tissue of the psyche..." Here, again we see relationship instead of substance at work within the human psyche.

Anthony Stevens on "thwarting archetypal intent"

It is difficult to give a brief explanation of how archetypes work so I will turn to Steven's account here. He explains that "One of the greatest scourges of contemporary man" is "neurotic illness." The fundamental problem in most cases is that such people were deficient in parental care. He defines this as the "quality of care provided was such as to frustrate those archetypal imperatives," which in a normal childhood would lead to a mature self. These archetypes are concerned with the "formation of attachment bonds, the establishment of basic trust, and the development of a secure ego conceiving of itself as being both acceptable to others and capable of coping with the eventualities of life."

The worst dilemma is when a child's basic archetypal attachment needs and his aggression are aroused at the same time and by the same parent. Such a situation is "unendurable" for a child and he has to get rid of the aggression in some way. Later in life, such childhood coping mechanisms show up most clearly in strange sexual patterns. In bondage symbolism, for instance, "the sadist who trusses up his sexual partner is parodying the behaviour of his parents who habitually restricted his desire to be free and to explore; the masochist who has himself tied up is parodying his own acquiescence to the same parental restrictions. Sado-masochism is a ritual, a game for the discharge of impulses prohibited from achieving their normal goals. As such, it affords a dramatic and instructive illustration of the possible consequences of thwarting archetypal intent."

Stevens' client, C. presents us with a clear example. When C. came to see Stevens he was intelligent, articulate, well educated, not depressed or anxious and had numerous friends. He was, however, curious about the kind of men who attracted him, sexually; as they were always working class men and toughly masculine. His present relationship was with an army sergeant. He described the particular ritualized encounter: In the late afternoon the sergeant "would come home in uniform and conduct a thorough military-type inspection of their quarters. If he found anything dirty or out of place, he would give C. a sound dressing down, and order him to lower his trousers and bend over the back of a chair. He would then beat him on the naked buttocks with a long, flexible cane kept especially for this purpose." Stevens notes that C. found all this "deeply satisfying. He had no wish to give it up, but he wondered why."

After a number of sessions with C., Stevens found that his masochism arose from his need for a masculine figure who could "maintain order in...a masculine way" not like his fussy father and further, out of his desire for punishment—which he never got from either parent. (To keep this short I have cut out most of the case history as recounted in Stevens' book on pages 115 to 117.)

Essentially, Stevens explains that Jung's archetypes do fit into what Lorenz and other ethologists have learned about behavior but, "What Jung failed to do, however, was to develop the necessary biological argument to substantiate his view." Of course Jung was not a biologist and furthermore, modern ethology was just beginning when Jung was doing his most important work.

Dr. J. P. Henry, author of *Stress, Health and the Social Environment: A Sociobiologic Approach to Medicine* says "that the metapsychological foundations built by Carl Jung are proving to be soundly conceived. There is a rapidly growing body of evidence linking our mammalian inheritance of basic brainstem functions with man's unique religious, social and cultural achievements. Society has scarcely begun to consider the implications of these discoveries."

Jung himself wrote in "Mind and Earth":

> I would not speak ill of our relation to good Mother Earth...he who is rooted in the soil endures. Alienation from the unconscious and from its historical conditions spells rootlessness. That is the danger that lies in wait for the conqueror of foreign lands, and for every individual who, through one-sided allegiance to any kind of-ism, loses touch with the dark, maternal, earthy ground of his being.

Conclusion

The growing recognition of the archetypes within, through dreams, active imagination, myths and other techniques leads to, what Jung calls, "individuation." He writes that "it is an innate urge of life to produce an individual as complete as possible—for instance, a bird with all its feathers and colours and the size that belongs to that particular species. So...the urge of realization, naturally pushes man on to be himself, and he would most certainly grow into his own form, if there were not obstacles and inhibitions of many descriptions which hinder him from becoming what he is really meant to be." In another of Jung's books, he states: "The aim of individuation is nothing less than to divest the self of the false wrappings of the persona on the one hand, and the suggestive power of the primordial images on the other." The persona is the role in life, which the individual feels he must take on for one reason or another—parental pressure or other pressures in modern culture—thus denying the archetypes within. On the other hand there is the danger that the individual can fall under the power of one particular archetype and no longer be a complete human being at all. For instance, when a man suddenly falls in love with a woman who is the personification of his anima (the female part within), the resulting infatuation takes over his entire life with disastrous consequences. In a way this is falling back into the "substance" trap. Actually full development of the human comes out of the relationship of the conscious mind to *all* the archetypes within.

Play is of fundamental importance in beginning this process because only free play in early childhood can activate the archetypes. The great festivals and ceremonies of the year, carry on the process begun in childhood by allowing all the archetypes to manifest within each individual but balanced by the actions of the group as a whole through such rituals as trance dancing, drumming, chanting etc. Primitive cultures throughout human history provided for full human development without the enormous psychological problems of modern culture because all the archetypes within were allowed full expression in the great festivals. I go more deeply into this in the next chapter.

"It seems to me that modern ecologists have yet to <u>find</u> language that approaches the compact imagery of native peoples whose myths not only explain the workings of ecosystem ethics but locate the people in the story, instruct us."

Tom Jay

"The problem may be more difficult to understand than to solve. Beneath the veneer of civilization, to paraphrase the trite phrase of humanism, lies not the barbarian and animal, but the human in us who knows the rightness of birth in gentle surroundings, the necessity of a rich nonhuman environment, play at being animals, the discipline of natural history, juvenile tasks with simple tools, the expressive arts of receiving food as a spiritual gift rather than as a product, the cultivation of metaphorical significance of natural phenomena of all kinds, clan membership and small group life, and the profound claims and liberation of ritual initiation and subsequent stages of adult mentorship. There is a secret person undamaged in every individual, aware of the validity of these, sensitive to their right moments in our lives."

Paul Shepard

"[After the Plains' Tribes were forcibly moved to "Indian Territory"], the Cherokees, now settled in their new home...made such progress that Senator Henry L. Dawes of Massachusetts paid them a visit. He reported: 'The head chief told us that there was not a family in that whole nation that had not a home of its own. There was not a pauper in that nation, and the nation did not owe a dollar...Yet the defect of the system was apparent. They have got as far as they can go, because they own their land in common... **There is no selfishness, which is at the bottom of civilization.** Till the people will consent to give up their lands, and divide them among their citizens so that each can own the land he cultivates, they will not make much more progress.'

Wherefore in 1887, the 'Dawes Act,' or 'General Allotment Act,' was passed. Briefly, it provided that instead of a communal, tribal ownership, every Indian was to be allotted a piece of reservation under a fee simple title. They were not expected to increase; therefore the 'surplus' was to be purchased by the government for $1.25 an acre and thrown open for settlement.

The rush began..."

Frank Waters

CHAPTER SEVEN

"I just want to put one idea in the record, and that is, we should study the reasons for the persistence of these peoples all over the world in light of all the conditions militating against their persistence...I am certain that there is something for us peasant agriculturalists or, if you like, industrialists to learn from the values associated with the tribal life and with the determination of these peoples to preserve this way of life at all costs."
Sol Tax, in his final statement made at the end of the Man the Hunter conference.

"This was the beginning of my meeting with the Akaramas, and now, living within their lives, I have become what I have always been and it has taken a lifetime, all of my own life, to reach this point where it is as if I know finally that I am alive and that I am here, right now."
Tobias Schneebaum

"Conscience is not a colonial governor imposing alien norms...It is our nature itself, becoming aware of its own underlying pattern"
Mary Midgley

"A 'real' person in these terms is one who hasn't forgotten what & where things are in relation to the Earth. Earth-rooted...He has only to maintain a true eye for his surroundings & a contact with the Earth, to recognize himself as the inheritor of reality...The real person (reality-person, if fact) lives, like the 'primitive' philosopher as described by Radin, in a blaze of reality through which he can experience 'reality at white heat.' This is a part of the tribal inheritance (not Indian only but world-wide) that we all lose at our peril...

Here is the central image of shamanism & of all 'primitive' thought, the intuition...of a connected & fluid universe, as alive as a man is—just that much alive...So, something more than literature is going on here: for ourselves, let me suggest, the question of how the concept & techniques of the 'sacred' can persist in the 'secular' world, not as nostalgia for the archaic past but (as Snyder writes) 'a vehicle to ease us into the future.'"
Jerome Rothenberg

 LESSONS FROM PRIMITIVE CULTURES

Preview

And when the other day some of our friends here said, almost a little contemptuously, 'Don't let us go back to Paleolithic society.' I was tempted to ask them how far they thought they could express that idea without using one of the tools of Paleolithic society, namely language.

Lewis Mumford in Summary Remarks at the conclusion of the International Symposium on "Man's Role in Changing the Face of the Earth"

This chapter consists of a brief overview of some of the important basics in our life which we owe to the so-called primitives. Way back in 1939, Professor Oakes Ames wrote that every major drug plant and every major food crop had been discovered by primitive man: "In the five thousand years of recorded history man has not added a single major crop to his list of domesticates." Furthermore, we find that all these plants were fully developed by five thousand years ago; so developed that it is difficult to find the wild ancestors of such plants. This means that, actually, primitive peoples were developing these plants over a far longer time, both in the Old World and the New World. Ames' conclusion concerning the New World specifically, is that: "Biological evidence indicated that man, evolving with his food plants, discovered horticulture and agriculture in both hemispheres at a time which may well have reached far back into the Pleistocene."

Yet it's seldom mentioned where we originally got such knowledge. For example, "new" scientific research is praised for making breakthrough cures. As an example, let's look at the history of the drug reserpin, one such "new" discovery, which is very useful in treating high blood pressure. Actually, the drug is obtained from a plant known as Serpina Rauwolfia, the snake plant, which grew on the Indian slopes of the Himalayas. It had been used by local villagers for generations, to calm down "maniacal" people. There are many other modern discoveries of "primitive" cures; but I won't take the time to go into it here. What I will be doing in this chapter is giving some idea of the sophisticated inter-related "systems" by which primitives successfully lived within their own land (or ecosystem). (Incidentally, the word "system" is not new; it originally comes from the Greek word, systema meaning "what is holding together.") These primitive "systems" were organically developed through thousands of years of living in place; not by modern research methods trying to find a "substance" to sell. Because primitive "systems" were devoted to helping all life in that place to flourish we don't find such devastating side effects occurring as we find in modern research with its narrow "substance" perspective.

In fact, primitive systems in general are so sophisticated that as far as government goes, early Europeans tended to think that they lived in complete anarchy. For instance, Louis Armand Lahontan, who came to the New World in the seventeenth century, writing of his experiences among the Indians in what is now Canada, thought they lived as naturally as animals. He wrote so glowingly of this "natural" life that his writings led Rousseau to his concept of the "Noble Savage."

Stanley Diamond points out that in primitive societies, leadership is "communal and traditional, not political or secular." He continues:

The chief of a clan, or the patriarch of a family, are respected as the embodiments of clan, family or tribal heritage, [often] simply the oldest member of the group. Obeisance toward these figures is symbolic, a sign of respect for one's tradition and thus of self-respect. It is not the result of coercion or an institutionally manipulative social act.

Leadership may also be situational, and based on skill. Primitive societies abound in 'chiefs.' In any one tribe, there may be a hunting chief, work chief, dance chief, women's chief, age grade chief, and fishing chief. These leaders function only in specific contexts and for limited periods of time; usually their primacy is based on capacity in the particular activity; and, almost everyone in the society is, at one time or another, in a 'chiefly' position.

Only quite recently, has the academic world begun to acknowledge ritual as part of the "government" of primitive groups. Rappaport states that "some social scientists...have put forward hypotheses assigning a major role to religious or ceremonial features as adaptive factors in the interactions of human populations with their environments." Below I will go more into Rappaport's findings when I deal with the Tsembaga of New Guinea; but I will save the more detailed use of ritual for governing purposes for Part III.

As far as thermodynamic efficiency goes, Rappaport reports that primitive cultures are way ahead of modern "high energy technology." "Hannon has recently estimated the slash and burn horticulture of the Maring of New Guinea, in which the only sources of energy are the gardeners themselves, to be forty times as efficient as 'modern food delivery systems'...he claims that in modern agriculture and food processing 45 units of fossil fuel is used to deliver 10 units to the supermarket." To make this even clearer, Rappaport states that "South African bushmen and Australian aborigines are able to support a person on 1/75 to 1/100 of what it takes to support an American. That is, from the standpoint of the ratio of energy flux per unit of standing biomass, hunters and gatherers are 75 to 100 times more efficient than we are."

Essentially, primitive cultures cannot be manipulated as easily as so-called "civilized" people. In his book, Propaganda, Jacques Ellul observes that "propaganda cannot succeed where people have no trace of Western culture ...Actually, the most obvious result of primary education in the nineteenth and twentieth centuries was to make the individual susceptible to superpropaganda." Ellul reports on the experience and research of the Germans between 1933 and 1938 which showed that their ideological radio propaganda had no effects on illiterate people in remote areas.

It's important to realize that the human brain has been essentially the same for 40,000 to 50,000 years. But these ancient ancestors of ours as well as present-day primitives are both encouraged and allowed by their culture to use their brain in ways which our modern IGS refuses to tolerate. For example, Hans Duerr, referring to the fact that the experts believe that both shamans as well as the mentally ill have difficulties with "the differentiation between phantasy and nonphantasy," goes on to say: "Only the latter, however, suffer due to this lack of ability to differentiate because their cultures do not provide them with 'valid concepts' that would help them to create a meaningful relationship between their fantasies and their everyday experience. This is the reason why, in contrast to shamans, the mentally ill do not have any 'cultural significance'."

Some highly acclaimed "new consciousness" aspects of the brain are actually due to the functioning of the very old brains within us. Duerr explains that telepathic ability "is not a progressive evolutionary phenomenon, but rather a rudimentary property, which humans retained from their zoological ancestors." Concerning the entire range of these so-called extra sensory abilities, Stephan Schwartz states that "psychic functioning is no more exceptional than being able to see color. It is a normal aspect of human functioning that has been culturally repressed." In primitive hunting cultures it's important "to know where the gazelle is, because that's how to feed your family. On the other hand, psychic functioning begins to disappear...as man or humankind begins to urbanize." I can add first hand testimony to this from mountain climbing and back country skiing. In such activities in nature these "repressed" psychic abilities quickly return because your life depends on them.

Since we have essentially the same brain as that of our ancestors of 50,000 years ago, they, too, had the "problem" of conscious thinking or the rational hemisphere or rational thinking (whatever label you want to use here). This type of thinking has been with us for a very long time and, of course, is useful in a limited way but deadly when allowed to take over. Remember, Gregory Bateson wrote that the rational part of the mind, alone "is necessarily pathogenic and destructive of life..." The successful cultures of the past learned how to deal with that limited part of the brain so that it was still useful to them but could not gain control of the entire body-brain and thus inflict the problems we have now in our present modern culture. The methods used were rituals and seasonal Festivals as well as ritual use of alcohol and drugs. It is important to remember that there were no alcoholics or drug addicts in primitive cultures.

The final point I want to make here in this Preview comes from the work of Arthur Morgan. Among other things he is responsible for Antioch College's "study-work" program, which he inaugurated in 1921. His life-long search was to find what qualities go to make real community. While working on a biography of Edward Bellamy, he investigated the social system of the Inca civilization of ancient Peru, and this, in turn, involved him in the study of Thomas More's *Utopia*, which he found out was "largely based on the order established by the Incas." Eventually he wrote *Nowhere Was Somewhere*, "written to supply evidence for the idea that supposedly utopian 'romances' are commonly based, sometimes in large measure, on actual past societies." In this book, Morgan remarked that what all the "cynical critics" of utopias label as "impossible" and "contrary to human nature [actually] have been applied to pictures of society which were generally true descriptions of actual societies operating with a high degree of effectiveness, over a vast area, and for a long period."

Examples of How Rituals "Embody" a People

I was being given rituals, part of the living body of the people.
The anthropologist, Stanley Diamond in Africa

To provide some idea of how rituals serve to "embody" a people within their total ecosystem I will first give a brief account of the research of three modern anthropologists, each working in a different part of the world. The last account dates from the nineteenth century in the Western U.S. In each of these accounts you can see how their myths provide the story which fits them into the pattern of their native land.

THE TUKANO

The Tukano Indians live in the central part of the Northwest Amazon River basin along the Vaupes River. G. Reichel-Dolmatoff explains that they view their universe as a circuit of energy in which the entire cosmos participates. The Sun-Father, a masculine power fertilizes a feminine element, the earth. This Sun-Father created a limited number of plants and animals and put them under the care of a "keeper of the game." The Tukanos', world was given to them by the Sun-Father and is a restricted, specific stretch of land "limited on all sides by permanent landmarks." The basic circuit of energy consists of "a limited quantity of procreative energy that flows continually between man and animal, between society and nature." Reichel-Dolmatoff notes that this Tukano concept "bears a remarkable resemblance to modern systems analysis. In terms of ecological theory, the Tukano thus conceive the world as a system in which the amount of energy output is directly related to the amount of input the system receives."

The Tukano have very little interest in exploiting resources more effectively but are greatly interested in "accumulating more factual knowledge about biological reality and, above all, about knowing what the physical world requires from men." There are specific rules and mechanisms concerning hunting and fishing. For instance, they associate particular species of animals with certain constellations and a "species can only be hunted *after* its constellation has risen over the horizon." It is believed that the animal cries when it realizes that its time is coming near. The various myths, rules and rituals prevent a person from hunting or fishing just because he needs food; hunting is allowed only after an "anxiety-charged period of preparation, the purpose of which is to avoid over-hunting." Even the gathering of natural resources such as thatch for a roof or fibres and wood requires obtaining permission from the spirit owners of each resource.

The shaman considers that illness results from a person's upsetting some aspect of the ecological balance and deals with it as a "symptom of a disorder in the energy flow." Reichel-Dolmatoff claims that the Indians are "quite explicit about the ecological aspects of such matters." In fact, most of their shamanistic activities could be viewed "as rituals concerned with resource management and ecological balance."

In the Tukano culture, nature is not a physical entity apart from humanity; therefore there is no talk of confronting nature or even harmonizing with nature. "Man can unbalance it by his personal malfunctioning as a component, but he never stands apart from it," Reichel-Dolmatoff explains. He concludes his study on the Tukano by pointing out that most ethnologists and anthropologists have tried to explain culture in terms of linear cause-and-effect models. Gregory Bateson, in his studies on the Iatmul tribe was the first one to "sense the need for a systems theory model"; although he wrote of the New Guinea natives long before such a formal system was developed. Reichel-Dolmatoff calls attention to the fact that it is only very recently that some anthropologists have come to accept "as the only kind of explanatory model which can be used to handle ecological relationships the kind of overall systems model which was adopted by 'primitive' Indians a very long time ago."

THE TSEMBAGA

Roy Rappaport states that among the Tsembaga of New Guinea "ritual mediates critical relationships between a congregation and entities external to it." In this particular case, ritual regulates the relationships between people, pigs and gardens. It protects people from the competition of their pigs for basic resources and also indirectly protects the environment by helping to maintain large areas in virgin forest. Special rituals protect populations of small wild animals from being decimated by reserving their protein for tribal members who need more protein such as nursing mothers. In addition, when there is a sudden misfortune or emergency, pigs are ritually sacrificed; thus providing high quality protein to those who most need it.

The ritual cycle is culminated by the year-long *kaiko* festival. This occurs approximately every twelve to fifiteen years, depending on the pig population. Unlike the Tukano, the Tsembaga do not necessarily understand ritual as a regulating mechanism but see it more as having to do with the relations of the people to various spirits. Rappaport, however, observes that the "latent function" of the rituals has to do with allocation of scarce protein. Rappaport, as well as Reichel-Dolmatoff mentions the systems aspect of ritual and explains that the rituals of the Tsembaga affect the size of the pig population, the amount of land under cultivation, the amount of labor expended, the frequency of warfare and other components of the system.

THE ARAPESH

The Arapesh are another New Guinea tribe, living in a mountainous area which is so rugged that there is practically no flat land. Very small garden enclosures are separated by miles of climbing. The work is arduous and by our standards inefficient. Up to six men with assorted wives and children may move over difficult terrain for miles, climbing from plot to distant plot; but enjoying each other's company as well as sharing the work. The Arapesh plants his fruit trees on someone else's distant land and takes his pig to another far-away hamlet so that someone else's wife feeds it. Food not only provides nourishment; it incorporates intensive social intercourse and ritual participation.

The anthropologist, Dorothy Lee, explains that the Arapesh "multiplies his exertions and minimizes his subsistence so as to achieve a maximum of social warmth."

A laborer on a New Guinea plantation needs a minimum of seven lbs. of yams plus some meat; but an Arapesh, working on his own fields, spending about a third of his time on high energy climbs over steep mountain paths, and working hard on ceremonials "lives a meaningful life and procreates healthy children on three lbs. of yams a day and almost no meat." Here we find ritual behavior literally cutting down the demands of human beings on their environment for food. Lee observes that the Arapesh conceive of themselves as "belonging to the land, in the way that flora and fauna belong to it."

THE TIKOPIA

My fourth example also has to do with Dorothy Lee; but in this case, she is drawing on Raymond Firth's work with the Tikopia people. The importance of this study lies in the fact that the island of Tikopia is very small (only 2 x 3 mi. roughly) and lies 120 miles from other inhabited islands. The population in 1928 when Firth first arrived in Tikopia was 1288. Thus the island is tiny, with a considerable population, and isolated; but, as Firth states, "the mode of life of the Tikopia is very rich and vivid; the people are cheerful and animated, lead an active, busy existence, and while they spend much time in the preparation of their food, devote also a great deal of attention to ceremonial and religious affairs." Thus Tikopia provides an excellent example of how ritual provides a meaningful life even in the most extreme social conditions.

The story of Dorothy Lee's discovery of what we modern people can learn from Tikopian culture, began one Christmas Eve, as she "was suddenly astonished" to find that she was thoroughly enjoying adding extra embroidery onto a doll-blanket she was making for her three year old daughter and she didn't even like to embroider. She says: "At this moment of discovery, I knew that I was experiencing what it meant to be a social being, not merely Dorothy Lee, an individual...I realized that some boundary had disappeared." She wasn't doing it just to please her daughter but "rather within a relationship unaffected by temporality or physical absence." It was the love of the family which "contained social value."

"This was a tremendous discovery for me... my mind went immediately to the Tikopia, about whom I had been reading, and I said to myself, 'This is the way the Tikopia work.' I had been puzzled about the motivating forces in the life of the Tikopia." She had studied Firth but didn't necessarily agree with his choice of words: "obligations, duty, etc." for what motivated them, because the situations he described "brimmed with joy." She now understood that the "Tikopia did not need external incentives." Rather, she realized that the "limits of her self" had changed and she began to realize that the Tikopia "self" was different from our usual concept of self.

She went back to an intense study of Firth and found "a social definition of self. I found that here I could not speak of man's relations with his universe, but rather of a universal interrelatedness, because man was not the focus from which relations flowed." For instance, in Tikopia, an embrace or touching was not an "expression" of affection—"starting from the ego and defined in terms of the emotions of the ego, but rather as...a sharing, as a social act."

I do not have the space to go fully into Firth's data which she uses, but instead will just give her findings. For instance, in our culture we keep our bodies so separate that "only in sexual relations do we allow physical mingling." "But the Tikopia help the self to be continuous with its society through their physical arrangement. They find it good to sleep side by side crowding each other" mixing generations and sexes indiscriminately. Work among the Tikopia is always social. If a man has to work alone, he will take along any child that's available not necessarily his.

When they prepare a meal, "the whole household works together. Nothing is within reach, and children fill this gap, fetching and carrying and running errands, forming a bridge between adult and adult."

Their closeness with the land is emphasized in the use of the word, *fenua*, for land. When a man marries he and his wife are known by the name of their house plot of land. The phrase: "*Fenua* has made speech," indicates that the land itself has given them their words. The word, *fenua* is also used to refer to the placenta. Lee states that this "continuity with land-society" causes disasters when the natives leave to work elsewhere. In fact, recruiting for plantation labor was prohibited in Tikopia after "repeated experience showed that almost all the men died when away from home." The land belongs to the dead, so the people walk carefully and in "awareness on the land of their fathers."

Each step of increasing socialization is always celebrated in itself whether anything else is accomplished or not. For instance, there is a celebration and gift-giving when a young boy first goes out on a boat with the men for torch-light fishing. He doesn't even hold a torch or use a net, but merely paddles with the men. Yet this is celebrated!

Birth control and infanticide are both "carried on in the name of society, so that there should be enough for all." In Dorothy Lee's final summation, she points out that with this definition of self, (we could call it "extended identity"), "work can take place among the Tikopia without coercion, without the incentive of reward or the fear of punishment, without the spur of individual profit; because work as participation is meaningful."

THE BLACKFEET

Just before the turn of the century, Walter McClintock travelled to visit the Blackfeet (an Algonquian people) to find out how they lived. He stayed with them four years and was made part of the tribe. He visited them off and on for fourteen years. The last time was 1896. At the beginning of his book, published in 1910, McClintock quotes Catlin, who wrote in 1832 that the Indians on the upper Missouri River were "the finest looking, best equipped" of all the Indians he painted. McClintock stayed with a Blackfeet group who lived in the vicinity of what later became Glacier National Park.

McClintock reports that the Blackfeet called the Rocky Mountains the "Backbone-of-the-world." The Sun and Moon and other natural beings such as rocks, plants, animals, "including the elemental processes...are seen as 'persons', but in a category other than human, hence 'other-than-human persons' or 'grandfathers', " according to Jay Vest. Vest recently (1986) completed a paper, written at the request of the present Blackfeet tribe in their efforts to keep the Forest Service from granting leases for oil and gas exploration in the land granted to the Blackfeet by the 1895 Agreement with the U.S. Vest goes on to explain that, for the Blackfeet, the usual "conceptual distinction of 'natural' and 'supernatural' is non-existent; the phenomena of the world are not natural objects in the contemporary sense at all, but 'persons' of the 'other-than-human' class of being, and therefore personal as in 'our grand-fathers'. Hence the 'land' as an ecosystem is personal and 'honored' as 'grandfather' of the people."

The sun is venerated by the Blackfeet not as a Supreme Being or High God, but as "an ultimate animating life principle that they associate with the Sun and with the principals of creation including the collective ecology of the earth." In general, "in keeping with the Algonquian tradition, the Blackfeet religion personifies the ecological processes and elements—e.g., 'Above Persons', 'Underwater Persons', 'Thunderer', 'Wind Maker', —as well as animals, plants, rocks, and soils of the 'land'. The 'land' is therefore respected collectively as the 'grandfathers' of the Blackfeet people and is sacred within the context of their traditional religion." When the Blackfeet signed their 1895 Agreement with the U.S. they "did not think they were selling their lands, but rather sharing them with another nation."

What forced them to sign this Agreement, long ago, was that they were starving. McClintock stated that the extermination in 1893 of the last of the great buffalo herds by the whiteman gave the death blow to tribal organization and our government had to provide relief from starvation.

With this brief background of the Blackfeet "religion," I want to give an example of how power was allocated within the tribe. McClintock writes about a time when the members of the Medicine Pipe society had to choose a new member in place of Lone Chief, "who had kept the Pipe for four years and was ready to give it up." The Pipe Keeper fulfilled both a healing and a governing role in the tribe. McClintock's main friend in the tribe tells him: "It is a difficult matter to secure an acceptable member, because the society can only take in prominent men, who can afford to pay well for the Pipe, and to give the customary feasts and ceremonials." Those that know they can't possibly do this, "who are unwilling to be chosen can sleep away from their lodges." The Society assembles, singing Owl songs and drumming and sending representatives out with Lone chief as leader to try to find the proper man to take his place. They found the man, Mu-koi-sa-po and began the ceremonial transfer of the Medicine Pipe "just as the sun rose from the plains." There were many rules the new man and his wife needed to learn about their new life as "keeper of the Pipe." The society of Crazy Dogs were the ones who kept order in the tribe.

McClintock gives a beautiful description of daily life in his friend, Bring-down-the-Sun's camp, which gives one the feeling of the peace and contentment of their daily life. As it takes up seven pages, I will just give a few of the highlights here. He begins the account as he walks over to see the spring used for their water supply and finds wild strawberries, chokecherries and sarvis berry bushes "growing high above my head and laden down with ripe fruit." In the woods, he lists the five species of birds he recognizes and "many varieties of warblers." He finds the tracks of the tribal children mixed in with the beaver tracks along the stream. Nearby is a deep pool where the old chief and all his family took an early morning plunge each day. Here the children and young people had gathered, playing games. One young girl is poling a raft. He describes the "arching cottonwoods," the tipis and the blue sky all reflected in the still water.

He climbs above the camp to "Lookout Butte" which had been used for many generations by this group of people and their ancestors "as a place of meditation and prayer." By following the green cottonwood trees growing along the river he could trace the Crow Lodge River westward "to its very source among the snow-crowned summits of the Rocky Mountains." Then, turning the other direction he could see it vanishing far out on the prairie. He could see the Indian camp below "with its white lodges and brightly blazing outside fires." The continuous beating of drums came to him as they got ready for the Crow Beaver Ceremonial to be held the next day.

McClintock closes his description by describing how "seated in this ancestral place of meditation, and under the spell of my peaceful and beautiful surroundings...a strong doubt entered my mind as to whether the white races, in the pride of their civilisation, [sic] fit their natural environments much better than this patriarchal settlement of Blackfeet." He praises the "character, contentment and loyalty to the community interests" of this "simple life and few wants of the average Blackfoot family, before the invasion of the white race."

Conclusion

In the last two decades, since the Man the Hunter conference in 1966, volumes have been written concerning the many aspects of primitive culture which provide more humane living than our present IGS. In this brief conclusion I cannot possible do justice to all these aspects; instead I will simply list what I think are the most important lessons we can learn from primitive, or what I would rather call, traditional cultures.

Perhaps the single most important characteristic of primitive cultures as over against civilization is that of reciprocal relationship—at all levels and between all entities: human and non-human or rather, "other-than-human," as Jay

Vest puts it. In his paper, "Algonquian Metaphysics and Wildness" he states:

> When these Native Americans refer to their 'grandfathers,' they reference a wide array of 'other-than-human,' persons including animals, plants, rocks, and ecological processes. In acknowledging entire natural ecosystems to be their 'grandfathers,' the Algonquians demonstrate an all-inclusive moral system that therefore sponsors environmental ethics. Hence, within this world view and ethos, the land—collectively all animals, plants, soil, etc. —is not a sellable commodity, but rather the sacred 'grandfathers' of the people.

The Pueblo people, talking about the animals say, "Yonder on all sides, our fathers." Jaime de Angulo, who lived among the Pit River Indians of Northern California explains that among the Pit River people, "The total society generates, and the children belong to that society...Everybody really exists in a continuous world of generations, of being the children of the world they are living in, so you're a very bad child indeed if you do not venerate Father Tree, or any other aspect of your parent world."

Extending this concept further brings us to "totemism." Barry Lopez, who lived with the Eskimo for some time, says that they told him that a particular animal "is our totem because it knows how to do something well that we need to know." In an earlier chapter I discussed how early humans learned from the gourd and bear. Totemism is also used in many cultures throughout the world to structure human kinship within the tribe.

Briefly, if your identity is based upon relationship, you can extend it—in many directions. If, your identity is based upon things (as in our culture) you have to hold onto it and guard your ego boundaries.

Growing out of relationship, is the equally important matter of sharing. After many years of working in various primitive cultures, Ruth Benedict began trying to define a "good culture." During this time she sent her grad student, Abraham Maslow out to live among the Blackfeet, a high-synergy culture, to check our her idea. Summarily stated, he found that private possessions were accumulated only so they could be given to others.

Benedict put her ideas together in 1941 but the ms. was lost until 1970, when it was finally published. Essentially she states that nonaggression is high in societies where "the individual by the same act and at the same time serves his own advantage and that of the group...Nonaggression occurs not because people are unselfish and put social obligations above personal desires, but when social arrangements make these two identical." A conspicuous sign of a high synergy culture is what Benedict calls the "syphon system." Wealth is continually channeled away from any single point of concentration and spread throughout the group. She states that in such a culture, "if a man has meat or garden produce or horses or cattle, these give him no standing except as they pass through his hands to the tribe at large." The Plains Indians "give-away" is one example. Marshall Sahlins devotes a chapter in *Stone Age Economics*, to the same concept under "spirit of the gift." This phrase comes from Marcel Mauss' famous essay. Near the end of this essay he "recapitulated his thesis by two Melanesian examples of tenuous relations between villages and peoples: of how, menaced always by deterioration into war, primitive groups are nevertheless reconciled by festival and exchange."

Among primitive groups, in general, leadership is fluid and frequently changing with either seasons or purposes. For instance, among Pueblo tribes there is a clan leader for particular seasonal festivals in the winter; another leader for the summer festivals, etc. In Plains Indian tribes there was a chief for war and still another chief for peace. Leadership is acknowledged by the group as a whole because of the ability of the leader. While in civilized societies, human leadership is always ideological. Manipulation is accepted and tolerated by the followers.

As Sahlins states, the hunting-gathering culture "was ...the original affluent society. By common understanding an affluent society is one in which all the people's wants are easily satisfied." In Australia, in nineteenth century studies, the aborigines' subsistence activities took only two to four hours a day. The well-known Kung Bushman figures show that they spend two to three days per week in subsistence activities. The rest of the time is spent doing the same things leisured people prefer in all places and times: hunting, dancing, playing games, conversing and flirting, as Paul Shepard explains in his book *Tender Carnivore and Sacred Game*. Shepard continues: "It is no accident that these are precisely the 'true vocations' of primitive hunters, who, like the aristocrats, make no distinction between leisure and life."

This brings us to another important aspect of primitive culture. Most of the time, most of these activities are combined to some extent. Each aspect of tribal life takes in many different facets of living. In our culture, if you are sick you go to a doctor; if you want entertainment you turn on the television or go to a film or out to a party in another part of town. If you are neurotic enough you go to a psychiatrist to be cured. If you want to get outside with other people, you drive 50 to 100 miles and go hiking with a club; or you go hundreds of miles to go skiing with another group of people. While some of the most intense bonding takes place at your work place; this bonding cannot be allowed to interfere with your "private" life at home. Human bonding is dissipated in many different directions; hence it becomes ineffectual. While in a primitive culture it is all right there all the time. If someone is sick, the shaman or medicine man is called in and a ceremony is begun where everyone in the tribe joins in. Thus healing and entertainment and bonding goes on. Working is always communal so that bonding and entertainment and production are combined. If everyone is out of sorts due to the season, everyone joins together in a seasonal festival and human and non-human celebrate together; thus many levels of bonding take place. See Part III for further details on rituals and festivals.

Opening Dialogue
concerning
"natural phenomena as being identical with the religious Reality"

In the 4th century A.D. in China:
J.D. Frodsham: "Landscape was not just the symbol for the Tao—
the term was at this period as much a Buddhist as a Taoist expression—it is the Tao itself."
This is clearly shown by:
Sun Ch'o (320?-80 A.D.) "When the Tao dissolves itself it becomes rivers. When it coagulates
it becomes mountains."
William La Fleur: "So the contemplation of landscape is the contemplation of Reality itself."
Concerning the poet, Hsieh Ling-yün, (385-433 A.D.):
J.D. Frodsham: "Ling-yün's own experience of dhyana techniques would have convinced
him that, since the landscape was perhaps the most perfect manifestation of the Buddha,
contemplation of it constituted a religious exercise...thus the very embodiment of the Truth."
William La Fleur: When Buddhism reached Japan, it "was forced to accommodate itself to
the long-standing...high attribution of religious value to the natural world...The wider application
of this...in verse such as Saigyō's, [the 12th century A.D. Buddhist poet], results in an intense
and complete valorization of physical and natural phenomena as being identical with the
religious Reality."

"The Confucians say that people are complete when joined to other people. The Chan
Buddhists say that people are complete when the parts of their being are divinely joined
together. The Taoists say that people are complete when joined to the Tao. The Tao manifest
in the world is Nature. By Nature is meant the way things go: the nature of the landscape,
the nature of human relationships, the nature of the self...Chuang Tzu devotes much of his
writing to Nature."

Tony Robbin

"It might seem as if there were a real Governor, but we find no trace of his being. One might
believe that he could act, but we do not see his face. He would have [to have] sensitivity
without form. But now the hundred parts of the human body, with its nine orifices and six
viscera, all are complete in their places. Which should one prefer?
Do you like them all? Or do you like some more than others?
Are these servants unable to control each other, but need another as ruler? Or do they
become rulers and servants in turn?
Is there any true ruler other then themselves?"

Chuang Tzu

"Plunging in with the whirl, I come out with the swirl. I accommodate myself to the water,
not the water to me."

Lieh Yü-Khou

CHAPTER EIGHT

"The Ruler of the South was call Shu. The Ruler of the North was call Hu. And the Ruler of the Center was called Hun-tun (Chaos). Shu and Hu were continually meeting in the land of Chaos, who treated them very well. They consulted together how they might repay his kindness, and said, 'Men all have seven openings in order to see, hear, eat, and breathe. He alone doesn't have any. Let's try boring him some.' Accordingly they dug one hole in him every day and at the end of seven days Chaos died."

Chaung Tzu

"When you use the word 'chaos,' it means there is no chaos, because everything is equally related—there is an extremely complex interpenetration of an unknowable number of centers."

John Cage

"The West teaches us that being is dissolved into meaning, and the East that meaning is dissolved into something which is neither being nor non-being: In the Same which no language except the language of silence names."

Octavio Paz

"[There are] two entirely different world-views according to whether one places special emphasis on the initial point of the process, namely, the birth, i.e., coming into being of new things, or on its final point, namely, the death and disappearance of old things. [Taoism and Neo-Confucianism, which grew out of it] chooses the first alternative. Hence it is fundamentally optimistic. Universal change in the context of [this] philosophy means the never-ceasing procreativeness of Heaven. Change here means life. In the I Ching *we read: 'Ever-new life, that is (what is meant by) the change.'*

Completely different is the position taken by Buddhism. Instead of putting emphasis on the initial point of the above-mentioned process, it emphasizes its final phase, i.e., the inevitable decline, decrepitude, destruction and death. Buddhism, avoiding all self-deception, starts from a clear recognition of the negative aspects of the universal change. It is a religion which primarily intends to teach the way of deliverance...In this respect, Buddhism at least in its initial stage, is extra-ordinarily gloomy and pessimistic. [Christianity, basically is concerned with the same thing, 'the last things'—death, and heaven or hell.]

But the main point is that in [Taoism and Neo-Confucianism] the incessant change of all things is not understood as impermanence or the ephemerality of existence. Change is the very manifestation of the unchangeable. Change is *the eternal Law. Change* is *the unchangeable...The...fundamentally optimistic nature of [this] philosophy is determined by this...interpretation of the change of all things...The movement which affects the very core of everything inevitably leads it toward its end...but...the end is directly connected with a new beginning. The universal change is not a movement toward death. Quite the contrary, it is rather a movement toward life, a new life...[It] is fundamentally optimistic because it sees in the universal change the never-ceasing creative activity of the universal life-force. As the* I Ching *says:*

> *The Way is everyday new.*
> *This is its glorious function.*

This glorious function of the Way is...typically exemplified by the periodical return of the four seasons...spring, summer, autumn and winter; then again spring..."

Toshihiko Izutsu

"Change is gushing life."
> *from "The Great Treatise" commentary on the* I Ching.
Commenting on this Hellmut Wilhelm says: "verbatim: life-giving life; the procreating of pro-creation; the begetting of birth. And this calls to memory a much-cited passage from the Great Treatise: 'The greatest virtue between heaven and earth is to live'."

Hellmut Wilhelm

 Taoism

Personal Introduction

Thirty years ago, reading widely in my efforts to understand the continuing destruction of nature going on all around me in this culture, I discovered volume two of Joseph Needham's *Science and Civilization in China*, just published in England. For some years I had been aware that only Chinese and Japanese paintings depicted nature as I saw it in the mountains; therefore, I felt that they knew something we in the West didn't know. Fortunately volume two was on Taoism so I was lucky to get my first introduction to Taoism from the very man whose dedicated work since 1952 finally forced Europe to pay attention to the fact that, largely due to Taoism, China gave us practically every major invention used in our European culture. Toward the end of the book, on page 478, I found the following sentence, which Needham wrote about a modern Chinese philosopher, who stated:

> ...that while European philosophy tended to find reality in *substance*, Chinese philosophy tended to find it in *relation*.

Needham continued by quietly stating that this "might throw light on many characteristic features of the thought of both civilizations."

Instantly I realized this provided the key to much that I was searching for. I've been going deeper into this matter ever since. But my real insights did not begin until 1970, when I first started studying Tai Chi and, later, began teaching it. Tai Chi teaches Chinese organic philosophy through the body itself and thus dissolves all the dichotomies inherent in Eurocentric thinking so there is no longer a split between human and nature or between the body and the mind.

Now, after all these years of gradual, deepening understanding of the Taoist way, I can state categorically that all these frantic last-minute efforts in our Western world to latch onto some "new idea" for saving the earth are unnecessary. It's been done for us already—thousands of years ago—by the Taoists. We can drop all that frantic effort and begin following the way of Lao Tzu and Chuang Tzu.

Preview

The Taoist approach to living is the culmination of all the "old ways," which I have been discussing so far in Part II of this work: ethology, archetypes, animal teachings, and lessons from the primitives. Because of the early development of writing in China all this was written down; therefore today we can have immediate access to it, uncorrupted by later developments in Chinese history. Essentially, according to Wing-Tsit Chan, "Taoists were keenly interested in nourishing, preserving, and restoring the original nature of man."

Taoists were not "other-worldly mystics" or "occult beings"; they were much like us in that they were intellectuals, who realized the necessity of returning to the original human nature and to find that out, they turned to nature herself. Needham tells us that in the old temple to Lao Tzu in Kunming, "if one ascended through all the lower halls with their various images one came at last to an empty hall where there were no images, nothing but a large inscribed tablet with the characters, *Wan Wu chich Mu*—Nature, the Mother of All Things."

But, today, for many people there remains the question: "Is it possible for humans to live according to the 'old ways' or do we have to continue the present course of the Industrial Growth Society, now spreading its tentacles over most of the globe, wiping out the last tiny remnants of original societies at an even faster rate than we are wiping out the last remaining species of animals?" Yes, it is possible. Exactly this same situation confronted intellectuals who loved nature long ago in China. Of course, it was on a much smaller scale—only imperial China was involved not the entire world. But these intellectuals in long-ago China had a great advantage over us. They still had immediate access to both "wild nature" and the "wild hill tribes."

This, in short, is the legacy of what is called Taoism. The very form of the land itself in China is what "afforded" these intellectuals the opportunity to lay down the "way" so brilliantly. The map for the population under the Han Dynasty shows that 2000 years ago, the main population of China was confined to thin bands of settlements along river valleys. Here there was a complex, "hydraulic" civilization based on irrigation but between these valleys were steep, complex small mountain chains. This territory was occupied by tribal peoples, still living in the original primitive way. That long ago there was no modern transportation, hence no planes to invade the "wilderness" and destroy it.

The early iron age in China (sixth century B.C.) was a time when bronze-age proto feudalism was beginning to decline. "Wars and diplomatic efforts took place among the various feudal states, each of which had the ambition to conquer all the others, as Chhin ultimately succeeded in doing." This breaking up and reforming of feudal courts "led to turmoil among that small middle class of specialists which had previously occupied for generations reasonably secure posts at State capitals." This included scribes, secretaries, experts in rites and sacrifices and musicians etc. Some individuals among this class of specialists left the warring feudal courts because they felt that the only way to begin to find out how to live rightly was to go into nature and there try to figure out the patterns that Nature had given to humans. These sages knew, of course, that Nature was too complex for human reason to fully comprehend. They felt that by not imposing their own preconceptions on Nature, but by a receptive yielding attitude they would be able to observe and eventually begin to understand. Needham has pointed out that Taoist temples were called *kuan*, which means "to look." Taoists not only observed non-human nature but also the true "primitives" who still lived a cooperative, undifferentiated village life in the isolated small mountain ranges between the civilized river valleys. This juxtaposition of an increasingly organized hydraulic civilization with primitive tribal groups continued in China for thousands of years. In contrast, here in the U.S., the first missionaries, the Jesuits, arrived in the heartland of America in the middle of the seventeenth century; while Ishi, called the last truly wild Indian, died in 1916 in California. Thus everywhere on our continent tribal primitive culture was essentially wiped out in less than three hundred years. Furthermore, whites only began to realize what Indian culture had to offer in the latter half of the nineteenth century. By that time the railroads had cut the great Plains' cultures to pieces.

Taoist intellectuals, refugees from the feudal courts, always had access to "primitive" culture—another way of doing things. They could see how much simpler and more fulfilling life was when lived in a tribal village where nature and human worked together. This contributed to the Taoist concept of "*wu wei*," which has been translated as "do nothing" but, actually, according to Needham, means "do nothing contrary to nature." Also, according to Needham this attitude of *wu wei* contributed to the Taoist beginnings of science.

JOSEPH NEEDHAM AND HIS SCIENCE AND CIVILIZATION IN CHINA

It is well to observe the force and virtue and consequences of discoveries. These are to be seen nowhere more conspicuously than in those three which were unknown to the ancients, and of which the origin, though recent, is obscure and inglorious; namely, printing, gunpowder, and the magnet. For these three have changed the whole face and state of things throughout the world, the first in literature, the second in warfare, the third in navigation; whence have followed innumerable changes; insomuch that no empire, no sect, no star, seems to have exerted greater power and influence in human affairs than these mechanical discoveries.

Francis Bacon, famous English philosopher, who is often given credit for the beginnings of modern science, wrote this in 1620. Little did he know that each of these three "ancient discoveries" had been given to Europe by China. It's taken three hundred more years for us to realize, thanks to Joseph Needham, that practically every single major discovery was first made by the Chinese. Needham explains: "It is often forgotten that one of the fundamental features of the great break-through of modern science in the time of Galileo was the knowledge of magnetic polarity, declination, etc...Nothing had been known of it...in Europe before the end of the twelfth century, and its transmission from the earlier work of the Chinese is not in doubt. If the Chinese were...the greatest observers among all ancient peoples, was it not perhaps precisely because of the encouragment of non-interventionist principles, enshrined in the numinous poetry of the Taoists." In another place Needham notes: "With their appreciation of relativism and the subtlety and immensity of the universe, they were groping after an Einsteinian world-picture without having laid the foundations for a Newtonian one."

To summarize very briefly all that Needham documents I will quote from Robert Temple:

...modern agriculture, modern shipping, the modern oil industry, modern astronomical observatories, modern music, decimal mathematics, paper money, umbrellas, fishing reels, wheelbarrows, multi-stage rockets, guns, underwater mines, poison gas, parachutes, hot-air balloons, manned flight, brandy, whisky, the game of chess, printing, and even the essential design of the steam engine, all came from China.

One of the most fascinating of the early discoveries of China concerns "manned flight with kites" or in our present day terminology, hang-gliding. Needham quotes at length the famous Taoist, Ko Hung (283—343 A.D.), who writes about gliding on the "hard wind," after going up "using the clouds as steps." This refers to using an ascending current of hot air to rise thousands of feet simply by "spiraling up with it" as I see hang-gliders doing as they rise off 13,066 ft. Mt. Kendall here in Silverton. The early Taoist gliders were not made of high-tech, man-made fabrics and supports but of silk and bamboo. A single continuous strand of silk runs for several hundred yards and has a tensile strength of 65,000 pounds per square inch; while bamboo is still used as scaffolding for building skyscrapers in Japan. It turns out that many of the Taoist terms which seemed fanciful were in fact just what they actually experienced, as they "wandered in the void." For example, Lieh Tzu said: "I could no longer tell whether I was carrying the wind along or whether the wind was carrying me."

I've gone to such length into Taoism's connection with early Chinese discoveries in order to help erase some of the many misconceptions concerning Taoism as a "spacy" or "other-worldly" mind trip. Essentially, Taoism had long been dismissed by most European thinkers because, in the last century when European intellectuals began arriving in China, they found that the superstitious village priests were practising what was called Taoism; hence they dismissed the whole thing. At the same time, of course, translations were being made of the ancient classics of Lao Tzu and Chuang Tzu but no connection was being made between these classics and Taosim as an on-going practice down to today's modern times. Furthermore, in these early translations many important terms were given Christian translations thus further confusing the matter. Not until Needham's work of the last thirty years was Taoism recognized as a major world system.

By the age of thirty one, Dr. Needham, renowned in the field of Biochemistry, had published his three volume *Chemical Embryology*, which defined this new field of study, and was teaching at Cambridge University in England. An accidental conversation in the halls of Cambridge with Chinese graduate students changed his life. When Needham heard from them that the Chinese had discoverd the compass centuries before the West and saw a reference to the compass, written in 1088 by Shen Kua he began his monumental work on *Science and Civilization in China*. Later he wrote: "I shall never forget the excitement which I experienced when I first read these words. If any one text stimulated the writing of this book more than any other, this was it."

In 1942 he was asked to go to China, as an envoy from the Royal Society, where he remained for the duration of the Second World War as Scientific Counsellor at the British Embassy in Chungking. During this time he had access to previously unknown sources of Taoist works. The Taoists knew that whichever side won the on-going war (the Japanese were invading China and the Communists were organizing), they would lose out. So all the resources of hidden Taoist monasteries were opened to Needham. When he returned to Cambridge in 1948 the writing of *Science and Civilization in China* began. Some fifteen volumes have since come out with ten more scheduled.

Since I first read volume two in 1956, I've been getting

these volumes from libraries and taking notes. But, fortunately, just in time, Needham has opened all his research to Robert Temple to do a popular book, published in 1986. This has saved me much laborious gathering together of material. As I mentioned before in Part I, Temple sums it up when he writes: "Without the importation from China of nautical and navigational improvements such as ships' rudders, the compass and multiple masts, the great European Voyages of Discovery could never have been undertaken. Columbus would not have sailed to America, and Europeans would never have established colonial empires."

Why then, didn't the Chinese rip off the world in the same manner as the European colonial powers? This particular question has been asked in many different academic fields. Essentially this question has to do with the differences between the early science of China and the Western scientific explosion of the seventeenth century. In Chinese science, coming as it did out of Taoism, humans learned by paying attention and looking at nature itself without imposing human will onto it; while, as Needham remarks Western scientific findings were the result of mathematization, (essentially a grid imposed by humans onto nature) and laboratory experimentation. Turn back to Bateson's story of the dog in the laboratory, which is part of the opening pages of this work, for more insight into laboratory experimentation.

We cannot find our way out of the destructive trap of science as done in the present Industrial Growth Society—destructive both to humans and to the earth—until we approach it in the Taoist way, by seeing an entire region as a living interacting organism. The IGS way, of course, is to concentrate on one bit of "data," separated out from all the rest.

I can't take the time here to go any deeper into this difficult problem other than to remark that the same Taoist thought which created the beginnings of science in China also was the underlying reason for the Chinese not destroying the earth. As Needham points out: "...the sciences of China and Islam never dreamed of divorcing science from ethics." But, in Europe it was quite different. Needham, now 86, continues in his "Introduction" to Temple's book, "Science needs to be lived alongside religion, philosophy, history and aesthetic experience; alone it can lead to great harm." He writes of the "unbelievably dangerous powers of atomic weapons" developed by modern science and hopes that "maniacs will not release upon mankind powers that could extinguish not only mankind but all life on earth."

In 1976, when Needham was brought from England to give the John Danz lecture at the University of Washington, I was able to hear him speak. He said that it had probably been necessary for European science to go through the long complex development of dualistic thinking before they could get back down to real science, which he summed up by saying: "Yet who shall say that the Newtonian phase was not an essential one for Europe?" Only in the last few decades have we begun doing science in the way the Chinese always did—as relationship rather than substance.

Since Needham opened up the Western world to the importance of Taoism there have been three international conferences on the subject. The first one was held in Bellagio, Italy, in 1968, the second one in Japan, where most of the leading experts on Taoism live and the third one in Switzerland. I will be making use of some of this material below in the main text of this chapter.

THE I CHING

Underlying all Chinese thought, including Taoism is the classic work, the *I Ching*, providing 64 hexagrams as a guide for living. Wilhelm states that to begin to understand how the *I Ching* works for us, it is necessary to "take up in detail the early history of the Chou [1030 to 722 B.C.] who at the time the early strata of the book took form were still close to the dazzling starlight of the high steppes, though their economy had recently shifted to an emphasis on agriculture, under which a trusting reliance on nature had to be complemented by artificial, communally directed irrigation projects. Such experiences produced a mind open to the primary questions of human existence."

Here we see how the openness to nature of existence on the steppe with its winds and seasons and all-embracing sky led people to see the recurring patterns of stars and the patterns of seasons, which provide the origin of such statements in the *I Ching* as "he is to be in accordance with heaven and must follow the earth." The numinous feeling of "heaven and earth" from which all comes is ever-present in the *I Ching*. In the commentary on the I Ching, called the Great Treatise, we find this account:

> When in early antiquity Pao Hsi ruled the world, he looked upward and contemplated the images in the heavens; he looked downward and contemplated the patterns on earth. He contemplated the markings of birds and beasts and the adaptations to the regions...Thus he invented the eight trigrams.

This legendary sage represented the two forces of the world, (later in China known as yin and yang) by either a broken line or an unbroken one. Seeing a turtle, he arranged the eight trigrams as an octagon, the same pattern as the turtle's shell. Each trigram represents different natural forces: heaven, earth, thunder, water, mountain, wood, fire and lake. From its very beginning the *I Ching* was a "perception of the movement and circumstance created by natural forces."

The word, *I* in the *I Ching* means "change," but it means more than that. As Wilhelm tells us, "[T]he concept *I* as such connotes not only the dynamic aspect of life, but also what is firm, reliable, and irrevocable," underlying all of life. In other words, the basic patterns of life, here on *this* earth, under *this* sky with its sun and moon and stars; as well as the seasons, which show us the patterns of interaction between our turning earth and the rest of the universe. "The Great Treatise" of the *I Ching* states that "Change is gushing life." Wilhelm points out that this literally means: "Life-giving life, the procreating of procreation; the begetting of birth." All of this is summed up by the famous passage from the Great Treatise: "The greatest virtue between heaven and earth is to live."

Origins of Taoism

There are two roots to Taoism. One goes directly back to the ancient shamanic practices of primitive societies in China and the other goes back to the sophisticated intellectuals of the Warring States period who left their feudal courts to learn directly from nature. To explain the impact of this Warring States period on the Chinese mind I must go very briefly into Chinese history.

The first historical Chinese dynasty was the Shang (1520 B.C. to 1030 B.C.). It was conquered by the feudal Chou dynasty, which continued until broken up by the long period of warfare which brought deep changes in political and social structures. This general period of unrest is called the Warring States Period (480 B.C. to 221 B.C.), the fifth to the third centuries B.C. Perhaps the easiest way to grasp the effect of this turmoil on the intellectuals of the time is to compare it to the effects of the first World War on the English ruling class. Britain had long ruled the world and felt that this state of affairs would continue but the war shattered their complacent belief that they could control things in a "civilized" manner. With the outbreak of the War many of the best of the sons of this ruling class died, others committed suicide and still others began to question the legitimacy of the entire society. At any rate, the British ruling class never recovered.

A similar upheaval occurred in China during the Warring States period. Out of this confusion and questioning came many different movements but here we are concerned solely with Taoism. Some of the intellectuals left the feudal courts to withdraw into nature and there seek to learn the Order of Nature. They felt that human society could never be brought into order until there was more understanding of Nature because human society was really only a small part of the whole of Nature. Here, away from the civilized courts they learned not only from natural beings of the environment—plants and animals, mountains and rivers—but also from the primitive societies still existing in the hill areas.

Lao Tzu, the legendary founder of Taoism has been identified with various historical personages. Whoever he was, he seems to have been connected with the southern state of Ch'u. Lying on the southern edge of the civilized Middle Kingdom, it was a wild land of marshes, rivers, forests and mountains inhabited by many people of a non-Chinese origin with "strange customs" where "shamanic practices thrived."

The word *Lao* in Lao Tzu's name, simply means old or venerable and was often given to legendary sages. The book credited to him is the *Tao Te Ching* which has been translated as the "Sacred Book of the Tao." The word, *ching*, means "moral canon" and was generally applied to books which have teachings of outstanding moral value. This book was written not long before 300 B.C. when, in Greece, "Aristotle was old and Epicurus and Zeno were young." Needham explains that: "As political stability was more and more achieved in the unified empire of the Han, (202 B.C. to 220 A.D.), the sense of strain of the Warring States period disappeared." The historians of the Han dynasty, who began classifying the sytems of thinking of the previous dynasties gave the title, *Tao Te Ching,* to Lao Tzu's book. These same historians gave the name, *Tao*

meaning "way," to the system of thinking which developed out of Lao Tzu's work.

Chuang Tzu, the other figure most often associated with Taoism was "a shaman philosopher, or in other words, a visionary shaman elevated to the level of a philosopher." He was an historical person who existed about the middle of the 4th century B.C. He lived in a place called Meng, which was probably in the area of present day Honan, south of the Yellow River. Chuang Tzu once served as "an official in the lacquer garden."

The influence of Taoism continued throughout Chinese history in spite of the overall popularity of Confucianism. Although Taoist writings attack knowledge—Confucian academic knowledge—Taoism was never just a form of mysticism. On the contrary, not only was it a philosophical and religious movement but it was at the root of all early Chinese science, producing discoveries which, as Needham documents, occurred sometimes thousands of years before such discoveries got to Europe. The influence of Taoism peaked in the Sung dynasty (960 A.D. to 1279 A.D.), when it was called Neo-Confucianism, with Chu Hsi as its major proponent. During this time basic Chinese ideas were systematized in an effort to combat the growing influence of Buddhism.

According to Needham, Taoism continued to influence Chinese thought right up until modern times. Summing up this influence he wrote: "Taoism was religious and poetical, yes; but it was also at least as strongly magical, scientific, democratic and politically revolutionary."

With this brief historical introduction to Taoism, I will now go more into particular aspects of Taoism which are most important for us, today, trying to regain our natural relationship to the earth.

Lao Tzu and the Tao

Lao Tzu seems mysterious and impenetrable only if one is stuck in Eurocentric thought; so before going further it is necessary to point out that our Western theory of knowledge has all along assumed that its own kind of knowledge is universal to all of mankind. "As a matter of fact, however, it is only one kind of knowledge, other kinds being present in other cultures," as Chang Tung-Sun points out. For instance, the Western philosopher, Kant "thought that he was treating the universal categories employed in the thinking process of all mankind, while as a matter of fact he has treated the forms of thought characteristic only of Western culture."

Hughes, in translating the commentary on the *I Ching*, titled "The Great Learning" explains this further:

> The main distinction between a western and a Chinese tradition [is] the western has tended to see reality as substance, the Chinese to see it as relationship. Behind the metaphysical idea of 'substance' lies the logical idea of 'identity'; and western philosophers laid down as a basic principle of thought that a thing cannot both be and not be at the same time. Chinese philosophy on the other hand, laid down that a thing is always either becoming or de-becoming, if the term be allowed. It is all the time on the way to being something else. Thus the idea of 'identity' is blurred.

In western thought a thing is either good or bad. In Chinese thought, first of all since there is no subject, there is no "thing." Secondly, there is no locking into an identity. So there is no dichotomy of good or bad. Rather Chinese thought emphasizes the relational quality between above and below, good and evil, something and nothing.

Fundamentally, Lao Tzu is not trying "to assert the existence or non-existence of any substance, entity, Idea etc." Instead, he sees into the essential nature of all things in terms of Tao or "nothingness (no-particular-thing-ness)."

Obviously, we are getting deeply into language traps here so I will use the experience of climbing a mountain to clarify "no-particular-thing-ness." When walking up a trail in the valley, you see each individual peak rising up above the trees. You often cross innumerable creeks, as well. As you begin climbing out of the valley, you suddenly find more mountains rising up behind the first mountains you saw. You continue climbing until you are at the top. There, you suddenly discover that all those individual mountains were actually part of the one mountain. They were outlying peaks, joined by ridges— all culminating in the summit you are standing on. Are there a number of different things or one thing? The same with the creeks. Each seemed like an individual separate creek. From the summit, however, you see that all those individual creeks were coming out of different gulches on the main mountain mass, draining from the same mountain slopes and running off in slightly different directions—only to all join together eventually to make one creek.

In the Chinese view of the world, all those individual things (which in Western thought are named and thought of as separate) are in no way so. From the Taoist point of view it is seen and recognized that each is a different manifestation of the whole and changing all the time as well. Just as a nearby mountain changed shape as you climb higher up on your own mountain. Wei-hsun Fu explains that the ordinary man, "shackled by his self-created human bondage" sees a "car, a blonde, a paycheck etc." He sees only that and cannot see "the as-it-isness or (the totality of) all things," underlying each manifestation. I would add that, the ordinary man sees only each individual mountain peak from the main valley and never climbs high enough to see that each of these separate peaks is only part of the long ridge of the main massive summit.

Here we see still another aspect of the underlying theme of this work—substance versus relationship. We can see that the Western world's concentrating on substance is similar to a person seeing a particular mountain peak from the main valley and studying each peak separately and accumulating massive amounts of data without ever having glimpsed the fact that each of these little peaks is part of the whole main mountain mass. While the Chinese with their underlying concept of relationship were able to discern that it's all connected together and furthermore, that everything is always changing.

The Tao is not mysterious or occult in any way once you grasp the fact that the Chinese language does not require a subject in the sentence. It only seems mysterious and elusive to us Europeans because in our language we cannot conceive of an action taking place without someone—person or thing— doing it. Actually, this is merely a problem within our language.

To make this clearer I will turn to the work of Benjamin Lee Whorf on the Hopi language. He states:

> We are constantly reading into nature fictional acting-entities, simply because our verbs must have [subjects] in front of them. We have to say 'It flashed,' setting up an actor, 'it' or 'light,' to perform what we call an action, 'to flash.' Yet the flashing and the light are one and the same! The Hopi language reports the flash with a simple verb, *ri pi*: 'flash' (occurred). There is no division into subject and predicate...Hopi can and does have verbs without subjects, a fact which may give that tongue potentialities as a logical system for exploring and understanding some aspects of the universe. Undoubtedly, modern science, strongly reflecting western Indo-European languages, often does as we all do, sees action and forces where it might be better to see states [or fields, as in modern physics].

Perhaps now, it is easier to understand that, as Fu tells us, the Tao is not an "entity, substance, God, abstract notion" or any other concept. Instead Tao is used "to denote Nature itself in terms of spontaneous self-so-ness (*tzu-jan*) of the world and of man." To further show how the Tao is concerned with the relationship of Chinese thought rather than the substance or subject of western thought, consider the season of spring. In spring the flowers bloom, the rivers run higher, the air is warmer; but there is no single thing which does all this. Some people simplistically say, "The sun is warmer because it's closer to the earth." Such is not the case, of course, because the sun is nearer the earth in the northern hemisphere in the winter. Rather than the sun being the subject, the one who causes spring, it is again relationship: the spinning earth in its course around the sun tilts more toward the sun in the season we call spring. Therefore the light of the sun lingers longer on the earth each day than before during the winter. With the increased sunlight, the snow in high mountains melts, causing the rivers to rise. More sunlight also causes flowers to grow etc. Here you will notice how difficult it is to keep from falling into the subject trap as I just used "sunlight" as a subject!

Returning to Charles Wei-hsun Fu, he further states that the Tao is neither materialism nor spiritualism. In fact, he explains that spiritualism is really "absolute idealism'— idealism carried to its ultimate abstract conclusion and therefore "merely human."

The Tao or "absolute" or whatever name you want to give it, cannot, simply because it is the whole, be described or manipulated in any way by human beings, who are merely parts within that greater whole. Any attempt to do so automatically means a splitting off from the real whole, into individual parts.

But to talk about it means "naming" it in a way. Hence there are two aspects to the Tao. One aspect of the Tao is it's "non-being" or "nameless Tao." This is Tao as it really is— the whole. The other aspect is from the point of view of the outward forms of Nature which human beings have given names to. This can be called Tao as "being." The "nameless Tao" is the totality of "things-as-they-are"—Nature itself. The outwardly manifest forms of Nature, as we have differentiated them by defining, is Tao as Manifestation.

Lao Tzu goes into this matter of the Tao as Reality and as Manifestation in the very beginning of the *Tao Te Ching*, with the famous lines: "The Tao that can be told is not the eternal Tao." Wei-hsun Fu explains that this opening chapter puts "in a nutshell the essential nature of Lao Tzu's...Tao." Because of its central importance to our human relationship to Nature as such I will quote from Fu's "new and philosophical" translation of this chapter. Read it very carefully and you will understand in spite of being caught in the European subject trap.

> The Tao that can be tracked (expressed in words) is not the invariable Tao;
> The name that can be named (given in concept) is not the invariable Name.
> [As] non-being [Tao] is named the origin of heaven-and-earth (the universe);
> [As] being [Tao] is named the mother of all things.
> Therefore: [Under the aspect of its] non-being [as hidden] as ever,
> One may see into the inner wonders of Tao;
> [Under the aspect of its] being [as manifest] as ever,
> One may see into the outer forms of Tao.
> These two (non-being and being) are of the same source, though differently named.
> They are both called 'deep and profound'
> All-deep and all-profound.
> [Here is] the gate to infinite wonders.

Both the nameless Tao (Tao as Reality) and the Tao that can be named (Tao as Manifestation) are actually two ways of saying the same thing. They are not categories but perspectives. Wu, in his book about Chuang Tzu, explains this further when he says that, "In such understanding there is no knowledge to process and convey. There is instead a deepening, a conversion of life outlook and attitude...The "message" is not ordinary conveyable information but an evocation of freedom, which amounts to a call back to oneself...When one comes home to one's naturalness, one understands the naturalness of the surroundings and lives accordingly." Needham goes even deeper here: "[F]or the Taoists the Tao or Way was not the right way of life within human society, but the way in which the universe worked; in other words, the Order of Nature."

Wu Wei

The Taoist concept of *wu wei* does not mean "do nothing" or "inactivity" as most early translators of the Taoist writings insisted. Rather, as Needham says, it means "refraining from activity contrary to Nature." Being "contrary to Nature" means "going against the grain of things." Needham refers to a book from the Han dynasty, written about the year 120 B.C. which states that "power may be exercised according to the intrinsic properties and natural trends of things...Now were there such a thing as leading the waters of the Huai River uphill to irrigate a mountain, such a thing would be personal effort, and actions contrary to Nature (lit. turning one's back on Nature). This could be called *yu wei* (action with useless effort). But using boats on water...making fields on high ground and reserving low ground for marshes—such activities are not [useless effort]. The sages, in all their methods of action, follow the Nature

of Things." Chuang Tzu calls the refraining from activity contrary to Nature, *wu wei* and further, he says "Let everything be allowed to do what it naturally does, so that its nature will be satisfied." Chuang Tzu's most famous statement on this subject is:

> (The operations of) heaven and earth (proceed in the) most beautiful (way), but they do not talk about them. The four seasons observe the clearest laws, but they do not discuss them. All things have their intrinsic principle, but they say nothing about them...The Perfected Man does nothing (contrary to Nature) and the Sage makes no invention (contrary to Nature). They look to Heaven and Earth as their model.

It is important to note here that in general when the word, "Heaven" or *Tien*, is used, the Chinese are not referring to heaven in the Christian or Western sense, but rather "the mysterious government of the blue sky at noon...a world of pure intensity." This concept seems to have come right down from the early Chou peoples who lived on the high steppes of Northern China.

Chuang Tzu's theme of *wu wei* continues throughout all the centuries of Chinese thought. It was felt that, "However fast the horses of logical rationalism might run, Nature would get ahead of them in the end, confounding them" thus justifying the Taoist "way." This statement refers to a Taoist story about two of the fastest horses, who began running due west in the morning so that the sun was behind them. All day, running as fast as they could, "they would find, when evening came, that it had got ahead of them."

There are two more stories along this line. One shows that the people who manage the dykes and channels of the nine rivers and the four lakes did not learn "from Yu the Great (a culture hero), they learnt it from the waters." The other story shows that those who are good at archery "learnt from the bow and not from Yi, the Archer."

Essentially, *wu wei* is not some mysterious, uncanny method but rather it is the way the universe works and the way that humans can fit themselves into it. To make this even clearer for those of us of European descent I want to repeat Jacquetta Hawkes' account of how only two generations ago, the people of the Cotswolds in England learned from nature how to do their stone quarrying. Only certain places in the Cotswolds have the special limestone needed to make roof tiles. Of these, the Stonesfield pits near Oxford are most famous. These tile beds are very thin so they are dug down into with shafts and horizontal tunnels. This part of the work was always done "between Michaelmas [mid- September] and Christmas." Once the "pendle" as it was called, had been quarried, it had to be put in clamps until the first sharp frost. This special limestone

could not be artificially split and the whole industry depended entirely on the help of frost. When it did come, and it was hoped for January, every man in the village rallied to spread out the slabs of pendle; if it fell suddenly during the night the church bells were rung to summon the villagers. They must often have hurried up the street while the bell was still ringing through the frosty air; then, dark figures in the moonlight, they attacked the clamps and strewed the big slabs on the stiffening grass. If the frost had done its work, the men gave the summer to shaping and piercing the thin sheets, each sitting in a little shelter of hurdles or waste stone. If the frost failed then the industry was at a standstill and the pendle had to be buried deeply in cool soil, for if once the 'quarry water' was allowed to escape the slabs became 'bound' and could never be split.

The demand for these limestone tiles is still great but now people strip them off the roofs of old cottages and barns to sell them. The old knowledge has been lost with the death of the last of the "old men [who] loved their work, knowing the character of their pits as intimately as those of their wives."

These stories about learning from natural beings such as rivers and lakes and from the bow not the archer and how the frost splits the stones for the English country people bring us to the vast subject of all that the lowly gourd has taught the human race and the Taoists in particular.

The Gourd

Way back in 1956 in volume two of Needham's work I first read the story of Lord Hun-Tun (chaos). Since then I've been trying to grasp the underlying meaning of "chaos." In 1978 I found N. J. Girardot's article, "Chaotic 'order' (hun-tun)...in the Chuang Tzu." Still later, in 1983 his book was published, with a properly academic title, *Myth and Meaning in Early Taoism*. The only clue that there's something unusual going on here is the small drawing of a gourd on the title page. The book begins with a properly academic investigation into the origins of the two Taoist classics. Not until page 169, after he has carefully and skillfully set up all the necessary documentation and references does he broach the main subject, gourds. Once I got this far, I continued reading it all night because it provided the answers to so many of the long-standing questions which I've been asking for the last twenty years. I am telling you all this because if you haven't yet asked the right questions, what he tells you will not at first seem very important. But, as Gregory Bateson says: "Information is a difference that makes a difference." And believe me this book does make a difference—and on many levels!

Very briefly, Girardot explains for us the sophisticated philosophical/religious/psychological/ritual system which developed organically out of what the gourd taught the early Taoists. Further, each aspect of these gourd teachings provides us with a "way" to get back into relationship with nature in our daily life.

BACKGROUND ON THE GOURD

Mankind emerges from a gourd; men escape from the deluge by drifting in a gourd; the gourd's vine serves as a skyrope ascending to heaven...The gourd lives in human consciousness as the 'mother' of both natural and cultural life...We may conclude that metaphorically the gourd is a womb, that it is the whole universe, or, stated more simply, the universal womb.

I used this quote by Lathrap back in chapter two but I repeat it here as the quickest introduction to the gourd. Remember, Europe is only a tiny part of the world. For all

the rest of the world, according to Carl Sauer, the gourd/fish poison complex was the origin of human culture. This area extended from Africa and South America throughout the Malayo-Polynesian area to South China. Throughout this entire area we find variations on essentially the same basic creation myth. A brother and sister take refuge in a safe container (a gourd) from a flood. All others drown. When the flood is over the brother and sister being safely deposited on land, ask the animals what they should do since all the other people are drowned. The tortoise and the bamboo tell them to marry one another. Out of this incestuous union a gourd is born. When the woman sows the seeds of this gourd in the ground, they become humans. This myth comes out of the root crop form of agriculture, where the gourd is the chief crop.

The gourd, has been used throughout the world for a "truly amazing inventory of different uses: as containers, as food, in medicine and surgery, as floats and rafts, pipes and snuff-boxes, cricket cages and bird houses, masks, games, charms, offerings, penis sheaths, musical instruments (especially rattles), drums and as a pervasive subject of myth and ritual."

The gourd is a tendril-bearing plant, developing a fruit with a hardened outer covering containing many seeds ordinarily attached in three places to the outer covering. The *Lagenaria*, meaning "bottle-like drinking vessel" most often produces the dumbbell shape, often referred to in myths and legends. The gourd is incestuous in that pollen from a male flower will fertilize a female flower on the same plant; hence the brother/sister creation myths. The flowers bloom at night and are pollinated by beetles, moths, butterflies and bats. The gourd, when mature, has the seeds of its future life safely enclosed within a watery, pulpy, undifferentiated mass—the chaos stage. As the gourd dries out, the "germs of life within the central cavity of the gourd signal their presence through sound: they rattle and roll." The gourd is then light enough to float, which is how it makes it way around the world and across the Atlantic. The hollow gourd floats along, landing wherever the ocean currents carry it. When the shell is broken, its "ten thousand" seeds are distributed to begin another generation of gourds. With this introduction we can go on into Lord Hun-Tun.

LORD HUN-TUN AND CHAOS

Chuang Tzu tells of Lord Hun-Tun, emperor of the Center who is host to the Lord of the North and the Lord of the South as they meet on his land. They decide to repay his hospitality by giving him the gift of eyes, ears, nose, mouth and anus because he has none of these openings in him. So they bore seven holes in him and he dies. This myth, coming out of the South China cultural complex, combines a number of mythological themes: primal chaos, time, the image of watery, fluid or embryonic states, symbolism of darkness, void, emptiness, and primal matter or flesh carved up into items. Essentially Lord Hun-Tun refers to a hollow container (void) out of which birth comes.

As noted above, Lao Tzu was from the state of Chu on the southern borders of the Chinese Empire; he therefore came out of this South China cultural complex where the gourd already meant all the above in local myths. In Chapter 25 of the *Tao Te Ching* we find "There was something chaotic yet complete." The gourd is complete but essentially chaotic until it dries.

In both the *Tao Te Ching* and the Chuang Tzu there is a basic concern with what "precedes the creation of duality in the world." Tao is equated with *hun*. While *hun* is often translated as "chaos" or "chaotic" it is not the random chaos of the Western tradition but rather the fertile, undifferentiated possibility of future creations. Girardot, summing up the connections between Tao and *hun* states: "The primary descriptive reference for the Tao in this cosmogonic sense is the term *hun* (or *hun-tun*), which is a primordial condition of totality or unity. It can also be called the mother, the great, the dark...It operates spontaneously and continuously to give birth and life to all things."

In Chapter 42 of the *Tao Te Ching* we find:

The Tao gave birth to the one.
The one gave birth to the two.
The two gave birth to the three,
And the three gave birth to the Ten Thousand Things.

There are many levels of meaning implicit in these words, considered the crux of early Taoism. The one being the one incestuous plant, where the two—male and female—combine to give birth to the gourd. The gourd, originally a shapeless mass (again, the One) as it dries, the seeds separate out and attach themselves in three places to the walls of the gourd. When the gourd is broken open these three places provide seed which give birth to the Ten Thousand. On another level, the One refers to the Great Beginning or the Tao; the two refers to Heaven and Earth and the three to Heaven, Earth and Man.

Going deeper into the Taoist interpretation, the watery void or emptiness is a swelling of the gourd as it grows, to the point where its center is a "hollow" or empty gap alive with ch'i energy. "It is the empty gap of the center that allows for the original movement, sound or flow of the life-principle." The gourd's fertility and usefulness depend on the "nothingness" within the fruit. This "nothingness" allows it to travel across oceans, to protect the seeds of future life. All possibilities lie within this "nothingness" as long as the gourd remains unbroken. Carved into by human to make utensils, it becomes "useful" but loses its original cosmic potentialities; just as Lord Hun-Tun died when bored into.

Chuang Tzu specifically describes the occasional, necessary return to the "chaos-time" or "the beginnings" of the uncarved gourd, when he writes of the step by step return of the Taoist master Hu Tzu (which literally means Master Gourd or Gourd Master): "I, [Hu Tzu] appeared to him as Not Yet Emerged from My Source. I came at him empty, wriggling and turning, not knowing anything about 'who' or 'what,' now dipping and bending, now flowing in waves." The modern, tree-planting poet, Robert MacLean shows us what this means in his life, immersed as he is in his surroundings of the Canadian woods for weeks at a time:

Tent tethered among jackpine and blue-
bells. Lacewings rise from rock
incubators. Wild geese flying north.
And I can't remember who I'm supposed
to be.

In a later Taoist work, the Yellow Court Canon, the "myriad things, returning lead to the Three, the Three to the Two, the Two to the One..." The many cut apart bits of the rational human being (likened to Lord Hun-Tun with seven holes bored in him), are put back together by Taoist practices so that the "paradise" form of the hollow bottle gourd is achieved. There are many stories of Taoist immortals who return to paradise by leaping inside a hollow gourd. The Taoist masters are called "gourd masters" and "pumpkin heads." In picturing these masters, the greatly enlarged head (gourd shaped) and belly indicate the gourd. For instance, Shou-lao, star god of Longevity, with a gourd shaped head, holds a dragon-headed staff with a gourd containing the elixir of life. The use of the basic *Lagenaria* shape in vases, paintings, and sculptures indicates the union of yang and yin (the two bulges of this gourd linked by the narrow waist) or Heaven and Earth or male and female, "linked by the empty yet pregnant force of *ch'i*."

Living with a gourd, I learned, just as the ancient Taoists learned, some of the secrets of the universe. After I read Girardot's book, I knew I must acquire a gourd. Naturally, they don't grow this high; but a friend bought me one down in Aztec, New Mexico. I put it up on top of my file cabinet where I could see it as I sat next to my Earth Stove on cold winter days, working on this book. Days and weeks went by while I watched the gourd. Slowly, something began to form in my mind but I was much too concentrated on writing to pay attention to it. Until finally—one day, I saw. Of course, no doubt about it! Here was the origin of the famous Tai Chi symbol.

In the morning when the sun comes in my little window to the east, the left side of the gourd is bright, the right side dark. As the sun moves through the day it finally shines in late afternoon through my southwest window. The right side of the gourd is lit up and the left side dark. The gourd mirrors the changing relationship of human, earth and sun as well as the yin (dark) and yang (light) of each day. In all my reading about Taoism I never found any reference to this origin of the Tai Chi symbol. People say it's two fish which I've always felt was nonsense as fish do not swim in that pattern next to one another. But a Taoist alone in his mountain hut with his bottle gourd sitting in the window would certainly—far sooner than I—see the yin and yang before him continually changing throughout the day.

CONCERNING CHAOS AND ORDER AND THE MEANING OF LIFE

To recapitulate statements made in Part I of this work, European tradition grows out of the Greek language with its emphasis on I, the human, the knower of all else—who must create order out of all the rest of nature or else there can be no order. European tradition also comes out of the kind of order created by the famous Greek games (some win; others lose) further reinforced by Christianity (some are saved; others are damned). In the Middle Ages, knights jousted—some winning; others losing—often for a kind smile or even less, a light in the eye of his lady-love, that he could never touch, as she was the wife of another. All of them being good Christians where it's important to suffer. If you suffer enough you win heaven. All of this points to the epic idea of conquest of "some existential chaotic foe." But, as Girardot remarks, "in Taoist literature where there is less attention to boring civilizational knights and gentlemen, the quest for a meaningfully authentic life is not a hero's price. A Taoist does not conquer life to *win* salvation but *yields* to the eternal return of things."

For the Taoists, "creation is not a once-and-for-all heroic act of a Creator outside of time and space," as it is in the West; therefore Salvation doesn't become such an epic, tragic problem. Instead "the early Taoist texts more modestly claim that the 'salvation' of man and society is a matter of the resynchronization of human periodicity with the cycles of cosmic time. This has a very primitive ring to it." Girardot is correct of course. It is primitive but always deep within us—the periodic need—at ritual or festive times, of putting the stages of human life back into phase with the ongoing cycles of the changing relationships of the seasons, the sun and the moon. These are the "world-renewal" times.

The real secret of life is to return to the "primitive chaos-order or 'chaos-mos' of the Tao." But in some ways we moderns feel that chaos threatens our planning of order. Chaos is often felt to be demonic. But the Taoists tell us that the "cosmos originally came from, and continually depends on, the chaos of creation time." Myths often show us this disguised or suppressed hidden connection, "linking chaos and cosmos, nature and culture." Sometimes this is called "the playing of the gods." Fundamentally it is the playing of human, earth, sky and gods in the great festivals. This is precisely why "play" is the crux of it all. True play in early life lets the child become a fully functioning human adult; true play in the great festivals allows human culture to happen. But true play cannot occur where there is fear of chaos.

I had just finished the above sentence when I took a break for lunch. It was late spring so I was running out of wood for my stove. After lunch I headed up the highway to a spot where I have been getting wood for some time. An avalanche had come down at this spot during the winter of 1984-85 and deposited a great pile of broken trees along the creek. The upper reaches of the avalanche were hidden by the hill rising above the creek. I knew that I had already taken all the avalanche deposited wood along the creek but I figured there would be some wood scattered up on the hillside above the creek.

When I climbed above the creek, I was confronted by a total jumble of ripped-off trees. This was the edge of the main avalanche path. All the trees from the main path itself had been ripped out completely and deposited below along the creek where I had been gathering wood for several years. Up above on the hillside, the wind wave from the impact of the avalanche had selectively taken out all the weaker standing live trees and smashed them in between the trunks of the still standing trees. There were large aspens, with leaves greening out as if they were still alive, lying across the top of large fir trees bent over almost to the ground. In some areas, enormous standing dead trees had been picked up and stuck right through a mass of living trees. A group of very old, standing dead aspen trees had newly uprooted living trees sticking out from them like needles in a pin cushion.

The entire scene was totally chaotic, seemingly making no sense at all. But, standing there, looking and perceiving it with all my senses, "order manifested itself." Having skied for forty years and been caught in avalanches, and lived here in this place for eight years, I was receptive to nature showing me the underlying, inherent order. I knew that this previous winter there had been an unusually heavy early snow—so early that we still had very warm days and freezing nights through the rest of October. This combination over a period of time causes the lower levels of the snow to turn to "depth hoar." The individual snow flakes, losing all sharp edges, turn into fragile skeletons of the original crystal. Only hollow spaces are left within the crystal. As more snow falls on top of this layer and the weight becomes greater, eventually the entire skeletonized structure collapses and the entire mass comes crashing down in an avalanche, carrying with it all the deposit of snow from the rest of the winter storms. Such an avalanche generates massive air waves both ahead of it and alongside as it sweeps by. This perfectly natural pattern of early season snow in Southwestern Colorado, due to warm days and freezing nights combined with massive amounts of snow on top; eventually gave way to gravity and swept down the mountainside depositing parts of trees and creating the "order" of this seemingly random mass of tree parts. The weaker of the standing trees had been uprooted and flung in at least two directions by the force of the wind—in front of the mass and alongside it. The standing dead trees, being lighter, had landed higher up in the living trees. None of this order would be apparent for a modern city person in the prevailing Industrial Growth Society. Only when one stepped out of that prevailing culture and lived within nature itself did this order manifest. The more our present culture tries to order and contain everything in the universe for its own purposes the more paranoid it becomes because the fear of losing control becomes greater and greater. We cannot recognize any "order" outside of our own cultural distortions. Meanwhile all about us in the real world of nature, order and disorder continue as always in the yin and yang rhythm of the Tao, completely unmindful of this tiny puny human with its distorted "ideas" of order. In the avalanche path, because the trees had been torn out, more sunlight reached the ground and new life in myriad forms was already bursting out of the earth. The Tao is truly the "sum of all orders."

The Taoist classic, Huai Nan Tzu, dating from the Han dynasty, refers to the paradise time of the "natural harmony of cosmos, society, and man..Then came the 'decadent age' when men gave into their inclinations 'to bore' into the one body of earth and man in order to regulate and control the world by artifical human standards: there was a rupture of the connection between yin and yang and the succession of the

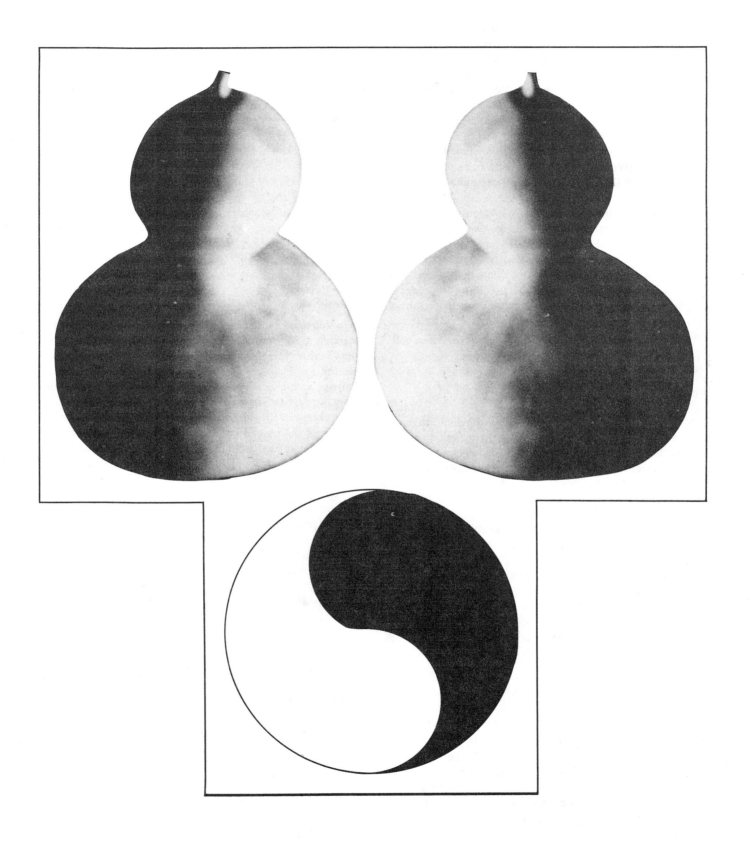

four seasons failed." But humans can again "learn how to rediscover the principles of balance and order." Another way to put this is that the discriminating mind of human beings cuts everything up into bits (bores into it) to analyze but forgets that the whole body/mind—a return to the chaos conditions of primordial unity—must be used to put things together again. Human action must be at the right time "to insure the return to, and maintenance of, the creative order and great transformation of all life." There needs to be a periodic return to chaos time (the example given in this Han classic is the period before the time of the winter solstice). These "world renewal" times are a "call back to oneself, to one's self-movement in and of the always-so. When one comes home to one's naturalness, one understands the naturalness of the surroundings and lives accordingly."

Girardot explains that the Taoist is a "Gourd Master who has learned the secrets of creation and stores the elixir of life within an empty calabash. Sacrificially cut in two, a calabash usefully serves as a ladle or dipper to feed the desires of ordinary social life; whole and empty, it is the container of wine and medicine, ecstasy and salvation. Chuang Tzu would have it that the best use of a gourd is to respect its original uselessness by 'making it into a tub so you can go floating around the rivers and lakes.'"

Taoist Animal Gods

Taoism seems to be the only major philosophical/religious system which never lost its animal gods. In ancient times, of course, the Chinese shaman put on his animal mask to communicate with the animal gods. Girardot points out: "By emphasizing the identification of human and animal nature, Taoism preserved more of an archaic religious consciousness where the mythological animal served as a link between the world of men and the world of the ancestors and gods." In the "Animal Frolics," a Taoist technique which pre-dated Tai Chi, there are specific forms for being the bear or the crane for healing purposes. This technique is taught even today.

Taoists retained their animal gods and animal teachers because from the beginning, as Needham notes, "the Taoist denial of anthropocentrism was diametrically at variance with those whose interests were focused on human society, and for whom man was the measure of all things."

Tai Chi

In Tai Chi we come to the wisdom of the belly. As said in the *Tao Te Ching:* "The sage is concerned with the belly and not the eye. He accepts the former and rejects the latter." This inner empty kind of knowing and doing that comes from the *Tan Tien*, the area just below the navel, resonates with the hollow, womblike condition of Lord Hun-Tun. This kind of knowing establishes direct contact with nature in all its forms of life.

When doing Tai Chi, cats will come up and sit in the center to absorb the energy; dogs will lie quietly by until you finish.

I have had a pine martin stand, watching us until we finished. I've also had a range steer bellow a challenge to me as he came around the bend in a dirt road where I was doing Tai Chi. As he neared me, he suddenly stopped short and lay down with his harem of cows and stayed right there until I finished.

Throughout the years of teaching Tai Chi, I have seen countless people change their lives as a result of becoming bonded with nature by doing Tai Chi. Their previous way of life had been much like the Confucian, who as Girardot explain, "through the exercise of his 'evaluating mind.' seeks a 'path to privilege' within an 'aristocracy of merit.' The Taoist, however, seeks a 'path to the mirror' wherein his mind reflects the larger nonhuman or 'chaotic' order of primordial life."

In this kind of knowing we see the connection between Taoism and the ancient shamanic ecstasy of the "way" sought by Taoists, where knowing with the belly "identifies the Taoist with the sacred madness of the ancestral gods of the creation time."

Taoist Sex

According to Taoism the energy of the universe operates through the interaction of yin and yang (female and male); thus Taoism developed the most sophisticated methods of any culture for dealing with sexual energy within and between humans and nature. Until recently, Taoist sexual techniques were dismissed as superstition, but these methods were rescued from obscurity when Joseph Needham devoted a considerable section of the second volume of his work to the subject.

Needham explains that, "The purpose of the Taoist techniques was to increase the amount of life-giving *ching* as much as possible by sexual stimulus...Continence was considered not only impossible, but improper, as contrary to the great rhythm of Nature, since everything in Nature had male or female properties. Celibacy (advocated later by Buddhist heretics) would produce only neuroses." Taoist sexual techniques were used to increase the energy not only between a particular man and woman, but within the human group as a whole and between the humans and their land. From these relationships came the exquisite sex/nature poetry of China. See chapter fifteen for more on this subject.

Conclusion

For Taoists, salvation is more a "matter of healing of man to the fullness of cosmic life" than it is a saving from this world, as it is in the Christian sense. The "true man" in the Taoist sense is one who is able to let go of the discriminating mind (rational mind which analyzes and cuts up things into bits) and thus feel the unity beneath all of the on-going changes of the Ten Thousand Things. This is in no way a homogeneous "wholeness" nor an effort to reach perfection. The "true man" is not perfect; nor does he impose his "idea" of order on the rest of the world. Wu explains:

The True Man's activities are at once a reflection of his nature and that of the things acted upon. In working on things, his hand somehow has a knack for it, but his mind can only wordlessly feel it, and he has to respond to it with his whole self. There is a natural match between the inner nature of such a man and that of the things aimed at; the deep meets the deep, Heaven meets Heaven...

No longer is there prostitution of one's original nature or dislocation of the original root-power, the power of being oneself.

Living according to the Tao requires a periodic return to a chaos-time where there is space in order to move, grow and create. A real culture, whether it be in a traditional, primitive society or in a modern group must provide the great festivals where the relationships of the group are deepened and newly formed out of the playful chaos of ritualized interaction among the gods, the mortals, the earth and the sky of your own place.

Herman Hesse, deeply influenced by the Orient, wrote:

"The future is uncertain but the road which [Dostoevski] shows can have but one meaning. It means a new spiritual dispensation. This takes us beyond Myshkin, it points toward magical thinking, to the acceptance of Chaos, to return to anarchy, back into the unconscious, into formlessness, into the beast, back far beyond the beast, back to the beginnings of everything." In other words, the "old ways."

Chuang Tzu shows us that there is a way of living where "this" and "that" are no longer opposed. This is called the "pivot of the Tao." He says: "The Ten Thousand Things all come from the same seed, and with their different forms they give place to one another. Beginning and end are part of a single ring and no one can comprehend its principle."

Robert MacLean shows us what this means in his poem:

DEATH AS A HELIX OF DRUNKEN OWLS

Sitting at the foot of a birch,
lungs capillaried with quartz:
root toes
bole spine,
leaf skull a window to wind.

In that darkness,
a luminous ring
with innumerable rooms where the dead
hibernate:
doorways opening into a centre hall
where a party's in full swing.

Owl changes into Rabbit
who pretends he's blade of Grass
hiding as Dirt which Worm
eats, flows into Cloud
into Snow into Rain back to Owl
bemused, blinks a lidded
Sun.

...All holding hands
blazing, I name 'yellow
marsh marygold.'

"For example, we arrange flowers in space whereas the Japanese arrange the ma or space between flowers. While we see a hole merely as the absence of objects, the Japanese perceive it as the relation between objects."

Barrington Nevitt

*"I carry occult and subtle power,
Carrying water, shouldering firewood."*
Zen Master, Koji

Chapter Nine

"When vision is thought of as a perceptual system instead of as a channel for inputs to the brain, a new theory of perception considered as information pickup becomes possible. Information is conceived as available in the ambient energy flux, not as signals in a bundle of nerve fibers. This ecological theory of direct perception cannot stand by itself. It implies a new theory of cognition in general. In turn, that implies a new theory of cognitive kinds of awareness—fictions, fantasies, dream, and hallucination."

James J. Gibson

"Thus, when I 'think', I reduce the field of my being, whereas, when I 'perceive', I belong, through my point of view, to the world as a whole."

M. Merleau-Ponty

 SEEING NATURE

Personal Introduction

When I was younger and still dutifully trying to fit into the culture of this Industrial Growth Society I made a real effort to try to like European art. I mean I really worked at it for a period of years, but Van Gogh was the only painter I could tolerate. I wouldn't go so far as to say that I was moved by his work, but I could certainly tolerate it. Then, quite by accident, I saw some of Georgia O'Keefe's paintings. Here was someone who could actually "see" nature. It surprised me and I wondered why she could do this but went no further into it because I'm not an artist.

Years later, when I first heard of Fenollosa (more on him below) I got a book about him from the library and found out why Georgia O'Keefe "saw" nature. She took classes from Dow and Dow was carrying out Fenollosa's work in the world since he was no longer allowed to do it. Thus Japanese art helped O'Keefe put down what she was seeing in nature.

I can't remember, of course, when I first saw reproductions of Japanese art it was so long ago. But from the very beginning they seemed true to nature as I saw it. When I began to climb mountains I was always seeing scenes which I could recognize as having been the immediate inspiration for art in China or Japan. More recently, as I have been taking people out into nature on workshops of various kinds I've been referring to "this Japanese scene" or that "Japanese waterfall." Then, about three years ago, taking an artist friend, named Raima up to see a "Japanese" waterfall, I said to her, "look at that Japanese print." The scene was an overhanging red ledge of rock, covered by a solid blanket of moss about 10 inches deep; below was a gorge with blue-green water rushing through. All of a sudden, both of us consciously realized something we had always known of course. This wasn't Japanese, because we were in southwest Colorado. But it certainly seemed Japanese to us. Why? As we talked, it became obvious—Japanese art had taught us Westerners how to see nature and that's why even generations later we still "see" the natural scene as "Japanese." Once we began talking about it, she recalled a book she'd read along these lines, titled *Japanese Prints and Western Painters*. Since she's not a rugged outdoor person, she had not been out in nature enough to fully understand what that book was telling her until I began taking her to beautiful natural waterfalls. Then a year later she told me of another book that she had just found. I later got it from inter-library loan. It is the account of a show in Munich concerned specifically with the Japanese influence on Western art. (More on this below.)

The second personal story I want to tell here in this introduction, has to do with Tai Chi. After only a month of lessons I went up to spend the summer on Mount Olympus on the Olympic Peninsula in Washington where I was part of an on-going glacier study team. I explain this elsewhere in more detail; here I just want to say that after doing Tai Chi for the first time up there I saw a mountain I had never seen before although I had been looking at that view for years and years. The more I did Tai Chi throughout the following years the more I saw how it was changing my "seeing." But I had no words for all this until David Abram sent me his article, "The Perceptual Implications of Gaia," and told me to be sure to look into one of his sources, Gibson's *The Ecological Approach to Visual Perception*. When I got the book I found that Gibson had figured it all out for me. Since then I've been able to help others to regain the natural "original human" way of seeing, which our culture destroys.

Preview

What I am going to do here is give a very brief summary of some of the most important aspects of seeing when it comes to our relationship to nature. I've neither the time nor the space to go into as it should be done but I give references for each aspect so that those who wish can pursue it further. First, I will go into how the Japanese were able to preserve their natural human way of seeing and then into Gibson's theory of vision.

Japanese Art

As shown in chapter thirteen later in this work, in more detail, Buddhism, in China, was influenced by the Taoist approach to nature so that it became Chan Buddhism. When Chan Buddhism reached Japan, it was further influenced by the native Shinto so that the end result, Zen Buddhism, was closely tied to nature. In China, as mentioned before, Taoist temples were called *kuan*, meaning "to see," such was the importance to them of seeing nature. The first Japanese to go to China to study Buddhism and bring it back to their native land, were thus deeply influenced by this necessity of turning to nature in order to see. For instance, when Dōgen left China to return to Japan, his master told him to avoid cities and keep away from government: "Just live in deep mountains and dark valleys." Dōgen returned to Japan and headed for the mountains of Echizen Province where he founded the Soto Zen school of Buddhism in 1224.

Before that, of course, the native Shinto religion of Japan had always been concerned with seeing. In an academic article written in 1913, a man named Schwartz, who climbed a Japanese sacred mountain in 1891, wrote that this gave him a "glimpse into the past relations of Shinto and Buddhism which amounts to a revelation of the former, by discovering most unexpectedly how much of what we have fully believed to be Buddhist has been simply baptized by it out of the older faith."

The first Europeans in Japan were the Portuguese who reached an outlying island in 1542. Seven years later, Franciscan missionaries arrived but the example of the Philippines, which was conquered by Spain in the sixteenth century after intense missionary activity, served as a warning to the Japanese. They banned the Spanish and other Europeans in 1639. Only the Portuguese were allowed to stay and they were allowed only one port for trading.

Japanese art had an effect on Europe dating as far back as this early contact. The Metropolitan Museum of Art catalog shows a piece of pottery made about 1735 at a "porcelain factory in Chantilly founded by the Prince de Cond, whose interest in Japanese porcelain influenced many of its products." However, the flood of Japanese prints and art, which totally changed Western European painting, did not occur until after the U. S. "opened" Japan in 1854.

Fenollosa, the American Who Saved Japanese Art

Chinese poets and painters were pouring out their souls to catch the spirit of morning dew upon bamboo groves or of white herons upon a snow branch, when Alfred was battling with savage Danes in the West.
Ernest Fenollosa

The event that changed Fenollosa's life occurred in the winter of 1877-78 when he was recommended to fill the first chair of philosophy in Tokyo University. He had been recommended by a Salem neighbor, Edward S. Morse, a Harvard trained zoologist who had first gone to Japan in search of brachiopods to test Darwin's theory. The Japanese were so impressed by Morse that they invited him to organize a department of zoology at the university and later, he was asked to find a philosopher for them.

Morse recommended Fenollosa because Fenollosa knew something about art and Morse was upset that the Japanese were throwing out all their own art to slavishly copy Western art. In December of 1884 the Japanese appointed Fenollosa to an official committee to study art education. He travelled to Europe with the Japanese members of the committee. The result was that the next spring the brush was restored in elementary schools and other principles of Japanese art were reinstated.

On the eve of his return to Boston in 1890, Fenollosa was given high court rank and decorated by the Emperor with the Order of the Sacred Mirror. The Emperor's parting words were: "We request you now to teach the significance of Japanese art to the West as you have already taught it to the Japanese." A tall monument was erected to Fenollosa in Tokyo which states: "To the merit of our Sensei, high like the mountains and eternal like the water."

Fenollosa became curator of the Japanese Department of the Boston Museum of Fine Arts. His collection of a thousand or more Japanese paintings eventually became part of the Museum. He resigned in 1896, having got a divorce from his wife, Lizzie, a member of the American ruling class at the time. He married his former assistant at the Boston Museum, a very lovely young woman, 12 years his junior. This scandal caused a sharp break with the gentility of Boston. "After leaving in 1896 he never again held an official position with a museum, university or American school of any kind; nor did he write again for the Atlantic Monthly...the official art world in the U.S. was very small in the '90s and its respectabilty was zealously guarded...Fenollosa must have realized that the notoriety of [his] divorce...would damage his career."

He supported himself by lecturing and fed his ideas on art education through Arthur Dow, who was then an art educator at Pratt Institute. Dow's influential book, *Composition*, containing the first extended outline of the Fenollosa-Dow theory of art education, was published in 1899. "In the course of Dow's thirty years of teaching he converted a generation of art teachers to Fenollosan principles, thereby re-educating the eyes of students from California to Maine, from Michigan to New Mexico." Georgia O'Keefe and Max Weber were the most famous of Dow's students. Later: the philosopher, F. S. C. Northrop wrote that O'Keefe's art was a "herald of the coming fusion of East and West."

When Ezra Pound discovered Fenollosa's writings in 1912, "his excitement over his 'treasures' as he called them, was intense. Fenollosa's papers were a 'ball of light' in Pound's hands, leading directly to "Cathay" and "Noh" and into the Cantos." In Fenollosa's essay on the Chinese written character Pound saw "a study of the fundamentals of all aesthetics." Pound was early involved in the Imagist movement but grew into a deeper poetic form after Fenollosa's influence. (See chapter seventeen of this work for Pound's influence on poets such as Gary Snyder.)

Western Art and Nature

The influence of Japonisme was what was needed to deliver us from the black tradition and to show us the bright beauty of nature.
Emile Zola
We have found the way to nature again and it lies through Japan.
A. Fendler in 1897

In the second half of the nineteenth century, "painting in France and elsewhere developed in a way which can largely be explained in terms of the growing understanding of the Japanese aesthetic. [This included] Manet himself, Whistler, Degas, van Gogh, Gauguin, Toulouse-Lautrec etc." Van Gogh especially tried to "dig down to the very roots of Japanese culture in order to be able to generate creative impulses of his own from the encounter." In 1886 Van Gogh wrote to his brother, Theo, who had introduced him to the world of Japanese wood cuts and prints, "In a way all my work is founded on Japanese art."

Even more directly, Degas used the figures in Hokusai's third volume of the *Manga*, as models for the postures in his paintings. "Without Degas's meticulous study of movement, it would hardly have been possible for the later Expressionists to depict action as they did." Toulouse-Lautrec also found models for his work in the *Manga*.

A still more lasting effect was due to the fact that children's books began to appear with original Japanese illustrations in them. This meant that "the children of the 1880s and 1890s grew up absorbing the elements of Japanese art." In other words, nature became visible to European children through Japanese eyes.

It's obvious that the Japanese see nature in a way that was completely closed off to Europeans until the influence of Japanese art. There are many historical reasons for this but there is also a practical physiological reason. European science had developed a completely unnatural way to account for how we see. This distorted attitude is still with us, but Gibson's work is finally beginning to change that attitude.

Gibson's "Ecological Approach to Visual Perception"

How we see determines our relationship to the world. It turns out that those of us in the West have, thanks once more to our Greek beginnings, been laboring under a totally invalid conception about seeing. It's not that we were born seeing wrong because, of course, we were born seeing in the manner our animal ancestors had developed for us over the course of millions of years. Some of us, even today, manage to hold onto the natural way of seeing in spite of our conditioning. But most lose this natural way sometime in the early years of childhood.

We've been told that vision depends on the eye, which is connected to the brain and that basically the brain does all the work in sorting out the image on the retina to make sense of what we see. Gibson, on the other hand, says that "natural vision depends on the eyes in the head on a body supported by the ground, the brain being only the central organ of a complete visual system."

James J. Gibson of Cornell University has been, as he says, "puzzling over [vision's] perplexities for 50 years." Long ago he began by learning "what is accepted as true about the physics of light and the retinal image" and other matters connected with the anatomy and physiology of the eye and the brain. "But the more I learned about physics, optics, anatomy, and visual physiology, the deeper the puzzles got." Experts in these fields could "create holograms, prescribe spectacles, and cure diseases of the eye...but they could not explain vision." His search began back in 1929, when he wrote a paper on the perception of drawings. Years later, he wrote that he has been puzzling about this matter ever since. During the war he was involved in training men to fly by the use of picture simulation materials. Beginning in 1947 he wrote a series of papers trying to explain the visual aspects involved in this training. Through the following years he continued his research, "abandoning one definition of a picture after another for twenty years." During these years of research he wrote 42 different papers and a number of books, culminating in his final book, which he spent ten years writing. By that time some of his former students had joined him in his research, further helping to clarify this complex matter of seeing. With this last book, he hopes that the "ecological approach to perception" will finally be understood, so that others can begin to profit from the long years of work.

What is at stake here is very important for healing our supposed "split" with nature, but clearing up two thousand years of invalid concepts concerning seeing is not a simple matter. This is why Gibson has had to spend all those years in research and writing. His latest book must be read carefully and with full attention, in order to clear out all that "they" have been telling us about seeing, all these years. But for me, the book clarified some things that had been happening to me, as far as seeing goes, but for which I had no understanding, because I had no words.

As a rock climber, from time to time, some of this way of seeing had come to me because, every time I see a rock face I automatically begin tracing out a possible route up it. Thus I could see things which could not be accounted for by current vision theory. In skiing untracked powder snow the same thing occurs. Then, finally, when I began doing Tai Chi, from time to time rather unnerving things would happen as far as the interactions between me and the surrounding land forms. But I could not put any of this together until I read Gibson's book.

Gibson begins by showing how we developed our vision through past evolutionary history in response to the play of the sun's light during the day and throughout the year. An essential point of his theory concerns ambient light. In daylight, part of the radiant light of the sun reaches the earth in parallel rays (as physics puts it) but other parts are scattered because they are transmitted through our atmosphere. This light is further scattered when it reaches the ground or the surface of other substances. "Radiation becomes illumination by *reverberating* between the earth and the sky and between surfaces that face one another." Gibson says that this could be thought of as rays, completely filling the air; furthermore, each point in the air is a point of intersection of rays coming in all directions. "It would follow that light is ambient at every point. Light would come to every point; it would surround every point; it would be environing at every point." This is ambient light. He summarizes the differences between radiant light, (which physics is essentially concerned with) and ambient light (or light as we experience it).

Furthermore, as the human body moves through the landscape certain things happen, which enable seeing. None of the laboratory experiments where the person is put into a chair with the head locked in place, while being shown different things has anything whatsoever to do with seeing outside in the real world. Fundamentally this is why the whole of seeing has become so complex.

The difficulties began when Plotinus, a follower of Plato, saw the eye of a dead ox. Peeling off the back of this eye and holding it up in front of a scene, he "observed a tiny, colored, inverted image of the scene on the transparent retina." Ever since then the image has been thought of as "something to be seen, a picture on a screen," Gibson remarks. He continues, "You can see it if you take out the ox's eye, so why shouldn't the ox see it? The fallacy ought to be evident." But from this original fallacy, came the further misunderstanding that the image came into the eye but needed the brain to make sense of it. This of course, goes right back to the underlying idea that the human, the knower, must make sense of the outside world or else there was no sense or order in it. A long time after Plotinus, some 350 years ago, Johannes Kepler, "was mainly responsible for the extraordinary intellectual invention" of forming an image of an object on the back of the eye. This has to do with focused rays of light etc. which I won't take the time to go into here. This has been the accepted way of explaining vision ever since. Recently there have been other theories along the same line. Gibson points out that in such theories "the eye sends, the nerve transmits, and a mind or spirit receives." And all these theories imply there is a mind separate from the body.

Gibson, however states: "It is not necessary to assume that anything whatever is transmitted along the optic nerve in the activity of perception. We need not believe that *either* an inverted picture or a set of messages is delivered to the brain. We can think of vision as a perceptual system," with both the brain and the eye as part of the system. The whole process is circular not just a "one-way transmission. The eye-head-brain-body system registers the invariants in the structure of ambient light."

Gibson's theory takes off from what is called visual angles. The eye forms the apex of the angle and the object, looked at, forms the base of the angle. But observation usually involves movement because all observers are animals. Plants don't observe; only animals do so because animals move about. "The point of observation normally proceeds along a path of locomotion, and the 'forms' of the array change as locomotion proceeds." What we really see is not depth but *"one thing behind another."* As you move along, walking toward the mountains, the nearby hills rise up higher and higher, thus covering more and more of the distant hill. Until finally the distant hill is cut off completely. The distant mountain sinks down as the nearby hills rise up. Also as you move along, the nearby trees go by you rather rapidly, moving in the opposite direction. Eventually as you continue along on your walk, the distant mountain, which was hidden since you first saw it, suddenly slides out from behind the nearby hills. And you see it once again. "The blue mountains are constantly walking," as the Japanese master Dōgen wrote. There is a continuous interaction between you and the surrounding environment. Vision is not a physically passive, internal, brain event as most eye research has told us. Instead it involves "active, exploratory systems within us attuned to dynamic meanings already there in the environment."

The light on the objects around one changes continually as one walks along. So there are two sources of changing light, one caused by you moving along, the other by the moving source of illumination, the sun. "The motion of the sun across the sky from sunrise to sunset has been for countless millions of years a basic regularity-of-nature. It is a fact of ecological optics and a condition of the evolution of eyes in terrestrial animals. But its importance for the theory of vision has not been fully recognized."

The puzzles of light and shade come from the "moving source of illumination," the sun. Whenever the sun moves, the direction of the light falling on trees, hills, houses etc, is altered and the shadows themselves move. All of this gives us further information about the objects surrounding us. The east side of a green tree in the morning, with the sunlight shining directly on it from the east, looks different, later in the day, when the sun is setting and hence shining on the other side of the tree. The green is much darker. The yin and yang of Chinese thought comes from the varying relationships between the sun and the mountain. In the old form of the Chinese characters *yang* is represented by the sun with its rays, together with the character *fu*, meaning hill or mountain. The character for *yin* was a coiled cloud along with the character *fu*. According to the definition in *The Erh Ya*, a dictionary of the Chou period, *yang* describes "the sunny side of the mountain" and *yin*, "the side in the shadow." This relates directly to the changing relationship of the sun and the mountain. In the morning, when the sun is behind the mountain, the trees are dark—almost black; in the afternoon, when the setting sun shines directly on these same trees, they are bright and glowing with light.

As a rock climber I've long known the importance of watching the cliff at different times of day to see where the cracks run and how the holds slope etc. This becomes second nature. Many facets of a cliff are obvious if you are a climber even if you have never been near it. These aspects, however are often completely hidden from other people, who have not learned to watch the sun's changing light on the face of the rock.

Watching a mountain grow as it rises against the sky is sometimes quite startling. Looking up at Humboldt Peak, from directly below, it doesn't seem so high, but as you climb Broken Hand, across from it, Humboldt continually grows and grows. In other words it moves up against the sky or fills more of the sky as the viewpoint changes with increasing altitude on Broken Hand. Paying attention to the space between objects in nature is something which Europeans ordinarily fail to do. Japanese art, however depends on this space. "For example, we arrange flowers in *space* whereas the Japanese arrange the *ma* or *space between* flowers while we see a hole merely as the absence of objects, the Japanese perceive it as the relation between objects." Once you learn to see the space between the moving leaves of a tree, an entire new world begins opening up.

Another thing that is important to remember is that as you stand, looking out over the scene, "about half of your surrounding world is revealed to the eyes and the remainder is concealed by the head." When the head turns, whatever was in back of the head comes into view. Gibson points out that this seemingly obvious fact, which we often ignore, "is fundamental" to vision. He explains: "Information exists in a normal ambient array, therefore, to specify the nearness of the parts of the self to the point of observation—first the head, then the body, the limbs, and the extremities. The experience of a central self in the head and a peripheral self in the body is not therefore a mysterious intuition or a philosophical abstraction but has a basis in optical information." Further, "the optical information to specify the self, including the head, body, arms, and hands, *accompanies* the optical information to specify the environment." They coexist. "When a man sees the world, he sees his nose at the same time...which of the two he notices depends on his attitude...The supposedly separate realms of the subjective and the objective are actually only poles of attention. The dualism of observer and environment is unnecessary."

THE CONCEPT OF AFFORDANCES

Besides teaching us how to see, Gibson's book provides us with a much-needed word, *affordances*. First, he explains the environment around us as being filled with particular surfaces, which we learn about from the way we move through them and they move by us and secondly, from the way the changing light of the sun illuminates them differently throughout the day and the year. But he also describes what the environment *affords* us animals, such as terrain, shelter, water, fire, tools etc. Since, we've already seen that there is information for the perception of surfaces, he asks whether there is information for the expectations of what they afford us. "Perhaps the composition and layout of surfaces *constitute* what they afford. If so, to perceive them is to perceive what they afford. This is a radical hypothesis, for it implies that 'values' and 'meanings' of things in the environment can be directly perceived."

The *affordances* of the environment are what it *offers* the animal, what it provides or furnishes, either for good or ill.

Afford, as a verb is found in the dictionary but Gibson made up the word, affordance. He explains that this word refers to both the environment and the animal (including the human) "in a way that no existing term does. It implies the complementarity of the animal and the environment." This is precisely why I think this word is so important. In our culture, we tend to think that humans have discovered all these amazing things; in some ways we believe that these things didn't even exist until humans found them. I've been trying to break down this latter presupposition throughout this work; first, by showing how the affordance we call the gourd gave us agriculture, and later, with other examples. Once you begin using this word, you will find that every day you will realize how nature provides affordances for us to use. It's all there before us—it's not dependent on humans to figure it out. This is a giant step forward in overcoming our culturally induced split from nature.

These affordances "are the way specific regions of the environment directly address themselves to particular species or individuals. Thus, to a human, a maple tree may afford 'looking at' or 'sitting under', while to a sparrow it affords 'perching', and to a squirrel it affords 'climbing'. But these values are not found inside the minds of the animals. Rather they are...a reciprocal interchange between the living intentions of any animal and the dynamic affordances of its world...The psyche...is a property of the ecosystem as a whole."

The concept of affordances allows us not only to get rid of the dichotomy of subjective-objective, but it helps us to understand how invalid this dichotomy is.

Direct Perception

Gibson defines direct perception as "the activity of getting information from the ambient array of light," resulting from looking around and moving around. It is not mediated by neural or mental pictures. It is direct. When the terrain is flat and open, the horizon is the "ambient optic array." It seems to make a great circle between the upper sky and the lower earth. Most often, however, these farther reaches of the earth are hidden by nearby surfaces such as hills, trees or buildings.

The famous vanishing point of Renaissance perspective came out of the human as the center of the universe; so all things get smaller and smaller as they lie at greater and greater distances. It also has to do with converging parallels which occur in a city or other humanized environment. "It involves setting up a piece of glass as if it were a window and then, with one eye exactly fixed in front of the window, drawing lines on the surface to coincide with the projections of occluding edges of the layout." Out in nature, in unfamiliar terrain, how is one supposed to know whether that tiny hill is a big hill lying in the distance or a small hill up close. There's no way by just standing there, that you can figure this out. But by beginning to walk toward the hill you will soon see it grow bigger as it rises higher up above the distant terrain. Or if it is truly far away you may see it slide behind a nearby hill as that nearby hill rises up. There is no problem about what is far and what is near if you move through the environment and look.

We can see now that vision is not concerned with merely the eye, somehow considered as an organ of the brain. "But," as Gibson makes clear, "the truth is that each eye is positioned in a head that is in turn positioned on a trunk that is positioned on legs that maintain the posture of the trunk, head, and eyes relative to the surface of support. Vision is a whole perceptual system, not a channel of sense. One sees the environment not with the eyes but with the eyes-in-the-head-on-the-body-resting-on-the-ground." In short one must "perceive in order to move, but we must also move in order to perceive."

Knowledge of the environment "develops as perception develops, extends as the observers travel, gets finer as they learn to scrutinize, gets longer as they apprehend more events, gets fuller as they see more objects, and gets richer as they notice more affordances." All of this knowledge can only come from looking, listening, feeling, smelling and tasting. This kind of knowledge only gets deeper and deeper and there's no end to it.

In his conclusion, Gibson states that the ecological approach to visual perception "begins with the flowing array of the observer who walks from one vista to another"; who moves around some obstacles and moves toward other objects so as to see them better and to see what they afford to him. It's important to remember that the information in light coming from all the myriad things out in the environment, does not have to resemble it or copy it at all. "*Nothing* is copied in the light to the eye of the observer, not the shape of a thing, not the surface of it, not its substance, not its color, and certainly not its motion. But all these things are specified in the light." The information coming to us is an interaction between the moving human, the moving earth around the sun and the object we are looking at.

Further Insights into Affordances

The indescribable innocence and beneficence of Nature—of sun and wind and rain, of summer and winter—such health, such cheer, they afford forever!

Henry David Thoreau

...everything offers itself as the most immediate, exact, and simple means of expression...It actually seems as if the things themselves came to me, and offered themselves...

Nietzsche

Throughout Part II of this work, I have shown how specific aspects of nature have continually provided affordances for us. In this sense I am carrying the word, affordance, a step beyond Gibson's use. Two affordances which I discussed earlier are the gourd, which led humans to agriculture and the bear, who showed us transformation and rebirth. This concept of affordances can be very helpful as we try to move out of the exploitative "using" of nature, common to European cultures. In contrast to this exploitative manner, Paul Shepard explains: "The attitude of hunting/gathering peoples the world over is similar to that described by Charles Hill-Tout, a nineteenth-century ethnologist, of the Lillooet Indians: 'Not a single plant, animal or fish, or other object upon which he feeds is looked upon as something he has secured for himself by his own wit and skill...or as mere food and nothing more...He regards it as something which has been voluntarily and compassionately placed in his hands by the good will and consent of the spirit.'" Or, to be more specific, we could say, "by the good will and consent of nature or any one of its myriad beings," depending on the specific affordance involved.

This is not a simple thing—to overturn the hundreds of

years of conditioning—which has led us to think that we, humans must figure out how to do all of it or it won't work. However, it's very, very obvious from the state of the earth's environment that we moderns simply don't know how to do anything on our own without causing irreparable damage to all life on earth. So it's about time we begin using a word, which will permit us to recognize that throughout time, non-human aspects of nature have been the affordances for much of the developments, inherent in valid human culture.

To give a specific modern example, New Alchemy's approach to productivity, is to keep nature's affordances in mind. For instance, there are plants that fix nitrogen so that we can grow other plants. "There's plants that will extract phosphorous from the soil more efficiently than others... There's animals, like geese, that you can use to weed certain crops." Each of these natural beings are affordances, which can better enable us to feed ourselves. John Quinney sums it up very well, when he says: "And what's nice about using biological resources in that fashion is that you don't incur any environmental costs. You can provide nitrogen fertilizer from ammonium nitrate, but that uses large amounts of energy and it pollutes and everything else, or you can get the plants to do it, using legumes or some other non-leguminous plants."

In Part III I will be giving directions for ritual structures to enable us modern humans to once again begin to allow the non-human beings in each place to afford us the knowledge needed to live in that place. This way of doing things was always true in the "old ways," as practiced for 99 % of the time humans have been on this earth.

"Through rites [Li] Heaven and earth join in harmony, the sun and moon shine, the four seasons proceed in order, the stars and constellations march, the rivers flow and all things flourish, that love and hatred are tempered and joy and anger are in keeping."

Hsün Tzu (298-238 B.C.)

"The extraordinary importance of this technical term li may be guessed from the fact alone that the entire philosophy of the Sung dynasty Confucianism is known as the 'science of li' (li hsüeh)."

Toshihiko Izutsu

"Gathered up, all things are unified in the one supreme Principle of Being. Separated from one another, every one of them has each its own supreme Principle of being."

Chü Hsi (1130-1200 A.D.)

*"I have often been impatient with colleagues who seemed unable to discern the difference between the trivial and the profound. But when students asked me to define that difference, I have been struck dumb. I have said vaguely that any study which throws light upon the nature of 'order' or '**pattern**' in the universe is surely nontrivial."*

Gregory Bateson

*"When in early antiquity Pao Hsi ruled the world, he looked upward and contemplated the images in the heavens; he looked downward and contemplated the **patterns** on earth. He contemplated the markings of birds and beasts and the adaptations to the regions...Thus he invented the eight trigrams in order to enter into connection with the virtues of the light of the gods and to regulate the conditions of all beings."*

I Ching

*"Let us then imagine archetypes as the deepest **patterns** of psychic functioning, the roots of the soul governing the perspectives we have of ourselves and the world. They are the axiomatic, self-evident images to which psychic life and our theories about it ever return."*

James Hillman

*"Told one day by someone that the Chinese had no science, [Jung] replied indignantly that they had already possessed one uniquely their own for thousands of years, a science based on a total acausal principle of approach, a profound observation and exploration of the **pattern** of meaning unfolded throughout time in the universe, utterly beyond and before our own conceptions of first cause and its effect. The I Ching was for him the greatest textbook of this classic Chinese science."*

Laurens van der Post

*"Li, then, is rather the order and **pattern** in Nature, not formulated Law. But it is not pattern thought of as something dead, like a mosaic; it is dynamic pattern as embodied in all living things, and in human relationships and in the highest human values."*

Joseph Needham

 INTER-LUDE

Death, work, domination, love and play, these are the elements of the patterns which we find in human existence, so enigmatic and ambiguous.
Eugen Fink

Li is a concept pregnant with ethico-religious connotations. The mere fact that it has been rendered as 'ceremony,' 'ritual,' 'rites,' 'rules of propriety,' 'good custom'...and a host of other ideas including that of natural law suggests the scope of its implications.
Wei-ming Tu

Inter-lude means "between the plays" (Latin, *ludus*, play and *inter*, *between*). Further meanings of *inter* include "between the parts; reciprocal *inter*relation; shared by or derived from two or more"; hence the meaning for this transitional piece. Part II gave the "old ways" deep inside of us; now, Part III provides "ways" to fit ourselves into these old ways—following both aspects of nature's patterns, those deep inside of us and those outside, in the natural environment around us.

The basic idea of Chinese *feng-shui* was that humans prospered if they aligned themselves with the forces of nature rather than going against them. The basic concept here is *li*, usually translated as pattern. The earliest meaning of *li* came from the pattern in which fields were laid out for cultivation in order to conform to the topography of the land; hence the earth was considered the ordering principle of a particular place. Later, the word *li* came to refer to the patterns in things—the markings in jade or the grain in wood. The Neo-Confucianist, Chu Hsi used the word, *li* for the principle of cosmic organization which ran through all levels of Being. The Chinese did not feel that either God or law was the ordering principle; rather they visualized the universe as a hierarchy of parts and wholes working in harmony—each according to its own *li* or pattern, but all fitting together in the great pattern. Wei-ming Tu notes that the "[C]oncept of *li* is actually much more inclusive than either the Christian concept of law or the Indian concept of *dharma*."

The ancient Chinese, *Chi Ni Tzu* book explains: "Thus all together the five directions [north, south, east, west and center] (with their corresponding *chi*, elements and planets) constitute the *kang-chi*." Providing further explanation here, Needham quotes from still another classic: "The Yin and Yang constitute the Tao of Heaven and Earth; their sum is called *kang* and their cycle of recurrence is called *chi*." He continues, "This is nothing less than the dynamic pattern of the universe... There is a web of relationships throughout the universe, the nodes of which are things and events. Nobody wove it, but if you interfere with its texture you do so at your peril." This is the "web woven by no weaver."

The Chinese "do not ask of an entity how well it measures up to the pure form prescribed for it, but rather what is its relationship to other entities." It's important that "Every entity have a place [in] the pattern of existence." Human self-realization comes out of participating fully in all of life around you, because it depends on relationship with all aspects of your place.

That's where play comes in—play as taking part in the great festivals, which bring all the beings of place together to play and thus recreate their world. The "something more than" which comes out of true festivity is the result of the free interactions, the play, of all the beings—not anything imposed from outside, either from a god above or from human laws. During the festival time, the *li* within humans, reflecting the *li* without, "serves as the very 'raw material' out of which

LUDE

man fashions his distinctively human creations—his music, art, cultural forms..."

Free-play in nature such as back-country skiing, mountain climbing, wild water running etc., when not competitive, can lead to similar results. When in play or in festive celebrations these "root-traces" come together, they show us the pattern for living the "story" and this story we live must accurately reflect the root traces both within and without to make a good culture. When that happens, "the entire landscape comes alive, filled with relationships and relationships within relationships."

Within each place on earth a particular pattern develops from the interactions of sun, gravity and space—the framework into which each fits. To show how this occurs, consider a tree on the edge of a cliff. It began growing in a sheltered spot within or under rock. As it grew taller, gravity began pulling it down and over the edge, but as it continued growing it grew up toward the sun. Sometimes a tree becomes too tall for the sheltering rock, under which it began, and then it grows horizontally out, reaching for the space to continue its growth. These complex patterns, which the tree forms, in relating to sun, gravity and space—all together conforming to the *li* of its place—create the beauty which the Japanese call "bonsai trees." Humans, too, can begin to fit just as beautifully into the pattern of their place, but not through conscious willing; instead, it's more like playing. "Story" grows out of this type of play. As the festival grows through time, the story develops. The story of a society is the way that people fits into its place. The place gives us the *li*, the pattern, and the story is how we fit into that pattern.

The story was his [the Bushman's] most sacred possession. These people knew what we do not: that without a story you have not got a nation, or culture, or a civilization. Without a story of your own to live, you haven't got a life of your own.

Laurens Van der Post

"Ceremony is an enactment of the story people live by," according to Elizabeth Cogburn.

So there is a work to be done in the matter of knowing where we are, the old American quest, which I share with all of you, for an identity, a sense of place. To know the place well means, first and foremost, I think, to know plants, and it means developing a sensitivity, an openness, an awareness of all kinds of weather patterns and patterns in nature.

Gary Snyder

Following the *li* implies following the patterns, the "root-traces" within us as shown in Part II and the patterns we begin to recognize in all of nature outside of us. This is facilitated by rituals and the Great Festivals. The more familiar you become with the patterns both inside and outside in nature, the deeper the play becomes.

The ear for the story and the eye for the pattern were theirs; the feeling was theirs; we came out of this land and we are hers.

Leslie Silko, Laguna Pueblo

Part III
Following the Root-Traces:
The Return

"Our goal should be not the emulation of the ancients and their ways, but to experience for ourselves the aspects of human existence out of which arose those ancient forms which when we see them elicit such a feeling of something…longing. Otherwise the modern will remain forever superficial while the real will remain ancient, far away, and therefore, outside of ourselves."

Mr. Aoki, founder of Shintaido

ESSENCE OF THE SACRED

"Magic may be defined as the imposition of non-physical power to attain a specific end. Religion is the maintenance of abiding relationship."

Gertrude Levy (1948)

"A vast old religion which once swayed the earth lingers in unbroken practice there in New Mexico...In the oldest religion, everything was alive, not supernaturally but naturally alive. There were only deeper and deeper streams of life...So rocks were alive, but a mountain had a deeper, vaster life than a rock...For the whole life-effort of man was to get his life into direct contact with the elemental life of the cosmos, mountain-life, cloud-life, thunder-life, air-life, earth-life, sun-life. To come into immediate <u>felt</u> contact, and so derive energy, power and a dark sort of joy. This effort into sheer naked contact, <u>without an intermediary or mediator</u> is the root meaning of religion."

D.H. Lawrence

"The greatest virtue between heaven and earth is to live."

"The Great Treatise" of the <u>I Ching</u>

LIMITATIONS ON RELIGION

'Well-nigh two thousand years and not a single new god."

Friedrich Nietzche (1888)

"Noting that Israel was only about one hundred by sixty miles, Watsuji Tetsuro observed: 'That small tribe of Israel has forced Europeans to believe for over 2,000 years that the history of Israel, in fact, reads almost like that of the whole human species'."

Paul Shepard

Now, "A GLINT AT THE KINDLING" OF THE SACRED IN EUROPEAN CULTURE

"Nature begins to present herself as a vast congeries of separate living entities, some visible, some invisible, but all possessed of mind-stuff, all possessed of matter-stuff, and all blending mind and matter together in the basic mystery of being...The world is full of gods! From every planet and from every stone there emanates a presence that disturbs us with a sense of the multitudinous of god-like powers strong and feeble, great and little, moving between heaven and earth upon their secret purpose."

J.C. Powys

CHAPTER TEN

FOR US, "FUTURE PRIMITIVES," MOVING NOW TOWARD THE SACRED

"[The religious feeling] consists in man's consciousness of being an infinitesimally small part, but as a reasonable being, also a <u>responsible</u> member of a systemic entity immeasurably greater and of immeasurably <u>higher</u> value than he is himself."
Konrad Lorenz, quoting his friend, William H. Thorpe

"To evolution and to comedy nothing is sacred but life itself...As patterns of behavior, both tragedy and comedy are strategies for the resolution of conflicts. From the tragic perspective, the world is a battleground where good and evil, humans and nature, truth and falsehood make war, each with the goal of destroying its polar opposite. Warfare is the basic metaphor of tragedy, and its strategy is a battle plan designed to eliminate the enemy. That is why tragedy ends with a funeral or its equivalent. Comic strategy, on the other hand, sees life as a game. Its basic metaphors are sporting events and the courtship of lovers, and its conclusion is generally a wedding rather than a funeral. When faced with polar opposites, the problem of comedy is always how to resolve conflict without destroying the participants."
Joseph Meeker

"It is not that religion is so much a statement of belief but that at its most effective it enables us to suspend disbelief in the things that are larger than ourselves, whether they be deities or nature..."
Victor & Edith Turner

"When you are in love with the world, you worship—not because you are told to, not because you ought to, but instead because you want to, because you must. Worship is not compulsory. It is spontaneous. Worship happens, emerges organically; it cannot be demanded or commanded. You worship because it feels good. You do it for yourself, even as you direct your feelings toward an Other. When you love the world, you can't help it."
Vern Crawford

ON-GOING PRIMITIVE, OR ARCHAIC, OR CHINESE "SACRED"

"We believe that land and people are one. We believe that only people with an integral relationship to the land can survive. We consider the land as our church, thus the destruction of the land is equal to the destruction of the cathedrals of Europe and the temples of Asia. We view this preservation of our natural land as our right to freedom of religion and our right to freedom of worship."
George Barta, Sioux

"The Indian loved to worship. From birth to death he revered his surroundings. He considered himself born in the luxurious lap of Mother Earth and no place was to him humble. There was nothing between him and the Big Holy. The contact was immediate and personal."
Luther Standing Bear

"Since hunting has been man's preoccupation for a half million years or more, it is inevitable that whatever developments changed rituals into more complex religions took place in a hunting context."
Hamilton Tyler

"Our belief in this regard is that a re-viewing of 'primitive' ideas of the 'sacred' represent an attempt—by poets and others—to preserve and enhance primary human values against a mindless mechanization that has run past any uses it may once have had."
Jerome Rothenberg

"For the primitive, <u>symbols are always religious</u> because they point to something <u>real</u> or to a <u>structure of the world</u>. For on the archaic levels of culture, the <u>real</u>—that is, the powerful, the meaningful, the living—is equivalent to the sacred."
M. Eliade

 THE "SACRED"

Personal Introduction

My first experience of "the sacred" happened when I was quite small. I was probably five or six years old. Our street was the last street with houses on it until one came to the main road, seven blocks west. The street running along the north end of our block marked the city limits of Denver, with only farms outside that line. We children seemed to have limitless space to roam. On this particular day, I had gone across the street to my friend's house, but she couldn't play that morning so I walked along under the cottonwood trees by the irrigation ditch which ran alongside her house. Just behind the house was a small field of meadow grass. I lay down there on my back to watch the clouds and moving leaves of the cottonwood trees above me. Then I noticed the seed pods of the grass, just above my face, waving in the wind. Suddenly I was enveloped in a feeling of complete happiness. There didn't seem to be any separation between me and the gently waving grass pods or anything else around me. That's the only way I can explain it now; then, of course, I had no words at all. When I thought to look up again at the trees I came out of that state. I guess you could say that "thought" broke it.

I can clearly remember that it was such a startling experience that I wanted to try to figure it out before I had to talk to anyone. I walked back across the street to my house and got in our old car and lay down on the floor of the back seat, where no one could see me, to think about it all. Well, of course, I couldn't figure it out so I never ever talked about it. In fact it took more than thirty years before I could even find any words for it. That was after I read Kenneth Rexroth's *Autobiographical Novel*. In that book, he describes an experience which happened to him about the age of four or five, sitting on the carriage stone at the curb in front of his house in Elkhart, Indiana in the early part of this century. He writes: "A wagon loaded high with new-mown hay passed close to me on the street. An awareness, not a feeling, of timeless, spaceless, total bliss occupied me or I occupied it completely." He clearly states that he was not "overwhelmed" or "swept away" or any of that. "On the contrary, this seemed to be my normal and natural life which was going on all the time and my sudden acute consciousness of it only a matter of attention. This is a sophisticated description in the vocabulary of an adult but as a five-year-old child I had no vestige of doubt but that this was me—not the 'real me' as distinguished from some illusory ego but just me."

The latter part of his statement was crucial in helping me to understand my experience. In *Earth Wisdom* I go into more detail concerning this "child nature mystic experience," the only label we have for it. Here, I merely want to report that after several other similar experiences in the last few years, but especially through Tai Chi, I have come to understand that this experience has something to do with the sudden recognition that "the pattern" within is a continuation of "the pattern" without. The Chinese, word, *Li*, seems to be the best word we have for it.

Of course, being a Catholic child, there were fleeting bits of this feeling occasionally during a ceremony in church—but not the total feeling at all. I now know, that the feelings, coming from the best of the Catholic ceremonial life, have to do with "bonding," which is not exactly the same thing.

One further aspect, having done a number of "first ascents" of mountains both in Colorado and Canada, there is a "rush" of joy and wonder at being the first human to stand on that piece of earth. But again, it's not the same feeling. Then, at last, the same feeling that I had had as a child, but deeper and more all-encompassing occurred when I climbed down the cliff to the small pond on the Blue Glacier. (I go into greater detail about this experience in chapter thirteen.) That experience somehow defined "the sacred" for me and since then it happens more frequently. Because of my growing familiarity with how nature "affords" us this experience; I can now recognize places in nature, which will enable others to experience "the sacred," as well. I admit that I have not yet defined "the sacred" in any of the above. Essentially, of course, it cannot be adequately defined by words. Instead, what I will be attempting below is to somewhat clarify where "the sacred" is most likely to be encountered.

Preview

The dictionary defines sacred as "made or declared holy, dedicated or devoted exclusively to a single use, purpose, or person worthy of reverence or respect." The word itself comes from the Latin, *sacra*, literally meaning "sacred, holy, consecrated." The noun (sing.) is *sacrum*, meaning "a holy thing or place, a sacrifice or sacrificial victim"; the noun (plural) is *sacra*, meaning "holy things or places, especially sacred rites, worship or poems." You will notice that the implication here is human centered. "Made sacred" or "consecrated." This Roman anthropocentrism derives ultimately from the Greek language trap of "substance." In general it is "something done to."

Such is the generally acknowledged meaning here in our European culture. This is what Micrea Eliade and most other writers mean when they talk about the duality of "the sacred" and "the profane." That is the sacred as "substance"; I will be dealing with the sacred as "relationship" and will be going into the matter at greater depth below, after a brief historical documentation of the two different traditions: European, on one hand and the Chinese or primitive on the other. But first, here is a brief definition of the sacred from a modern pantheist:

> 'Sacred' seems similar to what I have been calling 'meaningful'...a state that, when activated, gives a special type of meaning to an event. It is a kind of awareness, not obtained by any act of will or logic, of patterns running through everything around us. Each 'meaningful' occurrence becomes part of a person's behavior so that one's life is changed...as these accumulate, one's life enters a pattern guided by that of everything else.
>
> Derham Giuliani

In the "Inter-lude," just before Part III, I dealt with the Chinese word, *Li*, in depth. That concept seems to be echoed here in a modern American's understanding, which came to him directly from an experience with an animal, the "ringtail cat." This is the same way that most human beings in the earth's history first encountered "the sacred": through an encounter with the original gods—the animals, the plants or the land itself.

In this chapter I will be investigating the origin of religion in what Gary Snyder calls, "the Great Subculture of Illuminati, which goes back as far as perhaps the Paleolithic" and which united "Ancient Europe, Asia, Africa." This is the real origin of religion; not the ancient religions of Egypt or the Near East which, of course, came much later in human history. Whatever organized empires or states try to do to religion, it continually wells up from the deep "original" experience of the sacred, still within us as our ethological inheritance from the original humans (nature within) and their relationship to all of nature (nature without).

The "Old" European Religions

Ancient Europe, of course, was still connected to the original religion, dating from the Paleolithic. The Paleolithic cave art in Southern France and Spain gives us a good idea of this original religion. The people of that time seemed to have believed in a Master of the Animals, who provided the game. There were rules for humans using the game and if they were broken, the game ceased to come. This Master or Keeper of Animals concept can be seen still operating in the Tukano in South America as mentioned in the primitive chapter. Mircea Eliade states that the Master of the Animals type of god is "the most divine figure in all prehistory" and the prototype of all subsequent gods. The famous shaman or sorcerer painted on the wall of the Trois Frères cave, with antlers on his head, is considered a Master of the Animals.

According to recent findings the present day Basques of the Pyrenees may well be the descendants of these original Paleolithic cave people. What is certain is that the Basque language, Euskara, which, for years experts had vainly tried to relate to other languages, is now "seen as a living remnant of the languages spoken in Western Europe during the Mesolithic and Neolithic times, millenniums before the relatively modern evolution of the Indo-European groups." Christianity came very late to the Basque country; even in the fifteenth and sixteenth century the population was still "pagan" with only a thin overlay of Christianity. Even today, elderly Basques still 'see' the goddess in certain trees, or in a gust of wind, or white clouds boiling up off the top of Mt. Otoyo.

Another clear insight into the religion of ancient Europe comes from the area which Gimbutas terms "Old Europe:" it extends from the Aegean and Adriatic, as far north as Czechoslovakia, southern Poland and the Western Ukraine. It takes in the Danube and Dnieper River valleys, up which these people moved. Located within this area are both the stalagmites in caves from the Neolithic period in Minoan Crete and the Mother Goddess worship of ancient Greece.

Summarizing her findings, Gimbutas states that "it is no mere coincidence that the venerated goddesses of the sixth and fifth centuries in Ancient Greece resemble the Gods of Life and Death of the sixth and fifth millenia B.C. Mythical images last for many millenia. In her various manifestations— strong and beautiful Virgin, Bear-Mother and Life-giver and Life-taker—the Great Goddess existed for at least 5000 years before the appearance of Classical Greek civilization. Village communities worship her to this day in the guise of the Virgin Mary...The persistence of the Goddess worship for more than 20,000 years, from the Paleolithic to the Neolithic and beyond, is shown by the continuity of a variety of conventionalized images."

Gimbutas notes that: "The teaching of Western civilization starts with the Greeks...But European civilization was not created in the space of a few centuries: the roots are deeper—by six thousand years. That is to say, vestiges of the myths and artistic concepts of Old Europe, which endured from the seventh to the fourth millenium BC were transmitted to the modern Western world and became part of its cultural heritage." The culmination of this "Old Europe" culture was from 7000 to 5500 BC. Among the most important symbols used in their pottery and clay figurines are the directional cross and the moon and bull complex. The cross, with its arms indicating the four cardinal directions "is a universal symbol created or adopted by farming communities in the Neolithic and extending into present day folk art." Gimbutas writes of so-called "bisexual" images consisting of a bird with a long, obviously phallic, neck. There are a number of drawings and photographs of these images in her book. In some, the figurines consist of nude female buttocks surmounted by a long narrow phallic neck. In other examples, there are "figurines with a clay ball in the belly" and "rattles in the shape of a pregnant woman." Obviously, the gourd is the source of each of these images; although the author does not mention this fact. I have included a drawing of an actual gourd split in half to show

the "protruding buttocks" and "long phallic neck." From these goddess figures we learn that the gourd was an important religious object in early Europe. Elsewhere in this work I discuss the use of the gourd as a religious symbol in the rest of the world.

C. G. Jung has gathered together some interesting facts concerning the transition from the older religions into Christianity. He writes that the crypt at the famous cathedral of Chartres was previously "an old sanctuary with a well, where the worship of a virgin was celebrated—not of the Virgin Mary, as is done now—but of a Celtic goddess. Under every Christian church of the Middle Ages there is a secret place where in old times the mysteries were celebrated. What we now call the sacraments of the Church were the *mysteria* of early Christianity. In Provencal the crypt is called *le musset*, which means a secret; the word perhaps originally from *mysteria* and could mean mystery place." Some of these crypts date back to the cult of Mithras, which is always connected with a spring. Jung explains: "In Rome a Mithraeum has been discovered ten feet below the surface of the Church of San Clemente. It is still in good condition but filled with water, and when it is pumped it fills again...the spring has never been found."

Classical Greek Religion

> But as to the origin of each particular god, whether they all existed from the beginning, what were their individual forms, the knowledge of these things is, so to speak, but of today and yesterday. For Homer and Hesiod are my seniors, I think, by some four hundred years and not more. And it is they who composed for the Greeks the generations of the gods, and have given to the gods their titles and distinguished their several provinces and special powers and marked their forms.
>
> Herodotus (843-432 B.C., famous Greek historian)

Here, at the very beginning of Greek literacy we can already see the human-centered approach to the gods. The gods do not well up, powerfully out of nature; instead we have two men who give "to the gods their titles." The Greek alphabet had developed from the Phoenician forms by the 8th century B.C. At about the same time the ballads of the Trojan wars, which had emerged in oral form in the 10th century, were compiled and written down by Homer in the Iliad and the Odyssey.

For hundreds of years, an educated European, trying to figure out the origin of religion, had to first struggle free from Christian dogma only to find himself caught in the trap of the classical Greek, human-centered approach to the gods. As the noted Classical scholar, Gilbert Murray wrote in 1925:

> The things that have misled us moderns in our efforts toward understand-ing the primitive stage in Greek religion have been first the widespread and almost ineradicable error of treating Homer as primitive, and more generally our unconscious insistence on starting with the notion of 'Gods'... The truth is that this notion of a god far away in the sky—I do not say merely a First Cause who is 'without body parts or passions', but almost any being that we should naturally call a 'god' is not a part of primitive mentality. It is a subtle and rarefied idea, saturated with ages of philosophy and speculation.

The first scholar to try to go deeper into Greek religion than the usual Homeric stage was a woman, Jane Harrison. Acclaiming her work, Murray writes: "In 1903, came what I can only call a work of genius." He considered her book, *Prolegomena*, an epoch making book, clearing away preconceptions from the approach to Greek religion and focus-ing attention on Ritual: on what the actual practices were of the Greeks at their festivals. "What a people does in relation to its god is the safest guide to what its religion is... The *thing done*, the rite, is before the myth which explains it—ritual before theology." Her chief interest was in religious origins. All that she did was "pioneer work."

The great age of English archaeology was just beginning, with Sir Arthur Evans excavating at Knossos in Crete and Sir James Frazier working on the Golden Bough. Out of this early work of men such as Evans and Frazier, came the understand-ing that the beginnings of the anthropomorphic conceptions of gods entered Greece with the Achaeans, whose Olympian Zeus was a mountain god with human form. Soon, all over the lands that the Achaean people moved into, "the local gods began taking shape in the new human pattern." Gilbert Murray wrote: "A god with an epithet is always suspicious like a human being with an 'alias'." For example, the Classical Greek god, Zeus Meilichios developed from the the original Meilichios, who is still a real snake in some carvings, and thus a represen-tation of the underworld powers.

Jane Harrison documents this change to gods in human form and assumes that it must be a step "higher" in religion but she is not sure but that something important was lost when humanity took this step. "Sometimes the animal form of the god lives on in mythology; more often perhaps it survived in the supposed 'attribute' of the god." For example, beside Apollo is a stag, an animal "sacred to" him. Sometimes Zeus is riding a bull and still another god carries a sacred bough. In each of these stone carvings or coins of ancient Greece what we actually see here is the animal or plant which was the god before Greek religion became "merely human." Near the end of her book, *Themis: A Study of the Social Origins of Greek Religion*, published in 1912, Harrison gives us a beautiful tribute to the "original gods":

> In art this exclusion of animal and plant life from the cycle of the divine is sometimes claimed as a gain. Rather it leaves a sense of chill and loneliness. Anyone who turns from Minoan pottery with its blossoming flowers, its crocuses and lilies, its plenitude of sea life, its shells and octopuses and flying fish, anyone who turns from all this life and colour to the monotonous perfection of the purely human subjects of the best red-figured pottery, must be strangely constituted if he feels no loss. He will turn eagerly for refreshment from these finished athletes and these no less ac-complished gods, to the bits of mythology wherein animals still play a part, to Europa and her bull, to Phrixos and his ram, to Kadmos and his snake, and he will turn also to the 'attributes' of the humanized Olympian, he will be gladdened by Athena's owl; glad too that Dionysos' Dendrites still deigns to be a tree...The mystery gods it should be noted here, though it has been observed before, are never free of totemistic hauntings, never quite shed their plant and animal shapes. That lies in the very nature of their sacramental worship. They are still alive with the life-blood of all living things from which they sprang.

Classical Roman Religion

Anyone wading through classical works on the gods, finds it very confusing the way Greek and Roman names are used for the same god: for instance, Minerva for Athena, Cupid for Eros, and Neptune for Poseidon. Jane Harrison explains: "We now know that till they borrowed them from the Greeks, the Romans never had in the strict sense of the word any *gods* at all. They had vague daemonic beings, impersonal, ill defined and these beings they called not *dei* (gods) but *numina* (powers)." These numina did not have any merely human characteristics; instead they were "associated with particular places and were regarded with vague feelings of awe." Each numina "presided over some particular locality or activity of man." Naturally, they were very numerous. As the Romans took on more and more of Greek culture, their gods, too, became merely human gods. (See my *Earth Wisdom*, chapters six and eleven for an overview of the classical gods.)

When the Roman emperor, Constantine the Great (306 -337) adopted Christianity and it became the religion of the Roman Empire, belief in the old gods was no longer tolerated. Death and persecution wiped out many people who refused to give the old gods up. In many learned treatises right down to this day, this obliteration of the gods often focussed on the death of the Great God Pan. The Roman writer Plutarch, (46-120 A.D.), first told this story in his "On the Disappearance of Oracles." Plutarch writes that the father of a person who lived in his town was a passenger on a ship sailing near the

Echinades Islands. The wind dropped when, "Suddenly from the island of Paxi was heard the voice of someone loudly calling Thamus, so that all were amazed." Thamus was the Egyptian pilot of the boat. He was called twice but did not answer; however the third time the voice called, Thamus answered "and the caller, raising his voice, said, 'When you come opposite to Palodes, announce that Great Pan is dead'. " The wind picked up and they sailed on. When opposite Palodes, Thamus shouted out the words as he had heard them: "Great Pan is dead." There was a "great cry of lamentation" of many, many voices. The story was spread by the passengers and reached Caesar, who instigated an investigation, but no results came from it. Christianity made use of this story by Plutarch as a kind of "magical" acknowledgement by all the old gods that the ancient gods were dead and only the Christian god lived.

In his paper on this story of Pan, Borgeaud remarks about the many scholars and writers throughout the Christian era who have speculated on this story and ends up by stating that: "The death of the great Pan which, from the Christian point of view . . . presents an enigma to be resolved, does not belong to ancient mythology." Plutarch's text was probably in actuality a piece of "anti-imperial propaganda." Borgeaud explains that, "far from working with a prolongation of a Graeco-Roman myth, Christianity thus makes use of, and invests with a meaning proper to its own mythology, a scrap which is bereft of meaning, an enigma which had been refused by ancient polytheism."

The Christian use of this story plays off the meaning of the Greek word, Pan, which means "all." Plutarch's story, dating from the second century, predates the time of Constantine by roughly 150 years; yet, according to the Christians, this was a clear prophecy that all the pagan gods were gone; only the one Christian God remained. It's important to remember that it was not monotheism (one God) as such, that led to the European split between humanity and nature. After all there have been some monotheistic cultures which never lost their unity with nature. The decisive point was the "one god," Judeo-Christian concept lashed onto the "substance" model of Greek thought. This was further reinforced by the Greek concept that "man is the measure of all things," thus the subject that can know. Nothing else can "know." Further, with the spread of Christianity throughout the Roman world, and, eventually to all of Europe, the Latin translations of the Gospels had a literary influence as well as religious influence. This literary influence set "the stage for the Christian allegorical treatment of pagan literature that was to dominate European literature." This influence persists to this day. Intellectuals for the past two thousand years have not been able to achieve credibility if they did not put their ideas into the framework of the Greek/Christian culture. I will be referring back to this problem again in this chapter.

I need not go any deeper into what Christianity did to all the gods throughout the world as it spread its missionaries to every country. Furthermore, these missionaries often went right along with the European conquerors. In more recent times, such missionaries paved the way for the spread of capitalism. In the last few decades many writers have dealt with specific aspects of this subject in detail. I especially recommend Paul Shepard's book, *Nature and Madness*, which gives an especially good account of the destruction wrought by the Judeo-Christian belief system on the natural world.

The European "Spiritual" Search for Religious Meaning

For brevity in tracing this "search," my account must necessarily bypass several hundred years and jump forward to Petrarch (1304-1374). Petrarch's writings contain the beginnings of "the motives that appear in the thought of the fifteenth century"; furthermore, he was the one who "first definitely linked the name of Plato with the ideals of Italian humanism." After his death, the revival of Greek learning, which he had hoped for, was pushed forward and the prestige of Plato grew among Italian scholars. Eventually, the Medici founded the Platonic Academy in Florence. Marsilio Ficino (1433-1499), "the earliest Platonist of the Renaissance," while still a child was taken into the household of Cosimo de' Medici to be trained as a philosopher and student of the theories of Plato. He became a leader in the Academy and Cosimo entrusted him with the translation of manuscripts of Plato and Plotinus, which Cosimo had been collecting for some years.

Ficino had not yet begun translating the Platonic documents, when, in 1460, Cosimo brought him a manuscript of what was later called the Corpus Hermeticum, reputed to be the very words of Hermes, the ancient Egyptian. This document was destined to set off the "spiritual" quest for the origin of religion, which occupied so many scholars throughout the next centuries. Mircea Eliade, foremost scholar of the comparative study of religion, in his paper, "The Quest for The 'Origins of Religion'," reports: "Both Cosimo and Ficino were thrilled by the discovery of a primordial revelation, that is, the one disclosed in the Hermetical writings." At that time they had "no reason to doubt that it represented the very words of Hermes the Egyptian, that is, the oldest revelation accessible—one which preceded that of Moses and which inspired Pythagoras and Plato as well as the Persian Magi." Ficino and others wrote of the "harmony between Hermetism and Hermetic magic and Christianity."

Going even further, in order to show his protection of the "exalted and occult Egyptian tradition," Pope Alexander VI had a fresco painted, filled with Egyptian (Hermetic) images. Eliade explains that all this excitement marked the "Renaissance man's longing for a 'primordial revelation' which could include not only Moses and *Cabbala* but also Plato and, first and foremost, the mysterious religion of Egypt and Persia." For two centuries this, "obsessed innumerable theologians and philosophers."

This "religious and cultural myth of the 'primordial Hermetic revelation'," however, was destroyed in 1614 by the learned Greek scholar, Isaac Casaubon. He "proved on purely philological grounds, that, far from representing a 'primordial revelation', the *Corpus hermeticum* is a collection of rather late texts—no earlier than the 2nd or 3rd centuries of our era—reflecting the Hellenistic-Christian syncretism."

This Hermetic excitement began the quest for the "true" origin of religion which went on for the next three centuries.

This quest had little to do with any real searching for origins but was far more concerned with "Egyptianism" and other "Eastern mysteries." Real scholarly efforts to look at religion did not begin until the middle of the nineteenth century. Eliade notes that in "1856, Max Müller published his *Essays in Comparative Mythology*, which can be considered the first important book in the field of Comparative Religions." Eliade infers that it is no accident that the materialism of that century and the growing interest in oriental and other supposedly archaic "mystery" religions coincided. The belief was that through science "man will come to know matter...and master it ever more completely. There will be no end to this progressive perfectibility." This "progressive perfectibilty," of course, included "spiritualism." According to Eliade, this movement began in 1848 in Hydesville N.Y. when members of the Fox family heard mysterious knockings. The Fox sisters became the first "mediums"; thus began the "seance" craze. The Theosophical Society, was founded in 1875, by Helena Blavatsky. In her writings she gave "an occultistic revelation" in terms that modern people could understand. By reading her work "you knew finally that there is an unlimited progress and that not only you but all humanity one day will reach perfection." This, of course, sounds remarkably like modern New Age theory. But, as Eliade explains—that if there is any one thing most characteristic of all Eastern traditions, it is "precisely, an anti-evolutionistic conception of the spiritual life."

Back in 1864, Müller, writing about mythology among the Aryans, felt that the Rig Veda came out of "a primordial phase of Aryan religion" and thus indicated "one of the most archaic" stages of religion. Out of that study, as well came his belief that "myths were born from a 'disease of language.'" But only a few years later, in the 1870's the French Sanskrit scholar, Abel Bergaigne "proved that the Vedic hymns, far from being the spontaneous and naive expressions of a naturalistic religion, were the product of a highly learned and sophisticated class of ritualistic priests." Again, as in the case of the Hermetic ms., we find that philological analysis shows that this is not "primordial" religion.

Eliade goes through the entire progression of writers in this field including R. Otto's study of "The Holy," the contributions of Freud and Jung from their study of the "unconscious" and others. I will not take the time to go into that whole process; instead, I will proceed directly to Eliade's very important conclusions. To begin with, he notes that after all that searching into the original beginning of religion, the historian of religions "knows by now that he is unable to reach the 'origin' of religion...it is no longer a problem for the historian of religions." Although he concedes it might still be considered a problem worth working on by philosophers or theologians. What is important is "the grave crisis brought on by the discovery of the historicity of man." This caused "a profound humiliation for the Western consciousness. Western man considered himself successively God's creature and the possessor of a unique Revelation, the master of the world, the author of the only universally valid culture, the creator of the only real and useful science, and so on. Now he discovered himself on the same level with every other man, that is to say, conditioned by the unconscious as well as by

history—no longer the unique creator of a high culture, no longer the master of the world."

Very positive results have come out of this realization. Eliade notes that the acceptance "of man's historicity helped us to get rid of the last remnants of angelism and idealism. We now take more seriously the fact that man belongs to *this* world, that he is not a spirit imprisoned in matter. To know that man is always conditioned is to discover that he is equally a creative being." For those who study religion, "history," essentially means that "all religious phenomena are conditioned ...A religious phenomenon is always also a social, an economic, a psychological phenomenon, and, of course, a historical one, because it takes place in historical time."

Neoplatonism

To return to my discussion of the Platonic Academy in Florence, which opened this section. The Academy provides the essential clue to exactly how Platonic "ideas and ideals" were so deeply infiltrated into the European intellectual mind that even today, they persistently surface again and again—in modern movements such as the New Age and the so-called Aquarian Conspiracy. Through the Academy, Neoplatonic theories influenced the Italian Rennaisance; not only, by means of ideas but through the work of such artists as Michelangelo, Leonardo da Vinci and Botticelli.

Neoplatonism came out of Alexandria in Egypt. Plotinus of Alexandria (204-270), is generally considered the founder. Plotinus believed in an "eternal world of glory which is a world of thought and imagination." The early Christian doctors of the Church were greatly influenced by this philosophy, "which was exceptionally free from worldliness." As mentioned above, Ficino, the "earliest Platonist of the Renaissance," greatly influenced others with his writings.

In the Neoplatonic hierarchy of being, at the top is "the ineffable Godhead, perfect in simplicity, unity, and stability." In other words, the perfect "substance." Jumping way down this hierarchical ladder, we find "the material world" which "is the region of darkness and corruption...all things that exist in the material world are dim shadows of the eternal realities." This, of course, means everything here on this earth.

The peculiar character of the Florentine version of Neoplatonism "appears in its insistence on man's power to seize reality by his own efforts." Thus, all "human art, science, and speculation are the means whereby we lay hold upon reality and bring it within our sphere of consciousness." For Ficino, love is the "substance" [my word here, of course] that permits humans to partake in the knowledge of God. Ficino continues in his praise of the human: "His desires are so limitless that he cannot be satisfied with the world he knows but must needs, like Alexander demand others. He is undisputed lord of the earth (Est utique Deus in terra) linking it to heaven by his activities and so rendering the very soil he cultivates almost divine." If this sounds vaguely familiar to you, it is essentially the very heart of New Age and other modern "earth spirituality" trips. It is still us humans who are going to do all this; never a word about "the powers" of the earth affording us humans "the sacred."

Leonardo's notebooks show strong Neoplatonic influences as well. For instance, the idea that man is a kind of "divine" being "who rivals and disputes with nature, and even excels her by adding to her the qualities of his own mind." One final quote from Michelangelo: "Earthly beauty is only evil if it is allowed to distract the soul from its upward pilgrimage. It may be loved and rightly loved, as the type of the pure incorporeal beauty of the spiritual world." This was the fundamental stance for hundreds of years of European art, where the natural beauty of this earth can be "used" only to point the way to the divine beauty of the spiritual world. Only much later, when Japanese prints began to circulate through Europe did European artists begin to look at the beauty of this earth.

In Florentine Neoplatonism, which led the way to the Renaissance and the "humanist" movements, you can see the beginnings of many of the problems which continually erupt in European thinking when it comes to "this world," here where we dwell. I cannot take the time to document all of these problems; instead I will just use the example of Jung and the importance of Chinese thinking on his work with the unconscious.

INFLUENCE OF CHINESE CONCEPTS ON JUNG

In his autobiography, *Memories, Dreams, Reflections,* Jung writes that in 1928 when he received the manuscript of a Taoist-alchemical treatise entitled *The Secret of the Golden Flower* from Richard Wilhelm in China, "I devoured [it] at once, for the text gave me undreamed-of confirmation of my ideas about the mandala and the circumambulation of the center." He emphasizes: "That was the first event which broke through my isolation...I could establish ties with something and someone." Furthermore, in Jung's Foreword to the book he writes: "I shall only emphsize the fact that it was the text of *The Golden Flower* that first put me in the direction of the right track." Again, when Jung gave an address at the funeral of Richard Wilhelm he said: "Anyone who, like myself, has had the rare good fortune to experience in a spiritual exchange with Wilhelm, the divinatory power of the *I Ching*, cannot for long remain ignorant of the fact that we have touched here an Archimedean point from which our Western attitude of mind could be shaken to its foundations."

It is astonishing that, in spite of all Jung learned from *The Secret of the Golden Flower* and from Richard Wilhelm and his own unconscious he still remained so trapped within the framework of the Eurocentric tradition, that he consistently maintains that we, Europeans must only go through such European methods as alchemy or "Gnosticism," and not dabble in Eastern concepts. Yet, Jung, himself, knew that the reason he was able to put together all that he was "feeling" as far as the unconscious goes, was not the result of his European studies but the result of Chinese thought. The fact that, in spite of his own debt to Chinese concepts, he still insists on Eurocentric methods is indicative of the power, which limited Eurocentric, thinking, still has over even the most intelligent of men.

Primitive Religion as Power

For the primitive, *symbols are always religious* because they point to something *real* or to a *structure of the world*. For on the archaic levels of culture, the *real*—that is, the powerful, the meaningful, the living—is equivalent to the sacred.

M. Eliade and J. Kitagawa

When the early European ethnologists began to study a particular Indian culture, they would invariably ask the name of their god. Sometimes they got a specific name, but then later, that same informant would often give a different name; furthermore, sometimes there seemed to be no god at all. This greatly puzzled the ethnologists because, to the European mind, if there was no god then nothing was sacred.

A typical example of this attitude is shown in the "first thorough ethnographical description of an Indian tribe," the study by Lewis Henry Morgan on the Iroquois in 1851. In this study, Morgan states that the Great Spirit is the first and foremost of all their gods and is the "creator, ruler and preserver." Modern scholars in the field of Iroquois culture find that there is no such concept for the Iroquois.

Probably, the beginnings of a real attempt to understand "the sacred" from the point of view of the Indians themselves dates back to 1902 with Hewitt's paper on "Orenda and a Definition of Religion." He stated that, among the Iroquois, *orenda* meant "mystic potence," which he thought could be found in all religions. Some thought this was similar to the *manitou* of the Algonkian Indians. Others felt that *manitou* meant a supernatural being; thus, a spirit.

Perhaps the best attempt to understand these concepts came from the work of Alice Fletcher, working with Francis La Flesche, a member of the Omaha tribe. (1911) She stated that "*Wakonda* is the name given to the mysterious all-pervading and life-giving power to which certain anthropomorphic aspects are attributed." She clearly states that:

There is...no propriety in speaking of Wakonda as "the great spirit." Equally improper would it be to regard the term as a synonym of nature, or of an objective god, a being apart from nature...The European mind demands a kind of intellectual crystallization of conceptions, which is not essential to the Omaha, and which when attempted is apt to modify the original meaning. Wakonda stands for the mysterious life power permeating all natural forms and forces and all phases of man's conscious life. The idea of Wakonda is therefore fundamental to the Omaha in his relations to nature, including man and all other living forms...Visible nature seems to have mirrored to the Omaha mind the ever-present activities of the invisible and mysterious Wakonda...The rites pertaining to the individual reveal clearly the teaching of the integrity of the universe, of which man is a part.

Hultkrantz (1967) states that this definition "drew much attention from the scientific world." But, even after this essentially correct understanding of the basic Indian concept, experts continued to argue the matter. Some saying that religion has to include "a belief in spirits," others saying no.

Eventually, the dominating European idea of religion penetrated into the ranks of the Indian medicine men. It's not surprising, considering the fact that to get any credit among the whites, the Indian medicine men had to speak within the Indo-European confines of a substance language. This basic fact makes it almost necessary to refer to "gods" or "spirits."

When it comes to American Indian religion, it is necessary to keep in mind the fact that such religions have been either destroyed or co-opted since the 1600s when the Jesuit missionaries first went up the Mississippi River.

To give just one example of hitherto unrecognized Christian influence on Indian religion take the noted Lakota, Black Elk. The book, *Black Elk Speaks*, by John Neihardt, was first published in 1932. Reprinted often, it had a very wide influence in the 1960s and early 1970s. Many considered it the definitive statement on Native American Religion. When I read it—back in 1968—I was very suspicious of the emphasis on the "Great Spirit"; but I felt it was due to Neihardt's Christian influence. Only recently has the full story come out. It turns out that Black Elk was, for all of his life, a Roman Catholic catechist. That's not quite a priest but the next thing to it. A catechist is one who teaches his people the Catholic doctrine and gets them ready for baptism and other sacraments. According to modern Pine Ridge Sioux elders, Black Elk is remembered "primarily as a Roman Catholic catechist, not as a Lakota holy man."

In the book, *Black Elk Speaks* there is no mention of his life from the battle of Wounded Knee (1890) until the time he goes up Harney Peak in 1931. Black Elk "had been a Christian for 27 years when he was interviewed by Neihardt, and 43 years when he was interviewed by Brown, although neither mentions this aspect of Black Elk's religious life." In 1980, Steinmetz talked with John Lame Goose about Black Elk. Lame Goose said: "He never talked about the old ways. All he talked about was the Bible and Christ. I was with him most of the time and I remember what he taught."

While we need not throw out all that Black Elk tells us about particular Indian ceremonies, we must be very cautious when it comes to statements about the roots of "the sacred" in Indian life. I will not take the time here to give further examples, but see Reference Notes for more bibliographic information.

Once more, I want to emphasize here that this is why I find it much more useful to refer to Taoist writings instead of American Indian. As mentioned in part II of this book, the Taoists had direct access to the primitive before such cultures were destroyed; furthermore, they had a written language 3000 years ago. This combination guarantees a better insight into the original human concept of "the sacred" than we can get in any other written materials. To reiterate concepts which I discuss in detail back in the Taoist chapter of Part II, I want to quote Needham's summary here:

> It was not that there was no order in Nature for the Chinese, but rather that it was not an order ordained by a rational personal being [our Christian God concept] and hence there was no conviction that rational personal beings would be able to spell out in their lesser earthly languages the divine code of laws which he had decreed aforetime. The Taoists, indeed, would have scorned such an idea as being too naive for the subtlety and complexity of the universe as they intuited it. [They felt that] the universal order was intelligible because they themselves had been produced by it... "Heaven, Earth, and Man have the same Li."

We find no idea here that we, humans, because we are made "in the image of God," can figure it all out. Instead we see the pattern within the on-going whole. We humans were produced from within this pattern; therefore we fit within the on-going relationships of the whole.

The Japanese word, *kami* (sometimes translated as gods), may be useful here. "Usually the term, *kami* refers to all beings that are awesome and worthy of reverence, including both good and evil beings...the religion of the ancient Japanese...accepted the plurality of the *kami* as separate beings and objects, its basic affirmation was the sacrality of the total world (cosmos) permeated as it was by the *kami* (sacred) nature." Here we see again the concept of sacredness or power permeating the world.

To further clarify this concept of "the sacred," I want to quote from a very recent paper (1986) which sums up the research which Jay Vest did at the request of the present Blackfeet tribe in Montana, who are trying to keep their rights to worship in the Badger-Two Medicine area of Glacier National Park. These rights were guaranteed to them by the U.S. in 1895. Vest had already done extensive research on the Algonquian tradition; the Blackfeet are an Algonquian people. To begin with Vest points out the error of considering that the Manitou is a supreme Being, when he states: "There is an implicit claim [among Europeans] that the Manitou notion is understood indigenously as an expression of 'substance' comportable with a Western derived ontology." He states plainly that this is not the case. Furthermore, he explains that "the 'Supernatural' is a Western conceptual distinction which is not recognized among these religions." Concerning the Blackfeet concept of the Sun, Vest explains:

> Metaphysically, the Sun is recognized to be both an "other-than-human person" and the ultimate animating life principle: this ontological position is one of becoming rather than stasis, and therefore is significant for environmental ethics. Moreover, it is not to the Sun as a static being in the world (as the Western Tradition views it) to which the Blackfeet pray, but to a being who is in the world as a person, who is both present and in process...They pray to an "other-than-human person" who also represents "the timeless principle of life." This principle [*Li* in Chinese] of life "is shared by the Sun with all creation ... and it is this power that the people beseech in dreams, prayers, songs, and ceremonies. With this metaphysical reflection upon Blackfeet Sun worship, we should conclude that the Blackfeet, like other Algonquians, do not worship a Supreme Being or High God, but venerate an ultimate animating life principle that they associate with the Sun and with the principles of creation including the collective ecology of the earth.

Jaime de Angulo gives us an even clearer statement concerning primitive religion as power. Jaime was probably the best linguist of the modern world. After learning seventeen California Indian languages in fifteen years, he returned, in 1921, to his beloved Pit River Indians to record their literature and began to translate the *Dilasani qi*, the old-time stories of these people. Writing about these stories, he explained:

> In this early, primitive stage of civilization, ideas are still immanent in objects, and have not yet been separated either through identification or projection. In these stories we find the Tinihowi—the primitive religious spirit—reflected throughout...the life of these Indians is nothing but a continuous religious experience...The spirit of wonder, *the recognition of life as power*, as a mysterious, ubiquitous, concentrated form of nonmaterial energy, of something loose about the world and contained in a more or less condensed degree by every object—this is the credo of the Pit River Indians. Of course they would not put it precisely this way. The phraseology is mine, but it is not far from their own.

Jaime de Angulo and Nietzsche:
The Views of Two Extraordinary Europeans on the Sacred as Power in Nature

I am going further into Jaime's life because he and Nietzsche are the two outstanding examples of Europeans, who with no help from their culture found their way back into "the sacred"— Nietzsche, in the middle of the nineteenth century and Jaime in the early years of our century.

Jaime, born in Paris of exiled Spanish parents, came to America in his teens. In addition to his prodigious linguistic ability, Jaime had many other exceptional talents. Shortly after he got to this country, he enrolled in the now defunct Cooper Medical College in San Francisco and got his first medical degree in 1912 from Johns Hopkins. The following year he became a partner in a cattle ranch and met the Pit River Indians for the first time. With the outbreak of the First World War, he volunteered and was sent to Ann Arbor "to attend an early course on psychiatry for army doctors. He graduated, then stayed on as instructor at the school for the remainder of the war." After the war he drove a herd of horses from the ranch, down the five hundred mile central valley of California, to homestead on the Big Sur. Here, in 1919, he met the anthropologists, Alfred Kroeber and Paul Radin, who had rented a nearby cabin for the summer. Kroeber had Jaime up to the University of California to teach the following year. He taught one course in Jungian Psychiatry, the other on the Mind of Primitive Man.

The combination of natural linguistic ability, psychiatric training, anthropological background and his natural "wildness" provided Jaime with his unique insight into the meaning of the "sacred" for the Pit River Indians. He was able to set aside most of his European conditioning; eventually, he became what the Pit River Indians call "a wanderer." Explaining further, Jaime wrote: "The Indian never courts pain. It would never enter his head to imagine that by making himself miserable and pitiful in the eyes of the Powers he might gain their sympathy and aid. This is not his conception at all." Instead, as a wanderer, a seeker, one "becomes as wild as possible." "Climb awful mountains, climb down the rim of crater lakes...When you have become quite wild, then perhaps some of the wild things will come to you ... and take a fancy to you...When this happens, the wandering is over, and the Indian becomes a shaman."

In his search for the sacred, Jaime had the advantage of living in the somewhat wild lands of early California and associating with primitive people—somewhat damaged by early California mining activities in their vicinity, but nevertheless a primitive society. Nietzsche, the other outstanding example of a European who found his way back to the sacred, had a much more difficult time. Eventually he went insane—whether merely from syphillis or from the strain of attempting this search all alone it's hard to say. Nietzsche was born in 1844 and was a student of classical philology. According to the dictionary, philology is the study of literature and relevant disciplines. At 25 he became a professor in that field. Of course he was deeply immersed in Greek classics; thus Greek gods. His *only* contact with the primitive was the little he could get from reading the Swiss historian, Bachofen, who was interested in myths and symbols in primitive folklore. Since Nietzsche lived his entire life in Europe he never had any direct contact with the primitive.

He resigned his teaching post to begin his search. This eventually resulted in a plan to write a great work, *The Will to Power: Attempt at a Revaluation of all Values*. To begin this work he had to "overturn Platonism." Such an effort, of course, meant throwing out all European values, based as they are on Platonic ideals. With nothing clearly apparent to replace them, his suffering was intense at times. I will not take the time to go more deeply into his main work. Here I just want to indicate the particular events surrounding his finding of "the sacred."

"I shall now tell the story of Zarathustra," is how he begins his account. "The basic conception" came to him, "6,000 feet beyond man and time...I was that day walking through the woods beside the lake of Silvaplana; I stopped beside a mighty pyramidal block of stone which reared itself up." This was summer in Switzerland, with the clear light of the high mountains. The next winter he spent along the bay of Rapallo in Italy, not far from Porto Fino. I have spent some time near Porto Fino and know well the exquisite quality of the light there. Nietzsche wrote: "In the mornings I climbed in a southerly direction into the heights along the glorious route to Zoagli, past pine-trees and with a vast view of the sea; in the afternoons...I walked around the entire bay from Santa Margherita to Porto Fino...It was on these two walks that the whole of the first Zarathustra came to me, above all Zarathustra, himself, as a type: more accurately, *he stole up on me*..."

It's obvious now, more than a hundered years later, who this Zarathustra was. The combined exhilaration and danger which Nietzsche experienced, while climbing alone around these steep seaside rocks in that glorious light enabled Zarathustra to come to him. With his Greek classical education, he had to name the god; but it is interesting that the name was not Greek—but coming out of the Persian language. The name, Zarathustra refers to the Persian, Zoroaster, founder of the Persian-Iranian religion in the first millenium B.C. Zoroaster had each of his great visions while on top of mountains in the clear mountain light. Thus it is natural that the light itself could bring Zarathustra to Nietzsche.

He recounts that later, "In the summer, returned home to the sacred spot where the first lightning of the Zarathustra idea had flashed on me, I found the second Zarathustra...The following winter, beneath the halcyon sky of Nice, which then shone into my life for the first time, I found the third Zarathustra—and was done...Many hidden places and heights in the landscape of Nice are for me consecrated..." He continues with "The *body* is inspired: let us leave the 'soul' out of it...I could often have been seen dancing; at that time I could walk for seven or eight hours in the mountains without a trace of tiredness." For this experience, Nietzsche, elsewhere in his work, uses the German word, *rausch*, which Heidegger translates as "rapture"—meaning something "rushes over" and "sweeps us away."

Here we see that light itself is "the sacred"; but Nietzsche, with his background of classical Greek was forced to "name the god; while for many primitive cultures it is light itself or the sky which is "the sacred."

There's a great deal of misunderstanding about Nietzsche's "overman." In no way does it actually refer to any kind of super-man. "The Overman as species is in fact 'the superior species of *everything that is*.' Zarathustra says yes and *amen* in a 'tremendous and unbounded way', he is himself 'the eternal affirmation of *all things*.'"

In another place Nietzsche writes: "I, however, am one who blesses and affirms if only you are around me, you *pure, luminous sky*! You abyss of light!—then into all abysses do I carry my consecrating affirmation."

Thus we see that essentially Zarathustra came to Nietzsche from the sun's light. The light itself enabled Nietzsche to frame the words which greatly infuenced European thought to begin its climb out of the Greek language trap, which had held this thought captive for two thousand years. Here is the poet, Wallace Stevens on this subject. He points out that the dying of the gods of Christianity and Greece and all the other mono-systems of imperialism is not the end of everything. Instead, "the source of comparison having been eliminated, *reality is returned*, as if a shadow had passed and drawn after it and taken away whatever coating had concealed what lay beneath it." (The italics are mine.) The reality, which is returned to us, is the reality of earth and sky out of which the gods first manifested. That reality it now returned to us, unmarred by fighting Greek gods or the wrathful Jehova or the suffering Christian God. Reality can be clearly seen once again and we can begin once more to learn how to live within "the sacred."

In his collection of the poetries of primitives from all over the world, *Technicians of the Sacred*, Jerome Rothenberg writes:

> So, something more than literature is going on here: for ourselves, let me suggest, the question of how the concept & techniques of the 'sacred' can persist in the secular world, not as nostalgia for the archaic past but (as Snyder writes) 'a vehicle to ease us into the future.'

Conclusion

As Jane Harrison shows us, most of the Greek gods were originally animals. Later, after they became "merely human," the early carvings showed them in their human aspects; but with the original animal standing alongside The shamanic tradition among primitives is concerned with getting in touch with the animal helpers: not spirits but animals. In Part I of this work I discuss how the gourd taught us humans about agriculture and "afforded" us other practical necessities of life. In Part II, I discuss how the bear taught us transformation and healing herbs and how, for the Taoists, the gourd, "afforded" understanding of deeper matters connected with the nature of life. These and other learnings from our animal ancestors are still operating within us—in the limbic animal brain. Below I will go further into these aspects of the sacred.

It is well known by now that the left hemisphere can inhibit communication from the right hemisphere. But, it turns out that both these hemispheres of the neo-cortex may well be capable of suppressing communication from the limbic system,

(the animal brain). Moreover, psychic health and personality integration may well depend on the maintenance of open communication between the limbic system and the neo-cortex. Henry and Stephens, in their work on stress, explain that the neurophysiological purpose of dreaming is to promote integration of processes occuring in the limbic system with those of the cerebral hemisphere.

Even more to the point for this chapter, Henry refers to Otto's famous study of "the holy" in which Otto states that an experience of the holy frequently involves a sense of powerlessness and is often accompanied by autonomic arousing with pallor, sweating, shivering, and sometimes fainting. Henry quotes a personal communication to him from Jung in which Jung discusses possible "physiological concomitants of a numinous religious experience" and states that if one could locate such an experience physiologically, "the brain stem would be the most likely spot." Jung describes the psyche as reaching down from the "daylight of the mentally and morally lucid consciousnss into the nervous system that for ages has been known as the 'sympathetic.' The latter maintains the balance of life through the mysterious paths of sympathetic excitation, not only giving us knowledge of the innermost life of other beings, but also has an inner effect on these essentially physiologic processes." In his concluding paragraph, Henry declares that the "foundations built by Carl Jung are proving to be soundly conceived. There is a rapidly growing body of evidence linking our mammalian inheritance of basic brain stem functions with man's unique religious, social and cultural achievements. Society has scarcely begun to consider the implications of these discoveries."

Weston La Barre, in *Flesh of the Gods*, provides further evidence when he states: "The sacred world...is the ground of our conscious being, the basis of our apperception, our specific humanity, and each learned personality. [Concerning] the subjective world...every last shred of it is based either on inherited animal adaptations or on individual life-experience of the world."

Further understanding comes from the anthropologist, Roy Rappaport in his discussion on ritual. To begin with, he states that "ritual is not simply an alternative way to express certain things, but that certain things can be expressed only in ritual...ritual is without equivalents or even alternatives." Proceeding further, he explains that "Invariance...is characteristic of all rituals, both human and nonhuman, and it may be that both the sacred and the supernatural arose out of the union of words with the invariance of the speechless rituals of the beasts from whom we descended." Most important of all, he states: "It may be that the basis of the numinous is archaic, antedating humanity, and it may further be that religion came into being when the emerging, discursive, conventional sacred was lashed to the primordial, non-discursive, mammalian emotional processes that in their later form we call 'numinous'." Here we can see very clearly the animal origin of "the sacred."

To fully understand the depth of these connections between the animal and the sacred, it is necessary to give Gregory Bateson's definition of our much vaunted human consciousness: "Consciousness is just a sampling of the events and processes of the body and of what goes on in the total mind. It is organized in terms of purpose. It is a short-cut-device to enable you to get quickly what you want; not to act with maximum wisdom in order to live, but to follow the shortest logical or causal path to get what you next want, which may be dinner; it may be a Beethoven sonata; it may be sex. Above all, it may be money or power." Mind in the large sense includes not only each part of the triune brain within us; but all the pathways and messages which carry information to us from without. As Bateson says, "There is a larger mind of which the individual mind is only a subsystem. This larger Mind is comparable to God and is perhaps what some people mean by God." But he says that whatever you call it, "it is still immanent in the total interconnected social system and planetary ecology." Another way to look at this is to realize that the lines we draw between us and the environment, "are purely artificial fictitious lines. They are lines across the pathways along which information or difference is transmitted. They are not boundaries of the thinking system. What thinks is the total system which engages in trial and error, which is man plus environment."

This leads us back to the concept of most primitives, that "the sacred" is power. This "power" flows through animals, plants, waterfalls, mountains, humans etc. in endless abundance. But when a civilization comes along and stops this flow by lodging it in a "god," then the abundance ceases. This may be difficult to understand because our language needs a substance type of "god." But one can think of it, as I often do when skiing—that it's not me skiing. I'm not doing it; instead, *It* skies me. A great composer once answered those who asked how he could play so wonderfully, by saying that he didn't play the music; instead it played him. Whenever something is going very well with no effort, I think most of us have the feeling that it's not us doing it; but that "the powers" are skiing us or playing us. That's "the sacred" as power.

In certain traditional cultures, this state of flowing with "the powers," goes on most of the time. Daily life is lived within this flow. Once in a while the people must leave this "flow" of the sacred and go out to do some specific task—one which essentially calls for a concerted use of the "rational" consciousness. Then, special rituals are done, special precautions are taken. The leading men or medicine men or shamans must rouse up the people to take on the "danger" of this concerted, rational, one-pointed effort. This kind of effort takes place in a primitive society getting ready for warfare or among the Hopi, long ago when a selected group travelled the long, dangerous journey to get salt, or, in some other tribes it took place when they travelled to dig the turquoise. All of these consist of concerted, single-pointed efforts—undertaken for a short time for a specific purpose. When such actions are over, those taking part must undergo specific rituals to get them out of that "dangerous" state of mind and back into the "flow" of the "sacred" ongoing, daily life within their own place.

In our modern Industrial Growth Society, the exact opposite situation takes place. We live most of our life in the "rational, one-pointed concerted effort" to get something accomplished and only very rarely and then sometimes by accident do we ever experience the flow of "the sacred." Small children are wrenched forcibly out of their brief experience of this flow early on. Sometimes it's giving them lessons—swimming lessons, skiing lessons etc.—with the excuse that they can learn all these things easier when they are young. Of course a small child can learn anything—almost overnight but lessons are not what child-life is for. Then, by the age of six, they are forcibly removed from any possibility of the flow; they start to school. They are bombarded daily by specific, rational tasks which they must complete correctly to get the approval of parents, teachers and peers. In the school room they are never allowed to wait for the whole of nature (both within and without) to do it for them; to "play" them.

Thus children become victims of conscious willing. While trapped in this state they can never experience "the sacred." The conscious mind alone or I could say the rational hemisphere, specifically does not have access to this state because it's very nature is to take apart and analyze. The importance of the symbol is that it can bridge this gap between conscious and unconscious. Jung explains:

> Symbolism is the very essence...since the symbol derives as much from the conscious as the unconscious. It is able to unite them both, reconciling their conceptual polarity through its form and their emotional polarity through its numinosity.

Here again, we find that Jung's work agrees with neurological facts. (I will go further into this throughout Part III.) Here, I just want to emphasize that, as Jung pointed out, symbols at this level "cannot be thought up but must grow again from the forgotten depths, if they are to express the deepest insights of consciousness. Coming from these depths they blend together the uniqueness of present-day consciousness with the ago-old past of life."

THE SACRED AS RELATIONSHIP

The essence of "the sacred" is relationship. It has to do with conforming to the patterns (Chinese, *Li*) in nature because the patterns in nature are both within us (evolved through millenia) and without—in nature outside of us. In a good culture there is little dissonance between these two patterns. If such dissonance arises it is resolved through seasonal festivals. D. H. Lawrence, who spent his life exploring these relationships, says:

> The true God is created every time a pure relationship takes place...Blossoming means the establishing of a pure, new relationship with all the cosmos. This is the state of heaven. And it is the state of a flower, a cobra, a jenny-wren in spring, a man when he knows himself royal and crowned with the sun, with his feet gripping the core of the earth.

Because of our substance problem, which we inherited from the Greek language problem, we tend to think that God is some substance or thing which we worship. But, as Lawrence so beautifully states; instead, "the sacred" is whenever the relationship between human, land, animals, or plants occurs. The Ituri Pygmies say that the forest encompassing them is the body of God. That doesn't mean the forest, the body of God, is one thing and they are another thing. They are the forest encompassing them and the whole of the forest, including the people, is God. For example, in their daily life if a quarrel arises in one of the grass huts at night, the head man will shout out "Shut up. You are disturbing the forest."

It's very difficult to pin "the sacred" down in a few words to make a definition which has meaning for us in this fragmented, unholy culture. But I will try here. The most succinct definition I can give you now, at this time is: First, we humans cannot put it together. It's all together all the time. Secondly, when we manage to still the rational hemisphere or conscious mind long enough to recognize that—that is when we feel "the sacred." "The sacred" is the word we use to label that experience. Or, to put it another way, the word we give, the label we give to our recognition of what is always going on, or on-going, always, is "the sacred." I first worked out a preliminary form of this definition in June of 1984. I've been refining it and discussing it with others ever since.

Doing Tai Chi daily, has greatly clarified "the sacred" for me. One of my Tai Chi students, who studied with me for several years is Jackie. When I asked her how she felt, physically, when she was doing Tai Chi, she said that she felt it in the trunk of her body—not in the arms or legs. It was a total feeling—not merely "peace"—more of a feeling of "being at home." Again, in other conversations with Tai Chi students, some mention "a sense of being a part of the whole of life and realizing it."

In July of 1984, Bill Plotkin Ph.D., one of my colleagues, a "psychologist/wilderness guide" who leads vision quests, came up from Durango for a meeting where we discussed my "new" definition of "the sacred." He was very interested and took copious notes as we discussed it. Then he asked, "What about Mircea Eliade and his dichotomy of the "sacred and the profane?" That particular question at that crucial time helped me realize that in a traditional culture, the people are aware that sacred reality is the reality—it's always accessible to them; it's always on-going and they go in and out of it to do specific tasks but it's always there and easily entered. While in our culture the "out of the sacred" state is the only state we consider as real and the occasional times modern humans experience "the sacred" is considered occult or weird or supernatural.

During the course of many conversations on "the sacred" I came to a startling realization. The reason why a number of people so glibly label certain things "sacred" or "spiritual" or "occult" is that in labelling that brief experience of such a feeling with those terms, they safely cut it off from daily life. Then they can say that a particular vision quest or a certain ritual ceremony or that particular guru gives them the feeling of "the sacred." It only happens at that particular place or time. Thus they are safe from having the personal responsibility to make any changes in their lives. It's a great cop-out!

This feeling of "the sacred" going on all the time, is what Kenneth Rexroth meant when he wrote of sitting on the curbstone as a small child having this "awareness, not a feeling, of timeless, spaceless, total bliss occupied me or I occupied it completely." Our natural birthright is to feel this way—most of the time. Probably, many of us experienced this as a child but there were no words for it. Sudden glimpses occur in later life; but, again, without words it's lost. Once one begins doing Tai Chi, it can happen often enough to begin talking about it. As Donna said, after doing Tai Chi with me in the mountains: "What this time [in] the mountains taught me is that I can re-write myself and give myself permission for reverence." Even in our modern IGS life, once that happens to you, then, you begin to move more into that "sacred" mode in your daily life.

It is possible to begin to live in a "sacred manner" even within this present Industrial Growth Society by setting up ritual structures in our lives where we can feel nature moving deep within us, in response to the patterns of all of nature without. The remainder of Part III is concerned with how to do this.

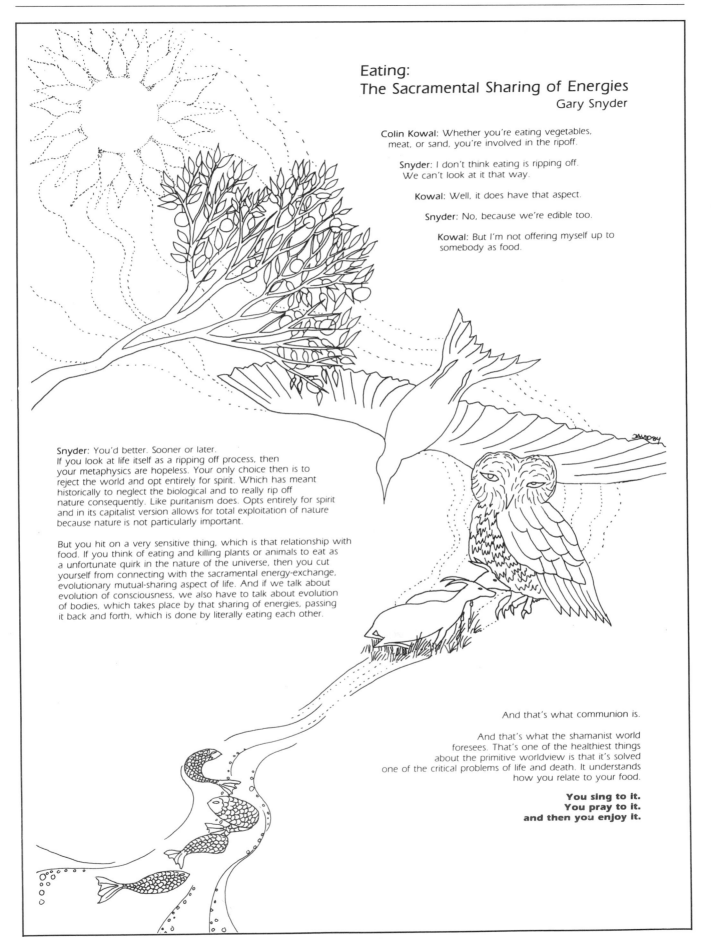

Eating:
The Sacramental Sharing of Energies
Gary Snyder

Colin Kowal: Whether you're eating vegetables, meat, or sand, you're involved in the ripoff.

Snyder: I don't think eating is ripping off. We can't look at it that way.

Kowal: Well, it does have that aspect.

Snyder: No, because we're edible too.

Kowal: But I'm not offering myself up to somebody as food.

Snyder: You'd better. Sooner or later.
If you look at life itself as a ripping off process, then your metaphysics are hopeless. Your only choice then is to reject the world and opt entirely for spirit. Which has meant historically to neglect the biological and to really rip off nature consequently. Like puritanism does. Opts entirely for spirit and in its capitalist version allows for total exploitation of nature because nature is not particularly important.

But you hit on a very sensitive thing, which is that relationship with food. If you think of eating and killing plants or animals to eat as a unfortunate quirk in the nature of the universe, then you cut yourself from connecting with the sacramental energy-exchange, evolutionary mutual-sharing aspect of life. And if we talk about evolution of consciousness, we also have to talk about evolution of bodies, which takes place by that sharing of energies, passing it back and forth, which is done by literally eating each other.

And that's what communion is.

And that's what the shamanist world foresees. That's one of the healthiest things about the primitive worldview is that it's solved one of the critical problems of life and death. It understands how you relate to your food.

**You sing to it.
You pray to it.
and then you enjoy it.**

"Intelligence is natural. Stupidity requires explanation."
Luis Machado

"The use Bowlby has made of the idea that attachment is predominantly an anti-predator device, a special adaptation to life as a baby...One can then no longer assume that it is simply the way we start acquiring social behaviour, or that it is bound to be related to food. But equally one cannot assume that this function implies any more about the method of development of the attachment than that it must develop reliably in the context in which it evolved... the situation in which babies develop has been exceptionally constant throughout our evolution, right back into our earliest hominoid phase some twenty-five million years ago and beyond throughout our higher primate ancestry of some forty million years."
N. Blurton Jones

"Primitive, or archaic ritual is thus sacred play, indispensable for the well-being of the community, fecund of cosmic insight and social development...In this sphere of scared play the child and the poet are at home with the savage."
J. Huizinga

"In every true man there is a child hidden."
Friedrich Nietzsche

Chapter Eleven

"The special places of childhood are not sacred, but the memory of them is necessary for attaching sacredness to place."

Paul Shepard

"The whole of growth through the first twenty years is our 'coming into being,' or ontogeny... Among those relict tribal peoples who seem to live at peace with their world, who feel themselves to be guests rather than masters, the ontogeny of the individual has some characteristic features. I conjecture that their ontogeny is more normal than ours... and that it may be considered to be a standard from which we have deviated. Theirs is the way of life to which our ontogeny was fitted by natural selection, fostering a calendar of mental growth, cooperation, leadership, and the study of a mysterious and beautiful world where the clues to the meaning of life were embodied in natural things, where everyday life was inextricable from spiritual significance and encounter, and where the members of the group celebrated individual stages and passages as ritual participation in the first creation."

Paul Shepard

"Parents are the earliest ritualizers in their children's lives... [Whatever powers] the ceremonies of the adult years call on... they sanction the adult, for his mature needs include the <u>need to be periodically reinforced in his role of ritualizer.</u>"

Erik Erikson

"A man is whole only when he plays."
Schiller

 CHILDHOOD PLAY AND ADULT RITUAL

Preview

In "Eight Ages of Man," Erik Erikson one of the leading figures in Human Development states that in the first stage—that of early childhood—Basic Trust must take place. Our culture's narrowly human (anthropocentric) outlook makes it very difficult for a child to experience such basic trust. For instance, the mother may be doing what she thinks is best for her baby; but sometimes, in her efforts to "do right," she overemphasizes the bonding so that the child is hopelessly imprinted on her or else she instills in the child an urgent necessity to "succeed" at everything, seemingly to meet her demands. Actually all she is trying to do is help the child be a "successful" person in our culture. But real living involves much more than this limited view of our present-day Industrial Growth Society. Real community, since humanity began, involves all aspects of the place: human and non-human; therefore; to learn basic trust the child must encounter nature as well as humanity. Most people, today, forget the power of this encounter in childhood; but the modern Greek novelist, Kazantzakis vividly remembers his first encounters with the non-human. In the first account below, he tells of the earliest memory of his life:

> Still unable to stand, I crept on all fours to the threshold and fearfully, longingly, extended my tender head into the open air of the courtyard. Until then I had looked through the windowpane but had seen nothing. Now I not only looked, I actually saw the world for the first time. And what an astonishing sight that was! Our little courtyard-garden seemed without limits. There was buzzing from thousands of invisible bees, an intoxicating aroma, a warm sun as thick as honey. The air flashed as though armed with swords, and, between the swords, erect, angel-like insects with colorful, motionless wings advanced straight for me. I screamed from fright, my eyes filled with tears, and the world vanished.

Next he tells of his first encounter with the sea:

> I remember, a man with a thorny beard took me in his arms and brought me down to the harbor. As we approached, I heard a wild beast sighing and roaring as if wounded or uttering threats. Frightened, I jumped erect in the man's arms and shrieked like a bird...Suddenly—the bitter odor of carob beans, tar, and rotten citrus. My creaking vitals opened to receive it. I kept jumping and pitching about in the hairy arms that held me, until at a turn in the street—dark indigo, seething, all cries and smells...the entire sea poured into me frothingly. My tender temples collapsed, and my head filled with laughter, salt, and fear.

Obviously, the narrow, merely human approach of our culture, leaves no room for such powerful encounters with nature as part of its story.

At its deepest level, Erikson's Basic Trust, includes confidence "that you will become part of the story." Much of the destructiveness and anger evinced in our culture comes from not being included in the story. In fact, one of the factors contributing toward childhood autism is either they get no response from their world or they are not allowed to respond at their own speed and in their own time. So the child gives up altogether. The child in a traditional culture is permitted to be "part of the story" whenever the time is right for that child. The following accounts are from traditional cultures in North America: the first, is from the Yurok tribe in California:

> Children grow when they grow, as they learn to see, learn to learn, according to their spirits. A famous man of the last century learned very early to observe the men of his village carefully. After a while,

using his toy bow, he killed a bird with valuable feathers. He made a small wooden storage box, as he'd seen done, put the feathers in this, and showed the men. One of them made him a real hunting bow, a small and light one, and from then on he was free to join hunting parties, with all of the rights and responsibilities of a hunter. He had done what a man does and, in this respect, was treated like a man. He was six at the time.

The second is about the Blackfeet tribe in the 1920s, as recounted by Abraham Maslow:

> He was about seven or eight years old, and I found by looking very close that he was a kind of rich kid, in a Blackfoot way. He had several horses and cattle in his name, and he owned a medicine bundle of particular value. Someone, a grownup, turned up who wanted to buy the medicine bundle, which was the most valuable thing that he had. I learned from his father that what little Teddy did when he was made this offer—remember he was only seven years old—was to go into the wilderness by himself to meditate. He went away for about two or three days and nights, camping out, thinking for himself. He did not ask his father or his mother for advice, and they didn't tell him anything. He came back and announced his decision. I can just see us doing that with a seven-year-old kid.

In each of these accounts we see basic trust on all levels: that of the parents, that of the culture, that of the child and furthermore, trust between the culture itself and the on-going natural environment around it. This is the crux of the matter. Essentially in a traditional culture the children are always "wanted children." There is no such thing as an unwanted child. Much of the wisdom of the tribe was devoted to "walking in balance with the earth." Human population was never allowed to upset this equilibrium.

Early ethnologists in North America found that the child spacing and child rearing practices growing out of this approach to the earth showed remarkable similarities in tribes as far apart as the Arctic and the southwestern desert. For instance, John Murdock wrote: "Infanticide is frequently practiced among the Eskimo of Smith Sound, without regard of sex...The affection of parents for their children is extreme...the children show hardly a trace of the fretfulness and petulance so common among civilized children, and though indulged to an extreme extent are remarkably obedient. Corporal punishment appears to be absolutely unknown." The Pima Indians in the southwest, according to Frank Russell, regulated birth in this manner: "Babies were nursed until the next child was born. Sometimes a mother nursed a child until it was six or seven years old and if she became pregnant in the meantime she induced abortion by pressure upon the abdomen...the youngsters are seldom whipped." In the Assiniboin tribe, according to Edwin Denig, the children were never hit or corrected in any way. "Notwithstanding this they are not nearly as vicious as white children, cry but little, quarrel less, and seldom if ever fight." He continued by saying that infanticide is very common among the Assiniboin, the Sioux and Crow. Cushman reported that, "Children were never whipped among the Choctaw, Chickasaw and Natchez Indians." Infanticide or abortion together with the lack of punishment of children; and yet the fact that they were quiet, "good" children, proved a continual source of amazement to these early researchers. Among these tribal people however, the birth of a child was not an "accident" left up to the individual parents, but instead, was regulated by ritual or contraceptive herbs or abortion, so that the particular child would fit into the overall health and stability of the entire ecosystem—the tribe plus the rest of the community consisting of the soil, the animals and the plants. This is shown in the chant from the "Reception of the Child" ritual among the Omaha, which is printed below at the end of this chapter. Contrast the above "traditional" handling of children within the overall needs of the entire ecosystemic community with what is going on within our culture today. The most apalling statistic here concerns child abuse: "Each year, more children under the age of 5 die because of child abuse than die of disease. Figures vary from 50,000 to 100,000 deaths."

In some cultures the food/reproduction/energy cycle is so attuned that there is no need for conscious birth control. The Kung of Africa have lived in the Kalahari desert for at least 11,000 years. Up until roughly twenty years ago they were living their traditional culture. But because of the drop in the water table due to "development" in the surrounding cultures they have been forced to move near the farming villages of the settled Bantu. This culture change—which caused the women to lose their equal status, the children to become aggressive and the once stable population to explode in growth—was heavily researched by many anthropologists. Population stability among the Kung had been mostly due to the scarcity of fat in their diet which delayed the onset of menstruation. First babies were formerly born when the mother was nineteen. They were nursed for four years and the mother rarely conceived during that time because nursing women need one thousand extra calories per day; thus there were not enough calories left over for ovulation to take place. This essential fact in most tribal cultures that all children are wanted leads to a sense of belonging which we don't have in our cultures today. Wildred Pelletier (modern Odawa tribe) talking about the fundamental difference between the white man's world and his experience living on the Reserve in Canada, said: "I guess what I've learned—and it's taken me a long time—is that if you live in white society the most difficult thing to do is simply be yourself... And that's because in white society just being born is a putdown...that infant, as he grows up, learns he's under pressure to become somebody."

As mentioned above rage and destruction at all age levels—small child, teenager and adults come from being left out of "the story." And it's getting worse as a result of the media, which continually floods us with stories that we have no access to. Poor people want to get into the wealthy story— that's why it's easy to persuade them to buy all that "stuff," which they see on television commercials. And the wealthy people, in turn, who use poor people to maintain their story—as servants, as workers on all the lower levels of city maintenance etc., find they have no inherent meaning in their lives, either; because, as Gary Snyder says, "All creativity is 50% maintenance." He is being continuously asked the question: "Where does your inspiration come from?" He patiently points out that it comes from routinely doing the necessary chores involved in living in his "place," such as chopping wood and tending the garden; but generally his interviewers don't believe him!

Before ending this Preview I want to quote Sylvia Ashton-Warner who taught the Maori in New Zealand. She wrote, "I see the mind of a five-year-old as a volcano with two vents: destructiveness and creativeness. And I see that to the extent that we widen the creative channel, we atrophy the destructive one...for, as Erich Fromm says, 'Life has an inner dynamism of its own; it tends to grow, to be expressed, to be lived. The amount of destructiveness in a child is proportionate to the amount to which the expansiveness of his life has been curtailed. Destructiveness is the outcome of the unlived life'."

This chapter is about the most important thing in childlife, play, and what it means to allow the child to become "part of the story" through ritual. As Julien Puzey remarks: "What makes a good culture is easy access to the story."

Play

But how do we begin moving toward a real culture? All we have to do is raise one generation of children right—according to the pattern laid down by hundreds of thousands of years of our mammalian ancestors, which set the stage for human life. This gradual development over aeons of time led up to one fundamental difference between all animals and humans. No, it's not consciousness—every species has its own consciousness. The reason we don't recognize that is because it's so different from human consciousness. This one major difference is—quite simply—that the human animal is the only one that is capable of playing throughout its entire life span!

When scientists began to study early human development "they steered clear of so frivolous a phenomenon as play." A highly respected research worker at Brown University in 1947 published a carefully researched paper, which concluded categorically, "that, since play could not even be properly defined, it could scarcely be a manageable topic for experimental research"; however, the growing field of work on primate ethology changed all that. When looked at in its natural setting play became "more and more central as one moves up the living primate series from Old World monkeys through Great Apes, to Man—suggesting that in the evolution of primates, marked by an increase in the number of years of immaturity, the selection of a capacity for play during those years may have been crucial." Thus, while early childhood development experts were wondering if play was a useful category to study; "primatologists were pondering its possible centrality in evolution!"

It turns out that Tinbergen's ethological methods can be applied to children at play as readily as to chimps in the forest. This new approach to play "begins to suggest why play is the principal business of childhood." Let's take a closer look at play as it was developed for us by the higher primates.

"For most primates the context of normal life is a social group—in all its complexity and stability. This group is a small world with few intrusive events. A majority of monkeys live their entire life in the group of their birth; hence they know it and its location well. This is the setting of play: a rich blend of social relationships and ecological pressures, dangers, times of plenty and scarcity, and seasonal changes in both environment and group." This is what humans still need when they are children; this life of diversity, rooted in basic stability provides the depth of meaning, necessary in life. Another researcher writes that it is important to remember that these "animals do not play because they are young, but they have their youth because they must play."

All higher vertebrates "are typical unspecialized creatures of curiosity." This same curiosity can be found in birds as well. For instance young ravens "exhibit their most intensive phase of curiosity behaviour immediately after fledging—at a time when they are still fed by their parents. If they become hungry, they follow the parental bird in an insistent manner, and they only exhibit interest for unknown objects when they are satisfied. Secondly, when the raven is moderately, though still demonstrably, hungry, the appetite for unknown objects prevails over that for the best available food. If one offers a tit-bit to a young raven actively engaged in investigating an unknown object, the tit-bit is almost always ignored." What this means is that the bird does not want to eat, it wants to know whether the object is "theoretically" edible. Bally regards it as the major characteristic of play that behavior patterns really belonging in the area of appetitive behaviour are performed "in a field released from tension...It is only through curiosity behavior that objects come to exist in the environment of an animal as in that of man."

For most animals this "curiosity behavior" occurs mostly when young; while in humans it can continue throughout life unless thwarted by the culture. "All purely material research conducted by a human scientist is pure inquisitive behaviour—appetitive behaviour in *free operation*. In this sense, it is play behaviour...Nietsche states that the inquisitive child is *hidden* within the 'true human being'; but in fact it completely *dominates* him!"

"GREETING RITUALS" BETWEEN BABY AND MOTHER

The earliest and most important play between mother and baby has been termed "greeting rituals." The mother comes into the room, smiles, calls the baby by name, picks her up and cares for her. The baby responds with its own rituals. These are developed very soon by the baby and he insists on the order of these rituals. Erikson explains:

> There is much to suggest that man is born with the need for such regular and mutual affirmation and certification: we know, at any rate, that its absence can harm an infant radically, by diminishing or extinguishing his search for impressions which will verify his senses. But, once aroused, this need will reassert itself in every stage of life as a hunger for ever new, ever more formalized and more widely shared ritualizations and rituals which repeat such face-to-face "recognition" of the hoped-for. Such ritualizations range from the regular exchange of greetings affirming a strong emotional bond to singular encounters of mutual fusion in love or inspiration, or in a leader's "charisma." I would suggest, therefore, that this first and dominant affirmation, this sense of a *hallowed presence* contributes to man's ritual making a pervasive element which we will call the 'Numinous'...The result is a sense of *separateness transcended*, and yet also of *distinctiveness confirmed*.

Each of the elements involved in the sense of sacred can be seen in this first "greeting ritual." Further, each of these involves opposites which appear to be reconciled:

1) Reciprocal needs of two organisms or minds which are not equal.

2) Very personal on one level but results in a group feeling, thus giving a sense of oneness and distinction.
3) Playful yet formalized.
4) Although it becomes familiar through repetition, it always seems to bring a surprise of recognition.

Dealing with ambivalence is one of the prime functions of ritualization, for while we love our children we also find them, at times, very demanding of our attentions. And likewise as our children grow, they will at times find us possessive and making too many demands. This is why ritualized affirmation becomes *indispensable* according to Erikson. He admits all this seems to be a "large order to burden an infant's daily awakening," but it turns out to be a fact that the "deepest and most devastating" disturbances can be traced back to a thwarting of early rituals of mutual recognition. Hope is the most basic quality of human life, according to Erikson, and this "emerges unbroken from early familiarity and mutuality and which provides for man a sense of a personal and universal continuum."

GREGORY BATESON ON PLAY

All mammals play; furthermore, interactions between different species in play gives us further insight into the importance of play. The predator/prey relationship is also relevant here. For instance, kittens play with the prey they catch until the mother teaches them how to kill. Referring to the relationship between a dog chasing a rabbit, Bateson defines play at a very deep level indeed. Looking at this relationship from either the dog's or the rabbit's point of view, makes the matter very complex, but when we throw out the thought that the dog is one creature and the rabbit another and "consider the whole rabbit-dog as a single system," then we find that the relationship, which is involved is the key to the matter. By running, the rabbit "invites" the dog to chase it; because, as a predator, the dog's inbuilt mechanism is to chase a running creature. In turn, the dog can "invite" a chase. Everyone who owns a dog knows this overture. My little border collie would put her entire front legs on the ground, rear end high up, chin on the ground with her eyes looking up at me. Meanwhile her back legs were bent under her body, ready to push her off in the chase. The relationship here involves her invitation, my response, which is to automatically lunge at her in a mock attack; followed by her response to run, looking back over her shoulder to be sure I am chasing her.

Bateson once decided to see what a female dolphin would do if he got in the water with her and gave her no stimulus whatsoever. "So I sat, with arms folded, on the steps leading down into the water." She came alongside him just a few inches away. Nothing happened on either side so she moved away and swam slowly around him. Then, "a few moments later, I felt something under my right arm. This was the dolphin's beak, and I was confronted with a problem: how to give the animal *no clues* about how to deal with me. My planned strategy was impossible." As soon as he relaxed his arm she pushed further under it. "In seconds, I had a whole dolphin under my arm. She then bent around in front of me to a position in which she was sitting in my lap." Naturally, swimming and playing together followed.

In such cross-species games each of the participants remains itself: the dog is still dog; the human still human; the dolphin still dolphin. Each still has its own "character"—its own way of looking at the universe—but something has definitely happened. Bateson points out: "Patterns of interaction have been generated or discovered...there has been a natural selection of patterns of interaction." Another way to put it is that the two species involved have worked out a way of "fitting together," developed from on-going natural selection of interactions. The overall system of dog-human or dolphin-human has become more "integrated and consistent." Bateson calls this A *plus* B, I call it the "something-more-than." No new information comes from outside during this play but only from "within the system." The interaction itself creates information about the dolphin for the human and information about the human for the dolphin. The boundaries have changed.

This is what play does. To be precise, play is not any particular action but rather the name for a "frame for action." In play the regular rules for reinforcement don't hold. Any mother who has tried to stop children's play to get them to come to lunch, only to find that before she knows it, she is included in the play understands this. Exploration is another category which defies ordinary reinforcement rules. Exploration is always self-validating whether what happens is pleasant or unpleasant for the explorer. Mountain climbing is a form of exploration. Bateson refers to his friend, Geoffrey Young, who climbed the Matterhorn with only one leg. Young felt that one of the main disciplines of climbing was "victory over self." Bateson rightly says that such terms as "victory over self," "Discipline" and "self -control" are "mere supernaturalisms—and probably a little toxic at that." Of course he's right. "Super," meaning above nature is definitely toxic, because it implies that we humans are above nature. This attitude is dangerous both to humans and nature. "What happens is much more like an incorporation or marriage of ideas about the world with ideas about the self." This leads to extensions of the boundary of the self. Essentially, of course, that's what play and ritual are about—extending the boundaries of self; but before going further into Bateson's concepts here, it is necessary to explore children's play in nature.

Children's Experience of Place

Very little research has ever been done on how children experience their own place. Piaget never even thought to look into this; furthermore, there has been no detailed, modern, research done on how children use outdoor spaces except for playgrounds. This total blindness to one of the most important aspects, to the children, themselves, of their childhood is amazing; but fits in with the attitude that nature is unneccesary for humans. The only in-depth study of children and place was done by Roger Hart, who did a two year study involving all the children of a small town in the northeastern U.S. All of the town's 86 children, up to age twelve were studied; while detailed work was done on the children in eight families.

Each child was questioned during school hours, on places they liked, disliked, feared or found dangerous. He found that when he and the children were actually out in the field they were much more likely to think of their "highly-valued land-uses and less likely to focus on people's homes than when they are interviewed in a school setting."

"Which places are you most likely to go to when you are alone?" was another question. Some of the most important places in a child's environment are experienced when alone, contrary to what urban planners think. Children search out quiet places to be alone. These places very frequently have water, dirt or sand and are sites for quiet introspection or "dabbling" aimlessly. Such activity is all too easily dismissed, but it may well be extremely important to a child's development.

FAVORITE NATURE PLACES

Climbing trees were valued from an early age. "It was clear in the place preference data how much more valuable trees were to the children than any play equipment."

Easily the most popular play location was beneath the "large maple in the front of the house." The main reasons given by the children for using this tree so often, concerned the shade from the tree and the good dirt beneath it. The children were very well-informed about the location and state of ripeness of all the fruit-bearing bushes and trees within their range. "Discovering a new edible resource or picking the first berry were among the most meritorious of events within this small band's system of recognition. The knowledge of these resources...was most reminiscent of my brief observations of a shifting cultivator's intimate knowledge of naturally-growing trees and plants within his range of movement."

Children all over the town "developed strong affection for particular trees." Hart saw certain children return repeatedly to the same tree during his two years of research in the town. Concerning a birch tree, seven year old Joe explained: "I like to climb up it and look out at spaces because it's high...Yeah, it's like a lookout tower." His parents said that "of all places outside of his bedroom, the birch tree was the place he most considered to be his own."

On May 6th, Hart wrote of a very sad experience in his research journal: "Johnny is really upset. He arrived at his home from school fifteen minutes before me and now with his eyes tearing he is sitting on the three foot stump of what had been a very old tree when he left for school. With little control in his voice he shouts, 'That was our tree, we used to play under it all the time—it's not fair, we didn't even know they were going to do it.' "

The next important natural feature after trees was dirt. These patches of dirt, often under trees, were "highly valued" both by boys and girls. Children from age three to twelve, either alone or with friends, played for hours in these dirt patches, "building miniature landscapes, often to suit their toy cars and trucks." Boys usually constructed large scale places such as highway systems and towns; girls most often built houses and then decorated the interiors. By the sixth or seventh grade, children seemed to quit playing in the dirt. If found playing in it, they would tell him that it was boring but that they had to be there to help the little kids. Hart states, "The possibility that societal attitudes to imaginative play among youth results in a rather sudden and 'unnatural' erosion of this activity."

AFFORDANCES

Hart found that both girls and boys of the poorer families "found great satisfaction in finding [natural] objects and putting them to some original use." In fact all children under the age of six regardless of income, found "immense satisfaction in discovering uses for things by themselves. Only through over-provision and a failure of the parents and the school to encourage resourcefulness, is this important skill lost."

LACK OF MEANING IN DISTANT PLACES

Throughout the two years of the study, Hart discovered that places outside the child's direct experience did not interest the child. "Near towns such as Grandville and Middleton are equally as far or near as New York, Boston or Washington." Furthermore, there was no difference between towns, cities, states or countries as far as the children were concerned. Each of these were simply places "out there." Whenever it turned out that they had actually gone to one of the nearby towns they usually said that that particular town was located in the same direction that their car had left town for the other city.

For instance, eight year old Johnny told Hart, "Where the President lives is over the sandbank, in Washington. You know, the sandbank across the street from us (his home), and so that's the United States."

Quoting another researcher Hart, says that young children, aged six and seven, who were bussed to school in rural England, "suffered serious problems of social and emotional adjustment in comparison to their peers who walked to school each day." Lee "hypothesized that the bus journey took them beyond their known (representable) world into a space which they had had no opportunity to articulate through their own bodily locomotion through the environment."

CONCLUSIONS ON THIS STUDY

Hart explains that the seemingly purposeless activity and day-dreaming, "has some most important 'inner' value of the kind described by Edith Cobb." In my book, *Earth Wisdom*, I discuss Cobb at length. Here I can only quickly summarize by explaining that Edith Cobb found, in her research on the lives of some 300 people considered as "geniuses" from the Middle Ages on, that "genius" invariably comes out of a nature mystic experience in early childhood. Her definition of genius is "an involuntary phenomenon, at biocultural levels, beginning with the natural genius of childhood and the 'spirit of place'." This most often takes place during "the little-understood, prepubertal, halcyon, middle age of childhood, approximately from five or six to eleven or twelve... when the natural world is experienced in some highly evocative way, producing in the child a sense of some profound continuity with natural processes."

Back to Hart's conclusions on his research. He states that the children valued the "froggy ponds" very highly, but not mainly for getting frogs. Most often, the frog ponds were used by children when they were alone; but they are so popular that the "same special or secret pond or stretch of brook is commonly shared at different times by different children."

Hart notes that children spent a lot of play time, changing

the "landscape in order to make places for themselves and for their play"; further, he states that this making special places is a "particularly important aspect of children's place experience and one which has not been recognized in previous surveys of children's play."

Another important conclusion in his study is that children need freedom to roam; but, as he notes, this need has not been discovered in any of the "countless studies of children's land-use by planners." In fact, Hart writes that, "It is notable that the most important qualities to the children of this town—sand, dirt, small shallow ponds or brooks of water, slight elevations of topography, low trees and bushes, and tall unmanicured grass—are systematically removed from all new residential areas, even the highly applauded new towns."

Play, Ritual, and Relationship

Gregory Bateson says "If we define play as the establishment and exploration of relationship then greeting and ritual are the affirmation of relationship. But obviously mixtures of affirmation and exploration are common." Just here is why the baby and mother's daily ritual greeting and the later, "peek-a-boo" games are so important. These greeting games build trust for the child to extend play to other spheres: 1) ritualized interplay, beginning with the mother/baby greeting games, leads to relationship; 2) play in nature leads to child/nature bonding and 3) play leads to ritual in adult life.

Erikson, discussing playful ritualization in man, explained that it is as hard to define as play itself, and states that perhaps such things as "playfulness" is "defined by the very fact that [it] cannot be wholly defined." He continues:

> There is a reconciliation of the irreconcilable in all ritualizations, from the meeting of lovers to all manner of get-togethers, in which there is a sense of choice and ease and yet also one of driving necessity: of a highly personalized and yet also a traditional pattern; of improvisation in all formalization; of surprise in the very reassurance of familiarity; and of some leeway for innovation in what must be repeated over and over again. Only these and other polarities assure that *mutual fusion* of the participants and yet also a simultaneous *gain in distinctiveness* for each.

BONDING AND NATURE MYSTIC EXPERIENCES IN CHILDHOOD

Essentially, bonding is extending one's boundaries to include others—human and non-human. During the first year or so of life, the child is bonded to the mother. The next stage is bonding to the earth. In traditional cultures this comes about as a part of living in nature. In modern times such bonding becomes more difficult because the small child has much less direct contact with nature; however it doesn't take a very large piece of nature for this to occur.

In the last chapter, I discussed Kenneth Rexroth's experience, sitting on the curbstone while a load of ripe hay went by. As an adult, trying to explain what occurred, he said that "an awareness... of timeless, spaceless, total bliss occupied me... this seemed to be my normal and natural life which was going on all the time and my sudden acute consciousness of it only a matter of attention." He further explains that as a five-year-old child he "had no vestige of a doubt but that this was me—not the 'real me' as distinguished from some illusory ego but just me." This type of experience has been called a "childhood nature mystic experience."

As noted above, in his conclusions on his research into the child's experience of place, Roger Hart refers to Edith Cobb. In her book, *The Ecology of Imagination in Childhood*, she gives many different accounts of these "childhood nature mystic experiences," dating from Giordano Bruno (1548-1600) on. She does not include that of the writer, C.S. Lewis; and, since he gives a particularly clear example, I will repeat it here: "As I stood beside a flowering currant bush on a summer day there suddenly arose in me without warning...a sensation..." He notes that it "is difficult to find words strong enough for the sensation which came over me; Milton's 'enormous bliss' of Eden...comes somewhere near it...It had taken only a moment of time; and in a certain sense everything else that had ever happened to me was insignificant in comparison." In her book Cobb documents similar occasions in autobiographical recollections from Africa, Asia, Europe, and the Americas. Her conclusions is that "These vivid experiences, described retrospectively by adults, appear to be universal and suggest some universal link between mind and nature as yet uncodified but latent in consciousness in intuitive form."

Conclusion

Rexroth's experience involved ripe hay. He mentions that he had read of the same kind of experience in the works of authors as different as Richard Jeffries, H.G. Wells, and Rousseau, "including the new mown hay." Ripe grass is so often mentioned in such experiences that some have looked for a hypnogenetic principle in ripe grass but none has been found.

In a new book about the famous Taoist, *Chuang Tzu: World Philosopher at Play*, there is a discussion about the name Chuang. It is often said to mean "serene" or "calm" but Wu points out there is no such meaning under the word, *chuang* in Chinese dictionaries. He continues: "Its original meaning is instead 'lush tall grass'." All he says is that maybe this is a more "appropriate" meaning for his name; but in the light of all the childhood experiences related above, it may well be that Chuang Tzu took this name because he had just such an experience in ripe grass at some time in his life. From this supposition we can see more clearly why Chuang Tzu lays such emphasis on play and childlike behavior. As Wu states elsewhere in his book, Jean Piaget "saw the self growing *out of game playing into moral judgment*" while "the reverse was true for Chuang Tzu—morality is something to be grown out of in order to play as the child." In fact this is precisely where real living occurs, "in and through the True Man, who 'plays' (*yu*) in life with the truth of things." In other words, not imposing human restrictions on the on-going life of all of nature; but rather, joining in the play of all of life. In Chuang Tzu we find this passage:

> They said to each other, 'Who can join with others without joining others? Who can do with others without doing with others? Who can climb up to heaven and wander (= meander, play, *yu*) in the mists, roam the infinite, and forget each other in life forever and forever?' They looked at each other and smiled...and...they became friends.

In Chuang Tzu's meandering/play, mutuality fulfills every individual being—human and non-human so that they are enabled to freely "play" out various modes of being and become friends with one another.

If a child does not have the chance to play freely in nature — even under a tree or in a vacant lot—then the efforts to sort out his place in "the story"—who he is in relation to all the adults in the on-going story around him, can become very threatening. In other words the "not-I" is too much in relation to her own small self. But in the childhood nature mystic experience the child *knows* that he is part of the whole and that the whole of nature accepts him as part of it. Any time in life the child or adult can draw on this understanding.

One of my Tai Chi students, Jackie, telling me of her childhood experience in a vacant lot in Ohio, explained in that place she always felt "at home." Everything seemed to "fit together." Donna, who attended one of my workshops, wrote me that in nature as a child she felt "chosen" and that "Nature was the one thing we could be totally selfish about and have totally and give away as totally to everyone else."

It is obvious that the most important thing we can do is see that small children have an opportunity to be bonded to nature. One way of insuring this is to have a festival where the small child can experience bonding with the whole community—in Aldo Leopold's definition—"the community includes the soil, the water, the animals and the plants as well as the people." The remainder of the chapter will be concerned with this type of festival.

"To Fly as Birds:" Huichol Indian Children's Ceremony

"When we beat the drum, shake the rattles and fly the children to Wirikúta"

INTRODUCTORY BACKGROUND

In 1900 Carl Lumholtz, Norwegian pioneer ethnographer of the Indians of the western Sierra Madre of Mexico, first told the world about the children's ceremony that he called "feast of the green squashes." He was particularly impressed by the use of what he called "god's eyes." This is not at all what they mean to the Huichol, but ever since, the European world has used this term. This "eye" is a cross make out of bamboo splints or straw, interwoven with different colors of yarn. It is made in the form of a square but the square is set diagonally in the ground or on the child's head. The straw is wound around the sticks from the center outward. One stick is much longer than the others so that the "eye" can be stuck in the ground upright. If the sticks are of equal length they are supposed to be attached to the roofs of the god-houses.

The Huichol name for the "eyes" is *tsikúri*. It is, in fact, a sacred protective symbol for the children. Actually, the best way to think of these "eyes" is that they symbolize the relationship of all the gods and the place itself, woven together to protect the children. I will be referring to this woven symbol as a "four sacred directions" symbol; because woven into them are the main gods of place for the Huichol.

Lumholtz wrote that these symbols were tied to the children's heads in an upright position by means of a hair ribbon. Also tied into the hair ribbon is a shaman's plume. The "four sacred directions" symbol refers above all else to Mother East-Water, creator of squashes and of all flowers, who takes care of children. She is also the mother of the culture hero, the Divine Deer Person. This being is also the shaman's spirit helper and companion animal as well as guide and protector of peyote pilgrims. In the mythic beginning time he helped the first shaman Tatewarí (Our Grandfather, the divine Fire), put the world in order. The Divine Deer Person was the one who made the first "four sacred directions" symbol for the protection of children.

The children's feast is called wima'kwari ("to beat the drum") and is held in October after the men hunt deer and gather squashes. Lumholtz' original account says that the shaman sits in the door-opening of the temple which faces east, where the sun rises and beats the drum and sings from early morning until sunset. The children are brought to the temple and placed on both sides of the shaman. Tied to each child's head is a shaman's plume and the "four sacred directions" symbol. Each child also has a gourd rattle in its hand. The gourds are filled with small stones from ant-hills. To the right of the children is a pile of squashes to be cooked and on the left, the jars to cook them in.

At the end of the first day the children are carried to their homes and the singing and dancing continue all night. Before sunrise the cooked squashes are taken out of the jars and given to the children, first, and then the adults. The adults use a drink made from peyote. Lumholtz remarked on the "noise" made continually by the drum and rattles. According to the myth, the squash was once a girl whose name was Riku'ama, called that because of the rattling noise she made. He says "perhaps this was originally suggested by the rattling noise which the dry seeds make inside of the squash when shaken."

"This ceremony...persists to the present time virtually without modification. It plays a more or less crucial role in the transmission from generation to generation of some of the essentials of the indigenous intellectual culture. It is thus in a very real sense decisive in the process of enculturation." Enculturation as a whole is a more or less continuous process involving other rites and daily living. But, it is particularly in this ceremony of the drum and green squashes, "in which they participate annually for the first five years of life as actors and thereafter as participant observers, that the young Huichol boy or girl learns 'how one goes being Huichol.'" Furst explains that this feast is not merely a harvest festival, although it includes that aspect. Primarily the feast is "to impregnate the young minds with the...tradition and a kind of subjective map of the geography of the sacred, through the device of a metaphorical celestial journey to the home of the Mother Goddess and, beyond it, the place of the Divine Deer—Peyote, the magical land called Wirikúta, which lies some 300 miles to the east of the present Huichol homeland in the north-central high desert of San Luis Potosi." The Huichol actually call this ceremony "Our Mother Ceremony." Another modern researcher, Myerhoff agrees with Furst in general and notes that the purpose of the ceremony is "to relate, in lengthy chants, the essentials of the peyote origin myth, which stands at the very center of Huichol intellectual culture, and to provide an

'inner map', a cognitive and spatial plan transmitted from one generation of Huichols to the next."

The "Children's Feast" as a Model

With this brief review of the "Feast," given above I can go more into why this ceremony is such a crucial one for us, today, as we begin to bond with our land. First, it is important to realize that although this children's ceremony refers to a specifically Huichol sacred pilgrimage, similar ceremonial journeys are held all over the world in places where traditional cultures bond with their land; for instance, in Japan, the Shugendō cult (part Shinto, part Buddhist), have their "opening the peak" ceremony and in this country many different Plains Indian tribes had similar ceremonies which are generally referred to under the name of "Hako" ceremonies.

To reclaim our "original human" relationship with the land, the first step is to help this generation of small children bond with the land in their own place. In this ceremony, we are not borrowing bits of culture from other peoples; instead, we are using the same ritual objects—the gourd and the drum—which our ancestors used, for at least the last 50,000 years. Using the drum and the gourd, we set up a ritual journey to a local place, near enough so that when the children are old enough, they can join the adults on the sacred journey to the "holy places."

A particular historical aspect of this ceremony concerns the very beginnings of the "new world rip-off" by Europeans. San Luis Potosi, where Wirikúta lies, the goal of the Huichol sacred journey and the former homeland of the Huichol, was the site of the famous "mountain of silver," which the Spanish exploited. Silver from this mountain helped lay the foundation for modern capitalism and added immense wealth to European royalty. In the process, thousands of South American Indians were killed; thus the Huichol were forced to flee their own place in the San Luis Potosi area. Ever since, for some 300 years, they return from time to time on a sacred journey because the "sacred peyote" grows there. But the peyote is not the only factor creating their sacred landscape. This is shown in some of the chants sung by the shaman to the children as they "fly as birds." The land in itself has become sacred by virtue of the ceremony through the years.

Every traditional culture has myths, but what is particulary powerful here is that the young hear the myth, take part in the journey by shaking their rattles (which supposedly sound like the wind rushing through their wing feathers) and also "ride the drum," as the shaman sings them on the journey. This is done each year, with the adults present, for the first five years of their life; thus they are "part of the story" from the very beginning. There is no anxiety in the Huichol culture, as there is in ours, about how to become "part of the story."

Huichol Cosmology

Furst remarks: "[T]he people residing in the different regions of the Huichol country do feel and express an intense emotional bond with their particular part of the indigenous environment."

Furthermore "more than any other sizeable indigenous Middle American population, the Huichols have successfully resisted Christianization of their religion and ritual life." The only really obvious influence Christianity has had is that of the famous "Virgin of Guadalupe," whom the Huichol consider an Indian woman. They believe that the indigenous sky deity, Our Mother Young Eagle Woman, and the Virgin of Guadalupe are the same being.

Many Huichol gods embody natural forces and others are the "Masters" or "Owners" of the different animal and plant species. These sacred beings are called Grandfather Fire, Our Father Sun or generically Our Grandfathers, Our Mothers etc. Rain comes from sacred springs or lakes, rises into the sky in the form of clouds and then returns as rain to the earth, our Mother, in a never ending cycle which requires ceremonies on the part of humans to continue. Furst says that the Huichol world-view is "essentially shamanistic…animistic, in some aspects typical of incipient subsistence farming societies but in some of its underlying assumptions more so of hunters and gatherers." Thus it fits the "old ways" as given in Part II of this work.

Ramon Medina, who died in 1971, was very important to all those who studied the Huichol. The two anthropologists, Furst and Meyerhoff both travelled with him on the ritual peyote journey, 300 miles to the sacred land. Much of the information on the "children's feast" comes from Medina, who explained to Myerhoff that in this flight "as transformed birds" during each of their first five years of life, the young Indians become prepared for taking the real pilgrimage. Whether or not the individual Indian makes the real pilgrimage, they all believe that this journey to the "sacred land" is the essence of their tradition. Medina, as he sang the journey, put in some of his experiences, his own hopes for the future and other variations which is as it should be.

In the ritual journey chant, each root, plant, flower, tree, animal, mountain, water and other natural beings act and talk in the narrative as real persons. This seemed odd to the anthropologists but to me as a mountain climber it seems perfectly normal—they are real persons. The mountain either lets you climb or it doesn't. The weather either cooperates or it doesn't. When an early researcher, Preuss (1907) remarked that "this person appears to symbolize water," the Huichol shaman replied, "One says it is Water Person."

The ritual pilgrimage is not something of the past or the future but something that is happening here and now. The singer, with the help of his drum and the assistance of the Divine Deer Person succeeds in lifting himself and the children out of their everyday life into a sacred journey to a distant "holy" place.

Preparation for the "fly as birds" Pilgrimage
1) Choosing "the way" for the pilgrimage
Before the first children's ceremony, you will have to decide where the pilgrimage will take place. Then all the adults involved must travel with you on the pilgrimage, noting as you go all important places. Particular places may become important during this first journey either because it is a particularly beautiful spot or because a humorous event happened there or a dramatic event occurred or a special species of bird was noted, etc.

The places where I have set up such pilgrimages in the past have been either in the mountains or the suburbs of large cities in the western U.S., where there were still ravines or wild bits of vacant spaces. However the pilgrimage can be set up anywhere that there is some access to natural vegetation out of sight of buildings or people. (In chapter thirteen, Sacred Land, see the Hako section for additional information on pilgrimages.) If there is no place near you out of sight of buildings or people, then you will have to drive some distance until you can find such a spot. Today in Mexico, the Huichol pilgrims actually do travel part of the distance by car or truck. If you must go by car, that also must be considered part of the ritual journey. If at all possible it is best to walk the entire journey. The journey should be fairly long because, eventually, you will be taking these children on the actual pilgrimage when they are ten years old or so. It should be somewhat strenuous for them. Two to four miles, round trip, is probably what you should aim for.

One further aspect here concerns the "sacred" goal of the pilgrimage. For those who say, "Yes, but we don't have a sacred mountain or a sacred waterfall or a sacred tree." The important thing here is to know that you do have such a place. For example, let's consider the matter from a single aspect of the sacred—that of healing. Negative ions promote healing and well-being. These negative ions are prevalent at the tips of tree branches, at waterfalls, at ocean beaches and on tops of mountains. Such places have been recognized as "sacred" by every traditional culture in the past. Temples and shrines were usually built in such spots. Negative ions are present at such places as waterfalls and ocean beaches because the kinetic action of the moving water strips the ions off the water molecules. The presence of negative ions on mountain tops and from vegetation is too complex to go into here. (See my book, *Earth Wisdom* for more information on this subject.) Essentially, the point here is that you do have a "sacred" place nearby. Nature provides it; all you have to do is recognize it.

2) Choosing the time of year
Ideally, the pilgrimage should be held in either the spring or fall. If in spring it should also be a "first fruits" festival as well. This is the time when nature gives us the first edible plants. Whatever edible natural plant first comes up in your area, should be first displayed on platters in the ceremonial site and eaten later in the ceremony. In our town, dandelions are the first plant. These were not originally native, of course, but they are now. Our high altitude edible plants do not come out of the ground until late June. Fall is also a good time because there are edible wild berries or nuts. See below for further details concerning the actual use of these edible plants in the ceremony itself.

3) Totem animals
You must decide on the totem animal for each of the four sacred directions. If you are new to ritual, the simplest thing is to use the directional animals from the book, *Seven Arrows*, because Storm provides sufficient background to easily

incorporate them into this ceremony.

During the "fly as birds" ceremony, each totem animal helps with the journey. For the Huichol, their main animal is "Divine Deer Person." Occasionally, their shaman chants: "Follow the Divine Deer Person, follow Divine Deer Person." In the framework for the ceremony below I have not included particular totem animals, but as the "storyteller" puts in the specific directions for your own place, these totem animals should be included.

4) Preparation of the site where the "fly as birds" pilgrimage takes place

This should be indoors for privacy and comfort. The "storyteller" sits on a low seat. The children sit on cushions on the floor: boys on one side; girls on the other. The small babies sit with their mothers. As soon as a child can sit up, it can join in this ceremony. The mother lets it hold its own rattle until it is tired and then shakes the rattle for the child until it is ready to take it up again. The "story teller" should be a man; he can do his own drumming or have another person, called "keeper of the drum," do the drumming.

There is food set out and will be put before the children at particular times during the ceremony. If possible there should be a small fire where sacred "Grandfather Fire" is present for the children and to warm the drum head from time to time.

5) List of items needed at the site:
1. drum
2. cushions for each person—child and adult
3. stool for the "story teller"—This special stool is considered very important by the Huichol.
4. flower petals in a basket (see below for use)
5. "sacred water" in a gourd bowl. If possible this water should be collected on the adult journey from a special place on the pilgrimage and saved for this ceremony.
6. A special cord or string to tie all the cotton balls of the children together in a long line.

6) Preparation of the children

Each child should have a headband to hold the "shaman's plume" (this can be a bird feather or a particular leaf but not a flower). Also in the headband is the "four sacred directions" symbol. These should be made ahead of time and the group as a whole decides what they want to include in them. One possibility is yarn symbolizing the four directions: using *Seven Arrows* symbolism, this would be white (north), black (west) yellow (east) and green (south). As soon as the group has developed enough experience with the ritual journey it can choose the sacred colors connected with the directions of its own place. Essentially, this has to do with the "color" of the directions in each region. But this takes time to register on modern people. For instance, if storms always come from one direction that color could be black; if the sun sets, leaving a red glow on a hill or mountain, west would be red, etc. This "four sacred directions" symbol shows the protection each of these Four Great Powers of the directions exerts over the child.

Each child must have a gourd rattle. In Part I of this work,

we saw how important gourd rattles were to early humans. Not only did they "afford" a way to carry water and food and also provided the first musical instruments, gourds also helped the pre-hominids to become human. In this "fly as birds" ceremony, gourds, which helped us become human, "affords" the small child the chance to begin participating in "the story." As soon as the baby moves its hand, the gourd rattle responds with sound. The slightest movement brings immediate response. This, of course, is why babies were given rattles in most cultures—including our own up until a generation ago. I'm not sure exactly when rattles fell into disfavor in this culture. Now they are replaced by "high tech" plastic gimmicks, which dangle above the crib to keep the baby amused. But none of these gimmicks give the immediate feedback to a baby that a hand-held rattle does.

For those who have not used a gourd rattle in a ceremony, it is difficult to explain how important they are. But I will give an example. Often when a "sweat" is being conducted, the first session will be completely silent. The second session will begin silently, but now everyone has a gourd rattle in their hand. Within moments, some slight emotion or even nervousness on the part of one person, will cause his rattle to sound. Others join in automatically and soon the group finds they are moving the rattles in synchronous rhythm. In other situations, where chanting is beginning and newcomers are frightened or rigid with uncertainty, hand them a gourd rattle and very quickly they are able to relax and quit worrying about "what I am supposed to be doing." The gourd is doing it for them.

In the Huichol "fly as birds" ceremony, the sound of the rattle is said to represent the rustling of the children's wings and this sound accompanies that of the drum, "on whose vibrations the shaman and his helpers lift them magically into the sky." Physiologically, we could say that the *entrainment*, provided by the synchronous sounding of the rattles, does "carry" the children into the story. (See the "Way of the Gourd" in chapter sixteen for further information.)

Each child must have a small ball of cotton. (See below for its use.) The Huichol use cotton because it is native to Mexico. Another object may be substituted here, native to your own place.

7) Final instructions concerning the setting

The place where the ceremony is held should have a fireplace or at least a wood-burning stove. Grandfather Fire must be present. There should also be a gourd bowl filled with the "sacred" water. The drum is near the "story-teller," who is seated on his stool. If another person will be doing the drumming, he or she is called "Keeper of the drum," and sits nearby. The "storyteller" and the "Keeper of the drum" are already there when the children enter.

The chant pilgrimage should last several hours. It takes time to get entrained with drumming so that it becomes effortless. The children can go to sleep whenever they want. It is especially fine to wake up, hearing the on-going drum. They will wake up and join in again with no effort, once the drumming and rattling have been going on for some time. California Indian song cycles lasted just as long as the actual physical journey—sometimes for days. But most of us aren't quite ready for that yet.

The "fly as birds" Ceremony

PRELIMINARY REMARKS

Using the structure of the Huichol ceremony, I will be drawing on my own experiences here in the San Juan Mountains, in providing a framework for your use of this ceremony in your own place. Through the years these experiences have included the following: first, an all-day journey with fourteen third grade children, which deeply influenced their lives up to the present time. They are now juniors in high school. Second, a journey to a sacred waterfall, which involves first crossing an ice-cold stream. I have taken different groups of adults on this pilgrimage for four consecutive years on my annual Taoist Autumn Equinox Celebration. Third, a pilgrimage to a small pond with a giant tree, completely hidden from sight even though it is just above the town.

During the ceremony, if the occasion comes up, the children should be referred to as "children of the mountain" or "children of the river" or "children of the waterfall." If the most powerful place in your area is a cave or a rock then they are "children of the cave" or "children of Inyan, the Rock" (Inyan is one of the four aspects of the Sioux concept of Wakan Tanka, erroneously translated as "the Great Spirit.")

At times below, I have made the account into a form of rough chant. When you do this ceremony you will automatically find yourself doing the same to keep in rhythm with the drum and the rattles. Words in boldface type are actual quotes from the Huichol ritual. The person leading the children in the journey is called the "storyteller" below. In the actual Huichol ceremony it is the Shaman or *mara'akame*, to be precise.

> In this ceremony the children are provided with 'an inner map' on which the sacred places and events of the . . . pilgrimage are indelibly etched. By their vicarious (but in their own minds, those of their relatives, and of the shaman, nonethless real) flight as transformed birds in each of the first five years of life, the young Indians become increasingly prepared for direct participation in the sacred pilgrimage, which Huichols . . . tend to view as the sine qua non for the survival of their culture.
>
> Peter Furst

OPENING OF THE CEREMONY

The "storyteller" is already seated and the drum is sounding softly before the children enter the room. One of the mothers should lead the group in and make a ritual circle round the space before they sit down. The children sit down on cushions on the floor—boys on one side of the "storyteller"; girls on the other. Mothers with small infants may sit either place. Parents may need to help their young babies hold the rattle at first. They will not need to help them keep rhythm; because once the drum and rattles are going well, babies automatically synchronize.

A helper walks round the seated children. Each child hands his or her ball of cotton to the helper, who ties each ball on the string—one below the other. When the string is complete, the helper ceremoniously presents the string to the "storyteller." This string of cotton balls symbolically connects each child with the "storyteller" on the mythical journey.

THE "FLY AS BIRDS" CEREMONY BEGINS

"Storyteller" and all adults join in:

We are all,
We are all the children of,
We are all the children of,

The mountain (or the waterfall) etc.

And there is no one,
There is no one,
Who regrets what we are.

Storyteller: We are all going to fly together—fly like birds—fly in the direction where our Father, the sun comes up in the morning (or goes down in the afternoon). To take off from the ground together we must flap our wings strong. Strong like the beat of the drum. Everyone shake your rattles hard so that your wings will be strong when we all fly together. (Wait while everyone gets synchronized to the drum before continuing. The children soon feel that in shaking the rattle, their wings are lifting them into the air.)

Now the sound lifts us into the air, we are flying like birds over to where the sun comes up. We are going to where your fathers and mothers went on their journey to the sacred mountain last year. And where they will go again this year. See, look down, we are going over the trees on the edge of town. We are going over them, we are leaving them behind. (Be very specific about where you are going as you leave the building you are in and begin the journey. If on the real pilgrimage, the people must travel first by car before they begin the walk, this is mentioned before the actual synchronization of drum and rattles. Just tell the children we are getting into the car, we are driving out the road. Soon we are where your parents got out of the car to walk to the sacred mountain. And then go on from there in the visualization.)

The drum helps carry us through the air, helps our wings to hold us up. The drum was given to us by our brother, the deer and by our sister, the cottonwood tree (or aspen). This is the deer's hide and this is the tree, (as you point to the wood itself.) The deer and the tree gave us this drum so that we may all fly to the sacred mountain. It took your parents all day to get to the sacred mountain but we are flying so that we can travel the whole journey in just a short time. You can see where your parents walked and where you will walk with your parents in a year or two—on this sacred journey.

Now we are coming to the place where the path gets very steep so we fly slowly over it. We are roped together here so that no one can fall. (The "storyteller" lifts the string with the cotton balls on it. He lifts it a bit so that each child can see his or her ball on the string, safely tied together. On the journey to the sacred waterfall we had all fourteen children tied onto a rope at one difficult place and this impressed them greatly.) We fly over this hard place where the rocks are steep, where our brother, the marmot helps us. He shows us how to climb as well as he does. And then, we are over it! We flew right over the hard part. We are now safe again. We can land in the grassy, warm meadow filled with flowers and rest. See here are the flowers. (The helper throws out flower petals over the heads of the children.) Now we are safe and warm and it is very beautiful and we rest.

Are you ready to go on? Now we go higher still and we can see down below, the place where your parents had to wade across the water. We have to cross the water too. The water is cold but it is so clear and shining we can see all the little green and red and blue rocks down there. They are so pretty we want to take them with us but we can't. If we did we couldn't fly anymore so we have to leave them, now. When you are old enough to walk to the sacred mountain then you can pick them up. Now we are flying over the cold water. Hear the rustling of your wings as we fly over. (Mothers shake your rattles harder and the children quickly join in.)

We fly further. We fly to where the big pine tree lives. The tree, our brother is even taller than this room and we fly alongside of it and we see all the glittering needles in the sun. (I always read a bit from D. H. Lawrence when we get to this great pine tree: "The tree gathers up earth-power from the dark bowels of the earth, and a roaming sky-glitter from above. And all unto itself, which is a tree, woody, enormous, slow but unyielding with life, bristling with acquisitive energy, obscurely radiating some of its great strength. It vibrates its presence into my soul...Its raw earth-power and its raw sky-power, its resinous erectness and resistance, its sharpness of hissing needles and relentlessness of roots, all that goes to the primitive savageness of a pine tree, goes also to the strength of man. Give me of your power, then, oh tree! And I will give you of mine.")

We see the glittering needles and maybe, if we look close we can see a little bird hidden in there.

Then we come to where the water falls over a steep rock. This is a very sacred place. Here we slow down our flying and go carefully behind the waterfall and here we are! Safe and dry, looking out through the shining water. Looking out at all the trees and the sky out there and we are safe looking through the water. Just like a dipper bird. (We have water ouzels here which fly under the water—something which always amazes children.) We see all the shining drops of water falling down. But we are safe, safe here in the earth. Here is some water from that sacred waterfall. Here in this gourd bowl. (The helper takes the bowl in hand and walks around among the children scattering a few drops of water just as a waterfall would do.)

"Look, here you are blessed, here you are cleansed, all of you. I bless you with the water from the (sacred waterfall). I bless you in the Four Winds."

(The "storyteller" calls on each of the directions.) The blessing comes to you from the North, where the cold wind comes from in the winter, the blessing comes to you from the east, where our Father the Sun rises up in the morning, the blessing comes to you from the South, where the big river flows, the blessing comes to you from the West, where our Father the Sun goes down at night. (Turn toward each of those directions.)

We now fly on. We fly over the path where your mothers and fathers walked last year. We fly on until we come to the magic place where the "little ones" live. Here we see all the tiny cups lined up in a row — all set out in a row. (This is where lichen grows; the fruiting bodies look just like cups). The little people all hide when we fly over because we are so big. But we see their cups all lined up waiting for them.

Now we are flying high—so high. We are flying like eagles. (Here all join in chanting: "We All Fly Like Eagles.")

Now we come to a very scary place. We have to go through a narrow place between two rocks. We must fly very carefully. Your rattles must be strong here. We need help from our rattles to fly through here! Now, we are safely through. We have arrived at the "Sacred Mountain" (Or sacred river etc.)

Here we are now, very happy, very content...
We have seen everything.

Of our Mother (the mountain)
Where Our Mother is,

Where the flowers are,
Where the Divine Deer persons are,

Which our Grandfathers, Our Grandmothers,
(Saw) Now we have arrived here,

Resting, resting.

Here everyone stands up and makes a circle round where they have been sitting. All children carry their rattles. One of the boys carries a leaf of the local plant, which can be eaten this time of year and a girl carries another leaf or a nut or berry. They circle round the room and near to Grandfather Fire. The song they chant together is the Arapaho chant: "We Circle Around the Boundaries of the Earth."

I CIRCLE AROUND

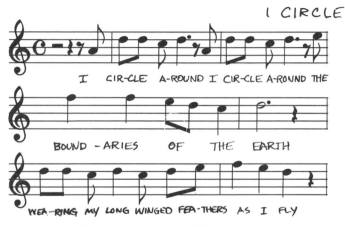

CONCLUSION OF THE CEREMONY

Then all return to their places. Flower petals are thrown over all. The "storyteller" very carefully winds up the string with all the cotton balls on it and stores it in a special box until next year. All the children see his care of them in this gesture. Then everyone shares a feast of the food carried by the children and available this time of year from your own place. The children actually carry only a few bits of the "first fruits" food; the rest has been prepared for eating and is served up from the platters.

The ceremony is over. "The children have been flown to (the sacred place) and they have returned safely; in another year, they will hear it again, and again in the following year. The sacred places will be named, the ancient landmarks pointed out. By the time they embark on their own pilgrimage, they will travel along a road they have long since learned by heart...All the sacred places are named as the singer sets the bird-children down in one named spot after another and lifts them up again into the sky on the vibrations of his drum." Furst is describing the Huichol ceremony here but it is just as true of our children as they take part in the ceremony. The "storyteller" chants the bird-children on their journey; but. actually, through him, the land itself is speaking to the children, telling the children about their own sacred land.

Conclusion

As mentioned often above, the central aspect of the Huichol culture is the "sacred pilgrimage." This yearly pilgrimage has kept their culture strong enough to stand up to all the pressures of the modern Industrial Growth Society as well as the Christian missionaries. If we are serious in our attempt to learn once more how to live as a traditional culture in balance with the land, we need to begin this "pilgrimage tradition." The best way to structure such a pilgrimage so that it does, indeed, become sacred within a few short years, is to follow the example of the Huichol and take the small children on the "fly as birds" pilgrimage, led by the "storyteller."

Another valuable effect of this children's ceremony is that at least once each year certain natural things are validated as sacred. If one of these children does have a "nature mystic experience" it is validated at the next "fly as birds" ceremony; therefore it is easier to hold onto. Moreover, it is validated by the group without using any words and might even be incorporated in "the story" at the next year's ceremony.

During these pilgrimage type rituals, which I give, often someone will tell me, "Now I remember." A particular experience during our pilgrimage will trigger a long ago nature experience which had been lost to their conscious mind for years. But remembering it, they suddenly find they have the power back, which had been lost in their lives. As mentioned above in discussing this "childhood nature mystic experience," once this occurs, you know that you can trust all nature, that you are not alone in the world. You can draw on sources of power much deeper and much bigger than yourself. Such a deep trust permits action without arrogance. This is the feeling expressed by such statements as "it skis me" or, in music, "it plays me."

In the daily life of children, who will experience this ceremony, there will be occasional times when the goal of the pilgrimage, the sacred spot far away or high above may be pointed out to them. For instance, when the parents and children are gathering berries in the fall. Each time this spot is pointed out or even the direction of the sacred place is shown, it adds more to its allure and promise. Yet, at the same time does not provoke anxiety. The child knows she will be able to walk there, sometime, because she's already been there, "flying as birds." All of this is part of the sacredness of land. In *Nature and Madness*, Paul Shepard writes: "Place to Australian aborigines is not a detachable quality or an abstract way of making location a relative commodity. It is continuous with the identity structure of the adult. It is embedded there as a result of a combination of daily life and formal ceremony during the first fifteen to twenty years of life. It is not unreasonable to suppose that something like it gave shape to the religious life and the personality of the prehistoric hunter-gatherers of Eurasia and Africa."

CHILD BONDING, CONSCIOUSNESS AND PLAY

Essentially, all bonding has to do with animal behavior because, as we have seen in Part II, bonding involves the older brains as well as body knowledge. After the initial bonding to the mother, comes the stage of bonding to the earth. By the age of seven, the corpus callosum, the network of cells connecting the two hemispheres of the brain, completes its growth enough so that the brain areas can begin to specialize: verbal and linear aspects to the left hemisphere and body-knowing and earth knowledge (primary process) to the right hemisphere. After this is accomplished, the mind can process information according to three different functions of consciousness which are separate but interdependent. One type of consciousness is that of the self as a unique individual and separate from the world; the second type is that of consciousness of one's body supported by and in interaction with the world (primary process); and the third type, which Jung called the collective unconscious and which Bateson calls mind-at-large or the "general field of awareness."

During the ages between seven and about eleven or twelve is the time when play is of the utmost importance. The child must play outdoors as much as possible with essentially the same group of children so the hierarchy can be established, painlessly. The best play places are similar to what humans have always preferred since we were primates, newly out of the trees. Places to hide, safely, and look out at others, places to climb, simple natural items to make things out of—rocks, sticks, dirt, mud. At the same time the child needs to see non-human beings: animals, trees, mountains, rivers. Long walks with a child is the best parent/child interaction. Let the child set the pace and stop when she stops. Don't volunteer information but do answer any questions.

In his book, *The Tender Carnivore and the Sacred Game*, Paul Shepard gives these three "ecological needs" for children under ten: "architecturally complex play space shared with companions; a cumulative and increasingly diverse experience of non-human forms, animate and inanimate, whose taxonomic names and generic relationships he must learn; and occasional and progressively more strenuous excursions into the wild world where he may, in a limited way, confront the non-human." All of these experiences are necessary for a child to develop a healthy sense of his identity. Harold Searles describes identity as "not only a honing of personal singularity but a compounding wealth of ever more refined relationships between the person and increasingly differentiated parts of the rest of the world." And he very definitely states that "world" includes the nonhuman as well as the human.

Jung points out that in our culture we so often demand that an adult "violently sunder" himself from his original childhood "in the interests of some arbitrary persona more in keeping with his ambitions." Of course what happens when this occurs is the repression of all that really matters to the person with consequent psychological damage. Jung points out that "Religious observances, i.e., the retelling and ritual repetition of the mythical event, consequently serve the purpose of bringing the image of childhood, and everything connected with it, again and again before the eyes of the conscious mind so that the link with the original condition may not be broken." This, precisely is one of the powerful purposes of the child ceremony, "fly as birds," as given above.

Such ceremonies not only reunite the adults with the childhood archetypes but also overcome the narrow dichotomies of Western culture: good-bad, mind-body, spirit-matter, positive-negative, man-earth etc. Our narrow rational ego attaches a good or bad value to one half of each of these pairs of opposites. Further, the adult then tries to deny the bad or negative half while identifying with its positive opposite. Meanwhile in the deeper layers of the mind—the unconscious—there is no such split. All these aspects are reunited there, because it was the ego consciousness itself, which created these opposites. They were not there before the ego consciousness split them. If children and adults through the years take part in ceremonies together, it is no longer necessary to repress the most important part of one's psyche. Each year there is a time which all can look forward to when complete expression is allowed of *all* that the individual *is*.

"In a completely pre-literate society the oral tradition is not memorized, but remembered. Thus, every telling is fresh and new, as the teller's mind's eye re-views the imagery of origins and journeys or loves or hunts. Themes and formulae are repeated as part of an ever-changing tapestry composed of both the familiar and the novel. Direct experience, generation by generation, feeds back into the tale told. Part of that direct experience is the group context itself, a circle of listeners who murmur the burden back or voice approval, or snore. Meaning flashes from mind to mind, and young eyes sparkle...

The many motifs of oral literature found world-wide, which at least prove that humanity enjoys the same themes over and over, are not heard as part of some comparative study demonstrating the brotherhood of man, but as out of the minds, hills, and rivers of the place— maybe through the mouth of a bear or salmon. A people and a place become one."

Gary Snyder

PRAYER, FROM THE RECEPTION OF THE CHILD RITUAL

Ho! Sun, Moon, Stars, all you that move in the heavens,
*   Hear me*
Into your midst has come a new life! I ask your consent!
Make smooth its path that it may reach the brow of the first hill!

Ho! Winds, Clouds, Rain, Mist, all you that move in the air,
*   Hear me!*
Into your midst has come a new life! I ask your consent!
Make smooth its path that it may reach the brow of the second hill!

Ho! Hills, Valleys, Rivers, Lakes, Trees, Grasses, all you of the earth,
*   Hear me!*
Into you midst has come a new life! I ask you consent!
Make smooth its path that it may reach the brow of the third hill!

Ho! Birds great and small that fly in the air,
Ho! Animals great and small that dwell in the forest,
Ho! Insects that creep among the grasses and burrow in the ground
*   Hear me!*
Into your midst has come a new life! I ask your consent!

Ho! all you of the heavens, all you of the air, all you of the earth:
*   Hear me!*
Into your midst has come a new life! I ask your consent,
*   I implore!*
Make its path smooth—then shall it travel beyond the four hills!

Omaha Tribe

"[Rituals] mend ever again worlds forever breaking apart under the blows of usage and the slashing distinctions of language."

Roy Rappaport

"There is a rapidly growing body of evidence linking our mammalian inheritance of basic brainstem functions with man's unique religious, social and cultural achievements. Society has scarcely begun to consider the implications of these discoveries."

Dr. J.P. Henry

"The purpose of ritual is to wake up the old mind in us, to put it to work. The old ones inside us, the collective unconscious, the many lives, the different eternal parts, the senses and parts of the brain that have been ignored. Those parts do not speak English. They do not care about television. But they do understand candlelight and colors. They do understand nature."

Z Budapest

CHAPTER TWELVE

"...a man without ritual cannot live; an undertaking without ritual cannot come to completion; and a state without ritual cannot attain peace."

Hsün Tzu (298-238 B.C.)

"I am...asserting that to view ritual as simply a way to fulfill certain functions that may as well or better be fulfilled by other means, or as an alternative symbolic medium of expressing what may just as well—or perhaps better—be expressed in other ways is, obviously to ignore that which is distinctive in ritual itself. Moreover, it becomes apparent through consideration of ritual's form that ritual is not simply an alternative way to express certain things, but **that certain things can be expressed only in ritual.**

[R]...ritual is without equivalents or even alternatives...that which can be expressed only in ritual is not trivial. It is, I think, crucial, and because of it I take ritual to be the basic social act...in fact, that social contract, morality, the concept of the sacred, the notion of the divine, and even a paradigm of creation are intrinsic to ritual's structure."

Roy Rappaport

"[In ritual] you get out of the narrow confines of the neo-cortex and into the 'great mind'."
Elizabeth Cogburn

 AN OVERVIEW OF RITUAL

Personal Introduction

Because my book, *Earth Festivals* (1973), was a pioneer work in helping modern people re-learn how to do the ancient earth rituals, at workshops people often ask me the question: "How did you get into ritual?" There is never enough time at a workshop to give the whole story so I will take the time here to recount it.

I did not "get into" ritual. What happened was that ritual engulfed me before I had a word for it or knew anything about such a process. For years I had been skiing steep, deep powder and fully knew the bliss of such interaction with snow, gravity, and the humans in the group. (See *Earth Wisdom* p. 55.) But all that seemed perfectly understandable at the time and I needed no explanation. The first event which caused me to really wonder was a day at Alta when it was snowing graupel. Now graupel is the quintessential ultimate in skiing. I've never heard of any ski area having enough of it to ski except Alta, Utah—and even there but rarely. In all the seventeen years I lived there, we had enough graupel snow to ski it only three times. The incident I am about to recount took place on the second occasion. Graupel consists of round, hard pellets just like marbles—it rolls ceaselessly and cannot stop. It combines the best of powder and of corn snow (spring snow). Thus one can ski anywhere—down vertical slopes and through thick trees, effortlessly. Even more marvellous is the fact that each run down the same slope is the "first run." By that I mean all previous tracks are erased as the snow has been gently rolling down the hill the entire time so there is untracked powder again and again and again. Graupel only occurs in the most miserable weather conditions possible. It is always just about 32 degrees—barely freezing. So it's both cold and wet. The wind is screaming in, horizontally, and it's impossible to see a thing unless you ski in the trees because they give definition to the whiteout.

Practically no one skis in this kind of weather unless they happen to know about graupel snow. Sitting inside a ski lodge, looking out the window, it seems utterly miserable. On this particular day the big ski race of the year, called the Alta Cup, was scheduled. Lodges were packed but no one was on the slope at all except the six of us. The race was cancelled, of course, and because of the wind only the lower lift was running. This was long ago and the lower lift was a single chair lift. Going up the lift was torture. The wind cut across horizontally, with such fury, that we held onto the metal rod connecting the chair with the cable for life and buried our faces deep inside our hoods. But once on top it was total bliss all the way down. All together all the way. No one ever falls in graupel. Of course you can't even ski graupel unless you can keep your skis together. The rolling snow separates them too easily. So only experts ever try to ski it.

We had been up and down enough times to know how really good it was and that it would continue for awhile so on this particular ride up the chair I had the chance to ponder about what in the world is going on here. Looking at my friend on the chair ahead, clutching the metal rod, head buried deep between his shoulders, I thought that if someone watched a film of this scene; they would think we were suffering unbearably, when actually this is sheer bliss. Why? Well I couldn't figure it out; although, I knew it had something to

do with the effortless flow of all of us together each time down the mountain. No thinking was ever needed; no concern as to whether that turn could be done before hitting the tree. So all are moving together with no thought. And of course we aren't *doing* it at all. All of us had agreed that none of us could ski this good—ever. So the mountain and the snow were doing it for us. These are the actual words many of us used. I was the only woman in the group. The others were either on the lift crew or ski patrol; so this kind of group would not be speaking poetically; they meant it when they said the mountain and the snow were doing it. Actually, it's the only words for such an experience.

My second story is even more amazing but much shorter in the telling. We were skiing powder snow, several years later. There was only the lower lift in the area called Albion Basin then. There was no upper lift and the lower lift was classified as "lower intermediate." So there was no one on the connecting, flat rope-tow back to the main area on stormy days. Those who skied the high steep powder slopes of Yellow Trail or Greeley Hill had the mountain to themselves when they got onto the flatter approaches to this rope tow; in order to grab it and let it carry them back to the main lift, for another ride up to the high country. We had been down several times so were aware of how the snow was, how fast we would be going etc. This time we came off the high powder, stopped to grin at one another in sheer delight and all took off at once heading for the rope tow. There were eight of us, going as fast as we could in a straight run for the tow. As the first guy grabbed the moving rope, I had a brief flash maybe I should check my speed a bit and see that we don't all crash but it was obvious we weren't. The next guy grabbed hold of it and then Charlie, ahead of me, then I grabbed it and all those behind me—just one after the other as if it had been choreographed or planned. It was such perfect timing with no effort. In such a situation, "objectively," any number of things could go wrong. Eight people moving as fast as possible and reaching out for a moving rope without even thinking about it! But, because we knew the snow and knew the terrain we let *it* do the deciding and it was perfect. When we got back to the main chair terminal we all stopped and grinned again and said, "Wow! Wasn't that amazing?" We had all felt it. We didn't try to explain it. How could we?

Humans rarely, if ever, get a chance to move this way; but birds, taking off together from a tree, do it. Barry Lopez, writing about the wild geese at Tule Lake, gives us the best description: "what absorbs me in these birds...is how adroitly each bird joins the larger flock or departs from it. And how each bird while it is a part of the flock seems part of something larger than itself. Another animal. Never did I see a single goose move to accommodate one that was landing, nor geese on the water ever disturbed by another taking off, no matter how closely bunched they seemed to be. I never saw two birds so much as brush wingtips in the air...They roll up into a headwind together in a seamless movement that brings thousands of them gently to the ground like falling leaves in but a few seconds." And that's the crux of our skiing experience—that phrase, "a seamless movement that brings...them gently to the ground like falling leaves..."

Long after this experience with the rope tow, I found that D. H. Lawrence, while returning to England, near the point of death from tuberculosis, had dictated this beautiful fragment to his wife, Frieda, as he watched the porpoises (dolphins) from the bowsprit of the ship. In this quotation, he is speaking through his fictional character, Gethin Day. To him, it was "a spectacle of the purest and most perfected joy in life" that he had ever seen. They were changing places all the time, "and ever the others speeding in motionless, effortless speed, and intertwining with strange silkiness as they sped, intertwining among one another." He watched spellbound, their perfect balance:

[M]ingling among themselves in some strange single laughter of multiple consciousness, giving off the joy of life, sheer joy of life, togetherness in pure complete motion, many lusty-bodied fish enjoying one laugh of life, sheer togetherness, perfect as passion. They gave off into the water their marvelous joy of life, such as the man had never met before. And it left him wonderstruck. 'But they know joy, they know pure joy!' he said to himself in amazement. 'This is the purest achievement of joy I have seen in all life...Men have not got in them that secret to be alive together and make one like a single laugh, yet each fish going his own gait. This is sheer joy—and men have lost it, or never accomplished it...It would be wonderful to know joy as these fish know it. The life of the deep waters is ahead of us, it contains sheer togetherness and sheer joy. We have never got there.'

There as he leaned over the bowsprit he was mesmerized by one thing only, by joy, by joy of life, fish speeding in water with playful joy...What civilization will bring us to such a pitch of swift, laughing togetherness, as these fish have reached?

With this masterpiece from Lawrence, I think you can begin to see what I was trying to explain above in my two ski stories. But now I know where this feeling comes from. In ritual it's called "tuning." I'll explain it in more detail, later on in this chapter; but, essentially, it has to do with the older brains in us: animal (limbic) and reptile. Bonding develops out of this "tuning" and bonding is the real basis of all society—both human and animal. When one experiences this "tuning" and the bonding that grows out of it, there is a feeling of deep gratitude or "grace." And you always know it's not just you—it's the "more than" involved.

This is what "festival" does. Josef Pieper writes: "Thus, when a festival goes as it should, men receive something that it is not in human power to give. This is the by now almost forgotten reason for the age-old custom of men wishing one another well on great festival days." What we are wishing for is the "true fruit of the festival: renewal, transformation, rebirth...Of course rapture is always a shattering of man's ordinary, 'normal' relationsip to the world." It was some years after the above ski experience, before I found Pieper's little book, *In Tune with the World* (1965). One other important answer, which this book gave me, accounts for that overflowing gratitude which always accompanies such a feeling. This overflowing gratitude is what produces the absolutely stupid, silly grins that we always flash at one another when these moments occur in skiing or climbing. We all agree that we never see these grins anywhere else in life. Pieper again, "There can be no festivity when man, imagining himself self-sufficient, refuses to recognize that Goodness of things which goes far beyond any conceivable utility...he truly receives it only when he accepts it as pure gift. The only fitting way to respond to such gift is: by praise." Pieper is referring to praise of God in Christian worship. But it's much deeper than that. When Pieper writes: "Joy is the response of a lover receiving what he loves."; this is the joy one feels when these experiences occur in nature. All this a gift for you, now, at this moment! "To celebrate a festival means: to live out, for some special occasion and in an uncommon manner, the universal assent to the world as a whole," is the way Peiper sums it up and he quotes Nietzsche: "To have joy in anything, one must approve everything." Pieper continues: "Underlying all festive joy kindled by a specific circumstance there has to be an absolutely universal affirmation extending to the world as a whole..." This is the heart of all nature festivals. One experiences for that time the universal goodness of nature as a whole.

To return to my own experiences in moving toward ritual. Often in climbing and skiing I had such experiences of joy. None so totally "tuned" together as in the rope-tow experience, because it's not often many people can move so cleanly together in dangerous circumstances. But I began to recognize the feeling. Also, of course, I knew that most people are not willing or able to go to such beautiful (and often dangerous) places in nature to experience what they—as mammals—need the most. But, in my early experiences in planning "disguised" nature rituals for children in a preschool program for the Catholic Church, I found that such rituals could occasionally enable the adults and children together, to experience both the "tuning" and the gratitude. Later, after I left the Church, I was freed to return to the original earth festivals and I've continued to learn ever since.

Preview

Essentially, you have no choice in this—it is not whether you do ritual or don't do ritual; because one cannot be here on this earth with other fellow mammals/humans and not do ritual. It's the way nature designed us to communicate with one another. Your choice lies in what kind of ritual. If you want to do rituals designed to keep humans apart, to encourage competition and anger and hatred then there's that kind of ritual. For instance, there's the high shoulders, head ducked between them, looking at the ground ritual. Everyone knows that guy is either mad or depressed; but, anyway he certainly doesn't want anyone talking to him! That's for sure. That's ritual movement and it comes out of our animal heritage. Our human culture, in itself, specializes in rituals which split off parts of one's own nature from other parts and hides the most powerful parts. However, the ritual I am dealing with in this chapter concerns putting all parts of the human together deep inside the individual, for putting humans together in society and for facilitating human interactions with nature. I call it "sacred ritual."

THE ROOTS OF SACRED RITUAL IN THE AMERICAS

Such "sacred rituals" not only keep alive the "old ways" but also facilitate rapid change, effortlessly, in a society. The Plains Indians' high culture lasted only some eighty years—from the time enough Spanish horses went wild to begin using them for buffalo hunting to the coming of the steam trains, which destroyed it all. Yet their "way" was so powerful and produced such an integrated culture that we now think that this is the way Indians always lived. To show how "sacred ritual" helped them make this transition, from the original "woodland" culture to the high plains culture, I will use the findings about their culture hero, "Sweet Medicine." But first, returning to "Our Mother, the Gourd" I will show how the very beginnings of the high cultures of South America were linked through the gourd. It was by gradual dispersion from the South American centers that this high culture diffused northward, first to Mexico and then still northward up the rivers into North America.

Carl Sauer points out that the pattern of root crop agriculture is far older than the seed crop pattern in the semiarid zones of the Middle East, which came down to us, Europeans, as our agriculture. Root crop agriculture began in the New World in the flood plains of tropical forests along such rivers as the Amazon. The Quetzalcoatl type god is the link between this tropical origin and the cultures of the High Andes. Lathrap points out that most of these later styles of culture "can be derived from Chavin by a series of gradual progressive modifications." This huge ceremonial center of Chavin de Huantar is located on the western tributary of the upper Maranon, the major headwaters of the Amazon River. This valley comes down from the eastern slope of the Cordillera Blanca, the highest section of the Peruvian Andes. Chavin itself is more than 3000 meters (9000 ft) above sea level. This is a high glaciated valley but its art style shows creatures native to the riverine flood plains of the Amazon Basin.

The famous "Obelisk Tello" is the most outstanding sculpture in Chavin, dated from between 800 to 1000 BC. This Obelisk is a cayman— somewhat like a crocodile—but this cayman has in its mouth a gourd. The cayman has a very restricted range, the flood plain of the largest rivers in the Amazon system. This Great Cayman of the obelisk has a bird (probably the great monkey-eating eagle) on the uppermost part of its snout. Lathrap says that the Obelisk Tello is a "sort of trinity, with the whole standing for 'The Great Cayman', as Creator and Master of the Fish; and with the two discrete depictions standing for a sky deity and a deity of the water and the underworld respectively." Both aspects deal with useful cultivated plants. The gourd, seeming to come out of its mouth, comes from a vine which has both male and female flowers on the same plant. The Cayman is dragging along a pepper plant (Capsicum). His penis exudes a manioc plant with the characteristic eyes of this plants. The eyes below the ground send out roots and those above the ground send out stalks. The manioc is propagated by cutting off a piece of a plant and putting it in the ground. The basic theme of the Cayman Obelisk is fecundity and the processes of propagation and Lathrap argues that the monument is not so much a depiction of ordinary

nutritional plants as a "celebration of the prior agricultural system which allowed the Chavin elite to achive its current dominance." This prior agricultural system was obviously from a very different geographical setting—the tropical lowlands along the Amazon. But the Chavin people took along their gods to this high Andean glacial valley; thus their gods insured cultural stability. Celebrating *all* the gods insures both easy transitions in changing times and connections with long-ago roots in the past.

It's easy to see that this "Great Cayman" with its bird on the top of its snout, it's gourd coming out of the mouth and its crocodile-like tail is reminiscent of Quetzalcoatl—the plumed serpent of the Toltec and older cultures in Mexico. One can see the linking of different cultural strategies in Quetzalcoatl as well. Present day southwest Indian cultures have links back to these South American "old ways." Other North American Indian cultures have influences from these same "old ways" by way of dispersion up the Mississippi and its tributaries.

Returning to the Plains Indians use of ritual, I will go into some detail concerning the Cheyenne Indians. Their history begins in Minnesota as Woodland Indians. They began moving westward across the Missouri under their Sacred Mountain and the Black Hills and out onto the high plains, leaving behind their cornfields and earth lodges. They were a poor people then. The Mandans and Arikaras transported them across the Missouri in buffalo rawhide bullboats. On the West side of the Missouri they were still building earth lodges in a fortified village above Standing Rock in North Dakota and planting fields of corn, beans and squash. According to Powell it was "near the pipestone quarries in a land of lakes" that the Cheyennes and Suhtaoi first met. The latter were called the Buffalo People. The Suhtaoi were the ones who gave the Cheyenne the sacred Buffalo Hat. Along with the hat came related ceremonies of the Sun Dance, Sweat Lodge, and Buffalo ceremonies. As the Buffalo Hat ceremonies grew in importance, the older agricultural ceremonies diminished; the hunting and world-renewal rites began to take over. This change-over of emphasis in the rituals was accomplished by such culture heroes as "Sweet Medicine," (Sweet Root Standing). He is the one, the Cheyennes believe, who brought them the arrows and the other buffalo ceremonies mentioned above.

Sweet Medicine's name comes from the sweet root of the plant *Actaea argutta* also called white baneberry. Indian women drank a tea of this to encourage the flow of milk in nursing mothers. "Sweet Medicine's teaching is the spiritual milk by which the Cheyennes have grown in wisdom." The many different names for this culture hero indicate the various roles he had in bridging the woodland and the high plains culture; the growing corn and buffalo hunting and also the male/female roles in nourishing the culture through its transitions. These names include: Erect Horns (referring to the sacred "Buffalo Hat" and rites); Red Tassel (meaning a stalk of corn in bloom); It Goes in (root of plant and penis of humans); Sweet Root Standing; Rustling Corn Leaf (the sound made by corn leaves as they rub); Sweet Medicine (plant used by nursing mothers).

In the Cheyenne Sun Dance ritual, the Arrow Lodge priests begin the four songs which have to do with the "world renewal" aspect of this ceremony. These were recorded in 1908. The words are as follows: First, "The solid sky, the cloudy sky, the good sky, the straight sky."; Second, "The earth produces herbs. The herbs cause us to live. They cause long life. They cause us to be happy."; Third, "The good life: may it prevail with the air. May it increase. May it be straight to the end." and Fourth, "Sweet Medicine's earth is good. Sweet Medicine's earth is completed. Sweet Medicine's earth is washed and flows." Here we see the relationship between the earth, the sky, the plants, the water and the humans as all are involved, together, in the sacred "world-renewal" rite.

With the arrival of steam trains, providing easy access, the Plains Indian culture was finished. At least 7,500,000 buffalo were shot between 1872 and 1874, thus destroying the sacred base of the Plains Indian culture as well as their source of both food and most other necessities in their daily life. Each of these meanings was inherent in the buffalo for the Indians; but for the invading Europeans, all these meanings were reduced to one—merely a "substance," either for selling or for "having fun." Originally, the whites stripped off the skin and sold it for buffalo robes; later, only the tongue was taken out to sell for gourmet eating. Shooting "for fun" was rampant. In all these cases, the greater part of the buffalo was left, as "waste," lying there on the ground.

Introduction to Various Aspects of Ritual

Ritualization is grounded [in the life of those involved] and yet permeated with the spontaneity of surprise; it is an unexpected renewal of a recognizable order in potential chaos...

It minds instinctual energy into a pattern of mutuality, which bestows convincing simplicity on dangerously complex matters...

Thus the decay or perversion of ritual does not create an indifferent emptiness, but a void with explosive possibilities...

Erik Erikson

The use of the gourd in ritual, of course, best shows us what Erikson means when he says "recognizable order in potential chaos." Part II showed how the gourd afforded the symbol for the development of Taoism. Now in Part III, the gourd becomes one of the prime affordances for ritual. The gourd provides an example of just what Erikson means in this introductory quote, when he says: "unexpected renewal of a recognizable order in potential chaos." The undifferentiated chaotic mass of the immature gourd, becomes an "unexpected renewal...of order," when it is mature and its seeds are able to sound for us as we use it in ritual as a gourd rattle. Because of the gourd rattle's ability to induce "tuning" among humans, it becomes one of the principle ways of producing order through ritual. (See Chapter 16)

This quote from Erikson is part of a talk, that he gave at the first important conference on ritual and related matters, held in 1965. The conference, "A Discussion on Ritualization of Behaviour in Animals and Man" was organized by Sir Julian Huxley to bring together important people from many different fields.

Modern study of ritual began with detailed observation of the elaborate mutual courting display of the Great Crested Grebe. Huxley in 1914 reported that these displays functioned as an emotional bond between the mated pair. His significant discovery here was that "the coordination of social behaviour, is effected by means of signals which symbolize a particular behaviour pattern." Later, he found that such displays were also to do with threat. About 1935 Konrad Lorenz began his work on what later came to be called "ethology." (Lorenz credits Whitman and Heinroth with being part of the "heroic" early age of ethology in the early decades of this century.) In 1948 Tinbergen began his work in ethology. In fact, Huxley in his opening talk at this meeting, reports that Lorenz calls him one of the founding fathers of this new science of ethology. According to Huxley ritualization in both animal and man serves four main functions: a) "to promote better and more unambiguous signal function," both between the individual humans or animals and also between species; b) "to serve as more efficient stimulators or releasers of more efficient patterns of action in other individuals; c) to reduce intraspecific damage; and d) to serve as sexual or social bonding mechanisms."

There is considerable confusion involved in the use of the words, ritual, ritualization and other related words. One dictionary defines ritual as "the established form for a ceremony"; another dictionary defines rite as "a formal procedure in a religious observance." In both this conference on "The Ritualization of Behaviour in Animals and Man" and a later, important conference of the American Ethnological Society on "Forms of Symbolic Action," there was considerable discussion about a definition of ritual, which would please both the ethologists and those studying human behavior. No final decisions were made. To be brief, I will oversimplify this complex matter, by saying that, there are three main categories: 1) biological ritualization, in animals and its further biological development in humans, 2) general human ritualizations such as "habitual, repetitive, stereotyped, compulsive or obligatory; or as acts of displaying, posturing, gesturing, or signalizing; or as methods of formalizing, routinizing, conventualizing etc."; and 3) "sacred ritual"—that which enables humans to celebrate or evoke the "sacred"—in the largest sense. This last category is the one I am most concerned with in the remainder of Part III. (See Chapter 10 for more on the "sacred.")

Most important of all, according to Huxley, rituals are "needed to help in the most comprehensive task before this generation—the achievement of a new and effective adaptative patterning of thought and belief about man's place and role in nature." This is "sacred ritual." The conference, "A Discussion on Ritualization" took place in England in June of 1965; yet even today, more than twenty years later, the importance of rituals in human life is still not generally recognized.

The last point of Huxley's discussion, which I want to emphasize here is that he points out rituals are "essential for all transcendent experience." In the present chapter, I will not go into animal rituals, in general, as that was covered back in Part II. Here we will be specifically involved in human "sacred ritual." But before closing this introduction, I do want to give you two examples of animals performing rituals. One could be termed "meditation" and the other is a community "rain dance." Both these rituals, together, may help you understand that, essentially, our human rituals developed out of the hundreds of thousands of years of rituals done by our animal ancestors.

CHIMPANZEE RAIN DANCE

Jane van Lawick-Goodall is famous for her research among chimpanzees. This is her report of a rare ritual event among the chimps. When the first heavy drops of rain began to fall the chimpanzees climbed down out of the tree and climbed up a steep grassy slope toward the ridge. When they reached the ridge the seven adult males stopped and just then with a sudden clap of thunder right overhead the torrential rain began. Just at that moment one of the chimpanzees stood upright and began rhythmically swaying back and forth. Suddenly he "charged, flat-out down the slope toward the trees he had just left." When he reached them he swung around the trunk of one to break his run and leaped into the lower branches and sat there. Right away two others ran down after him. One broke off a branch as he ran, waving it in the air and finally throwing it ahead of him. Others in the group broke off branches on the way down. As the last two got down the slope, the one who began the ritual jumped down and ran up again, followed by the rest of them. They continued this ritual for about twenty minutes. Jane Goodall says: "As the males charged down and plodded back up, so the rain fell harder, jagged forks or brilliant flares of lightning lit the leaden sky, and the crashing of the thunder seemed to shake the very mountains."

The young chimps and the females climbed up into the trees as soon as it all began and stayed there, watching. When the males climbed up the slope the final time, they came down out of the trees, joined the males and all disappeared over the ridge. One male stopped for a moment with his hand on a tree trunk and looking back at the scene before he too went over the ridge. Goodall continued to sit there "staring almost in disbelief at the white scars on the tree trunks and all the branches littering the ground." This was all that was left "to prove that the wild 'rain dance' had taken place at all." During the following ten years she only got to see this ritual twice more. But she does remark that often male chimpanzees do react to heavy rain by performing an individual rain dance. Apparently the group one is rare.

This ritual Jane Goodall witnessed was a "dance"; the other ritual is a waterfall meditation. Harold Bauer was following a male chimp through the forest when the animal stopped beside a waterfall. Falling twenty-five feet down the cliff it crashed into a pool with such force that the mist hung in the air for about seventy feet around it. Konner, writing of Bauer's experience, says: "The animal seemed lost in contemplation of it. He moved slowly closer, and began to rock, while beginning to give a characteristic round of 'pant-hoot' calls. He became more excited, finally beginning to run back and forth while calling, to jump, to call louder, to drum with his fists on trees..." Bauer found that this animal came back to the waterfall on other days to repeat the ceremony; as did other males. They did not need to cross the stream there but came just to see the waterfall; "it was something they had to look at, return to, study, watch, become excited about: a thing of beauty, an object of curiosity..." What they really felt we will never know but it is obvious that they were attracted to it.

Actually, the physiological aspects of these two events are the same for both the chimps and us humans. Just before a rainstorm positive ions fill the air which, in general, are somewhat depressing. When the storm first breaks, the refreshing influx of negative ions does make for celebration. Waterfalls are surrounded by negative ions because of the kinesthetic action of the force on the water molecules. So, waterfalls, too, tend to make a mammal feel better. What we have here is a relationship of factors of landscape, air molecules and mammalian interaction.

CONNECTIONS BETWEEN CHILDHOOD PLAY AND RITUAL

In the previous chapter I discussed the importance of what Erikson called "daily rituals of nurturance and greeting" between mother and child. This first and most crucial ritual for humans comes to us from our primate ancestors. We can see it operating in other species of mammals as well.

In summing up his study, Erikson writes that, although this seems to be "a large order to burden an infant's daily awakening" it is a fact that all elements involved in the sense of sacred can be found in this first "greeting ritual." Since this mother-child relationship in humans is "but a variant of the primate or even mammalian pattern," as Rappaport says. "It may be that the basis of the numinous is archaic, antedating humanity, and it may further be that religion came into being when the emerging, discursive, conventional sacred was lashed to the primordial, non-discursive, mammalian emotional processes that in their later form we call 'numinous'." Here we see that the original mother-child "greeting ritual" is the base on which "sacred ritual" is built.

The best way to show the crucial importance of play as a child for the later development of both ritual and the numinous is to recount what Jung discovered—by necessity. This crisis in Jung's life occurred around 1912 when he realized he had to break with Freud. This caused him great interior uncertainty and turmoil. He could not figure out what to do to sort it out, even though he had considerable training in the new findings of psychology. Finally when nothing else would work he began to play with rocks and mud just as he had done when a small child. For a middle aged (thirty-six year-old) professional man to play like this, years ago when psychology was hardly heard of yet, took great courage. In those long-ago days there wasn't even a word for this type of action. Now we label it "regression in the service of the ego" and call it therapeutic. Jung does say that it was a "painfully humiliating experience." But he had no choice so he proceeded to play with rocks again and through these "childish games" he was reconnected with the dream of his childhood of the underground phallus and thus found a way to re-enter this most important area of his mental life. Jung later stated that the "moment" he took up these "childish games" was "a turning point in my fate."

A. Plant, a Jungian analyst writes that "Regression, as we now call it, with its varied symptomology such as leaden inertia, or alternatively, oceanic blissful states and infant-like play and rhythmic activity can be, as is now common knowledge among analysts a precursor to new developments and insights...in short, rebirth." Although Plant does not discuss ritual in any way all of the above fits some of the states of ritual and the outcome of ritual as well. Plant remarks that one of the most important clinical features which usually occurs in regression did not seem to happen to Jung since Jung has no reference to "dependency." Searching for an answer to this, Plant states: "It is possible that the relation to stones... which were for him highly animated even 'numinous' objects that would not let him down and yet connect him with his past—his and theirs—may have replaced dependence on another human being to some extent." Here we can see the importance of bonding to nature in a child's early life. In Jung's case this play with nature continued throughout his entire life.

This "play with nature in early childhood" is the heart of both play and ritual in later life. It is also the secret of fully mature adult humanity and creativity.

KONRAD LORENZ ON RITUAL

The best brief description of what ritualization is about from the point of view of the study of human and animal behavior, comes from Konrad Lorenz. He states: "The first and probably most important characteristic of ritualization is... A phylogenetically adapted motor pattern which originally served the species in dealing with some environmental necessities acquires a new function, that of communication." From this communication two new, "equally important" functions may arise. The first of these is that aggresssion may be discharged without hurting fellow members of the species. This is what occurs in ritualized fighting found in birds, fish and mammals. The second function is "the formation of a bond which keeps together two or more individuals. This is achieved by most co-called greeting ceremonies." Such ceremonies are not "the expressions of a bond; indeed they themselves constitute it." Along with the ritualization comes bright colors and fancy displays—anything which produces increased visual or auditory stimulation. For example in animals this includes such things as the horns on deer or the white rump on the elk. Once an elk is alerted and turns to run, the white patch on its rump flashes an immediate signal to all the others. I've seen this happen. When that white rump flashes—immediately, all the rest are running. There's not a second of hesitation. These communicative signals are also shown in the bright plumage of birds, in the beautiful forms and colors of Siamese fighting fish fins and in the gorgeous peacock's tail. "All evolved under the selection pressure of the communicative function performed by some particular ritualized movement."

In a later work, Lorenz gave some "essential common functions... of phylogenetic and cultural rituals." The first three are relevant for us here: " 1) The first and oldest function is that of communication. 2) The second, which in the case of phylogenetic ritualization probably derived from the first, consists in the 'channeling' of certain behaviour patterns into specific areas as a result of their ritualization, in the same way one can channel a river in the direction one requires. In phylogenetic ritualization it is principally aggressive behaviour that is channeled in this manner; in the cultural process it is virtually the whole of social conduct of both phyletic and cultural ritualization. 3) The third basic function of both phyletic and cultural ritualization is the creation of new motivations which actively influence the complex of social conduct."

Summing this up for human rituals—whether coming out

of evolution or cultural aspects—these perform the same functions of communication, that of channeling aggression and of channeling bonding.

It is important to remember here, that there has not been any organic change in the human brain during the last thirty thousand years. The difference between modern and Paleolithic Man is "one of cerebral training and not of biological or anatomical advance. In later Paleolithic Man there was already all the room for memories, all the associative capacity, the reasoning power, the ability to learn, and the perceptive acuity of modern man." The main difference is that primitive man used all his capacities in relationship with all of nature while modern humans concentrate on the artificial world which we have created for ourselves.

JUNG'S TRANSCENDENT FUNCTION

Sacred ritual takes us out of this narrow, artificial human world and opens us up to the vast unlimited world of nature—both outside in our non-human environment and inside, in our own deeper layers of the older brains and cellular body knowledge. For us in modern times, one of the most important, immediate effects of ritual is that it reduces the more or less continuous inhibition, which the left hemisphere of the neo-cortex exerts over all the rest of the brain. Thus there is increased communication between both hemispheres of the neo-cortex and between that more recent part of the brain and the "older" brains. Jung gave this activity the label of "transcendent function;" because it transcends the narrow limits of the ego.

According to Stevens, "the transcendent function resides in the mutual influence of conscious and unconscious, ego and Self." According to Jungian practitioners, active imagination which includes dream, symbols and art is the best way to activate the transcendent function. Jung felt that such practices as astrology, magic and alchemy also worked toward integrating the two modes of hemispheric functioning. But the best way of all, of course, to integrate all the parts of the brain is through sacred festivals or ceremonies.

Initiation and Rites of Passage Rituals

Adolescence is the time when the young person must be permitted and encouraged to break away from parents; while the parents must begin to give up their role of "parental archetype" in the life of their child. To permit both of these factors to take place at the same time is one of the main purposes of initiation rituals. In most traditional cultures the initiation rituals marked a clear demarcation between childhood and the adult role. Adolescent rebelliousness and suicide in our time is caused partly by the lack of valid initiation rituals. An event which takes place all at once in traditional cultures, now takes years of continuous struggle between the adolescent and the older people within his environment.

Van Gennep, in 1908 wrote the classic work on the subject of initiation. He showed that such rites include three stages: separation, transition, and incorporation. Included in these stages was the recital of tribal myths, which during the initiation rituals, gave divine meaning to the young person's life by relating him personally to the myths or totems of the tribe. Such rites contribute to social cohesiveness by linking the individual to the group and at the same time permit group participation in the important events in the individual's life.

Initiation rites are part of a larger class of rituals, called "rites of passage," which are utilized at each change of role during the entire lifetime. Erikson has given a very concise summary of what these rites accomplish: "They strive, within an atmosphere of mythical timelessness, to combine some form of sacrifice or submission with an energetic guidance toward sanctioned and circumscribed ways of action—a combination which assures the development in the novice of an optimum of compliance with a maximum sense of fellowship and free choice."

Generally, in traditional cultures such "rites of passage" were part of the larger festivals, which added to their sacred power.

Reconciliation of the "Shadow"

"Guilt, and the fear that guilt produces, are at the root of the Shadow problem...As opposite poles of the morality archetype, good and evil are ineradicable characteristics of the human condition. To pretend that we can embrace one and eliminate the other is to breed personal division and public disorder." Jung felt that these two moral poles were capable of reconciliation by becoming aware of the "Shadow" side of the personality and by understanding the "psychic tension" that these opposites generate. This cannot be accomplished rationally or intellectually but only symbolically. This, again is part of the "transcendent function" accomplished by sacred rituals.

Explaining how difficult this is for the modern person, Jung wrote: "The intellect has no objection to 'analysing' the unconscious as a passive object; on the contrary such an activity would coincide with our rational expectations. But to let the unconscious go its own way and to experience it as a reality is something beyond the courage and capacity of the average European." Feeling that dreams were very helpful in bypassing the ever-present control of the intellect, Jung wrote: "In the dream, through association of unconscious contents, the momentary life of consciousness can once more be brought into harmony with the law of nature from which it all too easily departs, and the patient can be led back to the natural law of his own being." Jung felt that his work as a psychotherapist was to achieve a reconciliation between the patient and the "two million year-old man that is in all of us."

Unlike Freud, Jung thought of the essence of ego consciousness as *limitation*. He wrote: "Even though it reaches to the farthest nebulae among the stars...all consciousness separates; but in dreams we put on the likeness of that more universal, truer, more eternal man dwelling in the darkness of primordial night. There he is still whole, and the whole is in him, undistinguishable from nature and bare of all egohood."

The Neurophysiological Basis of Ritual

Jung's pioneering efforts opened up the study of the deeper layers of the human consciousness. Not only was there the conscious and unconscious aspects, but within the unconscious, itself, "there was a personal unconscious [which] is only the top layer resting on a foundation of a wholly different nature: the collective unconscious." He described the psyche as reaching down from the "daylight of the mentally...lucid consciousness into the nervous sytem that for ages has been known as the 'sympathetic.' The latter maintains the balance of life through the mysterious paths of sympathetic excitation, not only giving us knowledge of the innermost life of other beings, but also has an inner effect on these essentially physiological processes."

Only in the last two decades has there been research into the fascinating realm of these "essentially physiological processes." Because these physiological processes have a great deal to do with the effects of ritual I will go into some of the research in this area. In order for you to understand the terminology used in this kind of research I will have to define a few terms which, of necessity, will make this section fairly technical.

The *cognitive imperative* refers to the drive in birds, animals and humans to order their world "by differentiation of adaptively significant sensory elements and events, and to the unification of these elements into a systemic, cognitive whole." Too much environmental novelty frustrates this drive and may lead to anxiety and eventual systemic breakdown. On the other hand too little novelty leads to boredom. In general the brain strives to balance novelty and redundancy and fit new environmental stimuli into events already modelled in the organism's *cognized environment*. The *cognized environment* can be defined as the "totality of neural models of space and time, while the *operational environment* is that part of space and time that affects the organism's survival in one way or another." To simplify this a bit you might say that the cognized environment is what we think is going on; while the operational environment is what is really going on out there in nature. In general there is some overlap of the two kinds of environments but in most cases, a particular culture may not be aware of all the elements of the operational environment which affect it. This is where myth comes in. I will go further into this aspect of ritual toward the end of this section.

One of the primary biological functions of ritual behavior is to make it easier, by means of "the cybernetic flow of information" for individuals to become synchronized for group action. This action might be directed toward some environmental challenge that cannot be met by individual action. To enable a ritual to work there must be two levels of coordination. On the individual level there must be the integration of the sensory-neuroendocrine-motor subsystems of the nervous system and an appropriate balance between the sympathetic and parasympathetic systems governing levels of arousal. To facilitate interaction of individuals within the group itself there must be synchronization of the individual subsystems of each organism.

Human ritual develops out of the rituals of non-human organisms and still shares some aspects with them. Certain facial gestures, nonverbal displays and emotional body postures are still used by humans even though they are not consciously aware of the meaning of the postures. To ignore the non-human origin of certain ritual actions could be considered a form of anthropocentrism. We do share many ritual patterns in common with the non-human and recognition of this fact will help us to bridge the artificial split our European culture has put between us and nature.

Ritual necessitates the sharing of information, yet often information about physiological or genetic predispositions is not available to the individual's own consciousness so it cannot be passed along verbally. Ritual behavior, however, is especially suited to provide an indication to others of this kind of information, which although nonverbal and below the level of ordinary consciousness, nevertheless does have an effect on an individual's behavior. This below-conscious sharing of information is quite often achieved through ritual trance. Bourguignon found this type of ritualized trance behavior in 437 societies, 89 percent of the 488 societies for which adequate ethnographic data are available. Using this evidence as a basis, Goodman asserts that "we are dealing with a capacity common to all men." Ritual trance has been neglected in Eurocentric culture for a long time but, modern sacred rituals are once again incorporating this important aspect into our life.

There has been some work on the effect of repetitive stimuli on the brain to facilitate ritual trance but this is not sufficient to explain all the effects. The organs of the body are homeostatically interconnected by the nervous system as well as the brain. The one common affliction which provides the most convincing proof that the brain does not control the bodily organs is seasickness. The autonomic nervous system (ANS) consists of both the parasympathetic (PNS) and the sympathetic nervous system (SNS). The SNS mobilizes the organism for fight or flight. The entire SNS can be excited by stimulation of only a few nerves, thus readying the muscle structure for running or any other physical action, and stopping or reducing of activity in organs not immediately needed for escape or fighting. Neural stimulation of this system sets off the release of adrenal hormones and neurohumors.

The parasympathetic nervous system (PNS) responds only to more generalized stimulation of its components. Sweats, emetics and purgatives (all methods used in sacred rituals) excite the PNS. General stimulation of this system results in pleasurable states such as sleep, digestion, grooming in animals and relaxation. Too much or too intense stimulation can cause fainting and stomach disorders.

Gelhorn and his colleagues refer to a condition called *tuning*. Tuning may be accomplished by stimulation of either the SNS or PNS, or use of drugs that activate or block one or the other systems of mental activity. Methods used to facilitate ritual trance result in tuning.

Two systems have been named which reflect the "oscillating needs of an organism, inexorably shifting from energy-expending behavior to energy-conserving behavior." The first is the ergotropic, the startle or "what-is-it?" response, associated with the SNS and it expends energy. The second is the trophotropic, which conserves energy as it relaxes skeletal muscles, synchronizes cortical rhythms and is associated with the PNS. Generally speaking, if one of these subsystems (PNS or SNS) is stimulated, excitation of the other is inhibited.

Gelhorn and Kiely have devoted extensive research to the effect of tuning on the nervous system of animals and humans. They have found that in meditation there is at first intense stimulation of the trophotropic system as there is less sensory input in the effort to banish all thought and desire, eventually, reaching baseline homeostasis with only enough intrusion of the other system, the ergotropic, to prevent falling asleep. If the meditation is long and deep enough, there occurs spillover from the trophotropic to the ergotropic side with eventual strong participation of both systems. Ritual behavior starts from the opposite neural position. Strong activation of the ergotropic system, brought about by such actions as drumming, chanting, dancing or the use of gourd rattles, produces such strong activation of the ergotropic system that eventually the ergotropic system becomes supersaturated so that the trophotropic system is activated, resulting in participation of both systems. If stimulated long enough the next stage, that of tuning is reached where the simultaneous strong discharge of both autonomic systems creates a state of stimulation of the median forebrain bundle, generating not only pleasurable sensation but, in especially profound cases, a sense of union or oneness with all those present. This illustrates the neurophysiological basis of bonding.

Recent research proves that such techniques as meditation and ritual trance provide valuable release from stress. Mixed trophotropic-ergotropic discharge forcibly disrupt the usual neurobiological equilibrium which can provide the setting for allowing different patterns to form and thus eventually produce totally different behavior. Rites of passage and rites of intensification actually change neurphysiological functioning, thus discharging the emotional tensions which have built up. The further advantage of such rituals is that they enable the individual, under controlled conditions, to re-experience the intense emotional responses which he had to original stress situations thus bringing about the necessary physiological readjustments.

In sacred rituals many different techniques are used at once: visual and auditory stimulation (especially drumming), scents, dancing, and repetitive actions; thus providing the necessary redundancy so that the message goes through at all levels and to all participants regardless of their experience or genetic makeup. Those of us who set up sacred rituals have found that once the verbal response is blocked by ritual action, those with high intellectual propensities can learn from others of lower intellectual ability but more effective motor responses. Often the more abstractly intellectual the person is, the more deeply that person is moved because other aspects of behavior than the cognitive are allowed expression through ritual and thus integrated into their reponse.

Strong rhythm or repetition "of itself produces positive limbic [often labelled animal brain] discharge resulting in decreased distancing and increased social cohesion." This basic effect of ritual is just as present in human ritual as it is among animals and birds.

The specific aspect of human ritual which is not possible in non-human rituals is the myth. Myth supplies an answer to a problem raised at the conceptual level while the ritual which comes out of the myth applies a solution on the action level. The human drive of the cognitive imperative—the need to explain unexplained external stimuli in the operational environment (the rest of nature)—usually takes the "form of a myth in nonindustrial societies and a blend of science and myth in western industrialized societies."

For human beings the process of resolution requires more than just the myth. Ritual action, including the body, must also be involved in order to reach the nervous system and physiological functions. Such resolving of difficulties cannot come from cognitive unification alone because the left hemisphere of the neo-cortex, which has to do with rational thinking, by its very nature splits events up into individual bits thus creating logical paradoxes. It cannot, therefore, solve these paradoxes. The nondominant or right hemisphere is identified with the trophotropic system and the dominant or left hemisphere is identified with the ergotropic energy-expending system. As noted above, rhythmic activity or other ritual behavior supersaturates the ergotropic system to the point that the trophotropic system is stimulated. When this occurs it also allows both hemispheres of the neo-cortex to be maximally stimulated which further contributes to the ineffable bliss of such feelings. Such solutions to logical paradoxes and polar opposites have been called "the union of opposites," "conjunctio oppositorium," "union of self with God"—depending on which metaphysical system one uses to describe this state.

From their research on ritual d'Aquili and Laughlin conclude that when ritual works, "It powerfully relieves man's existential anxiety, and at its most powerful, relieves him of the fear of death and places him in harmony with the universe...Indeed, ritual behavior is one of the few mechanisms at man's disposal that can possibly solve the ultimate problems and paradoxes of human existence."

The type of research, which I've been explaining above, answered some of my questions related to particular skiing experiences long ago. It provided me with neurophysiological labels to help me talk about such experiences. For instance, the ritual "tuning" that enabled each of us, without thinking, to grab onto a moving rope one after another. And why that feeling gave us such a surge of great joy. We were doing what animals are "supposed" to do and what millions of years of evolution built into our brain/body continuum leads us to want to do. When the rhythmic activity of the ergotropic energy-expanding system was so activated by our continuous skiing for hours, it spilled over into the trophotropic system (which has to do with relaxation and bonding). Thus both systems were fully activated and that's real living!

In these modern times it might seem that such an experience could only happen in "play" or leisure. Not necessarily, because in real work it can still occur. Hal Hartzell's account of an epic experience of the Hoedads, an Oregon tree planting coop, shows how this can happen. Trying to finish off the planting they work very late into the twilight and cold, wet and hungry, stagger to the "crummy" (ancient bus that carries the planters). And it won't start! "Leaving 12 people in the grasp of the first stages of hypothermia." But

it was just a few hundred feet to the downhill slope. In an epic struggle—with first water in the gas and then one piece failing and then another, they finally get it up the hill. In his account of this mythic struggle we can read how, out of a very hopeless situation, comes the bliss and the incredible bonding that occurs when the "collective mind and body began to work" as Hartzell puts it. That's when it's sacred and obscene and humorous all at once—and that's real living. Just any kind of work doesn't produce these effects; only work with real meaning. But the Hoedads believe in their work, even though planting trees for a huge corporation may seem a hopeless thing to do; at least some of the trees might be allowed to live through the next cutting and that's better than no trees! That's why I've included Hal's full account in the "Back of the Book" section of this work. Be sure to read it.

Back to the neurophysiological aspects of ritual. While I've used the research terminology, because we do need words to talk about such matters, don't be misled into thinking these "latest findings" are the whole answer to any life process. For instance, such headlines as "Endorphins connected with stress-related cancer" or "Lack of endorphins in alcoholics can be corrected" and all the others you see in the popular press are merely part of the "substance" trap. Research is done on how this particular brain chemical performs this particular action with never a thought that the entire brain/body system was designed by nature to work together and to work within the larger context of nature itself—the natural environment. No one of these brain chemicals is the single cause of anything. Remember it's not the "substance" approach, coming out of Greek thinking; but the "relationship" approach, coming out of Chinese thought, that is the ecological approach. Below I will turn to Taoist concepts of ritual.

Rituals of "the Way"—The Taoist Approach

After that brief tour through the modern "substance" approach to neurophysiological aspects of ritual, it's a refreshing change to turn to rituals as done by the Chinese for thousands of years. As noted in the "Inter-Lude" which introduced Part III, the discussion there on the Chinese concept of Li, mentioned that the word also means rituals. At the earliest stage of Chinese thought on the matter, "the Li could be described generally as communication with or acknowledgement of a sacred, other-than-human reality upon which 'this world's' well-being somehow depended." By Confucius' time, "the very distinction between the sacred and the profane had ceased to be a crucial one." A later follower of Confucius, Hsün Tzu, wrote: "Through rites Heaven and Earth join in harmony, the sun and moon shine, the four seasons proceed in order, the stars and constellations march, the rivers flow and all things flourish...that love and hatred are tempered and joy and anger are in keeping...He who holds to the rites is never confused in the midst of multifarious change; he who deviates therefrom is lost."

In such rituals all aspects of the human being as well as all aspects of nature are allowed free play. Elements of joy and suffering, magic, humor, poetry, music, art "all consort together in symbiotic bliss." Thus we see that: "In a ritual," according to Girardot, "what was created was the 'chaos-order' or 'chaosmos'... the true meaning of the 'natural' order of the world where everything follows the spontaneous internal ordering principle of the primordial Tao." Ritual recreates the natural order of life which is one of constant "alternation, creative transformation and biological metamorphosis." This is the "world-renewal" aspect of ritual. Chuang Tzu uses the idea of a potter's wheel to show that "both cosmic and human time are essentially cyclic and must always return to the beginning to initiate a new creation."

Joseph Needham states: "A vast mass of folklore is available from Han and pre-Han texts" about "the position of totemism and ritual dances, the secret societies of the first bronze-founders... drums, potlatch, ordeals, rain magic." In these ancient, pre-Han texts we can find written documentation about important aspects of what I've been calling sacred ritual.

The Potlatch or "Give-Away" Ritual

I want to go into more detail about the potlatch here. It is not generally known that the potlatch was "of great importance in the most ancient Chinese society." Of course in the various Indian cultures in this country, such as the Plains Indians and the NW coast Indians, potlatch was important. The word comes from the Nootka word, *patshatl* meaning 'giving'. In both ancient China and in the New World, the prestige of a leader depends on the amount of food or other commodities which he can distribute to the community as a whole at periodical or seasonal feasts.

In most traditional cultures potlatches occur at births, initations, marriages, change of tribal leadership, rites of passage from one state in life to another as well as at such yearly feasts as "world renewal rites." In China, before the Han dynasty (pre-206 B.C.) such critical occasions in society were celebrated by "ritual observances known collectively as *li*." Cooper, in his article, "The Potlatch in Ancient China," explains: "While the *li* as we know them from the Confucian classics, as for example in the records of rituals (Li Chi) had already become a code of behavior and ritual actions for an aristocracy of the feudal Chou conquerors, it is clear that the roots of these practices may be traced to the predynastic tribal (rank) organization of the Shang and Chou peoples." (In other words, the tribal rituals.)

One ritual described in the Li Chi, called *hsiang yin chiu* ceremony involves ceremonial drinking and seating according to age. The proceedings during this ceremony are summed up in the Li Chi. Because distinction between low and high is made clear,

There is harmony and joy without disorder;
There is happy feasting without turbulence or confusion;
The observance of these... things is sufficient to secure the rectification of the person and the tranquility of the state.
When that one state is tranquil, all under heaven will be the same.

Confucius comments: "Therefore when I look at the *hsiang yin chiu*, I know that the kingly way is easy." Cooper remarks that Confucius is "marvelling at the social regulation achieved by this seemingly primitive ritual of the country folk when all the coercive authority of state power in his own time

achieves nowhere near equivalent results." Watson, writing of this type of social organization, states that "it is enough for the ruler to attune himself to it, and take no active measure for political order to be restored. Such harmony with the principle [li] can only be achieved by minute attention to the rites and ceremonies collectively designated *li*." These rites and ceremonies occur in the potlatch-like ceremonies of the primitive tribal cultures.

Another similar type of festival was called *cha* and was held in the Hall of Light—Ming T'ang. This is considered to be similar to the "assembly houses" of the tribal peoples of Taiwan, Southeast Asia and the Pacific Islands. W. E. Soothill, in his major work on the Ming T'ang describes it both as "a gathering place of the clans" from very early times and as a "thatched hut used in primitive days by the tribal wise man... who within its precincts read the stars, appointed times and seasons, performed the necessary rites, prayed for rain, ordered peace and war according to the auguries."

Summary of Potlatch Rituals

The French sociologist, Marcel Mauss, the authority on potlatch, suggested that the potlatch might well serve as a marker for a broad stage of human political evolution prior to the emergence of the state. Now that we are in the devolutionary era, when nation states are no longer working, it is important to begin making use of this "give-away" ritual. In it lies the secret of harmonious living. Anarchy does not work (no primitive group ever operated in such an unritualized manner) nor does egalitarian mass meetings. There must be hierarchy in human relations as there is in all mammalian societies. But there must also be rituals which easily allow different allocations of hierarchy for specific functions. Furthermore, such rituals must at the same time validate and give full credit to those "in power" at specific times.

In colonial times in America, the white leaders were always trying to find out who the "chief" was so they could get his signature on their document and that would mean the entire tribe, under his control, agreed to the document. But in most cases there was not a "chief" who had this kind of control; instead, there were peace chiefs, war chiefs, chiefs in charge of hunting deer, in charge of hunting rabbits (the "rabbit boss"), in charge of gathering camas or gathering huckleberries, etc. In the Southwest to this day one can see the remnants of this system at tribal rituals. In Hopi seasonal rituals, a particular clan is in charge of the spring rituals and another clan is in charge of the winter rituals. Each of these chiefs had specific power for a particular function but the rituals set it up so that no one leader could take over all the power.

Ruling Class Rituals in Modern America

Contrast this method of human relationship with the modern Industrial Growth Society. First of all, it is <u>necessary</u> to understand that rituals are essential for our present "ruling class" here in the United States. But what these rituals do is bond only within the "ruling class" itself; not outside of it; therefore the powerful politicans, corporation leaders and war leaders are bonded to one another, just as powerfully as the entire tribe is bonded in a "primitive" society. One of the tools used to achieve this bonding is the creation of the ruling class as an "in-group" with all the rest of us the "out group."

Fortunately, William Domhoff, of the University of California at Santa Cruz, made an in-depth study of these rituals. It was published in *The Bohemian Grove and Other Retreats : A study in Ruling Class Cohesiveness*. On the opening page of his book, Domhoff refers to the fact that this ritual has been taking place in a redwood grove sixty-five miles north of San Francisco for nearly a hundred years. He immediately puts us into the scene: "You are one of fifteen hundred men gathered together from all over the country for the annual encampment of the rich and famous at the Bohemian Grove...you are about to be initiated into the 'Cremation of Care' ritual." This consists of carrying an open coffin with a lifelike body in it, symbolizing the body of Care. The body is put into a boat and ferried to the foot of the shrine. Here, with much pageantry, "Care" is burned. "Care has been banished [from their lives], but only with a cast of 250." This includes torchbearers, fire tenders, woodland voices etc. The band strikes up "There'll be a Hot Time in the Old Town Tonight" and "the men begin to shout, to sing, to hug each other, and dance around...They have been freed...for some good old-fashioned hell raising."

The meaning behind this ceremony lies in the fact that each of the rich and famous men here, knows that every one of the other rich and famous men present in the gathering, will look after his interests so that he need have no care. So much for what the ordinary American thinks of as democracy and voter rights. Basic decisions are made here in the redwoods with maudlin college fraternity type rituals. The whole thing began back in the last century in San Francisco, when all the mineral wealth from the Sierras and even further east, was flowing into that town. The wealthy wanted to get together with the artists, the "bohemians" hence the name, Bohemian Grove.

Present day Bohemian Grove get-togethers allow no women in the Grove but high class prostitutes are available at bars in towns about a mile and a half away. Domhoff tells of a group of four famous men who chipped in together to hire a prostitute for one of their friends on his seventieth birthday.

Domhoff's careful study of the 1968 membership list and the 1970 guest list showed that men came from every part of the U.S. (Domhoff's book, "Who Rules America" gives a complete list.) In summary, most of them are corporate leaders. At least one officer or director from 40 of the 50 largest industrial corporations was present. For instance, the 1968 list included Stephen D. Bechtel chairman of the infamous Bechtel Corporation; top men from all the major banking houses in California; and Richard Nixon, president of the US. The 1970 Grove guest list included Edgar F. Kasier of Kaiser Industries and Henry S. Morgan of the famous investment banking house. "More intriguing are several of the government-business pairings, Paul Rand Dixon, chairman of the Federal Trade Commission, was the guest of oil man and Democratic fat cat Edwin W. Pauley while Walter J. Hickel, Secretary of the Interior at the time and deeply involved in negotiations concerning the Santa Barbara oil spill, was the guest of Fred L. Harley, president of Union Oil, the company responsible for the spill." One more piece of information to show how important this gathering is. "In 1942, the Bohemian Grove was the site at which leaders of the atomic-bomb project decided which experimental nuclear plants to build in their search for a usable atomic weapon." None of the American public knew anything about this proposal back in 1942 nor about the later decisions, when the "ruling class" decided to make atomic power respectable by building nuclear power plants.

In his final summary, Domhoff draws together his findings on the "ruling class" when he states that it is "made up of the owners and managers of large corporations...comprising at most 1 percent of the total population, members of this class own 25 to 30 percent of all privately held wealth in America, own 60 to 70 percent of the privately held corporate wealth, received 25 percent of the yearly income, direct the large corporations and foundations, and dominate the federal government in Washington." Domhoff makes it clear that "it is not only shared economic and political concerns which make this consensus possible. The Bohemian Grove and other upper-class social institutions also contribute to this process...members of socially cohesive groups are more open to the opinions of other members, and more likely to change their views to those of fellow members. Social cohesion ...creates a desire on the part of group members to reconcile differences with other members of the group. It is not enough to say that members of the upper class are bankers, businessmen, and lawyers with a common interest in profit maximization and tax avoidance who meet together at the Council on Foreign Relations, the Committee for Economic Development, and other policy-planning organizations. We must add that they are Bohemians, Rancheros, and Roundup Riders." (The latter two organizations are "wild west," horsy excursions of the "ruling class" but, essentially, imitate the Bohemian Grove).

The Bohemian Grove rituals are an illuminating example of "substance" carried to its ultimate. Ritual, which, since humanity began, has served to increase relationship among all the humans involved and between the human group and other beings—animals, plants and the natural environment; in the Bohemian Grove, is used to cement bonds for one reason only—money and power. Other aspects of the Bohemian Grove are just as interesting. First, the men don't do any ritual actions together; essentially, they just sit and drink and watch the pageant of burning "Care." This means that in their daily interactions during the "camp-out," money and power are the only criterion for achieving recognition. It's not who is strongest, physically, or who can swim the river, flowing through the Bohemian Grove; but who has the power and money *outside*, there in the "real world." Second, there are no women allowed on the grounds. Later, at night, some of these "ruling class" men will go the mile and a half to the motels and hire a prostitute for the night. This is again based on the single substance, money. Third, there is no relation to the land itself; it's treated merely as "scenery." Fourth and worst of all, there is no relationship to any humans back in the corporation, who work under them, or to the humans in other parts of the world who will die because the corporation is using up their resources.

One final lesson from the Bohemian Grove rituals. If

you're inclined to think that rituals are just something they did in primitive cultures and that they aren't very important or useful in these modern days, Bohemian Grove shows you that, on the contrary, they are still just as powerful as they ever were. The difference is that in the "old ways," the ritual is for the entire human group and the natural environment which encompasses them; while the "ruling class" rituals are strictly limited to the single purpose of bonding those men whose goal in life is power and money.

Victor Turner on Ritual

Research of the anthropologist, Victor Turner, has radically changed the entire study of rituals. He talks about "a new way of looking at ritualization ... that has been challengingly thrust upon anthropology by natural and biological sciences, notably ethology." He reports that at the famous London conference on ritualization a few years ago, "The ethologists...were in complete agreement both as to the definition of 'ritualization' and on its evolutionary importance...But the anthropologists...could not agree even on the definition of 'ritual'."

It was Turner's work on the religious life of the Ndembu in Africa that radically changed him. He wrote: "After many years as an agnostic and monistic materialist, I learned from the Ndembu that ritual and its symbolism is not merely epiphenomena or disguises of deeper social and psychological processes, but have ontological value, in some way related to man's condition as an evolving species...I became convinced that religion is not merely a toy of the race's childhood, to be discarded at nodal points of scientific and technological development, but is really at the heart of the matter."

I will briefly discuss some of Turner's main concepts because they are very important for all those who are beginning to incorporate sacred ritual into their life.

THE RELATION BETWEEN "UNIVOCAL" AND "MULTIVOCAL" SYMBOLS

"Bonding," Turner explains, "is often a matter of overcoming (at conscious and unconscious levels) of contradictions, conflicts and disparities between nature and culture and within culture itself—for few human systems of ideas, norms and beliefs are internally consistent, save those of certain philosophers who achieve internal harmony by leaving much that is essential and vital out of account."

Turner makes a distinction between univocal symbols and multivocal symbols: univocal symbols have only one proper meaning (money is a good example); multivocal symbols have many, many meanings, clustering around two poles. In the story recounted in the myth or in the actions of ritual, an interchange occurs between these "poles of meaning." Norms, values and ideas cluster at the "ideological pole"; while the physiological aspects of the body, including emotion, cluster at the other pole. The gourd is a perfect example of a multivocal symbol because it symbolizes, at the same time aspects of life, related to: sex, eating, useful utensils, mother of the world, fishing uses, poetry, art, sacred, land etc. Turner says that ritualization occurs when both these poles are present in a culture's

major symbols and "deritualization takes place when the bond between the poles is broken, for whatever historical reasons." When this happens all the many aspects of the symbol "are released from their connectedness and centrifugally diverge to start upon separate futures as concepts, rules and beliefs." In other words, when a many faceted symbol such as the gourd is lost and replaced by a univocal symbol such as money, "many of the concepts of the 'ideological' pole become the univocal notions of philosophical and scientific thinking." Of course, the myriad other important meanings of life are lost from this univocal symbol.

What multivocal symbols accomplish is that the culture's values and ideas located at the "ideological" pole become saturated with emotion, while the "gross and basic emotions," associated with the physiological pole, become "ennobled or sublimed" through contact with social bonding notions and values of the "ideological" pole. "The irksomeness of moral constraint is thereby transformed into the 'love of virtue' ...socially negative and destructive images and impulses may be...[turned] into the service of the social order."

COMMUNITAS

Turner's most famous concept is the term, "communitas" for the state achieved when a ritual works. Turner writes: "For me, communitas emerges where social structure is not." It cannot be easily defined but "it involves the whole man in his relation to other whole men." He uses the Latin word, "communitas" to distinguish this particular kind of social relationship from the more usual way of common living. He adds that, "The distinction between structure and communitas is not simply the familiar one between 'secular' and sacred'. It is rather a matter of giving recognition to an essential and generic human bond, without which there could be no society."

Communitas fits the stage of "liminal" in Van Gennep's classification of preliminal, liminal and post-liminal (also called rites of separation, margin (or limen = threshold), and reaggregation). In the liminal state of release from the usual rules and norms it is possible to "elicit creative and innovative responses." This is the aspect of play. Turner states that "the serious games which involved the forms and designs (icons, figurines, masks, sand-paintings, effigies, emblems and the like) are often, in traditional socities, reserved for authentically liminal times and places." All the amazing forms which such art takes—dragons, monsters, etc. stimulate the powers of persons in the liminal state, "revealing to them the building blocks from which their hitherto taken-for-granted world has been constructed." The original nature of the human playing freely within nature is permitted to take over during traditional rituals. Such rituals are held either outside in nature or else in a place where nature's symbols are obvious.

In 1982, only a year before his death at age sixty-three, Turner and other members of the Anthropology Department at the University of Virginia got together to do an "ethnographic performance," as a "teaching tool" in the basement of Turner's house. The event turned out to be much more deeply moving than anyone expected. Dr. Stanley Walens, an authority on the NW coast Indians used Franz Boas' translations of the text of the Hamatsa Cannibal ceremony, as a basis for the event.

Walens' account of what happened in Turner's basement is written with the usual scholarly caution but one of the participating students told how it affected many of those taking part in it: "As the ceremony progressed I felt not so much the antagonistic rivalry that was overtly expressed in the ceremony beween the bear clan and the killer whale clan, but the fact that we were collectively doing something really important—something essentially correct. There was so much power flowing all over the place in the longhouse (the Charlottesville basement) that night! The spirits were really at work that evening and we had to keep everything in line so all that power wouldn't destroy everything."

Walens, himself, wrote: "One has the feeling that rituals are magical, that for some reason as yet unknown to science they can communicate to people, not despite their artificiality, but because of and through their artificiality. Rituals are efficacious and we wonder how." Walens finished his discussion with these deep insights:

> It is not that religion is so much a statement of belief but that at its most effective it enables us to suspend disbelief in the things that are larger than ourselves, whether they be deities or nature...Just as at a ritual we may have a momentary inkling that there was something greater present than simply a bunch of people playing at ceremony, so in our acting of the cannibal dance we have an inkling of something which transcends the limitations of a particular moment in the history of the anthropology department at the Univ. of Virginia. Compare this finale with Dalton's [the student, mentioned above] leap into what he took to be the Kwakiutl view of the Hamatsa ceremony: 'The potlatch ended, in fact, with the assurance that the Kwakiutl would continue to keep the world in order in a pledge for next year's ceremony. The bitter rivalry that was expressed in the early parts of the ceremony gave way to a final reconciliation and a true feeling of oneness with the forces of the universe'.

World Renewal Rituals

The Northwest Coast Hamatsa ritual, mentioned above, was, supposedly, merely an Anthropology Department experiment but it became something, "really important—something essentially correct," as one student remarked. Truly, they were doing something really important because the Hamatsa ritual belongs to the "World Renewal" type of ritual. All over the world, traditional cultures performed these rituals.

In China, for instance, according to Schipper, a Dutch scholar who lived in Taiwan for ten years to study Taoist rituals, "The liturgy tradition of Taoism can be thought of as the literary valorization of the age-old Chinese folk tradition of individual and corporate renewal through ancestral veneration, ritual celebration, and shamanic healing." In the Western part of the North American continent, the Sun Dance performed a similar role. Hall, in his study of the Shoshoni Indians of Wyoming, explains their ritual:

> The Sun Dance was a ceremony which lasted for three to four days, in which the participants expressed their gratitude to the Supreme Being, but it was also a sacrificial dance, a prayer to be delivered from illnesses...and a prayer to be blessed with food and good health during the year to come. Thus, the Sun Dance was, among other things, a 'new year's ritual'. The Supreme Being, 'our father', was the foremost deity, connected with heaven, sun, and moon. Mother Earth was called upon in the Sun Dance. A long line of spiritual beings in animal form and spirits who were in some other way tied to nature...were also involved.

The purpose of such "world renewal" rituals is "to revive the *topocosm*, that is, the entire complex of any given locality conceived as a living organism." Continuing his explanation, Theodore Gaster states: "What is revitalized, is not merely the human community of a given area or locality but the total corporate unit of all elements, animate and inanimate alike, which together constitute its distinctive character...To this wider entity we may assign the name *topocosm*, formed (on the analogy of *microcosm* and *macrocosm*) from Greek, *topos*, 'place', and *cosmos*, 'world order'. The seasonal ceremonies are the economic regimen of this topocosm." The topocosm includes not only all aspects of a particular place at the present time; but its past and its future as a "continuous entity."

The basic pattern is "based on the conception that life is vouchsafed in a series of leases which have annually to be renewed." This renewal is achieved not just through "divine providence alone but also through the concerted effort of men; and the rituals are designed primarily to recruit and regiment that effort." These activities have two main divisions. The first is an "emptying" and the second, the Plerosis or "filling." The "emptying" symbolizes the eclipse of life and vitality at the end of each lease; thus, lenten periods, fasts and other "expressions of mortification or suspended animation." The "filling," of course, shows the revitalized life coming with the new lease. This involves rites of "mass mating, ceremonial purging of evil and rites to promote fertility, produce rain, encourage the sun etc."

This world renewal pattern is found in all of the ancient Near Eastern cultures: Babylonians, Assyrians, Israelites, Egyptians and Hittites. During the twenty two years that Gaster worked on his book he was able to document this seasonal pattern of world renewal, first, in the formal myths of the above mentioned ancient cultures, later on, as it re-appeared in both the Christian Bible and in the Greek choral odes and finally he traced it clear up to the present in modern literature, growing out of Christian and Greek themes.

In a later chapter, I will go more into Gaster's work. Here I will just give a few examples, taken out of context, for brevity. Associated with each seasonal ritual is a particular plant, which later became a "god." For instance, Attis was originally the pine, Dionysus was the grape vine, etc. The pruned vine, especially, was often personified as Dionysus. The famous Christian writer, Clement of Alexander speaks of Christ as "the great grape-cluster, the Logos that was crushed for us." In many of the psalms of the Bible there occur words in exactly the same pattern as the "hymns" of the ancient festivals. For instance Psalm 93, concerning Yahweh subduing the rebellious streams, states that His dispensations of the world is fixed and immutable and that He has installed Himself in an abode of sanctity. Gaster shows that precisely this same pattern of words occurs in the ancient Babylonian epic of Marduk, in the ancient text concerning the Canaanite god, Baal, and in the Hittite Puruli Festival, concerning their weather god. Gaster shows that this pattern continues right down to medieval times in a hymn by Adam of St. Victor, 1130 AD, for the feast of Michael the Archangel. The underlying sacred being for all the above was, originally, a weather god.

The noted classical scholar, Gilbert Murray, in the

introduction to this book tells of a country woman, his colleague met in Greece, who remarked to him: "Of course I am anxious. For if Christ does not rise tomorrow, we shall have no corn this year." This is a modern remnant of the old "world renewal" rituals.

The importance of Gaster's work for all of us beginning to "reinhabit our place" is that he shows us how these ancient cultures, from which we inherited our European culture, have precisely the same pattern of renewal of place "as a living organism"; although this authentic human/land relationship was hidden for millenia beneath a vast mass of Judeo-Christian worship of an anthropomorphic god in the sky.

Kroeber, the anthropologist who worked with Ishi, has done the most work on "world renewal" rites in the New World. The California Indians called such rituals "world's restoration" or world "repair" or world "fixing." Each tribe had specified places—from ancient times—for each particular rite. One tribe along the Klamath called the rite "refixing the world." Harrington reported that the rituals began with a ceremony on the Klamath River below the mouth of the Salmon River, called "working the earth." The object was to "propitiate the spirits of the earth and the forest to prevent landslides, forest fires, earthquakes and drought." I will go more into these California Indian rituals in a future chapter.

"Mutuality" in Festivals

Returning to the two main divisions of "world renewal" rites: the "emptying" and the Plerosis or "filling" aspect. In the Mediterranean region, where many of the ancient cultures began, there was a long, dry time, the "emptying"; before the early winter rains began, bringing back the vegetation and thus renewing life. The "world renewal" rites there, were concerned with the coming of the life-giving rains, the Plerosis or "filling" aspect. Jubilation comes out of the relief, which occurs when the new lease on life is accomplished during the ritual. The word "festival," originally referring to the ritual meal eaten in common at the time of the seasonal crisis, as Gaster expains, "came in time to acquire the meaning of an essentially *joyous* celebration and ultimately to serve as the most appropriate designation of the seasonal ceremonies as a whole." This ritual meal, the "festival," is the origin of "communion." "The words 'communion', 'community' and 'communication' are interrelated in ways that tell us something important about the nature and purpose of feasts and feasting." Communion is a celebration of "community or participation in a social group whose members communicate with one another by means of shared images, words, and concepts," Jungian analyst, William Willeford explains in his paper, "Festival, Communion and Mutuality." It can also involve "emotional interaction that is largely preverbal or subverbal...and such interaction, too, is communication. The chief characteristic of this second kind of communion—and communication—is mutuality."

This word, "mutuality" has much deeper levels than most of us recognize. Willeford gives an example of a man who picks up a woman in a bar and goes home with her and spends the night. It may be bad or it may be pleasant enough; but if it was only shared sex, it probably did not have much meaning for either of them. But, when two people "meet and see in each other the best of which each is capable—undistracted by the kinds of 'inferiorities' they share with everyone else," we have another level of relationship, immediately. "Having the best of oneself *seen* in such a way is an experience of abundance, as is *seeing* the best in another." Unlike the first young man above, the man and woman in the second case, "know *their* abundance to be of something remarkably and uniquely good."

Friends of this couple think they must have some special secret: "so much goes on between you, even when you are just sitting quietly together." This is not merely their secret at all. But it is a "secret about human life and the possibilities it holds." They know that "what they have discovered is part of something larger than their private world." Many, if not most relationships do not have this remarkable "sense of abundance" but some do. This matter of the "more than" involved in such mutuality, "concerns us all if we are ever to be more than fragments of ourselves." I will skip over the intervening parts of Willeford's paper, to concentrate on his discussion of mutuality and its connections with Festival.

Referring to Shakespeare's use of elements from festivals, he quotes Barber, who says that these elements bring about a surge of "the vitality normally locked up in awe and respect" and this brings about "a heightened awareness of the relation between man and 'nature'—the nature being celebrated on holiday." Here we can see one of the essential aspects of festival. It changes the ordinary consciousness of daily life by "enhancing our awarenes of mutuality." This gives the participants a "sense of abundance" Willeford goes into the psychological aspects of this "abundance."

The "heightened awareness of the relation between man and nature," which Barber talks about above, happens because, festivals lessen the distinction between nature and spirit, "so that nature becomes nature-as-spirit and spirit becomes spirit-as-nature...the experience it offers is one of abundance...as a quality of mutuality."

The response to this abundance is gratitude. This gratitude may be directed to the overflowing abundance of nature or to a specific god in the case of particular religions. Always, one of the primary aims of festival is the giving of thanks. In his summary, Willeford affirms that: "Mutuality is a vital need, expressive of the self that knows what is good for itself. Festival—with its abundance—celebrates the trust and hope that this need will be fulfilled." Festival awakens "the natural man" so that the usual dichotomy between nature and spirit is lessened. "In the process, the 'thinking of the body' becomes a means of apprehending the symbolic content of the festive occasion." Willeford does not go any deeper into this concept; but, of course this "thinking of the body," is the ritual actions done as part of the Festival. That is what awakens "the natural man" within us, because the discriminating rational part of the neo-cortex is bypassed; thus freeing the older brains to express themselves through the non-verbal ritual actions of the body.

I want to make it very clear that in Festivals, mutuality extends far beyond the merely human: it includes the land itself with its plants and animals. In other words all the beings of the place. True Festival or ceremony is about "the conduct of life; ultimately the conduct of the earth and everything on it, of all motion and change, of the cosmos...Land and nature, myth and ritual, cyclic pattern and continuum, ceremony and the sacredness of story are all basic elements that distinguish the Indian mode of literature from any other." I am quoting here from the Preface to a symposium of American Indian scholars and others concerning the book, *Ceremony*, by Leslie Silko of the Laguna tribe. Actually, reading this book provides the best training for anyone beginning true Festivals in their own place. I will go further into the book in the next chapter; here I want to quote what Paula Gunn Allen said during the symposium: "The healing of Tayo and the land is a result of reunification of land and person...This understanding occurs slowly as Tayo lives the stories—those ancient and those new. He understands through the process of making the stories real in his actions, for the stories and the land are also about the same thing." (My underlining here for greater emphasis.)

The Animals in Traditional Festivals

Contrary to the usual ideas in anthropology research, animals are not included in the Festivals merely to insure a supply of food; but for other, much deeper reasons. For a brief summation of the importance of these other ways of thinking—so difficult for Eurocentric cultures to understand—I will be referring to Hans Duerr's book, *Dreamtime*. He begins by pointing out that those who think that Stone Age art was only concerned with hunting magic, ignore the fact that dangerous animals such as lions and bears are also included; not just game animals in that art. He continues: "The saiga antelope was the most important game animal at least during the coldest periods, and one would think that its reincarnation should have been of the greatest significance to Ice Age hunters." But it is not found in this cave art.

Another example: "Australian natives carry out their 'increase ceremonies' for noxious and dangerous species, for mosquitoes and evil nocturnal birds."

This seems strange to us because in our Eurocentric culture we generally think of non-human beings only in terms of their usefulness or in terms of our fear of them. Traditional cultures did not think this way, in fact to many of these people, everything was sacred, as I noted earlier. Duerr explains that particular rituals "are not carried out before the hunt or when a particular animal is needed, but rather 'when the species is especially plentiful or fat'." Further, "a ceremony for the wind...is not carried out when wind is needed, but rather when it is already blowing or if it is stronger than usual during the year."

Referring to our idea of rain dances as manipulating the environment and other such events, Duerr summarizes: "After forgetting the sense of their rituals as being participation in cosmic events, many societies themselves began interpreting them as 'magic' acts, which in turn were classed as 'proto-techniques' by Western scholars." This is very important to remember for those beginning renewal rituals. Criticism that one can only do a ritual honoring the bear or the wolf or the deer if one is part of a hunting tribe is clearly nonsense. We honor the bear, the wolf or the deer for the same reason archaic tribes did; because, through this ceremony, we take part in the "cosmic events" of renewing the whole of the land.

Gary Snyder has some wonderful things to say about animals as part of the whole of the land. He is talking about how right now village and tribal peoples in Africa and India have large so-called dangerous animals near at hand, in the jungle just beyond the garden or in the woods where the path goes to another village. They are comfortable with this state of affairs and don't go out and kill all the dangerous animals to be 'safe'. Snyder says: "Human welfare goes beyond mere survival. What most of us desire for ourselves and others is a vivid life, a life that is real, with work, sharing, occasional ecstasy, and occasional deep contemplation. The bear, as the Ainu say, is the God of the Mountain. His energy, vigor, and alertness are pure expressions of the power of the wild forest. To meet him is not just an occasion of fear, but of delight and awe." Snyder claims that we need to learn to accept bears as part of the "risky beauty of life." If a rancher loses a few head of cattle to a bear he is paying "taxes" to nature and "the whole society should help him bear the burden by paying the rancher back for his loss."

GREEK GODS AND GODDESSES WERE ORIGINALLY ANIMALS

More than sixty years ago, way back in 1912, Jane Harrison, was one of the first to study the real origins of Greek gods. In her work, she showed that a bull god eventually became Zeus, that the concept of Apollo came from the stag, and that Artemis had aspects of the plant *artemisia*, (sagebrush). She continues: "The shedding of plant and animal forms marks of course the complete close of anything like totemistic thinking and feeling. It is in many ways pure loss. The totemistic attitude towards animals...is full of beautiful courtesies...The well-born, well-bred little Athenian girls who danced as Bears to Artemis of Brauronia, the Bear-Goddess, could but think reverently of the great might of the Bear."

TOTEMISM

It is very helpful to have the well-known classical scholar, Jane Harrison explain that totemism still lingers in the Greek gods. Such information is especially useful for those still trapped in the "glory that was Greece" mentality; because, after her explanation, it becomes clear that totemism is not merely a trait of "savages."

Levi-Strauss, in his book, *The Savage Mind*, showed that totemism is not an institution but a way of thought. Classification of plants and animals provides a model for "precisely delineating individual, kin, and tribal society...Applying classificatory thought from the natural to the cultural is totemism." Perhaps the best introduction for modern people to this ancient way of thought is provided by H. Storm's book, *Seven Arrows*, which I will be discussing at more length in the next chapter.

Robin Ridington, an anthropologist at the University of British Columbia in Canada, is the man who had the foresight and courage to bring Storm up to Vancouver to work with his class. Out of that encounter came the story, "Jumping Mouse."

A friend, living near Vancouver showed me a mimeographed copy of that story and it helped me formulate the various processes I had been working on with children; ultimately, this resulted in my book, *Earth Festivals*. While my book was in the process of being typeset, Storm's book, *Seven Arrows*, came out. The central piece of the book is "Jumping Mouse."

In an important paper, "The Inner Eye of Shamanism and Totemism," Ridington makes some very important points, which I want to bring out here. He writes: "Mythical cosmologies are not the attempts of savages to explain in fantasy where empirical knowledge of reality is absent, but are rather the opposite—statements in allegorical form about knowledge of the interrelations between what we would call natural (objective), psychic (psychological), and cultural (learned adaptational) aspects of reality. Myth and science are polar opposites, not because one is wrong and the other right, but because myth portrays reality as it is experienced while science postulates a reality that is thought to exist but can never be experienced." Here, again, we see science involved with substance—"rational thought," in this case; while totemism is a structure that allows all sorts of combinations of relationships, such as we see in real living.

Ridington's conclusion is very important: "Mythic and totemic systems reveal to men a cosmic structure that synthesizes and organizes their individual and collective experiences. They do not 'give meaning' to life but rather disclose the meaning that is its intrinsic property."

A Brief Word About Healing Rituals

Just in the last few years, Eurocentric institutions have finally begun to admit the validity of traditional cultures' healing rituals. American medical doctors allow Navajo "sings" for curing and Australian "men of high degree" are now allowed into the hospitals to help cure their fellow aborigines. A very important statement concerning this matter was made at the First National Congress of Peruvian Psychiatry held in Lima. Dr. Carlos Alberto Seguin, world-renowned Peruvian social psychiatrist said: "From the point of view of our specialization, I dare say—after many years of experience—that we have much to learn from our 'colleagues', the 'native curers', the 'sorcerers', and 'healers'... We have much to learn, not just about pharmacology...the use of psychotropic plants and drugs, but also in an area that psychiatry is 'discovering' in our times, for example: group dynamics, group psycho-therapy, family therapy as well as the manipulation of social and communal problems. These are novelties for us, but native practitioners have always manipulated them with enviable ability."

Here in the U.S., the ethnopsychiatrist Torrey, concludes from a cross-cultural survey of traditional therapists that "witchdoctors and psychiatrists perform essentially the same function in their respective cultures." He feels that the integration of traditional and modern therapy will have to take place and goes on to talk about the "resistance he perceives on the part of modern practitioners: Medicine can and will change ...And this can be done despite the hoary traditions of medicine and psychiatry, feet firmly planted in the medieval guild system,

voices echoing 'You just can't do that!' with each footstep down the hall of innovation."

Healing rituals have always been an integral part of most big Festivals in traditional cultures.

The Deeper Levels of Communication in Ritual

I've mentioned the work of Roy Rappaport before. In Part II, I told of his work with the "kaiko" ritual series and earlier in this chapter I discussed him again. In his book, *Ecology, Meaning, and Religion*, he has touched on levels of ritual that no one else has considered. While the book as a whole is very important, it is much too complex to try to summarize; but I do want to go into some of his discussion on communication. He states:

> First, whatever else may happen in some human rituals, in all rituals, both human and animal, the participants transmit information concerning their own current physical, psychic, or sometimes social status to themselves and to other participants.

That statement concerns the actual events of that particular ritual. The other important aspect is that ceremonies "make references to processes or entities...outside the ritual, in words or acts that have...been spoken or performed before." This relates to the "enduring" aspect of rituals. While Rappaport is specifically referring to the written liturgies of organized religions, which he labels "canonical"; in ceremonies or rituals to do with the land itself, such as World Renewal Rites, the enduring aspect is probably the main aspect of the ritual because the land and its beings are surrounding the ritual site. The landscape forms such as mountains are "enduring" in themselves. Hence these enduring land forms are both more long lasting and more impressive than any written liturgy.

I'm often asked the question: "Is it possible to do valid rituals alone?" First of all in a nature ritual, one is never alone. All the other beings of nature are present: either sun or moon, trees, plants or animals. To consider that you are alone when you are in nature is simply a remnant of Eurocentric thinking. To draw on Rappaport again, he says: "given the extent to which in solitary rituals various parts of the psyche may be brought in touch with each other it is reasonable to take ritual to be auto-communicative as well as allo-communicative." "Auto-communicative" means communiction within the self. Even in group rituals this aspect is present. "In fact, the transmitters of ritual messages are often, if not always, their most significant receivers." Again, what is happening here is communication between the rational neo-cortex and other parts of the human brain/body.

Referring to reason, Rappaport states that, even if it is "not always downright treacherous, it is often narrowly self-serving." Actually, the "rational" way of thinking in economics, which is what guides most of the modern world, now causes human to be against human for greater money-making and humanity to be against nature. Rappaport states: "If rationality in the economic sense is what conscious reason can come to it may be suggested that reason alone could not provide a secure and sound basis for real social life even if it could be freed from the nonrational. Fortunately it can't be, for the nonrational is not only the home of rage and fear, but also of art, poetry, and whatever it is that people mean by the word 'love'."

Human beings are part of larger systems upon which their very life depends. "But the wholeness, if not the very existence, of these systems, may be beyond the grasp of their ordinary consciousness...Participation in rituals may enlarge the awareness of those participants in them, providing them with understandings of perfectly natural aspects of the social and physical world that may elude unaided reason." Here we have the importance of rituals for changing the Eurocentric attitude toward nature into the more normal human response as shown by tribal peoples, everywhere.

The human neo-cortex, alone, can never arrive at the truth. Rappaport shows us this once again in his statement above. Ritual therefore, gives us a new insight into truth. It is not something out there to be searched for, or worked towards, or fought for. Rather truth appears out of the interactions of all those present—human and nonhuman—during the time of the Festival itself. The more one enters into the play of the Festival, the deeper one penetrates into this truth. Here again we see the wisdom of Chuang Tzu who said that all endeavours of civilization destroy human nature. Authentic human life must not be a series of tries, but one in which "the ultimate trying is not to try," and that is the "play" of the Festival in traditional cultures.

Conclusion

Living in a "sacred" manner, means living in accord with the flow between the "old ways" inside our human body and the "old ways," the enduring processes in the natural environment outside of us. The more the energy circulates within this flow and the less the energy is "leaked off" to the Industrial Growth Society, the better it will be for both us humans and all of nature around us.

In the first part of this chapter, I went into some detail concerning the "sacred buffalo" in Plains cultures and the "gourd" in the even more ancient South American cultures. These two examples give you some idea of how, even the seemingly trivial aspects of life—what you wear, or what you eat out of, or the buffalo horn or the gourd you drink out of—can contribute to the overall sacredness of that life, if you have a ritualized culture. Thus there is no complete separation between sacred and profane; all actions in life become part of the sacred. And all rituals become "sacred rituals": the biological ritualization, which we inherited from the animals, the "habitual and repetitive gestures and signals of humans," and the "sacred rituals" themselves, work together. We've got a long way to go! But the first step is to pay attention to the earth under your feet—the land you live on. In the next chapter you'll find some ways to begin.

"We're just starting…to begin to make songs that will speak for plants, mountains, animals…When you see your first deer you sing your salute to the deer…Such poetries will be created by us as we reinhabit this land with people who know they belong to it…They will be created as we learn to see, region by region, how we live specifically (plant life) in each place…"

Gary Snyder

"The spirit of that wild little slope to the Mill would come upon me, and there in the suburb of London I would walk wrapped in the sense of a small wet place in the valley of Nethermere. A strange voice within me arose and called for the hill path; again I could feel the wood waiting for me, calling and calling, and I crying for the wood, yet the space of many miles was between us. Since I left the valley of home I have not much feared any other loss. The hills of Nethermere had been my walls, and the sky of Nethermere my roof overhead. It seemed almost as if, at home, I might lift my hand to the ceiling of the valley, and touch my own beloved sky…whose stars were constant to me…But now the skies were strange over my head, and Orion walked past me unnoticing, he who night after night had stood over the woods to spend with me a wonderful hour…when does the night throw open her vastness for me, and send me the stars for company? There is no night in a city."

D.H. Lawrence

"When 28 percent of the GNP goes for transport—forcing us to work one out of every four days, or one out of every four work hours, just to pay for 'high speed' transport…"

Lee Swenson

"We are so little at peace with ourselves and our neighbors because we are not at peace with our place in the world, our land. American history has been to a considerable extent the history of our warfare against the natural life of the continent. Until we end our violence against the earth—how can we hope to end our violence against each other? The earth, which we all have in common, is our deepest bond, and our behavior toward it cannot help but be an earnest of our consideration for each other and for our descendants.

As long as a man relates only to other men, he can be a specialist with impunity… But…Once he is joined to the earth with any permanence of expectation and interest, his concerns ramify in proportion to his understanding of his dependence on the earth and his consequent responsibility toward it. He realizes, because the demands of his place make it specific and inescapable, that his responsibility is not merely that of an underling, a worker at his job, but also moral, historical, political, aesthetic, ecological, domestic, educational, and so on."

Wendell Berry

"…Until I can know what other men know when they say, 'this is where I live,' I will know nothing of worth—and when I can say that & feel it deeply, I'll know most of what I'll ever be able to know. 'This is where I live.' What a thing to know!"

Lou Welch

CHAPTER THIRTEEN

Part I

"If there can be such a thing as instinctual memory, the consciousness of land and water must lie deeper in the core of us than any knowledge of our fellow beings. We were bred of the earth before we were born of our mothers. Once born we can live without our mothers or fathers or any other kin or any friend or human love. We cannot live without the earth or apart from it, and something is shriveled in man's heart when he turns away from it and concerns himself only with human affairs."

Marjorie Kinnan Rawlings

"The first thing to do is to choose a sacred place to live in."

Tahirassawichi

"In a single gram of earth there is an astounding number of small organisms: among other things 30,000 protozoa, 50,000 algae, 400,000 fungae and 2.5 billion bacteria."

Arne Naess

*"The nation may topple,
But the mountains and rivers remain."*

Tu Fu (712-770)

Part III: Setting up Structures for Land Rituals

"We are the land...that is the fundamental idea of Native American life: the land and the people are the same."

Paula Gunn Allen

"In a fist of working forest duff are more small lives than the human population of Earth."

Kim R. Stafford

 SACRED LAND

Personal Introduction

In general, modern people begin to recognize that there is such a thing as "sacred land" when traditional peoples, still living on their land, tell us that it is "sacred" to them. But, can other types of land be "sacred?" I get many questions like this; so I will explain how I began to get an understanding of "sacred land." It started when I was privileged to encounter such land—long ago—before I had ever heard the term. At the time I was part of the "Blue Glacier Project."

ON THE BLUE GLACIER

For sixteen years I spent part of each summer on Mt. Olympus in the middle of the Olympic Wilderness in Washington state. I was cook and water carrier and anything else which needed doing for the glacier study project run by the University of Washington. Ed LaChapelle, at that time my husband, ran the project. The first summer of the project we were camped in tents on the lower moraine of the Blue Glacier.

Because our son was only 18 months old, my life and his was restricted to the moraine itself; which gave me unlimited time between chores to sit in the sun and watch the mountains and plants growing between the rocks. Day after day, for the entire month, I scanned the horizon and everything else within the incredibly beautiful setting of blue ice, white snow, rocks and flowers; however, it was not until the last day that I saw the waters of a pond glistening in the sun. It was clear across the glacier on the lower slopes of a mountain. (I can't give more details here because, as everyone knows, now, to protect any beautiful spot in the natural environment, it's best not to say much about the location.) There was no way to get there in the remaining few hours before we left; because the men were all occupied with the packing of scientific instruments and other gear so no one would be able to watch my son. But this gleam of water fascinated me. I determined that someday I would find out how a pond could be in that seemingly impossible location.

The following summer was the International Geophysical Year. A hut was built up on the Snowdome where a plane could land to supply the Project. The Snowdome is an immense snowfield lying between the mountains. To the west it drops off in cliffs facing out to the Pacific Ocean. Our hut was on a rock outcropping on the edge of this snow field. We began to call this rock outcrop "Panic Peak," because of the sheer dropoffs on all sides except where the gentle talus slope led down toward the hut.

Almost every afternoon we would all climb to the top of "Panic Peak" and watch the sun set into the Pacific Ocean, some 7000 ft. below us. During the day, any spare time I had from my chores, I would climb up and search out the wildflowers to identify them. It was such a wilderness those first few years, that I found a flower, so rare that it grows only in the Olympics above 8000 ft. There are very few peaks in the Olympic range that high. But years went by before I could think of trying to get down to my "once seen" little pond.

Then, the year my son was six—four years after I had first seen it—I decided he was strong enough to make it down and back. So I put him on a rope and we descended the face of

Panic Peak in search of the water. It was a rough climb but small children are very agile. We got off the cliff, finally and onto a flat place. We walked toward where the glacier would be. Within a few steps we were off the talus rocks and onto moss. A heart-stopping hush came over us. There's no other way to describe it.

Now, I had been climbing for fifteen years, having started as a teenager, and I'd seen many awe inspiring mountain areas and I'd done first ascents in Canada, with the thrill of knowing you are the first human in that spot. But this was different. And when the hush descended on us I had not yet realized we were the first humans ever to be there. That's what is interesting. The hush that means 'sacred' to me had come *before* I knew no one had ever been there before.

Back to the experience, itself. As we walked toward the little pond I realized that the star moss had never been disturbed. All around the pond the rim was encircled by a cushion of star moss about 8 to 10 inches thick. There was no break at all. Nor was there a cut or depression in the moss anywhere. Of course, where we were standing, it was pressed down; but nowhere else was there a mar to the continuous, unbroken surface of star moss. Then, it came over me with a rush that we were the first humans there; not only that, we were also the first large mammals for a very long time. I don't know the rate that this moss grows but it is very slow. Since that experience I've watched for it in other places in the Olympic rainforest and over a period of ten years I've not seen it make any noticeable advance. Any large mammal that ever came within sight of this pond would have come to drink. As anyone knows who spends time in the mountains, the drinking places of animals along streams or ponds is very noticeable. But no one had been drinking here. Then I stood absolutely still and carefully surveyed the entire area. This *was* paradise. High altitude flowers scattered among star moss and a perfect blue jewel of a pond rimmed by star moss. All of it nestled between a vertical cliff of brown rock (down which we had just come) and a lateral moraine, which hid the rest of the world except at one break where we could look out and up at the blue crevasses showing mid the white ice of the tongue of the glacier. That's my first recognition of "sacred land."

When I began to think, again, after the wonder of just breathing it all in; I realized that, truly, we were the first humans ever to see it. Indians did not come into the center of the vast "rainforest" of the Olympic Peninsula. Their legends referred to a magic, huge, boundless lake in the center. That was the only explanation for the huge rivers pouring out of the interior; actually, glaciers are the source of the water. There was no need for Indians to go into the dark forests. There was plenty of fish and shellfish to eat and a much easier life along the ocean beaches. The first whites never ventured very far from the lower rivers. It was much too fearsome and strange a country. The Peninsula was not crossed by white people until modern times, when a Seattle newspaper sponsored the expedition. When mountain climbers began to penetrate the interior, they came only to climb the big peaks—Mt. Olympus being the highest in the range. They follow up along the moraine to get high enough to avoid the tangled, crashing ice of the lower glacier and then move on up the steep snow to the

Snowdome. From this vast snow basin they have access to all the high peaks. No climber would ever try to cross the jumbled ice of the glacier tongue. Yes, we were the first humans ever to stand on that sacred land!

But how to account for that particular physiological feeling? The interesting point I want to make here is that my six year old son was just as hushed and reverent as I was. Yet, he had just been untied from the climbing rope. Normally when free from the rope, he would run and jump with sheer exuberance. But not that time; instead he stood in hushed wonder! For years I had no words for the experience. Finally, just a couple of years ago, reading David Abram's "Notes from Thami Valley," I found some words. He writes: "I want to ask, finally, if it is possible that our ecstatic or mystical experiences grow precisely out of our receptivity to solicitations *not* from some other non-material world but from *the rest of this world*, from that part of our own sphere which our linguistic prejudices keep us from really seeing, hearing, and feeling—from, that is, the entire non-human world of life and awareness." With this clue I now think that, possibly, when plants are growing in such a sheltered spot were no large mammals ever come, who might accidentally rip or tear the fabric of their growth, they may put off such a sense of well-being and—'health'—is the only word I can think of, that this somehow registered in our bodies. After all, long eons ago, we were plants before we were animals. I can tell you exactly where this "feeling" registered. It was in my wrists and in the lower abdomen (which in Tai Chi is called the *tan tien*). But at that time I had not yet heard of Tai Chi.

Back to that "feeling" we had—of the "the rest of the world." What we were experiencing was not "plant devas" or "elementals" or "fairies" or elves or any of those abstractions. Perhaps the best word for what we were experiencing is what the primitives call wakonda, orenda or mana—all meaning, "the powers"—the *connection* between my son and I and "the powers," present there. Giving particular names, such as "plant devas" etc, allows us to "objectify" the experience; in other word, to make it into a "substance." But, actually, it was a relationship between those "powers" present in that place and us.

Although I had experienced occasional flashes of this feeling during my climbing experiences, before encountering the pond, they came and went so fast—partly because of the danger of climbing—that I could never hold on long enough to think about it. But here in this "sacred" place I had the chance to ponder what was happening. At the time my child "nature mystic" experience in the grass did not occur to me; but later I realized the connection. To attempt the impossible, by putting words onto my experience, I feel that if one is able to stop the merely human reactions in such a place long enough, then one is able to join in the "play" or "li" of the ongoing natural relationships of all the living beings of that place and, of course, this is the sacred.

I mentioned Tai Chi briefly, in connection with the "feeling" at the pond. It was not until years later that I heard of it and was able to begin studying it. That led to the next stage of my learning about sacred land.

TAI CHI

On the Blue Glacier, each summer, I learned more of the mountains and saw "northern lights," and the atmospheric phenomena called "the glory" and full moons, bright as day with all that snow. Every summer I continued to spend time on top of Panic Peak, just sitting and looking until I felt that I knew every mountain in sight. But after I had taken only four lessons in Tai Chi, I found out differently.

Each year, the first few days after our arrival there's no time at all; because it's necessary to get everything in order so that the scientific studies can begin as soon as possible. But by the fourth afternoon, I was finally able to take enough time to go up to the top of Panic Peak. I was eagerly looking forward to trying my beginning Tai Chi and see what would happen up there. From the top of Panic, the cliff drops straight down two thousand feet to the White Glacier and beyond that, the Pacific Ocean. In the other direction is Mount Olympus and turning, still more, there is Mt. Rainier, over 14,000 ft. high, the highest peak in Washington.

I felt it would be a powerful experience but I was not at all prepared for what actually happened. First I had to level a platform out of the loose, fine talus rock and then I began doing the first Tai Chi forms. It was magnificent! But what I learned I certainly did not expect in any way. As I moved through the form I was suddenly jarred out of the bliss. I saw a mountain I had never seen before! For all those years I had been "looking, looking breathlessly," as Don Juan says. And I had never seen this mountain. But it was there, all the time. That made me begin to realize the depth of Tai Chi. Moving through the slow revolutions of the form you are freed to see as never before. A mountain peak I had never seen in some thirteen years became visible to me. I've been doing Tai Chi now for fifteen years and teaching it for ten years and it continues to surprise me. Essentially, Tai Chi relates our own "inner" nature to the larger nature "outside" of us.

Before I leave this discussion of Tai Chi I want to say that, perhaps, the best way to explain what happens when one does Tai Chi out in nature is to think of it this way: There's a certain feeling that everyone who climbs or backpacks a lot is familiar with. You get it after you've been out several days. It comes over you, gradually; but then, one day, you suddenly realize that you are "in nature" again. Well, doing Tai Chi you can step out of a car and begin Tai Chi and by the time the ten minute form is over, you have that feeling, which normally comes only after days of backpacking.

BREAKING THROUGH

In the early seventies we moved to Silverton Colorado where I wrote *Earth Wisdom*. Through that book, I got involved with the program called Breaking Through, which furthered my learning concerning sacred land. Rick Medrick is the head of Outdoor Leadership Training Seminars here in Colorado. One of his river guides gave him my book just after it was published. He wrote me immediately as we had so many things in common and arranged to meet with me the next time I was in the Denver area. From our discussions there, we began Breaking Through: a combination of back packing, two days white water rafting, and taking people (who have never climbed before) up the most difficult 14,000 ft. peak in the state—Crestone Needle. But what makes this different from other outdoor programs is that every day we do Tai Chi and rituals, as well. This enables those who go on the program to climb unroped and unafraid, Tai Chi style. Through the years this has developed into a pilgrimage. From this yearly pilgrimage, I have learned more about sacred land. I go further into this later in the chapter.

When we began this program, called Breaking Through, neither Rick nor I had any idea how deep these pilgrimages would get—of course, we didn't even know we were doing "pilgrimages," at first. That first year of the program, although I facilitated rituals for the group within nature; it was still basically just mountain climbing, white water rafting and nature walking—wonderful as these are in themselves. But, by the following year, Rick's love of his place—the Crestone Peaks—and my growing love of it, too, combined so that we were freed to fully live this pilgrimage into what was becoming truly sacred land. In return, we experienced the "abundance" which always comes from real festival or real pilgrimage. All who come on Breaking Through experience this "abundance" as well. The "abundance" comes out of the "more than" of the deep relationship between us, humans, and nature in this sacred place. Each year we're learning more about sacred land!

Preview

Many of you have experienced this "hush of the holy"—even, if only briefly—when you are out in nature. But the important questions here are: "How do we set it up so that a group can experience this together out in nature?" "How can we regain what traditional cultures had—the knowledge that they lived within sacred land?" And, perhaps most important of all, "How can we do this in the present destructive, Industrial Growth Society, that surrounds us on all sides?" Beginning once again to do the rituals that connect us with the land is the only way we can survive—either us or the many "endangered" species left on earth.

In this chapter I will first give basic background from many sources concerning the very same structures, which we discovered in Breaking Through and from my Autumn Equinox Taoist Celebrations, held each year. Then, I will outline how you can begin to use such structures on the earth of your own place.

"LAND, EARTH, SOIL, DIRT: SOME NOTES FROM THE GROUND"

I'm using Tom Jay's title of his magnificent essay on all the above. When I began this chapter I had some difficulty with the word, land. Sacred land seemed alright but land didn't. Both of my previous books have the word, earth in the title; but there's so much propaganda from the IGS about "whole earth" and other abstractions that it now makes me uneasy to use it. Tom Jay reclaimed "earth" for me; as well as showed me why the word, "land" made me uneasy. I've reprinted the entire essay in the "Back of the Book" section; be sure to read it.

Jay tells us that earth is from er, an Indo-European word, "a fundamental word with many meanings...it refers to the character of the land. We cannot yet 'buy earth,' we find that hard to say. Historically, earth has meant or still means: the world, cosmos, soil, [etc.]. Currently the word's meaning is shrinking...Earth is more than a green ball hurtling through eternity. Space flight is sucking the blood from a once healthy word." Talking about soil, he writes:

> The people are born, live and die, they dwell. The soil enters their stories secretly as background and gradually transforms itself into the theater of their myth...Soil digests and remembers...gradually a myth appears. It appears as a strange echoing. Solitary people hear it first. Animals and plants tell them. The echo twists them into wisdom, the doom of seeing. These witnesses report the tale until it is *true*...Myths are *nehgebur* stories, tales of the 'near fellow dwellers,' stories of the soul in place. The gods are embodiments of our daily local connections, the secrets that settle us here. Without a myth that tells us where we are, we are lost in our heads, head tripping. In a true myth, a *tree* story, we are both places at once, paradoxically sane. Inside out, one glove fits either hand

Once you begin to use the rituals and structures, given in this chapter, you will find that you will begin learning from your own sacred land, as traditional peoples have always done.

PART I: GENERAL BACKGROUND

Daily Rituals of Nurturance and Greeting between Humans and Nature

Once again, because of the essential nature of the human, I must refer to this all-important ritual structure. In both earlier chapters in Part III, I went into different aspects of it. Here, in this chapter it is even more important. To recapitulate, Erikson pointed out the importance of the daily rituals of greeting between mother and baby. He admitted that this seems to be "a large order to burden an infant's daily awakening"; but, he went on to say that all elements involved in the sense of sacred can be found in this first "greeting ritual." He further states that it is "but a variant of the primate or even mammalian pattern." Erikson, as a psychologist, felt no need to go into the deeper levels of this pattern; but it is obvious that "daily rituals of nurturance and greeting" are at the heart of our relationship to nature, as well. All traditional cultures knew and practiced this.

Fortunately, we have a description of a pre-human daily ritual greeting; a first-hand account by Jung himself. In 1925 Jung went to Africa and visited a tribe who lived on the slopes of Mt. Elgon. He writes: "The sunrise in these latitudes was a phenomenon that overwhelmed me anew every day." He took a camp stool and an umbrella and sat under an acacia tree just before dawn to watch the sun as it came up. As the horizon began to glow white from the oncoming sun, "gradually the swelling light seemed to penetrate into the very structure of objects, translucently, like bits of colored glass. Everything turned to flaming crystal. The cry of the bell bird rang around the horizon. At such moments I felt as if I were inside a temple. It was the most sacred hour of the day. I [was] in a timeless ecstasy." Near his observation point was an enormous cliff inhabited by baboons. "Every morning they sat quietly, almost motionless, on the ridge of the cliff facing the sun, whereas throughout the rest of the day they ranged noisily through the forest, screeching and chattering. Like me, they seemed to be waiting for the sunrise." They reminded him of the great baboons of the temple of Abu Simbel in Egypt, "which perform the gesture of adoration." These baboons tell the same story: "for untold ages men have worshipped the great god who redeems the world by rising out of the darkness as a radiant light in the heavens."

The Elgonyi people, where Jung was staying, told him of their daily ceremony—(a "daily ritual or nurturance and greeting"). "In the morning, when the sun comes, we go out of the huts, spit into our hands, and hold them up to the sun." They held their hands in front of their mouths, spat or blew into them, and then lifted their hands high, palms facing toward the sun. When Jung asked him why they did this, the old man just said "We've always done it." And further, the old man told Jung that all peoples, the Kevirondos, the Buganda, and all tribes "as far as the eye could see from the mountain and endlessly farther, worshiped *adhista*—that is, the sun at the moment of rising." Spit, offered to the sun, is considered by many traditional people to contain the "personal mana, the power of healing, magic and life."

They seemed to be offering their breath, which, in Arabic is *ruch*, in Hebrew, *ruach* and in Greek, *pneuma*—all meaning wind and/or spirit. Jung says: "this wordless, acted-out prayer...might equally well be rendered: 'Lord, into thy hands I commend my spirit'." He tells how "profoundly moving" for him it was to find way up on the mountain at the sources of the Nile this "reminder of the ancient Egyptian conception of the god, Horus (the principle of light)." It seemed to him that this primordial African experience "had flowed down to the coasts of the Mediterranean along with the sacred waters of the Nile," and influenced all the other conceptions of god with this "moment when, with the typical suddenness of the tropics, the first ray of light shoots forth like an arrow and night passes into life-filled light."

We all feed on sun. The flow of food which underlies all life begins with the sun's light arriving at the surface of a green leaf here on earth. Only plants make food directly from the sun; the rest of us here on earth are "plant parasites." All traditional humans recognize that the sun gives them both life and light. We are all "children of the sun" as the Pawnee Indians say; that is why it feels good to us, as humans to daily greet "father Sun."

Ritually greeting the sun as it rises, was done by many Plains Indian tribes in this country. Australian aborigines also greet the sun; in fact, these traditional people have probably the most sophisticated rituals of "nurturance and greeting" as far as the earth of their own place is concerned, of any peoples on earth.

Earth Rituals of the Australian Aboriginals

"Gradually I experienced the central truth of Aboriginal religion: that it is not a thing by itself but an inseparable part of a whole that encompasses every aspect of daily life, every individual, and every time—past, present and future. It is nothing less than the theme of existence, and as such constitutes one of the most sophisticated and unique religious and philosophical systems known to man...In a sense, everything within the Aborigines' environment is holy, not in some vague, pantheistic sense but in terms of concrete ties which the rituals use and revitalize." Thus, Richard Gould sums up what he learned while living with the Yiwara in the Australian desert.

This intimate relationship with nature in their place is begun in childhood, when, the names and locations of waterholes are given to them during initiations. This is done by songs, dances and designs on sacred boards. The route of named waterholes is given in song cycles of the dreamtime events that occurred there. Later, the initiates visit the places connected with these sacred traditions. While there, they absorb every detail. Each of the smallest things they see there is linked with the sacred songs. Gould continues: "Even while departing, from time to time he casts a glance back over his shoulder, 'back sighting' on the waterhole so that he will recognize it if he returns. The usefulness of this kind of knowledge to the desert people is obvious." Of course to any mountain climber this is also obvious. If you don't backsight, you won't be able to get off the mountain in a fog or a storm or at night. Gould points out that through the rituals and cult systems such knowledge is transmitted from one generation to the next. "Their ceremonial life is deeply involved with their subsistence and daily living." And that's why mountain climbing is so ritualistic as well. Getting off the mountain in an emergency situation (because you have done all the necesary rituals, such as backsighting) means you don't die but continue to live.

Specific natural locations in the place are celebrated by the Australian aboriginals by means of special rituals. I will give details of only one such ritual but this will show the complexity and inter-relatedness of these rituals. Gould went with the men of a particular cult to their sacred waterhole. It was located in a natural depression in a limestone ledge. On one side of the waterhole there was a series of "natural ripples or parallel grooves." These are thought to be the chest scars of the totemic "Two water-snakes" who came here in the Dreamtime, when they collected a great amount of sweet yellow wama and had eaten too much. "They became sick at this place and vomited out the contents of their stomachs onto the ground. The wama they vomited out turned to stone [became rock in the Dreamtime], becoming the piles of yellow rock where the men sprinkled penis blood today." These ancestral beings still live in the rockpiles. The older man of the group had been born near this rockpile and so had his son. "This place is their 'dreaming'." He calls the rockpile, "my father." He and his son claim descent in the male line from the "Water-snake...living within the rockpile." Other members of the group claim descent from other "sacred rock piles."

Each member of this cult has certain sacred duties which include keeping the area around the rockpiles clean and seeing that they remain intact as well as performing the actual ritual. In doing the ritual "they temporarily re-enter the dreamtime and the rockpile becomes part of their own being. Even when they are not performing the ritual, a direct kinship tie always exists between the men and the rockpiles." Although anthropologists generally refer to this kind of ritual as "increase" ceremonies, Megitt has correctly pointed out that there is more to it than this limited view: "It is worth noting...that the participants are simply concerned to main tain the supplies of natural species at their usual level, to support the normal order of nature." (Here, we can see the same type of ritual action as in the Chinese Li ceremonies to keep their relationship with nature in harmony.) In this particular Australian ceremony, they are helping to nurture the wama, so that it continues its fertile growth.

The most important part comes after lighting the ritual fire at the rockpile. Then, "each man steps up to his rockpile and, using a small, sharpened stick, jabs at his subincised penis until the wound is reopened. When blood flows freely from the wound it is sprinkled over the rockpile. Each man stands by his fire for a few moments to let the heat dry and slow the flow of blood." This entire action is done with "extreme reverence and meditation." This may seem grotesque to those not familiar with the gratitude a human can feel toward a rock. I've noticed, in common with other mountain climbers, that when coming down off a particularly harrowing rock pitch on a long mountain climb and suddenly noticing the blood dripping off a cut in my hand or arm; I feel that this little gift of my blood is truly appropriate. It somehow shows my gratitude toward the rock for allowing me to get safely down. Sometimes we joke to one another about "our gift" to the rock.

In the Australian aboriginal ritual, of course, there's a much deeper meaning connected with the penis blood. They are re-opening an old wound made as part of their original initiation. This is ritually done many times throughout their life. Some researchers feel this is tied in with a form of ritual contraception as well. If a man has just re-opened his wound he's not going to be doing sex for awhile, that's for sure. Instead of using that energy for sex he's used it in a larger renewal dimension—for contributing life to the entire place.

Before they leave the waterhole they ritually decorate it with the red ochre they've brought along. It is ground and mixed with water and spread over the rock rim of the pool. It covers the entire rim except one spot where they put serpentine designs for the Water-snakes. Gould says "It is an impressive sight— the black mud and red ochre designs in the desert area." Rain and wind will deface it but they will come again another year "to carry out their sacred duties once again." This "Water-snake" is often called "Rainbow-snake" and is associated all through Australia with rain and water.

All the landmarks in a particular area are connected with totemic beings who were transformed into the natural landmark "during the dreamtime." But the individual waterholes, trees, sandhills, ridges and all other landmarks are still alive and influencing the present. The Australian aborigine is related by kinship ties to each of these beings. "Thus the sight of virtually every landmark, no matter how insignificant it may seem to the foreign visitor passing through the desert, brings deep, emotional satisfaction to the aborigine." The concept of Dreamtime breaks down the separation of man and his physical environment and the rituals bring "Deep feelings of belonging to a harmoniously ordered universe." The individual aborigine's relationship to his "dreaming," carried on within the appropriate cult-lodge, becomes "the core of his social and spiritual identity."

In order to ground this last statement so that we can feel it in our own brain and body, I want to refer back to Jung's concepts. Back in Part II of this work it was explained how the contents of the "collective unconcious" are "impersonal and collective...forming an omnipresent, unchanging, and everywhere identical quality or substrate of the psyche per se...thus the self can appear in all shapes from the highest to the lowest, inasmuch as these transcend the scope of the ego personality." Jung found that in both the dreams and in active imagination of Europeans, many different animals come out as part of the self. Other natural beings which occur are plants (most often flowers and trees); the inorganic forms are most often mountain, lake and rock. These appear from within us when given half a chance. They are still there. The patterns are in our genes; therefore, it is not difficult to re-activate them and build them back into our daily life so that we can restore communication again between us and nature. (See "Personal Totem Pole" in the index, for a ritual to communicate with our own animals, inside us, developed by Steve Gallegos.)

In summary, to begin to heal the "split" between us and nature, inflicted on us by our culture, the crucial action is daily rituals of "nurturance and greeting" between us and the natural beings of our own place.

The "original" gods: Trees, Rocks, Mountains and Water

Each of the gods of classical Greece and Rome, was originally a particular aspect of nature. While most traditional cultures have kept enough continuity so that it is still possible to see the connection between the gods and nature; in Europe, this continuity was deliberately broken so often that the connections are no longer clear. Here I will try to re-connect some of the more important aspects of the gods with nature. Let's begin with the Greek gods because there's been a recent revival of the names of these early gods but in most cases it's become a further level of abstraction from the original Greek abstraction. Herodotus (484-432 B.C.), the famous Greek historian, who is often called The Father of History, has this to say:

> But as to the origin of each particular god, whether they all existed from the beginning, what were their individual forms, the knowledge of these things is, so to speak, but of today and yesterday. For Homer and Hesiod are my seniors, I think, by some four hundred years and not more. And it is they who have composed for the Greeks the generations of the gods, and have given to the gods their titles and distinguished their several provinces and special powers and marked their forms.

(My underlining for emphasis.) There have been numerous books written about the coming of the patriarchal concept from the Aryan sky gods onto the original matriarchal Greek goddessess. But, actually more to the point is the destruction of local gods and goddesses by putting them under a single classical anthropomorphic new god or goddess; thus co-opting the on-going cycle of local people, local place and deity. This helped focus people's energy onto the newly emerging "Greek culture."

When we look back still further into the origins of these deities, we turn to Crete. I cannot take the time here to go into great detail about most of these early gods and goddesses; however, the Mountain-Mother of Crete is important for the earth goddesses. Jane Ellen Harrison (1924), one of the first to write sympathetically about these early Cretan deities, said it was almost "too good to be true" when she first saw a portrait of the Mountain-Mother on a clay impression of a signet ring which Sir Arthur Evans had found in his excavations in Crete. She wrote: "On the summit of her own great mountain stands the Mother with sceptre outstretched... for solemn guardians they have given the fierce, mountain ranging lions, placed heraldically to either side. To the left of the goddess is a Minoan shrine with 'horns of consecration' and pillars, the symbols that connect her with plant and animal life, for the pillar is but the tree shaped and stylized." She explains that "this supremacy of the Mother marks a contrast with the Olympian system where Zeus the Father reigns supreme. It stands for the Earth Worship." She states that the "mountain naturally enough in Crete stood for Earth, and the Earth is Mother because she gives life to plants, to animals, to man." But this is no "whole earth" goddess. She is local; she stands on her own mountain. Harrison tells us that this original Earth goddess was invoked by priestesses as follows: "Earth sends up fruits, so praise we Earth, the Mother."

Harrison shows how this original earth goddess was still present even though classical Greek thought had brought in the sky gods. For instance, the shrine at Delphi eventually became dedicated to Apollo, a sky god. But even then the priestess began her prayer to all the divinities of the place with these opening words:

> First in my prayer before all other gods
> I call on Earth, primeval prophetess.

The Cretan Great Mother was never admitted to Mt. Olympus but she "had great influence on Greek thought and religion. Many of her sacred animals and attributes, much of her nature in general she lent to the women divinities of the mainland." These are the well-known goddesses Hera, Demeter, Athena, Aphrodite etc. But Artemis is the nearest of all to the "Lady of the Wild Things," the original Cretan concept. On the Acropolis at Athens was an area dedicated to Artemis Brauronia. Here young girls were sent for *arkteiap* or "bear service." In one of Aristophanes' dramas of later time he has a chorus of women sing of their benefits when they were little girls. Among other things they sing: "*I was a bear* in the Brauronian festival." Harrison explains: "[T]he little girls of Athens wrapped in yellow bear skins would dance or crouch bear fashion before the goddess. A goat was sacrificed to Artemis and till the next festival the little girls were safe from marriage. They had accomplished their bear-service." By the time of Aristophanes saffron robes were substituted for the bear skins.

Artemis is most famous as the goddess of the hunt. Harrison quotes a classical writer, Arrian in his *Treatise on Hunting* where he tells us that hunters must pay homage to Artemis "She-of-the-Wild," must pour libations, crown her, sing hymns and offer first-fruits of the game taken. "Great stress is laid... on the purity and sanctity of the garland and the place it was culled." Harrison explains that these enclosures were places for growing medicinal herbs. She says that Dr. Rendel Harris in his book, *Ascent to Olympus*, "has drawn attention to the importance of these herbal gardens in ancient religion and he tells us the very herb to which Artemis owes her name, the *artemisia*, a wormwood, sometimes called mugwort." Even up to the early years of this century, "garlands were made on St. John's Eve [summer solstice] of this and other magic herbs and they 'dispelled demons'... The herb Artemisia grew abundantly on Mt. Taygetus, the favourite haunt of Artemis." Here we have a local goddess, possibly originally a bear who was connected with the local mountain. Being English, Harrison does not give the more usual name for this herb in our country—sage. As mentioned in Part I of this book, sage grew everywhere early man was found. So this use of *artemisia* (sage) as a sacred herb in rituals may date back to the paleolithic in the Mediterranean region.

Romans had no names for their gods until they borrowed them from the Greeks. They had vague beings which they called *numina* (powers). Harrison says "These vague *numina* were associated with particular places and were regarded with vague feelings of awe... The real specialization of the *numen* was not in his character but in his function... and he presided over some particular locality and activity of man." Here we see the more usual primitive concept of "power" residing in some particular aspect of nature rather than the making of a god in human form as in Greece. The more primitive Etruscan influence was still strong in Rome even into the classical times.

THE ETRUSCANS

Who were these people who had no gods but worshipped the "powers" in their local place? They were the native tribal peoples—generally called Etruscans; but, actually, they had their own tribal names. The nostalgia for that lost world is shown in the liquid mourning sounds of all the natural beings crying out: "For you the grove... mourned, and the... glassy waters/And the clear lakes..." In this manner the Roman classical writer, Vergil mourned what his people had done to the land in their "colonizing" wars against the native people of the Italian Peninsula so that the Roman Empire could rule the world. This is the underlying meaning of the famous Latin classic, the *Aeneid*. Vergil spent the last eleven years of his life writing it but died before it was fully revised.

Classical scholars of past generations presumed that Vergil's epic glorified the beginning of the "great Roman Empire" with the reign of Augustus but; actually, Vergil was taking the opposite stand. Quoting Commager, an authority on Vergil: "Historically, we may grant that the development from the huts... to the marble buildings of the Forum marked a triumph of civilization over primitive simplicity, and the Eighth Book (of *the Aeneid*) dwells upon the contrast between the two. Yet we feel not so much a sense of progress as one of loss; we are constant witnesses to the violation of the land. An extraordinary simile compares Aeneas in the final battle to a tempest bringing ruin to the crops and trees."

In this final battle, Aeneas' spear misses his chief enemy Turnus, and hits an olive tree in a sacred grove, symbolizing the destruction of the tribal people's sacred relationship to the land of old Italy. Another recent scholar writes: Aeneas will defeat Turnus and the people of the 'old ways' but Vergil knows the price that is paid by the victory of the order of positive law over natural law." (My underlining for emphasis.)

Vergil died nineteen years before the birth of Christ but

he could already see what the "civilized" world had lost. His epic concerns the mythological founder of Rome, Aeneas. After Troy was taken by the Greeks and burned, he fled with his son and his father. His father dies on the way but after many perils he and his son reach Italy. Latinus, the reigning king, receives the exiles hospitably and promises his daughter Lavinia, in marriage to Aeneas. But Lavinia's mother has already promised her to Prince Turnus who refuses to give her up. Latinus orders the rivals to settle the matter in battle. Turnus is killed, Aeneas marries Lavinia and thus begins Rome. Latinus, Turnus and others are actual historical figures.

Nearly all the warrior followers of Turnus—the tribal peoples—are associated with sacred springs or groves. Turnus has a sister who was formerly a nymph of the Numicus River but by Emperor Augustus time she had been domesticated into a small spring in the Forum; just as the mysterious wood of Avernus, entrance to the underworld had been cut down to furnish material for Agrippa's shipyard. The sacred forest was destroyed to build ships to help Rome "conquer the world."

The last verse in Book Six of the epic, is the crucial one: "There are twin gates of dreaming [sleep]: the one is said to be of horn, here is an easy exit for true visions; the other is made of polished ivory, perfect, glittering, but through that way the Spirits send false dreams into the world above. And here Anchises, when he is done with words, accompanies the sibyl and his son and he sends them through the gate of ivory." Anchises is Aeneas' dead father. The distinction between these two gates is important for us today. The symbolism of the "gate of horn" refers to the powers of animals, to the caves deep in the earth, which are places of rebirth, and to religion as the maintenance of abiding relationship. Through the "gate of horn," the human being continues in an abiding relationship, through the "old gods," to the earth itself, the source of all life. The "gate of ivory" refers to Emperor Augustus' attempt to establish himself as a god, to inaugurate a new era of worship of the Empire.

A few generations before Vergil, the Marsi people had lived in independence as Roman allies. In the Marsic war of 91-88 B.C., they had been defeated and lost their independence. For Vergil, the Marsi represented the original people and the true Roman spirit. Parry says "His feeling for them had something in common with what Americans have felt for the American Indian." Vergil uses actual place names from the Marsian hill country east of Rome for the nostalgic verse quoted above.

The "Gate of Horn," which is the pivotal point of Vergil's epic, also refers to the Eleusinian Mysteries of Greece, held under the powerful horns of Mount Kerata above Eleusis. For the sophisticated writers of the classical period such as Vergil, the mystery rites of Eleusis tended to re-establish the lost unity of human beings with the Mother Goddess, Earth herself, "whose body — no longer every day and night or for time everlasting, but only during the period of purposeful communion with her—was the complete refuge for men." In his epic, Vergil has Aeneas land at Cumae in Italy after his escape from Troy. At Cumae is a temple with a gate carved by Daedalus who came from Crete. Vergil uses the figure of

Daedalus to connect Cumae directly with the old Minoan Mother Goddess religion of Crete.

There is one more stage, which I must take you through, before you can see the deep connections here. For this last stage we must go way back to the very land forms of Crete itself for this is where the entire Mother Goddess concept began for the Europeans.

ORIGIN OF THE "MADONNA" IN THE CAVES OF CRETE

There are two essential aspects of the Mother Goddess—afar, she is the Mother Mountain. But worshipped close up she dwells in the cave.

Here I will be referring to the work of the great British archaeologist-scholar, Sir Arthur Evans, who made discoveries in Crete, which were to change current thinking completely regarding the early Mediterranean civilizations. Because of Evans' work, the power and extent of the Minoan civilization were revealed after thousands of years of semi-legend.

His great breakthrough in this field came when he connected the objects engraved on the Minoan seal-stones, collected in Crete, with the natural landscape forms, worshipped in prehistoric times in Crete and still powerful to the local peasants. He points out that the Greeks had transformed the earlier objects of worship into "perfect human shapes" but that often the carving of the human type god still contains the original natural object from which that god developed. For instance, Apollo is often shown leaning against the column which was originally the limestone pillar in the caves in Crete, worshipped as a fertility symbol—a giant limestone phallus or penis. The Greeks inherited the Cretan gods: "The great caves, such as are found in the Cretan limestone districts, provided, moreover, in their stalagmite pillars cult objects within what themselves were natural shrines of primitive Religion." In just such a cave the Greek goddess gave birth to the Cretan Zeus, according to the myth.

Evans, who excavated the famous cave of Eileithyia near the ancient city of Knossos in Crete, explains: "We have here the clearest evidence as to the character of the cult itself. In the middle of the cave rises a stalagmite pillar, which, in the half darkness, might itself suggest a standing female figure in long robes, and the religious attributes with which it was invested are at the same time evidenced by the surrounding of the pillar by a temenos of rough masonry." This stone enclosure, the temenos, dates from Neolithic times. Eileithyia was the goddess of childbirth for the Greeks and from the Homeric age onward she was associated with this cave sanctuary. On page nine of Sir Arthur Evans' book there is a photograph of the cave of Eileithyia. The stalagmite, which he is discussing above, is madonna shaped with a protuberance just where an infant would be held in her arms. This basic nurturing form of mother with child lies deep in the uncon-scious; thus from the very beginning humans have invested such forms in nature with "power." In this particular photo in Evans' book, one can see a ridge of stone round "the head," very much resembling the later haloes round the Christian madonnas. Here we have the origin of the entire "madonna in a rock grotto" complex which has continued right down to the present time.

As a child attending a Catholic church, I was fascinated by the madonna in the rock grotto. Such madonnas are still installed in the grounds of modern Catholic churches. When we were children there were May Day processions where each small girl carried flowers to put at the feet of "Mary." But Jesus was born to Mary in a stable not a rock cave, according to what the nuns told us so I was always puzzled, but delighted, by Mary in the rock cave. The grottoes at some deep level have always attracted people—from the ancient classical era, through the Middle Ages right up to the present time. It's not Mary, the Madonna, but the rocky grotto itself which is the real sacred being.

Sir Arthur Evans' photograph gives us the origin of the Madonna/Earth Mother Goddess figure, beginning with the original Neolithic Cretan feeling of the sacred character of the caves with the stalagmite figures and the carving of such figures on their seals and temples. The next stage came when the Cretans, who emigrated to the Greek mainland, encountered the northern sky god influence, which eventually developed into those Greek gods, made into "perfect human shapes." At this time, the Cretan influence would tend toward carving madonna-type figures. These Mother Goddess types acquired Greek names but were still often worshipped in actual caves. Demeter is associated with a cave at Eleusis, for instance. When the upper class Romans, influenced by Greek culture, began forming their own gods (from the original *numen* or powers of the Latin people) the madonna shape again re-appeared. As mentioned above, in Vergil's *Aeneid*, he writes of Daedalus as a Cretan who carves the gate of the temple.

The next stage in the development of the madonna occured not long after. Remember, Vergil's epic was just nineteen years before the date assigned by the Christians for Christ's birth. This was the reign of Augustus. According to the biblical story, Mary and Joseph were on their way to register for the census of Augustus when Jesus was born. So the later Roman converts, always carrying within them the madonna image naturally turned to that form for the statues in the churches. The full development came with the gigantic Gothic cathedrals of the Middle Ages—many of them dedicated to Mary. In still more recent times, every big city in the United States had its cathedral enshrining Mary in her grotto. Usually the figure of Mary is crushing the snake under her foot—perennial reminder of the Christian underlying fear of the natural world.

After this brief account of how, in Europe, both the early empires and Christianity repeatedly broke the original human connection with nature as sacred, I will now turn to another part of the world where the sacred relationship to nature remains evident no matter which religion the people adopt.

The Japanese Relationship to the Sacred in Nature

Sacred mountains and caves throughout the world are discussed in detail in my previous book, *Earth Wisdom*. Here I will concentrate particularly on the Japanese relationship to the sacred in nature; not only because it has remained unbroken from the most primitive times right down to this day; but also, early Japanese myth and poetry came directly out of this sacred relationship. (See Part II of this work for more information concerning the apparent contradiction between the concept of "sacred" land in Japan and their success as a modern industrial nation.)

CATEGORIES OF SACRED SPACE IN JAPAN

"Flying Mountains and Walkers of Emptiness," these two phrases from a twelfth century mountain Buddhist text, have been used by Allan Grapard as the title for his paper on sacred space in Japanese religion. There are three distinct categories of sacred space. The first and oldest form is found in the early Shinto myths and rituals. This was the actual space around the *kami* or divine being of nature. The second category was developed after Buddhism reached Japan and it emerged out of the "dynamic interaction" between Shinto and Buddhism. This sacred space was a more extensive geographical area, "usually consisting of the territory covered by a pilgrim during a pilgrimage or of the territory onto which a Buddhist mandala had been projected." It was considered that this area was a place where Buddhahood could be realized. The third category was Japan itself as a sacred land, dating back to the early writings in the eighth century *Kojiki*; but becoming more important during the Kamakura period when Japan faced the threat of a Mongol invasion from the sea.

The sacred site can be either the *kami* itself—the sacred tree, rock, waterfall, etc. or a "certain object which was precisely the point of contact for the divinity with the earth." If this point of contact is a stone, it is set within a rectangular bed of white pebbles. Four bamboo or wooden pillars are erected at the corners, connected by straw ropes and hung with the paper decoration (*gohei*) which mark any sacred object in Shinto. These sites seem to be connected to one of the following: the beauty of an area; the "power" of an area such as a volcano or an earthquake site; or a waterfall; an important historical event; a myth; or a dream.

Mountains are the most prominent *kami* . There are three sites associated with the mountains. If the mountain as a whole is sacred, then there is no main shrine at all only a veneration hall on the mountain. Central sites of shrines are located at the entrance to valleys going into the mountain; and close sites are near the village from which you can see the distant mountain.

MOUNTAIN BUDDHISM AS IT DEVELOPED OUT OF SHINTO

Kukai (774-835), who founded the Shingon sect on Mt. Koya, was a mountain worshipper from his youth. He felt that not only rituals made a place sacred but "an internal process leading to Awakening, [which] by allowing the subject to see the world in entirely different terms, can also transform the space to sacred." Yamabushi, from *yama*, meaning mountain and *bushi*, meaning sleep—those who sleep in the mountains— is the general term for those who wander in the mountains as sacred places. This process became known as "mandalization." "Just as one entered a painted mandala, performing the rituals, they would enter the mountains, thereby penetrating the Realm of the Buddha." This is one aspect of how Shingon Buddhism was grounded by tying it right back into the on-going Shinto concept of the mountains as *kami*. Yamabushi go from peak to peak venerating the Bodhisattvas and Buddhas residing on each peak. As the Buddhist document, *Shozen engi* states:

"Alongside the peaks of the Buddhas, they tread Emptiness." Not only do the Yamabushi find the peaks sacred but also the natural elements on the mountains such as hot springs, waterfalls and medicinal herbs. The *Shozen engi* provides further instruction: "Those who tread those spaces and cross these rivers must think that each drop of water, each tree of these mountains is a drug of immortality, even if they suffer from a heavy past of misdeeds."

There are at least 80,000 Shinto shrines in Japan; thus indicating the many *kami* venerated throughout the country. Kitagawa, a Japanese scholar on religion says that *kami* refers "to all beings that are awesome and worthy of reverence, including both good and evil beings." This is similar to the general approach in primitive societies that the sacred is the "powers." Kitagawa continues by stating that Shinto "accepted the plurality of the *kami* as separate beings...its basic affirmation was the sacrality of the total world (cosmos) permeated as it was by the *kami* (sacred) nature."

In order to clearly show the difference between the abstractions of Europe and the immediacy of the Japanese approach I will contrast Eliade's statement about symbolism with how the Japanese feel about it. "When a tree becomes a cult object, it is not as a tree that it is venerated, but as a hierophany, that is, a manifestation of the sacred," according to Eliade. In other words there's a god who lives in the tree (Greek) or a spirit or a deva or elemental (current New Age terms) but there's no way the tree itself is sacred. Kitagawa, on the other hand states: "in early Japan, which held to a monistic world of meaning, symbols were not understood symbolically. The epistomological basis of the nonsymbolic understanding of the early Japanese was their aesthetic, magico-religious apprehension of the primeval totality as well as everything within it not as representations of *kami* but as *kami*." In other words *kami* were sacred or divine in themselves. Kitagawa quotes from the *Manyoshu*, "the collection of myriad leaves," the earliest Japanese collection of poems; the title actually means "collection of myriad leaves." In these two bits of poems the mountain itself is the god, the kami.

> Mount Futagami...
> When I come out and gaze upon it
> In the rich and blossomed spring,
> Or in the glorious leaf of autumn—
> How sublime it soars
> Because of its divinity...

Another one concerns snow-covered Mt. Tachi

> Lofty beyond the mountains,
>   bright in the rising sun
> Mount Tachi, a kami standing...

Kitagawa points out that *Manyo* poets "sang to and about rivers, oceans, celestial and atmospheric phenomena, animals, birds, insects, and flowers as living beings possessing intimate relations with men and women [there is] mutual participation that evokes reverence and affection on both sides."

In Japan the word for mountain pass is toge, coming from the word tamuke, meaning "to offer," because travelers always offered something to the god of the pass for the safe journey through. This offering at the pass is common also in Korea, Mongolia and Tibet. I can add it's also common among a number of mountain climbers today in this country.

I've been dealing with mountains as beautiful or awe-inspiring. Another aspect of mountains is concerned with them as watersheds or sources of streams and fertility. "The mountain god comes down from the mountain in early spring to guard the rice field and returns to the mountain in the fall. Villagers observe the rituals of welcoming and sending off the deity." This is similar to the Pueblo relationship to the kachinas in our own Southwest. Ichiro Hori states that, in Japan "it seems that the mountain goddess was originally the goddess of reproduction both of plants and animals, as well as human beings. These mountain goddesses were first worshiped by the hunting tribes, then by the farmers. There is some evidence that the sacred mountains occupied by mountain ascetics [*yamabushi*] were [entered] at first by leaders among the hunters. And there is an intimate connection between mountain ascetics and hunters."

In his "Sacred Tree in Japanese Prehistory," Hosoi, another Japanese scholar states that "trees were the original shrines of Shinto and that trees were not added to primitive god-houses... but that god-houses were provided for trees." Putting this in more familiar European terms, they did not build temples to the god and then plant trees around it; instead, they "provided" temples for the trees, who were the gods, the *kami*.

CONCERNING THE "ORIGINAL" HUMAN CONCEPT OF NATURE AS SACRED

In this entire section on the Japanese relationship to nature as sacred, we see that their "flying mountains," waterfalls, trees and all the other *kami* have come down fairly intact right to this day; thus providing a much clearer connection for us to the real "perennial wisdom." Not what Huxley meant by it, when he used the phrase: essentially civilized ponderings over the ultimate questions, by poring through documents from the last couple of thousand years of European Platonic idealism; but instead, the wisdom from "ancient Europe, Asia, Africa whose world was united by what Olson called the 'pleistocene' and [Gary] Snyder, 'the Great Subculture of illuminati' which goes back as far as perhaps the late Paleolithic."

The fact that our immediate European heritage broke the connection so many times by increasing levels of abstraction and 'idealism': Greek intellectualism, Roman empire building, and continual Christian crusading monotheism makes it a difficult and laborious task to trace the threads of the sacred relationship to nature which still lie deeply embedded within us. The facts about the origin of the madonna concept from way back in the Neolithic limestone caverns of Crete, but still operating within us today shows the natural human response to the shelter of the cave, the power of rock and the natural origin of water sources deep within the rock. All of these draw forth our respect, reverence—you might call it worship. But we can't talk about this natural sacred relationship in our culture because it's deeply ingrained in us that to "save our soul" or to "be religious" or even to learn how to be a whole integrated human being; we have to turn to other-worldly "ideas" of god in the sky or to narrowly anthropocentric "ideas." Nature herself is not considered important enough to take into consideration when it comes to such matters. Not so for the Japanese. They have kept their contact with the real sources of life much clearer though the ages. This is why their writings are so helpful for us now that we are trying to find our way back into the real "perennial philosophy."

Enlightenment

Although the Buddha himself achieved enlightenment at the precise moment when, after meditating all night under the pipal tree, he saw the Morning Star, Venus shining before him; when he died his followers immediately began to abstract his teachings into a formal system. Buddha said that "enlightenment" was possible for "all sentient beings." When he died his followers began debating who are "sentient beings?" Is it possible for animals to be enlightened? They decided that animals were not "sentient beings." But when Buddhism got to China and was influenced by Taoism, thus becoming Chan Buddhism, it was acknowledged that animals were "sentient beings"; however, the discussion still continued concerning the "Buddhahood of Plants and Trees." By the time Buddhism arrived in Japan, where it had to accomodate itself to "the ancient and continuous recognition of the presence of *kami* throughout the natural world it was forced to adjust," still more. "The discussion that began [in China] with the question of the possibility of salvation for plants and trees eventually led to the position that there was a salvation for man which derived *from* plant and trees." This was the work of the Buddhist poet-monk, Saigyō (1118-1190).

SAIGYŌ

Saigyō lived in the declining days of the great Heian period, which developed after the capital of Japan was established in Kyoto. Poetry was the accepted way of communicating and nature was woven into everyday life. Even their architecture contributed to this easy access. For instance, the sliding shoji doors where one could step right out into nature. Particular aspects of nature thus became the key to the seasons in their poetry: the blooming of certain flowers, the flights of certain species of birds, etc.

Saigyō left the court life in Kyoto at twenty-three to become a Buddhist monk. At that time, he changed his name to Saigyō, which means "West-Go" and began his travels into nature. He felt he needed to get away from social customs and learn from nature itself. This is reminiscent of the original Taoists who left the Chinese court in order to learn directly from nature. The crucial event, which changed Saigyō's life, was when he was on a pilgrimage and stopped by the side of the road to drink from a spring. He wrote:

> 'Only for a moment's stop'
> I'm in a roadside willow's shade,
> Where pure water of a spring
> Flows by ... as has the time now
> Since my "moment's stop' began.

Although he stopped for a moment only, this pause has lasted much longer. He has "lost all sense of time and all concern about pushing on toward a destination." In the total immersion in the moment of being here beneath the willow by the flowing stream he has suddenly recognized "enlightenment." As La Fleur explains: "we might say that it was in going 'to the side of the road' that he found 'the Way'." He has found the sacred without going to the temple or shrine. He "has been drawn into the world of nature" and he finds the sacred right there in that place. Nature "saves him."

La Fleur spends some time, defining the exact meaning of "salvation." He discusses Eliade's work as well as other scholars of religion and ends up with this definition: "Salvation consists in discovering and identifying the 'sacred' and unification with it." Once Saigyō had discovered the saving power of nature, he found it often: when he was "united with the moon, when he yielded his life to the sky, when he gave over the remains of his body to the safekeeping of a pine tree, and when his heart and mind were 'taken' by the blossoms of spring. The action involved is always one of giving, yielding, and surrendering—as if it is the Absolute to which he is giving himself." One of Saigyō's favorite places was Mt. Yoshino, to view the cherry blossoms:

> Each and every spring
> The blossoms give my mind
> Its needed solace;
> For more than sixty years now
> The time has been passed like this.

The golden aspen leaves in the fall provide precisely this same experience for me. Once one has visited the aspen leaves in a "sacred manner" for a couple of years in a row; it's enough to just walk into the grove and the sacred feeling overcomes one and the hush comes over the world. This experience grows deeper and deeper with each passing year. Although there is no way to describe this feeling since I am not a poet; all I can tell you here is to begin this process and you will soon experience precisely what Saigyō is talking about. I know this is true because through the years I have helped many others to start the process.

In no way does Saigyō seek "union" or "oneness" with the moon or the cherry blossoms or the willow tree. Instead they are "salvation" for him, precisely, because they accept their own impermanence; therefore he can learn from them. La Fleur explains: "In this sense the forms of nature are to man as a 'master' or demonstrator of the way." The aspen tree has helped me to understand this because it does not greedily hang onto the leaves, which it has spent all summer producing from the light of the sun and the water its roots draw up from the ground. Instead at the final moment in the fall, its leaves become a glory of gold and fly off to enrich the soil below. This is the spontaneity and freedom that Saigyō aimed for in his life. Centuries later, the great haiku poet, Bashō explained that he found in Saigyō, "a mind both obeying and at one with nature throughout the four seasons."

One more poem of Saigyō's is important for this concept of nature as salvation:

> Making my way through
> Miyataki River's fast
> Moving, waist-high rapids
> There's sensation of being
> Made pure to the base of the heart.

"The significant thing here is that the water is not understood as an external 'symbol' pointing at an internal cleaning. Rather, it seems to penetrate the body of the poet and reach inside to cleanse a heart which is felt to be physically inside. The verb in the last line, *sumu* means both 'to be purified' and 'to reside.' Thus the action is one of penetration or entry into the place in the body where the heart is...It is, therefore, the phenomena of nature that constitute the sacred reality."

Saigyō often uses the term *fukaku*, "deeply," as in the frequent phrase *fukaku irete* "deeply entered into." This phrase of the poet's often recurs to me while out in nature and is one of the reasons for the sub-title of this book: "rapture of the deep."

Nature is not permanent and civilization transitory for Saigyō. Rather, the difference is that the beings in nature accept their impermanence while civilization does not. Because they accept their transitory nature they can "assist him in his acceptance of his own." Natural beings are a "master" for him to learn from in this sense. "They are ahead of man both in their acceptance of truth and in the spontaneity of life they have on the basis of this enlightenment." Natural beings are "more than symbols of the way; for Saigyō they are the essence of Truth itself. Contact with them is to be in the presence of the Absolute. The things of nature become, in this attribution of value, not only mediators of Truth, but its very being."

In his poems Saigyō "fashioned the closest possible link between nature and Buddhist teaching...he has great importance for our understanding of the history of religion in East Asia," is La Fleur's conclusion. I want to add here that this is precisely why I felt it necessary to go so deeply into the poetry of Saigyō. As noted above, in Europe, religion became more and more abstracted from it's beginnings in the relationship of Paleolithic and Neolithic human beings to the natural beings of their place: mountains, caves, trees, etc; while, here we find that, culminating in Japan, religion found its way back to its beginnings in nature. Or rather, it never lost its connection and so still is part of that "Great Subculture of illuminati" as Gary Snyder so clearly puts it.

Saigyō's verse celebrates the beings in nature, not his own ego for being so "sensitive" as to see these things. The latter has been the dominant theme in European poetry. But for Japanese haiku, as Le Fleur explains, "We might say that the phenomenon and the self are both equally elevated when not in competition or contention." This is the underlying meaning of the famous lines from the Buddhist, *Genjōkōan*:

> That the self advances and confirms the
> myriad things is called delusion.
> That the myriad things advance and confirm
> the self is enlightenment.

Saigyō talks to the various beings in nature, such as the moon or cherry blossoms as his companions. This is an aspect of what Buddhists call "codependent origination," the fact that "in no thing is there a trace of that being's having its existence in and of itself alone." It took another eight hundred years before we in the West began talking about such matters—until the surge of ecology in the sixties.

In the sixteenth century, the poet Bashō, the great master of haiku remarked that he followed the "way" as shown by Saigyō in his poetry, Sesshū in his paintings and Rikyū in his art of tea: "One spirit activates all their works. It is the spirit of *fuga*; he who cherishes it accepts Nature and becomes a friend of the four seasons. Whatever objects he sees are referred to the flowers; whatever thoughts he conceives are related to the moon." This kind of mind is not supernatural, mysterious, numinous or any of those categories. It is not symbolic nor does it point to something beyond itself. It is rather egoless "Mind-at-one-with-all" or, in Gregory Bateson's terms: "Mind-at-large." In other words not limited by the boundaries of our skin but recognizing all the inter-relationships between us and nature. As the tree-planting Canadian poet, Robert MacLean wrote:

> Tent tethered among jackpine and blue-bells.
> Lacewings rise from rock incubators.
> Wild geese flying north.
> And I can't remember who I'm supposed to be.

We're only "supposed" to be when caught in the trap of the ego. When freed by our "masters"—the natural beings whether Saigyō's willow, or Bashō's flowers or MacLean's lacewings and wild geese; we, too are within nature and can simply *be*—totally— in relationship to whatever else we are with at that moment. And the depth of such relationship is in itself rapture:

> The Green mountains ...
> Deeper, and still deeper.
>   Santoka

This *is* "the way"—remain in your own place on the earth and go "deeper and still deeper." You will find it is truly "sacred land."

PART II: PLACE AND BIOREGION

Wherever you live, the place where you live is alive, and you are part of the life of that place. No matter how short a time you've been there, or whether or not you're going to be leaving it and going to another place, it will always be that situation throughout your life. The place that you end up being in is alive and you are part of that life. Now what is your obligation and your sense of responsibility for the sustenance and support that these places give you and how do you go about acting on it? That is the entire bioregional premise...
Peter Berg

Personal Introduction

When I began filing away material for this book, I labelled the folder for this chapter "Sacred Land." I couldn't even bring myself to use the word, earth. That word has been so grievously and totally misused by the media, by "newagers," and by upward rising, fame seeking, self-styled "shamans." The phrase, "whole earth" has become merely an abstraction, just another "Platonic idea." You could talk about the "whole earth" on television or in the slick new environmental magazines and never pay the slightest attention as you wasted the natural resources of your own "place."

To make this even clearer I want to the tell the story of certain events, connected with the drouth, which we had here in the West during the winter of 1976-77. Here in my own place we never got any snow until February 19th. We had day after day of glorious San Juan sun—shirt sleeve weather—through December and January and well into February. The high mountains were dusty! By spring there was little reserve water in the mountains throughout the entire West. In April, I drove to Claremont California to meet with others to begin the New Natural Philosophy Program of International College.

New Dimensions Radio wanted to tape me so I drove further up north to San Francisco. Marin County had strict water rules enforced; because the drouth had created a true water crisis. The people I met were all supposed to be "environmentally aware," but I want to tell what I learned from Kathy. We were all in her kitchen. She had just turned on the faucet to fill her glass with water; when turning to me, she began talking about how much she loved mother earth. The water continued to run, unheeded down the drain as she continued her conversation. Finally, she turned back to the water faucet and filled her glass. Variations of this scene occurred over and over while I was in Marin County. I began to realize that "mother earth" was just another abstraction to these people. While continuing to talk about their love of Mother Earth, this abstract deity, they ignored nature in their own place.

As mentioned above, Tom Jay helped me re-cognize the true meaning of earth. It's the ground under our feet and the more deeply we live our life on that ground the more it truly becomes "sacred land." Jay explains: "Land's meaning for us is *owned topography*. Land is a concept, not a locality." But living in and on that land, doing the ceremonies and listening to the beings of that place it becomes truly "sacred land," not merely owned topography. This chapter is designed to help you begin to live your way toward this reality. And there's no other way to do it but by living it. I had finished the first half of this chapter and was just beginning to wonder how I could possibly put all that I know about Peter Berg's "reinhabitation of place" and the whole bioregional movement into some kind of order when—once again—nature showed me "the way."

While working on this chapter in late November, I realized that for the quality of the book and for my own sanity I'd better take time out from writing to go out skiing once a week. This is the account of how I learned from nature during two of these ski expeditions. On the first one, we climbed up on our backcountry skis and Ramer bindings to just about 12,000 ft. and came down in glorious powder snow. After such an experience, "you know what it is to be alive," as Walking Jim Stolz sings. Such snow makes it very clear: if you conform to the earth itself, you have bliss; if not, you fall. Looking back we noticed, with surprise. that the pattern the curve of our tracks made, as each of us had gone over a small rise in the snow was identical. Then, we both said, "of course." Letting the gravity and mountain and snow turn you with no ego control over the way you go, your turns are going to be the same because the same natural events guided them.

In fact the snow was so good, I just had to go, again, the next day. My usual skiing partner, Steve, had to leave for Denver. There's no work here for him in Silverton. He commutes up to Denver every few weeks for ten days at a time to work as a photo technician so he can continue to live in Silverton. In the morning I went up to Tim Lane's place, because he was taking a day off just to ski so I knew he would be climbing up high. Tim is the last "daily-in-the-field, avalanche

researcher" in the country. Avalanche forecasting has become just another computer science most other places. Tim had found two separate layers of depth hoar the day before but not too much of it so things were relatively stable. We decided just to go up the trail already set to an area called "Sam." That suited me fine because, with trying to pull all the aspects of this book together, my "head wasn't on straight," as I explained to Tim so I wasn't able to give my full "attention" to skiing as one should when in steep powder snow.

We climb up and up, crossing inviting steep tree slopes with wonderful snow just pulling me toward it; but we still climb up and up and across a steep bowl of snow in the hot morning sun. So hot it was just like glacier lassitude—one can barely move. Finally we arrive at the top of the bowl. We take off our skins, scrape the ice off the edges, take a quick bite to eat and we are off downhill. We've discussed the way but no decision was reached—too much to choose from. In this bowl below us are old tracks from Tim and friends, several days before. To find untracked snow, Tim heads for the far edge.

When I come up with him we are standing on the ridge looking into the further, untouched bowl. He says: "Well, we've never been there; might as well try it." It's so compelling I agree. He takes off, traversing in a direct line across the slope as fast as he can go. I wait, nervously looking up, hoping nothing is going to come down because we are entering it well below the top. We both have shovels and Pieps but there's a lot of snow above us. Nothing moves. Then he reaches the little ridge and begins skiing down it. Beautiful snow and he's flying! Within minutes he's way down to the only tree left by the avalanches and the agreed upon spot and waits. He whistles for his avalanche dog, Cholo, who tears straight down through the deep snow to him. Seeing how long it takes the dog to reach Tim and how small the dog becomes in the distance, I begin to fully realize how huge this basin is and how much snow is above us and I begin paying attention! All thoughts about writing leave my head completely.

I move cautiously out along the windblown edge of the ridge I've been standing on—very conscious that it could fracture into a hard slab slide at any moment. But it doesn't. Then moving just as fast as Tim, I follow his track, traversing across the middle of it and arrive safely on the other little ridge and the snow hasn't moved it all. It's going to be ok. I peel off down the ridge in perfect snow. No effort at all just moving with gravity and snow and sun—bliss—it always is. But at the same time there's total attention, watching to see if there are any tell-tale sudden little cracks in the snow beginning to form. I reach Tim and we are ecstatic—both of us—with that crazy, insane grin I never see anywhere except in steep deep snow. But at the same time we are still very alert, totally attentive to the snow. We discuss what's the best way to go next. We are in the bottom funnel of a massive snowfilled bowl. And this is no ski resort; no avalanche guns have routinely knocked the avalanches down every week. In fact, no one has ever skied this bowl before! Total attention is mandatory. I know I don't want to go down any deeper into the shadowy, dark funnel. We joke together that if we go down there they won't find any of our bodies, including Cholo's, until next June.

We move out onto the sunny side of the funnel with sticky wet snow clinging to our skis—but safe. Then we scrape off the edges and continue through thick trees looking for a place, open enough to get a few turns in on our way down. Finally we get to an opening Tim has seen from below and we fly off again effortlessly—this time feeling there's no need to be so totally attentive. But after I start I know that's not really true. It's so steep that I'm flying through the air after each little rise. When I get down to Tim he says, "That's steep!" and I agree, but so exhilarating that we continue on down the slope which means we walk all the way back along the flat to his little house.

On the way we come to an old mine hole—looking fearsome and dark, as we look down through the elegant white snow festooned around the opening. Thinking how quintessentially yin and yang this sight is, I merely say, "that's mythological!" Somehow that opens us up to try to talk about what we had just experienced high up on that risky slope. Tim says, "How did you feel?" And I don't answer right away. So he continues: "Not afraid but..." And I say, "Yeah, just total attention. Life and death depending on it." And I suddenly realize that this is the way humans lived for most of our existence on earth—living fully with total attention to your place—and truly that's what "it means to be alive." And that's what sacred land is all about—our gratitude to the whole place for giving us such bliss and letting us walk away alive. We'd give our lives for these San Juan Mountains. It's not heroism it's just deep gratitude and respect for the privilege of being here in such luminous light and space.

Living "in a blaze of reality" is the way Stanley Diamond explains primitive cultures. Gary Snyder tells us: "Wildness is the state of complete awareness. That's why we need it."

And that's what we felt while skiing that "wild" snow basin. Essentially, the above account shows the difference between the "whole earth" mentality and reinhabitation of place. A mammal cannot bond to the whole earth—it's too big—and he or it or she can't walk over the whole earth every few days. And we humans are mammals. If you don't walk on your own earth in a "sacred manner," you can't bond to it. It's that simple. That's why in this chapter I will be giving some structures that have been used since we were still apes in the trees to help us humans bond to our earth so that it truly becomes "sacred land."

Introductory Background on "reinhabitation of place" and "Bioregions"

In the Autumn 1976 issue of *Coevolution Quarterly*, I first read of Peter Berg's *Planet Drum*, in "Future Primitive" by Raymond Dasmann. He was writing about "ecosystem people" vs "biosphere people." "Ecosystem people" include "all members of indigenous traditional cultures and some who have seceded from, or have been pushed out of, technological society; in the latter are those who are tied in with the global technological civilization." Ecosystem people "are dependent upon that ecosystem for their survival. If they persistently violate its ecological rules, they must necessarily perish."

Biosphere people "draw their support, not from the resources of any one ecosystem, but from the entire biosphere." Biosphere people "can exert incredible pressure upon an ecosystem that they wish to exploit, and create great devastation—something that would be impossible or unthinkable for people who were dependent upon that particular ecosystem." This is the most succinct statement of what place and bioregions are about that you will find anywhere. Toward the end of the article he used the phrase, "future primitive," which came from the essay of the same name, written by Gerry Gorsline and Linn House and printed in Planet Drum.

I was working on my first book, *Earth Festivals*, at the time, so I ordered it from the address, mentioned in the references. I got a reply from Peter Berg, telling me that the bundle, "North Pacific Rim Alive," was out of print but he sent parts of it and xeroxed "future primitive" for me. I later printed it in my second book, *Earth Wisdom*.

The first bundle I got was "Continent Congress" sent out in 1976, the year of the United States Bicentennial Celebration. In his masterful, "Amble Toward Continent Congress," Peter Berg first outlined the horrors of European invasions and then called for a new kind of "congress."

> What's new about the New World is the terrestrial piracy of global monoculture. Massive and inexorable imposition of a roughly unified alien world-view over regions as diverse as South America, Australia and the Pacific Islands—a total area of the Earth's living surface vastly larger than Mother Europe— would follow until the 'unknown' planet was completely under the carpet...Globalism, monoculture, and displacement (human beings bereft of their own and other species) are fatal... There needs to be a Continent Congress so that occupants of North American can finally become inhabitants and find out where they are. (The 1976 Bicentennial Celebration...will be a hollow burp to salute 200 years of mindless gluttony, a travesty on the planet unless it becomes an opportunity to recognize reinhabitation of North America). This time congress is a verb. Con*gress*, come together. Come together with the continent.

Such was Peter Berg's original call, which, for a brief moment seemed to have been validly answered for the land by the North American Bioregional Congress in 1985; but, unfortunately, wasn't. More of that below. Here I want to continue my story of Peter Berg.

The next bundle Planet Drum put out was "Backbone—the Rockies" about my own mountains. By this time I had also seen several books, which Planet Drum put out and I began to wonder who or what is Peter Berg that he can contain so many facets within one human being. In 1981, while staying down on the Monterey Peninsula for a few weeks, I called Peter Berg, hoping to get a chance to talk to him. We arranged to meet during the one hour that he had free on the day I would be in San Francisco.

As it turned out we talked for seven hours. Early on, I asked him what had happened in his life to make him realize the importance of place. His story began back in the fifties when he was a statistician for the American Bankers Association in New York City. He had a house and a car and all the stuff one is "supposed" to have. One day he was riding to work on the subway when he saw a sign. He read: "If you don't know who you are they will tell you." Well he looked again and it didn't say that at all. It was one of those strange, subconscious misreadings. But he thought about it and he realized that he didn't know who he was. So he sold his house and car and quit his job and set out to find out who he really was.

Back in those days you didn't hitchhike; instead you rode the rails. He ended up in the Berkeley freight yards. After a stay in California he wandered on down through Mexico. Way down in a very rural, very poor area he suddenly got extremely ill. He was almost dying by the time a poor Mexican family took him in. They nursed him back to health and tried to teach him how to live there. Rabbits were their main source of protein, but all they had to shoot them was an old muzzle loading gun. He couldn't learn how to shoot it very well at all. In fact he couldn't learn how to do anything right that was needed to live there. "I learned I had no grace at all," Peter said, looking steadily at me. So he figured he had best learn how one lives "with grace" on this earth. He headed back up to San Francisco and finally joined the San Francisco Mime Troupe since he still didn't know who he was.

During the rock festivals in the sixties, Peter and several friends within the Mime Troupe began feeding everyone who needed it as well as taking care of the worst drug freakouts which occurred. They called themselves "the diggers." This part of his story was especially fascinating to me; because during that time, hearing about how "the diggers" took care of everyone I wondered who they were. All I knew was that they must be from California because that's what the Spanish called the California Indians.

Then, at this stage of the conversation, Judy brought out *Living Here*, a little booklet which Planet Drum had sent out a few years back. She asked if I had seen it because it has more about "the diggers." I was delighted to see this again because someone had walked off with my copy long ago. I said, "I've always wanted to know who wrote it because it has the best writing about how it is to live in place that I have ever seen." She said quietly, "Peter did," and gave me the book. I've reprinted the opening page of this great little book below.

The "digger" period ended when Peter realized that all they were doing was just helping the "most damaged" people produced by this IGS. So he took time out to try to figure out what can possibly be done to turn things around so that humans can begin to live again. And he came up with his concept of "reinhabitation of place." Find the place you love enough to fight all the battles necessary to protect all the natural beings and just stay there and do it.

I've related this long story to show that Peter's concept of "reinhabitation of place" is not something just suddenly dreamed up; but that it's the *only* way he could figure out after years of trying all the more usual ways to bring about change in the structure of this society so that it was less damaging to humans and the earth. I have not the space here to cover all the aspects of "reinhabitation" that we talked about that day; instead I will go more into how Planet Drum began: "The real start of Planet Drum was at the 1972 Environmental Conference in Stockholm where there were 10,000 people in the streets from all over the planet: Japanese Minamata disease (mercury poisoning) victims, American hippies, Swedish anarchists, all sorts of folks. They had no forum and no telling way to express their concerns...They were a potential cultural

force for changing the societal definition of the relationship between human beings and the planetary biosphere, but there was no forum for them." The United Nations was not interested. Nation states are no longer valid and neither is "one world."

The main question is: "What are the ways for people living in unique natural places to have a kinship to each other that works and provides them with a forum? Out of that concern came bioregions. Planet Drum promotes the notion of bioregions as the places where people live and bioregionalism as cultural and social regard for those places. Reinhabitation, or becoming native again, is the way to carry out that perspective." Planet Drum's logo is a very different kind of drum than we are familiar with. It's a Samish (Lapp) shaman drum: made out of reindeer hide stretched over walrus ribs. It's a flat round drum with designs painted in various places on the surface. It's played by drawing a piece of reindeer antler across the stretched hide. When the designs begin vibrating you can see the resonance between various events, animals and humans. The essential concept of Planet Drum is that when we each develop our own bioregional culture the living beings—human, plant and animal within one particular bioregion—will resonate in harmony with other similar bioregions on earth and then we will have the harmony of planet earth. One kind of bioregion will resonate with bioregions similar to that one so that there isn't one single monoculture of "whole earthism" but the resonating harmony of many cultures.

In explaining where he got the concept of bioregions, Berg says:

> I had the good luck of running into the work of a planetary ecologist named Raymond F. Dasmann who had just completed an obscure study for an obscure agency called 'Biotic Provinces of the World.' And so I got hold of him and said I think these ideas you're working on are right. There are real 'natural' countries that make up the planetary biosphere. Do we start to planet by identifying the places where we live as biotic provinces—in biological terms rather than geopolitical terms? What we decided together was that in fact you could describe and define real biological entities, geographic entities, but that these biotic provinces were too large and they left people out. Human beings weren't part of them. So we took some of the constituent ideas. A bioregion would be a place that has a continuity of watersheds, river valleys, continuity of landforms, of climate, of native plants and animals, and that had in the past, by at least some people, been defined as a home place. In North America, there were native language areas, for example...those tribal areas are very much described also in climatic, watershed, native plant and animal, landform, soil terms. The ranges of those languages are roughly what we would call bioregions now.

Actually, the first event to use the word "bioregional" took place in April 1979 in San Francisco: "Listening to the Earth: The Bioregional Basis of Community Consciousness." About a thousand people were there. When you walked through the door you located yourself in your home watershed with a pushpin on a map of Northern California.

At first Planet Drum put out "bundles": a bunch of drawings, essays, poetry etc. within a large envelope—all celebrating a particular regional culture. With the growing interest in bioregionalism they began the newspaper, *Raise the Stakes*. The first issues contained the work of individuals, writing about the places where they lived. Then, as the network grew people found others in their place and began to form bioregions. In issues 7, 8 and 9 congresses were developing. "By issue 10, according to Peter Berg, RTS geared up for the first North American Bioregional Congress."

FIRST NORTH AMERICAN BIOREGIONAL CONGRESS

What happened there, unfortunately, was a strong emphasis on 'politics', presicely the narrowly "human centered" way we got into the present destruction of the earth. The OACC (Ozark Area Community Congress) sponsored it and limited most of the activities to a narrow political approach. Fortunately (for me), in writing David Haenke, beforehand, and offering to help set up rituals, I discovered this predilection and did not go. Others were not so fortunate. Ron Rabin of the tree-planting organization, Children of the Green Earth, told me of how difficult it was to get the "authorities" to allow them to do the only public ritual done during the entire congress. This was a tree planting ritual for children and was conducted by Ron and a wonderful human being from Africa, Robert T. Mazibuko who has implemented tree planting there for some time. Others later told me of sneaking around in the early morning, trying to get a small natural ritual done before all the human centered politics began.

Stephen Duplantier, long a member of Planet Drum and part of the group who helped put out one of the original "bundles," "Continent Congress," back in 1976, wrote a very subtle little piece in the NORTH AMERICAN BIOREGIONAL CONGRESS PROCEEDINGS, the book put out by this first bioregional congress. The title of Duplantier's piece is: "What Color is Our Work?" He starts out by pointing out that "Combining 'politics' with 'green-ness' (the color of photosynthesis) is an admirable attempt to put a natural face on the unnatural monster of POLITICS (from *polis*, city, a counter-natural, overwrought and therefore anti-ecological agglomeration of humans which survives by preying off other humans and surrounding ecosystems)." He continues by explaining that there are many other colors in nature: white for fungi, blue for the sky, etc. and vehemently explains that, "These are not trivial questions...If ecology's lesson about the interlocking importance of all the pieces of an ecosystem is not heeded then we are open again to the human mistake of monovalent thinking."

Precisely what is "not trivial" here is that the only way there is to allow other beings into our human councils is by ritual: dance, drum, bardic poetry and ritualized interactions of all kinds. This is what Gary Snyder called for when he was asked to speak at the Center for the Study of Democratic Institutions in Santa Barbara. He said: "This Center—is of the order of a kiva of elders. Its function is to maintain and transmit the lore of the tribe on the highest levels. If it were doing its job completely, it would have a cycle of ceremonies geared to the seasons, geared perhaps to the migration of the fish and to the phases of the moon." Pointing out how animals spoke to people in the ancient cave paintings, he continued:

And when, in the dances of the Pueblo Indians and other peoples, certain individuals became seized, as it were, by the spirit of the deer, and danced as a deer would dance, or danced the dance of the corn maidens, or impersonated the squash blossom, they were no longer speaking for humanity, they were taking it on themselves to interpret, through their humanity, what these other life-forms were. That is about

all we know so far concerning the possibilities of incorporating spokesmanship for the rest of life in our democratic society.

This is the way other beings on this earth can communicate to us—through our moving bodies—not through our narrowly human ego-consciousness (which is all that speaks when we communicate with the words and written papers of human politics).

Here I will end this overly-long introduction by quoting Peter Berg's great "Borne-Native in the San Francisco Bay Region."

We who live around the San Francisco Bay-Sacramento River Estuary, all species ranging this watershed on the North Pacific Rim, feel a common resonance behind the quick beats of our separate lives; long-pulse rhythms of the region pronouncing itself through Winter-wet & Summer-dry, Something-flowering-anytime, Cool Fog, Tremor and Slide.

The region proclaims itself clearly. It declares the space for holding our own distinct celebrations: Whale Migration & Salmon Run, Acorn Fall, Blackberry & Manzanita Fruit, Fawn Drop, Red Tide; processions and feasts which invite many other species, upon which many other species depend. The bayriver watershed carries these outpourings easily. They are borne, native, by the place. their occurrence and the full life of the region are inseperable.

Human beings have lived here a long time. For thousands of years, the region held their celebrations easily. They ate enormous quantities of shellfish, acorns, salmon, berries, deer, buckeyes, grass seeds, and duck eggs. They cut countless tule reeds for mats, boats and baskets, burned over thousands of acres of dead grass, made trails everywhere, cleared land and packed down soil with villages. They netted fish from boats, strung fish traps across creeks and rivers, and dug up tidelands looking for oysters. The region probably never held a species that had a greater effect upon it, but for thousands of years human beings were part of its continuous life. They lived directly in it, native.

Bioregions

A bioregion can be defined as "a geographical area linked by particular plant, animal, soil and climatic characteristics and by the human influences that bear on that region." This is a much more natural way to define areas on the earth. As Raymond Dasmann remarked: "In the United States we are cursed with state and county boundaries drawn with straight edges by people who did not know the land. Would it not make more sense to re-orient them toward ecological realities." If we were to begin thinking this way, according to Dasmann, "many serious land use blunders" could be avoided. When people try to transplant land-use practices developed within one biotic province to another vastly different biotic province the land is seriously damaged. The knowledge of how the plants and animals respond in one set of climatic conditions makes for a sense of identity to that place. According to Peter Berg, it "refers both to geographical terrain and a terrain of consciousness—to a place and the ideas that have developed about how to live in that place...there is a distinct resonance among living things and the factors which influence them that occurs specifically within each separate place on the planet. Discovering and describing that resonance is a way to describe a bioregion."

Jung's work with the collective unconscious adds even

more depth to this statement of Peter Berg's. Way back in 1927, Jung wrote:

> Just as, in the process of evolution, the mind has been moulded by earthly conditions, the same process repeats itself under our eyes today…he who is rooted in the soil endures. Alienation from the unconscious and from its historical conditions spells rootlessness. That is the danger that lies in wait for every individual who, through one-sided allegiance to any kind of -ism, loses touch with the dark maternal, earthy ground of his being.

Bioregional living in Peter Berg's view, means "learning to live-in-place in an area that has been disrupted and injured through past exploitation. It involves becoming native to a place through becoming aware of the particular ecological relationships that operate in and around it. It means undertaking activities involving social behavior that will enrich the life of that place, restore its life-supporting systems, and establish an ecologically and socially sustainable pattern of existence within it. Simply stated, it involves applying for membership in a biotic community and ceasing to be its exploiter."

But what about how to "make a living" in the place where you want to live? Berg says that "Reinhabitory consciousness can multiply the opportunities for employment within the bioregion. New reinhabitory livelihoods based on exchanging information, cooperative planning, administering exchanges of labor and tools…and watershed media emphasizing bioregional rather than city-consumer information could replace a few centralized positions with many decentralized ones. The goals of restoring and maintaining watersheds, topsoil, and native species invite the creation of many jobs to simply un-do the bioregional damage that the invader society has already done." He points out: "Jobs that require annihilating living things or manufacturing monotonous garbage breed self-contempt. Constant exposure to other people or television without an opening into the naturally evolving graces of the planet is oppressive and demeaning. There is a feeling that one's life is being used up…Connections with perpetuating sources of all life are lost and replaced with an all-pervasive doubt whether society can control its ultimately destructive course."

Gary Snyder says that the bioregional movement is an "effort to become aware in place and to have a clear sense of where we are. The psychological side is 'who am I?' The bioregional side is 'where am I?' Who? and Where? are not such different questions…It's a more concrete and personal sense of relationship to the whole of your surrounding terrain and the mutuality that exists in it than people in this country, with their high mobility, tend to feel." The bioregional program is "first, don't move. Find a place to live, live there, take responsiblity for where you live, learn what's going on there and become involved, both in terms of human politics and in terms of natural politics…You can't make a culture if you don't stay put."

THE SECOND NORTH AMERICAN BIOREGIONAL CONGRESS

Peter Berg began Planet Drum way back in 1974. All of us who have been involved with the bioregional concept for a long time, initially felt that the first North American Bioregional Congress would continue the direction which

Planet Drum had pioneered. Instead, as mentioned above, it went the narrowly human political direction. The reason for responses ranging from stunned disbelief to outrage is that we finally were beginning to allow the non-human beings of each place to have a say in human decisions about that place and then, suddenly, we find ourselves right back in the anthropocentric trap.

NABC II was held in Michigan in the summer of 1986. Although the preliminary information, seemed to imply an attempt to let the other beings in; apparently that's not what happened to any great degree. I am relying here on letters from people in different bioregions, most of whom I've never met but who have been ordering books from me for some time. Amy Hannon of the Katúah bioregion, wrote about travelling to NABC with David Abram and continued: "At the conference we found ourselves dissatisfied with the various committees for their neglect of the creatures and formed a new committee: M.A.G.I.C. (Madcap animism, geomancy and Inter-Species Communication). David carried this off in most elegant fashion." Hopefully, with so many good people beginning their own bioregions the situation will continue to improve and we, humans will find ways to include more and more of the non-human beings in our councils.

CONCERNING THE BOOK, *DWELLERS IN THE LAND*

The other treatment of bioregionalism on the national level was Kirkpatrick Sale's *Dwellers in the Land: Bioregional Vision*. It was most surprising to find in this book only two one-line references to Peter Berg and Planet Drum along with the use of the word "bundles" on page 160 with no reference at all. But this didn't bother me nearly as much as the overall general attitude of here's another way for us humans to do it. Particularly unsettling was his approval of a new bioregional industry: making parquet floors out of mesquite in Texas. He says that Max's Pot was trying to find some use for the mesquite trees growing so freely in the savanna of the Colorado River that "they are regularly eradicated as a weed."

Finding that mesquite parquet floors are produced in Argentina, Max's Pot began a similar industry. The trouble with this is that mesquite seeds were a prime food for all the native peoples in those areas. Desert areas are not so loaded with natural food for humans that we can afford to use them as the base for a bioregional small-scale industry. Feeding us humans in a marginal area is the first consideration if we are trying to "reinhabit" a bioregion. Water is the prime factor and mesquite, of course, grows natually there. Of course someone is sure to remark that the present Industrial Growth Society is regularly eradicating them as weeds. Further, I know that pinon (the prime food for other natives throughout the Southwest) is regularly chained, ripped out by the roots, and burned by the BLM to increase grazing for cattle. But that fact doesn't make it any less important for us to find a way to help people begin using such important food plants for food instead of for consumer goods.

This matter of indigenous, local food in each bioregion is not trivial either; instead it's an essential part of living there, validly. For instance, the famous anthropologist, Ruth Benedict, writing about a chief of the Californian Digger Indians reports:

One day, without transition, Ramon broke in upon his description of grinding mesquite and preparing acorn soup. 'In the beginning,' he said, 'God gave to every people a cup, a cup of clay, and from this cup they drank their life. .They all dipped in the water,' he continued, 'but their cups were different. Our cup is broken now. It has passed away.'

Our cup is broken. Those things that have given significance to the life of his people, the domestic rituals of eating, the obligations of the economic system, the succession of ceremonials in the villages, possession in the bear dance, their standards of right and wrong— these were gone, and with them the shape and meaning of life. The old man was still vigorous and a leader in relationships with the whites. He did not mean that there was any extinction of his people. But he had in mind the loss of something that had *value equal to that of life itself*, the whole fabric of his people's standards and beliefs.

This was in 1934 and now, of course, the entire culture is gone. But what we are trying to do, now, in the bioregional movement is begin, once more, to "live-in-place" as native peoples all over the world once did. In the fall issue of *The Permaculture Activist*, in the bulletin board section, David Bainbridge wants information because he "is making a concerted effort to reintroduce acorns to the American food system." He is looking for sweet, flavorful ones. He lists the scientific name for the best he's found but is still looking for better ones. He says: "Remember to mark the tree clearly if you find it— nothing like trying to find the landmark oak again in a big forest." He would like to hear from people who would collect acorns for sale. This is a step in the right direction.

It's not that *Dwellers in the Land* is all that bad; it's just that it's totally misleading. I'm sure Kirkpatrick Sale thought he was doing a good thing, but to anchor bioregionalism right back down in the narrowly humanistic trap does no service to the land. Michael Helm, in his review for Planet Drum's *Raise the Stakes*, says it so well: "Whoa! What Kirk Sale has done here is take the idea of bioregionalism, mat down its cowlick, put it in its Sunday best Greek clothes and make it intellectually *respectable*." But, as Helm says, we don't need that kind of book. "What we need are working stories that challenge and extend our multi-species identity, that tell of the struggle we face daily, that add to the dream and the mystery. The trouble with Sale's book is that it is finally too *humanist* to be exciting anymore."

Power points and sacred land within your own bioregion

In the last few years there has been a number of articles and books about geographical places designated as power points: the general idea being that either some kind of occult knowledge is necessary to find such places or only the ancient peoples were capable of locating them. Actually, any group of people truly inhabiting an area over a period of time, will begin to recognize the power points within their own area. You recognize power points by the effect they have on your body and/or mind as you move through your own area with "attention," over a period of years. This is how the chimps, as well as prehominids and early humans all over the earth recognized such spots, originally. Just begin to pay attention in your own place and compare your feelings with others who care about the place and you will soon notice a general consensus. The geophysical reasons for power points are many: sometimes it's the crossing of two fault lines below the surface; sometimes it has to do with the pressure of rocks on one another. Most rock has some quartz in it. The molecular structure of quartz is spiral and it is piezo-electric. "That is, it expands slightly if given a slight charge of electricity. If placed under pressure—as it would be if charged while inside another stone—alternate edges of its prism give off positive and negative voltages on what can reach a dramatic scale: a force of 1,000 pounds applied on each face of a half-inch crystal of quartz creates 25,000 volts." Some of the effects at places such as Stonehenge result from the minute quantities of electricity generated by the pressure of a large mass of rock placed across the two support rocks. (See *Earth Wisdom,* pages 3 to 30 for more information.)

FENG SHUI

Tai Chi is the best way of all to sense the power of particular spots. While doing Tai Chi one becomes so sensitized to the earth itself that I presume it was used by the early *feng shui* practitioners long ago in China. This word is generally translated as wind and water. It consists of siting houses and tombs according to the energy patterns of the land itself. The compass was developed in China hundreds of years before Europe by *feng shui* experts, not for sea-going navigation but "for determining the indications of the topography." It was a very sophisticated system but there are great gaps in our knowledge concerning it because in 1602, the Italian Jesuit, Matteo Ricci, converted to Christianity, Li Ying-Shih, a distinguished scholar particularly skilled in geomancy, (as the European translators called it). Ricci burned all Li Ying-Shih's books because he considered the geomantic art "diabolical," according to Needham. Needham proceeds to quote Ricci's account of the burning:

> He had a rather good library and it took him three full days to purge it of books on subjects prohibited by our (churchly) laws, books which were very numerous, especially on divinatory arts, and the most part in manuscript, collected with the greatest assiduity and expense. So at this time, all of these, amounting to three trunks full, were committed to the flames, either in his own courtyard or publicly outside our own house.

Needham reports that some of this geomantic art became merely superstitious but "the system as a whole undoubtedly contributed to the exceptional beauty of positioning of farmhouses, manors, villages and cities throughout the realm of Chinese culture." In Reference Notes, I list some of the better books to consult on Chinese geomancy.

It's interesting that the Oxford dictionary defines geomancy as "divining from throwing a handful of earth out and seeing how the patterns go." Rather than trying to learn about ancient geomancy, it's much more effective to begin to pay attention to the patterns of the land in your own place and live accordingly.

CONCERNING SACRED LAND IN YOUR OWN BIOREGION

"Sacred land" need not necessarily be at the same site as power points. Sacred land involves a much deeper and more inclusive relationship between the humans and the land. Often I refer to sacred land in my own place in terms of such dramatic things as steep mountains or deep snow. That is the nature of mountains. But for each bioregion there will be other forms of sacred land.

For many years, when I lived part of each year in Washington state, I took my son and other boys to Shi Shi Beach on the Olympic Peninsula. This was before it was "discovered" in the mid-sixties and we usually had it to ourselves. This is certainly "sacred" land. Everyone who visits it agrees. In fact, after it was "discovered" someone carved a plank pulled out of the ocean with the words "Don't look back" at the top of the trail. If you did stop to look back here, it was extremely difficult to walk away. What saves it from developers is the fact that it has several hundred inches of rain a year. This wild beach is neither dangerous nor mountainous but it is definitely sacred. One other place, just as sacred, is the Ventana Wilderness behind the Big Sur coast in California. Again, it's not real mountains; it's more like hills; but these hills consist of very steep grass, dropping down in some places 5000 ft. straight to the water below. I love Jaime de Angulo's description of this country. He's writing about walking along a trail on these steep grass slopes, and says that when you take a step "one foot is on the trail and the other foot, 5000 ft. above the Pacific ocean." One can live in the mountains here where I do very well without a tribe, but I would never want to live either on Shi Shi Beach or in the Ventana Wilderness without a tribe. Each of these places is so powerful that to live there very long, one needs to know the ceremonies of the long lost tribes to feel at home. Again, quoting Jaime: "How can a thing be so wild that it is so full of life and charming variety, of young trees and deer grazing in the gay clearings, of the chatter of bluejays, and the red trunks of the madronyos. And yet it is so wild in there that you cry with the loneliness of it. You feel a creeping panic in your heart. Perhaps it is because we are civilized and do not understand these things. We have other gods, and we can no longer pray to the tree."

I do not know the answer for the Ventana Wilderness either. But I do know that if you live deeply enough in a place you love and do the ceremonies long enough, the land there teaches you. Thus you will discover the powerful places in your own bioregion. Furthermore, I can guarantee that if you and your children begin doing the "fly as birds" pilgrimage, as given in chapter eleven, by the time these children grow up and have their own children that place will truly be sacred.

In the next section, I will discuss setting up structures to begin to learn from the earth itself in your own place. Before I do that I want to go into the matter of what physically constitutes a bioregion. Often it is a watershed: the area drained by a particular river or system of rivers. Sometimes it is a plateau or a valley or a particular stretch of land along the ocean. Occasionally, it is a point where the climate definitely changes. A few years ago, at a preliminary meeting to begin to define a bioregion along the Front Range here in Colorado, everyone in the room agreed that the climate along the Front Range changed radically at a point called Monument Hill between Denver and Colorado Springs. At this point there is no big mountain; it's just a hill. But during the winter, on one side there will be reasonable weather and on the other, a blizzard. Such a place provides a definite boundary for a bioregion.

Another important point in locating your bioregional boundaries: don't be confused by the lines on the map of states, counties or countries, either for that matter. For example, many people talk about the "four corners area" here in the West. They try to give it standing as a natural unit. Of course it's not that at all. It's merely where the lines drawn for four states meet. If you knew the history behind the political in-fighting here, you would hardly take where these lines meet seriously. To find out some of the outrageous battles between mining interests, politicians, cattle ranchers etc. that caused this "four corners" read David Lavender's book, *The Southwest*.

The real bioregions in this area have to do with the San Francisco peaks in Arizona, which produce much of the water in the area; or the San Juan River that drains into the Colorado; or the drainage of the Rio Grande, which eventually goes into the Gulf of Mexico; or the San Juan or San Miguel Mountains. These are the powerful entities that formed the life of the ancient peoples. If we begin once more to do the necessary ceremonies they will weave our present-day lives into the fabric of sacred land just as they did for the "old ones" here in the Southwest:

Then weave for us a garment of brightness:
May the warp be the white light of morning,
May the weft be the red light of evening.
May the fringes be the standing rainbow.
Thus weave for us a garment of brightness.
That we may walk fittingly where birds sing.
That we may walk fittingly where the grass is green.
Oh our Mother the Earth, Oh our Father, the Sky.
                                    Tewa chant

"Ask yourself, how would you tell people where you live so that they could find your house without mentioning a street name, a road name, a town, a country, or a state. When you've figured out how to describe where you live, you've made the first step in bioregional awareness. You see the place you live, city or country, with fresh eyes for a moment, not just a counter on a political map, but a map on an incredibly old, slowly changing land form with the ebb and flow of different plant, animal, and human communities following climate changes. Then you see yourself and society as a tiny part of that, and you might say to yourself, 'Ah, this is the story I'm really in, not the one in the newspaper or on the TV.' That's when life starts getting interesting."

Gary Snyder

PART III: SETTING UP STRUCTURES FOR LAND RITUALS

Introduction

How can we begin to reweave the fabric of our broken, fragmented world? The first step is to fully acknowledge that we humans can't do it. The Tewa Chant, above, asks that the greater beings of our place do it for us: the white light of morning, the red light of evening and the rainbow; therefore, the first step is to set up structures which will invite the changing light of the sun or the moon or the storm or the sudden clearing; the light of the different seasons; and the various animals or plants that come with those seasons in each place. Once we do this, we begin to recognize the relationship between nature within us, the "inscape" and nature outside of us, the landscape. By ritual use of these structures through the seasons we begin to discover that there's no one thing that causes everything else; we find that truly everything in the bioregion is interrelated. The entire bioregion is a single organism or, in Needham's words, "the web that has no weaver." All beings in the bioregion follow their own pattern laid out for them by the climate-season-landforms-water etc. of the place. But by following that greater pattern (*li*), they develop most fully and thus they follow their own individual *li* as well.

FOUR USEFUL STEPS IN
BEGINNING TO CELEBRATE NATURE RITUALS

1) Always allow a natural being to set the time for your celebrations. A good way to do this is to begin the celebration at sunset or moonrise or at the equinoxes or solstices. This procedure allows natural beings to take part in our human decision making.

2) When the group of people gathers together for the first time to do a nature ritual do not have them give their names or interests or occupations as an introduction; instead have them all sit down on the ground or, if inside, on the floor in a circle. Beginning with yourself, as "one" and the next person as "two," the following person as "one" and the next person after her is "two." Continue this counting all the way around the circle. When the ritual introduction begins, all the "ones" turn to the person on their right and all the "twos" turn to the person on their left and the introduction proceeds within these couples only, because it takes time for each person to fully tell their own "story." This procedure is set up ahead of time so that there is no possibility of confusion which might cause them to become "stuck" in the human mode when the next step occurs.

In the ancient Greek mysteries a person was considered "one who knows" if they had done certain ritual actions; furthermore, this ritual action was their introduction to the others in the group. For example: "I have eaten from the drum" or "I have drunk from the ram's horn." This type of introduction establishes, from the beginning, a ritual connection between each person and nature.

Each person tells the story of a particular time in his or her own life when a natural being "spoke" to them. I often tell of the wind in Capitol Reef. We were camped in a shallow depression on top of a sandstone cliff. Our sleeping bags were laid out and the tent was up, when we heard the wind roaring up the face of the cliff. Taking a rope along, we walked over to the edge, tied ourselves to the only large tree there and then leaned over. The wind "took us." The force of the wind rushing up that cliff was so great that there was no room for fear or wonder—it just enveloped us in deep chords of majestic sound; then it swirled us round until we were breathless, dropped us and roared on up higher toward the sky and we roared back with glee. Then another surge of wind came and lifted us again. It was a storm front coming in and, although it was April in the desert, it snowed later that night. During a lull in the wind we untied and crawled back along the sandstone to our sheltered tent. Thus, "I have spoken with the wind" is my ritual phrase.

Have each person in the couple turn toward the other and tell of a time in their life when a natural being encountered them on its terms. This procedure immediately lifts the occasion out of the merely human realm. I have found, later, that people have been "allowed" for the first time in their life to tell of something that has always been very important for them but not recognized in our normal culture.

3) After a group has been celebrating natural rituals for a time you should begin figuring out who the group is in relation to a natural entity. You will become "People of the Wind" or "People of the Forest" or "Wolf People." This helps develop the group bonding by focusing around something in nature they can relate to as a whole group. Then, later when two or more groups get together for a seasonal ritual or a Hako type ritual, each group is distinct but without the hubris of a merely human relationship. This type of relationship is called totemism. As a group becomes more identified with their natural totem they become more aware of its place in the bioregion and what it does for them and, at the same time they become more dedicated to preserving it.

4) Early on be sure your group also begins relating to the "Trickster" of your bioregion or place. In the Great Plains, the Great Basin, the Colorado Plateau, the Southwest, and California he is "Coyote." In the Northwest he is "Raven" or "Mink"; but in a small area in Washington he is "Bluejay." Among the ancient Algonkian Indians he was the "Hare." The importance of the "Trickster" figure for us is that he helps us get out of our European "tragic hero" complex.

Much destruction of the land comes from a human being who has a great "idea" and carries it through like a real hero no matter what the cost to himself or those around him or to nature. We got the "tragic hero" from the Greeks and still follow that mode. Most cultures in the world never had a tragic hero; only comic or picaresque heroes. They sneak around the edges and get things done without much damage and they are always humorous.

These four basic steps should help you get out of our limited human consciousness as you begin moving toward nature rituals and ceremonies. Paul Shepard explains, "Place to Australian aborigines...is continuous with the identity structure of the adult. It is imbedded there as a result of a combination of daily life and formal ceremony during the first fifteen to twenty years of life." This was true of most hunter-gatherer cultures and other traditional cultures as well. In fact, for the Hopi, *Techwa Ikachi*, meaning "Land and Life," is their greatest god.

"Medicine wheels reflect the delicate problem of keeping a human community in accord with the rhythmic order of the universe."

Joseph Campbell

General Background on the Medicine Wheel

I have been using Medicine Wheels and henges for fourteen years. I first realized the importance of the Medicine Wheel from the book, *Seven Arrows*.

I began using the concept first with children and later with adults. The more I used it; the more I learned of its depth. I will go into this more in the section on The Way of the Medicine Wheel, below. Using this concept, I began to realize some of the deeper learnings involved in henges and, eventually began using them.

Even before the time of the early humans, the higher apes made use of forest clearings for their meetings. Humans first used clearings in forests; but in later times as these forests were cut down, they met in "sacred groves": remnants of the original forest, preserved by the fact that their ceremonies were held there. With the advent of big civilizations and more tree cutting, most of the groves were destroyed. Then, in Greece, for instance, they set up wooden pillars to define the sacred area. Finally this became the carved marble pillars of Greek temples. It is important to remember that Greek temples were not merely enclosures to focus attention on the god inside; but also, to line up the human observer's view between the posts so that it focused on the distant landscape—mountain or sea—the real god.

In China, temples were always sited in groves of trees; but care was taken that a few trees always remained. This is why there are still gingko trees in the world. The gingko is actually a very ancient form of tree. There are none left in the wild: the only remaining ones were found around temples. They have now been propagated and their use has spread to other parts of the world. In Japan, to this day, you will always see a few immense old cryptomeria trees around Shinto shrines. These giant trees are the only ones remaining from the time, long ago, when most of Japan was forested.

Most rituals depend on a laying out of sacred time and space. Sacred time often has to do with solstices and equinoxes and the phases of the moon. The word, temple, can be traced back to the Greek word, *temnos*, to cut off a sacred area. In Latin, this became the word *templum* (space) which has come down to us in the words, template and tempus, meaning time. From all these interlocking meanings we can see that the word, temple, can refer to both sacred space and sacred time. An understanding of these concepts achieved through ritual, focuses energy on the place itself, as deliminated by land and sky. In many cultures the sacred space at the center of their "world" had an opening upward toward the heavens and another opening downward to the underworld and the world of "the ancestors."

Such a space is a centering point and a vertical axis. In different cultures it has been referred to by such terms as: the world mountain, Mt. Meru, the Ziggurat, Jacob's Ladder, the maypole, the shaman's pole or the sundance pole. Both stone circles and temples were further developments of the original sacred pole. In the central spot a pole was driven into the ground. A rope was tied to it and a circle marked off by holding the rope taut and walking around the pole. The pole was also a gnomon for a sundial and its shadow falling across the circle at dawn and sunset gave east and west. From each of these two points, east and west, an arc was drawn to form what the Hindus call a "fish" and the Christians, the "sign of Christ."

FEAR OF WILDERNESS

Some people have the illusion that simply by taking humans out into the wilderness they will "see" the beauty and realize the importance of saving the environment. This is nonsense. When the pioneers first came here it was "natural." The Indians had never destroyed it in their thousands of years of occupation. Yet the whites "feared" it until they could "tame the wilderness" by destroying it. This European fear of the wilderness, induced by the centuries long Christian attitude toward wilderness as the abode of the devil, still exists.

In the spring of 1986, the *Wall Street Journal* printed an article by a staff reporter who went on a camping trip in the Gros Ventre Wilderness in Wyoming's Bridger-Teton National Forest. His article was on the controversy surrounding Getty Oil's efforts to drill there. He described himself as a flabby 50-year old who had always done his sightseeing in the West from a car. Since his guide was a local person trying to save the wilderness from exploitation the reporter tried to see it from both his view and his guide's view. He was honest enough to describe some of his deep feelings about the place.

One day this reporter wandered alone among the small lakes. He was struck by the intimidation he felt in the wilderness. The dizzying dropoffs that surrounded him on the mountain summits, the deep silences and the high, piercing sounds of night winds across the granite cliffs—all of these made him uneasy.

> He decides that that is because he is of no importance whatsoever here. Down below, his entire world is tailored to fit his convenience; he sees accomodations to his humanity everywhere he looks, and he takes them all for granted, like the lord he is in that country. But the Gros Ventre doesn't accomodate him in a single way. It doesn't care whether he is hot or cold or even whether he lives or dies. It goes about its mighty works with an overwhelming indifference to the tiny, ridiculous figure that has come to see them. So a last purpose for wilderness: it teaches humility.

This fear of the wilderness probably accounts for some of the "sheer vindictiveness" of the politicians, newspaper editors, civic boosters, and civil servants who positively hate the wilderness and its defenders.

I have found that the more a person fears to look at the depths within his own self, the more afraid that person is of the "wilderness" outside. This is true both in climbing and in river running. When a breakthrough does occur: when the person learns through ritual to trust nature there's always a breakthrough on the inner level as well. This is why such events are always accompanied by such gratitude and joy. As I mentioned before, one of the reasons I began doing rituals is to set it up so that people who are unable or unwilling to endure the so-called hardships of travel in nature can have a similar experience. We don't need to take them out into the wilderness; they can experience the real wilderness inside them through ritual when done outside in nature in their own place.

IMPORTANCE OF RITUAL IN SAVING NATURE

This brings me to the last important point I want to make here about ritual structures. If you truly love the natural beings of your place you have no choice about ritual. You must begin to set it up in some way in order to save the nature you love. Today, there are too many people in the world and too few bits of nature left anywhere. I'm not talking about wilderness now; I'm talking about trees, bushes, birds and animals in any bioregion. The Industrial Growth Society is set up to consume and use up all resources. But a ritual experience of nature can turn that right around because it operates on such deep levels. I have seen real changes in the lives of many people accomplished by ritualized experiences in nature. Of course, these people then have to quit their fancy jobs; sometimes sell their big houses; often get a divorce. But there's no confusion in their minds any longer about where the real values are. The one thing we have on our side in our efforts to save a piece of real nature is that deep down inside us, we are still the "original human." That "original human" can be reached quite suddenly and sometimes with only minimal ritual out in nature.

GENERAL USE OF MEDICINE WHEELS AND HENGES

Forms of medicine wheels and henges have been used by humans from the Paleolithic—20,000 years ago; no one race of human being has any monopoly on these forms. Such structures are essential for beginning a sacred relationship to nature because they are mandalas—even more important for nature than myth. "Whereas the myth tends to master the world man encounters by relating the objects of the world—be they personal, material, or conceptual—to one another in temporal terms, that is, by narrating how this or that came about, the mandala relates the things in the world—in all its spheres and layers—to one another in spatial terms." Medicine wheels are essentially mandalas; thus, in using the medicine wheel one can physically see and feel how all the natural beings in your bioregion relate to you.

Concerning myth itself, it has finally been recognized by scholars that myth, too, comes out of the land itself. Kaiser states: "the formation of myths is connected to the geographical conditions which a people encounter...the mythic representations of people are bound up with their experience of the landscape." This is of the utmost importance for bioregional people; because, many "experts" on myths erroneously state that particular myths have the same meaning for everyone regardless of where they live; therefore the place itself is not particularly important to our psychic life.

Returning to the concept of the mandala, the Sanskrit word mandala means "circle." It has three basic properties: a center, symmetry, and cardinal points. The center is the human centering herself or himself within the total surroundings of place; while the cardinal points are fundamental in almost every traditional human culture. For example, here on our continent, the Sioux, Black Elk explained to his biographer,

Neihardt, about "the sacredness of having the four directions meet in his body."

CONCERNING MYTH IN PLACE-ORIENTED CULTURES

[Y]ou're going by in a car, going by a mesa (faces west and gestures to the right) with pink and yellow stripes of sandstone and about 300 ft. up the side of it there's a cave up there.

You're going along with a Zuni and the Zuni says '*That's the cave, you remember that story about Aatoshle ogress that's the cave where she lived when that little girl wandered into her cave to spend the night.*

Right there.'

Or going by another mesa a little farther down the road on the left side (faces west and gestures to the left) the one where the people went during the world flood, it's about oh, 500, 600 ft. above the surrounding counryside.

That's where the people went during the world flood those stripes those stripes on the side of the mesa are the rings the water left as it went down...

Right there that's the place.

This is Dennis Tedlock, telling about travelling with Zunis in New Mexico. He continues: "So that begins to give you a sense of what place means in stories...So I hope you begin to get the picture here that myth is coming to the surface all the time whenever you happen to look for it.

They're looking for it all the time it's a whole habit of life.

It's what it means to be continuously and every day and in this moment always connected up with the whole past."

For at least a hundred thousand years human beings performed an annual seasonal ritual. This was the hunter-gatherer, nomadic journey through their bioregion—the food trek. From their ancestors and the animals and plants they had learned precisely the right time of the year to be in a certain spot—perhaps to pick ripe melons or to gather monongo nuts (if they were the Kalahari on their 11,000 year old ritual journey). The Sioux, Vine Deloria, says that his ancestors knew to begin their journey back to their winter place when a certain flower bloomed in the foothills of the Rocky Mountains.

CIRCUMAMBULATING AROUND
SACRED MOUNTAINS AND ROCKS

Some cultures made special ritual journeys of many miles simply to circumambulate, "walk around," a "sacred" natural land feature. This is still done by pilgrims from India who journey hundreds of miles and then begin the arduous trek around Mt. Kailas, the most sacred mountain in the Himalayas.

Turning to the European/Near Eastern heritage, there is the city of Jerusalem, now cluttered each year with "tourists," not real pilgrims, from many different religions. All of this began with "The Rock"—the top of what is now called Mt. Moriah, but was formerly called Temple Mount. This rock could be seen from far out in the surrounding area and impressed wandering tribes with its power. Later peoples were equally impressed so that some of the most important myths of these organized religions were located in this spot. Here is where Abraham was about to sacrifice his son, Isaac to please his god, Yahweh; when Yahweh told him that he could kill a goat instead. Abraham, patriarch of the Jewish religion, became equally important to the Christians when the Christian religion developed out of the Jewish prophets. Moslems consider Abraham as the "Patriarch Prophet of God." In fact

Mohammed himself is associated with "the Rock": "On the summit of Mt. Moriah is the Noble Rock from which the Prophet, at God's command, ascended to Heaven after his nocturnal journey from Mecca to Jerusalem...God through his emissary the Archangel Gabriel one night summoned the Prophet to journey from Mecca to Jerusalem." (The journey was made on a winged mare named Al Buraq.) "On reaching Jerusalem, the Prophet prayed along with the prophets of the past, including Abraham, Moses and Jesus, at the place where the Dome of the Rock now stands. Accompanied by Gabriel, he then rose from the Noble Rock up a stairway of light and through the seven stages of Heaven. Finally...before the Divine Presence...received instructions for himself and for the followers of Islam. The Prophet then returned to the Rock and again mounting the mare was returned to Mecca by dawn. It was toward Jerusalem that Moslems first turned their faces in prayer." Only later, "after another of the Prophet's revelations," did they turn toward Mecca.

When the Moslems first got control of Jerusalem they built a simple wooden mosque on the rock; later Caliph Omar built the first big mosque on the sight. It grew more sumptuous and, at one time, the outer dome was gilded in gold. "With exacting design the four main portals of the shrine are oriented precisely to the points of the compass, with the south entrance facing Mecca...Enclosed and protected within its walls is the Noble Rock, an immense, solid mass of stone that looms with impressive grandeur in the dim light." The original dome was destroyed by an earthquake; the new one is now covered with golden aluminum.

Mecca itself, the goal of pilgrimage for all good Moslems is *the sacred place* because of the Kaaba shrine; built around the famous "black stone," which is a meteorite. To this day devout Moslems perform the ritual circumambulation around the sacred stone. Of course earlier traditional cultures, long before the Moslems, also ritually circled this "sacred" black stone.

Much has been written about the famous Megalithic monuments in Europe, but it is not as well known that this Megalithic culture which probably began in Asia Minor spread across the Mediterranean to Africa, along the southern shore of Asia; up the northeastern seacoast and over to Alaska, Japan and the islands of the Southwest Pacific. Everywhere it spread the people built stone monuments; often just a ring of stones; but, sometimes the rock was so inspiring that they built great structures. As Jaquetta Hawkes explains: "It was only because the blocks were there that the religious architects of the Bronze Age were able to build Avebury and Stonehenge on such a magnificent scale. With their rough tools and tackle they were capable of shaping the blocks, of moving and raising them, in itself an astonishing feat, but they could hardly have detached them from solid rock." These are the famous sarsen stones. The country people in later times felt that these rocks seemed strange because they were hard angular rocks lying here and there on top of the soft yielding curves of chalk; they called them sarsen after the Saracens which they fought in the Crusades. These stones now lie on the surface of the downs, the hardest fragments surviving from a layer which once covered the chalk but which has been worn away. These great grey rocks "afforded" the Megalithic peoples the opportunity to build their holy rock circles.

"*Inyan*—the rocks—are holy," Lame Deer said. "Every man needs a stone to help him...Deep inside you there must be an awareness of the rock power, of the spirits in them, otherwise you would not pick them up and fondle them as you do." For the Oglala Sioux, one of the four powers which together are called *Wakan tanka* (sometimes translated "The Great Spirit) is "the Rock" which *was* even before earth's creation and is the oldest of all. Natural rock monoliths in the Sioux country are the emblems of Inyan, the Rock. Standing Rock in South Dakota and *Inyan Kara*, which the white man named "Devil's Tower," in Wyoming, are two of these "sacred" rocks.

The power of the Rock is chanted in this Omaha tribal chant:

> Verily, one alone of all these was the greatest,
> Inspiring to all mind,
> The great white rock,
> Standing and reaching as high as the heavens,
> enwrapped in mist,
> Verily as high as the heavens.
>
> He! Aged one,
> You Rock!
> Aged One,
> He! Unmoved from time without end, truly
> You sit
> In the midst of the various paths of the coming
> winds
> In the midst of the winds you sit
> Aged one...
> He! This is the desire of your little ones
> That of your strength they shall partake
> Therefore your little ones desire to walk closely by
> your side
> Venerable one!

Simon Ortiz, the great Acoma poet tells us that these great Rock Gods are still with us in these few lines from his poem, "Having Left Round Rock":

> those gods standing solid forever
>   since millions of years no one ever considers
> anymore

and then later in the poem, after someone questions him about how in the world anyone could possibly live out here in this "stone beaten by wind and sun," he writes:

> i look at the rearview mirror
> and the gods are standing solid
> and to the side toward monument valley more gods
> these people here in the dancing heat
> they see gods coming out of the earth
> like the First People.

The aborigines in Australia don't explain at all they just say: "You see that rock? It has power." Always these traditional peoples are either circling around their rock or dancing before their rock so that they partake of the power of the rock. That is why today, we build a medicine wheel of rocks so that we, too, may begin to learn the power of rock and what it teaches us about our relationship to the rest of nature.

USES OF THE MEDICINE WHEEL ON OUR CONTINENT

The inspiration for much of the present-day use of the

medicine wheel comes directly from the Cheyenne, H. Storm's book, *Seven Arrows*. The living record of the traditional Indian use of the medicine wheel is in the Bighorn Montains of Wyoming at 8700 feet, just above timberline on a flat-topped shoulder of Medicine Mountain. It is a roughly circular shape, about 74 to 80 feet in diameter, "outlined by white and cream-colored limestone slabs." The largest diameter is 87 feet; "only slightly smaller than that of the large sarsen ring of Stonehenge." From the small circle in the center, there are many straight lines of rocks leading out to the rim of the larger circle. Then outside the main circle there are rock cairns. Dr. John Eddy, a solar astronomer at the High Altitude Observatory of NCAR in Boulder, discovered the alignments of these cairns. One spoke of the wheel extends past the rim for thirteen feet and ends in a small cairn. "The view from the cairn...across the center of the central cairn, and on to a low ridge to the northeast coincides with the direction of summer solstice sunrise." In other words the particular spot where the sun reaches its northernmost rising point on the horizon. Other cairns mark the sun's rising point on the equinoxes: when the sun rises exactly east and sets exactly west.

Krupp states that there are at least 50 medicine wheels and related stuctures. "Nearly all are found on the east flanks of the Rockies or on the open plains below; most are in the north, on the grassy prairies of Canada. Some wheels seem to be only a few centuries old; others are very ancient." The Majorville Cairn in Alberta, Canada is now dated at 4,500 years old; "making it about the same age as the pyramids of Giza," in Egypt.

The other famous medicine wheel, located on Moose Mountain in Saskatchewan, has been dated back to around 440 B.C.

Medicine Wheels were used by only a minority of the Indian cultures on this continent. Instead, many traditional people throughout the world lived within their medicine wheel. By that I mean they had "mandalized" the surrounding hills and mountains so that they moved daily within this giant medicine wheel. White people never bothered to learn any of this from the Indians before they were moved out to reservations. Now the land is so obscured by buildings, highways and conflicting telephone lines that it's not easy to relate to the surrounding hills or mountains without a ritual structure to align you.

Before leaving this subject of "mandalization" of one's own place, it might be useful to take a brief look at the practices of the *yamabushi* (those who sleep in the mountains) of Japan. Their practice, which has been called "mountain Buddhism," is part Buddhist; part Shinto. Coming out of this combination, they felt the Buddha was within; further, they identified "the realm of Buddha with the realm of man." Continuing his explanation, Grapard writes:

> The mandala, or representation of the residence of the Buddha, could therefore be none other than this natural world. A new perspective was opened up on the world: it could be seen, not as a world of suffering, but as an 'actualization of the mandala.' The site of practice became a natural mandala, a large geographical area endowed with all the qualities of a metaphysical space.

These mountain ascetics walked from peak to peak, performing rituals and meditations. "Their walk in those pure spaces was regarded as a process along the Middle Path, that of Emptiness... The *Shozan engi* states: 'Alongside the peaks of the Buddhas, they tread Emptiness'. These practitioners established connections not only between each summit and each divinity, but also between each site's natural virtues (water, hot springs, medicinal herbs) and each divinity's qualities: 'Those who tread those spaces and cross these rivers must think that each drop of water, each tree of these mountains is a drug of immortality, even if they suffer from a heavy past of misdeeds'. "

Once you begin using the medicine wheel to "mandalize" your area, each landscape form becomes important. For example, today, from the freeway near Albuquerque, the Navajo "sacred mountain," Mt. Taylor is such a low-lying form on

the horizon that most passing drivers never even notice it. But once seen, when it is standing out black against the sky, lit by slanting sun rays, the form is so astonishing in its pure symmetry that it's never forgotten. Everytime I drive near that region I stop to see this distant mountain.

Building a medicine wheel in your own place, aligns you with the power of the surrounding natural elements of your landscape so that they stand out—even when distant. Thus you become involved in an on-going, constantly changing, relationship with your own land throughout the year.

The "Way of the Medicine Wheel"

CHOOSING THE SITE

Your medicine wheel should be located in an area where each member of the group has ready access to it. In other words, ideally it should be within walking distance of most of the people, so that individuals can move through it whenever they feel the need. It should be in a location, where trees or a fence screen it from passersby. In a small town or out in the country it is easy to find such a location, but in a city it is difficult. The following specific directions are for those living in the city. Essentially, the area must be flat and with an open sky above it. It should not be covered by trees or by the shade of a large building. One of the most important things you will soon begin to learn by using the medicine wheel is that the color of the sky changes thoughout the day and the year. Even in the city, once you become sensitive enough, you will see color changes. Do not locate the medicine wheel in a park. First, you will have strangers wandering through and second, your stones will be disturbed. In the back yard of a house is the best location in a city area. Sometimes in a city there is an area along a local river which is flat and large enough. Some of these places are not official parks so if your stones are low and inconspicuous they will be left alone. In this latter case, you only want the four directional stones and the center stones—no pathways between so that it is not too conspicuous.

It is not necessary to plot the four cardinal directions with mathematical precision: just make sure that the rocks are placed in the general direction of east, west, north and south. You can take a compass reading for these directions if you wish but it is not necessary. Henge locations are much more crucial. The reason you can't demand precision here, is that from the center of your wheel, you should be able to site over the direction stone to something natural if at all possible: a tree, a distant view, a mountain or where the sun sets sometime during the year. The worst possible location is one where a street with moving traffic can be seen in the distance. Even the blank side of a building is preferable to moving traffic.

The medicine wheel, as given to us by Storm in *Seven Arrows* sets up a situation which links the "inner" world within us (inscape) to the "outer" world of nature (landscape). The four directions primarily mark the cardinal directions of your own place; but also, they stand for the four elements (earth, air, fire and water), the four seasons, the four winds of your own place and the four types of human personality according to Jung: feeling, thinking, sensation and intuition. One of these ways of being is predominant in each person; but to become whole one must learn to see in the other three ways as well. Besides his own native Cheyenne tradition, Storm had studied Jungian psychology; thus, he was able to incorporate both these aspects into his medicine wheel.

Each of the four directions on your site should be marked ahead of time before the ritual construction. The rocks you will be using should also be on the site. If rocks are easy to acquire, have a number of them so people have a choice. It is important to have local stones, but in a city that's not easy! Sometimes one can use large rocks from the bed of a nearby river, after cleaning off all the oil and garbage. Often, it's possible to find large rocks at nearby construction sites. The rocks for the four cardinal directions should definitely be from your own local place. The other rocks could be brought in from elsewhere or each person taking part in the ceremony can bring one that means something to them—especially rocks they have picked up during hikes on mountains in the vicinity or in tranquil places somewhere in the bioregion.

FURTHER BACKGROUND ON THE FOUR WINDS AND THE FOUR DIRECTIONS

Recent research by James McNeley, who teaches at Navajo Community College, involved field interviews with Navajo informants and library research, conducted from 1970-1972 at Many Farms, Arizona in the central part of the Navajo Nation. He worked with ten Navajo elders and consulted the most reliable of the older translations (Matthew, Haile, and Wyman); but, as he explains: "The task of comprehending the elder's points of view would have been impossible without the assistance of the young bilingual Navajos who worked with me as interpreters, transcribers and translators."

McNeley's *Holy Wind in Navajo Philosophy*, is very important because not only is it in keeping with how the wind actually speaks to us in desert areas but it clears up previous misconceptions of white scholars.

I am going further into McNeley's work here because it will help you to understand the winds in your own place: how they bring the weather; how they change the seasons and how they influence you. Most important of all, his work provides an understanding of the changing relationships involved.

What is important about his newly revised "model of the Wind concept" is that it shows us that Navajo psychology is "less ego-centered than existing views, arguing that the Navajo conceive of thought and behavior as being strongly externally determined rather than originating primarily within the individual." It also fits the Chinese *li* concept—patterns of relationship within each place. Therefore it helps us validate our inner convictions of relationship to all the powers of our place; rather than the old Eurocentric emphasis on the autonomous individual.

Translations of Navajo terms may seem confusing, but that's because of our "substance" addiction. In Eurocentric thought, wind is wind and that's all there is to it. For the Navajo, Wind in its totality is comprised of many different Winds—sometimes, under one name and sometimes under another—depending on other aspects of the variable relationships going on in nature; thus, there can be frequent shifts from singular to plural as well as changes of names. These names have to do with color symbolism, the specific direction that the wind comes from, whether it is inside or outside the person, its appearance, the influence it might have on the person or place and which direction it turns as it moves in whirlwinds or "dust devils," as whites call this phenomenon.

The wind is within us as well, because we are made of the same elements as the greater, natural beings in the world: "This vegetation with which we live, this that we exist on top of, (the Earth), those mountains, what the Sun is made of, we were made in the same way as these." This is beautifully stated in River Junction Curly's version of the Blessingway: "With everything having life, with everything having the power of speech, with everything having the power to breathe, with everything having the power to teach and guide, with that in blessing we will live." Each of the natural beings of our place "affords" us the means to live our life there.

As in many other traditional cultures, the Winds of the four directions are associated with certain qualities of light and particular mountains. For the Navajo, White Wind is associated with the white of Dawn; Blue Wind with the blue of the Sky, Yellow Wind with the yellow of twilight, and Dark Wind with the night. For those of you who live in the eastern part of the country, it may seem strange to call twilight, "yellow." For us living out west in the clear mountains that's exactly the color and the brighter the yellow, the more certain it will be clear for several days in succession.

Each of these powers within the Earth and the Sky work together and can bring blessings to the people on earth if the necessary conditions are fulfilled. In a footnote, McNeley says that this can cause "real ambiguity," but admits that this "ambiguity may reside in our lack of complete data and understanding." While none of us wants to claim complete understanding of the Navajo feeling for the Winds, their concepts do provide us with words for our own understanding of our relationship to natural beings. European languages so often fail us here. In his section on Navajo Psychology, McNeley states that the European concept of "the soul of an individual...imparting life to the individual," fails to translate the Navajo concept. It's more like an "essentially unitary Wind" and the individual "may more accurately be thought of as participating in this Wind existing everywhere thereby deriving from it the powers of life, movement, thought, speech, and behavior of which it is the source." But, just here McNeley is caught in the European "substance" trap. Wind is not "the source"; there are many inter-related sources of life in your place. The medicine wheel helps us to identify these many sources. It focalizes distant sources of life for the bioregion: Mountains or hills on the horizon, generally unnoticed, become living presences for those ritually using the medicine wheel.

I've been using Navajo concepts here to help you understand how the medicine wheel can "afford" us deeper relationship with the other beings of our place. More than three hundred years ago in China, the painter Shih-T'ao said it much more elegantly than I:

> Mountains and rivers compel me to speak for them;
> They are transformed through me and I am transformed through them.

When I help people begin making medicine wheels, I often use this Apache chant so they can begin to "see" their own hills or mountains as beings speaking to and with them:

> Big Blue Mountain God,
> You of the blue clouds
> There! Standing before me
> With life!
> Great Blue Mountain God.
>
> Big Yellow Mountain God in the south,
> You of the yellow clouds
> Holy Mountain God
> Standing toward me with life.
>
> Big Mountain God in the west
> You of the white brightness
> Holy Mountain God,
> I am happy over your words,
> You are happy over my words.
>
> Big Black Mountain God in the north
> You of the black clouds
> The way of the North, Big Black Mountain God
> Holy Mountain God
> I am happy over your words,
> You are happy over my words.
> Now it is good!

RITUAL CONSTRUCTION OF A MEDICINE WHEEL

Below, I give a pattern for ritually laying out the medicine wheel. This pattern is a composite of various ceremonies I have done through the years. Sentences within quotation marks are actually quoted from other works; words within brackets consists of directions to the person facilitating the ritual. All the rest of the sentences below are said by the ritual leader to the group.

A) Opening of the ritual

[Leader] "There is Power in the Earth—power and life. But we are blind to them because we do not share enough, with the Land and with each other." Today we are going to build a medicine wheel to invite the other beings of this land into our meeting; together we can begin to circulate the Earth Power among all of us present, human and non-human.

[Ritual greeting from the Leader] "Be welcome, strong heart and weak, light and dark, blood and bone and thew and mind and soul, for good and all. Set Peace about you and within you. This time is concentrated to the service of the Earth."

[Response of all present] "Let there be healing and hope, heart and home, for the Land, and for all people in the service of the Earth."

[Leader] "We are the preservers of the Land—votaries and handservants of the Earthpower; sworn to the healing of the Earth from all that is barren and unnatural, ravaged, foundationless, or perverse. And sworn and dedicated as well, despite any urgings of the ego—to the Oath of Peace. For serenity is the only promise we can give that we will not desecrate the Land again. Hope comes from the power of what you serve, not from yourself."

[Response as above.]

B) Body poem

[Leader] The sacred number for many traditional peoples is four. It is four for the Indians here on our continent of Turtle Island. We will be doing many things in fours today. First, we will center ourselves within this place by paying homage with our body to the four great beings of our universe: [Have everyone spread out so there is enough room between each person to extend the arms full length.]

1. Carry the Sun. Imagine you are holding the sun right in front of you. Make your arms round and full to hold the entire sun. Your hands will be down below your waist, fingertips meeting, in order to hold the sun. Inhale as you raise your arms all the way up over your head and as far back as they go. Exhale as you carry the sun forward and back down to the horizon. Do this four times.

2. Raise the Moon. Imagine you have the two crescents of the moon balanced one in either hand. [The hands are down at hip level with the backs of the hands close to the hips and the palms facing outward from the body.] Inhale as you raise these two crescents of the moon, balanced in your two hands. Raise them up to meet overhead for the full moon. Rise clear up on your toes as the crescents meet for the full moon. Exhale as the moon crescents go down toward the ground to set. Do this four times.

3. Bring in the four winds. Hold your hands naturally in front of you. Then raise them and sweep both arms to the left [about halfway between waist and shoulder or whatever feels good]. Inhale as you sweep your arms around laterally as far as possible keeping your feet flat. Then exhale on the return as you sweep them the other way. Four times.

4. Centering the self in this place. Think of the six vertebrae of your neck. Count them. Let your breath flow easily as you rotate your head around each of the vertebae. Start with rotating round the top vertebra—a small circle. Then around the next vertebra, a slightly bigger circle and on down. Now reverse the direction and come back up. Four times.

Now, turn toward the sun for a ritual greeting. Raise your face toward the sun, close your eyes, turn the palms of your hands toward the sun so as to feel the warmth and breathe in the sun. Now open your eyes and we will finish with a Chinese, Tai Chi closing.

Bend your knees slightly so that your spine is straight to carry the energy better. Lift your hands, that have been gathering the sun's radiance, on up over your head. [The hands are in front of the body, palms up.] Raise them up over your head. Then, turning the palms out, make a big circle, sweeping your hands down, gathering in all the energy around you and bringing it all together here just below the navel, where our other brain is, the center of our being. The hands are slightly cupped here, to hold all the energy. Now raise your two hands, still cupped slightly, to the heart level; turn your palms over and lower your hands gently down on either side as you straighten the knees. Stand for a moment, feeling the powers from all the great beings flowing through you.

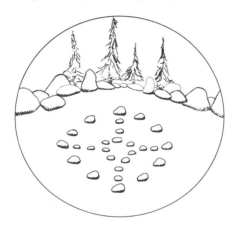

C) Constructing the medicine wheel

[Each person picks up one of the smaller marking rocks and walks around the circle you have laid out. When the circle is formed, each person evens up the distance between one another. Then everyone puts down their rock in that spot. This is the outer perimeter. Make an opening for the entrance, facing East big enough to walk through easily. Everyone continues sunwise around the circle to this opening and exits there.

Put someone into the center of the big circle—a child, if possible. Then seven people pick up a stone and re-enter the opening and make a smaller circle of seven rocks around that person.]

[Leader] This is the sacred center space marked by seven rocks—one for each direction; one for mother Earth; one for father Sky and one for the harmony (*li*) which holds everything together.

[These seven people and the center person exit through the opening. Now, from the pile choose the four biggest rocks to mark the cardinal directions. North should be white if possible; south, green; east, yellow and west black. (These are the four colors of the Cheyenne as Storm gives them.) After you have played and worked with your medicine wheel and the four winds have told you their colors in your place you can change them. It is good to start with Storm's concepts because they have been widely used by people in the last ten years so are becoming familiar. If possible, the ground should be

scooped out a bit or weeds cleared to make a hollow for each rock to rest in. Each rock should actually be buried within the earth a bit.

Now everyone picks up some of the smaller rocks and re-enters the circle to place the rocks marking the four paths between the cardinal direction rocks and the center circle.]

A PATTERN FOR THE FIRST CEREMONY

[After you complete your medicine wheel, have everyone move into the wheel and walk around the inner and outer circles and along the paths for a few moments. The Tai Chi walk is very helpful for the combination of attention and respect that is needed here. The back is kept straight; the knees very slightly bent. The right foot is put out heel first; then slowly the weight is moved over onto the foot until it is flat on the ground. Then the other foot is put out, repeating the same procedure. Breathe in when the heel is first put down and out as the weight moves over onto the foot. This very ancient walk soon permits the lower brain (in the *tan tien* or abdomen) to register natural effects which are not yet perceptible to the upper brains. After a few moments tell everyone to stop where they are and face inward to the center of the circle.

Explain that you will be giving the first introduction to moving through the medicine wheel. Using a gong to signal the stops is very helpful. If you do not have a gong then use a large stainless steel mixing bowl and hit it with a wooden spoon. The necessary resonating sound will be produced. Hold the bowl upside down, balanced by holding one finger in the center of the bowl.]

A) [Here I will give the essentials of what seems to work best for beginners. You can adapt it in any way that works for your place. Begin with Storm's words] "Let us teach each other here...of each of the Ways on this Great Medicine Wheel, our Earth." To the North on the medicine wheel we find the white buffalo who stands for wisdom. In the South is the mouse and the color is green for growing. This is the place for innocence and trust, for seeing things from close up as a mouse does. In the West we find the Black Bear. This is the direction for those who spend a lot of time looking within themselves; trying to figure things out from within. In the East is the Eagle; the color is the gold of the morning star or the sun rising.

Each of us was born, seeing from one of these directions on the medicine wheel; thus that direction will remain the easiest from then on. But anyone who sees from only one of the four great directions is only part of a whole human being. A person who sees only from the North, has wisdom but cannot see things close up and cannot feel. Someone who sees only from the East will be able to see things far—will be able to lay great plans—but cannot see the small details. She will have the clarity of an eagle, but never be close to things. This person will feel separated from life. A man or woman who sees only from the West will go over and over the same thought in their mind and will always be undecided. If a man sees only from the South, he will see the details close up; everything that actually touches his whiskers but can never understand the bigger things. To live a complete life each of these people must learn to move around the medicine wheel and see things from other perspectives.

In the center of the medicine wheel are the seven arrows or mirrors or ways of learning. These are sometimes called seven arrows because four of the rocks stand for the four great directions of this place. Another rock stands for the earth; another for the sky and the last rock is the harmony which holds all together. We are going to see how each being in this place within nature mirrors others.

Turn now to the person nearest you. The shorter one of you will do any kind of movement you wish; the other one must mirror your action. Then move onto the next person. The shorter one here does an action; the other imitates. Continue until you hear the gong and then just stop right where you are—wherever it is on the medicine wheel. You can be humorous, serious, athletic or artistic. [Let this continue for a few moments. Then sound the gong and explain the actions for the second half of this ceremony.]

B) Moving through the seasons: preliminary instruction
[This ceremony consists of moving through three seasons on the medicine wheel. This will consist of two seasons before the present one and the present season itself. The actual ceremony I am basing this account on was held in the fall; therefore, I will be using the seasons of spring, summer and fall as an example. The first thing to do is re-form the medicine wheel.

[Leader] Everyone move out so that someone is standing in each part of the wheel including the paths and the center. [Allow them to re-form.]

[Leader] I will read the narrative of the medicine wheel and the seasons to you—beginning with spring. After spring comes summer and then we will finish with autumn, the season we are standing in now. I will explain the three actions we will be doing:

1) When I say the word, **mirror**, and the gong sounds, you **mirror** one another as you did before. You will be freely circulating anywhere within the outer circle of the wheel. Continue doing that until I say the next of the these words.

2) The second word is **medicine wheel**. When you hear that word and the gong sounds, stop the action you are doing and re-form the medicine wheel as we just did. Then stand there in the place you are and feel how it is in that direction. If you are in the north feel the buffalo; feel what wisdom is like. If you are in the south, feel yourself as a mouse and how it is to see everything very clearly, close up. If you are in the west, feel the power of the buffalo and look deep inside yourself. If you are in the east, feel the all-seeing vision of the eagle and how it is to be way up in the sky—so high you can't really see all the little ordinary day-to-day things in front of you. When I say, "Now walk the medicine wheel," you will once more begin circulating freely anywhere within the outer rim of the wheel.

3) The third word is **touch**. When you hear that word and hear the gong reach out and touch anyone near you. It can be on the hand, the arm or the back if their back is to you. Just a light touch and then continue walking the wheel.

C) Ceremonial narrative
[Leader] We begin when the **medicine wheel** (sound the gong) of the earth has turned to spring. Spring is here! "The earth has received the embraces of the sun and we shall soon see the results of that love! Every seed has awakened and so has all the animal life. It is through this mysterious power that we, too, have our being. We therefore acknowledge to our relatives the plants and animals, the same right as ourselves, to inhabit this land." The first peace, the peace which is most important, is that which comes within us when we realize this relationship—between one human and another and between us humans and other beings in this place; and between us and the universe and all its Powers. Many teachings come to us when we relate to all the other beings in this place. Now resume walking the medicine wheel.

These teachings begin with the **touching** (gong) of our brothers and sisters. Next it speaks of the **touching** of the world around us: the animals, the trees, the grasses and all other living things. Then we begin to hear the song and the chants which other beings teach us. And we begin to become whole people. "Let us **Touch**. Let us, each to the other, be a Gift as is the Buffalo. Let us be Meat to nourish each other, that we all may Grow, each of us, as we are in our Perceiving of ourselves as Mouse, Coyote, Weasel, Fox or Prairie Bird. Let me see through your Eyes."

In many ways this circle can best be understood if you think of it as a **mirror** in which everything is reflected. Each person in the Circle is a **mirror** to every other person. As you begin to do this, you will learn to see through the eyes of your brothers and sisters, and to share their perceptions.

Any other person or any animal or plant can be a **medicine wheel** (gong) to teach us. The tiniest flower can teach us, as can a wolf, a story, a mountain top. Each of these is a **medicine wheel**— just as you are too. Black Elk tells us that "the Power of the world always works in circles." The sky is round and the earth is round. "The sun comes forth and goes down in a circle. The moon does the same, and both are round. Even the seasons form a great circle in their changing, and always come back again to where they were."

We are now standing in our summer **medicine wheel**. The whole earth becomes green. It is the time of innocence and trust. This is the time of the "give-away." The Cheyenne, Storm says: "All things within this Universal Wheel of the earth know of their harmony, with every other thing, and know how to Give-away one to the other, except man. Of all the Universe's creatures, it is we alone who do not begin our lives with knowledge of this...According to the Teachers, there is only one thing that all people possess equally. this is their loneliness...This is the cause of our growing, but it is sometimes difficult...Loneliness is a teacher of giving. Man, of all the animals is the only one that feels loneliness. But his loneliness teaches him the Give-away." Resume walking the wheel.

This is the time to give—each to the other. Let us **touch** (gong) and give-away each to the other. Those who walk together learn from one another in the **mirror** (gong) of the medicine wheel. This is the sign of the mirroring. It is what happens when one meets Seven Arrows. Seven Arrows will reflect only what you feel and think. The seven stones in the middle circle of the **medicine wheel** (gong), symbolize these Seven Arrows. Four of these Seven Arrows are the four directions. "The Mother Earth is the fifth **mirror**, the sky, with its moon, sun and stars, is the Sixth **mirror**. The seventh of these arrows is... the universal harmony which holds all these things together."

Now we have become the Autumn **medicine wheel**. This is the season of Autumn. People think of it as being a sad time because the leaves fall off the trees onto the ground and decay. But, actually, for the tree it is a time of joy, of completeness— of coming to fulfillment—the time of the Give-away from the tree to the earth. The tree, with the help of the sun, has been working all summer to bring all of its leaves to their fullest growth—to their completion. And now the joy of giving away all that power and energy back to the earth. The tree took the gift of the sun—its energy and the gift of water and transformed these gifts into leaves and then gave these gifts back to the earth to enrich it so that other plants could grow. Leaves make the topsoil which is the basis of all life on earth. This lavish gift of golden yellow leaves in the fall gives us true wealth— life itself.

Some people think of autumn as a time when trees are bare; but, actually, they are covered with all the things that they will unpack and unroll in the spring, the buds. Flowers do not die in the fall; actually they are born then. That is when the seeds are formed. The future is right here now in the shape of the seeds of the future. Sometimes inside of us we seem to smell of decay, encumbered by the faded remains of the past but if only we could see how many fat shoots are pushing up out of that old tilled soil in us. These seeds in us are germinating in secret, getting ready the living bud which will one day burst into flowering life. If we could only see all that secret life deep within us, we would not be so filled with distrust and sadness. Instead we would know that the best thing of all is to be a living person, one who grows. But we cannot grow without a living relationship with all the other beings around us in this place. This relationship is beautifully explained by D. H. Lawrence:

What man most passionately wants is his living wholeness... not his own isolate salvation of his 'soul.'... For man, the vast marvel is to be alive. For man, as for flower and beast and bird, the supreme triumph is to be most vividly, most perfectly alive. Whatever the unborn and the dead may know, they cannot know the beauty, the marvel of being alive in the flesh... the magnificent here and now of all life in the flesh is ours, and ours alone, and ours only for a time. We ought to dance with rapture that we should be alive and in the flesh, and part of the living, incarnate cosmos. I am part of the sun as my eye is part of me. That I am part of the earth my feet know perfectly, and my blood is part of the sea... So that my individualism is really an illusion. I am a part of the great whole, and I can never escape. But I *can* deny my connections, break them, and become a fragment. Then I am wretched.

What we want is to destroy our false, inorganic connections, especially those related to money, and re-establish the living organic connections, with the cosmos, the sun and earth... Start with the sun, and the rest will slowly, slowly happen.

Here, today in this medicine wheel we begin our connection with the sun on its yearly journey through the seasons.

D) Closing

Now we will complete today's medicine wheel ceremony. Everyone move into the center circle area and cluster around the seven stones. I will give you a few moments while you close your eyes and recall how you felt in each position on the medicine wheel. How did you feel when you were the buffalo of the north, the mouse of the south, the eagle of the east or the bear of the west? Do you feel you are seeing things from afar like the eagle or close up like the mouse; or do you need to look within like the bear; or do you feel you are wise like the buffalo but need help to feel for others? [allow a few moments] Now, open your eyes and move directly out along one of the paths to the direction of the animal who sees as you do right now: north to the buffalo, east to the eagle, south to the mouse, or west to the bear.

[When everyone has arrived in their directional spot] Now join hands in a circle with the others who have chosen that same direction. This is your clan for now. This is the completion of our first medicine wheel together.

FURTHER INFORMATION FOR BEGINNING MEDICINE WHEELS

There are several possibilities for future ceremonies now that the clans have been chosen. In this first ceremony, if there is enough time left, each clan can gather natural items around the site and decorate their direction stone to manifest how they feel there. Then the entire group can move through the medicine wheel and see the shrine of each clan.

Another possibility is that the clan in the direction of the next earth festival could be in charge of that celebration: buffalo for the winter solstice, eagle for the spring equinox, mouse for summer solstice and bear for autumn equinox. These clans are not permanent, of course. As people grow to see more ways, they will move into another clan. Eventually, after more ceremonies the clans may take the name of an animal that belongs in your bioregion.

The directional colors are very important. While, it is wise to keep Storm's colors for use in medicine wheels involving people from other places, for your own place, eventually, colors should be chosen that mirror the color people feel emanates from that direction. This color has to do with atmospheric conditions or states of mind, which the wind from that direction brings. Remember some directions may be considered bad or harmful by your group. This has to do with the approach of storms and with positive ions brought by certain winds. (See *Earth Wisdom*, page 56 and 57.)

INDOOR MEDICINE WHEELS

If you are in a location where you cannot find a suitable place, outside and must therefore hold your medicine wheel inside a building, here is a ritual way of bringing the earth of your place into your medicine wheel. This practice of bringing a bit of your own earth into the ceremony has been done not only by Indians in our continent but is done each year by the people of Siena in modern day Italy. Siena is a ritualized city and has been so since the Middle Ages; their essential ritual is a horse race round a circular piazza within the city itself:

Approximately one week before the day of the palio, workmen of the city of Siena begin to bring yellow earth to the Campo. It takes a day of so to complete the miraculous transformation of a beautiful medieval piazza into a unique theater-racetrack-arena. The placement of the earth in the piazza is regarded as a sign that the palio is truly near at hand. In folk speech, there is a popular idiom which may be used at any time during the year whenever someone needs to be cheered up. The sad person is told not to worry because soon there will be 'la terra in piazza.' During the evening after the earthen track is in place, one can observe Sienese of all ages coming to the Campo where they take great delight in touching the earth. They come to...press [or tread] the earth in the square...and there is a certain sense in which pressing the earth is a joyful act of communication with something basic, something fundamental, perhaps life itself. The past has returned and a future event, the palio, about to become present.

This is in modern day Siena, a city of about 50,000 people.

The Sioux, Lame Deer, in 1972, explained that the chief symbol of the four quarters of the earth is Umane. It represents the "unused earth force." Dorsey in his nineteenth century report of research among the Sioux has this to say about it:

The 'U-ma-ne'—The mellowed earth space, U-ma-ne in Dakota, and called by some peculiar names in other tribes, has never been absent from any religious exercise I have yet seen or learned of from the Indians. It represents the unappropriated life or power of the earth, hence man may obtain it. The square or oblong, with the four lines standing out, is invariably interpreted to mean the earth or land with the four winds standing toward it. The cross, whether diagonal or upright, always symbolizes the four winds or four quarters.

To use this sacred earth inside for your medicine wheel (or any other ceremony), you should go out into an area within your place or bioregion where the earth has not been disturbed by man for some time. Dig up a shovelful and bring it back to the location where you will be having your ceremonies. The best thing is to set aside a small corner of the room where it can remain. In that case you will put a piece of wood or a piece of cardboard, covered by plastic down on the floor first. Then spread out a small, low mound in the shape of the Umane. The mound should be piled up several inches above the floor. With a piece of living twig off a tree, draw the four lines extending from the corners. Sprinkle the surface with water just a bit to begin to settle it. Then you can cover it with a box between ceremonies. Also each time before a ceremony sprinkle it again.

If there's no space for a permanent Umane, there's another possibility. Using the earth from your place, make a sand painting of the Umane symbol. On a piece of wood, trace out the diagram of the Umane and spread glue over the entire diagram. Then spread a thin layer of the earth over the glue and leave until dry. When thoroughly dry, brush off the extra earth. This can be stored for future use.

Another use of "sacred earth" comes from Japan, as noted in the 1883 volume of the *Transactions of the Asiatic Society of Japan*: when a Japanese country person went on a long journey, he carried a bit of the local earth with him to mix with water to keep him well in a strange land.

OTHER PATTERNS FOR CEREMONIES WITHIN THE MEDICINE WHEEL

Tossing the stones of
the circle
"we" built
"we" shared
as circles
en circled
in midst
of this
this hour   glass canyon
of time.
"We" growing
out of I
sinking
in
to deeper than
the mind
can reach
into the
god aw fullest depths
where self
resides
between
what's known
and yet to be seen
Jessie F., April 11, 1982

Jessie had never before been involved in a ritual out in nature until this four day medicine wheel ceremony held in Hourglass Canyon in Utah; the depth of his response to the teachings of the medicine wheel is shown in his poem. Jessie's poem moves us toward the story that our own medicine wheel ceremony can give us. Paula Gunn Allen tells us that, "the Ceremony is the ritual enactment of a specialized perception of cosmic relationships, while the myth is a prose record of that relationship." Since the ceremony outlined above provides a pattern for your beginning rituals, it necessarily emphasizes the human beings more than the other non-human beings of the place. Each of the patterns below will begin to allow the *li* of the other beings to teach us as well.

As the people in each "clan" develop greater knowledge of the animal of their direction—if using Storm's system: buffalo, bear, eagle and mouse—or if your place or bioregion has begun to recognize the teachings of the local animals, you can begin building small shrines during the ceremony in the direction dedicated to that particular animal. People can bring items which honor "bear" or things they have found on walks that speak to them of the eagle or the mouse.

As soon as you feel people are ready, you should begin using gourd rattles. As mentioned before the gourd "afforded" us the chance to become humans and, at every stage of human history, the gourd has been the prime method of communicating within human society itself and between humans and other beings. See chapter sixteen for more on how to use the gourd.

At the end of your second medicine wheel ceremony close with Wavoka's Ghost Dance chant, "I Circle Around."

From the very beginning of your use of the medicine wheel you will find the boundaries of your "self" expanding, as you begin to recognize your relationships with other beings. Silas Goldean goes deeper into this in his essay, "Principle of Extended Identity":

This principle holds that to know one's self you must be able to sense, establish, and sustain relationships beyond the self...The extension of identity is a way to explore what makes us possible. I seeks life beyond and within our own. Lovers. Friends. Owls. Bobcats. Saxifrage. Sun...The moon on the water spilling. It seeks the pattern of connections and the resonance of associations. It makes distinctions in order to assimilate the differences...

I cannot define identity...[but]...What makes us possible must certainly be part of what we are...The practices used for extending identity are richly diverse and have been developed and employed from the Paleolithic to the present, most notable in the Great Spirit/shamanism tradition...most practices share a simple tenet: Pay Attention. Attune the mind with attention. Attend the relationships and associations alive among the self and other forms of life. Use imagination to explore the binding curve that joins us together...

I think the current cultural fit of egocentricity is primarily a response to the isolation caused by displacement...we have increased our mobility so much we are seldom really anywhere...This increased mobility has slowly resulted in a monotonous homogenization of American culture, a state of mind strongly abetted and sustained by the centralization of information and information sources—the same information from fewer and fewer sources, almost all of it channelled through media originating beyond our immediate locale...we're everywhere at once, but in actual sensual fact, we're not any where at all...

To have an identity or self in any lively sense of the word means understanding the contingencies of other identities and appreciating the relations connecting life to life...The only way to grasp this is to live somewhere long enough to attend the complexity of living relationships. You can't fuck on a dead run. You can't join the owl's spirit by watching it on the Wide World of Animals. You can't appreciate the seasonal qualities of moonlight without spending seasons with the moon.

Time is a function of place. If you seek the owl's spirit, you have to see one every once in a while, and to see one you must learn where to look and how to wait. You can't do that at 55 miles per hour on the freeway; can't talk to one on the C.B. Place encourages patience. You see it over and over again until you really begin to see it. And in doing it, you learn what is involved in that doing—the landforms and plants and watercourses...

There has been a recent surge of Industrial Mysticism...[those] who think it would be the 'natural' extension of the 'human adventure' to create space colonies...I think they would all be stone-fucking-crazy within a year, not just because of the rat-cage mentality they would take with them, but because they would miss the hundreds of subtle planetary cues the Earth provides the human organism: scents; changes in the quality and duration of light; magnetic shifts; cloud formations; a sense of horizon and panorama scaled to our neural coherence—those, and a hundred others, and probably twice that many we don't even suspect. The planet— and more specifically, the place we live on it—is our main source of spiritual and biological information, and to do without it for any length of time would affect us in much the same way that starvation influences morality.

It seems to me that a watershed offers the ideal neural and social scale for the exploration of human identity; it is complete enough to yield a pattern of relationships, and large enough to be inexhaustible. Practiced in place the extension of identity becomes the realization of community, and as place turns into home, the heart opens like a seed.

We have used medicine wheels occasionally on our Breaking Through adventures where we take people mountain climbing and river rafting while doing Tai Chi and rituals out in nature. (See "Resources" for more information on this program.) We generally make a medicine wheel within the first two days at our beginning camp place in the Wet Mountain Valley. From this site we can see—way off in the far distance—the rock needles on the ridge of 14,000 ft. Crestone Needle which we eventually climb. Crestone Needle is to the

west from our camp site—the direction the sun sets. One year we set up the medicine wheel in the early afternoon so that we could use it at twilight.

We walked west toward the setting sun from our camp-site. As the sun began to sink behind the mountains we walked through the wheel until each person reached their chosen direction on the wheel. Then standing there, silently—in awe at the glory of the sunset—we were visited by night hawks. The whooshing, whirring sound they made as they plummet down, wings folded, going after insects was suddenly joined by a coyote chorus from the next ravine just south of us. When the coyote chorus broke off abruptly, we walked the wheel one final time, chanting: "We circle around the boundaries of the earth." Our boundaries were extended far, far into the sky, where most of us had never ever dreamed of being, as we were carried by the plummeting sound of the night hawks.

The Breaking Through program is held in summer. But each of you who begins to use your own medicine wheel for rituals throughout the year, will soon find that it lets each of the four seasons speak to you directly.

"TURNING THE CHILD" CEREMONY
INTRODUCING THE CHILD TO THE FOUR WINDS,
"WALKING ABOUT THE RIM OF THE WORLD"

This ceremony is adapted from an Omaha ritual for young children, both boys and girls. It is a way to introduce the child to the pattern of the medicine wheel as it mirrors the earth itself. The ceremony is directly related to the natural forces of the wind and the earth. Long ago, in the Omaha tribe, all the children, when they were old enough to walk steadily on their own, were symbolically "sent into the midst of the winds"—that element considered essential to life and health by many Indian societies. In the old days this ceremony welcomed the child into its place as a member of the tribe. The baby name was thrown away and a new name proclaimed to "all nature and to the assembled people." The only requirement was a new pair of moccasins, which were ritually put on the child to show that it was prepared for the journey of life and the journey will be a long one." Indeed, the journey would go to the fourth and last hill of life.

For our modern ceremony, the parents of a child between toddler and kindergarten age, should make or buy a pair of moccasins for the child. The moccasins and a ritual gift for the earth (sage or juniper or cornmeal) are brought to the ceremony. The only change in your medicine wheel, itself, is that a fairly large flat stone is put in the middle of the center circle of rocks for the child to stand on.

"The ceremony of Turning the Child took place in the springtime, after the first thunder was heard, When the grass was well up and the birds were singing, 'particularly the meadow lark', the tribal herald proclaimed that the time for these ceremonies had come."

[Parents and children assemble at the East entrance of the medicine wheel. The one who is in charge of the ceremony, called "the leader" will stand just within the entrance. Each child is brought up to the entrance by the parent but the parents do not enter; they remain outside. The parent gives the leader the gift for the earth saying], "I desire my child to wear moccasins. I desire that my child walk long upon the earth." [Then the parent drops the child's hand. The child, carrying its new moccasins enters alone. As soon as the child is across the entrance the leader takes it by the hand and leads it by the path to the center circle of stones. When they arrive at the stone, all of the parents waiting outside and the leader and child chant together, calling on the four winds:]

> 'Four Winds, come and stand, stand here
> In four groups shall you stand
> Here shall you stand, in this place stand."

[At the close of the ritual chant, the leader lifts the child onto the central flat stone in the circle of rocks. The child is put onto the rock facing east. Then he or she lifts the child and turns it completely around from left to right; putting the child back down on the rock facing south. He then lifts the child again, turning it and setting it back down on the rock facing west; then he lifts it once more, turns it and sets it back down on the rock facing north. The final time he lifts the child, turns it and places it down again facing east. During this action the entire group chants:]

> 'Turned by the wind goes the one I send yonder;
> Yonder he goes who is whirled by the winds;
> Goes, where the four hills of life and the four winds
> are standing;
> There, in the midst of the winds do I send him,
> Into the midst of the winds, standing there.'

[Followed by a loud, rapid beat on the drum to make the thunder sound.]

This ritual symbolized the four winds that come to strengthen the child, to help him in the difficulties he encounters as he travels over the four hills of life: infancy and childhood, youth, maturity, and old age. The Omaha believed that this ceremony enabled the child to grow in strength. It also symbolizes for us, now, relinquishing some of the control we exert over our life, letting the Powers of nature have some say in our life and that of our child's.

[After turning the child, the leader puts the new moccasins on the feet of the child. Then she lifts the child down from the rock; taking him by the hand, together, they take four ritual steps out along the pathway back to the entrance. This symbolizes the entrance to a long life. When they reach the entrance, the leader announces the new name of the child and, calling on the other beings of the place says]: "You hills, you grasses, you trees, you creeping things both great and small, hear me! This child has thrown away its baby name. Ho!"

[The new name is decided upon ahead of time. The parents—perhaps by talking with the child—decide on a new name to be given the child in the ritual. A name connecting the child with some aspect of nature or animals or plants would be suitable. If he or she likes the name it can be kept in use; otherwise it can be dropped.

Each child of the group is ritually taken one at a time onto the central stone and the ritual procedure, as given above, followed.]

The ceremony ends with dancing within the medicine wheel. The newly named children, dance in their new moccasins and are swung around by each adult and passed on from one adult to another during this dance.

Truly, in this dance, "the four winds walking on the rim of the world" join us in the Round Dance of the earth, the sky, the god and the mortals in our own place.

THE DANCE

Always, the medicine wheel is the location for the sacred dance, in which we make space for the other beings of our place to join us. The "round dance," for the earliest Greeks, "was the ring of the gathering Fourfold [earth, sky, gods and mortals]. Heidegger says: "A boundary is not that at which something stops but, as the Greeks recognized, the boundary is that from which something *begins its presenting.*"

"Digging still deeper in the 'geology' of Being, [Heidegger] traces these words for 'place' to the more elemental *chao, source of our* word for *chaos,* and meaning: 'to gape, to split open, to become receptive to, and to open'. The place, therefore, as the gathering of a region whose depth is an utterly open expanse." The philosopher, David Levin has been quoting here from Heidegger. Levin continues by saying: "Perhaps a thoughtful experience of the hermeneutical round-dance would open us to possibility of experiencing that openness of Being as a field of dancing energy..."

Notice here that Heidegger refers to chaos as meaning "to gape, to split open" etc., reminiscent of *hun-tun* and the chaos of the gourd, in Taoism, with its connotation of "the myriad things," coming out of the hollow void of the gourd.

Back to Levin, who continues: "The human beings whose hearts have gathered them for a round-dance are *mortals* gathering in a sacred ring, inviting the 'gods' to join with them, there in the place at the center of their heart, for a celebration of cosmic order, and at a time when earth and sky may come together." Here we see that what Heidegger was trying to explain in his seemingly "difficult" work and further, what Levin wrote in his conclusion to his 349 page book, in which he goes further into Hiedegger's position—all of this becomes much clearer when experienced in the ceremonial dance within our medicine wheel. Out of that dance, comes the full "presencing" of all the beings of our place during the Festival times.

MEDICINE WHEEL GATHERING: WINTER SOLSTICE

Below, I am reprinting the ritual invitation for this ceremony sent out by Amy Hannon to those participating with her in celebrating her place, Greenville, in the Katúah bioregion. (North Carolina). Although I have never met Amy, she has used my books for years and kept in touch with me concerning the activities of their ritual group. Her ritual invitation will show you other ways of celebrating your own place.

> Medicine Wheel Gathering
> Winter Solstice
>
> Make the circle
> Remember the cosmic concept
>
> Praise and thanksgiving
> to the Sun and the Moon
> the water, the fire, the wind
> and the soil
> the animals and the plants
> Praise to the North and to Winter

Poems - Song - Dance
Turn the Wheel
Give away fire light

Greenville Town common
by the six holly trees

Conclusion

By ritual use of the medicine wheel, we sharpen our perceptions of the natural world around us. Standing in the medicine wheel we begin once more to feel the wind as it moves us; to feel the subtle differences it makes within us; to begin to recognize the deepest reciprocal give-away of all—the interchange taking place all the time between all the beings of our Earth within the atmosphere itself. In spite of all the media hype concerning Lovelock's Earth hypothesis (accidentally mis-named Gaia) there is still a core of great importance within it. Briefly, geochemist Lovelock states: "The entire range of living matter on Earth, from whales to viruses, and from oaks to algae, could be regarded as constituting a single living entity, capable of manipulating the Earth's atmosphere to suit its overall needs and endowed with faculties and powers far beyond those of its constituent parts." Here, coming from a modern scientist, we have the "Powers" long recognized by native peoples throughout the world. Of course, Lovelock had no knowledge of traditional people's use of the word, "Powers"; yet that very word is the only one he could find for his use. The fact that he could turn right around and speculate that we could transfer this Earth atmosphere to Mars, merely shows that he is still caught in the narrow Eurocentric trap of "substance." But that typical aberration does not really matter because he has awakened many people to the fact that the Earth and its atmosphere together is a reality that "*encompasses us*, a phenomenon we are immediately *in* and *of*," as David Abram expresses it. "It is no 'mere formula'—it is our own body, our flesh and our blood, the wind blowing past our ears and the hawks wheeling overhead. Understood thus with the senses, recognized from within, [our Earth] is far vaster, far more mysterious and eternal than anything we may ever hope to fashion."

Abram's conclusion to his article for the British journal, *The Ecologist*, is so useful for the ritual use of the medicine wheel that I am going to quote extensively from it here:

I have suggested that the most radical element of the [Living Earth] hypothesis, as presently formulated, may be the importance that it places on the air, the renewed awareness it beings us of the atmosphere itself as a thick and mysterious phenomenon no less influential for its invisibility. In Native American cosmology, the air or the Wind is the most sacred of powers. It is the invisible principle that circulates both within us and around us, animating the thoughts of all breathing things as it moves the swaying trees and the clouds. And indeed, in countless human languages the words for spirit or psyche are derived from the same root as the words for the wind or the breath. Thus in English the word 'spirit' is related to the word 'respiration' through their common origin in the Latin word 'spiritus', meaning 'breath'. Likewise our word 'psyche', with all its recent derivations, is related to the ancient Greek 'psychein', which means 'to breathe' or 'to blow (like the wind)'.

Spirit...is simply another word for the air, the wind, or the breath. The atmosphere *is* the spirit, the creative awareness of this planet. We all dwell within the spirit of the earth, and this awareness circulates within us. Our individual psyches...are all internal expressions of the invisible awareness, the air, the psyche of this world. And all our perceiving, the secret ongoing work of our eyes, our nostrils, our ears and our skin, is our constant communication and communion with the life of the whole. Just as in breathing, we contribute to the ongoing life of the atmosphere, so also in seeing, in listening, in real touching and tasting we participate in the evolution of the living textures and colours that surround us, and thus lend our imaginations to the tasting and shaping of the Earth. Of course the spiders are doing this just as well...

And, of course the bear, the buffalo, the mouse and the eagle are doing it just as well too—and that's why we can learn from each of them. That's why we can learn from any being on this earth. As Storm says, we "mirror" one another in the great medicine wheel of the earth.

An even deeper level of this "mirroring" or learning comes to us from the anthropologist Roy Rappaport in his *Meaning Ecology and Religion*, where he tells us: "Humans are gifted learners and may continually enlarge and correct their knowledge of their environment, but their images of nature are always simpler than nature and in some degree or sense inexact, for ecological systems are complex and subtle beyond full comprehension...Given the complexity of natural ecosystems...we can never predict fully the outcome of anything we do. Because **knowledge can never replace respect as a guiding principle in our ecosystemic relations**, it is adaptive for cognized models to engender respect for that which is unknown, unpredictable, and uncontrollable."

But, the dominant Eurocentric economic view insists that the "ecosystem is composed of three general sorts: those that qualify as 'resources', those that are naturally useless, and those that may be regarded as pests, antagonists or competitors. These two views of the world obviously suggest radically different ways of living in it."

That is precisely why we do rituals—so we can regain the understanding that all traditional peoples had—respect for "The Powers." That is why, in rituals, we always let the natural Powers have the say in setting the time of the ritual: equinoxes or solstices or full moons and that is why we set up structures such as the medicine wheel which acknowledge the presence of "The Powers." When we are climbing mountains, we climbers always say "if the mountain allows us" or "if the rain gods hold off till we get off the ridge."

This respect and mode of consulting the non-human can be extended to everything we do. In fact, "this balancing of one's personal behavior and 'success' with rituals relating to natural elements and other people acts as *figures of regulation* and is a force for stability at the highest level of human understanding. It does so not by understanding the specifics of every homeostatic process (the nitrogen cycles, for instance) but by providing a framework for interpreting careful observations and undertaking corrective actions...No one owns a bioregion in the sense of property, but everyone owns a personal stake in its well-being." This is part of the give-away of all the beings, including the human beings in the great medicine wheel of each one of our bioregions. As a Menominee Indian once said: "to fulfill my part in the Medicine Wheel— in that spoke. If I do my share, the whole wheel is going to turn evenly."

The Kogi Indians of northern Columbia consider their "bioregion" to be a vast loom into which all the beings are woven. The Earth itself is an immense loom on which the sun weaves the Fabric of Life. Solstices and Equinoxes provide the four directional corner posts of the loom. "Spiraling back and forth, the sun weaves day and night...light and darkness, life and death." The sun also weaves on the smaller loom of their own place, the Sierra Nevada mountains. It weaves between the four main ceremonial centers and includes all the beings of their place—human and non-human.

The medicine wheel allows "The Powers," the gods of our own place to weave for us...

> a garment of brightness,
> That we may walk fittingly where the birds sing,
> That we may walk fittingly where the grass is green,
> Oh our Mother the Earth, Oh our Father the Sky.

Setting up your own Woodhenge

HISTORICAL BACKGROUND

"In late Neolithic and Chalcolithic [Copper age] times—a period of seven or eight centuries which is now known to have started at around 2500 BC—a characteristic type of monument was built in large numbers all over the stonier regions of Britain and Ireland and Brittany." In this single sentence, Euan MacKie gives us the essential facts about megalithic structures, and since so many books have recently been published about them, it's not necessary, here, to go very deeply into their history. Few of these books, however, mention that it was the rock itself which "afforded" the people the opportunity of building such structures. Some were built of glacial "erratics" (large boulders, left behind when the ice retreated), but others were built of sarsen stones. As mentioned in the medicine wheel section above, these sarsen stones lie about on the surface of the softer chalk downs. They are the surviving fragments of a layer, which once covered the chalk, but during the passage of geologic time was worn away. They are large angular gray blocks; very different from the yielding curves of the chalk on which they lay. Jacquetta Hawkes, in her great book on her much-loved British countryside, titled simply *A Land*, tells us more about these sarsens. "Because they had already been quarried by water, frost and wind they provided the best possible material for masons with a rough equipment of stone mauls and antler wedges. It was only because the blocks were there that the religious architects of the Bronze Age were able to build Avebury and Stonehenge on such a magnificent scale."

Although such names as G. S. Hawkins or Keith Critchlow are more familiar, the man who spent his life studying the great megalithic monuments is Alexander Thom. MacKie tells us how all this began. "At dusk after a fine summer evening in 1934 Alexander Thom, then Professor of Engineering at the University of Oxford, was sailing his boat into Loch Roag (in the Outer Hebrides) to find an anchorage for the night. The full moon was just rising in the east and, as it came up over the nearby low hills, the standing stones were starkly silhouetted against its yellow disc. It must have been a striking sight and from that moment Professor Thom's interest in these strange prehistoric megaliths was kindled, to be followed up by more than forty years of painstaking fieldwork and measurement throughout the length and breadth of Britain."

Standing stone structures are found not only in parts of Europe and the Near East but also in many other parts of the world such as India, and some Pacific Islands. In Japan, "the erection of stone pillars for cultic purposes appeared in the Middle Jomon period; and, when Jomon culture reached its late phase, a great number of stone circles of different sizes dominated the scene in the northern region of the mainland." The stone circles at Oyu in Akita prefecture include a number of sundial arrangements. The Neolithic Jomon period in Japan began about 7000 BC; while late Jomon occurred about 1500 BC.

I will not take the space here to go into the conflicting ideas and theories of modern researchers about what the ancient peoples were trying to do with their henges. Many of these researchers are caught in the usual Eurocentric trap of trying to pin it all down with one formula—usually mathematical. Because henges, by their very nature, relate to so many points in the sky and on the land, one can make almost any mathematical formula fit the thesis one is promoting. Essentially, however, we are building our henges for the same reason that most traditional peoples built their henges: to help us see the changing relationship of the sky and earth which creates our world through the seasonal year. The Chinese called it seeing the fading yin and growing yang of one season and the growing yin and fading yang of another season. Knowing this cycle will happen again each year when the "edges of the year meet" (Ashanti in Africa), makes for great serenity. It seems natural for traditional human cultures to set up structures which help them relate to the changing earth/sky patterns. Humans "must approach Cosmos via the Physiognomy of their own Homeland, or they work against Nature."

Many of the famous henges are made entirely of stone, but occasionally, particular sections were made of wooden posts, long since rotted away. For instance, in the 1960s, it was discovered that the Neolithic structure of Woodhenge had a ditched 'ritual' enclosure where holes had been dug to hold wooden posts.

While Stonehenge has had more publicity; it is probably true that the great Avebury Monument was more important: the entire ritual complex covers more than two miles. Part of it was made of wooden posts. When Stukeley first saw it in 1719 he noted that "the country people have a high notion of it...They still call it the Sanctuary. The veneration for it had been handed down thro' all the successions of times and people." But then a few years later in 1724, he reported with grief that two thirds of the temple had been plowed up by two farmers. He wrote: "The loss of this work, I did not lament alone; but all the neighbours (except the person that gained the little dirty profit) were heartily grieved for it." It was so damaged that it was lost sight of until the 1930s, when excavation began. Cunnington found the cavities of two stone rings and, in addition, six concentric rings of post holes, dug about 2500 BC to receive timber uprights. At the very center of this area was a single slender post hole.

In his book on Avebury, Dawes states that "the life of the

henge came from the living land. Among primitive peoples everywhere, landscape is still recognized as a divine functioning body...The temple [Avebury] served to amplify and render more accessible the sacred qualities of the *genius loci*." Quoting from earlier research, Dawes remarks that to the Romans, the domestic snakes "were the male and female forms of the family or clan's power of continuing itself by reproduction. At every wedding, a bed, the *lectus genialis*, was made for the *genius* and *iuno* of husband and wife and its presence in the home was a sign of matrimony." Then going even further back, Dawes shows that in the Neolithic age, at Avebury, the two enormous, winding processional ways, defined by 100 pairs of standing stones, were the entrance for this "power" into the Avebury circle. In Roman times these "Lararia serpents were not regarded as *portraits* relating to one generation, but as passing, on death, to their successors. This helps to explain why the Avebury monuments were still receiving active veneration in AD 1300, long after the Neolithic peoples had vanished. Eventually, in adapting to modern times, the genius had to give up its body, and now [the word, genius] appears in the dictionaries as 'high intellectual ability measured by performance on a standardized intelligence test, i.e. 140+ or even 180'."

Avebury Henge was "no sculpture in the sense of being a finite completed object. It was brought to completion *at the right time* by human participation." Different parts of the vast Avebury complex were activated during the particular seasonal festival relating to that part of the structure. So you can see that Avebury with its circles of wooden posts is a fitting example for our own wood henges today.

FINDING THE PROPER LOCATION FOR YOUR OWN WOODHENGE

If you have already set up and used a medicine wheel you will now have some idea of the patterns of sun and land forms in your own place throughout the year which will make a henge structure much easier to design. While the medicine wheel is designed to indicate the four cardinal directions and the sacred center; the henge must show the risings and settings of the sun for the four major earth days: solstices and equinoxes; thus it takes a great deal more preparation and planning. To build a Woodhenge you must have access to an open space with a distant view in at least one direction.

In most cases the henge cannot be made large enough to duplicate the effects of the famous Stonehenge in Britain, where the sun seems to set right behind the stone; instead our henges will be pointing toward the particular land form where the sun sets in our place or bioregion. Actually, this is an advantage because it helps tie us to our own land. The place where the henge sets must be flat. That in itself will dictate the size of the henge. If at all possible, there should be a distant view in at least one direction. Ideally, you should be able to see the sunset point at either the summer or winter solstice. These are most important because they mark the turning point of the light of the sun. But if none of your possible sites fit these ideal requirements don't despair. Use what you have.

SITING THE HENGE THE "NATURAL" WAY

The simplest and most natural way to design the henge is, first, to decide the location and then measure the narrowest part of the available space there and put in a temporary stake to mark the center. Supposing your space is roughly 20×40ft. (this is a small henge). Your center point would be one half of the narrower dimension—10 ft. With this center point, the finished henge will be only 20 ft. in diameter. Tie a 10 ft. long string to this center stake and, pulling it taut, walk around the center point to mark out the circle. You can use a sharpened stick to scratch the line in the ground. Set this center stake up a year ahead of the date you plan to build the henge. Then through the year at each of the great earth festival days you site in the sunrise and sunset point.

You will need one other person for this siting because you must have a foresite and a backsite. The observer stands at the backsite (the post marking the center of the proposed henge). The foresite person (carrying a sharpened stake) stands along the outer rim of the circle in the general direction where the sun has been rising. At the first flash of the rising sun, the observer tells the foresite person to move left or right as the sun rises. This is done by prearranged hand signals so there's no confusion. In this way you get the final spacing of the entire sun as its middle clears the horizon. The sun does not rise or set directly straight up; it moves at an angle. (Actually, to be technical the earth is doing the moving here.) Before the foresite person moves he or she should pound the sharpened stake into the ground to mark the place.

For the setting sun the procedure is the same, but for safety, both persons should use a double thickness of totally black exposed photographic film over their eyes for the final few moments of watching the sun. Of course, it is always possible that bad weather will obscure the sky on any one of the important dates. If this happens, you can fill that direction in by compass reckoning from your known sites.

SITING THE HENGE USING THE COMPASS AND MODERN DATA

It is possible by complex sitings and the use of an Ephemeris to line up your site without having sited in on the earth festival days, but the more natural way is to let Nature help you. If you want to put up your henge sometime before an entire year has gone by that is relatively simple. Just site in the alignments as given in the paragraph above at the time of one of the solstices or the equinoxes. Then measure from that point for the other important alignments. For this you will need to consult the book, *Sun Angles for Design* by Robert T. Bennett (see Reference Notes for further information on this book). The book can generally be found in the reference room of most libraries. Or if you live far from any city you can send for it on inter-library loan. For amateurs like us, it is much easier to use Bennett's book than an Ephemeris. Since the book is written to help people line up the siting of houses to make use of solar energy, it provides very clear diagrams of the sun's journey through the sky, aligned with the compass degrees. It has many dates throughout the year but fortunately, for henge building, it has the dates of the solstices and equinoxes. Of course it cannot have every degree of latitude but it does have the degrees of latitude for representative major cities. Look up the city nearest to your latitude. While this is not scientifically exact because your place may not be on the precise latitude of the nearest big city, it is helpful enough for henge buildng. (See References Notes for how difficult it is to compute precise alignments by formula.)

When you find Bennet's book, xerox the "sun angle chart" nearest your latitude. Then, back on the henge site, use a compass to site in the degrees of the azimuth the book gives for the rising and setting of the sun in your location. Frederick Adams designed his first henge in 1968. During the years since then as he designed henges for others in the Los Angeles area, he has worked out the following instructions:

1) Mark a center point on a board and draw a circle slightly larger than your magnetic compass.
2) Center the compass in the circle, and place the board at the selected center of your henge site.
3) Rotate the compass so that the needle points to 15 (because in the Los Angeles area magnetic north is at 15). North on your compass is now True North. Polaris, the North Star, will be within 1 degree of this direction.
4) On the board mark lines at North, South, East, West, and at the following degrees on the compass: 61, 119, 241 and 299. If convenient, use the same center point and measure the degree points with a large protractor for greater accuracy.
5) Remove the compass and run a cord from a nail at the center point of the board, through each marked point to the boundary of the henge.
6) Mark each alignment spot with a stake so that each spot is clearly marked for putting in the posts when you actually build the henge.

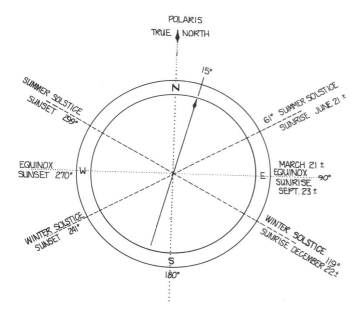

The above directions are for Los Angeles. For your own area, get a topographical map to find the declination for your area. It's printed at the bottom of the map. If the declination is to the east of true north, you subtract the declination from the compass points given in Bennett's book. If the declination is west of true north, you add the declination to your compass reading.

I've successfully used the above directions in many different areas. In my own area, however, because the entire north is blocked off by a mountain we've never done a complete henge.

Now your henge site is set up for the ritual building of the henge. It may be that your site does not have distant views in most directions; therefore the sun will be rising and setting over nearby trees or distant houses or buildings. That's alright because the sun's movement will still be obvious and the changing, slanting light of the sun will be focused for you by the henge. Through ritual, the distant house or building will become part of the ritual journey of the sun.

RITUALLY SETTING UP YOUR HENGE

The best ritual time to actually set up your henge is on the day of one of the four major earth festivals: solstices or equinoxes. Another possiblity is one of the cross-quarter days, which includes May day and Samhain (Hallowe'en). You will divide your group into four clans so that each clan will be responsible for setting up the posts for one of the directions of the henge. You can also set up posts for other important alignments for your group. For instance, if the general location of the place where you will be taking your children on their yearly "pilgrimage" with gourd rattles is visible this should certainly be marked with a post. All posts will be decorated or carved at the ritual setting up.

> Dancing and singing the mighty Landforms, miming the Seasonal Rites of other species of life: animal, vegetable, mineral and meteoric, generate a supreme Ceremonial Art [which] sanctifies everyday Life in Nature on the Mandala of the Year, of which our Henge serves as the principal Regional-Cosmic Dial. The Year itself becomes a continual revelation, epiphany, and individuation in the Jungian sense…In painting, sculpture, costume, poetry, music, drama and dance, we develop the imagery of our own Native Plants as Charms for the different posts which align with canyons, mountain ridges, central valleys, streams and inclined plains radiating into the Continental Vastus, as well as with Heavenly Bodies.

Once your henge is set up people will be drawn to it in time of joy (to celebrate with the greater beings) or in time of sadness (to be inspired by the gods of the place). Sometimes just to sit in the henge and see the distant valley or mountain where the group goes on pilgrimage is enough. Such connections between symbolized land and actual land is healing in itself, as shown by the Laguna Indian, Tayo in the book, *Ceremony*:

> He remembered the black of the sand paintings on the floor of the hogan; the hills and mountains [here] were the mountains and hills they had painted in sand. He took a deep breath of cold mountain air; there were no boundaries…

The above directions set up the preliminary arrangements to make the henge, but for the great rituals connected with building the henge see the next chapter because Henge building contributes to bringing the sky into your life.

The Hako Pattern for Pilgrimages through the land

BASIC BACKGROUND

As indicated before in this work, the roots of any human behavior, which deeply move us, lie far back—with our animal ancestors. This is true of the "Hako" pattern of ritual pilgrimages as well. While studying African tribal people, Garner (1896) heard them talk about "one of the most remarkable habits of the chimpanzee...the *kanjo* as it is called in the native tongue. The word...implies more of the idea of 'carnival'. It is believed that more than one family takes part in these festivities." After making a kind of drum out of damp clay and waiting for it to dry, "the chimpanzees assemble by night in great numbers and the carnival begins. One or two will beat violently on this dry clay, while others jump up and down in a wild grotesque manner. Some of them utter long rolling sounds as if trying to sing...and the festivities continue in this fashion for hours." Two modern ethologists, V. and F. Reynolds say that "apart from the drum, [this account] describes quite well what occurred in the Budongo Forest in its extreme form as we heard it six times." It happened only twice at night; the other four times it was during the day. This event "consisted of prolonged noise for periods of hours, whereas ordinary outbursts of calling and drumming lasted a few minutes only." While no one claims to know the essential meaning of this chimp ceremony, Reynolds does state that "twice it seemed to be associated with the meeting at a common food source of bands that may have been relatively unfamiliar to each other." In this chimp ceremony we can see the earliest beginnings of a ritual form which continued to take place among early humans and, in some form, still continues today among traditional peoples.

Human groups of hunter-gatherers moved in regular patterns, following game and the seasons. Occasionally these different groups met, often by accident. "But, indications are that at special times—when game was assembled in one area, when certain edible fruits and nuts were ripe for gathering—a concentration of bands took place." This still occurs among the Kalahari when gathering mongongo nuts. On our continent, because the California Indians were "spared the blight of agriculture," as Carleton Coon succinctly puts it: when they had harvested enough acorns they would cache the surplus and travel, visiting other bands along the way: singing, dancing and chanting. Ritual encounters among the different groups resulted in various forms of the "The Hako." The intensity of these encounters helped hone the languages of certain California tribes so that these languges were among the most sophisticated in the world. Language itself became their art form.

This kind of interaction developed among the Plains Indians into a particular ceremony, where one tribe travelled formally through their land to meet with another tribe. During this journey, they ritually greeted each of the other beings they encountered: trees, rivers, mountains and rocks. All were part of the "community." The Pawnee called this ceremony The Hakkow, meaning "breathing mouth of wood," the feathered wands carried by the leaders. From this word, *hakkow*, ethnologists came to call such ceremonies by the generic term, "Hako."

The Omaha called it *Wawan*, "to sing for someone." The ceremony had many different aspects including the binding together of two different groups: one called "The Fathers" and the other, "The Children." But, essentially the ceremony had to do with the whole of the community including the non-human beings. The Pawnee priest, Tahirussawichi explains this aspect:

> We take up the Hako in the spring when the birds are mating, or in the summer when the birds are nesting and caring for their young, or in the fall when the birds are flocking, but not in the winter when all things are asleep. With the Hako we are praying for the gift of life, of strength, of plenty, and of peace, so we must pray when life is stirring everywhere.

Black Elk, describing a similar ceremony among the Lakota Sioux, called *Hunkapi*, "The Making of Relatives," tells of the culture hero, Matohoshila who says, "We have established a relationship of peace, not only among ourselves, but within ourselves and with all the Powers of the Universe." The Hako, at its deepest levels, provides us with a ritual structure for bonding with all the beings of our own place.

PERSONAL INTRODUCTION

Ten years ago I began using the Hako pattern for ritual journeys into nature because I felt it would help people to begin to feel a real connection with the non-human beings of their own place. I had no idea then of the depth of commitment the ceremony opens up after it is done in the same place for a number of years.

The first time I did a Hako ceremony with a large group was in 1979. Fred Hodkins was on the planning committee for the Association of Humanistic Psychology Annual Meeting in Denver. At that time he was still a minister. He had heard such enthusiastic remarks about my book, *Earth Festivals*, from the women who used it for their church school that he called me to ask if I would give a talk on ritual for the entire group and a workshop for a smaller group. Knowing that I would be dealing with highly trained psychologists and therapists of various sorts, I realized I would have to approach ritual through a psychological perspective. Fortunately for my focus, I had just had the most remarkable experience I've ever had with a great being of nature that previous winter. I tell of this experience, to do with the atmospheric phenomena called the "jet stream," in the following chapter. With this opener I was able to bypass a lot of psychological bullshit and open people up to the power of nature; thus many of them were inspired to come along on the "Hako" ritual pilgrimage with me.

My talk and the ritual together provided such a unique experience for this audience that during the next few days of the meeting, men from a number of different psychological disciplines made appointments to talk to me, privately. What I discovered was that they thought this was a very powerful new approach and were sure it would be very successful; therefore, they wanted to be remembered when I established this approach and went "big time." In fact, the response immediately after that talk was so unexpected that Fred, half jokingly said: "Remember I discovered you." Well none of the expected drama happened, because what I am doing is not a new gimmick for helping people or making me rich. Instead it's a very ancient "way" of connecting humans and nature so that we can live as nature intended us as programmed in our genes. Hence it's not commercially marketable as is a "quick cure." What it requires is a total change of life—a movement toward goals which are not generally acknowledged in the Industrial Growth Society.

One of the men who waited patiently to talk to me after the big crowd left was Rick Medrick, head of the Outdoor Leadership Training Seminars in Colorado. Because his projected plan had come directly out of his intense ties with his own mountains, I agreed to meet again to talk at length about it. For some years he had thought about doing something he was calling BREAKING THROUGH. They had tried it just once. That experiment made him realize they needed something more than mountain climbing and river running; they needed ritual. This is where I came in and I agreed to try it. That summer we did the first BREAKING THROUGH with rituals and we began to learn from the mountains and the river.

Each year on BREAKING THROUGH, we follow the same route on our ritual journey. I began to recognize just exactly what the land form does to people in each place. The resulting human/earth bonding astounded us. The more skilled Rick and I become at recognizing what the land wants from us the easier it becomes; because it's not us; its the mountains and the river who do the bonding. We spend two days in a secluded valley, giving our people the necesssary skills and beginning rituals; then two days white water rafting on the Arkansas River; followed by four days in the alpine Crestone Peaks area. I teach Tai Chi every day and we do rituals whenever the mountains or rocks or trees tell us to. The final ritual is a "talking staff" after climbing Tai Chi style, and unroped, the most difficult 14,000 foot peak in the state. (I explain the "talking staff" later on, in chapter sixteen.) Without the experience of this yearly pilgrimage on BREAKING THROUGH, I would not have known how to set up my next "pilgrimage."

Roaming the "in-between" areas here in the mountains above Silverton, I had found such exquisite places that I felt guilty keeping them to myself. We are very lucky here. Although the roads in the valleys are filled with tourists and the high tundra filled with four-wheeled vehicles, in-between there's nobody. I found myself ritually returning to each of these areas at the proper time of year. That happened because there's no way to resist the pull of such places when once seen. So, five years ago I set up the first "Taoist Autumn Equinox Celebration." We listed it in Rick's brochure the first year; but since then it's grown mostly by word of mouth. I can only take twelve people each year because that's how many can fit on the rock where I do the tea ceremony for our honored guest, the sacred waterfall.

With this one event I've "ruined more people's lives" than anything else I do. That's a phrase I use when someone wants to study Tai Chi with me. I warn them by saying you probably will be sorry beause it will "ruin your life." And it usually does—meaning they can no longer take the Industrial Growth Society seriously—and that means quitting the usual, normal job and other traumatic events. Of course, once all this happens, none of them would ever go back to being half-dead. But the change is not easy. I think the quickest way to show the depth of what people experience in these sacred places of my land is to, once again, quote Donna, who was along on the 1985 Autumn Equinox. She said that the mountains had given her permission to be reverent; that's what nature does, when ritually approached. It allows us to return to the "original religion"; and once that's done all the systems of organized religion just "leave you."

I've gone into these two events in some detail to show how I've discovered that the Hako does provide the fundamental pattern for restoring the connection between humans and nature. When you give a group of people the chance to fully live as hunter-gatherers always lived, daily moving together through the place, where the trees and rocks and waterfalls are 'sacred'—worshipping the beauty and chanting the songs these natural beings give you—then you "remember" deep inside that "this is how it always was." And then you are home!

Once I began to discover the power of "the Hako" ritual, I started reading more about the early ethnographers' research into the ceremony. The main source for this ceremony is Alice Fletcher's study with the Pawnee ritual leader, Tahirussawichi, published in 1904. Concerning this study, Hartley Burr Alexander wrote: "The ceremony which has thus been described, chiefly in the words of an intelligent and reverential custodian of the mystery, is the most complete and perfect extant example of a type of religious rite worldwide in its development." He calls it "perhaps the most beautiful of all Indian rites, not in its displays, which are slight, but in the wealth of poetic interpretation which it brings...A vision of the world is established in a ceremonial mode." He says that it is similar in its effects to the most famous of all Greek ceremonies: The Eleusinian Mysteries. (See my *Earth Wisdom*, pages 37 to 41 for more about this connection.)

During the years that I've been using variations of the Hako, I continued my research into why and how it worked. Obviously I cannot reconstruct for you each step of this learning process. The best I can do here is give a few of the highlights from various disciplines which helped me to understand the reasons for the depth of this experience in nature.

Beginning with Jungian insights connected with "depth psychology," Bowlby explains: "[A]ll the instinctive systems of a species are so structured that as a rule they promote the survival of the species within its own environment of adaptedness...On some occasions the relevant part of the environment is recognized by perception of some relatively simple character, such as a moving flash of light; far more often, however, recognition entails the perception of pattern. In all such cases, we must suppose, the individual has *a copy of that pattern in its* Central Nervous System [my italics] and is structured to react in special kinds of ways when it perceives a matching pattern in the environment." Going back even deeper into this phenomenon—to the findings of ethology—Konrad Lorenz says that our cognitive apparatus is itself an objective reality which has acquired its present form through evolutionary adaptation to the real world: "[W]e have developed 'organs' only for those aspects of reality which, in the interests of survival, it was imperative to take account, so that selection pressure produced this particular cognitive apparatus."

As the Jungian analyst, Stevens points out: "Jung, for all his Platonic idealism, was clearly on to a similar notion as Lorenz concerning 'the facts of objective reality' in his conception of the phylogenetic psyche as being 'objective.' What Jung failed to do, however, was to develop the necessary biological argument to substantiate his view." Of course Jung could not have done this, as Stevens admits. First, Jung was not a biologist and, even more relevant, the new field of ethology was just beginning. Jung fully accepted that the archetype had an instinctual component; but what really interested him was just how the archetype found symbolic expression in consciousness. As he wrote to Harding: "The picture changes at once when looked at from the inside, that is, from within the realm of the subjective psyche. Here the archetype presents itself as numinous, that is, it appears as an *experience* of fundamental importance."

In his special wilderness edition of the Canadian ecophilosophy journal, *The Trumpeter*, Alan Drengson writes: "If Jung is correct and there is an archetype of Sacred Space within us, then when we go to such a place…we accept the possibility that some kind of transformation may occur. This acceptance may not be conscious, but is there, and it makes change, growth or healing possible."

For me this helps to understand the power of "the tree" or "the rock" when experienced by the "collective mind and body" of a group travelling together on a ritual journey, such as the Hako. Because what we are really dealing with here is bonding—moving together in such a manner that the human is once again bonded to the earth in the same way as our ancestors were in the "old ways." When this happens we again experience sacred land because we have truly walked on it "in a sacred manner." The "something more" of ritual is created together by humans and non-human in that particular place.

While working on this chapter last December, preparations for Christmas (the only festival the IGS allows people these days), were frantically going on all around me here in our town. Essentially that means buying trips—driving clear to Farmington, New Mexico where the biggest shopping mall is. It's one hour or 50 miles over two high mountain passes to Durango, our closest town and then another half hour to Farmington. On our way out of town in the opposite direction, to climb up to timberline and ski down through untracked powder in the bliss of our high altitude sun we talk over this strange phenomenon—everyone else driving down 65 miles into the smog and darkness of the lowland inversion caused by this big high pressure system up in the mountains. As we start to climb up, I'm still mulling over the writing of this chapter, over festivals, in general and particularly over the strange phenomenon of Christmas shopping, when suddenly a phrase jumps into my mind and keeps recurring over and over—until finally I recognize it. I hadn't heard or thought of these words for more than thirty years: "We adore thee, Oh Christ and we bless thee" and the response, "Because by thy cross thou hast redeemed the world." And suddenly I was back as a child in Catholic school. During Lent, children were expected to stay after school and do "the Stations of the Cross" with the priest. He carried a large gilt cross accompanied by two altar boys with candles and the children followed, as they went from station to station. These stations are pictures of various parts of the journey Christ went through on his way to be crucified: carrying the cross, falling with the cross, nailing

on the cross and hanging from the cross, etc. At each station the priest and all others genuflect (kneel down) and rise. The priest says the above phrase and all the children respond. Then he reads out some prayer and they move onto the next station. Now years later I realize that too was a bonding. Walking down the aisle, kneeling, rising, looking at the candle, reciting the sort of chant together and moving on to the next station. All this ritual moving bonded the children to the powerful figure of the priest and to the whole image of how good it is to suffer for the world: in essence making them good Christians. But nowhere in this debased, late remnant of the old pilgrimages is there any mention at all of it being spring, the season of Rogationtide when for hundreds of years in Europe, the boundaries of the villages were marked off by priest and people.

Probably this concept of ritually marking the boundaries, dates clear back to the Roman festival of the Lupercalia. The city of Rome was originally settled by shepherds. On the Lupercalia, the young men carrying the fleece of sheep would run around the boundaries of the hill where Rome began, hitting all the young women they passed with the fleece to insure fertility for humans and their sheep. This fleece was called *februa*— which, of course, is the origin of the name of the month we call February. In Ireland within living memory there was a wide-spread custom called "tura"; consisting of a local pilgrimage at certain important dates around all the stones and megaliths of the area. The season of Rogationtide occurred throughout the middle ages in all parts of Europe and continued up until rather recently. In some rural places it was still in practice until the second World War. The ritual part of the ceremony takes the form of a perambulation around the fields or the town led by the priest carrying sacred emblems and crosses. A number of stations are made, and at each of them rogations or prayers of supplication were offered for the fertility of the earth and the aversion of bad influences. Here is a description, dating back to the Middle Ages:

> Now comes the day wherein they gad about, with cross in hand
> To bounds of every field, and round about their neighbor's land;
> And as they go, they sing and pray to every saint above…
> That he preserve both corn and fruit from storm and tempest great
> And them defend from harm, and send them store of drink and meat.

Here we can see some remnants of the "old ways" in Europe when tribal peoples wandered through their territories, greeting their forest gods. But, of course, by the Middle Ages the ritual journey had become completely human centered. What the Hako ceremony provides for us is a ritual journey acknowledging all the beings of the place not just humans and their belongings. As Aldo Leopold said: "We abuse the land because we regard it as a commodity belonging to us. When we see land as a community to which we belong, we may begin to use it with love and respect."

PREPARATIONS FOR THE HAKO CEREMONY

1. The "hako"

The two "hako" are the most important ritual symbols carried on the journey. The Pawnee made them from two pieces of ash wood, each about 3 feet long. The pith was burned out to leave an opening for the breath to pass through. However,

since they also have a downy feather at one end which moves in the breath it is not absolutely necessary to have a hollow tube.

I will give a fairly complete description of the Pawnee hako so that you can decide how much of the symbolism is suitable for your own place. Feathers and bones of animals which were important to the life of their place were tied on by the Pawnee. It is important for us modern people, making these "hako," to use only feathers that have been "given" to us by "those-who-walk-upon-the-air," the birds. In other words, use only feathers that you have found in your own place. Unless you find a bird run over on the highway do not try to imitate the main pendant on the Pawnee hako (see drawing). If you do find a road kill, then you can ethically take that many connected feathers; otherwise use only three feathers placed as a triad to symbolize the feather pendant. Since this ceremony is to acknowlege the other beings of our place, to kill any of them for the ceremony would be putting yourself right back into the Industrial Growth Society "substance" trap. We don't need the feather as "substance" here, but the feather as showing relationship between the earth and sky of our place. Indian life was so set up that every part of any animal they killed for food was used for some purpose; but they controlled their human population so that other peoples (the animals and the birds) could live. Since we no longer do that, we have no right to take the life of any other creature for any purpose other than necessary food.

The two tubes or wands of wood were rounded and smoothed. One was called "the breathing mouth of wood with the dark moving feathers" and the other, "the breathing mouth of wood with the white moving or swaying feathers." The first stem was painted blue to symbolize the sky. (Sky is one of the Four Great Powers of the Plains Indians and was called *Skan* by the Sioux.) A long straight line, running the entire length of the wood, was painted red, the symbol of life. Three split feathers were fastened to the stem as to an arrow. A fan-shaped pendant of ten brown feathers were hung onto the stem. "These feathers represented the Mother and led in certain of the rites."

"The blue paint represented the clear, cloudless sky" and "soft blue feathers were fastened around the mouthpiece end. These blue feathers also symbolized the clear sky, and it is this end which was always upward toward the...Powers." They fastened feathers of the duck to the other end. "The duck is familiar with the pathless air and water and is also at home on the land, knowing its streams and springs."

Red and white streamers were tied on to represent the sun and the moon, day and night. These were made of red cloth, dyed horsehair and white cotton cord; "but it is said that formerly soft deerskin strips painted red and twisted hair from the white rabbit were used."

The second stem was different from the first in two ways: it was painted green and the fan shaped pendant was made of seven white feathers to "represent the male, the father." The green "represents Toharu (Vegetation) the covering of Mother Earth." A red groove was painted the entire length. Blue feathers were also fastened at the breathing hole on this stem too. Woodpecker feathers were tied at the head of it. The Pawnee put the feathers of birds, which they considered as leaders, on the hako. You could use feathers from the birds of your own bioregion, which you consider "the leaders": chief of the day; chief of the night; chief of the trees; and the chief of the water.

Once made, these stems should be treated with great reverence at all times. Miss Fletcher wrote: "I have many times remarked the reverence felt toward the feathered stems... during the entire time that I was engaged with Tahirussawichi on the ceremony he never allowed the feathered stems to be placed on the floor" or anywhere but "on the skin they were wrapped in." She continues: "I have seen manifested among the tribes not only reverence toward these sacred symbols, but an affection that was not displayed toward any other objects. Few persons ever spoke to me of them without a brightening of the eyes. 'They make me happy', was a common saying." In our modern Hako ritual these stems, the "hako," will soon assume this role because they come to represent so many things for the people of the place: the joy of the pilgrimage together, all the animals and birds and plants they saw on the journey, their childhood chant journey with the gourd rattles and many other events: reverent or humorous or joyful.

It is not likely that you will have ash wood for the stems. You can use willow but it cannot be hollowed out easily. I often use willow because it is sacred to the Chinese and everywhere it grows it symbolizes life and water. It is also hardy. If you cut two pieces of willow they will grow back more easily than any other plant. You do not have to have the hollow wand, because, as mentioned above, the downy feathers at the end move in the slightest breath from wind or human. The most important thing to remember in making these two hako, is first, that you should try to use only those things which come from your own place.and second, use only "give-aways" from nature for each part. In fact, one of the on-going elements of delight on these hako journeys is to find just what is needed during the journey itself to complete your hako stem. Remember, these two hako are the essence of your place.

2. Corn

In the Hako, the Pawnee leader also carried an ear of Mother Corn. This was a perfect ear of white corn with the tip end painted blue for the sky and four equal lines running halfway down the ear to represent the four paths along which the great Above-Powers descend. For our bioregional Hako, try to use a local edible plant, instead of corn, to lead you on the journey. However, if you do not yet know any of the most important foods for Indians in your area or if they are all totally destroyed in your area, use a piece of a branch from a local tree or a pine cone.

Returning to the Mother Corn ear of the Pawnee. "Two straight sticks from the plum tree were bound to the corn by a braid of buffalo hair. One extended above the corn and one below." The latter one was pointed on the end so that it could be thrust into the ground to hold it. "To the other stick was tied a white, downy eagle feather. This feather had a double significance: It represented the high, white clouds that float near the dome of the sky where the powers dwell, thus indicating their presence with the corn. It also stood for the tassel of the cornstalk. The feather here refers to the male principle, the corn to the female. The plum-tree wood was chosen for the sticks because the tree is prolific in fruit...and so signified abundance. Buffalo hair represented the animal which supplied food and clothing for the people." For our modern hako we could use the hair of some animal in our place. Often, sad to say, the best source for this is once again, a "road kill."

3. Gourd rattles

In the Pawnee ceremony the leaders also carried two gourd rattles which "represented the gift of food to humans and the breast of the mother. Around the middle of each a blue circle was painted from which depended four equidistant lines of the same color. The circle represented the dome of the sky, and the four lines the four paths descending therefrom to earth." In our modern ceremony each person should have a gourd rattle decorated with any symbols of the place, which that person wants to put on the gourd. There are many reasons for each person having his or her own gourd. (See gourds in chapter sixteen.) But the main reason is that it connects the Hako with the children's chant journey. What the gourd does on the hako journey is help the human to communicate with tree, rocks etc. Also it integrates and coordinates emotions among the humans and other beings as well as encouraging chanting.

If you don't have enough gourds for your first year, plastic vitamin or medicine bottles from the drug store with about one fourth inch of dry split peas make a good substitute. Split peas are good because they last without breaking down into powder and have sharp edges so their sound is fairly authentic.

4. Final note

For the journey, as given below, I will be combining events from various Hako type journeys, which I have conducted during the past few years. I will combine directions, descriptions of powerful types of places you may encounter and anecdotes from actual experiences of people on these journeys. Do not consider that all of this happened in one single Hako ceremony. I will be giving a number of different aspects—poetic, legendary, natural history etc.—about each of the great natural beings you are likely to encounter. I'll not be saying much about the animals or birds you will encounter because there are so many different species involved.

DIRECTIONS FOR BEGINNING THE HAKO JOURNEY

Wealth of relationships not segregation nor inflation of the individual is regarded as the highest human value by the Chumash.
(a California tribe)

The white man does not understand the Indian for the reason that he does not understand America. He is too far removed from its formative processes. The roots of the tree of his life have not yet grasped the rock and soil...But in the Indian the spirit of the land is still vested; it will be until other men are able to divine and meet its rhythms. Men must be born and reborn to belong.
Luther Standing Bear

Luther Standing Bear is absolutely correct; however, in a ritual we are born and reborn each time and, after a few years of the Hako the roots of our tree of life will sink deeply into the rock and soil of our own place.

1. Directions for the Leader

The leader of the ceremony carries the feathered stem, which is painted blue. It has brown feathers tied on, so it is the female and the leader. It represents the night, the moon, the north, and stands for kindness and helpfulness. It will take care of the people. It is the mother. The assistant leader carries the other stem. It is the green stem with white feathers. "This feathered green stem represents the male, the day, the sun, and the south." Basically, the stems, the two hako, reconcile male and female or sun and moon. The blue stem, symbolizing the male sky, has brown feathers for the female tied on. The green stem, symbolizing the earth, has white feathers for the male tied onto it.

[The leader explains the down at the end of the hako by quoting the Pawnee priest] "The down grew close to the heart of the (bird) and moved as the bird breathed." It represents the breath and life of those "who-walk-upon-the-light-the-birds." They are our guides because they can go through all the elements: fly through the air, walk along the ground and some, such as the "dipper" bird can fly through the water. Other birds swim through the water. "The white down also represents the fleecy clouds of the sky and the life of heaven: ever moving as if it were breathing...it represents the great power, the blue sky (Skan) which is above the soft, white clouds." As the "breathing stems" guide us today they will be breathing in some of the breath from all the life we encounter on our journey. They will gather all this breath together for us and focus it so that when we use the "breathing stems," the hako, at the end of our journey today, the "Power" of all these beings will give us words so we can communicate with them. [Throughout the journey, whenever it is appropriate, call attention to the moving down feathers, as the hako "breathe."]

The leader carries the "Mother Corn" or "Mother plant" of that place. Before the journey begins the leader holds aloft the two hako stems and turns to the four directions to invoke the Powers of those directions. Then handing one to the assistant the leader addresses the plant. [Leader] "Mother (Corn) leads us again as we walk over the land. She leads us now, because she was born of Mother Earth and knows all places." [This symbolically turns the leadership over to the non-human.] The Pawnee leader of this ceremony who gave it to us, explained that "The first act of a man must be to set apart a place that can be made sacred and holy...a place where the lesser powers dwell."

[Then, using his own words the leader explains that on this ritual journey they will greet all the beings of the place: trees, animals, rocks, mountains, clouds etc. At each place we stop to read special words to acknowledge the power of this being for us or we will chant or sing to the being. It is important that the leader emphasize that "the sacred" to most traditional peoples included laughter as well as reverence. Before a Shinto ceremony the Shinto priest says: "Let us all now laugh."]

2. Outline of the journey.

It is important to have the rough outlines of the journey laid out ahead of time. Start the journey with a meeting with the non-human sufficiently exciting or complex so that everyone's mind is focused immediately on the journey and not still preoccupied with everyday problems. A river crossing is excellent where everyone must wade through the water. Or if there are hills or mountains or rocks near the beginning, start by leading the people through a narrow place where everyone is strung out by ones or twos and following the leader without knowing exactly what is ahead. Another possibility is leading them through thick trees in a zigazag manner as in a labyrinth. The idea here is to get everyone paying attention to the land itself. Do not try to do any sort of ritual at this first natural site. Ritually speaking, they must cross the threshold into the liminal state before any readings are done.

3. Talking

Everyone is encouraged to talk while moving along; but the talk should be about the here and now and not about politics, religion, etc., etc. Then when the group comes to a particularly important part of the journey, the leader gathers them together first and everyone enters this place shaking their rattles. This quiets the chatter and focuses expectation on the non-human, which they can expect to encounter.

4. Using gourd rattles.

> I didn't think I'd
> shake the pumpkin
> not just here & now
> not exactly tonight...

This Seneca Indian song about the pumpkin, which is what they called the gourd rattle is translated by the contemporary poet, Jerome Rothenberg. He continues: "Now, I had not shaken the pumpkin before, had not sung before or sung before to a rattle: I had not done any of these things and it would have seemed foolish to me then to have done them. It did seem foolish but at a point I was doing them and it no longer seemed foolish, seemed necessary if anything..."

Exactly! That's why I put his remarks here. When one first uses the gourd rattle it seems like it might be weird and out of place. But after a few shakes, the body takes over and ignores the confused mind and within a very short time, it seems the most "natural thing in the world"—which, of course, it is. We humans have been doing it for several thousand years. Using the gourd rattle in a group, while walking outside, one quickly finds out that the old Taoists were right to always carry a gourd along. Using the gourd helps us to "see"—to have that "generalized perception that can come into play only when the distinction between 'inside', and 'outside', between 'self' and 'things', between 'this' and 'that' has been entirely obliterated. Chuang Tzu's symbol for this state of pure consciousness which sees without looking, hears without listening, knows without thinking, is the god Hun-Tun (Chaos), the gourd."

THE RITUAL HAKO JOURNEY

[Learning how to read the land is a different kind of literacy than that which we learn in schools. It's much deeper and the connections are all there—all we have to do is learn to pay attention. Below, I list the natural beings you are most likely to encounter, together with the readings I have found helpful as well as incidents from Hako journeys I have led.]

Trees

When you come upon a tree which impresses the group, pause there a bit and use the Sioux ritual greeting: "O you people, who are always standing, who pierce up through the earth, and who reach even unto the heavens, you Tree People." If the tree is a pine tree you can read D.H. Lawrence's great tribute to the Ponderosa Pine which grew outside his cabin near Taos:

> [This] tree is a strong-willed, powerful thing-in-itself, reaching up and reaching down. With a powerful will of its own it thrusts green hands and huge limbs at the light above, and sends huge legs and gripping toes down, down between the earth and rocks, to the earth's middle.
>
> This big pine tree is like a guardian spirit...its column is always there, alive and changeless, alive and changing. The tree has its own aura of life. And in winter the snow slips off it, and in June it sprinkles down its little catkin-like pollen-tips, and it hisses in the wind, and it makes a silence within a silence...
>
> It is just a tree...And we live beneath it, without noticing. Yet sometimes, when one suddenly looks up and sees those wild doves there, or when one glances quickly at the inhuman-human hammering of a woodpecker, one realizes that the tree is asserting itself as much as I am. It gives out life, as I give out life...the tree's life penetrates my life, and my life the tree's. We cannot live near one another, as we do, without affecting one another.
>
> The tree gathers up earth-power from the dark bowels of the earth, and a roaming sky-glitter from above. And all unto itself, which is a tree, woody, enormous, slow but unyielding with life, bristling with acquisitive energy, obscurely radiating some of its great strength...The piny sweetness is rousing and defiant...the noise of the needles is keen with aeons of sharpness. In the volleys of wind from the western desert, the tree hisses and resists...its column is a ribbed, magnificent assertion.
>
> I am conscious that it helps to change me, vitally. I am even conscious that shivers of energy cross my living plasm, from the tree, and I become a degree more like unto the tree, more bristling and turpentiney...
>
> Its raw earth-power and its raw sky-power, its resinous erectness and resistance, its sharpness of hissing needles and relentlessness of roots, all that goes to the primitive savageness of a pine tree, goes also to the strength of man.
>
> Give me of your power, then, oh tree! And I will give you of mine.

If your Hako takes place in the fall, here is a reading for the golden aspen:

> The constant Aspen's unfolding gold. Only
> Once to touch the limbs like stems electric
> When they are charged with love, like gold.
> Is enough for me to be no longer heavy celibate
> Instead to be all air, unafraid as Adam
> Electric king of the leaves.

If you come across aspen or alders on your Hako journey you should thank them for their "give-away" to the other trees and the soil. Both of these trees fix nitrogen from the air. "Alders produce four times the nitrogen of other North American trees. And, being generous, the Alder is deciduous. It puts the nitrogen in little capsules (called leaves) and then drops them on the ground to return to the forest floor or enter nearby streams. In streams, these time-released nitrogen capsules eventually supply over 50% of the energy needed by young coho salmon in Oregon. On the forest floor, the decomposed leaves strengthen young and old Douglas fir." And then when the young Douglas fir has grown tall and strong enough the alder "return their bodies to Earth" so the fir can have more room to grow. The aspen do the same for the alpine fir and spruce in our mountains.

If appropriate, you can explain how many of our words, concerned with books, are related to trees.

> [T]he word book is from Old English, *bece*, the beech tree. The first books were runic beech rods. A book's pages rustle like leaves. We leaf through a book. A page was originally a trellis, words on a page like leaves on a trellis. The word, library, comes from the root word *LUBH* that means leaf or tree bark. Script and writing grow from roots meaning to scratch on bark. Trees still sway in our terms, old forests haunt our speech.

Move on through other trees, continuing on the ritual journey. If you hear sounds from the trees: rustling of branches, clicking of limbs or the susurrous sound of wind in the pine needles; have everyone stop and close their eyes and listen. After a few moments begin shaking the gourd rattles. Continue for a minute or so. Have them open their eyes and begin the Huichol chant.

Continue as long as they wish. As you continue on your journey, repeat the line, "The trees know..."

Rocks

When you get to a rock of any size at all, stop and pay homage to it. If your area does not have many rocks maybe you can find an area where the people will be standing below a rock on a hillside so that it stands against the sky. That's all you need to explain that The Rock is one of the four Great Powers, which make up Wakan Tanka, often erroneously translated as "the Great Spirit." The other three Powers are the Earth, the Blue Sky, (*Skan*) and the Sun. In 1917, Sword, an Oglala priest, explained:

> Yes, the Rock is the oldest. He is grandfather of all things. Which is next oldest? The earth. She is grandmother of all things. Which is next oldest? *Skan* (the Blue or Sky). He gives life and motion to all things. Which is the next oldest after *Skan*? The Sun. But He is above all things.

While the group is standing before the rock the Leader recites the Omaha chant:

> Truly, one alone of all is the greatest
> Inspiring to all mind,
> The great white rock [put in the color of your rock]
> Standing and reaching as high as the heavens...
> Truly as high as the heavens.
> Ho! Aged One
> Rock
> Aged One
> Ho, Unmoved from time without end, truly
> You sit,
> In the midst of the paths of the coming winds
> In the midst of the winds you sit
> Aged one...
> Ho! This is the desire of your little ones
> That we may take part in your strength
> Therefore we your little ones desire to walk closely
> by your side
> Venerable One!

Then the group can slowly walk around the rock, gourd rattles shaking to gather up the rock's power. Circumambulate the rock for the sacred four times. Before proceeding you can tell them what the Sioux, Lame Deer said: "Every man needs a stone to help him...people are always picking up odd shaped stones, saying it's just because they please them. But I know better. Deep inside you there must be an awareness of rock power...otherwise you would not pick them up and fondle them as you do." You can encourage everyone, as they walk along on the Hako to pick up a rock, which appeals to them.

If you find a cave or a deep rock overhang, go into it with the rattles to chant, summoning the very rock itself to answer you. You can use a Paiute chant from the Ghost Dance ceremony:

> The rocks are ringing,
> The rocks are ringing.
> They are ringing in the mountains,
> They are ringing in the mountains.

Birds

Proceed on the way. When you see birds acknowledge them by the Winnebago phrase: "Those who walk upon the light, the birds." And begin the chant again, "Nobody Knows."

The Light of the Sun

Be particularly aware of the lighting as you move along. Watch for a place where the sun's ray's slant through narrow rocks or trees branches. If the group enters such a place have everyone stop and just stand silently in the rays of the sun for a moment. Then read from the Pawnee Hako Ceremony: "Shakuru, the Sun...is the first of the visible powers to be mentioned in the ceremony. It is very potent; it gives man health, vitality, and strength. Because of its power to make things grow, it is sometimes spoken of as atius, father." We will shake our gourd rattles toward the sun to thank the sun for all that he gives-away to us.

As you proceed along, if you find that the sun slants through the high arched branches of trees, stop again and explain that the great period of building cathedrals in Europe began when they had cut down the last of the great primeval forests. "A metaphor of forms and spaces within [these cathedrals] suggests nostalgia and profound emotion linking cathedral and the post-Pleistocene primeval forest," according to Paul Shepard. The human longing to experience again the slanting rays of the sun through the high curved ribs of the tree was the inspiration for Gothic cathedrals. Furthermore, Filarete, a specialist on medieval architecture tells us that, "The pointed arch, the definitive shape in Gothic architecture, is inherited from primitive Teutonic structures. The Gothic arch is the shape of two upright saplings tied together at the top as in a neolithic hut. The cathedral congregation, facing the east window, is a reenactment of a Teutonic tribe facing the barbaric sun-god Balder through the door of the hut."

Walking through our mountains here near Silverton, whenever I see this "cathedral lighting" among the trees, I tell about this connection between forests and cathedrals Recently, one of my friends, Steve, wrote a beautiful piece concerning this connection:

> There is a large, flat meadow of aspen along the course of Lime Creek through which I often walk. The trees are mature and tall, their lower branches having long since withered, died and fallen. The slender white trunks of the trees rise from ths floor, radiant and luminous. Although the forest is dense, there is no sense of confinement or darkness; the distinct impression is one of open, glowing space. The lines of the trunks soar upward where they join the curving branches of the forest crown, a lofty region where individual trees lose identity in the vaulted ceiling of the forest roof. Light filters through the leaves, softened, and against this subdued background, finds itself magnified in those places where it passes through openings in the canopy unimpeded, brilliant rays striking the heights and sometimes descending to the very roots of the forest...
>
> Light filters through the high branches of the aspen wood much like the light of the clerestory. White aspen trunks soar upward into the heights of the forest crown much like the responds which decorate the interior space of the cathedral. The forest glows. The forest soars. The forest was before the cathedral, and will most likely remain long after the cathedral has gone. The Gothic cathedral is a magnificent expression of the forest, an elegant distillation, a wondrous abstraction, but it is not the forest itself.

Rivers and Streams

During the Pawnee ritual Hako journey, they sing one chant when they see the river in the distance. As they reach the edge of the water, they sing: "Behold, the water now touches our feet! River we must cross. Oh Kawas (the brown feathers on the hako represent this sky power) hear! We call you. Oh come, and give us permission to pass through the stream." Then as they wade deeper into the stream: "Behold, the water now covers our feet. River we must cross." When they have forded the stream they pause at the bank. "We are wet with water...but we must not touch our bodies where we are wet to dry ourselves, for the running water is sacred. So we sing the song to call on the Wind, Hotoru, to come and touch us that we may become dry."

> Hither winds, come to us
> Come oh winds come
> Now the winds come to us
> Lo the winds round us sweep
> Safe now are we
> By the winds safe.

Before you leave the banks of the stream read this ancient Taoist story:

> Confucius was taking a walk with his disciples along the bank below the Lu Chiang waterfall. In the raging torrent, where even a turtle would not have survived they saw a man's head bobbing in the waves. The disciples dashed forward to help, but the man climbed out quite unconcerned. 'Have you a tao', Confucius asked, 'to tread in the water like this?' 'No', the man replied, 'I began in what is native to me, grew up in what is natural to me, matured by trusting destiny. I enter the vortex with the inflow and leave with the outflow; follow the Way of the Water instead of imposing a course of my own; this is how I tread it'.

After you finish the story, have everyone chant "Nobody Knows," once more because now we understand even more that "the rivers knows."

Wind

If you go through a tree area and the wind is blowing enough to really move the trees, read from John Muir's description of a wind storm in the Sierras long ago. He was fascinated by the different movements and sounds of the various kinds of trees:

> Young pines, light and feathery as squirrel-tails, were bowing almost to the ground; while the grand old patriarchs, whose massive boles had been tried in a hundred storms, waved solemnly above them, their long arching branches streaming fluently on the gale, and every needle thrilling and singing and shedding off keen lances of light like a diamond...Even when the grand anthem had swelled to its highest pitch, I could distinctly hear the varying tones of individual trees...and even the infinitely gentle rustle of the withered grasses at my feet. Each was expressing itself in its own way—singing its own song and making its own peculiar gestures.

Call attention to the wind breathing through the hako and stirring the down attached to their mouths.

Mountains and Hills

If you will encounter any hills or mountains on your journey, then it should be arranged ahead of time that someone play a few bars of music on the flute when they are first sighted through intervening trees or rocks; or when you have just come around the bend of an intervening hill. When the flute music ends just have everyone stand and gaze at the mountain or hill while you read the chant for mountains from the Hako ceremony:

> Mountains loom upon the path we take;
> Yonder peak now rises sharp and clear,
> Behold! It stands with its head uplifted,
> Thither go we, since our way lies there.

Then part way up the hill you will be climbing, the leader reads the second verse:

> Mountains loom upon the path we take;
> Yonder peak now rises sharp and clear,
> Behold! We climb, drawing near its summit;
> Steeper grows the way and slow our steps.

At the top:

> Mountains loom upon the path we take;
> Yonder peak that rises sharp and clear,
> Behold us now on its head uplifted;
> Planting there our feet, we stand secure.

> Mountains loom upon the path we take;
> Yonder peak that rose so sharp and clear,
> Behold us now on its head uplifted;
> Resting there at last, we sing our song.

Everyone can then sit down to rest and look around. Before people begin to wander to look at whatever they want, gather them all together, looking out over the earth below and recite the praise of Mother Earth from the Hako ceremony:

> Behold! Our Mother Earth is lying here.
> Behold! She gives of her fruitfulness.
> Truly, her power she gives us.
> Give thanks to Mother Earth who lies here.
> Behold! On Mother Earth the growing fields!
> Behold the promise of her fruitfulness!
> Truly, her power she gives us.
> Give thanks to Mother Earth who lies here.

SACRED GOAL OF THE JOURNEY

You might want the mountain summit to be the goal of the sacred Hako journey. But you also might want a sheltered little valley behind the mountain as the site. This depends on your land forms. What you want for the goal is a place with power but also that seems sheltered, contained and where the earth seems to surround one with peace. In *feng-shui* terms such a site is a small hollow or clearing that is protected on three sides, the fourth opening out on an expansive or panoramic view. If you do not have a spot with a view then you can choose a clearing in the trees where the trees seem to protect the spot. If possible there should be one particular focus for the view (even from the clearing). This can be a particularly beautiful tree or a rock or an especially harmonious grouping of rocks and trees. It's nice to have a small stream flowing through but not necessary at all; the contained, secure sense is the most important.

This sacred goal should be decided before the journey begins. Then, on the actual journey, when the group is nearing the spot, the assistant unobtrusively, goes ahead to the final destination to tie a short rope between two trees to form an entranceway into the site. In Japan, Shinto shrines always have a straw rope hanging between two posts or trees as the entrance to the *kami* or god within—the rock or tree or waterfall. Then, when a ceremony begins, the Shinto priest formally unties the rope to let the people through. This constitutes the "opening of the ceremony." The curve of the hanging straw rope was later copied to make the famous *tori*, the curving cross beam in front of the wooden gates of shrines.

When your group arrives at this "sacred goal," the leader explains this "straw" rope and then ritually unties the rope so all can enter the sacred place. As the leader walks through the entrance he or she says:

> Mother corn (or your native plant food) has guided us to the entrance . . .
> She has crossed the threshold and entered . . . She represents the power
> that dwells in the earth which brings forth the food that sustains life:
> so we speak of her as 'mother breathing forth life'.

All then enter, following "Mother Corn."

Circumambulating the boundary

Once you arrive at the sacred spot everyone should be ritually gathered together. You will circumambulate the spot—going around the boundary, using the gourd rattles chanting any chant you wish. This is to demarcate the sacred spot and focus the energies. Go around four times. Then the leader stands in the middle and carefully, reverently places the two feathered hako stems on a forked branch in the very middle of the space. This is where they will be during the time the group spends at this sacred spot; providing a focus for the group. After they are arranged you can once again explain the symbolism of the hako as they unite male and female, father sun and mother earth etc. As you explain this you can use as examples all the beings of this sacred spot where you are.

Lunch and rest and wandering

Many events can take place here. Lunch should be laid out and eaten here with attention paid to giving-away the first pieces of fruit or cheese or whatever to the gods of the place so they share in the feast. Then everyone should be free to wander in the vicinity or sleep or play or whatever for some time.

If it is impossible to have even a very tiny fire here, then before people take off to wander a bit, tell them to bring back something with them that seems special to them—either a rock or piece of wood etc. These are arranged in the central area in front of the two feathered hako stems resting on the forked branch.

Talking staff council

Calling everyone together again, have them all sit in a circle around a tiny fire, whether it's warm or not. In the hot Australian desert at temperatures of 100 degrees, the aborigines still have a tiny fire going even if there's no cooking to be done. From the time I've spent out in nature, I know how important "Grandfather Fire" is to focus the energy of the group within the natural spot. If you are not allowed to have a fire here, then have people arrange the natural items they brought back (as mentioned in the paragraph above).

Everyone should have their gourd rattle in hand. [Leader] The Blackfoot Indians say that "A man may be walking along and hear a bird, insect, stone or something else singing; he remembers the song and claims it as especially given to him." The poet, Jerome Rothenberg tells us that "Anything, in fact, can deliver a song because anything—night, mist, the blue sky, east, west, women, adolescent girls, men's hands & feet, the sexual organs of men & women, the bat, the land of souls—is alive. Here is the central image of shamanism & of all 'primitive' thought, the intuition of a connected & fluid universe, as alive as a man is—just that much alive."

Begin the chant, "Nobody Knows." After a couple of times around of the Huichol chant, have volunteers call out anything they want to put in—for instance, "the cloud knows" etc. This can be serious or humorous or sexual or poetic or all the above at once. Let this continue until it becomes obvious that all of nature is involved in the chant—that nature "knows" more than we do.

Then put the rattles aside and introduce the "talking staff." (See chapter sixteen for how to do this.) Mention before the council begins that the "breathing stems" of the hako will give us words for what we experienced on our journey as we walked to this place in a "sacred manner." Using the talking staff rules, let everyone tell of their experiences during the ritual journey or how they feel right now, here in this "sacred" spot.

When the "talking staff" has gone around three times, the ceremony is brought to a close by ritually circling the enclosure with rattles in hand and chanting "We circle around the boundaries of the earth." Point out before the chant starts how this journey has enlarged our personal boundaries.

RETURN JOURNEY

On the return trip there's not much necessity of planned rituals as the whole journey has by now become ritualized so that almost everything anyone does becomes part of the on-going ritual. This is the "more than" which takes place when a ritual is going well. There will be spontaneous poems, chants, and sexual remarks. Remember that the two hako are male and female and sexual humor within a sacred event provides still another element of reconciliation. As you return, there are a couple of times when you should stop and provide another ritual moment. At the place where you first saw the mountain or hill in the morning, you should stop and have everyone sit and face toward the mountain or hill while you read Li Po's poem:

Flocks of birds have flown high and away.
A solitary drift of cloud, too, has gone wandering on.
And I sit alone with the peak, towering beyond.
We never grow tired of each other, the mountain and I.

You can insert the name of your mountain or hill before "Peak" if you know it. If your hill is so small it does not have a name on the map you should be sure someone has come up with a name before you leave the lunch spot.

When you cross the stream again—either the one on the journey or the first one you crossed as you began—read a bit from Gary Snyder's poem. I always end such ritual journeys with this poem. Just say that the poem came to him as he waded across a stream in the northern Cascades, barefoot, pants rolled up with his boots in his hand, listening to the "rustle and shimmer of icy creek waters…creek music, heart music" and the sun so inspiring him that he sang out,

I pledge allegiance…
I pledge allegiance to the soil
of Turtle Island
And to the beings who thereon dwell
one ecosystem
in diversity
With joyful interpenetration for all!

The ending of the Hako journey

When it's growing late in the day and you are nearly back to your starting point and the sun is so low in the sky that its rays touch only the tops of the trees or the hill standing above you, recite the words of the Pawnee priest:

The ray of Father Sun, who breathes forth life, is standing on the edge of the hills. We remember that in the morning it stood on the edge of the trees in the east, now it stands on the edge of the hills that, like the walls of a lodge, enclose the land where the people dwell.

At the very end of the journey, when you have crossed the final stream or come out of the narrow rock walls or through the final trees, everyone chants the Tewa chant, which we've used before in this chapter:

Then weave for us a garment of brightness:
May the warp be the white light of morning,
May the weft be the red light of evening.
May the fringes be the standing rainbow.
Thus weave for us a garment of brightness.
That we may walk fittingly where birds sing.
That we may walk fittingly where the grass is green.
Oh our Mother, the Earth, Oh our Father, the Sky.

Ritual Closing

[Leader] Today the "breathing stems of wood" have led us on this sacred journey. They have breathed with us and with all the other beings of this sacred place. They have helped us to find the words we need to communicate with one another and with the other beings of our place. Today, the earth, itself, and the sky and the "Powers" of this place and we human beings, as well as all the other beings with whom we share breath, have together woven the sacred fabric of our world, this place. "For as my body is clad in the cloth, and the flesh in the skin and the bones in the flesh and the heart in the whole, so are we, soul and body clad in the living fabric of all of nature surrounding us—here in this place."

Conclusion

FURTHER INSIGHTS INTO THE HAKO CEREMONY

The ceremony as given above ends with the return from the sacred journey. On this first journey you will be setting up the pattern. The Hako as done by the Pawnee had another ceremony within it, where the visiting tribe called the Fathers and the other tribe called the Children, joined together while the leader performed a series of ritual actions over a small child from the Children tribe. The essence of this part of the ceremony is a prayer that all the beings of the place—natural and human—continue to live in health and strength. Hartley Burr Alexander explains: "The signs of these promises are put upon this little child, but they are not merely for that particular child but for its generation, that the children already born may live, grow in strength" so that the tribe may continue. Hartley Alexander, of course, is a white anthropologist. But to understand the real power of the Hako Ceremony in its entirety we have to try to understand it from the traditional point of view. As Jaime de Angulo points out: "[W]e can't understand a social structure where the tribe as a whole has children…We still have the term generation for 'my generation', my generation was the 'jazz generation'. In that way we can understand what generation is. The total society generates, and the children belong to that society…Everybody really exists in a continuous world of generations, of being the children of the world they are living in, so you're a very bad child indeed if you do not venerate Father Tree, or any other aspect of your parent world."

The word, engendering means, according to the dictionary, "to produce, give existence to living beings." Looked at from Jaime's point of view, it is obvious that humanity alone cannot engender children—instead it is the entire living environment which produces the child and keeps it alive—the air, soil, plants and animals of its immediate environment. We are the children of our particular place on earth. That is why the land is sacred and sex is sacred and eating is sacred; because they are all parts of the same energy flow within that place. That is why traditional Indian ceremonies repeatedly acknowledge "all our relatives"—including the non-human.

The Hako journey can be used as the ritual journey for the children in their "fly as birds" journey; it can be used as a "world-renewal rite" (see the following chapter) and each year that the people travel along this ritual journey, it becomes deeper and more sacred. They begin to *know* that the source of the sacred is in their own place, on the mountain or in the headwaters of the river.

Often we who have remembered the heritage deep inside us and are once again returning to the natural human rituals in nature, are criticized by both whites and Indians. We are not supposed to "usurp their claims with glib, sentimental comparisons between native attitudes and ours, nor by self-consciously inventing reinhabitory rituals for land worship which won't stand up in court. [As if that's the whole purpose of them.] Most of us remain strangers in a strange land, canoeing down rivers whose voices are mute to us. The earth is not our mother nor the sky our father." I am quoting here from Peter Nabokov's "America as Holy Land." All I can say is that it's too bad he never listened to the water as he canoed down the river, as the water "afforded" him the joy of following its patterns.

Of course if one persists in acting like a narrowly Eurocentric white man or an "apple Indian" for that matter, then nature remains mute forever. But as soon as one relinquishes control and lets nature herself "afford" you the chances for living, as soon as you begin to pay attention and learn to follow the patterns or *li* of your own place, you rejoin "all our ancestors" going clear back hundreds of thousands of years—to the apes who did just such rituals as the Hako journey—going clear back to the Paleolithic cave rituals in the Pyrenees (30,000) years ago. We've been hunter-gatherers for 99% of human history. Why is it that we are supposed to stay stuck in the last 400 years of Eurocentric stupidity? Or, as Gary Snyder puts it, the "temporary anomaly" of the last 400 years. The long past is still encoded in our genes. As Carleton Coon said: "Only in the last 10,000 years has man begun to domesticate plants and animals." Ten thousand years is only four hundred generations, "too few to allow for any notable genetic changes...we and our ancestors are the same people." And, as soon as we do the old rituals out in nature, Mother Earth and Father Sky give us "permission to be reverent" once more and we are "home," where we've always been.

Wilfred Pelletier, a modern Odawa Indian agrees, when he writes:

> [They] are finding out, both Indians and whites. They're going back to the land, more and more of them...They'll learn from the land, all they need to know, all there is to know. If they stay there long enough, they'll learn that they *are* the land...
>
> Wherever you are is home. And the earth is paradise and wherever you set your feet is holy land...You don't live off it like a parasite. You live in it, and it in you, or you don't survive. And that is the only worship of God there is.

Within a remarkably short time a ritual journey such as the Hako, when undertaken each year, begins to dissolve within the participants, the boundary between civilization and wilderness, allowing them to:

step across the fence separating their 'civilization side' from their 'wilderness side'...These are the people who can look their 'animal nature' in the eye...and in this way can develop a consciousness of their 'cultural nature'.

We may have to admit then that our person contains within itself, significantly more than is admitted by our everyday culture...That which we include in our personality will then expand to the same extent as we, our everyday person, surrender our more or less firm boundaries.

We begin to include other beings, those which we used to think were outside of us; hence no part of us. But after the Hako ritual we begin to include these beings within our boundaries. As Hans Duerr explains: "Our soul does not *leave* our body, but the limits of our person no longer coincide with the boundaries or our body that we might see on a snapshot." We don't fly like witches or new age "out of body" trippers. "What happens instead is that our ordinary 'ego boundaries' evaporate and so it is entirely possible that *we* suddenly encounter ourselves at places where our 'everyday body,' whose boundaries are no longer identical with our person, is *not* to be found."

As the Laguna Indian, Tayo, found at the end of his long journey:

> ...at that moment in the sunrise, it was all so beautiful, everything, from all directions, evenly, perfectly, balancing day and night, summer months with winter. The valley was enclosing this totality, like the mind holding all thoughts together in a single moment...He cried with relief at finally seeing the pattern, the way all the stories fit together...to become the story that was still being told. He was not crazy; he had never been crazy. He had only seen and heard the world as it always was: no boundaries, only transitions through all distances and time...

The rising sun is throwing its light up against the clouds along the horizon so they were glowing translucent and yellow. Long shadows ran out from the tamarac and the willow along the river and Tayo realizes that, "The ear for the story and the eye for the pattern were theirs; the feeling was theirs: we came out of this land and we are hers." And as he crosses the river the sun's lower rim clears the horizon.

BIOREGIONAL CULTURE AND LAND RITUAL

Peter Berg asks: "How much 'ecological wisdom' do we really want? Bioregionalists answer, 'All we can get!' They see their lives as intertwined with ongoing natural processes, part of the life of a bioregion, and human society as ultimately based on interdependence with other forms of life. They use these principles to make choices about which work activities to undertake and to confront late industrial society's depredations." I am quoting this from "Upriver Downriver #7"—a paper from Northern California's bioregion. Such papers are beginning in various regions throughout the country where people are beginning to ask such questions and seek for answers from the non-human as well as the human in their own place.

Katúah: Bioregional Journal of the Southern Appalachians is another fine journal. They speak proudly of their mountains: "The Applachians are the oldest mountains on the continent. In the eons of their youth, it is hypothesized that they stood as tall as the Himalayas. Now, rounded and worn with age, they are a deep storehouse of wisdom, strength, and endurance. They are the elders of the land, and their energies are more subtle and demand more attunement than the raw pride of the mountains to the west glorying in their physical strength."

Peter Berg tells us that: "There is a distinct resonance among living things and the factors which influence them that occurs specifically within each separate place on the planet. Discovering and describing that resonance is a way to describe a bioregion." Katúah continues:

[I]n discovering the land as she is in the place where we live, we discover ourselves in the process. There is a necessary connection here...If we make a gesture to the earth, the earth gestures back—this is the source of the magic...

The geological formations underpinning the land, the spring rains every year, the winds sweeping in from the west, the tangled undergrowth of a rhododendron slick, the juncoes playing among the forest trees—these are among the forces that shape our bioregion... These forces also shape the landscape of our consciousness...We are here to learn and grow and, like the great trees of the forest, to develop roots and become part of this place.

In this way the process of transformation begins. It is a healing process, a voluntary marriage of ourselves to the land. As we help the land to repair the damage done by a careless humanity, so does she help us to repair the damage done within our hearts and minds by a bankrupt system...

The bioregion does not have to be organized or proclaimed. It is already there, waiting for us to discover it. It is a process begun long ago, waiting only for us to plunge into its stream.

Here's the beginning of a piece called "Map Meditations" from *Katúah*: "I was driving back on I-40 from Raleigh, and I started to get this excited feeling as I drove into the foothills. I began to feel that certain feeling of being in the mountains

again as I started to climb, and I knew I was coming home. The mountains were in front of me looking magnificent. You know the way they do sometimes, with big clouds gathered all around the top and the sunlight slanting through..."

And that's just how I feel about my mountains way out west here in the southern Rocky Mountains. And that's the real "one World"—we in mountain bioregions know how one another feel and you in the river bioregions can know one another through your love for the river—all over the world those who know and love their mountains or their river can feel, together, that love. But since I am a mountain person I want to end this chapter on sacred land with an ancient Chinese legend about mountain-love.

There was a Chinese scholar who, like scholars of most lands, was blessed with few of this world's goods, and, unlike a great many of them, was noted for his zealous devotion to the service of his country's gods. One night he heard the voice of an invisible being that spoke to him thus: 'Your piety has found favor in the sight of heaven, ask now for what you most long to possess, for I am the messenger of the gods, and they have sworn to grant your heart's desire.' 'I ask', said the poor scholar, 'for the coarsest clothes and food, just enough for my daily wants, and I beg that I may have freedom to wander at my will over mountains and fell and woodland stream, free from all worldly cares, till my life's end. That is all I ask'. Hardly had he spoken when the sky seemed to fill with the laughter of myriads of unearthly voices.

'All you ask', cried the messenger of the gods. 'Know you not that what you demand is the highest happiness of the beings that dwell in heaven? Ask for wealth or rank, or what earthly happiness you will, but not for you are the holiest joys of the gods'.

"The sky is the vaulting path of the sun, the course of the changing moon, the wandering glitter of the stars, the year's seasons and their changes, the light and dusk of day, the gloom and glow of night, the clemency and inclemency of the weather, the drifting clouds and blue depth of the ether. When we say sky, we are already thinking of the other three along with it."—(The Earth, the Sky, the gods and the mortals.)

Martin Heidegger

"Truth as revelation is not located in the mind, a responding to an object or as that to which an object responds, but in the world itself. Since the world is the interrelation of earth, sky, gods and mortals, this interrelation, the mirror-play is the primary revelation, the primary truth."

Vincent Vycinas

"When Bashō, the seventeenth-century poet usually considered to be Japan's best, thought about his debt to past masters, he chose Saigyō as the classic poet to whom he owed most. Bashō wrote that the reason for this selection was that he found in the twelfth-century poet, 'a mind both obeying and at one with nature throughout the four seasons'."

William R. LaFleur

CHAPTER FOURTEEN

"I however, am one who blesses and affirms if only you are around me, you pure, luminous sky. You abyss of light—then into all abysses do I carry my consecrating affirmation."

Friedrich Nietzsche

"Science...Progress. The world marches on Why shouldn't it turn?"
Rimbaud

"I am no longer caught in a moving flow, but becalmed in a place or sea that has depth and content, a life and meaning all its own. At these moments of utter peace I feel absolved from the necessity of hurrying through space to reach a point in time...For time seems then a living, organic element that mysteriously helps to fashion our own shape and growth."
Frank Waters

*"Far away in the depth of the mountains
Wandering here and there I carry no thought
When spring comes I watch the birds;
In summer I bathe in the running stream;
In autumn I climb the highest peaks;
During the winter I am warming up in the sun
Thus I enjoy the real flavor of the seasons..."*
Shih T'ao (1641-1717)

 BRINGING THE SKY INTO YOUR LIFE

Personal Introduction—The Sky in My Life

For years I had wanted to spend the night among the golden aspens in the fall—to see the late sun slanting through them and wake up with the early morning sun glittering through the quaking aspen leaves and shining down onto me. "Quaking aspen" is what all the old-timers in Colorado called these beautiful trees.

The year I finally moved back to Colorado, where aspen trees grow, it was late October when I arrived here in Silverton. Of course, the aspen leaves had already dropped by then. All through the following year I looked forward to fall when I would finally be able to spend a night among the golden aspen.

During that year whenever I drove to Durango on the highway, I would look for a good spot among the aspen. Finally I saw an overhanging, limestone ledge which seemed to have a deep cave beneath it, thus ensuring shelter if I needed it in the middle of the night. So that fall, I drove down the Lime Creek road and parked the car in a spot I hoped would be near my "cave." It was far better than I thought! Not only golden aspen but a great grove of rather rare, red aspen. Laying out my sleeping bag, I got everything ready for the night and then sat down among the golden and red aspen, which were back lit by the setting sun. Back lighting allows each leaf to radiate the most light from the sun. The sun was about to set over 12,900 ft. Engineer Peak. The light on the leaves was glorious—better than I could have imagined! The sun kept on setting and the glowing light continued to radiate. Time had stopped! When I finally took my eyes off the glowing leaves to look directly at where the sun was, I realized that it had not set on the top of Engineer, where I thought that it was setting. Instead the sun was rolling down the ridge of the mountain. Then I looked at my watch and I looked at the rest of the world in darkness and I felt privileged—chosen by the gods. I was surrounded by golden light while the rest of the world was dark. The sun rolled down the ridge for twenty minutes! Until it finally vanished behind a low sweeping ridge of the mountain. It left me astounded. It seemed like a miracle. If one wrote in a "holy book" that the sun rolled down the mountain for twenty minutes it *would* be considered a miracle. But it was actually a natural phenomenon caused by the interrelation of the mountain, the sun, my special chosen place by the cave and the turning earth: the line of the sun's descent coincided exactly with the angle of the ridge of the mountain.

That was one of my first powerful lessons in the *li* (patterns) of this special place here in the San Juan mountains where I live. By the time I had lived here two more years, I realized that twice every year—once in spring and once in fall—I can see the sun roll down the ridge of Sultan Mountain right out my front window. It only rolls down for eight minutes on Sultan but that's pretty exciting anyway. And it always surprises me. I'll be busily doing something, thinking the sun was on the way down and suddenly I'll realize it's getting brighter, not darker, as it moves out from behind a little knob on the ridge and continues on down the mountain.

During all the years since then, I've been continually surprised and delighted by the power of our sun. In the winter, it can get as low as 40 degrees below zero at night, but half

hour after the sun rises I can sit outside in the southeast corner of the house and be *warm* without even a sweater—just a cotton shirt. Every day all winter, unless it's actually snowing, I can eat lunch outside in that same corner. But when the sun sets at night the temperature drops 20 degrees immediately. We thank our Sun—deeply and often. Sun worship goes on around here all the time even if the Fundamentalist Christians would never admit such a thing.

In our high clear air, the stars and planets are wondrous indeed and things happen here regularly which I never saw before, during all my years of climbing. The reason is that I am living here at this altitude in a house; thus, I have the chance to watch closely when planets set. When one is out climbing and it gets dark enough for the stars to show up you've no time to watch them set; because if you don't get down soon you spend a long cold night waiting for dawn to let you see your way down the cliffs. But here, safely in a house or walking through the streets of our little town, it's another matter. One night, while I was walking five blocks across town, great white Venus rose and set nine times. Because stars don't radiate light out from them as the sun does, Venus was gone in a flash. One minute a great white star glowing and the next minute totally gone—snuffed out instantly. And a minute later there it was again. What was happening was this: I was walking along Greene street, which parallels a ridge to the West of town and Venus was on its way down, but passing through branches of trees. Each time it went behind a branch it was gone—no light emanating from it at all. Every time it moved lower, from behind the branch, there it was in full glory. I realized that if a person, who never looked at the sky, saw that great light suddenly disappear only to reappear again that person would surely think it was a vehicle from outer space.

I guess you could say my first step toward "enlightenment" came from the Morning Star, Venus. I'm not the only one to claim that; see below for other people it has deeply affected. My particular "enlightenment" happened long ago, when I was still living in Alta, Utah at the ski area, where my former husband was snow ranger. One year a wealthy couple built a beautiful little A-frame chapel so the Catholic priest could come up from Salt Lake to say mass every Sunday for the few Catholics in the valley and for the skiers staying at the lodges. I was a devout Catholic at the time. The Blessed Sacrament was kept on the altar in the little locked wooden shrine. In the Catholic Church when the Blessed Sacrament is kept in the church, people are supposed to "visit" there and pray. So the couple who built the chapel asked me to be sure to do that each day, when she was not living in her "winter home" up on the hill. Their regular home was in California.

I would ski down very early in the morning as soon as I got up and then come back up on the little rope tow to our house. I had bought what is called a "layman's divine office." This is a simplified version of the "divine office" that priests say each day. I would carry that book down each morning to read the "daily office" out of it while I was in the chapel.

One bright crystalline morning, with the mountains covered with surface hoar reflecting the light of the stars, I skied down and went into the chapel. That day I read a long, glowing litany praising the Son of God, coming down to be the "Light of the World." It was early January and the church was still glorying in the Christmas story. The litany consisted of a whole series of phrases comparing Jesus Christ with the stars. Several times this phrase was repeated: "O Wondrous Star in the East, Light of the World, come to save mankind." Finishing the page for the day, I got up off my knees, turned out the light and, as I went out the door, suddenly, there was the "Wondrous Star in the East." There was Venus—huge and magnificent, just rising from behind the mountain. All of a sudden many things clicked in my head which hadn't been allowed to come together before. I began to fully realize the true origin of religion. And to begin to realize how the Christian Church had co-opted the old natural religion. It didn't change me at that particular moment, but, that vision of Venus certainly began the process.

The experience which most powerfully brought the sky into my life happened only a few years ago—after I'd been living here in Silverton for several years. We were having a most unusual winter—far more snow than normal. Another big storm had begun on the 17th of December and days later it was still snowing. Several friends were staying here with me, but since the highways were closed from avalanches, no one could travel to the ski area. On December 20th when I got up I looked out and saw that it wasn't snowing at that moment; although from the looks of the clouds it would begin again soon. I got all my winter gear on, grabbed the shovel and rushed outside. I put the ladder up and got onto the roof. My house is an old one—left over from the mining days, when it was a one-room shack. The roof is not too strong. As I got up on the roof I suddenly realized the entire sky directly overhead was blue. Then I saw something I've never seen before—and I've been watching the sky all my life—since my father was a great sky watcher. Right above me in the blue space—crisscrossing in every direction were beaded bands of clouds. They were translucent, glowing beads. Covering the whole area directly above Silverton was a gigantic track. Both edges were clearly defined by these bright bead-like translucent clouds. They were sharp edged against the blue sky. Between the two sharp, beaded edges the entire track was filled with random short bead-like lines. And the whole thing was moving so fast, all I could do was watch open-mouthed as it raced by overhead, bringing in the next storm clouds right behind it. It had come from the southeast direction and disappeared over the shoulder of Storm Peak to the northwest. It seemed to be moving faster than any jet plane I've ever seen. It was gone before I could even shut my mouth. No one else in the entire town was out—not a car moving because all the roads were still unplowed—so no one else saw it. It was already snowing again before I got down the ladder. No one inside had seen it either because the insulation was still up in the windows. The whole thing seemed like a vision. At first I had no idea what it was. I just knew that primitive people would have called it "the track of the storm god."

The next day I called my friend who is an atmospheric scientist at National Center for Atmospheric Research in Boulder. When I described the whole thing he said, awed: "Why, you must have seen the jet stream." He looked up the records and told me that between the 19th and 20th of December

it was above Durango and it was very low, 500 millibars—that's about 18,000 ft. Our mountains around town are 13,900 so it would look close to me. The maximum speed at that level is about 100 knots (110 MPH).

The jet stream screams around the earth as a tremendous wind—most often 500 to 600 mph. Ordinarily, the tip of Mt. Everest is the only part of the earth which juts up into the jet stream. This Great Being, the Jet Stream has enormous influence over our lives, though practically no one ever gets to see it. The first time humans ever really encountered this Being was in 1944 when a high level bombing mission (30,000 ft.) was attempted over Tokyo in the winter. One hundred eleven planes left Saipan. Only twenty four actually got through to bomb the target. The pilots said that it was as if a wind came out of a hose with jet force, straight at them. Hence the name. After a few more of these disasters, the U.S. quit high level bombing and came in at a low 4900 ft.—very dangerous for the planes as they made easy targets. In fact, this was one of the little known reasons for dropping the atomic bomb on Japan—to get the war over quickly and not have to face another winter when the jet stream screams over Japan.

Oddly enough the atom bomb testing after the war showed more about the jet stream and about how small the earth is. In 1961 the Soviets did some testing in Siberia on September 10. Carried by the jet stream until it reached the arctic coast of Canada, the cold air began to sink slowly and the fall-out was over the New York region on September 17 to 20 (only seven days later). Another example was when the U.S. exploded a test bomb on May 4, 1962 on Christmas Island. Due to an even freakier jet stream this was dropped out in thunder shower activity over Wichita, Kansas and St. Louis and showed up in the milk of cattle by May 13—only 9 days later!

Ordinarily, of course, no one sees the jet stream. Usually it's seen only by looking at photos from satellites. But because it happened to be unusually low and our skies are very clear I was privileged to see it. The jet stream is a Great Being because it is the life-giving circulation of our planet. Without it the tropics would fry and the northern hemisphere would freeze. When I saw this Great Being going overhead I had no fear or wonder just incredible awe; followed by gratitude to be so privileged to witness such a thing. It's worship. Sort of a combination of "Praise be" and "why me." This, of course, is the type of experience that primitive peoples had much oftener, because they had not yet built so many walls (both physical and mental) between them and nature.

This type of experience lies at the root of religious feeling. The philosopher, Heidegger explained that it was not man who is the primordial ground of the gods of his world, but Nature. Gods are Nature's transcendent powers which, when colliding with the responsive openness of humans, become disclosed in the human world. For a culture to experience such an event, the human beings must live and work, together, in contact with the earth and the sky. The humans and the earth and the sky together bring about the fourth aspect of Heidegger's *Fourfold*, the gods.

Without an intimate relationship with the earth and the sky and the gods, human beings cannot live fully. In the modern

IGS we are limiting our full development by cutting ourselves off from these infinitely greater aspects of our being.

Preview

> The Khasi tell a myth, according to which an enormous tree used to shade their land in the dim and distant past. The ancestors of the Khasi wanted to make gardens and needed the rays of the sun that could not penetrate the jumble of leaves of the tree. So they felled it. But as the tree thundered to the ground, the sky dissolved and disappeared above. Now they were able to enjoy the fruits of the earth, but the navel cord to the sky had been torn forever.
>
> Hans Duerr

In many parts of the world today the sky is so badly obscured that it seems almost hopeless to consider that we might once again live in daily relationship to it. But, once you set up ritual structures that allow you to pay attention to the the influence of the sky on your life, your relationship with the sky becomes obvious. The first part of this chapter will deal with the sky itself; the second part with the relationships between the sky and the earth which give us the seasons.

PART I: THE SKY

> When the Chinese speak of the relationship of heaven and earth creating their world, they use the word, *Tien*, for heaven. 'They are aware of all that is enclosed within the hallowed conception of *Tien*, which is not the heaven we know, but the mysterious government of the blue sky at noon. It is a world...of...pure intensity.'
>
> Robert Payne

Background on "The Sky" from Traditional Cultures

The "Blue Sky," *Skan*, is one of the four great Powers for the Sioux. The other "Powers" are the Rock, the Earth and the Sun. Only through the union of Mother Earth and the Sky was life possible. For the Skidi Pawnee, the blue sky was associated with Tirawahat, "this expanse" or "our father here above." On the other side of the world, in Tibet the Buddhist scripture, *Sadhanamala*, states that when one has reached the Supreme Illumination of Buddhism, absolute nirvana, "he should understand that the sole nature of all things can be qualified only as absolute identity, similar to pure crystal, as the clear autumnal sky at midday." Here, again, we see recognition of the highest power as blue sky.

There is a certain quality about the autumnal blue sky that makes it qualitatively different than the sky at any other time of year. Our San Juan mountains, on the same latitude as Tibet, share this unique blue. It is caused by day after day warm sun, coming at the end of summer. By the end of summer, the upper air is warmer and more stable; therefore, convection doesn't rise as high so there is less cloudy weather. With less convection, the dirty air from the congested lower elevations doesn't mix easily with the air of the higher mountains. Furthermore, the slanting rays of the sun, which occur in autumn, are not as hot as the direct rays of the summer sun so the objects on the ground are not daily heated up as much as they are in summer. This also lessens convection. With the warm upper layer of air on top of the colder air there can be no mixing of layers. The longer the warm fall days last, the clearer the blue becomes due to subsidence; the dirt particles

keep dropping down from the still warm air. Until there is the "clear light of the void" as the Buddhists call it: "An ultimate blue...deep dark in the north over Tibet—a blue bluer than blue, transparent, ringing" is the way Peter Matthiessen describes it in his book, *Snow Leopard*. With subsidence, there comes a stillness, too, so that one is mesmerized by the deep blue and the intense stillness. Just sitting there in this blue stillness is total bliss. That's how I recognized *Skan*, Blue sky, as a Power or a god, long before I knew how the Indians felt about it. The Utes, who long ago hunted here in our San Juan Mountains, called themselves "the Blue Sky People."

Very early in the process of begriming the sky by the current Industrial Growth Society, way back in 1928 (that's a year before the so-called Depression), D. H. Lawrence, exiled from the clear blue sky of Taos in the Southwest by his tuberculosis, was working on a book while staying in Italy. He has his heroine, Connie, writing a letter from Italy back home to England: "How nice it was here, in the sunshine...compared to that dismal mess of the English midlands! After all, a clear sky was almost the most important thing in life." At the time he wrote this, very few people realized the truth of this, but now, with clear blue sky a rare wonder, it's become far more obvious.

To find the most profound description of the power of the sky I must turn, again to the Japanese poet, Saigyō:

> The wisps of smoke from Fuji
> Yield to the wind and lose themselves
>   In sky, in emptiness
> Which takes as well the aimless passions
> That through my life burned deep inside.

In order to make clear what Siagyō is saying here I must refer to the translator, La Fleur. He states that the word, "yield" here (*nabiku*), refers to "a 'yielding' by something or someone actively but gently wooing...the smoke gives itself bit by bit into the erotic power of the wind and is absorbed into the sky (*sora*)." When Saigyō writes about sky he "intends it to mean also all that is implied in the Buddhist notion of *sunya*." The Japanese character for sky (*sora*) can also be read as (*ku*) and in that case is a "precise equivalent of the Buddhist Void"—the Absolute. The sky here is not just a symbol pointing to something beyond. "For Kukai and for Saigyō there is no beyond. The sky—is itself both the symbol and the symbolized. It is the absolute which theorists call 'sunya' but, which is, in fact, nothing, other than the phenomenon itself." Thus, as La Fleur says, the sky itself offers salvation for us human beings.

Without the clear sky above us, humans shut out the rest of the universe. No wonder we are lonely. When we begin to recognize the sky itself as a Great Power, we may be able to make the necessary changes from the Industrial Growth Society so that we can once more be blessed by this Great Power in our daily life.

> I think over again my small adventures,
>   My fears,
>   Those I thought so big,
>
> For all the vital things
>   I had to get
>   And to reach,

And yet,
   There is only one great thing—
      The Only thing—

To live,
   To see the great day that dawns,
   And the light that fills the world
                              Old Inuit Song

Sun Rituals

The Sun is one of the Four Great Powers of the Sioux. Of course the sun has been worshipped by most other cultures throughout human history, as well. An ancient Egyptian litany to the sun went as follows:

...fire-ruler, creator of light, fire-breathing, fiery-heated, shining spirit, rejoicing in fire, beautiful light, lord of light, fiery-bodied, giver of light, sower of fire, confounding with fire, living light, whirling fire, mover of light, hurler of thunderbolts, glorious light...holder of fiery light, conqueror of the stars...

Worship of the sun, of course, goes way back before human beings. Not only did apes worship the sun, in their own fashion, as Jung explained, but back in Part II of this book I told how Leyhausen found that the cats in the cities of Europe have strict schedules laid out for their place in the sun. These sunning places are so important that intricate social rituals have evolved around the time of day each cat gets to use place.

John Lilly, who has done a great deal of research into dolphin and human behavior wrote about the importance of the sun in his book, *Dyadic Cyclone*. He writes: "Each of us [his wife and he] has noted that sufficient sunlight also changes our state of being, in some very fundamental way. Our bodily limits are expanded by adequate sunshine. When either because of necessity or other work or because of a rainy period we are unable to get the sun, we notice a very slow but detectable deterioration in our bodily and mental performance. Once we can get back into the sun, we find that it gives us a lift in a very particular way that nothing else seems to be able to do. It is as if the human animal is so constructed that it periodically needs ultra-violet and infrared radiation of its blood and its skin in order to stay in the best of health. There is some very fundamental biochemical research needed here to find out what these changes involve."

D. H. Lawrence gives us a powerful tribute to the sun, in his description of the coming of day as he walked along, cleaning the irrigation ditch leading to his ranch near Taos. He stood, looking far out over

the vast amphitheatre of lofty, indomitable desert, sweeping round to the ponderous Sangre de Christo mountains on the east, and coming up flush at the pine-dotted foot-hills of the Rockies! What splendour!...Never is the light more pure and overweening than there. Those that have spent morning after morning alone there pitched among the pines above the great proud world of desert will know, almost unbearably how beautiful it is, how clear and unquestioned is the might of the day. Just day itself is tremendous there...in New Mexico the heart is sacrificed to the sun and the human being is left stark, heartless, but undauntedly religious.

The Pawnee Hako ritual, which I wrote about in the previous chapter, has a specific sun ritual. It occurs the second day after the visiting group arrives at the village of the "children." This provides the framework for a powerful ritual for a modern group as the ritual follows the course of the sun throughout the day. The explanations below, unless indicated otherwise, are by the Pawnee priest, Tahirussawichi:

Whoever is touched by the first rays of the sun in the morning receives new life and strength which have been brought straight from the power above.

We speak of the sun as Father breathing forth life, causing the earth to bring forth, making all things to grow. We think of the sun...and his ray as the bearer of this life. [You have seen this ray as it comes through a little hole or crack.] While we sing, this ray enters the door of the lodge to bring strength and power to all within.

We sing this verse four times as we go around the lodge. [Chant 'We Circle Around'] When we reach the west we pause.

As the sun rises higher, the ray, which is its messenger, alights upon the edge of the central opening in the roof of the lodge, right over the fireplace. We see the spot, the sign of its touch, and we know that the ray is there...Father Sun is sending life by his messenger to this central place in the lodge.

As we sing we look at the bright spot where the ray has alighted, and we know that life from our father the Sun will come to us by the ray.

We sing this verse four times, and when we have completed the second circuit of the lodge and have reached the west we pause.

As the sun rises higher...the ray is now climbing down into the lodge. We watch the spot where it has alighted. It moves over the edge of the opening above the fireplace and descends into the lodge, and we sing that life from our father the Sun will come to us by his messenger, the ray...

Now the spot is walking here and there within the lodge, touching different places. We know that the ray will bring strength and power from our father the Sun as it walks within the lodge. Our hearts are glad and thankful as we sing...

The hako are laid down upon the holy place. [The Pawnee priest explains that the first four verses of the chant are sung in the morning...When the spot has reached the floor we stop singing and do not begin again until the afternoon.]

In the afternoon...we observe that the spot has moved around the lodge, as the sun has passed over the heavens...After a little time we see the spot leave the floor of the lodge and climb up toward the opening over the fireplace, where it had entered in the morning...Later, when the sun is sinking in the west, the land is in shadow, only on the top of the hills toward the east can the spot, the sign of the ray's touch, be seen...

The ray of Father Sun, who breathes forth life, is standing on the edge of the hills. We remember that in the morning it stood on the edge of the opening in the roof of the lodge over the fireplace; now it stands on the edge of the hills that, like the walls of a lodge, enclose the land where the people dwell.

When the spot, the sign of the ray, the messenger of our father the Sun, has left the tops of the hills and passed from our sight...we know that the ray which was sent to bring us strength has now gone back to the place whence it came. We are thankful to our father the Sun for that which he has sent us by his ray...At the west we sing the sun down, and sing the songs that belong to that direction.

The sun ritual, which I do most every morning unless it is cloudy, can be done even in a city because the important thing is to follow the red light of the early morning sun down a mountain or even a building. Determine where the sun's first rays fall by looking out your windows which face west. Then choose the type of music which you feel most expresses the joy that the rising sun's rays bring to you. I suggest Andean flute music. There is a record which has become such a classic that it continues to be available at good record stores. It's called "La Flute Indienne." It comes from France but the name of the company is Barclay. Volume 1 has "Pescadores" from

Ecuador, which is perfect for watching the sun rays grow as they cover more and more of the land. It begins with seagulls and then a single flute, but as the sun grows stronger the guitars come in, and somehow, lift your spirits even further toward the rising sun. Make a tape loop of this one song and then have it on the tape player, ready, so that you can start it when you see the light from the sun, beginning to rise in the east, as it first begins showing on the top of the hill or tree or mountain to the west. You need only play a few minutes of the tape once you get into the daily rhythm of the ritual and you, too, each morning will begin to feel as the Inuit:

> There is only one great thing
> The Only thing
> To live,
> To see the great day that dawns,
> And the light that fills the world.

A SUN TRIGGERED LIGHT SHOW

In "Kinetic Art with Sunlight," P. K. Hoenich, of the Faculty of Architecture in Israel, tells about his method of creating moving "art" by the use of sun rays and the rotation of the Earth. He begins by saying "I have had ample time to reflect upon the problems of art. More than 40 years ago I frequented the art schools then in vogue..." Later he went through many styles in his painting but now, "I have returned to abstract design, realizing kinetic art by means of Sun rays." He began working on this in 1956, the article was written in 1967 and published in the British art journal, *Leonardo*.

He makes use of the Sun as the fixed source of light and the rotation of planet Earth is what moves a row of reflectors. "The composition of the projection is dependent on the forms of the reflectors...If we wish to project a picture with Sun rays we must mount the rows of reflectors in such a way that they will reflect rays from sunrise to sunset. As the course of the Sun is different during the four seasons, the rows of reflectors will be effective differently during the year. A single form will not necessarily be produced by a single reflector and various reflectors may unite in a single complex form." Any opaque, bright surface can be the projection screen—such as the wall of a house, a wooden fence, your own totem pole in front of the house etc.

He points out that these Sun projections are only visible when the Sun shines. "This is quite often an advantage, as the impact is stronger with pictures for which you wait expectantly, than with those that are always visible. The hesitating, veiled appearance of a Sun projection, when the Sun is still partly hidden behind clouds, and its crescendo, coinciding with the breakthrough of the Sun, are a breathtaking event."

Hoenich notes that the Jesuit Abbe Castel (1688-1757) "has been mentioned as the first to project pictures with Sun rays. I personally think that most probably this possibility was known already in antiquity." Yes, of course it was, because some of the megalithic stone works were set up so that a ray of sun entered only on the winter solstice. Another example is the recent find in our own Southwest of slabs of sandstone on top of a butte in Chaco Canyon, where Sofaer saw a shaft of sunlight pass through the narrow opening between three large stone slabs and, precisely at noon, pierce the center of a spiral carv-

ing on the wall. The shaft of light resembled a dagger, set up so that the winter solstice dagger of sun enters and focuses on a particular place on the sandstone rock.

The Megalithic structure of Newgrange, some 26 miles north of Dublin, Ireland, has a sophisticated winter solstice device. The structure was built about 3300 BC, roughly 500 years before Stonehenge in England. A very old local legend claimed that the back of the underground vault was lit by the sun on only one special day of the year. This seemed to be impossible because no light, coming in the door of the passage, could possibly reach this inner chamber because of the uphill slant of the floor. An archaeologist, Professor O'Kelly, found that a curiously carved "false lintel" concealed a sort of window or "roof-box" as he called it. Two blocks of quartz—one still in place and another, lying nearby—were a perfect fit for the "roof-box." Guessing that this might let the sun's rays through, on Dec. 21, 1969 he stood in the back of the tomb, and, sure enough, a few minutes after dawn on winter solstice the sun's rays came right through the "roof-box," down the passage, across the main chamber and into the back of the tomb.

Unfortunately Hoenich's short article does not give him the space to provide more details. The photos of his reflection device show that it is mounted on a cross arm between two wooden posts. The cross arm is bolted to the two side posts with screws. This makes it possible to change the angle of the reflector so that it can catch the sun rays at whatever angle they are coming for that time of the year or, for that matter, any particular time of day.

I see this technique as providing an interesting way to mark the summer and winter solstices—in particular. If a reflector is set up so that the only time the sun's rays hit it directly, is when the sun sets at its southernmost point then you have a dramatic winter solstice effect. If set up properly this will happen each year but only at the winter solstice sunset.

I have not personally found the time to experiment with this technique. Hoenich says specifically: "No part of my work is patented." Two of his books have been published on his Sun Ray art, both out of print, but in a footnote to this article he says: "Author will supply, upon request, addresses of libraries which have copies."

Stars

VENUS

The Morning Star, Venus, has deeply influenced humans since the beginning. It is mentioned in ancient records from China, Egypt and Babylonia, but here I have space for only a few aspects of the relationship between humans and the Morning Star. Beginning with Christian aspects, it is interesting to notice that, since Christians did not consider the stars to be gods or powers they paid very little overt attention to the starry sky itself. But, that doesn't mean the stars had no effect on them. For them, all the power of stars was concentrated on one star—the mysterious star of Bethlehem. The only Biblical reference to this star appears in the Gospel of St. Matthew. The wise men say: "We have seen his star in the east and are come to worship him." From that single reference in the Bible has come all the mass of stories, legends, songs etc. dealing with this one star. The Library of Congress recently issued a bibliography about the star of Bethlehem which lists 277 titles! That's an amazing tribute to "substance" in the Eurocentric tradition vs "relationship" in other cultures: the "one" star which comes to announce the "one" god here on earth is the subject of 227 books.

Most of the cultures on earth felt that many different star beings were powerful. What is not so well known is the connection between the Buddha and Venus at the actual moment of his enlightenment. "Tradition has it that this took place at the end of a night in the full moon of Vaishakha [our month of April]...Shakyamuni's enlightenment took place at dawn, or as it is customarily described in the scripture, 'when the morning star appeared'...With the approach of dawn, the eye of his wisdom gained sublime clarity, and when the morning star began to shine, he sensed his life bursting open, and in a flash discerned the ultimate reality of things. In that moment of enlightenment he became a Buddha."

Black Elk's relationship to the Morning Star is similar to that of the Buddha—a source of enlightenment—as shown by his salutation: "O Morning Star, there at the place where the sun comes up; O you who have the wisdom which we seek, help us in cleansing ourselves and all the people, that our generations to come will have Light as they walk the sacred Path. You lead the dawn as it walks forth, and also the day which follows with its Light which is knowledge...that they may know all that is holy." Black Elk usually called it the "daybreak-star" and he always got up early in the morning to watch for the coming of this star. When it appeared he said: "Behold the Star of understanding."

Returning to our European heritage: In Vergil's *Aeneid*, Venus appears at the moment when Aeneas leaves Troy. "The morning which breaks here is symbolic—the glorious history of Rome just begins." In the Greek classic, *The Odyssey*, the morning star rises when Odysseus reaches his island home.

Venus, as either The Morning Star or the Evening Star, appears repeatedly in literature. For example Walt Whitman wrote: "What subtle tie is this between one's soul and the break of day?...Preceded by an immense star, almost unearthly in its effusion of white splendour." Tolkein was born in the Bushman country of South Africa, "And his own journey, his particular inward journey, began when, as a boy of 8, he saw the evening star in the sky over Africa, that part of Africa which was ancient Bushman country."

But the European writer with the closest ties to Venus is D. H. Lawrence. He referred to it in many of his works throughout the years, not always mentioning it by name. I am quoting several of his descriptions because they show so well the power this star exerts over humanity even when there is no religious meaning assigned to it. In his second novel, *The Trespasser*, Helena and Siegmund are lying in the sand, looking out over the water, waiting for the moon to rise. "Each was looking at a low, large star which hung straight in front of them, dripping its brilliance in a thin streamlet of light along the sea almost to their feet. It was a star-path fine and clear, trembling in its brilliance, but certain upon the water." To Siegmund it seemed like a lantern hanging at a gate to light someone home, and he wondered what would he find if he followed the "thread of the star track."

In an early short story, "Witch a la Mode," a young man comes back to the town of a former girl friend. As he enters the town, "the young man, looking west, saw the evening star advance, a bright thing approaching from a long way off, as if it had been bathing in the surf of the daylight, and now was walking shorewards to the night. He greeted the naked star with a bow of the head, his heart surging." While living in Sicily, Lawrence wrote: "...oh, regal evening star, hung westward flaring over the jagged rock precipices of tall Sicily."

Throughout the intervening years, Lawrence wrote often of Venus but he used it with greatest effect in his novel, *The Plumed Serpent*, where it became the symbol of balance and equilibrium. It is "central between the flash of day and the black of night. The mystery of the evening-star brilliant in silence and distance between the downward-surging plunge of the sun and the vast, hollow seething of inpouring night. The magnificence of the watchful morning-star, that watches between the night and the day, the gleaming clue to the two opposites." In this passage he shows the influence of the many times he watched the evening sky over the desert near Taos.

Both in the desert or here in the high clear air of Silverton along toward twilight, search as diligently as one can, there is no star in the sky—until suddenly, it is there, like magic, where nothing was before. It requires just enough darkness before it can be seen; and, then it is gone a short time later because it has set. Thus it provides the symbol for that moment of perfect relationship.

The Skidi Pawnee had the most sophisticated knowledge of the stars of any American Indian tribe. Their basic creation myth concerns White Star Woman, the Evening Star who lives in the west. The Great Star of the East, Mars, which the Pawnee called the Morning Star had to journey through the sky to the west overcoming all the difficulties on the way before he could meet with her and creation begin. Von Del Chamberlain, a Planetarium director who wrote *When the Stars Come Down to Earth: Cosmology of the Skidi*, explains that "we can expect both evening and morning conjunctions between Venus and Mars about every 6.4 years...Therefore, the Skidi would have seen Mars make the east-to-west migration every 2.14 years." These would be the unsuccessful journeys for Mars (their Morning Star). But, "about every 6 1/2 years they would have been reminded of their celestial parentage as the Great Star (Mars) and the Bright Star (Venus) stood together in the evening sky at the end of the journey of the Great Star." In figuring this chronology out, Chamberlain used the Zeiss Model VI Planetarium instrument in the Albert Einstein Spacearium of the National Air and Space Museum to watch a long, continuous run of planetary events. He "ran the planetary gear system back to 1800, and then ran it forward 200 years and studied planetary events in relationship to what has been written about the Skidi Morning and Evening Star rituals." Special rituals occurred in the Skidi culture when this conjunction of the two stars took place.

PAWNEE STAR CULT

In addition to these two most important stars, the Skidi have four "world-quarter stars." Chamberlain shows that the Big Black Star of the Skidi is our Vega, their White Star is our Sirius, their Yellow Star is our Capella and their Red Star is our Antares. "The Black and Red stars roughly mark the rising corridor of the sun, moon, and planets through the year." Chamberlain explains that the association of these four stars with the seasons also fits: "Capella transits at sunset in spring; Antares is one of the dominant stars of summer; Vega transits just after sunset in autumn; and Sirius rules the winter sky...From the plains, these stars could be conceived of as pillars or posts seemingly supporting the heavens."

Fletcher (the same one who did the research on the Hako ceremony) studied the Pawnee star knowledge as well. She wrote: "The influence of a star cult was manifest in the construction of the earth-lodge of the Pawnee. The circular floor of this dwelling symbolized the earth, and the dome-shaped roof the arching sky. The four posts which supported the framework of the roof represented the four stars of the leading villages [and the four world-quarter stars] and on occasion were painted their respective colors." Another researcher, Weltfish explained that, "The house was a microcosm of the universe and as one was at home inside, one was also at home in the outside world...Through the roof of the house the star gods poured down their strength from their appropriate directions in a constant stream." Each Pawnee earth-lodge had a circular hole in the center of the roof.

The Pawnee earth lodge was built so that the rays from the rising sun "would stream through the east-facing doorway to fall upon the buffalo skull on the altar at the west side of the lodge, directly opposite the doorway." This was possible only for a number of days near the two equinoxes, but the equinoxes were more important for their ceremonial cycle than the solstices.

The Field Museum had a Pawnee star rattle: a gourd rattle with the four world-quarter stars painted in their ritual colors. Dorsey wrote that such rattles were part of sacred bundles and were used in the bundle ceremonies. The Skidi world tree "had its roots in the sky, with its branches extending to the earth. Evening Star and Moon were Mother; Morning Star and Sun were Father."

The Pawnee called the Pole Star, (our Polaris), "the star that does not move." The Pole Star was the central pole and therefore the symbol of unity for most shamanistic cosmologies throughout the world. The Konyak and the Chukchee call it the Nail Star, the Samoyed call it the Sky Nail. It was called the Golden Pillar by the Mongols and the Iron Pillar by the Kirgis. The Chinese call it the "Great Ridge Pole" (*Tai Chi*).

BEGINNING STAR RITUALS

In your own region it is good to begin tracking the time of the year by where the stars stand in your own place. Here in Silverton, we first see Orion coming up late at night from behind Kendall Mt. in early winter. He is lying down. Later, in the spring, he stands triumphant and glorious, filling most of the sky over Sultan in the early evening. By careful watching of the sky in your own area, you will be able to notice similar movements of the stars against the background of your own land.

In the Hako Ceremony of the Pawnee, there was a particular ritual devoted to the Morning Star, which included a song for Dawn. You could adapt parts of this for your own ritual. In explaining this ceremony to Fletcher, the Pawnee priest, Tahirussawichi told her:

> We sing this song slowly with reverent feeling, for we are singing of very sacred things. The Morning Star is one of the...powers. Life and strength and fruitfulness are with the Morning Star. The Morning Star...is painted red all over; that is the color of life...On his head is a soft downy eagle's feather, painted red. This feather represents the soft, light cloud that is high in the heavens, and the red is the touch of a ray of the coming sun. The soft downy feather is the symbol of breath and life.
>
> The star comes from a great distance, too far away for us to see the place where it starts. At first we can hardly see it; we lose sight of it, it is so far off; then we see it again, for it is coming steadily toward us all the time. We watch it approach; it comes nearer and nearer; its light grows brighter and brighter...We see him standing there in the heavens, a strong man shining brighter and brighter. The soft plume in his hair moves with the breath of the new day, and the ray of the sun touches it with color. As he stands there so bright, he is bringing us strength and new life.
>
> Now we look upon him he grows less bright, he is receding, going back to his dwelling place whence he came. We watch him vanishing, passing out of our sight. He has left with us the gift of life...
>
> Now in the distance we see the Dawn approaching; it is coming, coming along the path of the Morning Star. It is a long path and as the Dawn advances along this path sometimes we catch sight of it and then again we lose it, but all the time it is coming nearer.
>
> The Dawn is newborn, its breath has sent new life everywhere, all things stir with the life Tirawa has given this child, his child, whose mother is the night...
>
> We sing this song with loud voices; we are glad. We shout, 'Daylight has come! Day is here!' The light is over the earth...We call to the Children; we bid them awake...We tell the Children that all the animals are awake. They come forth from their places where they have been sleeping. The deer leads them. She comes from her cover, bringing her young into the light of day. Our hearts are glad as we sing, 'Daylight has come! The light of day is here!'

The Moon

The moon's cycle is actually very complex but its regular rhythm of waxing full and waning away to nothing divides up the year for us into 12 fairly even groups of days which we call months. Both moon and month come from the same root words which mean "to measure." The moon has no light of its own; it merely reflects the sun. The dark of the moon means it is in the same direction as the sun so we don't see a moon. When the moon moves east of the sun, a thin crescent of moon shows up in the west just after the sun sets. About a week later it is half lit by the sun. This is called a "quarter moon" though, because it is only a quarter way through its cycle. Then, when the moon is opposite the sun it is a full moon. In one month, moonrise can oscillate between two extremes on the horizon, just as the sunrise does in a year. But moonrise can only take place a certain distance on either side of the points where the sun rises at the solstices. It takes 18.6 years to complete the entire pattern which occurs between sun and moon and earth.

The controversy continues to this day over whether the

full moon really affects humans or not. Most cultures fully realize that it does. But Western science has a difficult time with this concept, since the moon is actually always in the sky and it's real volume never changes—just the reflection of light changes. I cannot take the space to go further into this complex matter here so I will just summarize data from a recent research project, which used an 18-year computerized data base of 4,000 psychiatric patients. "Psychotic patients are known to be most pathological under the influence of the full moon during summer and fall. Their symptoms also peak during the new moon of spring and winter." Further, most suicides occur in the spring or fall. Paul Mirabile, who conducted the study thinks that these mood swings may be caused by some combination of the changing light cycle and a changing relationship to gravity. "Mental illness may show itself when the delicate balance of these two systems is thrown off."

Traditional cultures all over the world have been aware of this power of the moon and certain rituals are timed to coincide with either the new moon or the full moon. Ancient China furnishes us with the most complete written account of such a complex moon ritual system. The "Yue Ling" is a monthly calendar inserted into the Book of Rites, but actually it is more ancient that the Book of Rites itself. In this calendar each month has its protector, its note of music, its symbol, its first sign of new life in nature: bird, plant or animal—all to enable the human being to fit more easily into the cosmic rhythm. I will just give a few examples here from a translation of this document:

> During the first month of Spring the celestial energy descends while the terrestrial one ascends. Heaven and earth communicate...mountains, ravines, slopes, marshes, plains and the quality of land are verified...During the second month of spring... sparrows are coming...During the third month of Spring, the sun diffuses its heat...the Son of Heaven [the sun] expands his kindness to all...the turtle-dove coos...In this month the master of music and his disciples give a concert... [In the cold of winter] men close all the places which have to be kept warm. When comes again the spring of the following year, Man and the universe are thrilling; soon Spring, light, heat will come again, life will begin anew.

Concerning the use of the "Yue Ling," Bergeron writes:

"After having penetrated into all the zones of the universe, man has centered them upon himself, he has drawn upon all the vital energies that they have accumulated; he has assumed them, and by this very act he has participated in the Great Harmony."

Today, it is difficult for us to ground the names of our months in our local place because our months are mostly named after Roman gods. This, of course, involves two levels of abstraction, because the Romans had no names for their gods until they got them from Greece. As Jane Harrison points out the Greeks denoted gods by name; the Romans called them numen or powers until influenced by Greece. Then they translated the Greek names and put them onto their own gods.

For instance our first three months are called January (after Janus, the Roman god who looks both ways), February (after februa, the goat skins used in the Lupercalia) and March, (after Mars, the god of war).

Why should we still call on those old gods of the Romans? Let's begin to recognize the "powers" of our own place by putting their names onto the respective months when each of these "powers" appears in our place. Planet Drum's "Rocky Mountain Bundle" contains a medicine wheel which shows the names of the months which particular tribes in the Northern Rocky Mountains used.

One of the best ways to get to know your own place is to watch the animal and vegetable life of the place as the year unfolds. Which plant first appears in the spring? What plant blooms latest in the year? When does the snow come? The more you learn to pay attention to this seasonal rhythm, the more you realize there is to learn and the deeper you get into the life of your own place. This, of course, constitutes real culture. Such "knowing" is present in a Japanese haiku such as the one printed below, under Summer Solstice, where Bashō uses the cicada to invoke the whole intense summer heat and all that goes with it. This "knowing" will become the work of the poets in each of our bioregions: to catch the words— which anyone in the community may come up with at a festival—and weave them into the fabric which constitutes the on-going life of that place.

"The Sun, as the great centre of power and the upholder of all things, was the Blackfeet's supreme object of worship. He saw that every bud and leaf and blossom turned its face towards the Sun as the source of its life and growth; that the berries he ate reddened and ripened under its warmth; that men and animals thrived under its sustaining light, but all perished when it was withdrawn. He saw that in the darkness and cold of winter, nature retired into silence and sleep; that when the sunlight and warmth of spring returned, all nature awakened and put on its robe of green; the bears left their hibernating dens and the beavers their winter lodges. The Sun made the grass to grow and the trees to be covered with foliage for subsistence of the birds and animals, upon which men, women and children and everything that had breath to worship the all-glorious, all-powerful Sun-God who fills the heavens with life and beauty. To them, he is the supreme source of light, of life, and of power."

Walter McClintock

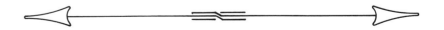

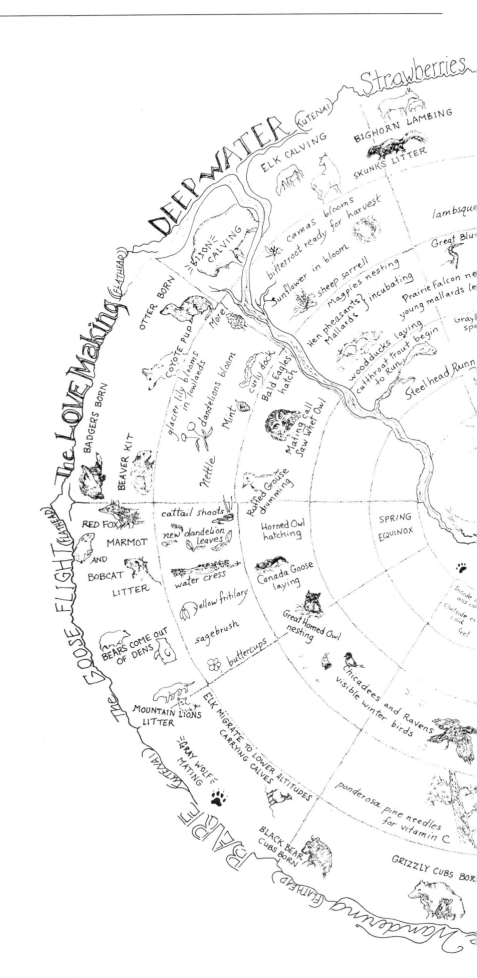

ROCKY MOUNTAIN LIFETIME

Naming the months in the "old way"
— A pattern for your own bioregion —

ipen (KUTENAI)
ripe service berries (KUTENAI)
MULE DEER FAWNING
GRIZZLIES MATING
BIGHORN AND LAMBS MOVING TO HIGHER PASTURES
service berry
ELK AND CALVES MOVING TO HIGH GRAZE
wild strawberry
sweet clover
raspberry
BISON BREEDING
fireweed
graycheeked rosyfinch and water pipit nesting
nesting
Red-tailed Hawks leave nest
Prairie Falcons fledge
salmon fly
trout feeding hungrily
blueberry
wild onion
Pintail blue winged teal migrate
thimbleberry
golden currant
huckleberry
mountain ash berries redden
Berries Ripen at Night (KUTENAI)
Harvest of Ripe Things (FLATHEAD)
elderberry
yampa root
choke cherries
whitefish spawning
Hawks migrate
AUTUMN EQUINOX
Grasshoppers abundant
Aspens and Maples turn color
cutthroat migrate to lower altitudes
Snow Geese Arrive Some Years
Rosehips
oregon grape
tamarack turn
Acorns
Mallards migrate
Snowy Owls arrive some years
pine nuts to eat
bearberry
BEARS BEGIN TO HIBERNATE
ELK BUGLING AND MATING (KUTENAI)
LEAVES FALL OFF
DEER LAMENTING (KUTENAI)
still available
BIGHORN RUT
ries
the FIRST PRA

*These events are clues and cues for sustenance,
celebration and new views of inter-species regard.*

"If you want to find yourself, you must enter the appropriate context—nature. To enter the context of nature, you must live in and with the seasons—acutely!!!"

Frederick Adams

PART II SEASONAL FESTIVALS

Introduction to the seasons

Fundamentally, the changing relationship between the sky and the earth throughout the year produce the patterns, *li*, which we, here on earth call the seasons; but with the sky so darkened by the products of human greed, this is no longer as obvious as it was to all the previous generations of humanity. That is another reason why we must return to the seasonal round of festivals.

The solstices and the equinoxes are the four prominent alignments of sun and earth: each of these is the beginning of one of the four seasons. At the Spring Equinox the equatorial plane of the earth is in direct line with the sun which makes day and night of equal length. During the winter the North Pole has been tilted away from the sun but with the Spring Equinox it begins tilting in toward the sun. Thus the sun's rays shine more directly on the northern hemisphere and we get warmer weather. By the time of the Summer Solstice (around June 21), the sun has reached its northernmost setting point on the horizon. On that day it spends the longest time in the sky during the year. On the following day it begins its journey back along the horizon to its winter setting point. Summer Solstice is considered the beginning of summer; although for centuries in Europe it was called "Midsummer's Day" and the important evening of the day before the longest day of the year was called "Midsummer's Eve." Again at Autumn Equinox, we have equal day and night and this is the beginning of autumn. When the sun reaches its farthest setting point on the southern horizon we have the shortest day of the year. This is Winter Solstice and the beginning of winter (around Dec. 21). The word, solstice comes from two Latins words: *solstitium* meaning *sol*, sun and *sistere*, "to stand still." Although the sun doesn't really stand still, it seems that it does, because one day it's approaching this point, the following day it sets right on this point and the third day it's moved back so little that it is not noticeable without some obvious landmark.

Here in Silverton the sun seems to "stand still" for seven days. Our Winter Solstice setting point is on a bench of snow covered rock along the left ridge of Sultan Mountain. The sun has been moving down this ridge from the summit of Sultan, for days before the solstice. Then about three days before the solstice it sets right behind the bench. On Winter Solstice and for the following three days, the sun sets every day directly behind this bench. Each day during this time, when one glances at it with the naked eye, it seems to be placidly sitting on the bench. Watching it with a double layer of exposed film, one can see minute movements of the sun during this time because of the protuberances on the ridge.

The other four important seasonal days of the year are often called "cross-quarter" days. Although the relationship between the earth and the sun are marked by the obvious equinoxes and solstices, and thus each season begins; the full force of the season doesn't affect us until sometime later on in the season. Summer comes around June 21st but it doesn't really get unbearably hot until late July or early August in most places and in winter, although Winter Solstice is December 21st, it doesn't really get unbearably cold until sometime in January. The ancient Celtic peoples marked the four main seasonal days by lighting huge bonfires, but they also lit ritual fires on four other nights through the year. These nights were about half-way between the main seasonal days. On our present calendar these dates are February 4, May 6, August 8 and November 8; thus the year is divided into eight sections. I will go further into the holidays based on these cross-quarter days below.

Most traditional cultures had festivals to mark each of these eight important stages of the year. In the last few hundred years these festivals have gradually been eliminated so that, now in the U.S. we really have only one festival left, Christmas. Loading all the expectations and hopes and needs onto this one festival is the Eurocentric predilection toward "substance" carried to its ultimate logical insanity. In the last decade researchers have begun to question this matter: I list some of the best sources in Reference Notes. Just recently they have actually coined an official acronym for the problem: SAD for Seasonal Affective Disorder. According to Laurel Lagoni, a human development specialist at Colorado State University, "research has shown that the body secretes a hormone called melatonin during periods of darkness [during the year]. Melatonin causes edginess and fatigue, disturbs sleep and increases appetite. But sunlight suppresses the hormone, even a brief period of sunlight such as during an afternoon walk."

Traditional cultures knew about this "edginess" and "disturbed sleep" in the winter; hence the Iroquois "False Face" ceremonies; the riotous behavior of late winter festivals such as the Lupercalia in Roman times and other festivals which I describe below.

BEAR TURNS THE YEAR

For many traditional cultures in the northern hemisphere, the bear turns the year. Two conspicuous constellations of the northern hemisphere are Ursa Major and Ursa Minor, (Ursa meaning bear). Together, the two constellations are called The Great Bear. The brightest star in Ursa Minor is the Pole Star or Polaris. Traditional symbols for the turning Great Bear include the cross and the swastika (the four revolving seasons, the four directions), and what might be the most basic of all symbols, the spiral. The Great Bear is the ever-turning mandala in the sky. Thus the Pole Star is the "still center of the world," round which our world turns.

The Great Bear and the hunter, Bootes, who make up the prey and pursuer, pivot around the North Star during the course of the night.

THE WAY OF THE HEAVENS
THE FOUR SEASONS

The ever-changing relationship between our spinning earth and the sun as the earth revolves around the sun through the year gives us our Seasonal Festivals here in the Northern Hemisphere.

This diagram indicates the growing sunlight followed the waning sunlight on the earth as the Seasonal Festivals progress. For other ancient names of these festivals see the text.

Designed by Michael A. Darr for Sacred Land *© 1988 Dolores LaChapelle*

The sky is swept by this great arm of lights, the drama of the chase from horizon to zenith, circling from right to left, dominating the visual field, awesome in its energy. In the Paleolithic era it was not Polaris but another 'north star' that was the hub of the revolving universe. The 'pursuit' was like a great gear on an invisible axis, driving the whole stellar panorama through the night, bringing the rising sun, whose brightness was therefore also the bear's doing: the ultimate food chain. Hunters have always known that the chase liberates the energy that turns the world...The hunt is not a frenzied pursuit but the stately procession of final things, energy gained and spent, transferred, assimilated, and dissipated, only to be renewed again by the holy sun.

Paul Shepard

In some cultures the Bear is the hunter-bear pursuing the calf; in other cultures the Great Bear is pursued by the human hunter. "The path of these figures around the Pole Star is so much a part of northern life that the Soviet ethnologist G. M. Vasilevich says that the young people of today read it like a watch, and can tell the time of night to the minute by the position of these constellations."

LEARNING FROM EARTH/SKY RELATIONSHIPS

Each season teaches us humans some particular aspect of the earth/sky relationship. Dennis Tedlock points out:

The thing about that, that's another good point too, a book you can take down off the shelf any time you please, 24 hours a day twelve months a year.
Or any year.
In an oral culture there are some kinds of words that you allow yourself to hear only maybe at certain seasons.
Or at certain times of day maybe even only once a year and other things that you hear only every fourth year, and other things that you hear only every eighth year.
And that's part of the whole secret of making a story really *fit here now* in *this place.*
It's got to fit the calendar, too.

Seasonal Festivals

HISTORICAL BACKGROUND

In the seasonal festival, the humans take part along with the earth, the sky and the gods of that particular place in the weaving of the sacred fabric of life. This is the *topocosm*—the on-going inter-relationship of the earth with all its plants and animals and the sky with its rain, and snow, stars, moon and sun and the gods that manifest, within this interaction, as well as the humans, who also dwell within this living organism of place. Also the *topocosm* includes not only the present community of that place, but also the on-going and "continuous entity" of which the present community is but "the current manifestation."

"In most parts of the world," according to Dr. Gaster, "seasonal rituals follow a common pattern. This pattern is based on the conception that life is vouchsafed in a series of leases which have annually to be renewed." This renewal depends not only on the non-human beings of the place but on the human as well. The rituals are of two specific kinds: *Kenosis*, or Emptying, and *Plerosis*, or Filling. "Rites of Kenosis include the observance of fasts, lents, and similar austerities," all indicating that the topocosm is in a "state of suspended animation...Rites of Plerosis include mock combats against the forces of drought

or evil, mass mating, the performance of rain charms and the like, all designed to effect the reinvigoration of the topocosm."

Gaster tells us that the word, *topocosm*, is related to the words: microcosm and macrocosm. The Greek, *topos*, means "place" and *cosmos*, means "world order." Thus "seasonal ceremonies are the economic regimen of this topocosm" Even today, we have a faint remembrance of this concept of the on-going *topocosm*, in "Alma Mater," as meaning all the context of the college one has attended. But the non-human is always left out of such concepts.

The ancient beginnings of our European literature go back to "a religious ritual designed to ensure the rebirth of a dead world." With his training in archaeology and philology, Gaster traces phrases used in the Bible and in modern literature, clear back to their origin in the ancient Hittite (roughly 1600 B.C.), Babylonian (2000 B.C.), Canaanite (1800 B.C.) and Egyptian eras. He then shows how these same phrases re-appear in the Greek plays and in the Christian Bible. This, of course, involves deciphering, not only ancient manuscripts, but cuneiform inscriptions.

Gaster states that there are four major elements in this "seasonal pattern" of rituals. First, come rites of "MORTIFICATION, symbolizing the state of suspended animation," which comes at the end of the year, "when one lease of life has drawn to a close and the next is not yet assured." Second, come "rites of PURGATION," where the group tries to rid itself of all bad influences both physical and moral, which have accumulated and therefore might threaten the "desired renewal of vitality." Third, come "rites of INVIGORATION," as the community tries to get together all the energy it can summon, so that life will continue in that place. "Last come rites of JUBILATION," which follow from the relief when they know that "the new year has indeed begun and the continuance of their own lives and that of the topocosm is thereby assured."

In Mortification rites tears are often shed, but that doesn't mean that mourning is necessarily involved. Among the Toradjas, Galelarese, and Javanese peoples of Indonesia, "tears are regarded—as are blood, sweat, semen, and urine elsewhere—as effusions of the 'soul-substance', so that the shedding of them serves as means of reinvigorating the earth." This was likewise true of the ancient Babylonian New Year ceremonies as well as the ancient Canaanite. Furthermore, "a specific allusion to it may be recognized in the familiar words of Psalm 126:5-6 in the Bible."

They that sow in tears shall reap in joy.
He that goeth forth weeping,
bearing the trail of seed,
shall doubtless return with rejoicing,
bearing his sheaves [of grain]

Purgation rites are done all over the world. For example, among the Eskimo of Point Barrow the evil spirit, Tuna, is expelled annually at the moment when the sun reappears. In most places purgation of bad influences is done by fire. For example, among the Incas and even in the south of France until modern times, bad influences were expelled by blazing torches.

These examples are enough to give you an idea of the basic pattern of seasonal rituals. There is much more information in Gaster's book. (See Reference Notes.) Below I will give you some idea of the basic pattern in each of the eight major seasonal festivals, as well as the remnants of this pattern, still hidden within the current holidays.

PART III THE WAY OF THE HEAVENS: THE FOUR SEASONS

In this way the yin and yang annually meet each other in the north at the winter solstice, when the yin is dominant and the yang subordinate, and again in the south at the summer solstice, when the reverse is true. They are annually opposite each other at the spring equinox, when the yang is in the east and the yin in the west, and again at the autumn equinox, when their positions are reversed; on both occasions they are exactly equal in strength. All this, constitutes 'the course of Heaven', [which] when it has been completed, begins again.

Tung Chung-shu (179—104 B.C.)

The first step in regaining our place in nature, is to insist on celebrating the major seasonal festivals on the very day indicated to us by the changing relationship between the earth and sun. The Sioux, Vine Deloria tells us:

Unless time is understood as sacred, experienced in all its fullness, and so dominant a consideration of the life of a people that all other functions are subservient to it, it is impossible to have a complete and meaningful ceremonial life.

He continues by pointing out that the U.S. government, "seeking to make the people abandon old ways and adopt new practices which were carefully orchestrated by a new sense of time—a measured time which had little to do with cosmic realities. It is debatable which factor was most important in the destruction of tribal ceremonial life, the prohibition of performances of traditional rituals by the government or the introduction of the white man's system of keeping time."

At the great seasonal festivals, as Leo Frobenius puts it:

[A]rchaic man *plays* the order of nature as imprinted on his consciousness...the change of seasons, the rising and setting of the constellations...the course of the sun and moon. And now he plays this great processional order of existence in a sacred play, in and through which he actualizes anew, or 'recreates,' the events...and thus helps to maintain the cosmic order.

Frobenius draws even more far-reaching conclusions from this "play": "He deems it the starting-point of all social order and social institutions too."

The Season of Autumn

Now, what of that celestial movement which decrees the succession of those mysterious moods of the Earth Being we call The Seasons? That movement gives us a new sense of Land Sky Embodiment, ever deepening through the spiral of the Seasons.

Frederick Adams

I begin with autumn because here in Silverton, the aspen leaves turn golden and the clear light of the blue sky is at its best. It is all warm and golden and a kind of hush lies over everything. This seems to be a stillness of balance between the end of summer and the beginning of winter. In traditional agricultural countries of the more temperate zones it was the time of gathering in of the harvest and thus a giving thanks time.

The Chinese celebrate certain times of the year when the earth is most yin or most yang. One of these is the Full Moon Festival in September, when summer heat gives place to autumn coolness. This full moon is considered the time when the female or yin principle begins to take over the upper hand in Nature. Concerning this full moon, the Chinese say: "At no other time is she so bright and brilliant. Then, and then only, the Chinese say, 'she is perfectly round'." The feast is "usually at midnight—the hour when the moon illumines the highest palaces. General festivities continue for three days. The evenings are devoted to moon-viewing parties which date from the time of Emperor Wu Ti (100 BC)."

In the Near Eastern area, where some of the roots of our European culture originate, autumn was the beginning of the agricultural year. Along the Mediterranean and in the Near East, the planting takes place in the autumn in hopes of fall or winter rains. Gaster writes: "Every autumn, at the beginning of the agricultural year, when the earth stood in imminent need of water, the ancient Hittites held a festival they called Puruli." A still earlier form of the word, dating from the Hattites is Vuruli, meaning "earth." It was the "Festival of the Earth" and so important, that it is recorded on 32 clay tablets. Briefly it has to do with the weather god, who, with the aid of the goddess Inaras succeeded in subduing a "contumacious dragon." The goddess has her temple at the "outlet of the subterranean waters (those which the dragon had previously controlled)." This has to do with both the irrigation waters and the hoped for rain. The "dragon really represents the nether waters, supposed source of rivers as well as springs, which have annually to be 'tamed' or subdued lest they flood the earth instead of fructifying it." This "dragon" much later became identified with the devil in Christian thought. This came about through the transmission of culture from the Near East to the Jews, and thence to Christian thought.

In places such as England where the beginning of the agricultural year is in the spring, even as late as 1903 in Suffolk, a dragon was paraded through the streets. In Sicily on St. George's day, April 23, an "enormous effigy of a dragon, complete with moveable tail and eyes," was carried through the streets. Both of these late remnants have to do with the subduing of the rain dragon so that it will help, instead of harm, humans. In other words, give rain and not floods. Notice the date of St. George's day. This saint's day was assigned to April in order to take over the ceremonies from the previous pagan celebrations of defeating the dragon.

At the feast of Michaelmas, a harvest feast in England, there is usually a fight between St. Michael, the archangel and the dragon, again dating back to the very ancient Hittite approach. St. Michael is called the "dragon-slayer."

There are two different approaches to fall festivals—one a battle with bad influences or devils and one a calm, peaceful balance. Autumn Equinox is the main Festival day of this season: it is a day of balancing all the forces within and without; while Hallowe'en, the cross-quarter day, partakes much more of the aspects of encountering "darkness" without and within the human. At the Autumn Equinox we have equal day and equal night which is a balancing of the relationship between earth and sun.

Concerning the sun's journey in the fall, Henry Beston writes:

> All these autumn weeks I have watched the great disk going south along the horizon of moorlands beyond the marsh, now sinking behind this field, now behind this leafless tree, now behind this sedgy hillock dappled with thin snow. We lose a great deal, I think, when we lose this sense and feeling for the sun. When all has been said, the adventure of the sun is the great natural drama by which we live, and not to have joy in it and awe of it, not to share in it, is to close a dull door on nature's sustaining and poetic spirit.

HALLOWEEN

Halloween is the "cross-quarter" day between Autumn Equinox and Winter Solstice. It is based on the old Celtic Samhain, "summer's end." The Celtic people brought their cattle in from distant places to a nearby field in preparation for the coming of winter, which brought the people together, as well. There was anxiety because of the increasing darkness of on-coming winter. The Samhain festival dealt with this "darkness" both inside the people and outside. Giant bonfires were built and people leapt over the fires to prevent evil influences on themselves. Sometimes cattle were driven between fires to keep them from harm. Early "world-renewal" rituals always included the dead along with the living. Food offerings were put on the graves, which is how the dead were welcomed into the festival. The Christian church put the feast of All Saints on October 31 to take over some of the energy of this feast for the dead, and on November 1, the feast of All Souls, which refers to all the other Christians, who have died but aren't considered saints. Under World Renewal Festivals below, I will give more details of a modern Samhain type ritual in Washington state.

Gary Snyder, writes about "How we do Mayday & Halloween on the western slope of the Sierra Nevada" in the bioregional paper, *Upriver Downriver*. He says: "At Halloween there is sometimes a deer or goat to barbecue, and animal—or demon—masked dancers...games, feats, and races follow." Explaining the importance of these two festivals, he remarks: "But to get together two times each year for the spirit of the place, the place we all love and share, for holy craziness, for each other, for the myth of human beings making love to animals, more than anything else, I think, helps keep us together, helps keep us sane. These two dates...survivors from the stone age...should be widely appropriated all over Shasta Nation. It could become a way we can keep in touch, place to place, ear to the Maypole."

Another important aspect of Halloween, dating from long ago, is what has been called "status reversal." It's important that age and sex-role reversal occur once in a while. By making the low, high and the high, low it shakes up the hierarchical structure, which always tends to rigidify. This kind of celebration resolves the tension. Also in some Indian tribes it regulated which clan had the political power for that season. Remnants of this still exist in the Hopi ritual cycle. A particular clan is in charge of the rituals for that season. When the next season comes, a different clan takes over. In the old days this shift in political power happened "naturally," by tying it in with nature. This was such a subtle thing that early white people in this country, assumed the Indians had no organization—

that it was anarchy. Anarchy never works. To live in harmony there has to be someone or some group in charge. Konrad Lorenz said: "Without hierarchy there is no social order possible." But the hierarchy should be kept shifting around. Some Indian tribes had peace chief and war chiefs—another way to handle this matter. Halloween gives bioregional groups a chance to experiment with this shifting type of political power.

Halloween is increasing in importance in this country and it's no longer considered merely a festival for children. In Boulder, Colorado it is about the biggest festival of the year. Durango, the nearest "big town" to Silverton is beginning to notice Halloween as well; but, unfortunately, it's already becoming merely a commercial venture.

The Season of Winter

Many of the most important festivals of the year cluster around the time of the Winter Solstice. In the north of Europe the Lussi festival, celebrated on December 13, a festival of light, dates back to pagan times. According to the research of Hammarstedt: "Lussi herself appears in Nordic popular belief as a beneficent virgin goddess of love who, dressed in white and surrounded by light, reveals herself at the darkest period of the year, distributing an elixir of life from a bowl...Offerings were made to her near a tree...She was, though virgin, the mother of the personified forces of nature, elves and fairies, and in pre-Christian belief she was probably regarded, under another name, as all-mother." When these northern people were converted to Christianity, this festival was renamed by means of the "apocryphal Christian legend of Saint Lucia, who on December 13th, A.D. 304, was surrounded in Syracuse by burning pine torches and, when these failed to ignite her, finally suffered martyrdom at the hands of the executioner." Hammarstedt concludes his dissertation on the Lussi Festival with these words: "Even to-day this goddess survives, in a manner, in thought, speech and writing, although most people are unconscious of her. She is now called Nature."

In recent times, in Sweden, the youngest daughter of the household wearing a wreath of burning candles on her head, goes through the house serving coffee and singing songs. This is followed by a festive breakfast for the family and the animals are given extra fodder.

In ancient Rome the Saturnalia began on December 17th and lasted for seven days. It was observed in honor of Saturnus, traditionally regarded as the first king of Latium who supposedly introduced agriculture to the people. It grew out of an earlier rustic festival to celebrate the safe bringing in of the harvest, but by classical Roman times it became associated with feasting, gambling, exchange of wax tapers and presents. It was also a time when social roles were reversed. Slaves were served by their masters at the feasts. In other parts of Italy there was a mock king who, after a time of feasting was ritually killed "to renew the life of nature at the winter solstice."

YULE FEAST

Sometime after the cattle were brought in to nearby fields at Samhain, and as it grew closer to severe winter weather, decisions were made about how many cattle could be carried through the winter with the available fodder. The rest were slaughtered, followed by a feast of the meat as the people gathered around giant bonfires. Eventually this feast was "fixed in the Germano-Celtic calendar in the middle of November, under such designations as Jiuleis, Giuli, and in Scandinavia, Yule, a name which still perplexes philologists." Later when the northern tribes had penetrated into the Roman world, it was celebrated in the darkest period of the year from mid-December to mid-January. Under Christian influence it became part of the Nativity rites. Summing up all the influences on this feast, E. O. James states: "Therefore, Yuletide became a highly complex observance combining Nordic pagan elements with those derived from the Christian calendrical tradition with its Graeco-Roman background." A Yule log was put on the hearth on Christmas Eve and kindled with the remains of the previous year's Yule log which had been carefully saved throughout the year for this purpose. Once the Yule log was lit it had to kept alight until Twelfth Night (Jan. 6th the feast of the Epiphany when the wise men arrived with gifts for Jesus.) The ashes of the Yule log were scattered over the fields to make them productive.

CHRISTMAS

Christmas, the official birth of Jesus, was assigned to December 25th to take over the celebrations of the birth of Mithras which had been celebrated on this date by the Romans. The religion of Mithras had been introduced into Rome by returning soldiers of the Roman Legion. It's origins come from Iranian sources combined with some Babylonian astrology. Mithras had originally been an Indo-Iranian god of light, but in the Roman cult he became "the invincible god of celestial light," the sun. There was a bull sacrifice and a sacramental communion of bread, water and wine. "These esoteric rites were celebrated in small *mithraea* constructed wholly or partially underground." But often the rites were in caves or grottoes.

The actual date of the Nativity is not mentioned anywhere in the Gospels, of course. No reference is made to such a festival until the fourth century when the Philocalian calendar was compiled in Rome in 336 and December 25th was set as the date of the birth of Jesus. In the Eastern Roman Empire the main celebration was January 6th. But the December 25th date was officially fixed by Pope Liberius "to counteract the Saturnalia and the Mithraic ritual in honour of the birth of the Sun." December 25th, in the old calendars, coincided with the Winter Solstice. Later calendar reforms resulted in the Winter Solstice occurring on December 21st to 23rd.

In the modern world, unfortunately, all the festivals have been loaded onto this one day—December 25th. All the myriad things, which only a true festival can accomplish, are all "supposed" to happen on this one day. The result, of course is disaster! There are too many expectations without any real grounding in the power of the returning sun with its blessings on people and place. Besides sheer loneliness, there is increased violence within families and even suicide on this day. An article in the *Christian Science Monitor*, "Tis the season to be lonely," takes a determined look at this problem. Melvin Maddocks starts out with the homeless people at Christmas: "The shoppers, laden with their parcels of gifts, step around homeless people as if they were an impediment, like a lampost...while the loudspeakers in the mall trill of 'goodwill to men'." He continues by telling about how Christmas is supposed to be "a celebration of communion." He asks, "How come, then, the famous loneliness of this season, annually reviewed by social observers under such headings as 'Christmas blues'?" He notes that we also "step around...those closest to us," too. He quotes R. D. Laing who argues that not only for those in extreme "mental misery" but also for those characterized as normal, "camaraderie, solidarity, companionship, communion" can be "almost impossible." Maddocks closes with the remark that getting out of this "lost centre of loneliness is like climbing out of a sand pit. Is it because we lack rituals?... And all the villages have become so big!"

Maddocks does hit on two of the main problems here— no rituals and huge populations but he misses the root of the problem: "Psychology without ecology is lonely," Tom Jay succinctly tells us in "The Salmon of the Heart." Until more people begin to realize that we must include the earth, the sky and the gods in our celebrations, there'll be no "climbing out of the sand pit" of loneliness.

Following the underlying theme in this book, I want to point out here that this modern aberration of putting all the festivals, previously occurring throughout the four seasons of the year, onto one festival day, Christmas— the birthday of the son of an other-wordly, monotheistic type of god, constitutes the ultimate "substance" approach to life. Here we have everything loaded onto one "substance," Christmas, which by some sort of devious magic is supposed to bring the result, labelled "happiness." Contrast this system with the "normal" human pattern throughout millenia of celebrating the changing relationships of earth and sun throughout the four seasons. In celebrating these changing patterns in nature we also allow and even encourage the humans to celebrate the ever-changing yin and yang aspects within each person. There is a correlation here beween "inner" landscape and "outer" landscape.

Notice that in the opening quote for Part III of this chapter, yin and yang vary throughout the year. In winter the yin is dominant and the yang subordinate, but in the summer it's the opposite; and at the equinoxes they change places. Here again we see the emphasis on the relationship between earth and sun, yin and yang, rather than the yin, as "substance" or yang, as "substance." In analyzing this relationship, "we can see two aspects: static and dynamic. The static can be summarized as a spatially hierarchical (dominant and submissive, upper and lower) and a temporally sequential (from winter to summer or from summer to winter) relationship. A spatial relationship connotes a temporal relationship and vice versa. The dynamic relationship can be equated with the 'Tao,' the way in which the binary poles dialectically exchange and reciprocate in supplementing and alternating with each other." This is, of course, true in human relations as well.

It's useful here to repeat the original definitions of yin and yang, because now that these terms are being used more often here in the West, they have become rigidified into substances. In the old form of these Chinese characters yang is represented by the sun with its rays, together with the character *fu*, meaning hill or mountain. The character for yin was a coiled cloud along with the character *fu*. According to the definition in the Erh Ya, a dictionary of the Chou period, yang describes "the sunny side of the mountain" and yin, "the side in the shadow." This relates directly to the changing relationship of the sun and the mountain: thus, in the morning, when the sun is behind the mountain, the trees are dark; in the afternoon, when the setting sun shines directly on these same trees, they are bright and glowing with light. This same pattern extends to the earth as a whole in its relationship to the sun.

WINTER SOLSTICE

At the Winter Solstice the yin reaches its fullest development; the yang has completely disappeared. "The world is filled with yin energy—darkness, potential creativity etc. But, actually the moment the Yin reaches its apogee; the Yang already starts to make its return; the Yang energy, no matter how faint and imperceptible it may be, is already there." Thus, no static position is possible; by the very fact that something has moved as far as possible in one direction it is compelled to turn around and go the other way. In human life this is very hopeful; when things look darkest they have already, secretly so to speak, begun to move in the other direction toward a new, as yet unperceived happiness.

Winter Solstice is one of the seasonal "transitional moments" in Taoism, the moment of "chaos" before the "new beginnings" within the human world and in nature as well. That is why it is considered so precarious. In ancient China no one travelled on this day for fear of upsetting this delicate transition from yin to the beginnings of yang. In ancient China, according to the *Li Chi:*

> The initial point [of the Twelve Branch system] is placed in relation to the north, the winter solstice, midnight: it is symbolized by the character *tzu* which signifies 'the infant,' 'an egg,' 'a seed,' 'semen'. [It is] The Time of Origins, the initial point, the winter solstice, north…is the place where the two cosmogonic sexual principles, whose inverse and antithetical action constitute the continuity of time, coexist without separation.

At such a crucial time everyone tried to get back to their own place to take part in the energy of that particular place and to add their human energy to the needs of the place. On the Winter Solstice, "when the edges of the year meet" the sun "turns around" and begins its journey to its "summer home." The original and only source of food is the sun. Every creature feeds on the sun. The most important rhythm in our body is the circadian rhythm of light and dark, regulated by the sun. We are all children of the sun. There is an involuntary hush of our being as we approach the longest night of the year:

> We are all children
> and the night is starry
>
> > In the hush…
> > In the space of silence…
> > The pine trees,
> > on this holy night,
> > are still and serene.
>
> Inhale the stars, inhale
> the beauty of this planet.
> the fragile miracle
> of our present.

> We are all children
> and the night is starry.

Because Winter Solstice is the longest night of the year and there is less sun than any other day of the year, in archaic times it was felt that if proper attention and respect was not paid, the sun might not turn back toward his summer house and it would just get colder and darker and darker. In these so-called modern days, we are finding out that due to human, short-sighted stupidity, the sun is losing some of its power—at least as far as we here on earth are concerned. In many places the smog is getting worse. Here in the Four Corners area, where we used to have "the last clean air in the conterminous United States," as Ed Abbey puts it, the sun has been darkened so much that we can see the brown smudge on the horizon from the tops of our San Juan mountains. This brown smudge is due to the infamous Four Corners power plant and associated activities. "The sun is becoming darker," Loloma, a Hopi artist told Stan Steiner. "Everyday there is less light." Loloma was talking about a Convocation of Indian Scholars at Princeton University, to which he had been invited. Everyone got up and made speeches about the problems of Indians and the future of America, but Loloma thought that they were ignoring the true problem. He told Steiner: "I stood up. And all I had to say were seven words," Loloma remembered with a smile. "In the East, there is no sun!" He sat down. First, there was silence; then they all applauded.

Thus Winter Solstice, for us modern people, becomes a very important time to ritually recognize the power of the sun in our lives.

This Winter Solstice recognition of the sun's returning power was so important to many cultures, that they designed certain structures to enhance it. As noted above, the megalithic, New Grange had the "letter-box" opening, so that only on Winter Solstice, the sun's rays could penetrate the interior.

Later on, in Christian Europe, homage to the Winter Solstice continued, although not recognized by the Christian hierarchy. In the ancient hill town of Vezelay, France there is a Romanesque style basilica, built in the twelfth century by unknown master masons and artisans. This basilica ranked with Rome, Jerusalem and Compostello as points of pilgrimage. "The basilica's generous nave is a cadence of high, rounded arches of alternating cream and brown colored stones which spring with amazing lightness from the columns," that show the usual festoons of foliage. What is unusual about this nave is that "at the winter solstice, the light streams through the upper windows of the nave and strikes, precisely, the upper capitals of the soaring columns just as they are about to converge with the round arches. At the summer solstice, on the other hand, the light, coming from the highest point in the sky, streams down into the nave and creates footprints of itself precisely down the middle, marching from the entrance to the altar."

William Merlin points out that the "solstices celebrated at Vezelay's basilica do not just penetrate it [they were] basic to its design." He explains that the building was aligned before it was built in order to focus the solstice sun down the center aisle leading to the altar. In other words, the sun itself was enthroned on this Christian altar.

In China, part way up the Sacred Mountain of the West, Mount Omei, the "Monastery of Holy Myriad Years Longevity" was built in 268 A.D. During the reign of Wan'li (1575-1619) he had the monastery rebuilt and enlarged. The building "was designed to exhibit in brick the procession of creation." It was so oriented that "the sun's rays strike the jewel in the god's forehead, twice a year at the solstices, through a small orifice in the dome."

Among those of us here in the United States who are beginning to celebrate the great Earth Festivals, Winter Solstice is becoming an important time whereby we can celebrate both our own place and at the same time relate to friends who are celebrating the sun's shortest day of the year in other places. This powerful communing with the sun on Winter Solstice links people together in a real way in contrast to abstract Christmas "joy." Here is a letter from a woman who lives in West Virginia, who was on one of our Autumn Equinox Celebrations here in the San Juan mountains: "In a note to Peggy [one of the other participants from Florida] I was saying there was something special in knowing that while we were out celebrating the Solstice it felt deeply meaningful to know she was acknowledging these same events, and you were out there in Colorado at the same time...I've never before felt so connected with people around a natural sort of happening that cuts across all distance. It's a wonderful feeling—another gift!" It is a great gift to be sharing in the relationship of sun and earth on this day and, because of its importance, you may choose to celebrate Winter Solstice as a World Renewal Festival.

CROSS-QUARTER DAY BETWEEN
WINTER SOLSTICE AND SPRING EQUINOX

Spring comes early along the Mediterranean and in the Near East where our European heritage developed. With it comes the return of life and increasing power of the sun. Lupercalia, (Wolf Festival) marked the end of the old Roman year and the beginning of the new. The priests, called Luperci, descendants of the oldest clan on the hill, gathered at the cave of Lupercal, where Romulus and Remus, legendary founders of Rome, were nurtured by the she-wolf. Goats were sacrificed and offered to the god, Faunus. Then, with the blood of the newly killed goat, ritually smeared on their foreheads, youths, stripped naked except for loin cloths made from the skin of the slain goats and with strips of goat skin (februa) in their hands, ran around Palatine Hill—whipping everyone but especially women to insure fertility and good luck for the coming year. This was the "beating of the bounds" of the settlement to trace a magic circle to shut out evil influences, sickness and other harmful things—such as wolves, who might kill their flocks. The name of February for our second month, comes from februa, these strips of goat skin.

The early Romans were pastoral people who kept sheep and goats; but the interesting thing is that Faunus, the god of the feast, was also the supernatural "power" associated with the woods and he had some of the attributes of the god, Mars, to whom the wolf was sacred. So it seems that at a more ancient level, the Festival was concerned with a wild wolf god of the forests, later becoming the one they sacrificed to, in order to protect their goats and sheep.

Lupercal was not the god—that was a late Classical Roman abstraction of the wild god Faunus. The goddess Fauna, his sister, was the goddess of animal life, especially those in a particular region. The great god, Faunus became the faun of late Classical Roman times, a lesser deity of fields and herds having human shape, with pointed ears, small horns, and sometimes a goat's tail—thus becoming more goat-like rather than wolfish. After the Christians triumphed, they turned this "faun" into the devil.

Later still, after Emperor Constantine established Christianity in Rome, Pope Gelassius (492-496) put the feast of Candlemas on February 14th to counteract the wildness of the pagan Lupercalia. Sometime after that, Candlemas was moved up to February 2nd, as a thanksgiving for the ending of a plague. Thus it co-opted the ancient pagan Feast of Lights, celebrated with lighted torches and fires to welcome the return of the goddess from the underworld and the rebirth of nature in spring. There's a very tenuous connection between the reason for Candlemas and the custom of carrying lighted torches. Candlemas is the Feast of the Presentation at the Temple. Jewish women were supposed to present their firstborn baby boy at the Temple forty days after the child's birth. So forty days after Christmas, when Mary brought the baby Jesus to the temple, Simeon, an old man who had long awaited the coming of the Messiah, said that now he could die because he had seen Jesus, "the Light for the enlightenment of the Gentiles." Thus Christ as the Light of the World was the pretext for carrying torches at Candlemas. This Christian feastday is still an important holiday in rural parts of Europe.

The basic sun-symbolism is ever-present behind such phrases as the above in the church's liturgy. Another one for this time of the year is "Today He comes as 'King of the new Light'." At the Winter Solstice, the sun turns back on its course and begins to move toward summer. There is a delay of several weeks before the change in the earth/sun relationship becomes noticeable. By the time of this cross-quarter day in early February, the sun's heat is becoming more powerful and it can truly be said that the "King of new Light," the sun is here.

The old pagan, "return of the goddess celebrations," were continued in Europe under a thin veneer of Christian ideas. For instance, in Scotland, the sacred fire of St. Bride or Bridget was carefully guarded and on the eve of Candlemas a bed made of grain was surrounded with candles as a fertility rite, symbolizing the victorious emergence of the sun from the darkness of winter.

There is a combination of delight at the returning sun and continuing uneasiness, connected to the lingering darkness and cold of winter. That is why the cross-quarter day for this time of the year is often associated with a wild carnival spirit, where these accumulated emotions are given full play. The Church decreed a forty day period of Lent to precede the resurrection of Jesus, which is called Easter; thus the last day before this forty day period was usually a wild celebration. This is the origin of Carnivals in Southern Europe and South America. Shrove Tuesday is another name for this holiday.

"Spring is still spring. The atom bombs are piling up in the factories, the police are prowling the cities, the lies are streaming from the loudspeakers, but the earth is still going round the sun, and neither the dictators not the bureaucrats, deeply as they disapprove of the process, are able to prevent it."

George Orwell

The Season of Spring

Spring Equinox marks the day when the sun's path crosses the earth's equator from the south toward the north. The word "equinox" comes from the Latin word meaning "equal night." Night and day are the same length. Both the dark side and the light side of the earth become equal in area, from pole to pole during the equinox. The north pole which has been tilted away from the sun during winter, gradually begins tilting in toward the sun after the equinox so that the sun's rays fall more directly onto the northern hemisphere and the weather begins to get warmer day by day. In the southern hemisphere we have just the opposite. It's true that on Spring Equinox dark and light are equal but the south pole now begins to tilt away from the sun and so it becomes gradually colder in such places as Australia and New Zealand.

At the Autumn Equinox, despite the glory of the leaves and the stable warm weather in most places, there is an underlying bit of dread at the approach of the cold of winter. Around the time of the Spring Equinox there can often be bad weather, but the general feeling is one of joy, "the sun advancing, the disk rising each day to the north of where it leaped from yesterday's ocean and setting north of yesterday's setting, the solar disk burning, burning, consuming winter in fire." The sun is heading toward his "Summer House" as the Hopi say.

Jubilation is the prevailing emotion, dating clear back to the Puruli Festival of the ancient Hittites as shown by this passage cut into clay tablets:

So Telipinu returned to his house. He took thought for his land. The window said good-by to soot; the house said good-by to smoke. The shrines of the gods were restored to good state. The hearth said good-by to the ashes (that were piled upon it). He released the sheep which were in the fold; he released the oxen which were in the stall. Mother (once again) nursed child; ewe nursed lamb; cow nursed calf...In the presence of Telipinu an evergreen was set up, and from it was hung the fleece of sheep. Enwrapped in that fleece were the fat of sheep, grains of corn, fruit of the vine, (symbolizing) increase of oxen and sheep, continuance in life and (assurance of) posterity.

This same rite of erecting an evergreen tree and suspending fleece from it was later used in the Babylonian rituals and "in many other ancient cults and even to have survived into modern times." The main feature of the Asiatic "mysteries" of Attis celebrated at the Spring Equinox was the bringing in of a sacred pine log on which they hung fleece.

Gaster points out that what we have in all these ceremonies is "a symbolic representation of the death and resurrection of the year spirit or genius of fertility, the erection or adoration of the sacred tree going closely together with the...felling of it. This comes out especially in the more explicit symbolism of earlier examples from Egypt and Mesopotamia." Often these sacred trees were burned later. "Similarly, at the Scottish Beltane festival, at the beginning of summer it was customary in many parts to fell a tree and cast it upon the sacred fire,

while an analogous disposition of the maypole is recorded from Prague, Wurtemberg, and other European centers."

As usual the Christian Church has put an important Church holiday near the Spring Equinox just as it did for the Autumn Equinox, the autumn cross-quarter day and on the Winter Solstice. This time it's the Feast of the Aunnunciation which occurs on March 25th. The Spring Equinox dates around the 21st to the 23rd of March. The Christian feast day has to do with the annunciation by the angel to Mary that she was to be the mother of God. On March 25th, ancient Rome celebrated the Carnival of Hilaria in honor of the Great Mother Goddess, Cybele. So we see both a Mother Goddess festival and the Spring Equinox supplanted by a church feast-day dedicated to Mary.

The New Year Festival of the ancient Mesopotamians was celebrated on the full moon immediately following the Spring Equinox, out of which grew the Jewish Passover and the Christian Easter. Spring Equinox festivals were associated with the beginning of new life and the return of the sun; so it was natural that the Church would put the date of Christ's resurrection (Easter) on the Sunday nearest the full moon after the Spring Equinox. Here we have another curious situation. For most of human history, the return of new life in the spring has been celebrated by dancing/singing/feasting with the gods, but, a mentioned above, the Christians designated the forty days before Easter as Lent. The forty days supposedly refers to the time Jesus spent in the desert; but more important for the early Church, was that Lent begin sometime near the time of the Roman Lupercalia celebrations. This also has a great deal to do with Lent being so self-punishing as over against the "orgies" of the Roman Lupercalia. So during the brief span of Christian history this early spring-time has been concerned with "What I'm going to give up for Lent" and other self imposed sufferings. It is true that the great seasonal festivals always have a time of purgation preceding them but not such a long time as 40 days without some continuous on-going ritual happenings during that time.

MAYDAY

This is the cross-quarter day festival occurring between Spring Equinox and Summer Solstice. As noted above, the rituals to do with Attis concerned erecting a pine tree. In later Roman times, Cybele, the Great Goddess and Attis were part of the same ritual where a pine tree was set up near the temple of the Great Mother on Palatine Hill in Rome. Cybele was responsible for the fertility of the fields and so flower offerings were brought to her. Later, when celebrations in honor of Mary, the mother of Jesus were put on this day there were processions of people carrying flowers to Mary, whose statue was in the rock cleft. (The rock "cave" dates back to the original Mother Goddess figure of the limestone formation in the Cretan caves.)

In the British Isles, the Celts lit ritual bonfires at the beginning of May. This was continued until the Eighteenth Century. These fires were known as Beltane fires, and on Walpurgis Night, the Eve of May Day, there was dancing round the fire. The name comes from the "Gaelic *tein-eigin* 'need-fire' and *Beil*, possibly connected with the Celtic god Belenos whose worship was widespread in Gaul and perhaps in Britain. Beltane and Belenos both mean 'bright fire' and the practice of lighting sacred fires, often on hills, at this time was for the purpose of stimulating the sun as the life-giving agent at the commencement of summer." The fires were also a precaution against "witchcraft and other sinister forces rampant at the beginning of summer."

Later on in Europe, during the Middle Ages, young men and women spent the night together in the woods: sexual intercourse was considered to add to the fertility of nature. On the morning of May Day they carried a tree back into the village. This Maypole was set up on the village green and long streamers attached which entwined around the pole as they danced. "These may be a survival of the bands of wool on the Attis tree in Rome." There was a May Queen, who was brought to the dancing green on a decorated cart; as well as a May King, often a chimney-sweep, clad in a wooden framework covered with leaves, and called The Green Man. He played the role of Attis.

On the other side of the world in Japan there is a similar "maypole" type structure to do with renewal of life in the spring. In the Shugendō religion (a combination of Buddhism and Shinto) there is the "opening of the peak ceremony" in the spring. In the main hall there is a large white object suspended up high with red and white streamers hanging down: white for the bones and red for the blood. The essential idea here is the going into the peak, mother earth herself, to be reborn. This ceremony is only for the Shugendō monks, but once they have "opened the peak" others can go into the mountain area during the summer. (For more information on this "opening the peak" ceremony, see World Renewal Festivals.)

Today, the Maypole is being used as part of land-based rituals. One way is to have a particular color of streamers for each species of plant or animal. Those wishing to "become" that animal or plant for the Maypole dance, take hold of the corresponding color. The entertwining of the streamers is very simple if a fundamental rule is followed—otherwise it is complicated. The entire circle around the pole is formed into couples. One person in each couple turns to the left and the other person turns to the right. Then a leader for left facing people and a leader for right facing people is designated. Thus, one half the group is moving to the right round the Maypole, the other half to the left. All those moving left just follow the actions of their leader—when the leader lifts the streamer over the head of the next person he encounters all those do likewise; when the leader allows the person facing the opposite direction to put their streamer over him, all his followers do the same. This same procedure of following their own leader is done by all those moving right. The entire group dances round the Maypole, while this weaving is going on. The final result is quite beautiful—and for a land ritual—very important because we can see there before us on the Maypole, with all the streamers woven together round the pole in a beautiful design, how the lives of all the beings of that place are woven together.

The Season of Summer

What a stillness!
Deep into the rock sinks
The cicada's shrill
                              Bashō

SUMMER SOLSTICE

Some years ago three of us were climbing in the Alps. We had climbed up to the Hornli hut, high up on the ridge of the Matterhorn in order to finish the climb the next day. As twilight deepened all the climbers in the hut suddenly got up and went outside and stood around, waiting expectantly. Then on a far distant mountain we saw a fire suddenly blaze up. Our hutmaster immediately lit the fire at our hut and soon, far down the valley, another fire was lit. It was a moving ceremony there in the wilderness of rock and snow. I asked the hutmaster and some of the Swiss climbers what it meant. They said, "That's what we always do on St. John's Eve." Actually, of course, it's what most humans have done on the Summer Solstice for millenia. But none of the climbers knew about that and, at that time, I did not know about Summer Solstice either—only about Midsummer's Eve—which is the same date. But what's the connection between St. John and Summer Solstice? A Catholic theologian and liturgist makes it plain: "The birth of Jesus is observed on December 25 at the time of the winter solstice, while the birth of his forerunner is observed six months earlier at the time of the summer solstice. Christmas is a 'light' feast: the same is true today [on St. John's Eve]. The popular custom centering around 'St. John's Fire' stems from soundest Christian dogma... St. John's Fire symbolizes Christ the Light; John was a lamp that burned and shone..."

How about that? It "stems from soundest Christian dogma." Never mind the fact that for millenia before there was such a thing as Christianity, human beings had been lighting fires on this important day when the sun turns around and begins the journey toward his "winter house." It is at this crucial time that humans felt the energy of the sun needed to be renewed as it was to begin its long journey back to winter. Actually, winter really begins on Summer Solstice day. This is when yin energy, although totally hidden in the brightness and warmth of summer, begins to grow, increasing in strength until Winter Solstice. Although this change does not seem quite as perilous as the change-over from yang to yin in the winter, that is because humans feel better when it is warm and sunny; while in the winter they feel anxious at the growing cold and dark. The Celts lit bonfires at Summer Solstice for just this reason: "to protect from witches and other evil influences, and to ensure the well-being of the sun in its course in the heavens." In fact the word "bonfire" comes from the fact that sometimes bones were thrown into these fires to keep witches away. Summer Solstice fires were lit by many of the early cultures in Europe.

Traditional cultures throughout the world lit fires to encourage the sun on this important day. In the New World, the Sun Dance was done at the Summer Solstice time to encourage the sun with the energy of the men dancing. It was a "world renewal rite": to renew the energy of the sun, the vegetation and the people. Essentially, the Sun Dance is not a very old custom. It developed only in the late nineteenth century, as the tribes saw their culture disintegrating because of white encroachment. The Sun Dance actually combines various older rites. Now it is usually held on July 4th instead of Summer Solstice because it provides a long enough holiday for everyone to travel to one site. In fact, although few grasp the fact, many of the important aspects of Summer Solstice celebrations have devolved onto July 4th. But without the sacred aspects of relating to the land and sun, such practices become merely drunken parties with no sense of "abundance" or "rebirth" just hangovers and remorse.

Different cultures throughout the world have a special festival when the sound of thunder is first heard. Thunder and lightning and the coming of fertilizing rain, signal a periodic return to the "chaos time" and the resulting new creation or rebirth. This was true in ancient China and much of the Taoist writings about Lord Hun-Tun, "chaos," has to do with thunder. "The magic and ritual power of drums was associated with the power to reproduce the thunder of the creation time." Ritual drums of this type were an "hourglass" form, based on the sacred gourd. The Ute Indians in our own Southwest had their bear dance when the first sound of thunder was heard. In the ceremony they had notched sticks which were scraped to make the sound of thunder. Ritual sexual coming together was part of the renewal of the new creation in these thunder ceremonies in both the ancient Chinese rituals and among the Ute. The Utes still have a "bear dance" but it has lost its cosmic meanings and become more an event staged for tourists; therefore it's no longer timed by the "first thunder."

SUMMER CROSS-QUARTERDAY

The old Irish celebration of Lammastide in August was associated with the worship of Lug, the sun-god. In Roman Italy the feast of Diana was on August 13th, "at the height of the summer when the fields were golden, the trees laden with fruit, and the vines with bunches of ripening grapes. Then was the moment to rejoice for the beneficence of the bountiful Mother, greeted...as Our Lady in Harvest." Naturally, the Christian church put a Mary Festival on this date, the Feast of Assumption of the Blessed Virgin Mary, when she was "taken up into Heaven." Parsch writes that on this day "the Church celebrates the most glorious 'harvest festival' in the Communion of Saints." At Lauds on this day the Divine Office reads: "Who is this that comes forth as the rising dawn, fair as the moon, bright as the sun, awe-inspiring..." Notice how all the praises of Mother Nature herself have here been loaded onto Mary. Parsch admits: "Since ancient times vegetables have been blessed on this day, yet its relation to the feast is not readily evident...Most probably some pre-Christian Germanic harvest festival was Christianized and associated with her assumption." At the Introit of the Mass for this day a phrase is used, coming from the Bible: "The woman, clothed with

sun, the moon at her feet, a crown of twelve stars about her head." Again there is reference to the ancient Mother Goddesses and perhaps the 12 stars could be related to the moons or months.

In Celtic countries Lammas Day was celebrated on August 2nd. There were chariot races in medieval times and the "Telltown" marriages in honor of Lugh. These were trial marriages of "a year and a day," which could be dissolved by a ritual in the same place where they were performed. The man and woman stood back to back and then walked apart, one to the north, the other to the south. Lugh probably dates from the early Bronze Age invaders of Ireland, who brought male gods in to replace the matriarchal goddesses.

We have no holiday at this time in our country: partly because our harvest is later than the Mediterranean countries and partly because July 4th takes over most of the summer holiday activities.

Another aspect of this August Festival is that the yin power is growing stronger all the way through the summer and in the European countries this came out as a recognition of bountiful Mother Nature

Summary of the Seasonal Festivals

We have now come full-circle through the seasonal round back to Autumn Equinox. It should be clearer now, how the original festivals based on the relationship of earth and sun throughout the year, were covered over by Christian holidays and thus made into abstractions relating to a "spiritual" life in the hereafter of heaven, rather than grounding humans into the on-going creative life of their place on earth. Instead of creative interaction between all aspects of place: earth, sky, gods, animals, plants and humans the energy was leaked off to this otherwordly religion, Christianity, and the power of place was dissipated. It has been said that "All the arts are homeless without festivals" and, through the years as we grew further and further away from the true round of the year, the arts became more abstract and narrowly human centered. There were no words to express our relationship to nature. Poetry lost it heart.

Only recently has it begun to regain "heart." In an article about Gary Snyder, one of the greatest of our present-day earth centered poets, Scott stated that: "To regain the power poetry once had, poets must rediscover the ancient rituals that reenact its one universal subject, the seasonal cycles of life and death. Thirty years earlier Robinson Jeffers had decided to do so by writing tragedies, but Snyder did so [in the Imagist manner] by using mere brief metaphors and allusions to the myths that personify seasonal cycles." The Imagist movement grew out of the work of Pound; what is not generally known is that he was deeply influenced by Fenollosa's writing on Japanese poetry. Japanese haiku comes out of a specific, concrete relationship to nature in a particular season; as Bashō shows us in the opening poem for the Summer Solstice, which I quoted above. I will go more into the importance of this "bardic" poetry for grounding us in our own place in chapter sixteen.

"'Within and around the earth…within and around the mountain your authority returns to you'. (Tewa) This 'power circle' is the consciousness of a people reacting with the energy of the place, building up the energy, circulating it through the system again and again with each seasonal 'earth festival' so that the connections between human and non-human grow deeper with the passing years."

PART IV: WORLD RENEWAL FESTIVALS

Introduction

Festivity is the origin of all civilization and all culture.

Jean Wahl

Using this quotation as his starting point, Vincent Vycinas says that: "On the day of festivity, [the community] receives its standards for dwelling with which it finds its way in its world." Going still deeper, Rudolph Otto explains: "In the primeval time, as the Greek mythos says, in the Golden Age…gods and men lived together in trusted alliance and sat together at meals. Such a time comes back repeatedly in every sacrificial meal as festivity." The actual food which is eaten during the meal brings about the meeting of gods and humans. Kerenyi explains this for us, by referring to the Odyssey where the suitors wish to eat up the *zoe* of Odysseus. This word means "not only the life of men and of all living creatures but also what is *eaten*…The same meaning attached to *bios*, the characteristic life of men. Where men draw their nourishment chiefly from plants, the nutritive plants—not only grain but the tuberous and fruit-bearing plants as well—are individually perishable, destructible, edible, but taken together, they are the eternal guarantee of human life."

The material which I have quoted above gives some idea of the depth and wide-ranging meaning of World Renewal Festivals. The Chinese concept of *Li* as "following" or "treading" a pattern gives still another aspect of these Festivals. In this sense, according to Wei-ming Tu:

Li is understood as a movement leading towards an authentic relationship…If we seriously take the notion of *li* as a movement, the dichotomy of self and society has to be understood in a new perspective. The self must be extended beyond its physical existence to attain its authenticity…perceiving the self as a continuum, an extension of its physical existence to the embodiment of the universe as a whole…The process must take the individual as its starting point, but complete self-realization implies the inclusion of the universe as a whole. In practice the given structure of an individual is necessarily an integral part of his self-realization, and yet for him to be fully developed he must transcend any limited version of the given structure, such as egocentrism, nepotism, ethnocentrism, and anthropocentrism.

In the Chinese classic, the *Li Chi*, "sage rulers observed meet and just patterns implicit in the world and sought, in turn, to devise formal rules of conduct that would enable men to make these same patterns explicit in their own lives." In World Renewal Festivals, not only sages but all who live in that place are enabled to "observe meet and just patterns." This is the real meaning of the phrase from *Hsūn Tzu*, which I have quoted before:

Through rites Heaven and Earth join in harmony, the sun and moon shine, the four seasons proceed in order, the stars and constellations march, the rivers flow and all things flourish.

By following these "meet and just patterns," which we are able to see while doing the rites or rituals, we begin to learn how to fit into that larger pattern of nature in our own place; thus we flourish as well.

In different parts of the earth, humans have celebrated their World Renewal Festival at different seasons. In Egypt, in ancient times, the Nile was at its lowest; therefore the most crucial time—in May. In June the first beginnings of the annual flood began to arrive—consisting of vegetable matter; then a month later, real soil with potash and minerals and finally the main flood of water, continuing until October. The star, Sirius was important to them because it rose before the sun on the day the Nile flooded highest, around the middle of July. They arranged their festivals accordingly. In Sumeria the calendar began with the spring floods as well. Only later, did the Chaldeans draw up the first zodiacal calendar in order to make their natural seasonal calendar fit the Babylonian gods

Here, in the southwestern part of our continent, "The Niman ceremony or 'Home Dance' conducted by the Kachina society in July, marks the return of the kachinas to the San Francisco Mountains and emphasizes the maturation or ripening process. At parting the Kachinas give the children gifts, including sweet corn from the first planting which symbolizes and anticipates the main harvest in September."

Each of these festivals has to do with the food, which the humans eat as well as the relationship of earth and sky, which brings about this food. At World Renewal Festivals we align ourselves once again with patterns in our own place—the on-going *Li* of the land—so that we can create our world for the following year. Not a one time creation by one god—the substance trap again—but an on-going creation produced by the inter-relationship of all the beings of that place.

To many people, this will seem a strange statement: to say that the non-human should be allowed to make decisions about how we humans will run our world—especially today, when the human "considers, judges and treats everything in relation to himself." But, actually, according to Vycinas:

The earth on which we walk and dwell is mysteriously impenetrable and undisclosable in spite of its obviousness. By scraping a flower petal or by splitting a ponderous rock, we end up with nothing. The obvious things of nature in all their obviousness escape our penetrating insights; by an attempt to disclose the earthliness of a thing, we merely lose it instead of possessing it. The only thing which remains in our hand after the attempt to control the earth and things is our formula, or subjective system by which we seemingly had conquered them. The earth 'shows itself only when it remains undisclosed and unexplained'. The disclosure of the earth is only possible by bringing it into openness as that which conceals itself.

I've quoted this fairly long piece from Vycinas because this, essentially, is what the Festival does for us. Dancing, chanting, drumming and other ritual actions diminish the rational, planning, "in control" part of our brains; thus opening up the other parts of the brain: not only the artistic, spatial other hemisphere, but also the older brains and the body-knowledge inherited from our most ancient ancestors—clear back to our animal ancestors. In that state the earth not only speaks to us, but at times, can even speak through us to other people, who might not be as open to the earth. The latter possibility is especially the poet's role—or, as Vycinas calls him, the "poet-priest."

But a "poet-priest is not truly a poet without the resonance of a community; and gods, without having entered the world of [the community] are distant gods; either they are have-been gods or the gods of the future." Only in a community which includes the earth and its living beings: the animals and plants can we recognize the gods. "The gods of the past are the gods of the future." They are the gods "who formerly were here and who come back when the time is right," as the poet, Hölderlin said. He lived in the 1840s, in the midst of the most complacent Eurocentric culture, yet he was able to see that these gods, "the ones of the future, shine and speak joyfully from afar."

"When the world speaks to us, without our being able to speak to it, we are deprived of speech, and hence condemned to be unfree," Gunther Anders tells us. True festivity, however, enables us to speak to the earth. We "enter again that process of becoming—as if to begin anew the old work of formation. [The] fundamental process of constructing a world of possibilities: not a single sacred work of genesis but a space in which all words can come to light," as Jerome Rothenberg tells us.

"Between the times," when the everyday world is interrupted by Festival and the "renewed" world not yet begun, everything is beyond the bounds of "normal" life. It is the "chaos-time" of Lord Hun-Tun, the gourd. All sorts of possibilities for living for all the beings of our own place can come out of the World Renewal Festival time. Hans Duerr tells us that:

> [B]etween the times...normality was rescinded, or rather, order and chaos ceased to be opposites. In such times of crisis, when nature regenerated itself by dying first, humans 'died' also, and as ghostly beings ranged over the land in order to contribute their share to the rebirth of nature. [But] in the course of time, knowledge became lost that 'outside of time' the boundaries dissolved between the living and the dead, between those in the mountain and those walking in the sun, between wilderness and civilization. With knowledge gone, the experience itself also faded. The last of the [medieval] night travellers might still have been aware of the fact that they flew away with 'fraw Holt' or went to the mountain...but why it was that they were doing this, they became less and less aware.

Soon, then, such "non-rational" states became something to be feared and to be suppressed by church and state. Later still, historically, psychology was developed to "cure" these suspicious kinds of consciousness. And, as the European world became still more "rational" these types of consciousness were even more suppressed with the consequences that we see today—where people are bored, powerless and, as a result, frantic consumers of every piece of junk the international corporations can produce for them to buy—anything to fill the great empty hole in the middle of their being. And all this frantic production destroys the very being of our earth.

World Renewal Festivals, show us the way—both for ourselves and for our land as well—to get out of the destructive trap of the present Industrial Growth Society.

World Renewal Rituals of Northern California

Between 1900 and 1942, the anthropologist, Kroeber did research on the Northern California Indians' "world-renewal" rituals. Other names for these rituals include, "world's restoration" or "repair" or "fixing." The ritual included first-fruit observances, new fire, prevention of disease and calamity for another year. Everything they did during the festival was done at a "specific site" in the area. In our modern "World Renewal" rites we could include repair of a particular damage done to the ecosystem by corporate greed.

The "core" of the World Renewal rites involved the "recitation of a narrative or dialogue formula" repeating the words of the "prehuman spirit race" whose actions made the world of the California Indians. In this respect it is similar to the Australian Aborigines repeating the ritual actions each year at specific sites, which had been done "long ago" in the Dreamtime.

From the context of the California Indian rituals, this "prehuman spirit race" can be considered to be the ancestors of the animal, especially salmon, or the tree, the water, the rock, etc. They are not "spirits" such as we have in our European tradition; but ancestors of the present natural Beings of that particular place.

The ritual words of "dialogue formula" are "recited in segments at a series of specified spots in a fixed order, by a single priest. He is purified by prolonged abstention from water, profane acts, sexual contact, semi-fasting and sweating." He uses either tobacco or burns angelica root as incense. What we have here is a rigorous ritual purification and cleansing so that the priest, unencumbered by human bias, could "see" clearly the needs of the land.

The Karok "refixing the world" was done at three places along the Klamath River. The first salmon ceremony took place on the Klamath River below the mouth of the Salmon River. According to Harrington the year began with the ceremony in September, literally called "working the earth," the object being to propitiate the spirits of the earth and the forest to prevent landslides, forest fires, earthquakes and droughts. Today, we would be more concerned with the damage done by humans ripping off the resources of the land.

Then in the spring, when the salmon "begin to run up the Klamath," the priest retires into the mountains and fasts. When he returns all the people leave the site so that he is left alone to ritually catch the first salmon and ritually eat it. No Indian could take a salmon either before this ceremony or for ten days after the ceremony.

Structures were built to focus on the local sacred mountain. In some places the structure was built of rocks in the bed of a stream so that the next high water washed it away. It was U-shaped and sited so that it directly faced the mountain. The "priest," as Kroeber calls him, who builds the structure must hold his breath from the time he picks up each rock until he lays it on the structure. He fasts completely during this time.

Another interesting rite was called "Dancing up the Ridge." This was along the Klamath River. The people start up the open side of the hill. "They stopped where the dead weeds and grass had been scraped [by the 'priest']. Spott and others took out two woodpecker headbands and five headrings (ornamented with white deer-belly fur, woodpecker heads, and black feathers); also some headfeathers, of white plumes and small feathers on sticks. Seven dancers put these on." Then they danced at this first site. "These seven danced again, in the same relative position and wearing the same ornaments" at the four following places on the ridge. The other eight or ten in the party, old and young men, sat down when these seven men danced; sometimes in front, sometimes behind them. The dancers in these five dances going up the ridge always faced toward the river.

The Rivet Mountain ridge, where this "Dancing up the Ridge" ceremony took place, runs northward some three or four miles to its summit, which is perhaps 2500 to 3000 feet above river. This ridge, projecting into the river, forces the Klamath River to make a big bend which changes its course from SSW to NW; thus the ridge has the river on both sides of it. Kroeber explains exactly how each dance was done, but here I will just continue with the journey. "Now going up the hill some way and stopping to rest once, they made the next stop for a dance among some oaks. There was a pile of rocks a foot or more high, and in front of this (on the river side) the cleared space for the dancers. During this dance, the little group of spectators held their hands to their faces or eyes, and wept...Going uphill again after this...The third dance was among some trees. There was no crying during this...The fourth dance under some firs, through which the dancers looked down into the valley. Instead of a pile of rocks, there was one rock. This was movable but fitted on rocks beneath, so it was probably in its natural site." Then came a fifth place and then the "approaching the top" place where more dance regalia was brought out. This brief description shows how the ceremonial journey proceeded. I cannot take the space here to go more into these rituals, but see Reference Notes for the complete bibliography concerning these California Indian World Renewal Rituals.

Skidi Pawnee Rites

The Skidi Pawnee have bundle songs in which the priests re-create their world. Murie says: "This creating of all the things was through the clouds, the lightning, the thunders, and the wind storms. So it is that when the first thunders sound in the west, the priests open the sacred bundles to sing creation songs. Further, the idea is that the songs are to be replenished with new power." The keeper of the sacred bundle lived in a special lodge in each Pawnee village. "The bundle was kept hanging in a special place in that lodge; it was considered dormant, as though sleeping. At the proper ceremonial times, when the bundle was taken down and opened by the priest, it was thought of as alive, awake, and powerful."

When any article in the sacred bundle wore out it was replaced and so were the animal skin wrappers of the bundles. The Thunder or renewal ritual carried out each spring, was

concerned with "meteorological gods." Here is Murie's description of such a ritual, undertaken during a thunder storm:

> Tirawahat...present in all things, especially the storm...He arose and walked about...He spoke softly (low thunder). Then he went out of the door and spread his arms wrapped in dark heavy clouds. He looked about (lightning) and took a deep breath (rolling thunder). He shouted (thunder), threw back his robe (rolling clouds), and sent lightning out in all directions to vitalize the earth.

Here the thunderstorm, itself, rolling across the land, is the god in the process of renewing the earth.

Shugendō — "Entering the Peak" Ritual

BACKGROUND ON THE SHUGENDŌ RITUALS

Moving clear across the Pacific Ocean to Japan, the world renewal rites of Shugendō show similarities to the rites of the California Indians. Moreover, what is most helpful for us, these rites still take place each year. Thus, we do not have to depend on some turn-of-century research by ethnographers, steeped in the European Christian tradition, and try to read through their necessarily biased accounts to get at what the ritual meant to those doing it. Modern Japanese scholars have done research on Shugendō, of course, but here I must rely on the work of an American, Byron Earhart and that of Dr. Carmen Blacker, from England. Both were permitted to attend the autumn peak ritual pilgrimage on Mt. Haguro.

Both Blacker and Earhart express their appreciation for the help which Togawa Anshō consistently gave to them. Blacker reports that he was an "invaluable guide during the entire event, explaining symbolism which would otherwise have been incomprehensible." Anshō's writings on the Haguro sect are "based on a lifetime of research and experience"; furthermore, his "knowledge of the doctrine and practice of the Haguro yamabushi is unrivalled."

Both Blacker and Earhart were able to continually compare notes and meanings during the actual ritual time with the karate master, Miyake Hitoshi, now teaching at Keio University, who actually took part with them on the ritual journey. Thus we have the advantage of English speaking writers, not only doing the ceremony itself, but having access to Japanese scholars, who also took part in the ritual journey.

Shugendō developed out of the religious activities associated with sacred mountains since prehistoric times in Japan. By the sixth or seventh century these original sacred mountain rites had become "overlaid with the symbolism and belief of especially Buddhism and religious Taoism." As an organized movement it flourished from about the twelfth century onward. "Shugendō means the 'way' of practicing or mastering magico-ascetic powers." The usual term for the Shugendō practitioner is *yamabushi*, "one who sleeps in the mountains."

Archaeological discovery of prehistoric activities at the foot of the mountains represents the earliest datable evidence of this practice. Particularly interesting is the fact that they found stone representations of jewels, swords and mirrors—"the three symbols indicating both the royalty of the imperial family and the most sacred obects of the Shinto shrine." The curved "jewel" which is called the *magatama* has always looked suspiciously like an animal claw to me; fortunately, in Blacker's book, *The Catalpa Bow*, there is a photograph of what is called, for lack of a better word, a "rosary" of one of the practitioners. Hung on this rosary are "bones, claws and horns of male and female animals." In a footnote, Blacker says: "The earliest *magatama* of the Jōmon period are simply claws and teeth perforated at one end, but by the end of the Jōmon period they are found carved from stone." Naturally, to a hunting people living in wild mountains the claws of the large animals are particularly potent "power" objects.

The *yamabushi* might be termed the priests of the religion and the ordinary believers are the families living below the mountains. The *yamabushi* "form a bond between the people of a certain district and a particular sacred mountain." The *yamabushi* had the right to "guide these people to the mountain, provide lodging for them on the way and at the mountain, and later to distribute periodic charms or blessings to them in their village homes."

The *yamabushi* take part in ascetic practices and rituals within the mountain. They acquire religious power in their own person but also learn the "various religious forms which enabled them to mediate these powers." When they come down out of the mountains to visit the people in the villages, they give out blessings or perform healing or exorcism rituals. In general this revolves around a seasonal schedule so that the *yamabushi* come out of the mountains at certain times of the year down to the plains and then return back up to the mountains. There are rituals for both aspects of this seasonal practice.

Earhart writes: "The timing of the festival is just before and just after the period of work in the rice field. It is quite likely that this alternation between spring and fall is linked with the widespread faith in the spring descent of the mountain kami (god) from the mountain to become the rice-field kami and fall ascent or return to the mountain." In some ways these Japanese festivals are similar to the Kachinas of the southwest Indians in our own country: who arrive suddenly out of the mountains and are welcomed by the dances and then depart back up to the mountains.

The four annual rituals are called: spring peak, summer peak, autumn peak and winter peak. Actually, the complex spring and summer rituals are no longer done. In pre-Meiji times, before Japan was "opened" by the U.S., the climax of the summer peak ritual was the celebration of "saito goma." The *yamabushi* went to a spot on the summit of the mountain, called the saito grove, piled up small branches and burned them...praying for the peace of the country and the prosperity of crops. This fire on the mountain top was a signal for the villagers below. When they saw the fire blaze up, each family lit a fire at their gate. The purpose of the fire was to greet the souls of their ancestors. The souls of the dead live in the mountain and come down to visit their descendants at the time of the ritual.

As the California Indians did in their "world renewal," so also these *yamabushi* must do particular rituals at certain sites on the mountain. In the main seasonal ritual, the autumn peak, which is a kind of initiation or rebirth for young novices and others, there is ongoing sexual symbolism connected with the mountain being the "womb" and the humans being reborn within it.

THE AUTUMN PEAK RITUAL

In 1963, both Earhart and Blacker went on the autumn peak ritual held on Mt. Haguro in Yamagata prefecture. She describes the procession as it starts out from the village toward the gateway at the foot of the mountain. The five main *yamabushi*, each of whom represented one of the cardinal directions and the sacred center, were wearing garments of the colors of those directions: black for north, green for east, red for west and yellow for the south. The sacred center color is white. The ritual items needed for the week-long rituals were also carried. The most important ones are the "powerfully symbolic *oi*, representing the mother's womb, carried near the middle of the line" and the "*bonden*, decorated with a mane of white paper streamers," which went in front. In addition to the regular pilgrims, *yamabushi* living in the village at the foot of the mountain, there was a karate master from Osaka who was a part-time *yamabushi*, five women who were "professional ascetic healers come to consolidate their power," some farmers from the valley, and four "students." These youths "performed the pilgrimage as a mild form of initiation. In many villages it was the custom for youths to pay their first visit [to the mountain] at age 15. In effect, this symbolized becoming a man."

The procession stopped at two specific sites of worship before proceeding to Kogan-do where "the real beginning of the fall peak [takes place] and gives the clue to the meaning of the whole ritual period." The leader, the white clad person of the center, shoulders the *oi*, (the symbolical womb) places the white hat, the *ayaigasa*, symbolizing the placenta, which covers the embryo in the womb upon his head, and "walks forward to the steps of the shrine holding the tall *bonden*, in his hands. He turns the *bonden* around three times and throws it up on the steps of the shrine." This ritual actually imitates the mythical acts of the kami, (gods), Izanagi and Izanami in the creation myth. The sexual intercourse of this "primordial couple" up in the sky caused the Japanese Islands to form. The leader putting the female *oi*, the womb on his shoulders, wearing the "placenta" and carrying the male phallus, which he then throws indicates "the 'conception' or re-conception of the participants in the fall peak...Together the three tools depict the initial act of reproduction. The fall peak represents a general theme of death and rebirth...the rite of the *bonden* marks the decisive point of ritual conception which introduces the drama of the fall peak."

After a few more stops, the procession marches two or three miles into the heart of the mountain where the main temple stands, which will be their base for the week. Suspended from the ceiling of the shrine room is the *tengai*. It is a circle formed by three paper fans. Hanging down from this circle are red and white cloth streamers and flax threads. Thirty-three old coins are strung on the flax. The red strings represent arteries, the white ones, veins, and the flax represents bones. All of these hangings together "represent the umbilical cord by which the embryo is attached to the mother's womb." The coins represent the thirty-three heavens of Buddhist cosmology. All these hangings are tied up to the ceiling at this time of the beginning of the rituals; "they are latent." At the end of the fall peak, they are all let down as they have "become active; thus signifying that the humans are once again re-born out of the mother mountain."

After everything is cleaned up and arranged, the first night service is held there in the main temple. The service began with a roll call of all the participants by the special names they had been given just for this "fall peak" ritual. They started by chanting a fast Heart Sutra (Buddhist). After that came the *Hokke Sembo* chant. "It was very beautiful, on three wailing notes... with invocations to all the Ten directions, the east, the south-east, the south, the south-west, the west, the north-west, the north, the north-east, above and below." Carmen Blacker writes: "There was a haunting quality about the chant which pursued me for days afterwards. I would wake up in the morning with it ringing in my ears, and it followed me in everything I did for at least a week after the retreat ended." The invocations are ostensibly to the buddhas of the Ten Directions but, of course, originally they were the ten directions from this particular locality, for all the centuries that this was part of the original Shinto mountain religion. You will notice a similarity here with American Indians in the "above and below."

I do not have space to go into all the ritual journeys they took, during the week to hanging waterfalls, cliffs, etc. The end result, of course, was a bonding which provided great exhilaration. There are many things about this ritual mountain journeying, which neither Blacker nor Earhart recognize, having no prior experience. For instance, Blacker writes of the final ritual journey which involved a long trip down the course of a river and then six or seven miles back up the mountain to the temple. She says: "I remember feeling surprised that throughout the day I had felt no suspicion of tiredness at all." Although she could not know it, this is the normal feeling after such an intense bonding experience in nature. See below for more on this.

Here is Blacker's description of the final descent of the mountain: "The packing, sweeping... disposed of, a clamour of conch shell blasts and a stentorian voice calling, *'Tatsu!'* announced our departure. The procession of five coloured *sendatsu*, the red umbrellas, the great black axe, the *oi* covered with the white hat, the purple banners followed by the rest of the blue-and-white company, marched down the stone steps of the temple and into the cryptomeria forest." At the Haguro shrine they all "tramped up the ten wooden steps representing the ten stages on the path to Buddhahood" and at the top chanted. The leader in loud formal tones cried out that "the top of the steps represented our birth into the world from the mother's womb. We must therefore all give the... first cry of a newly born child, 'all together and as loud as possible'. Everyone thereupon roared 'Wa' at the top of his voice, and clattered down the steps."

He then announced there was only one more pilgrimage involved—that to a holy spot called Akoya and everyone had to go. This involved going down a precipitous steep slope, "clutching hold of the branches of tough saplings. At the bottom was a waterfall rushing down a sheer face of rock, and away among the boulders. Under this waterfall the Founder had stood

in the days of yore." They all went into the water but only the karate master stood under the waterfall, doing hand mudras etc. Blacker says he "looked strangely demonic," but after he came out of the water, this quality "dropped off him like a garment, and in an instant he was a human being once more." It is odd that when for an instant we drop our merely human facade and let the other beings in us show, people consider that we look "demonic." But to return to her account. She states: "By the time we had hauled ourselves up to the top again by the sapling branches, an extraordinary exhilaration had descended on the party. We almost ran, in fading light, down the hundreds of stone steps through the forest, and through the red gate at the bottom which marks the end of the mountain and the beginning of the village." Here we have a wonderful description of the euphoria coming from the bonding between human and human and between the human group and nature which comes at the end of such a religious encounter.

Blacker sums it up for us: "In a week we had undergone death, conception, gestation and rebirth in the heart of a mountain which stood for a mother's womb. At the same time we had passed through the realms of hell, hungry ghosts, animals, titans, men, devas, bodhisattvas and finally Buddhas on a mountain which represented a mandala or sacred cosmos. After such an experience the company was in theory endowed with powers beyond the ordinary human allotment. The professional women ascetics retired to their temples convinced that they had received a new dispensation of strength to carry out their tasks... the professional *sendatsu* were raised in the rank of Shugendō hierarchy. Even the farmers declared an increase in... spiritual strength as a result of their ordeal."

I have gone into considerable detail about this "fall, entering the peak" ceremony because it has so much to teach all of us who are just beginning to relearn or remember such ceremonies for tying us to our own place. Remember all of the above is not some ancient forgotten ceremony. This took place in 1963 with modern people—mostly Japanese but some westerners as well. Notice also that the "root-traces" of the old ways, traditional hunter rituals, keep reappearing from time to time; although somewhat hidden by a Buddhist overlay. Just as in the West we can discern "root-traces" of our own old ways hidden beneath layers of classical Greek, Imperial Roman and Christian overlays.

The essential core of a World Renewal Festival is brilliantly explained by Anshō Togawa, talking about the more important, Spring Opening the Peak ritual. Since he has spent his entire life in both actual experience of the Mt. Haguro rituals and in research on them, his insight into the real meaning of such rites is absolutely unique in modern times. He explains that:

Heaven and earth and the natural seasons 'move' according to a prescribed order, and according to this 'movement,' new phenomenon or 'root-traces' are born... the spring peak is seen more clearly as the re-creation of the seasons out of this primordial potentiality.

This "potentiality" lies in the sacred Mt. Haguro for the people of that region. They draw on it by the ritual journey into the womb of the mountain; there to be given new birth for the coming year. But this rebirth is not for the humans alone; it is for all the other natural beings of the place as well. In such rituals we follow the "root traces" down into the ground of our own being as well as that of nature. By doing this we discover the underlying *Li* or pattern of each aspect of nature in the particular place; and therefore we learn how to live rightly within that place during the coming year.

Concluding remarks on World Renewal Rituals and Festivals

World Renewal rituals may well go back to paleolithic times. For example, such rituals may have been connected with paleolithic cave art. "Some of the paleolithic caves, such as Le Combel, for instance...suggest the thesis that the cult caves of the Ice Age were uteri of the earth goddess. The initiate was conducted into a cave so that he would 'die' and then be born again to a new life. There is sufficient evidence to assume further that rituals were carried out in these uteri in which the initiate participated in 'separating' the animals from the cave walls, thus aiding in their birth from the womb of the earth." Generally, it has been assumed that the cave art had to do with "magic for hunting." But microphotography shows that many of the alleged arrows and spears piercing the animals are reeds or branches. Many of the animals show copulating positions. Duerr states categorically that "spears or harpoons, or objects thought to be weapons of that kind, are found in less than 10 percent of known animal representations. In Gabillou, which has about 150 animal drawings, there are only two associated with these objects."

Those inclined to the idea of "hunting magic" have always wondered why these Ice Age hunters also painted dangerous animals such as lions and bears; while some animals which would have been the best source of food, such as the saiga antelope are not painted at all. Duerr says that the Australian aborigines "carry out their 'increase ceremonies' also for noxious and dangerous species, for mosquitoes and evil nocturnal birds, for spotted rock snakes and death otters, for centipedes and fleas...This appears strange to us because in our culture we are much more used to thinking along the lines of *exploitive usefulness* than was ever the case in 'archaic' societies." Of course, these "increase rituals" were part of what I am talking about here under the heading of "world renewal" rites and, as such, dealt with the life of the entire place not just that which was immediately useful to humans.

It is important for us to remember in our own "world renewal" rites, today, that we should always consider that any natural being, which makes up the *Li* or pattern of our place, is part of the renewal rites. This is because we do not necessarily know what is most important for the on-going life of the entire bioregion of our place so we give respect to that which we don't fully understand. To give an overly simple explanation here. Long ago when Aldo Leopold was first working to promote "wild life" in New Mexico he thought that the more deer, the better; thus wolves should be killed. After being there long enough to learn about the place itself, he realized that because of too many deer, the plants were destroyed and the deer themselves suffered. Then, looking into the eyes of a dying wolf, he realized that the wolf was just as important for the health of the deer as was a plentiful supply of grass and that the two were inter-related.

Another insight into World Renewal Rituals comes from the Inuit or Eskimo world and has to do with Sila:

> [There is] a power we call Sila which is not to be explained in simple words. A great spirit, supporting the world and the weather and all life on earth, a spirit so mighty that (what he says) to mankind is not through common words, but by storm and snow and rain and the fury of the sea; all the forces of nature that men fear. But he has also another way of (communication); by sunlight and calm of the sea, and little children innocently at play, themselves understanding nothing. Children hear a soft and gentle voice, almost like that of a woman. It comes to them in a mysterious way, but so gently that they are not afraid, they only hear that some danger threatens. And the children mention it (casually) when they come home, and it is then the business of the (shaman) to take such measures as shall guard against the danger. When all is well, Sila sends no message to mankind, but withdraws into his own endless nothingness, apart. So he remains as long as men do not abuse life, but act with reverence toward their daily food.

After a year or two of doing "World Renewal" type festivals, your group will begin to understand at what particular time during the year, your own place needs a World Renewal Festival. By that time you will have a better idea of what works for your group and can set up your own ritual around whichever one of the eight seasonal festival dates most fits the needs of the natural beings in your place. Below I give two examples of modern World Renewal Festivals: one from Australia and one from Chinook Center on Whidby Island in the state of Washington.

World Renewal Festivals of the present time: from two widely separated bioregions on the Pacific Ocean

RENEWAL OF THE DREAMING, SPRING EQUINOX — AUSTRALIA

from

The Deep Ecologist, Warracknabeal, Victoria, Australia
January, (1986)

On a property named "Casurina" near Maldon, Victoria, thirty people gathered to re-connect with the Mother Earth and what Aboriginal tribal Elder, Guboo Ted Thomas, calls the Great Spririt.

We camped out on land which has undergone whiteman's devastation by hoof and axe. We came together to learn how to help bring our land back to a state of balance.

Guboo Ted is an elder of the Yuin Tribe of the south coast of NSW. He is primarily concerned about people's spiritual contact with the environment. He describes Renewing the Dreaming as "the re-establishment of our innate spiritual relationship with the Earth, using as a starting point the sources of power at selected sites. It is a movement toward reviving identity with the natural environment for the birth of a truly Australian culture." [He talked of the special blessings his people received from the land and that we too could receive if we let experience flow from our heart.]

Guboo (meaning Good Friend) guided us on this weekend through various ceremonies, activities and sharings in a way which left all of us more in touch with that innate and intimate awareness of our environment, which to the tribal Aborigines (as distinct from the dispossessed and alienated Aborigines) is second, or perhaps first, nature.

[We watched the sun set, receiving its blessing for the night and for our dreams, accepting the importance of the day and the night. Earlier we had walked from the camp site past the Hand tree, its four fingers stretching skyward, the thumb to the left. From there we walked toward a grove of trees, stopping as Guboo told us it was a place for women to go. As we waited, the ground to the right of us sparkled and shimmered as the afternoon sun touched the tiny heads of the sun-dews. It was magic...Later we shared our writings and joined together in the sunset blessing and humming bee, creating a chorus of sound.

The knocking of the clapping sticks woke me up at dawn. Many of the group stood in a horseshoe gazing east waiting for the sun's rays to clear the distant treetops. Guboo related the dawn to the symbolism in the Aboriginal flag. The yellow circle, the sun, dispelling the night and linking with the red of the Great Earth Mother, blood returning to its origin in the earth.]

The sunrise ceremony was a particulary powerful one. Psychologically, the rising of the sun has such a powerful affirming effect on a western consciousness which cries out for hope and for a new dawning of what is good and true. In an era in which the mind is all too easily dominated by catastrophe, holocaust and eco-disaster, the rising of the sun can give us a blessing for the whole day—a promise of renewed hope and strength.

During the day we walked over the land and tuned in to the plant, animal and mineral life as we went. It is astonishing to find that even in this abused and down trodden piece of land, when we really looked at what was there, we found myriads of plants which were both food and medicine. Every square foot had some thing to offer.

Over the weekend, the beauty of the landscape became more and more apparent. I found that my pre-conceptions that this was just a waste land of little interest were fundamentally wrong and prejudicial. What I really experienced once I dropped these pre-conceptions was the absolute beauty and force of nature on this land. And this coincided with my feeling more "at home" with the environment and myself and the other people.

[Sunday afternoon was the children's time. There was maybe a dozen ranging from eleven to 9 months and they worked out their interactions with a minimum of adult help. The most fun and the most trouble focused around two stray puppies. Guboo dedicated the Casurina tree to them and the children of Victoria and we directed our thoughts to those in Dandenongs celebrating the Spring festival.]

At the end of the weekend as I drove out at dusk, after the sunset ceremony, and headed back through the arch of old gum trees lining the moon-lit road, I realised that I had only just begun to awaken to the depth and richness of the lives of the first Australians and the life of this ancient continent. Australia is unique in never having had a full-blown war fought on its soil, and in still having, an albeit tenuous, connection with one of the oldest peoples on earth. As such, we have a unique opportunity to learn from those Aborigines such as Guboo Ted who are in touch with the Dreaming; in touch with their primitive ancestors who retain the prime truths on mankind's unity with the environment, his community and transcendence.

(Most of the above account is by Michael Gardiner; however, I inserted the material between brackets from a second account of the same ceremony, written by John Martin, the editor of *The Deep Ecologist*.)

SAMHAIN FESTIVAL—CHINOOK CENTER, WHIDBY ISLAND, WASHINGTON, U.S.A.

Whidby Island is a small island in the Strait of Juan de Fuca, part of the Pacific Ocean.

Introductory notes: The basic orientation of all festivals is provided by the inter-relationships between the two circles: the circle of the four seasons (sacred time) and the circle of the horizon around us: the "Powers" standing in each of the four directions (sacred space), mediated to us by the "holy winds" that walk about the "rim of the world." The pivot of these two circles is the power of the relationship between Mother Earth under our feet and Father sky above our heads.

Aboriginal means "native to a region" (from the Latin, *ab*, "from" and *origine*, "the beginning"). Sacred has to do with "the power" that flows through all the cosmos. In most major civilizations it gets lodged in "one god" above all else. But in Aboriginal cultures still in touch with their roots in the land it does not take this aberrant direction. Instead it has to do with the flow of power through the plants, animals, land, humans, gods, earth and sky. As long as this flow of energy circulates unimpeded it is sacred—whether it is flowing through food, sex, birth or death. The one who tries to stop this flow arbitrarily or to control it for one's own ends is the one who brings doom onto himself or his people or the earth of his own place. The human mind, having come out of nature, follows the same patterns as nature. "Heaven, earth and man have the same *Li* (pattern)."

The major earth festival days rectify or re-align this flow of power so that it does not get too badly out of balance due to human arrogance.

Opening remarks at the Festival

Ritual Leader: "Be welcome, strong heart and weak, light and dark, blood and bone and mind and soul, for good and all. Set Peace about you and within you. This time is consecrated to the service of the Earth."

What we are going to do today is first, get to know each Being on this land, right here where we are now. During the morning we will become better acquainted with the tree people, the rock people and all the other peoples. In the afternoon we will build a wood henge to honor all the beings of this place and tonight at the Samhain fire we will celebrate together, both human and non-human.

Samhain [really pronounced So-ahn] is a Celtic festival. The Celtic people seemed to originate about where Yugoslavia is today and moved west reaching France, Belgium, parts of Italy, Ireland and Scotland. They were a bronze age culture which flourished until about the fifth century B.C. when they were defeated by Roman armies and retreated to the fringe areas such as Ireland. When Ireland became Christian the early Irish monks wrote down the old Celtic legends so we do know a lot about them.

In Celtic mythology the two chief gods were Dagda—the "all competent," the "good at everything" and Morrigan, the "great queen," goddess of fertility and the earth. The relationship between these two, Dagda, the tribal personification of all skills and Morrigan, the Earth Goddess personified their world for the Celts. These two aspects were united for the common good at Samhain each year. It was the time of reconciliation between the tribal god and the earth mother. For this one day, the "in-between time"—the period between the end of summer and the beginning of winter, all feuds and problems were suspended so all could meet in harmony. At Samhain the cattle were brought back from the distant pastures because winter was coming on. Special rites were held to counteract the blight of winter with its fears, by merriment, dancing, singing, feasting and the dead were included in all these activities. In most "traditional" cultures the dead are considered as part of the community; thus, food is brought to their graves and wine poured out to them. But when people lost the sense of their dead being connected to their place they began to fear the dead. Now, instead of respect and honor, we have only fear of "ghosts" on Hallowe'en, the modern remnant of Samhain.

At World Renewal Rituals, the entire "sacred hoop of the world" is there: nothing is left out. Freeman House writes of the "richness and complexity of the primitive mind which merges sanctity, food, life and death—where culture is integrated with nature at the level of the particular ecosystem." And **nothing** is left out. An Eskimo shaman, Ivaluardjuk, says: "The greatest peril of life consists in the fact that human food consists entirely of souls." This awesome responsibility and the heightened awareness which goes along with it, works toward a sense of dynamic harmony with the "rest of the world." We, in the modern world, are so little at peace within our own selves or in our relations with one another because we are not at peace with our "place," our land. The Earth, our Mother is our closest bond and until we end our violence against the earth how can we hope to end our violence against each other? In both war and peace we've been waging continuous war on nature. Whether we destroy a watershed and pollute the water in a single bombing or through the so-called "normal" destruction, caused by the Industrial Growth Society at work, really amounts to the same thing; the only difference is a matter of time.

When the first white men came to this land, they did not come to "Virgin Land"; but rather to inhabited land, or rather, cohabited land (inhabited by the Indians and all the other life forms). The turnabout was from "reverenced" land to "ravaged" land. In the last few hundred years European colonists and their descendants—and that's who we are—have ravaged the land from the Atlantic coast right up here to the Pacific coast. As one bioregion was ripped off they kept moving west. Now we are at the edge of the continent; there's no place left to go. We must make a stand right here and begin to learn how to "reinhabit" the land, as Peter Berg calls it. How do we do that? We learn from the place itself: the land and its animals. We don't live on the piece of land, drawn on paper by straight lines, which makes this Washington state. Instead we are standing on living soil which belongs to the bioregion called "the North Pacific Rim." This same type of geology, volcanoes, forests and climate extends from Northern Oregon on up through here and to western British Columbia and on up the coast of Alaska over through the Aleutians and down through the Japanese Islands. It's the same country.

So we can learn from the "aboriginals," the original people, living in this region: our own Northwest Indians; the Inuit of Alaska, the primitives in Japan: the Ainu. And we can learn from our own ancient Celtic tradition: the Irish. They, too, lived on a northern island in the ocean, so it is a similar bioregion. Now the fascinating thing is that all the peoples I mentioned above had the same totem animal: the salmon! The totem animal sums up the energy flow for an area. Traditional people say that their totem animal is one who knows how to do something they need to know in order to live. The salmon shows us here in the Pacific Northwest how to live in this particular bioregion.

The NW Indians, the Haida, have drawings which show Wasgo—a creature of two worlds— land and sea; the Kwakiutls have Kanikilak, who went about the world transforming animals into people, people into animals or sometimes changing both into mountains or islands or trees. Today, at Chinook, here at the edge of the world, is our place of transformation. And today, now, at Samhain is the time for transformation.

This is the day between the end of summer: the light half of the year and the beginning of winter: the dark half of the year. Today on this day "when the edges of the year meet," we are here to learn to move softly over the ground; discover fire and become inside the balance. Survive and be strong within the earth. Discover new gods, mysteries, pray for help and somehow be given new eyes.

Opening ceremonies
[First came the "Body Poem" (See page 192). This was followed by a ritual greeting to the Sun.]
Leader: Everyone face the sun, raise your face toward the sun, close your eyes. Turn the palms of your hands towards the sun. Just stand and breathe in the warmth of the sun's rays.

"Great Being! Your illuminating splendors overflow the world. We honor you, we thank you, you have touched us with your radiance!"

Now open your eyes and we will finish this greeting with a "Tai Chi" closing. Bend your knees slightly so that your spine is straight but the center on your body is lowered toward the earth. Now follow me. Lift your palms, which just gathered in all the sun's radiance up over your head. Keep the palms turned out toward the sun while doing this. When your arms are completely extended up, let them sweep out and around, gathering in all the energy around you from the sun and bring it all together here just below the navel (where our fourth brain is), the center of your being. [Hands are cupped here to hold the energy.] Now raise the energy to heart level [hands still

cupped.] Turn your palms over and push them slowly and gently down alongside your body as you stand up straight.

Hako type pilgrimage through Chinook's land
[For how to do the Hako ritual journey, see page 208. When the journey was completed, there was a very brief session, sitting out at the site of a great tree, the last natural being we greeted, of the introduction ritual where each person introduces himself as "I have talked with the wind" or "I have . . ." See page 186. End this, with Black Elk's ritual phrase]:
"Grandmother Earth hear me! The two-leggeds, the four-leggeds, the wingeds, and all that move upon you are Your children. With all beings and all things we shall be as relatives; just as we are related to you, O Mother."

Lunch

Wood Henge
[After lunch, we built a wood henge (see page 202). Followed by clan formation and shrine building by clans. This took all afternoon.

There was only a half hour allowed to get cleaned up or a change of clothes and we all moved up to the main farmhouse where we had the "salmon communion."]

Salmon Communion
[Preliminary directions: Before I came to Chinook I wrote, explaining my plans for the salmon. The salmon was caught in August and frozen. It was thawing when I first saw it. The head had been cut off before freezing so I had David Whyte, Chinook's bard, draw a head for it which would go under it on the platter, after it was cooked. The room where we met was lit only by candles scattered here and there. People were sitting on the floor or on various chairs around the room. After everyone arrived the salmon was ritually carried in and placed on the central coffee table and it did look beautiful! It was surrounded by chard from the garden and local flowers and ferns. The salmon lay in state there on the central table as we began the ceremony and I explained what we would be doing.

We began with the ritual opening I had used in the morning but by now they knew the response.]
Leader: "Be welcome, strongheart and weak, light and dark, blood and bone and mind and soul, for good and all. Set Peace about you and within you. This time is consecrated to the service of the earth."

Response: "Let there be healing and hope, heart and home, for the Land, and for all people in the service of the Earth."

Leader: "We are the new preservers of the Land—votaries and handservants of the Earth Power; sworn to the healing of the Earth from all that is barren and unnatural, ravaged, foundationless or perverse. And sworn and dedicated as well, despite any urgings of the ego—to the Oath of Peace. For serenity is the only promise we can give that we will not desecrate the Land..."

[Introductory remarks] We can't force things to change or "use" others to bring about change. All that leads to the way of the "Despiser." We have to start learning how from the Land itself—what is "the way" to heal it. But how does it teach us?

For those of you in the North Pacific Rim bioregion, salmon is the one who will teach you. [Then a reading from Freeman House' "Totem Salmon"]:

> Salmon is the totem animal of the North Pacific Range. Only salmon, as a species, informs us humans, as a species of the vastness & unity of the North Pacific Ocean and its rim. The buried memories of our ancient human migrations, the weak abstractions of our geographies, our struggles toward a science of biology do nothing to inform us of the power and benevolence of place. **Totemism is a method of perceiving power, goodness & mutuality in locale through the recognition of & respect for the vitality, spirit & interdependence of other species.** In the case of the North Pacific Rim, no other species informs us so well as the salmon, whose migrations define the boundaries of the range which supports us all.
>
> For time without increment, salmon have fed & informed bear, porpoise, eagle, killer whale. For the past twenty to thirty thousand years, salmon have fed & shaped the spirit of Yurok, Chinook, Salish, Kwakiutl, Haida, Tsimshian, Aleut, Yukagir, Koryak, Chuckchi, & Ainu—to name a few of those old time peoples who ordered their daily lives and the flow of generations according to the delicate timing and thrust of the salmon population.
>
> Asian & North American salmon range & feed together in great thousand mile gyres, in schools numbering in the millions, all around the North Pacific, then divide into families & split off from this great species celebration to breed & spawn in specific homes in the great rivers & innumerable streams of the North Pacific Rim. The great rivers, the Columbia, the Fraser, the Skeena, the Stikine, the Yukon, the Anadyr, the Amur, are spawning homes for the ubiquitous salmon and drainage route for vast portions of the planetary watershed.

The fascinating thing, as mentioned this morning, is to find out that in both the other areas of the world, which have a similar bioregion, it is salmon who is the teacher for the primitives of Japan, the Ainu and for the Celts in Ireland. In Ireland, there was a sacred well, reputedly located under the sea. The hazels of wisdom grew at the well and their magic nuts fell down into the water. The sacred salmon, living in the area, would eat the nuts and thereby acquire their supernatural wisdom.

The salmon was used as a symbol in the stone carvings of the Pict people who were in Ireland long before the Celt. The famous Celtic culture hero, Finn traditionally obtained his wisdom when he sucked the burn he got on his thumb when he was cooking the salmon.

How does the salmon teach us humans? Before we can find that out, we have to know a bit why the salmon is so prolific off the coast of this area. The extreme western parts of Oregon, Washington, and B.C. have very young rocks that are actively being lifted up as well as active volcanic action. What this means is that there is a very different kind of nutrient cycling, a very different kind of life-sustaining system west of the Rocky Mountains, the continent is breaking up, moving forward into the Pacific. The rivers move nutrient rich materials into the ocean creating an ideal place for spawning salmon. The combination of high nutrients and deep ocean coming in near to the shore creates high diversity both in the ocean and on the land.

West coast tribal peoples took advantage of this diversity. Each coastal mountain valley provided upland areas or coastal plains for deer and elk browse and game birds; tidal areas for shellfish; and river for salmon; forested lands for bear and small mammals and beaches and estuaries for migrating birds.

If one particular food failed them—say shellfish they could live off deer. Now in modern times, with industry creating a monocultural Douglas fir ecosystem that diversity is lost. Humans lose, too, when species diversity is lost. That's where "reinhabitation" comes in. If you stay in one place long enough and learn to love that place, the place will give you the same living instructions that it gave to indigenous people.

The indigenous people learned from the salmon. We can too. If we reclaim the area so that salmon can again flourish, we have reclaimed the soil, the plants etc. to their original health. It's as simple as that. How do we learn to relate to salmon as a god, as a teacher and as food? According to our modern culture such things can't possibly fit together. But Gary Snyder tells us how.

[Read "Eating: The Sacramental Sharing of Energies," see page 129.]

[The Salmon in its beautiful bed of chard and flowers was passed around from person to person. Each plucked a bit from the salmon with their fingers and passed it on to the next. Wine was poured for everyone. Laughter and jokes and serious remarks were exchanged as each person passed the salmon on. By the time we had finished eating it, everyone was in a very festive mood. Someone shouted, "We need a song for salmon." A woman said a first line in a half-joking, half serious chant manner: "Oh, let's sing a song for the salmon." She stopped and thought for a moment and then continued: "that pretty, soft, pink fish." Everyone spontaneously repeated it after her and that became the refrain. Someone else added a bit and then everyone got into it. Deep profound lines were added; comic humourous ones. And every so often we would all spontaneously sing the refrain: "That pretty, soft, pink fish." David Whyte added: "At $4.50 a pound." That became another refrain. It was a wonderful example of spontaneous linked verse or you could call it ethnopoetics, modern style.

This "Song for Salmon" was completely spontaneous and unplanned. So, as the song dwindled off, I read from Gary Snyder for the closing of the Salmon Communion:] "We're just starting in the last ten years, to begin to make songs that will speak for plants, mountains, animals and children. When you see the first deer of the day you sing your salute to the deer, or your first red-wing blackbird. Such poetries will be created by us as we reinhabit this land with people who know they belong to it; for whom 'primitive' is not a word that means past, but primary and future."

Samhain Fire: Culmination of the Festival
[Preliminary preparation. We had laid the wood for the two fires the day before. It was done the way the Taos Pueblo Indians lay their fires for their Winter Solstice Festival, now disguised as Christmas eve. It was built like a log cabin with logs piled alternately so that the bright fire shows between the dark logs and so that it burns, well and gloriously. Two fires were built so that the people could run between them—safer than jumping over the fire. Since Samhain is also a balancing of male and female energies, each man had to grab the hand of the woman nearest him and run through. And then, because there were more men than women, he had to run around the fire and grab the hand of the next woman. It proved to be

exciting enough just running between such big fires. Also before the fire ceremony we had put a double row of luminarias (candles in oiled paper bags filled with sand) leading up from the main path through the meadow to the fire site.

We all walked together from the farmhouse to the fire meadow. The way led along an old road through deep dark woods. We had only a few flashlights. This was a time for jokes about ghosts and scary things; filled with laughter. This was the yin, following after the yang of the bright joyous "salmon communion." When everyone had arrived at the bottom of the luminaria-lighted path, there was a sudden hush at the beauty of it.]

Leader: We approach the lighting of this fire quietly, introspectively, from the "looks within place." [A Seven Arrows term, which they had learned that afternoon from henge building.]

[Everyone walked up single file between the luminarias and gathered before the pile of logs. Before lighting it a few words were said about the symbolism of the fire: the bright fire showing between the dark log. This light and dark standing for male and female and yang and yin. The ritual running between fires adds human energy to the fires and thus brings about the "union of opposites" in a time of reconciliation between people and nature and the yang of summer and the yin of coming winter. The fire purifies everyone before the time of darkness. Then all the men stood to one side of the fires; all women to the other side. The fire was lighted. It flamed up immediately as planned. Everyone was awed and there was some fear. As soon as it had died down sufficiently, I had David grab Autumn's hand (they were to be married soon) and run through. Everyone else ran right behind. It was very tense and exciting. Everyone was ready to sing out and we had a glorious final song.]

Closure
[The ferry for the mainland left at 9:00 P.M., which provided a wonderful ending. Everything built up to a powerful high and then, by necessity, ended suddenly so that there was no dwindling down of energy. We all made a big circle round the fire and sang the closing song. Kristi shouted out at the end]:

"Through purgation and purification to jubilation" [And everyone raced off to catch the ferry. There was certainly the overflowing abundance which true festivity provides!] (See Reference Notes for further information.)

Beauty is our reaction to the perfect miracle of the undamaged, mutually consummating reconciliation of yin and yang..."

Frederick Adams

"To change ideas about what land is for, is to change ideas about what anything is for."
Aldo Leopold

"Thus it is that the Hindu groom tells his bride, I am the Sky, you are the Earth"; that the tribal Nagaras of Gujerat give the groom and bride the divine titles of Shiva and Parvati, god and goddess; and that in Babylonia the king impersonated the god of heaven by bedding his queen, the personation of earth, on top of the ziggurat, the image of the world, and so married society to nature."
Francis Huxley

 SACRED SEX

Personal Introduction

The concept of "sacred sex" did not occur to me until 1979. In that year I began work on a manuscript about D. H. Lawrence, which grew out of an event dating back to 1976, when I was completing my first book, *Earth Festivals*. At that time I saw a quotation by Lawrence which so exquisitely portrayed the Morning Star that I added it to that section of my book. I had never before considered Lawrence of any importance, but if he could write in such a manner about Venus, he obviously had a deep connection with nature. Because this quotation came from his novel, *The Plumed Serpent*, I got the novel through inter-library loan and began reading it. Immediately, I realized that he knew far more than he should have known being the son of a lower class British coal miner back at the turn of the century. I was very curious, how could a man of his background figure out all this way back in the 1920s. So I began reading everything he had ever written. And found all the answers—they were obvious; it's simply that few academics have ever read Lawrence, recognizing that nature was the most important thing in his life.

During the course of this reading, I found that Lawrence was trying to work his way toward an entirely different conception of sex than that of any other modern writer. Although, so far as I know, he never used the words, "sacred sex"—those words precisely describe his orientation. In my search for information for my Lawrence book I got the book, *A Discourse on the Worship of Priapus*, first published in 1786. In this book I learned that Christianity was one of the few religions in the world that did not include "worship of the generative powers." Wright states the ancient, "worship of the reproductive organs," ritually solemnized "the fertilizing, protecting, and saving powers of nature." Even in Europe, "we have clear evidence that the phallus, in its simple forms, was worshipped by the medieval Christians, and that the forms of Christian prayer and invocation were actually addressed to it." This was mostly in Italy and Southern France, where pagan influences remained much longer than the rest of Europe.

In the midst of working on my Lawrence manuscript, I flew out to California to give lectures at two colleges: University of California at Santa Cruz and Sonoma State. My main subject had to do with rituals and the environment, but during each of the question periods, students continually came up with questions to do with sex and nature. In answering these questions, I found myself formalizing and putting together things I had hardly even dared to put together in my own thoughts yet. Without their questions, I would not have been motivated enough to go deeply into such difficult matters. I want to thank the students at both these colleges for their part in all I learned.

I finished the book on Lawrence in time for the fiftieth anniversary of his death. Unfortunately, the trustees of International College, my publisher, were in the midst of a fight with their president, who wanted to keep the press. The press lost, he resigned and eventually, the college closed. In the succeeding years I've sent the book around to various publishers with no success. I've discovered an interesting fact, however: people in the English departments of colleges find him most distasteful. For example, from one well-known university, I got a letter back saying: "I think Lawrence's writing is execrable." Personally, I feel that the reason for this antagonism is that in his best writing, Lawrence was chanting rather than writing in prose and chanting is *not* intellectually respectable; for that matter, neither is a deep love of nature.

When Tobias called me to contribute an essay for his projected book, *Deep Ecology*, I organized some of my Lawrence material and sent it in to him under the title, "Sacred Land, Sacred Sex." I used the words "sacred sex" here because, due to those four years of research, I discovered that without sacred sex, it's not possible to have sacred land.

Because sex is such a basic drive in every human life, I will go very briefly into how, why and what I learned in my own life. First, in the overall pattern of this book, I have been dealing with the Eurocentric position of "substance" as ultimate reality versus the Chinese position where relationship is considered to be the ultimate reality. But, when it came to sex I had early on absorbed the idea that it wasn't even granted the status of a substance; it was merely a problem. You see, I was brought up as a Catholic and when a Catholic girl approaches the teenage years, the entire weight of the church imposes the ideal of virginity. Hence sex becomes **the problem**. For years I fought the battle to "preserve my virginity" against all attacks on it. But, after getting out of college I went to Aspen, Colorado to teach so that I could live in the mountains. This was long ago, before it became famous or infamous (depending on how you look at it). Aspen, at that time, was the nearest thing to a real culture, that I've seen in any town in this country. (I go more into this in *Earth Wisdom*, p. 119-120.)

This was before skiing became so popular and no one knew yet, that it would soon become part of the consumer industry. The town had a large number of former Tenth Mountain Troop men taking a year off to ski before they had to go to work at a "normal" job. The other important male group, was the European ski instructors. I dated the first category, but often, the second category would stop by the house to talk to us three virgins, simply because we stood out notoriously in such a town.

After a couple of years of expending energy fighting this "noble" battle to preserve my virginity, I decided I'd better get married and solve "the problem" so I could get on with more important things in life. I married a fellow mountain climber because I figured at least I would be able to keep on climbing which is what really mattered anyhow. And, of course, it did not solve "the problem"; it merely made it far more intense. The man I married had been living with a girl for about a year before we married so was used to easy, normal sex. And I was used to fighting tooth and nail for my virginity, while doing intense sex up to, but not including, the final act. This combination was doomed, of course. We stayed married because our life style was so similar and his work allowed us to continue living in mountains, but we could not talk about all this because my ex-husband's style was never to talk about deep, personal things. With no communication possible on either the sexual level or the verbal level, the toll on me was heavy. I was caught in a triple bind. I never had an orgasm—how could I with all my problems of Catholic purity, but plenty of interesting men that I skied and climbed with were more than ready to fill this need. But, being a Catholic I could not have intercourse outside of marriage without committing a mortal sin; furthermore, being a Catholic, marriage is for eternity so I could not just get a divorce and marry again. The final aspect of the problem was that I couldn't even commit suicide because that's a mortal sin, too and I would go to hell. Now, years later, this triple problem seems ridiculous because I am no longer a Catholic. That I had total belief in such a system seems amazing now. But back then I did believe all of it. Obviously, there was a lot of stress and anger and frustration with no end in sight.

Finally an avalanche saved me. I had allowed a skiing friendship to become too close because I felt it was "safe." He had arranged for a job for his girl in California at one of the lodges and sent for her. So I figured our closeness would end when she arrived, but she got there and he still loved me. On top of that stress, we did not have any new snow for more than a month. For a powder snow skier this is devastating. This was at Alta, of course, where I lived for about sixteen years. Finally it snowed. The first clear day we were out skiing it. By the last run, we had skied every slope; only one was left. No one skied this slope except ski patrol and instructors. Some years after my avalanche, it was put in a special category—you ski this slope and you either pay a $300 fine or go to jail. Neither Snowbird nor Alta want to try to control it.

So, last run we take off for this one remaining slope—several ski patrol, a climbing friend from Canada and me. My binding came off just over the ridge from Alta and I stopped to put it back on. Meanwhile all four men had skied on down the first open slope and were waiting in the trees for me because I was the one who knew this slope best and therefore could find the only route through the cliffs below. So I started down the open slope and it avalanched. I tried the usual ploy. When an avalanche begins, if you can slam your skis down hard, often you can ski out of it; but this slope proved too steep for that. I slammed my skis down, but no hill was under them. I was in the air! Turning over and over. I thought you don't live through this—flying through the air, but it's good I'm dying. I'm tired of this on-going sexual battle. Then I landed and I wasn't dead! What a shock. I had to think about getting some part of me out so they wouldn't have to probe for me; because if my husband, who would be called out on the rescue, had to probe I'd never be allowed to ski powder again. So I got one hand out before the snow quit moving. The moment it stopped, it settled into solid concrete; however, I could move my hand so I knew it was out of the snow and then I passed out. Since three of the other men were ski patrol, they dug me out quickly and I went on down the hill on a toboggan to the sheriff's car and to the hospital.

I knew something was wrong because I couldn't move my legs. I was afraid I was paralyzed. Then they gave me an anaesthetic and I was out. The next morning I woke up, delighted to find myself in a body cast—delighted because I could move my toes. I wasn't paralyzed after all! Being in a body cast is no big deal if you can move your toes. Then, the next thought. Well here I am still alive so nothing's solved after all. Then came the breakthrough. I had been willing to die a martyr's death for my Catholic faith—die, rather than commit a mortal sin by doing sex. But "they" hadn't let me die. So I don't have to do any of that anymore. It was that simple. And, the Catholic religion just "left me." Friends could not believe it was that easy for me. But it was that easy because the avalanche had made the decision for me. As one of my women friends said: "Some people are so stubborn it takes being thrown down a mountain to wake them up." While near death experiences more often make a person a "believer" in Christianity; my experience freed me from that belief.

Of course, after that breakthrough a divorce followed, inevitably, some years later. By that time I had been involved in a number of real relationships. In some of them I was able to explore techniques, which come out of Tantric sex or what's sometimes called sexual yoga, and they work because they are concerned with breathing and energy flows—not merely with genital sex. Since all these relationships began while either skiing or climbing, they were usually with younger men so I fully understand that Paul Shepard is correct when he documents in his book, *The Tender Carnivore and the Sacred Game*, that in most primitive cultures it's older women and younger men and later, after the woman has died or when it comes time to take a second wife, it's the older man and a younger woman. The idea of throwing two young people together and making them work out all the problems with no previous experience on either side is not done in most cultures.

Now, because of my love of these San Juan Mountains, I have effectively cut off all possibilities of an ongoing, continuous relationship. Although I have deep and long-lasting relationships with certain men, none can live here in this mining town and survive, economically; so we visit together once in a while elsewhere. Men need "peer groups" far more than women. And there's none here for that type of man. So, for me, with my love of mountains, it's place above all else. Given this fact, I rather favor the idea of "seasonal husbands." This pattern fits the primitive concept where the woman has the lodge or tepee; the men come and go, depending on the circumstances. Up in western Canada in a particular place where people are beginning to learn how to "reinhabit" their valley, a few years ago there was a woman who had four different "husbands." Every year, each would arrive in his own season and leave at the end of that season; to make way for the next man. But she got to stay right there in the place she loved!

What I've learned throughout all these years is that real sex is sacred but also, there's no sacred sex without sacred land. And this concept is just beginning here in our western culture; while in most other cultures that has been the ongoing basis of the very life of the people. So what I am trying to do in this chapter is give a few insights into this radically different way—for us westerners—of viewing sex. Essentially, of course it's not sex as a thing or substance (which is the way Eurocentric culture usually considers it) but sex as relationship with **all** of life in a particular place.

Preview

Oh, what a catastrophe, what a maiming of love when it was made a personal, merely personal feeling, taken away from the rising and the setting of the sun, and cut off from the magic connection of the

solstice and equinox! This is what is the matter with us, we are bleeding
at the roots, because we are cut off from the earth and sun and stars,
and love is a grinning mockery, because, poor blossom, we plucked
it from its stem on the tree of Life, and expected it to keep on blooming
in our civilized vase on the table.

D. H. Lawrence

We're all "bleeding at the roots" because we're all suffering
from the effects of treating sex as a substance. In fact the
biggest "substance abuse" of all is monogamy. **One** person
will satisfy all your needs **forever**! You don't need anyone
else or the earth or the sun or the stars! When put this clearly
it's obvious nonsense, but this is precisely the real meaning
of the concept of "romantic love" and its supposedly
"correct" outcome of monogamy. The present fad of "serial
monogamy," where one marries and then divorces and moves
on to marry another etc., is just as bad, if not worse. All the
energy is continually devoted to trying to make this particular
monogamous marriage "work" and then the next one and then
the next. No energy is fed back into the whole of either the
culture or the place. Of course that's one of the reasons for
the monogamous "ideal": it keeps the economy of the Industrial
Growth Society going very well. There's no end to the "things"
needed to keep it going: new hair styles, new make-up, new
fashions, new appliances, new furniture and new house, to
begin the "new life" one more time!

Too often, modern "love" proves to be another form of
"addiction." Instead of a relationship where two people help
one another to grow, within an ever larger context, we find
that many relationships are based on a need for the security
of having someone always there; which means "spending as
much time as possible with someone totally sensitized to one's
needs...the individuals [are] hooked on someone whom they
regard as an object; their need for the object, their 'love', was
really a dependency," according to Peale and Brodsky, in their
book, *Love and Addiction*. Julien Puzey provides still another
level, when she points out: "Anytime anything becomes an
end in itself it becomes addiction. When the sexual act in itself
becomes the 'end' you're in trouble, and, as with any addiction
it intensifies, and the returns are less and less."

It is important to realize that dependency is not an "attribute
of drugs," but rather an "attribute of people." This dependency
extends to addictive love. Phil Donahue, states it very strongly
and clearly in *The Human Animal*, where he states: "At a
neurophysiological level, 'attachment is essentially an addictive
phenomenon involving opoids'." Scientific research has found
that "falling in love" causes the brain to produce substances
called opoids, which are indeed similar to opiates. But
fortunately, "romantic love" and sex are too different things.

Sex is really the most natural thing in the world! In all
species of animals, sex is used to produce young to continue
the species. In the higher primates it began to be used for bonding within the group as well. We humans inherited ritualized
sexual techniques for bonding from our ancestors, the chimps;
naturally, we have elaborated on these techniques. In most
primitive cultures such sexual rituals have become integral
parts of the great festivals.

As shown in the previous chapter, World Renewal Festivals
always include human sexual rites: the renewal of life cannot
occur without sexual contact. It is important to remember that
the hoped for "abundance" coming out of the sexual rituals
within the World Renewal Festivals is not limited to the human
participants alone, but is extended to all of life in that place—
that all life in that place may "blossom" to its fullest.

"Every form of life has the equal right to live and blossom,"
is one of the most important objectives of deep ecology, as
stated by Arne Naess, in 1972. Fifty years earlier, D. H.
Lawrence used the same wording when he wrote that all living
beings must "move toward a blossoming." Of his contemporaries, only the perceptive Scandinavian novelist, Sigrid
Undset, grasped the importance of Lawrence's work. She
explained: "Lawrence symbolized his civilization at the
moment when it reached a crisis...of population and an
economic crisis." Writing, just before the second World War,
she continued: "Much of what is happening in Europe today
and yet more that will doubtless happen in the future are the
brutal reactions of mass humanity to the problems which the
exceptional man, the genius, D. H. Lawrence, perceived and
faced and fought in his own way." Even today, in our Eurocentric world, few see as clearly as Lawrence did, the sexual roots
of the problems facing the world.

In most traditional cultures human sexual activity was part
of the on-going whole of all of life in that particular place.
It had specific effects on the whole: positive when it contributed
to the overall fertility of life as humans added their sexual
activity to the ritual "increase ceremonies" of animal or plant
life in that place and negative, when humans failed to keep
the number of children within the limits of what that place
could feed without damage. In the latter case, naturally, humans
destroyed the basis of their own on-going life. Few traditional
primitive cultures did this for very long. They either died out
or moved elsewhere or learned the rituals to enable them to
stay. This is the basis of "sacred sex." As mentioned above,
Thomas Wright tells us that: "Western culture is the only one
which has no on-going concept of sacred sex." Primitive
groups all over the world, as well as Taoists had the concept
of "sacred sex."

Sexual strategies inherited from our animal ancestors

First of all, most of our sexual gestures can be traced back
to care of the young as developed in birds and mammals. As
Marge Midgley explains, "It provided an excellent repertory
of gestures that could be used to soothe anger, to beg for help,
and in every way to oil the wheels of society. Creatures that
have to deal with helpless and demanding young must be
capable of genuine kindness and tolerance. This makes it
possible for fellow-adults to tap these resources if they behave
in a childlike way."

Courting birds approach each other with gaping beaks
just as young birds in the nest gape for feeding. Kissing,
according to Eibl-Eibesfeldt, developed out of the animal
mother chewing up and passing food to the young. In his book,
he has a modern ad for biscuits, showing a young man passing
food to the young woman, lip to lip, which takes advantage
of the sexual attributes of this action. Furthermore, flirting
behavior patterns are nearly universal all over the world.

Eibl-Eibesfeldt has photographed these patterns in cultures as different as Eskimo, African, and modern people. These behavior patterns are so nearly identical that he feels it is a biological pattern inherited from our animal ancestors.

The higher primates made the break-through from the usual mammalian pattern in which all the females come into heat at the same time of the year, thereby creating intense rivalry among the males during this limited time. Usually the dominant male secures a harem of females thus leaving the other males to wander alone or rove in "bachelor" bands. Such activity effectively breaks off any continuity of relationship among all the members of the herd or band. In the higher primates all this is changed. With females coming into heat throughout the year, at any one time, some females are always available; copulation thus becomes an on-going activity. In fact, Schaller says that gorillas show no sexual jealousy whatsoever. Mating becomes a year round possibility; therefore sexual activity becomes a method of creating closer bonding rather than a temporary breaking-up of society as in most mammalian species.

In most species of animal, when the female comes into heat (or estrus) she suddenly begins to solicit males, using alluring scents and postures. This cycle of estrus is controlled by the release of ovarian hormones, mainly estrogen. The words, "estrogen" and "estrus" both come from the Greek word for "gadfly"; thus implying that females are suddenly driven "crazy" by this "temporary buzzing in their endocrine system," as Sarah Hrdy, aptly puts it. Although the rigid sexual cycle, according to season is broken down, when it comes to the higher primates; in most species, females do have a particular time when they come into heat and are thus most interested in sex. But human females can become interested in sex at any time. Carl Sauer suggested that the weakening and loss of the estrus cycle "is probably a feature of domestication, and it may have occurred early in the history of man, eldest of the domesticated creatures."

A further aspect of the estrus cycle is that, in some species of higher primates it is obvious when the female is in heat; in others it is not. It seems that conspicuous estrus signals, such as the flamboyant red swelling of the female baboon, is linked with a "multimale breeding system." Several males can breed with a single female within the troop. This "advertising" that she is fertile and ready, saves her the effort of individually soliciting attentions. Hrdy states that: "Years of looking at primates from a male viewpoint has led many scientists to believe that insemination is the only rationale for sexual behavior among non-human animals." But from a female's angle, there are other purposes involved: former male consorts can assist the female in rearing the young and secondly, "males who have mated with a female are less likely to harm her infants."

Under the difficult living conditions of the Atlas Mountains in Morocco, the Barbary macaques provide an example of the usefulness of having other males help with the young. The females come into heat for a brief time and exhibit the bright red swellings mentioned above. "A female at mid-cycle copulates every 17 minutes and mates at least once with each adult male in the troop." David Taub, the researcher who studied these primates, believes that this promiscuity helps in the survival of the young because more males will carry and protect each infant and, most important, keep them warm in the cold mountain winter. Each male helps take care of several different infants, so more infants survive.

On the other hand, there is an advantage in not showing estrus signs for some other primates. Solitary females, such as the orangutan and females in one-male bands, mate with the locally dominant male but can also copulate with other males when they meet unfamiliar males from other groups. The female might or might not want to mate with these other males so it is not wise to advertise that she is "in heat." Female humans also do not show any overt signs of their place in the ovulation cycle. Either of these two strategies may well be advantageous for greater bonding both within the primate band and between two different primate troops.

"Understanding Chimpanzees," the first major international conference on chimpanzees to include biologists, anthropologists and psychologists as well as primatologists was held late in 1986 by the Chicago Academy of Science. From the point of view of how sexual encounters facilitate bonding between troops of chimpanzees, the discussion by Nancy Thompson Handler of Stonybrook was very useful. She worked with a troop of pygmy chimpanzees in Africa. On one occasion she was already at a certain spot in the forest, when two different groups of pygmy chimps happened to encounter one another. They all climbed into a big fig tree and engaged in a mass copulation. She remarked: "If this is what a reunion is for pygmy chimpanzees I think chimps have a great way of saying hi."

Among animals, styles of mating range from polyandry, through monogamy, to polygyny. Biologists are only recently beginning to understand the factors which favor one style over another for any particular species. Essentially it involves a complex interaction between basic genetic structures and the way that species gets its food and survives. For instance in birds, where the female carries the egg inside her body, it seems as if the male could just take off and go his own way to mate again if he wants. But in most species the male stays right there. The reason most bird species are monogamous—at least for one breeding season—is that the effort required to keep the eggs warm during the prolonged incubation time as well as the constant feeding of the young birds in the nest, needs the cooperation of two adult birds.

For our primate ancestors, sex came to serve as a bonding mechanism within the troop. In early hominid society the females usually did the daily food gathering and the males did the occasional big hunt for meat. Since, they carried over the primate use of sex as a bonding agent as well as for procreation, sexuality in general contributed to the bonding of the group. No one has explained the importance of this link between food-sharing and sexuality as well as Richard Leakey, son of the famous team of Mary and Louis Leakey who made the discoveries of early humans in Olduvai Gorge. He wrote: "Most probably, then, heightened human sexuality evolved as emotional cement...in the uniquely interdependent child-rearing bond of Homo sapiens. If our ancestors had not invented the food-sharing economy of gathering and hunting around three or so million years ago, we would be neither as intelligent as we are today, nor so interested in each other's sexuality."

Nature's Strategy of Automatic Birth Control

It's obvious by now that mothers under stress generally do not produce children who can grow up into balanced individuals at peace within themselves and with their natural environment outside. Both psychiatric and social worker case studies prove this over and over. Granted, occasionally really bizarre stress can produce "geniuses" and other aberrant behavior where the individual stands out and is recognized, but seldom does such a person produce anything of real value to the on-going life of others in the group. In most animal species—except for the human animal—stress in the mother can automatically prevent conception and, even more surprising, terminate a pregnancy already underway.

Here I can only take the time to give a few examples of how this works. I will be drawing mostly on the work of Wolfgang Wickler, the well-known European ethologist, who wrote *The Sexual Code: The Social Behavior of Animals and Men*. Such situations as overpopulation, aggression within the group, too much cold, and even underfeeding can produce stress which is "characterized by the fact that the suprarenal gland cortex produces more hormones than usual, which means that there are fewer growth, thyroid, and sex hormones in the body than in the normal state." Studies on how this effects population have chiefly been done on mice, rats, rabbit and tree shrews, both because it is easy to keep these animals in captivity and they breed easily.

Tree shrews are especially important for these studies because it is very easy to see when they are under stress; whereas other animals have to be killed and their organs examined, to prove stress. Under stress, the tree shrew's tail hairs stand on end and the tail becomes very bushy. Normally, the hairs lie flat and the tail seems to be smooth and slender. Young animals, who show stress often by tail-bristling, grow much more slowly than others who live in an undisturbed environment. If the animal's tail bristles for about 60% of the time, "the animal loses a third of its weight within a few days." Adult animals can regain this weight in a short time but young animals so disturbed never reach their normal weight. If the tail is bristling most of the time, the animal dies.

Proceeding with the sexual aspects of these studies, Wickler explains that in young male tree shrews, "whose tail hair stands on end for more than 40 percent of the twelve hours, the testicles do not, as they normally would, pass through the inguinal canal into the scrotum but remain in the body." The scrotum skin doesn't turn dark colored either. If the animals are moved into a safe environment it can take a week before the scrotum darkens and the testicles enter the scrotum once more. Female tree shrews simply do not produce offspring if their tail-hair bristles for half the day.

Wild rabbits exhibit what is called the Bruce Effect. For instance, if a strange male rabbit is introduced near the already pregnant female, his smell alone causes her to abort. "The fertilized eggs of the embryos that have developed in the uterus of the mother are destroyed." This can happen even up to the last few days before birth. Wickler states that over half the pregnancies among wild rabbits in New Zealand are ended in this way.

Another excellent source for nature's strategies of limiting progeny is the book, *Biological Mechanisms of Population Regulation*. Under stress induced by overcrowding, aggressive interactions increase. Such interactions result in "diminished secretions of gonadotropins and increases adrenocortical activity"; thus limiting reproduction. Further, in "years of peak densities there may be complete cessation of reproductive function, whereas in years of low densities the young may continue to mature throughout the breeding season."

Mating and Sexual Reproduction

Using many different case studies, Wickler shows that "mating is not necessarily linked to sexual reproduction." Many species of fish discharge their eggs or sperm just anywhere and swim off leaving to chance that the eggs and sperm connect. While the "butterfly fish," on the other hand, proves to be one of the few species in the world to live in permanent monogamy. The reason is that this fish is very tiny and yet does not swim in large schools (groups) as most small fish do. In the huge ocean it is thus very difficult to find another butterfly fish to mate with. When once found the two of them stay together in permanent monogamy simply because they may never again be lucky enough to find a mate.

The other conspicuous example of monogamy is shown in the pair-bonding of the graylag goose. This is a life-long monogamy based on "redirected aggression." When the young gander begins the search for a mate, he swims and chases after the young female he is interested in. At the same time he looks for the chance to run off and attack other young ganders to show how bold and strong he is. After chasing the other gander off he returns triumphantly to his intended bride. She joins him in his excitement and they perform the famed "triumph ceremony." This consists in dipping their necks, lowering and pointing their heads as if they were going to attack, but they direct the threat past one another and chatter wildly to one another. Thus begins the life-long bonding ceremony. Each year, thereafter, in the spring the bond is renewed between the two. After each skirmish the male returns, triumphantly, telling the female all about it. Furthermore, the female goes out and entices a strange male to chase her. She lures him back to within reach of her mate and then her mate can triumphantly chase the interloper off again. Here we see aggression maintaining bonding in one of the few long-lived monogamous relationships within the animal kingdom. This strategy is often used as well by human pairs trying to maintain the intensity of the relationship.

Monogamy is not necessarily superior to any other form of pair-bonding such as polygamy or seasonal bonds. Each of these types "correspond to the typical living requirements at the time of the species in question. Permanent monogamy can be a transitional stage," in the evolution of any species. He further points out that one cannot say that any of the various current forms of marriage among humans is "biologically right" and all the others are "wrong." What matters is whether "the marital form in question is adapted to the over-all life structure of the respective tribe or nation."

Wickler's main purpose in writing his book was to help the average person recognize that there is no "natural law" that all humans must follow when it comes to mating and reproducing. In his Preface he states: "It was the encyclical Humanae vitae that occasioned this book. For the encyclical very clearly shows where theology is deficient in knowledge of nature and why the instructions it has given under the aegis of natural laws are suspect." This encyclical of the pope reaffirmed the basic Catholic position that intercourse is only for procreation because that's the "natural law." Wickler's book should be read by everyone who fell into that trap. Wickler devotes several chapters to the bonding nature of sex and sums it up by stating: "As we have seen, what is commonly called the foreplay to mating often does not have the aim of creating new life, but of binding the partners of a pair more firmly together. An incipient or fully performed act of copulation can still serve this purpose even if ejaculation, the ejection of the sperm into the female sexual passages is lacking."

Several examples of animal behavior are furnished here. The Indian flying fox must copulate three to seven times before an ejaculation can occur. Some monkeys such as rhesus monkeys and baboons also must have a series of copulations before ejaculation can occur. This is why the dominant male baboon can afford to have the females of his harem copulate with other lower-ranking males. This strengthens the bonds of the troop because, afterwards, the other male will run up and "present" to the leader. The leader mounts briefly, thus providing the necessary social satisfaction. Wickler explains that in the games of classical Greece, "the victor among the young competitors is also said to have had the right to placatory anal intercourse with his defeated rival." Thus, here are two examples of sexual activities leading to bonding within the group. Below I will give further examples from various human cultures but here I want to quote Wickler's very important summation at the end of his book because it can help every person, trying to live a "natural" life to cut through the confusion of what one is "supposed" to do concerning the sexual aspect of life:

> Theology has shown itself unable to determine what is natural and what is contrary to nature in love life...The morality of the marital act does not depend on the potential fruitfulness of each individual act, but on the requirements of mutual love in all its aspects. The consequence of this statement is that the form of his love life is the responsibility of each individual, that the married couple must decide for itself which methods are acceptable to it and that these methods can differ from marriage to marriage. Furthermore, each individual must also decide for himself—again given the requirements of reciprocal love in each marriage—what is permissible to him or her in the way of extramarital, so-called 'flirtation' as a social bond. In both cases the decision also depends on the consideration of other members of the society who are all more or less affected by it, which makes the question no easier.

Ecosystem cultures and biosphere cultures

Now that I have "grounded" sex within its biological origins, I want to turn to a consideration of the two different strategies found necessary by different peoples as the earth became more populated.

First, it is necessary to briefly review what I covered elsewhere in this work. Until quite recently agriculture was considered to be an enormous step forward for the human race, one which vastly improved mankind's life; but, during the last few years, new areas of research have made this idea seem very dubious indeed. Beginning with the 1967 conference on "Man the Hunter," proliferating research since then has clearly shown the advantage of the hunting-gathering life over both the agricultural life and modern industrial culture. Until quite recently, modern hunting-gathering cultures in the most marginal land, such as the Kalahari desert, worked an average of two days a week to secure all their food, leaving vast amounts of leisure for the preferred human pursuits of dancing, music, flirting, conversation and art. Recent research has proved that hunting and gathering provide both higher quality and more palatable food than agriculture; furthermore, crop failures cannot wipe out the entire food supply because that supply is so diverse. Only ten thousand years ago a few groups began agricultural practices, yet by two thousand years ago, the overwhelming majority of human beings lived by farming. What happened to cause this incredible shift to agriculture all over the earth in only 8000 years? Although clues have been accumulating during the past few decades not until 1977 did the answer become clear when Mark Cohen's book, *The Food Crisis in Prehistory*, was published.

Drawing on more than 800 research studies, Cohen shows that human populations grew so large that hunters caused the extinction of great numbers of species of large mammals by the end of the Pleistocene, thus forcing large numbers of human beings to resort to agriculture. Some research points to the fact that climatic changes, during which living became more difficult for some animal species, also had a part in this extinction. Cohen points out that the only advantage that agriculture has over the hunting-gathering life is that it provides more calories per unit of land per unit of time and thus supports denser populations. He explains that fifty species of large mammals were extinct by the mid-Pleistocene in Africa, two hundred species in North and South America by the end of the Pleistocene and, in Europe, the enormous herds of grazing animals were gone by about the same time. Mythologically, we can say that the hunters realized that the Mother of all Beasts no longer sent her animals among them for food.

To deal with this new situation, over a period of several thousand years, human beings developed several strategies— some of which led to "biosphere" cultures and others to "ecosystem" cultures. One of these strategies, agriculture, required more work than hunting-gathering, thus encouraging larger families of children to provide more workers, which, in turn, meant more intensive agriculture and so on in an ever increasing spiral of scarcity, hard work and destruction of soils. Eventually this led to enslaving other peoples as workers. These conquerors, the "biosphere" people, as Gary Snyder succinctly explains, "spread their economic system out far enough that they [could] afford to wreck one ecosystem, and keep moving on. Well, that's Rome, that's Babylon," and every imperialistic culture since then, including the present Industrial Growth Society.

Biosphere cultures assumed that Nature was no longer the overflowing, abundant Mother, giving all that humans needed. She had withdrawn her plenty; the never-ending stream of animals was gone. Nature was not to be trusted anymore; therefore humans must take affairs into their own hands. Within the short time period of the last five hundred years of the era encompassing the 10,000 year spread of agriculture, all the world's so-called "great ethical systems" arose, beginning with Confucius and Buddha (approximately 500 B.C.), through the Hebrew prophets and Plato and ending with Christianity, in the beginning of the present era (the year 1 A.D.). What we really have here is the establishment of religious systems based on "ideas" out of the head of individual human beings—Buddha, Moses, Jesus, St. Paul and others.

Turning now to "ecosystem" people, we find that instead of taking up agriculture these people moved off into marginal areas—high mountains, deserts, deep jungles or isolated islands and learned to pay attention—to watch carefully and to revere all of life for it was their body, their life. They developed rituals which acknowledged the sacredness of their land; thus enabling them to remain aware of the sacred cycles of taking life to live but also of giving life back so that the whole of the land could flourish not just one small segment of that whole—the human beings. Because their economic basis of support consisted of a limited natural region such as a watershed, within which they made their whole living, it took just a little careful attention to notice when a particular species of animal or plant became scarcer and harder to find. At such times they set up taboos limiting the kill. They began to understand that they could destroy all life in their environment by excess demands on it if there were too many human beings there; thus they came to understand that sex, too, was part of the sacred cycle. Misused it caused destruction not only within the human tribal group but on all life around them. Used with due reverence for its power it brought increased energy and unity with all other forms of life.

In the primitive cultures which developed out of the "ecosystem" way of life, based on "sacred land, sacred sex," much of the wisdom of the tribe was devoted to "walking in balance with the earth." Human population was never allowed to upset this equilibrium. As mentioned elsewhere in this work, among tribal people, the birth of a child was not an "accident" left up to the individual parents, but instead, was regulated by ritual or contraception or abortion so that the particular child would not disturb the overall stability of the entire ecosystem—the tribe plus the rest of the community consisting of the soil, the animals and the plants. (For more details on primitive methods of birth control see page 132 in this work as well as Notes and References.)

Although some of the more sophisticated methods of birth control were lost when entire cultures were destroyed, modern women, trying to live closer to nature, are beginning to rediscover some of them. For example, an article in the Katúah Bioregional Journal, titled, "Alternative Contraception," states: "Herbalist Susun Weed has shared the information with us that Queen Anne's Lace (or Wild Carrot) is possibly the best contraceptive there is." It's been used for generations by women in certain traditional cultures.

> In her book, Susun mentions these hairy little seeds as a morning-after contraceptive. The directions she gives are to take one teaspoonful the morning after a fertilizing intercourse and continue for five days. Queen Anne's Lace seeds work by making the inner wall of the uterus slippery so that no egg will implant. How beautifully simple!
>
> Since writing her book Susun has learned of a group of white women in Alaska who have been using Wild Carrot seeds with great success for eight years. They were eating up to half a teaspoonful of the seeds everyday. They would sprinkle the seeds on their food and keep a bowl of them sitting on the table so they could take a few seeds each time they walked by. Two of the women decided they wanted to have children while they were using this method, so they simply discontinued using the seeds and conceived promptly.

Sexual type of bonding in ecosystem cultures

For "ecosystem" people it is not possible to speak of the human being as being related to the universe, but rather of a universal interrelatedness. Humanity is not the focus from which the relations flow. For instance, Dorothy Lee, in her study of the Tikopia natives found that "an act of fondling or an embrace was not phrased as a 'demonstration' or an 'expression' of affection—that is, starting from the ego and defined in terms of the emotions of the ego, but instead as an act of sharing within a larger context."

To show how this works in the deeper, sexual sense, I will give three detailed examples: in the Ute Bear Dance, sex was used to bond the widely scattered hunting bands into the tribe as a whole; in the Eskimo game of "doused lights," sex was used as an emotional cathartic and in the final example, a modern Odawa Indian shows that the sharing of sex can still contribute to the bonding of the tribe.

Although I mentioned the Utes earlier in this connection, here I will go into more detail. During most of the year, the Ute tribe was split up into small kinship groups hunting in widely separated parts of the high Rocky Mountains. Once a year the entire tribe met for the annual spring Bear Dance. They waited for the first thunder, which they felt awakened the hibernating bear in its winter den and awakened the spirit of the bear within the people. A great cave of branches, the *avinkwep*, was built with the opening facing the afternoon sun. At one end of the cave a round hole was dug to make an entrance into a small underground cave. Over this area a resounding basket was placed with the notched stick resting on top. When played this made a sound like thunder "spreading out over the awakening land and rumbling in the spring air." The singers closed in around this thunder and the dance began. Because the female bear chooses her mate, the woman chose which man she would dance with by plucking his sleeve. For three days the dance continued. The spirit of the bear filled the *avinkwep*. From time to time a couple would leave the dance and "take their blanket up into the brush of the hillside to let out the spirit of the bear and the thunder of spring that had grown too strong in them." Many healings took place during this Bear Dance. At noon of the third day the Dance ended and gradually over a period of days the big camp broke up as the small hunting groups went out into the hills. A woman who plucked the sleeve of a man during the Bear Dance might

'77 - Sig. Kvaløy

visit the bushes with him for an hour, or for the entire night or might stay with him for the entire year's hunting until the next Bear Dance, or even for "many moons." Here ritualized sex served the function of putting the individuals together again within the tribe as well as back in connection with their land through their totem animal, the Bear.

Peter Freuchen tells of an Eskimo game, "doused lights," where many people gathered together in an igloo. All the lights were extinguished so that there was total darkness. No one was allowed to say anything and all changed places continuously. At a certain signal each man grabbed the nearest woman. After a while, the lights were lit again and now innumerable jokes were made concerning the theme: "I knew all the time who you were because..." This game served a very practical purpose if bad weather kept the tribe confined for such a long time that the bleakness and loneliness of the Arctic became difficult to face. The possibility of serious emotional trouble is ever-present because such weather can mean little food or an uncertain fate, but after this ritualized sexual game is over, when the lamp is lit again, the whole group is joking and in high spirits. "A psychological explosion—with possible bloodshed—has been averted." Freuchen explains.

In the book, *Eskimo Realities*, Edmund Carpenter has included a drawing made for him by Pakak, an Igulik. It shows the wife-changing game. Women wait in the snow house and men stand ready to choose, while masked dancers stand beside the lamp block, singing. This "wife-changing game" is another aspect of the the ritual use of sex to help the tribal group in a difficult time.

Wilfred Pelletier is a modern Odawa Indian who left his island reserve in Canada and became a success in the white man's world, but he found it lacking so returned to his reserve. He says that his own introduction to sex was provided by a relative. "I still look on that as one of the greatest and happiest experiences of my life. From that time on, it seems to me that I screwed all the time, without letup. Not just my relatives, who were not always available, but anywhere I could find it, and it always seemed to be there... On the reservation people were honest about their feelings and their needs, and as all the resources of the community were available to those who need them, sex was not excluded. Sex was a recognized need, so nobody went without it. It was as simple as that."

In his book, *Position of Women in Primitive Societies*, Evans Pritchard, lists five characteristics of sex in primitive cultures. Here I merely give a brief summary of each of these: 1) There is plenty of lovemaking, but no romantic love. 2) There are no unmarried adult women. 3) Every girl finds a husband and furthermore, is usually married at an early age. 4) Polygamy is permitted and practiced in varying degrees. 5) Custom enables widows to remarry without difficulty.

Closer to our immediate European heritage, Dawes, in his book on Avebury, states that: "Traces of these patterns persisted in the remoter parts of Ireland till the 18th century." That was the time when the puritanical influence of the Jansenist heresy was introduced into Ireland by exiled French priests; who refused to give up this heretical doctrine.

Concluding Remarks Concerning Ecosystem Cultures and Sex

Throughout the years that I've been using some of the above material in workshops, I find that most of the questions seem to cluster around these two points. How does "sex within a ritual work" and "how is it possible that everyone gets to have sex that needs it?" It's a difficult matter to give precise answers here for a number of reasons. One factor is that the participants in a traditional ritual do not know how to write, but even more to the point, they don't feel it necessary to even verbalize such sensations; so you can't quote them. Our best source of information is Europeans who have been open enough to drop their prejudices *and* superiority *and* willfulness; so that such experiences can come to them.

The first account is by a woman anthropologist, F. Donner and concerns the anthropologist herself, her friend, Ritimi from the tribe and Ritimi's husband, Etewa. Because of certain circumstances the three of them had to travel through the jungle together. They spend the night in a small, rough shelter. Donner hears soft moans and then Ritimi's soft voice asks Donner if she wants to try it. Surprised by this, Donner opens her eyes and looks right into Etewa's "smiling face." She watches them. "Then Etewa, not in the least embarassed moved out of Ritimi and knelt in front of me. Lifting my legs, he stretched them slightly. He pressed his cheeks against my calves; his touch was like the playful caress of a child. There was no embrace; there were no words. Yet I was filled with tenderness. Etewa switched to Ritimi again, resting his head between her shoulder and mine." Ritimi then said, "Now we are truly sisters."

The second account is by Tobias Schneebaum, who was fortunate enough to first, find a group of primitive people in South America that he had been searching for, by "keeping the river on his right" and then stay with them long enough to become part of their life. In this passage he is writing about an initiation ritual for young men. It's the final day and the youths are being ritually marked by putting a sliver of ebony through the lower lip. Following that, each youth is scrubbed clean with a bundle of fibers and thistles and painted. Then he is a man. Before the last youth is painted, the day is over. Throughout the day, the women have been inside the hut, coming out from time to time with bowls of the native liquor for the men. By nightfall everyone is laughing. They all crawl into the smoky light of the hut. Some of the women were already waiting in the partitions set aside for each man. Others were still standing around the central fire. Each of the "newly made men" and some of the older ones went up to the women, and, without saying a word, embraced and copulated. Schneebaum's best native friend lay on top of the woman whose child he had just fathered. "We others found arms stretched up in welcome. Strange, inevitable, holy, to feel that soft flesh beneath my hands and body."

In each of these account the people have been together all day out in nature: in the first account, moving through the jungle together and in the second account, "doing a ritual" together. Sex, then, becomes natural, inevitable and sacred because it's part of the whole inter-relationship of humans and nature in that place.

Taoist Sex Rituals

Before I go into Taoist rituals it is necessary to recall the fundamental difference between the "creation" story of most of Asia and the European Christian "creation." As shown earlier in this work, the basic southern Asian story concerns a brother and sister safely carried through a flood or other disaster in a "hollow container." When the disaster is over they find they are the only people so they copulate and begin the human race. The "hollow container" is the gourd, of course and the human copulation is incestuous because the gourd vine has both male and female flowers on the same vine. The gourd is the "mother of the human race." The "unassailable fact is that the gourd... has existed in human cultural history as a prototypical botanical symbol for the idea of creation." Lathrap goes even further when he says: "[W]e may conclude that metaphorically the gourd is a womb, that it is the whole universe, or, stated more simply, the universal womb." The growing gourd on the vine suddenly and dramatically swells, containing within, its seeds embedded in a pulpy mass. As the gourd ages it changes from this "chaos" stage into a hard, hollow container and the "germs of life" within are freed from their undifferentiated pulp to rattle around, thus signalling their presence within the "safe" container. The Lagenaria, or bottle gourd, in particular, with its two swellings above and below, joined by the constricted middle, "emulates the balanced cosmic form of heaven and earth, yin [female] and yang [male] linked by the empty yet pregnant force of ch'i [energy]."

Variations of the gourd creation story occur throughout the Pacific from Hawaii through the South Sea Islands to Southern Asia, China, Japan and Africa. Over here in the tiny projection of the vast Eurasian continent, which we call Europe, we have a totally different story. A male god up in the sky created all of nature out of ideas in his head and on the last day he made a man and out of that man's rib he made a woman. Immediately, we have "ideas and ideals" and "off the earth" spirituality. I want to give one more example to ground the difference involved in these two creation stories.

Living in Switzerland for one winter, we went occasionally to Austria or the Italian Tyrol for mountain climbing. Everywhere we went in the high mountain towns we saw a crucifix standing alongside the road near the villages or near the fields. Village children pass these crucifixes several times a day on their journeys to school and elsewhere. They see a bleeding male god looking down upon them with suffering resignation. Contrast this with the Dosojin which every Japanese child passes by daily. Along all the roads in Japan and near the rice fields, there are carved stone Dosojin—a male and a female so closely entertwined that they are called by the one word, Dosojin. Sometimes they have their arms around one another; sometimes their hands are up one another's sleeves (symbolizing intercourse) but, always they have blissful smiles of joy. Daily, the Japanese child sees that it takes male and female to make the rice grow, to make humans grow and, furthermore, it's all joyful!

Translating these two stories onto a more philosophical plane, in the European tradition, we have a male god up in the sky who created everything once and for all. True spirituality or true meaning of any kind only comes from that one source. God's creation continues with every new and more dramatic human breakthrough in science, technology, art etc. etc., but it all comes indirectly from this male god up there. And over here in a tiny corner lies the problem of human sexuality. Without it, of course we would have no more people but it's not very important when it comes to the "real stuff"—philosophy, science etc. Sex is somewhat suspect, and nasty anyway, because it has to do with the body and not just the brain; but it's necessary for making more humans. Now in the South Asian tradition, sex is at the beginning of it all and continues in every facet of every development of tradition and life. The "myriad things" come out of the interaction of yin (female) and yang (male); the energy of the universe operates through the yin and the yang. But this is no mere dualistic system in contrast to a monotheistic European system. Rather this is a continually changing pattern; because if something moves along the yin continuum and gets more and more yin, eventually it turns back and begins to moves toward the yang pole. Everthing is fluidly inter-related. In this Asian philosophical system, sex is not stuck way over in the corner as a kind of aberration but is central in all aspects of life.

It is natural, then, that Taoism developed the most sophisticated methods of any culture for dealing with sexual energy within the human community itself and between humans and nature. Briefly to recapitulate what was said back in chapter eight, until recently, Taoist sexual techniques were dismissed by Western thinkers as mere superstition, but with the publication of the second volume of his massive *Science and Civilization in China* by the Cambridge scholar, Joseph Needham, all that has changed. Since the purpose of these techniques was to "increase the amount of life-giving *ching* as much as possible by sexual stimulus...Continence was considered not only impossible, but improper, as contrary to the great rhythm of Nature, since everything in Nature had male or female properties." These sexual techniques were used to increase the energy not only between man and woman but within the group as a whole and between the humans and their land.

"THE TRUE ART OF EQUALISING THE CHHI'S"

This is the name of the most important Taoist sexual ritual. It was also called "Uniting the Chhi's" of male and female and it dates back to at least the second century A.D. Most of what we know of these ancient rituals comes from a convert from Taoism to Buddhism who wrote the *Hsiao Tao Lun*, "Taoism Ridiculed," in much the same fashion as pagan converts to Christianity wrote essays ridiculing pagan customs.

The ritual of "Uniting the Chhi's" occurred on either the nights of the new moon or full moon, after fasting. It began with a ritual dance, "coiling of the dragon and playing of the tiger," which ended either in a public group ritual intercourse or in a succession of unions involving all those present, held in chambers along the sides of the temple courtyard. According to K. Schipper, this "union of the ch'i," as he translates it, involved a "correlation with calendrical periods"—thus was practiced at the major seasonal festivals.

A fragment of the highly poetic book of liturgy for this ritual called the *Huang Shu* has survived. During the Ming dynasty, most of these Taoist sexual ritual books were destroyed. Fortunately some were preserved because they had been translated by the Japanese in about the tenth century.

In both the Chinese sexual rituals and in primitive tribal rituals, sex itself was made numinous. In the Chinese rituals it is not clear what deities were involved, but Maspero says that they seem to have been: star-gods, the gods of the five elements, or the spirits residing and controlling the various parts of the human body.

Buddhist ascetism and Confucian prudery were both scandalized; so there were no public Ho-Chhi festivals after the seventh century. Private practice continued well into the Sung dynasty in Taoist temples, and, among certain classes of lay people, until the last century. While Needham was in China in 1945, gathering together Taoist documents that were endangered by the revolutionary struggles, he visited many old Taoist monasteries, dating back as far as 554 A.D. This enabled him to get considerable insight into the ideas behind Taoist sexual techniques. When he asked "one of the deepest students of Taoism" at Chhengtu, "How many people followed these precepts?" The answer was: "Probably more than half the ladies and gentlemen in Szechuan."

THE "SACRED MIDDLE"

To understand why the Taoists devoted so much attention to sexual techniques it is necessary to understand the importance of the structure of the pelvic region with its central bony mass, the sacrum. Because Western culture puts so much emphasis on the rational mind, (specifically, the rational, left hemisphere of the neo-cortex), the Taoist insistence on the importance of the lower mind, located four fingers below the navel (tantien in Chinese and hara in Japanese), seemed utter nonsense until quite recently. For instance, in the nineteen twenties when D. H. Lawrence emphasized the "solar plexus" he was ridiculed; but, in the last two decades with the growing popularity of such disciplines as Tai Chi, Aikido and other martial arts as well as therapies such as Rolfing, the pelvic area is coming to be recognized as truly our "sacred middle"— the area within us where the flow of energy takes place between us and the cosmos. The functions of sex, prenatal life, birth, assimilation of food as well as deep emotions all take place in this area. The "sacred middle" refers to the sacrum, the bony plate which gets its name from the same Latin root as the word, sacred. The lower five vertebrae, which in the adult become fused into a single, curved, shield-shaped plate, make up the sacrum. Because the muscles of the entire pelvic girdle are attached here, this is the area which makes us human. The enlarged human brain developed only after we achieved true upright posture. Furthermore, all the muscles involved in walking, standing and sitting converge here. Of these muscles, the psoas muscles are the most important for determining the human, upright position; while the pubo-coccygeus muscles, which attach the legs to the inner sides of the spine and run on up to fasten the pelvic rim to the front of the ribs and the breastbone, literally hold us together. Both these large strong sets of muscles crisscross in the pelvic area, circling around the sexual organs.

Much of the corrective work accomplished through

Rolfing has to do with breaking down the overly rigid abdominal muscles so prevalent in our culture. The psoas musles are then freed to function as they as supposed to; thus permitting the body to realign itself correctly with gravity. It has been proven through laboratory experiments that rolfing these muscles cuts down and often completely eliminates the state of underlying anxiety so prevalent in our culture. This connection between what we generally conceive of as a "mental" condition and the actual facts of its cure through manipulation of muscles within the pelvic region, defies the usual Western logic; yet the Chinese have always considered the tantien, the pelvic region, as the location of the "other" brain. Not only is the tantien the seat of strong emotions, but, when trained by Tai Chi, it can also sense these emotions in other people as well as register energy currents within the earth. For example, modern experiments with dowsers prove that the pelvic area is the particular physical location within the dowser's body which indicates water beneath the earth.

The most ancient of the martial arts, Tai Chi was developed in the Taoist Shaolin monastery in the mountains of China. Each of its 108 forms deals specifically with the muscles discussed above. It is these same muscles, which Tai Chi liberates, that are crucial for the practice of Taoist sexual techniques. For a man these muscles are essential in the Taoist technique of orgasm without ejaculation; for a woman, during the moment of vaginal orgasm, the coccygeal muscles, when trained properly, can of themselves, with no immediate conscious effort, prevent the entry of semen and thus provide an automatic method of birth control, when needed. This latter technique may be the answer to some of the puzzling reports of early anthropologists, such as Jane Belo in the south Pacific, who could find no contraceptive use among women, yet these women had children only by their own man even though they had sex with others in the tribe while their own man was away fishing.

Bob Klein, writing about the Tai Chi exercise called "push hands," says that it is "effective training for making love." He continues: "Sex is no place for the performance of mechanical techniques. It requires a giving into the flow of energies, a giving up of the feeling of isolation. Sex should not be something one 'does' to someone else, but should be a form of 'not doing' in which two 'Body-Minds' unite and play spontaneously in the 'field' of energy." It can also be considered as "exchanging energy with another person. This energy must be freely given."

This energy is connected to the area in the crotch, where the major puboccoygeal muscles cross. Development of these muscles automatically prolongs orgasm for both men and women.

For men, the Chinese saying is: "Ejaculate when you want to have children otherwise it is best to retain the semen and use it for nourishing the internal organs." Orgasm need have nothing to do with ejaculation. Certainly today, in our overcrowded world, most of the time, men do not need to ejaculate. In fact, there is a sort of rule of thumb for how often a man can safely ejaculate and not deplete the other important glands in the body. Take your age and multiply by 2. For example, if you are 30 years old $\times$ 0.2 = 6 days. So every six days you can ejaculate and stay even. If you go longer than six days then you will be building up nourishment for the other organs.

How does orgasm occur without ejaculation? It's really quite simple. You or your partner press the *tu-mo* acupressure point. This tube-like arrangement goes from the anal opening between the legs up to the penis. You can feel it easily when the penis is erect. Along this tube, halfway between the anal opening and the scrotum is the *tu-mo*. Press this point when about to orgasm and there is no ejaculation—once you get practiced at this technique, you will get even fuller orgasms. Because this technique is so important, both for sexual bonding and for birth control, I will give more precise details here. If you press too close to the scrotum, the semen will go into the bladder. While this is not harmful, it is not useful for nourishing the other organs. When learning how to do this it is recommended that you urinate into a glass jar after having sex. If it appears cloudy then semen is in it and you are pressing too near the scrotum. If allowed to stand overnight you will see the semen settle to the bottom of the jar. So the next time, press a little closer to the anal opening.

The actual pathway by which the saved "semen" enters the other parts of the body can occur in two ways. According to Chinese medicine there is a connection between the prostate and other glands. (This is not admitted by Western science, of course.) This is one way—the other way is that the semen is absorbed by the blood stream from the prostate and carried elsewhere. It is recommended that shortly after orgasm, when you have held the *tu-mo* point to prevent ejaculation, you do a brief exercise. Tighten the anal sphincter muscle and draw it up into the body—squeezing hard. This helps the prostate to come back to its normal size and promotes the flow of the semen out of it into the blood stream and elsewhere. It also prevents prostate trouble later in life.

It is very useful, when learning these Chinese techniques to also adopt their poetic landscape terms for the sexual organs. First, use of these "poetic" names, liberates the sexual organs from their usual Western pejorative connections and, secondly, it ties them to the land itself out of which we come. For men, "the gate of destiny" is the scrotum; "the dark barrier" is the *tu-mo* point, which must be pressed to send the semen back into the body; "the jade peak" is the penis. Other names for the penis are "positive peak" and "yang peak." Women's sexual organs in general are called: "anemone of love," "cavern," "cinnabar crevice," "golden furrow," "jade cavern," "jade gate," "mysterious cavern," "mysterious valley," "pleasure grotto," "precious crucible," and "secret cavern." The womb is called "Cinnabar Cave," the opening to the womb is called "Flower Heart" and the lips of the vulva are called "Strings of the Lyre."

SIMILARITIES IN TAOIST AND PRIMITIVE SEXUAL TECHNIQUES

Ritualized sex in both primitive societies and in Taoism comes out of entirely different roots than sexual activities in Western culture, where the emphasis has always been on procreation. In the latter culture, male ejaculation is of great importance because it is tied in with fertility and the male ego. In ritualized sex, however, the main concern is "dual cultivation" and bonding within the group and with nature.

Neither of these functions needs ejaculation to succeed hence male ejaculation becomes unimportant. This attitude completely eliminates some of the most important male emotional problems due to such things that Western culture labels "premature ejaculation" and "impotence'—two categories, actually created by an overemphasis on ejaculation. Freed from the constant "sex in the head" preoccupation with ejaculation, the "jade peak," as the Chinese call the penis, naturally acts as it was designed by nature to act, unless there is physical disability.

In ritualized sex, which is not confined to the genital area, the entire body and the brain receive repetitive stimuli over a considerable period of time. This leads to "central nervous system tuning," which I explained earlier in this work. I will briefly summarize it here. Generally speaking, if either the parasympathetic nervous sytem or the sympathetic nervous sytem is stimulated, the other system is inhibited. Tuning occurs, however, when there is such strong, prolonged activation of one system that it becomes supersaturated and spills over into the other system so that it, in turn, becomes activated. If stimulated long enough the next stage of tuning is reached where the simultaneous strong discharge of both autonomic systems creates a state of stimulation of the median forebrain bundle, generating not only pleasureable sensations but, in especially profound cases, a sense of union or oneness with all. This stage of tuning permits right hemisphere dominance; thus solving problems deemed insoluble by the rational hemisphere. Furthermore, the strong rhythm of repetitive action as done in sexual rituals produces positive limbic (animal brain) discharge, resulting in increased social cohesion; thus contributing to the success of such rituals as bonding mechanisms. All these benefits, which follow on "tuning" apply even more powerfully in ritualized sex; such "tuning" however, cannot come about through the usual quick orgasm of Western style sex, programmed as it is for procreation only. Such an orgasm resolves only the immediate sexual tension. Ritualized sex requires considerable time to allow for full "tuning" of all the interconnected systems in the body. Li T'ung Hsuan in his seventh century's commentary on the "thousand loving thrusts" of the jade peak, connects its movements with all of nature: "Deep and shallow, slow and swift, direct and slanting thrust, are by no means all uniform...A slow thrust should resemble the jerking motion of a carp toying with the hook; a swift thrust that of the flight of the birds against the wind."

Taoist sexual techniques sensitize the entire body: whereas, in Western culture we have forced most of the passion of living into the narrowness of genital sexuality. But any time there is a total response, the whole being is there, and because the whole being is sexual, sexuality is always there in any total response. It can occur in any relationship—with an animal, with a flower, with the world itself. Some of the criticism of D. H. Lawrence comes from his total response to nature. Walking one day with his stuffy Edwardian editor, Ford Madox Ford, they were talking of literary matters; when, suddenly, according to Ford, Lawrence went "temporarily insane." He knelt down and tenderly touched the petals of a common flower and went into an "almost super-sex-passionate delight." Ford admitted that this was "too disturbing" for him. Westerners, in general, don't like it when one links sex and nature in such an intimate way. Because Lawrence is the only great English-speaking writer that I know about, who is capable of this kind of response to nature, I will go further into his work below.

Jaime de Angulo on Ritualized Sex in Certain Indian Tribes

While written accounts of Taoist sexual practices date back to over a thousand years ago, when it comes to ritualized sex among primitives in this country we have no written material from the people themselves since they were not literate. Anthropologists have written on such matters but they can deal only with surface manifestations. Fortunately, because of a most unusual combination of personal talents and circumstances in his life, Jaime de Angulo has contributed some unique insights into the Indians' own understanding of the place of sex in their world. I have mentioned him before in this work so here I will just touch briefly on the relevant events in his life which gave him this insight.

To begin with, he got his M.D. from Johns Hopkins in 1912 and was a psychiatrist for the U.S. army. When Jaime was working on a ranch in California he became friends with the Achumawi ranch hands; thus beginning his linguistic studies. Later he lived with the Pit River Indians. In 1915 he met Alfred Kroeber and Paul Radin, both outstanding anthropologists at the time. Recognizing Jaime's linguistic talents, Kroeber got him to teach two courses at Berkeley: one in psychiatry and the other on the mind of primitive man; but Jaime did not stay at the university very long because he wasn't academically inclined. He learned seventeen new Indian languages in the next fifteen years and became known as something of a shaman.

The combination of his shamanic knowledge and his academic knowledge of psychiatry and medicine along with his amazing linguistic ability gave him access to areas of Indian thought denied to other white men. The poet, Robert Duncan was de Angulo's typist during the last years of his life. In an interview with Bob Callahan of Turtle Island Press, Duncan explains a few aspects of what Jaime had discovered. Duncan reports that Jaime got the idea from the Indians "that you could cross over not just between the living and the dead, as in Shamanism, but also from one sex to another. He found the Indian understanding reasonable enough. We get confused about something like homosexuality. But sex and gender are not the same thing...At one point when I confused sex and gender, Jaime said you're Western in your thinking, you think that male and female are genders. For Indians there can be five genders in a language, five genders in a tribe."

In English we have only three genders: male, female and neuter. According to a number of sources there can be as many as eleven to fifteen genders in some tribes: in other words, eleven to fifteen different ways of being male or female. The most commonly known example of crossing from one sex to another, is the *contraire* in certain Plains Indian tribes.

Influenced by "Thunder," such a man could marry a warrior and was considered a sacred personage.

In various workshops which I've given through the years, whenever I mention Jaime's knowledge of these sexual roles, there are questions about the nature of these roles. Jaime did not elaborate, of course; however, Margaret Mead did touch briefly on this subject in writing about "Psychologic Sex Gender and Sex Role Assignment." First, she mentions that in our culture there are "only two approved sex roles" for children, while in some primitive or traditional societies there are far more. To give some idea of the possibilities here, she states that:

> The commonest sex careers may be classified as:
> 1. Married female who will bear children and care for her children.
> 2. Married male who will beget and provide for his children.
> 3. Adult male who will not marry or beget children but, who will exercise some prescribed social function, involving various forms of celibacy, sexual abstinence, renunciation of procreation, specialized forms of ceremonial sexual license, or exemption from social restrictions placed on other men.
> 5. Persons whose special, nonprocreative ceremonial role is important, roles in which various forms of transvestism and adoption of the behavior of the opposite sex are expected, so that the external genital morphology is either ignored or denied, e.g. shamans, etc.
> 11. Age-determined sex roles, as where homoerotic behavior is expected of adolescents, or withdrawal from all sex relationships expected from older heads of households etc., or license is expected before marriage and fidelity afterward, or chastity before marriage and indulgence after marriage, or where widows are expected neither to remarry nor to engage in any further sex relationships.

Mead points out that any or all of these adult roles may occur in the same society. She states: "In summary, it may be said that sex role assignment may be far more complex in other cultures than in our own, and it would be a mistake to build too much of a theoretical structure on contemporary American educational efforts to induct every child into an active and exclusively heterosexual role within the bonds of legal, monogamous unions."

Returning to the interview concerning Jaime de Angulo, Bob Callahan remarks: "With de Angulo, almost for the first time, we are getting a text on Native America which is sexually charged, we are getting an American Indian mythological text which is sexually sophisticated in terms of the individual identity of the characters. I mean it was there all along, but now we got this unusual man picking right up on it."

> Duncan replied: Oh yes. Again, Jaime's definition of sex is not specifically male or female. It's not locked to gender in that way. It's who you can actually fuck. Now that might be a tree, a rock...We've confused generation with reproduction and production; and so, as we also have private property thrown in there as well, we confuse children with 'our' children. And we can't understand a social structure where the tribe as a whole has children...We still have the term generation, 'for my generation', my generation was the 'jazz' generation. In that way we understand what generation is. The total society generates, and the children belong to that society...Everybody in [Jaime's] stories really exists in a continuous world of generations, of being the children of the world they are living in, so you're a very bad child indeed if you do not venerate Father Tree, or any other aspect of your parent world.

The word, engendering, means according to the dictionary, "to produce, give existence to living beings." Looked at from

Jaime's point of view, it is obvious that humanity alone does not engender children; instead it is the entire living environment which produces the child and keeps it alive—the air, soil, plants and animals of its immediate environment. We are the children of our particular place on earth. That is why the land is sacred and sex is sacred and eating is sacred; in Taoism, they are all parts of the same energy flow. American Indians repeatedly acknowledge "all our relations" in their sacred sweats—the hot rocks, the water which is thrown on the rocks, the sage—all are part of the same family.

D. H. Lawrence on Human Sexuality and Nature

Because Lawrence's work is so often misunderstood, the best way to introduce this aspect of his work, is to go clear back to the 1920s. Rolf Gardiner, English farmer, forester and pioneer of the Land Service Camps for Youth, thought that the young science of ecology should play an "increasingly important role in the counsels of reformers." Having read one of Lawrence's books in 1919 he wrote:

> Lawrence became the torchbearer, the torch leader of my youth. He went ahead exploring the dark, dispelling the limits of our shabby, exhausted vision of things, breaking away from the abstractions of finite ideas, worn-out concepts, barren words and tired symbols...It always seemed to me that country spoke through Lawrence. It was indeed the dark, fecund forces of Nottinghamshire which threshed through his earlier books filling them with...the secret hidden gods of country to speak to us and claim us...The spirit of the place, (Italy, Australia, Mexico) this dominated him and fed him with power. All his books throb with this dark exciting spirit of place...teaching us to sense and experience afresh the intense power of the gods in the earth...He knew that we could draw power from the earth and live significantly if we worked in communion with the authorities of the past in the earth, in particular landscapes...I have felt for a long time that some vindication of Lawrence's teaching, of his vision must be made, and not by literary critics, but by people trying to live his vision.

Lawrence's native place was in the county of Nottinghamshire. All his biographers write of the mining there but few even mention that Sherwood Forest is in this county. Here Lawrence and his young friends could enter "under the splendid oak and ash, elm and beach and alder to Robin Hood's Well and Maid Marian's Dancing Green," in the words of one childhood friend. I have documented elsewhere the fact that Lawrence had a childhood "nature mystic experience." This sense of being part of the whole stayed with Lawrence throughout his life and all his work is an effort toward communicating that feeling, which he first experienced in his "beloved home valley."

The other aspect of his childhood, generally overlooked and almost equally important as "place" was his contact with what was essentially a "primitive tribal" group. His father was of the "last generation of Englishmen who escaped compulsory schooling" as Lawrence explained. His father went "down pit" at the age of nine. He and his "mates" worked together, poached rabbits on the land owner's estates, hunted mushrooms and drank together. As Lawrence wrote later, "the miners worked underground as a sort of intimate community." The darkness and danger "made the physical, instinctive, and intuitional contact between men very highly developed... very real and powerful." Lawrence's father was very handsome with wavy black hair, "a very melodious voice...graceful dancing ...a gallant manner and overflowing humor and good spirit." In other words, a true primitive! The young Lawrence felt the power of this way of life. Against that overflowing life was his mother's way—the "genteel tradition." Although he followed her rules and almost died because of those rules, his father's early influence stayed deep within him.

Lawrence's first editor, Ford Madox Ford, found Lawrence's writings entirely different from other English novelists. Ford said that when Lawrence writes of nature, these passages "run like fire through his books and are exciting—because of the life that comes into his writings...you have the sense that there really was to him a side that was supernatural...in tune with deep woodlands, which are queer places." Like any true primitive, Lawrence lived in "a blaze of reality" in his contact with nature.

Another contemporary of Lawrence's, Cecil Gray, the Scottish composer, who lived near the Lawrences in Cornwall, actively disliked Lawrence, but admitted that where Lawrence "realized himself completely, was in the world of nature...and with trees." Gray states: "In all literature there is little, if anything to compare with the extraordinary depth and delicacy of Lawrence's perceptions of Nature in all its forms and manifestations. He was a faun, a child of Pan...That was the essential Lawrence; there he was truly great."

Marrying Frieda enabled him to write about the power of sex. Before he met Frieda, she (although already married to Professor Weekly) had been involved with Otto Gross, once one of Freud's most remarkable students. At one time, Freud, himself, remarked that Jung and Gross were his ablest students. Gross was the leading proponent of "the erotic movement," which held that love outside marriage was the only way in which modern man could be linked with "the natural fountain of all." Gross once wrote that Frieda had "removed the shadow of Freud from his path." He later wrote directly to Frieda that she was "the woman of the future." By this he meant that she was an example of how people would be in the future when they were no longer damaged by all the conditions he fought against. He continued by saying that she was "the only person who *today* has stayed free of chastity as a moral code and Christianity and Democracy and those heaps of nonsense." He then goes on to marvel at how she, "the golden child," has been able to keep the "curse and the dirt of two gloomy millenia from your soul with your laughter and love."

She obviously was attracted to Gross but his power frightened her. He later died in an insane asylum. When she met Lawrence, she found that he could see the same things in her as Gross had, but Lawrence was "safer." The sexual torments Lawrence went through in the years before he met Frieda is shown in a poem titled "Manifesto." This poem begins with the fierceness of hunger for food and warmth for the body and the hunger for knowledge; he continues: "But then came another hunger/very deep, and ravening." It is more frightening even than the hunger for food: it is "the hunger for woman." But not just any woman. And then he describes the fullness of life which Frieda brought him. From this time on Lawrence realized that in some deep way woman, sex and nature were connected.

In his most famous novel, *Sons and Lovers*, written after he met Frieda there is a love scene with Clara Dawes, a divorced woman (partly modelled on Frieda). They have made love beside a canal and as their consciousness returns, he says:

> They had met, and included in their meeting the thrust of the manifold grass stems, the cry of the peewit, the wheel of the stars...To know their own nothingness, to know the tremendous living flood which carried them always...If so great a magnificent power could overwhelm them, identify them altogether with itself, so that they knew they were only grains in the tremendous heave that lifted every grass blade its little height, and every tree, and living thing, then why fret about themselves? They could let themselves be carried by life...

In a letter to Lady Ottoline Morrell, Lawrence gives the clearest explanation of what he meant by the "power" of woman. He wrote that the earth needs the prophetess type of woman, and that she should not trust merely her brain or her will but that "faculty for receiving the hidden waves that come from the depths of life, and for transferring them to the unreceptive world."

Lawrence, as described by Kenneth Rexroth, was "one of those individuals...who give off an unbelievable charge of radar. If you were sitting in a room and he came in behind you the whole place reverberated as if enormous dynamo poles had been put against either wall." Lawrence was pursued by many women and he sometimes told Frieda that she was to keep them away from him.

In a number of his works Lawrence called for a new kind of relation between the sexes, even a new kind of marriage. In *Women In Love*, he has Birkin criticize stuffy—what we would now call "addictive love"—and marriage: "the world all in couples, each couple in its own little house, watching its own little interests, and stewing in its own little privacy." Again, much later he wrote this about current marriage: "What a feeble lot of compromises! It's no good talking about it: marriage ...will last while our social system lasts, because it's the thing that holds our system together. But our system will collapse, and then marriage will be different—probably more tribal...as in the old pueblo system..."

Concerning sex itself Lawrence wrote: "It is no good being sexual. That is only a form of the same static consciousness. Sex is not living till it is unconscious: and it never becomes unconscious by attending to sex. One has to face the whole of one's conscious self, and smash that." Way back in 1908 when Lawrence was trying to work his way toward his "phallic vision," he wrote that most people marry "with their soul vibrating to the note of sexual love...but love is much finer, I think, when not only the sex group of chords is attuned, but the great harmonies, and the little harmonies, of what we call religious feeling (read it widely) and ordinary sympathetic feeling."

A hundred thousand years of genetic programming by our animal ancestors has instilled in us an organic, inevitable flowing and mingling of sexual energies, which previously occured naturally, through intense living out in nature. But today, in our civilized life this "inevitable" flow seems to surface only when working together outside in natural surroundings. In all of Western literature no one but Lawrence has ever given us a fitting description of this flowing together of sacred land, sacred sex. He had often helped out at harvest time in his beloved "home valley," before he had to leave to teach in town. Then, after meeting Frieda, he wrote in his novel, *The Rainbow*, about Will and Anna harvesting oats under a serene, full moon. "A large gold moon hung heavily to the grey horizon, trees hovered tall, standing back in the dusk, waiting." Will and Anna walk through the gate into an open field where some sheaves of oats had been left lying on the ground by the reapers, while still others were already standing in shocks. They begin putting up the sheaves. And the rhythm of working in nature takes over. The tresses of the oats hiss like a fountain as each alternately stacks the oats. "There was only the moving to and fro in the moonlight, engrossed, the swinging in the silence, that was marked only by the splash of the sheaves, and silence, and a splash of sheaves." And they moved ever nearer as they went down the rows until at last they meet and he takes her in his arms, "sweet and fresh" with the night air and the grain. "And the whole rhythm of him beat into his kisses...they stood there, folded, suspended, in the night." Here there is no mere "sex in the head," but a great flowing together of the moon, the ripe sheaves of oats, male, female and the tall, standing trees.

After he almost died in Mexico he returned to Europe and wrote *Lady Chatterley's Lover*, in one last effort to explain his "phallic vision," but all he got was criticism for writing a "pornographic" novel when he was dying. So in 1929, the year before he died, he wrote an essay, published after he died, called, "Apropos of Lady Chatterley's Lover." It contains his beautiful final statement:

> The last three thousand years of mankind have been an excursion into ideals, bodilessness, and tragedy and now the excursion is over...it is a question, practically, of relationship. We must get back into relation, vivid and nourishing relation to the cosmos...The way is through daily ritual, and the reawakening. We must once more practice the ritual of dawn and noon and sunset, the ritual of kindling fire and pouring water, the ritual of the first breath, and the last...We must return to the way of 'knowing in terms of togetherness'...the togetherness of the body, the sex, the emotions, the passions, with the earth and sun and stars.

Conclusion

Finding our way back into "vivid and nourishing relation to the cosmos...through ritual" is just beginning in our country; therefore it is important to emphasize two things here. Traditionally a "world renewal festival" always includes a joyous free mingling of the sexes; but, with our Eurocentric emphasis on sex as "substance"—something to be willed and limited— we are not yet in a position where we can expect a ritual use of sex to be either "free" or "joyous." So probably for at least the near future, the sexual energy (which, by nature, is always there) will be shared in the form of dances, maypoles, flirting and teasing (traditional ways of primitive cultures to handle the potentially explosive sexual energy between people who for kinship reasons are not allowed to marry). Each of these activities do share the energy and re-new it just as well as full genital sex if the sexual energy involved is glorified, fully acknowledged and, equally important—laughed with and at. Anyone who has been to a seasonal ritual at one of the pueblos knows how important the "clowns" are during the dance. Often they have a huge, mock penis or are dressed in the most ridiculous female attire and they often catch an unsuspecting tourist and mime intercourse, outrageously. This is what we, too, must begin allowing to happen in order to keep the important sexual energy flowing within the human group and between human and non-human in the great festivals.

According to Gaster, "The institution of sexual promiscuity at seasonal crises survives in European folklore in the attenuated form of compulsory kissing or 'lifting' on certain days of the year." He writes about "hocking day" at Hungerford in England. On the second Thursday after Easter the men go through the streets "lifting" or "hocking" the women and exacting a kiss from each. The custom of kissing under the mistletoe at Christmas is another remnant of the old sexual promiscuity at the Winter Solstice.

The second important aspect concerns the importance of ritualized birth control. As I mentioned before in one of the earlier chapters, seasonal rituals have to do with the "increase" of all beings in the place—human and non-human—in a manner that keeps the balance within the ecosystem. This obviously involves controlling human births; but looking at it from the point of view of ritual, has never even occurred to most people. The Guajiro, who live in Venezuela at the present time, however, have made this control of human births an integral part of their female initiation rites.

As soon as a girl notices the first bleeding of menstruation she is rushed immediately to a small separate enclosure. She is given a "medicine" in the middle of her first night of seclusion. This medicine, called huawapi, "is designed to control and space pregnancies so that she will have three, or, at the most, four children during her lifetime." During the first month of her seclusion she will be given this medicine, which is a local herb, three times a day. "Later, as a married woman, when she gives birth, she will take this medicine again, for three days after delivery, but for no longer, for if she does she will become sterile." Many other teachings are given to her while she is secluded so that she knows she is special, but I have not space to go into them here.

The great seasonal festivals, as done in traditional primitive cultures, also balance out the male and female in each person. This is very important for preventing the difficult anima and animus battles between the unconscious of men and women. C.G. Jung gave these labels to us. They come from the Latin word, *animare*, which means "to enliven." He felt that "the anima and animus were like enlivening souls or spirits to men and women." The animus is the male aspect inside a woman and the anima is the female aspect inside the man. In our culture these other aspects are seldom given a chance to develop fully so that when the person reaches middle age there is a real crisis. "In the case of the anima, it is she who lies behind a man's moods. When a man is possessed by the anima he is drawn into a dark mood, and tends to become sulky, overly sensitive and withdrawn. A poisonous atmosphere surrounds him, and

it is as though he is immersed in a kind of psychological fog." If he would or could express his feelings things would be alright. But if he cannot do that, "the anima gets them...He is possessed by rage, and his anger is in constant danger of [exploding], for it is as though the anima stands poised to drop her flaming match into the waiting can of gasoline, and the man will erupt in an engulfing and uncontrolled emotion." In a woman, the animus (her male aspect), "typically expresses himself in judgments, generalizations, critical statements." The woman becomes very depressed because these judgments from her own interior "destroy her sense of her own value and worth." The novelist Emily Bronte called the anima, "The Great Prosecutor" and the anima has also been called the "Duty Demon." The woman possessed by the animus, projects it onto the man in her life and wants to get back at him because she feels he is the one who has hurt her. What eventually happens is that these two unconscious aspects of the husband and wife take over and thus vicious battles can begin over the most trivial statement while neither of the conscious persons can understand why it happens. Traditional seasonal festivals allow balancing of these energies by such actions as the men wearing women's clothes or women wearing men's clothes and both groups doing humorous burlesques of one another's actions.

In traditional cultures neither sex is as locked into a role structure as much as our Eurocentric cultures demand. In traditional cultures, when a woman is through bearing her children she automatically becomes an elder who is consulted by all the tribe because she "knows." Likewise, a man as he grows older, very often takes an even greater part in the ritual of the tribe and thus his anima or female intuitional aspect has a chance to grow. Thus the individual becomes a better person and the tribe gains from the greater understanding of the elders—both men and women.

If, instead of looking at sex as "substance," a *thing* done between two humans, we begin to look at it as relationship in the largest sense, then it grows and grows. Outside in nature, the sexual act may lose its limiting boundary of being "merely" between a man and a woman. It grows deeper until the power of the older "animal" brain is tapped and even the still older "reptile" brain. Out of this "extended identity" you feel your Self growing ever larger and ever deeper until the Self is "opened in the bloom of pure relationship to the sun, the entire living cosmos...This is the state of heaven. And it is the state of a flower, a cobra, a jenny-wren in spring, a man when he knows himself royal and crowned with the sun, with his feet gripping the core of the earth." This is Lawrence's lyrical outpouring of joy to the power in his own life of his sacred land on Lobo Mountain. "For me," he wrote in 1925, describing how it is to look far "away at the mountains in shadow and the pale-warm desert beneath, with wings of shadow upon it: For me, this place is sacred. It is blessed." In your own life, as well, the power of your sacred land can lead to sacred sex where, you, too, will experience "rapture of the deep."

"It seems that the Ndembu doctor sees his task not as curing an individual patient, but rather of remedying the ills of a corporate group. The individual's symptoms are seen as a signal that 'something is rotten' in the corporate body. The patient will not recover until all the tensions and aggressions in that group's network of relationships have been brought to light, then exposed to ritual manipulation."

Victor Turner

"Taoism, however, remembers the story of man as being essentially mythological in nature. It leaves room for the sacred madness, freedom, imagination, and creativity of man's primitive nature. Knowing the true story of man provides a way of personally reliving that story."

N.J. Girardot

"Some of the healing that goes on…is this putting all the chaotic and traumatic events of a life into [the story]. My interest in story is as something lived in and lived through, a way in which the soul finds itself in life."

James Hillman

"Hear the voice of the Bard!
Who Present, Past and Future, sees;
Whose ears have heard
the Holy Word
That walk'd among the ancient trees."

William Blake

"Why Fenollosa wrote the damned best piece on language since when, is because, in setting Chinese directly over against American, he reasserted these resistant primes in our speech, put us back to the origins of their force not as history but as living oral law to be discovered in speech as directly as it is in our mouths."

Charles Olson

CHAPTER SIXTEEN

"Eskimos are more interested in the creative activity than in the product of that activity. Art to them is a transitory act, a relationship…"

Edmund Carpenter (1978)

"Our purposeful creation of such things as Art or Architecture belies our ignorance of their and our deeper natures. If we grow through a certain act or experience and reach deeper into the vast potentials of our nature, that in itself is good. Beyond that, what is produced and remains is like the cast-off skin of a molting snake—a sign, but only that—of its growth. If we are truly growing, our every act and every surrounding will be permeated with the beauty of that growth, and there will be no need or desire to cling to and hold separate some things as Art."

Tom Bender

"Experienced chanters…quickly re-find the way to effortlessness each time; the switch from thinking to unthinking is done with ease, but the beginner must guard against effort, against the activities of the intellect, returning to the original phrase whenever the mind interjects some idea that interrupts the completely unguided changes in the chant."

Jean Liedloff

"In India he witnessed a Kathakali dance with its 'demonically clever and incessant drumming that shakes up the very dormant plexus solaris of the European'…A score of different nuances from the sentimental to the obscene, from the monstrous to the blood-curdling, arose in the dance and would have become grotesque but for the insistent rising and falling of the drums which drew upon mysterious powers and created 'a new reality rising from the bowels'."

C.G. Jung, quoted by Vincent Brome

"Conflicts within the group are resolved by talking, sometimes half or all the night, weeks on end. After two years with the San, I came to think of the Pleistocene epoch of human history (the three million years during which we evolved) as one interminable marathon encounter group."

Melvin Konner, who lived with the Kung (San) of the Kalahri for 20 months.

"[B]ut what is truth, what is wisdom? Wisdom is that particular emergence from your own spontaneity of an identification with what you know of the universe around you…T'ai chi does not mean oriental wisdom or something exotic. It is the wisdom of your own senses, your own body and mind together as one process."

Al Huang

SEVEN "WAYS" TOWARD HUMAN/EARTH BONDING: BOUNDARY CROSSING BETWEEN WILDERNESS AND CIVILIZATION

ESCAPE
When we get out of the glass bottles of our ego,
and when we escape
like squirrels turning in the cage of our personality
and get into the forest again, we shall shiver
with cold and fright.
But things will happen to us
so that we don't know ourselves,
Cool, unlying life will rush in,
and passion will make our
bodies taut with power.
We shall stamp our feet with new power
and old things will fall down.
We shall laugh, and
institutions will curl up
like burnt paper.

D. H. Lawrence

Personal Introduction

To help you begin using these ritual "ways," I will provide a brief account of when I first experienced each of them. Sage provides the most immediate boundary crossing—out of our narrow personal, merely human, ego into the whole of life; thus it is an integral part of all ritual. Growing up in Denver near the foothills of the Rocky Mountains, where the small, soft, mountain sage grows, I encountered it during the first years of my life so the power of it has always been with me. Later, on hikes in the mountains we always broke off a piece as we went by and stuck it behind our ear so we wouldn't lose it and, at rest stops along the way, we would just take it out and smell it because it made us feel good.

I had heard that Indians were supposed to use sage in their ceremonials and I thought that was appropriate. Years later, when we began celebrating the solstices and equinoxes we found that passing a piece of sage around for everyone to rub over them, provided a good transition from our everyday life to the celebration. Little did I know then how ancient this custom is—it's been with us since before we were human. I will go into this more below.

The first of the seven "ways" I encountered, was the gourd rattle. The story is a long one but has to do with how I first experienced many other ritual techniques too. Having read about the power of trance dancing to the drum, in rituals all over the world, I knew this was the way that humans had held it together for at least 40,000 years, but I never thought I would actually be able to experience such a dance. Then I heard of Elizabeth Cogburn.

Ten years after the avalanche, recounted earlier in this work, when my back finally gave out from the fact that one leg was an inch shorter, I was living in Colorado once more so I went to Tom Wing in Boulder to be Rolfed. We soon found a great deal to talk about with our common interest in nature and ritual. He told me of Elizabeth because she had "blessed" their house for them. I wrote her immediately, but they were already filled up for the "Sundance" at Summer Solstice. I had her put my name down for the following Winter Solstice.

Fortunately, I was able to meet her before then. Chris Cappy, Director of Feathered Pipe Ranch in Montana, had a special session concerning the earth. My book, *Earth Wisdom*, had just recently come off the press. He contacted me in Boulder and I flew up to give workshops there. He also had arranged to have Elizabeth, Joan Halifax, Brooke Medicine Eagle, and Wabun, the wife of Sun Bear. This was the first time all of us had met together. We learned a lot from one another in addition to the teaching we did for the people who had come to the workshop. I found that Elizabeth had the most to teach me.

Out of the dynamics of the workshops, it happened that Elizabeth held a "talking staff" council for the staff of Feathered Pipe Ranch. We walked up the dirt road in silence to the site, with Elizabeth drumming. She had a few gourd rattles with her and handed them out to some of us. Walking up the road, I found myself automatically shaking the gourd and getting a response. This surprised me; but I had no time to think on it. When we reached the site up in the pine trees, we all sat on the ground to discuss the very important matter of whether a tree should be cut to allow the younger one to flourish or whether it should be left, tangled in with the younger one. So, immediately after my first meeting with the gourd rattle I experienced my first "talking staff" council. More below on this.

Back to the gourd rattle. I drove down to Taos for the Winter Solstice, held in an old adobe house way above town, where Elizabeth's mother lived. As part of the preparation for the dance we visited Lawrence's cave. It's called that because a scene in one of his short stories is set there. We all walked up a dirt road through pine trees, carrying our gourd rattles. I watched Bob Cogburn, Elizabeth's husband, feeling out the places we walked through by first shaking the gourd over them to receive the information it gave him.

The cave has a tremendous icicle hanging down before the opening. When we gathered in the cave we could see the solstice sun, setting through this icicle. It was powerful! Walking back out through the twilight, our gourd rattles immediately fell into the same rhythm. The bonding this produced was surprising. We had to drive about 20 minutes to get back to the house. As we unloaded the cars it began to snow! And there had been no snow yet that year. It was a most auspicious beginning of the trance dance.

Elizabeth had just acquired her magnificent ceremonial drum (roughly four feet in diameter). We had learned from her during the day how to let the drum "play itself" by using the beaters properly. And I loved the sound, but I was not prepared for what happened that night. As we walked into the long room where the dance was to take place I remember thinking: "I know this will be fine but it's going to be difficult for me to let go enough to really go all night long." Well, as I stepped across the threshold and the big drum began, my feet began to move. I had nothing to do with it. My feet did it all. And before I knew it dawn came and the Winter Solstice night was over!

Although I had done some chanting through the years, I did not begin to experience the full power of it until a few years ago. The only event I regularly schedule here in Silverton is the Autumn Equinox Taoist Celebration. At that time Jackie Miller, a musician and teacher, was still living here. She was in my Tai Chi class and, since she was interested in ritual, I invited her to come along on the Equinox. I gave her a tape of the chanting done by "The Circle" group in California and told her we might try a few of them. So on Dragonback Mountain, we chanted the sun down as it set behind backlit, golden aspen on Autumn Equinox. In that setting, all of us fully experienced the power of chanting!

A growing understanding over a period of about three years led me to fully realize that bards are absolutely essential for helping a group of people get back in touch with the earth. I will go more fully into this below.

Tai Chi is my personal "way" for increasing human/earth bonding. Although I've been doing Tai Chi, daily, for sixteen years and teaching it as well for the last ten years; I am continually amazed at the deeper and deeper connections with all of nature that it brings about! Of course Tai Chi cannot be taught in a book, but I will give more details below concerning its power of connecting human and nature.

Preview

When you first "think about" using any of these "ways" they may seem strange, weird—even freaky. After all there's been two thousand years of concerted propaganda and continuous invective from our Christian culture concerning the use of these "pagan" devices. They might even put you into the hands of the "devil" himself! No wonder there's a certain amount of anxiety connected with these "ways." But once you quit thinking about it and take a gourd rattle into your hand, within moments it's leading you into deeper connections with the other humans present and the natural environment. Very soon, it becomes "the most natural thing in the world" and you will wonder how you ever did without it. You'll find this happens with each of these "ways."

When you use sage, you invoke the entire past of our human race. Sage (*artemesia*) grew all around the Mediterranean, including Africa in the period when the early humans developed. When you use the gourd rattle you invoke most of the ancient cultures around the entire world from South America to China and Japan, to Europe. Human beings in each of these areas used the gourd in daily life and for ritual. Our ancestors, the chimps and other higher primates still drum on hollow logs when they are excited or during their rituals. Some form of drum has been used by every human culture throughout the world—even in the Arctic. The drum has always invoked the dance to further bond humans and nature. Human chant grew out of the exclamations of the higher apes. It was facilitated by the gourd rattles, of course. The "talking staff" can be traced clear back to the "baton" painted on the walls of the Upper Paleolithic caves in Southern France. It is certain that bards appeared very early in human history, because the bard is the one who puts together the drum, gourd rattle and chanting of all "the people" into words and recites it back to his people so that they can continue to build their culture.

Essentially each of these "ways" involves playing. While ritual gives us permission to play, it is by following one of these ways, that we remember how to play. Just in the last decade or so, we find intellectuals not just observing the rituals of primitives and then writing learned papers on the event or merely "doing" the ritual to please the "natives"; but actually participating in the ritual and learning directly from the ritual.

Through this participation, these Eurocentric people relearn the techniques, which our primitive ancestors spent thousands of years refining for us. Of course, still caught in the "substance" trap, some of these anthropologists and their followers then decide that he or she, the human being, now has "the power" and could do what they wanted with it. They were incapable of recognizing that the power resides in the whole of nature/human interaction and is dispensed to us through these "ways" and others like them. These "ways" are non-human; fabricated by humans out of the natural being: the drum from wood or the rattle from the gourd. For example, in the case of the drum, it is always expressly acknowledged that the wood of the tree shows you how to make the drum. To fabricate the ritual object the human must follow the pattern of the wood. The wood of the tree "affords" the drum to human beings; the gourd "affords" the humans a drinking vessel, a pot, a ritual rattle etc.

Back in Part II of this book I introduced Gibson's term "affordances" when I was talking about "seeing." Gibson wrote about what the "environment *affords* animals": the terrain, shelter, water, fire, tools etc. The "*affordances* of the environment are what it *offers* the animal, what it *provides*." As mentioned before Gibson made up the word affordance, from the verb, "to afford." He explains, "I mean by it something that refers to both the environment and the animal in a way that no existing term does. It implies the complementarity of the animal and the environment." Again, the reason we don't have such a word is quite simple. Since the time of Plato it is the human being who arrogantly sees objects, defines terms, says what is useful and what is bad—in short runs the world. Since all other beings in the world are only "used" by humans there's no need of such a word. But now that we, in deep ecology, are trying to express what we already know deep inside us, we need this word. It's not a great word but it's all we've got right now.

The tree affords the drum, the gourd affords the rattle—for us. This is truly the relationship between human and nature. Nature affords us all we need to live if we don't fall into the trap of the "arrogance of humanism," thinking we know all the answers when we've only been here some 700,000 years, or "one cosmic instant," as Livingston puts it. Our ancestors, the higher apes have been around far longer than we; the wolves have been here thirty million years and the whales, fifty million years. Remember, too, that gourds crossed the Atlantic and back before there were any humans around at all.

The "ways" in this chapter are "affordances," which give you the opportunity to begin getting in touch with the earth so that once more you can live as deeply as our ancestors did long ago. After all it was by following these "ways" that we first became human. But then, by overspecialization of the rational part of the neo-cortex, the merely human part of the brain, we threw ourselves out of this living relationship with all of nature. Looked at in this manner, it seems obvious that today, we modern humans cannot find our way back into nature no matter how much rational planning or human decision making we put into it; because this is exactly how we threw ourselves out in the first place. But the ancient human ways of chanting and bardic poetry—both of which draw on all the older brains—can help us. Even more helpful is to allow the non-human: the gourd, the drum, the sage to afford us the way. If you do that you will find that "it's the most natural thing in the world" to live fully, with all four brains and each cell of the body in total relationship to "all of life" that surrounds us here on earth. As the Japanese Zen master, Dōgen put it, more succinctly seven hundred years ago:

> That the self advances and confirms the myriad things is called delusion.
> That the myriad things advance and confirm the self is enlightenment.

"West of the mountain…The overcast remained high, distantly threatening. From wispy, slate-blue rain clouds big drops still spattered down irregularly. A single raindrop touches a sage leaf, and a rare perfume is created! For me, the odor is nostalgic, rich, beautiful, and lonely: it evokes memories of things I have never experienced…history, the Old Days, hard times, a spare and precious freedom."

John Nichols

SAGE IS ESSENTIAL IN ALL RITUAL

"In the northern Mediterranean region [which includes North Africa, Spain, Italy, Greece, Iran, and Syria] evidence is now extensive for the existence of a cool, dry steppe for the period from before 35,000 years ago to about 11,000 years ago." Herbert Wright, in his paper in the book, *Origins of Agriculture*, continues by saying that "before about 11,000 years ago the vegetation was a steppe dominated by *Artemisia* [sagebrush], with a climate cooler and drier than today. The conclusion is that the climate of the late Pleistocene in this area was drier than that of today."

For most of the Pleistocene, the vegetation was "an *Artemisia* steppe, in which grasses or chenopods were generally common." The transition from the Pleistocene to the Holocene about 11,000 years ago, "was marked by a profound and relatively abrupt climatic and vegetational change thoughout the northern Mediterranean" and many other parts the world as well.

The typical Mediterranean species of trees and shrubs of today were not present then. "Their abrupt expansion 11,000 years ago signaled the return of the inter-glacial-style Mediterranean climate to the Mediterranean region."

When these somewhat moister conditions arrived, the dry *artemesia* style steppe retreated further north, to the foothills of the Zagros Mountains, and such places, where humans, at a later time, began cereal grain agriculture. Humans and sage moved north together.

In Southwestern Asia, as well, there was a dominance of sagebrush steppe in this same Pleistocene period.

From all the above you can see that as the human race began during Pleistocene times in Africa, the odor of sage was everywhere present. The persistent odor of sage accompanied humans as slowly, over generations, they moved further north and into the Paleolithic cave area of Spain and France. Then, as the climate changed the persistent odor of the sage steppe moved further north into the areas where humans later learned to grow cereal grains. Throughout all this period of human development, sage was always present.

No wonder that Artemis, one of the most important Greek goddesses has the same name as this plant. The noted Classical scholar, Jane Harrison in her book, *Mythology*, writes that Harris, tells us about "the very herb to which Artemis owes her name, the artemisia." It grew abundantly on Mt. Taygetus, the favourite haunt of Artemis.

Paul Shepard says that Artemis means bear. The syllable, *art*, in the word certainly has a connotation of bear. Here again we have a herb which bear first showed humans. "Artemis, whose name means 'bear', is the goddess who absorbs some of the sacred bear's ultimate qualities as the animal image itself disappears," Shepard explains. Harrison says that, historically, two strands go to the making of this goddess. One is the "Earth-Mother" from Crete and the other, the maid magician, the Healer of the North.

Sage is one of the great healing herbs. It has a stimulating effect on uterine circulation and will help in suppressed, crampy menstruations, particularly following illness or some emotional or physical trauma. This may have some connection with the fact that the name of Artemis keeps coming up in the stories of rapes of Greek goddesses. Sage is also good for nursing mothers and Artemis is considered a protectoress of mothers in childbirth. It's also a classic stomach tonic and gets rid of worms, which would be a prime reason for bears to use it, after the long winter hibernation.

The Greek classical author, Hippolytus says, "Artemis seems to beckon from the future, to call me toward who I am now to become."

Sage truly has been with us from the beginning, teaching us. It truly beckons toward the future as well as we begin to learn once more, from the natural beings through ritual.

Sage was used by American Indians in sweats all over the American continent. It's use is growing among all of us doing rituals. Sage is not merely one of the "ways," it is the fundamental ritual affordance and should be used in *all* rituals—large or small. In sweats, sometimes the participants sit on sage. It is used in other ways such as hitting various parts of the body with it or merely rubbing it on the wrists. Before any kind of ritual or ceremony, sage should be distributed among the people as the transition marker from every-day life in this Industrial Growth Society to living in the "once and future" of ritual time.

The power of sage is shown in a recent account of efforts to stop uranium mining in the Grand Canyon. Mary Sojourner, 47 years old, was arrested "for believing that the Grand Canyon and its surrounding forests and high desert are no place for [French owned] uranium mines." In the Coconino County jail, she met one of the native inhabitants, Judy, eighteen years old, "busted that afternoon for one of those sad little crimes with not so little consequences, for shoplifting crayons for her little nephew, both of them no longer living at home; home gone to 'one of those big companies,'" as Judy said. [probably Peabody coal]

When Mary gave her some of the sage she had brought in from the mine site, Judy "crushing the sage, said, 'It smells like home'."

Truly, sage is the "smell of home" and has been so since the first humans clear back in the Pleistocene era.

THE "WAY" OF THE GOURD

The intuitive observer...seeks to enter with his whole being into the lawless profusion...He surrenders to the inner logic of growth, evolution and maturity, a realm which system and experiment are powerless to unlock. Instead of petrified laws and formulas, he discovers symbolic events and types of living, breathing reality.

Leo Frobenius

"Our Father the Cayman, Our Mother, the Gourd"

The gourd, in many ways, is the "mother" of the human race. According to Lathrap: "The bottle gourd as a cultivated plant furnished the womb in which all more elaborate agricultural systems developed. Stated more precisely: the artificial propagation of the bottle gourd and certain other technologically significant crops such as cotton and fish poisons imposed particular disciplines on man and in the context of these behavioral patterns all of the other nutritionally significant agricultural systems arose."

Here I will briefly review some facts on gourds, which were covered earlier in this work. Paleolithic fishing/gathering communities, which lived along river banks began to use the gourd as a container and a dipper, for fish net floats, and the bitter gourd, for fish poisons. When a group moved on or split off into two groups each faction took along the gourd plant to begin life anew. Carl Sauer explains that plants were first grown for body paint and other ritualized uses before they were grown for food. Before overpopulation of the world, plant food was much more easily available. The rare item was the plant that produced particular necessities of life—which, of course, always included ritual. Primitive groups made sure they had a supply of such plants by cultivating them. They knew they could always find something to eat.

The gourd plant probably began in Africa. In their mythology, the horizontally halved gourd symbolizes the entire universe. The upper half is the sky and the lower half the ocean. The earth is a smaller gourd floating within the lower half.

The gourd crossed the Atlantic ocean by itself, long before humans. Heiser says it could have happened "fifty thousand or a hundred thousand years ago, or even earlier." Thus in South America, as well, the gourd became the "mother" of the humans. Bottle gourds can float in seawater for a year, be stored for six more years and still have viable seeds. Reed reports: "Since bottle gourds have been picked up on the coasts of Norway and Ireland, they seemingly floated there from South America or Mesoamerica or came from western Africa, in which case they must have crossed the Atlantic twice, first

following the Atlantic South Equatorial Current and the Caribbean Current into the Gulf of Mexico, and then following the Gulf Stream to Europe." Likewise throughout the islands of the Pacific and reaching clear to China and Japan the gourd is known as the "mother." In the Hawaiian, "Prayer of the Gourd," it is addressed as "The gourd is this great world, its cover the heavens."

It was "one of man's most important plants before the invention of pottery" and in many parts of the world the early pottery itself was modelled directly after the gourd shape. Throughout the world the gourd was used as containers, plates, cups, and spoons. Futhermore when cracked or broken it can be repaired by sewing it together as is still done in Africa, South America and Hawaii. It is used to make floats and rafts, for pipes, to make cricket cages and bird houses, and as penis sheaths. It was the first musical instrument in places as widely separated as Africa, South America and Asia. Gourds were used as masks by American Indians such as the Cherokee in their Booger Dance as well as Apaches, Zunis and Hopis. Furthermore, the gourd has not only been the basis of myth and ritual throughout the world, it provides *the* single most important ritual item—the rattle. The Cherokee name for the gourd rattle is "life-force maker."

Cultivated squashes and pumpkins come from gourd ancestors. The growth of the annual species (Cucurbita) is magical. They can reach 300 lbs. in one year while the bottle gourd can grow to 9 feet in length and 6 feet long in one year. These factors further contribute to its symbolical meanings.

As mentioned in the chapter on Taoism, the gourd's hollow space filled with the "germs" of life link it to Lord Hun-Tun—the chaos out of which creation comes. When the gourd is cut or carved, "it freely yields its ambivalent natural life to man so that the human world may be created." Its power lies in its emptiness, "a wu-wei that accomplishes all things." Girardot calls it an "earth egg"; but as a creation symbol it is even more powerful than an egg which needs a "mother hen" to hatch it. The bottle gourd, however, "in its emptiness and self-yielding...emphasizes the mystery of spontaneous self-generation out of 'nothing'."

Without the hollow within the gourd, no sound could be produced. The seeds must have space to move about to produce the sound. Humans learned resonance from the gourd.

"Multivocal" symbolism of the gourd

Considering all the above statements, we can say that the gourd is the quintessential "multivocal" symbol. Because of its relevance here, I will summarize what I explained, in depth, back in chapter twelve of this work. As Victor Turner noted, such symbols bring together multiple meanings clustering at two opposite poles: one with "gross, physiological references" and the other, "oriented toward a 'cognitive-ideological' focus." The second pole involves much more than "ideological" or "ethical" matters. "True empirical ideas, results of valid experience and experiment, may also be found there. Ritualization occurs when these semantic poles are present in a culture's major symbols...and deritualization takes place when the bond between the poles is broken, for whatever historical reasons."

When the bond is broken, the many meanings of the symbol are no longer connected so they begin to diverge and go their separate directions, becoming concepts or rules or beliefs. Turner summarizes by stating: "When ritualized systems of symbols, whether liturgical, theological or mythical are 'unbound' many of the concepts of the normative-cognitive pole of their dominant symbols become the univocal notions of philosophical and scientific thinking." In Eurocentric cultures this happened long ago, as explained in Part I of this work; therefore the gap between the two poles has widened almost irrevocably until modern culture can no longer find "meaning" in anything. While in the Taoist tradition, for instance, there has never been any break, whatsoever, no matter what historical disasters ocurred in the political structure of China.

Taoism continually reverts to the basic gourd symbolism; thus never breaking the connection between the two poles. Both philosophy and technology remain connected with the sexual as well as the animal natures within human beings and, even more important, remain connected to the earth and its seasons through the ever-present gourd symbolism in art, ritual and poetry. Urns painted with gourds were found in graves of the Yang Shao culture dating clear back to 2000 B.C. And, as we have seen back in Part II, the ever-present Tai Chi symbol developed out of the gourd's relationship to the changing light of the sun throughout each day.

Girardot sums up the many connections held together by the multivocal symbolism of the gourd, when he states: "Within the cultural sphere it is the cut and carved ornamental emptiness of the gourd that is the basis for the creation of the utensils of the civilizational order. Suspended, uncarved and whole, the gourd is the Taoist model for mystical unity and naturalness; when carved, its utility is the model for the foundational arts of human civilization." In essence, the gourd tells us the story of the "cyclic, inexhaustible creativity of the world and man, a creativity that ultimately depends on emptiness."

"Shaking the gourd" evokes all these meanings. It doesn't matter whether you ever heard these philosophical meanings, they come to you, effortlessly, through the gourd in your hand. Here I will give a few directions for beginners in the use of the gourd rattle. (See Reference Notes for directions for making simple gourd rattles.)

Directions for beginning to use gourd rattles

When a group gathers together for a ritual, especially when ritual is new to them, there's always a certain amount of uneasiness, doubt, and other rational mental traps. Using gourd rattles dispels this uneasiness. Everyone sits in a circle on the ground or the floor, the gourd rattles are passed around and the chanting begins to the steady rhythm of the rattles. Those who don't know the chants or are afraid to open their mouths can't resist shaking the gourd rattle. They might try to resist; but the rattle in their hand soon begins moving to the rhythm of the others, much to their surprise. This is the "ancient one" within us responding to the old rhythms. After an hour or two of chanting even the most dubious persons begin to join in.

It helps to have subdued light—preferably only candle or firelight. Direct eye contact is to be avoided. In fact, one of the clues that someone is trying to be a "guru" or take over the energy of the group comes when someone deliberately and persistently tries to establish eye contact early on. Chanting with rattles is often done with eyes closed.

Following the American Indian practice, often the first action during a major seasonal festival is a ritual sweat. While I will not take the space here to go into this too much because they vary with the occasion, essentially there are four rounds. In between each round the door flap is opened to let in air or let those out who are too hot. Often, the best way to start is to have total silence during the first round. Second round, still silence but gourd rattles are passed out and, soon the rattles begin and synchronize effortlessly. Then on the third round, chanting and on the last and fourth round, those who wish to speak may do so. By the last round you will find that most people are speaking from the heart and not just from the surface.

Using gourd rattles is very good for keeping people together on ritual walks or pilgrimages out in nature. The ritual leader sets the pace and, of course, the rhythm communicates through the rattle. Others pick this up and, automatically, it synchronizes the speed of the walking without undue effort. Ordinarily on a trail out in the woods—even on a ritual walk—some people feel they must show off how fast they can walk and others tend to dawdle and go slower and slower. Keeping both groups together often becomes a problem; but the rhythm of the gourd rattles keeps everyone together. Of course this is only necessary at the beginning; later you will want to walk in silence to absorb the sounds of nature.

For such events as "full moon rituals" or "sunrise" or "sunset" rituals, gourds are very important. Ideally the entire walk to the site to watch the moon rise should be done with no talking—just with the sound of the rattles. Using the rattles helps enforce the silence because no one feels called upon to make conversation out of nervousness or politeness. When you get to the site, total silence is sometimes very powerful: just watching the horizon where the moon will appear. When its lower rim clears the horizon then the chanting and shaking the rattles begins. The feeling is that the rattles help the moon to rise and then jubilantly, celebrate after it has risen.

To close this section on the "way" of the gourd I want to quote once more the famous Seneca Indian chant, which is part of a medicine society ceremony called "shaking the pumpkin." It's worth repeating here, the remarks the translator, Rothenberg made when he used the rattle for the first time:

I didn't think I'd
shake the pumpkin
not just here & now
not exactly tonight

"Now, I had not shaken the pumpkin before, had not sung before or sung before to a rattle: I had not done any of these things & it would have seemed foolish to me then to have done them. It did seem foolish but at a point I was doing them & it no longer seemed foolish, seemed necessary if anything..."

THE "WAY" OF CHANT

We begin to regard language too casually, thereby taking it for granted, and we forget the sacredness of it. Losing this regard, we become quite careless with how we use and perceive with language. We forget that language beyond its mechanics is a spiritual force.

When you regard the sacred nature of languge, then you realize that you are part of it and it is part of you, and you are not necessarily in control of it.

...

The song as expression is an opening from inside of yourself to outside and from outside of yourself to inside, but not in the sense that there are separate states of yourself. Instead, it is a joining and an opening together. Song is the experience of that opening, or road if you prefer, and there is no separation of parts, no division between that within you and that without you, as there is no division between expression and perception.

...

My father...he sings...The feeling that I perceive is not only contained in the words; there is something surrounding the song, and it includes us. It is the relationship that we share with each other and with everything else...Indeed, the song was the road from outside of himself to inside—which is perception—and from inside of himself to outside—which is expression.

Simon Ortiz, poet of Acoma Pueblo

The group affords the chant—it is not the product of authorship.
Julien Puzey

Artistic skill is the combining of many levels of mind—unconscious, conscious, and external—to make a statement of their combination.
Gregory Bateson

While in the great seasonal Festivals we find ourselves once again living within the whole of nature and grasp—all at once—meanings which we never understood before, we cannot hold onto them without words. As Susanne Langer explains: "Without words our imagination cannot retain distinct objects and their relations." Without words we cannot share with others the particular emotion that we experienced and without sharing we cannot hear from them what they experienced either. Thus the clarity of such an experience cannot be carried over into daily life to provide the grounding needed for real living. It all becomes merely a fuzzy glow of "good feelings."

Chanting is the "way" we find the words. In fact, chanting goes much deeper than that. It turns out, as shown in Part II, that through chanting we, humans began to speak. This is the basis of being human: out of speech came all the later human culture. Langer postulates a primitive human who has just seen something extraordinary letting out an involuntary sound. Another human present may, in fact, make the same sound. "The two creatures would look at one another with a light of understanding dawning under their great brow-ridges." They would repeat the sound, grinning with delight. More might join in with this new game. The sound would soon become rhythmical; thus even more "fun." As Langer remarks, "Such a wonderful 'fashion' would become immensely popular."

But words do not stand alone in speaking. "They tend to integrate, to make complex patterns, and thus to point out equally complex *relationships* in the world." Here we come to the crux of it: "for as soon as an object is denoted it can be *held*, so that anything else that is experienced at the same time, instead of crowding it out, exists *with* it, in contrast or

in unison or in some other definite way." In this manner an entire complex relationship of event and emotions and who was there, all can come together with one word. For instance the word, "River" could bring back the excitement of a dangerous crossing, which person almost drowned and who was the rescuer. All of this is recalled with one word. I have greatly abbreviated Langer's account, here, but I hope you can see how this same process can continue in chanting, today.

When a group has experienced a ritual event together, more things happen all at once than any one person can possibly comprehend. But much of this registers subliminally. Getting together to chant, letting out tones and primitive ohs and ahs, rhythmically, can focus some of these happenings. Partly because someone remembers, that is exactly the sound they made; others pick up on it and soon there is a word where no word was before. Others recognize that the word works for what they want to say, too. The entire group then picks it up, and rhythmically playing with that word, or a string of words, a chant begins. And their world is created anew—again. This is the unexpected joy.

Brenneman helps us here when he writes: "Groans and tones are exclusively instinctual in their nature while chant begins to move out of the instinctual area as it moves toward the point where unconscious and conscious modalities meet, i.e., as it moves toward consciousness." Essentially such "groans and tones" come out of instinctual or automatic needs of the human organism. They are related to such things as sudden joy, anger or fear or sexual desire. But when sounded in the group and rhythmically picked up on by others, such sounds turn into words and eventually into chant, automatically. No conscious thought is necessary at this stage. In fact, it can end the entire process. Conscious thought comes in later, as the group plays with what has been given to them by the chant process and refines it.

Chant is the mechanism which facilitates communication between our conscious brain and the older brains within us (the source of real creativity). At the great seasonal festivals when the group has been out together in their own place, things are picked up at the unconscious level directly from the land and plants and animals which are not registered, consciously, at all. Too much is going on at once. But, afterwards when the group begins to chant together, much of this unconscious material can surface and become conscious and embeded in the chant. Then with these words, given to us by the chant, we begin to recognize the *Li*, the pattern, of that place and how the plants and animals mirror it and thus how we humans can begin to fit into it.

That is when we begin learning our songs from nature. In the Blackfoot tribe in the old days, Wissler writes: "A man may be walking along and hear a bird, insect, stone or something else singing; he remembers the song and claims it as especially given to him." Once you begin chanting, you'll find that this is the "most natural thing in the world."

Jerome Rothenberg explains: "Anything, in fact, can deliver a song because anything—night, mist, the blue sky, east, west...the sexual organs of men and women...etc. is alive. Here is the central image of shamanism and all 'primitive' thought, the intuition of a connected and fluid universe, as alive as a man is—just that much alive." This is exactly how the "techniques of the 'sacred' can persist" in our world today, "not as nostalgia for the archaic past but (as Snyder writes) 'a vehicle to ease us into the future'."

Types of chanting

So far I've been writing about chant as it's always been done—by primitive or traditional groups throughout human history—where it is concerned with work, play, sex and the sacred all at once. In later times chanting often became more specialized and devoted to specific ends:

Spiritual chanting. Essentially, the purpose of this type of chanting is to disassociate the brain from the other aspects of your body so that you can rise to so-called "higher" levels and focus on an abstraction—whether a god or otherwise. You do get out of the rational hemisphere and that is a step in the right direction. But once you get into the unconscious, this type of chanting uses that very unconscious to reach the so-called spiritual level thus cutting you off deliberately from this earth and all its beings. The origin of this "spiritual" chanting as used in Hinduism and later, in Buddhism came from the individual clans chanting the Vedas, long ago in the sub-continent of India. But as these Aryan invaders got more organized, the priestly class separated more from the others and the chants became more and more narrowly spiritual. When the Hindu and Buddhist sects migrated to this country during the sixties this type of chanting was very popular. The real danger is, that in the hands of a skilled manipulator, all these chants become mechanisms for focusing the energy of the group onto the leader. After you have done the real traditional earth chants you will recognize this tactic immediately by the effect it has on you, but until you have more experience in chanting, be aware of the danger.

In our European heritage we have Gregorian chanting as done by monks and nuns of the Christian church for hundreds of years. This too, originally came out of the on-going primitive tradition, but again, got side-tracked by "specialists" into serving higher "spiritual" purposes. It can have healing aspects, but definitely does not ground you on this earth.

Healing Chants. Still another type of chanting is used for healing. Shamanic types, who healed themselves developed this type of chanting. Some of it deals with very concrete energy fields in the body and thus promotes healing. If you wish to learn this type of chanting you should go to a person who can teach you because it's not easy to develop on your own. Futhermore, because of the power of this chanting it is dangerous to learn on your own as sometimes you are in levels where only a skilled person can help you.

Work Chants. Traditional cultures "conducted such collective tasks as hoeing, paddling, ploughing, reaping, and hauling to a rhythmic chant which has an artistic content related to the needs of the task, and expressing the collective emotion behind the task." To us modern Americans, the most familiar examples of this type of chant come from black laborers who kept their work chants long after the slaves were freed. Chanting is what kept them sane. You will find when your group begins chanting, that work chants will again surface whenever people are working together at something strenuous.

The deeper aspects of earth chanting

Once you get into the "way" of chanting you will discover that it connects all the many aspects of life which, in our culture, never seem to fit together. There is no way that I can go into all of these connections here; instead I will devote a few paragraphs to what I feel are three of the most important aspects: ecology, psychology and Chuang Tzu's teachings from Taoism.

The anthropologist, Roy Rappaport, explains the difference between the actual natural environment in which people live and what their "thinking about" that environment leads them to believe. He works from the word, "cognized" which means "to know." He defines the "cognized model" as a "description of people's knowledge of their environment and of their beliefs concerning it." The "operational model," on the other hand describes the same ecological system, including the people and their activities but from the point of view of real ecology, which deals with the actual relationships within a particular ecosystem. Rappaport explains that the public affairs in the present Industrial Growth Society "are guided more by the assumptions of formal economics than by those of any other discipline." While economics claims to be based on descriptions of processes coming out of "precultural and quintessential human nature"; actually, of course, rather than having anything to do with real human nature, these processes are simply "operating instructions for establishing and maintaining conditions that will reproduce" humans who are merely consumers of things. This basic attitude of "industrialized capitalism, which must expand to remain stable" has now reached the proportions where it is obvious that such a system must violate nature to continue. Essentially then, the premises underlying everything we hear from the media, everything we learn in school, practically everything we are exposed to in this entire culture, lead to dehumanized people and destroyed natural environment, inevitably—not by accident. When stated this way it becomes obvious why it proves so difficult to save even a tiny bit of the natural environment. The entire culture is against it! How do we go about changing the basic way in which we know, when all day, every day, everything around us programs us the wrong way?

Rappaport provides us with the glimmerings of the direction to take to get out of this trap when he writes: "But, as the impoverishment of meaning deadens life and threatens its continuity, so may the richness of life be enhanced and its continuity abetted by cognized models that permit distinctions to multiply, metaphors to prosper, and the experience of unity to flourish." A "true cognized model" leads people to "act in ways that are in harmony with natural processes." Cognized models develop both from what we hear and what we say; and that's why chanting is so important. Rappaport writes that the "degradation and abandonment of ritual" at the present time "contributes to social and environmental problems." I agree, of course, and this work deals with those problems at a deep level. But right here I want to be very specific about the way to begin to move out of the narrow, meaningless life as mere "economic man." Chant can do it for us. It's that powerful!

By chanting I mean not only that you begin learning chants and chanting together with friends on festival days and full moon days, but even more important, you let chant change your very thinking by opening yourself to chanting whenever it wants to come—in your daily life. I know from personal experience that getting into the habit of chanting whenever your deep unconscious self wants to do it, will tell you how to make decisions that day; will tell you what is really bothering you; and will keep you in touch with the greater world of nature even in the city. This seems like a large order, but give it a try. I never believed it myself until it began to happen a few years ago. Then, writing this book, I was able to "scientifically" prove it to myself. When I was stuck—usually because I had too much data and too much I thought needed to be said—a chant would come into my head and it would tell me what I needed to say in that place in the book in order to provide the most help to those trying to save nature. Remember, you don't always have to chant out loud. In fact often you'd better not!

The chant that I recommend most strongly for daily life is: "Nobody knows."(See page 281 for this chant.) This chant prevents rash decisions, acting on merely human ideas, and perfectionism. It literally begins turning your life over to all of nature around you. It not only provides you with a censor of the nonsense heard on television but also a coyote-type trickster to laugh at it. The next time you hear something from the Industrial Growth Society's media, begin chanting "The trees know, the birds know, the river flows." You'll be amazed at how clear it becomes that it's "merely human" nonsense that you are hearing.

The Jungian, psychologist, James Hillman, assures us that "myth and poetry, so altogether verbal and 'fleshless' nonetheless resonate with the deepest intimacies of organic existence." He praises this "soul speech" and "its self-generative spontaneity, its precise subtlety and ambiguous suggestion." It cannot be replaced by either modern "communication media, by contemplative spiritual silence or by physical gestures and signs." Most important of all, "The more we hold back from the risk of speaking because of the semantic anxiety that keeps the soul in secret incommunicado …the greater grows the credibility gap between what we are and what we say." This splits us—both within our own self—and from all of nature. As you all know, sometimes it is very difficult to say something real. But when the group gets together to chant familiar chants, sooner or later one of the chants will remind you of what you most need to say. And then as this chant is repeated you can throw in a word you need. Others pick up on it and soon it becomes a matter of common understanding. This difficult thing that you could not explain, becomes known by all and can be spoken about and the fear leaves. More than that, you often find that others in the group share this very fear or hope and that brings about the overflowing abundance of joy which continually happens in chanting.

In chanting one can be totally oneself and yet totally with all the others. For once, there seems to be no dichotomy; and one is "surprised by joy." Often I say to myself, "Tonight it doesn't seem like it's going to happen. Not tonight; not the way I feel." And then the chanting begins and it happens yet again. Since I've begun chanting I've often wondered, philosophically, how this can be explained. It turns out that Chuang Tzu can help us to understand this matter. At first, it seems that being totally oneself would be egoism and that would mean that your ego would be over against all the other egos and there would be conflict. That's because in our culture, egos are lived as exclusive of one another. These exclusive egos naturally clash with one another and problems result. So it's not so much the ego that's the problem as the "exclusiveness" of the egos. "Chuang Tzu says, in essence, that egos are mutually exclusive, not because they are born so, but because they are molded so, or rather, intruded into becoming so." At birth, the ego is neither exclusive nor inclusive; "they are born non-exclusive." We need to find our way "back to this non-exclusive togetherness." Wu explains: "In Chuang Tzu's mind, becoming oneself need hardly imply coming into conflict with others. Self-becoming means, instead, for each to become truly himself, which could well mean for each to become himself *together*."

In Chapter 8, Chuang Tzu contrasts "*chien pi*, looking at others, with *tzu chien*, looking, not at oneself, but of oneself." To look at oneself means treating oneself as an object. Immediately there's a "suicidal dichotomy. For one can only look *at* what is separate(d) from one, an object. Looking at oneself then requires that one be separated from oneself." Of course it's impossible to really look at oneself as if you stood outside so what you are really doing is looking at yourself as reflected back by what others think of you—similar to when you are looking at the mirror reflecting an image back to you. "And so self-look is an unjustifiable intrusion of others into oneself." It therefore destroys "the natural self."

What we call selfishness is bad because it is really "a look at oneself in the light of others." One begins to want what others think is important: wealth or fame etc. One begins losing sight of the real self entirely; thus, relying totally on what others think one should want. This mentality leads to everyone competing for the same things so, obviously, some are excluded. "Morality," Wu explains, "is an exclusion of oneself to please and benefit others. Such acts not only harm oneself; they hurt others also. For morality (and to some extent talent also) is a means of enticing others, that is, an intrusion into others. Such an intrusion into oneself and others spells exclusion of both. Exclusion of the self is suicide, and exclusion of others, conflict."

The answer is that one must not indulge in selfish "looking-at-oneself, that is, allowing others to mirror into oneself." One must become neither intrusive nor inclusive, but instead, "return home to the self-world of a being-of-oneself, a doing-of-oneself, and a sensing-of-oneself. It is this sort of 'naive' or natural egoism that Chuang Tzu advocates, a non-intrusive selfishness which does no violence either to oneself or to others." This doing violence is what causes anger and conflict. Chuang Tzu's version of natural egoism is a "sure cure for conflict, and this means that being one-self naturally is the way to an authentic sociality." Because one is true to one's own self, one does not have to "use" others in any way. If everyone is totally being oneself there results a mutual sense of worth that builds up in everyone concerned, which leads to the unexpected gift of joy, that can happen in chanting.

What is it that happens in chanting that sends one out reinspired—that makes it feel as if all aspects of your world: nature, self and others are working together with no effort? The feeling of abundance generated by chanting spills over into your daily life and it, too, becomes more real. Chuang Tzu talks about "the piping of men, the piping of earth and the piping of heaven" and resonance between each of these pipings. Wu explains further: "For the Real is that which is 'not-*yet* to begin not-yet to begin,' the piping of heaven that rustles forth the piping of earth, that in turn engender the piping of men." That seems to truly happen in chanting. Things happen that you never knew you knew, events occur that you never dreamed of and you really feel there are no words for it all. But then, as the chanting continues and everyone is "saying-it-anyway-though-unsayable" it all comes together and you are saying it—chanting it together. Creating it by saying it and all together doing it. "Such is the capturing of the Pristine world of Full life . . . that leaves no records," Chuang Tzu tells us. This is on-going, creative, real culture changing with the seasons and by the seasons; yet deeply grounded in the earth, always.

The Earth poet, Gary Snyder, explains: "We're just starting, in the last ten years here, to begin to make songs that will speak for plants, mountains, animals and children. When you see your first deer of the day you sing your salute to the deer, or your first red-wing blackbird—I saw one this morning! Such poetries will be created by us as we reinhabit this land with people who know they belong to it . . . They will be created as we learn to see, region by region, how we live specifically (plant life!) in each place."

Chanting to connect with all of nature

For those just beginning chanting as a "way" to connect with the natural world, I want to show you how chanting worked, for us, on three different occasions out in nature. The first story concerns a friend of mine, Bill Plotkin, a psychotherapist who lives fifty miles from here in Durango, Colorado. We've worked together in a number of outdoor ritual settings. He conducts Vision Quests several times a year. This particular Vision Quest happened to have only one woman; the rest were men. When they reached the desert, the preliminary rituals went fairly well but when they began to get their things together to go off for their solo time, the men began punning and joking (as is usual among men when there is tension). While punning and joking can be an important asset in certain ceremonial times; it is not helpful at this point in the Vision Quest. Bill told me that he just didn't know how to get this situation together quick enough to send them off in the proper frame of mind/body to accept what nature might give them.

In his inner turmoil, he felt a longing to be absorbed by the canyon and he remembered a feeling he once had out in nature: it was a sheltering—one might say—nourishing feeling. Physically, while thinking back on it, he told me that it felt like an arm around his shoulder. He wondered how to give that feeling to them at that moment. Then he remembered a nearby place which my son, David, who also leads Vision

Quests, had shown him the previous year. He asked everyone to be silent for the opening walk into the wilderness and led them in single file toward that place. On the way they stopped once. Crystal, the only woman present, led them in a few Tai Chi movements for centering. Bill had them practice the Om chant, because it's the one most people are likely to know.

When they got to the spot, the rock formations curved out a bit at both ends and they made a circle within this arc, facing out to the open desert with the rocks at their back. Bill had the first person chant the first word, the second person chanted the second word etc. around the circle. This "got them right out of the punning and into the real," is the way Bill explained it. Since their packs were already with them, they picked them up and went off, each in his own direction to look for the place for the solo time.

The second chanting event I want to share with you occurred on our annual Taoist Autumn Equinox. The previous year was the first time we had chanted during this event; therefore, the following year we were more familiar with the best specific sites for chanting. This event occurred on the second day, after our climb of Dragonback Mountain to watch the sun set on Autumn Equinox. Throughout that day on the mountain we chanted often. When we returned to town, everyone cleaned up, ate dinner and returned to the Center. The session began quite spontaneously. The chant, "Ancient One," had just come to one of the participants, Julien, that morning at breakfast. (For this chant, see p.280) During the day, Jackie who helps with the Festivals here, had been able to get the chant into music. So we were going to put it all together and chant it. It turned out to be so powerful and tapped so much of what had happened to us out on the mountain that we just kept going. Most of the people had never chanted before. We had only two drums, but everyone had rattles of some sort. And as the chanting continued everyone opened up more and more, the chanting got more powerful and the circling of energy became easier and easier. All felt the growing joy. Then, at a break in the chanting, Rosie, a participant from West Virginia, just broke out with sheer joy. She said something like, "I had always hoped everyone could do music together all at once with no one trying and no one forcing and here we are doing it. I can't believe it. It's never happened before." What she said was actually much closer to poetry than this; but no one wrote it down. Rosie's ancestry is Welsh I found out later. This chanting experience put her back into touch with her Welsh bardic heritage, which she didn't even know she had; but once it surfaced it became "the most natural thing in the world."

We all glowed that she had so beautifully put into words what we all felt. The energy was so good that no one could go home. We finally went outside and chanted along the Animas River. I want to make it clear that we had been out on the mountain all day. Most of these people were from sea level and none of them strong hikers. But the chanting gave such energy that they weren't even tired at midnight.

The third occasion took place on BREAKING THROUGH. I mentioned this annual workshop I do, earlier in this work. The summer of 1986 was the first time I decided to do chanting. I was loathe to begin because it involved still more items to pack along, but I got enough medicine bottles together and put half an inch of split peas into each one. This made light, unbreakable substitutes for rattles. We had a very disparate group that year. When we all gathered at the river base on the Arkansas River I really wondered: "How will we ever get this group together?" First of all we had an unusually high ratio of introverts (thus too few extroverts). Too many extroverts can be very difficult, but too few means not enough interplay among them to get everyone laughing. In addition to this unbalanced ratio we had one single teenager and a male at that. Furthermore it had not been his idea at all; his father had given him several alternatives and this seemed the least unpleasant to him. Ordinarily we don't take teenagers on BREAKING THROUGH for a number of reasons, primarily to do with safety.

We all got into the van and drove to the ranch site where we always begin. It gets us into the mountains quickly and we can see the high 14,000 foot peaks, which we climb later, in the distance; yet it's warm at night so that people are comfortable on their first night in the Rockies. We do a number of getting acquainted techniques and bring in firewood and all work together getting dinner going. All of this helps to get everyone talking together. After dinner the first night is usually the most difficult, because everyone is still getting acquainted and thus unsure and uneasy. I brought out the bag filled with "medicine bottle rattles" and just walked around the circle passing them out, remarking: "We'll be doing chanting tonight." I was purposely abrupt. Although the BREAKING THROUGH brochures say that there will be ritual and Tai Chi, some of the people going on it are there mainly for the mountain and white water rafting aspects. Then we began. And it worked. The sounding rattles of the three of us who had done it before, reached the depths inside everyone there in the fire-lit darkness and they couldn't resist joining in. Our teenager nervously looked around for a few minutes, but everyone was doing it and no one was looking at him so he joined right in and had a great time. Soon people asked for certain chants to be repeated, asked about where these chants came from and commented about how good it felt. And chanting became a part of our lives for the next week.

Spontaneous bits of chant came out on scary parts of the climb. Someone would chant out "The trees know, the birds know" as we became temporarily confused on the route. I have told this event in some detail because I want to show that when you first introduce chanting to a group, the less said the better. Still lingering in the mind of many people is the thought that chanting and rattles are "primitive" and somehow dangerous and just "not done." But once they begin, it always becomes easier and easier because it's built into our body/brain from at least a hundred thousand years of doing it.

Basic Earth Chants

Below are the words and music written out for five of the chants I've found most useful when out in nature. Each of them has its roots in a very old traditional culture but some of them have been changed a bit by us. In general music has strict copyright rules but chant neither should nor can be copyrighted. If it is a real true chant then we learned it from the "old ones"—

American Indians, Huichols, and sometimes the plants, the animals and the earth herself will give us a chant. Those coming directly from the old cultures were recorded by ethnographers mostly in the nineteenth century and can be found in government publications. If someone deliberately and consciously tries to make up a chant, it is not a true chant. It might be used for awhile but it drops out of use rather quickly because it has no roots. This type of chant could possibly be copyrighted but it would be unethical, if not illegal, at the deepest level because the person claiming copyright would be lying; since a chant, by definition, cannot be just made up by one human or even a group of humans. It can, of course, come out of a real culture over a period of generations; or it can come to any of us directly from nature when we "allow" it to happen.

Actually, chanting is very Taoist, something is not there at one moment, and shortly it takes form and finds expression and it's there. No one person does it, no one talks about it, no one tries but there it is! The simplest procedure is to just keep chanting the same chant until people spontaneously begin throwing in words. These words begin circling around and forming the new meaning, the new way of living which everyone takes away with them from the chant session. The melody of the old chants always works best for this process.

I CIRCLE AROUND

I CIR-CLE A-ROUND I CIR-CLE A-ROUND THE
BOUND-ARIES OF THE EARTH
WEA-RING MY LONG WINGED FEA-THERS AS I FLY
WEA-RING MY LONG WINGED FEA-THERS AS I FLY I
CIR-CLE A-ROUND I CIR-CLE A-ROUND THE
BOUND-ARIES OF THE EARTH

This chant and all those below transcribed by Diana Harper Paioff.

This chant is actually from the Arapahoe tribe but it comes out of the Ghost Dance tradition. In the western United States there was an eclipse of the sun in January of 1889, which brought about the vision of the Paiute sheepherder, Wavoka. "When the sun died," he said that he went up to heaven and saw God and "all the people who had died a long time ago." God told him to tell the people that they must not fight, steal, or lie and he "gave me this dance to give to my people." This was the start of the Ghost Dance movement. They were to dance five days and five nights. When they fell into trance they saw their dead relatives returning and saw also the vast herds of buffalo coming back. The movement spread rapidly throughout the West. At the battle of Wounded Knee, many Sioux were killed and the movement lost its impetus but it's chants and dreams still linger on. It is thought that the chant is the returning dead coming down to rejoin those below here on earth.

When chanted for some time, the chant begins to dissolve the "boundaries" we've artificially set up around our single individual person in this Eurocentric culture. The longer you chant the more the boundaries of the self extend. But this is not some airy, spacy "spiritual" concept. It occurs only because you are grounded in that particular place where you are circling around, circling around, chanting and chanting. "To have an identity or self in any lively sense," Silas Goldean writes,

> means understanding the contingencies of other identities and appreciating the relations connecting life to life...such an understanding requires [roots] in much the same way that flowers require roots. Identity is not an airy generalization; it is grounded in the specifics of daily living...blood and soil and sun. The only way to grasp this is to live somewhere long enough to attend the complexity of living relationships. You can't fuck on a dead run. You can't join the owl's spirit by watching it on the Wide World of Animals. You can't appreciate the seasonal qualities of moonlight without spending those seasons with the moon...
>
> Practiced in place, the extension of identity becomes the realization of community, and as place turns into home, the heart opens like a seed.

As you "circle around, circle around the boundaries," your self extends to include the trees around you, then the mountains surrounding the trees and then the sky curving over all. This is Aldo Leopold's "land ethic" which simply enlarges "the boundaries of the community to include soils, waters, plants, and animals, or collectively: the land."

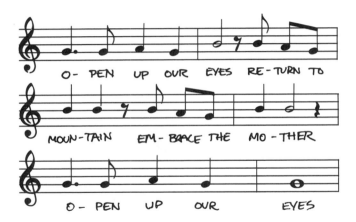

This chant came through Julien, one of those participating in the Autumn Equinox celebration. It came to her as we spent the day: first climbing up Dragonback Mountain; then doing Tai Chi on the rock ledges, looking out over the high snowfields above timberline and the golden aspen filling the valleys below; then chanting among the aspen; stumbling through the downed trees over to the cliffs, where we sit in the only "safe place" and chant, while we watch the setting sun slide out of sight behind the golden mountain. After that we hurried down through slide rock so we could reach the valley before darkness caught us on the mountain. That's why

> We are so weary
> We have travelled far

Through all this she was conscious of the "ancient one" deep inside who showed her how to do things she'd never done before—slide down talus slopes for instance, swing from aspen branch to aspen branch, to keep from falling off the mountain on a steep traverse. Once safely down to the valley we repeat the closing movements of Tai Chi and

> Return to Mountain
> Embrace the Mother   (two Tai Chi forms)

All the events of this full day

> Open up our eyes.

Here's an example of how nature herself gives you the chant. During the day from time to time, we talk of deep, philosophical matters as well. In this sense, "Ancient One," comes from when I mentioned Jung's remark about "the 2 million year-old man in all of us" and how our difficulties "come from losing contact with our instincts, with the age-old unforgotten wisdom stored up in us." Mother Earth is present, as well, in every part of this chant.

This chant, used in the peyote ceremony of the Huichol Indians in Mexico, has even more levels of meaning than the other chants listed here. To begin with it is chanted on the ritual journey back to Wirikura where they gather the sacred peyote, "the place of the Ancient Ones, where it all began." According to Huichol mythology, when they reach Wirikura, all "divisions dissolve" and that includes the division between humans and animals and plants and between humans and particular parts of the land. In fact, the animals and plants and the land teach the humans; that's why "the trees know," "the birds know," the "river flows." Victor Turner explains that in the state of "communitas" achieved in Wirikura, "they become, transiently... founders, initiators, unencumbered by the cultural baggage they normally rely upon and prize." Hence, "where I'm going nobody knows" comes to mean no human knows what will happen there, what new meanings will infuse their daily life when they return.

NOBODY KNOWS

"The sacred is a natural condition for the 'true Huichol.' It flows in and out of the mundane." Just as "the river flows." This chant is also used in the "fly the children" ceremony, when the tiny children journey, gourd rattle in hand, through the air to Wirikura. (See chapter eleven) To a small child, the "trees know, the birds know" much more than he or she does.

I've found that this chant provides the easiest vehicle for dissolving the boundaries between the human and the rest of nature. When chanted for a long time outside, around the fire, the "merely human" rational hemisphere readily relinquishes control and it's not difficult at all to understand that "the trees know" and, that, if we approach them with sufficient reverence the trees will help us to know as well.

A second level of this chant concerns the times in one's life where there is "an agonizing situation of conflict from which there seems no way out"; not for the conscious mind anyway where everything has to be either one way or the other. Things have to be either yes or no. "But," as Jung says, "out of this collision of opposites the unconscious psyche always creates a third thing of an irrational nature, which the conscious mind neither expects nor understands." How could it? The conscious mind can know nothing beyond the opposites so it cannot know what lies in the depths which unites them. But when the solution to a conflict is so longed for and hoped for, the conscious mind begins to have "some inkling of the creative act, and of the significance of it." But it is frightened of this unknown new thing, deep inside. Often the more the solution is longed for, the more frightening the uncertainty becomes. That's when you chant: "Where I'm going nobody

knows" and the rest of it over and over. Very shortly it becomes obvious that while you don't consciously know, the deep nature inside of you knows just as much as nature outside of you—the tree or the bird knows. This chant puts you into a state of receptivity without anxiety and thus the resolution of the conflict follows. Then comes the joy and thankfulness. As Jung remarks, "all uniting symbols have a redemptive significance."

A third level of the chant occurs when it is used on a ritual walk out in nature or on a pilgrimage. Such events are, by nature, full of many conflicting emotions—humor, a bit of fear at strange natural things, joy, wonder, etc. This chant provides the perfect transition between any or all of these emotions. It reinforces humor, when everyone laughs in thinking about what the "deer droppings" know, that we don't know. It focuses wonder; for example when standing before a strange rock outcrop that almost speaks to you. Then when things get totally outrageous and the punning is going just great but something truly unexpected and awesome suddenly comes in view, just beginning the chant changes the feeling back to the sacred without any jarring whatsoever. It all "flows."

This chant is very powerful when used as a healing chant—either when alone or in a healing group. It readily allows the sick or injured parts of a person to begin to furnish you with information your conscious brain ordinarily resists and thus begins the healing process.

The last aspect I'm going into here concerns the usefulness of the chant in groups out in nature. After everyone learns it and feels good chanting it, each person can interject something of nature which they encountered that day and want to share with the group. This becomes fun and deep at the same time. "The clouds know," "the columbine knows," the "mud knows" etc. The possibilities are both endless and surprisingly creative in the long run. In fact, often this chant gives people the first glimmerings of how a true place oriented culture develops spontaneously, right now!

The last two chants concern how we learn from specific animals—the eagle, who is either a god or a messenger of the gods in many primitive groups around the world and the bear.

"We all fly like eagles" is a natural for chanting on the way up a mountain or on top. Here I will just go into how we use it on BREAKING THROUGH. After we have been together for some days at the ranch and white water rafting on the Arkansas River for two days we pack into the high country. The first mountain we go up is "Broken Hand"—a fairly short climb, with alternating rock cliffs and beautiful flower-filled tundra. After we've been hiking up the steep trail on the approach to the mountain for an hour or so we come to a magnificent rock overlook. A sweeping ramp of green tundra leads right out onto it. But when you get to the edge you have a sudden drop off right down several thousand feet. Here Rick leads us in his "eagle rising" which he developed out of Tai Chi. It's quite easy to follow. After the ritual nine times repeating the raising and lowering of our "wings," it concludes with the Tai Chi final movement where our open hands are pushed down toward the earth while our body rises up. And "we all fly like eagles." Incredible sensation! After that we chant "We all fly like eagles" as we continue on up the mountain. The chant stays with us the rest of the day—to be used when someone is suddenly a bit afraid in a difficult spot or when someone is suddenly "surprised by joy." The wonderful thing is that with this chant your emotions are instantly shared by all the rest.

WE ALL FLY LIKE EAGLES

I do not need to go any further into the many levels of this chant as they become instantly obvious once you learn it.

BEAR CHANT

Our chant developed out of a few lines from the famous Sioux bear chant, which Frances Densmore recorded long ago. Some years ago when I climbed in the Canadian Rockies, we would see bear on the trail ahead or crossing near us. It was thrilling but not scary because we carried rattling tin cups tied to our pack so we wouldn't suddenly surprise them. This was what the old timers told us to do and it seemed to work. Though now, with so many tourists in Canada many bears are addicted to garbage and it's a whole different thing. Here in the San Juans, we've had several sightings of bear around Silverton in recent years; although I've not actually seen one. But even when I just see bear sign, my home country suddenly seems real wilderness! It jolts me right awake and I suddenly become totally alert and alive. Bear adds another dimension whenever we encounter him.

This has been so since humans were first on this earth. "Around the northern hemisphere, wherever he migrated, man found the paw prints of the bear," Paul Shepard writes in his book, *The Sacred Paw*. He seems to be "humanlike; yet close to the animals and hence to the source of life." The sacred paw of the slain bear was an important symbol in most human societies. Bear has for so long influenced our unconscious that there are forty-four meanings in fourteen different categories for the verb, "to bear," ranging from "bearing children" to "bearing responsibilities." As Shepard notes, "we can...see that, deep in our unconscious where language 'means' in multiple ways, the bear's sacredness is still part of our lives."

After reading Shepard's book some of us began talking more about bear and I brought out my notes from the Bureau of American Ethnology and found the Sioux bear chant. The next time we got together to chant I showed them to my friend, Jackie. She began mulling the words over on her walks in the nearby hills and came up with this chant. It does seem to invoke bear for us whenever we need to feel his power in our lives.

Three of these chants are on "The Circle" chant tape which can be bought from Way of the Mountain Center: I Circle Around, Nobody Knows and We All Fly Like Eagles. The other two chants: Ancient One and The Bear Chant are on a tape made during one of our Autumn Equinox chant sessions. It's just a spur of the moment tape; but, in case you don't read music, at least you can learn the chants from it.

THE "WAY" OF THE DRUM

The chief drummer at a dance in the Benue-Cross River area (Africa) maintains a running commentary on the dance, controls the linedancers with great precision, calls particular persons by name to dance solo, tells them what dance to do, corrects them as they do it, and sends them back into line with comment on the performance. He does this by making his drum talk, even above the sound of four or five other drums in the 'orchestra'.

R. G. Armstrong

In the Introduction to this chapter I told how, despite my misgivings about an all-night trance dance, my feet began to move as soon as I crossed the threshold into the room and the sound of the big ceremonial drum went through me, moving me, literally. I will go more into the actual dance in the section below; here, I want to explain the after-effect of the drum. The dance ended at sunrise. The procedure was for everyone to take a brief time to wind down and then a short nap, followed by the breakfast feast and then the ritual weekend would be ended. I was overdue on meeting a writing deadline and knew I'd better leave, immediately, because I had a six hour drive back and should get to work. So I just walked out, unobtrusively, after clearing it with Elizabeth, got in the car and began driving north from Albuquerque toward Silverton. Then came the surprise, that big drum stayed with me—sounding just as loud in my head as it had during the dance—for two whole hours. In fact, it stayed with me until I stopped to fill up with gas. That's the power of the drum.

Background on Drumming

Since that day I've searched out everything I could find about the use of drumming in ritual and the neurophysiological events going on in the body/brain to bring this about. Below I will give some insights into what I discovered.

DRUMMING BY OUR ANCESTORS, THE CHIMPS

Drumming came to us from our ancestors, the higher primates. Many accounts of chimps drumming on hollow logs have come to us from research in Africa, but the most sophisticated chimp "drum" of all concerns the chimps of the Budongo Forest. It could be called an earth drum. The chimps carried damp clay from the bank of a nearby stream and spread it out over porous earth (somewhat like a peat bog). The researchers could see the finger-prints of the apes, still preserved in the clay after it dried. When the clay dried, the peaty stuff underneath acted as a resonance cavity and the ground itself became a drum. At night the chimps came together and "the carnival begins." Several chimps beat on the dry clay drum while others "utter long, rolling sounds, as if trying to sing. When one tires of beating the drum, another relieves him, and the festivities continue in this fashion for hours."

SHAMANIC DRUMMING

The classic book on shamanism by Eliade, *Shamanism: Archaic Techniques of Ecstasy*, has considerable material on shamanic use of the drum and he refers to the shaman "riding" the drum to ecstasy. But I found more succinct insight from an article by Eliade in *The History of Religions*, where he refers to a Russian study of Siberian shamans. In the ceremony, "animating the drum," when the Altaic shaman sprinkles it with beer, the shell of the drum "comes to life" and, through the shaman, relates how the tree of which it was a part grew in the forest, how it was cut, brought to the village and so on. When the shaman sprinkles the drum skin, it comes to life and tells of its past as an animal. It ends the account by "promising the shaman that it will do him many services." This animal is often connected with the origin of the tribe. By drumming, the shaman "rides" the drum to the cosmic tree; but also by way of the "re-animated" skin of the drum, the shaman is able to take part in the nature of the original ancestor.

Eliade states that the "oldest forms of shamanism in western Europe" can be found in the caves of Lascaux (about 25,000 years old). It can be considered that our European ancestors used the drum at least as far back as that date. The drum has been used by practically every culture from the Arctic to the tropics.

NEUROPHYSIOLOGICAL ASPECTS OF DRUMMING

In The British Anthropological Journal, *Man*, Rodney Needham investigates why the drum is the single most commonly used item in rituals. From the time of that original article, there have been a vast number of other papers replying to him, criticising him or giving further facts. In fact I discovered that a full-scale academic battle had been going on for some time concerning the drum, which encompassed the fields of anthropology, biology and sociology. I won't take the time to go into the whole thing here; instead I will just list the findings that are relevant to our modern day use of the drum in ritual. It is very interesting, however, that none of these men ever took the obvious step of actually playing the drum themselves to see what effect it had on them. Instead there was laboratory research done on its effects by the biologists and quotations of research pro and con among those in other fields; as well as tabulating the effect on the "natives" in various parts of the world.

First of all, percussion is the important aspect here. The word percussion comes from the Latin *quatere*, to shake or strike. Percussive musical instruments such as drums cause vibrations within the human body just as thunder does. Percussive sound can be used to clearly indicate or mark a change. In voodoo in Haiti for instance, "It is the drummers who largely provoke dissociation; they are skillful in reading the signs, and by quickening, altering, or breaking their rhythm they can usually force the crisis on those dancers who are ready for it." This is stated in anthropological terms; for us, it is important to realize that drumming is the major factor in "affording" the possibility for the dancers to reach the trance state, together, and thus provide the bonding for the culture.

For a long dance there is a specific rhythm, which can carry the entire group all night long. If this rhythm is interrupted for very long by some other rhythm, the effect can be so jarring and unpleasant that the critical rational factor of the brain jumps right in and takes over control of the dancers. See below for further information on this aspect.

For ritual in general, the drum serves as a very efficient "marker" because "a change of rhythm is far more specific than a change of melody in denoting change of mood." Also the sudden change in rhythm, which a drum can produce, is a far better indicator than such things as gestures. Sight is more limited; it's not as pervasive as sound. In primitive cultures there are no deaf ritual specialists, but there are a number of blind ones.

The reason drumming can have such a powerful effect on us is that it produces "steep-fronted" sounds in a "wide range of audible acoustic frequencies." This is because a wide range of frequencies "stimulates the whole basilar membrane of the ear, transmitting impulses along many different nerve pathways to effect a larger area of the brain than would a note of a single frequency." Especially important in this age of so much noise that the human ears are damaged, is the fact that a drum beat contains mostly low frequencies. "The low frequency receptors of the ear are more resistant to damage than the delicate high frequency receptors and can withstand higher amplitudes of sound." I can say for sure that not only is there no damage to the ears, there is a positive soothing effect. There are many people that I know who drum for meditation, simply because it does have the overall effect of putting together many different parts of the brain as well as effortlessly preventing the rational, "merely human," aspect of the brain from taking over control.

The effect of repetitive stimuli on the brain, as mentioned above, cannot account for all the effects of ritual drumming. As shown in chapter twelve, the other effects come from "tuning." To review this briefly, here, the ergotropic system is the startle or "what-is-it" response associated with the sympathetic nervous system and readies one for fight or flight. The trophotropic system relaxes skeletal muscles, synchronizes cortical rhythms and is associated with the parasympathetic nervous system. It has to do with pleasurable states such as sleep, grooming in animals and relaxation. Generally speaking, if one of these subsystems is stimulated, excitation of the other is inhibited. Seemingly, both cannot operate at the same time. But, strong activation of the "fight or flight" system brought about by such actions as drumming, chanting and dancing produces such a strong effect on the ergotropic system that eventually the system becomes supersaturated and the other system, the relaxing system, is activated resulting in both systems, working at the same time. This condition is labelled "tuning" of the Central Nervous System by Gelhorn and colleagues. If stimulated long enough the next stage of tuning is reached where the "simultaneous strong discharge of both autonomic systems creates a state of stimulation of the median forebrain bundle, generating not only pleasurable sensation but in especially profound cases, a sense of union or oneness with all those present."

The criticism of Neher, who takes a biological approach in his article in *Human Biology*, seems to come mostly from those who disagree with his reporting of how many cycles per minute produce certain effects. It is not necessary to enter here into this controversy, because on the drumming tape, which Elizabeth Cogburn produced, there are samples of most of the important rhythms for rituals. By listening to what that particular rhythm does for you, you will know which ones are useful. (See Resources for ordering information).

CONNECTIONS BETWEEN THUNDER AND DRUMMING

There seems to be some connection between the effects of thunder and the effects of drumming for human beings. Thunder certainly has a powerful effect on many animals as well as humans. In some ways it can be fearful; but for most primitives it contributes to a sense of well-being also. Thunder signals spring to some cultures; brings rain for fertility in the fields; and ends hot drying winds for others. The Ute tribe in the western U.S. used to hold their "bear dance" when they heard the first thunder, because that signalled the beginning of spring as well as the time the bear comes out of winter hibernation. In a whole different part of the world, the Bimin-Kuskusmin deliberately time their rituals to coincide with the "predictable mountain thunder."

Thunder is a god in many cultures throughout the world.

In fact, Jehovah, the Jewish God who later became the Christian God, was originally a Cannanite storm god of the north. The drum and thunder do have similar vibratory effects on humans, but whether a particular culture interprets these effects as good or bad depends mostly on the culture itself and its relation to the whole of nature in its place.

Another aspect of drumming concerns the fact that we humans begin life in a syncopated world. The fetus floating in the womb, is surrounded by amniotic fluid, which carries sound far better than air. The baby's heartbeat is twice as fast as the mother's. These two steady beats, superimposed one upon the other produce a syncopated rhythm. This is the baby's entire world for many months. The drum is important to us in ritual dance because we are freed to move once again with the syncopated heartbeat of the world.

The fetus floating in the womb, with the thunderous sound of the two heartbeats rolling in on it, and the human out in nature with thunder sounding all around are in a similar situation. In both of these safety and danger coincide—a real union of opposites. A person in any traditional culture knows that thunder means rain—without which nothing lives—this is the fertilizing effect of the "sky father" on the womb of the "earth mother." Still the immediate sound of thunder fills one with awe. Likewise in the womb, there is loud sound all around but the very sound means on-going life—the heartbeat—as the fetus, safe in the womb, grows toward its birth into the outside world.

I'm not saying there is any direct connection here, but in the unconscious there may well be a connection. This would account for some of the fascination, fear, awe and yet wonder and attraction, which thunder holds for all humans.

European attitudes toward the drum

For many Europeans, as they set about conquering the so-called lower races, the drum was always that "infernal tom-tom" of the natives. They could hear no difference in drumming for war or drumming for celebration of new life in the spring. It was all the same to them. Some people still feel that way. They become uneasy when they hear the steady sound of a drum, because they fear it and will not accept it. The more one tries to withstand the rhythm of a drum, the more it bothers one.

I've found that one of the best ways to stop someone from manipulating the group, either for gaining attention or for control, is to bring out the drum. A steady, contemplative drum beat transmits so many impulses directly to the brain—all in a reassuring heart beat pattern—that each person in the room is temporarily freed from the on-going, continuous anxieties inherent in this culture and thus can no longer be easily manipulated. The manipulator, on the contrary, finds these same drum beats disorienting. He or she can no longer stay focused within their usual pattern of manipulation and soon must leave the room. Their excuse is the drum makes their head ache or the sound is "driving me crazy." Actually, the drum beat is interfering with their normal rational "control" over their own inner processes and everything outside, as well.

For those of us who now use the drum, it seems that "it's the most natural thing in the world." We forget that, in western

European cultures, it's only in the last fifty years, that a Western writer had anything good to say about the drum. Before that, it was simply either that infernal "tom tom" or a piece of data in an anthropologist's reports. Oddly enough, we find that the notoriously self-willed Mabel Luhan of Taos seems to lurk in the background of each of the men who, later, wrote favourably about the drum. Over a period of years she invited or lured a number of remarkable men to Taos. Years later, she explained what she had in mind quite plainly: "I wanted Lawrence to understand things for me. To take *my* experience, *my* material, *my* Taos, and to formulate it all into a magnificent creation." In this passage she refers only to Lawrence, but that was, of course, what she expected from C. G. Jung and Robinson Jeffers as well.

C. G. JUNG ON THE DRUM

In his autobiography, *Memories, Dreams, Reflections*, C. G. Jung wrote about the power of the drum that he felt when he attended a ceremony in a temple in India, which began with five men drumming together: "The drum speaks the ancient language of the belly and solar plexus." Some time after he went to India, he visited Taos at Mabel's invitation and, of course, heard the Taos Pueblo drumming, which further increased his respect for the drum.

D. H. LAWRENCE ON THE DRUM

When Mabel brought Lawrence to Taos, at first he lived in her compound; but later, he and Frieda, his wife, lived up at the little ranch, on the slopes of Lobo Mountain, which Mabel had given to Frieda. Mabel's Taos Indian husband, Tony Luhan helped Lawrence repair the ranch house and, in the twilight, after work was done for the day, Tony and his Indian friends would sing to the soft thudding of the drum around the fire while the Evening Star hung in the west over the ranch.

Later, when Lawrence wrote *The Plumed Serpent*, a novel about a cultural revolution brought about by a highly educated Mexican, that he names Don Ramon, he has him replace the ringing of church bells with the drum beat. The heroine in the book, Kate, sitting on the lake shore, hears the drum beat and thinks: "But the world was somehow different; all different." No ringing of church bells and no clock striking, "just the drum." In these few sentences Lawrence hints at the enormous changes implicit in moving from rigid clock time with metallic bells to drums timed to the natural rhythms of the day: dawn, first sun showing, sun highest in the sky and sunset. Kate decides that, "The drums seemed to leave the air soft and vulnerable, as if it were alive...no clang of metal..." Don Ramon's verses say, "Metal for resistance/ Drums for the beating heart."

Lawrence was in India on his way to Australia, the year before he first went to Taos. He has his heroine, Kate remembering when she first heard the drum in Ceylon: "The sound that waked dark, ancient echoes in the heart of every man, the thud of the primeval world...acting on the helpless blood direct." Later on, in *The Plumed Serpent*, Lawrence writes about how the bells call attention to the Christian Church standing there focusing all power onto itself; while the drum connects humans with their "circumambient universe" and with nature's changing cycles.

Lawrence described the full relationship created by ritual dancing to the drum, in his book, *Mornings in Mexico*, where he writes: "The drums keep up the pulsating heart-beat...and for hours, hours it goes on: the round dance...in the dark, near the fire...the pine-trees standing still, the everlasting darkness, and the strong lifting and dropping, surging...the pulsing, incalculable fall of the blood, which forever seeks to fall to the centre of the earth..back to the great central source where is...unspeakable renewal."

Just before Lawrence died, Mabel Luhan had sensed the underlying similarity of certain aspects of the work of Lawrence and Jeffers and hoped to bring them together. She did bring Jeffers to Taos. He, too, found the atmosphere around her not conducive to his work and soon left. He wrote only one poem about the Taos country, titled "New Mexican Mountain." Mabel had seen to it that he attended the Taos ritual where he watched the Indians "dancing up the corn." He notes in the poem that the young men were very reluctantly dancing with no heart in it; while the old men tried to urge them on. But "only the drum is confident." Then he continues the poem by describing the white tourists, all watching with "hungry eyes," trying to find out how to be "human again." But, "only the drum is confident." He ends the poem by saying that only the tribal drum, Taos Mountain and he, himself, "remember that civilization is a transient sickness."

Yes, the drum is "confident." By following "the way of the drum," it links us directly with our real human nature in all its deep aspects and therefore can link us once again to our land.

Lord Hun Tun and the drum in Taoism

The "Lord Hun-tun and chaos" theme of Taoism gives added depth to the power of the drum. The creation process, in general, is signaled by "wind, rain, thunder, and darkness." Furthermore, "transformation is due to the magical powers of a bell, cauldron, or drum": each of these is "analogous to the creative power of the primordial...gourd." All these aspects are part of the Taoist elaborations on the basic Hun-tun theme, which is related to early bronze working as well as the gourd. For a primitive culture, bronze working would be considered a shamanistic art concerned with the transformation of matter. In the early "barbarian" cultures of South China the bronze drums had a special ritual role. According to Girardot: "The magic and ritual power of these drums was associated with its power to reproduce the thunder of the creation time, and the 'hourglass' form of the drums seems to have been based on the cosmological prototype of the sacred...gourd."

Because the gourd makes such an excellent resonator, it is linked with the making of all types of musical instruments in China as well as many other parts of the world. They are used in marimbas, the original banjo in Africa, zithers, lute and lyres. Drums in Hawaii, the near East and India still have the basic hourglass shape of the Lagenaria gourd. The gourd rattle is sometimes called "the drum beaten from within."

The hollow cavity or "chaos gap" of the gourd makes it possible for the creative power of sound to resonate. This basic aspect of the gourd came to be relevant for all types of creation in Taoist thinking: "In the central hollow place at the Beginning, the Sound and Light of creation thunder forth: *hun-hun-tun-tun*." Here we can see why the drum "affords" us the perfect marker for the creation time of ritual.

Concerning the drum's leading role in ritual, an ancient Chinese classic, the Book of *Shen-tzu*, states: "The [sound of the] drum does not take part [as one] of the five notes, and yet it is their ruler." Creel explains that "the percussive sound of the drum does not correspond in pitch to any of the five notes, and yet it gives rhythm, emphasis, and definition to the music, thus 'ruling' the five notes."

Present-day use of the drum

In this section I will give a few examples of the growing use of the drum; not only for ritual but as therapy for children. Because my first contact with the ritual drum was through Elizabeth Cogburn's "long dances," I will conclude with a few remarks about her work with the drum.

THE DRUM IN CHILDREN'S THERAPY

A new form of music therapy was pioneered by the late Dr. Paul Nordoff, an American composer and Clive Robbins, a special educator in the field of handicapped children. It proved useful for severely handicapped children: some autistic, some mongoloid and some brain damaged, as well as for less severe cases. Nordoff would sit at the piano and improvise music. The child is asked to stand by a drum, and is given sticks and asked to beat to the music. "As he becomes active, he becomes deeply, personally involved in the rhythmic activity...he is listening, alert, responding to the music, and controlling what he is doing."

If a child is unable to relate his beating to the music, then the therapist changes the rhythm to correspond to the child's rhythm. "The child is then usually able to make a tentative relationship to the music." This gives a "confidence that he has never felt before."

In my own ritual work with people, we have found that emotionally disturbed children or one having trouble within the family context are helped enormously by chanting and drumming in a semi-ritualized group situation. Sometimes it is fascinating to watch the parents of a child at this time. As the child really gets into the drumming and no longer needs to play up to the all-powerful adults in its life, the adults sometimes become dissatisfied and bored and often decide it's time to leave. But, if they pay attention to this, they can find that the drum "affords" the family a chance to balance the relationships within that family; just as the drum has done for thousands of years in the past for most human cultures.

JAPANESE KODO DRUMMERS

When I was living in Japan during the winter of 1971-72, the year the winter Olympics were held in Sapporo, I was able to see the first big performance of the Kodo Drummers of Sado Island. The group had just begun in 1971, but I didn't know that at the time. The curtain opened to a stage filled with three tiers of Japanese men dressed only in white loin cloths and white headbands, drumming. The silences were just as effective as the drumming. Essentially, their drumming is based on ancient Shinto drumming to first, call up the gods for the festival, then converse with the gods, and finally, to send them back to the mountains or their other dwelling places.

The drummers live on Sado Island, 200 miles northwest of Tokyo. Before sunrise, the drummers run along the beach. Then, after attending to their chores, they drum most of the remainder of the day. Their master drum-maker, Yoshiyuki Asana, comes from a family that has been making drums since 1609. He makes the giant "o-daiko," a huge drum hollowed out from an enormous log, three feet wide and four feet long. It can weigh close to 1000 pounds and is played with sticks the size of small logs. The big drum sounds like a heartbeat, as do all taikos. "More specifically, the sound the drums produce is like a mother's heartbeat as heard from the womb: warm, gentle, nurturing, the first sound we ever hear." The name, Kodo, means "heartbeat."

"Kodo's music has been described as having the 'natural strength and violence of a hurricane.' It is explosive, thunderous and electrifying, critics say." But, for those who know ritual, it truly does call up the gods—those inside us and those outside in nature. The author of the first article on Kodo in English, John Perreault, writes: "You can feel the drum between your ears, against your chest, in your diaphragm and belly, along your spine." And he's right. It's easy to see how such a powerful drum can hold a culture together.

The Kodo drummers played at the Los Angeles Olympics recently, and a few minutes of their drumming was put on television, which greatly increased their popularity. They do tour in this country occasionally and you should make every effort to attend. Just recently a 30 minute video of the Kodo Drummers was made. (See Resources for how to rent it).

In Denver, there is a Taiko group of young Japanese people (both men and women) who drum together to "get back to our Japanese roots." They perform at local events in Denver. They use hand made drums and drums made from discarded wine and whiskey barrels as they haven't the money to invest in imported drums. "Members say the power of their performance comes from the 'strength of the 'ki' [*tantien* in China], the Japanese center of life. Located in the lower stomach, it is considered the soul from which spiritual and physical force flows." You can see that drumming, for these young people is far more a ritual event than a performance event. Toni Yagami, speaks for all of them when she said, "We're holding on to our culture real tight."

I'm fairly certain there must be other groups throughout the country, beginning to drum since being inspired by the Kodo drummers. In fact, I know this is one of the best ways for teenagers to begin to get grounded in their place. I recommend that anyone really trying to help our teenagers to find a way back out of their rootlessness, caused by this Industrial Growth Society, read the information in the Reference Notes and begin a Taiko group.

Other groups using the drum

In addition to Wicca groups (good witches) and pagan ritual groups, more in-line religious groups are beginning to return to our natural human heritage of drumming. Two examples: Theresa Havens, a Quaker does drumming at her Temenos Center and Mother Tessa Bielicki, a Carmelite contemplative nun of the tradition of St. Theresa of Avalon and St. John of the Cross also drums at her workshops.

Drumming in Elizabeth Cogburn's New Song Group

Although I go into more detail on the origins of this group in the Way of the Dance section, I do want to explain how the drum came to them. Trained in dance, Elizabeth knew how to inspire people to improvise with dance. She felt this should be just as possible with the voice. "But without a hundred years of tradition behind them, they knew they'd have to find the 'new song' and thus was born the name of the ceremonial community she heads." Living in New Mexico, where her husband taught at the University, she began to "concentrate on learning the art of drumming, or in native terms, getting to know the drum—for, in native terms, the drum is a sacred being; one builds one's relationship with this 'being', the drum, by entering into an agreement to combine human efforts with the drum's essence and thereby *co-create* the sound field for the dance." A genuine drummer showed up and served as her teacher. They'd sit all night with the drum, playing a simple one-one-one pulse, the heart beat of the universe.

Beginning first with ceremonies at the full moon, she says, "We used to greet the full moon rising over Taos and drum straight through to the sunrise." She learned, in those early moon rituals, the truth of the drum: "All the songs of the universe are contained in the one-one-one-one beat; the drum will show the way to the dance and to the song."

While the big ceremonial drum is used at all "long dances," one side of it is played only at the annual Sun Dance in June. Before the journey into the wilderness area where the Dance is held; everyone gathers at her place in Albuquerque. People have come by plane and car from all over the country. That first evening, when everyone has finished eating, they gather in the Lodge at the edge of the Garden. After everyone has quieted down, "the Big Drum is taken from its heavy black case and placed so that the head played only at Sun Dance faces up. It is then fed (i.e., sprinkled with) cornmeal and smudged with sage and cedar smoke. At this time, the shaman [Elizabeth, for her group], instructs the participants to image in their minds those of the dancers who are still enroute to speed them on their way. The drummers begin to drum, and everyone dances and shakes the rattles in the lodge, and a great surge of energy can be felt emanating from the group. When the Drum is quiet and the dancing ends, the Big Drum is officially open." This "Opening of the Big Drum Ceremony" begins the two-week ritual of the Sun Dance.

For the "long dances" which are held at other major earth festival days throughout the year and in other locations, the Big Drum is also ritually treated; furthermore, before the dance begins Elizabeth gives detailed instructions on how to "become a companion to the Big Drum." The important thing here is to remember that the drum is a real "being"—a being that "affords" us the opportunity of the dance. Without it, the dance would not "happen." So one must be respectful and "ask"

the drum for it's help and cooperate with what it wants to do. This is done by "letting the drum play itself." True, we hold the beaters in our hands, but we let them fall loosely onto the drum and the drum sends the beater back up into our hand, ready for our next move of letting it fall again. But the drum, itself, is the one setting the rhythm and the depth of the drumming. If one can let go enough to permit this "affordance" to occur, then you can drum for hours tirelessly. The drum synchronizes all four drummers and all the dancers. If someone tries to retain rational control and "beat the drum" with that control, immediately, dissonance comes between the drummers. The dancers are jarred out of their dance and everyone becomes very uneasy. At this point, Elizabeth must walk over and remove the drum stick from the hand of the unaware person and show them once again how to let the drum take over. Then, serenity and harmony returns to our world of the dance.

During a night-long dance there are always four people at the drum. Drummers can change at any time providing the new drummer stands near the one whose place he is taking, long enough to feel the rhythm and thus not interrupt the on-going flow. Generally the drummers among them develop a wordless chant; but this is not necessary.

The drum must be just below the knees of the drummers: held there by the four drummers holding the straps on all four sides of the drum or by an open drum stand. The drum stand must allow both heads of the drum to vibrate—the one below and the one being played on. With the drum in this position it is easy to let the drum sticks "fall" onto the head of the drum.

In her directions for playing the drum, Elizabeth says that one should "sit with a straight back, loose belly and loose crotch." There should be only a small space between your hand and the drum so that the striker falls only a fairly short distance—about 4 to 6 inches. The way the striker is held is very important. It is held firmly between the little finger and the palm of the hand—but firmly, only there. The remainder of the striker moves freely up and down along the palm of the hand, between the thumb and fingers, giving it about a two inch play. With this controlled yet loose play, the drum can send it back up to you; hence the drum "plays" itself. The drummers should be relaxed in their arms and shoulders and let the sound flow. This is the "way of the drum" which "affords" us humans the "way of the dance."

THE "WAY" OF THE DANCE

I do not believe that the original purpose of the rain dance was to make 'it' rain. I suspect that that is a degenerate misunderstanding of a much more profound religious need: to affirm membership in what we may call the *ecological tautology*, the eternal verities of life and environment.

Gregory Bateson

...for hours, hours it goes on: the round dance...the ceaseless downtread, always to the earth's centre...For the whole life-effort of man was to get his life into direct contact with the elemental life of the cosmos, mountain-life, cloud-life, thunder-life, earth-life, sun-life. To come into immediate *felt*-contact, and so derive energy, power, and a dark sort of joy.

D. H. Lawrence on Taos Pueblo dancing

The dances are pivots in a system of transformations which change destructive behavior into constructive alliances. It is no accident that every move, chant and costume of the *kaiko* dances are adapted from combat: a new use is found for this behavior. Quite unconsciously a positive feedback begins: the more splendid the displays of dancing, the stronger the alliances; the stronger the alliances, the more splendid the dancing.

Richard Schechner on the Tsembaga *kaiko*

Kohler on chimp dancing

As with almost every other aspect of real human life, we inherited the dance from the higher apes also. Writing about the chimpanzees he worked with, Kohler states: "The resemblance to a human dance became truly striking..." Two chimps would play and wrestle near a wooden post in the enclosure. Their movements would begin to get more regular and they would start going in circles round the post. "One after another, the rest of the group approach, join the two, and finally they march in an orderly fashion and in single file round and round the post." Soon they are trotting with a "special emphasis on one foot." They move their heads in time to the rhythm and other variations occur as they "joyously" move around the circle. This "dancing" took place often and Kohler remarks: "It seems to me extraordinary that there should arise quite spontaneously, among chimpanzees, anything that so strongly suggests the primitive dancing of some primitive tribe."

The "trance dance" or "long dance"

While there is no limit to the types of dancing that have been used in rituals, here I will just go into the form which I believe is absolutely essential; it has been called "trance dance" or "long dance." While there is certainly a change of consciousness, I hesitate to use the word "trance" because of all the invalid ideas about trance. A better way to think of this "long dance" is that all the aspects of the mind: conscious and unconscious, as well as the sympathetic and parasympathetic nervous systems are "tuned" together within the individual so that bonding occurs both throughout the group and with nature in that place.

That's a large order; obviously, you aren't going to be able to set up such a long dance without some previous experience. The best place you can get such experience in this country is at one of the long dances put on by Elizabeth Cogburn of the New Song Group. (See Reference Notes for more information about her work.) The most important event of the year for this group is the annual Sun Dance. (1988 will be the seventeenth year). It is always held in the mountains of New Mexico (her home country). But one must have attended at least one regular long dance before taking part in the Sun Dance, which involves three days and nights of steady drumming and dancing. Below, I will give a brief explanation of the basic structure of the long dance followed by my own experience of such dances.

Sarah Dubin-Vaughn has just recently completed a manuscript dealing with "The New Song Ceremonial Sun Dance Ritual—1983 and 1984." This is her doctoral dissertation for a Ph. D. in Transformational Psychology. I refer to this work below. (See Reference Notes for further information.)

Elizabeth states that, "the purpose of the celebration is first and foremost *to renew the well-being of the people*." Talking about her "orchestrating of basic energy patterns that pertain to the Long Dance," she explains that different drumbeats create different energy patterns which, in turn, create different kinds of consciousness. "The elaboration grows organically instead of being forced by neocortex inventions. The generic emotional expression emanates from the limbic system [of the brain], and just as the sense of play comes from the same source, this expression can explore many options. One can say, 'here's another way to go about it,' and be able to move back and forth to check out different facets of the life we're making. There's always a great air of play and discovery."

BASIC STRUCTURE OF THE LONG DANCE

The essential structure of the long dance involves preliminary preparation as Cogburn provides instruction in drumming and tuning the body through the "Body Poem," which is based on Tai Chi. In order to take part in the long dance each person must vow that once they begin they will continue until dawn or sunrise (whichever has been decided). That doesn't mean you have to dance every moment. It means that you stay there in the room and stay within the sound of the drum. You can leave, temporarily, for necessities and you can sleep, if necessary, but that's done in the same room, sitting up. No conversation is permitted as it drains away the energy. Light snacks and fruit juice are provided.

The dance itself consists of three major "rings." The outermost ring surrounding the dance ground itself is called the "witness ring, where all those beings, both seen and unseen, may watch, or witness, the Dance. Immediately inside the witness ring, on the outermost rim of the Dance Ground, is the single-file, 'yang' circle, or ring." Here the dancers move clockwise, while facing in the direction they are moving. The ring inside this outermost 'yang' circle is the 'yin' circle... where the dancers move counterclockwise. These dancers face inward toward the center of the circle and they move slowly sideways, hips and shoulders swaying. "Inside the three rings, there is a large area, the 'inner courtyard,' where theatrical events, dramas, both comic and sad, are played out through individual and group dances." This is not done by acting out in the usual sense; instead, it's more like inner events flowing into outward expression. A person can move freely from one to another of these areas as they wish during the dance.

The dance begins with Elizabeth leading a spiral, holding the Pipe before her with its stem pointing forward. When the spiral is tightly wound around her she lifts the Pipe, suddenly, high into the air toward the sky. As she lowers it, the person at the outer end of the spiral leads the line outward until the spiral is unwound and the dance begins. Essentially everyone moves as they wish, but always in time with the drum. The closing ceremony is short and consists of the reforming of the circle, then the spiral inward and out, "finally the releasing of the energy to the universe through the Pipe."

RELATING TO ALL OF LIFE IN THE DANCE

"Riding the drum" during the long dance, one effortlessly relates to all aspects of life—both inside and outside. This is how we *know* there is really no separation between the human and other forms of life; in spite of what all the "experts" tell us. When the body begins to move a certain way, all of a sudden, you are the coyote or the buffalo or the bear. There's nothing mysterious about this. We communicate with other animals by means of the animal (limbic) brain within us. It's just that in ordinary, "merely human," consciousness we don't pay attention to those levels of the brain. But, in the dance, these animals move us from within. This is what Gary Snyder meant when he said: "when, in the dances of the Pueblo Indians, and other peoples, certain individuals became seized, as it were, by the spirit of the deer, and danced as a deer would dance...they were no longer speaking for humanity, there were taking it on themselves to interpret, through their humanity, what these other life-forms were." This is how we let the other people, "what the Sioux Indians called the creeping people, and the standing peoples, and the flying people—into our councils of government."

Here is an example of how the Indians, long ago, let the other peoples into their councils. This chant comes out of the dance of the Buffalo Bull Men of the Osage tribe.

> I rise, I rise.
> I whose tread makes the earth to rumble.
>
> I rise, I rise
> I, in whose thighs there is strength.
>
> I rise, I rise
> I, who whips his back with his tail in rage.
>
> I rise, I rise
> I, in whose humped shoulder there is power.
>
> I rise, I rise
> I, who shakes his mane when angered.
>
> I rise, I rise.
> I, whose horns are sharp and curved.

My own experience of a Winter Solstice Long Dance

The first time I took part in an all-night long dance was in the adobe house of Elizabeth's mother on the hillside above Taos. There were people there from a wide range of professions: teachers, anthropologists, lawyers, artists, students and a few dancers. We had spent two days together in preparation for the dance. I knew none of them beforehand except Elizabeth. During the time together I began to like some people, while others did not interest me. But during the dance, I found that, as I encountered each of these people, somehow during the brief, nonverbal interchange of the dance, we sorted out what had taken place between us in the last few days so that I felt bonded to everyone present. In talking about the dance the next day many of us found this to be the most startling aspect. And this aspect is what makes the long dance just as much a necessity for an on-going group of people today, as it was for our ancestors for hundreds of thousands of years.

The following day after this first Winter Solstice dance, we all loaded into cars and drove off to Albuquerque, where Elizabeth and Bob live, for some more ceremonial instruction. On December 31st, New Year's Eve, we had the second long dance. Before the dance began, the decision was made to finish at dawn. The night went even faster and more effortlessly than before. When dawn came, however, small pink clouds began slowly moving over the top of sacred Sandia Mountain, with everyone turning, spontaneously to watch them, while continuing to dance in place. Not one person stopped. As the sun began to rise, the drumming, the shaking of the gourds, and the dancing intensity increased. Just as the sun's lower rim cleared the mountain everyone stopped moving and all sound stopped instantaneously. There was not one extra beat of sound. The entire group had been ritually synchronized to the point where it was enabled to act as a unit, unthinkingly, in the same manner as a flock of birds suddenly turning at the same time. Everyone was exuberant with both joy and overwhelming thankfulness that we had been "given" this possibility. Thus we had our "share in the superhuman abundance of life...the true fruit of the festival: renewal, transformation, rebirth."

The ritual dancing, which I've discussed above, was entered into in full conciousness of the power of what we were doing. In other words it was true ritual, even though we are just beginning to regain such a culture, here in modern America. Before closing this section, however, I want to explore the depth of experience, which can come to modern people, even though the ceremony may begin as an imitation ritual. I am referring, here, to an article by Victor Turner, the anthropologist who has done more for ritual studies than anyone else.

After a lifetime of studying rituals among cultures in Africa and elsewhere he got together with some students, other professors and friends to attempt a ceremony. Dr. Stanley Walens, an authority on the Northwest Coast had condensed the long series of rituals composing the Hamatsa ceremony into a shorter form for the occasion. Turner's students prepared the ceremonial space [in the basement of Turner's house in Charlottesville] and everyone took part in the general preparations of making props, body painting, etc. After the ritual was completed everyone was totally surprised at the depth of the experience. One of the students, Douglas Dalton said: "As the ceremony progressed I felt not so much the antagonistic rivalry that was overtly expressed in the ceremony between the bear clan and the killer whale clan, but the fact that we were collectively doing something really important—something essentially correct. There was so much power flowing all over the place in the longhouse (the Charlottesville basement) that night! The spirits were really at work that evening and we had to keep everything in line so all the power wouldn't destroy everything!"

Walens, himself wrote: "One has the feeling that rituals are magical, that for some reason as yet unknown to science they can communicate to people, not despite their artificiality, but because of and through their artificiality. Rituals are efficacious and we wonder how...[This question leads him into talking about religion.] It is not that religion is so much a statement of belief but that at its most effective it enables us to suspend disbelief in the things that are larger than ourselves, whether they be deities or nature or the sacred corpus of anthropological theory. Just as at a ritual we may have a momentary inkling that there was something greater present than simply a bunch of people playing at ceremony, so in our acting of the cannibal dance we have an inkling of something which transcends the limitations of a particular moment in the history of the anthropology department at the University of Virginia." And he ends by quoting the student, Dalton: "The potlatch ended, in fact, with the assurance that the Kwakiutl would continue to keep the world in order . . . The bitter rivalry that was expressed in the early parts of the ceremony gave way to a final reconciliation and a true feeling of oneness with the forces of the universe."

If this much depth of meaning can come out of an experiment in an anthropology department; how much greater will it be for all of you who are beginning to relearn the rituals, which, obviously, still lie within us, from hundreds of thousands of years of practice.

THE "WAY" OF THE TALKING STAFF

Art . . . is the origin of the essential provenance of a work, which is neither a mere thing nor a piece of equipment but a place where truth occurs.

Heidegger

Introduction

This quote from Heidegger explains, precisely, the importance of the Talking Staff: it is "where truth occurs"—the truth within us, between humans and between human and nature. Yet few people have even heard of the Talking Staff. In this section I will attempt to give you some of its possibilities.

My second encounter with the Talking Staff took place in front of the fireplace in the long room of Kathleen Summit's adobe house on the hillside above Taos. It was Winter Solstice time—and in those days, 1979—Elizabeth Cogburn held her all-night long dance for that festival in her mother's house. That Talking Staff Council had been convened to share our experience of the Winter Solstice Long Dance. (The structure and rules will be given below.) Here I will just say that the person who has the Staff is the only one who has the right to talk. All others must be silent and *listen*, with their heart. Before the Staff had gone around once, I realized that here was a marvellous technique for preventing people like me—verbally, very quick—from interrupting the flow of thought of those who preferred to take their time. In fact, Elizabeth had to stop me—by a gesture—once before the first round was finished, but I wasn't the only one she had to warn. Quite early on, I was astounded by the depth of experience which the Staff "afforded" us. From that time on, as I participated in numbers of other Talking Staff Councils with Elizabeth and later, as I held them myself; I continued to wonder at the power of the whole process. I began collecting research from many different academic fields, which might have a bearing on the process.

From my own experience leading people out into nature to experience the earth in a ritual manner I soon realized that the Talking Staff was probably the single most important "way" to help them realize the depth of the bonding which had taken place—both among the individual humans and between the humans and the earth. In the chant section I referred to Bill Plotkin, a psychotherapist who specializes in Vision Quests. He experienced his first Talking Staff Council here at our Way of the Mountain Center in Silverton. Elizabeth Cogburn, drove through on her way north to give a workshop and stopped to spend the night. I gathered together the six other people in town who were doing rituals with me at the time so she could "meld" our Talking Staff to hers. (More on this below.) Bill experienced his second Council on BREAKING THROUGH, after the climb of 14,000 ft. Crestone Needle Peak. The following day I gathered everyone together for the Talking Staff. Bill was simply astounded at the events which followed. We talked about it later and both of us began gathering "data." He planned on writing an article for a psychology journal. Through the years since then we have shared information and discussions; therefore, I will be referring to his experiences from time to time throughout the discussion below.

He has not written the article yet; the areas on which the Talking Staff draws are so immense. But last spring, while I was working on the manuscript for this book, we had a long meeting to try to correlate our information. During this process, inadvertantly, we had still more experiences to draw on. Several different people who had been on his recent Vision Quest just happened to drop by his house. When they heard what we were doing, they stayed. They, too, wondered about how the Talking Staff works. They had just shared the Talking Staff experience on a Vision Quest with Bill and were still wondering at the depth it provided.

Origin of the New Song Talking Staff

Perhaps the best way to begin, is to tell the story of how Bob Cogburn, Elizabeth's husband, aquired their first Talking Staff. Because of many requests he wrote the experience up for the New Song Village Journal for their December 1985 issue. Back in 1972 he and Elizabeth and their friend, Tom Erhlich (who gave workshops in drumming and creating "sound fields") decided to call their first Sun Dance. For some years they had been talking about how to "hold a community celebration of the sacredness of life, of renewal and transformation, that worked" for us modern people of the white culture. They planned for a three day celebration with two days of preparation and the final dance itself on Summer Solstice. The site was high above the Rio Grande River gorge near Taos. They realized that they would need a center pole to focus the dance and drumming. Since the nearest trees were twenty miles away, the three of them decided to go to the forested area a day ahead of the celebration.

Bob writes: "Now you must understand what novices we all were." He felt that Elizabeth, with her "shamanic power" was assured and that Tom seemed sure, as well. But he, himself, feeling very unsure, decided to make up for that with "bravado." As Bob explains, just before a major festival, is a "very tricky" time. All of us involved in rituals fully realize that. Accidents happen, personal egos are threatened, etc. There are reasons for all this but I won't take the time to go into it here. When they got to the site, each of them chose a tree immediately but, of course, it was three different trees. In the ensuing squabble, Bob wrote that he no longer cared which tree they got, but "I did want to be heard and taken seriously and I thought we all must be feeling the need of that." Pondering all this, while walking through the trees, he remembered the opening scene in "The Anger of Achilles," Robert Grave's translation of the *Iliad*, which he was reading at the time.

The *Iliad* opens with the Greeks holding a Council of War before the walls of Troy. The conflict is "between two men of power, in whose passions and decisions the fate of the whole group is involved." One is Achilles, the Greek hero and the other is King Agamemnon. Although each of these two men thinks it is only himself concerned in the struggle for power; actually, "their acts and thoughts disturb the conduct and affect the fate of the society in which they move." As the quarrel gets more bitter, Achilles decides to withdraw from the battle for Troy and so takes a vow on the "gold-studded wand which gave him the right of uninterrupted speech":

> By this dry wand no more to sprout
> Or put green twigs and foliage out
> Since once the hatchet, swinging free,
> Cross-chopped it from a mountain tree,
> Then trimmed away both leaves and
> bark—
> By this same wand, which men who
> mark
> Ancient traditions praised by Zeus
> Have set to honourable use
> In ruling their debates: I vow
> That all you Greeks assembled now
> Before me—mark these words...

Bob remembered, "a compelling image of the talking staff, a ceremonial staff representing the right to speak and to be heard without interruption. Casting about I found a dry cedar limb and tied my bandanna to one end. As I started back I saw three fine blue jay feathers and felt they appropriately represented the three of us in our squabbling, so I inserted them in a crack at the top of the staff. Thus I returned with the first talking staff of our new tradition, explaining its function to Elizabeth and Tom."

By now they were primarily interested in resolving the situation, too, so, as they passed the staff around the circle, each was able to express his or her "perceptions and feelings." Bob writes: "When my turn came and I noticed that they were actually listening to me, my clutched up feeling that my visions weren't regarded as being important like theirs melted away." Soon, they were all three able to go out and meditate under each of the three previously chosen trees "until we found a common perception of that tree's willingness and suitability for the sacrifice." They all three immediately agreed on the same tree. As Bob writes, for the Talking Staff to work, "we must give ourselves to that which is beyond our personal selves." In this case it was by letting the tree, itself, decide.

At the 1979 Sun Dance it was decided to use Elizabeth's Medicine Pipe for the Talking Staff, "bringing with it a deep sense we are indeed making medicine as we make our way to the Heart of the Matter before us." Elizabeth writes:

"You can feel the Band literally forming itself, 'coming together around' compelling questions, dreams, experiences, situations."

How I began using the Talking Staff

At the Spring Equinox celebration here in Silverton in 1980, we inaugurated our own Talking Staff. Some years before, on the desert I had found a curved piece of very old juniper, twisted and worn smooth by many seasons under the wind and sun. I had each person bring with them something of nature which they had found during the previous week in their walks near Silverton. We tied these bits of bone and feather and rock onto the juniper. Then, when we began passing the Staff we discovered that the curve fit beautifully right around the *hara (tan tien)* where the lower, fourth brain, lies in the abdomen. This fit gives one a wonderful sense of support when trying to articulate something difficult to put into words. We began the ceremony with light snow falling; but before the Talking Staff had gone around once, a great hole opened in the clouds directly overhead and we had the full moon during the remainder of our ceremony. Just as we were packing up to walk back down the hill to Silverton, the next wave of snow blew in and we couldn't see a thing all the way back to town. But what an auspicious start for our Talking Staff—bringing the moon out!

A few days later Elizabeth drove through town on her way north. She "melded" our new Talking Staff to hers with a small ceremony. First she "fed" both staffs by sprinkling some of her Taos mixture of shredded cedar and sage and cornmeal over them. Then, holding both Talking Staffs together she raised them high as she said the invocation before passing them around. Then both staffs went around together on the first round. As they came back to her; she kept hers and our Staff continued around for the other two rounds.

From then on I have kept some of her original mixture and added bits of our local plants to it. With this mixture, I have inaugurated numbers of new Staffs around the country.

It was some years before I did the first Talking Staff for BREAKING THROUGH. At first I felt that, since this was an advertised workshop out of COLORADO OUTDOOR LEADERSHIP SCHOOL and thus a commercial venture I should not introduce such a "sacred" ritual object. I did bring some of the mixture with me each time—just in case.

Finally, one year I decided that nature "gave" us permission. It was only the second day; we were still on the ranch. Because of the large group, Rick took one half and I took the other, for beginning rock scrambling. I took our group to my favorite rock area. We had only just begun climbing when sudden, tremendous black clouds began rolling in. I called everyone down onto the ground and we got our ponchos on just in time. There was a great deal of nervousness as they saw the clouds drawing near. I assured them that the lightning wouldn't hit us there as the rocks towered way above us and the safest place to be is in open country in a small hollow, which is where we were. I also told them that I had climbed in numerous lightning storms. I didn't really know we were safe, of course, but all that assured them enough so that they could relax and enjoy it. Then the summer snow came rattling against our hoods, but no one cared if we got wet. The lightning and thunder was right around us—crashing and flashing in every direction. I was worried that some of these Easterners would be afraid. But it was too powerful for fear. It was beautiful and sublime and awesome all at once. I looked around. Not a person was trembling; instead they were openmouthed at the power. The storm was over in about fifteen minutes and the sun was out again. With wet rocks, we couldn't climb so we started back up the road to our main camp. Everyone was radiating joy: the lightning and thunder had bonded us in such a deep way. I decided then that this group deserved the Talking Staff.

Days went by before I got a chance to introduce the Staff. In fact it was the day after we climbed Crestone Needle. I used Rick Medrick's beautiful hickory walking staff, as it would be reassuring to have that in one's hands after all the successful climbs Rick had taken it on. On Broken Hand Peak, a bird had flown directly overhead at such speed we could hear the whirr-r-r of its wings. It dropped us a feather. And we found another feather on Crestone Needle—only one feather on each of the peaks. I tied these two feathers onto the staff with my bright red and black boot laces and left the long ends dangling. I introduced the Staff by telling of Elizabeth's first staff. Then I ritually went around to each person and gave them a bit of the cornmeal/juniper/sage mixture. I had explained that part of it was from the SW desert and some from the Crestone area. Next, I took the Staff, and holding one end on my heart area I raised the other end to the sky and turned to face the four directions: calling on the Sun's rising place out over the Wet Mountain Valley to the East; south, calling on Broken Hand Peak; West, calling on Crestone Needle where the sun sets; and north, calling on Humbolt Peak. I called on each of the mountains and the valley of these directions to stand witness at our council. Then I sprinkled some of the mixture gently the length of the staff and passed it on for each person to anoint it with some of the mixture from their own hand. This was done silently. When it returned to me, I raised it straight up to the zenith and brought it down and gave them the question: "What did you learn from the mountain?" I gave my answer first and then passed it around. When it got to one young woman from New York, who had been my best Tai Chi pupil of the group, she began talking; but soon tears were pouring out of her eyes and down on the Staff she was so moved. This broke the group through. The second round was even deeper and, on the third round, we had a major breakthrough. One of the men was from California and was an EST trainer. Rick and I felt there was little we could do for him with all the built-in presuppositions that meant. But when the Staff came to him, he, too, was so moved that he confessed, "I've been a real asshole!" And spoke of his feelings of superiority and how Crestone Needle had changed him. And, as he spoke, tears welled up in his eyes. He was deeply moved!

Background on the Talking Staff from our Animal Ancestors and Early Man

We do find that our ancestors, the chimpanzees also use a "staff" and, in circumstances somewhat similar to Achilles

using it in support of his efforts against King Agamemnon in the *Iliad*. From time to time a dominant male chimp will pick up a stick and march about with it. He may be asserting his superior position before the other, younger males, as Jane Lancaster mentions. However, the chimp's stick can never be used to facilitate talking as chimps do not communicate chiefly by vocal means. Their main communication is by body language.

The "batons," found in the Upper Paleolithic caves in France may have been used as "staffs" in ritual; although Alexander Marshack has pointed out that they probably served as markers for keeping track of seasonal sun and moon. Of course it may be that he who kept the record, by that very fact, was a leader of ritual. In the Tuc d'Audoubert cave in France, there are dancing heel prints, possible ivory and bone bullroarers and "so-called batons made of bone." The staff has been a mark of leadership for many cultures down through to our time; but, of course, we do not know how many of these staffs were used by the leader to facilitate communication with his followers. Without that aspect they cannot be termed talking staffs.

General Background Concerning the Talking Staff

In this section I will give some particular aspects, which may contribute to the Power of the Talking Staff. Turning first to C. G. Jung, he explains that sometimes a personal problem, which might seem merely subjective, "coincides with external events that contain the same psychological elements as the personal conflict." Then it "acquires a dignity" that it lacked before. This is important because, often we feel that inner trouble is somehow humiliating and degrading. This is why people rarely feel free to speak out about deep matters. But when something makes it plain that there is a connection between the personal problems of a number of people, "it brings release from the loneliness of the purely personal, and the subjective problem is magnified into a general question of our society." In the case of the Talking Staff, when it frees one person to talk of their own deep feelings; others, who secretly share that feeling, find that an enormous weight is removed from their life. They are no longer alone! In the resulting relief, the next time the Staff is passed around, they, too are able to speak out about this problem. As others join in speaking of this, there is no longer merely concern or worry; instead there is positive affirmation.

For further insight here, I want to mention Lévi-Strauss' description of a shaman's cure: "The shaman provides the sick woman with a *language* by means of which unexpressed, and otherwise unexpressible, psychic states can be immediately expressed...And it is the transition to this verbal expression which makes it possible to undergo in an ordered and intelligible form a real experience that would otherwise be chaotic and inexpressible." This is precisely what the Talking Staff does for us; whether used in rituals or out in nature. For instance, when I use the Staff, I have been out in nature hiking or climbing with a group of people for several days in succession. Those in the group have come to trust the group for support when they are frightened or for approval, when they have done something they never tried before. And, in the background always is the feeling that the mountain "afforded" them the opportunity to climb it. They know that alone they would never have done it. Moving along together in nature allows wonderful opportunities to begin deep conversations without the fear that happens in one-to-one conversations. The whole group hears and contributes—sometimes humor; sometimes remarkable insights. Together the group achieves symbolic words for certain states of mind, which further facilitates speaking about these states. Without the Talking Staff all of this might be lost. But, when the day is over and the Talking Staff is brought out; the state of alert "listening" and heartfelt "talking" involved, allows people to talk of matters they've never before had any words for at all! That's the shaman's "language by means of which unexpressed...psychic states can be immediately expressed."

Another insight comes from the process of focusing. Eugene Gendlin, tells us that "Focusing moves inward, drawing on information from the deeper, wiser self [the older brains and the body itself]." If done with the proper attention, "usually within half a minute or so, the felt shift or bodily release occurs." This "felt shift" may actually be whole-brain knowing. "That is, the brain's analytical left hemisphere, dominant for language, names that which, heretofore, was inarticulate and diffuse, known only to the holistic, mute right brain." Generally, new insights seem to come first through the right brain, which has more connections to the older limbic (animal) brain. For instance, if the group has been engaged in ritual together or in nature, hiking or climbing together, they have been moving together for some time. All sorts of information is exchanged by moving bodies, which the conscious brain does not even register. But it's all there inside. Then, later when the group is sitting with the Talking Staff, it needs only a bit of a trigger and all of a sudden this accumulated body/old brain knowledge is accessible because *the* word has suddenly appeared. I know this is true from climbing and skiing for so many years. But, before the Talking Staff there was no mechanism for all of us sitting together in a state of alert receptivity to "await" the words for the events of the day. A bar full of skiers just isn't quite the same thing! So these bits of amazing information would be hastily exchanged while climbing up the hill from the lift to the bar. Once inside, normal American culture takes over and we are suddenly all "mute" about real things.

So far I've been mostly dealing with talking; but, obviously, for the Talking Staff experience, listening is just as important. "Because it is capable of arousing such passion for one's life, listening is a revolutionary act," according to Carl Faber. He says that normally, all of our experiences just "flow through us, we become sewer pipes." It doesn't register at all. People may have worked hard for years, tried to be good friends to others, and yet feel that they have accomplished nothing. The feeling brings intense loneliness. But real listening—the kind that we do with the Talking Staff can change all this. Faber says, "In reality, the facing of truth gives everyone you are involved with an opportunity to see their lies, meaninglessness, and lack of fulfillment. Instead of destroying them in a monstrous act of selfishness, you are really giving them the gift of a chance to live. There is no way that a lie for you can be truth for other people." When one person dares to say

"true" things about themselves with the Talking Staff's help, it suddenly opens up all the others to recognize their own lies. Even more, the continuing exchange as the Staff goes around the circle helps them to find a way out of the on-going life they have been living. "Listening allows them...to feel what life is meant to be, not the acceptance of what they are not."

Too often, in normal everyday life, people listen only in ways that "stop other people from feeling and talking...We meet them with impatient, self-righteous, intolerant, perfectionistic, and defensive attitudes. We interrupt them to assert our ideas and feelings." Or we joke or make sarcastic comments. All this cannot happen with the Talking Staff. No one can reply as you finish—until the staff gets around to them. By that time they don't even want to make any of those remarks because the "words from the heart" of others in between in the progression of the Staff around the circle, have made them understand you better.

Faber says that: "Sometimes the loneliness people feel comes also from their failure to listen lovingly to themselves." This is why Beno Kennedy's question when he starts the Talking Staff around is so important: "Do you love yourself enough to listen with the ears of your Heart to the other voices of yourself speak?"

MUTUALITY

In the "way" of the Talking Staff, listening becomes just as important as speaking. As each person speaks from the "heart"; all the others listen in a manner seldom permitted in our current IGS culture. This mutual interaction has two aspects. First, you speak from the innermost depths, taking as much time or as many false starts as is needed to communicate what is important, knowing that no one will interrupt you. Then, having opened up those depths (perhaps for the first time in your life), you find there's no need to defend what you just said because there can be no questions. You pass the staff on to the next person and begin listening just as intently as you have been speaking. This is the second aspect of the mutual interaction. As the Staff moves on around the circle, you understand more of what you just said and you find that others are moving in that direction so by the time it gets back to you, there's a sense of delight and abundance which spills out in your next statement. This is picked up by others on the next round. Soon the entire group is feeling a sense of the overflowing abundance which comes out of true festivity. Here, I want to go further into that feeling of abundance and its roots in mutuality by turning once more to Willeford's important paper, "Festival, Communion and Mutuality," where he deals with the psychological aspects of this sense of abundance.

In chapter eleven, I refer to Winnicott's famous paper about the relations between mother and infant. Willeford begins his study by quoting from this same paper, where Winnicott states that "ego-organization [occurs] only if someone is there adding up personal experience into a total that can become a self." Willeford continues: "In other words, ego-organisation and the sense of self-identity are largely built up through non-consummatory experiences of mutuality." Earlier on in Part III, I quoted Willeford's statement about seeing in each other the best of which each is capable: "Having the best of oneself *seen* in such a way is an experience of abundance, as is *seeing* the best in another." Admitting that this kind of experience rarely occurs in a relationship between a man and a woman, he states that it can occur more often through festival. But, in festival itself we rarely have the chance nor is it fitting to talk about what is going on. But with the Talking Staff, afterwards, we do use spoken language; and, as Willeford says: "We are creatures of language, which—through its resources of metaphor—extends the known into the unknown and makes the unknown known, and thus gives us mastery over the world."

But that's "utilitarian mastery" and we are right back in the trap of the IGS culture. But when you begin the Talking Staff Council by calling on the Great Beings or gods of the place, they are present, with you, in the Talking Staff Council. And just as the rock cliff "afforded" us the hand hold, thus showing us how to climb in that particular place on the mountain, and thereby giving us life not death; so also, the greater beings of the place, "afford" us deeper understanding of living in that place. If we remember, as traditional cultures acknowledge, that there is a mutual relationship between the human and non-human aspects of the world—the trees, animals, mountains, rock, the "rest of the world," through the "ancient one" deep within us, then we can draw on even deeper levels of seeing the best in others and thus further the sense of abundance.

Once we accept the non-human aspects of the environment in such a mutual relationship, we find that there is no "merely human" personal ego: our true Self extends out into the whole of surrounding nature. This is the abundance which "it is not in human power to give" and we are in the realm of "the sacred."

How to set up the Talking Staff Ritual

Note: There is a basic difference between the Talking Staff Ritual and the ritual passing of other objects around the circle to facilitate communication. In Wicca groups, for instance, they pass around a quartz crystal or a bowl of clear water, etc. In all these rituals, only the one holding the ritual object can speak at that time; no one else can talk. Each of these objects can give a person the freedom to speak undisturbed by anyone else and thus provide for the intense "listening" of the others. This, in itself, can allow the mutuality of the group to develop. However, what all these rituals lack is the incorporation of the non-human into the group council, which the Talking Staff Council, as developed by Cogburn, provides for. Below I will give some basic guidelines to this process.

FINDING THE STAFF

It is essential that the piece of wood chosen for the staff have an integral connection with your place. Ideally, it should come from a tree which is native to that area. If that is not possible, choose one from a species that has been growing for a long time there. If you can find a fallen branch, choose it rather than cutting one. Cutting a branch from a living tree should be a special ritual in itself. The Talking Staff for my place is from a desert juniper not from a local tree; but it is from our Southwest area. My reasons for using it have to do with its connection to the original site for my Way of the Mountain Center and also with its curved form.

The tree connects the earth of the place with the sky above it. Within the tree the light from the sun and the nurturing ingredients from the soil meet and photosynthesis takes place and the tree grows. Its roots extend and connect all around it. From all these meanings, the "tree of the world," (*Yggradsil*) and the "axis mundi" concepts grow.

> In the heart of truth there is a tree. Truth is from the Indo-European root DERU or DRU which means oak or tree. Truth's cognates are: truce, trust, tryst (now a lover's rendezvous but originally it meant waiting for game in the trees), durable, dryad, and druid. A druid is one who sees the tree...In fall a tree sheds its leaves to the ground where various organisms compost (de-compose and re-compose) them into soil, *humus*. Humus is the root for human, humble, humility etc. The tree nourishes itself on its death. The tree cycles all this energy, *informing* it. Roots feed leaves in spring; leaves breathe in light and carbon dioxide to feed the roots and breathe out the air that *inspires*

These words of Tom Jay show us why the Talking Staff comes from the tree.

PREPARING THE STAFF

The first time the group meets to inaugurate the Talking Staff, ask everyone to bring a natural object from your own bioregion which has real meaning for them. Have strong twine or thin leather strips available for tying. These pieces of twine or leather should be quite long—maybe 2 feet or more. I've found that, as the Staff is passed, people stroke these strings. The fingers naturally seem to want to travel along them, searching out the "way" to say what is needed. As part of the actual ceremony you can have each person tie on their offering to the Staff.

It is good to have on hand a bit of the mixture, from another group, which carries the Talking Staff. Here, I will refer to this staff as the "mother" Staff and to the new Talking Staff, as the "daughter" Staff. This mixture should contain broken up bits of native plant material from the place of the "mother" Staff: cedar, balsam pine needles, eucalpytus leaves, etc. Any plant item which seems aromatic to those who live there. Generally sage is not part of this mixture because it is passed separately to begin most ceremonies. Usually cornmeal is included and sometimes tobacco because both these items are sacred to the native inhabitants on this continent. If you have secured some of the mixture from a "mother" Staff, you should add some of your own local mixture to it.

What we are doing here is establishing physical connections between different groups who are ritually learning to "reinhabit" their own place. When first bringing out your new Talking Staff, you can ritually recite its human lineage.

Our Talking Staff here in the San Juan Mountains is the "daughter" of the New Song Ceremonial Talking Staff and connected, because of that, with Talking Staffs in Minneapolis, New York and New Mexico. The Talking Staff I use for BREAKING THROUGH is the daughter of our San Juan Staff and grand-daughter of the New Song Ceremonial Talking Staff.

The natural plant mixture is important as it helps to ground the Staff in the place and to connect it with the natural beings who "gave" the mixture to us. It incorporates those beings in our council and adds that much more depth to our talking council. If a group regularly uses their Staff, this anointing with the mixture does not have to be done each time; only the first time.

The leader walks around the circle, placing some of this mixture in each person's hand. Then the Staff is passed around and each person rubs a bit of the mixture along the length of the staff. When the Staff returns to the leader, further directions are given.

DIRECTIONS FOR USE

1) Explain the purpose of the Staff and how it came to your group. Give the question or the topic which the Council is discussing here with the help of the Staff. This can be quite general such as "What did you learn on the Mountain today?" or very specific or it can be: "Speak whatever is in your heart now, at this time."

2) The Staff is passed around the circle three times. When it comes to you, hold it for a moment and rub your hands along it to feel the power of this tree staff. Touch the strings dangling from it which connect us humans to all the non-human on the string: the plants and bones of animals etc. Take the time to feel what your heart needs to say here in this place, now. If you don't feel like talking, don't; there is no necessity to talk at any time. Just pass it on to the next person. Some people may not feel free enough to talk until the third time around.

3) When you speak: You speak a) to the issue before the group; b) from the Heart and c) briefly—in other words don't ramble but do speak as long as you need to say what you need to say. (These are Elizabeth's basic rules.)

4) Tell only the truth as you see it —now— as you hold the Staff. After the Staff has been around once and comes again to you, you may find that you see the truth differently; well, then, say it differently.

5) Speak with full knowledge of all the beings around you including the natural beings. Speak only from the depths opened by nature—nature within you and outside of you.

6) The Staff itself, imbued as it is by the power of all of us and by the power of the mountains around us or the trees or the river, helps one speak of that which is deep and real. It helps bring up to the conscious level that which is hidden—maybe even from us until we begin speaking. This is why Beno Kennedy introduces the Staff with the words from his dream: "Do you love yourself enough to listen with the ears of your Heart to the other voices of yourself speak?"

7) The person who holds the Staff is the only one who can speak. No one may interrupt for any reason. Another person may answer but only when the Staff reaches them. The only exception to this rule is when someone is speaking so low that the words can't be heard. Then someone may say quietly, "Louder" or "We can't hear you." Keep this remark very simple and non-threatening.

8) If anyone heartily agrees with what the person holding the Staff has just said you may say, "Ho!" Anyone in the group may say "Ho" at that time. It is surprising how this works! No one may express disagreement aloud until they get the staff.

PASSING OF THE STAFF

After all the preliminaries are done—the explanations and rules and everyone has anointed the staff, then the leader begins the ceremony. Each person develops their own ritual here, but, always, it should include open acknowledgement of the great beings of nature, standing around the site. What I do on BREAKING THROUGH is this: after the Staff comes back to me from everyone "anointing" or "feeding" it, I stand up holding the end of the Staff on my heart and lifting the other end slantingly toward the mountains. As mentioned before, I turn to face the four directions, calling upon the East: the place of sunrise, out over the Wet Mountain Valley; the West, the place of sunset and Crestone Needle Peak; the south, Broken Hand Peak; and the north, Humboldt Peak. Then I raise it high in the air toward the zenith and lower it toward the ground. Then I sit down, holding it across my knees and give the question or topic and give my comment on that question. Then I pass it to the next person.

Some of us who use the Staff do not talk about establishing eye contact; others specifically do talk about it to the group. Personally, I feel that in my work, since sight is connected with discrimination, in a way it cuts one off from things. Hearing pulls things together as in an aural culture. Sound pulls things together; sight cuts things apart. Dogs and small children cannot tolerate being stared at; neither can primitives. Since in the Talking Staff Councils we want to reach the depths I feel that purposely establishing eye contact with the group is not useful. In 1985, after our Autumn Equinox celebration was over, a few of the people stayed over another day and I had a chance to talk about this aspect. Donna, a psychotherapist from West Virginia, said that in therapy work it is important to establish eye contact early on because it makes for good communication. She said: "The Talking Staff seemed to violate all of this. But worked superlatively." She wondered about that. After thinking on it awhile, Donna said that somehow in the Talking Staff Council, to look up "would be to invade the boundaries—you would not want to do that. It's important to have privacy when you are baring your soul in that way." So in the Talking Staff Council she purposely did not look up at the person as they were talking. During this conversation Donna said: "Hearing is healing!"

Bill Plotkin, as mentioned before, is also a psychotherapist. He does use direct eye contact from the beginning in his Vision Quest Talking Staff Councils. I feel that perhaps this is necessary in that particular setting because the people need to have confidence in Bill, their leader, before they venture into something as threatening as being alone in the wilderness. Bill always brings in the surrounding natural beings at the opening invocation just as I do. Everyone is sitting on the floor at their first meeting before they travel off to the site in nature for the Quest. Before he passes the Staff around he takes it in hand and goes around the inside of the circle, kneeling in front of each person, looks them in the eye and says the ritual phrase I mentioned above: "Do you love yourself enough..." He tells his people that "the Staff gives you access to parts of the Self that are normally hidden." He sometimes refers to it as "a dialogue with the unconscious." He instructs his people to "Wait until the Staff comes to you. Let yourself be surprised at what you say. Let the Staff tell you what to say." Bill does not limit passing the staff to the usual three rounds, but, instead lets the staff continue making the rounds until "no one needs to talk anymore." This depends on the amount of people and how much time you have.

Each summer Bill helps to lead a major desert Vision Quest for people from all over the country. It lasts for two weeks. On this particular occasion, they were ten days into it and "the experience hadn't jelled yet." He was "puzzled and disconcerted" because this had never happened before in the desert. Always people had responded to the power of the place and become "fully" real. So he called a Talking Staff Council. He began with the statement that he felt "they were not worthy to be there" in such a powerful place. This opened things up and the Council went on for 18 hours—taking time out to eat twice. One person—with years of experience behind him in setting up therapy for people—had been moved to tell of how totally desolated he was, long ago, when his first wife left him. Later, he told Bill he had never shared that with anyone before. In talking about this occasion, Bill said: "The talking staff gives a person the chance to share the burden...the opportunity presented by the Staff to finally feel free and open and trusting enough to "share the burden" of something one may have carried around all their life without ever daring to before." And once you do share something, it no longer has the terror or power over you.

Talking Staff Council on BREAKING THROUGH

I chose this particular Council to describe in some detail for two main reasons: first, it shows how the power of self-disclosure released the other men who were present to tell of events in their lives, hitherto never shared; second, it shows how through the Talking Staff, individuals can begin to talk about the effect of the greater beings, the mountains and rivers, on their life.

On this particular BREAKING THROUGH there were roughly equal men and women, but to fully explain the unique Talking Staff experience, which occurred, I will be dealing mainly with the men as I recount the events leading up to it.

After the preliminary two days on the ranch, where we get acquainted with one another, learn how to function in cooking and cleaning up as well as rock climbing, Tai Chi style, we move to the Arkansas River for two days of white water rafting. Following that we backpack into our high mountain site, located just below timberline (around 10,000 ft.). On the following day we climb Broken Hand. When we arrive on the mountain itself, we follow a trail up to the Green Ramp. Here we do "eagle rising," which I explained in the "Way of Chant" section. Briefly, standing on the flat green grass ramp with a cliff dropping off below us, we do a Tai Chi style movement that leaves all of us feeling as if we had turned into eagles flying high up in the sky. Then we take a short break and continue the climb.

Usually everyone is exhilarated by the experience of nearly

flying and the walk up to where the rock cliffs begin, passes swiftly. The cliff area actually consists of short pitches of steep rock and then broad green ledges covered with alpine flowers, but from below it looks like an all rock cliff. After the first and hardest cliff of the entire climb we gathered above the rock pitch to share remarks about the rock. In such places either Rick or I always remark how fine it was that the rock let us climb it and even helped us along by "affording" that handhold just when we needed it. Looking back, we realized that two of our members had stayed behind at the "eagle rising" place. Since both were experienced climbers, we felt there was no problem as it was a good place to sleep or rest and we could pick them up on the way down.

After our usual hour summit sleep in the sun, we joyously began the descent and noticed that our two members were making their way back to camp, as well. When we all got there, George Sessions told us that, after the combination of exposure and the totally unfamiliar "eagle rising" he had decided that, without a rope he didn't want to continue the climb. It turns out that, although George had done many of the early first ascents in Yosemite years before, he had not done rock climbing much since, due to his work. You may have recognized the name. George is the one who began Deep Ecology here in this country. Another factor is that always before, when climbing rock he had been leading a rope. Approaching strange rock cliffs without a rope was something he had never done in his life. Generally, people on BREAKING THROUGH are not really climbers so they don't notice the lack of a rope. (We always carry a spare rope in a pack for emergencies, of course.) As George was explaining this to us, I noticed the respect the younger men showed to George for admitting his fear.

The next day George and two other members climbed the other 14,000 ft. peak, Humboldt, while we climbed Crestone Needle. We always spend a good long time on top, exhilarated by the view directly down onto the lake and the fearsome crags leading over to Crestone Peak. For an hour we have been lying around in the sun with good conversation, laughter, singing, eating, etc. In other words doing what humans have most liked to do for the past 50,000 years. On top of that we have had some fear and excitement on the climb up so the combination makes for real bonding and great joy. Then, Rick and I get everyone up off their soft, comfortable rock and under way for the descent. At first there is a real shock of surprise. After all that relaxation, our people are suddenly climbing along a very narrow rock ridge, with the lake several thousand feet below them and drop-offs on both sides. I have seen the grins suddenly disappear as we begin the descent. But we have the route carefully programmed by now and—almost as soon as we are on the narrow ridge, we are off it, in a nice, safe, rock-enclosed gulley. And everyone finds that their feet are moving as if they knew what to do. I always take a minute here to let everyone realize their feet are doing fine; it's their head that's in trouble and we talk about that and joke about the "ancient one" deep inside that knows how to do this. Anyone having real trouble is put directly behind either Rick or I and we tell them the old Swiss guide saying: Put your foot right in the place where mine just left. Soon everyone is exhilarated again. It does work. Even going down on steep cliffs.

Everyone arrived back in camp, tired but very pleased with their success. Crestone Needle is clearly visible from camp, looking absolutely vertical from there, but we can't even see the top of Humboldt as it towers vertically above us.

The next morning everyone has three hours of solo time to go off and be alone in this high alpine area. Then we return to the campsite and have our second and last, Talking Staff Council of BREAKING THROUGH. We leave in the afternoon and everyone begins the journey to their homes.

I will not go through the entire Talking Staff Council; instead I will begin near the end of the second round. One of the younger men said, with great feeling: "I've never before met so many tender older men." Many said "Ho!" feelingly, in strong agreement. With this disclosure, others felt free to tell how much being with these four men had done for them. (We had four men over 40, including Rick and George.) Then, one young man explained how much it had helped him to have George admit publicly, with no effort, that he had been afraid on Broken Hand. It turns out that this young man had never in his life had the courage to admit he was afraid and had kept it to himself. Now, knowing it was "ok" to admit fear because George, a famous climber, had done so, just changed his life. There were tears in the eyes of many of us while listening to his account. Then, on the last and third round, things got even deeper. As the Staff got to a man from Arizona, he began telling us of his commander in the Viet Nam war—how much this commander had done for them and how much he thought of him. And then, with a catch in his voice, he said that his commander had been killed over there in Viet Nam and he had never been able to tell anyone how much this man meant to him. And then a real glow came over his face as he shared this with us, because now, finally he had been able to tell someone. In telling this "story," somehow he had released some of the pent-up sorrow he had carried so long. His deepest sorrow now became part of our shared "story" here in the mountains. From that moment this man became a different person—no longer so closely guarded, but freely willing to take the chance of being open and his smile grew bigger and bigger.

I cannot take the space here to tell more of this Council, as I want to go further into the power of self-disclosure. These people have learned trust on all the previous days of BREAKING THROUGH. Trust not only in Rick and Mike Adams, Rick's main rock climbing instructor, and I, to get them safely through scary situations on the mountains and the river, but trust in the river itself that it will show them the way through the rapids if they let it. And trust in the rock that their foot does hold on the scary place if they stand up straight and don't lean in from fear. The rock is trustworthy. After all these days of learning to trust their "world" around them, they begin to feel it's "safe" to disclose deeper things to the group as a whole. There's a reciprocity in "self-disclosure." Once someone takes the risk of disclosing something very deeply buried within them, others are freed to share their burdens, long hidden. Through the days of shared living on the river and the mountain and shared feelings through the Talking Staff we all become bonded together in a truly tribal group. The river becomes a real being to us—one that responds to us and we learn to trust it. The first glimpse of the high mountains brings disbelief.

"You mean I'm supposed to go up that?" Then comes the wonder of finding the mountain lets you climb it. There's no bravado or "I conquered the mountain." It's always respect and wonder that the mountains let us climb them.

All of this becomes real for each member of the group through the sharing of each "story" through the Talking Staff. And through this sharing we find that each of the different stories become one story, "our" story, here in *this* place—the Crestone Mountains.

Becoming part of "the story"

"Jung said that he learned from the start how in every disturbance of the personality, even in its most extreme psychotic form of schizophrenia...one could discern the elements of a personal story," the great story-teller, Laurens Van Der Post explains, as he tells us how important "story" was to Jung. Laurens continues: "That story was the personality's most precious possession, whether it knew that or not, and the person could only be cured—or healed, as he put it...by the psychiatrist getting hold of the story. That was the secret key to unlock the door which barred reality in all its dimensions within and without from entering the personality and transforming it." Jung felt that the story held not only the original trauma but also the "potential" for further development of the personality. Laurens continues: "This arrest of the personality in one profound unconscious timeless moment of itself called psychosis, he would tell me, occurred because the development of the person's own story had been interrupted...All movement of the spirit and sense of beginning and end had been taken away from it and the story...stood still."

Each patient Jung worked with showed him "how a personal story was clamoring to be carried on and lived." But how could this be facilitated when the story had been interrupted so radically. Jung felt only through "constantly reiterated, truthful and face-to-face encounter between patient and psychiatrist." All aspects of psychiatrist and patient must dialogue "at the deepest level."

This brings us to crux of the matter. Stanley Diamond, for instance, tells us that there is no schizophrenia among primitive people. Why? The answer, of course, is quite simple: through "constantly reiterated, truthful and face-to-face" on-going rituals and myth based on the great beings or gods of that place and their changing relationships through the seasons, the individual "becomes" part of the on-going story of his people since the moment he was born. There's no effort involved, if begun soon enough. That's why, for all of us trying to learn how "to reinhabit our place on earth," the "fly like birds" Huichol ceremony, as given in chapter eleven, is so important for babies and young children. Furthermore, in a primitive society, if a person has some deep conflict or difficulty he or she does not go "insane"; instead, one becomes a shaman through this very difficulty and by virtue of that standing, helps the rest of the group "live" their story to a greater depth.

In passing the Talking Staff round the circle, sitting there midst all of the surrounding natural beings, we become able "to read everything that's around" us. And that's a "different kind of *literacy*" as Dennis Tedlock tells us. This, of course, is what myth is all about. Concerning the Zuni, Tedlock says:

> So—I hope you begin to get the picture here that myth is coming to the surface all the time—whenever you happen to look for it.
>
> They're looking for it all the time—it's a whole habit of life.
>
> It's what—it means to be continuously and every day and in this moment always—connected up with the whole past.

As Tedlock points out the things one really learns are the things one "*realizes*," not just takes on faith. "And," as he says, "that is hermeneutic phenomenology—which is quite a mouthful—all it really means—in the end—probably is learning to—tell the story, it means reducing your—distance between you and that story..."

Sitting, centered within the surrounding natural beings, passing the Talking Staff around and around, one begins to enter that story. Speaking, then, becomes "relational": "In speaking the individual is opened to that which is a we, is opened to a spirit which is not under the individual's control." This, in turn, leads to a new self-understanding. (Now we are at the very heart of both hermeneutics and the sacred.) Such an experience is "the encounter which shows the individual his or her mutuality with all existence" and thus the further dimensions of Self. Even deeper, this "Self-knowledge alone is capable of saving a freedom threatened not only by all rulers but much more by the domination and dependence that issue from everything we think we control." But in the Industrial Growth Society, if we don't "control" all of it; it must be chaos. Which brings us back full circle to the chaos of Taoism and Chuang Tzu.

Chuang Tzu and Chaos

In writing of the Talking Staff experience, I am dealing with the real meaning of communication. The root word, *communicare*, means "to make common to many," "to share, impart" or to "participate." We ordinarily think of communication as giving a message, but its deeper meaning concerns an evocation of experience. The knowledge that comes from undergoing experience is called "understanding." "In such understanding there is no knowledge to process and convey. There is instead a deepening, a conversion of life outlook and attitude... Understanding cannot be conveyed; it must be evoked." Kuang-ming Wu is explaining the effect of Chuang Tzu's words on us; but it also describes the "communication" which the Talking Staff "affords" us. As the Talking Staff proceeds around the circle and people are stating their "heart" words: "Concepts crack open, the inside radiates. The words do not so much grasp the objects as they evoke responses. They do not talk about the subject matter, but render it present by moving the subject."

There is no message as such but an on-going openness to "explore presences without disturbing them." As Chuang Tzu says: "...walking among the beasts without alarming their herds, walking among the birds without alarming their flocks." When we explore deeply within ourselves, we are called back to our true self: "When one comes home to one's naturalness, one understands the naturalness of the surroundings and lives accordingly." Through the Talking Staff one becomes "a communicated one, a shared one, shared in the awakened way of life, a changed person, who looks at things in depth and freshness..." In other words a person who listens to the "ancient one" deep within; and listening to this "ancient one" within, you begin to listen to the "ancient one" all about you, speaking in the leaves of the trees, the shifting light of the fire, the distant howl of the coyote.

"Ceasing to impose itself upon itself, the self can now afford to open itself outside" is the way Wu puts it. He continues: "This one's *being*-open responds to everything, and thereby invites every being to actively open itself." Every being has "the equal right to live and blossom" is what Arne Naess proclaims as the heart of Deep Ecology. By letting things *be* as they are without pushing them around or harming them, one is freed to become oneself. This is where truth appears. As Chuang Tzu says: "the True Man, who 'plays' (*yu*) in life the truth of things." Chuang Tzu does not talk about Taoists he talks "only of 'friends' one to another, and in the name of *Hun-Tun* (in the Circle that is at once no circle and many a circle), 'treat each other very well'." Remember, Hun-Tun is the gourd! And Chuang Tzu is not too sure whether he is the butterfly, dreaming of him or Chuang Tzu, dreaming of the butterfly. "Chuang Tzu's meandering mutuality fulfills every individual being, so that they are enabled to freely 'play' out various modes of being and become *friends* with one another," Wu tells us. He continues: "In such mutualities each one grows into oneself."

At her first Talking Staff council, Donna said: "I feel as if I've come home." This coming home has to do with returning to one's own nature, which, as Wu tells us is for "each self to return to its root, returning to the Primitive through non-doing...[and] to be at home in one's nature is to be at home in nature..."

Coming home to the self frees one to respond fully to every being in nature and the freedom of being allowed this full response contributes to the joy which the Talking Staff affords us. Once more I must quote Wu's words here because he understands Chuang Tzu so clearly:

> No longer is there prostitution of one's original nature or dislocation of the original root-power, the power of being oneself. One is whole in his innate lucidity, responding, adapting, changing with the seasons...what one exudes from within happily meets what one confronts outside. This is where deep answers the deep..."

And where you are always part of "the story."

THE "WAY" OF THE BARD

Mountains and rivers compel me to speak for them; they are transformed through me and I am transformed through them.

                                    Shih-t'ao (1641-1717)

The Talking Staff "affords" each of us the "way" to become part of the story of our own place. The Bard takes all of these individual stories—each human story within the on-going story of the place itself—and combines them into a vast epic. He can do this because he is registering more than the "merely" human; he speaks for the land itself. One of the greatest of our modern bards, Gary Snyder says:

> As a poet I hold the most archaic values on earth. They go back to the late Paleolithic: the fertility of the soil, the magic of animals, the power-vision in solitude...the love and ecstasy of the dance, the common work of the tribe. I try to hold both history and wilderness in mind, that my poems may approach the true measure of all things and stand against the unbalance and ignorance of our time.

For a very long time in our European culture we had no bards. In his *Republic*, Plato "killed" the bards to clear the way for intellectuals; only recently have we begun to grasp the full depth of the disasters which Plato's "ideas" and "ideals" have brought both to the natural world and to human beings. But now, beginning with the pioneering work of Snyder, we have a new generation of bards coming up, who can show us how nature and human consciousness are but different aspects of the one consciousness. They put the mind and body together in one complete whole.

In the West, the Welsh bards held out longest; they were still writing their epics as late as the ninth century; disguising them under a thin veneer of Christianity. The modern Welsh poet, Dylan Thomas has a bit of the bard in him; but he couldn't hold it together all alone in this wasteland and had to drink himself to death. Robinson Jeffers is sometimes considered a bard but the near destruction of his humanity, brought about from the forced rootlessness (by his father) during his teenage years, prevented him from seeing human and nature as two aspects of the "one consciousness" and he became bitterly anti-human.

So, essentially we owe the revival of the bardic tradition to Gary Snyder. And it dates clear back to 1950 and 1951 when he had ten poems published while at Reed College. In reviewing Snyder's work, Robert Scott writes: "These early poems show that from the start, he agreed with Robert Graves' book, *The White Goddess*, published in 1948; our patriarchal industrial society destroys the emotional and matriarchal source of life. To regain the power poetry once had, poets must rediscover the ancient rituals that re-enact its one universal subject, the seasonal cycles of life and death. Thirty years earlier Robinson Jeffers had decided to do so by writing tragedies, but Snyder did so [in the fashion of] the Imagists by using mere brief metaphors and allusions to the myths that personify seasonal cycles."

Scott adds that in giving him permission to publish the poems he had collected, Snyder wrote: "These poems, I guess, show that I (and all of us) read Pound and Eliot. Plus the Mother Consciousness first stirred up by Robert Graves."

It all seems to go back to Ezra Pound and then stop. But who came before Pound? That answer is not easy to come by; but it was Ernest Fenollosa's "Essay on the Chinese Written Character," written at the beginning of this century. It was not until he found this essay that Pound began his real work. Writing about its importance, Pound states:

> Fenollosa's essay was perhaps too far ahead of his time to be easily comprehended. He did not proclaim his method as a method. He was trying to explain the Chinese ideograph as a means of transmission and registration of thought. He got to the root of the matter, to the root of the difference between what is valid in Chinese thinking and invalid or misleading in a great deal of European thinking and language.

Just here we find the crucial step which may eventually lead to reclaiming our European language system from the "invalid and misleading" thinking concerning human and nature, which we have inherited from the ancient Greek language problem and Plato. (See chapter one of this work.) Notice further that our "salvation" comes out of the Chinese/Japanese written language by way of Pound and then directly into the new "bardic" tradition through Gary Snyder.

International communication expert, Barrington Nevitt further explains: "Paradoxically, the synchronic structure of the Chinese ideogram reinforces the audile-tactile sensory awareness of its users, just as the diachronic structure of the printed European languages intensified the visual sensory bias that the Greek phonetic alphabet created. Poet (Greek *poietes*, meaning "maker") T. S. Eliot dedicated poetry to Ezra Pound, (the best maker)." Pound was one of the founders of the school of poetry called "Imagism," edited the first anthology of Imagist poetry (1914), and translated a great deal of poetry from the ancient Chinese and Japanese. His major work is the *Cantos*.

"At the turn of the century, American poetry was in a dismal state," writes Lawrence Russ. "One young scholar and poet by the name of Ezra Pound, however was soon to set off powder kegs." Pound succeeded in making American writers pay attention to "poets as 'primitive' as the *Beowulf* bards and as foreign as the Chinese Li Po." In one of Pound's earliest bits of writing (1910), he speculates on the Provencal troubadours and connects their songs with the pagan rites of May Day and wonders: "...surely we come to this place where the ecstasy is not a whirl or a madness of the senses, but a glow arising from the exact nature of perception." Here we are at the heart of bardic poetry.

"Many writers blazed the trail, but two in particular radically transformed the spiritual life of American poetry: Robert Bly and Gary Snyder." "Snyder," another critic, Parkinson, writes, "has effectively done something that for an individual is extremely difficult: he has created a new culture." Although in some ways, an innacurate statement, because fishermen and forest workers from California and the Northwest as well as mountain climbers and other maverick types also had a hand in shaping this culture, still Snyder has certainly been its outstanding spokesman. Snyder's poetry is now finally generally recognized. Another younger poet, the Canadian, Robert MacLean is not as well known. After eight years as a tree planter, MacLean right now is living in Japan (just as Snyder did when he was younger).

With MacLean we have a wholly different way of looking at the world. The only way I can succinctly explain MacLean's type of consciousness is to quote Gregory Bateson, who pointed out that for the few who achieve what he calls *Learning III*, "the concept of 'self' no longer functions as a nodal argument in the punctuation of experience...personal identity merges into all the processes of relationship in one vast ecology or aesthetics of cosmic interaction." In other words, the concept of "self" just leaves you and, as MacLean writes:

> Tent tethered among jackpine and blue-bells. Lacewings rise from rock incubators. Wild geese flying north. And I can't remember who I'm supposed to be.

Nearing the top of a rarely climbed mountain—going up

a long, steep, green ramp of tundra—everything falling away below me—more mountains coming into view with each step—walking becoming flying, his words came to me... "And I can't remember who I'm supposed to be." And, suddenly, I realized: "Yes, I had forgotten all about who I'm *supposed* to be." MacLean gives us the words we never had before for what we experience in nature.

As I travel to various places to give workshops I find there are more young poets out there beginning to learn how to be a bard for—and—in their own place. I feel that an important first step for any bioregional group is to search for the young man trying to be a bard within that region and support him by recognition and money if at all possible. For without a real bard you won't be able to find the "soul of your place" for at least another generation. As Tom Jay, writes of his place, western Washington:

> The salmon is the soul of the world. Indeed the salmon is at least the soul of this biome, this green house. He is the tutelary spirit that swims in and around us, secret silver mystery, salmon of the heart, tree-born soul of our world."
>
> This essay depends in part on the notion that, salmon-like language bridges subject and object world, inner and outer: Language is the path, the game trail, the river, the reverie between them. It shimmers there, revealing and nourishing their interdependence. Each word *bears* and *locates* our meetings with the world. A word is a clipped breath, a bit of spirit (*inspire, expire*), wherein we hear the weather. Our 'tongues' taste the world we eat. At root, language is sacramental.

I want to tell you a bit about one more bard—Nanao Sakaki. He is a close friend of Gary Snyder. In fact Gary met his wife, Masa, at one of the communes associated with Sakaki in Japan. Sakaki was asked to talk to a poetry class at Naropa Institute in Boulder in 1985. I've long appreciated Nanao's poetry and asked one of the young bards that I know (who was attending the class) to let me know what Nanao was like. Andy wrote me that at a colloquim there, he [Nanao] was asked who his greatest influences had been. Andy wrote:

> It was very interesting. Most of the writers picked somebody like William Carlos Williams, Ezra Pound and Gertrude Stein. But Nanao? He flashes an appealing smile and says, 'The bear, maybe the bear. Maybe coyote.' Then he laughs. 'Maybe fir tree.' The students as well as the staff thought him odd, but of course it's due to ignorance that he is not understood. Nanao does a lot of walking...Nanao's poetry is a voice of contact beyond the communication of human to human. It's a poetry of listening.

THE TAI CHI WAY

This is the last of the seven "ways" in this chapter and the greatest of all the ways to cross the boundary between wilderness and civilization. It "affords" you the deepest experiences of "extended identity" with all of nature as well as "mutuality" among humans. In fact, in the "Animal Frolics," an early form of Tai Chi, still taught for health, you learn to walk as a bear or move as a sea serpent. The only information I've been able to find on the animal origin of the discipline of Tai Chi, however, comes from Bob Klein, who has a degree in Zoology and has been teaching Tai Chi since 1975. He writes that Tai Chi "reconnects the mind to the body, the consciousness to the sub-consciousness and the individual to the environment...reunites the individual with the source of life itself—

the Earth." In his Introduction, he states that his book, "is an expedition into a nature-oriented perspective and lifestyle whose origins reach back into prehistoric antiquity." Essentially, as he explains, Tai Chi is "a slow relaxing series of movements based on animal behavior." This gives important verification for what I've discovered. Klein has a degree in Zoology so has considerable experience with animal behavior.

You can't learn Tai Chi from a book so what I will do here is give you three separate descriptions of what happened to me over a period of years, while doing Tai Chi out in nature as I have done since the beginning of my studies. Each experience gave me a progressively deeper insight. As far as I can find out, few people get the chance to regularly do Tai Chi out in wild nature over a period of years. Done inside, Tai Chi is amazing enough, but outside things happen to you for which there are no words. Doing Tai Chi outside you know that it connects us directly to the animal and to the mountains and rivers and rocks as well.

I've been doing Tai Chi for seventeen years now and teaching it for fifteen years. I began studying it because we were going to leave Alta, Utah where my husband had been the snow ranger. I thought "I'll die without powder snow." And there is no powder anywhere in the world like there is at Alta. Unfortunately, that's true! That summer, on a wild beach in Western Washington, I saw two friends doing Tai Chi. Watching them from a rock above, I realized that those movements would probably give one the same feeling as skiing powder. Fortunately living in Seattle half the year, I found a good Chinese teacher, who came down from Vancouver, Canada once a week to teach us. I was only able to get four lessons before mid-summer arrived, when I went up to the glacier on Mt. Olympus to help out with my husband's avalanche work.

As soon as things were organized in the hut I headed up Panic Peak to do Tai Chi. This is a small rock "nunatack" left from the glacier scouring. On one side it drops right off to the Pacific Ocean; on the other we see Mt. Rainier. I scraped the gravelly rocks away to make a flat place just below the summit and began the slow, circling movements of Tai Chi. When I finished I was amazed. I had seen a mountain I had never seen before! Now, you must realize that I had been walking up to the summit and sitting on it and looking, looking—for something like sixteen years. I had watched sunrises and sunsets and storms and thought I knew every mountain. And I saw a new mountain I'd never seen before! Now, that I had seen it doing Tai Chi, I looked again and yes, it was truly there. I realized that Tai Chi certainly helps you see better. I began using it as a "seeing" tool. Even for art shows—when no one was looking. Returning to Seattle in the fall, I continued the lessons until moving here to Silverton full-time.

Doing Tai Chi one is continually amazed by new discoveries. But I am going to skip a number of years and tell you about doing Tai Chi on Golden Horn, a local mountain near Silverton which is just under 14,000 ft. This particular event happened in 1984. I climb the mountain at least once a summer and had done Tai Chi on it for the first time about five years previously. The location is superb. Golden Horn, named for its bright yellow "popcorn" rock—exploded volcanic stuff—looks like it will be a technical rock climb. But when you get on it, it's much easier until the final tower which has intense exposure for a short time. The tower is vertical gray rock. Part way up this tower, the glacier had carved out a perfectly flat platform and covered it with very fine gravel. It's just the right size for two people to do Tai Chi! There's nothing above you as you face out doing Tai Chi and all the world below you. Mountains in every direction, river drainages and waterfalls and snowbanks and flowers. Every time I do Tai Chi there it leaves me in a state of bliss. One year we had a pine martin watching us. He was so enthralled he didn't even leave, when we finished and turned around to look right in his eyes. So in 1984 I expected no more than that. In that year I took my sister and a friend from Silverton, who had been taking Tai Chi from me for two years, Jackie Miller.

My sister sat in the sun as we began the movements. As we finished I was stunned. Jackie was "blissed out." When I didn't say a word, she asked me "What's going on?" For a few moments I couldn't even answer and then I said, "I don't know. When I find some words for it I'll tell you." For miles down the trail I mulled it over. It wasn't until we got back to Silverton that I was able to tell her. As I finished the last movement, looking out over all those mountains, a feeling came to me of "infinite sadness." But not ordinary sadness. Not something bad or sorrowful. Just "infinite sadness" as if I had lost something—something very important. Had I not been Rolfed I probably would never have been able to put words to it.

As mentioned earlier in this work, I was Rolfed to heal the after-effects of the avalanche I was in. My Rolfer was Tom Wing in Boulder, who studied directly with Ida Rolf. As I mentioned earlier, we had a lot to talk about each time because he, too, is into ritual. At the end of the last of the ten sessions, the Rolfer does a special sort of final adjustment. Up to then I lay on the table and Tom worked on me. For this final adjustment, he told me to sit up straight and he got behind me on the table. He reached around my body with both arms and did a strange little jerk which effectively put my entire backbone in its correct position (that it was born in). Then he sat quietly without saying a word for a few minutes. When he got off the table, he asked me, "How did you feel?" Again, words were difficult. But I explained that I sort of felt as if I had suddenly realized all that I had lost—that I sort of had a remembrance of something much deeper and bigger that I had been a part of and had lost. He told me that most people who are Rolfed have a great cry after this adjustment. If anything has been wrong in their life or they have a hidden sorrow they just cry and cry, therapeutically, but that when Ida Rolf, herself had Rolfed him, he hadn't done that either. He had felt as I felt. Ida and he talked about it but came to no conclusions because so few have this experience. Over the years Tom had figured out that what he felt when his entire body was re-aligned the way it was born to be, was this: one suddenly feels all the connections with the animals, with the deeper non-human inside which we lost when we became humans. This gives one that strange, "almost remembering sorrow."

Now, with that explanation I can tell you that up on Golden

Horn, as I finished Tai Chi and looked out over the infinitude of the mountains, I suddenly realized that for that brief time of doing Tai Chi I had not been separate—I had been moving with all I saw out there. I suppose you could say that the rational, human brain had been totally bypassed. But, as I completed the movements, the "merely" human brain took over control again. With that sudden shift, I realized the enormous loss of that sense of "being at one with everything," which the human brain causes us to lose in some way. I realized that I was back again in normal consciousness and that being human had disconnected me from the immediate, felt contact with all of nature.

The next few times up Golden Horn, in doing Tai Chi I always had that same feeling of "infinite sorrow." Don't get me wrong by thinking it was bad. It was still bliss but it was something added on to bliss not counteracting it. Sort of a connection I could almost remember.

Then this last summer, I climbed it with another friend, now moved from Silverton, who had taken Tai Chi from me for only one winter. It was the first time I had ever climbed it in less than perfect weather. There was a total heavy black overcast above us everywhere. But we could see the sunlight between that black pall and the horizon. We just pushed through for the summit hoping that we would get back off the ridge before the lightning arrived. Coming down from the summit, with the storm not actually upon us yet, we decided to do Tai Chi on the platform. He had heard me talk of it so often that he couldn't pass it up.

Before I continue I must explain that once one begins doing the form of Tai Chi, the knees are slightly bent; because one cannot walk with the spine straight unless the knees are bent. The spine is kept straight to allow the energy to circulate freely. Tai Chi ends with a movement where your encircling arms draw together all the energies which have been generated during the 108 forms. All of this is focused in the slightly cupped hands held just at the *tan tien* level (just below the navel). Then the hands are raised to heart level, turned palms down and pushed down toward the earth. At the same time, the legs are straightened. Always, this Tai Chi ending gives one a sense of completeness—almost—abundance.

Just before the final Tai Chi form, explained above, there is a complete 360 degree turn and a final kick (the "lotus kick"). As I spun around in this turn, I suddenly saw my friend for the first time since beginning the 108 forms. Seeing him there, was a real shock. I rather hastily completed the final movement. Of course the usual bliss was not there—after that sudden shock. Then I stood there, trying to figure it out. Thinking back, I realized that the last thing I consciously remembered, was seeing a single shaft of sunlight coming down out of the lowering pall of black clouds right onto the sloping green tundra leading up to the top of Bear Mountain—the very route another friend and I had used to climb the mountain that previous summer. Then I recalled being so drawn into that incredible green light—and that is the last thing my conscious, "merely human" brain remembered. My feeling was that I had been moving through the forms in both places at once. Definitely, I was on the rock platform but just as definitely I was in the glowing, green light. And that green light was what I had suddenly missed when I turned and saw my friend. I was no longer within the green light. That was the shock.

About that time the summer snow began pelting us and the wind roared in and we raced off the ridge, glissaded down a much too steep snow slope for a beginner such as he, but survived to walk away in the rain shower, now safe from the lightning playing on the ridge above us.

All the way back down the trail, I mulled over that experience. I recalled reading of shamans "travelling" over the mountains and valleys of their place and seeing the approaching caribou, although they were still miles away. I thought of the Taoist sages in their "light bodies" riding on the phoenix and the crane. But most of of all I felt very, very good! The only thing I knew for certain was that I had been moving through the Tai chi forms in *both* places—on the rock platform and in the glorious green light of the alpine trundra some five or six miles down the mountain from the rock platform on Golden Horn. The odd thing was, it seemed like the "most natural thing in the world" to me even though it made no rational sense at all. It finally came to me that during Tai Chi, my "identity" had "extended" as far as that glorious green light, miles down the valley.

I want to make it very plain that this was no "out of body" experience, at all. I was in my body but my body took in miles of terrain. Now that this has happened to me, I wonder if maybe the "out of body" experiences one reads about is because the person was not grounded enough in the earth to realize that they were being given the privilege of "extended identity."

It was not until six months later—while writing this book—that I came across anything more which could help me understand this experience or help me explain it to anyone else. I ordered the book, *Dreamtime: Concerning the Boundary Between Wilderness and Civilization*, which I've mentioned before. Soon as it came I sat down to skim through it. Near the end of the book in chapter ten, "The Half-truths of the Coyote or Castaneda and the Altered States of America," Hans Duerr is trying to explain just how Castaneda went wrong in interpreting the very real experiences which Don Juan had set up for him. Castaneda is saying to Don Juan that the coyote really talked. Don Juan says in reply: "Now, look who is talking like an idiot." He goes on to say that after all these years of learning Castaneda should know better. "Yesterday you *stopped the world* and you might have seen." Castaneda insists that the world is the same today and yesterday, but Don Juan points out that all those things happened yesterday "simply because something had stopped in you." Duerr explains that Castaneda "had allowed the boundaries to dissolve within himself that prevented an understanding between humans and coyotes in ordinary life, and in doing so, something hidden behind that boundary showed itself." Well, that made me sit up and pay attention. Duerr explains that "an ordinary person" thinks such experiences are delusions; and an "ordinary witch is a human who thinks that *basically* animals talk and their failure to do is a mere appearance. Both are able to see, even though differently, but they cannot *see*...He who can *see*, however, recognizes the truth and the simultaneous limitations of both points of view." To really see you have to "smuggle yourself in between the worlds" of the ordinary people and the witches.

"For between the worlds, 'on the fence', it becomes possible to recognize that the 'true believers of science', as also the 'true believers in magic', are simultaneously right and wrong." Magical animals don't talk like in fairy-stories, but their "talking" is not delusion either, as psychology would label it. Duerr says that such magical animals can be seen only with "the eyes of the heart" as the Sioux Indians say. Then, the next sentence is the one that spoke to me about what happened up there on Golden Horn:

> The boundaries of our person expand, and we become aware of things that remain invisible and unreachable for our ordinary eyes...a *brujo* need not be able to fly like a bird in order to arrive at a different place within seconds, for it seems that a sorcerer can change the boundaries of his person so much that he can be simultaneously within his everyday body and *also* at another place, where his body is not...We are apparently dealing more with a 'lifting of boundaries', in which there is a dissolution of barriers developed during the processes of civilization and individuation...[Further] some of the boundaries that modern individuals are encapsulated in, as compared to archaic humans, disappear.

To get to back to this state—as was normal for our archaic ancestors—"to be able, for instance, to 'speak' with plants, a person needs what the Indians call 'reverence'. Humans must become *unimportant* before the other beings of nature."

Through the years as I've been doing Tai Chi out in nature, each time I finish the concluding move I have a sense of overwhelming reverence. Lately, I find as I teach it out in nature, my students are picking up on this reverence sooner and sooner. Instead of years of practicing Tai Chi before this reverence comes to them, in certain places it happens almost instantaneously. To quote Donna again, after she had done the first Tai Chi of her life here on the Autumn Equinox, beneath the golden aspen she told me: "Tai Chi gives me permission to be reverent."

Somehow Tai Chi "affords" us humans the unique opportunity of fully experiencing our individual human nature while taking part in the abundance of all of surrounding nature. In terms of Western logic this can't happen, of course; but it can, if we think in terms of Chuang Tzu's goal of repossessing "man's true treasure," which is a way of *seeing* "that can come into play only when the distinction between 'inside' and 'outside,' between 'self' and 'things,' between 'this' and 'that' has been entirely obliterated. Chuang Tzu's symbol for this state of pure consciousness which sees without looking, hears without listening, knows without thinking, is the god Hun-Tun ('Chaos')." Here, once more we find Lord Hun-Tun, the gourd, showing us "the way."

APPENDIX: SKILLFULL STRATEGIES

This appendix offers "skillful strategies" for those people asking, "Yes, but how do I begin?" I get this question often at workshops; therefore, I fully understand the problem. If you have begun to grasp the need to change, but there's no one else near you who shares this understanding; often one is stymied at the very beginning. The most important thing to remember is that you can't do everything at once; you must begin small and allow the process to grow, trusting to the "original human" still in each of us. Rituals help at every stage, so begin using them as soon as you are able.

Remember, since we are mammals, we can't even communicate without rituals; therefore, everyone is using them already even though unaware of it. However, these present day social rituals come to us out of the Industrial Growth Society, thus they are destructive to both humans and the earth itself. At a deeper level, the "original" human rituals are still within us so you can, consciously, begin using those rituals which not only put people together, but put people together with their own land.

From my experience in answering the question—"how do I begin?"—I offer the following practical beginning strategies: At the individual home and family level

Strategy #1

I used to think that the nuclear family was most damaging to the adults involved, I now know it's much worse on the children. As any therapist can tell you, people spend the rest of their life trying to cure what their parents did to them. For most of human history, the child had access to numbers of adults in its daily life. Up to roughly sixty years ago, according to Margaret Mead, there was generally, an uncle or a grandparent living in the house. Now, in the nuclear family, the child must try to please these two "all powerful" adults. It's impossible on both sides—there's too much at stake. However, if the child has continual, easy access to other adults, this "pressure cooker" atmosphere is eased.

Trying to start a community, however, is not the answer in most cases, because it's very difficult and takes a long time. Unless you are very dedicated, don't try it. Instead, if you have children, find two other families within walking distance, who also want their children to grow up without being neurotic. If you can't find two families already living near you, then search for such families and when you find them, move near enough together that the children can walk between the houses. This must be done long before they are teenagers.

The ground rules are quite simple. No one of the sets of parents owns their children. The children are free to move into whichever house suits them best at that time. For instance, if a child gets up in the morning and things are all wrong, he is free to walk down the street and walk right in and begin breakfast, with no questions asked. Furthermore, he can stay at that house until the time is right, for him, to move back to his own house.

The parents, of course, will have to meet from time to time and sort out some of the things that happen. This is the difficult part, of course. But if you keep clearly in mind that the children are not yours to own, that they are natural beings and will develop naturally, unless thwarted by you, it will be easier. Another thing to remember is that it doesn't matter if the other adults aren't "perfect" by your standards. The main thing is that the child has ready access to other adults; not that they are perfect models.

Strategy #2

The next step in this "beginning tribal" arrangement is for the three families, jointly to hire an "uncle." In most primitive tribes, the father is not the disciplinarian; instead, it is the mother's brother (the uncle of the child). We can't quite do that within our present Industrial Growth Society, but we can do the next best thing. Hire an "uncle." This might be a young man—maybe still in college or working part time or an artist or writer, who needs free time. He is hired jointly by the three families. He must be paid a living wage. After all, that will be cheaper than therapy for your children later, when they are teenagers or adults. All the children, especially boys, should have ready access to him, during the hours agreed upon between the "uncle" and the families. He is there to talk to, to do things with, to complain to: sometimes to go somewhere with, etc. For those who have tried this, it makes an enormous difference for their children.

If the families can be open enough to have the "uncle" sit in on their joint meetings they'll learn a lot about "family dynamics" from his feedback. A Talking Staff proves very useful in such a situation, when children and parents are meeting together.

Strategy #3

If you have teenagers and there's problems developing, remember that according to Erikson, "fidelity" is the most important need of a teenager—finding something to be faithful too. In these confused times that's difficult. Remember that the earth is the most powerful being we know. So my immediate recommendation here is give your "problem" teenager a subscription to *Earth First*. (See Resources for the address.) They will find something big enough to be faithful to, the earth itself, and he or she will find ways they can help "save the earth" and thus give meaning to their life. If you do this, on no account should you politely ask them what they think of it or question them about anything they might read in it. Privacy is essential to teenagers.

Strategy #4

Obviously, after reading so much about the gourd in this work, you can begin by throwing out most of the plastic in your household and replacing it with gourds. Immediately, you cut down on the pollution of the environment and engender respect for daily items in yourself and your children. Furthermore, you will cut down on your expenses and also on exposure to the hidden noxious side effects of plastic.

You can buy gourds at country markets and then the next year, begin growing your own. They can sometimes take as long as two years to dry properly, for the big ones. You just hang them in an airy place and let nature take its course. They can be left outdoors during the winter but be sure of good drainage around them. Gourds last indefinitely. They were passed on to the children as inheritances until this last century. They are easy to decorate and can be sewed together if they break and still hold liquids. The best book for explaining all this is:

Gourd Craft by Carolyn Mordecai. Crown Pub. 1978. Unfortunately, it's currently out of print but you can get it through inter-library loan.

Use them for ladles, cups, bowls, to store items in etc. They can be easily washed but not in dishwashers, of course. The amount of water dishwashers use is invalid anyway.

At the neighborhood level

Strategy #5

Three families, beginning to live "as nature intended" them to, will soon be making changes in the neighborhood. The best advice I have for you here is to get the following book. It's expensive so you may have to go to the reserve room of a library to see it. I've found, after years of trying, that seldom will a library send it out on inter-library loan.

The Timeless Way of Building by Christopher Alexander
Oxford Univerity Press, 1979

It took him twenty years to write this book and it's slowly changing people's lives. On page 360 he gives a list, which he labels: "Here is a language for repairing common land inside a neighborhood":

activity nodes	high places
network of paths and cars	dancing in the street
green streets	holy ground
main gateways	public outdoor room
accessible green	street cafe
	small public square

You'll find, once you begin reading this book, that deep inside, you always knew this was what you needed.

Ritualizing your town

Strategy #6

I want to show you what ritual can do for a modern town. Siena, Italy, with a population of about 50,000 has the lowest crime rate of any Western city of a comparable size. Delinquency, drug-addiction and violence are virtually unknown. Class is not pitted against class, nor old against young. The reason for this unique situation in Siena, as well as for its remarkable stability, is that Siena is a tribal city, with a ritualized life dating back to the thirteenth century. I will go into these rituals of Siena in some detail because there is much to learn from this example.

The "clans" of the city, called *contrada*, function as independent city states. Each of these contrada has its own flag, its own territorial boundaries, its own discrete identity, church, songs, patron saint and rituals. Each contrada is named after an animal—either real or mythical—just as done in primitive totemistic clans. Furthermore, each contrada has a ritualized relationship with all the other contradas. Chicciola, the snail, feuds with Tartula, the turtle, Brucco, the caterpillar with Giraffa etc. Particular topographical features of each contrada's area are ritualized and mythologized.

Rituals for forming bonds between the child and its contrada begin at birth when a flag is sent to be flown from the window of the newborn's house so that the child is officially claimed for the contrada. In contrast to our culture, where each child is expected to make its own place in the world as he deals with first, school and later, a job, a child of the contrada is "enmeshed in a criss-cross of bonds," just as in a primitive society.

Nicholas Hildyard, in his report on Siena titled, "How an Ideal City Works," acknowledges that "to us the idea of ascribed status is anathema. It is considered reactionary." Actually, this "liberal" viewpoint "creates a situation where social relations are barely sustainable." Our cities are proving this to us.

The famous horse race, the Palio, serves two main purposes. In the intense rivalry surrounding the race, each contrada "rekindles its own sense of identity." Every other contrada is either an enemy, an ally or neutral. The Palio also provides the Sienese with an outlet for their aggression and as such is a ritual war. The horse race grew out of games, which were actually mimic battles and were used to mark the ends of religious festivals.

Everyone knows when the Palio is about to begin, because workmen of the city bring yellow earth from outside the city walls, into the Campo inside the town. "It takes a day or so to complete the miraculous transformation of a beautiful medieval piazza into a unique theater-racetrack arena..In folk speech, there is a popular idiom which may be used at any time during the year whenever someone needs to be cheered up. The sad person is told not to worry because soon there will be 'la terra [earth] in piazza'." Sienese people of all ages can be seen touching this yellow earth of their land with great delight.

The Palio is truly a religious event. On this one day of the year the contrada's horse is brought into the church of its patron saint. In the act of blessing the horse, the Contrada itself is blessed. This horse race is the community's greatest rite. "In the Palio, all the flames of Hell are transformed into the lights of Paradise," according to a local priest, Don Vittorio.

There is considerable historical precedent for such a tribal city. Athens in the sixth century B.C. was divided into four tribes, united by real or fictitious ties of blood. In Rome there were three tribes, subdivided into gens, which operated as autonomous religious, educational and judicial units. In his conclusion, Hildyard states: "If future cities are to work they must be organized along the same lines as Siena." In other words they must be ritualized.

At the next larger level: the bioregion

Strategy #7

To begin to pay attention to what your own place needs from you, you must begin to focus, consciously, on the fact that, fundamentally, you live in a bioregion not in a state or a country. (See Resources for addresses concerning bioregions.) As each group of people begins to acknowledge their bioregion and name it, one of the most powerful things you can do is to begin including your bioregional name within your address.

I first saw this done, when David Wheeler of the Katúah

Bioregion in the Southern Appalachians, wrote me. In the return address on the envelope, below his name and Route and box number, was this:

(city) (state)

Katúah Province,
(zip)

I was immediately aware of the possibilities here for bioregional people not only to pay attention to their own natural region, but to recognize one another, simply by seeing such an address anywhere. At my request, he asked his postmaster and found that it is alright to put the name of the bioregion anywhere, but the best place would be after the state initials or on a line below the town and state and above the zip code. The postmaster said either way would cause no trouble to the post office. Obviously, with zip codes all they really look at anymore is the zip code. I have a friend in a small town in New Mexico, who lists his address as simply his last name and the zip code of the little town—nothing else.

If you come from a very small town and don't want to hassle your small post office, then just put the bioregion name on the same line as your street address or box number but with five or more spaces between the number and the bioregional name:

P.O. Box (no.) "Katúah"

(city) (state) (zip)

Preserving nature around your town

Strategy #8

An example for your own area—around the edges of your town, is provided by Jefferson County here in Colorado. This county has done the most outstanding job of any place I've seen. They have been a model for other towns throughout the country. For information write: Jean Saum, Public Information Specialist, Jefferson County Open Space, 1801 19th St., Golden, Co. 80401. This is an underfunded local government organization so enclose a stamped return envelope and be willing to pay costs for any material sent. You could get immediate information by buying their annual OPEN SPACE CALENDAR. This has color photos of some beautiful little spots in their Open Space, along with some of the things they do. The calendar is very local and specific. Write for cost and postage.

Government on the large scale

Strategy #9

It will take years to "devolve" back to useful, local government, but it will grow out of the bioregional movement, eventually, from the ground up. If the "devolution" is deep enough we will not have to resort to what the greatest president we ever had in this country and one who loved his own native earth of Virginia, intensely, Thomas Jefferson, felt was necessary:

God forbid we should ever be 20 years without such rebellion. What country can preserve its liberties if its rulers are not warned from time to time that this people preserves the spirit of resistance. Let them take arms...What signify a few lives lost in a century or two. The tree of liberty must be refreshed from time to time with the blood of patriots. It is its natural manure.

(letter from Jefferson to John Adams' son-in-law)

Pilgrimages

Strategy #10

Last of all, to begin to save the land itself we need to promote pilgrimages instead of tourism. In most cultures of the past, pilgrimages served to bond people together and to give them respect for the land they were travelling through. The most famous rite in ancient Greece, the Eleusinian mysteries involved a pilgrimage. There was a day-long procession with singing and dancing from Athens to Eleusis, beginning with a climb over the pass of Daphni, thence down to the Gulf of Eleusis, passing among numerous sacred landscape forms. After ritually bathing in the sea, the pilgrimage continued around the shore to arrive at Eleusis at night, where during the central rite an ear of wheat, the goddess Demeter's gift to humanity, was ritually displayed.

In Asia, Mt. Kailas and Lake Manas, two of the holiest places of pilgrimage for Hindus are located on the farther side of the Himalayas in western Tibet; yet throughout the centuries devout pilgrims from India have made the journey to this region, the source of the five great rivers of India, including the Ganges, the Indus and the Brahmaputra.

In China, the basic structure of the universe was symbolized by a central pole region and four peripheral regions. On earth these were the Five Sacred Mountains, which have been venerated for thousands of years. In ancient times the Emperors made tours to the four quarters of the empire every five years and performed the Imperial Feng and Shan Ceremony at each of the five sacred mountians. Veneration of these mountains continued right down to modern times.

In Victor Turner's book on ritual, *Dramas, Fields, and Metaphors*, he has devoted an entire chapter to pilgrimages. He states that "reports from all over the world indicate that, if anything, larger numbers of people than ever are visiting pilgrim centers...Pilgrimages are, in a way, both instruments and indicators of a sort of mystical regionalism." Although he covers the major sites of pilgrimages in Europe, he devotes more attention to a detailed analysis of the Mexican pilgrimage centers. Turner observes that these centers are frequently connected with natural features such as hills, mountains, caves, wells and springs. Some of the more important Christian centers are located at the major pre-Columbian centers of pilgrimage. The land forms dictate the pilgrim route rather than the particular pagan or Christian gods associated with the shrines.

In Europe as well, the goal of some Christian pilgrimages was the site of a particular natural feature, which had been previously dedicated to a pagan god. For instance, one of the most famous pilgrimage centers of all—that of Chartres, is located on an old sanctuary with a well, where a Celtic goddess was once worshipped.

A real pilgrimage, of course, should be done on foot and takes time. In that way, the land itself, is appreciated rather than becoming mere backdrop scenery as is the case with travelling by plane or car.

Conclusion

The above is merely a brief introduction to some particular aspects of living more validly on this earth of ours, but with this start, you will be able to incorporate much more of the ritual aspects of this work into your life, naturally.

RESOURCES

I had planned a much more extensive section on Resources, but space precludes it; thus I am restricted to only a few of the most important listings in each category. However, through my on-going "Way of the Mountain" newsletter I can keep such resources up-dated for you. Below you will find the most useful listings in each category; but they are not necessarily the *only* ones available. In general I don't give prices except for the current year of journals because of the fluctuation of costs.

Mountain experiences and workshops

Addresses for brochures concerning the two events, frequently mentioned in this book:

1) BREAKING THROUGH—mountain climbing, ritual, Tai Chi, deep ecology etc.
Outdoor Leadership Training Seminars
P.O. Box 20281
Denver, CO 80220 (phone 303-333-7831)

2) AUTUMN EQUINOX TAOIST CELEBRATION
Way of the Mountain Learning Center
P.O. Box 542
Silverton, CO 81433

Experiencing ritual

1) Elizabeth Cogburn's NEW SONG CEREMONIALS
Elizabeth Cogburn
6741 Edgewood Dr. N.W.
Albuquerque, N.M. 87107

2) MEN'S QUEST WORKSHOPS
Joseph Jastrab
68 Mountain Rest Rd.
New Paltz, N.Y. 12561

3) VISION QUESTS IN THE SOUTHWEST
Bill Plotkin
1941 E. 2nd Ave.
Durango, CO 81301

4) A LIVING COMMUNITY which facilitates learnings concerned with PLACE AND FESTIVAL. (Celtic Christian background. I give occasional workshops there: they call me their "favorite pagan.")
Chinook Learning Center
Box 57
Clinton, WA 98236

How to begin living validly in the city

Workshops and a self-sufficient ecologically valid "townhouse" as a model. Write for information.
Farallones Institute
1516 Fifth St.
Berkeley, CA 94710

Drums

You can make your own rattles but a good drum is much more difficult. Here are addresses of the drum-makers whose drums I like best:

1) Greg Colfax, (Makah Indian). The most powerful "shaman type" (flat drum) I've ever heard was his. When I wrote for particulars to list here, he wrote: "I need to speak to my customers to see exactly what they want and to find out the climate the drum will live in so that it be made for that climate." His drums sell for $85 for 15″ on up. He is just beginning to make some 36×8″ "four person drums" for $400. Address: Greg Colfax, Box 327, Neah Bay, WA. 98357 (ph. 206-645-2564). He is a skilled Makah carver and makes rattles, totem poles, boxes, etc. He adds: "I don't mind carving ritual gear for non-Indians who wish to use them in new rituals."

2) Elizabeth Cogburn has provided "long dances" for people up in Vancouver, B.C. One of the men who began making drums for this group is now turning out good drums. 15″ drum $85 (U.S. funds). Address: Renato Carboni, 101-628 East 8th Ave., Vancouver, B.C. Canada V5T 1T1.

3) The old stand-by for drums is the Taos Indian Drum Company, but I suggest you go in person for their drums as some are good and some are not so good. Taos Indian Drum Co., P.O. Box 1916 D, Taos, N.M. 87571.

4) For learning how to make your own, contact Terry Keepers, 1314 8th St., Boulder, CO 80302, who gives classes two or three times a year. He is connected with a men's kiva group, which grew out of Cogburn's New Song Ceremonials.

Books and journals

1) *The Way of the Mountain Annual Newsletter* (7th year) provides on-going information and sells books and cards on "deep ecology, place and the old ways as well as other Earth-centered topics." Artwork in this volume will be for sale in poster format, as well, in the next issue. Write for free copy.

Way of the Mountain
P.O. Box 542
Silverton, CO 81433

2) Bioregional journals

Learning about your bioregion is the first step to a living relationship with the earth. My list begins with Peter Berg's, *Planet Drum*, which began the whole bioregional movement.

They have lists of bioregions in existence and forming. Membership ($15) gives you their regular *Raise the Stakes* paper, discounts on all their publications and "person-to-person replies to all requests for information, regional contacts, etc."

a) PLANET DRUM
   P.O. Box 31251
   San Francisco, CA 94131

If you want to see what a bioregion can do, here are the two best journals I've seen:

b) KATÚAH: BIOREGIONAL JOURNAL OF THE SO.
   APPALACHIANS
   P.O. Box 638
   Leicester, NC
   Katúah Province 28748 ($10 sub; $1.50 single issue)

Special note on Bioregional addresses: When David Wheeler of Katúah, first wrote me, he had his bioregion on the return address. I am impressed with the importance of this tactic to bring about awareness and identification with your bioregion. Wheeler checked with his post office. The name of the bioregion can go anywhere before the zip code. Wheeler uses "province"; one could use "country" in the sense that it's long been used here in the West, ex. "big sky country" for Montana.

c) UPRIVER DOWNRIVER
   P.O. Box 1051
   Arcata, Ca 95521
   (Sub. $6 for four issues)

Eleventh issue just came out. They "think of it as an extended correspondence among people who live in northern California, a place we regard as a distinct biologic/cultural region. We consider the region a community of life and therefore feel it is important to resist the further destruction of its natural systems and to begin repairing the damage already done."

3) EARTH FIRST! JOURNAL

It does much the same as the above for the entire United States and further afield. This journal has tapped into people's deepest hopes to save the animals and plants and trees on this earth, giving them specific ways to do it. The real meaning of land has become not territory to defend but earth to save.
Earth First!
P.O. Box 5871
Tucson, AZ 85703 (sub. $20 a year)

Note for parents of teenagers. If your teenagers are rightfully having problems finding something worth living for, give them a subscription to Earth First! The prime need in adolescence is "fidelity," according to Erik Erikson, who has defined the virtues for each age of man. He writes: "Fidelity is that virtue and quality of adolescent ego strength which belongs to man's evolutionary heritage, but which can arise only in the interplay of a life stage with the individuals and the social forces of a true community." This, of course, is precisely one of the reasons for the fact that suicide is the leading cause of death among young males right now. The IGS is not a true community. A true society "recognizes the young individual as a bearer of fresh energy and the individual so confirmed recognizes society as a living process which inspires loyalty as it receives it." Today, only those serving the earth itself have such community; in the rest of society, youth is a threat and kept out of the job market and safely "in school." One more Erikson quote: "Fidelity...is the strength of disciplined devotion. It is gained in the involvement of youth in such experiences as reveal the essence of the era they are to join..." Precisely, here is the importance of Earth First. As the philosopher, Seyyed Nasr says: "What is forgotten is that in both the state of war and peace man is waging an incessant war upon nature...it is no more than a chimerical dream to expect to have peace based upon a state of intense war toward nature...Whether one pollutes water resources in a single bombing or does so over a twenty-year period is essentially the same; the only difference is the matter of time." Through Earth First, your teenager can join the earth herself in this on-going warfare between the earth and the IGS. The earth needs him or her and he or she needs the earth. Furthermore, other women besides me agree that Earth First has the most nurturing, caring men we have ever met. Which brings me to a final Erikson quote. "...the test of what you produce is in the *care* it inspires." Only the earth herself could inspire such care. "Earth First is not the name of an organization. It is a commitment to a priority." So give your teenager Earth First!

4) Tai Chi books

Tai Chi is the quickest way to get out of the narrow, "merely human," Eurocentric philosophy into the ever-deepening relationships of the Chinese "philosophy of organism." It works because in doing Tai Chi, the body itself teaches you what you always, already knew but forgot. The best way to see what it does for you is in Al Huang's video. (Listed below in the film section.) The best book I've found is by a zoologist, who teaches Tai Chi, Bob Klein, who explains that Tai Chi taps the million-year-old animal knowledge within us from our mammalian past. I wrote to him to find out more about his next book for this "resource" section. In his reply he said, "I began learning T'ai-chi from animals before I knew T'ai-chi existed." We've been selling his *Movements of Magic,* for two years. His new book, *Movements of Magic V.II* (spring 1989), goes even deeper— "including the Taoist Forest Wine Ceremony, interpersonal relationships, learning Tai Chi from animals etc." You can order his first book from Way of the Mountain Center. He has produced two videos. Write: Tai Chi-Chuan School, Robert Klein, Dir., 87 Tyler Ave., Sound Beach, N.Y. 11789.

5) Books and tapes on specific aspects of ritual
   a) In Part III, I quote from Sarah Dubin-Vaughn's paper, "The New Song Ceremonial Sun Dance Ritual 1983 and 1984." She has some copies available at $20 including postage. (It will eventually be put out by International Microfilms.) Her address: 483 Pine Needles Dr., Del Mar, CA 92014.
   b) I also quote from Steve Gallegos' book: *The Personal Totem Pole": Animal Imagery, the Chakras and Psychotherapy,* just out. You can get it from Moon Bear Press, Box 15811, Santa Fe, NM 87506. ($12)
   c) To learn how to drum: Elizabeth Cogburn's tape, "Finding the Pulse," available from Way of the Mountain Center.
   d) To see how a bard can bond human and land: Robin Williamson's tape, "Glint at the Kindling," available from Way of the Mountain Center.
   e) My own book, *Earth Wisdom,* is still in print. Order from Way of the Mountain Center. My book for beginning rituals, *Earth Festivals,* is now out of print, but write for information on securing a xeroxed copy.

Films and Video
The best way to see how the "old ways" work is through film. There are two superlative films for this. (See below.) First, I will list two excellent ones on video and commercially available for rental at any video outlet.
1) THE GODS MUST BE CRAZY—Made in South Africa. And yes, of course, it's "racist" but it's against white Eurocentrism, not the blacks as the fuzzy-thinking liberals think. The scenes of the blacks, which the liberals condemn, show the blacks, using white man's law to solve problems; thus, disclosing the limitations of IGS laws. The hilarious comedy has to do with how our white culture makes sex such an on-going problem. The entire film gives excellent insight into true primitives. I've seen it many, many times and still learn more each time.

2) EMERALD FOREST—Filmed in the Amazon, the small son of an American technocrat is taken by the "Invisible People" and grows up among them. He's a grown man when his father finds him and the son refuses to return to so-called "civilization." The underlying theme is the dangerous destruction of the Amazon rain forest. One of the Indians say: "They are taking off the skin of the Earth. How will they breathe?" Excellent insights into true primitive living if you overlook some of the foreground actions.

Video to rent or buy by mail:
1) The most powerful film you'll see that shows the validity of the "old ways" for children. **Dreamspeaker**, based on the novel by Cam Hubert, who lived with the Nootka. We've been selling it for years. A small "disturbed" boy runs away and eventually is taken in by an old Nootka Indian, who cures him by myth and real living. But then the IGS world catches up with the boy; thus causing such a sad ending that some people cry for hours; some for days—just from reading the book. I highly recommend this film, which has won numerous awards. (Color) The director is with the Canadian Film Board.
Write:
CBC Enterprises
P.O. Box, Station A
Toronto Ontario, Canada M5W 1E6
(available on film or video)

I want to thank Bert Horwood for finding this information for me.

2) **Drumming**
You'll feel the full power of the drum when you see this one—the Kodo drummers of Japan in action. You see them drum the sun up, playing their giant drums on the sand, their daily life, and drumming the sun down at the end of the day. "From the quiet and tranquillity of the early moments of the prologue until it suddenly breaks onto a new plane of intensity, I am embraced in the enormous vibrations of the *O-daiko,* [drum] and just as I feel a catharsis of the spirit my eyes become blurred with tears." (Jap. review) color, 28 min. #4629-1465. For rental or purchase of film or video, write:
Kinetic Film/Video
255 Delaware Ave. Suite 340
Buffalo, N.Y. 14202 (ph. 716-856-7631)

3) **Tai Chi**
You can't learn Tai Chi from this film but you will experience how it feels to do it. Incredibly beautiful scenes of Al Huang doing Tai Chi along the Pacific Ocean. The film begins with Tai Chi at sunrise and includes his dynamic teaching at Esalen, doing Tai Chi with people in various natural areas, and closes with Tai Chi at sunset. The film-maker Kai De Fontenay worked with him for two years to get this footage. The video is not for rent but the sale price is only $75 and well worth it. Color. Write:
Living Tao Foundation
P.O. Box 846
Urbana, IL 61801 (ph. 217-337-6113)
Ask for information on their other Tai Chi videos of Al Huang.

Films on the "old ways" to rent by mail

1) Documentary films of the Kung (San) by John Marshall.

a) BITTER MELONS—daily life of a small group with the music on Ukxone's hunting bow. Young boys play animal games, men and boys dance the "ostrich courting dance," etc. ($55 film rental, $35 video)

Documentary Educational Resources
101 Morse St.
Watertown, MA 02172 (ph. 617-926-0491)
D.E.R. is the most helpful film distributor I've ever worked with. Ask for their list because they have many other good films including Balinese trance dancing, etc.

b) John Marshall's "The Hunters"—concerns four men tracking a giraffe, shooting it with a poison arrow, following it for a long time until it lies down sleeping and then killing it. Shows the religious importance of hunting. Distributed by Films, Inc. of Chicago, IL but I have no current address.

c) THE BUSHMEN OF THE KALAHARI—An excellent documentary of the Kalahari, made when John Marshall returned 20 years later and tried to find his "tribe." Graphically shows the changes brought about by so-called "modern" improvements, etc. One scene documents exactly how domesticating animals created irreversible changes. They have only one horse, but they must gather many melons to break open, to give the horse enough water to live; meanwhile the people are almost dying of thirst. This is a National Geographic Society film. Address: 17th and M Sts. N.W., Washington D.C. 20036.

2) **The two best films to show the "old ways"**

a) WHITE DAWN, a Hollywood production (1974) with a cast of St. James Bay Eskimos. The setting is long ago when three whalers are cast up on the ice and found by Eskimos. They call them "dog children" and try their best to make these three into human beings, but eventually had to kill them in order to survive as a people and you *know* they had to kill them. (110 min. color)

Films Inc.
5625 Hollywood Blvd.
Hollywood, CA 90028 (toll free 800-421-0612)
or eastern office
440 Park Ave. So.
N.Y., NY 10016 (800-223-6246)

b) PEOPLE OF THE WIND, an English documentary, directed by Anthony Howarth. He travelled with one of the last great nomadic tribes—the Bakhtiari of western Iran over the Zagros Mountains, on their 200 mile annual spring migration to bring the sheep to summer pastures. It shows, as no other film does, how bonding takes place, automatically, by real living. Also how important the small children are on the journey, carrying the lambs on their shoulders over 15,000 ft. passes. James Mason narrates it. Filmed in the Zagros Mts. The last listing I have for rental is Unifilm West Coast Office, but they are now out of business. I would appreciate anyone knowing current rental information on this film, writing me so that I can list it in my annual newsletter.

BACK-OF-THE-BOOK

On Wilderness: About crossing the artificial boundaries—set up by the decaying Industrial Growth Society—between human beings and the "rest of the world." Each of the selections below gives a particular aspect of this all-important endeavor: Jay Vest on the "will-of-the-land"; Dave Foreman on the fact that without wilderness, evolution comes to an end; David Abram on contacting the vast non-human "rest of the world"; tree planter, Hal Hartzell on how bonding comes out of real work in the natural world; Tom Jay on reclaiming the necessary words and Daniel Menkin on how men can reclaim their natural role as ritualizers. (We hear a lot about women and ritual but it's just as natural and even more important for men.) In the final piece, Sigmund Kvaloy tells us how Deep Ecology grew out of defending the land and waters of Norway from the destructive activities of the IGS. (You will find further information on each individual author as well as his copyright and references in the Reference Notes.)

WILL-OF-THE-LAND
WILDERNESS AMONG EARLY INDO-EUROPEANS
Jay H. Vest

The traditional theme of sacred natural places, free from desecration by humans and their technology, is an ancient land-use ideal. These sacred natural places were wilderness in the deepest sense. Contemporary scholarship, however, implies that only members of our modern cultures can appreciate such wilderness. Western historian Roderick Nash, for example, suggests that "wilderness had no counterpart in the old world" and that "if paradise was man's greatest good, wilderness, its antipode, was his greatest evil." The implication is that wilderness is "instinctively understood as something alien to man—an insecure and uncomfortable environment against which civilization had waged an unceasing struggle."

Perhaps in terms of the modern belief in a dichotomy of wilderness versus civilization, this is true. But there is a primal reverence for "wild" nature that predates the medieval/renaissance view of the world, a view that extols human chauvinism or the arrogant belief in the intrinsic value of civilization.

The problem with contemporary scholars' historical treatment of wilderness is that they do not investigate the values of primal peoples. Nash concentrated his historical review of the wilderness concept on medieval Europe and ignored pre-Christian inhabitants—the early European cultures that thrived outside the rule of imperial Rome.

The ancient Celts, a sub-group of the Indo-European race, worshipped nature: for them it was alive with the same creative force humans share. Their conception of *Will Power* or *will-force* was extended wholly to nature—even solid earth. This notion of 'will' is akin in origin to the term 'wild'. Nash tells us that 'wilderness' means 'wild-dēor-ness'—the place of wild beasts, the root probably being 'will', meaning self-willed or uncontrollable, from which came the adjective 'wild'. 'Wild-dēor' denotes creatures not under the control of humans. 'Ness' in Middle English was apparently retained only in place names.

Nash maintains that 'ness' suggests a quality producing a certain mood in an individual who assigns it to a specific place. However, considering the Middle English application of 'ness' to place names, it may well have been combined with 'wild' in an entirely different sense from that Nash suggests, meaning 'willed-land'. If the 'der' of wilderness represents 'of the', then in 'wilderness' there is 'will-of-the-land' and in 'wild-dēor' there is 'will of the animal'. The primal people of northern Europe were not bent on dominating all environments and the 'will-of-the-land' concept demonstrates a recognition of the land for itself.

Wilderness then means 'self-willed land' or 'self-willed-place' with an emphasis upon its own intrinsic volition. A wild animal is a 'self-willed animal'—an undomesticated animal—similarly wildland is 'self-willed-land'. Indo-European nature worship evidences a tradition of sacred places—wilderness in the deepest sense, imbued with *will-force* and spirit.

With Roman Christianity, an imperialism emerged where the wild took on connotations of a desolate waste filled with demons, and the primal Indo-Europeans, in failing to acknowledge the God of the Bible, were defined as barbarous. Nature and nature worship were consequently perceived as evil. 'Heathen' means 'dweller on the heath', and 'pagan' originally meant a rural or rustic person'. As Christianity became the religion of the towns, the rural people who retained the ancient deities became known as 'pagan heathens'. They worshipped on the heath or in the grove—that is, in the wilderness.

Among ancient Indo-European cultures are many examples of wild sanctuaries. The Celts held sacred certain groves known as *nemetons*—related to the Breton *nemu*, 'the heavens'—reflecting the Celtic belief that the real and the surreal were two facets of a whole. The sacred grove continued in its wild—willed or uncontrollable—condition, and thus the will-of-the-place, its spirit, manifested itself. Such groves were the site of worship, particularly on earth festival days. When these festivals were discontinued, usually because of imperial compulsion, the primal culture disintegrated.

In these sacred groves the Druids, the spiritual leaders of the Celts, developed their lore, wisdom and ecological ethics, glimmerings of which can be gleaned from Arthurian legend. The archetypal Druid, Merlin, explains to Arthur what it means to be king: "You will be the land and the land will be you; if you fail, the land will perish, as you thrive, the land will blossom." Kinship with the land and its continued health are central themes of the Celtic world view.

The American concept of wilderness is new and innovative only within the confines of the Western tradition of utilitarianism and humanism. Since the earliest of times, wildlands have been treated as sacred space free from alteration by humans.

The fact that the wilderness concept has resurfaced in America demonstrates our species' determination to avoid separation from the wild source that gave us birth. It further confirms the notion that primal peoples had a much more sophisticated world view than previously believed; they had their own environnmental ethic. Certainly, by worshipping in wilderness *nemetons*, the people manifested a love, respect and admiration for the 'wild'. These are elements that are tantamount to any sort of ethic, whether humanistic or environmental.

Still the preservation of wilderness remains fundamentally a religious movement demonstrating axiological regard for Nature and giving wilderness highest veneration. That wilderness literally means **will-of-the-land**—a fact of cosmological significance—demonstrates a profound conclusion for a philosophy of wilderness where the metaphysic is Nature in process and not some abstract supernatural reduction of inconceivability. While this Nature Awe metaphysic deserves further explication, it does provide us with the **will-of-the-land** notion, a significant alternative for thinking through our ecological interrelatedness and ethical obligations to Nature.

DREAMING BIG WILDERNESS
Dave Foreman

It has been over 20 years since the passage of the Wilderness Act. During these two decades, conservationists have waged a protracted struggle to preserve **a portion** of the United States remaining in an essentially wild condition. I emphasize "a portion" because wilderness preservation groups have not asked for protection of all roadless or undeveloped lands even though they amount to only 3 or 4% of the total land area of the United States outside of Alaska. In the Forest Service's second Roadless Area Review and Evaluation (RARE II), conservationists asked that only 35 million acres of approximately 80 million acres of roadless lands on the National Forests be protected. It has been a similar story with the holdings of the Bureau of Land Management. Even in Alaska, where the Alaska National Interest Lands battle stands as the outstanding conservation achievement of the 1970s, environmental groups never considered proposing that **all** of the wild lands of Alaska remain wild. It has always been taken for granted that the implacable forces of industrialization will continue to conquer the wilderness. Environmentalists, as reasonable advocates within the mainstream of modern society, have gone out of their way to appear to be moderate and willing to compromise. We have acquiesced in the clearcutting of old growth forests, massive road building schemes on our public lands, mineral and energy development in pristine areas, and the destruction of "problem" bears. We have accepted that some wild lands will be—and should be—developed. We merely ask that some of these areas—generally the scenic ones—be spared.

In short, wilderness conservationists have lacked vision since the passage of the Wilderness Act. We have accepted the dominant social paradigm, the inevitability of continued industrialization and development of open spaces, the utter hopelessness of preserving **real** wilderness. We have had no vision for such noble but vanishing species as the condor, the grizzly, the wolf. We try to hang on to their diminishing habitats, their puny populations as museum pieces, but not as growing, vigorous, **living** parts of the functioning world.

It is time to have vision, to dream of the world the way it should be, rather than the way it is handed us by Louisiana-Pacific, the Forest Service, Sen. Jim McClure, and Ronald Reagan. It is time to ask deeper questions: Is 2% of the 48 states adequate for our National Wilderness Preservation System? Are 20 condors sufficient? Six hundred grizzly bears? A handful of minuscule remnants of the cathedral old growth forests of Oregon?

Have we logged too much virgin forest? Have we built too many roads? Have we damned too many rivers? Have we driven the griz, the wolf, the cougar, the bighorn, the bison from too many places? Have we drained too many wetlands? Was the extermination of the passenger pigeon, the plowing of the Great Plains all a monstrous mistake?

Are Wilderness Areas only museum pieces of land on display? Or are they the world of life; vibrant ecosystems where natural processes still reign and evolution runs its course?

If we fail to ask these deeper questions, if we neglect to dream these dreams and articulate our vision, then the wilderness crusade is lost. Remnants of the wild, with truncated floras and faunas, will haunt future generations with the shadow of what once was real.

Real Wilderness is something far different than that which forms our current National Wilderness Preservation System. To Aldo Leopold, a wilderness was an area large enough for a two week packtrip without crossing your tracks. To Doug Peacock, wilderness contains something bigger and meaner than you—something that can kill you.

We can have real wilderness tomorrow in the United States. And we can have it without necessarily disrupting our national economy, without "locking up" crucial "resources." But it will require some courage, some vision:

1) A new profession, a new science needs to be developed. Wilderness reclamation. The methods and techniques to recreate native ecosystems, to reintroduce extirpated wildlife, and to repair damaged landscapes need to emerge.

2) East of the Rockies, large ecological wilderness preserves need to be recreated: a Great Plains National Park with free-roaming bison, elk, pronghorn, grizzlies, and wolves; a large deciduous forest preserve in the Ohio Valley with elk, wolves and cougars; a million-acre roadless chunk in New England with wolf, moose and other former inhabitants; a similar preserve in the southern Appalachians; and a revitalized Everglades/Big Cypress in Florida.

3) In the West, roads should be closed, ravaged clearcuts rehabilitated, and livestock grazing removed to create some thirty preserves of a million acres or more. Merely through the closure of a few dirt roads, a 3 million acre Wilderness

could be established in the slick-rock canyon country of the Escalante/Kaiparowits/Capitol Reef/Henry Mountains area of southern Utah. Closure of the Magruder Corridor dirt road would give us a five million acre Central Idaho Wilderness. Minor dirt road closures would produce intact roadless areas of one to four million acres in the Owyhee Canyons complex (Idaho, Oregon, Nevada) the Black Rock Desert (Nevada), Cabeza Prieta and Kofa (Arizona), and Death Valley (California).

4) The grizzly will not survive restricted to the dwindling Yellowstone and Bob Marshall/Glacier ecosystems. New populations must be re-established in the Gila wilderness of New Mexico, the Weminuche of Colorado, the High Uintas of Utah, the Kalmiopsis of Oregon, the North Cascades of Washington, Central Idaho, the Marble Mountains and Siskiyous of California, and the Blue Range of Arizona. The wolf should be returned to these areas and others. A million and a half acres in the Los Padres National Forest northwest of Los Angeles should be totally closed to any human use or entry in order to preserve the condor. Large animal carcasses should be regularly deposited there for the big birds. In suitable areas of southern New Mexico, Arizona and Texas, the jaguar, ocelot and jaguarundi cat should be reintroduced. Bighorn sheep, elk, bison, pronghorn, otter, eastern cougar and other once widespread species should be widely propagated in former habitats.

5) Commercial livestock grazing should be phased out on the Western public lands. Only 3 % of the nation's red meat supply comes from the public lands and the federal government spends more on managing this private grazing than it receives in return from the grazing permittees. Grazing has been the single most important factor in the devastation of intermountain ecosystems:

the widespread decimation of bear, wolf and mountain lion; destruction of native vegetation and populations of elk, pronghorn, bighorn and bison; and severe damage to watersheds and riparian systems.

6) And, finally, conservationists must develop a new (old) reason for wilderness, a new understanding of the place of humans in the natural world, a new appreciation for the other nations which inhabit this beautiful blue-green living planet. Why wilderness? Because it offers an escape from the rat race of San Francisco or Washington, DC? Because it's pretty to look at? Because it's a place to hike, backpack, or float rivers? Because it protects watersheds for use downstream?

No. Because it is. Wilderness for its own sake. Because it's **right**. Because it's the real world, the repository of three and a half billion years of organic evolution; because it's our home. The grizzly has a right to live for her own sake, not for any real or imagined value she may have for human beings. The spotted owl, the wolverine, Brewer's spruce, the fungal web in the forest floor have a nature-given right to follow their own intertwined evolutionary destinies without being meaningless pawns in the arrogant games of industrial humans.

What right does a man with a life span of seventy years have to destroy a two thousand year old redwood to make picnic tables? To kill one of 30 female breeding grizzlies in the Yellowstone region because she ate one of his sheep? To rip through a five thousand year old creosote bush on a motorized tricycle for some kind of macho thrill? To damn Glen Canyon and Hetch Hetchy?

Until we learn to respect and accept these other nations as our equals, we will be strangers and barbarians on Earth. Wilderness, **real** wilderness is the path home.

Dave Foreman is the editor of Earth First! The Radical Environmental Journal.

NOTES FROM THAMI VALLEY IN NEPAL
ON "THE REST OF THE WORLD"
David Abram

In 1980, I received a generous fellowship from the Watson Foundation to support a year's research into modes of perception utilized by traditional sorcerers in the equatorial islands of Indonesia and the mountain heights of Nepal. One aspect of this grant was especially unique: I was to journey into rural Asia not as an anthropologist or sociologist, but rather as a magician in my own right, in hopes of gaining a more direct access to the native practitioners. By approaching them not as an academic researcher, but as a magician from the West, I would explore from the inside the relation between these traditional magicians and their magic. Here I will not write at great length about my encounters with the shamans. It suffices to mention that my unorthodox approach was ultimately quite successful, that my own magical skills brought me into the company of several exceedingly powerful and bizarre individuals of the sort known as "dukuns" in Indonesia or "djankris" in Nepal. Indeed, it was while staying in the household of one of the djankris that I experienced a unique shift in my own sensory awareness.

On one of the first walks along the narrow cliff trails that wind from his village high in the Himalayas of eastern Nepal, my host had casually pointed out to me a certain boulder that he had "danced" on before attempting some especially difficult cures. It was a large rock thrusting out several feet beyond the cliff's edge, its surface alive with pale white and red lichens. I recognized the boulder two days later when hiking back alone to the village from the yak pastures above and I climbed out onto the rock to sit and gaze at the snow-covered mountains across the valley. It was a ringing blue Himalayan morning, clear as a bell. Between the gleaming peaks, two lammergeier vultures floated on the blue sky, wings outstretched, riding invisible currents. Without thinking, I took a silver coin out of my pocket and began an aimless sleight-of-hand exercise, rolling the coin over the knuckles of my right hand. One of the huge birds swerved away from the snow peaks and began gliding over the valley, heading in my general direction. I stopped rolling the coin and stared. At that moment the lammergeier halted in its flight and just hung in the air, motionless for a moment against the peaks, then wheeled around and headed back toward its partner in the distance. I pondered for several seconds, then on impulse began rolling the coin down my knuckles once again, letting its silver surface catch the sunlight as it turned, reflecting the rays back into the sky. Instantly the bird swung out from its path and began soaring back in a wide arc. As I watched it approach, my skin began to crawl and come alive, like a community of bees all in motion. The creature loomed larger—a sort of humming grew loud in my ears—and larger still, until it was there: an immense silhouette hovering just above my head, huge wing feathers rustling ever so slightly as they mastered the breeze. My fingers were frozen, unable to move—the coin dropped out of my hand. And then I felt myself stripped naked by an alien intelligence ten times more lucid than my own. I do not know for how long I was transfixed—only that I felt the air streaming past naked knees and heard the breeze whispering in my feathers long after the Other had departed.

It was dusk before I returned to the village, stunned and wondering at this strange initiation. Elements of my own magic (the coin-rolling exercise) and the djankri's magic (the sacred boulder) had been woven together by the sunlight into an unlikely meeting, an experience suggesting that the deepest magic has its source not in humanity itself, but in the meeting, the encounter of the human with what is not human. I had had intimations of this teaching many times in the past, but I had never felt its implications as clearly as I did that evening, and as I have ever since. After a dinner of potatoes dipped in salt and ground peppers, I took out my field notes, settled down in a corner, and began to write some conclusions. (What follows in the next section is excerpted from my research notes written in the Thami Valley, Eastern Nepal.)

It would be good if I began writing more often, rather than merely recording observations, for I have made some grand progress in that task, set for me some months ago by a Javanese witch, of thinking sensually—thinking, that is, with the senses, or sensing with the thoughts. It is a sort of clairvoyance, really, since we usually imagine thoughts to take place in some nterior space (we say that we think thoughts "inside" or that we are being "inward" when we are thinking) while the senses are in direct contact with the exterior world. But to have one's **thoughts** in direct contact with an exterior, open space—thoughts not just processing and interpreting data from the other senses but thoughts which themselves are feeling their way through the shifting contours and textures of an open world—how is this possible? What would it feel like to "taste" the world, to "savor" the world with one's thoughts?

Perhaps it's best to begin with this fact: there is indeed, an interior into which I commonly close myself when I think, but it is not "inside" my particular body or brain. It is, rather, the "inside" which my brain shares with all other brains that think in the same fashion. It is like a cave that opens among the sounds of the world, an auditory hollow that slowly begins to define its limits and to isolate itself. It is, in other words, this verbal space, the house of human language, this one region of awareness which is inhabited strictly by us humans, and which we therefore feel to be an "inside" or an "interior" in relation to the "outside" world which we appear to share with so many other forms of life. We readily perceive that this planet has given birth to many species, to so many styles of awareness, so many ways of being, yet our everyday thoughts as human-

beings currently inscribe themselves within a region of awareness which seems strictly our own and which presumptively shuts out all other styles of consciousness. Today we see and hear all the rest only in the terms of this privileged space—all the other animals, all the trees and oceans and rocks and storms, all that lacks a human tongue, including the Earth itself, we view only from within our insider's space of purely human discourse. "If it cannot be put into words, then it does not exist," we say, efficiently banishing all other types of awareness from the picture. What arrogance! That to be human is a unique thing is quite certain, but surely it is also unique to be a crow, or a frog, or even a night-blooming cereus for that matter. To be able to think with words is a neat power indeed—but that crow can actually fly!

By way of analogy: a person who is gifted with a certain type of intelligence is not thereby rendered unable to understand, empathize, and communicate with the rest of humanity. If she chooses to shut herself up within her particular sensitivity and to communicate solely with those few who share her gift, well then so much the worse for her and her potentially wondrous sensitivity, which will become swollen and distorted. In a like manner, our collective gifts as homo "sapiens" hold a wonderful promise, but we betray that promise when we hide behind those gifts and use them as a barrier between us and all that lives. We have such potentially grand powers for empathy and communication, since there is something in us of every animal, and also something of plants and of stones and seas, for we are woven of the same fabric as everything on the Earth, and our textures and rhythms are those of the planet itself.

And yet we have staked out and established a space that contains only what we believe is unique and privileged in ourselves. All who cannot speak our type of language are necessarily mute and dumb, not really alive; nothing is mindful but ourselves—all else is inert, determined, and therefore fit only for our observation and manipulation. We have closed ourselves into a universe of human verbiage.

How strange this is, and sad—and how clear it is why we have come to a crisis in our particular history which is also a great crisis for the planet. How can we ever become fully human when we refuse to admit that this human is a species of animal—when we have forgotten how to be genuine animals?

The magicians that I have traded with during the last nine months—like that monsoon magician of the rice paddies, or this mountain shaman whose medicineless cures have failed only once since I arrived—these are persons who struggle to regain those memories. That is what sets the magician's path at some distance from that of the mystic; while others seek to move out of their bodies, the magician fights to return to his body, to recover a place in this material world from which he feels somehow cut off and estranged. Thus the successful sorcerer is hardly a transcendent being — he is an animal, human, a creature of Earth. And his magic, far from being a supernatural power, grows out of an almost proto-human attentiveness to Nature itself—out of his ability to listen not only with his verbal mind, but with his animal mind, his plant mind, his soil, rock, river, and deep Earth mind. For the sorcerer knows that the verbal space, this human gift, only makes sense for those who have learned how to enter that space, how to grow into it out of the silence; how to grow into the head from the body itself.

And yet, and yet; there are so many, these days, who speak of communication with supernatural powers and other, a-physical worlds, so many who write that our destiny as conscious beings lies not with the planet but elsewhere, on other more spiritual worlds or in other dimensions. The new-age lecture halls resound with such assertions backed up with accounts of profound mystical experiences, of deeply spiritual sensations, of magic. I have an elegant intuition about all of this, an intuition born from certain sensations experienced as a young boy drawn to the study of conjuring back in the States, and then again, here, among the shamans of Asia. For I, too, have had some extraordinary mystical experiences in my life, some powerful bursts of oceanic awareness, although somehow these shifted states were always caught up in the material world that surrounds; they did not take me out of this world into that purely spiritual region of disembodied freedom and light about which so many of my cohorts speak and write. No, for the young magician those experiences always revolved around a heightened and clarified awareness of the organic world that enveloped him. Far from drawing him outside his domain, his "spiritual" or "ecstatic" experiences never failed to make him that much more startlingly aware of his corporeal presence, here, in the midst of a mysteriously shifting but none-the-less thoroughly physical world. And so there grew in me, steadily, a sense that the so-called spirit is really the breath of the material world; indeed, that there is no spirit more spiritual than the dance of light on the water's surface, or the wind rustling in the leaves. What the conjuror is ever straining to express with his vanishing coins and color-changing cards is that the world of the most mysterious and mystical transformations is **this** world, right here, under our noses. And yet still I am confronted by news of another world, more eternal than this one (can it be?), an utterly transcendent, non-physical realm to which all truly mystical revelations give us access. From this I am forced to conclude either that my own ecstasies and visionary experiences have in fact nothing to do with the genuinely religious path—that they are in fact false ecstasies and unreal revelations still basely "attached" to the "physical plane" as my neighbors tell me, or else that there is some sort of mundane clarity in my own ecstatic experience which is lacking in the experience of those who feel the need to postulate the existence of some other, wholly transcendent source.

Which brings me back to my aforementioned intuition about all our mystical encounters and revelations from elsewhere. Can it be that such experiences are, indeed, in-timations of another, larger world than the one we usually in-habit with our everyday thoughts and perceptions, but that the larger world to which we gain access is none other than this very Earth, this very sphere within which we move, seen now, however, for the first time clearly? Is it possible that at such times we actually do break out of a limited, constricted world, although that limited world is not the material landscape that surrounds us, but is rather our particularly limited and prejudiced human way of perceiving these surroundings, that stuffy house into which we lock our sensibilities by considering all other forms of life and existence to be without consciousness, inert, and determined? I want to ask, finally, if it is possible that our ecstatic or mystical experiences grow precisely out of our receptivity to solicitations **not** from some other non-material world but from **the rest of this world**, from that part of our own sphere which our linguistic prejudices keep us from really seeing, hearing, and feeling—from, that is, the entire nonhuman world of life and awareness, from the sphere of whales with their incredible alien intelligence, of goats and apes and the fantastically organized and industrious insect colonies, of flowers and hurricanes, of lightning and earth-quakes and volcanoes. It is the living, breathing, conscious Earth of creatures who are being bred and "harvested" as meat in our mechanized farms, of great schools of fish choking in polluted waters, of whole rain-forest universes, whole inter-communicating systems of elements, insects, plants and animals that are falling apart and dying from our fear, our species-amnesia, our refusal to recognize awareness anywhere outside our own brain. It is the live, breathing space of a planet whose sacred fluids are being sucked dry and whose breath is being poisoned by one little part of itself, a planet that is feeling sick, a world-space that has been made unhealthy by one of its favored children.

The other animals have given us much, and they have been patient with us, as have the plants, the rivers, and the land itself. Many creatures have donated their lives to our quest—many have undergone excruciating pain in our laboratories before being "sacrificed"—yet still their relatives are unaware of our purposes. The fish find it more and more difficult to swim in the stinging waters, while the passage upstream is blocked by freshly built dams; birds spin through a chemical breeze, hunting in circles for that patch of forest which had been their home. They are not alone in their dizziness, for things are worsening throughout the biosphere. Naturally, then, the mountains, the creatures, the entire non-human world is struggling to make contact with us; the plants we eat are trying to ask us what we are up to, the animals are signaling to us in our dreams or in forests, the whole Earth is rumbling and straining to let us remember that we are of it, that this planet, this macrocosm is our own flesh—that the grass is our hair and the trees are our hands and the rivers our own blood—that the Earth is our real body, and that it is alive. And so every-where, now, our "interior" space of strictly human discourse begins to spring leaks as other styles of communication make themselves heard, or seen, or felt, and all over, in so many different ways, we feel intimations of a wholeness that is somehow foreign to us, and we see the traceries of another reality. It is indeed a time for magic, a magic time. But it is no supernatural thing, this magic. We are simply awakening to our own world for the first time, and hearing the myriad voices of the Earth.

Hoedads Inc.
Hal Hartzell

The winter of '74 certainly put the Hoedads to the test. There was one incident, about the second time the Cougar Mountain crummy almost died on the unit, that characterized the winter experience. Cougar Mountain and the Cheap Thrills were working together, about six from each crew. Gerrie Mackie, a Cheap Thrill, and me, a Cougar Mountain, collaborated on a true story, since we were both there:

We had worked hard all day. It became clear that with a little extra effort we could finish off the unit. The two crews worked together into the twilight and made it up to the landing in the dark; cold, wet, tired and hungry. More so than usual because of the final push.

Cougar Mountain's green crummy would not start, leaving 12 people in the grasp of the first stages of hypothermia. It was a few hundred feet up, out of the unit, before the road started down hill. It was against government regulations to give rides to treeplanters, so the inspector drove off. There was crankiness, yelling and then depression. But then the collective mind and body began to work.

Rust calmed everyone down, enough to start working together on the problem which was his talent. While hands held a weak flashlight under the hood and tinkered, voices chanted mechanical deductions. Fire? Electricity? No, the battery was alive, the cables were tight, juice flowed to the dashboard and the lights. Fuel? It was coming through the line, making it to the carburetor. Better check the gas though. Another 20 minutes went by while people searched for a siphon hose or reasonable facsimile. None was found.

Next we disconnected the fuel line and let the gas pump squirt the gas into a jar; soon a quart of amorphous liquid was available for inspection. The problem was clear: the gas was murky. Scrambling for gas from suspicious suppliers in the embargo and too many weeks in the rain forest had produced a fuel mixture that was about one-third water. Knowing the problem and finding the solution were two different things.

Some crummies have a drain plug on the tank for this eventuality. Not this crummy. No siphon, no plug. The cold, dark and hunger dragged on. People shivered and complained, but the greater part of the crew organism was attuned to getting the hell out of there, no matter how stubborn the resistance. Even the stupid suggestions became worthy of consideration. The only way to get that water out of the tank is to punch a hole in the bottom of it with a screwdriver and a hammer; drain the gas and water into a container and then replug the hole. We did that with a sheet metal screw robbed from somewhere on the crummy. We separated the gas from the water, but still the starter motor ground and ground. The fuel would not take. Assumptions were re-examined with anguished deliberation. One thing left to try, "If the gas won't get to the carburetor by itself, we'll get it there ourselves." It had been a dismal two hours up to this point.

A solution was found: fluid was pumped out a quart at a time, allowed to settle, and the nearly pure gas was extracted and set aside. Then it took everybody to get the crummy up the hill. One rode on the front fender and poured small amounts of gas straight into the carburetor, knowing full well that too much could flood the engine or worse. The hood was up and the battery was down, due to all the starting and pumping. The lights could not be used. Someone sat at the driver's seat to work the pedals. Another stood in the driver's door to look ahead and work the wheel. Others were stationed along the edge of the road to provide verbal guidance. The night was pitch black.

It worked. The crummy lurched up the hill, pint by pint and foot by foot. Another hour passed. We finally reached the top of the hill and another problem arose: the electrical system had drowned because of the open hood in the driving rain. Nothing to do but wait for it to dry out.

Just about then, Lew Melson showed up with gas and food. A couple of Cheap Thrills lumbered in a housetruck. They had been worried back in camp some 30 miles away and had sent out a rescue party. Most rode freezing back to camp in the pickup. Some stayed in the housetruck. In the middle of the night the crummy's lights started up. Rust fired up the engine and drove the green crummy back to camp. It was waiting for the crew in the morning.

Land, Earth, Soil, Dirt:
Some Notes from the Ground
Tom Jay

Years ago, the morning after an evening of beer drinking and poetry reciting, a hung-over clot of revelers were walking back from breakfast. Robert Sund, whom I had met the night before, lagged behind the rest of us, preoccupied. He had stopped and was staring into a corner, a crack where two concrete buildings met. Curious, we went back; he looked up from a small cranial shaped pile of moss and said something like, "That's our only hope." We laughed nervously, a little shaken, it struck us all. . . The moss was patiently turning the building to soil, to dirt, to earth. That moment has haunted me since and the *idea* (the idyll) of soil and its import has become a recurrent meditation for me.

I want to look at soil as a metaphor, as a self-darkened lens that bends light, dividing, revealing, obscuring. Try to imagine soil as the context, the textural background of other images, other ideas: culture, personality, language.

A good place to start is in the words we use about soil. By examining, exhuming the stories hidden in them, their roots, we reveal the *etymon*, the words' true word, the root meanings of our attitudes toward soil. We say "back to the land," "mother earth," "good ground," "dirty," but only vaguely know what we're saying. In the world it is the roots that hold the soil. Perhaps it is the etymons, the wordroots, that hold the soil of our souls.

LAND

Land is from the Indo-European (I.E.) root *lendh*, openland. This sense still adheres to the cognates of *lendh*. Old English (O.E.) has *land*, meaning specifically open land. French has *lande*, heath, moorland, especially infertile moorland. Our word lawn comes to us from French *lande*. Old Slavic has *ledo*, wasteland. German has among others *landau*, water meadow (land + owh [water]). Old Celtic has *landa*, a valley. Welsh and Cornish have *lann*, an enclosure. Land is a relatively abstract term that refers to boundaries. Its basic idea is open or closed space. Its root does not refer to any other specific aspect of landscape except its open-ness or closed-ness. Land's meaning for us is *owned topography*. The idea of property is the word's context. To express other qualities of landcape it requires qualification, *dark* land, *green* land. Land no longer constellates an image. We can "land" anywhere. There is a land romance, some of us went "back to the land." But it is telling that we went back to the land (an abstraction) not to the Palouse, the Olympic Rain Forest or even the heath, desert, or forest. Part of the failure of the back-to-the-land movement was that their speech did not adequately inform their impulse. Land was a concept, not a locality.

EARTH

Earth is from I.E. *er*, earth is its own root; a fundamental word with many meanings specific and abstract. It is the planet. It refers to the substance, one might say the character, of the land. We cannot yet "buy earth," we find that hard to say. Historically, earth has meant or still means: the world, cosmos, soil, surface, country, chemical oxide, the place between heaven and hell, electrical ground (British), a grave, as burrow, a shelter. Currently the word's meaning is shrinking, so soon its image for us will be only the planet. The historical nuances, the shades of the word's meaning are lost to us. Losing these nuances, earth becomes dessicate, a label. It loses its ability to connect us to things; it loses its "ethics," its character. Earth is more than a green ball hurtling through eternity. Space flight is sucking the blood from a once healthy word.

DIRT

Dirt is from Old Norse (O.N.) *drit*, excrement. Drit is from O.N. *drita*, to shit. It is telling that we use a word with that root to describe soil. It still has its excremental undertone, "your hands are dirty." It expresses our alienation from soil's true qualities to call it dirt. Even earth is contaminated by "dirt." We do *dirt*, using it as a synonym for soil or earth. We should maintain its specific connections to excrement. Earth and soil are not shit. An earthy mind and dirty mind are different gatherings.

GROUND

Ground is from O.E. *grund*, foundation, earth. Ground means bottom; a "groundling" was originally a name for a fish that lived on the bottom of ponds. Ground means fundamental, basic. We run aground; we are well grounded in thought. Many disciplines use the word. (Carpentry, naval terminology, philosophy, engineering, art, etc.) Ground is cognate with O.E. *grynde*, abyss. So ground is cousin to depth and mystery. It is also used in reference to soil and landscape. We work the ground, the groin (also from *grynde*, abyss) of the earth. Perhaps we confuse soil and ground because soil grounds us, soil is *fundamental*.

SOIL

Soil is "the root metaphor," "our only hope." Soil is an earthy, grounding term that is not land. Soil is not easily owned or domesticated. It suffers our antics with motherly patience. Soil's history as a term is fascinating. In time it has meant: a wild boar mire, a pool of water used as a refuge by hunted deer, sexual intercourse, composition of the ground, mold, staining, to purge a horse on green feed. Etymologically, soil has two roots; I.E. *su*, to produce young. Cognate words are sow, succulent, socket, hyena, and hog. Pigs were sacred to the earth goddess. Pigs and snakes were her favored images. The sense that comes to us from this root is mire or stain but behind these senses in the roots wild pigs are balling and birthing at the mired edge of ancient oak forests; deer are dying near a hidden pool. "Soiled" we touch the sacred suckling succulent sow.

Soil's other sense (ground-earth) comes to us from Latin *solum*, ground floor, threshing floor; and our *solium*, throne. The I.E. root is *sed*, to sit, to settle. Soil's cognates are: nest, nestle, eat, soot, cathedral, sole. Soil is where we stand (sole), a throne of bones where light nests, where we settle. Soil is a kind of bicameral word. Like a good two-house legislature, it converses with itself. The two root meanings, *fertility* and *seat* have intertwined since Middle French, when the words became identical in sound and spelling. Indeed, the sow is enthroned in soil. Soil is the throne, the nest that bears young, the queen's room. Soil is the land in hand, smelled and seen.

The science of ecology affirms the etymological complexity of soil. From *Ecology and Field Biology* by Robert Leo Smith:

> Soil is the site where nutrient elements are brought into biological circulation by mineral weathering. It also harbors the bacteria that incorporate atmospheric nitrogen into the soil. Roots occupy a considerable portion of the soil. They serve to tie the vegetation to the soil and to pump water and its dissolved minerals to other parts of the plant for photosynthesis and other biochemical processes— vegetation in turn influences soil development, its chemical and physical properties and organic matter content. *Thus soil acts as a sort of pathway between the organic and mineral worlds.*

In short, soil is the bridge between the living and the dead, it is both in one, a living death, a paradox.

Geologist Robert Curry explains the crucial connection between soil and human life:

> All life, without exception, is dependent upon outside sources of nutrients for their support within a substrate upon which they nurture themselves. In all non-marine systems, the ultimate substrate is soil. Even marine systems are dependent upon weathered minerals derived by soil-forming processes throughout geologic time on land.
>
> Soil is not an inert inorganic blanket of varying thickness on the land that can be diffentiated into subsoil and topsoil. Those naive terms belie a basic misunderstanding that permeates the agricultural advisory services of this country. Soil is generally recognized by soil

scientists to be a dynamic, living assemblage of precisely biogeochemically segregated micro-and micro-nutrient ions held in a series of remarkable storage sites. These nutrients are provided by slow weathering over geologic time and are translocated and reprocessed by soil organisms and plant activity. In general the living biomass beneath the ground equals or exceeds that above ground. Soil is thus not a mineral geologic resource but a biospheric resource that, although renewable, can reform only at extremely slow geologic rates of tens of centuries. *The nation's soil represents its basic energy conversion resource upon which its efficiency and capability for feeding its populations is directly and virtually completely based.* The soil nutrients, within their delicately segregated geochemical levels, represent precisely and literally the sum total of the long-term sustainable economic capital of the nation. The sustainable gross national product, to use a crude literal analogy, is defined and limited by the soil nutrient capital.

To paraphrase Curry, we might say soil is fate. This notion resonates with soil's connections to seats of power, the sow goddess, soil our destiny, our destination.

Soil is the land in hand, a specific place.—Soil embodies the meeting, is the meat of weather and rock; re-members them into trees and kingfishers, salamanders and salal. Each location knots that meeting differently. Your county soil survey becomes a kind of earth phrenology—soil is a live being, a dark leaf breathing water and light.—Soil is myriad neural serpents writhing knotted on an infinity of their discarded skins.—It is its own renewable research, a porcine cannibal lover, phoenix, shit-eating alchemist, Ouroboros enshrined, an honest mother.—Persephone, Goddess of Spring lives underground, ensoiled. She rises in spring, wife of wise Hades, King of Wealth. Her name means "bringer of destruction." Perhaps she is a personification of soil, the living death, Demeter's virginal daughter married to the king of the dead. Plants and animals follow her back into the light.—Soil blurs the distinction between the living and the dead, *humbling* us. Soil is the pious Confucian son tending the graves of the ancestors. It is husband and wife in one dark body. Soil is the dwelling wave, the resource. Resource from *re-surge* which is in turn from *subregeae*, to rule from below. Soil is the resurrecting, hidden ruler.

SOIL AND PLACE, HEART AND BODY

Three word-witnesses to our notion of place:

l) *Human*, humble and homage all derive from Latin *humus*, earth, soil, ground, region, country. A human is earth-born, shares the quality of humus. It is well to remember that to our ancestors humus was local and that "humanity" was born, arose from, a specific locale, a place. The people over the hill might not be quite human, in the sense of your local humus. Our language knows we're earth-born even if we think we're heaven sent.

2) *Home* is from O.E. *ham*, house with land. Old Norse was *heimr*, world, village and *heima*, home. The I.E. root is *kei*, to lie, bed, couch; beloved, dear. Home's cognates include: hide, haunt and cemetery. Home means the haunted place, our beloved, a firm farm, a welcome bed, the graveyard. Home is where we live and die.

3) *Kith*: kith and kin. . .We all know what/who kin are. They are our family, our familiars. We forget what *kith* means. Kith derives from O.E. *cunnan*, to know, hence our cunning. From *cunnan* we also have couth, what is known. O.E. *cuth*, known, had a derivative *cyth*, native land, one's known land, hence *kith*, familiar land, neighbors and by confusion relatives, kith and kin. Interesting that place, kith, had equal standing with kin. Blood was evidently not thicker than watersheds. Kith is a strong word slumbering in an anachronism. Maybe some earth poet can wake it up.

——-

Place is a popular term among poets and writers these days. It evolved from Latin *platea*, a wide street or city square. The I.E. root is *pla*, to widen or flatten. Cognates include plain, plane, platitude, explain, plan, Plato and plot. But place for us is not something flat; it is to the contrary intricate, deep and inclusive. Neighborhood from O.E. *nehgebur*, "near fellow dweller," is closer to what we mean by place. To plot, plat and plan the *nehgebur*, the *kith*, into mere places is to abstract them until the "near fellow dwellers" become numbers. Our places, our locales are expressions of the soil; what is coaxed from soil by weather.—This Puget Sound soil-person-place is 15,000 years old, barely budded . . . wise child. What are we doing here in its lap, this couth humus, this *nehgebur* hood? Are we human yet?

Humans are born with predilections; born liking red, bells, booze, clams and flags. We are like the seeds of plants in that way, *informed*, expectant kerneled bets that a *kind* of weather will appear; that we will arrive in *cyth*. If we land in the right place we grow, our stories unfold resounding. For plants and animals it is literal, they are organs of neighborhood. An acorn in the sea, an armadillo in Antarctica are lost. For humans it seems less crucial, there may be many soils for us, many living deaths we might call home, be human in.

Soil in language; language in place.

l. Language is a soil, the poet planted, hard-shelled tender seed. The soil rots his shell, feeds him, feeds on him. The living dead surround him, worm by him in the dreamy dark, caress of million-year-old minerals, old bones, broken stones, recycled dreams; light beckons and burns him, withering; but if he is in the right language, the right weather of words, it rains; he blooms.

2. Language is a specific soil, a locale, a place, a neighborhood. Words' roots hold the soil, the leaves, the living surface of the soil, speech, catch the light and return it to the soil treasure (Pluto's Thesaurus). Words are animals working, birthing and dying. ("Sometimes a poem is writ to let one word breathe:"—William Stafford.)

Literatures are the ecosystems of language, the neighborhoods of soil. Each soil climaxes in a poem, or some perfected form that consecrates diversity, stability and adaptability, a form that envisions community (mutual promise, giving and obligation). The old languages, Finnish, Sioux, Icelandic are deep soils. Their roots intact, nutrient budgets secure. They flower in distinct possibilities; simple poems, rhymes of reverence, hot crossed puns.

American is a modern language. We are busy electrifying and mechanising our speech with robot words, input, feedback, interface. We are polishing our speech into a chrome abstraction, smooth and easily cleaned; the roots cut by its quick abstract edge, the disposable razor. The old roots suffocate beneath the gloss of our cleverness, the ancient loam beneath the condos. Our speech polishes but doesn't plow. Weather is our enemy, not our *neighbor-hood*, our home. The living death of language no longer mires, moulds or suckles our thoughts.

Language is soil because the nutrients, the *durable* images, are stored inside it. *Cultivation* releases nutrients. Poets plow language. A verse originally meant a turned furrow, a plowed line.

3. Language in place, ensoiled, blooms culture. Culture in root means to plow, return, cycle. Understood etymologically, culture is soil homage. Culture grows out of and dies back into language in place. Culture is the soil's sacrifice; it consecrates the ground, soul and soil the same dark being.

Western society has abandoned the older notion of culture, the husbanding of human life in place. Our culture does not arrive through the discrimination of the different songs the wind rings in the several pines of the Sierras, or the terror of the child lost in the rain forest, or the shape of a fisherman's pipe; no, we buy our culture. It is a consumer item, an *uncouth* import.

In our wealth or was it greed, we forgot we are humus, we took to the wind, restless and weedy, thistledown with a cross and sword. We learned to grow anywhere, choke out the natives. (Aboriginal peoples die of homesickness.) We came to favor shallow roots, learning to grow in places we wasted. This may be what we really are, but our language once lived in a neighborhood where the word for tree and truth were the same (I.E. *dru*, whence truth, tree, trust, druid, etc.)

4. Each speech has an accent, the odor of composted history. If left alone, our patterns of speech become localized, "dried" by the heat, made pungent by rain. But our electric neighborhood ignores locality; dialect is now electrified, blind as a volt, our tongues are in the air, groundless. T.V. is our tree.

5. The soil is where we return our dead. It is the home of the ancestors. This sense of soil is lacking for most of us. We are careless. I have not witnessed the lives of my kith and kin. True to the American dream we scattered, seeking private versions of wealth, ignoring Hades' dark treasure. I am less for my lack of witness. Human life grows in weight and intensity as people stay in one place. The ancestors form a wedge behind us, press us forward on the edge of that weight. Depending on our ability to bear the weight, to balance it, our located word is good or it breaks and the weight falls away. We lack ballast, a ship of fools, our speech empty, ghastly, groundless. Without the ancestors, without the soil of souls, we are potted plants, doomed in real weather.

When we speak of living here we should remember that perhaps the most imporant thing we'll do here is die and that our deaths may be the first step in steadying our children's steps. Our graves will anchor them while they work the waves of the cedar green sea.

Maybe our minds are kinds of soil. Maybe my mind is a soil where only certain things can grow, glacial till, ice-scoured clay, and only willows claim my rocky soil. Or yours perhaps is an old forest or lake bed, deep with dark

inexhaustible revenues of death; its fertility may make you frivolous and lazy.

——-

If the word roots are true we might expect our souls, our psyches, to grow in something like soil. Psyche is from the Greek for night moth. Moths pupate in the dark of the soil, sleeping like Arthurian knights in amber armor...The Salish (the people here) dug those pupa up, roasted them and ate them with delight. It is perhaps no accident that the Salish were great fire dancers.

——-

Even the sea is a kind of soil as Curry hinted, quick silver soil (And soil is like the sea only slower.)

——-

(The living biomass beneath the soil is approximately equal to the living biomass above ground.)

——-

Oil is condensed soil, burning Persephone's jewels, we're sure to catch hell for it.

Myth-Soil-Story:

When people first come to a *neighborhood* it takes a while to settle in, maybe seven generations to become kith and kin. The people act out their story; drama, trauma, dream (root-wise drama is doing work; trauma is a wound; dream is a cry of joy). The people are born, live and die, they dwell. The soil enters their stories secretly as background and gradually transforms itself into the theater of their myth. The tales become indistinguishable from the neighborhood.

Mythic time is when kith and kin are aspects, visions of the same experience. Soil digests and remembers the neighborhood coincidences; gradually a myth appears. It appears as a strange echoing. Solitary people hear it first. Animals and plants tell them. The echo twists them into wisdom, the doom of seeing. These witnesses repeat the tale until it is *true*. It becomes *religious*, a word whose root sense is "the ties that bind," "the ligaments that return us." This is the way the soil humanizes the people.

Contrary to modern psychological theory, myth isn't only psycho-logical but eco-logical as well. Myths are *nehgebur* stories, tales of the "near fellow dwellers," stories of the soul in place. The gods are embodiments of our *daily* local connections, the secrets that settle us here. Without a myth that tells us where we are, we are lost in our heads, head tripping. In a true myth, a *tree* story, we are both places at once, paradoxically sane. Inside out, one glove fits either hand.

——-

We can live *true* to ourselves and this place, human, humbled by it. We can begin in our speech and work to compost a myth, a story wherein our deaths will *matter*, "where we can take on the mystery of things as if we were god's spys."

One Circle in the Night
Daniel Menkin

As the drumming slowly faded, one by one we dropped our instruments and gazed upward into the crystal winter night. This was to have been a ceremony of sorts, interviewing a potential new member for our men's group. But any pretense of structure dissolved in the peace and majesty of this balmy interlude in a New England winter. "Your drumming . . ." said Ron, ". . . it's very powerful. It has been a long time since I've done anything like this. But how does it fit into what your group is about otherwise?"

A silence allowed us to stoke the fire in the pit before us, and when the sparks had fled into the night, it was Bernie who reached for the Talking Staff and replied. "What we are about—how can I tell you when we haven't even figured it out yet? We come together to support each other in our unfolding as men, to explore the deep male mysteries that Robert Bly talks about. But what we're about—well, its kind of like making poetry together, creating a spontaneous intunement that comes out of different mouths at different times. But we each keep listening inwardly and outwardly to somehow 'hear' what is right to contribute and when. The drumming together at the beginning is great for letting go of our day-to-day mind habits. I can't speak for the others, but it really helps me come to a much deeper, older, wiser consciousness than I normally carry."

After another poke at the fire, Daniel took the Talking Staff and continued. "This piece of cedar came from a place that has deep spiritual associations for me. I am not a woodworker, but it meant a lot to try and carve this into a ceremonial tool for this group. Whoever holds it is the voice for all of us at that moment, and we give a special sort of attention to him. Lots of times I'm eager to put in my two cents worth when a brother is speaking, but by having to wait until the Talking Staff is relinquished, it encourages me to go deeper into just being here, helps me let go of being so concerned with what 'I' want to put out there."

Since we were dispensing with any sort of interviewing formality at this meeting, the motion of the Talking Staff eventually found the rhythm of a check-in circle, a relating of our successes and difficulties since our last time together.

Even though we had been only meeting for a few months, there was already a warm awareness of each brother's life focus, his current challenges, and his relational situations. Here we were creating a safe place to explore our deeper yearnings and conflicts, and it was good to hear of each brother's inner adventures during the last few weeks.

When the staff reached Ron, he held it for quite a while before he spoke. Finally, in a deeply thoughtful voice, he said, "I'm really impressed with the respect I am feeling here tonight. It's very rare to be with men who obviously care for each other and are able to show it without all the boisterous macho stuff that usually passes for male friendship. But tell me, how did you guys get this group started—what got this process going anyhow?"

It was Michael who reached for the Talking Staff and tenderly warmed it over the glowing fire. We had been taking turns doing that all evening as an improvised way of spiritually "charging" the new instrument. The fact that it's warmth made it feel almost alive in our hands certainly helped deepen our feelings of awareness as we spoke. "Back in the summer, Daniel wrote a vision statement, a calling to like-minded men who might want to form a peer-lead support group together. It didn't get too much response until a few months ago when Kenneth showed it to several of us at a reunion meeting here. Bernie picked up the ball and organized the first meeting, and we've been going ever since. Our weekend retreat out in the woods last month deepened our commitments a lot, and now we're ready to incude a few more people."

As the Talking Staff waited near the fire, we each had some space to dance with the silence, to remember the good times and close sharing that had come from our in-tune, moment-to-moment being together. And yet, as the silence continued, it was obvious that there was a discipline at work here also, a deep respect and willingness to honor our stillness as a circle. Though we were reluctant to trap it in words, we each were there to participate in the deep male mysteries, to re-connect with a wisdom beyond this local time and culture. We have been careful to avoid becoming cultish, yet there is aa delightful openness to experimenting, to playing with new forms of experessing the ancient truths that love to dance in the midst of a circle of men come together to see Truth.

And the dance is joyous!

Complexity and Time
Breaking the Pyramid's Reign
Sigmund Kvaloy

Sigmund Kvaloy tells us about the "roots" of deep ecology, growing out of the Norwegian "ecophilosophy" movement and explains the difference between "normal" human society and the "temporary anomaly" of the present Industrial Growth Society. This article came out of a lecture he gave to the British Schumacher Society, which was later printed in the British publication, *Resurgence* (Autumn 1984). In addition to being a Norwegian philosopher and environmental activist, Kvaloy is a farmer, musician, airplane mechanic, artist and mountaineer. His insight into Buddhism, as given below, comes out of the Himalayan Mountain Buddhism of the Sherpa village, which has adopted him as a clan member.

Modern Ecophilosophy started some 15 years ago. For a brief

spell, bright ideas were launched in various countries. Since then, there has been a lot of action, but very little philosophy. We have gained a good deal of experience. Now we need to sit down and philosophize. Otherwise, we'll keep on doing unnecessary, sometimes very serious mistakes even moving in the wrong direction.

Of course green philosophers have been at work during this period, but they have generally not been people of concrete action—so few viable ideas have appeared. The socio-ecological crisis of our time is throwing us into something completely unprecedented. It's global, and it is deeper and more up-rooting than most people—even among the greens—have the imagination to grasp.

TWO KINDS OF SOCIETY

Much of the thinking of the Norwegian Ecophilosophy group has been formed through posing two basically different sorts of social organization against each other. We have called them *Industrial Growth Society* (IGS) and *Life Necessities Society* (LNS), the first one being based on steady or accelerated growth in the production of industrial articles and the use of industrial methods. The second one is based on producing life necessities and always giving priority to that. There is only one historical example of the first kind of society, our own, which is tending to become global. Most other human societies have been of the second kind.

IGS is an abnormal kind of society, which can exist only for a historical second. Judging from various indications spanning 1-2 million years, the LNS is the human kind of society, and it will remain so. We have no faith in the saving capacity of the computer. Rather the opposite: the computer and its data-collecting networks and its educational systems will have as its most conspicuous function a treatment of symptoms and a hiding of real causes, and so will permit a build up of the crisis. The result will be a more devastating crash.

HYDRO-POWER AND ECOPOLITICS

A green movement started very early in my country. Its beginnings were in the 1930s, giving the Norwegian labour movement a special flavour. Half of its popular basis was small farmers and fishermen, not industrial workers. Norway was industrialized very late compared to the rest of Europe.

Norwegians have always been very curious people, they have travelled a lot, and our authors started very early to describe and analyse the effects of industrialization in different countries. It was as if we were sitting there, on top of our mountains, and looking southwards towards Europe, watching the new order of things approach, with fear and excitement. I grew up with that double sentiment. In my own lifetime, I experienced the complete transition from an almost medieval agricultural, self-reliant society to modern superindustrialism replete with computers, relaxation in Mallorca, and complete dependence on world market forces.

One reason for our very late industrialization, was the lack of resources. The only thing we had in any abundance was the combination of steep mountains and a lot of rain. In other words: hydroelectricity. Today Norway has, per capita, more electricity than any other nation in the world, almost twice as much as Canada which is number two in the world statistics. But this has meant a direct collision with the Norwegian folk soul. The people of Norway once settled along the rivers. They utllized the rivers in many different ways and became dependent on them for their material existence. Their organization as a nation consisted of many small, almost independent sub nations along our extremely long and rocky territory. Their soul was a soul of rivers and waterfalls and deep fiords.

NECESSARY CONFLICT

Throughout the first half of this century people went along with hydroelectric projects, feeling that electricity and industry would compensate for river losses. But after the war all that changed. The schemes grew out of all proportion and far beyond the needs of the people. That's when Norwegian electricity became the bridge for international industry, and for Western Jet-Set civilization. Then North sea oil came along and worked neatly as the second stage of this two stage rocket now threatening to fire Norwegian society off into empty black space.

This is the period when the cultural collision became apparent. That conflict has hardened tremendously during the last few years and I have come to see it as my duty to intensify but also to clarify that conflict. It's not possible to reach a future that is creative without social, economic and political conflict.

We need to develop a new paradigm, a new world picture; a new mode of perceiving, thinking and living, some people would call it a new myth. We need something that will give us a collective strength equal to the security with which our opponents operate, and which the self-verifying IGS system gives them every day. Without this, we are at their mercy, and we are easily split asunder and brought to confusion.

COMPLEXITY VERSUS COMPLICATION

The propaganda of IGS tells us that LNS is a simple, primitive and even standardized sort of society, while IGS is complex. Actually it is the other way around. The complexity of IGS is just an appearance. A closer look reveals something else.

The main reason for the common misunderstanding—on which the propaganda thrives—is that in IGS, a *multifarious division of labour* is confused with spiritual, social and cultural complexity. These are, of course, entirely different parameters. The different jobs that had to be done in the older society could, in principle, be taken care of by any individual. Each person came near to self-sufficiency and self-reliance, given a minimum of natural resources. To be so fit, this required of her or him the development of a broad spectrum of talents— intellectual, institutional, emotional and practical. Modern women and men have been robbed of the kind of work that brought this out, of work as the everyday catalyst to the enfoldment of human complexity. The potential of each individual's complexity has instead been administratively cut up and handed out to a thousand different career specialists. The IGS makes life *complicated* instead of complex.

I'll use my childhood to illustrate this. I lived on a Norwegian mountain valley farm. Contrast this with a glimpse into a present-day situation: it's my son who has gone to bed in an apartment in modern Oslo. When a child goes to bed all the impressions of the day are digested. The only time when there is peace for that, is in bed, before sleep comes. When I look back I have a lot of fabulous memories of the room in the old log house where every single piece of timber had been individually shaped and I knew whom among my own relatives had done it. I knew where in the forest they had cut the timber, spots I could visit myself and still see the stumps. We didn't have electricity and we were not to use candles or oil lamps unnecessarily, so in my room I just had natural twilight which was different every night and my experiences and impressions of play and work were new every day. Every night there would be something new with me to give life to all those fantastic visual patterns that surrounded me on the walls and ceiling, the natural pattern in the wood, always impressing upon the mind the rhythms of living growth. They inspired adventure stories that grew incessantly in my mind, bridging waking existence and dreams.

The situation today is different. Look at my son's room, which is "bed-and-media chamber". On the surface it looks colourful; closer scrutiny reveals it as an expression of the mass production of IGS. We have a Buddha here, pointing to "spiritual values" and a "cosmopolitan attitude", a Buddha printed in 4 million copies on washable, glossy plastic, made in Tokyo. Every item in the room is expressive of the standardization and commercialization of the world of this growing child. There is nothing here that challenges him to be self-creative, to use his own hands and senses in direct interplay with the naturally complex material and spiritual world.

LIVING WITHOUT SPLITTING

Well, the child of the log house grew up, and was one day sitting on top of a Norwegian mountain looking southwards. As mentioned, it was not solely frightening; like so many growing boys I was excited at the technical miracles and the promise of mastering enormous forces; it was a new version of what we had been told the old Norwegians could do in their time of magic and giants. Like so many of my own age, I was split down my mental middle; one part wanted to take over the farm that had been in the family since before the Viking era; the other part thought the greatest adventure of all must be to leave not only the farm but the earth and to fly on a rocket ship to Mars or Alpha Centauri. But my eyes were not good enough to navigate an airplane that was later to become a starship, so I settled for a career as a designer of rocket engines. My best friend was the son of the village blacksmith. In the smithy, we produced three rockets. Design No. 3 went straight through the roof of our barn and landed across the river—that was like crossing the Atlantic. Later, at the Technical College of the Royal Norwegian Air Force, I learned that rocket careers today require you to be part of a 'Technical Order System'. So the adventure was wiped off the pages of the latest science fiction book, the one I was writing myself. In the nick of time—before the social investment became too heavy for withdrawal, I left the Air Force and entered the philosophy department at the University of Oslo. Actually I went there to find out about double personalities, but to my disappointment, no such idea was on the curriculum.

A LABORATORY FOR ECO-POLITICS

To make a long story short, after some years in New York, India and Nepal, I joined the Norwegian ecopolitical tradition on an all-day, all-night basis. If you vividly feel that the roof may cave in any moment, it's just not possible to sit still at an institute of philosophy, analysing some Greek concepts presupposing the world to stand still. So, in 1969 on the 24th of June, a group of friends met and founded what we later called The Ecopolitical Ring of Cooperative Action—the RING, for short. All activists are welcome, but none other. It still exists, and nowadays there are members in many countries, in America and India. In Norway we represent ECOROPA and Friends of the Earth and *The Ecoloigist*. We put out our own journal devoted to ecopolitical philosophy, called *The Ring*.

That first autumn we lacked practice and training, so we called on top experts of the Norwegian IGS to come every week to our meetings and be informative, but what they did not know was that their primary function was to act as our training objects. That was our laboratory. I am stressing it, because it proved very successful. At each 'laboratory session' they were one and we were many, which meant that we dared to confront them and make mistakes without losing our nerve. Not only did we pick up courage this way, we discovered their one vulnerable spot, they were specialists, meaning they could be beaten by generalists. They were extremely good within their own narrow field, knowing next to nothing outside that field. The world is full of such people. We are governed by persons who don't know where we are heading. So we built our own training programme to become *super-amateurs*, meaning people who both know a little within all relevant social and ecological fields, who love their work and who put all their effort and talent into learning that work. The *main* trick of 'super-amateurship' is the training to combine logically and understandably across the specialists' fields and to tie all that to the main theme that interests people.

During this period we invited the head of the Landscape Protection Office of the Norwegian Hydro-electric Dept. He had a surprising argument. He had been around Norway in his car and had taken lots of photos of farms, houses, courtyards and fences, and he tried to prove through this series of pictures that the common people of Norway completely lack aesthetic sensibility. If our group's main argument against dams and hydropower was aesthetic, our case was doomed. You are just a tiny, exclusive elite, so his argument ran, and most people, in any society, are primarily concerned with material security and growth, if they are economically compensated for ugliness, then ugliness is OK. To prove this he showed an old, well built log house where the walls had been broken through and enormous panorama windows put in, even at the corners.

We were at a loss to counter his allegations. The next week's meeting we had to be alone to discuss his argument. Our conclusion was twofold. First, his selection of pictures was clearly biased. The situation wasn't that bad. But of course few people today are creative, they are passive consumers of the mass media. One cannot speak much of an artistic folk culture. If you go back half a generation you find an artistic folk culture. Secondly, the deterioration in taste coincides with industrialization. His documentation of a national low ebb in aesthetic sensibility testified to a deterioration that he himself, the designer of 'nicer' power stations, had contributed to. His contribution had been one of making a quick superindustrialization of Norway more acceptable. He was an IGS cosmetologist.

COMPLEX WORK

Let's go back to a time when aesthetics were part of daily

life. I will relate a story found in Snorri Sturlason's *The Sagas of the Norwegian Kings*. Its theme is the building of the most famous of the viking ships, the *Long Serpent*. It was built for the equally famous king, Olav Tryggvason, a few years before the end of the first millenium A.D. The ship was the largest known at the time, around 180 ft. long and considered the most beautiful. One of the foremen of the building crew was a man named Torberg. During the construction of the ship Torberg was called home, something serious had happened there, and his help was needed. The king let him go.

That tells us something important about that society which is strikingly different from our own. The difference is twofold. This man Torberg was actually one of the main designers and construction engineers of the ship, but he was not a specialist in ship-building. He was a farmer, but we learn from other sources that people along the coast were never just farmers, they were fishermen, hunters in the mountains, traders, blacksmiths, iron ore miners and refiners, carpenters, semi-nomads herding cows and sheep and goats among mountain pastures, local parliamentarians, and they built boats, large and small. They were persons that could in principle do anything. Torberg was a generalist or a 'super amateur'.

Point two: Torberg was permitted to go to his farm, in spite of his role as a key man on the most prestigious ship. In that society the farm was regarded as the foundation. The king knew that disregarding this order of things, he would risk losing the support of the farmers of Tröndelag.

Well, Torberg had to stay away for quite a while.

When he came back, it was evening, but he eagerly went to the ship. By then, the sides had been boarded up to the rim, including the rim plank. The king and a crowd of people were expressing pleasure and excitement. But Torberg did not share their happy mood. The following morning the king and Torberg arrived to find everybody standing around. What's up, asks King Olav, why aren't you working? And the men say: something terrible has happened; someone has ruined one of the top rim planks. Hearing this, the king flies into a rage and promises death to the one who is guilty of such an atrocity and gold to the one who tells who the guilty one is. Torberg says quietly,—well, you don't have to go far to find the one who is now first to be given gold and thereafter lose his life, it was I who did it. Everybody was as if struck by lightning.

And the king says, I have to keep my promise, if you can't make the damage good right now. Whereupon Torberg runs over to the ship and he uses his axe and starts slicing off wood to level out all the cuts he had made during the night, and since the ship is really the *Long* Serpent I guess they let him keep at it for a couple of hours.

Now, to understand the story we have to keep a few things in mind, like for instance: the top rim board is always made out of very hard wood. In addition, Torberg must have worked very fast during the night when he made the incisions, in order to finish the whole rim before being discovered, so I think he'd just cut straight down on the plank, he hadn't stopped to chop sideways. And he had been cutting into the wood at right angles to its growth lines and that way you never get very deep. Adding it all up I doubt if he had gone deeper than half an inch, at the most. So that's the thickness of what he was

slicing off, and I am sure that we today would not have noticed the difference when he was finished—not on a 180 foot ship! But the saga reports differently: "Then everybody saw that the ship was even more beautiful," it says. And not only that, the crowd immediately noticed the difference between the two sides of the ship, and the king made him polish down the other rim plank as well. *Now*, finally the ship was perfect, and Torberg was made Honorary Chief Builder of The Long Serpent, and he was given a name by which he could be remembered: Torberg *Skavhogg*— "the one who shapes wood by axe". We get the full significance of the story if we keep in mind one more thing: The saga of the life of Olav Tryggvason is a long and detailed one, and it tells us vividly that Torberg was taking a grave risk. He knew quite plainly that his life was at stake.

But Torberg could not bear living the rest of his life knowing that he had taken part in building the Long Serpent and that the ship was less than perfect. Playing against death, he *had* to show everybody what a perfect form is, but he knew what kind of audience he was performing for, so when it was cut out for them, *all of them* were immediately convinced. He knew they would be, if he was given the chance. What *we* would single out as a purely aesthetic value, had at least as much force in Torberg's society as economic necessities in ours. The enormous difference between those two societies becomes even clearer when we remember that ours is an extremely rich society in the material sense, while Torberg's was full of physical toil with very little economic reward. And Torberg's act was not by his contemporaries regarded as strange or unreasonable. Rather the opposite. He was made a historical figure because he was one of those who set a norm of excellence for everybody to be guided by.

Now, the story of Torberg Skavhogg is just one of many of the same nature in Norwegian history. Many other nations and cultures have similar stories.

In the economy of those cultures everyday challenges are complex and children are included in work. Parents or adults are careful in selecting work for the children so that their experience *is often one of success*.

This is a situation I have seen on many occasions in Sherpa culture in the Himalayas. There is a social seriousness in the challenges that a child has to cope with. Every child knows that she or he is a highly regarded member of society. The child is given responsibility and is even relied upon for initiative when unprecedented situations arise, and the jobs are so varied that the whole range of talents of this human being are in principle developed, the intellectual, intuitional and emotional. So when this person grows up a high level of self-reliance and resourcefulness is achieved, and on top of that the ability to discern between ugly and beautiful.

EXPERIMENTS WITH TRUTH

Briefly, I will mention a few campaigns and direct actions we went into and which taught us a lot.

Our first action came in 1970 in *Eikesdal*. Local cooperation came easily and naturally, because there had already been two hydropower schemes implemented in the valley, and the emptiness of promises had become clear to everybody. The action had been under preparation one year. Our aim was to stop the hydro-electrocution of the Mardola Water Fall—the third highest in the world when the springtime thawing of snow in the mountains makes it plunge 2,000 feet in one leap into an extremely lush forested valley by the Eikesdal lake. The picture of that waterfall later became the symbol of the whole ecopolitical movement of Norway, and is the emblem of the Ring.

One element in the Mardola action is an abridgement on Gandhi, I don't know if he would have approved. We used steel chains to anchor ourselves to the rocks so that the police could not move us. A 70 year old Eikesdal farmer, Olav Utigard, made the chains from old cow anchors. Some of us were mountain climbers so we used drill pitons. We drilled into the rock and sat on the pitons so the police could not get at them. We fastened ourselves so that no one could cut the chains without hurting our bodies. Norwegian policemen hesitate to hurt anyone, so that was successful. The chains represented our vital ties to Mother Earth. They couldn't be severed without lethal damage. Olav Utigard himself and several of the other farmers sat with us in the chains. The action and the larger campaign around it became very involved and we learned more from it about Norwegian society than we would have in seven years at a university seminar. We came out as different people. The Mardola action was sensational. It was reported in the *New York Times* and *Der Spiegel* and on television. About 500 persons joined it, some from France, America and Holland. We lost the waterfall but we started a movement. Right after that, and inspired by it, we went into a series of actions; to save a beautiful forest near Oslo, to stop a new international airport on good farming land, to stop a road through a kindergarten and another through a suburban settlement, to stop several new military target ranges, etc.

Through these practical actions we worked on a new philosophy of society and man-in-nature. From 1969 we called our way of thinking *eco-philosophy*. We held ecophilosophical seminars in the mountains—in and out of the chains. Our experiment had proved to ourselves that Gandhi is right when he says "the goal is the way and the way is the goal". It's detrimental to your effort to concentrate on some pre-conceived achievement. Living here and now makes you strong.

My great source of inspiration has been *The Gita According to Gandhi*. Gandhi makes the Gita relevant to the 20th century. But in any century its bright guiding star is the Norm of Selfless Action. The source of knowledge is to be found, not at some university, but at the centre of social and political conflict, in the *selfless* search for Truth. But what is this "life-truth"? You may find guidance in Gandhi, in Martin Luther King, in the Vietnamese Buddhist monks who burned themselves to death, in Torberg Skavhogg. But you have to help yourself through your own action. It's not laid out before hand. That why *you should not hanker for the fruit of your action*. This is very strange to Europeans. We always act as if the world is a map, a piece of space where definite goals are plotted. To us it is crazy that we should be striving without the aim of the fruit of our action. What else could inspire activity?

It is impossible for us to say that an aim will materialize as we define it. If, for instance, in the Mardola river project you get very close to reaping the fruit, but in the end you lose the river, commonly, you are shocked into inactivity because "everything is lost". That's where Parliament and Big Industry may sit back and let out a sigh of relief and say; finally we have peace, those demonstrators have been robbed of their wind, so, let's get on with the next electrocution!

Pre-figuring a future point of win-or-lose was what we started to get out of through the Mardola action. We liberated ourselves from the chess-board. In life obstacles are just inspirations to experimentation. [See Bateson's "lab-dog" story in this volume]

In 1970 the parliamentarians, as usual, let out their sigh of relief, happy to be rid of the demonstrators. But to their consternation there wasn't any good riddance this time. The next day we were there again campaigning for the next river, plus putting brakes on North Sea oil drilling, and to keep Norway out of the European Common (growth) Market which we won. The movement reached the less activist-oriented parts of the population, creating the *Future in Our Hands* organization four years later; that one has since grown very large and spread to the other Scandinavian countries, and to England as well.

INNERDALEN AND ALTA

Mardola was only the first in a series of nonviolent direct actions and unconventional campaigns. All the big ones were river actions, the most notable of which were at *Innerdalen* and *Alta*.

Innerdalen "The Inner-most Valley" is (was, now I regret to say) a beautiful, extremely fertile mountain valley in Mid-Norway, that was to be completely inundated as a hydroelectric dam. In this valley we were finally able to stage a pure, Gandhian action, plowing and harvesting crops, keeping cattle, producing milk, butter and cheese. We organized a 'green University' and a 'green factory workers occupation', proclaiming the dam workers as 'strike breakers'. The latter was to provoke discussion with the labour movement. It was at meetings in Innerdalen that we conceived the idea of a Green Workers International.

The *Alta* campaign comprised a lengthy series of direct actions, repeated arrests and a morass of court cases, aimed at protecting the river Alta and the last unspoiled territory of the *Same* (Laplanders) reindeer herders.

That campaign reached its culmination in the winter of 1980-81, with large-scale direct action under arctic conditions. The temperatures went down to 40 degrees centigrade, and the actionists chained to the rocks as in Mardola—housed in heated tents. The international participation was this time much larger, besides Scandinavians, people from West Germany, France, Holland and Belgium took part. The resistance, named 'nonviolent winter guerrillas', was broken when the authorities sent a ship with 600 policemen to Alta. Specially trained technicians used fly-wheel cutters to break the extemely heavy chains, and asbestos and steel sheets to protect the demonstrators from the terrible wounds that this technique might otherwise inflict. The campaign included a one month hunger strike, staged in

Oslo by five young *Same* men, a *Same* women's occupation of the Government Building, and a *Same* Women's delegation to New York and Ottawa to seek support from American Indians and Eskimo organizations, a support that was whole-heartedly given. One of the very positive results of the Alta campaign has been a contribution to the international cooperation between the various aboriginal organizations. One of the young *Same* fighters, Nils Somby, who lost his left arm in trying to blow up a hydropower construction site bridge in Alta, fled the Norwegian police and was adopted by a Canadian Indian tribe. He lives in Canada now with his family.

One result of a decade of Alta campaigning has been a substantial reduction of that hydropower scheme. Another result has been the positive transformation of the lives and outlook of a lot of the participants. Many of them have told me that "for the first time I experienced meaning in my life". That is noteworthy. For the first time they were part of a process where it became natural to forget their egos, to identify completely with other human beings.

MEANINGFUL WORK

Moving from one river to the next, the horizon was widened step by step. Above all we learned the meaning of work. This is a topic that E. F. Schumacher stresses and treats lucidly in his chapter "Buddhist Economics", in his book, *Small is Beautiful*. In Buddhist thinking *man needs work as much as he needs food*. In Western thinking work is a means, not an end in itself. Because in the IGS economy the ideal worker is an appendix to the machine. In IGS work loses its meaning.

Search for *meaningful work* is the basis for our initiative to form the Green Workers' International. We define the concept through five characteristics:

1. It is an activity necessary for a human being's material survival.
2. It's *fruits* (material objects and services) do not damage, but, rather *enhance life*.
3. It poses such challenges that the potential *complexity of talents* and *capabilities* in the individual are brought to bloom.
4. It demands *loyalty* as well as cooperation.
5. It engages *children* and other social groups.

IGS deprives us of meaningful work. That might be its most damaging aspect. A wonderful aspect of meaningful work is that a society built upon that foundation will thrive on meager energy resources. Energy affluence actually destroys meaningful work. Meaningful work presupposes a specific kind of economy, which requires the enhancement of sensitivity towards fellow human beings and nature.

TIME AND SPACE

We in the West are handicapped at predictive activity because our minds have such a weak sense of *time*. I mean "human" or "natural" time, as distinguished from clock time or the time of physics, which is time reduced to space, or to projections on paper and on the computer. Our perception and personalities are static. We need to regain time, and train our sense of process. With no training of that kind we are unable to predict the future. Being equipped with computers makes us worse, because it makes us think we're coming to grips with time, while actually a static piece of apparatus, a machine, has been interposed between us and the creative process of life.

We often ask the question "what does the future hold?" That is a meaningful question only if the future is a storehouse. A computer can piece together a million indications of, say, what's buried in a cave; it can help us become better archeologists, but archaeology doesn't help us in uncovering the future.

We are building the future, on the basis of or *often in spite of*— what's buried in our history. Some of us are trying to build a society that is qualitatively different from past and present society; a complex instead of a complicated society. But, of course, we *have* to take our ideas from earlier experience.

Some of the greens say that we can and should start by *changing ourselves first*, and through *that* get ready to change the system. That's still building on the view of man as a soul separated from his body and from his environment. That's observing the river, from a safe river-bank. [The other way is] you step into the river, and are—grabbed by the current, and are *forced* to learn how to swim. It's then that you have a chance of being shaken so that you're changed and through that you change the system. That's when you learn to accept that nothing is permanent, that everything is time, and time is creativity. Only then will initiative and responsibility replace passivity.

The West is space fixed. The East—has temporalized space.

Let me illustrate the separation by referring to the house-building cultures of the two traditions. In the Himalayas, there is a valley called "The Plow Furrow". I have visited the place six times, and I and my family are adopted members of three local clans. I have seen tourists and mountaineers from the West come through this valley, and stop briefly, take one look at the village and say, well look at these poor people. They strive to build houses with right angles, perpendicular walls, conforming to geometrical perfection, and look how these ideals are always beyond their reach! They are toiling, but frustration is always their lot.—And of course! Because these primitives don't have the simplest knowledge of mechanics, they lack the proper instruments and tools, and they are always short of time. We have to help them, said Sir Edmund Hillary, and brought in an aluminum school, *shining* with Graeco-American principles.

But these tourists and helpers haven't a clue. The Himalayan farmers, are not aiming for geometric-Platonic perfection which has to do with perceiving the world as immobile space overlaid with illusionary movement, even with detesting movement and time. It is misleading to use the word 'architecture' about Himalayan houses. We should talk about 'life with one's house': the house is part of one's personality. It is always changing; change is its nature. The house, together with everything near and relevant to it, human beings, animals, plants, all this is behaving like one organic, rhythmically changing form.

The Sherpa and Tibetan houses are living beings of which the builders take responsibility on an every-day basis. The house is meant to be repaired every day. It is built light so that the forces of nature, like wind, are permitted to show their force, but in such a way that it's always the parts that are quickly, almost effortlessly rebuilt. The roof blows off in strong winds, the way it's meant to, but that means that the much more important skeleton of the house remains untouched, and the family puts the roof back. I've watched it happen on several occasions. Putting the roof back is like putting your hat back. You don't feel terrible having to do that. This is the strategy formed by necessity in a non-affluent society.

Western architecture is an expression of a 'stop-time aesthetics'. The modern house is a member of a class, I label 'paper constructions', because when that kind of house is built it shares an important characteristic with the clean drawing on paper done by the architect. If you smoke a pipe, like I do, and as an architect you have a bad day and happen to put your sooty thumb on the just finished drawing, leaving a black stain, that's intolerable, and you just have to throw it in the dust bin. The same is the case with a modern house. If one day the passers-by observe a crack in the wall—a scar on that pure, smooth face—they can't bear it because it's part of a structure where the cracks of time are supposed not to have relevance. Western architecture is built to make you believe that time is stopped and that withering or death is no more. To keep that illusion going, however, presupposed a global robber economy, a systematic plundering that is now finally emptying the earth's last resources at an exponential pace, scooping up energy and materials and people around the globe to desperately preserve stuctures that are contradicting time, the process of life. Man is here living by contradicting himself at his existential roots. On the personal micro-level something like this would be called insanity, probably labelled as schizophrenia.

In contrast to this, to regain sanity, I propose the *philosophy of positive decay*. Accepting decay means accepting life. It's another word for eco-philosophy.

The Process Paradigm of Buddhism

The key element of Buddhism, is that the world is suffering, (*Dukkha*: 'revolving on a crooked axle'), they mean *we are time but think we are space*. It's the element that unlocks Buddhist philosophy. We think we are space and act accordingly, which means we are continuously colliding with ourselves and everybody else. We are part of a time flow, of a stream, of chains of events with no beginning and no ending and in this stream our individuality disappears. By natural inclination we seek individual permanency. We are *inclined* to do that, but as human beings we are born with a freedom to rid ourselves of that inclination. Even the name we are given at birth fortifies the inclination. Holding on to our name from one minute to the next is pulling us into the trenches of the war against time. When we are born as human beings we start by discovering our body, as often as not by getting hurt, we don't get milk when we need it, we burn our fingers or cut ourselves on a knife. Having a human perception and self-consciousness we react self protectively, and step by step an individuality bound to a body becomes the most vital thing

in the world to care for. But we can't protect our body, nor even our mind! To exist individually means to be a loser. This kind of thinking is consistent with the IGS, with a socio-economic system demanding that individuals fight each other. We build protective walls around our person, we seek economic security, social status, honour, a pyramid on top of our grave. But everything has to come down because we are but eddies in the time stream. The worst of our 'reductionisms' is that of reducing time reality to space—an illusory world. And the more we do it, the greater the crash when time breaks through.

Eye Versus Ear

Let us once more look at two basically different cultures, contrasting them. We'll first focus on the **Industrial Growth Society** which is based on mechanical mobility instead of time. IGS is a pyramidal society. As it progresses its administrative and political networks tend toward perfecting the pyramidal shape. The development is fourfold.

1. It is aiming for *linear expansion of the production of industrial commodities and services and the use of industrial methods*—standardized mass production, concentrated in a few, urbanized centres, carried out by specialists on all levels;
2. It is based on *individual competition*, in every human field of endeavour.
3. Its main resource for expansion is *applied science*.
4. Its main method of governing is quantification.

I'll use the usual Western approach to vision as a symbol here. [Kvaloy drew a straight line.] Now fix your eyes on the tip of my pen as I move it from the left to the right side of the drawing. You manage to do that easily, I'm sure, and you're equally successful in reversing the process, following the pen as I move it back to the starting point. This ability to reverse and repeat, to control a movement in space, is a specific ability of our organ of visualization. It is our primary organic-perceptive instrument for fixing us to space and thereby controlling our world. It is in this way different from the other sense organs, that are predominantly sensing time flows. Take hearing. You cannot, for instance, stop my flow of words and reverse them; you cannot go back and hear once more what I said a while ago. You cannot reverse that kind of process. And because of that *you have to raise your awareness to a higher level—to be really present*, in conscious and active synchronization with what's happening. Otherwise you'll slide out of participation, you'll be individualized. The eyes, in contrast, are conducive to the private study of books etc. You may be attentive or not, as you choose. You have control because of isolation. You're abstracted from the world, from the life stream.

Because of its seeming security, we think that eyesight is the most important. In keeping with Buddhism, controlled space is illusory. But that illusory world is fortified through material and competitive success, especially if you are part of the IGS and have at your disposal the science and technology of that socio-economic system. But our sense of hearing may help us to regain awareness of what time is. Time makes the space usable and discernible to a living being. All our activity has its roots in time. Time makes us active, so that we can act in space, with our senses and with our hands. But we are taught to reduce time to space.

THE COSMIC JAZZ BAND

Our technology and our commercial power centres have launched a massive attack on hearing and on sound to reduce them to space phenomena. They do it with tape recorders and record players. The most crazy thing I know is when jazz fans are listening to the same improvization by Charlie Parker one thousand times over, trying to copy his improvized solo in detail. It's so crazy, because improvized jazz is actually one of the very few outlets for time awareness in our culture. Jazz offers us real creativity and organic existence, the opportunity of genuine personal creativity. We may use as the contrast here classical orchestra music, and this is not a contest between two types of music but between two types of society.

The cello player is governed from the outside. You look at sheet music, you follow the metronome, you count and subdivide bars, you listen to recordings, you try to copy and you are alone. Alone, but secure, in a controlled environment, where everything unfolding is according to plan. Maybe you have a conductor in front of you, giving orders that you have to comply with. You know that if you don't comply, there is no security any more. Chaos threatens, which means time would take over.

The small, well-integrated jazz band is a different world, a flow where every member has the same importance, where there's no conductor, and where creativity happens all the time.

Why are there so few individuals that are good at playing both kinds of music—that can function in both kinds of society? Because going from one to the other is so radical a shift that it is like changing personality. Coordination in 'jazz band society' is done through an internal sharing of the rhythm of a total creative flow. If you try to keep time by counting, keeping track of bar lines in jazz, you are lost. To achieve that undefinable quality called 'swing' the part-takers have to share the ability to swim in a river of rhythm. It's more like being in your breathing and stomach—like meditation—than in your head. This is, partly, the basis on which jazz functions so well as an international language. Because it employs directly the natural rhythms that we all share as children of nature. Jazz musicians all over the world know some 150-200 standard, rhythmically ordered chord sequences, but they don't know them as mathematics or grammar, they have internalized them in their 'body and soul'. These internalized sequences have become like a refined interpretation of their own breathing-life.

You may go to New York or Bristol or Tokyo or Addis Ababa or Moscow and without any practice beforehand you may join a jazz band and somebody just gives a short signal and right away all of you, Japanese, English, Norwegian, Russian or African are out swimming in the same river. We are more than one.

Our psychologists, have been wrong in one of their basic pre-suppositions. When they talk about a human being whose mental life is chaotic, they always stress the importance of him or her getting back into his or her self. Their aim is to build one individual identity. And all success is based on the possibility of defining one and only one personality structure as a skeleton for the healthy and sane individual.

Well, instead of this notion we can conceive of a human being as a being who at birth is like a very complex root system which is trying not to fix a permanent personality structure, but to grow a multiplicity of personalities. I have in mind a *dynamic* and *multi-directional* but *organically ordered* pattern. Contrasting this, we, 'the civilized' peoples, live under pyramidal systems that demand of us that we must be one single, rigidly identifiable person. That's the only way we can function as controllable 'elementary particles'.

The only author I have found in Western literature who has taken a full step toward questioning this basic assumption is H. G. Wells. It's a deviation from everything else that he wrote. Toward the end of his life he had the idea that he ought to be a member of the Royal Society, and for that purpose he wrote a doctoral dissertation. It was published in 1944 as an appendix to an essay collection, and it's got the fantastic title, "A Thesis on the Quality of Illusion in the Continuity of the Individual Life in the Higher Metazoa, with Particular Reference to the Species Homo Sapiens." I've never heard of anyone who is aware of it. I guess those who read it at the time thought the idea was untenable or just plain crazy. (He got the doctor's degree but not the Royal Society.) He has this idea that this one individual centre that we turn back to all the time is wrong. Maybe the human personality structure is like a stage instead of a centre, a stage where a series of actors are performing. We recognize only one of them, the others are suppressed. But sometimes we go to bed at night having very interesting plans for the next day; in the morning they all seem totally irrelevant to us. We feel like being part of an entirely different universe, where other things matter. The sleep has mixed up our various identities.

Well, I think a lot of interesting ideas and observations would come out of looking at the world from this angle. The most rewarding places to look for healthy multiple person structures are semi-nomadic societies, because they are made up of people who live two or more parallel lives, in integration with more than one environment. I'll mention a couple of examples. One is from my own country, from communities on the Western and Northern coast up until about 70 years ago. The men of these communities were stationary in one place with their farms and neighbours and then every winter for three months they left home on a sailing vessel, to go fishing at the *Lofoten* islands far away to the North. One of my grand-fathers lived like that in his youth. They often had very rough weather, and this little, open, square-rigged viking type boat wasn't easy to handle. But they were masters at it, and the only way they could manage, was through total mutual integration. The six of them, together with the boat and its rigging, became like one organism.

These men had to be members of two extremely different sorts of society with two different ways of social integration. They were also meeting nature in two different ways. They could do it so well because they developed two personalities. The theory of permanent ego-centredness does not cover that phenomenon. And, mind you, these two personalities go deeper than role playing; they were dynamic; always shifting, adjusting and growing, sometimes by the situation brought to order on each other, and there might be conflict between the two personalities.

These men in the tiny nutshell of a boat—40 to 50 feet long—riding the storm, had actually lost their egos in that situation. *One* of the part-personalities of each man combined with the similar one in each of the others, producing—with the boat, the waves and the wind—an over-individual, organically functioning form, one that was flexible in time, or rather: creating these men's time. A storm would be the final catalyst to complete this fusion. And this situation—if nothing else—should convince us that the personalities here at work were constituents of a world other than the one from which these men had put to sea, the 'geometrical' farm community of 'secure separateness.'

What I am talking about is, of course, different from 'split personality'. I am speaking here about a really radical utilization of an enormous potential for complex, deep 'permeating' or interpenetration, an urge we all have from childhood, but which we are not permitted to follow in our society. And the clinging to isolated individuality, a hardening of the membrane, is the root of suffering. IGS is a society demanding that we close up our membranes, so that we may be used as bricks in the pyramid.

But the *ecopolitical* struggle needs people with soft, semi-permeable membranes! And not only that; right now it needs people who are trained to be two, who are *utilizing* that potential. I am here getting back to my starting perspective. Let's look at what ordinarily happens if we re-enter nature and start living on a farm as I have done and which by now a number of Norwegian ecopoliticians and eco-philosophers have done. They did it, saying we have to do, ourselves, what we teach. And we can still manage to be eco-activists. But what happens?—We don't hear a word from them after that, from most of them. They are out of that political fight. I think I understand why.

I know through my own experience. For instance working in the forest, often alone and in winter, even when there's a blizzard blowing the cap off my head, I find my work so rewarding it seems to me almost like a terrible thing, to go back to the house at night and sit down to read parliamentary acts and talk on the telephone to some bureaucrats in Oslo and bang on the typewriter in order to try and protect our own river.

To be able to do it I have to build a bridge to my other, urban personality. I have hit on some tricks to facilitate that shift, like turning on the radio and listening to Berlin or Moscow or London, or I put on a record with Western urban music. Instead of eating oatmeal porridge, I put a pizza in the oven, and instead of local beer I pour myself a drop of bourbon. I light a cigar instead of my homemade pipe. These are pleasant things, so that moves me softly onto the bridge. Doing it directly, without this sort of mediation, is too painful to be bearable. I happen to have a double background, so I can do it. Most farmers can't and *that inability* is used as a weapon against them by the established powers. My neighbour farmers are bulldozed into the ground by academic formality

and legalistic pyramidism!

What I try to do, right now, is to devise training courses for many personalities. Our chance lies in something along these lines. We must work directly with soil and forest and sea—not all of us—but as many as possible. We have to contribute directly to the green texture which must be our over-riding concern, *but if we only do that*, we are lost. The next you know, your river is dry and you're buried under concrete. Even though it is painful, we have to develop an urban busybody too. And we do have the capacity to do it, without losing the other, the 'green' stem of our dual-world tree. That's what I have been trying to argue. The 'many personality existence' is demanded of us, living in this age of mankind's most pervasive and deep-going transition.

Let's look momentarily at another illustration of man's capacity for radical complexity: I have done altogether seven expeditions to a valley in the central Himalayas where I am acquainted with people whose behaviour is best explained by assuming they have *three* different, annually operative person-structures, repeated sequentially. That's a utilization of their complexity potential brought forth by the very diverse demands posed by *their* environment and *their* resources, meagre and widely spaced. These are, of course, again the kind of people who thrive in houses with no right angles, people living by creating time. Their existences are:
1. As village-based farmers part of the year,
2. as high-altitude cattle herders another part, and
3. as caravan traders across the Himalayas visting Lhasa or other important trading centres once or twice annually.

A reincarnate lama, head of a monastery, ritually regarded as god-son of mine, has five personalities, a product of *his* training to be deeply knowledgeable in all human interest fields. That actually makes him an unusually stable *and* courageous person. He consists of a little *society*, prepared for anything, within his own mental-physical range. And his community expects him to be many, and feels safer through knowing that he spans that range.

DEMOCRATIC REVOLUTION

A pyramidal society can exist only so long as its members accept an existence as that pyramid's elementary particles or indivisible building blocks, accepting that they themselves are small pyramids, micro-copies of the big one. It can exist only if it may rely on identifying each member in a standardized way. Today computers are facilitating that sort of control. As soon as a member deviates from his pyramidal identity the psychiatrists are there at hand, and because they are his own accepted authorities, he is easily convinced of where he belongs, often putting his own effort into getting back into his one and only self. And that self keeps him insecure, frightened, and in need of Big Brother, suffering and contributing to others' suffering. It's a self-perpetuating, affair, keeping the great pyramid going, through Egypt, Babylonia, Rome, the British Empire, and the Third Reich. But modern technology and globalization is now finally winding up that story. Our task is to cushion the great crash, to build a green basis for the complex, time-creative society.

We *have* covered some distance in the Western world in building democratic institutions in society; but we have not begun to even conceive of the possibility of democracy in the individual's inner world. For this inner world we have the capacity and even an urge to create a whole society of personalities. I'm not speaking of some fixed set of entities, but something like a group of personality trends, given us by nature to cope creatively with a vast variety of situations.

So in the perspective I'm outlining, any person has a lot of different personality tendencies that are always budding, or trying to bloom or actually evolving and some of these are supporting or complementing each other, some are in conflict. And all this means that such a person, if he is *aware* of his inner, radical complexity range, can with extraordinary courage and confidence meet challenges from new social or natural processes. Let's say, you meet a situation and a person deviating from your normal social setting; you would be able to relate, because even this extraordinary human character conforms to one of the actors on your inner stage, one you already know.

. . .

Liberation Generates Courage

Anyway, this is what I mean: if you are aware of this ability you have of utilizing your personality complex and building bridges to put the right part of your resources to use in the right place, your courage to act will be up to the challenge. Going into it deeply you should discover that you are psychically invulnerable because you no longer have just one single personality with its specific vulnerability. We know that our life is movement. But we also have personality resources to cope with a much wider range of environments and challenges than most people are conscious of. We have in us the potential to integrate deeply with situations extremely far from our normal ones.

We have this because we have 'inner members' that embryonically have the various resources. We should just let them come forward and take responsibility, to unfold their own person-structures. Through that the hard shell between us and the world would be broken and we could become true, co-operative partners with all fellow human beings in the endlessly creative life stream. And you'll accept *all kinds of people, because you find them all in your inner society. Recognizing and then permitting your inner democratic revolution to happen furthers the democracy in your environment. And finding all the elements of nature within, your feeling for the earth's ecosphere will be lifted to a new level.*

. . .

'I' exists in several geographical places at the same time because personality is defined through participation which is not confined to one spot. Right now, one of my part-personalities is speaking here at Bristol University, another is working the Sätereng farm in Tröndelag, Middle Norway. The activity that defines one member of my personality group goes on there, where it is partly carried on through the activity of my son Oystein and Tashi, a Sherpa from the Himalayas who is staying at the farm, and by some of our neighbours as well. Another of my part-personalities is at work in Oslo in the Ecopolitical Cooperative Ring. One part is still active in The Plow-Furrow, the remote Himalayan valley. That's because I've spent so much time there, taken an active part in village life, been adopted with my family into three Sherpa clans. I as Tsering Dorjee, my local name, is still a somewhat dynamic element in The Plow-Furrow affairs, and the villagers know I am concerned and have responsibilty as a clan member and that my body again will be seen among them. That keeps Tsering Dorjee's presence alive . . . But the most intensely active member of 'my bunch' is now here at Bristol, I guess. In any case, that one draws on experiences of all the other part-personalities through variously open channels: the Sigmund Kvaloy/Tsering Dorjee complex is not a split personality!

If this sort of person-structure, this kind of complex human activity-presence, was cultivated as the dominant paradigm—there would not be any suffering in the Buddhist sense, because there would not be any individual to inflict suffering upon. Activity does not suffer. And there would, for instance, not be any 'I', afraid of dying. Activity does not die, as long as there's someone to carry it on. Person-death would cease. Nirvana in Buddhism is not Heaven or a state to be achieved after physical death; instead, Nirvana is our situation, our way of life from that moment when we are liberated completely from the prison of the individual struggling to hold on to his individuality. And Nirvana means releasing the brakes on time—to be free to swing, as partaker in the cosmic jazz band.

NASS RIVER

Tent tethered among jackpine and blue-
bells. Lacewings rise from rock
incubators. Wild geese flying north.
And I can't remember who I'm supposed
to be.

I want to learn how to purr. Abandon
myself, have mistresses in maidenhair
fern, own no tomorrow nor yesterday:
a blank shimmering space forward and
back. I want to think with my belly.
I want to name all the stars animals
flowers birds rocks in order to forget
them, start over again. I want to
wear the seasons, harlequin, become
ancient and etched by weather. I
want to be snow pulse, ruminating
ungulate, pebble at the bottom of the
abyss, candle burning darkness rather
than flame. I want to peer at things,
shameless, observe the unfastening,
that stripping of shape by dusk.
I want to sit in the meadow a rotten
stump pungent with slimemold, home
for pupae and grubs, concentric rings
collapsing into the passacaglia of
time. I want to crawl inside someone
and hibernate one entire night with
no clocks to wake me, thighs fragrant
loam. I want to melt. I want to swim
naked with an otter. I want to turn
insideout, exchange nuclei with the
Sun. Toward the mythic kingdom of
summer I want to make blind motion,
using my ribs as a raft, following
the spiders as they set sail on their
tasselled shining silk. Sometimes
even a single feather's enough
to fly

Heartwood - FINN HILL ARTS

REFERENCE NOTES

Deep ecology is not merely another academic discipline; instead it's an effort to reclaim our birthright as a natural part of "all life." To do this requires restoring access to many "ways of knowing" which are part of our natural human heritage; but lost in the last few hundred years. Hence the voluminous notes below. I've tried to make these Reference Notes easy for the general reader to use as well as provide all the information necessary for academic use. Obviously, I will not always be able to follow accepted academic formulas in these notes.

For a particular entry in the Reference Notes, I first list the page in the main text, where the quotation appears. Next, the opening words of the material I am quoting are listed within quotation marks. This is followed by the author's name in boldface, while the rest of the listing is in regular type. Further information is provided after the words, **Add. notes:**

If I feel that a particular subject needs further documentation, I list that subject in small capitals at the beginning of the listing.

Opening Quote:

— "Man is not the supreme...": **R. Murray Schafer**, *The Tuning of the World*. Philadelphia: Univ. of Pennsylvania Press, 1980, p. 112.

Beginning Stories

— "Now, Farewell and Hail." **P. L. Travers**. *Parabola* 10 (1985): 23-24.

— "The Dog in the Lab." **Gregory Bateson** and **Stewart Brand**. In Stewart Brand, *Two Cybernetic Frontiers*. New York: Random House, 1974, pp. 25-26.

— "The Lesson of the White Mist." In **John Blofield**, *Taoism: The Road to Immortality*. London: Allen & Unwin, 1978, p. 77-79.

Preface

8 "To change ideas...": **Aldo Leopold**. In Susan Flader, *Thinking Like a Mountain*, p. 33.

— "Where angels fear...": **Gregory Bateson**, *Mind and Nature*, p. 213. **Add. notes:** While I was working on the ms. for this book, Mary Catherine Bateson put together her father's last writings. The book was published under the title, *Angels Fear:Towards an Epistemology of the Sacred*, in May, 1987.

— "entrenched positions of...": **Donald Tuzin**, "Miraculous Voices."

— "revalue all values...": **Friedrich Nietzsche**, *The Will to Power, Attempt at a Revaluation of All Values*, first projected in 1884. **Add. notes:** This volume was never written. Throughout his later writings Nietzsche kept referring to it. (See pages 9 to 12 of Hollingdale's introduction to his trans. of Nietzsche's *Ecce Homo*.) There is, of course, considerable debate about what Nietzsche really meant. Here, I am referring to Heidegger's interpretation, concerning the aspect of "overturning Platonism," which is what I found myself doing in my work. Heidegger writes: "For Platonism, the Idea, the super sensuous, is the true, true being. In contrast, the sensuous...not being. To overturn Platonism thus means to reverse the standard relation...When the inversion is fully executed, the Sensuous becomes being proper, i.e., the true, i.e., truth." (p. 154) and again on p. 201, "It means that it is the true, it is genuine being." In still another place, p.209, Heidegger states: "But the sensuous world is 'apparent world' only according to the interpretation of Platonism. With the abolition of Platonism the way first opens for the affirmation of the sensuous..." Nietzsche wrote: "The true world, attainable for the wise...man—he lives in it, he is it." (*Twilight of the Idols*, September 1888). This is quoted in Heidegger's work on p., 201. All the above quotations from Heidegger are from his book, *Nietzsche* Vol. 1.

— "Knowledge represents...": **Hans Duerr**, *Dreamtime*, p. viii.

9 "While European philosophy...": **Joseph Needham**, *Science and Civilization in China*. v, 2, p. 478. **Add. notes:** His reference is Chang Tung-Sun, "A Chinese Philosopher's Theory of Knowledge." *Etc: A Review of General Semantics*, 9 (1952): 203-226. Another treatment of this concept, stating that the Chinese "concentrate more on categories of relationship than on categories of substance," can be found in E. R. Hughes, "Epistemological Methods in Chinese Philosophy", p. 86. In C. A. Moore, ed. *The Chinese Mind*. Honolulu: East-West Center Press, 1967,

pp. 86 ff. (I go further into this matter in chapters one and eight.)

— "Greek language...": **Barrington Nevitt**, "Pipeline or Grapevine." *Technology and Culture*, 21, (April 1980): 217-226.

— "HEIDEGGER IN THE MOUNTAINS" CONFERENCE: **Dolores LaChapelle**, "The Blue Mountains are Constantly Walking," a report on this conference, published by Way of the Mountain Center, 1981.

Introduction

10 "Does it serve...": **"For the children yet to come."** *Katúah, Bioregional Journal of the Southern Appalacchians* 11 (spring 1986): 1.

— INDUSTRIAL GROWTH SOCIETY: **Sigmund Kvaloy**, "Complexity and Time." *Resurgence* 106 (Sept/Oct 1984): 12-21.

— "For God's Sake...": **Stewart Brand**, *Coevolution Quarterly* 10 (summer 1976): p.32-44.

11 "deep ecology"...down to "autonomy and decentralization": **Arne Naess**, "The Shallow and the Deep Long Range Ecology Movement." *Inquiry* (1973), a Norwegian (English language) publication. U.S. address: P.O. Box 258, Irvington-on-Hudson, N.Y. 10553.

— "If you vividly"...down to "will remain so...": **Kvaloy**, "Complexity and Time."

12 "I thought until...": **Arne Naess**, "Essentials of a New Philosophy of Nature." Unpublished paper, 1978.

— GENERAL BACKGROUND ON SESSIONS: **George Sessions**, "A short informal summary (from memory) of my philosophical development as it pertains to the deep ecology movement." (Typescript, 1986) Sessions sent this to the Australian scholar, Warwick Fox, who needed background information for his dissertation.

12–13 "immediately instituted"...down to "Hughes, LaChapelle and the rest." **Sessions**. Ibid.

13 "But in deep...": **Arne Naess**. In Stephen Bodian, "Simple in Means, Rich in Ends: A Conversation with Arne Naess." *The Ten Directions*, (Summer/Fall 1982).

14 "Smith agreed...": **Sessions**, "A Short Informal Summary."

— "It is very peculiarly...": **Kirkpatrick Sale**, "Anarchy and Ecology — A Review Essay." *Social Anarchism* 10 (1985).

— "It's not the kind...": **George Sessions**. Letter to LaChapelle, October, 1987.

— FORM LETTER ABOUT TITLE: **Michael Gosney**, Publisher. Letter to LaChapelle.

15 BILL DEVALL'S BOOK: Devall is working on the ms. for a book to be titled, *Simple in Means, Rich in Ends: Practicing Deep Ecology*, to be published by Gibbs Smith.

— THE TRUMPETER, VOICES FROM THE CANADIAN ECOPHILOSOPHY NETWORK: **Alan Drengson**, editor. Address: Lightstar Press, 1138 Richardson St., Victoria, B.C. V8V 3C8 Canada. **Add. Notes:** Alan Drengson uses a new term, "wilderness scholar," for those who have spent a great deal of time in the mountains or wilderness and are also doing academic type research. He uses this term for himself—he has climbed and hiked in the Olympic Peninsula and Canada; for Jay Vest in Montana (more on him later in this work) and for my work. Because we are beginning to move in a totally new direction in this culture, we need people who can "read" the "wilderness" not just human works. There are more "wilderness scholars" out there, but I have no information on them.

— THE DEEP ECOLOGIST: **John Martin**, editor. Address: 10 Alamein Ave., Warracknabeal, Vic. 3393 Australia.

— WARWICK FOX: A young Australian philospher, who has, among other articles, written, "Approaching Deep Ecology." (Occasional Paper #20) in which he clarifies and defends deep ecology. Fox argues that deep ecology represents an alternative to the "normal (i.e. environmental value theory) approach to ecophilosophy [and that this alternative] should be accepted on phenomenological, philosophical, and political grounds." Copies may be ordered from Centre for Environmental Studies, Univ. of Tasmania, GPO Box 252C, Hobart Tasmania 7001, Australia. Write for costs.

— "Certain kinds...": **Arne Naess**, "Essentials of a new philosophy of nature."

—— "The Basic Points…": **David Rothenberg**, *Wisdom and the Open Air*. Unpublished.

—— "This place is sacred.": **D. H. Lawrence**, *St. Mawr*. New York: Vintage Books, Random House, (no date).

—— "can be a catastrophic…": **Mary Dickson**, "Environmental Illness—A Growing Concern." *Catalyst* 5 (1986): 8-9. (Salt Lake City, Utah)

—— Vitamin C and AIDS: **Frank Murray**, "Vitamin C: A Clue for AIDS Treatment." *Better Nutrition* 47 (Oct. 1987).

—— Healing Aids Naturally: In *For the Love of Life* 18 (Fall 1987). (Published by the Theosophical Order of Service, Jean Gullo, Editor, P.O. Box 41584, Tucson, Az. 85717.)

—— "back in 1982…": **Tom Monte**, "Treating AIDS with Diet." *Mountain Ark Trader* (Oct/Nov, 1987): 20-21.

—— Breakdown of the Immune System: For more in-depth information concerning the political, scientific, etc. squabbling involved in the cover-up of AIDS, see **Randy Shilts**, *And the Band Played On: Politics, People, and the AIDS Epidemic*. New York: St. Martin's Press, 1987. **Add. notes:** The virus is now officially called "Human Immunodeficiency Virus" or HIV (p. 593). Originally the best temporary cure seemed to be "HPA-23, which [interfered] with reverse transcriptase, blocking the virus from replicating itself. In this sense, HPA-23 was not a cure. It merely kept the virus from running wild and destroying the immune system." (p. 475). In France, where HPA-23 is available, they now think that "isoprinosine, a drug believed to act as an immune system booster," may be more useful. My point here is that the functioning of the human immune system is the problem and this can't be "cured" by a "substance" approach; instead the entire environment is involved: inside and outside the human body. A further word about the conflicting times concerning the number of years a patient lives. Shilts' book explains that it takes five years before AIDS shows up, once it has been contacted; after that the usual survival rate is two years.

—— "deeply entered into…": **Saigyō**. William LaFleur, "Introduction." In LaFleur, trans. *Mirror for the Moon*. New York: New Directions, 1978. **Add. notes:** Bashō, the most famous Haiku poet, said that Saigyō, had a "mind both obeying and at one with nature throughout the four seasons." (p. xiii) "Saigyō insisted that through all this he had discovered in nature what he called a 'depth' completely beyond the ken of people passing their lives in society." (p. xv) "All things are fully interdependent. 'Depth' in nature, then, was not a Platonic realm of being somewhere behind concrete phenomena but a discoverable play of free interrelatedness. Saigyō found this play best expressed in nature." (p.xxv).

—— "You could not…": The translation I have used here is a combination of Charles Kahn's and Heidegger's. **Charles H. Kahn**, *The Art and Thought of Heraclitus*. Cambridge: Cambridge Univ. Press, 1979.

—— "essentially biological…": **Kahn**, Ibid., p. 127.

—— "The Tao of Heaven…": **Needham**, *Sci. and Civil.* v. 2, p. 561.

—— "We mean that…": **Maurice Merleau-Ponty**, *The Visible and the Invisible*. Evanston, Ill: Northwestern Univ. Press, 1968, p. 136.

—— "The world is universal…": Ibid., p. 137.

—— "the great frontal…": **Abraham Maslow**, *The Farther Reaches of Human Nature*. New York: Viking Press, 1971, p. 163.

—— "Rapture [rausch] is feeling…": **Heidegger**, *Nietzsche: v. 1, The Will to Power as Art*. New York: Harper and Row, 1979, p. 105. **Add. notes:** I will go into the word, rapture, more at length here by quoting further from this volume. The translator explains that he used "rapture" here "from the past participle of *rapere*, to seize…No single English word—rapture, frenzy, ecstasy, transport…delirium—can capture all the senses of Rausch. Our word, 'rush' is related to it; something 'rushes over' and sweeps us away…I have chosen the word rapture because of its erotic and religious background." (p. 92) In Heidegger's text he quotes Nietzsche, *Twilight of the Idols*, 1888, (VIII, 122-123): "If there is to be art, if there is to be any aesthetic doing and observing, one physiological precondition is indispensable: *rapture*…All the variously conditioned forms of rapture have the requisite force: above all, the rapture of sexual arousal…the rapture that comes as a consequence of all great desires, all strong affects; the rapture of the feast, contest, feat of daring… rapture under certain meteorological influences, for example, the rapture of springtime… Back to Heidegger: "For our summary, which is to simplify our previous

characterization of Nietzsche's art, we can limit ourselves to the two predominant basic determinations, rapture and beauty. They are reciprocally related. Rapture is the basic mood, beauty does the attuning… Rapture as a state of feeling explodes the very subjectivity of the subject. By having a feeling for beauty the subject has already come out of himself, he is no longer subjective, no longer a subject…The aesthetic state is neither subjective nor objective." (p. 123) My underlining above to help explain the philosophical aspects of my title.

17 "invocation, which sets…": **J. Stephen Lansing**, "The Aesthetics of the Sounding of the Text." In Jerome and D. Rothenberg, *Symposium of the Whole*, p. 241-256.

—— "The god concerned…": **P. J. Zoetmulder**, *Kalangwan: A Survey of Old Javanese Literature*. The Hague: Nijhoff, 1974, p. 175 and 173.

—— "way langö…": **Lansing**, "The Aesthetics of the Sounding of the Text."

—— About the Number Seven: Seven has been given a "magic" or "sacred" quality whereas actually there is a neurophysiological reason behind it all. In experiments, if someone throws out a number of small objects, it is possible to instantly recognize the number of objects up to six. "Somewhere between 6 and 8, the reports became inaccurate." Miller, writing on the "significance of the number 7 as a limit on our capacities [reports] that for unidimensional judgment this span is usually somewhere in the neighborhood of seven." G.A. Miller, "The magical number seven, plus or minus two." *Psychological Review* 63 (1956): 8ff. And E. Kaufman et al, "The discrimination of visual number," *Amer. Jour. of Psychology* 62 (1949): 498-504.

—— Idealism: Konrad Lorenz, writing about how this "preposterous" (to a biologist) concept came about, says: "Greek philosophy did this…Thus a branch of learning came into being [which] had the paradoxical consequences that images formed by our perceiving apparatus were taken for reality and the real objects to be imperfect, fleeting shadows of perfect imperishable ideas…Platonic idealism…" Lorenz, *Behind the Mirror*, p.15.

—— "But in deep ecology…": **Arne Naess**, In Bodian, "Simple in Means."

—— "All I wish…": **Donald W. Lathrap**, "Our Father the Cayman, Our Mother the Gourd."

18 "Many of the ills…": **Ralph Borsodi**, "Plowboy Interview with Dr. Ralph Borsodi." *Mother Earth News* 26: 6-13.

—— Human Time Span Compared to 24 Hours: This method has been used by many authorities, including John Livingston, see below. I have put together my own version, here.

—— "I will be here…": **John A. Livingston**, *One Cosmic Instant*. New York: Dell, 1973, p. 227.

—— "The archetypes are…": **C.A. Meier**, "Wilderness and the Search for the Soul of Modern Man." In Vance Martin, ed. *Wilderness: The Way Ahead*. 152-161 **Add. notes:** In another place in this article, Meier states: "The archetypes are within us, and some of them represent the *chthonic* part of our soul, by which we are linked to this Earth, nature and wilderness."

—— "our major…": **Edgar Anderson**, *Plants, Man and Life*. Berkeley: Univ. of California Press, 1967, pp. 132-133.

—— "Heaven and earth and…": **Anshō Togawa**. In H. Byron Earhart, "Four Ritual Periods of Haguro Shugendō."

—— Ritual and Information: **Roy Rappaport**, "The Obvious Aspects of Ritual." In *Ecology, Meaning and Religion*, pp. 172-221

19 "I know too…": **Jack Goody**, "Preface." In *The Domestication of the Savage Mind*. Cambridge: Cambridge Univ. Press, 1976.

—— Influences on my Work: **Add. notes:** New developments in science—some based on fractal geometry—are covered in James Gleick, *Chaos Making: A New Science*, (Viking, 1987), involving recognition that patterns are the same at micro and macro levels; thus providing a way for modern science to deal with chaos. As usual, the Taoists were thousands of years ahead with their concepts of *li*, (pattern) and Lord Hun-Tun (chaos). The works of Prigogine and Jantsch (*The Self-Organizing Universe*) are also useful here.

The work of Gregory Bateson has greatly influenced my work. As I began to grasp how deeply I was going, in my first book, *Earth Festivals*, I figured the world wasn't ready for it yet and was going to stop work. Then, Bateson's *Steps to An Ecology of Mind*, came out and I realized someone else was there before me; so I continued. The publisher of my second book, *Earth Wisdom*, sent him a copy at my suggestion and I was gratified to have the film maker who was working with Bateson, the year before he died, write me and say that he told her: "This book is well worth reading." She added, "Believe me, he said that about very few books." Kai de Fontenay was trying to show Bateson ideas through film.

PART I

21 "The last three thousand...": **D.H. Lawrence**, "A Propos of Lady Chatterley's Lover." In *Phoenix II*, p. 510.

Ch. 1 Greek Language Problem

Note: What I have tried to do in this chapter is make the actual text as simple as possible so that it is readily understandable to all types of readers. Below I provide complete references to facilitate deeper research.

pp. 22 and 23 Opening Quotes

—— "[In the West] the idea...": **Chang Tung-Sun**, "A Chinese Philosopher's Theory of Knowledge."

—— "[T]here were...": **Joseph Needham**, *Sci. and Civil.*, v. 2, p. 284.

—— "Here is poetry...": **Robert Payne**, *The White Pony*, p. ix.

—— "But this concrete...": **Ernest Fenollosa**, "The Chinese Written Character as a Medium for Poetry."

—— "[Bacon] speaks of...": **B. Farrington**, *Francis Bacon; Philosopher of Industrial Science.* New York: Schuman, 1949, p. 146. Quoted in Needham, *Sci. and Civil.*, v. 2, p. 93.

—— "The greatest recent...": **Nietzsche**. (Aphorism 343) **Add. notes:** According to Heidegger, "In 1886 Nietzsche added to the four books of *The Gay Science*, a fifth, which is entitled, "We Fearless Ones." Over the first section in that book (Aphorism 343) is inscribed "The Meaning of Our Cheerfulness." Heidegger's explanation, which I use in the quote, is from: Martin Heidegger, *The Question Concerning Technology and other Essays*, New York: Harper and Row, 1977, p. 61.

24 "The very process...": **Barrington Nevitt**, *The Communication Ecology*, p. 5. **Add. notes:** For the quickest insight into this entire process, consult these sources in the works of Barrington Nevitt: (1) "Pipeline or Grapevine." *Technology and Culture*, 21 (April 1980): 217-226; (2) *ABC of Prophecy*, pp. 12-14 and 51-54; and (3) *The Communication Ecology*, pp. 58-61. As mentioned elsewhere in this work, Nevitt, in 1920-31, was involved in design, construction and maintenance of radio receivers and transmitters for private and commercial use and trained as a bush pilot in Canada. In 1932-33 he was employed as research and development engineer in Leningrad, USSR. I will not try to go through his entire resume: sufficient to say that through "residence in Europe and Latin America, [he] gained working knowledge of the principal European languages." He has been an advisor to most major European countries at some time or other. Recently he has been visiting professor for Informatics and System Science at Stockholm Univ. and the Royal Institute of Technology, Sweden and was an associate of Marshall McLuhan's from 1964 to 1980 at the Centre for Culture and Technology, Univ. of Toronto.

—— NO MEANING IN INDIVIDUAL LETTER OR SYLLABLE: **Nevitt**, "Pipeline or Grapevine." This reference reads: "Learning to read and write with the Greek phonetic alphabet transformed corporate consciousness into the private psyche and created the illusion of objectivity that separated thought from feeling. Although the Greek phonetic alphabet was derived from morphemic alphabets of Semitic origin, it was the first alphabet that had neither visual nor acoustic semantic meaning for its users... Greek phonetic literacy is the foundation of Western civilization: it created our archetypal forms of philosophy, science, art and education. The Greeks abstracted Nature from the chaos of 'nature in the raw'."

—— SYLLABLES OF JHVH: **Walter J. Ong**, *The Presence of the Word.* New Haven: Yale Univ. Press, 1967, p. 12-14 and 175-191.

—— "abundant, rich...": **Dr. L. Wieger, S.J.**, *Chinese Characters.* New York: Dover reprint, 1965, p. 239.

—— "arrogance of humanism...": **David Ehrenfeld**, *The Arrogance of Humanism.* Oxford: Oxford Univ. Press, 1978.

—— "got to the root...": **Ezra Pound**, *ABC of Reading.* New York: New

Directions, p. 19.

—— FENOLLOSA'S EXAMPLE: Ibid., p. 19-22.

—— "Any language...": **Barrington Nevitt**, *ABC of Prophecy*, p. 54.

25 NORTH SEMITIC SCRIPT & BEGINNINGS OF GREEK WRITTEN LANGUAGE: **David Diringer**, *The Alphabet.* New York: Philosophical Library, 1948, pp. 216-217, 451, 458, 461, 575. See especially pp. 159-162. **Add. notes:** "While the Greek names have no meaning in Greek, the Semitic names are words in Semitic languages... The Greeks, when they borrowed their alphabet took over the names with the letters." Diringer, p. 159.

—— IONIC ALPHABET ADOPTED AT ATHENS & DELPHIC ORACLE: **Diringer**, p. 362.

—— WHORF ON THE HOPI LANGUAGE: **Benjamin Lee Whorf**, "Time, Space and Language." In Laura Thompson, *Culture in Crisis: A Study of the Hopi Indians.* New York: Harper Bros., 1950. **Add. notes:** While each of Whorf's own books are useful in understanding this basic difference between languages, this essay is the most concise.

—— "In phonetic reading...": **Eric A. Havelock**, *Origins of Western Literacy*, p. 22.

—— "in the midst....": **Nevitt**, *The Communication Ecology*, p. 3.

—— PLATO DESTROYING THE BARDS: Ibid. See also, **Eric Havelock**, *Preface to Plato*, p. 38-39 and p. 294.

—— "frame words to express...": **Havelock**, *Preface to Plato*, p. 199.

—— SETTING THE STAGE FOR PLATO: Ibid., p. 158.

—— "a crippling of the mind...": Ibid, p. 4.

—— "buzzing confusion of nature...": **Nevitt**, *ABC of Prophecy*, p. 13.

—— CAPACITY TO KNOW, ETC. IN TOTAL DISTINCTION FROM CAPACITY TO SEE, ETC.: **Havelock**, *Preface to Plato*, p. 206.

26 "Pure subjectivity..." down to "we must...": **Toshihiko Izutsu**, "Naive Realism and Confucian Philosophy." **Add notes:** Izutsu here is referring first, to the "pure subjectivity" of Buddhism. To that, he contrasts the way things work in the world by describing the Neo-Confucian (Taoist) approach beginning with "we must...". Although Izutsu is referring to Buddhist/Neo Confucian thought here, I have found no better explanation of the difference between the "subjectivity" of Plato and the "relationship" aspect of the world, than this quote.

—— "the majority can never be intellectuals": **Havelock**, *Preface to Plato*, p. 256.

—— "this 'object'...Latin term, 'abstraction'...": Ibid., p. 256.

—— THE OBJECT: **Gregory Bateson**, *Angels Fear*: "...I can know nothing about any individual thing by itself, I *can* know something about *relations between things*...but which I distort by referring the special character of the relationship entirely to one of the components in it. In so doing, I distort what I could know about the relationship into a statement about a "thing" which I *cannot* know. It is always relationship between things that is the referent of all valid propositions." (p. 157) Again, on p. 50, he states: "[M]ind is an organizational characteristic, not a separate 'substance'."

—— "If he...": **Havelock**, *Preface to Plato*, p. 267.

—— "If Lake Erie...": **Gregory Bateson**, quoted in Stewart Brand, *II Cybernetic Frontiers.* New York: Random House, 1974, p. 10.

—— "You cannot induce...": Ibid., p. 25-26. For the entire story see "Beginning Stories."

—— "that which was beyond...": **Vincent Vycinas**, *Earth and Gods: an Introduction to the Philosophy of Martin Heidegger*, p. 145.

—— "identified as...": **Charles H. Kahn**, *The Art and Thought of Heraclitus*, p. 127.

Ch. 2 Agriculture

p. 29 Opening Quotes

—— "[A]griculture is not easier...": **Mark Nathan Cohen**, *The Food Crisis in Prehistory*, p. 15.

—— "A number of...": Ibid., p. 26

—— "Soil and slope are...": **Carl Sauer**, "Theme of Plant and Animal Destruction in Economic History."

30 "All I wish to do...": **Donald W. Lathrap**, "Our Father the Cayman, Our Mother the Gourd: Spinden Revisited, or a Unitary Model for the Emergence of Agriculture in the New World." In Charles A. Reed, ed. *Origins of Agriculture.* The Hague: Mouton Pub., 1977, pp. 713-751. This volume of 1013 pages, is part of the *World Anthropology Series*, general ed. Sol Tax.

30 PRIMITIVE PLANT FIBERS & FISH POISONS: **Carl Sauer**, *Agricultural Origins and Dispersals*, p. 24.

— USES OF THE GOURD: **Charles B. Heiser**, *The Gourd Book*, pp. 71-228.

— CULTIVATION OF THE GOURD: It began as early as 40,000 years ago in Africa. "[T]he bottle gourd was brought under cultivation in Africa...We must necessarily assume that this...took place sufficiently early to meet the timetable of its arrival in Thailand and Ayacucho. Given that constraint, I consider it not unlikely that the "Neolithic" experimentation sketched above started by 40,000 B.P. [before present]." **Lathrap**, ("Our Father the Cayman", p. 725). **Heiser** (*The Gourd Book*, p. 81) says that cultivation began at least 9000 years ago in Thailand. Cultivation began 10,000 years at Tamaulipas, according to **Richard Mac Neish**, "Preliminary archaeological investigations in the Sierra de Tamaulipas, Mexico." *Trans. of the Amer. Philosophical Society* 48: 1-210. **Lathrap**, in "Our Father the Cayman." (p. 22), states: "The real shocker is the occurrence of fragments of rinds from bottle gourds from levels at Pikimachay Cave in the Ayacucho Basin dating earlier than 13,000 B.P."

— "The gourd, besides...": **Girardot**, *Myth and Meaning in Early Taoism*, p. 213.

— "We may conclude..." and "The bottle gourd...": **Lathrap**, "Our Father the Cayman."

— DISTRIBUTION OF THE GOURD: **Charles A. Reed**, "Origins of Agriculture: Discussion and Some Conclusions." (This information is provided on p. 932 of the article.)

— CROSSING THE ATLANTIC: Ibid., p. 933.

— MALE AND FEMALE FLOWERS: Ibid.

— "TRASH HEAP" OR "DUMP HEAP": Ibid., p. 934.

31 "I presented them...": **Edgar Anderson**, *Plants Man and Life*. (First published in 1952). Berkeley: Univ. of California Press, 1967, p. vii and viii.

— "nothing but...": Ibid., p. 136.

— "I played hooky...": Ibid.

— "It's not an orchard...": **Edgar Anderson**, "Reflections on Certain Honduran Gardens." In Edgar Anderson, *Landscape Papers*. Berkeley: Turtle Island Foundation, 1976, p. 69.

— DESCRIPTION OF THE GARDEN: **Anderson**, *Plants etc.*, p. 140-141

— "non-human...": **Mark N. Cohen**, "Population pressure and the origins of agriculture: an archaeological explanation from the coast of Peru." In Reed, ed. *Origins of Agriculture*, p. 135 to 177. Cohen's reference here is (Jolly 1972:59).

— "were inherently...": **Lathrap**, "Our Father the Cayman", p. 729.

— "In the controlled...": Ibid., p. 730.

32 "A wide...": Ibid., p. 731.

— "Great Cayman of the sky": Ibid., p. 734.

— GROUP TOO BIG: **Gregory Bateson**, *Naven* (2nd ed.). Stanford: Stanford Univ. Press., 1958.

— "would proceed...": **Lathrap**, "Our Father the Cayman", p. 737

— "flushed upstream...": Ibid., p. 738.

— TELLO OBELISK DISCUSSION: **Donald Lathrap**, "Gifts of the Cayman: Some Thoughts on the Subsistence Basis of Chavin."

— "We tend...": **Lathrap**, "Our Father the Cayman", p. 715.

— "agriculture provides neither...": **Cohen**, "Population pressure and the origins of agriculture."

— "occasioned by...": **Sol Tax**, "General Editor's Preface." In Reed, *Origins of Agriculture*, pp. vii-ix.

33 "In November...": **Richard B. Lee and Irven DeVore**, "Preface." In R. B. Lee and I. DeVore. (eds.) *Man the Hunter*, p. vii.

— "For the first time...": **Nancy Oestreich Lurie**, "The voice of the American Indian: report on the American Indian Chicago Conference." *Current Anthropology*, 2 (Dec. 1961): 478-499. **Add. notes:** Lurie states: "Among those vitally concerned with the future of the American Indian was Sol Tax who with his students had been working for many years on techniques for effective community development." Sol Tax "had developed a concept of community action emphasizing self-determination, which he termed Action Anthropology (Tax, 1959; Gearing et al., 1960)." But he felt there should be a "representative sample of the half million or more Indians in the U.S." Out of that, developed the American Indian Chicago Conference (AICC). The final registration showed 467 Indians from 90 bands and tribes had taken part.

Tax's early work among tribes was with the Apaches in 1931 and the Fox Indians in 1932-34. He went on to work in Mexico and other places throughout the world. I won't take the space here to list all his teaching and research work. He was Assoc. Ed. *American Anthropologist* 1948-52; he founded and edited *Current Anthropology*, 1957-74, Gen. Ed. *World Anthropology* 1975-80. He was the co-ordinator of the Am. Indian Chicago Conference in 1961.

This Conference began in April of 1960 when Tax learned that a Foundation had money available for a conference if Tax would consider directing a study of Indian problems. Tax felt that "in line with the action anthropologist's commitment, any policy recommendations that a conference might make would have to be formulated by the Indians themselves." Once he got the Foundation to agree to these terms, it "led six months later to the conference." (The ref. here is David Blanchard, "The Emergence of an Action Anthropology: Sol Tax." In Robert Hinshaw, ed. *Currents in Anthropology: Essays in Honor of Sol Tax*. The Hague: Mouton Pub., 1979, p. 435.)

"In all these contexts Tax invited, indeed insisted upon, more grass-roots participation in deliberation and feedback in decision making and publication of findings than most would have deemed either logistically feasible or desirable...": Robert Hinshaw (p. x)

Concerning "action anthropology": "Tax (1952) first put the ideas to paper. He wrote that an anthropologist while at work in a community should embrace two coequal purposes: to discover new knowledge and to be useful to the community in which he works...pivotal guidelines: the action anthropologist should carefully avoid any exercise of power..." (Gearing, quoted in Hinshaw, *Currents in Anthropology*.)

A citation accompanying the honorary Dr. of Law degree conferred on Sol Tax by Wilmington College in 1974, states "Incurably optimistic...Sol Tax repeatedly has allied himself with the exploited and the disadvantaged. From Chicago-ghettos to the fragmented societies of Native Americans, he has served time and time again as catalyst in relating human needs to those in positions of power and authority. Sol Tax never has been hesitant in speaking the truth to power." (Hinshaw, p. vii)

33 FOREST SERVICE AND BUREAU OF LAND MANAGEMENT: **William A. Douglass**, "Basque immigrants: contrasting patterns of adaptation in Argentina and the American West." In Robert Hinshaw, ed. *Currents in Anthropology*, pp. 287-304.

— THE CONFERENCE: The IXth International Congress of Anthropological and Ethnological Sciences (the *Origins of Agriculture* volume came out of this conference). According to Sol Tax, this Congress "was planned from the beginning not only to include as many of the scholars from every part of the world as possible, but also...eventual publication of the papers." This volume thus provides an insight into agriculture different from the usual, narrow "Eurocentric" approach.

— "changes...in store...": **Sol Tax**, "General Editor's Preface." In Reed (ed), *Origins of Agriculture*, p. vii-ix.

— "After thousands...": **Herbert E. Wright**, "Environmental change and the origin of agriculture in the Old and New Worlds."

— "The wild cereal...": Ibid.

— "opportunists...": **Hawkes**, "The ecological background of plant domestication."

34 "To primitive man...": Ibid.

— "The propitious combination...": **Wright,** "Environmental change."

— "the primitive ancestral forms...": **Vavilov**, quoted in Hawkes, "The ecological background."

— "I must tell...": **Norman E. Borlaug**, quoted in J. H. Hulse and D. Spurgem, "Triticale." *Scientific American* 231: 72-81.

— "After years of research...": Ibid.

— "aggravated environmental...": **Kent V. Flannery**, quoted in Reed, "Origins of agriculture: discussion and some conclusions."

— "The important cultivated...": **Reed**, "Origins of agriculture: discussion and some conclusions."

35 "for many plants...": **Vavilov**, quoted in Hawkes, "The ecological background of plant domestication."

— "for most...the only possible..." **Lathrap**, "Our Father the Cayman."

— "The very process...": **Nevitt**, *The Communication Ecology*. p. 5.

— **Add. notes:** Before leaving this chapter concerning agriculture and indirectly, human eating patterns, I want to include information, which indicates that the popular theory that prehistoric human hunting caused the extinction of large animals is not necessarily true to the facts.

In *The Food Crisis in Prehistory* (New Haven: Yale Univ. Press, 1977), the author Mark Nathan Cohen, states: "The major critique of human hunting as an agency in the extinctions has been provided by Hester (1967) and Guilday (1967). One major focus in their critique has been to point out that man seems to have appeared in North America after many of the major groups were already extinct, or at least after many of them were already greatly reduced in numbers. A similar argument has been put forward by Kurten (1965), who notes that many of the extinct species show a progressive diminution in the size of the individuals; this, he argues, is suggestive of ecological stress. To the extent that this diminution is contemporary with human hunting it might result from the negative selective effects of such hunting on large animals (Edwards 1967). But by Kurten's reconstruction the trend is often evident well back into the Pleistocene, suggesting that stresses leading toward extinction had a long history prior to human arrival." (p. 183) On page 184, Cohen continues: "Even more striking, as Hester points out, is the fact that of all the extinct species only mammoth and bison occur with any regularity or in significant numbers, in Paleo-Indian sites; and many of the extinct species, including some potential prey, have no provable association with Paleo-Indian hunters at all. This latter point can be confirmed by references to the bestiary of Pleistocene extinctions provided by Martin and Guilday." (1967). One more important fact: "Among others, Hester (1967), Slaughter (1967), and Guilday (1967) have all argued for the significance of post-Pleistocene environmental changes as a key ingredient in the extinction of the megafauna. They postulate a general deterioration of the North American environment related primarily to the decline in effective moisture...this particular type of climate change could have acted selectively against large mammals, particularly herbivores." Furthermore, this would have had the greatest effect on animals with long gestation periods.

It seems to me that those authorities trying to make early humans responsible for this extinction are caught in their own narrow, modern human trap, coming from lack of attention to *place*. They fail to realize that any human being living "in place," notices what's going on in the food supply, daily and continually. Specifically, rituals deal with this attention to place. (See chapter seven for more on this subject and all of Part III.) Cohen's bibliographic list of references for the above:

Guilday, J. E. 1967. "Differential extinction during late Pleistocene and recent times." In Martin and Wright, eds., pp. 121-40.

Hester, J. J. 1967. "The agency of man in animal extinctions." In Martin and Wright, eds., pp. 169-92.

Kurten, B. 1965. "The Pleistocene Felidae of Florida." *Florida State Bull., Biol. Sci.* 9:215-73.

Martin, P. Sch. and Guilday, J. E. 1967. "Bestiary for Pleistocene biologists." In Martin and Wright, eds., pp. 1-62.

Martin, P.Sch and Wright, H. E. eds. 1967. *Pleistocene extinctions: the search for a cause.* New Haven: Yale Univ. Press.

Ch. 3 Addiction, Capitalism...

pp. 36 and 37 Opening Quotes

— "[T]he annual per person...": "Health Quiz." *Better Nutrition 47* (October 1987:34.

— "The doctrine...": **Carl Sauer**, "Theme of Plant and Animal Destruction in Economic History."

— "So also in the American...": **Joseph Needham**, *The Grand Titration: Science and Society in East and West*, p. 132
"Harold Innis' later...": **Ronald Keast**, "It is written—but I say unto you: Innis on Religion." *Journal of Canadian Studies* 20: 20. **Add. notes**: Innis has "probably the greatest reputation ever achieved by a Canadian academic." Concerning the field of communication—"At his death, he was just beginning to open it up, and it was left to McLuhan to carry it farther." Arthur Lower, "Harold Innis: As I Remember Him." *Journal of Canadian Studies* 20 (winter 1985-6): 3-11. As mentioned before, McLuhan and his colleague, Barrington Nevitt took as their starting point, the pre-Socratics—before the influence of Plato.

— "The Wasichus did not kill...": **Black Elk**, quoted in John G. Neihardt, *Black Elk Speaks*. Lincoln: Univ. of Nebraska Press, 1961.

38 *Sergeant Lamb's America*: **Robert Graves**—historically accurate novel about a Dublin man in the services of the English Army.

— "good one...": **Andre Gunder Frank**, *World Accumulation*. New York and London: Monthly Review Press, 1978. **Add. note**: Frank, a Chilean economist, worked on this book since 1967. At the time of its publication he was in exile in Germany—at the Max-Planck Institute in Starnberg, Germany.

— "Indeed, the booty...": **John Maynard Keynes**, *A Treatise on Money*. 2 vols. London: Macmillan, 1930.

39 "the best thing...": **Christopher Columbus**. In Frank, *World Accumulation*, p. 41.

— "We Spaniards...": **Hernando Cortez**. In FRANK, *World Accumulation*, p. 41.

— DIFFERENCES IN ECONOMIC EXPLOITATION: Ibid., p. 45.

— NAMES FOR SPAIN: **Manuel Fernandez Alvarez**, Univ. of Salamanca, "Introduction to the History of Spain." In Bradley Smith, *Spain: A History in Art*. New York: Doubleday & Co. (no date), pp. 1-16.

— EARLY HISTORY UP TO 2ND PUNIC WAR: Ibid.

— SPAIN'S MINERAL WEALTH TO ROME: **Will Durant**, *Caesar and Christ*. New York: Simon and Schuster, 1944.

— WITH SPAIN'S RICHES, ROME CONQUERED THE KNOWN WORLD: Ibid.

— "Silver and lead...": **Alvarez**, "Intro. to the History of Spain."

— AFTER ROME UNTIL 1492: Ibid. **Add. notes**: For insight into the cultural superiority of the Moors over the local people see P. M. Holt, ed. *Cambridge History of Islam* v. 1. Cambridge: Cambridge Univ. Press, 1970. This provides another reason for the Spanish hatred of the dark-skinned peoples in the New World.

— "was the richest...": **Alvarez**, "Intro. to the History of Spain."

— "Spain served as...": Ibid. **Add. notes**: "When the Catholic Sovereigns ended the war of reconquest from the Moslems, the Reconquista... Columbus arrived...It was at this moment that the concept of manifest destiny...sank deep into the Spanish conscience. The Spaniard felt he had a godly mission to carry out..." (Alvarez).

— EUROPE JUST BEFORE COLUMBUS' DISCOVERY OF THE NEW WORLD: **Barbara Tuchman**, *A Distant Mirror: The Calamitous 14th Century*. New York: Alfred Knopf, 1978. **Add notes**: For years I've been collecting information on the disastrous state of Europe at this time, but here I have used Tuchman's work as background to provide a brief introduction. I've used her data down to and including the Hundred Years War ending with the Treaty of Etaples.

— BLACK DEATH AND THE "CULT OF DEATH": Ibid, p. 587-588.

40 "At the Council...": Ibid., p. 591.

— ENORMOUS QUANTITIES OF PRECIOUS METALS WHICH SPAIN ACQUIRED: Of course no one really knows the total amounts. Here I will just give two insights. Before the Spanish Civil War in the 1930s, Spain had the "fourth highest gold reserve in the world." During the war, the republic decided "to remove this treasure 'to a safe place'." Eventually, it was taken to Russia. Here are the figures: The total Spanish monetary gold before the civil war was $788 million. This was *700 tons of gold*. There's no way to know how much of this remained from the colonial period, of course. The quantity shipped to Russia was $500 million. Later, $155 million was shipped to Paris to add to the $85 million already there. (Hugh Thomas, *The Spanish Civil War*. New York: Harper and Row, 1963, p. 448 and 974.)

The other example is a recent find of a Spanish "treasure ship." The *Atocha* was sunk in 1622 in a hurricane off Key West. According to recent research done in the Archives of the Indies in Seville, by Dr. Eugene Lyon, the "ship was carrying 160 pieces of gold bullion, 900 silver ingots, over 250,000 silver coins, and 600 copper planks..." After fifteen years of searching it was found in 1985. ("Research in Spain Leads to Treasure Find." *The News, Univ. of Denver* 24 (winter 1986.) The important thing to note here is that this was just one of Spain's shipments of new world riches back to the home country.

— INDIAN POPULATION DECLINED BY 95%: **Woodrow Borah**, "America as Model: The Demographic Impact of European Expansion upon the Non-European World." Reprint no. 292, Center for Latin American Studies, Univ. of California.

— "principle contribution...": **Frank**, *World Accumulation*, p. 24.

— "Not long after...": Ibid., p. 48.

— SUGAR IN ITALIAN CITY-STATES, CANARY ISLANDS ETC.: Ibid., p. 35-36.

— SUGAR IN BRAZIL: Ibid., p. 49.

40 THE PLANTATION SYSTEM: Ibid., p. 50.
41 YEAR'S SUPPLY OF BREAD IN BRITAIN: **Ernest Mandel**, *Marxist Economic Theory*. 2 vols. New York: Monthly Review Press, 1970, pp. 107 and 148.
— EASTERN EUROPEAN PEASANTS AS SERFS: **Frank**, *World Accumulation*, p.74.
— "It was precisely..." Ibid., p. 78.
— SPANISH MANILA GALLEON TRADE: Ibid., p. 88.
— NEW ENGLAND AND THE BEGINNINGS OF THE TRIANGULAR TRADE: Ibid., p. 95.
— RELIGIOUS PERSECUTION: Ibid., p. 100.
— "NATURAL LAW" SHIFTED TO "NATURAL RIGHTS": **Leo Strauss**, *Natural Rights and History*. Chicago: Univ. of Chicago Press, 1953. See especially the section beginning on p. 81.
— "no arts; no letters...": **Thomas Hobbes**, *Leviathan*. (ed.), Michael Oakshott. Oxford: Basil Blackwell, 1960, p. 82.
— "Land that is left...": **John Locke**, *Two Treatises of Government*, (ed.) Peter Laslett. Cambridge: Univ. Press, 1960, p. 316.
42 "Bacon's concern...": **Frank**, *World Accumulation*, p. 101.
— "enlightened rationalism...": Ibid., p. 180.
— "It is well to observe...": **Francis Bacon**, *Novum Organum*, book 1, aphorism 129. Quoted in Needham, *Sci. and Civil.* v. 1, p. 19.
— HOW MUCH EARLIER IMPORTANT INVENTIONS WERE FIRST MADE IN CHINA: **Robert Temple**, *The Genius of China: 3000 Years of Science, Discovery and Invention*. Introduction by Joseph Needham. New York: Simon and Schuster, 1986. These figures came from the charts used as endpapers in this volume. **Add. notes:** Needham gave Temple total access to all his files, accumulated during the past 30 years, thus providing for him ready access to Needham's vast research.
— "The only really important...": **Needham**, *Sci. and Civil.* v. 1., p. 243.
— "It is just as much...": **Temple**, *The Genius of China*, p. 9.
43 "there was little or no...": **Joseph Needham**, *Sci. and Civil.* v. 3, p. 167.
— "creations of many...": Ibid.
— "Renaissance, the Reformation...": Ibid., p. 166.
— "concentration on one...": Ibid., p. 164.
— "No, indeed...": **Chheng I-Chhuan**, quoted in Needham, *Sci. and Civil.* v. 3, p. 164.
— "develop anything...": **Needham**, *The Grand Titration*, p. 311.
— "One can only hope...": **Joseph Needham**, "Introduction." In Temple, *The Genius of China*, p. 8.
— UNITARY OPERATIONAL THINKING: **Herbert Koplowitz**, "Unitary Operations: A Projection Beyond Piaget's Formal Operations Stage." Originally available from Cognitive Development Project, Dept. of Physics and Astronomy, Univ. of Mass. Amherst, Ma. 01003. I've been informed it's no longer available. Koplowitz is a Canadian, but I've no current address for him.
— "What was to emerge...": **William Barrett**, *The Illusion of Technique: A Search for the Meaning of Life in a Technological Age*. London: William Kimber, Pub. 1979, p. 8.
44 "What then did I formerly think...": **Rene Descartes**, "Meditation 2". In P. T. Geach and G. E. M. Anscombe. trans. *Philosophical Writings*. Indianapolis: Bobbs-Merrill, 1971, p. 67.
— "He concluded...": **Mary Midgley**, *Beast and Man: The Roots of Human Nature*. Ithaca: Cornell Univ. Press, 1978, p. 209.
— "Descartes divided...": **William Grey**, "The Value of Wilderness." *Environmental Ethics* 1 (winter 1979): 309-319.
— "In rejecting...": Ibid.
— "What, then, is...": **Barrett**. *The Illusion of Technique*, p. 129.
— "I want to get away...": **Midgley**, *Beast and Man*, p. 260.
— 'If you put God outside...": **Gregory Bateson**, "Form, Substance, and Difference." *General Semantics Bulletin* 37 (1970).
— "...the ideas which dominate our civilization...": **Gregory Bateson**, "The Roots of Ecological Crisis." In *Steps to An Ecology of Mind*. New York: Ballantine Books, 1972, p. 492-3.
45 "transferred from France...": **Frank**, *World Accumulation*, p. 104.
— "By a well-managed...": **Glyndwr Williams**, *The Expansion of Europe in the Eighteenth Century*. London: Blanford Press, 1966.
— EFFECT OF GOLD DISCOVERIES IN MINAS GERAIS: **Frank**, *World Accumulation*, p. 116.
— "prepared that country...": Ibid., p. 104.
— "It is significant...": **Lewis C. Gray**, *History of Agriculture in the Southern United States to 1860*. v. 2. Gloucester, MA: Peter Smith, 1958, p. 302.
— "USEFUL" LIFE OF SLAVES: **Frank**, *World Accumulation*, p. 128.
— "A large-scale slave...": **Paul Bohannon and Philip Curtin**. *Africa and Africans*. Garden City, New York: Natural History Press, 1971, p. 264.
— "Those Africans...": **Basil Davidson**, *The African Slave Trade: Precolonial History, 1450-1850*. Boston: Atlantic, Little Brown, 1961, p. 201-202.
— "No single state...": Ibid., p. 238.
— FEUDALISM IN INDIA: **Bhowani Sen**, *Evolution of Agrarian Relations in India*. New Delhi: Peoples Publishing House, 1962, pp. 47 and 51. Quoted in Frank, *World Accumulation*.
— DECLINE OF MOGHUL POWER: **Frank**, *World Accumulation*, p. 145.
— BATTLE OF PLASSEY AND DESTRUCTION OF THE FORT AT PONDICHERRY: **Frank**, *World Accumulation*, p. 145 and 148.
— "Money! Money!...": **Narenda Krishna Sinha**, *The Economic History of Bengal from Plassey to the Permanent Settlement*. v. 1. Calcutta: Firma K. L. Mukhopadhyay, 1961-1970, p. 221. Quoted in Frank, *World Accumulation*.
46 "British colonialists...": **A. I. Levkovsky**, *Capitalism in India: Basic Trends in Its Development*. New Delhi: Peoples Publishing House, 1966, p. 10. Quoted in Frank, *World Accumulation*.
— "The connection...": **William Digby**, *"Prosperous" British India: A Revelation from Official Records*. New Delhi: Sagar Publication, 1969, p. 31.
— "possibly, since the world...": **Brooks Adams**. In Digby, *"Properous" British India*, p. 31.
— "As your Ambassador...": **Ch'ien Lung**, quoted in Franz Schurmann and Orville Schell, *The China Reader, I: Imperial China*. New York: Vintage, 1967, p. 108-109.
— "The practice..." and "In the 1790s...": **Sinha**, *The Economic History of Bengal*, p. 233.
— "This [opium trade] grew...": **John K. Fairbank**, *Trade and Diplomacy on the China Coast*. Stanford: Stanford Univ. Press, 1969, p. 62-64 and 75.
— "Although the tide of...": **Frank**, *World Accumulation*, p. 162.
— "The Chinese...": Ibid., p. 27.
— ENCLOSURE ACTS: Ibid., p. 177.
— GRAZING SHEEP FOR WOOL: Ibid., p. 258.
— "[O]nly the destruction...": **Karl Marx**, *Capital*, p. 748.
— "On the final leg...": **Daniel P. Mannix and Malcolm Cowley**, *Black Cargoes: A History of the Atlantic Slave Trade, 1518-1865*. New York: Viking Press, 1962, p. 160.
47 FOOD STAPLES TO FEED SLAVES: **Eric Williams**, *Capitalism and Slavery*. New York: Capricorn Books, 1966, p. 108.
— "Why, did...": **Guy Stevens Callender**, *Selections from the Economic History of the United States, 1765-1860*. New York: Augustus M. Kelley, 1965, pp. 122-123.
— "In Britain the parliament...": **Frank**, *World Accumulation*, p. 202.
— ECONOMIC INTERESTS HURT BY THE NEW TAXES: **Chester W. Wright**, *Economic History of the United States*. New York: McGraw-Hill, 1941, p. 193.
— "Whatever the British advance...": **E. I. Hobsbawm**, *The Age of Revolution, 1789-1848*. New York: Mentor, 1964, p. 47.
— "it was the capital...": **Williams**, *Capitalism and Slavery*, pp. 102-3.
— ESSENTIALS OF STEAM ENGINE DEVELOPED BY CHINESE: **Temple**, *The Genius of China*, pp. 64-66.
— "these European designs...":Ibid., p. 65.
— "the advantage of Britain...": **E. I. Hobsbawm**, *Industry and Empire*. Harmondsworth: Penguin Books, 1969, p. 49.
— "was the greatest triumph...": Ibid., p. 60
— "The seven 'useful' years...": **Frank**, *World Accumulation*, p. 243.
— EYEWITNESS ACCOUNT OF THE EASTERN COASTLINE: **Paul Metcalf**, *Apalache*. Berkeley: Turtle Island Foundation, 1976, pp. 1-3 and 5.
48 "$29,000, stainless steel...": **B. Kuttner**, "Coke, Cars & Capital." *New Republic* 187 (Nov. 15, 1982).
49 COCA CHEWING AND CHRONIC HIGH ALTITUDE SICKNESS: **Andrew Fuchs**, "Coca Chewing and High-Altitude Stress: Possible Effects of Coca Alkaloids on Erythropoiesis." *Current Anthropology* 19 (June 1978). **Add. notes:** In the "Conclusion", the author states that Indian coca chewers in the Andes use the drug to alleviate "symptoms of hunger, thirst, fatigue,

cold, and pain...the antimuscarinic ingredients in the leaf act upon critical areas of the posterior hypothalamus to depress erythropoiesis. By so doing they are antagonists to the hypoxia which stimulates excessive red blood cell production..." Excessive red blood cell production can cause Chronic High Altitude Sickness among male Indians beginning around the age of 40. Females are not prone to this because menstruation rids them of excess red blood cells. (E. Heath and D. Williams, *Man At High Altitude: The Pathophysiology of Acclimatization and Adaptation.* Edinburgh, Scotland: Churchill Livingston, 1981.)

49 "America's No. 1...": **U. S. House committee on narcotic control**. Quoted in Charles J. Hanley (Assoc. Press Writer) "Narcotics War Deadly Fight." *Albuquerque Journal*, Sunday May 26, 1985.

— "Like any successful 'multinational'..." down to "the narcotic traffic is now stronger than the state.": Ibid.

— "I felt as if I'd...": **Kathleen McAuliffe**, "The Black Box: Brain Tuner." *Omni* 5 (Jan. 1983): 45-48 ff.

— "In sharp contrast..." down to "that drugs...The body heals itself...": Ibid.

— "major conceptual..." down to "Many of these...," **Candace B. Pert, Michael R. Ruff, et. al.**, "Neuropeptides and their Receptors: A Psychosomatic Network." *The Journal of Immunology* 135 (August 1985): 820s-826s.

50 ANIMAL USE OF DRUGS: **Ronald K. Siegel**, "Jungle Revelers." *Omni* 8 (March 1986).

— "Several Indians...": Ibid.

— "Western man is the first..." down to "Because this difference...": **Sylvia Wynter**, "Ethno or Socio Poetics." *Alcheringa*, New Series 2 (1976): 78-94.

— "based on steady or accelerated...": **Sigmund Kvaloy**, "Complexity and Time." **Add. notes**: The entire essay is reprinted in the "Back of the Book" section in this work.

51 "By a process of addiction...": **Gregory Bateson**, *Mind and Nature: A Necessary Unity*, p. 174.

— "consume unreplaceable natural...": **Gregory Bateson**, *Steps to An Ecology of Mind*, p. 496.

PART II

53 "You cannot go back...": **Paul Shepard**, Lecture at University of Utah, Salt Lake City, Utah—February 13, 1985.

Ch. 4 Ethology
pp. 54 and 55 Opening Quotes

— "The human body...": **John Lilly**, *The Dyadic Cyclone*. New York: Simon and Schuster, p. 74.

— "Civilization is thus...": **A. T. W. Simeons, M. D.**, *Man's Presumptuous Brain: An Evolutionary Interpretation of Psychosomatic Disease.* New York: E. P. Dutton & Co, 1961, p. 78.

— "As far as one can...": Ibid., p. 281. **Add. notes**: Simeons studied medicine at the University of Heidelberg with post-graduate studies in Germany and Switzerland and worked in Africa and India on tropical diseases for a number of years. This book grew out of his work on psychosomatic disorders at the Salvator Mundi International Hospital in Rome.

— "[M]ere purposive...": **Gregory Bateson**, "Style, Grace, and Information in Primitive Art." In Anthony Forge, ed. *Primitive Art and Society.* Oxford: Oxford University Press, 1974. (Reprinted in Bateson, *Steps to an Ecology of Mind*, pp. 128-152.)

— "[I]t should not be forgotten...": **Dr. E. Estyn Evans**, quoted in "Industrial Revolution and Urban Dominance." In William L. Thomas, ed. *Man's Role In Changing the Face of the Earth*. Chicago: University of Chicago Press, 1956. p. 435. **Add. notes:** This 1193 page volume came out of the conference of the same name, held at Princeton in June, 1955, "the first large-scale evaluation of what has happened and what is happening to the earth under man's impress," and was the beginning of much of the important work in this field ever since. The article above was part of the "Symposium Discussion: Restropect." Dr. Evans was Head of the Geography Department at Queen's University, Northern Ireland.

— "The symbols...": **C. G. Jung**, *Essays on a Science of Mythology*, p. 92.

56 "I was a student...": **Paul Leyhausen**, *Motivation of Human and Animal Behavior*, p. xi.

57 "The sea eye...": **Paul Shepard**, *Man in the Landscape: A Historic View of the Esthetics of Nature*, p. 19.

— "An affinity...": Ibid.

— "What we didn't...": **Konrad Lorenz**, quoted in Alec Nisbett, *Konrad Lorenz: A Biography*, p. 20.

58 LORENZ' EARLY LIFE: Nisbett, *Konrad Lorenz*, pp. 13-67.

— "I would be nowhere...": **Konrad Lorenz**, quoted in Nisbett, *Konrad Lorenz*, p. 69.

— "has involved...": Ibid., p. 78.

— EISENBERG'S MISTRANSLATION AND FURTHER CONSEQUENCES: Ibid., pp. 82-89.

— "The 1940 paper tried...": **Konrad Lorenz**, quoted in Nisbett, *Konrad Lorenz*, p. 90.

— "at exactly...": Ibid., p. 89.

— "a significantly...": **Leyhausen**, *Motivation*, p. xii.

59 "SOCIAL ORGANIZATION AND DENSITY TOLERANCE IN MAMMALS": Ibid., pp. 120-143.

— "centripetal tendencies" down to "Eventually a despot...": Ibid.

60 "the biological study...": **Niko Tinbergen**, "On the Aims and Methods of Ethology." Quoted in Gerard Baerends, ed. *Function and Behaviour: Essays in Honour of Prof. Niko Tinbergen*. Oxford, Clarendon Press, 1975, p. xii.

— "behavior patterns...organs": **Niko Tinbergen**, "Ethology."

— HUXLEY AND HEINROTH: Ibid.

— "father of modern ethology...": **Huxley**, In Tinbergen, "Ethology."

— THREE STAGES OF INTEREST IN ETHOLOGY: Ibid.

— ETHOLOGY SHOULD BE APPLIED TO HUMAN BEHAVIOR: Ibid.

— "that of causation..." down to "Animal behaviourists...": Ibid.

61 "Is this how...": **Bernard Hellman**, quoted by Konrad Lorenz, "The Fashionable Fallacy of Dispensing with Description." Lecture at the XXV International Congress of Physiological Sciences, Munich, July 25-31, 1971. English translation in Richard Evans, *Konrad Lorenz: The Man and His Ideas*. New York, Harcourt Brace & Jovanovich, 1975, pp. 152-179.

— "The 'constructor'..." down to "a simple excess of it.": **Lorenz**, "The Fashionable Fallacy."

— "My late friend Ronald Hargreaves" down to "antagonistic factors": **Konrad Lorenz**, "The Enmity Between Generations and Its Probable Ethological Causes." English translation in Evans, *Konrad Lorenz*, pp 218-269. Hargreaves was a psychiatrist at Leeds in England.

— "labelled by such words...": **Konrad Lorenz**, "The Fashionable Fallacy."

— "Ronald Hargreaves's double question...": **Konrad Lorenz**, "The Enmity Between Generations."

— "they smile and laugh...": **Irenaus Eibl-Eibesfeldt**, *Love and Hate*, p. 12. **Add. notes**: Eibl-Eibesfeldt worked with Lorenz beginning in 1949 and then later went with him to the Max Plank Institute for Behavioral Physiology in Seewissen, near Munich. He developed a camera which had the usual lens attachment in front, but no lens. At the side of the camera was the real lens; hence no one knew that he was photographing them. With this set-up he was able to film behaviors in widely varying cultures all over the world thus indicating their similarities.

62 "We found agreement...": **Eibl-Eibesfeldt**, *Ethology, The Biology of Behavior*, p. 416.

— "coy behavior...": **Eibl-Eibesfeldt**, *Love and Hate*, p. 50.

— CARE OF THE YOUNG AND FUTURE BEHAVIOR: Ibid., p. 125.

— HUMAN INFANT: Ibid., p. 22.

— COURTSHIP IN BIRDS: Ibid., p. 111.

— KISSING: Ibid., p. 137.

— "The unconventional decision..." down to "This type of evidence...": **Nikolaas Tinbergen**, "Ethology and Stress Diseases." *Science* 185 (5 July 1974): 20-26.

63 "appears to be...": **Jerome S. Bruner**, "Introduction." In Jerome Bruner, Alison Jolly, and Kathy Sylva, eds. *Play—Its Role In Development and Evolution*. New York: Basic Books Inc., 1976, p 13-14.

Ch. 5 Relationships Between Animal and Human
pp. 64 and 65 Opening Quotes

— "We are not...": **Midgley**, *Beast and Man: The Roots of Human Nature*, p. xii.

—— "The appreciation of the separate...": **Barry Lopez**, *Of Wolves and Men*, p. 285.

—— "We patronize...": **Harry Beston**, *The Outermost House*. New York: Holt Rinehart and Winston.

—— "The brain as an...": **Donald Griffin**, *Animal Thinking*. Harvard Univ. Press, 1984. **Add. notes**: Because we humans are mammals, relationship, as Gregory Bateson notes, is more important than anything else. Essentially, then, it doesn't matter whether an animal "thinks" in the same way we do or not. You only need to know the relationship between you and the animal, but, while animals *always* make the status of a relationship very clear; humans usually fail this fundamental mammalian test.

—— "...the numinous emotion...": **Roy A. Rappaport**, "The Obvious Aspects of Ritual." In Roy Rappaport, *Ecology, Meaning, and Religion*, p. 212. (See chapter eleven for more on Erikson's statement.)

—— "[A]n archetype...has the divine quality...": **C. G. Jung**, "Psychological Analysis of Nietzsche's Zarathustra." In "Notes on Seminars" Spring 1934-Winter 1939. Edited by Mary Foote. Zurich multigraphed typescript. Copy in Zurich at the C. G. Jung Institute and a copy in the Kristine Mann Library of the Analytical Psychology Club of New York. (For the continuation of this quote, see chapter six.)

—— "It is not the case that man...": **Chu Hsi**. Quoted in D. Bodde, "Harmony and Conflict in Chinese Philosophy." **Add. notes**: Chu Hsi [1130 to 1200 A.D.] is considered one of the greatest of the Neo-Confucian philosophers.

66 OLDER BRAINS: **Paul D. MacLean**, *A Triune Concept of the Brain and Behaviour*. Toronto: Univ. of Toronto Press, 1973.

67 JUNG'S THEORY ABOUT ANIMALS IN DREAMS: **Dr. Anthony Stevens**, *Archetypes: A Natural History of the Self*, p. 269.

—— SNAKE DREAMS CONNECTED TO BRAIN STEM ACTIVITY: **C. G. Jung**, *Coll. Works* v. 9, pt. 2, paragraph 396.

—— "In India there...": **Peter Steinhart**, "Fear of Snakes." *Audubon*, March 1986, pp. 6-9.

—— "You discover...": **Voltaire**, quoted in Midgley, *Beast and Man*.

—— "The question is not...": **Jeremy Bentham**, quoted in Midgley, *Beast and Man*.

—— "The earliest..." down to "In tracing...": **Paul Shepard and Barry Sanders**, *The Sacred Paw: The Bear in Nature, Myth, and Literature*. p. 71.

—— "The boundary of Dawn...": **Heraclitus**. In Kahn, *The Art and Thought of Heraclitus*, p. 51. **Add. notes**: Kahn translates fragment #XLV as: "The limits of Dawn and Evening is the Bear; and, opposite the Bear, the Warder of luminous Zeus." I have used another translator's words in two places—boundary for "limits" and Watchman for "Warder"; because this is more fitting for place oriented people.

—— "At night, the Great Bear...": **Shepard**, *The Sacred Paw*, p. 67.

68 DRACHENLOCH CAVE: Ibid., p. 187.

—— "supplies the first...": **Emil Bachler**, quoted in Shepard, *The Sacred Paw*, p. 188.

—— FORTY-FOUR MEANINGS FOR "TO BEAR": Ibid., p. xvii-xix.

—— "the bear no longer...": Ibid., p. xix.

—— HERBS AND THE BEAR: Ibid., p. 100-103.

—— ARTEMIS AND DEMETER: Ibid., p. 116-117.

—— BEAR DREAM OF JUNG'S PATIENT: **Jung**, *Coll. Works*, v. 9, Pt. I, par. 342, p. 195. **Add. notes**: One of these dreams is worth recounting here. The woman dreamed that she went through a door into a tower-like room and climbed up the steps. The steps go up to a temple on the top of a wooded mountain. "It is the shrine of Ursanna, the bear-goddess and Mother of God in one." Remember, bear's Latin name is *Ursus*. Animals are standing around here and to get into the temple one must be changed into an animal. A circular space in the center of the temple has no roof and it is possible to look straight up at the constellation of the Bear. There is a "moon-bowl" on the altar with smoke rising. The image of the goddess is very unclear, but the worshippers, who have now become animals, must touch the goddess' foot with their own foot. Jung points out that in this dream the "bear-goddess emerges plainly."

Dr. Stevens, in his book, *Archetypes: A Natural History of the Self*, says that in volume 9, Jung most closely connects his "archetypes" with what later was termed "ethology."

—— EARLY HUMAN SOCIAL ORGANIZATION: **George B. Schaller and Gordon R. Lowther**, "The Relevance of Carnivore Behavior to the Study of Early Hominids." *Southwestern Journal of Anthropology* 25 (winter, 1969).

68 "Early man was...": **John A. Livingston**, *One Cosmic Instant*, p. 109.

—— "probably parent...": **Lopez**, *Of Wolves and Men*, p. 17.

—— HUNTER RELYING ON WOLF TO FIND CARIBOU: Ibid., p. 80.

—— "comings and goings...": Ibid., p. 103.

—— "At a tribal level...": Ibid., p. 105. **Add. notes**: Another fine book on wolves is R. D. Lawrence, *In Praise of Wolves*. New York, Henry Holt & Co., 1986. On pages 89 to 96 he explains just exactly how he enters wolves' territory and lets them make the moves to become acquainted with him; thus setting up a lasting relationship wherein he can enter this territory again much later and know they will recognize and accept him. What is fascinating about the process is that it is so similar to how N. Tinbergen makes the acquaintance of a small child (as recounted in my previous chapter). Also similar to the way Doug Peacock, the grizzly expert, encounters a male grizzly, whose territory he has accidentally encroached upon. He has been "rushed" by numerous male grizzlies but was not attacked because he knew the "rituals" for mammalian interaction. (Personal communication from Dave Foreman.) What I am getting at here is that we, humans, are so much a part of the mammalian species that when we do not let our human consciousness get in the way, we "remember" the essential mammalian behaviors for relationships. Furthermore, these behaviors are the "correct" ones; not as confused and inept as our conscious, human ones.

—— "The coyote survives...": **Gary Snyder**, *The Old Ways*, p. 68.

—— "but...most of the time...": Ibid., p. 69.

69 "god, man & animal...": **Jung**, "On the Psychology of the Trickster Figure." In Paul Radin, *The Trickster: A Study in American Indian Mythology*. New York: Schocken books, 1972.

—— STORY OF THE COYOTE: **Dick Dorworth**, "Coyote Song." *Mountain Gazette* (December 1976.)

—— "Salmon is the totem...": **Freeman House**, "Totem Salmon." In "North Pacific Rim Alive." *Planet Drum*, Box 31251, San Francisco, California.

—— "Indeed the salmon...": **Tom Jay**, "The Salmon of the Heart." In *Working the Wood Working the Sea*. Port Townsend, Washington: Empty Bowl, pp. 100-124.

—— "TOTEMISM" IN LONG'S ACCOUNT: **Abe Hultkrantz**, "North American Indian Religion: A General Survey: Part I." *History of Religions* 6 (1966). **Add. notes**: Hultkrantz' complete account is in four parts— the first two parts concern "totemism."

—— "TOTEMISM" FROM 1866 ON: **Hultkrantz**, "North American Indian Religion: Part II." *History of Religions* 6 (1966)

70 "the world's most..." down to "the language brain...": **Paul Shepard**, *The Tender Carnivore and the Sacred Game*, p. 170 and 203.

—— "Only when...": **Bruno Bettelheim**, *The Uses of Enchantment*. London: 1976., p. 78.

—— "What actually takes place...": **Hans Duerr**, *Dreamtime: Concerning the Boundary Between Wilderness and Civilization*, p. 65.

—— PERSONAL TOTEM POLE: **Eligio S. Gallegos**, *The Personal Totem Pole: Animal Imagery, the Chakras, and Psychotherapy*. Santa Fe: Moon Bear Press, 1987. **Add. notes**: While working on the ms. for this work, I had Gallegos's original printout (1985), which he sent to me. Since the book has been published, all the paging has been changed so I can't give precise pages, here. The statement by Suzuki, which Gallegos uses is from R. H. Blyth, *Zen in Western Literature and Oriental Classics*. New York: E. P. Dutton, 1960. (The book may be ordered from Moon Bear Press, Box 15811, Santa Fe, NM 87506 $12)

—— TAOIST "ANIMAL FROLICS": **Kenneth Cohen**, "Taoist Shamanism." In *Laughing Man* (Bubba Free John publication), pp 48-52. **Add. notes**: Cohen now teaches at Univ. of Colorado and has a center in the mountains west of Boulder. Address: Ken Cohen, Nederland, Co.

71 "Snowy owls...": **Hans Duerr**, *Dreamtime*, p. 106.

—— EAST INDIAN STORY: **Alan Drengson**, "Social and Psychological Implications of Human Attitudes Toward Animals." *The Journal of Transpersonal Psychology* 12 (1980).

Ch. 6 Archetypes

pp. 72 and 73 Opening Quotes

—— "...the 2 million year...": **C. G. Jung**, "Roosevelt 'Great' in Jung's

Analysis." *New York Times* (October 4, 1936).

— "Every night...": **Dr. Anthony Stevens**, *Archetypes: A Natural History of the Self*, p. 271.

— "The archetype—let us never...": **Jung**, "The Psychology of the Child Archetype." *Coll.Works*, v. 9, Pt. I., p. 160. I added the boldface for emphasis. **Add. notes:** Quotation sources from the *Collected Works* of Jung are indicated by the volume number, followed by the number of the paragraph from which the quotation is taken, (if I noted it in my research). Usually I also list the page number.

— "The archetypes are as it were...": **Jung**, "Mind and Earth." *Coll.Works* v. 10, pp. 29-49.

— "...an archetype...always based upon the animal...For instance, the glow-worm...": **Jung**, "Psychological Analysis of Nietzsche's Zarathustra." **Add. notes:** I repeat this quote again because it has great truth in it, in spite of the fact that Jung equates wisdom with human self-consciousness.

— [archetypes] "They are essentially...": **Jung**: *Contributions to Analytical Psychology*. New York: Harcourt, Brace & Co. 1928, p. 118.

— "Archetypes are about relationship...": **Julien Puzey**, "Deep Ecology, The Root and the Return: Outline of an Experiential course." Silverton, Colorado: Finn Hill Arts, 1987. **Add. Notes**: Essentially, archetypes are patterns of relationships rather than substances (or categories). That's why people in European cultures have such difficulty understanding them.

74 "This was the best..." down to "Yes, I thought...": **C. G. Jung**, *Memories, Dreams, Reflections*, p. 78.

— "The mountain...": **C. G. Jung**, *Man and His Symbols*, pp. 221-225. This book was first published in 1964.

— "he suddenly expressed...": **Vincent Brome**, *Jung*, p. 269.

— "I think that's the last time...": **Jung**. In Brome, *Jung*, p. 270.

— PAINTING OF MT. KAILAS: **Miguel Serrano**, *C. G. Jung and Herman Hesse: A Record of Two Friendships*, p. 107.

— "I am sitting...": **Jung**, *Memories, Dreams, Reflections*, p. 20.

— "Now I know the truth...": **Jung**. In Serrano, *Jung and Herman Hesse*, p. 104.

— "Intellectuals think...": **C. G. Jung**, source unknown. I've seen this quoted by others as Jung's words but cannot trace it back to his works.

75 "panic fear.": **C. G. Jung**, *The Undiscovered Self*.

— "The conscious mind allows...": **Jung**, *Coll. Works*, v. 14, par. 51.

— "even though it reaches...": **Jung**, *Coll. Works*, v. 10. par. 304.

— STUDY "ATTACHMENT BONDS IN INFANCY": **Stevens**, *Archetypes*, pp. 1-12.

— "Moreover, the nurses...": Ibid. p. 4.

— "her neat theoretical..": Ibid., p. 2.

— "the primary reward...": Ibid, p. 3.

— "mother-infant attachment bond...": **Dr. John Bowlby**, quoted in Stevens, *Archetypes*, p. 3. **Add. notes:** Bowlby's work on "attachment" was an important part of the beginnings of research on "bonding." Bowlby showed that essentially it is play between mother and child which forms the "bond." (See chapter 11 in Part III of this work, for more concerning the importance of play). Not only is play necessary for the development of the child, but also for the on-going life of the adult. Play as an integral part of festivals and ceremonies, is essential for human interaction as well as bonding to nature. Bowlby's most famous paper is J. Bowlby, "The nature of the child's tie to his mother." *International Journal of Psycho-Analysis* 39: (1958): 350-373. His most important book is *Attachment*, vol. 1 of his two volume work. New York: Basic Books. No publication date on these volumes; however they were originally published in England in 1969.

— "fury would be...": **Stevens**, *Archetypes*, p. 3.

— "sour grapes" down to "Alone among...": Ibid. p. 8-9. **Add. notes:** Stevens defines ethology as "the study of behaviour patterns in organisms living in their natural environments." All the fury and opposition came about because Bowlby applied these methods to humans. This type of reaction still occurs, today.

76 "simple and more consistent..." down to "drawing developmental...": Ibid., p. 11.

— "inner psychic..." down to "Jung's ideas...": Ibid., p. 13-15.

— "to develop what is...": Ibid., p. 16.

— "unbiological...": Anthony Steven's paraphrase of **Irene Champernowne**. Ibid, p. 16-17.

— "This was a...": Ibid., p. 17.

— JUNG'S DREAM IN 1909: **Jung**, *Memories, Dreams, Reflections*, p. 158-161. The words within quotation marks are Jung's actual words.

— WILHELM SENDING JUNG THE CHINESE MS.: **C. G. Jung**, "Foreword to the Second German Edition." In Richard Wilhelm. trans. *The Secret of the Golden Flower*, pp. vii-viii.

— "I have chosen the term...": **Jung**, *Coll. Works*, v. 9, Pt. I.

77 "one great experience...": **Jung**, *Memories, Dreams, Reflections*, p. 107.

— "My heart suddenly began...": Ibid., p. 108.

— "the Jungian archetype...": **Stevens**, *Archetypes*, p. 39.

— "The first element...": **J. Jacobi**, *Complex, Archetype, Symbol*. London: Routledge & Kegan Paul, 1959.

— "Because of their typical...": **Jung**, *Coll. Works*, v. 8, par. 277.

— "represents or personifies certain..." down to "This original form" : **Jung**, *Coll. Works*, v. 9, Pt. I, par. 271, p. 160.

— "the roots which the psyche has sunk not only in the earth...": **Jung**, "Mind and Earth." In *Coll. Works*, v. 10, pp. 29-49.

— "The symbols of the self arise in the depths of the body...": **C. G. Jung**. In C. G. Jung and C. Kerenyi, *Essays on a Science of Mythology*, p. 92.

— "no 'rational' substitute...": **Jung**, *Coll. Works*, v. 9, Pt I, par. 272, p. 161.

— "an inherited mode of psychic functioning, corresponding to that inborn way...": **Jung**, *Coll. Works*, v. 18, par. 1228. **Add. notes**: I've added the italics here to emphasize "way" as pattern—connected with the Chinese concept of Li, occurring later in this work.

— "to concentrate on relatively few..." down to "gigantic Promethean debt...": **Jung**, *Coll. Works*, v. 9, Pt. I, p. 162-163.

78 "knows nothing beyond the opposites...": Ibid., p. 168.

— "In the unconscious mind both opposites...": **Lawrence N. Gelb**, "Man and the Land: The Psychological Theory of C. J. Jung." *Zygon* 9 (December 1974): 288-299. **Add. notes**: This provides more insight into the European "substance" trap. It is the nature of the conscious mind to "know nothing beyond the opposites: good and bad, spirit and matter (earth)" etc.; hence nothing comes together into a meaningful whole. But, as Gelb says "in the unconscious mind" both opposites "are reunited." They are always united in reality and in the unconscious. It is the conscious mind itself that creates the opposites. This is essential to remember. Also it's been said, I think by Gregory Bateson, that there are no paradoxes out in nature; only in the human mind. Of course, that's why festivals and ceremonies are so important; they allow the unconscious mind to show us this wholeness.

Gelb also writes; "Just as man created the spirit-matter, mind-body dichotomies, he also created an opposition between himself and the earth, the environment with which he was formerly at one." Now that the human is destroying the earth to such an unprecedented degree, Gelb, somewhat caustically, writes: "To destroy the earth is to destroy himself. And with the end of species man, all the opposites are ended."

While, as Anthony Stevens says, we "must be willing to sacrifice the arrogance of ego-consciousness and abandon the subjective attitudes characteristic of left hemisphere imperialism", we don't just throw them out. They are needed by the fully functioning human being. Instead, as Stevens says, we need, "a more equitable balance" and "a widening and enriching of awareness." (p. 293).

— "No archetype can be reduced...": **Jung**, *Coll. Works*, v. 9, Pt. I, par. 301, p. 179.

— "One of the greatest..." down to "formation of attachment...": **Stevens**, *Archetypes*, p. 110.

— CHILD'S BASIC NEEDS AND AGGRESSION AROUSED: Ibid., p. 133-134.

— "the sadist who...": Ibid., p. 134.

— STORY OF CLIENT C.: Ibid., p. 115-117.

— "What Jung failed...": Ibid, p. 59.

— "that the metapsychological foundations...": **J. P. Henry**, "Comment." This "Comment" was printed, immediately following Ernest Rossi, "The Cerebral Hemispheres in Analytical Psychology." *Journal of Analytical Psychology* 22 (Jan. 1977). The "Comment" is on pp. 52-57. **Add. notes**: As noted in the text, Henry is the author, along with P. M. Stephens, of *Stress, Health, and the Social Environment: A Sociobiologic Approach to Medicine*. New York: Springer-Verlag, 1977. In the Preface they acknowledge primitive cultures and note that what such cultures did to maintain stability in human relations "may be as much a part of man's biologic inheritance as his speech." It's a fairly technical book but very important.

— "I would not speak ill...": **Jung**, "Mind and Earth." In *Coll. Works*, v. 10, par. 103, p. 49.

— "it is an innate urge...": **Jung**, *Coll. Works*, v. 11.

Ch. 7 Lessons From Primitive Cultures
pp. 80 and 81 Opening Quotes

— "I just want to put...": **Sol Tax**, "Part VII: Hunting and Human Evolution.-Discussions, Part VII, c) Future Agenda." In Richard B. Lee and Irven DeVore, eds. *Man the Hunter*. Chicago: Aldine Publishing Co., 1968, p. 345. **Add. notes**: As the Preface explains, "Sol Tax asked us to organize a symposium on current research among the hunting and gathering peoples of the world." It was held at the University of Chicago in April 1966. In attendance were some 75 scholars from as far afield as India, Japan, Kenya etc. This conference, bringing together experts from many different fields, changed the entire perspective on our hunting/gathering ancestors. Sol Tax made this statement, which I quote at the end of the discussion and reflects the over-all feeling of the conference. Before, in general, "primitives" were studied as interesting examples of long-ago sub-humans; after this conference it came be realized that on the contrary we could and must learn from them, before it is too late, about how to live rightly on this earth.

At the time of the conference there were still many fully-functioning cultures left. Today, only some 20 years later, all of them have been violated to some extent by our Industrial Growth Society. While data which I use in this work on particular cultures was valid at the time it was gathered—often only a few years ago—it may no longer accurately reflect how that people lives today. But still in the memory of the older ones the real life continues and we can learn from them. As Peter Berg of Planet Drum says: "Such people would be more interesting to hear from than to destroy. We could learn from them about who we are and what we're doing here." ("Bioregional Culture": tape of Peter Berg, available from Finn Hill Arts.)

— "It seems to me that...": **Tom Jay**, "The Salmon of the Heart".

— "This was the beginning of my...": **Tobias Schneebaum**, *Keep the River on Your Right*. New York: Grove Press, 1970, p. 69.

— "The problem may be more difficult...": **Shepard**, *Nature and Madness*, p. 129.

— "Conscience is not a colonial...": **Midgley**, *Beast and Man*, p. 274.

— "After the Plains' Tribes were forcibly...": **Frank Waters**, *The Colorado*. New York: Holt Rinehart & Winston, 1974, p. 257.

— "A 'real' person...": **Jerome Rothenberg**, *Technicians of the Sacred*. pp. xx, 425 and 426.

82 "And when the other day...": **Lewis Mumford**, "Summary Remarks: Prospect." In William L. Thomas Jr., ed. *Man's Role in Changing the Face of The Earth*, pp. 1141-1152.

— "In the five thousand years...": **Oakes Ames**. Quoted in Anderson, *Plants Man and Life*, p. 133-134. Ames made this statement in *Economic Annuals and Human Cultures*. Cambridge: Botanical Museum of Harvard University, 1939.

— RESERPIN: **Simeons**, *Man's Presumptuous Brain*, p. 153.

— BARON LAHONTAN AND THE NOBLE SAVAGE: **Baron de Lahontan**, *New Voyages to North America*. Edited by Rueben Gold Thwaites (2 v.). Chicago: 1905. Mentioned in Carl Sauer, *Seventeenth Century North America*. Berkeley: Turtle Island, 1980, p. 253.

— "communal and traditional...": **Stanley Diamond**, *In Search of the Primitive*. New Brunswick: Transaction Books, Rutgers University, 1974, p. 135.

— "some social scientists...": **Roy Rappaport and Andrew Vayda**, "Ecology, Cultural and Noncultural."

— "Hannon has recently...": **Roy Rappaport**, "Energy and the Structure of Adaptation." *Coevolution Quarterly* (spring, 1974): 20-28. He is quoting Bruce Hannon, *Man in the Ecosystem*. Urbana-Champaign, University of Illinois, 1973. **Add. notes**: Rappaport's article provides an excellent introduction to a very important subject. In his abstract Rappaport states: "Issue is taken with the assumption that increases in the amount of energy harnessed by a society improves its adaptation."

— PROPAGANDA AND PRIMITIVES: **Jacques Ellul**, *Propaganda: The Formation of Man's Attitudes*. New York: 1965. The actual quote I use is Barrington Nevitt's summation of Ellul's statements. In "Pipeline or Grapevine: The Changing Communications Environment."

— "the differentiation between phantasy...": **J. Silverman**, "Shamans and Acute Schizophrenia." *American Anthropologist*. (1967). Quoted in Hans Duerr, *Dreamtime*, p. 310.

— "Only the latter, however...": **Duerr**, *Dreamtime*, p. 310.

83 "is not a progressive evolutionary...": **L. L. Wassiliev**, *Experimentelle Untersuchungen zur Mentalsuggestion*. Bern, 1965, p. 155. Quoted in Duerr, *Dreamtime*, p. 343.

— "psychic functioning is no more exceptional...": **Stephan Schwartz**, "Dowsing and Consciousness Panel Discussion," part of the Symposium on Dowsing and Consciousness at the 1985 Annual Convention of the American Society of Dowsers. In the *American Dowser Quarterly Digest* 26 (February 1986): 29. **Add. notes**: We get our color vision from our primate ancestors. It was useful for them to be able to tell if the fruit in the next tree was ripe. We still find yellow and orange colors "good." See Paul Shepard, *Man in the Landscape*.

— "is necessarily pathogenic...": **Gregory Batson**, "Style, Grace, and Information in Primitive Art." In Anthony Forge, (ed.) *Primitive Art and Society*. This quotation is reprinted on p. 146 in *Steps to an Ecology of Mind*.

— "largely based...": **"The Burden of the Utopians,"** *Manas*, v. xxx (1977), p. 1 (no author).

— "impossible" and "contrary to human nature...": **Arthur Morgan**, *Nowhere was Somewhere*. University of North Carolina Press, 1946. (Quoted in *Manas*.)

— "I was being given rituals...": **Diamond**, *In Search of the Primitive*, p. 71.

— THE TUKANO: **G. Reichel-Dolmatoff**, "Cosmology as Ecological Analysis: A View from the Rain Forest." *Man: Journal of the Royal Anthropological Institute II* (September 1978). **Add. notes**: I have to report that due to U.S. "substance" addiction this sophisticated ecological culture is crumbling. Some Tukano have become middle-men in the drug exchange thus opening themselves up to all the destruction of a consumer culture. They've become cocaine pickers and to some extent processors for the international drug business. A television special on cocaine showed scenes of these activities.

84 THE TSEMBAGA: **Roy Rappaport**, *Pigs for the Ancestors*.

— THE ARAPESH: **Dorothy Lee**, "Are Basic Needs Ultimate."

— TIKOPIA ISLAND: **Raymond Firth**, *Tikopia Ritual and Belief*. London: George Allen & Unwin, 1967, pp. 16 and 17.

— "the mode of life...": Ibid., p. 17.

— "at this moment of discovery..." down to "work can take place among the Tikopia...": **Dorothy Lee**, "The Joy of Work as Participation." In *Freedom and Culture*. **Add. notes**: The three books by Firth, which she refers to are: *We the Tiikopia*, *Primitive Polynesian Economy* and *The Work of the Gods, Parts I and II*.

85 "the finest looking...": The painter, **Catlin**, quoted in Walter McClintock, *The Old North Trail: Or Life, Legends and Religion of the Blackfeet Indians*. Lincoln: University of Nebraska Press, 1968, p. 2. (Reprint of the original 1910 volume.)

— BACKBONE-OF-THE-WORLD: **McClintock**, *The Old North Trail*, p. 13.

— "including the elemental processes...": **Jay Vest**, "Traditional Blackfeet Religion and the Badger-Two Medicine Wildlands", p. 5. Unpublished paper. **Add. notes**: We will be hearing a lot more about Jay Vest, hopefully, in the near future, because he is doing something no one else is attempting. Among other things, what he is trying to do is put essential Indian concepts into western philosophical terms so that they will be seen as philosophy in the full sense of the word. Also his "wilderness praxis" work is very hopeful for the saving of wilderness. It is part of his recently completed dissertation. He has worked in federal and state service as a forester, environmental coordinator, outdoor recreation planner and wilderness specialist. He holds degrees in philosophy: The Philosophy of Ecology and Interdisciplinary Studies: Primal Religions (Native American and Indo-European) from the University of Montana. See Vest's "Will-of-the-Land: Wilderness Among Primal Indo-Europeans" in the "Back of the Book" section in this volume.

— "an ultimate life principle..." down to "did not think...": Ibid.

— EXTERMINATION OF BUFFALO: **McClintock**, *Old North Trail*, p. 509.

— "It is a difficult matter...": Ibid.

— "just as the sun rose...": Ibid., p. 262. **Add. notes:** The entire chapter xix of McClintock's book is well worth reading for anyone seriously interested in how ritual governing of a tribe works.

— CRAZY DOG SOCIETY: Ibid., p. 243.

— DAILY LIFE IN BRING-DOWN-THE SUN'S CAMP: Ibid., p. 387-394.

86 "seated in this ancestral...": Ibid., p. 393-394.

— "When these Native Americans...": **Jay Vest**, "Algonquian Metaphysics and Wildness." Unpublished paper.

— "Yonder on all sides...": **Hamilton Tyler**, *Pueblo Animals and Myths.* Norman: University of Oklahoma Press, 1975, p. xi.

— "The total society generates...": **Jaime de Angulo**, quoted in Bob Callahan, *The Netzahualcoyotl News* 1 (summer 1979). Berkeley: Turtle Island Foundation, 1979.

— "is our totem...": **Barry Lopez** in a talk at the Women and Wilderness Conference, organized by Flo Krall of the University of Utah, October 22, 1981 in Salt Lake City, Utah.

— RUTH BENEDICT'S "SYNERGISTIC CULTURE": **Add notes:** For my complete account of Ruth Benedict's "synergistic culture", see *Earth Wisdom*, pp. 120-121. The article concerning the finding of her long lost ms. is T. George Harris, "About Ruth Benedict and Her Lost Manuscript." *Psychology Today* (June 1970). This complete ms. of Benedict's was published in *American Anthropologist* 72 (1970).

87 "was...the original...": **Marshall Sahlins**, "Notes on the Original Affluent Society." In Lee and DeVore, *Man the Hunter*, p. 85.

— WORK TIME OF AUSTRALIAN ABORIGINES AND THE KUNG: Ibid, p. 89.

— "It is no accident...": **Paul Shepard**, *The Tender Carnivore and the Sacred Game*, p. 150. **Add. notes:** In this chapter I have given just a very brief introduction into the whole field of what we can learn from primitive cultures. The word "primitive" is not helpful. Other words used for this concept have been "original human," "indigenous," "aboriginal" and "future primitive." Sylvia Wynter, from Jamaica, explains: "[W]e find that the quest of the primitive is a misnomer for the quest of *human being* now reified into a commodity." (*Alcheringa/Ethnopoetics*, 1976, p. 87.) For more information on the "original human," I recommend: *The Tender Carnivore and the Sacred Game* by Paul Shepard, *In Search of the Primitive: A Critique of Civilization* by Stanley Diamond, and for greater depth, *Man the Hunter* ed. by Lee and DeVore. *Pigs for the Ancestors* by Roy Rappaport provides the best analysis of how rituals work in regulating a culture.

Ch. 8 Taoism

Note: Because this chapter constitutes the deep core of this work, I provide more opening quotes than usual. It is important to realize that Taoism provides us with a way out of the Greek language trap and Plato. Once this is understood then Taoism is no longer a "fuzzy, mystical, Eastern idea," as most western academics think of it, but the way to once again begin to live according to the way nature designed us. What I've tried to do in this chapter is keep the text as simple as possible so that the general reader can follow the discussion. Here in the references I go deeper into each aspect covered in the main text.

A further note on Chinese terms in this chapter: In general I am using the older romanisation of Chinese characters, because that's what most of my sources use. The reason that the names for Chinese persons and places now look so different is that the previous romanisation was essentially based on the French language. If you spoke French the words came out sounding similar to the Chinese pronunciation; however, using this system, English speaking people were not pronouncing the words anywhere near the Chinese way. For example, Peking, as the English speaking people pronounce the French romanized word, versus Beijing, which is the way we all say it now. The latter is more true to the original Chinese pronunciation. Basically, now, instead of being French based it's English based so that the words we use are more nearly pronounced as in the Chinese pronunciation. In the older system, called the Wade-Giles system, Chuang Chou was the spelling used for the Taoist. In the new system, called the *pinyin* system, it is written, Zhuang Zhou. In Chinese words within my quotes from Needham, I have kept his extra letter "h" in Chinese words. which he had introduced as a substitute for the aspirate apostrophe. (Ex. he uses *chhien* for the more usual *ch'ien*.)

pp. 88 and 89 Opening Quotes

— "natural phenomena as being identical...": **William La Fleur**, "Saigyō and the Value of Nature: Pt. I." *History of Religions* 13 (November 1973): 93-128. **Add. notes:** I owe the inspiration for this entire "Opening Dialogue" to La Fleur's footnote No. 34 on page 122.

— "Landscape was not just...": **J. D. Frodsham**, "The Origins of Chinese Nature Poetry." *Asia Major* 8 Pt. 1 (1960): 68-104.

— "When the Tao dissolves...": **Sun Ch'o**. Ibid.

— "So the contemplation...": La Fleur, "Saigyō and the Value of Nature: Pt. I."

— "Ling-yün's own experience...": **J. D. Frodsham**, *The Murmuring Stream*, 1967, pp. 63-64, quoted in La Fleur, "Saigyō: Pt. I."

— "it was forced...": **La Fleur**, "Saigyō: Pt. I."

— "The Ruler of the South...": **Chuang Tzu**. I have combined two different translations of this story from Chuang Tzu, Ch. 7: 1: first, James Legge trans. *The Texts of Taoism*, v. 1. New York: Dover, 1962, pp. 266-267 and second, Burton Watson, The *Complete Works of Chuang Tzu*. New York: Columbia University Press, 1968, p. 92. **Add. notes:** The philosopher's name is Chuang Chou. The book, bearing his name, called the *Chuang Tzu*, probably contains his own essays and those of his followers, but, in general, quotations from this book are credited to Chuang Tzu.

— "When you use the word...": **John Cage**, *New York Times* 23 (May 25, 1969): 3.

— "The West teaches us...": **Octavio Paz**, quoted in *Claude Lévi-Strauss: An Introduction*. London: Jonathan Cape, 1971, p. 94.

— "The Confucians say that...": **Tony Robbins**, "All Things Are What They Are." *Main Currents in Modern Thought* 32 (October 1975): 20.

— "It might seem...": **Chuang Tzu**, chapter 2. J. Legge. trans. *The Texts of Taoism*, v. 1. Oxford: Oxford University Press, 1891, p. 179.

— "...two entirely different world-views..." down to "Completely different...": **Toshihiko Izutsu**, "The Temporal and A-Temporal Dimensions of Reality in Confucian Metaphysics." *Eranos Yearbooks* 43 (1974): 411-447. This statement appeared on pp. 413-414. **Add. notes:** This was a lecture which Izutsu gave at the Eranos Conference in Switzerland, titled "Norms in a Changing World." I consider Izutsu's clear differentiation between these two ways of viewing the world to be of such importance that I am giving the exact page on which each of the following quotations occur to facilitate finding them within the printed lecture.

— "But the main point...": Ibid., p. 415.

— "The...fundamentally optimistic..": Ibid, p. 417.

— "Plunging in with the whirl...": **Lieh Yu-Khou**. A. C. Graham. trans. *The Book of Lieh Tzu*. London: 1960, p. 44.

— "verbatim: life-giving life, the procreating...": **Hellmut Wilhelm**, *Heaven, Earth and Man in the Book of Changes*. Seattle: University of Washington Press, p. 189. **Add. notes:** Hellmut Wilhelm is the son of Richard Wilhelm, who sent his translation of *The Secret of the Golden Flower* to Jung. In Jung's Memorial Address in 1930, he mentions his "grateful reverence" for Richard Wilhelm's work and states that "the greatest of his achievements is the translation of, and commentary on, the *I Ching*." (*Secret of the Golden Flower*, p. 139.) *Heaven, Earth, and Man* contains seven lectures which Hellmut Wilhelm gave at Eranos conferences through the years; thus providing the culmination of two generations of work to help Europeans understand the *I Ching*.

90 "that while European philosophy...": **Joseph Needham**, *Sci.and Civil.*, v. 2, p. 478. **Add. notes:** For more on this very important statement, see the notes below for page 93.

— "Taoists were keenly interested in nourishing...": **Wing-Tsit Chan**: "Syntheses in Chinese Metaphysics." (This quote occurs on p.141 of his long paper.)

— "NATURE, THE MOTHER OF ALL THINGS": **Needham**, *Sci. and Civil.*, v. 2, p. 164.

— MAP FOR POPULATION UNDER THE HAN DYNASTY: **Caroline Blunden and Mark Elvin**, *Cultural Atlas of China*, p. 30. **Add. notes:** Further explanation of the map is given on page 37: "...distribution of population under the Han dynasty shows that, outside the north plain, the real China of 2000 years ago consisted of thin arms of settlement along river valleys. The higher ground in between was occupied by non-Han peoples..." and "Several of the non-Han states that emerged in the south and southwest now and later were also led by Chinese emigrés who had 'gone native'." Needham in *The Grand Titration*, p. 253: "...the ancient Taoist philosophers...harked back always to the ancient paradise of generalized tribal nobility, of co-operative primitivity, of spontaneous collectivism...They were probably stimulated in this by the persistence of pre-feudal relationships among some of the tribal peoples on the fringe of Chinese society, such as those who have been known as the Miao, Chiang, Lo-lo and Chia-jung in our own time, and are only now, after more than two millennia, being integrated into Chinese society as a whole."

—— "Wars and diplomatic...": **Needham**, *Sci. and Civil.*, v. 2, p. 3.

—— *Kuan*, "TO LOOK": Ibid. p. 56.

91 "do nothing contrary to nature": Ibid. v. 2, p. 68. **Add. notes:** The actual translation which Needham uses is "refraining from activity contrary to Nature."

—— "It is well to observe...": **Francis Bacon**: *Novum Organum*, book 1, aphorism 129. Quoted in Needham, *Sci. and Civil.*, v. 1, p. 19. **Add. notes:** I used this quote back in chapter three; I repeat it here again for emphasis.

—— "It is often forgotten...": **Joseph Needham**, *The Grand Titration: Science and Society in East and West*, p. 211

—— "With their appreciation of relativism...": **Needham**, *Sci. and Civil.*, v.2, p. 543.

—— "...modern agriculture, modern shipping...": **Robert Temple**, *The Genius of China: 3000 Years of Science, Discovery and Invention*. New York: Simon and Schuster, 1986, p. 9.

—— MANNED FLIGHT WITH KITES: Ibid, pp. 175-178.

—— SINGLE STRAND OF SILK—TENSILE STRENGTH OF 65,000 POUNDS: Ibid, p. 120.

—— "I could no longer tell...": **Lieh Tzu**, Ch. 2, quoted in Max Kaltenmark, *Lao Tzu and Taoism*, p. 88.

—— NEEDHAM'S 3 V. CHEMICAL EMBRYOLOGY: In the brochure distributed at the three Needham lectures, which the University of Washington sponsored: "Jessie & John Danz Lecturer: Explorations in Chinese Science" by Joseph Needham, June 28 to June 30, 1977.

—— "I shall never forget the excitement...": **Needham**, *Sci. and Civil.*, v. 4, Pt. I, p. 250. **Add. notes:** Temple provides additional information here."One day he [Needham] met and befriended some Chinese students, in particular a young woman from Nanking named Lu Gwei-djen, whose father had passed on to her his unusually profound knowledge of the history of Chinese science. Needham began to hear tales of how the Chinese had been the true discoverers of this and that important thing, and at first he could not believe it. But as he looked further into it, evidence began to come to light from Chinese texts..." Needham was 37 at the time. (Temple, *Genius of China*, p. 10)

—— ENVOY FROM THE ROYAL SOCIETY TO CHINA: **Temple**, *Genius of China*, p. 10.

92 "Without the importation...": Ibid, p. 9.

—— THE QUESTION OF SCIENCE IN CHINA: **Needham** provides the quickest insights into this matter in chapter 6: "Science and Society in East and West." of *The Grand Titration*, pp. 190-217. For instance on page 202: "Wealth as such was not valued. It had no spiritual power. It could give comfort but not wisdom, and in China affluence carried comparatively little prestige."

—— "...the sciences of China..." down to "unbelievably dangerous": **Needham**, "Introduction." In Temple, *Genius of China*, p. 8.

—— "Yet who shall say...": **Needham**, Jessie and John Danz Lecture at the University of Washington, Lecture One—June 28, 1977. Unpublished.

—— THE I CHING: **Add. notes:** Before beginning this section it is well to clarify the commentaries and appendices to the *I Ching*, which are known as the "Ten Wings" because the matter is confusing. Most of the ten parts of this "Ten Wings" are supposedly written by Confucius, but that is not necessarily true in all cases. The most important of these are the fifth and sixth which have been known since the early Han dynasty (202 B.C.-9 A.D.) as "The Great Appendix." This forms Appendix III in Legge's translations and in Wilhelm's translation it is called "The Great Treatise." Needham states that the "editions of R. Wilhelm, especially the English translation by Baynes (quite sound in itself), constitute unfortunately a sinological maze, and belong to the Department of Utter Confusion...Wilhelm, the only person from first to last who knew what

it was all about...presented the late commentary material as an amorphous mass with no indication" of dates or authors. Needham says it's the "more regrettable because the uniqueness of the work itself fully deserved the munificence of the Foundation which gave the typographical beauty of the English translation." So, if you've been totally confused by the maze of English translations of the *I Ching*, as I have, don't give up. Read Needham for background: *Sci. and Civil.*, v. 2, pp. 304—345.

E. R. Hughes' explanation is also useful. Explaining the hexagrams, he states: "The significant thing is that these symbols, i.e., the lines in the hexagrams and the trigrams, were regarded as centers of energy continually acting and reacting on each other according to their relative positions." These hexagrams "were linked...by a sort of science of symbolism to the yin and the yang [female/male] and the five elements: [earth, air, fire, water and metal]." Thus use of the hexagrams provided a "direct clue"...to the "nature of the universe with its correlation of phenomena in the heavens and phenomena on earth...One triumph of the system was what can only be called its ecological good sense. The plumage of birds and the pigmentation of animals' skins were guessed at as deriving from the nature of the terrain in which the birds and animals lived." (p. 86-87 of E. R. Hughes, "Epistemological Methods in Chinese Philosophy.") According to Joseph Needham, Hughes was the " foremost sinologist at Oxford." For more on Hughes see my notes to page 93, below.

—— "take up in detail...": **Wilhelm**, *Heaven, Earth and Man*, p. 6. **Add. notes:** Four different ways of divination "are at the bottom" of the *I Ching* (The Book of Changes): 1) omen interpretations of peasants; 2) "drawing by lot" using yarrow stalks; 3) divination from the cracks made by putting turtle shells or shoulder blades of animals into the fire (keeping track of these led to the "oracle bone" inscriptions out of which came early writing in China); and 4) divining by using some form of tablets (the Chinese word for the hexagrams is *kua*, meaning tablet). The use of bones in fires for divination was widespread among early hunting societies. Essentially, divining is a way of by-passing the narrow rational consciousness to allow information from the older brains to help in decision making.

Today, people use 64 yarrow stalks or three coins to throw the I Ching. The hexagrams are made up of sets of lines—unbroken ones are yang lines and broken ones are yin lines. This probably came out of the yarrow stalk divination. (See Needham, *Sci. and Civil.*, v. 2, pp. 304-309 for more on this.)

—— "he is to be in accordance...": Ibid, p. 153. **Add. notes:** Wilhelm adds that, in the early stratra of the *I Ching*, "heaven is still the name for the highest deity, a name the early Chou had in common with other peoples who came up out of the steppes." and "Earth is the primordial, often uncanny power of the arable soil, in its turn the keeper of souls that have returned to the eternal night." (p. 153)

—— "When in early antiquity...": **R. Wilhelm and C. Baynes**, trans. *I Ching*. New York: Pantheon, 1950, p. 328-329.

—— "[T]he concept *I* as such...": **Wilhelm**, *Heaven, Earth and Man*, p, 3.

—— "Life-giving life, the procreating...": Ibid., p. 189.

93 HISTORICAL BACKGROUND ON TAOISM: **Needham**, *Sci. and Civil.*, v. 2, pp. 33-35.

—— TAO TE CHING: **Max Kaltenmark**, *Lao Tzu and Taoism*, p. 12.

—— "Aristotle was old...": **Needham**, *Sci. and Civil.*, v. 2, p. 35.

—— "As political stability...": Ibid, p. 214.

—— CHUANG TZU: **Burton Watson**, *Chuang Tzu: Basic Writings*. New York: Columbia University Press, 1964., pp. 1-3.

—— "Taoism was religious...": **Needham**, *Sci. and Civil.*, v. 2, p. 35.

—— "As a matter of fact...": **Chang Tung-Sun**, "A Chinese Philosopher's Theory of Knowledge." *Etc.: A Review of General Semantics* 9 (1952): 203-226. **Add. notes:** This relatively little-known article is of fundamental importance. Because it's not easy to come by I am going to quote a few important passages from it : (1) p. 207: "Newtonian physics starts with matter in the form of concrete things. Hence the conceptions of absolute motion, and absolute space and time. But modern physics takes cognizance of concrete matter only as a point in the framework of time and space." [Hence more in keeping with Chinese thought.] (2) p. 210: "The traditional type of subject-predicate proposition is absent in Chinese logic." (3) p. 211-212: "As we know, Aristotle's philosophy was made possible entirely by the use of 'identity-logic.' For him the substance is merely derived from the subject and the verb 'to be'...from the subject, because in a subject-predicate proposition the subject cannot be eliminated. From the indispensability of the subject in a sentence, only a short step leads to the necessity for a 'substratum' in thought. For example, when we say, 'this is yellow and hard' yellowness and hardness are the so-called 'attributes' which are attributed to something, the something in this case being 'this.' The 'something' in general is the substratum. With a substratum emerges the idea of 'substance.' The idea of substance is indeed a foundation or fountainhead for all other philosophical developments. If there is any description, it becomes an attribute. An attribute must be attributed to a substance, thus the idea of substance is absolutely necessary in thought, in the same way as the subject is absolutely necessary in language. **This is the reason why in the history of Western philosophy, no matter how different the arguments may be, pro or con, about the idea of substance, it is the idea of substance which itself constitutes the central problem.**" (my use of boldface for emphasis) (4) p. 213:"The Chinese system of logic, *if we may call it a system, is not based upon the law of identity*...[it] puts no emphasis on exclusiveness, rather it emphasizes the relational quality between above and below, good and evil, something and nothing. All these relatives are supposed to be interdependent." (5) Essentially we might say, p. 215: "The Chinese are merely interested in the inter-relations between the different signs, without being bothered by the substance underlying them." (6) p. 217: "[T]he idea of causality is derived from that of substance." (7) p. 218: "The idea of the Supreme Being or a Creator is closely correlated with the idea of Substance...We may maintain that there are three fundamental categories in Western thought, substance, causality, and atoms. Religion has a foundation in substance. With causality science is developed, and from atoms materialism is derived."

Another aspect is made obvious by the way we use language. It's a well-known fact that the Eskimo have over twenty different words for snow. Less well known is the fact that Polynesian peoples do not have one word for the yam. They have instead, one word for a just-beginning-to-grow yam; one for a young yam, one for a green yam, one for a ripe yam, another for a yam used for one purpose, and still another when used for a different purpose. This is far from the word yam, as a substance, which is just yam. In the Polynesian languages each of the words for yam take into consideration the time of year, the length of the growing season, the time of harvest, the human uses of the yams and sometimes the needs of the yam itself. In other words, relationship. My colleague, Julien Puzey, in Salt Lake City, was trying to explain this to her class in deep ecology and getting nowhere; when suddenly an Indian in the back of the room, who had not said a word the entire quarter spoke up and said: "The rain is on the yellow corn." And he said nothing more; he didn't have to. It was all there (for a tribal society): the season, the stage of growing of the corn (mature), the promise of food for the winter, and, of course, all the mythological connotations of corn and rain. Julien also has a new definition of genius: "Genius bypasses wasted motion and substance by directly perceiving necessary and sufficient relationship."

93 "The main distinction...": **E. R. Hughes,** *The Great Learning and the Mean-in-Action*. New York: E. P. Dutton, 1943, p. 52. **Add. notes:** *Mean-in-Action*, is usually translated, the Doctrine of the Mean. The Chinese title is *Chung Yung, chung* meaning "centrality." In The Sung dynasty (1127 to 1279 A. D.), *The Great Learning* was made the first of the "Four Books" and the *Mean-in-Action*, the second. (The originals of both books were written between the sixth and first centuries, B.C, revised by Taoist influenced, Neo Confucianists of the Sung Dynasty.) The "Great Learning" (Ta Hsueh) is dated by Needham to about 260 B.C. The best explanation of what this "learning" is about is quoted in Needham v. 2, p. 25: "...I realized that Meng Tzu is talking about the heaven-nature and what he calls the goodness of human referred to its (innate) uprightness and greatness. He wished to encourage it. That is what the Ta Hsueh calls (developing) sincerity." (Tai Chih, thirteenth century A.D.) The great Neo-Confucian, Chu Hsi "rewrote" the "Great Learning." (p. 392 of Needham, v. 2.)

Hughes wrote this book in 1939, just before the outbreak of WW II; hence it was largely overlooked. While this book does provide more

insight into the substance problem, it's real importance here is that he gives facts about how Chinese thinking got to the West and in these facts we find the true beginnings of most of what is valid in western thinking concerning nature: particularly to do with Leibniz, Rousseau, and further, Leibniz's influence on Spinoza. The latter leads in a direct line down to "deep ecology." because as, Arne Naess maintains, his main philosophical influence was Spinoza. Leibniz began his "passion" for information on things Chinese in his early twenties, (which would be 1666). Spinoza lived until 1677.

Confucius, Sinarum, Philosophus Sive Scientia Sinensis, written by Jesuit missionaries who had been in China: Intorcetta, Rougemont and Couplet, was published in Paris in 1687 and was widely read all over Western Europe—in Italy, Spain, France, Belgium, Holland and England. (p. 4) Here again I will give specific quotes and the pages from Hughes' book.

(1) p. 12: Concerning Leibniz: "from his early twenties to the last of his seventy years had a passion for information on China, and took every opportunity he had of forgathering with the Jesuit missionaries...there are some particularly close resemblances between Leibniz' special theories and what he could find in *Confucius, Sinarum Philosophus*. That he read this in the year it was published we know from a letter of that year." (2) p. 17: Leibniz and Rousseau; "for it was through their minds more than any one else's that Confucianist philosophy came." (3) p. 18: About Leibniz: "In fact, China became a major interest of his life, and for more than forty years he studied and did all he could to stir up the world to an interest in their philosophy...He was also in correspondence with some of the Jesuit missionaries." There were reasons why Leibniz could not acknowledge his debt to Chinese writings. (4) p. 20: "[T]he major explanation of his silence may well lie in the fact that in the long and bitter struggle between the Jesuits and their enemies over Chinese religion, it was the Jesuits who were beaten. In 1704 the pope and the Inquisition decided finally that the Scholars' Religion" was not acceptable. (5) p. 15: To Voltaire the most widely read author in western Europe, [*Sinarum* was] a continual source of inspiration...In Confucianism, the "Scholars' Religion" as the Jesuit Fathers had taught him to call it, he saw the living archetype of that "Natural Religion." (6) p. 19: "...when Leibniz read this work he was actually imbibing Confucianism very largely through the Sung adaptation of it." (This was essentially the Neo-Confucianism of Hu Chi, greatly influenced by Taoism.) The "Scholars' Religion" was "hailed as a useful corroboration of theories about 'Natural Religion'." (Background information on E. R. Hughes: He was a missionary in the interior of China from 1911-1929, Prof. of Chinese language and literature at Oxford from 1941-1947 and visiting professor of Chinese at Claremont Graduate School in California. He died in Oct. 1956.—from bibl. information in Moore, ed. *The Chinese Mind*.)

What I want to make clear here is that most of the European thinkers, which modern eco-philosophers point to as possible antecedants for modern western ecological thought, were deeply influenced by Neo-Confucian thought as coming out of China through the Jesuits at this time.

Concerning Leibniz specifically, Needham points out that the "philosophies of *organism*" whether that of Lloyd Morgan and Smuts with their emergent evolution or of certain ideas in biology or of "Whitehead himself and the full organic view of the world. If these ideas are traced backward in the thought of Europe they lead to Leibniz and then they seem to disappear." And, again he writes "from Whitehead back to Engels and Hegel, from Hegel to Leibniz...the theoretical foundations of the most modern 'European' natural science owe more to men such as Chuang Chou... and Chu Hsi than the world has yet realised." (See Needham, *Sci. and Civil.*, v. 2, pp. 496-505 for the complete discussion). On p. 340 of the same volume, Needham goes into Leibniz and mathematics. From 1697 to 1702, Leibniz was in continuous correspondence with Fr. Bouvet, a Jesuit missionary in China, who was particularly interested in the *I Ching*. Needham explains, on page 341, "The discovery that the I Ching hexagrams could be interpreted as another way of writing numbers according to the binary system, if the unbroken lines were taken to represent 1, and the broken lines to represent 0, seems to have been in the first place the idea of Bouvet rather than of Leibniz." Again, on p. 344, Needham says: "the binary or dyadic arithmetic of Leibniz...has been found to be, as Wiener points out in his important book on "cybernetics", the most suitable system for the great computing machines of the present day;" and again, p. 344: "It is thus no coincidence that Liebniz, besides developing the binary arithmetic, was also the founder of modern mathematical logic and a pioneer in the construction of calculating machines." (See Needham, v. 2, pp. 340-345.)

94 "to assert the existence or non-existence...": **Charles Wei-hsun Fu**, "Lao Tzu's Conception of Tao."
— "shackled by his self-created human...": Ibid
— "We are constantly...": **Benjamin Lee Whorf**, "Time, Space and Language." I am once again using this quotation, first used in chapter one, because it gives the most concise example.
— "entity, substance, God...": **Charles Wei-hsun Fu**, "Lao Tzu's Conception." pp. 367-391.
— "absolute idealism—idealism carried...": Ibid.
— "non-being' or 'nameless Tao...": Ibid.

95 "in a nutshell the essential nature...": Ibid.
— "The Tao that can be tracked...": Ibid.
— "In such understanding...": **Kuang-Ming Wu**, *Chuang Tzu: World Philosopher at Play*, pp. 32 and 34.
— "[F]or the Taoists...": **Needham**, *Sci. and Civil.*, v. 2.
— "refraining from activity...": Ibid, p. 68.
— "power may be exercised...": Ibid, p. 68. Needham is quoting from the ancient Chinese document, *Huai Nan Tzu*. E. Morgan. trans. *Tao the Great Luminant: Essays from 'Huai Nan Tzu'.* Shanghai, Kelly & Walsh, 1933, pp. 220, 224-225.
— "(The operations of) heaven and earth...": **Chuang Tzu**, J. Legge trans. *The Texts of Taoism*, v. 2. Oxford: Oxford Univ. Press, 1891, p. 60.
— "the mysterious government of the blue sky...": **Robert Payne** (ed.) *The White Pony*, p. 24.
— "However fast the horses of logical...": **Needham**, *Sci. and Civil.*, v. 2, p. 73.
— "they would find...": **Master Lu**, *Lu Shih Chhun Chhiu (Master Lu's Spring and Autumn Annals)*, 239 B.C. Needham used the translation by *Hellmut Wilhelm: Gesellschaft und Staat in China*. Peiping: Vetch, 1944, p. 434. In Needham, v. 2, p. 73.
— "from Yü the Great...": **Shen Tao**, *Shen Tzu*, dating from the Warring States period, just prior to Chuang Tzu. In Needham, v. 2, p. 73.
— "learnt from the bow and not from...": **Kuan Yin Tzu** (from the Thang dynasty about the 8th century A.D.). In Needham, v.2, p. 73. **Add. notes:** I have given a number of these examples because they are actually "affordances,"—non-human beings which "afford" us humans the opportunity to learn or do. See chapter nine for more on this important concept.

95-96 STONE QUARRYING IN ENGLAND: **Jacquetta Hawkes**, *A Land*. London: Newton Abbot, 1978, pp. 122-123. (First published in the early 1950s.)

96 N. J. GIRARDOT, "CHAOTIC 'ORDER' (*HUN-TUN*) AND BENEVOLENT 'DISORDER' (*LUAN*) IN THE *CHUANG TZU*." *Philosophy East and West* (July 1978). Girardot at that time was Professor of Religions in the Theology Dept. at Notre Dame.
— N. J. GIRARDOT, *MYTH AND MEANING IN EARLY TAOISM: THE THEME OF CHAOS (HUN-TUN)*. Berkeley: University of California Press, 1983. By that time Girardot had become Chair of the Religion Studies Department at Lehigh University.
— "Mankind emerges from a gourd...": **Ting-jui Ho**, *A Comparative study of Myths and Legends of Formosan Aborigines*. Taipei: The Orient Cultural Service, 1971. Quoted in Girardot, *Myth and Meaning*, p. 213.
— "The gourd lives in human consciousness...": **Donald Lathrap**, "Our Father the Cayman."
— "truly amazing...": **Girardot**, *Myth and Meaning*, p. 212.
— BASIC GOURD INFORMATION: Ibid, p. 223-224.
— "germs of life..." down to "ten thousand seeds...": Ibid.
— LAO TZU FROM THE STATE OF CHU: **Toshihiko Izutsu**, *A Comparative Study of the Key Philosophical Concepts in Sufism and Taoism*, p. 5. **Add. notes:** Izutsu points out that the spirit of the state of Ch'u runs through the entire book of Lao Tzu: "...what may properly be called shamanistic tendency of the mind or shamanistic mode of thinking. Ch'u was a large state lying on the southern periphery of the civilized Middle Kingdom, a land of wild marshes, rivers, forests and mountains...

inhabited by many people of a non-Chinese origin with variegated, strange customs...shamanistic practices thrived."

97 "precedes the creation...": **Girardot**, *Myth and Meaning*, p. 50.
— "The primary...": Ibid., p. 56.
— "The Tao gave birth...": Quoted in Girardot, p. 56. This is quoted directly from a Chinese publication—the English translation of the title is "Lao Tzu collated and explained."
— "It is the empty gap...": Ibid, p. 61.
— "nothingness...": Ibid, p. 62. **Add. notes:** This "nothingness" is what seems most to disturb Westerners. To explain further I quote: "Everybody agrees...that the future is what has not 'yet been' and is now nothing, and that the present, which was the future and becomes the past may be said to come from Nothing and go to Nothing. If we know deeply that everything comes from Nothing and goes back to Nothing, then all things may be taken as involved in a Great Nothing, or as floating out from the Great Nothing, only to sink into it again. Then not anything can really constitute bondage or disturb our spirit." (Tang Chün-I, "The Development of Spiritual Value in Chinese Philosophy.")
— "I [Hu Tzu] appeared to him...": **Hu Tzu**, quoted in Girardot, *Myth and Meaning*, p. 73.
— "myriad things returning...": **Yellow Court Canon**, quoted, Ibid., p. 285.
— "paradise" down to "linked by..." Ibid, p. 286.

98 "some existential..." down to "early Taoist texts...": Ibid, p. 15.
— "primitive chaos order...": Ibid, p. 3.
— "natural harmony of cosmos..." down to "to insure the return to...": Ibid, p. 154-155.

100 "call back to oneself...": **Kuang-Ming Wu**, *Chuang Tzu: World Philosopher at Play*, p. 34.
— "Gourd Master who has learned the secrets of creation...": **Girardot**, *Myth and Meaning*, p. 309.
— "By emphasizing...": Ibid, p. 260.
— ANIMAL FROLICS: **Kenneth Cohen**, "Taoist Shamanism." *Laughing Man*, pp. 48-52 (no date) Bubba Free John, organization, publisher.
— "The Taoist denial of anthropocentrism...": **Needham**, *Sci. and Civil.*, v. 2, p. 83.
— "The sage is concerned with the belly...": **Tao Te Ching**, Ch. 12 (trans. W. T. Chan), quoted in Girardot, *Myth and Meaning*, p. 266.
— "through the exercise of his 'evaluting mind'...": Ibid., p. 267.
— "identifies the Taoist...": Ibid., p. 268.
— "The purpose of the Taoist techniques...": **Needham**, *Sci. and Civil.*, v. 2, p. 149.
— "The True Man's activities...": **Kuang-Ming Wu**, *Chuang Tzu: World Philsopher at Play*, p. 124

101 "No longer is there prostitution...": Ibid, p. 125.
— "The future is uncertain...": **Herman Hesse**, *In Sight of Chaos*, pp. 63- 64. Quoted in Girardot, *Myth and Meaning*, p. 303.
— "this" and "that" and "pivot of the Tao...": **Chuang Tzu**, Ch. 2.
— "The Ten Thousand Things...": **Chuang Tzu**, Ch. 27. Quoted in Girardot, p. 305. (He used the Concordance to the Chuang Tzu and Burton Watson, *The Complete Works of Chuang Tzu*. New York: Columbia University Press, 1968, pp. 304-305.) **Add. notes:** Kuang-Ming Wu provides further insight: "Merleau-Ponty works his way up to a totality of the world; Chuang Tzu always plays *in* the world with a total (though indefinite) map of the non-being that 'beings' every being unobstrusively." Wu continues in a footnote: "Merleau-Ponty is related to Chuang Tzu as the early Heidegger is to the later. The early Heidegger investigated the structure of Dasein in order to catch glimpses of the structure of our being-in-the-world. The later Heidegger emphasized the essence of truth as the revealment of being in concealedness, from which Dasein's ontological forgetting is derived. Similarly, Merleau-Ponty worked his way up from an analysis of perception, and was planning on a reversal of ontological perspective, when he met his untimely death. Chuang Tzu was at home in the non-being in and behind the world, where he meandered at will in nonchalant joy." (*Chuang Tzu: World Philosopher at Play*, p. 92.)
— DEATH AS A HELIX OF DRUNKEN OWLS: **Robert MacLean**, *Heartwood*, Silverton, Colorado: Finn Hill Arts, 1985 (no paging).

Note: I am often asked about what to read in order to understand Taoism.

Below I list the sources I've found most useful in more than twenty years of studying Taoism. Many of the more popular books are entirely too "spiritual" and "other-worldly" to have anything to say about essential Taoism. See Bibliography for complete information on each.

Books:
1) J. Needham, *Science and Civilization in China*, v. 2. (for general background)
2) Kuang-Ming Wu, *Chuang Tzu: World Philosopher at Play*.
3) N. J. Girardot, *Myth and Meaning in Early Taoism*.

Individual articles:
1) Charles Wei-hsun Fu, "Lao Tzu's Conception of Tao." *Inquiry*, 16 (1973): 367-390. This is not easy but very important. The only paper I've found which explains the Tao from the point of view of the Chinese language itself. Essentially, "Both the nameless Tao thus-named and the real nameless Tao are two ways of saying the same thing, namely Tao as Reality; they are not categories but perspectives." The author then goes into Tao as Reality and Tao as Manifestation, as well as six other aspects of the Tao.
2) David L. Hall, "Process and Anarchy—A Taoist Vision of Creativity." *Philosophy East and West* (July 1978): 270-284.

For more information on international Taoist conferences, see the journal, *History of Religions* 9 (1969-70) and H. Welch, *Facets of Taoism*. There have since been two other conferences—one in Switzerland (1979) and one in Japan. See *History of Religions*.

Ch. 9 Seeing Nature
pp. 102-103 Opening Quotes
— "For example…": Nevitt, "Ecological Rationality Beyond Cybernetics."
— "When vision is thought of as…": **James J. Gibson**, *The Ecological Approach to Visual Perception*. Boston: Houghton Mifflin Co., 1979, p. 263.
— "I carry occult and subtle…": **Zen Master Koji**, quoted in Katsuki Sekida, *Two Zen Classics: Mumonkan and Hekiganroku*. New York: Weatherhill, 1977, p. 263.
— "Thus, when I 'think,' I reduce…": **M. Merleau-Ponty** *Phenomonology of Perception*. London: Routledge & Kegan Paul, 1962, p. 329.

104 JAPANESE PRINTS AND WESTERN PAINTERS: This book is by Frank Whitford. New York: Macmillan Co. 1977.
— DAVID ABRAM'S ARTICLE: **David Abram**, "The Perceptual Implications of Gaia." *The Ecologist*, (England) 15 (1985): 96-103.
— "Just live in deep…": **Ju-ching**, quoted in Eihei Dōgen, *The Way of Everyday Life*. Los Angeles: Zen Center of L.A. and the Institute for Transcultural Studies, 1978.
— "glimpse into the past…": **W. L. Schwartz**, "The Great Shrine of Idzumo: Some Notes on Shinto, Ancient and Modern." *Transactions of The Asiatic Society of Japan* 41 (October 1913).
— BRIEF ACCOUNT OF JAPANESE HISTORY "History Time-line." In Random House Encyclopedia, 1977, pp. 1829-1873.

105 "Chinese poets…": **Ernest Fenollosa**, quoted in Lawrence W. Chisolm, *The Far East and American Culture*. Westport Connecticut: Greenwood Press, 1976, p. 156. (This book was first published by Yale University Press in 1963.) **Add. notes:** Fenollosa made this statement in a speech before a Washington D. C. audience.
— BRIEF ACCOUNT OF HOW FENOLLOSA WENT TO JAPAN: Ibid., p. 30.
— OFFICIAL JAPANESE COMMITTEE TO STUDY ART EDUCATION: Ibid., p. 57.
— "We request you…": **Emperor of Japan**, quoted. Ibid, p. 86.
— "After leaving in 1896 he never…": Ibid., p. 121.
— "In the course of Dow's thirty years…": Ibid., p. 179. For more on this subject, see pp. 122 & 161.
— O'KEEFE AND WEBER: Ibid., p. 230.
— "herald of the coming…": **F.S.C. Northrop**, paraphrased in Chisolm, *Far East and American Culture*, p. 241.
— "treasures": **Ezra Pound**, quoted. Ibid., p. 224. Pound actually called them: "old Fenollosa's treasures in mss."
— "ball of light…": Ibid, p. 215.
— "a study of the fundamentals…": **Ezra Pound**, Ibid., p. 226. **Add. notes:** Because it contributes to the underlying premise of this work, concerning substance and relations, I quote Fenollosa: "Relations are more real and more important than the things which they relate." (p. 226 of Chisolm.) Chisolm is paraphrasing Fenollosa here: " 'Like nature,

the Chinese words are alive and plastic, because thing and action are not formally separated,' wrote Fenollosa. Because 'nature has no grammar' and does not abstract a noun or a 'quality' from its rich relationship to life…" (p. 226).
— "The influence of Japonisme…": **Emile Zola**, *Salons*, Paris, 1959. Theodore Reff, "Manet's Portrait of Zola." *Burlington Magazine*, (January, 1975): 34 ff.
— "We have found…": **Aemil Fendler**, quoted in Siegfried Wichmann, *Japonisme: The Japanese Influence on Western Art in the 19th and 20th Centuries*. New York: Park Lane (Crown Publishers Inc.), 1985, p. 87. **Add. notes:** This book was translated from the German edition, published in 1980. The book grew out of the exhibition: "Weltkulturen und Moderne Kunst", mounted to mark the Olympic games in Munich in 1972. Additions were made as a result of further research in the Far East in 1973-1977. Wichmann has been professor of Art History at the University of Karlsruhe, West Germany since 1968. The book is an oversize, 432 page text, with full page, full color reproductions of Japanese art as well as the European works, influenced by it.
— "painting in France and elsewhere…": Ibid, p. 25.
— "dig down to the very roots…": Ibid, p. 42
— "In a way all…": Ibid, p. 52. **Add. notes:** Van Gogh wrote to his sister, Wilhelmina: "For my part I don't need Japanese pictures here, for I am always telling myself *that here I am in Japan*. Which means that I have only to open my eyes and paint what is right in front of me, if I think it effective. In this same manner Japanese art can still help people see nature even today.
— "Without Degas's meticulous…": Ibid., p. 36.
— "the children of the 1880s…": Ibid., p. 74.
— JAPAN: **Add. notes:** Before leaving the subject of Japan, I want to add a few words. The most criticism I have had about my previous book, *Earth Wisdom*, concerns the fact that I wrote about the Japanese reverence for nature. My critics point to current abuses. I want to say that Japan has never had any natural resources except it's people. Here, I want to give some pertinent facts: First, "Statistically, more than 80 % of Japan's total land space is taken by unarable mountains and hills." (Y. T. Hosoi, "The Sacred Tree in Japanese Prehistory," *History of Religions* 16 (November, 1976): 95-119.) Secondly, for 300 years, up until the time the U.S. forcibly "opened" Japan in the middle of the last century, Japan kept its population the same. With the coming of Christian pressure against controlling births, their population jumped catastrophically; thus making it necessary that they copy the West in its industrial growth. Since WW II they have made concerted efforts to control their growth."Japan recently halved its birth rate in less than a generation—the fastest such decline in demographic history." (Ned Greenwood and J. Edwards, *Human Environment and Natural Systems*. Belmont California: Duxbury Prses, 1973). Essentially, had Americans, with their extractive approach to "natural resources," owned Japan, the entire country would long ago have eroded down into the Pacific. I say this because we had the extremely fertile, flat mid-West; yet we've managed to destroy most of the topsoil in only a few hundred years. Japan with its steep terrain took great care of the arable land they had, because they considered nature "sacred." I lived in Japan in 1972 for 3 months and did extensive travelling in the back country and I would say that the single largest piece of flat land is the site of Tokyo. Given all the above facts and having lived there I feel that the Japanese have not lost their essential "reverence" for nature. Once the population is again stabililized we will see a return of that attitude among more of the people.

106 "puzzling over…" down to "But the more I learned…": **Gibson**, *The Ecological Approach to Visual Perception*, p. xiii.
— SUMMATION OF HIS RESEARCH WORK: Ibid., pp. 1-3 and 273.
— AMBIENT LIGHT: Ibid., p. 49.
— "Radiation becomes illumination…": Ibid., p. 50.
— "It would follow…": Ibid., p. 51.
— "observed as tiny, colored…": p. 62.
— "was mainly responsible…": p. 59.
— "the eye sends…": Ibid., p. 6.
— "It is not necessary…": Ibid., p. 61.
— "The point of observation…": Ibid., p. 72.

107 "one thing behind…": Ibid., p. 77. **Add notes:** For a real insight into

the sophisticated concepts, which a primitive society has developed using this way of seeing, see Thomas Gladwin, *East is a Big Bird: Navigation and Logic on Puluwat Atoll.* Harvard University Press, 1970. Gladwin clearly shows how these people have just as sophisticated a way of knowing as anything our Western systems have developed. They use this system in sailing for days across the ocean with no land in sight. Gladwin spent two years learning from a Puluwat navigator. He did well in everything except the concept of "etak" which he could not handle. This, precisely, is Gibson's "moving array" and "visual angles." The quickest way to express "etak" is "a canoe pictured pushing through the sea with everything moving past it except the stars poised overhead." (p. 182). *East is a Big Bird* is a fascinating book which may well help you re-learn the natural way of vision, which our culture forces us to lose in childhood.

— "The motion of the sun..." down to "moving source...": Ibid, p. 87
— YIN AND YANG: For a more complete discussion on this, see my *Earth Wisdom*, p. 22.
— "For example...": **Nevitt**, "Ecological Rationality Beyond Cybernetics."
— "about half of your..." down to "is fundamental...": **Gibson**, *The Ecological Approach*, p. 112.
— "Information exists...": Ibid., p. 114.
— "the optical information to specify...": Ibid., p. 116.
— THE ENVIRONMENT AFFORDS: Ibid., p. 127.
— "Perhaps the composition..." down to "in a way that...": Ibid., p.127

108 "are the way specific...": **Abram**, "The Perceptual Implications of Gaia."
— SUBJECTIVE-OBJECTIVE DICHOTOMY: **Gibson**, *Ecological Approach*, p. 129. Specifically, Gibson writes: "An affordance cuts across the dichotomy of subjective-objective..."
— "the activity...": Ibid., p. 147.
— "But the truth is that...": Ibid., p. 205.
— "develops as perception...": Ibid., p. 253.
— "begins with the flowing array.": Ibid., p. 303.
— "Nothing is copied in the light.": Ibid., p. 304-305.
— "The indescribable...": **Henry David Thoreau**, *Walden*, (1854).
— "everything offers itself...": **Friedrich Nietzsche**, "Thus Spoke Zarathustra." In *Ecce Homo.* New York: Penguin Books, 1979, p. 103. I am combining two different translations here.
— "The attitude of hunting/gathering...": **Charles Hill-Tout**, quoted in Shepard, *The Sacred Paw*, p. 91.

109 "There's plants that will extract..." down to "And what's nice...": **John Quinney**, "New Ideas in Ecology and Economics," p. 5. A series by the Canadian Broadcasting Corporation May 29, June 4, 11, and 18, 1986. Presented by David Cayley. A printed transcript of this 4-part series is available through CBC Enterprises, P.O. Box 6440, Station A, Montreal Canada, H3C 3L4. Send $5.00. This particular broadcast was excellent but there is no date on it. In ordering it be sure you specify the one with Peter Berg, John Todd, Stuart Hill and John Quinney.

Inter-lude

pp. 110-111 Opening Quotes
— "Through rites..": **Hsün Tzu**, *The Book of Master Hsün*. H. H. Dubs. trans. *Hsün Tzu; the Moulder of Ancient Confucianism.* London: Probsthain, 1927.
— "When in early antiquity...": **"The Great Treatise"**, *The I Ching: Or Book of Changes*, trans.Richard Wilhelm (German) and Cary Baynes (English).
— "The extraordinary importance..." **Toshihiko Izutsu**, "The Temporal and A-Temporal Dimensions of Reality in Confucian Metaphysics." *Eranos Yearbooks* 43 (1974): 411-447.
— "Let us then imagine...": **James Hillman**, *Re-Visioning Psychology*, p. xiii.
— "Gathered up, all things...": **Chu Hsi**, *Philosophical Commentary on the Explanation of the Diagram of the Supreme Pole*. This translation is from T. Izutsu, "The Temporal and A-Temporal Dimensions." **Add. notes**: For the best explanation of the "Supreme Pole", see Needham, *Sci.and Civil.*, v. 2, pp. 460-472. Very briefly, this concerns "That which has no Pole! And yet (itself) the Supreme Pole!" Moving this "pole" produces the yin and yang. These two, interacting, produce the "five elements" and out of that come the "myriad things." Needham sees

this Sung philosophy diagram as "the conception of the entire universe as a single organism." Going deeper into Chu Hsi's work on this concept, Needham states: "For while the universe was all spontaneity and uncreatedness yet at the same time it was all order, that sublime order produced by the harmony of individual wills, the intuitive faithfulness of organisms to their own natures." (p. 470)
— "Told one day by someone...": **Laurens van der Post**, *Jung and The Story of Our Time.*
— "I have often been impatient...": **Gregory Bateson**, *Steps to an Ecology of Mind*, p. xvi.
— "Li, then, is rather...": **Needham**, *The Grand Titration*, p. 321. **Add. notes:** The quickest explanation of the different meanings of the Chinese words, *li*, are given by Needham on p. 331 of *The Grand Titration* "Three Chinese terms...are homophones and have therefore been distinguished by superscript letters. They are:

li a) good customs, ceremonial observances, ethical behaviour.
li b) organic pattern at all levels in the cosmos.
li c) calendrical science based on observational astronomy.

112 "Death, work...": **Eugen Fink**, "The Ontology of Play." *Philosophy Today* 18 (Summer, 1974): 147-161.
— "*Li* is a concept...": **Wei-ming Tu**, "Li as a Process of Humanization."
— THE CONCEPT OF LI: **Needham**, *Sci.and Civil.*, v. 2, pp. 280, 453, 473-485, 569, 581. Also, see Needham, *The Grand Titration*, p. 321.
— "The concept of *li* is actually...": **Wei-ming Tu**, "Li as a Process of Humanization."
— "Thus all together..." down to "This is nothing less...": **Needham**, *The Grand Titration*, p. 319-320. **Add. notes:** Other useful readings: James B. Robinson, "The Price of Harmony" *Parabola* 9; Wing-Tsit Chan, "Syntheses in Chinese Metaphysics"; and Herbert Fingarette, *Confucius—The Secular As Sacred.* New York: Harper & Row. 1972. The latter is only 84 pages, but very thought-provoking. Out-of-print, but get it through your library.

The Chinese had no need for a concept of law such as in the West. Needham has a good discussion of how we got laws—dating back to the Babylonian "conception of Laws of Nature [arising] in a highly centralized oriental monarchy" on down through the Greeks, the Christian God on to modern times in "Human Laws and the Laws of Nature," pp. 299-330, in *The Grand Titration*. Concluding, he states: "It is extremely interesting that modern science...found [it] possible...and even desirable to dispense completely with the hypothesis of a God as the basis of the Laws of Nature, [and] has returned, in a sense, to the Taoist outlook." In the last section of v. 2 of *Sci. and Civil.* he has a much longer and more detailed analysis. See pages 518—584.
— "do not ask...": **Ted J. Kaptchuk**, *The Web That Has No Weaver: Understanding Chinese Medicine.* New York: Congdon & Weed, 1983, p. 140. **Add. notes:** Kaptchuk trained in western medicine and in Chinese medicine. After providing basic explanations, he gives examples for specific diseases of how a Western doctor would treat a hypothetical patient and how the Chinese doctor would treat him. Provides a good understanding of the shortcomings of the "substance" approach of Western medicine.

113 "The entire landscape...": **Frank Herbert**, *Dune*, Appendix: "The Ecology of Dune." pp 505-511.
— PATTERNS FROM INTERACTIONS OF SUN, GRAVITY, AND SPACE: For detailed photos on both the micro and macro level, see **Peter S. Stevens**, *Patterns in Nature* (Atlantic Monthly Press Book, 1974). They show how trees branch, rivers branch and arteries branch in the same manner; while in another example soap bubbles and turtle shells have the same pattern. With 180 photos and lucid explanations, this book is a necessity for understanding patterns in nature.
— "The story was...": **Laurens Van der Post**, "Patterns of Renewal." Pendle Hill Publications, No. 121, Wallingford, Pa. 1979. **Add. notes:** For more on how primitive societies, in general, fit themselves into the on-going story of their place, see chapter seven, back in Part II of this work.
— "Ceremony is an...": **Elizabeth Cogburn**, in a talk during the Long Dance, in Aztec, N.M., May, 1987. Unpublished.
— "So there is...": **Gary Snyder**, *The Old Ways*, p. 79.
— "The ear for the story...": **Leslie Marmon Silko**, *Ceremony*. New York: Penguin Books, 1987, p. 255. **Add. notes:** In his conclusion to *Living*

the Sky: The Cosmos of the American Indian (Boston: Houghton Mifflin, 1984), Ray Williamson, an astronomer, explains how: "The sky turns, and in turning, measures out our lives. To live in harmony with the world and its cycles is the goal of traditional Native Americans. Their patterns for living derive from a deeply held attention to the rhythms of the sky and earth. The lessons of archaeoastronomy and ethnoastronomy instruct us that whether as architects, weavers, hunters, potters, or storytellers, traditional Native American men and women weave their perceptions of the celestial patterns into their lives in order to participate directly in the ways of the universe." (p. 319) Thus they follow the Li of their own place. For more on how to begin living this way, see chapter fourteen.

PART III

115 "Our goal should not be...": **Mr. Aoki**. Quoted by David Franklin, in a letter to Melissa Zink, 1985.

Ch. 10 The "Sacred"

pp. 116 and 117 Opening Quotes

— "Magic may be defined...": **Gertrude Levy**, *The Gate of Horn : A Study of the Religious Conceptions of the Stone Age and their Influence upon European Thought*. London: Faber & Faber Ltd., 1948, p. 35.

— "A vast old religion...": **D. H. Lawrence**, "New Mexico." *Survey Graphic* (January, 1928). Reprinted in *Phoenix*.

— "Well-nigh two thousand...": **Friedrich Nietzsche**, *The Anti-Christ*, 1888.

— "Noting that Israel was...": **Watsuji Tetsuro**, quoted in Shepard, *Nature and Madness*, p. 147. **Add. notes:** Watsuji Tetsuro wrote in the mid-twenties and thirties about many things which we are only now beginning to recognize."The two pillars of [his] thought were the concepts of human climate and man." I will be referring here to David Delworth, "Watsuji Tetsuro: Cultural Phenomenologist." *Philosophy East and West* 14: 3-22. Delworth writes of a chapter in his book, *Fudo*, "The Basic Principles of Climate" (1929 first drafted & revised for pub in 1935)."The piece is a creative response to Heidegger... Watsuji's concept of *fudo* translates *Dasein*'s 'there-Being' in the mode of '*ex-sistere*' into the concrete spatial-historicality of cultural existence." Delworth states that "Watsuji's position was well grounded in Nietzsche, Heidegger, and Soseki." In *Fudo*, he writes about "all the expressions of human activity, such as literature, art, religion, and manners and customs as *human-climatic* phenomena in his sense." I've only been able to find one of his books in English, *Climate and Culture*, published by The Hokuseido Press, 1961 (based on his lectures in 1928-29). There are others. Watsuji Tetsuro's work is useful for the emerging bioregional approach.

— "Nature begins to present...": **J. C. Powys**, *The Meaning of Culture*. New York, Norton, 1929, p. 180.

— "[The religious feeling] consists...": **William H. Thorpe**, quoted in Konrad Lorenz, "The Fashionable Fallacy of Dispensing with Description."

— "To evolution and comedy...": **Joseph W. Meeker**, *The Comedy of Survival: In Search of an Environmental Ethic*.

— "When you are in love with...": **Vern Crawford**, *The Days Afield*. (Autumn, 1985) This seasonal publication provides further depth for seasonal celebrations. Address: Vern Crawford, The Days Afield, 923 Harmony Ln., Ashland, Or. 97521.

— "We believe that land and people...": **George Barta**, quoted in Peter Warshall, ed. "The Voices of Black Lake." *Coevolution Quarterly*. (Winter 1977): 64-69.

— "The Indian loved to...": **Luther Standing Bear**, *Land of the Spotted Eagle*. Lincoln: Univ. of Nebraska Press, 1978.

— "Since hunting...": **Hamilton Tyler**, *Pueblo Animals and Myths*, p. 241.

— "Our belief in this regard...": **Jerome Rothenberg**, *Symposium of the Whole*, p. xii.

— "For the primitive...": **M. Eliade**, "Methodological Remarks on the Study of Religious Symbolism."

— "A wagon loaded...": **Kenneth Rexroth**, *An Autobiographical Novel*. p. 337.

118 CHILD NATURE MYSTIC EXPERIENCE: For further information, see *Earth Wisdom*, pp. 63-66. Edith Cobb gives a number of these experiences

in her book, *The Ecology of Imagination in Childhood*. New York: Columbia University Press, 1977.

— DEFINITION OF THE WORD, SACRA: *Cassell's New Latin Dictionary*. Funk and Wagnell, 1968. **Add. notes:** I want to thank Art Goodtimes, poet and Latin scholar, for helping me with these Latin definitions.

— MODERN PANTHEIST DEFINITION OF SACRED: **Derham Giuliani**, letter, May 11, 1985, in reply to my question of how he would define the word, sacred. **Add. notes:** Giuliani, Harold Wood, an environmental lawyer, and Enid Larson, an expert on chipmunks got together and started the Universal Pantheist Society, PO Box 265, Big Pine, Ca. 93513. Derham has been studying insects since before he could walk. His mother tells him that when he was still crawling, he would follow a line of ants across the floor. His research reputation is now so well established that he spends his entire life studying animals in the true sense—just watching them. He claims that if one learns to imitate the behavior of the animal you want to see and goes into the wild behaving in that way, taking cover where it would, being near to what it eats, moving as it moves, the animal becomes accustomed to you and goes ahead living as it always does, ignoring you. He's been called the "ring-tailed cat man," because that animal changed his life.

119 "the Great Subculture of Illuminati...": **Gary Snyder**, quoted in Jerome Rothenberg, "Pre-face to Origin," *Alcheringa*.

— MASTER, OR KEEPER OF ANIMALS: This concept was widespread among hunting peoples throughout the world. For more information see Ivar Paulson, "The Animal Guardian: A Critical and Synthetic Review." *The History of Religions* 3 (1964): 202-219. **Add. notes:** He states that for Pettazzoni, the Supreme Being of the lower hunting culture was identical with the master of animals. "Animal guardian," means both the guardian spirit and deity of the animals or the game. "Besides the genuine animal guardians, we must take into account the countless local and interlocal or multilocal nature spirits or nature gods of the bush, mountain, forest, and waters and other realms and elements of nature, who function generally as the protectors of the animals within their own realms." These are protectors of game. "The various deities who probably help the hunter in his hunt, or the fisher in his occupation, that is, the personal guardian spirits of man, the shaman-spirits etc. but who in no way function as guardians of the game, are therefore excluded from this definition. The genuine animal guardian is distinguished by a double function; on the one hand, he is a protector of the game; on the other, he is the helper of the hunter or fisher."

— "the most diverse figure in all...": **Mircea Eliade**, quoted in John Pfeiffer, *The Creative Explosion: An Inquiry into the Origins of Art and Religion*. New York: Harper and Row, 1982, p. 119. **Add notes:** For more in depth presentation of the original Paleolithic on-going religion, see Pfeiffer's book and Gertrude Levy, *The Gate of Horn*.

— "seen as a living...": **Roslyn M. Frank**, "The Basque Goddess." *Lady Unique Inclination of the Night,* Cycle 4 (Autumn 1979). Sowing Circle Press. (This venture resulted from a conference held in April 1978 at Santa Cruz under the Univ. of Calif. auspices.) Her sources for this statement are: Antonio Tovar, *El euskera y sus parientes* (Madrid: Minotauro, 1959). Jean Bernard and Jacques Ruffle. "Hematologie et culture, Le Peuplement de l'Europe de l'Quest." *Annales Des Economics, Societies et Civilizations* 31 (1976): 661-676. Roslyn Frank is Assoc. Prof. of Spanish and Portuguese at the University of Iowa. She spent 1979 collecting and researching in the Basque country of Northern Spain.

— OLD EUROPE: **Marija Gimbutas**, *The Goddesses and Gods of Old Europe 6500-3500 BC: Myths and Cult Images*. Berkeley, University of California Press, 1982, (new ed.).

— "It is no mere...": Ibid., p. 200.

— "The persistence...": Ibid., p. 9.

— "The teaching of Western..." down to "is a universal symbol...": Ibid., p 238 and p. 91.

— BISEXUAL IMAGES—FEMALE WITH PHALLIC NECK (GOURD SHAPED): Ibid., p. 135, 36, 108, and 204.

— "an old sanctuary with a well...": **C. G. Jung**, *Analytical Psychology, its Theory and Practice*, p. 129, 131 and 132. **Add notes:** For an excellent account of the gradual supression of the classical gods of Europe, see Hans Peter Duerr, *Dreamtime*.

120 "But as to the origin...": **Herodotus**, quoted in Jane Harrison, *Mythology*, p. xvii.

— HOMER: *Random House Encyclopedia*, 1977, p. 1832.

— "The things that have...": **Gilbert Murray**, *Five Stages in Greek Religion*. 1925, p. 24.

— "In 1903, came..." and "what a people...": **Gilbert Murray**, quoted in Jessie Stewart, *Jane Ellen Harrison: A Portrait from Letters*. London: The Merlin Press, 1959, p. 23. **Add. notes:** Today, the "idea" of an earth goddess seemed worthwhile, but there are two problems. First, the wrong goddess was chosen. Gaia is not an ancient goddess but essentially is a creation of Hesiod, based on the Greek word, *gea* meaning earth and secondly, the Gaia concept has become just another abstraction. One can talk about Gaia all one wants and not have to consider the earth itself at all. Jane Harrison, in her *Mythology*, writes about how various attributes of the ancient Cretan mother were transferred to the mainland Greek goddesses such as Hera, Demeter etc.; but "one lovely figure...comes straight to us from the Cretan Mother, that is the figure of Pandora, the All-giver. On vase-paintings, the Earth-Mother is often figured rising half out of the actual ground. On a red-figured amphora in a museum at Oxford above the uprising figure which we are accustomed to call Gaia, the Earth, is written the name *Pandora*. In origin there is no doubt that Pandora was simply the Earth-Mother, the All-giver, but an irresponsible patriarchal mythology changed her into a fair woman dowered with all manner of gifts...Hesiod in the Works and Day ...tells the story." Harrison says thus "the great Mother has become the Temptress maid." The true name of Pandora it turns out is Anesidora the "sender up of gifts, true epithet of the Earth-Mother." Her famous box is not a box at all. The word used by Hesiod is *pithos*, the large jars used to store grain, wine and oil. "When Pandora opens her box it is not the woman temptress letting out the woes of mortal man, it is the great Earth-Mother who opens her *pithos*, her store house of grain and fruits for her children." She shows that despite all the glamour of Hesiod's verse, "There gleams also an ugly and malicious theological animal." He "is all for the *Father* and the father will have no great Earth-Goddess in his man-made Olympus. So she who made all things, gods and mortals, is unmade and remade and becomes the plaything of man..." J. Harrison, *Mythology*, pp. 64-68.

The famous classical scholar, Gilbert Murray agreed with Harrison's explanation. In a more recent study, *Pandora's Box*, Panovsky points out that Jane Harrison told about it 50 years ago. He claims that the false story was carried down in art and literature through Plotinus (the Neoplatonist) into the middle ages, through Goethe, to the post impressionists of the twentieth century. Jessie Stewart, *Jane Ellen Harrison*, p. 30.

— "pioneer work...": **Gilbert Murray**, quoted in Stewart, *Jane Ellen Harrison*. **Add. notes:** Murray had promised Stewart a preface but died before he wrote it. He did, however, write a few lines to Stewart about the importance of Harrison's work. A further statement was that "Nobody can write on Greek religion without being influenced by her work." (p. xi).

— BEGINNINGS OF ANTHROPOMORPHIC GODS: **Susanne Langer**, *Philosophy in a New Key*, p. 168.

— "the local gods..." and "A god with an epithet...": **Gilbert Murray**, quoted in Langer, p. 168.

— "Sometimes the animal form...": **Jane Harrison**, *Themis: A Study of the Social Origins of Greek Religion*. Cambridge: Cambridge University Press, 1912, p. 449.

— "In art this exclusion of animal...": Ibid., p. 450.

— "We now know that till...": **Harrison**, *Mythology*, p. xv.

121 "Suddenly from the island of Paxi...": **Plutarch**, "On the Disappearance of Oracles." Quoted in Philippe Borgeau, "The Death of the Great Pan: The Problem of Interpretation." *The History of Religions* (1983): 254-283.

— "The death of the great Pan...": Ibid.

— ROOTS OF WESTERN LITERATURE: *Random House Encyclopedia*, 1977, p. 1836.

— "the stage for Christian allegorical...": Ibid, p. 1838.

— PETRARCH: **Robb Nesca**, *Neoplatonism of the Italian Renaissance*. London: George Allen & Unwin Ltd., 1935, p. 19.

— "the motives that appear...": Ibid. **Add. notes:** Nesca studied under Foligno of Oxford and then under several Italian professors, specialists on the subject. All translations of the original documents are Nesca's.

— "the earliest Platonist of the...": **William Rose Benét**, ed. *The Reader's Encyclopedia*. New York: Thomas Y. Crowell Co, 1948, p. 378.

— "Both Cosimo and Ficino..." down to "all religious phenomena are conditioned...": **Mircea Eliade**, "The Quest for the 'Origins' of Religion."

122 NEOPLATONIC INFLUENCE ON ARTISTS: **Nesca**, *Neoplatonism*, p. 218, 219, 245 and 248.

— "eternal world of glory..." and "which was exceptionally free...": **Benét**, *The Readers Encyclopedia*, p. 764. **Add. notes:** Others claim that "Plotinus, once considered to be the founder of Neoplatonism is now being interpreted as its greatest member—important but not all important..." (Philip Merlan, *From Platonism to Neoplatonism*. The Hague: Martinus Nijhoff, 1968, p. 2)

— "the ineffable Godhead...": **Nesca**, *Neoplatonism of the Italian Renaissance*, p. 64.

— "the material world" which "is the region...": **Ficino**, Ibid., p. 65-66.

— "appears in its insistence...": Ibid., p. 69.

— "His desires are so limitless...": **Ficino**, quoted in, Nesca, p. 73. **Add. notes:** Because this statement is particularly pertinent to the present human destruction of the earth, I will give the reference to the particular place in Ficino's works where this occurs: Ficino, *Theologia Platonica*, Bk. XVI, p. 378.

123 "divine...who rivals and disputes...": **Leonardo da Vinci**, quoted in Nesca, p. 222.

— "Earthly beauty is only evil...": **Michelangelo**, quoted in Nesca, p. 248.

— "I devoured it at once...": **C. G. Jung**, *Memories, Dreams, Reflections*, p. 197.

— "I shall only emphasize...": **C. G. Jung**, "Foreword." In Richard Wilhelm. trans. *The Secret of the Golden Flower*, p. xiv.

— "Anyone who, like myself...": **C. G. Jung**, "In Memory of Richard Wilhelm." Ibid., p. 140.

— "For the primitive...": **M. Eliade**, "Methodological Remarks on the Study of Religious Symbolism."

— "first thorough...": **Ake Hultkrantz**, "North American Indian Religion in the History of Research: A General Survey." Pt. I. *The History of Religions* 6 (November 1966).

— "orenda...mystic potence...": Ibid.

— "Wakonda is the name...": **Alice Fletcher**, "The Omaha Tribe." *Bureau of American Ethnology, Twenty-seventh Annual Report*, 1911.

— CONTROVERSY CONCERNING WAKONDA AND BELIEF IN SPIRITS: **Hultkrantz**, "North American Indian Religion."

124 "primarily as a Roman Catholic...": **Roger Echo-Hawk** (Pawnee), "Black Elk's Vision/Neihardt's Revision." *The Bloomsbury Review*, (April 1985): 3.

— "had been a Christian..." down to "He never talked about...": **Clyde Holler**, "Black Elk's Relationship to Christianity." *The American Indian Quarterly* 8 (winter 1984): 37-49

— "It was not that there was no order...": **Needham**, *Sci. and Civil.*, v. 2, p. 581.

— "Usually the term...": **Joseph W. Kitagawa**, "'A Past of Things Present': Notes on Major Motifs of Early Japanese Religions."

— "There is an implicit..." down to "Metaphysically, the Sun...": **Jay Vest**, "Traditional Blackfeet Religion and the Badger-Two Medicine Wildlands." Unpublished.

— "In this early, primitive...": **Jaime de Angulo**, quoted in Bob Callahan, *A Jaime de Angulo Reader*. Berkeley: Turtle Island, 1979, p. xii.

125 JAIME DE ANGULO: My main source for information on him is listed above, the *Jaime De Angulo Reader*. Elsewhere, in Michael Tobias, ed., *Deep Ecology*, I go more deeply into his life in my paper, "Sacred Land, Sacred Sex." (pp. 102-121). My other references for material in that essay are *The Netzahualcoyotl News*, #1 (Summer 1979). Berkeley: Turtle Island Foundation and D. L. Olmsted, "Introduction." In Olmsted, "Introduction to the Achumawi Dictionary." *University of California Publication in Linguistics*, v. 45. Berkeley: University of California Press, 1966. **Add. notes:** Olmsted devotes this "Introduction" to the work of de Angulo because his work has not been recognized by the academic system. There has not yet been a biography about this man, because he crossed too many boundaries to make such a biography easy. Turtle Island Foundation has printed a number of volumes of his work, taken from radio talks

gave over KPFA in the late 1940s. All the quotations I use here are from the book, *A Jaime De Angulo Reader*, pp. x to xiv.
—— Nietzsche meeting Bachhofen: **Heidegger**, *Nietzsche*, v. 1., p. 7.
—— "overturn Platonism": Ibid. See Heidegger pp. 154-202, for discussion on this concept.
—— "I shall now tell the story...": **Nietzsche**, "Thus Spoke Zarathustra: A Book for Everyone and No One." In R. J. Hollingdale. trans. *Ecce Homo*. New York: Penguin Books, 1979.
—— "In the mornings I climbed..." down to "It was on these two walks...": Ibid., pp. 100 and 101.
—— Zarathustra and Zoroaster: **Benét**, *The Reader's Encyclopedia*, p. 1120. For more details, see *Earth Wisdom*, pp. 14 and 15.
—— "In the summer, returned...": **Nietzsche**, *Ecce Homo*, p. 104.
—— Rausch, "rapture": **Heidegger**, *Nietzsche*, p. 250.

126 "The Overman as...": **Gilles Deleuze**, *Nietzsche and Philosophy*. (Hugh Tomlinson, trans.). New York: Columbia University Press, 1983, p. 177.
—— "the source of comparison...": **Wallace Stevens**, *Opus Posthumous*. New York: Alfred A. Knopf, 1957, p. 213.
—— "So, something more than...": **Jerome Rothenberg**, *Technicians of the Sacred*, p. 426.
—— Open Communication Between Limbic System and Neo-cortex: **J. P. Henry and P. M. Stephens**, *Stress, Health and the Social Environment: A Sociobiologic Approach to Medicine*, pp. 109 and 111.
—— Otto's study of "the holy": **R. Otto**, *The Idea of the Holy*. Now out of print, it was originally published in 1917, 2nd ed. 1950, p. 37.
—— "physiological concomitants...": **J. P. Henry**, "Comment" following Ernest Rossi, "The Cerebral Hemispheres in Analytical Psychology."
—— "the brain stem would be the most likely spot...": **C. G. Jung**, personal communication to J. P. Henry, quoted in Henry, "Comment", p. 53. The actual wording is as follows: Henry writes: "Jung's opinion of the possible physiological concomitants of a numinous religious experience such as the self was that 'if one could locate such a basic fact as the self at all, the brain stem would be the most likely spot. I am certain that the universally occurring symbols of the self point to a fairly reliable fact of a basic nature, i.e., a structure expressed through an organic pattern.' (personal communication)."
—— "daylight of the mentally and...": **Jung**, *Coll.Works*, v. 9, Pt. I, p. 19.
—— "foundations built by Carl Jung...": **Henry**, "Comment."
—— "The sacred world...": **Weston La Barre**. In Peter T. Furst, ed. *Flesh of the Gods : The Ritual Use of Hallucinogens*. New York: Praeger, 1972.
—— "ritual is not simply...": **Roy Rappaport**, *Meaning, Ecology and Religion*, p. 174.
—— "Invariance...is characteristic.": Ibid., p. 208.
—— "It may be that the basis...": Ibid, p. 212.
—— "Consciousness is just...": **Gregory Bateson**, *Steps to An Ecology of Mind*, p. 433.

127 "There is a larger...": Ibid., p. 461. **Add notes:** In *Angels Fear* (1987), Bateson's daughter has drawn together his last thoughts on the sacred. On p. 145 she has a "metalogue" with her dead father, where she exasperatedly remarks: "You just don't spell out what, finally, you mean by 'the sacred'...It's not easy for people to equate the 'pattern which connects' with the sacred..." Later, on p. 183, she explains: "Gregory had been building up a set of ideas about the nature of mental process, which he believed formed the basis for a new understanding of the epistemology of living systems." He thought that if such a new understanding was "widely shared, people would act differently on matters of ecological balance and war and peace. And he thought that the development of this sensitivity to natural systems had something to do with aesthetics and with the 'sacred'." I feel that during the long time span of humans on earth, most cultures recognized this connection also. Our Eurocentric culture forgot it. But the rapidly escalating destruction of nature is beginning to make people in the West ask the real questions once more. This chapter is designed to contribute to that questioning.
—— "are purely artificial..." Ibid., p. 483.
—— The Sacred as Power: Additional insight on this concept comes from **Jay H. Vest**, "Algonquian Metaphysics and Wildness: Ontological and Ethical Reflections upon an Ultimate Animating Life Principle." Unpublished. **Add notes:** Vest states that the the Ojibwa use of the term,

"grandfather," applies not only to "human persons but to spiritual beings who are persons of a category other than human [sun, tree, rock, thunder etc.]. In fact, when the collective plural 'our grandfathers' is used, the reference is primarily to persons of this latter class." If we look at it from a narrow Eurocentric, social science point of view we account for only one set of "grandfathers, the human ones." But if we look at it from the point of view of studying the Ojibwa religion we find another set of "Grandfathers." Vest points out here: "The crucial point is that no such dichotomization exists in this perspective of the Ojibwa world view." He quotes Hallowell, who explains that "In this perspective 'grandfather' is a term applicable to certain 'person objects,' without any distinction between human persons and those of an other-than-human class. Both sets of grandfathers can be said to be functionally as well as terminologically equivalent in certain respects." Vest continues: "The 'power' of human beings is derived from the enhancing properties of the other-than-human 'grandfathers.' The social relatedness between human persons and 'other-than-human persons' is of cardinal significance in recognizing moral and ethical norms in such societies."

Concerning "substance", Vest comments on the fact that "the ontology of the West has been shaped by the early Greek philosophies...[who] held that substance is the basic category of being..." Continuing, he points out that "there is an implicit claim that the Manitou notion is understood indigenously as an expression of 'substance' comportable with a Western derived ontology" and he show that this is invalid. As I have shown before in this work, primitive cultures in general, as well as the Chinese, are not caught in our "substance" trap.
—— "Symbolism is the very essence...": **Jung**, *Coll.Works*, v. 9, Pt. 2, Par. 280.
—— "The true god is created...": **D.H. Lawrence**, "The Crown."
—— Blossoming means the establishing...": **D.H. Lawrence**, "Reflections on the Death of a Porcupine."
—— Ituri pygmies—Body of God: **Colin Turnbull**, *The Forest People*. New York: Simon and Shuster, 1962.

128 "awareness, not a feeling...": **Kenneth Rexroth**, *An Autobiographical Novel*, p. 337.
—— "What this time...": **Donna G.** letter, October 4, 1985. She is a psychotherapist in the eastern United States.

Ch. 11 Childhood Play
pp. 130 and 131 Opening Quotes
—— "The special places...": **Shepard**, *Man in the Landscape*, p. 37.
—— "Intelligence is natural...": **Luis Machado**, politician-professor, who brought massive educational reform and enrichment to Venezuela, quoted in *Brain Mind Bulletin*, February 10, 1986.
—— "The use Bowlby...": **N. Blurton Jones**, "Mother-Child Contact." In N. Blurton Jones, ed. *Ethological Studies of Child Behaviour*. Cambridge: Cambridge University Press, 1972, p. 323. **Add. notes:** Bowlby is the one who did the early research (1950s) on attachment behavior, which indirectly led to the beginnings of the use of ethological research in human behavior. See chapter six for more on him.
—— "The whole of growth...": **Shepard**, *Nature and Madness*, p. 6.
—— "Primitive, or archaic ritual...": **J. Huizinga**, *Homo Ludens: A Study of The Play Element in Culture*. Boston: The Beacon Press, 1955. (first published in 1939). **Add. notes:** Huizinga, in 1933, while rector of the University of Leyden, chose as the theme for an important lecture: "The Cultural Limits of Play and the Serious." Out of that, came the book, *Homo Ludens*. Huizinga was a specialist on the Middle Ages.
—— "Parents are the earliest ritualizers in their...": **Erik Erikson**, "The Ontogeny of Ritualization in Man," pp. 338-349. From "A Discussion on Ritualization of Behaviour in Animals and Man," organized by Sir Julian Huxley, June 10-12, 1965. In *Philosophical Transactions of the Royal Society of London, Series B*, v. 251, 1966, pp. 247-523.
—— "A man is whole only when he plays..": **Schiller**, quoted in Eugen Fink, "The Ontology of Play." *Philosophy Today* 18 (Summer 1974): 147-161.
—— "In every true man there...": **Nietzsche**, quoted in Lorenz, *Behind the Mirror*, p. 149.

132 "Still unable to stand...": **Nikos Kazantzakis**, *Report to Greco*. New York: Simon and Schuster, 1965, p. 42.
—— "I remember...": Ibid.

— "part of the story": **Add. notes:** The Jungian Psychologist, James Hillman has a very important little piece, titled, "A Note on Story", where he says that from his perspective as a depth psychologist, "I see that those who have a connection with story are in better shape and have a better prognosis than" others without "story." He continues: "One integrates life as story because one has stories in the back of the mind (unconscious) as containers for organizing events into meaningful experiences. The stories are means of finding oneself in events that might not otherwise make psychological sense at all." Originally published in "Children's Literature: The Great Excluded." *Journal of the Modern Language Association Seminar on Children's Literature* 3 (1974). Reprinted in *Parabola* 4: 43-45.

132 "Children grow...": **Thomas Buckley**, "Doing Your Thinking." *Parabola* 4 (November 1979): 29-37.

— "He was about seven...": **Abraham Maslow**, *The Farther Reaches of Human Nature*. New York: Viking Press, 1971, p. 231.

— "Infanticide is frequently...": **John Murdoch**, "Ethnological Results of the Point Barrow Expedition." *Bur. of Am. Ethnol. Ninth Annual Report* (1887-1888), p. 417.

— "Babies were nursed...": **Frank Russell**, "The Pima Indians." *Bur. of Am. Ethnol. Twenty Sixth Annual Report*. (1904-1905), p. 185.

— "Notwithstanding this...": **Edwin Denig**, "Indian Tribes of the Upper Missouri, The Assiniboin." *Bur. of Am. Ethnol. Forty Sixth Annual Report* (1928-1929), p. 520.

— "Children were never whipped...": **H. B. Cushman**, "History of the Choctaw, Chickasaw, and Natchez Indians." *Bur. of Am. Ethnol. Forty Fourth Annual Report*.

133 "Each year, more children...": **J. Magid**, "Child abuse may be sorriest problem of all." *Salt Lake Tribune* (February 13, 1977).

— THE KUNG OF AFRICA: **James V. Neel**, "Lessons from a 'Primitive' People." *Science*, (November 20, 1970).

— "I guess what I've learned...": **Wilfred Pelletier**, *No Foreign Land*, p. 156.

— "All creativity...": **Gary Snyder**, "Poetry of Wildness." (cassette tape available from Finn Hill Arts.)

— "I see the mind of...": **Sylvia Ashton-Warner**, *Teacher*. New York: Simon and Schuster, 1963, p. 29. (The paging is from the Bantam ed.)

— "Life has an inner...": **Eric Fromm**, quoted in Ashton-Warner, *Teacher* p. 88.

— "What makes a good culture...": **Julien Puzey**, "Deep Ecology: The Root and the Return."

— "they steered clear..." down to "begins to suggest...": **Jerome Bruner**, "Introduction." In Bruner et al, eds. *Play—It's Role in Development and Evolution*. New York: Basic Books, 1976, pp. 13-23. **Add. notes:** The editors state: "The book's most frequent and most powerful theme is play. Play is a must of the first order for individuals (Piaget, Spitz, Murphy) and for mankind (Lorenz, Erikson etc.)...". (p. 172).

— "For most primates...": **Phyllis Dolhinow**, "At Play in the Fields." Special Supplement of the *Natural History Magazine* (December 1971). Reprinted in Bruner et al, *Play—It's Role*, p. 312 ff.

134 "are typical..." down to "All purely material...": **Konrad Lorenz**, "Psychology and Phylogeny." In *Studies in Animal and Human Behaviour*. Robert Martin. trans. Methuen, 1971. (Reprinted in Bruner, *Play—It's Role*, pp. 84-95.)

— "There is much to suggest that man...": **Erikson**, "The Ontogeny of Ritualization in Man."

— "large order to burden" down to "emerges unbroken from early...: Ibid.

— "consider the whole...": **Bateson**, *Mind and Nature*, p. 136.

— "So I sat...": Ibid., p. 137-138.

135 "Patterns of interaction..." down to "within the system...": Ibid., p. 138.

— "victory over self..." down to "What happens...": Ibid., p. 140.

— ROGER HART'S STUDY: **Roger Hart**, *Children's Experience of Place*. New York: Irvington Pub. Inc., 1979.

— "highly-valued land-uses...": Ibid., p. 156.

— "Which places are you most...": Ibid., p. 171.

— "It was clear in...": Ibid., p. 203.

— "Discovering a new edible...": Ibid., p. 318.

— "developed strong affection..." down to "of all places...": Ibid., p. 203.

— "Johnny is really upset...": Ibid., p. 283.

— "highly valued...: Ibid., p. 213.

— "The possibility that societal...": Ibid., p. 272.

136 "immense satisfaction...": Ibid, p. 219-220.

— "Near towns such as Grandville...": Ibid., p. 150.

— "Where the President lives...": Ibid., p. 91.

— "suffered serious problems..." and the quote from Lee: "hypothesized...": Ibid., p. 91.

— "has some most important...": Ibid., p. 205.

— EDITH COBB: See her *Ecology of Imagination in Childhood*. New York: Columbia University Press, 1977. Also see my *Earth Wisdom*. Silverton Colorado: Finn Hill Arts, pp. 63-65 and 106-107. Cobb's book is out of print now, but you can buy a reprint of the only article she ever wrote, (same title), from Finn Hill Arts.

— "same special or secret pond..." down to "particularly important...": **Hart**, *Children's Experience*, p. 205.

— "countless studies...": Ibid., p. 278.

— "It is notable that the most important...": Ibid., p. 349.

— "If we define play...": **Bateson**, *Mind and Nature*, p. 137.

— "playfulness...is defined...": **Erikson**, "Play and Actuality." In Bruner, *Play-It's Role*, pp. 688-704.

— BONDING TO THE EARTH: **Paul Shepard** has done a great deal of work on this subject. **Add. notes:** Each of his books is useful here but especially, *Nature and Madness*. On page 108 he states: "The archetypal role of nature—the mineral, plant, and animal world found most complete in the wilderness—is in the development of the individual human personality, for it embodies the poetic expression of ways of being and relating to others. Urban civilization creates the illusion of a shortcut to individual maturity by attempting to omit the eight to ten years of immersion in nonhuman nature. Maturity so achieved is spurious because the individual...is without a grounding in the given structure that is nature. His grief and sense of loss seem to him to be a personality problem, so that, caught in a double bind, he will be encouraged to talk out his sense of inadequacy as though it were an inter-personal or ideological matter."

Joseph Chilton Pearce's book, *The Magical Child* (E. P. Dutton, 1977) has some very worthwhile things to say on this; however, don't bother to read his next book, *The Magical Child Matures*. By this time Pearce had fallen into the East Indian guru trip. In this book, essentially, he says that it doesn't matter if you didn't bond to mother or earth as a child, because if you follow a guru he can take care of it all for you.

— "an awareness of timeless...": **Rexroth**, *An Autobiographical Novel*, p. 337.

137 CHILD NATURE MYSTIC EXPERIENCE: I cover this matter in more detail in *Earth Wisdom*. **Add. notes:** I want to quote from a letter, written to me by Greg Culp, after reading what I had written about such experiences: "I now understand why I need to read these things. Concepts and verbally recognizable experiences, perceptions which can be structurally understood in terms of cultural frameworks, is that which is imprinted in adult life. Whereas in childhood we perceive, absorb, flow into and become, the experience of environment, in acceptable adulthood we're encouraged to hack out piecemeal those portions of our experience deemed acceptable by some perverse consensus, which in turn takes its form not just from what is mutually beneficial, but incorporates the cultural anxiety, fear and neurosis. The experience of reading that which I could never put into words is the 'recognition' that that childhood mystical experience is real, must continue to be nurtured, and to be shared with others who may have forgotten."

— GIORDANO BRUNO: His experience is particularly important. Because of a childhood experience with two volcanoes he was able to stand up against the entire Christian church and was eventually burned at the stake. I discuss him at length in *Earth Wisdom*, p. 64-65.

— "As I stood beside...": **C. S. Lewis**, *Surprised by Joy*. London: Collins, 1965.

— "These vivid...": **Edith Cobb**, *The Ecology of Imagination in Childhood*, p. 88. **Add. notes:** Since beginning work on this volume, I found another "child-nature mystic experience" worth recounting here, for what it has to teach us. Jean Liedloff, in *The Continuum Concept*, writes of an experience she had when eight years old: "through the trees, I saw a glade. It had a lush fir tree at the far side and a knoll in the center covered in bright, almost luminous green moss. The rays of the afternoon sun slanted against the blue-black green of the pine forest. The little roof of visible sky was perfectly blue. The whole picture had a completeness, an all-there quality of such dense power that it stopped me in my tracks. I went to the edge and then, softly, as though into a magical or holy place, to the center, where I sat, then lay down with my cheek against the freshness of the moss…This, at last, was where things were as they ought to be. Everything was in its place—the tree, the earth underneath, the rock, the moss. In autumn, it would be right; in winter under the snow, it would be perfect in its wintriness. Spring would come again and miracle within miracle would unfold, each at its special pace…but all of equal and utter rightness." She tried to hold onto it through her life, but at times she lost "the Glade"; however the memory of it kept her aware of what "rightness" was. Her description of "the Glade" contributes another facet to the "child nature mystic concept." It's a recognition of the "rightness" of all of nature in that little spot. Finally, she discovered that kind of life, while living among primitives. Her book, *The Continuum*, is very important for anyone with a new baby. John Holt gave her the title. It's really about what Blurton Jones calls the "25 million years of human…extending clear back to our higher primate ancestry of some 40 million years" continuum of how a baby develops best and how to continue with your baby so it's part of that on going "continuum." She discovered the "right" way for babies living with a primitive tribe in South America."They were the happiest people I had seen anywhere." She only saw one baby there who did not fit and who, incidentally, showed her how right their life was. This was a baby "who sucked his thumb, stiffened his body, and screamed like a civilized baby." She found out that it had been separated from the tribe; taken away by the missionary and kept in a Caracas hospital for 8 months until his illness was cured. (p. 19) In another place, she writes: "Again, it is the intellect trying to 'decide' what a child can understand, when the continuum way simply permits the child to absorb what he can from the total environment, which is undistorted and unedited." (p. 106) Essentially what Liedloff says is that for the first 8 mo. of life the baby should be in the arms of someone, constantly and all the time. Then when the child is ready to crawl, he does that and no longer needs the first stage which is now completely lived through. If we consider Bowlby's idea that attachment is predominantly an anti-predator device, this makes sense. Real safety is in the arms of the adult.

—— "including the new mown hay…": **Rexroth**, *An Autobiographical Novel*, p. 337.

—— THE NAME, CHUANG: **Kuang-ming Wu**, *Chuang Tzu: World Philosopher at Play*, p. 101.

—— "saw the self…": Ibid., p. 107.

—— "in and through the True Man…": Ibid., p. 108. **Add. notes**: In light of what I said above about the "rightness" of Jean Liedhoff's experience in "the Glade," I will give Wu's entire quote here: "One experiences no 'external conformity,' but merely 'things' thing and is not thinged by things, letting them be as they are…This constitutes the listening to 'the piping of earth'… This fit, once attained, endures. One now realizes that one has already been listening to the 'piping of heaven,' where every effort and every comfort is forgotten, including the very fit to things. And this is where the truth of things appears.." The quote in my text continues from here. Wu is referring to Chuang Tzu's statement concerning "the piping of heaven" that rustles forth "the piping of earth," that in turn engender the "piping of men." (Watson's translation of *Chuang Tzu*, pp. 36-37, and 43.)

—— "They said to each other…": **Chuang Tzu**, trans. Watson, p. 97 and 86.

—— "When we beat the drum…": **Ramon Medina**, quoted in Peter T. Furst and Marina Anguiano, "'To fly as birds': myth and ritual as agents of enculturation among the Huichol Indians of Mexico." In Johannes Wilbert, ed. *Enculturation in Latin America: An Anthology*. UCLA Latin America Center Publication. Los Angeles: University of California, 1976, pp. 95-181. **Add. notes**: Again, I will put specific paging for the material in this article in order to facilitate locating it.

—— GOD'S EYES OR "FOUR SACRED DIRECTIONS" SYMBOL: **Furst**, "To fly as birds," p. 95-97.

138 DESCRIPTION OF THE FEAST CALLED WIMA'KWARI: **Carl Lumholtz**, quoted in Furst, "To fly as birds," pp. 97-98.

—— "This ceremony…" down to "Our Mother Ceremony": Ibid., p. 98-99.

—— "to relate, in lengthy chants…": **Barbara Myerhoff**, *Peyote Hunt: The*

Sacred Journey of the Huichol Indians. Ithaca: Cornell University Press, 1974, pp. 113-116.

—— SAN LUIS POTOSI—MOUNTAIN OF SILVER: See chapter three for more on this.

—— "first five years of their life…": **Furst**, "To fly as birds", p. 98.

—— "The people residing…" down to "Virgin of Guadalupe": Ibid., p. 99- 101.

139 "Masters of Animals…": Ibid., p. 107.

—— RAMON MEDINA: Ibid., p. 110-113.

—— SEVEN ARROWS: **Hyemeyohsts Storm**, *Seven Arrows*. New York: Harper & Row, 1972.

140 GOURD RATTLE FOR EACH CHILD: **Add. notes**: After I had done the first draft of this chapter I went on E. Cogburn's "long dance" at the Aztec kiva in New Mexico. There were fifty people taking part in the ceremony. The day following the dance there is a ritual closing. Everyone was seated in a giant circle on the ground. There was chanting to the drums and some had gourd rattles. Deborah Chapin had her daughter on her lap, 13 month old Aleah and was shaking the gourd. I was sitting directly across from them, watching Aleah. Quite soon Aleah reached up for the gourd, took it in her hand and began shaking it. A look of sheer surprise and joy came over her at the sound she was making. She quickly looked all around the circle at the others doing the same and continued, smiling broadly. And, of course, her rhythm synchronized, automatically, with all the others. I was delighted to see how easily this happened. It truly was the "most natural thing in the world."

—— WHEN THE DRUM IS BEATEN AND THE MARA'ÁKAME FLIES THE CHILDREN TO WIRIKTA: **Furst**, "To fly as birds", pp. 126-149. The entire ceremony is given on these pages.

—— "Keeper of the drum.": Ibid., p. 137. **Add notes**: This is not a ceremony merely "for the children." Quoting Jean Liedloff here, she says that anything done, should be "primarily by and for the grownups, and the children allowed to join in without unduly disrupting it. In this way, everyone will be behaving in a natural, unforced way with no strain on the parent's part to confine their mind to a childish level, nor upon the children to try to adapt themselves to what an adult believes is best for them, thus preventing their own initiative from motivating them smoothly and without conflict."

141 "In this ceremony…": Ibid., p. 111.

—— COTTON BALLS ON STRING: Ibid., p. 141-142. **Add.notes**: For the Huichol ceremony an arrow is stuck into the ground. A cactus fiber cord with a cotton ball for each of the children is attached to it. The other end of the cord is said to be supported by, "Elder Brother," the "divine deer person." The Deer and the shaman are "the ones who will bear the string of children," while they are on their "journey." In doing your own "fly as birds" ceremony refer, often, to a local animal, who helps the children during their journey.

—— "We are all…": Ibid., p. 111.

142 GOURDS REPRESENTING RUSTLING OF WINGS: Ibid., p.137. The text reads: "they are given small gourd rattles whose sound, said to represent the rustling of their wings, accompanies that of the drum on whose vibrations the shaman…lift[s] them magically into the sky."

—— "The tree gathers up earth-power": **D. H. Lawrence**, "Pan in America" In *Phoenix I*, New York, Viking Press, 1968, pp 22-31.

—— "Look, here you are blessed..": **Furst**, "To Fly as Birds", p. 128.

—— "Here we are now, very happy…": Ibid., p 170.

143 "The children have been flown…": Ibid., p. 148.

—— "Place to Australian…": **Shepard**, *Nature and Madness*, p. 132.

144 IMPORTANCE OF PLAY: **Add. notes**: To document the philosophical importance of play, there are three articles, which I recommend as especially useful: 1) Elizabeth Behn, "Integrative Issues and Methods: Toward An Understanding of Play." *Main Currents In Modern Thought* 3 (May/June 1975). The article begins with a quotation by Eugen Fink: "Human play…is the symbolic action which puts us in the presence of the meaning of the world and of life." Further along she quotes Fink again: "Death, work, domination, love and play, these are the elements of the patterns which we find in human existence, so enigmatic and ambiguous." 2) Eugen Fink, "The Ontology of Play." *Philosophy Today* (Summer 1974): 147-161. This is one of the few translations you'll find of Fink's work, which, as the editor states, "remains the most basic and comprehensive study of play available." This translation is from a section of Eugen Fink's work: *Oase des Glucks: Gedanken zu einer Ontologie*

des Spiels. Freiburg, Germany: Karl Alber Verlag, 1957. Trans. Sister Delphine Kolker of St. John's College, Cleveland Ohio. 3) And most imporant of all as an introduction, Lawrence M. Hinman, "Nietzsche's Philosophy of Play." *Philosophy Today* 18, (Summer 1974): 106-124. Sub-headings include "Play as the Highest Form of Human Activity", "Creative Play as the Overcoming of Nihilism" and "The World As Play: The Eternal Recurrence of the Same."

For an in-depth discussion, see **Gilles Deleuze**, *Nietzsche and Philosophy*. New York: Columbia University Press, 1983. Trans. Hugh Tomlinson, first published in France in 1962. Here is a quote from Deleuze: "But the creation of values, the yes of the child-player, would not be formed under these conditions if they were not, at the same time subject to a deeper genealogy. It is no surprise, therefore, to find that every Neitzschean concept lies at the crossing of two unequal genetic lines. Not only the eternal return and the Overman, but laughter, play and dance. In relation to Zarathustra laughter, play and dance are affirmative powers of transmutation...[then summing up], laughter and play are affirmative powers of reflection and development. Dance affirms becoming and the being of becoming; laughter, roars of laughter, affirm multiplicity and the unity of multiplicity; play affirms chance and the necessity of chance." (p. 193-194)

— "architecturally complex play space...": **Shepard**, *The Tender Carnivore and the Sacred Game*. **Add. notes:** See chapter five of his book, "The Karma of Adolescence", pp. 177-233. In addition to explaining important needs for small children, this chapter is the best thing ever written on adolescence. On page 225, Shepard states: "Adolescence is not a sickness that is inevitably traumatic but a highly specialized, profoundly rewarding period of human life, an evolutionary adaptation that developed during centuries of high human maturity in small, hunter-gatherer groups. All its characteristics have an internal logic and purpose."

— "not only as a honing of personal...": **Harold F. Searles**, quoted in Shepard, *Nature and Madness*, p. 12.

— "violently sunder...in the interests...": **C. G. Jung**, "The Psychology of the Child Archetype." This particular quote is from p. 162, par. 274. **Add. notes:** This was first published, 1951 in Zurich, in C. G. Jung and C. Kerenyi, *Essays on a Science of Mythology*. The English translation of this work was published in 1969 by Princeton University Press.

— "Religious observances, i.e., the retelling and ritual repetition...": Ibid., p. 162, par. 275.

— "[T]he oral tradition is not memorized...": **Gary Snyder**, "Foreword." In Donald L. Philippi, *Songs of Gods, Songs of Humans: The Epic Tradition of the Ainu*. Tokyo: University of Tokyo Press, 1979 and Princeton: Princeton University Press., p. vii.

145 "HO! Sun, Moon, Stars, all you that...": **Alice Fletcher and Francis LaFlesche**, "The Omaha Tribe."

Ch. 12 Overview of Ritual
pp. 146 and 147 Opening Quotes

— "a man without ritual...": **Hsün Tzu**, 2, p. 25. Burton Watson. trans. *Hsün Tzu: Basic Writings*, 2. New York: Columbia University Press, 1967, p. 25.

— "[Rituals] mend ever again worlds...": **Roy Rappaport**, *Ecology, Meaning, and Religion*, p. 206.

— "There is a rapidly growing body...": **Dr. J. P. Henry**, "Comment." In *Journal of Analytical Psychology*.

— "I am...asserting that to view...": **Rappaport**, *Ecology, Meaning, and Religion*, p. 174.

— "The purpose of ritual...": **Z Budapest**, a modern ritual facilitator, quoted in Margot Adler, *Drawing Down the Moon*. New York: The Viking Press, 1979, p. 193.

— "[In ritual] you get out...": **Elizabeth Cogburn**, in a talk at the "Long Dance" held in the kiva at Aztec, New Mexico, May, 1987.

148 "What absorbs me...": **Barry Lopez**, *Arctic Dreams*, pp. 154-155.

149 "a spectacle of the purest...": **D. H. Lawrence**, "The Flying Fish." In *Phoenix*. New York: The Viking Press, 1968.

— "Thus, when a festival...": **Josef Pieper**, *In Tune with the World: A Theory of Festivity*. New York: Harcourt, Brace & World, 1965, p. 30-31.

— "There can be no...": Ibid., p. 53.

— "Joy is the response...": Ibid., p. 18.

— "To celebrate...": Ibid., p. 23.

— "To have joy in anything...": **Nietzsche**, quoted in Pieper, *In Tune with the World*, p. 20. Being German, Pieper quotes from the German edition of Nietzsche: *Nachgelassene Aufzeichnungen aus den Jahren 1882 bis 1888*. Gesammelte Werke, v. 16, p. 37. **Add. notes:** Pieper's little 81 page volume is the best introduction to real festival that I've found. By reading it back in 1965 when it first came out I began to understand the importance of ritual and festival. Because I was still a Catholic and Pieper is a Catholic philosopher, it never occurred to me to ask where he got these ideas. Years later, rereading the book I found that all the quotations, leading into his main points are from Nietzsche.

— "Underlying all festive joy...: **Pieper**, *In Tune with the World*, p. 20. Further down the page Pieper quotes Nietzsche: "If it be granted that we say Yea to a single moment, then in so doing we have said Yea not only to ourselves, but to all existence." (*Wille zur Macht IV*, no. 1032. Gesammelte Werke, V. 19, p. 352.)

150 OLDER FORM OF AGRICULTURE—ROOT CROPS: **Carl Sauer**, *Agricultural Origins and Dispersals*, 1952.

— "...can be derived from Chavin...": **Donald Lathrap**, "Gifts of the Cayman."

— "sort of trinity...": Ibid.

— "celebration of the prior...": Ibid.

— CHEYENNE INDIANS: **Peter J. Powell**, *Sweet Medicine*, v. 1. Norman Oklahoma: University of Oklahoma Press, 1969, pp. xxii, 22, 24, and 26.

— SWEET MEDICINE'S name: Ibid., v. 1, p. 53.

— "Erect Horns...": Ibid., v. 2, p. 872.

151 "The solid sky, the cloudy sky...": **Arrow Lodge priests**, quoted in Ibid., v. 2, p. 488.

— STEAM TRAINS AND BUFFALO: Ibid., v. 1, p. 84.

— "Ritualization is grounded...": **Erik Erikson**, "The Ontogeny of Ritualization in Man." In "A discussion on Ritualization of Behaviour in Animals and Man." In *Philosophical Transactions of the Royal Society of London*, Series B. v. 251, 1966, pp. 338-349.

— HISTORY OF THE MODERN STUDY OF RITUAL: **Julian Huxley**, "Introduction." In "A Discussion on Ritualization of Behaviour in Animals and Man", pp. 249-272.

— LORENZ CREDITS WHITMAN AND HEINROTH: **Konrad Lorenz**, *Behind the Mirror*, p. 208.

— "to promote better...": **Julian Huxley**, "Introduction." In "A Discussion on Ritualization of Behaviour in Animals and Man.", pp. 249-272.

— "needed to help...": Ibid.

— "essential for all transcendent...": Ibid.

152 "charged, flat-out down..." down to "prove that the wild...": **Hugo and Jane van Lawick-Goodall**, *In the Shadow of Man*. Boston: Houghton Mifflin, 1971, pp. 52 and 53.

— "The animal seemed lost in contemplation...": **Melvin Konner**, *The Tangled Wing: Biological Constraints on the Human Spirit*. New York: Harper Colophon Books, 1983, p. 431-432. He is quoting from an unpublished ms. which Harold Bauer gave him. This scene has also been observed by other observers at the Gombe Stream Reserve in Africa and additional information was given Konner by Barbara Smuts and Irven deVore.

— "It was something they...": Ibid., p 432.

— IONIZATION: **Dolores LaChapelle**, *Earth Wisdom*, p. 56-57.

— "a large order...": **Erik Erikson**, "The Ontogeny of Ritualization in Man."

— "but a variant..." and "It may be...": **Rappaport**, *Ecology, Meaning and Religion*, p. 212.

— JUNG'S CRISIS WITH FREUD: **C. G. Jung**, *Memories, Dreams, Reflections*, pp. 170 and 174.

— "painfully humiliating...": Ibid., p. 174.

— "a turning point...": Ibid.

— "Regression as we now call...": **A. Plant**, "Jung and Rebirth." *The Journal of Analytical Psychology* 22 (April 1977): 142-157.

153 "The first and probably most..." down to "All evolved under...": **Konrad Lorenz**, "Evolution of Ritualization in the Biological and Cultural Spheres." In *Philosophical Transactions of the Royal Society*, pp. 272-284. (This has been reprinted in Richard Evans, *Konrad Lorenz: the Man and His Ideas*. New York: Harcourt Brace & Jovanovich, 1975, pp. 129 to

151.) The latter may be easier to get through inter-library loan.
— "essential common functions...": **Lorenz**, *Behind the Mirror*, p. 209.
— "one of cerebral training...": **Simeons**, *Man's Presumptuous Brain*, p. 58.
— "the transcendent function...": **Stevens**, *Archetypes*, p. 272.
— ACTIVE IMAGINATION: **Ernest Rossi**, "The Cerebral Hemispheres in Analytic Psychology."
— INITIATION RITUALS: **Stevens**, in *Archetypes* explains that "Initiation rituals possess biological, as well as psycho-social significance..." (p.149).

154 "They strive, within...": **Erik Erikson**, "Identity and the Life Cycle." *Psychological Issues* 1 *Monograph* 1, New York: International Universities Press, p. 144.
— "Guilt and the fear...": **Stevens**, *Archetypes*, p. 241.
— "The intellect has no...": **Jung**, *Coll. Works*, v. 12, par. 60.
— "In the dream...": **Jung**, *Coll. Works*, v. 16, Par, 351.
— "two million year-old man...": **Jung**, "Roosevelt 'Great' in Jung's Analysis."
— "Even though it reaches...": **Jung**, *Coll. Works*, v. 10, Par. 304.
— "there was a personal unconscious...": **Jung**, Ibid., p. 573.
— "daylight of the mentally...": **Jung**, *Coll. Works*, v. 8, p. 19.
— "by differentiation of adaptively...": **C. Laughlin, J. McManus, and E. d'Aquili**, "Introduction." In E. d'Aquili et al, *The Spectrum of Ritual: A Biogenetic Structural Analysis*. New York: Columbia University Press, 1979. p. 10.
— "totality of neural models...": Ibid., p. 13. **Add. notes**: d'Aquili refers to Roy Rapport, *Pigs for the Ancestors*, pp. 237-238. Rappaport's beginning work on these concepts is: 1) 1963, "Aspects of man's influence upon island ecosystems: alteration and control." In F. R. Fosberg, ed. *Man's Place in the Island Ecosystem*. Honolulu, Bishop Museum and 2) 1967, "Ritual regulation of environmental relations among a New Guinea people." *Ethnology* 6: 17-30.
— "cybernetic flow...": **Laughlin et al**, "Introduction," pp. 29, 30-32.

155 HUMAN RITUAL DEVELOPING OUT OF NON-HUMAN: **Konrad Lorenz**, "Evolution of Ritualization in the Biological and Cultural Spheres." *Phil. Trans. of the Royal Society*, B. 251, pp. 273-284.
— RITUALIZED TRANCE BEHAVIOR: **E. Bourguignon**, "Dreams and Altered States of Consciousness in Anthropological Research." In F. K. L. Hus, ed. *Psychological Anthropology*. Homewood, Illinois: The Dorsey Press.
— REPETITIVE STIMULI AND RITUAL TRANCE: **Barbara W. Lex**, "Neurobiology of Ritual Trance." In d'Aguili, ed. *The Spectrum of Ritual*, p. 117-151.
— TUNING: **E. Gellhorn**, "Central Nervous System Tuning and Its Implications for Neuropsychiatry." *Journal of Nervous and Mental Diseases* 147 (1968): 148-162.
— IF ONE IS STIMULATED, THE OTHER IS INHIBITED: **K. H. Pribram**, "Emotion: Steps Toward a Neuropsychological Theory." In D. Glass (ed) *Neurophysiology and Emotion*. New York: The Rockefeller Univ. Press, 1967.
— EFFECT OF TUNING ON THE NERVOUS SYSTEM: **Gellhorn and Kiely**, "Mystical States of Consciousness; Neurophysiological and Clinical Analysis." *Journal of Nervous and Mental Diseases* 154 (1972): 399-405.
— ACTIVATION BROUGHT ABOUT BY DRUMMING ETC: **d'Aquili and Laughlin**, "The Neurobiology of Myth and Ritual." In d'Aquili, *Spectrum of Ritual*, p. 177.
— "of itself produces positive limbic...": Ibid., p. 159.

156 "form of a myth in nonindustrial...": Ibid., p. 161.
— RATIONAL THINKING...SPLITS: **R. E. Ornstein**, *The Psychology of Consciousness*. San Francisco: Freeman, 1972.
— "union of opposites" ... "union of self with God"...": **d'Aquili and Laughlin**, "The Neurobiology of Myth and Ritual", p. 176.
— "It powerfully relieves...": Ibid., p. 179.
— HAL HARTZELL'S ACCOUNT OF THE HOEDAD EXPERIENCE: **Hal Hartzell**, "Hoedads, Inc.: Birth of a Cooperative." (See Back of the Book section for the entire story.)
— ENDORPHINS, BRAIN CHEMICALS ETC: Useful sources: 1) Roger H. Unger, "Endogenous Opioid Peptides." In R. Petersdorf et al, *Harrison's Principles of Internal Medicine*. New York: McGraw Hill, 1983, pp. 487-490. 2) Candace Pert et al, "Neuropeptides and Their Receptors: A Psychosomatic Network." *The Journal of Immunology* 135 (August 1985). (She has a new paper out on a possible cure for AIDS.) 3) *Brain*

Mind Bulletin, P.O. Box 42211, L.A. California has useful articles on the latest findings on brain research.
— "The Li could be described...": **Robert M. Gimello**, "The Civil Status of Li in Classical Confucianism." *Philosophy East and West* 14.
— "Through rites, Heaven and...": **Hsün Tzu**, 19. trans, Burton Watson, p. 94.
— "all consort together...": **Kuang-Ming Wu**, *Chuang Tzu: World Philosopher at Play*, p. 9.
— "In a ritual...": **Girardot**, *Myth and Meaning in Early Taoism*, p. 145.

157 "A vast mass of folklore...": **Needham**, *Sci. and Civil.*, v. 2, p.119.
— "of great importance..." down to "While the li ...": **Eugene Cooper**, "The Potlatch in Ancient China." *The History of Religions* 22 (Nov. 1982).
— "There is harmony...": **J. Legge**, trans. *The Sacred Books of China: The Texts of Confucianism*, Parts III and IV, the *Li Ki*. In F. Max Muller, ed. *Sacred Books of the East*. Oxford: Clarendon Press, 1885, v. 28, p. 442.
— "Therefore when I look...": **Cooper**, "The Potlatch in Ancient China."
— "it is enough for the ruler...": **William Watson**, *Early Civilization in China*. New York: Oxford University Press, 1966, p. 71.
— CHA IN THE HALL OF LIGHT: **Cooper**, "The Potlatch in Ancient China."
— "a gathering place of the ...": **W. E. Soothill**, *The Hall of Light: A Study of Ancient Chinese Kingship*. London: Lutterworth Press, 1951, pp. 78 and 88.
— MAUSS ON POTLATCH: **Marcel Mauss**, *The Gift: Forms and Functions of Exchange in Archaic Societies*. New York, W. W. Norton, 1967. (first published in 1924).

158 "You are one of fifteen...": **G. William Domhoff**, *The Bohemian Grove and Other Retreats: A Study in Ruling Class Cohesiveness*. New York: Harper, 1975, p. 1. **Add. notes**: He gathered material for the book from club members, present and former employees of the club, historical archives and newspapers. The particular biographical information is from the years 1965 to 1970.
— NO WOMEN BUT HIGH CLASS PROSTITUTES: Ibid., p. 27.
— LIST OF MEMBERS: Ibid., p. 41-42.
— "In 1942 the Bohemian Grove..." down to "But it is not only...": Ibid., pp. 59, 82, and 96.

159 "a new way of looking...": **Victor Turner**, "Forms of Symbolic Action: Introduction." In Robert F. Spencer, ed. *Forms of Symbolic Action: Proceedings of the 1969 Annual Spring Meeting of the American Ethnological Society*. Published by American Ethnological Society. Seattle: University of Washington Press, p. 15. **Add. notes**: This publication is just as important as Julian Huxley's Conference: "A Discussion on Ritualization of Behaviour in Animals and Man," which I discussed in the first part of this chapter. These two publications, together, give an excellent grounding in the basics of ritual.
— "The ethologists...": **Victor Turner**, Ibid., p. 7.
— "After many years...": **Victor Turner**, *Revelation and Divination Among the Ndembu*. Ithaca: Cornell University Press, 1967, pp. 31-32.
— "Bonding...": **Victor Turner**, "Forms of Symbolic Action: Introduction," p. 18.
— "poles of meaning...": Ibid., p. 21.
— "deritualization takes place...": Ibid., p. 18.
— "many of the concepts of the 'ideological'...": Ibid.
— "The irksomeness of moral...": Ibid., p. 21.
— "For me, communitas...": **Victor Turner**, *The Ritual Process: Structure and Anti-Structure*. Ithaca: Cornell University Press, 1969, p. 126
— "elicit creative...": Ibid., p. 127.

160 "As the ceremony progressed...": **A student**, quoted in Victor and Edith Turner, "Performing Ethnography." *The Drama Review* 26 1982: 33-50. Cambridge: M.I.T. Press.
— "One has the feeling that..." and "It is not...": **Stanley Walens**, quoted in Turner, "Performing Ethnography."
— "The liturgy tradition...": **K. Schipper**, quoted in N. J. Girardot, "Let's Get Physical: The Way of Liturgical Taoism," a review of *Le Corps Taoiste*, by K. Schipper, Paris, 1982. In *The History of Religions* (November 1983). **Add. notes**: Schipper is a European who studied Taoism for ten years and practiced it in Taiwan. Girardot says that Schipper's book is a good antidote "to the largely incoherent appraisals of Taoism...popular Wattsian and Blofeldian fabulations."
— "The Sun Dance...": **Clare Hall**, "An Ideological Dichotomy: Myths

and Folk Beliefs Among the Shoshoni Indians of Wyoming." This is the report on a Colloquium arranged by Clare Hall at Cambridge University in 1971. *The History of Religions* 2.

— "to revive the topocosm...": **Theodore H. Gaster**, *Thespis: Ritual, Myth, and Drama in the Ancient Near East*. New York: W. W. Norton Co., 1961 revision, pp. 17, 23 and 24. Originally published in 1950. **Add. notes**: In his Preface, p. 15, Gaster writes that he spent a total of "22 uneasy years...and [it was] written in conditions of very considerable difficulty and privation."

— "based on the conception that life...": Ibid. p. 17.

— WORLD RENEWAL PATTERN FOUND IN ANCIENT CULTURES: Ibid., p. 18.

— ATTIS THE PINE, ETC.: Ibid., p. 9.

— "the great grape-cluster...": Ibid., p. 420.

— PSALM 29 OF THE BIBLE: Ibid., p. 443-445.

— ADAM OF ST. VICTOR: Ibid., p. 461.

161 "Of course I am anxious...": **country woman**, quoted by Gilbert Murray, in Gaster, *Thespis*, p. 10.

— NAMES OF WORLD RENEWAL RITES: **A. L. Kroeber and E. Gifford**, "Kuksu Cult of Central California." *Anthropological Records* 13 "World Renewal: A Cult System of Native NW California." Berkeley, 1949.

— "festival...came in time...": **Gaster**, *Thespis*, p. 43.

— "The words 'communion'...": **William Willeford**, "Festival, Communion and Mutuality." *Journal of Analytical Psychology* 26 (October 1981): pp. 345-355.

— "meet and see in each other..." down to "concerns us all...": Ibid.

— "the vitality normally locked up...": **C. L. Barber**, *Shakespeare's Festive Comedy*. Princeton: Princeton University Press, pp. 5, 7, and 8. Quoted in Willeford, "Festival, Communion and Mutuality."

— "so that nature..." down to "In the process...": **Willeford**, "Festival, Communion and Mutuality."

162 "the conduct of life...": **Kathleen Sands**, "Preface: A Symposium." To, "Conference Concerning *Ceremony*, a novel by Leslie M. Silko, 1977." *The American Indian Quarterly: A Journal of Anthropology, History and Literature* 5 (February 1979). Published by the Texas Society for American Indian Studies and Research.

— "The healing of Tayo...": **Paula Gunn Allen**, "The Psychological Landscape of Ceremony." Ibid.

— "The saiga antelope..." down to "a ceremony for the wind...": **Hans Duerr**, *Dreamtime*. This is in his footnote #26, p. 180. See *Dreamtime* for his references here.

— "After forgetting the sense...": Ibid., p. 180.

— "Human welfare...": **Gary Snyder**, "Afterword." In Shepard and Sanders, *The Sacred Paw*, pp. 206-212.

— "The shedding...": **Jane Harrison**, *Themis*, p. 449.

— "precisely delineating...": **Lévi-Strauss**, quoted in Robin and T. Ridington, "The Inner Eye of Shamanism and Totemism." *History of Religions* 10 (1970): 49-51.

163 "Mythical cosmologies..." down to "Mythic and totemic...": Ibid.

— "From the point of view...": **Dr. Carlos Alberto Seguin**, "Peiquiatria folklorica." In *Peiquiatria Peruana* (Primer Congreso Nacional) Oscar Valdivia and A. Pendola, eds. Lima pp. 154-159. Quoted in Douglas Sharon, "Becoming a Curandero in Peru." In Johannes Wilbert, *Eculturation in Latin America: An Anthology*.

— "witchdoctors and psychiatrists...": **E. Fuller Torrey**, *The Mind Game: Witchdoctors and Psychiatrists*. New York: Bantam Books, 1972, p. 201. Quoted in Sharon, "Becoming a Curandero in Peru."

— "First, whatever else...": **Rappaport**, *Meaning, Ecology and Religion*, p. 179

— "make references to..." down to "given the extent...": Ibid., p. 178.

— "not always downright treacherous..." down to "Participation in rituals...": Ibid., p. 236-237.

164 "the ultimate trying...": **Chaung Tzu**, quoted in Kuang-Ming Wu, *Chuang Tzu: World Philosopher at Play*, p. 91. This is Wu's translation of *chih wei ch'u wei, ch'u wei wu wei*.

Ch. 13 Sacred Land

pp. 166 and 167 Opening Quotes

— "If there can be...": **Marjorie Kinnan Rawlings**, author of *The Yearling*. Quoted from her Journal on a 1986 PBS documentary on her life titled "Cross Creek."

— "The first thing to do...": **Tahirassawichi**, the Pawnee priest who worked with Alice Fletcher to give her the rituals of the Hako ceremonial journey. (See below in this chapter for more on the Hako.) **Add. notes**: The precise wording of this statement is from the poem by Ernesto Cardinal, "Tahirassawichi in Washington." (*Homage to the American Indians*. Baltimore: The Johns Hopkins University Press, 1973, pp. 63-66.) The poem is about the journey that he took to Washington in 1898 "only to speak about religion." Essentially this poem gives a very moving poetical account of the Hako; although the word is not mentioned in the poem. The poem ends laconically, with this line: "Tahirassawichi's words, I suppose, did not mean anything to the State Department."

— "In a single gram of earth...": **Arne Naess**, *Ecology, Society, and Lifestyle: Ecosophy T*. Cambridge: Cambridge University Press, (due off the press in 1988). This was first published in Norwegian in 1976. Naess sent me a section of it which was poorly translated into English. The quotation comes from that translation and his reference is Ehrlich 1970, p. 180. Essentially what Naess is doing with this sentence is enlarging the concept of community. The original Norwegian title had community instead of society in the title. In this quote he is pointing out the disturbance of the "community" of, say, one footprint of earth, when one steps on the ground.

— "The nation may topple...": **Tu Fu**. I have no further bibliographical information concerning the origin of this frequently quoted poem.

— "We're just starting...": **Gary Snyder**, *The Old Ways*, p. 42.

— "The spirit of that wild...": **D. H. Lawrence**, *The White Peacock*. Carbondale: Southern Ill. Univ. Press, 1966.

— "When 26 percent of the GNP...": **Lee Swenson**, Executive director of Farralones Institute, "Culture from the Groundup." *New Age* (March 1979): 58-61. **Add. notes**: These figures were correct back in 1979; obviously the percentage is much higher now with the escalating costs of transportation, but I could find no more recent figures, which in itself is indicative of the problem.

— "We are so little at peace...": **Wendell Berry**, *The Long-Legged House*. New York: Harcourt Brace & World, 1969, pp. 84-85.

— "...Until I can know...": **Lou Welch**, "I Remain." *Upriver Downriver* 8.

— "We are the land...that is...": **Paula Gunn Allen**, "The Psychological Landscape of Ceremony."

— "In a fist of forest...": **Kim R. Stafford**, *Having Everything Perfect*. Lewiston: Confluence Press, Lewis-Clark State College, 1986, p. 108.

169 "I want to ask, finally, if...": **David Abram**, "Notes from Thami Valley." See Back of Book Section for complete essay.

— THE GLORY: For more information on my experience of "the glory," see *Earth Wisdom*, pp. 10-14.

— BREAKING THROUGH: For more information write Outdoor Leadership Training Seminars, P.O. Box 20281, Denver, Colorado 80220

170 AUTUMN EQUINOX TAOIST CELEBRATIONS: For more information write Way of the Mountain Learning Center, P.O. Box 542, Silverton Colorado 81433.

— "The people are born, live and die...": **Tom Jay**, "Land, Soil, Dirt: Some Notes from the Ground." First published, 1987 in *Upriver Downriver*, a bioregional journal for Northern California. Address: P.O. Box 1051, Arcata, California, 95521.

— "a large order to burden...": **Erikson**, "Ontogeny of Ritualization in Man."

— "The sunrise in these..." down to "moment when, with the typical...": **Jung**, *Memories, Dreams, Reflections*, p. 268-269.

171 "Gradually I experienced..." down to "they temporarily re-enter...": **Richard S. Gould**, *Yiwara: Foragers of the Australian Desert*. New York: Charles Scribner's Sons, 1969.

— "It is worth noting...": **Megitt**, quoted in Gould, Ibid.

172 "each man steps up..." down to "the core of his social...": **Gould**, Ibid.

— "impersonal and collective...": **C. G. Jung**, *Coll. Works*, v. 9, pt. 2, pp. 7 and 223.

— "But as to the origin...": **Herodotus**, quoted in Jane Harrison, *Mythology*. England: Marshall Jones Co., 1924, p. xvii.

173 "too good to be true...": **Harrison**, Ibid., p. 59-61.

— "Earth sends up fruits..." down to "first in my prayers...": Ibid., p. 61.

— "had great influence..." down to "the little girls of Athens...": Ibid.,

p. 117. Also see Shepard, *The Sacred Paw.*

— "Great stress..." down to "the herb, Artemisia...": Ibid., pp. 125-127.

— "These vague *numina* ...": Ibid., pp xiv and xv.

— "For you the grove...": **The Aeneid.** Adam Parry, "The Two Voices of Vergil's *Aeneid." Arion* 2 (Winter 1983): 66-80.

— "Historically, we may...": **Steele Commager,** ed. *Vergil: A Collection of Critical Essays.* Englewood Cliffs: Prentice Hall, 1966, p. 10.

— "Aeneas will defeat...": **Allan Mandelbaum,** *The Aeneid of Vergil: A Verse Translation.* Berkeley: University of California, 1971, p. 271.

174 RELIGION...MAINTENANCE OF ABIDING RELATIONSHIP: **Gertrude Levy,** *Gate of Horn,* p. 35.

— "His feeling for them...": **Parry,** "The Two Voices."

— "The great caves...": **Sir Arthur Evans,** *The Earlier Religion of Greece in the Light of Creatan Discoveries.* London: Macmillan & Co., 1931, p. 5

— "We have here...": Ibid., p. 8.

175 SACRED MOUNTAINS AND CAVES: **LaChapelle,** *Earth Wisdom,* pp. 31-39.

— "usually consisting..."down to the quote from the *Shozen engi,* "Those who tread...": **Allan Grapard,** "Flying Mountains and Walkers of Emptiness: Toward a Definition of Sacred Space in Japanese Religion." *History of Religions* 20 #3: 195-221.

— "to all beings...": **Joseph W. Kitagawa,** " 'A Past of Things Present': Notes on Major Motifs of Early Japanese Religions."

176 "When a tree becomes...": **M. Eliade,** "Methodological Remarks on the Study of Religious Symbolism."

— "In early Japan..." down to "sang to and about rivers...: **Kitagawa,** "A Past of Things Present."

— THE WORD FOR MOUNTAIN PASS: **Ichiro Hori,** "Mountains and Their Importance for the Idea of the Other World in Japanese Folk Religion."

— "The mountain god...": Ibid.

— "Trees were the original...": **Y. T. Hosoi,** "Sacred Tree in Japanese Prehistory." *History of Religions* 16 (November 1976): 95-119.

— "ancient Europe, Asia...": **Jerome Rothenberg,** *"Pre-Face to Origin."* In *Alcheringa.*

177 BUDDHA ENLIGHTENMENT/MORNING STAR: **Daisaku Ikeda,** *The Living Buddha: An Interpretative Biography.* Burton Watson. trans. New York: Weatherhill, 1976.

— "the ancient and continuous recognition..." down to "we might say that it was in going...": **William R. LaFleur,** "Saigyō and the Value of Nature: Pt. 1." *History of Religions* 13 #2 (November 1973): 93-120.

— "Salvation consists in discovering..." down to "fashioned the closest possible link...": **LaFleur,** "Saigyō and the Value of Nature: Pt. 2." *History of Religions* 13 #3 (February 1974): 227-248. **Add. notes:** In the haiku, given on this page, the Japanese word, translated as "mind," is *kokoro.* While the Japanese were writing about this concept as far back as 700 A.D., we still have no word for it. This word, in itself, *kokoro,* contains the heart of our relationship to nature; but there is no simple way to define it. See T. and Toyo Izutsu, *The Theory of Beauty in the Classical Aesthetics of Japan.* The Hague: Martinus Nijhoff, 1981. I will give a few quotes from the book to show the depth of this concept: "The way Tsurayuki mentions the *kokoro* (mind) suggests that it is not to be understood as a particular state of subjectivity or of the consciousness which has already been activated toward artistic creativity. Rather, it is structurally posited by Tsurayuki as the ground not merely of poetic creation but of all psychological and cognitive activities or experiences of the subject." (p. 7) "Contemplative experience, first of all, implies...a total negation of, the cognitive focus unilaterally directed from the subject to the object, which further implies that the subject has to relinquish the logico-linguistic thinking whose most conspicuous characteristic consists in being causal, successive and linear." (p. 32) And one more, concerning the essential aspect that the aesthetic impulse comes from nature to the human, not the other way around."In the poetic 'field' of *haiku,* the centripetal dynamics of the positive linguistic expression emphatically suggests the existence of *yo-haku,* the non-expressed totality of Nature and human affairs in the phenomenal time and space surrounding [the particular natural thing] ... " (p. 73) This is the underlying meaning of Bashō's "Of the pine-tree learn from the pine-tree. Of the bamboo learn from the bamboo."

178 "That the self advances...": Zen master, **Dōgen,** *Genjōkōan.* This translation was given in Robert Aitken, "Gandhi, Dōgen and Deep Ecology."

Zero 4 (1980). Aitken. in his reference gives *The Way of Everyday Life,* with commentary by Hakuyu Taizan Maezumi. Published by the Zen Center of Los Angeles and the Institute for Transcultural Studies, 1978 (no paging). However, the translation in this book is not the same as the one Aitken used. I much prefer Aitken's translation.

— "codependent origination...": **William La Fleur,** *Mirror for the Moon: A Selection of Poems by Saigyō* (1118-1190). New York: New Directions, 1978, p. xxv. All haiku by Saigyō used in this chapter are from this volume.

— "One spirit activates...": **Bashō,** *Oi no kobumi.* trans. Suzuki, *Zen and Japanese Culture,* p. 258. **Add. notes:** Actually, "spirit" is the wrong word here, but it's probably the only way Suzuki could say it in our language. Again referring to Izutsu's, *Theory of Beauty,* p. 69, Bashō actually wrote: "there is observable one single thread stringing them together." And Izutsu continues, "By the 'one single thread' is meant here in this context the existential pursuit of the *fuga-no-makoto,* the 'genuineness of aesthetic creativity'." This, once again, refers to nature itself.

— "Tent tethered among...": **Robert MacLean,** *Heartwood.* Silverton Colorado: Finn Hill Arts, 1985.

— "The Green mountains...": **Santōka,** *Mountain Tasting.* John Stevens trans. New York: Weatherhill, 1980. Santōka is considered the last of the great haiku poets. He took the name, Santōka, which means "Burning Mountain Peak" in 1902. Living during the heavy military period in Japan, he wrote the most poignant poems I have ever seen on war. The title of this book comes from his statement: "Westerners like to conquer mountains; Orientals like to contemplate them. As for me, I like to taste mountains." (p. 27.)

— "Wherever you live, the place is alive...": **Peter Berg.** Quoted in David Cayley, "New Ideas in Ecology and Economics": a four part series by the Canadian Broadcasting Corporation (May 29 to June 18, 1986). A printed transcript is available from CBC Enterprises, P.O. Box 6440, Station A, Montreal H3C, 3L4 Canada ($5).

179 "Land's meaning for us...": **Tom Jay,** "Land, Earth, Soil, Dirt: Some Notes from the ground." *Upriver Downriver,* 1987.

— "you know what it is to be alive...": **Walking Jim Stoltz,** in the song, "All Along the Great Divide." On the tape, "Spirit is Still on the Run." Lone Coyote Records, Box 209, Big Sky Montana, 59716.

180 "in a blaze of reality...": **Paul Radin,** quoted by Stanley Diamond, *In Search of the Primitive,* p. 194.

— "Wildness is the state...": **Gary Snyder,** *Turtle Island.* New York: New Directions, 1974, p. 99.

— "ecosystem people...": **Raymond Dasmann.** I give complete bibl. information in the text. Here I will give further information. **Add. notes:** Dasmann first mentioned the concept of "biotic regions" in *Environmental Conservation.* John Wiley & Sons, 1959. There is a chapter devoted to "The Major Biotic Regions." He has a "map of the major vegetation regions" on p. 27 and diagrams, relating to "biotic regions as habitats for man" on p. 44. On page 9 he defines a *biotic community* as "an assemblage of species of plants and animals inhabiting a common area and having, therefore, effects upon one another." He continues: "A combination of a biotic community with its physical environment is called an ecosystem. Ecology is the study of ecosystems to determine their status and the ways in which they function."

— "FUTURE PRIMITIVE": For reprint of this, see LaChapelle, *Earth Wisdom,* p. 150.

— CONTINENT CONGRESS "BUNDLE": It was put out in June of 1976. It contained "Amble towards Continent Congress." Also in this bundle was "New Orleans Report," which included Stephen Duplantier's "Tractatus Geopsycorum" (begun in 1967 and "still in process"). The opening paragraph: "Of late a self-evolving mode of knowledge has undertaken to be revealed. **Geopsychics:** Def.: Characteristic phenomena that may be seen as an expression of the consciousness of a locale in its most unique stylistic and behavioural manifestation. The study of regional peculiarities: the ambiance of local phenomena."

181 "I had the good luck...": **Peter Berg.** In David Cayley, "New Ideas in Ecology and Economics."

182 OZARK AREA COMMUNITY CONGRESS (OACC): "Founded in 1976, the OACC is an alternative representative body for the Ozarks Bioregion, based on political ecology...We call it OAK because the Oak trees,

transforming sun energy, are the major living power source, creator, sustainer, healer, and regenerator of the land and water in the Ozarks; and the teacher of the way we can live sanely and abundantly here..." Quoted from OACC IV—brochure announcing their 4th congress—Sept. 1983.

— FIRST NORTH AMERICAN BIOREGIONAL CONGRESS: It was held May 21-25, 1984, north of Kansas City. The Congress Proceedings was published by New Life Farm Inc. and printed in the Ozark Bioregion. It is a beautifully designed and printed book of 87 pages. The address is New Life Farm, Box 129, Drury, Mo. 65638.

— CHILDREN OF THE GREEN EARTH: This organization was begun by Ron Rabin and Michael Soule to encourage tree planting—especially among children throughout the world. It was inspired by Richard St. Barbe Baker, the Man of the Trees. They put out an excellent paper for a number of years, but it is now defunct.

— "This Center...is of...": **Gary Snyder,** "The Wilderness." *Turtle Island* pp. 106-110.

— "We who live around...": **Peter Berg.** First published in a little booklet by Planet Drum. Later, reprinted as "Living Here, Frisco Bay Mussel Group: Borne-Native in the San Francisco Bay Region." In P. Berg, ed. *Reinhabiting a Separate Country: A Bioregional Anthology of Northern California.*, 1978, p. 125. (Published by Planet Drum.)

— "In the United States...": **Raymond Dasmann,** "Biogeographical Provinces." *Coevoution Quarterly* (Fall 1976): 32-37.

— "refers both to geographical terrain...": **Peter Berg,** *Reinhabiting a Separate Country,* p. 218. Berg adds: "We define bioregion in a sense different from the biotic province of Dasmann (1973) or the biogeographical province of Udvardy (1975). R. Dasmann, "A system for defining and classifying natural regions for purposes of conservation. (IUCN Occ. Paper 7, 1973, 47 pp. International Union for Conservation of Nature and Natural Resources, Morges, Switzerland.)" M. Udvardy, "A classification of the bioregional provinces of the world." IUCN Occ. Paper 18, 1975, 48 pp. (same address)

183 "Just as, in the process...": **Jung,** "Mind and Earth." The original paper was dated 1927. Now in Jung, *Coll. Works,* v. 10.

— "learning to live...": **Berg,** *Reinhabiting a Sep. Co.,* p. 217.

— "Reinhabitory consciousness...": Ibid., p. 220.

— "effort to become aware...": **Gary Snyder,** "Interview with Snyder." In the *Los Angeles Weekly* (March 1-7, 1985).

— "they are regularly eradicated...": **Kirkpatrick Sale,** *Dweller in the Land: Bioregional Vision.* California: Sierra Club Books.

184 "One day, without...": **Ruth Benedict,** *Patterns of Culture.* Boston: Houghton Mifflin, 1934, pp. 21-22.

— "is making a concerted...": **David Bainbridge,** published by Permaculture Institute, 6488 Maxwelton Rd., Clinton Wa. 98236.

— "Whoa! What Kirk Sale has...": **Michael Helm** "Review of *Dweller in the Land: The Bioregional Vision." Raise the Stakes* (Summer 1986): 12.

— "That is, it expands...": **Francis Hitching,** *Earth Magic.* New York: William Morrow & Co. 1977, p. 285. **Add. notes:** Hitching, a member of the Royal Institute of Archaeology, draws on reputable scientific research for this book. For further information on the subject of power points etc, see my *Earth Wisdom,* pp. 3-30. For an in depth study of particular aspects of power points see James Beal, "Electrostatic fields and brain/body/ environment interrelationships." A lecture delivered at The Rhine-Swanton Interdisciplinary Symposium: "Parapsychology and Anthropology." American Anthropological Association, 73rd Annual Meeting, Mexico City, November 1974.

— "He had a rather good library...": **Needham,** *Sci. and Civil.* in China, v. 4, pt. l, pp 243-244. **Add. notes on Feng Shui:** In this section of v. 4, Needham gives the best general background for feng-shui. He specifically attributes the use of the "south-pointer" in feng-shui sitings as the earliest use of the compass—some 800 years before Europe discovered it. One of the most concise, lucid attempts to make sense out of the bits and pieces left to us after Ricci's burning of the books, is Stephen Skinner, *The Living Earth Manual of FengShui Chinese Geomancy.* England: Routledge Kegan & Paul, 1982. Skinner, however, does get caught in the semi-magic late developments of the craft at times.

One of his main references is: Stephan D. Feuchtwang, *An Anthropological Analysis of Chinese Geomancy.* Editions Vithnagna B. P.

447 Vientiane Laos, 1974. The University of California at Riverside has the copy I got through inter-library loan. His sources are the 1726 edition of the Imperial Encyclopedia, the *Ku Chin t'u Shu Chi Ch'eng* in the British Museum, which draws on 18 separate works of Chinese geomancy. In the Chinese Library of the University of London there are six other treatises. Feuchtwang's book is probably the most in-depth treatment in English; however, it covers a great deal of esoteric material not particularly useful. He often uses Needham as a reference. Basically, if you really want to see a book in English, containing about all that's known, today, this is the book; but it's actually not particularly useful. My feeling is that you stay in one place and pay attention and you will soon know more about your place than you can get from these works, because they are so specifically oriented to China's particular landscape.

185 "How can a thing...": **Jaime de Angulo,** Bob Callahan, ed. *A Jaime de Angulo Reader.* Berkeley: Turtle Island Foundation, 1979, pp. 107-108.

— "Then weave for us...": **J. Spinden,** *Songs of the Tewa.* New York, 1933, p. 94.

— "Ask yourself, how...": **Gary Snyder.** In Geeta Dardick, "An Interview with Gary Sndyer: When Life Starts Getting Interesting." *Sierra* (Sept/Oct. 1985): 68-73. Dardick lives on San Juan Ridge in California, where Snyder lives.

— **Add. Notes on the importance of place:** One of the most helpful statements I've found for making it clear that "one-world assimilation of languages and cultures" and "internationalism" and all the current "one world" propaganda are essentially the "worse problem we've got" is contained in Gary Snyder's book, *The Old Ways,* p. 27-28. It's a long quote from Roy Rappaport's article, "The Flow of Energy in an Agricultural Society" in the special Energy issue of *Scientific American* (September 1971). Here, I will merely give one sentence: "What we have called progress or social evolution may be maladaptive. We may ask if the chances for human survival might not be enhanced by reversing the modern trend of successions in order to increase the diversity and stability of local, national, and regional ecosystems even if need be, at the expense of the complexity and interdependence of international world-wide organizations." And then he points out why so much is against this attitude in our present Industrial Growth Society.

As usual, **D. H. Lawrence,** said it best, way back before 1930, (the year he died). "Myself, I am sick of the farce of cosmic unity, or world unison. It may exist in the abstract—but not elsewhere...as soon as it comes to experience, to passion, to desire, to feeling, we are different...The **spirit of place always triumphs**...To me it is life to feel the white ideas and the 'oneness' crumbling into a thousand pieces, and all sorts of wonder coming through." (my boldface, for emphasis). H. T. Moore, ed. *The Collected Letters of D. H. Lawrence,* v. 2. New York: The Viking Press, 1962, pp. 796-797.

187 "MEDICINE WHEEL...": **Joseph Campbell,** *The Way of the Animal Powers.* London: Summerfield Press, 1983, v. 1, p. 222.

— JUMPING MOUSE: **Robin Ridington,** "The Anthropology of Experience." *Annual Meeting of the American Anthropological Association,* November 22, 1969. New Orleans, La.

— MEDICINE WHEEL FOR CHILDREN AND ADULTS: *See* **LaChapelle,** *Earth Festivals,* which is largely based on the teachings of the medicine wheel.

— FROM FOREST CLEARINGS TO GREEK TEMPLES: **LaChapelle,** *Earth Wisdom,* p. 36 ff.

— GINGKO TREE: **Professor Halle,** quoted in J. Gunnar Andersson, *Children Of The Yellow Earth: Studies in Prehistoric China.* Cambridge: MIT Press, 1973, p. 25. (This English trans. was originally published in England in 1934.) **Add. notes:** Because the story of how Chinese temples preserved the extinct Gingko tree is relevant to the theme of this chapter, I quote Halle here: "The last retreat of the remains of the Jurassic flora was to be found just in Eastern and Southern Asia. Especially interesting is the history of the gingko plants...Even as late as the Tertiary period—the period which immediately preceded the ice age—these forms existed in Europe, North America and even the Arctic regions, but now there only remains one species, the *Gingko biloba,* which is found in China and Japan. The Gingko tree is not even authentically known in the wild state, but it has been cultivated since time immemorial round the temples. Thanks to this circumstance it is still to be found as a living fossil, which fact has made it possible to interpret the remains, preserved in rock deposits, of a large plant group which was characteristic of the flora of the Jurassic age in the same districts."

This tree has yellow, deeply-lobed leaves which make it unusually attractive in gardens. I have seen it in private gardens in Seattle and lining the streets of downtown Sapporo on Hokkaido Island in Japan.

— TEMPLE: **Keith Critchlow,** *Time Stands Still.* London: Gordon Fraser, 1979, p. 22. Also see, Francis Huxley, *The Way of the Sacred*, Garden City: Doubleday, 1974, p. 20.

— WORLD MOUNTAIN, WORLD AXIS: **Mircea Eliade,** *The Sacred and the Profane.* New York: Harcourt Brace and World, p. 40.

— GNOMON: **Critchlow,** *Time Stands Still*, p. 30. **Huxley,** *The Way*, p. 165.

— "He decides that...": Staff reporter, quoted in Robert Spertus, "The dark side of wilderness." *Earth First* (May 1, 1985): 27.

188 "Whereas the myth tends...": **Hans J. Klimkeit,** "Spatial orientation in mythical thinking as exemplified in ancient Egypt: considerations towards a geography of religion." *History of Religions* 14 (May 1975): 273-281.

— "the formation of myths...": **Otto Kaiser,** *Die Mythische Bedeutung Des Meeres In Agypten, Ugarit and Israel* (Berlin, 1962). Quoted in Klimkeit. "Spatial Orientation."

— MANDALA: **C. G. Jung,** *Mandala Symbolism*, Bollingen paperback, 1972, p. 3. Other worthwhile books on the Mandala are: Jose and Miriam Arguelles, *Mandala*. Shambala, 1972. and Giuseppe Tucci, *The Theory and Practice of the Mandala*. New York: Samuel Weiser, 1973. Tucci was the director of an Italian archaeology expedition to Nepal in 1952 and 1956.

— "[Y]ou're going by in a car...": **Dennis Tedlock,** "Toward a Restoration of the word in the modern world." *Alcheringa*, 1976, pp. 120-132.

189 "On the summit of Mt. Moriah..." down to "With exacting design...": "The Dome of the rock: jewel of Jerusalem." (no author) *Jordan* 5 (Fall 1980). Published by Jordan Information Bureau, Washington D.C.

— MEGALITHIC CULTURE: **K. Dittmer,** a German authority on "Megalithkulturkreis." Quoted in F. Sierksma, "Sacred Cairns in Pastoral Cultures." *History of Religions* 2: 227-241.

— "It was only because...": **Jacquetta Hawkes,** *A Land*. England: David and Charles, Publishers, 1978, p. 132.

— "Inyan—the rocks...": **Lame Deer,** *Lame Deer, Seeker of Visions.* New York: Simon and Schuster, 1972, p. 275.

— "Verily, one alone...": **Alice Fletcher and Francis LaFlesche,** "The Omaha Tribe." *Bur.of Am. Ethnol. Twenty-seventh Annual Report* (1911), p. 570 and 572.

— "those gods standing solid...": **Simon Ortiz.** I have been unable to find the "in print" source of this poem.

— "You see that rock . . . .": **Carleton Coon,** *The Hunting Peoples*, Boston: Little Brown & Co., 1971, p. 194.

190 BIG HORN MEDICINE WHEEL: Information on it from "Rocky Mountain Lifetime," the medicine wheel in"Backbone—The Rockies" bundle from Planet Drum. Peter Berg and Linn (now Freeman) House were mainly responsible for it. And from Dr. E. C. Krupp, *Echoes of the Ancient Skies: The Astronomy of Lost Civilizations.* New York: Harper & Row, 1983.

— "The view from the cairn...": **Dr. John Eddy,** quoted in Krupp, *Echoes of the Ancient Skies.*, p. 143.

— "making it about...": Ibid., p. 142.

— "The mandala, or representation of..." down to "Their walk in...": **Allan Grapard,** "Flying Mountains and Walkers of Emptiness: Toward a Definition of Sacred Space in Japanese Religion."

191 MEDICINE WHEEL: **H. Storm,** *Seven Arrows.* New York: Harper & Row, 1972.

— "The task of comprehending...": **James McNeley,** *Holy Wind in Navajo Philosophy.* Tucson: University of Arizona Press, 1981, p. xvii.

— "less ego-centered...": Ibid., p. 4.

— "This vegetation with which...": Ibid., p. 27.

— "With everything having life...": **Leland C. Wyman,** *Blessingway. With Three Versions of the Myth Recorded and Translated from the Navajo by Father Berard Haile.* Tucson: The University of Arizona Press, 1970, p. 616.

— "ambiguity may reside...": McNeley, *Holy Wind*, p. 23.

192 "an essentially unitary wind...": Ibid., p. 52.

— "Mountains and rivers...": **Shih-T'ao.** (no further bibl. information available).

— "Big Blue Mountain God...": **Chiricahua and Mescalero Apache Texts.** Harry Hoijer. trans. Chicago: University of Chicago Press. I have re-worked this to fit the way mountains are.

— "There is Power...": **Stephen R. Donaldson,** *Lord Foul's Bane.* New York: Ballantine, 1978, pp. 231 and 233.

— BODY POEM: **Elizabeth Cogburn,** "The Body Poem." She told me it was an inspiration from John Muir, who currently lives in New Mexico. I have adapted hers somewhat.

194 "The earth has received..": **Sitting Bull,** quoted in Paul Jacobs and Saul Landau, *To Serve the Devil*, p. 3.

— "Let us touch...": **Storm,** *Seven Arrows*, p. 128.

— "The sun comes forth and...": **Black Elk.** Quoted in John G. Neihardt, *Black Elk Speaks*, p. 198-199.

— "All things within us...": **Storm,** *Seven Arrows*, p. 5 and 120.

195 "The Mother Earth is the fifth...": Ibid., p. 20.

— "What man most passionately...": **D. H. Lawrence,** *Apocalypse.* New York: Viking Press, 1966, p. 198-199.

— "Approximately one week...": **Alan Dundes and Alessandro Falassi,** *La Terra in Piazza.* Berkeley: University of California Press, 1975, pp. 53-54.

196 "The 'U-ma-ne'...": **G. A. Dorsey,** *Bur. of Amer. Ethnol*, v. 11, p. 451.

— LOCAL EARTH AS PROTECTION: **E. M. Satow,** Japanese Secretary to the British Legation at Yedo (old name of Tokyo), "The revival of pure Shin-tau." *Transactions of the Asiatic Society of Japan* 3 (1883).

— "Tossing the stones...": **Jessie F.** This poem was written toward the end of the "Heart of the Mother," workshop held in Canyonlands, April, 1982. Nancy Rumbel-Rabin and David LaChapelle, facilitators.

— "the Ceremony is the ritual...": **Paula Gunn Allen,** "The Psychological Landscape of Ceremony."

197 "This principle holds that...": **Silas Goldean,** "The Principle of Extended Identity." *Pantheist Practice.* (Available from Finn Hill Arts)

— "Walking about the rim of the world": **J. R. Walker,** "The Sun Dance and other ceremonies of the Oglala Division of the Teton Dakota." *Am. Mus. of Nat. Hist. Anthropological Papers* 16 pt. II (1917), pp. 78, 92 and 152-8. This phrase is quoted on p. 165 of Hartley Burr Alexander, *The World's Rim.* Lincoln: University of Nebraska Press, 1967.

— TURNING THE CHILD CEREMONY: **Alice C. Fletcher and Francis LaFlesche,** "The Omaha Tribe." **Add. Notes:** In her foreword she writes: "For more than 25 years the writer has had as collaborator Mr. Francis LaFlesche, the son of Joseph La Flesche, former principal chief of the tribe"

198 "round dance...was the ring...": **David M. Levin,** *The Body's Recollection of being: Phenomenological Psychology and the Deconstruction of Nihilism.* London: Routledge Kegan & Paul, 1985, p. 331.

— "A boundary is not that...": **Martin Heidegger,** "Building Dwelling Thinking." *In Poetry, Language, Thought.* New York: Harper & Row, 1971, p. 154.

— "Digging still deeper...": **David Levin,** *The Body's Recollection*, pp. 333 and 335.

— "The human beings...": Ibid., p. 335.

199 "The entire range...": **J. Lovelock,** *Gaia: A New Look at Life on Earth.* Oxford: Oxford University Press, 1982, p. 9.

— "encompasses us a phenomenon...": **David Abram,** "The Perceptual Implications of Gaia." (revised). It was originally published in the British, *The Ecologist* 15 (1985). Copies of the revised essay available from Finn Hill Arts.

— "I have suggested...": Ibid.

— "Humans are gifted learners...": **Rappaport,** *Meaning, Ecology and Religion*, pp. 100 and 101.

— "this balancing of one's personal...": **Peter Berg and George Tukel,** *Renewable Energy and Bioregions: A New Context for Public Policy.* San Francisco: Planet Drum Foundation. (Prepared for The Solar Business Office, State of California. September, 1980.), pp. 9 and 11.

— "to fulfill my part...": **Menominee Indian),** quoted by Stewart Brand, in *Psychedelic Review*, No. 9.

200 "Spiraling back and forth...": **Gerardo Reichel-Dolmatoff,** "The Loom of Life: A Kogi Principle of Integration." *Journal of Latin American Lore* 4: 5-27.

— "In late Neolithic...": **Euan MacKie,** *The Megalith Builders*, p. 93

— "Because they had already...": **Jacquetta Hawkes,** *A Land*, p. 132.

— "At dusk after a fine...": **MacKie,** *Megalith Builders*, p. 93.

—— "the erection of stone pillars...": **Hosoi**, "The Sacred Tree in Japanese Prehistory."

—— "must approach Cosmos via...": **Frederick Adams**, "The Henge: Land, Sky, Love Temples." *Feraferia* (1969): 3.

—— WOODHENGE: **MacKie**, *Megalith Builders*, p. 24.

—— "the country people...": **W. Stukeley**, *Avebury Described*,(1943 ed.), p. 31. Quoted in Michael Dawes, *Avebury Circle*, pp. 66 & 67. **Add. notes**: About **Druids**. Although there were Druids in pre-historic Britain they did not build Stonehenge. It was constructed around 2800 BC, nearly 2000 years before the Celts arrived in Britain. They were priests and poets of the Celts. The first account of them dates from the time of the Roman conquests of Britain, when Julius Caesar referred to them. Mention of Druids in modern times dates back to the 17th century. In 1666, John Aubrey, an antiquarian, wrote *Monumenta Britannica: A Miscellanie of British Antiquities*. He suggested that the stone rings of Britain were Druid temples but did not say much more about it. This ms. remained untranslated until 1980. But a copy of it had been seen by another antiquarian William Stukeley, who, using this scant evidence, published his *Stonehenge, A Temple Restor'd to the British Druids*, in 1740. Thus began the Druid legend. (Krupp, *Echoes of Ancient Skies*, p. 214.)

—— CUNNINGTON'S FIND: **Dawes**, *Avebury Circle*, p. 67.

201 "the life of the henge...": Ibid., p. 125.

—— GENIUS LOCI: Ibid., pp. 125, 137 and 142.

—— "the male and female forms...": Ibid., p. 125.

—— 100 PAIRS OF STANDING STONES: Ibid., p. 137.

—— "Lararia serpents were...": Ibid., p. 142.

—— "no sculpture in the sense...": Ibid., p. 149.

—— SITING THE HENGE THE "NATURAL WAY": **Frederick Adams**, "The Henge: Land." These directions come from my own experience, based on the work of Adams. Another helpful paper for henges is Adams, "Topocosmic Mandala." *Feraferia* (1969).

—— SUN ANGLES FOR DESIGN: **Robert T. Bennett**. Bala Cynwood, Pa., 1978. (No further address in the copy I've seen.)

202 FURTHER INFORMATION FROM ADAMS: **Add. notes**: When I wrote to Fred Adams asking him about any advice he could pass on to me for this work, I received a letter (December 12, 1985), in which he wrote: "The calculations of solstitial rising and setting points [of the sun] for a given latitude is certainly beyond the capability of the layman! At the outset, it involves spherical trigonometry, and is further complicated by special considerations of the (minute) variances in the shape of the Earth, parallax, atmospheric refraction (displacement), and so forth.

"If you want to review the 'hairy' difficulties, see W. M. Smart, *Spherical Astronomy*, Cambridge University, 1965. This involves taking the ablate spheroid of the earth as a 'geoid', i.e., as if the observer is at sea level—way out at sea— where there are no orographic variations in the horizon line...What we need is some kind of table that shows the lovely, progressive 'opening' of the 'Solstitial cross' from the Equator, no. and so. to the poles (latitude by latitude)...The best advice to give the 'Neo-neolithic' Landscape temple Builders is that she/he write or call her/his local observatory and request the azimuths for solstitial risings—settings relevant to her/his location by latitude. [if you live far from a big city, I suggest you use Bennett's book]. People moving into Feng-Shui Geomancy should also obtain good cardboard astrolabes and practice using them (it's easy, basically) IN ORDER TO FOUND THIS WAY OF THINKING—feeling—SENSING in their very souls and cytoplasms again.

"Now since people won't be doing all this at sea (I don't think), the *real* procedure involves selecting and siting against horizons that have symbolically desirable peaks & vales, slices & gaps, prominences, mesas & clefts. THIS IS A GREAT AND 'AHH-CONSUMING' SACRED ART (of course!). Again, to get used to this way of cosmic-seasonal sensing, I recommend those who are interested in apprenticing themselves to it, begin watching maxima and minima of sunlight edges where they fall, day by day, on walls & floors inside the house thru windows and doorways. Markings should be made." (End of Adams' letter).

The technique he gives is what the Skidi Pawnees did in their earth lodges, see my next chapter.

—— DIFFICULTIES IN USING FORMULAS: To further show the complexities of trying to make a formula that fits the entire earth instead of as in the "old ways," just siting in for your own sun risings and settings, I wrote the Naval Observatory and got a single formula, consisting of three pages. What this shows specifically is the advantage of the relationships involved in a "place" orientation over a "substance" formula of the "whole earth" mentality; because the Naval Observatory formula still won't be absolutely correct due to local mountains, buildings etc.

—— "Dancing and singing the mighty...": **Adams**, "The Henge: Land." **Add. notes:** Adams has unique insights to offer, but, of course, no one has ever published his work. I first heard of him when Viking sent me a review copy of Margot Adler's historical, *Witches, Druids, Goddess Worshippers and other Pagans in America today.* (1979.) Reviewing it for an early issue of *New Age*, I found that in the entire 455 page book, Fred Adams was doing the most worthwhile work for the earth itself so wrote him and eventually talked with him in California. We've been in correspondence since. Adler says right off at the beginning of her section on Adams and Feraferia (pp. 229-243): "Of the many groups I have encountered, Feraferia is one of the most difficult to describe. Feraferia— the name is derived from Latin words meaning 'wilderness festival'—is the most intricately formed of the Neo-Pagan religions in the U.S." Adams was also written up in the *History of Religions* journal, in Robert Ellwood, "Notes on a Neopagan Religious Group in America." 11 (August 1971): 125-139. Adams has remained true to his own place of origin, Los Angeles—not the "temporary anomaly" of the gross city but the land forms. He seems to always find a canyon on the edge for his home. All the more admirable, because instead of retreating to an unspoiled wilderness, he "re-turns" a tiny corner of the biggest mess of a city we've got into a "wilderness."

—— "He remembered...": **Leslie Silko**, *Ceremony*, p. 258.

203 "one of the most remarkable...": **Garner**, quoted in V. and F. Reynolds, "Chimpanzees of the Budongo Forest." In E. DeVore, ed. *Primate Ethology*. New York: Holt, Rinehart & Winston, 1965, pp. 408-409.

—— "But, indications are that...": **Richard Schechner**, "Towards a poetics of performance." In *Alcheringa* (1976): 42-64.

—— "spared the blight of agriculture...": **Carleton Coon**, *The Hunting Peoples*. Boston: Little Brown and Co., 1971.

—— NAMES OF THE CEREMONY: The basic Pawnee name for the ceremony is *Ruktaraiwarius*, meaning stick of wood, hung upon, coming, shaking or moving, and referring to the feathered stem actually being used in the ceremony. The word Hako is a composite term designating an article of the ceremony derived from *hakkow*, "breathing mouth of wood." Hako was the term Fletcher used for the ceremony, (p. 376). *Wawan*, meaning "to sing for someone," is the Omaha name. (Fletcher and LaFlesche, "The Omaha Tribe," p. 376.) **Add. notes:** In the early 1880s Alice Fletcher witnessed the Wawan ceremony among the Omahas. The Omahas, Ponkas and Dakota Indians told her that the Pawnee still preserved it entirely. In 1898 she saw it among the Pawnee and then did a further four years of work on it. Her entry to the old Pawnee men came from her long contact with the Omaha and Joseph LaFlesche. She also had the help of James R. Murie, an educated Pawnee. She first knew him as a school boy twenty years before. Murie, at her request, made a final review of her ms. in 1902. (For further information on Murie, see Reference Notes for the next chapter.) So we have here a more than usual reliable account as far as what the Indians were actually doing, but some of Fletcher's conclusions may have been influenced by the all-encompassing Christianity around her. The Hako ceremony not only bonds humans to the land but is a peace-making ritual between neighboring groups.

Tahirussawichi, who was the Kurahus (priest-leader of the ceremony), was a full Pawnee who had carried the Hako to the Omaha people and thus become acquainted with the leading men of that tribe. He was seventy years old at the time he worked with Fletcher. In 1898 she took him to New York to Washington D.C. He saw the capitol, the library of Congress and the Washington monument. Concerning the latter he said: "I will not go up. The white man likes to pile up stones, and he may go to the top of them; I will not. I have ascended the mountains made by Tirawa." The title, Kurahus means "a man of years who has been instructed in the meaning of sacred objects and ceremonies."

The Osage words for the ceremony is "bringing the drum." The drum was a section of tree with skin stretched over it. "It came to be used to accentuate the sound which originally came when singing by waving the hand to and from the mouth or beating the lips to make a series of notes." (An action debased when used in old Hollywood films). So we have here another aspect of the "breathing mouth" of the ceremony—that the "breathing mouth" of the humans gives praise to all the natural beings. The term Hako came to be applied to all the articles because, according to Tahirussawichi, "everything speaks: the eagle, Kawas, speaks; the corn speaks...so we say Hako—the voice of all these things."

The basic information in my account comes from Alice C. Fletcher, *Bur. of Amer. Ethn. Twenty Second Annual Report*, Pt. 2 (1904).

— "We take up the Hako...": **Tahirussawichi**. Ibid.

— "We have established a relationship...": **Matohoshila**, quoted in Joseph Epes Brown, ed. *The Sacred Pipe*. Norman: University of Oklahoma Press, 1963, p. 114.

204 BREAKING THROUGH: *See* "Resources."

— TAOIST AUTUMN EQUINOX: *See* "Resources."

— "The ceremony which...": **Hartley Burr Alexander**, *The World's Rim*, p. 126. **Add notes**: Tahirussawichi himself spoke of the many difficult times he had lived through: nearly killed in wars, wounded many times but how he had lived when so many were killed. "I did not fall but I passed on, wounded sometimes but not to death, until I am here to-day doing this thing, singing these sacred songs into that great pipe [the gramophone] and telling you of these ancient rites of my people. It must be that I have been preserved for this purpose, otherwise I should be laying back there among the dead." (Fletcher, "The Hako", p. 278.)

— "...all the instinctive systems...": **J. Bowlby**, *Attachment and Loss*, v. 1, pp 47-48.

— "[W]e have developed 'organs'...": **Konrad Lorenz**, *Behind the Mirror*, p. 7.

— "Jung, for all his Platonic...": **Anthony Stevens**, *Archetypes*, p. 59.

205 "The picture changes at once.": **C. G. Jung**, in "Foreward" to E. M. Harding, *Woman's Mysteries, Ancient and Modern*. London: Longmans, 1948, p. ix.

— "If Jung is correct...": **Alan Drengson**, *The Trumpeter* 3 (Winter 1986).

— "the collective mind and body...": **Hal Hartzell**, "Hoedads Inc." *See* "Back of the Book" section for the whole story.

— ROGANTIONTIDE: **E. O. James**, *Seasonal Feasts and Festivals*, p. 221.

— LUPERCALIA: Ibid., p. 220.

206 THE HAKO: All the quotations from the original Pawnee, which I use during the ceremony come from Fletcher, "The Hako: a Pawnee ceremony."

207 "The white man...": **Luther Standing Bear**, quoted in Barry Lopez, ed. "The American Indian Mind." *Quest* (September/October, 1978).

208 "I didn't think...": **Jerome Rothenberg**. trans. a Seneca chant in "Preface to a Symposium on Ethnopoetics." In *Alcheringa* (1976): 6-12.

— "generalized perception...": **Arthur Waley**, *Three Ways of Thought in Ancient China*. Garden City, N. Y.: Doubleday, 1956. London: Allen & Unwin, 1969, pp. 66-67.

209 "[This] tree is a strong-willed...": **D. H. Lawrence**, "Pan in America." In *Phoenix I*. New York: Viking Press, 1968, pp 22-31.

— "The constant Aspen's...": **Fr. Ruddy**, Seattle poet in the late 1960s. Unpublished.

— "Alders produce...": **Malcolm Margolin**, "Hurray for the Alder" In *The Living Wilderness* (Spring, 1974).

— "[T]he word book is from Old English...": **Tom Jay**, "Words Bear Nature's Wisdom." In *Upriver Downriver*.

— "Where I'm going...": **Huichol Chant**, from "The Circle" tape. (Available from Finn Hill **Arts.**)

— "Yes, the Rock is the oldest...": **Sword**, an Oglala priest, quoted in J. R. Walker, "The Sun Dance and other ceremonies of the Oglala divison of the Teton Dakota." *Am. Mus. of Nat. History. Anthropol. Papers* 16 pt. II (1917): 155.

— "Truly, one alone of all is the greatest...": **Fletcher**, "The Omaha Tribe", p. 570 and 572.

— "Every man needs a stone...": **Lame Deer**, *Lame Deer Seeker of Visions*, p. 275.

210 CAVES: FOR MORE INFORMATION ON SACRED CAVES: *See* **LaChapelle**, *Earth Wisdom*, pp. 31-43.

— "The rocks are ringing...": **Paiute**. In James Mooney. trans. "The Ghost Dance Religion." *Bur. of Am. Ethnol. Fourteenth Annual Report*, Pt. 2 (1892-3)

— "A metaphor of forms...": **Shepard**, *Man in the Landscape*, p. 172.

— "The pointed arch, the definitive...": **Filarete**, quoted in Gerald Hawkins,

Beyond Stonehenge. New York: Harper and Row, 1973, p. 43.

— "There is a large, flat...": **Steve Meyers**, "Lime Creek Odyssey: An Ode to Place." Golden Colorado: Fulcrum Press, 1988.

211 "Confucius was taking a...": **The Book of Lieh Tzu**, A. C. Graham, trans. London: 1960, p. 44.

— "Young pines...": **John Muir**, *The Mountains of California*.

212 HOLLOW VALLEY: **Kenneth Cohen**, "Challenge of the Earth: Chinese Geomancy." *Yoga Journal* (1980).

— IMPORTANCE OF FIRE FOR FOCUSING: **Amos Rapoport**, "Australian aborigines and the definition of Place." In *Environmental Design: Research and Practice*. Berkeley: University of California Press, 1972, Ch. 3.3, pp. 1-14.

— "A man may be walking...": **C. Wissler**, "Ceremonial Bundles of the Blackfoot Indians." *Anthrop. Papers of the Amer. Museum of Natural History* 7 (1912): 263.

— "Anything, in fact, can deliver...": **Rothenberg**, *Technicians of the Sacred*, p. 425.

213 "I pledge allegiance...": **Gary Snyder**. First published in the *New York Times* (July 4th). Reprinted in *Axe Handles*.

— "For as my body is clad...": **Dame Julian**, an anchoress of Norwich (about 1393). I have substituted "nature," for her "grace of God."

— "The signs of these promises...": **Alexander**, *The Rim of the World*, p. 103.

— "[W]e can't understand...": **Jaime de Angulo**, quoted in The *Netzahualcoyotl News* 1 (Summer 1969) Berkeley, Turtle Island Foundation.

214 "usurp their claims...": **Peter Nabokov**, "America as Holy Land." *North Dakota Quarterly* (Autumn 1980).

— HUNTER-GATHERERS FOR 99% OF HUMAN HISTORY: **Coon**, *The Hunting Peoples*, p. xvii.

— "Only in the last...": Ibid., p. 393.

— "[They] are finding out, both...": **Wilfred Pelletier**, *No Foreign Land*, p. 208 and 210.

— "step across the fence...": **Duerr**, *Dreamtime*, p. 87.

— "...at that moment...": **Leslie Silko**, *Ceremony*, p. 249 and 258.

— "The ear for the story...": Ibid., p. 267.

— "How much 'ecological...": **Peter Berg**, "Bioregionalists & Greens: Life-Place-Politics: from a working paper". In *Upriver Downriver*, 7

— "The Appalachians are...": **"Map Meditations: The Katúah Bioregion."** *Katúah: Bioregional Journal of the Southern Appalachians* 1 (Autumn 1983). See "Resources" for address.

215 "There is a distinct...": **Peter Berg**, quoted in, "Bioregions: The Trail to Home." Ibid, p. 2.

— "I was driving...": **"Map Meditations"**. Ibid.

— "There was a Chinese scholar...": quoted in **R. F. Johnstone**, *From Peking to Mandalay*. London: John Murray, 1908.

Ch. 14 Bringing the Sky

pp. 216 and 217 Opening Quotes

— "I however, am one who blesses...": **F. Nietzsche**, *Thus Spoke Zarathustra*. R. J. Hollingdale. trans. New York: Penguin Books, 1961, pp. 185-186.

— "Science...Progress...": **Arthur Rimbaud**, "Bad Blood." In *A Season in Hell*. Louise Varése. trans. New York: New Directions, 1945, pp. 7 to 19.

— "The sky is the vaulting path...": **Martin Heidegger**, "Building Dwelling Thinking." In *Poetry, Language, Thought*. Albert Hofstadter. trans. New York: Harper & Row, 1971, p. 149.

— "Truth as revelation is not located...": **Vincent Vycinas**, *Earth and Gods: An Introduction to the Philosophy of Martin Heidegger*. The Hague: Martinus Nijhoff, 1961, p. 235.

— "When Bashō, the seventeenth...": **LaFleur**, *Mirror for the Moon*, p. xiii.

— "I am no longer caught in the moving...": **Frank Waters**, *Pumpkin Seed Point*. Chicago: Swallow Press, 1973, p. 100.

— "Far away in the depth...": **Shih t'ao**. No printed source.

219 "O Wondrous Star in the East...": **Pius Parsch**, *The Church's Year of Grace*.

— JET STREAM AND BOMBING RUN ON SAIPAN: **Elmer R. Reiter**, *Jet Streams*. New York: Doubleday, 1967, p. 5.

— FALLOUT FROM BOMB TESTING AND THE JET STREAM: Ibid., p. 159-161.

— HEIDEGGER'S FOURFOLD: **Heidegger**, "The Thing." In *Poetry, Language*,

Thought, p. 178-181.

220 "The Khasi tell a myth...": **Hans Duerr**, *Dreamtime*, pp. 30-31.

—— "When the Chinese...": **Robert Payne**, *The White Pony*. New York: New American Library edition, p. 24.

—— THE FOUR GREAT POWERS OF THE SIOUX: **Sword**, an Oglala priest, quoted in J. R. Walker, "The Sun Dance," p. 155.

—— "this expanse...": **Von Del Chamberlain**, *When Stars Came Down to Earth: Cosmology of the Skidi Pawnee Indians of North America*, p. 48.

—— "he should understand...": **Giuseppe Tucci**, *The Theory and Practice of the Mandala*, p. 32.

—— CLEAR BLUE OF THE AUTUMN SKY IN MOUNTAINS: **Joost Businger**, atmospheric physicist at NCAR, Boulder, Colorado. Letter, 1986.

—— "An ultimate blue...": **Peter Matthiessen**, *The Snow Leopard*. New York: The Viking Press, 1978, p. 98.

—— "How nice it was here...": **D. H. Lawrence**, *Lady Chatterley's Lover*. New York: The New American Library, 1959.

—— "The wisps of smoke...": **Saigyō**. La Fleur, *Mirror for the Moon* and "Saigyō and the Value of Nature, Pt. 1."

—— "And I think over again...": **Old Inuit Song**. Quoted in Knud Rasmussen, *Intellectual Culture of the Copper Eskimo*. trans. W. Calvert. New York: AMS Press, 1976, p. 53. (Reprint of the 1932 ed.)

221 "fire-ruler, creator of light...": **Dieterich Papyrus**. In R. G. H. Siu, *Ch'i a Neo-Taoist Approach to Life*. Cambridge: M.I.T. Press, 1974, p. 205.

—— "Each of us...": **John Lilly**, *Dyadic Cyclone*. New York: Simon and Schuster.

—— "the vast amphitheatre...": **D. H. Lawrence**, "New Mexico." *Survey Graphic* (January 1928). Reprinted in *Phoenix*. New York: The Viking Press, 1968, pp. 141-150.

—— "whoever is touched...": **Tahirussawichi**. In Fletcher, "The Hako," p.136-139.

222 "I have had ample time...": **P. K. Hoenich**, "Kinetic Art with Sunlight: Reflections on Developments in Art Needed Today." In Frank J. Malina. ed, *Kinetic Art: Theory and Practice: Selections from the Journal Leonardo*. New York: Dover Publications, 1974, pp. 23-29.

—— CHACO CANYON: **Anna Sofaer**. "Solstice Project." In John O'Connor, "Exploring Science and Religions." The New York Times (July 16, 1982) There was also a PBS television documentary titled "The Sun Dagger." July 16, 1982.

—— NEWGRANGE: **Krupp**, *Echoes of Ancient Skies*, p. 122-124 and **Mackie**, *Megalith Builders*, p. 68.

223 "Tradition has it...":**Daisaku Ikeda**, *The Living Buddha: An Interpretative Biography*. Burton Watson. trans. Tokyo: Weatherhill, 1976, p. 61.

—— "O Morning Star, there at...": **Black Elk**, *The Sacred Pipe*. Baltimore: Penguin, 1971, pp. 40-41.

—— "What subtle tie is this between...": **Walt Whitman**, *Specimen Days*, 1892 ed., p. 70.

—— "And his own journey...": **Laurens van der Post**, "Where will all the stories go?" *Parabola* (Summer 1982.)

—— "Each was looking at...": **D. H. Lawrence**, *The Trespasser*. London: William Heinemann, 1955, chapter 16.

—— "...the young man, looking west...": **D. H. Lawrence**, "The Witch A La Mode." In *The Complete Short Stories of D. H. Lawrence*, v. 1. New York, The Viking Compass ed., 1961, pp. 54-70.

—— "...oh, regal evening star...": **D. H. Lawrence**, *Sea and Sardinia*. New York: Viking, 1963.

—— "central between the flash...": **D. H. Lawrence**, *The Plumed Serpent*. New York: Alfred Knopf, 1951, p. 90.

—— WHITE STAR WOMAN, EVENING STAR: **Chamberlain**, *When the Stars Come Down*, pp. 22-23. **Add. notes**: Because the Pawnee are not as well known as many other Indian tribes I will fill in some details here. Smallpox epidemics from 1803 to 1840 killed large numbers and by 1892 the entire Pawnee tribe had only 7859 people. All the traditional roles had lost their significance. Chamberlain quotes Lesser: "From cultural maturity as Pawnee they were reduced to cultural infancy as civilized men." Their population reached a low of 600 in 1900.

A great deal of Chamberlain's material comes from the work of James Rolfe Murie, whose mother was Pawnee and his father, white, who later deserted the family. But because Murie was intelligent, educated at white schools and yet came back to the Pawnee area, his writings and research in connection with the Bur. of Amer. Ethn. are to be relied on to a greater extent than casual informants. At the age of sixteen he was sent to school at the Hampton Normal and Agric. Institute in Virginia; the first Pawnee to graduate from an eastern school. After trying farming etc. he eventually became a clerk in a bank at Pawnee (1896) and worked at this job for 20 years.

When Alice Fletcher, a Smithsonian anthropologist with the Bur. of Amer. Ethn. began her study of the Pawnee she contacted him. As mentioned in the previous chapter she had met him when he was a student at Hampton. He became her assistant. The records of their correspondence are in the National Anthropological Archives (1898 to 1902). Murie eventually worked with Dorsey, another Bur. of Amer. Ethn. researcher for seven years until Dorsey completed his research and then Murie continued on his own. In 1910 he was appointed a part-time researcher for the Bureau, working on Pawnee ceremonies. In 1912, Clark Wissler, Curator of Anthrop. at the Amer. Museum of Natural History worked out a program for Murie to write descriptions of the Pawnee societies. This culminated in a paper by Murie which was to be published in 1914. Eventually in 1973, Douglas Parks discovered it and it was finally published in 1981.

Primarily descriptions of the old ceremonies came from an old Pawnee, named Scout through Murie, to Fletcher and Dorsey. Scout had been taught as a youth in Nebraska, by the last of the old priests. In 1901, when Scout visited Fletcher in Washington he was between 60 and 70 and Scout said that it had been 30 or 40 years since the ceremonies had been performed (about 1865). (Chamberlain, *When the Stars Came Down*, pp. 32-33, 40-41 and 37-38.) The importance of this work is that we have a traditional Pawnee who had taken part in the ceremonies when young, working with an educated and (later trained) half-Pawnee researcher, Murie, so this information is more valid than most research on Indian ceremonials.

—— "we can expect...": **Chamberlain**, *When the Stars Came Down*, p. 84.

—— "ran the planetary gear system...": Ibid., p. 84.

224 "The Black and Red stars...": Ibid., p. 104.

—— "The influence of a star cult...": **Alice Fletcher**, quoted in Chamberlain, p. 155.

—— "The house was a microcosm...": **Weltfish**, quoted in Chamberlain, p. 156.

—— "would stream through the...": Ibid., p. 92

—— "had its roots in the sky...": Ibid., p. 93.

—— NAMES OF THE POLE STAR: **Critchlow**, *Time Stands Still*, p. 52 and **Needham**, *Sci. and Civil*, v. 2.

—— "We sing this song slowly...": **Tahirussawichi**, quoted in Fletcher, "The Hako," p. 129-132.

—— MOON'S CYCLE: **Krupp**, *Echoes of the Ancient Skies*, p. 14.

225 "Psychotic patients are known...": **Paul Mirabile**, "Moon Cycles Affect Moods." *Brain Mind Bulletin* (May 28, 1984): p. 3.

—— YUE LING: Quoted in **Mother Marie-Ina Bergeron**, "Man: Hinge of the Universe." *Main Currents in Modern Thought* 29 (March- April, 1973).

—— "The Sun, as the great centre of power and the upholder...": **Walter McClintock**, *The Old North Trail: Life, Legends, and Religion of the Blackfeet Indians*. Lincoln: University of Nebraska Press, 1968. (originally published in 1910), p. 169-170.

228 "If you want to find yourself...": **Adams**, "The Art of Artemis: Biome Religion." Unpublished.

—— DIVISION OF YEAR INTO EIGHT SECTIONS BY CELTS: **Gerald S. Hawkins**, *Beyond Stonehenge*, p. 276.

—— "research has shown...": **Laurel Lagoni**, quoted in Joe Garner, "Gunnison: State's 3rd-Coldest Spot Fights Freezer Image." *Rocky Mountain News* (February 2, 1986). **Add notes**: The first popular book on the subject of how light of the sun and seasons influence humans was Gay G. Luce, *Body Time*. Pantheon, 1971. It is still in paperback and still the best introduction to the field. Unfortunately, many textbooks and scholarly articles concerning the nervous system, hormonal systems and brain/body interactions completely ignore the influence of the changing seasons.

—— "Traditional symbols for...": **Shepard**, *The Sacred Paw*, p. 61.

230 "The sky is swept...": Ibid., p. 67.

—— "The path of these figures...": **G. M. Vasilevich**, "Early Concepts About the Universe Among the Evinks." In Harry N. Michael. ed., *Studies in Siberian Shamanism*. Translations from Russian Sources. No. 4, *Anthropology of the North*. Toronto: Arctic Institute of North America,

University of Toronto, 1963, pp. 46-123.

— "The thing about...a book you...": **Dennis Tedlock**, "Toward a Restoration of the Word in the Modern World." *Alcheringa* 2 (1976): 120-132.

— "topocosm...continuous entity...": **Theodor H. Gaster**, *Thespis: Ritual, Myth, and Drama in the Ancient Near East.* New York: W. W. Norton & Co., 1977, p. 17. First published by Doubleday, 1950. The Foreword by Gilbert Murray points out that "Dr. Gaster has turned his vast learning to demonstrating, in fields far beyond my reach, the existence of a similar pattern, based on the same seasonal drama, in the extant remains of Canaanite, Hittite, Egyptian and Hebrew literature...has traced the essential structure backward to purely functional procedures..." In my own discussion here of Gaster's work, I have hardly scratched the surface. If his work was more widely recognized, we would be safely out of the Judeo-Christian trap and back into the original religion, relating us to the on-going earth and its relationships to the sky throughout the changing seasons. Gaster shows us how the very ancient "world renewal" rites to revitalize the topocosm of the place itself gradually became abstracted and spiritualized until finally with Christianity, it was held that the rite occurred only once with the resulting *new life* becoming an *after life* in a never-never place called *heaven*.

— "In most parts of the world..." down to "Rites of Kenosis...": **Gaster**, *Thespis*, p. 17.

— "seasonal ceremonies are the economic...": Ibid., p. 24.

— "a religious ritual designed...": Ibid., p. 9 and 18.

— "MORTIFICATION, symbolizing...": Ibid., p. 26.

— "tears are regarded...": Ibid., p. 33.

231 "In this way the yin and yang annually meet...": **Derk Bodde**, "Harmony and Conflict in Chinese Philosophy." The particular passage I quote occurs on p. 23. In the first part, Bodde is summing up Tung Chung-shu's thought; while the only actual quote from Tung Chung-shu is "the course of Heaven, [which] when it has been completed, begins again."

— "Unless time is understood...": **Vine Deloria**, "Order Out of Chaos." I have no futher bibl. reference on this.

— "[A]rchaic man plays the order of nature...": **Leo Frobenius**, quoted in Richard Schechner and Mary Schuman, *Ritual, Play and Performance.* New York: Seabury Press, 1976, p. 57. **Add. notes**: Frobenius (1873-1938) spent many years in Africa, gathering and translating African oral traditions and founded the Institute for Cultural Morphology in Frankfurt, which contains prehistoric and African paintings and engravings. According to Rothenberg, Frobenius "has profoundly influenced at least two major and largely unrelated directions in twentieth-century poetry—the American line of Pound and Williams/Olson and Duncan etc. and the African and French Caribbean line of Negritude poets." (*Symposium of the Whole*, p. 36) The best source for Frobenius is Eike Haberland. ed., *Leo Frobenius: An Anthology.*

— "Now, what of that celestial movement...": **Adams**, "The Henge: Land."

— "At no other time...": **Juliet Bredon and Igor Mitrophanow**, *The Moon Year.* Shanghai, Kelly and Walsh Ltd. 1927.

— "Every autumn, at the beginning..." down to "enormous effigy of a dragon...": **Gaster**, *Thespis*, p. 245 and 250.

— MICHAELMAS: **E. O. James**, *Seasonal Feasts*, pp. 226-227. James was Professor Emeritus of the History of Religion at the University of London and Fellow of King's College, London, with a lifetime study of religions.

232 "All these autumn weeks...": **Henry Beston**, *The Outermost House.* Viking Explorer Books, 1961 ed., p. 59.

— "At Halloween there is sometimes...": **Gary Snyder**, *Upriver Downriver* 7.

— HIERARCHY AND FESTIVALS: For the system of changing leadership for seasonal festivals, see books on Hopi cermonialism. A good beginning is Frank Waters, *Book of the Hopi.* Just about the best book, readily available, for how the Indians actually arranged for social order in daily life, is Walter McClintock, *The Old North Trail.*

— "Lussi herself appears..." down to "Even to-day...": **Edvard Hammarstedt**, "Lussi". In *Meddelanden fran Nordiska Museet*, 1928, pp, l-38. Quoted in J. Gunnar Andersson, *Children of the Yellow Earth: Studies in Prehistoric China.* Cambridge Ma.: M.I.T. Press, 1973, pp. 277-278.

— "fixed in the Germano-Celtic calendar...": **James**, *Seasonal Feasts*, p. 177.

233 "Therefore, Yuletide...": Ibid., p. 292.

— YULE LOG: Ibid., p. 294.

— "the invincible god of celestial...": Ibid., p. 197.

— "to counteract the Saturnalia...": Ibid., p. 229.

— "the shoppers laden with their...": **Melvin Maddocks**, "Tis the Season to be lonely." *Christian Science Monitor* (December 1986).

— "Psychology without ecology...": **Tom Jay**, "The Salmon of the Heart."

— "we can see two aspects...": **Shin-Pyo Kang**, "The Structural Principles of the Chinese World View."

234 "Yin—shade, the north side...": **Sun Tzu**, *Art of War.* (6th century B.C.)

— "The initial point...": **Marcel Granet**, *Etudes sociologiques sur la China.* Reprint ed. Paris: University of France, 1953. trans. Girardot, *Myth and Meaning*, p 185.

— "We are all children...": **Keith Cunningham**, poem: "Children of the Dromenon." Unpublished.

— "The sun is becoming darker...": **Loloma**, quoted in Stan Steiner, "The Sun is becoming darker: the ultimate energy crisis." *Akwesasne Notes* (early autumn 1974).

— NEWGRANGE AND WINTER SOLSTICE: **MacKie**, *Megalith Builders*, p. 68.

— "The basilica's generous nave...": **William Marlin**, "When ancient basilica becomes a sundial." *The Christian Science Monitor* (January 21, 1977.)

235 "was designed to...": **Rev. Virgil C. Hart**, *Western China.* Quoted in Mary Mullikin and Anna Hotchkis, *The Nine Sacred Mountains of China* Hongkong, Vetch & Lee Ltd. 1973, p. 128. (The journal of their journey to the mountains was written in 1935 and 1936.)

— "In a note to Peggy...": **Rosie Evans**, letter, Dec. 29, 1985.

— LUPERCALIA: **James**, *Seasonal Feasts*, pp. 177-179.

— CANDLEMAS: Ibid., pp. 232-233.

— SIMEON AND THE "LIGHT OF THE WORLD": **Pius Parsch**, *The Church's Year of Grace*, v. 5, pp. 370-375.

236 "Spring is still spring...": **George Orwell**, "Some Thoughts on the Common Toad." In S. Orwell and I. Anous. eds., *The Collected Essays, Journalism and Letters of George Orwell*, 4 v. New York: Harcourt Brace, 1968.

— "the sun advancing...": **Beston**, *Outermost House*, p. 150.

— "So Telipinu returned...": **Gaster**, *Thespis*, p. 314-315.

— "in many other ancient...": Ibid., p. 313.

— "a symbolic representation...": Ibid., p. 314.

— CARNIVAL OF HILARIA: **James**, *Seasonal Feasts*, p. 189.

— EASTER: Ibid., p. 216.

— CONNECTION BETWEEN MAYDAY AND CYBELE: Ibid., p. 184.

237 "Gaelic *tein-eigin*...": Ibid., p. 312.

— SEXUAL ASPECTS OF THE MAYPOLE: **Thomas Wright**, *The Worship of the Generative Powers During the Middle Ages of Western Europe.* (1866), Reprinted, New York: Julian Press, 1957, p. 93.

— "These may be a survival...": Ibid. p. 310.

— "opening of the peak...": **H. Byron Earhart**, *A Religious Study of the Mount Haguro Sect of Shugendō*, p. 139.

— "The birth of Jesus...": **Parsch**, *The Church's Year of Grace*, v. 4, p. 207.

— "to protect from witches...": **James**, *Seasonal Feasts*, p. 315.

238 SUN DANCE: For a table, giving 28 different aspects of the Sun Dance as used by 19 different tribes, see Leslie Spier, "The Sun Dance of the Plains Indians: Its Development and Diffusion." *Anthrop. Papers of the Am. Museum of Nat. Hist.* 16 Pt. 7 (1921): 473.

— "The magic and ritual power...": **Girardot**, *Myth and Meaning*, p. 182.

— DRUMS IN GOURD FORM: Ibid., p. 199.

— UTE BEAR DANCE: **Robert Emitt**, *The Last War Trail.* Norman: University of Oklahoma Press, 1954, pp. 29 and 35-38.

— LAMMASTIDE IN AUGUST: **Gaster**, *Thespis*, p. 48.

— "at the height of the summer...": **James**, *Seasonal Feasts*, p. 238.

— "the Church celebrates the most glorious...": **Parsch**, *The Church's year of Grace*, v. 4, p. 327.

— "Since ancient times...": Ibid., p. 239.

— LAMMAS DAY: **James**, *Seasonal Feasts*, p. 238.

— "To regain the power poetry once had...": **Robert Ian Scott**, reviewing Gary Snyder, *Uncollected Poems.* North American Review, (Fall 1977).

239 "Within and around the earth...": **Tewa prayer**. "This 'power circle' is...": **LaChapelle**, *Earth Wisdom*, p. 139. For the complete Tewa prayer, see Alfonso Ortiz, *The Tewa: World, Space, Time, Being and Becoming in a Pueblo Society.* Chicago: University of Chicago Press, 1969.

—— "Festivity is the origin...": **Jean Wahl**. Quoted in Vincent Vycinas, *Earth and Gods*, p. 295.

—— "On the day of festivity...": **Vycinas**, *Earth and Gods*, p. 298.

—— "In the primeval time...": **Rudolph Otto**. Quoted in Vycinas, *Earth and Gods*, p. 294.

—— "not only the life of men...": **C. Kerenyi**, *Eleusis*. Pantheon books, 1967, p. xxv.

—— "*Li* is understood as a movement...": **Wei-ming Tu**, "Li as a Process of Humanization."

—— "sage rulers...": **Li Chi**, quoted in Robert M. Gimello, "The Civil Status of Li in Classical Confucianism." *Philosophy East and West* 14: 202-211.

—— "Through rites Heaven and Earth...": **Hsün Tzu**: 19. Burton Watson, trans. *Hsün Tzu: Basic Writings*. New York: Columbia University Press, 1967, p. 94.

—— EGYPT: **James**, *Seasonal Feasts*, p. 32.

—— "The Niman Ceremony...": **L. Thomson and Alice Joseph**, *The Hopi Way*. Chicago: Univ. of Chicago Press, 1945.

—— "considers, judges...": **Vycinas**, *Earth and Gods*, p. 298. The quotation within Vycinas: "shows itself only when..', comes from Heidegger, *Holzwege Auflage*. Frankfurt am main: Vittorio Klostermann, 1972, p. 36.

240 "poet-priest...": Ibid., p. 294.

—— "When the world speaks to us...": **Gunther Anders**. No further bibliography.

—— "enter again that process of...": **Jerome Rothenberg**. No further bibliography.

—— "Between the times..." down to "The last of the night travellers...": **Hans Duerr**, *Dreamtime*, pp. 35-36.

240-241 WORLD RENEWAL RITUALS: **A. L. Kroeber and E. Gifford**, "World Renewal: A Cult System of Native Northwest California." *Anthrop. Records* 13. Berkeley: University of California Press, 1949.

241 "This creating of all things...": **James Murie**, article filed with a ms. by Helen J. Roberts at the National Anthropological Archives. Quoted in Chamberlain, *When Stars Came Down to Earth*, p. 44.

—— "The bundle was kept hanging...": **Chamberlain**, *When Stars Came Down*, p. 45.

—— "Tirawahat...present in all things...": Ibid., p. 48. Chamberlain is paraphrasing the Skidi ritual carried out in the spring concerning the meteorological gods. His ref. is Murie 1981: p. 43-52.

—— SOURCES FOR SHUGENDŌ RITUALS: **Carmen Blacker**, *The Catalpa Bow: A Study of Shamanistic Practices in Japan*. London: George Allen & Unwin Ltd., 1975. (She is a "Lecturer in Japanese" at the Univ. of Cambridge.) H. Byron Earhart, *A Religious Study of the Mount Haguro Sect of Shugendō: An Example of Japanese Mountain Religion*. Tokyo: Sophia University, 1970. Also I will be referring to his article, "Four Ritual Periods of Haguro Shugendō in Northeast Japan." *History of Religions* 5: pp. 93-113.

In addition, both the above authors express their thanks to Anshō Togawa and Dr. Miyake Hitoshi. Hitoshi, a karate master and part-time Yamabushi "studied and participated in the event at the same time, was also unfailingly generous in giving of his unrivalled knowledge of Shugendō ritual." (Blacker, p. 11). Earhart explains that Hitoshi is now teaching at Keio University and also says: "The three of us made notes and collected information together, trying to discover the 'meaning' of the innumerable details of action and expression within the fall peak." (Earhart, *Religious Study*, p. 114)

—— "invaluable guide...": **Blacker**, *Catalpa Bow*, p. 11.

—— "based on a lifetime...": Ibid., p. 344.

—— "knowledge of the doctrine...": Ibid., p. 221.

—— "overlaid with the symbolism...": **Earhart**, *Religious Study*, p. 1.

—— YAMABUSHI: *Yama* means mountain, *bushi*, added to it means "one who sleeps in the mountains." Ibid., p. 2.

—— "the three symbols...": Ibid., p. 8.

242 "bones, claws and horns...": **Blacker**, *Catalpa Bow*, p. 96 for her photo of the "rosary."

—— MAGATAMA: Ibid., p. 332. In a footnote: "The earlist magatama of the Jomon period are simply claws and teeth perforated at one end, but by the end of the Jomon period they are found carved in stone." Her source here is J. E. Kidder, *Japan Before Buddhism*, p. 69, 180-181. But most researchers on Japan and even the Japanese themselves seem reluctant to admit this. Her definition on p. 362 for *magatama* is "the claw or comma-shaped jewel found in prehistoric tombs and ritual sites." I can't

take the space to go further into it here but, as the Ainu were the primitives of Japan and they worshipped the bear god as the intermediary between human, mountains, and salmon and the ocean, possibly we have here a bear claw at the base of it all. The fact that Japan, a modern nation, has a bear claw, even though disguised, as its "crown jewel," certainly gives an indication of its on-going ties with "the primitive." For more on the interactions between Japanese and Ainu, see Gary Snyder, "A Note on the Interface." *Alcheringa* v. 3 (1977): 2-3.

—— "form a bond between the people...": **Earhart**, *Religious Study*, p. 3.

—— "The timing of the festival.": Ibid., p. 11.

—— FOUR SEASONS OF THE RITUALS: "The...summer peak is a 120-day period of rituals, ceremonies, and pilgrimages within all three of the mountains of Dewa Sanzan. For, although Gassan and Yudonosan are generally closed to visitors, during the winter and spring peaks, the beginning of the summer peak is marked by the ceremony of 'opening the door' to Gassan...The route from Haguro to Gassan is opened on the third day of the fourth month...The summer peak begins on this day and continues until the 'closing of the door' to Gassan on the 8th day of the 8th month." (Earhart, "Four Ritual Periods.") Earhart notes that "technically pilgrims could not enter the mountain until it had been ritually opened." (Earhart, *Ritual Study*, p. 103) In a footnote he states in "present day Japan the 'mountain opening' is essentially the opening of the mountain climbing season, but at various places rituals are still associated with this event." (Earhart, "Four Ritual Periods," p. 106). Blacker points out that the Winter Peak is more a "celebration to mark the emergence from ritual seclusion of two high-ranking yamabushi." (Blacker, *Catalpa Bow*, p. 218).

—— INITIATION: **Earhart**, "Four Ritual Periods."

—— DESCRIPTION OF THE PILGRIMAGE SETTING OFF: **Blacker**, *Catalpa Bow*, 219.

—— LIST OF PILGRIMS: Ibid., p. 222.

—— "performed the pilgrimage...": **Earhart**, *Religious Study*, p. 104.

—— "the real beginning...": Ibid., pp. 115-116.

—— TENGAI: Ibid., p. 139-140 and **Blacker**, *Catalpa Bow*, p. 222.

243 "It was very beautiful, on three wailing...": **Blacker**, *Catalpa Bow*, p. 223-224.

—— "I remember feeling surprised..." down to "the top of the steps...": Ibid., p. 231.

—— "clutching hold..." down to "by the time...": Ibid., p. 231-232.

—— "In a week...": Ibid., p. 233.

—— "Heaven and earth and the natural seasons 'move'...": **Anshō Togawa**, quoted in Earhart, "Four Ritual Periods."

244 "Some of the paleolithic caves...": **Duerr**, *Dreamtime*, p. 21.

—— "spears or harpoons...": Ibid., p. 182.

—— "carry out their increase ceremonies...": Ibid., p. 182-183.

—— ALDO LEOPOLD AND THE WOLF: **Aldo Leopold**, *A Sand County Almanac*, p. 130.

—— "[There is] a power we call Sila...": **K. Rasmussen**, *Across Arctic America*. Westport Conn.: Greenwood Press, 1968, p. 386. (reprint)

245 RENEWAL OF THE DREAMING: From two accounts: "Dreaming Impressions" by John Martin and "Renewal of the Dreaming, Spring Equinox, '85" by Michael Gardiner. In John Martin. ed., *The Deep Ecologist* 19 (January 1986), unpaged. The beginning section is by Gardiner.

246 SAMHAIN FESTIVAL—CHINOOK: This account is from my notes of the Festival so I no longer have all the references.

—— "Be welcome, strong heart...": **Stephen Donaldson**, *The Chronicles of Thomas Covenant, the Unbeliever*.

—— "sacred hoop of the world...": **Black Elk**, *Black Elk Speaks*.

—— "richness and complexity of the primitive mind...": **Freeman House**, "Future Primitive."

247 "where the edges of the year meet...": **Ashanti Tribe** in Africa. See *Stanley Diamond, In Search of the Primitive*.

—— "we are here to learn...": **Gino August Sky**, "Searching for the Miracle." *Clear Creek* (June 1972). His words are not within quotes in the text because I was the one who recited them.

—— "Grandmother Earth hear me!": **Black Elk**, Joseph Brown. ed., *The Sacred Pipe*, p. 105.

248 "Salmon is the totem animal...": **Freeman House**, "Totem Salmon."

—— "We're just starting...": **Gary Snyder**, *The Old Ways*, p. 42.

249 "Beauty is our reaction...": **Adams**, "Magic." 1957. Unpublished.

Ch. 15 Sacred Sex

p. 251 Opening Quotes

— "To change ideas about...": **Aldo Leopold,** quoted in Susan Flader, *Thinking Like a Mountain,* p. 33.

— "Thus it is that the Hindu groom...": **Francis Huxley,** *The Way of the Sacred,* p. 211.

252 D. H. Lawrence and the Morning Star: **D. H. Lawrence,** *The Plumed Serpent,* p. 178.

— "worship of the reproductive organs... the fertilizing...": **Thomas Wright,** *The Worship of the Generative Powers During the Middle Ages of Western Europe,* 1866, p. vi. **Add. notes:** Two very old texts were reprinted together in one volume, along with an introduction by Ashley Montagu, by Julian Press in 1957: the title above and Richard Payne Knight, *A Discourse on the Worship of Priapus and Its Connection with the Mystic Theology of the Ancients,* (1786). It's a valuable work because it shows how the ancient pagan worship of the generative organs continued under a thin veneer of Christianity even up to the time of the first World War. (Montagu, in "Introduction.") In general, both male and female generative organs brought not only abundance but good luck etc. Knight recounts how in the church of St. Cosmus and Damianus in Abruzzi, (then part of the Kingdom of Naples), wax models of the phallus were brought to the altar by women hoping for marriage and/or children. This was up until the year 1780. Another important aspect concerns "hot cross buns," which we still eat at Easter. "Children carried in the procession, at the end of their palm branches, a phallus made of bread, which they called undiguisedly a pinne, [penis] and which, having been blessed by the priest, the women carefully preserved during the following year as an amulet." (p. 88, Wright) This came from an old Roman custom, but "the Christians, when they seized upon the Easter festival, gave them the form of a bun...and to protect themselves, from any evil influences which might arise from their former heathen character, they marked them with the Christian symbol—the cross." (p. 87, Wright) At St. Jean d'Angely small cakes made in the form of the phallus were carried in the procession for the feast of Corpus Christi. Wright continues: "The custom of making cakes in the form of the sexual members, male and female, dates from a remote antiquity and was common among the Romans."

Another item, worth recounting here, concerns the *Shelah-na-Gig* carvings on ancient churches in Ireland. This carving depicts a woman, holding wide her labia to expose the generative organs "to avoid the evil eye." Knight gives some former locations of these in the county of Tipperary and one preserved in Dublin and still another at the Church of San Fedele at Como in Italy. He has plates of these opposite pages 32 and 44. This custom was followed in many parts of the world, for instance, the "Arabs of North Africa stick up the generative organ of cow, mare or female camel." From this, Wright traces the use of a "real horseshoe nailed up for the same purpose. In this way originated, apparently, from the popular worship of the generative powers, the vulgar practice of nailing a horseshoe upon buildings to protect them...a practice which continues to exist among the peasantry in some parts of England at the present day." (p. 49)

Wright reports that the ancients had two forms of what antiquarians (such as Wright) called the "phallic hand...in which the middle finger was extended at length and the thumb and other fingers doubled up." (p. 66) It is interesting that this gesture, which was originally a sign of the "fertilizing, protecting, and saving powers of nature," today is considered such a great insult that it's often the provocation for a fight.

Montagu (p. vii) says that we need a "thoroughgoing systematic treatment" of such beliefs, but no one has done it yet. He points out that the enormous literature on the subject is summarized in R. Goodland, *A Bibliography of Sex Rites and Customs.* London: George Routledge, 1931.

253 Older men and younger women: **Shepard,** *The Tender Carnivore and the Sacred Game,* p. 137.

— "Oh, what a catastrophe...": **D. H. Lawrence,** "A Propos of Lady Chatterley's Lover." In W. Roberts and H. Moore, eds. *Phoenix II,* 1968.

254 "spending as much time as possible...": **Stanton Peale and A. Brodsky,** *Love and Addiction.* New York: New American Library, 1976, p. 10.

— "attribute of drugs...attribute of people...": Ibid., p. 43. **Add. note:** This is clearly shown by the fact that almost all primitive societies had either drugs or alcohol but were not addicts. As soon as Europe got tobacco they became addicted. And this pattern is repeated for every one of these items. This, essentially goes back to "substance" versus "relationship." In a substance culture one can believe that a substance—money or love or a drug etc. can give what you need. In a relationship culture, such as the old Chinese culture or almost any "fully functioning" primitive society, this kind of thinking does not happen. In a conversation with Julien Puzey, concerning this matter she said: "Anytime anything becomes an end in itself it becomes addiction. When the sexual act itself becomes the end, you're in trouble, and, as with any addiction it intensifies and the returns are less and less."

— "At a neurochemical level...": Phil Donahue, quoting **J. Panksepp,** a scientist at Bowling Green State University in Ohio. In Donahue's book, *The Human Animal.* New York: Simon & Schuster, 1985, p. 128.

— "Every form of life has the equal...": **Arne Naess,** "The Shallow and the Deep, Long-Range Ecology Movements."

— "move toward a blossoming...": **D. H. Lawrence,** "Reflections on the Death of a Porcupine." Philadelphia, 1925.

— "Lawrence symbolized his civilization...": **Sigrid Undset,** *Men, Women and Places.* New York: Alfred A. Knopf, 1939.

— "It provided an excellent...": **Midgley,** *Beast and Man,* p. 333.

— Kissing, flirting etc.: **I. Eibl-Eibesfeldt,** *Love and Hate,* p. 122-128 and p. 152.

255 "estrogen...temporary buzzing...": **Sarah B. Hrdy,** "Heat Loss: The Absence of Estrus Reflects a Change in Sexual Strategy." *Science 83* (October, 1983): 73-83.

— "is probably a feature...": **Carl Sauer,** quoted in John Livingston, *One Cosmic Instant,* p. 113.

— "multimate breeding..." down to "advertise that she is 'in heat'. ": **Hrdy,** "Heat Loss."

— "If this is what a reunion...": **Nancy Thompson Handler** of Stonybrook, at the first major international conference on chimpanzees, held in 1986 by the Chicago Academy of Science, called "Understanding Chimpanzees." My source is a tape, ATC Series on National Public Radio, November 11, 1986. Segment #12, "Chimps I." Cassette tapes of this broadcast may be ordered directly from: National Public Radio, Custom Tape Service, Audience Services, 2025 M. St., Washington D.C. 20036.

— "Most probably, then...": **Richard Leakey,** *People of the Lake: Mankind and its Beginnings.* New York: Avon, 1978, p. 204.

256 "characterized by the fact..." down to "the fertilized eggs...": **Wolfgang Wickler,** *The Sexual Code,* pp. 64-66. Wickler, a noted ethologist is professor of Zoology at Munich University.

— "diminished secretions...": **Mark Cohen,** ed, *Biosocial Mechanisms of Population Regulation.* New Haven: Yale University Press, 1980, pp 85-86.

— "mating is not necessarily...": **Wickler,** *Sexual Code,* p. 88.

— Triumph ceremony of the Graylag geese: **Konrad Lorenz.** In Alec Nisbett, *Konrad Lorenz,* pp. 49-51.

— "correspond to the typical..." down to "the victor among the young...": **Wickler,** *Sexual Code,* pp. 279-280, xxi, 226 and 229.

257 "Theology has shown...": Ibid., pp. 283-284.

— Man the hunter conference: **Richard Lee and I. DeVore.** eds, *Man the Hunter.*

— Spread of agriculture in only 8000 years: **Mark Cohen,** *The Food Crisis in Prehistory,* p. 8.

— More calories per unit of land: Ibid., p. 15.

— Extinct mammals in Africa: Ibid., p. 100.

— Extinct mammals in North and South America: Ibid., p. 181. **Add. notes:** Concerning the fact that changing climate had a part in this, I want to note Wright's statement here: "For example, the replacement of 'big-game hunters' about 9000 years ago is usually attributed to the extinction of big mammals about this time, whether as a result of climatic change or of overexploitation by man himself. Although opinions differ... the paleontological and archaeological evidence is now abundant enough and dated well enough to state with some assurance that a major shift in fauna occurred throughout the New World, and that the human populations adapted to the shift more by changing their patterns of collecting food than by domesticating available plant and animals." (Herbert Wright, "Environmental Change and the Origin of Agriculture in the Old and New Worlds.")

— "biosphere...spread their economic...": **Gary Snyder,** *The Old Ways,* p. 21.

258 **Add. notes:** The most detailed study of the normal use of methods to control birth throughout the world was made by Sir Alexander M. Carr-Saunders, who took advantage of his widespread contacts with the British rulers throughout the world as well as written sources. The book was published in Oxford, England in 1922. Fortunately, Arno Press found a copy in the University of Illinois Library and did a reprint in 1974; therefore you can probably get it from inter-library loan as I did.

It gives us a clear insight into the fact that, until the present "temporary anomaly," most human groups have considered population control as a normal part of life. He notes that "everywhere groups...as we have seen, [are] confined to definite areas...There is—taking all the relevant facts into account—an optimum number. The advantages to any group of approaching this number are immense; a wide departure can only be socially disastrous." (p. 222) He credits tradition (including ritual) with keeping birth down. Here are a few examples, I've taken at random: "In the Kingsmill Islands a woman seldom has more than two children, and never more than three; when she discovers herself to be *enciente* [pregnant] for the third or fourth time, the foetus is discharged by a midwife." (1850) And again, among the Melanesians, "the old women of the village generally determined whether a new-born child should live; if not promising in appearance or if it was likely to be troublesome, it was made away with." (1891) A source on the Fiji people explains that "relatives of a woman take it as a public insult if a child should be born before the customary 3 or 4 years have elapsed, and they consider themselves in duty bound to avenge it in an equally public manner."

He gives an Appendix listing the birth-control methods of 183 "primitive" societies. For convenience he has grouped these under "prolonged restriction of intercourse" (often ritualized, of course), abortion, and infanticide. This figure includes 37 American Indian societies, 51 African, 55 New Zealand and So. Pacific etc. He includes 20 pages of fine print listing his written sources. Sir Alexander M. Carr-Saunders, *The Population Problem: A Study in Human Evolution* Oxford: Clarendon Press, 1922. (reprint New York: Arno, 1974).

— "In her book, Susan mentions...": **"Alternative Contraception"** *Katuah* (Spring 1987). Important! Queen Anne's Lace looks quite similar to the poisonous Water Hemlock *(Conioselinum)*—a deadly poison. Consult reliable authorities on how to tell the difference as the odor is the key. **Add. notes:** Susan B. Weed, the author of *Wise Woman Herbal for Childbearing Years and Healing Wise,* also gives workshops on herbal medicine etc. Address: P.O. Box 64, Woodstock, New York, 12498.

— "an act of fondling...": **Dorothy Lee,** *Freedom and Culture.*

— "spreading out over the awakening..." down to "take their blanket...": **Robert Emmitt,** *The Last War Trail.*

260 "A psychological explosion...": **Peter Freuchen,** *Book of the Eskimos.* Cleveland: World Publishing, 1961, p. 92.

— A DRAWING OF THE WIFE-CHANGING GAME: **Edmund Carpenter,** *Eskimo Realities.* New York: Holt, Rinehart and Winston, 1973.

— "I still look on that...": **Wilfred Pelletier,** *No Foreign Land,* pp 77-78.

— SUMMARY OF THE ROLE OF WOMEN: **Evans Pritchard,** *Position of Women in Primitive Societies.* London, 1965, pp. 45-47.

— "Then Etewa, not in the least...": **Florinda Donner,** *Shabono.* New York: Delacorte Press, 1982, p. 160.

— "We found other...": **Tobias Schneebaum,** *Keep the River on Your Right.* New York, Grove Press, 1970, p. 99.

261 "unassailable fact...": **Girardot,** *Myth and Meaning in Early Taoism,* p. 221.

— "[W]e may conclude...": **Lathrap,** "Our Father the Cayman, Our Mother the Gourd."

— "emulates the balanced cosmic...": **Girardot,** *Myth and Meaning,* p. 224. **Add. notes:** This Langenaria form is common in all Chinese and Japanese art and appears on vases, sculptures and decorations of all sorts. Taoist figures always have a staff with a Langenaria gourd fastened to it; yet few explanations of this art ever refer to the cosmic symbolism involved in the seemingly simple gourd.

— DOSOJIN: **Michael Czaja,** *Gods of Myth and Stone: Phallicism in Japanese Folk Religion.* **Add. notes:** Dosojin means "earth-ancestral-gods." They are everywhere in Japan, although over-looked by western authors. Japanese art authorities, generally, overlooked them as well, because after all, they had seen them everywhere, since they were children. How could they be important? They were not seriously studied until this book.

It's a lavishly illustrated book, but now out of print. The author, Czaja is an architect.

— "increase the amount of life-giving...": **Needham,** *Sci. and Civil.,* v. 2, p. 149.

— TRUE ART OF EQUALIZING THE CHHI'S: Ibid., p. 150. **Add. notes:** It is interesting to find that the Chinese phrase for this is *ho chhi hun chhi ho chhi. Hun* is the same word as in Lord Hun-Tun and the concept of "chaos" of the gourd etc. Needham merely says in his footnote here: "Note the survival of this ancient watchword of community life." He deals with *hun* and community earlier in his work, linking this with Lord Hun-Tun, but not the gourd as such. We owe that linking to Girardot's later work.

— "correlation with calendrical...": **K. Schipper,** "The Taoist Body." *History of Religions* 17: 355-386.

262 "one of the deepest..": **Needham,** *Sci. and Civil.,* v. 2, p. 147.

— INSIGHTS INTO THE "SACRED MIDDLE" FROM ROLFING: **V. Hunt** *et al,* "A Study of Structural Integration from Neuromuscular, Energy Field and Emotional Approaches." Boulder: Rolf Institute for Structural Integration. Another useful book is John T. Cottingham, *Healing Through Touch.* Boulder, Colorado, Rolf Institute, 1985. Address: P.O. Box 1868, Boulder, Co. 80306.

— TAI CHI: **Wen-Shan Huang,** *Fundamentals of Tai Chi Chuan.* Hong Kong: South Sky Book Co., 1973.

— PUBOCOCCYGEAL MUSCLE AND BIRTH CONTROL: I cannot give my source here because when my Chinese Tai Chi teacher from Canada explained it to us, he had us take a vow not to tell others of these techniques. However, if one practiced Tai Chi long enough, these techniques could be figured out for oneself.

— "effective training for making love...": **Bob Klein,** *Movements of Magic: The Spirit of Tai Chi.* North Hollywood, California: Newcastle Pub., 1984, pp. 57 and 125. Despite the title this book is genuine because Klein knows ethology. He has a degree from Cornell in zoology and maintains his work in that field. (See "Resources.")

263 *TU-MO* PRESSURE POINT: Again, I'm not at liberty to give the source here, because it was a private series of lectures by a Chinese Taoist. For written information consult the books of the Thailand master, Mantak Chia. They are helpful but, unfortunately, he feels it necessary to use a narrowly Western "substance" approach in explaining valid Chinese techniques. Mantak Chia and M Winn, *Taoist Secrets of Love: Cultivating Male Sexual Energy.* New York: Aurora Press, 1984. *Healing Love through the Tao: Cultivating Female Sexual Energy.* New York: Healing Tao Books, 1986.

— "THE GATE OF DESTINY," "CINNABAR CAVE" AND OTHER POETICAL NAMES: **Holmes H. Welch,** "The Bellagio Conference on Taoist Studies." *History of Religions* 9:107-136.

— TUNING: **d'Aquili ed.,** *The Spectrum of Ritual,* pp. 130-140 and 170-180.

— "thousand loving thrusts...": **Li T'ung Hsuan:** quoted in Jolan Chang, *The Tao of Love and Sex: the Ancient Chinese Way to Ecstasy.* New York: E. P. Dutton, 1977, p. 47. **Add. notes:** This book and Chang's other book, *The Tao of the Loving Couple,* provide the best beginning information for what's been called Taoist Sex. The famous scholar, Joseph Needham, wrote the Foreword to the first book, explaining how he first heard of these techniques in China and through the books of the Europeans, Maspero and Van Gulik. At the end of his Foreword, Needham writes: "our friend Chang chung-Lan (Jolan Chang) from Stockholm, whose book on Chinese—and Universal—sexology I here commend to the candid reader." Needham further states: "Though he deals mainly with technical matters, these must always be seen against that background of wider sapientia, startling though it may be for Westerners, the Chinese conviction that there can be no line of distinction between sacred and profane love."

Given the underlying theme of this book, dealing with substance and relationship, Chang's second book has a useful remark. This second book contains stories of people who came to Chang for help, after reading his first volume. This story concerns July and Tom, who, Chang says, "like most people, measured man-woman satisfaction in terms of orgasms and ejaculations. When a relationship is based on such a dubious foundation, it is hard to achieve true satisfaction." (p. 15) Chang has some remarks concerning new fads in Western sex, such as the "famous G spot" of a few years ago, and notes that the *Tao* discovered this "at least 2000 years ago and called it the *tide of Yin*." (p. 24) Here, instead of a "substance," the G spot, "discovered" by Grafenberg, we have the "tide of Yin," the tide of all life energy which carries along the man and woman. One concept, the Western attitude, concerns a "thing," the G spot, which the man manipulates to bring pleasure to the woman, while in the Taoist concept, the "tide of Yin" encompassing all of nature, carries the two humans along.

— "temporarily insane...": **Ford Madox Ford**, *Portraits from Life*. Boston: Houghton Mifflin Co., 1937, pp. 78-79.

264 "that you could cross over...": **Duncan**, *The Netzahualcoyotl News*. A recent book, Walter Williams, *The Spirit and the Flesh: Sexual Diversity in American Indian Culture*, provides further information on the *berdache* role.

— SEX ROLE ASSIGNMENTS: **Margaret Mead**, "Cultural Determinants of Sexual Behavior." In William C. Young. ed., *Sex and Internal Secretions*, v. 2. Baltimore: The Williams & Wilkins Co. (3rd ed.), 1961, pp. 1438-1479. **Add. notes:** I list only five of her eleven categories (using her original numbers). For the remainder see her original article.

— "With de Angulo, almost for the first time...": **Bob Callahan**, *The Netz. News*.

265 "Lawrence became the torchbearer...": **Rolf Gardiner**, *England Herself*. London: Faber & Faber, 1943, p. 88.

— "under the splendid oak and ash...": **May Chambers Holbrook**, "The Chambers Paper." In Edward Nehls. ed., D. H. Lawernce: *A Composite Biography*, v. 3. Madison: University of Wisconsin Press, 1959, p. 580.

— "beloved home valley...": **D. H. Lawrence**, *The White Peacock*.

— "last generation of...": **D. H. Lawrence**, "Enslaved by Civilization." In *Phoenix II*, pp. 578-581.

— "the miners worked underground...": **D. H. Lawrence**, "Nottingham and the Mining Countryside." *Adelphi*, June—August, 1930. Reprinted in *Phoenix*, 1968, pp. 133-140.

— "a very melodious voice...": **Ada Lawrence**, *Young Lorenzo*. New York: Russell and Russell, 1966, pp. 24 and 26.

— "run like fire...": **Ford Madox Ford**, *Portraits from Life*, p. 78 and 79.

— "realized himself completely...": **Cecil Gray**, *Musical Chairs*, p. 141.

— "natural fountain of all...": **Otto Gross**, quoted in Martin Green, *The Von Richthofen Sisters*. New York: Basic Books,1974, p. 10.

— "only person who...": Ibid., p. 47.

— "But then came another hunger...": **D. H. Lawrence**, "Manifesto." In V. de Sola Pinto and W. Roberts. eds., *The Complete Poems of D. H. Lawrence*. London: William Heinemann, 1957.

266 "They had met...": **D. H. Lawrence**, *Sons and Lovers*. New York: Viking Press, 1958, ch. 13.

— "faculty for receiving...": **D. H. Lawrence**. In Harry T. Moore. ed., *The Collected Letters of D. H. Lawrence*, v. 1, p. 326.

— "one of those...": **Kenneth Rexroth**, *An Autobiographical Novel*, p. 272.

— "the world all in couples...": **D. H. Lawrence**, *Women in Love*. New York: Viking Press, 1960.

— "What a feeble lot of...": **D. H. Lawrence**. In Aldous Huxley, *The Letters of D. H. Lawrence*. New York: Viking Press, 1936, p. 685.

— "It is no good being sexual..." and "with their soul vibrating...": **D. H. Lawrence**. In Harry Moore. ed., *The Collected Letters*, v. 1, p. 374 and p. 23.

— "a large gold moon...": **D. H. Lawrence**, *The Rainbow*, Ch. 4.

— "The last three thousand...": **D. H. Lawrence**, "A Propos of Lady Chatterley's Lover." London: Mandrake Press, 1930. (reprinted in *Phoenix II*, pp. 487-515.)

267 "The institution of sexual promiscuity...": **Gaster**, *Thespis*, p. 41.

— GUAJIRO GIRL'S PUBERTY RITE: **Maria-Barbara Watson-Franke**, "To Learn for Tomorrow: Enculturation of Girls and Its Social Importance among the Guajiro of Venezuela." In J. Wilbert. ed., *Enculturation in Latin America: an Anthology*. Los Angeles: UCLA Latin American Center Publication, University of Los Angeles, 1976, pp. 191-211.

— "the anima and animus...": **John Sanford**, *The Invisible Partners*. Paulist Press, 1980, p. 6. **Add. notes:** Jung's life was enriched by some deep relationships with women other than his wife. He wrote: "The pre-requisite for a good marriage it seems to me is the license to be unfaithful." (This is from a letter to Freud, Letter #175, 30 January 1910. In (Freud-Jung' Letters) That's about all he could say at that date, trapped within the commonly accepted "substance" definition of marriage.

— "In the case of the anima...": Ibid., pp. 35 and 36.

— "the anima gets them...": Ibid., pp. 43 and 47.

— "opened in the bloom of pure relationship...": **D. H. Lawrence**, "Reflections on the Death of a Porcupine."

— "For me, this place is sacred...": **D. H. Lawrence**, *St. Mawr*. In *St. Mawr and The Man Who Died*. New York: Vintage books, Alfred A. Knopf. This statement occurs on p. 140 in this edition.

Ch. 16 Seven "Ways"
pp. 268 and 269 Opening Quotes

— "Taoism, however, remembers the story...": **Girardot**, *Myth and Meaning*, p. 245.

— "Eskimos are more interested...": **Edmund Carpenter**, "Silent Music and Invisible Art." *Natural History* (May 1978).

— "Our purposeful creation...": **Tom Bender**, *Environmental Design Primer*, 1973, p. 81.

— "It seems that the Ndembu...": **Victor Turner**, "The Bite of the Hunter's Ghost." *Parabola* (Spring 1976).

— "Experienced chanters...": **Jean Liedloff**. *The Continuum Concept*. p. 134.

— "Some of the healing...": **James Hillman**, "A Note on Story." *Parabola* 4: 43-45.

— "In India he witnessed...": **Jung**, quoted by Vincent Brome, *Jung*, p. 231.

— "Conflicts within...": **Melvin Konner**, *The Tangled Wing*, p. 7.

— "Why Fenollosa wrote...": **Charles Olson**, *Human Universe*. New York: Grove Press, 1967, p. 18.

— "Hear the voice of the Bard...": **Walt Whitman**, *Songs of Experience*.

— "[B]ut what is truth, what is wisdom...": **Al Huang**, *Embrace Tiger, Return to Mountain—the essence of Tai Chi*. Moab, Utah: Real People Press, 1973, p. 35.

270 I owe the inspiration for the sub-title of this chapter to Hans Duerr's book, *Dreamtime: the Boundary between Wilderness and Civilization*.

— "When we get out of the glass.": **D. H. Lawrence**, "Escape" In V. de Sola Pinto and W. Roberts, eds. *The Complete Poems of D. H. Lawrence*, p. 482.

271 "*affordances* of the environment...": **Gibson**, *Ecological Approach to Visual Perception*, p. 127.

— "one cosmic instant...": **Livingston**, *One Cosmic Instant*, p. 96. He states: "The oldest known example of Homo erectus is our ancient acquaintance from Java, who lived more than 700,000 years ago."

272 "That the self...": **Dōgen**. Quoted in Aitken, "Gandhi, Dōgen and Deep Ecology." In Devall and Sessions: *Deep Ecology*, pp. 232-235.

— "West of the mountain...": **John Nichols**, *The Last Beautiful Days of Autumn*. New York: Holt Rinehart & Winston, 1982, p. 79.

— "In the northern Mediterranean region..." down to "Their abrupt expansion...": **Herbert Wright**, "Environmental Change and the Origin of Agriculture in the Old and New Worlds."

— SAGEBRUSH IN SW ASIA: **Charles A. Reed**, "Origins of Agriculture: Discussion and some Conclusions."

— "tells us that the very herb...": **Harrison**, *Mythology*, p. 127.

— "Artemis, whose name...": **Shepard**, *The Sacred Paw*, pp. 116- 117. **Add. notes:** The link here between bear and sage is probably due to the fact that humans first learned medicinal uses of many plants from the bear, as noted in *The Sacred Paw*.

— HEALING USES OF SAGE: **Michael Moore**, *Medicinal Plants of the Mountain West*. Santa Fe: The Museum of New Mexico Press, 1979, p, 162.

— "for believing that the Grand Canyon...": **Mary Sojourner**, "Grand Canyon Uranium Heats Up." *Earth First* (May 1987).

273 "The intuitive observer...": **Leo Frobenius**, "Paideuma." In Jerome Rothenberg, *Symposium of the Whole*, pp. 36-40.

— "The bottle gourd as a cultivated...": **Lathrap**, "Our Father the Cayman, Our Mother the Gourd."

— PLANTS FIRST GROWN FOR BODY PAINT ETC.: **Carl Sauer**, *Agricultural Origins and Dispersions*. **Add. notes:** Some of the items mentioned by Sauer, are tumeric for body paint and food coloring, fibers for cordage, bark cloth and yellow dyes from breadfruit, as well as drugs and fish poisons, etc.

— GOURD AS THE UNIVERSE: **Geoffrey Parrinder**, *African Mythology*. Paul Hamlyn, Pub. 1967.

— "fifty thousand or a hundred...": **Charles Heiser**, *The Gourd Book*, p. 114.

— "Since bottle gourds have been picked up...": **Charles Reed**, "Origin of Agriculture: Discussion and some Conclusions."

— "The gourd is this great world...": **Girardot**, *Myth and Meaning*, p. 208.

— "one of man's most important plants...": Ibid., p. 212.

— USES OF THE GOURD: **Heiser**, *The Gourd Book*, pp. 71-228.

— 300 LBS. CUCURBITA: Ibid., p. 34.

— BOTTLE GOURD SIZE: Ibid., p. 75.

— "it freely yields..." down to "in its emptiness...": Ibid., p. 224.

— "gross, physiological..." down to "When ritualized systems...": **Victor Turner**, "Forms of Symbolic Action: Introduction," pp. 9 and 10. **Add. notes:** Gregory Bateson has some more to say on this subject: "it is probably an error to think of dream, myth and art as being about any one matter other than relationship." Talking about art, he says: "If the picture were *only* about sex or *only* about social organization, it would be trivial. It is nontrivial or profound precisely because it is about sex and social organization and cremation and other things. In a word, it is only about relationship and not about *any* identifiable relata." (*Steps to an Ecology of Mind*, pp. 150 and 151.)

274 GOURDS ON ANCIENT URNS: **Andersson**, *Children of the Yellow Earth: Studies in Prehistoric China*, p. 275 and 336.

— "Within the cultural sphere...": **Girardot**, *Myth and Meaning*, p. 227.

— "cyclic inexhaustible creativity...": Ibid., p. 230.

— DIRECTIONS FOR MAKING GOURD RATTLES: Hang the gourds in a dry place for one to two years, depending on your climate. They are dry when the seeds rattle freely inside. Drill a small hole in the stem end. Add tiny sharp edged pebbles or small rocks from ant hills, or fragments of quartz. (some Indians put in tiny garnets). Insert a small stick or dowel into the hole and glue with any good wood glue. Decorate as you wish. For detailed information on making gourd rattles or other crafts, see Carolyn Mordecai, *Gourd Craft*. Crown Pub., 1978. It is currently out of print but can be secured through inter-library loan.

— "I didn't think I'd shake...": **Jerome Rothenberg**, "Pre-Face to a Symposium on Ethnopoetics." *Alcheringa* 2 (1976): 6-12.

275 "We begin to regard...": **Simon Ortiz**, "Song/Poetry and Language—Expression and Perception." In Rothenberg, *Symposium of the Whole*, pp. 399-407.

— "The group affords the chant...": **Julien Puzey**, Discussion, February 1987. Unpublished.

— "Artistic skill is the combining...": **Bateson**, *Steps to an Ecology of Mind*, p. 404.

— "Without words our imagination...": **Susanne Langer**, *Philosophy in a New Key*, p. 126.

— "They tend to integrate...": Ibid., p.135.

— "Groans and tones are...": **Walter J. Brenneman**, *Spirals: A Study in Symbol, Myth and Ritual*. University Press of America, 1979, p. 49.

— "A man may be walking...": **C. Wissler**, "Ceremonial Bundles of the Blackfoot Indians." *Anthrop. Papers of the Amer. Mus. of Nat. History.* 7 pt. 2 (1912): 263

— "Anything, in fact, may deliver...": **Rothenberg**, *Technicians of the Sacred*, p. 425.

276 GREGORIAN CHANT: "High frequencies cited in 'recharging' effects reported with Gregorian chant." *Brain Mind Bulletin* 10 (March 4, 1985):1.

— "conducted such collective...": **Christopher Caudwell**, *Illusion and Reality: A Study of the Sources of Poetry.* New York: International Pub., 1937 (fifth printing, 1963), p. 28.

— "cognized" and "operational": **Roy Rappaport**, *Meaning Ecology and Religion*, p. 98.

— "are guided more..." down to "operating instructions...": Ibid., p.138-139.

— "But, as the impoverishment...": Ibid., p. 141.

277 "myth and poetry...": **James Hillman**, *Re-visioning Psychology*, p. 217.

— "Chuang Tzu says, in essence..." down to "In Chuang Tzu's mind...": **Kuang-Ming Wu**, *Chuang Tzu: World Philosopher at Play*, p. 119 and 120.

— "*chien pi*, looking..." down to "sure cure for...": Ibid., p. 120 and 121.

278 "the piping of men, the piping of...": Ibid., p. 48.

— "For the Real is that...": down to "Such is the capturing...": Ibid., p. 57.

— "We're just starting...": **Gary Snyder**, *The Old Ways*, p. 42.

— TIBETAN "OM CHANT": For a quick introduction to what this chant means and how to use it, see LaChapelle, *Earth Festivals*, pp. 110 and 111. For more depth, see Lama A. Govinda, *Foundations of Tibetan Mysticism*. London: Rider and Co. The entire book is a thorough investigation of Tibetan religion by way of this chant.

279 "I CIRCLE AROUND" CHANT: **James Mooney**, "The Ghost Dance Religion." *Bur. of Amer. Ethnol. Fourteenth Annual Report*, 1896. Pt. 2, p. 970 ff.

280 "To have an identity...": **Silas Goldean**, "The Principle of Extended Identity." Available from Finn Hill Arts.

— "ANCIENT ONE" CHANT: **Jackie Miller** and **Julien Puzey** were the ones who put it in final form.

— "NOBODY KNOWS" CHANT: **Huichol** influenced chant which came to Stephanie L. on a trip of Robert Greenway's Wilderness Experience Class—Sonoma State College.

— "Wirikura...the place...": **Barbara Myerhoff**, *Peyote Hunt*, p. 142.

— "divisions dissolve..." down to "The sacred is the natural...": **Victor Turner**, "Introduction." In Myerhoff, *Peyote Hunt*, pp. 9 and 10.

281 "an agonizing conflict..." down to "all uniting symbols...": **Jung**, *Coll. Works*, v. 9, Pt. 1, pp. 167 and 168.

282 "WE ALL FLY LIKE EAGLES" CHANT: Traditional Chant, from the California group, "The Circle."

— "BEAR CHANT": **Frances Densmore**, "Teton Sioux Music." *Bur. of Amer. Ethnol. Bulletin* 61 (1918).

— "Around the northern hemisphere...": **Shepard**, *The Sacred Paw*, p. xii.

— CATEGORIES OF THE VERB, "TO BEAR": Ibid., p. xvii.

— "we can...see...": Ibid., p. xix.

— "The chief...": See reference below for p. 284.

283 "the carnival begins...": **Robert M. and Ada Yerkes**, *The Great Apes*. New Haven: Yale University Press, 1929. Quoted in V. Reynolds, *Budongo: A Forest and Its Chimpanzees*. London: Methuen, 1965. And V. and F. Reynolds, "Chimpanzees of the Budongo Forest." In I. DeVore, ed., *Primate Behavior*. New York: Holt Rinehart and Winston, 1965.

— "animating the drum..." down to "oldest form of shamanism...": **Mircea Eliade**, "Recent Works on Shamanism." *History of Religions* 6: 152-186.

— ARTICLE BY NEEDHAM: **Rodney Needham**, "Percussion and Transition." *Man* 2 (1967): 606-614.

— "It is the drummers...": **Francis Huxley**, "Anthropology and ESP." In J. R. Smythies, ed., *Science and ESP*. London: Routledge & Kegan Paul, p. 286.

— "a change of rhythm...": **Anthony Jackson**, "Sound and Ritual." *Man*, 3 (1968): 293-299.

— "steep-fronted..." down to "The low frequency...": **William C. Sturtevant**, "Categories, Percussion and Physiology." *Man* 3 (1968): 133-134.

284 TUNING: See chapter twelve, for more on this.

— BIOLOGICAL APPROACH: **Andrew Neher**, "A Physiological Explanation of Unusual Behavior in Ceremonies Involving Drums." *Human Biology* 34 (1962): 151-161.

— DRUM TAPE BY COGBURN: Order from Finn Hill Arts.

— CONNECTIONS BETWEEN THUNDER AND DRUMMING: **Donald Tuzin**, "Miraculous Voices: the Auditory Experience of Numinous Objects." **Add. notes:** Tuzin states: "My thesis is that a certain type of naturally occurring sound has a perceptual effect on some, possibly many, animal species that is intrinsically mysterious and thus anxiety-arousing; that this sensation is humanly interpreted and its accompanying anxiety cognitively resolved by referring it to the mystery that is allegedly inherent in the supernatural realm..." This entire paper provides much interesting background on the drum—some of it not necessarily accurate, but the footnotes and "Comments" by others make it very useful. Before I go further into Tuzin here, remember that humans began in the Rift valley in Africa, which is subject to thunder showers over the mountains.

Essentially, Tuzin is dealing with the almost unhearable sound of very distant thunder, as he experienced it among the Arapesh in New Guinea. I want to add one further personal insight here. In *Earth Wisdom* I recount our experience of "lightning headaches" in afternoon thunderstorms when climbing as teenagers. Tuzin does not go into this aspect, of course. Writing about these "sounds, which are not 'heard'...but affect the brain," he continues: "This...suggestion...entails that the special, pre-articulate feelings which validate religious belief by referring it to subjective experience are not primarily (if at all) creatures of cultural conditioning, but natural emanations or proclivities of the brain itself." I would add, especially the older animal (limbic) brain and the even older brain that has to do with homeostasis.

In fact, one of the "Comments," (p. 592) following the paper states: "The core of the mind-body problem is that there is *no* culturally independent way of separating mind from body (subjective from objective, etc). How the boundary is drawn, and where it is drawn, is itself a cultural datum. This is not merely a metatheoretical issue but also...a moral and political problem." ("Comment" by Geoffrey Samuel, Dept. of Sociology, Univ. of Newcastle, N.S.W. Australia.)

Drum Language—Another important aspect of drumming, is the "literature" created by drumming in Central and West Africa. One of the most sophisticated aspects, concerns the actions of a chief drummer at a dance. Through the "language" of his drumming, he "maintains a running commentary on the dance, controls the line dancers with great precision, calls particular persons by name to dance solo, tells them what dance to do, corrects them as they do it, and sends them back into line with comments on the performance. He does this by making his drum talk, even above the sound of four or five other drums in the 'orchestra'." (R. G. Armstrong, "Talking Drums in the Benue-Cross River Region of Nigeria." *Phylon* 15 (1954). Quoted in Ruth Finnegan, *Oral Literature in Africa*. London: Oxford Univ. Press, 1970. An abridgement is in Rothenberg, *Symposium of the Whole*, pp. 129-139.)

285 "I wanted Lawrence...": **Mabel Dodge Luhan**, *Lorenzo in Taos*. New York: Alfred Knopf, 1932, p. 70.

— "But the world was somehow...": **D. H. Lawrence**, *The Plumed Serpent*, p. 357-358.

— "The sound that waked...": Ibid., p. 359-360.

— "The drums keep up the pulsating...": **D. H. Lawrence**, "Indians and Entertainment."

— POEM, "NEW MEXICAN MOUNTAIN": **Robinson Jeffers**, *The Selected Poetry of Robinson Jeffers*. New York: Random House, 1959, p. 363.

— "wind, rain...transformation is due...": **Girardot**, *Myth and Meaning*, p. 190-191.

— "The magic and ritual...": Ibid., p. 199.

— "drum beaten from within...": **Heiser**, *The Gourd Book*, p. 186-189.

286 "In the central hollow...": Ibid., p. 310.

— "the percussive sound of...": **Creel**, *What is Taoism? and other Studies in Chinese Cultural History*. Chicago: Univ. of Chicago Press, 1970, p. 63.

— "As he becomes active...": **Clive Robbins**, "Outline of a Unique Music Therapy." In *For the Love of Life* (July 1985). Published by Theosophical Order of Service.

— KODO DRUMMERS: **John Perreault**, "Kodo Means Heartbeat." *Geo*, (November 1983): 52 ff.

— TAIKO GROUP IN DENVER: **Barbara Bellomo**, "Denver group reaches back to ancient Japanese ceremony." *Rocky Mountain News* (May 31, 1985).

287 "But without a hundred..." down to "We used to greet...": **Elizabeth Cogburn**, "Warriors of the Beauty Way: An Interview with Elizabeth Cogburn" by Ross Chapin. *In Context* 5 (Spring 1984).

— "All the songs...": **Elizabeth Cogburn**, quoted in Sarah Dubin-Vaughn, "The New Song Ceremonial Sun Dance Ritual—1983 & 1984: Shamanic Theatre and Ritual Art as a Better Game than War." Dissertation for the degree of Doctor of Philosophy in Transformational Psychology, International College, Los Angeles (Summer 1986). For more on Elizabeth Cogburn, see "Resource" section.

— "the Big Drum is taken...": Ibid., p. 69.

— OPENING OF THE BIG DRUM CEREMONY: Ibid., p. 69.

— "become a companion...": Ibid., p. 152.

— "I do not believe...": **Bateson**, *Mind and Nature*, p. 209.

— "...for hours, hours it goes on...": **D. H. Lawrence**, quoted in Mabel Luhan, *Lorenzo in Taos*, p. 343.

288 "The dances are pivots...": **Richard Schechner**, *Essays on Performance Theory*. New York: Drama Book Specialists, 1977. (See pp. 63-78 for his discussion of the Kaiko).

— "The resemblance to a human dance...": **Wolfgang Kohler**, *The Mentality of Apes*. London: Routledge, Kegan Paul, pp. 314-315. (First published in 1925.)

— NEW SONG CEREMONIAL SUN DANCE RITUAL: Unless otherwise noted, all the quotations in this section are from **Dubin-Vaughn**, "The New Song Ceremonial Sun Dance Ritual."

289 "When, in the dances of the Pueblo...": **Gary Snyder**, *Turtle Island*, pp. 108-109.

— CHANT OF THE BUFFALO MEN OF THE OSAGE TRIBE: **Francis LaFlesche**, "The Osage Tribe: the Rite of Vigil." *Bur. of Amer. Ethnol. Bull.* 39th Annual Report, 1917-1918: pp. 31 ff.

— "Share in the superhuman abundance...": **Josef Pieper**, *In Tune with the World*.

— "As the ceremony progressed..." down to "The potlatch ended...": **Victor and Edith Turner**, "Performing Ethnography." *Drama Review* 26: 33-50.

290 "Art...is the origin...": **Heidegger**, *Nietzsche*, p. 254.

— BILL PLOTKIN AND THE TALKING STAFF: **Bill Plotkin, Ph.D.** is a licensed clinical psychologist in Durango, Colorado who leads Vision Quests. He says that he guides people through both the wilderness, outside in nature, and the wilderness within.

— "hold a community celebration..." down to "We must give ourselves...": **Bob Cogburn**, "Talking Staff." *New Song Village Journal* (December 1985).

291 "between two men of power...": **Havelock**, *Preface to Plato*, p. 67.

— "bringing with it a deep sense...": **Elizabeth Cogburn**, quoted in Dubin-Vaughan, "New Song Ceremonial."

292 TALKING STAFF AND SELF DISCLOSURE: **Add. notes:** Referring here to Sidney Jourard, *The Transparent Self*. Van Nostrand Reinhold Co., 1971. Jourard feels that "Every maladjusted person is a person who has not made himself known to another human being and in consequence does not know himself." (p. 32.) Often such a person works very hard not to be known and this causes great underlying stress in his life and eventually physical illness. Jourard finds a reciprocity in self-disclosure, (p. 13). The more a person disclosed at depth, the more others open up likewise. Jourard states certain "conditions under which people are willing to make dimensions of themselves known to others. One of these conditions was *mutual* disclosure." (p. 17).

Another aspect of self disclosure was given by Jackie Miller. She used the phrase "the need to be known" and said that an important factor here is "the trust that the other will stay with you—be with you—throughout the self disclosure." In the Talking Staff ritual this is guaranteed because once the person joins the ritual they stay through to the end. Another aspect of the Talking Staff is that once someone has, in speaking out, managed to find just the right word for some state of being, this word becomes magical in that others now find **the** word, too, that they have been looking for. It seems that the particular work unlocks a door for others or we could say that the word seems to give a right to *be* that did not exist before.

— STICKS AND DOMINANT MALE CHIMPS: **Jane Lancaster**, "On the evolution of tool-using Behavior." *American Anthropologist* 70: 56-66.

— BATONS: **Alexander Marshack**, "Upper Paleolithic Notation and Symbol." *Science.* 178-817 (1972).

— "so called batons made of bone...": **John Pfeiffer**, *The Creative Explosion: An Inquiry into the Origins of Art and Religion*, p. 180. **Add. notes:** In Jacquetta Hawkes, *The Atlas of Early Man*, p. 21, there is a very clear drawing of one of these batons. She writes that they "were often highly ornamented" and may have served "some ritual purpose." (New York: St. Martin's Press, 1970).

— "coincides with external...": **Jung**, *Coll. Works*, v. 6, p. 119.

— "The shaman provides...": **Lévi-Strauss**, quoted in Meyerhoff, *Peyote Hunt*, p. 234. (her ref. is Lévi Strauss, 1963: p.198.)

293 "Focusing moves inward...": **Eugene Gendlin**, *Focusing*, p. xi.

— "Because it is capable...": **Carl Faber**, *On Listening*. Perseus Press, P.O. Box 1221, Pacific Palisades California 90272, p. 13.

— "flow through us..." down to "Sometimes the loneliness...": Ibid., pp. 6, 8, 13, 16 and 17.

— "Do you love yourself...": **Beno Kennedy**, quoted in E. Cogburn, "New Song Sun Dance, 1982: Announcement of the annual sun dance."

— LISTENING: **Add. notes:** Scott Peck, on the importance of listening, writes: "This knowledge that one is being truly listened to is frequently in and of itself remarkably therapeutic." In many of his cases, "dramatic improvement is shown during the first few months of psychotherapy," even before he's uncovered any of the origins of the problems. He says the main reason, he thinks "Is the patient's sense that he or she is being truly listened to, often for the first time in years, or perhaps for the first time ever." (M. Scott Peck, *The Road Less Traveled*. New York:Simon and Schuster, 1978, p. 129.)

— "In other words..." down to "We are creatures...": **William Willeford**, "Festival, Communion and Mutuality."

294 "In the heart of truth...": **Tom Jay**, "Words Bear Nature's Wisdom." *Upriver Downriver*.

297 "Jung said that he learned..." down to "constantly reiterated...": **Laurens Van Der Post**, *Jung and the Story of Our Time*, pp. 119 and 120.

— NO SCHIZOPHRENIA AMONG PRIMITIVES: **Stanley Diamond**, *In Search of the Primitive*, pp. 160 and 227-254. **Add. notes:** On p. 253, Diamond states: "...whether schizophrenia exists among primitive peoples. I believe that as an essence it does not, but the *process* is identifiable. That is, schizophrenia...is irrelevant in authentically primitive societies. The reasons for this are as follows..." He points out that first, the rights to all the necessities are "completely customary...Functionlessness is not a problem in primitive society." 2."Rituals at strategic points in the bioculturally defined life cycle permit the person to change roles while maintaining, and expanding, identity...". 3. "Rituals and ceremonies permit the expression of ambivalent emotions and the acting out of complex fantasies...". The 4th and last point has to do with kinship networks and he concludes, "*Social alienation* as we experience it in civilization is unknown." In a footnote on p. 253 he notes: "In 1939 George Devereux observed: "Schizophrenia seems to be rare or absent among primitives. This is a point on which all students of comparative society and of anthropology agree." (Devereaux, "A Sociological theory of Schizophrenia." *Psych. Review* 26 (1939), p. 317.)

— "to read everything..." down to "So- I hope you get...": **Dennis Tedlock**. "Toward a Restoration of the Word in the Modern World." *Alcheringa: Ethnopoetics* (1976):120-123.

298 "And,...that is hermeneutics...": Ibid., p. 130. **Add. notes:** Or, as Kuang-ming Wu says, understanding Chuang Tzu "demands nothing less than a transvaluation of hermeneutics." (p. 31). If for no other reason than the fact that it is so difficult to talk about these matters in a European language as I've said before. Furthermore, in general, since Plato, philosophers haven't even tried. Also this is why modern European philosophers, such as Heidegger who are trying to do this are so extremely difficult to read. It's easier to go directly to a Chinese. Read Wu's book, *Chuang Tzu: World Philosopher at Play* and then you'll know the full depth of the experience that the Talking Staff affords us.

— "relational: In speaking the individual is opened..." down to "Self-knowledge alone...": **Pat Johnson**, "The Task of the Philosopher: Kierkegaard, Heidegger, Gadamer." *Philosophy Today* 28 (Spring 1984): 13-19.

— "to make common to many...": **Oxford English Dictionary**.

— "to participate...": **Webster's Dictionary**.

— "In such understanding...": **Kuang-Ming Wu**, *Chuang Tzu: World Philosopher*, p. 32.

— "Concepts crack open...": Ibid., p. 34

— "walking among...": **Chuang Tzu**, quoted in Ibid., p. 214.

— "When one comes home to one's naturalness...": Ibid., p. 34.

— "a communicated one...": Ibid., p. 35.

— "Ceasing to impose...": Ibid., p. 104.

— "the True Man, who 'plays'...": **Chuang Tzu**, quoted in Ibid., p. 108. **Add. notes:** Barrington Nevitt explains further: "In this process, *understanding* is neither a point of view nor a value judgement." It comes about through seeing all the different modes of each person and how they relate. Patterns of perception merge and change in the very act of talking about them so that we explore them and discover new relationships in them. In such understanding, "we take no sides but many sides, also the inside. For *truth* is neither a label nor something to *match*. Truth is something we make with all our senses in a conscious process of remaking the world, as *that* world remakes us." Use of the "Talking Staff" out

in nature "affords" us real understanding of how this occurs. The above quotations are from Barrington Nevitt, "Via Media with Marshall McLuhan." (This article was in lieu of an obituary for his colleague, Marshall McLuhan.)

— "only of friends..." down to "Chuang Tzu's meandering...": **Kuang-Ming Wu**, *Chuang Tzu*, pp. 110 and 111.

— "each self to return to its root...": Ibid., pp. 115 and 116.

— "No longer is there prostitution...": Ibid., pp. 125 and 137.

— "Mountains and Rivers...": No further bibl. ref.

299 "As a poet...": **Gary Snyder**, quoted in Thomas Parkinson, "The Poetry of Gary Snyder." *The Southern Review* (July 1968): 616-632.

— FORCED ROOTLESSNESS AS A TEENAGER: **Melba Berry Bennett**, *The Stone Mason of Tor House*. Ward Ritchie Press, 1966, p. 27. **Add. notes:** As a long time friend of the family, she had access to their records. After the age of 12, his father sent him to Europe to school. Each year he put him in a different school in still another country, in his search of "the perfect" school. The boy was devastated—no friends and no roots—and was heading for destruction; fortunately, due to a good marriage his life was saved.

— "These early poems...": **Scott**, *Uncollected Poems*.

— "Fenollosa's essay...": **Ezra Pound**, *ABC of Reading*. New York: New Directions, 1965, pp. 19-22. (first published in 1934.)

— "Paradoxically, the synchronic...": **Nevitt**, *The Communication Ecology*. Toronto: Butterworths, 1982, p. 60.

— EZRA POUND: **William Rose Benét**, *The Reader's Encyclopedia*, p. 873.

— "At the turn of the century...": **Lawrence Russ**, "The Whole and the Flowing." *Parabola* 8 (August 1983): 82-87.

— "Snyder has effectively...": **Thomas Parkinson**, "The Poetry of Gary Snyder."

— "the concept of 'self' is no longer...": **Bateson**, *Steps to an Ecology of Mind*, pp. 304 and 306.

— "Tent tethered among jackpine...": **Robert MacLean**, *Heartwood*. Silverton Colorado: Finn Hill Arts, 1986. For complete poem, see Back of the Book section.

300 "The salmon is the soul...": **Tom Jay**, "The Salmon of the Heart."

— "It was very interesting...": **Andy Hoffman**, letter, August 1985.

— "reconnects the mind to the body...": **Bob Klein**, *Movements of Magic*, pp. vii and p. 1.

302 "had allowed the boundaries..." down to "The boundaries of our person...": **Duerr**, *Dreamtime*, pp. 109 and 110. **Add. notes:** I want to make it quite plain that there was not "spiritual" or spacy magic involved here with what I experienced. In order to explain further, I will quote once more from Duerr: "Our soul does not *leave* our body, but the limits of our person no longer coincide with the boundaries of our body that we might see on a snapshot...It is not so much that we fly. What happens is that our ordinary 'ego boundaries' evaporate."

— "that can come into play only...": **Arthur Waley**, *Three Ways of Thought*, pp. 66 and 67.

304 RITUALIZED CITY OF SIENA, ITALY: **Nicholas Hildyard**, "How an Ideal City Works." *The Ecologist* 9: pp. 320-326. Alan Dundes and Alessandro Falassi, *La Terra in Piazza: An Interpretation of the Palio of Siena*. Berkeley: University of California Press, 1975.

307 "Fidelity is that virtue...": **Erik Erikson**, "Youth: Fidelity and Diversity." *Daedalus* 91 (Winter 1962): 5-27.

— "What is forgotten...": **Seyyed Hossein Nasr**, *The Encounter of Man and Nature*. London: George, Allen and Unwin, 1968, p. 135.

SELECTED BIBLIOGRAPHY

This bibliography contains entries for books or articles which are referred to throughout the entire text. Full bibliography for all other sources can be found within the Reference Notes for that particular chapter.

Abram, David. "The Perceptual Implications of Gaia." *The Ecologist* 15 (1985): 96-103.

Adams, Frederick. "The Henge: Land, Sky, Love Temple." *Feraferia* (1969).

Alexander, Hartley Burr. *The World's Rim: Great Mysteries of the North American Indians*. Lincoln: University of Nebraska Press, 1953.

Allen, Paula Gunn. "The Psychological Landscape of Ceremony." In "Conference Concerning *Ceremony, A Novel." American Indian Quarterly: A Journal of Anthropology, History and Literature* 5 (February 1979).

Anderson, Edgar. *Landscape Papers*. Berkeley: Turtle Island Foundation, 1976.

—— *Plants, Man and Life*. Berkeley: University of California Press, 1967.

Andersson, J. Gunnar. *Children of the Yellow Earth: Studies in Prehistoric China*. Cambridge: The M.I.T. Press, 1973.

Bateson, Gregory. "Form, Substance, and Difference." *General Semantics Bulletin* 37 (1970).

—— *Mind and Nature, A Necessary Unity*. New York: E. P. Dutton, 1979.

—— *Steps to an Ecology of Mind*. New York: Ballantine Books, 1972.

—— "Style, Grace and Information in Primitive Art." In Anthony Forge, ed. *Primitive Art and Society*. Oxford: Oxford University Press.

Bateson, Gregory and Bateson, Mary Catherine. *Angels Fear: Towards an Epistemology of the Sacred*. New York: Macmillan, 1987.

Baynes, Cary. *The I Ching: Or Book of Changes*. Princeton: Princeton University Press, 1950. [R. Wilhelm, German trans. and Baynes, English trans.]

Bennett, Robert T. *Sun Angles for Design*. Bala Cynwood, Pennsylvania, 1978.

Berg, Peter. "Bioregionalists & Greens: Life-Place-Politics: from a working paper." *Upriver Downriver* 7.

—— *Reinhabiting a Separate Country: A Bioregional Anthology of Northern California*. San Francisco: Planet Drum, 1978.

Berg, Peter and Tukel, George. *Renewable Energy and Bioregions: A New Context for Public Policy*. San Francisco: Planet Drum Foundation. 1980.

Better Nutrition. Published by Communications Channels, Inc. Atlanta, Ga.

Blunden, Caroline and Elvin, Mark. *Cultural Atlas of China*. Oxford: Equinox Ltd., 1983.

Bodde, D. "Harmony and Conflict in Chinese Philosophy." In A. F. Wright, ed. *Studies in Chinese Thought*.

Bodian, Stephen. "Simple in Means, Rich in Ends: A Conversation with Arne Naess." *The Ten Directions* (1982).

Borgeau, Philippe. "The Death of the Great Pan: The Problem of Interpretation." *History of Religions* (1983): 254-283.

Bowlby, John. *Attachment and Loss*. 2 vols. New York: Basic Books.

Brome, Vincent. *Jung*. New York: Atheneum, 1978.

Bruner, Jerome, Jolly, Allison and Sylva, Kathy, eds. *Play—Its Role in Development and Evolution*. New York: Basic Books Inc., 1976.

Chamberlain, Von Del. *When Stars Came Down to Earth: Cosmology of the Skidi Pawnee Indians of North America*. Los Altos, California; Ballena Press; College Park Maryland: Center for Archaeostronomy, University of Maryland, 1982. (A Cooperative Publication)

Chang, Jolan. *The Tao of Love and Sex : The Ancient Chinese Way to Ecstasy*. New York: E. P. Dutton, 1977.

Chang Tung-Sun. "A Chinese Philosopher's Theory of Knowledge." *Etc.: A Review of General Semantics* 9 (1952): 203-226.

Chisolm, Lawrence W. *The Far East and American Culture*. Westport Connecticut: Greenwood Press, 1976.

Cobb, Edith. *The Ecology of Imagination in Childhood*. New York: Columbia University Press, 1977.

Cohen, Mark Nathan. *Biosocial Mechanisms of Population Regulation*. New Haven: Yale University Press, 1980.

—— *The Food Crisis in Prehistory: Overpopulation and the Origins of Agriculture*. New Haven: Yale University Press, 1977.

Cooper, Eugene. "The Potlatch in Ancient China." *History of Religions* 22 (November 1981).

Critchlow, Keith. *Time Stands Still*. London: Gordon Fraser, 1979.

Czaja, Michael. *Gods of Myth and Stone: Phallicism in Japanese Folk Religion*. New York: Weatherhill, 1974.

d'Aquili, E; Laughlin, Charles, and McManus, John, eds. *The Spectrum of Ritual: A Biogenetic Structural Analysis*. New York: Columbia University Press, 1979.

Dasmann, Raymond. *Environmental Conservation*. John Wiley & Sons, 1949.

Dawes, Michael. *Avebury Circle*. London: Thames & Hudson, 1977.

Deleuze, Gilles. trans. Hugh Tomlinson. *Nietzsche and Philosophy*. New York: Columbia University Press, 1983.

Delworth, David. "Watsuji Tetsuro: Cultural Phenomenologist." *Philosophy East and West*. 14: 3-22.

Devall, Bill and Sessions, George. *Deep Ecology*. Salt Lake City: Gibbs M. Smith, 1985.

Diamond, Stanley. *In Search of the Primitive*. New Brunswick: Rutgers University Press, 1974.

Diringer, David. *The Alphabet*. New York: Philosophical Library, 1948.

Dōgen, E. *Genjōkōan*. trans. Hakuyu Taizan Maezumi, *The Way of Everyday Life*. Los Angeles: Zen Center of Los Angeles and the Institute for Transcultural Studies, 1978.

Domhoff, G. William. *The Bohemian Grove and Other Retreats: A Study in Ruling Class Cohesiveness*. New York: Harper, 1975.

Donaldson, Stephen R. *Lord Foul's Bane*. New York: Ballantine, 1978.

Douglass, William A. "Basque Immigrants: Contrasting Patterns of Adaptation in Argentina and the American West." In Robert Hinshaw, ed. *Currents in Anthropology: Essays in Honor of Sol Tax*. The Hague: Mouton Pub., 1979.

Drengson, Alan, ed. *The Trumpeter, Voices from the Canadian Ecophilosophy Network*. Address: Lightstar Press, 1138 Richardson St., Victoria, B.C. V8v 3C8 Canada.

Duerr, Hans Peter. *Dreamtime: Concerning the Boundary Between Wilderness and Civilization*. Oxford: Basil Blackwell, 1985.

Dundes, Alan and Falassi, Alessandro. *La Terra in Piazza: an interpretation of the palio of Siena*. Berkeley: University of California Press, 1974.

Duplantier, Stephen. "Tractatus Geopsycorum." Continent Congress Bundle. San Francisco: Planet Drum, 1976.

Earhart, H. Byron. "Four Ritual Periods of Haguro Shugendō in Northeast Japan," *History of Religions* 5: 93-113.

Eibl-Eibesfeldt, Irenaus. *Ethology, The Biology of Behavior*. New York: Holt Rinehart & Winston, 1970.

—— *Love and Hate: The Natural History of Behavior Patterns*. New York: Holt Rinehart & Winston, 1972.

Eliade, Mircea. "Methodological Remarks on the Study of Religious Symbolism," in *The History of Religions—Essays in Methodology*. Edited by M. Eliade and J. Kitagawa. Chicago: University of Chicago Press, 1959.

—— "The Quest for the 'Origins' of Religion." *History of Religions* 1.

—— *The Sacred and the Profane*. New York: Harcourt Brace and World.

Emitt, Robert. *The Last War Trail*. Norman: University of Oklahoma Press, 1954.

Erikson, Erik. "The Ontogeny of Ritualization in Man." In Huxley, Julian. "A Discussion on Ritualization of Behaviour in Animals and Man." *Philosophical Transactions of the Royal Society of London, Series B*. 251 (1966):247-523.

Evans, Arthur. *The Earlier Religion of Greece in the Light of Cretan Discoveries*. London: Macmillan & Co., 1931.

Evans, Richard. *Konrad Lorenz: The Man and His Ideas*. New York: Harcourt Brace & Jovanovich, 1975.

Fenollosa, Ernest. *The Chinese Written Character as a Medium for Poetry*. San Francisco: City Lights Books, 1963.

Fink, Eugen. "The Ontology of Play." *Philosophy Today* 18 (Summer, 1974): 147-161.

Flader, Susan. *Thinking Like a Mountain*. Columbia: University of Missouri Press, 1974.

Fletcher, Alice. "The Hako: A Pawnee Ceremony." *Bureau of American*

Ethnology, Twenty-second Annual Report, Part 2 (1904).

Fletcher, Alice and LaFlesche, Francis. "The Omaha Tribe." *Bureau of American Ethnology, Twenty-seventh Annual Report* (1911).

Frank, Andre Gunder. *World Accumulation*. London: Monthly Review Press, 1978.

Furst, Peter, ed. *Flesh of the Gods: The Ritual Use of Hallucinogens*. New York: Praeger, 1972.

Furst, Peter T. and Anguiano, Marina. " 'To fly as birds': myth and ritual as agents of enculturation among the Huichol Indians of Mexico." In Johannes Wilbert, *Enculturation in Latin America*.

Gaster, Theodore H. *Thespis: Ritual, Myth, and Drama in the Ancient Near East*. New York: W. W. Norton, 1961.

Gibson, James J. *The Ecological Approach to Visual Perception*. Boston: Houghton Mifflin, 1979.

Gimbutas, Marija. *The Goddeses and Gods of Old Europe 6500-3500 BC: Myths and Cult Images*. Berkeley, University of California Press, 1982.

Gimello, Robert M. "The Civil Status of Li in Classical Confucianism." *Philosophy East and West*. 14.

Girardot, N. J. *Myth and Meaning in Early Taoism: The Theme of Chaos (hun-tun)*. Berkeley: University of California Press, 1983.

Hall, David L. "Process and Anarchy—A Taoist Vision of Creativity." *Philosophy East and West* (July 1978): 270-284.

Harrison, Jane. *Mythology*. London: Marshall Jones Co., 1924.

—— *Themis: A Study of the Social Origins of Greek Religion*. Cambridge: Cambridge University Press, 1912.

Hart, Roger. *Children's Experience of Place*. New York: Irvington Pub. Inc. 1979. (Distributed by John Wiley & Sons.)

Havelock, Eric. *Origins of Western Literacy*. Toronto: Ontario Institute for Studies in Education, 252 Bloor St. West, Toronto, Ontario M5S 1V6. Monograph Series 14,1976.

—— *Preface to Plato*. Cambridge: Harvard University Press. 1963.

Hawkes, Jaquetta, *A Land*. England: David and Charles, Publishers, 1978.

Hawkes, J. G. "The ecological background of plant domestication," in *The Domestication and Exploitation of Plants and Animals*. Edited by P. J. Ucko and G. W. Dimbleby. London: Duckworth, 1969.

Heidegger, Martin. *Nietzsche v. 1: The Will to Power as Art*. trans. David F. Krell. New York: Harper & Row, 1979.

—— *Poetry, Language, Thought*. New York: Harper & Row, 1971.

—— *The Question Concerning Technology and other Essays*. trans. William Lovitt. New York: Harper and Row, 1977.

Heiser, Charles B. *The Gourd Book*. Norman: University of Oklahoma Press, 1979.

Henry, J. P. "Comment." *Journal of Analytical Psychology* 22: 52-57.

—— *Stress, Health and the Social Environment: A Sociobiologic Approach to Medicine*. New York: Springer-Verlag.

Hillman, James. *Re-Visioning Psychology*. New York: Harper and Row, 1975.

Hinshaw, Robert, ed. *Currents in Anthropology: Essays in Honor of Sol Tax*. The Hague: Mouton, 1979.

Holler, Clyde. "Black Elk's Relationship to Christianity." *The American Indian Quarterly* 8 (Winter 1984): 37-49.

Hori, Ichiro. "Mountains and their Importance for the Idea of the Other World in Japanese Folk Religion." *History of Religions* 6 (August 1966): 1-23.

Hosoi, Y. T. "The Sacred Tree in Japanese Prehistory." *History of Religions* 16 (November 1976): 95-119.

House, Freeman. "Totem Salmon," in North Pacific Rim Alive Bundle. San Francisco: Planet Drum.

Hughes, E. R. "Epistemological Methods in Chinese Philosophy," in *The Chinese Mind*. Edited by C. A. Moore. Honolulu: East-West Center Press, 1967.

—— *The Great Learning and the Mean-In-Action*. New York: E. P. Dutton, 1943.

Huizinga, J. *Homo Ludens: A Study of the Play Element in Culture*. Boston: The Beacon Press, 1955.

Huxley, Julian. "A Discussion on Ritualization of Behaviour in Animals and Man." *Philosophical Transactions of the Royal Society of London*. Series B. 251 (1966): 249-272.

Izutsu, Toshihiko. *A Comparative Study of the Key Philosophical Concepts in Sufism and Taoism*. Tokyo: Keio University, 1967.

—— "Naive Realism and Confucian Philosophy." *Eranos Jahrbuch* 44 (1975): 379-413.

—— "The Temporal and A-temporal Dimensions of Reality in Confucian Metaphysics." *Eranos Jahrbuch*. 43 (1974): 411-447.

—— *The Theory of Beauty in the Classical Aesthetics of Japan*. The Hague: Martinus Nijhoff, 1981.

Jacobi, J. *Complex, Archetype, Symbol*. London: Routledge & Kegan Paul, 1959.

James, E. O. *Seasonal Feasts and Festivals*. London: Barnes & Noble, 1961.

Jay, Tom. "The Salmon of the Heart," in *Working the Woods, Working the Sea*. Edited by Finn Wilcox and Jeremiah Gorsline. Port Townsend: Empty Bowl, 1986.

Jones, N. Blurton. ed., *Ethological Studies of Child Behaviour*. Cambridge: Cambridge University Press, 1972.

Jung, C. G. *Analytical Psychology, its Theory and Practice*. New York: Pantheon Books, 1968.

—— *The Collected Works of C. G. Jung*. Edited by H. Read, M. Fordham, and G. Adler. New York: Pantheon Books, 1953-60; The Bollingen Foundation, 1961-7 and Princeton, New Jersey: Princeton University Press, 1967-78.

—— *Contributions to Analytical Psychology*. New York: Harcourt Brace, 1928.

—— *Man and His Symbols*. New York: Dell, 1979.

—— *Memories, Dreams, Reflections*. New York: Random House, 1961.

—— "Mind and Earth," in *Collected Works*, v. 10.

—— *The Undiscovered Self*. New York: Little Brown and Co., 1957.

Jung, C. F. and Kerenyi, C. *Essays on a Science of Mythology*. Princeton: Princeton University Press, 1969.

Kahn, Charles H. *The Art and Thought of Heraclitus*. Cambridge: Cambridge University Press, 1979.

Kaltenmark, Max. *Lao Tzu and Taoism*. Stanford: Stanford University Press, 1969.

Kaptchuk, Ted J. *The Web that Has no Weaver: Understanding Chinese Medicine*. New York: Congdon & Weed, 1983.

Kitagawa, Joseph W. "'A Past of Things Present': Notes on Major Motifs of Early Japanese Religions." *History of Religions* 20 (August and November 1980): 27 ff.

Knight, Richard Payne. *A Discourse on the Worship of Priapus and Its Connection with the Mystic Theology of the Ancients*. First published in 1786. Reprinted together with Wright's *Worship of Generative Powers* (1866) in 1957. (See Wright, Thomas, below for complete bibl.)

Knight, W. F. Jackson. *Vergil: Epic and Anthropology, Comprising Vergil's Troy, Cumaean Gates and the Holy City of the East*. George Allen & Unwin, 1967.

Konner, Melvin. *The Tangled Wing*. New York: Harper and Row, 1982.

Kroeber, A. L. and Gifford, W. E. "World Renewal: A Cult System of Native Northwest California." *University of California Publications in Anthropological Records* 13 (1949-1952): 1-135. Berkeley: University of California Press, 1952.

Krupp, E. C. *Echoes of the Ancient Skies: The Astronomy of Lost Civilizations*. New York: Harper & Row, 1983.

Kuang-Ming Wu. *Chuang Tzu: World Philosopher at Play*. New York: Crossroad Pub. and Scholar's Press, 1982.

Kvaloy, Sigmund. "Complexity and Time: Breaking the Pyramid's Reign." *Resurgence* 106 (September/October 1984): pp. 12-21. (England)

LaChapelle, Dolores. "The Blue Mountains are Constantly Walking." Way of the Mountain Occasional Paper. Silverton: Finn Hill Arts, 1981.

—— *Earth Festivals*. Silverton: Finn Hill Arts, 1976.

—— *Earth Wisdom*. Silverton: Finn Hill Arts, 1978.

LaFleur, William. *Mirror for the Moon*. New York: New Directions, 1978.

—— "Saigyō and the Value of Nature: Part I." *History of Religions* 13 (November 1973): 93-128. Part II (February 1974): 227-248.

Langer, Susanne. *Philosophy in a New Key*. Cambridge: Harvard University Press, 1941.

Lathrap, Donald W. "Gifts of the Cayman: Some Thoughts on the Subsistence Basis of Chavin," *Variation in Anthropology: Essays in Honor of John C. McGregor*. Edited by D. Lathrap and Jody Douglas. Urbana Illinois:

Illinois Archaeological Survey, 1973.

—— "Our Father the Cayman, Our Mother the Gourd: Spinden Revisited, or a Unitary Model for the Emergence of Agriculture in the New World, in *Origins of Agriculture*. Edited by Charles A. Reed. The Hague: Mouton,1977.

Lawrence, D. H. *Apocalypse*. New York: Viking Press, 1966.

—— "The Crown." *The Signature* (October/November 1915). Reprinted in *Phoenix II : Uncollected, Unpublished, and other prose Works by D. H. Lawrence*. Edited by Warren Roberts and Harry T. Moore. New York: The Viking Press, 1968.

—— "Escape," in *The Complete Poems of D. H. Lawrence*. Edited by Vivian de Sola Pinto and Warren Roberts. New York, Viking Compass Edition.

—— "The Flying Fish," in *Phoenix: The Posthumous Papers of D. H. Lawrence*. Edited by Edward D. MacDonald. New York: The Viking Press, 1968.

—— "Indians and Entertainment," in *Mornings in Mexico*. Edited by Richard Adlington. London: William Heinemann.

—— "New Mexico," *Survey Graphic* (January 1928). Reprinted in *Phoenix*.

—— "Pan in America." In *Phoenix*.

—— *The Plumed Serpent*. New York: Alfred A. Knopf, 1951.

—— "Reflections on the Death of a Porcupine." *Phoenix II*.

—— *The White Peacock*. Carbondale: Southern Illinois University Press, 1966.

Lee, Dorothy. "Are Basic Needs Ultimate," in Dorothy Lee, *Freedom and Culture*. Englewood Cliffs: Prentice Hall, 1959.

—— *Freedom and Culture*. Englewood Cliffs: Prentice Hall, 1959.

Lee, Richard B. and DeVore, Irven, eds. *Man the Hunter*. Chicago: Aldine Publishing, 1968.

Levin, David M. *The Body's Recollection of Being: Phenomenological Psychology and the Deconstruction of Nihilism*. London: Routledge Kegan & Paul, 1985.

Levy, Gertrude. *The Gate of Horn: A Study of the Religious Conceptions of the Stone Age and their Influence upon European Thought*. London: Faber and Faber, 1948.

Leyhausen, Paul. "Social Organization and Density Tolerance in Mammals," in *Motivation of Human and Animal Behavior: An Ethological View*. Edited by Konrad Lorenz and Paul Leyhausen. New York: Van Nostrand Reinhold,1973.

Liedloff, Jean. *The Continuum Concept*. Reading Massachusetts: Addison-Wesley, 1985.

Livingston, John A. *One Cosmic Instant*. New York: Dell, 1973.

Lopez, Barry. *Arctic Dreams*. New York: Scribner, 1986.

—— *Of Wolves and Men*. New York: Scribner, 1978.

Lorenz, Konrad. *Behind the Mirror: A Search for a Natural History of Human Knowledge*. Harcourt Brace Jovanovich, 1977.

—— "The Enmity Between Generations and Its Probable Ethological Causes," in *Konrad Lorenz: The Man and His Ideas*. Edited by Richard Evans. New York: Harcourt Brace & Jovanovich, 1975.

—— "The Fashionable Fallacy of Dispensing with Description," in *Konrad Lorenz: the Man and His Ideas*. Edited by Richard Evans. New York: Harcourt Brace & Jovanovich, 1975.

Lorenz, Konrad and Leyhausen, Paul. *Motivation of Human and Animal Behavior: An Ethological View*. New York: Van Nostrand Reinhold, 1973.

MacKie, Euan. *The Megalith Builders*. Oxford: Phaidon Press, 1977.

MacLean, Paul D. *A Triune Concept of the Brain and Behaviour*. Toronto: University of Toronto Press, 1973.

MacLean, Robert. *Heartwood*. Silverton: Finn Hill Arts, 1985.

Martin, John. *The Deep Ecologist*. 10 Alamein Ave., Warrackneabeal, Vic. 3393 Australia.

Mauss, Marcel. *The Gift: Forms and Functions of Exchange in Archaic Societies* New York: W. W. Norton, 1967.

McAuliffe, Kathleen. "The Black Box: Brain Tuner." *Omni*. 5 (January 1983): 45 ff.

McClintock, Walter. *The Old North Trail: Or Life, Legends and Religion of the Blackfeet Indians*. Lincoln: University of Nebraska Press, 1968.

McNeley, James. *Holy Wind in Navajo Philosophy*. Tucson: University of Arizona Press, 1981.

Mead, Margaret. "Cultural Determinants of Sexual Behavior," in *Sex and Internal Secretions*. v. 2. Edited by William C. Young. Baltimore: The Williams and Wilkins Co., 1961.

Meeker, Joseph. *The Comedy of Survival: In Search of an Environmental Ethic*. Silverton: Finn Hill Arts, 1982.

Merleau-Ponty, Maurice. *Phenomenology of Perception*. London: Routledge & Kegan Paul, 1962.

—— *The Visible and the Invisible*. trans. A. Lingis. Evanston: Northwestern University Press, 1968.

Metcalf, Paul. *Apalache*. Berkeley: Turtle Island Foundation, 1976.

Meyers, Steven J. *Lime Creek Odyssey: An Ode to Place*. Golden Colorado: Fulcrum, 1988.

Midgley, Mary. *Beast and Man: The Roots of Human Nature*. Ithaca: Cornell University Press, 1978.

Moore, C. A. ed. *The Chinese Mind*. Honolulu: East-West Center Press, 1967.

Murray, Gilbert. *Five Stages in Greek Religion*. Garden City: Doubleday, 1955.

Myerhoff, Barbara. *Peyote Hunt: The Sacred Journey of the Huichol Indians*. Ithaca: Cornell University Press, 1974.

Naess, Arne. *Ecology, Society and Lifestyle: Ecosophy T*. Cambridge: Cambridge University Press. (In Press).

—— "The Shallow and the Deep Long Range Ecology Movement." *Inquiry* (1973).

Needham, Joseph. *The Grand Titration: Science and Society in East and West*. London: George Allen & Unwin 1979.

—— *Science and Civilization in China*. Cambridge: Cambridge University Press. The first volume came out in 1954. The work will be complete in some twenty-five volumes. Fifteen have now appeared or are presently in press.

Nesca, Robb. *Neoplatonism of the Italian Renaissance*. London: George Allen & Unwin, 1935.

Nevitt, Barrington. *ABC of Prophecy: Understanding the Environment*. Toronto: CANADIAN FUTURES, 2 Toronto St., Toronto Ontario M5C 2B6.

—— *The Communication Ecology*. Toronto: Butterworth, 1982.

—— "Ecological Rationality Beyond Cybernetics." *Kybernetes* 9 (1980): 275-281.

—— "Pipeline or Grapevine: The Changing Communications Environment." *Technology and Culture* 21 (April 1980): 217-226.

—— "Via Media with Marshall McLuhan." *Kybernetes* 10 (1981): 235-240.

Nisbett, Alec. *Konrad Lorenz: A Biography*. New York: Harcourt Brace Jovanovich, 1976.

Parsch, Pius. *The Church's Year of Grace*. trans. William G. Heidt. Collegeville Minnesota: The Liturgical Press, 1954.

Payne, Robert ed., *The White Pony*. New York: New American Library. (no date)

Pieper, Joseph. *In Tune with the World: A Theory of Festivity*. New York: Harcourt Brace & World, 1965.

Pound, Ezra. *ABC of Reading*. New York: New Directions. (Originally printed in 1934).

Puzey, Julien. "Deep Ecology, The Root and the Return: Outline of an Experiential Course." Way of the Mountain Occasional Paper. Silverton: Finn Hill Arts, 1987.

Rappaport, Roy. *Ecology, Meaning and Religion*. Richmond, California: North Atlantic Books, 1979.

—— "Energy and the Structure of Adaptation." *Coevolution Quarterly* (Spring 1974): 20-28.

—— *Pigs for the Ancestors*. New Haven: Yale University Press, 1968.

Rappaport, Roy and Vayda, Andrew. "Ecology, Cultural and Noncultural," in *Introduction to Cultural Anthropology*. Edited by James Clifton. Boston: Houghton Mifflin, 1968.

Reed, Charles A., ed. *Origins of Agriculture*. The Hague: Mouton, 1977.

—— "Origins of Agriculture: Discussion and some Conclusions," in *Origins of Agriculture*. Edited by Charles A. Reed. The Hague: Mouton, 1977, pp. 879-956.

Rexroth, Kenneth. *An Autobiographical Novel*. New York: New Directions, 1969.

Rothenberg, Jerome. "Pre-Face to a Symposium on Ethnopoetics." *Alcher-*

inga/Ethnopoetics 2 (1976): 6-12.
—— Technicians of the Sacred. Garden City: Doubleday,1969.
Rothenberg, Jerome and Rothenberg, Diane. Symposium of the Whole: A Range of Discourse Toward an Ethnopoetics. Berkeley: University of California Press, 1983.

Sale, Kirkpatrick. Dwellers in the Land: Bioregional Vision. San Francisco: Sierra Club Books, 1986.
Sanford, John. The Invisible Partners. Ramsey New Jersey: Paulist Press, 1980.
Sauer, Carl. Agricultural Origins and Dispersals. New York: American Geographical Society, 1952.
—— "Theme of Plant and Animal Destruction in Economic History." Journal of Farm Economics 20 (1938): 765-775.
Schechner, Richard and Schuman, Mary. Ritual, Play and Performance. New York: Seabury Press, 1976.
Sessions, George. Ecophilosophy. Philosophy Department, Sierra College, Rocklin, California 95677. An on-going publication since its first issue in 1976.
—— "Shallow and Deep Ecology: A Review of the Philosophical Literature," in Ecological Consciousness: Essays from the Earthday X Colloquium University of Denver, April 21-24, 1980. Edited by Robert C. Schultz and J. Donald Hughes. Washington: University Press of America, 1981.
Shepard, Paul. Man in the Landscape: A Historic View of the Esthetics of Nature. New York: Alfred A. Knopf, 1967.
—— Nature and Madness. San Francisco: Sierra Club Books, 1982.
—— The Tender Carnivore and the Sacred Game. New York: Scribner, 1973.
Shepard, Paul and Sanders, Barry. The Sacred Paw: The Bear in Nature, Myth and Literature. New York: Viking, 1985.
Shin-Pyo Kang. "The Structural Principles of the Chinese World View," in Support for the Structured Method. Edited by Ino Rossi. New York: Dutton, 1974, pp. 198-207.
Silko, Leslie Marmon. Ceremony. New York: Penguin Books, 1987.
Snyder, Gary. The Old Ways. San Francisco: City Lights Books, 1977.
—— Turtle Island. New York: New Directions, 1974.
Stevens, Anthony. Archetypes: A Natural History of the Self. New York: William Morrow, 1982.
Stewart, Jessie. Jane Ellen Harrison: A Portrait from Letters. London: The Merlin Press, 1959.
Storm, Hyemeyohsts. Seven Arrows. New York: Harper & Row, 1972.

Tang Chun-I. "The Development of Spiritual Value in Chinese Philosophy," in The Chinese Mind. Edited by Charles Moore.
Tax, Sol. "General Editor's Preface," in Origins of Agriculture. Edited by Reed.
Tedlock, Dennis. "Toward a Restoration of the Word in the Modern World." Alcheringa/Ethnopoetics 2 (1976): 120-132.
Temple, Robert. The Genius of China: 3000 years of Science, Discovery and Invention. New York: Simon and Schuster, 1986.
Thomas, William L., ed. Man's Role in Changing the Face of the Earth. Chicago: University of Chicago Press, 1956.
Tinbergen, Niko. "Ethology," in Scientific Thought 1900-1960. Edited by R. Harre. Oxford: Clarendon Press, 1969.
—— "Ethology and Stress Diseases." Science 185 (July 1974):20-26.
Turner, Victor. "Forms of Symbolic Action: Introduction," in Forms of Symbolic Action: Proceedings of the 1969 Annual Spring Meeting of the American Ethnological Society. Edited by Robert F. Spencer. Seattle: University of Washington Press.
—— Revelation and Divination Among the Ndembu. Ithaca: Cornell University Press, 1967.

—— The Ritual Process: Structure and Anti-Structure. Ithaca: Cornell University Press, 1969.
Tuzin, Donald. "Miraculous Voices: The Auditory Experience of Numinous Objects." Current Anthropology 25 (December 1984): 579-592.

van der Post, Laurens. Jung and the Story of Our Time. New York: Random House, 1975.
Vycinas, Vincent. Earth and Gods: an Introduction to the Philosophy of Martin Heidegger. The Hague: Martinus Nijhoff, 1961.

Waley, Arthur. Three Ways of Thought in Ancient China. Garden City: Doubleday 1956.
Watson-Frank, Maria-Barbara. "To Learn for Tomorrow: Enculturation of Girls and Its Social Importance among the Guajiro of Venezuela," in Enculturation in Latin America: An Anthology. Edited by J. Wilbert, Los Angeles: UCLA Latin American Center Publication, University of Los Angeles, 1976, pp. 191-211.
Wei-hsun Fu, Charles. "Lao Tzu's Conception of Tao." Inquiry 16 (1973): 367-391.
Wei-ming Tu. "Li as a Process of Humanization." Philosophy East and West 22 (April 1972): 187-201.
Welch, Holmes and Seidel, Anna. Facets in Chinese Taoism. New Haven: Yale University Press, 1979.
Whorf, Benjamin Lee. "Time, Space and Language," in Culture in Crisis: A Study of the Hopi Indians. Edited by Laura Thompson. New York: Harper, 1950.
Wichmann, Siegfried. Japonisme: The Japanese Influence on Western Art in the 19th and 20th Centuries. New York: Park Lane (Crown Publishers), 1985.
Wickler, Wolfgang. The Sexual Code. New York: Doubleday, 1972.
Wilbert, Johannes, ed. Enculturation in Latin America: An Anthology. UCLA Latin America Center Publication. Los Angeles: University of California, 1976.
Wilcox, Finn and Gorsline, Jeremiah. Working the Wood, Working the Sea. Port Townsend: Empty Bowl, 1986.
Wilhelm, Hellmut. Heaven, Earth and Man in the Book of Changes. Seattle: University of Washington Press.
Wilhelm, Richard. trans. Secret of the Golden Flower. Foreword and Commentary by C. G. Jung. New York: Harcourt Brace and World, 1962.
Wilhelm, Richard and Baynes, C. trans. I Ching. New York: Pantheon, 1950.
Willeford, William. "Festival, Communion and Mutuality." Journal of Analytical Psychology 26 (October 1981): 345-355.
Williamson, Ray. Living the Sky: The Cosmos of the American Indian. Boston: Houghton Mifflin, 1984.
Wing-Tsit Chan. "Syntheses in Chinese Metaphysics," in The Chinese Mind. Edited by Charles A. Moore. Honolulu: East-West Center Press, 1967.
Wissler, C. "Ceremonial Bundles of the Blackfoot Indians." Anthropological Papers of the American Museum of Natural History. 7 Pt. 2 (1912): 263.
Wright, A. F., ed. Studies in Chinese Thought. Chicago: University of Chicago Press, 1953.
Wright, Herbert E. "Environmental change and the origin of agriculture in the Old and New Worlds," in Origins of Agriculture. Edited by Reed.
Wright, Thomas. The Worship of the Generative Powers During the Middle Ages of Western Europe. New York: Julian Press, 1957.
Wynter, Sylvia. "Ethno or Socio Poetics." Alcheringa/Ethnopoetics 2 (1976): 78-94.

USEFUL DEFINITIONS

This is not a complete glossary; rather it's a few of the more important words or new meanings of old words, which I think will be useful. One of the first steps in renewing our relationship with the earth is to reclaim the language. Some of the following entries concern two contrasting words. In such cases, the definitions for both are listed with the word which comes first, alphabetically. Some important words are not listed, because they are discussed at length within particular chapters in this work: for example sacred, *li*, land etc.

aboriginal native to a region or indigenous. Latin *ab-origine*, meaning: from the beginning.

"accumulation of capital" "Employing surplus-value as capital, reconverting it into capital is called accumulation of capital." (Marx) It used to be thought that the so-called "surplus value" in capitalism came from human work. We now know that essentially, it comes from ripping off nature herself.

affordance This is probably the most useful and important word in the entire text. Gibson defines it as "The affordances of the environment are what it *offers* the animal [including the human], what it provides or furnishes, either for good or ill...in a way that no existing term does it implies the complementarity of the animal and the environment." (Gibson, *Ecological Theory of Vision*, p. 127). This involves "a reciprocal interchange between the living intentions of any animal and the dynamic affordances of its world..." (D. Abram) See chapter nine.

alchemy Long ago Paracelsus (1493-1541) wrote: "Nature does not produce anything that is perfect in itself; man must bring everything to perfection. This work of bringing things to perfection is called 'alchemy'." This, precisely, is why alchemy is part of the problem; not part of the solution when it comes to human relationship to the earth. This is true whether it's ancient alchemy or newage alchemy.

analogous See homologous

anima Jung's term, based on the Latin word, *animare*, meaning to enliven. He felt that the anima and animus were like enlivening souls within. Anima refers to the female within the male. "As the archetype of life, the anima contains the element of meaning. It is not that she has the answers; rather, she embodies within herself the secret of life, and helps a man discover it by leading him to a knowledge of his own soul." (J. Sanford, *The Invisible Partners*, p. 67).

animism The attribution of a living soul to inanimate objects and natural phenomena. (First mentioned in English in 1871 in Tylor's *Primitive Culture*).

animus Jung derived this word from the Latin, *animare*, also. The animus is the male aspect within the female.

anthropocentric Considering man to be the most significant entity of the universe; interpreting or regarding the world in terms of human values and experiences. In this work I am using "merely human" or "narrowly human" as a substitute. The word "biocentric" has been used for regarding the world in terms of "all of life"; however this tends to be too abstract. We could begin to talk about meaning or values etc. related to "all of life."

anthropomorphic Described or thought of as having a human form or human attributes or ascribing human characteristics to nonhuman things.

"apple Indian" Red on the outside; white on the inside—meaning although an American Indian, the values have so changed that they are really IGS values—no longer oriented toward nature. A term in rather general use in Western U.S.

archetypes "Let us then imagine archetypes as the deepest patterns of psychic functioning, the roots of the soul governing the perspectives we have of ourselves and the world." (Hillman, *Revisioning Psychology*, p. xiii).

azimuth An arc of the horizon measured between a fixed point (as true north) and the direction of an object on the horizon. Another way to think of it is the azimuth is the distance in degrees east or west of true north. 360 degrees encompasses the total circle of the compass.

B.P. means "before present." Ex. "I am using a half-life for carbon 14 of 5,570 years to get nearly 5000 BC (or approximately 7000 B.P.). Both figures refer to exactly the same time." (Reed, *Origins of Agriculture*, p. 902).

Beltane Celts called the May festival, La-Bel Taine, meaning the Day of the Sacred Baal Fire.

bioregion This word was supposedly first used by Raymond Dasmann in *Environmental Conservation* (1959). Actually, in this book he wrote about "biotic regions", not bioregions. On p.9 he wrote: "A *biotic community* is an assemblage of species of plants and animals inhabiting a common area and having, therefore, effects upon one another. A combination of a biotic community with its physical environment is called an *ecosystem*. *Ecology* is the study of ecosystems to determine their status and the ways in which they function." Then, on p. 44 in his "Biotic Regions as Habitats for Man," he gives a diagram of these biotic regions.

bonding The beginnings of research into bonding came with Bowlby's work (1958). "He conceived of the growth of attachment as being dependent on a series of goal-directed behavioural systems which operate cybernetically in both mother and child. Thus, response patterns in the child, such as staring, smiling, crying, babbling and laughing, release parental feelings in the mother...To those who found it inconceivable that innate behavioural mechanisms could exist in human beings, Bowlby countered that one need have no greater difficulty in accepting the existence of these than in accepting the existence of innately determined physiological or anatomical systems of comparable complexity...[Bowlby's attachment theory] provides simpler and more consistent explanations of the data of human attachment formation than the psychoanalytic and learning theories which preceded it." (A. Stevens, *Archetypes*, p. 9-10). Bowlby, states that "attachment behaviour in adult life is a straightforward continuation of attachment behaviour in childhood." Further, attachment behaviour "plays a vital role...in the life of man from the cradle to the grave." (J. Bowlby, *Attachment*, p. 207-8). Bonding or "attachment" cannot occur without moving together in face to face interaction; hence the present crisis created by the ever growing use of television etc. In a fully functioning so-called "primitive" culture, every action contributes toward the bonding of the group. Another factor here is that if bonding has not occurred in childhood it is difficult, if not impossible, for it to take place in later life.

"Ch'an Buddhism" "'Becoming one with the universe' is the literal connotation of the character *ch'an*. It is composed of *tan* (one, singleness) and *shin* (sun, moon, and stars hanging from Heaven, hence the universe.)" *Tao of Painting*, p. 103.

chaos "[M]ythology generally affirms that the cosmos originally came from, and continually depends on, the chaos of the creation time...Even in those elite civilizational and literary mythologies that emphasize a seemingly decisive battle between chaos and cosmos, dragon and hero, monster and God, the chaos figures are in the final analysis 'depicted as the very source of creative power'." The English word chaos derives from the Greek *chaos*, primarily meaning the "yawning gap" or the "empty separation" between heaven and earth in the beginning time. Summing up, Girardot writes: "In early Taoism chaos, cosmos, becoming, time and Tao are synonymous for that which is without an Orderer but is the 'sum of all orders'." (Girardot, *Myth and Meaning*, pp. 3-5). J. Needham refers to this as an "organic view of the universe" or as the "philosophy of organism."

ch'i or **chi** R.G.H. Siu, a Chinese/American biochemical researcher, in his book, *Chi: A Neo-Taoist Approach to Life*, published by Mass. Institute of Tech. Press, states: "*Chi* has been variously translated as 'passion nature,' 'material principle,' 'constitutive ethers,' 'force, energy, breath, power,' 'ether or force,' 'the great breath of the universe,' etc." (p. 256-257) The word appears in Lao Tzu. The Neo-Confucianist, Chu Hsi (1130-1200) said that the universe is formed by the *ch'i* as activating essence, putting the *li* (principle) into concrete form. J. Needham states: "I need not again insist on the untranslatability of this work, which has connotations similar to the *pneuma* of the Greeks, and to our own conceptions of a vapour or a gas, but which also has something of radiant energy about it, like a radioactive emanation." (*Sci. and Civil*, v. 2, p. 369). Doing Tai Chi and actually feeling it is the best way to understand *chi*.

ching "*Ching* is the word for what later became a 'canon of writings.' In Confucius' time the character *ching* meant 'The warp set up on a loom.' But after Confucius' time there came the practice of recording a teacher's noteworthy dicta, and these records came to be called *ching*, i.e., warp teaching on which disciples could weave the woof of their amplifications. Finally, in mid-Han times (2nd century B.C.) came the establishment of State Confucianism and with it the colleges for explaining the Five Classics (*wu ching, wu*, meaning five)." (E. Hughes, "Epistemological Methods in Chinese Philosophy"). This is the underlying meaning of the word, *ching*, in the *Tao Te Ching* and the *I Ching* etc.

circle The word is derived originally from the Roman circus.

clan "Clan is an anglicized form of the Gaelic word for children, and reflects the underlying belief in the clan as representing the descendants of one person...The functions of the chief included almost all aspects of looking after the interests and welfare of his people—the children of the clan." (D. Watson, "A Brief History of the Origins of the Scottish Wildlands." p. 246 ff. in V. Martin, *Wilderness: the Way Ahead*). When Europeans began studying other cultures, they used this word for groupings in a particular society.

"Codependent origination" A Buddhist term. "In no thing is there a trace of that being's having its existence in and of itself alone. All things are fully interdependent." (W. LaFleur, *Mirror for the Moon*, p. xxv).

"Cognized environment" and "operational environment" "The term 'operational environment' was originally proposed by Marston Bates (1960:554), who quotes a def. of environment constructed earlier by Mason and Langenheim: 'The environment of any organism is the class composed of the sum of those phenomena that enter a reaction system of the organism or otherwise directly impinge upon it to affect its mode of life at any time throughout its life cycle as ordered by the demands of the ontogeny of the organism or as ordered by any other condition of the organism that alters its environmental demands'. " Rappaport continues: "The cognized environment may be seen as the class composed of the sum of the phenomena ordered into meaningful categories by a population." Of course, these two kinds of environments will not necessarily agree in all respects. Rappaport again: "[I]t is clear that no cognized environment will ever include all of the elements in any ecosystem." (Rappaport, *Ecology, Meaning, and Religion*, pp. 5-6).

"collective unconscious" "I have chosen the term 'collective' because this part of the unconscious is not individual but universal; in contrast to the personal psyche, it has content and modes of behaviour that are more or less the same everywhere and in all individuals." (Jung, *Coll. Works*, v. 9, Pr. 1).

"Communitas and community" Turner points out that Hillery (1955) examined 94 definitions of "community" and came to the conclusion that "beyond the concept that people are involved in community, there is no complete agreement as to the nature of community. Community is a 'social structure'... For me, communitas emerges where social structure is not." After explaining that Buber mistakenly uses community for communitas, Turner quotes Buber's definition: "Community is the being no longer side by side (and, one might add, above and below) but *with* one another of a multitude of persons. And this multitude, though it moves towards one goal, yet experiences everywhere a turning to, a dynamic facing of, the others, a flowing from *I to Thou*. Community is where community happens." (Buber, *Between Man and Man*, p. 51). Turner goes on to say that communitas "as an existential quality; it involves the whole man in his relation to other whole men. Structure, on the other hand, has cognitive quality; as Lévi-Strauss has perceived, it is essentially a set of classifications, a model for thinking about culture and nature and ordering one's public life." (Turner, *The Ritual Process*, pp. 127 and 298).

community See communitas.

"concepts" and "percepts" "Whereas percepts are the raw sensory experience of our direct encounter with existence, concepts are extracted from repeated percepts of past experience. Jokes are percepts, not concepts. We cannot reduce percepts to concepts, which are the foundation of science and philosophy for classification automatically converts present insight into rear-view-mirror hindsight...Today there is no word for 'percept' in any European language but English. 'Perception' on the other hand has become a 'buzz-word' ignoring ancient wisdom." (Barrington Nevitt, "Via Media with Marshall McLuhan.") Concerning perceive—"To perceive is to render something present to something through the body." (Merleau-Ponty, *Primacy of Perception*, p. 42) A questioner then remarked, "I would be tempted to say that the body is much more essential for sensation than it is for perception." M.-P. responded, "Can they be distinguished?" Konrad Lorenz writes: "For the moment a higher primate recognized for the first time that its own hand and the object it held in its grasp were both objects in the material world, and realized the relationship between them, its knowledge of the grasping process became conceptual thinking, and its awareness of the object that it grasped became a concept. Incidentally, the Latin word *concipere*, means 'to grasp'. " (Lorenz, *Behind the Mirror*, p. 151).

coniunctio was an alchemical term for the union of opposites that "confront one another in enmity or attract one another in love." (Jung) "The search for a synthesis which would reconcile opposites remained one of the driving forces in Jung's life and work." (V. Brome, *Jung*).

conscious "To be *conscious* in Latin is simply to share an understanding; it is a word used of conspirators, and from thence reflexively, to describe the aspects of the self working together. *Conscience* is originally just being fully and thoughtfully aware of something. It became specialized to the moral case merely because that particularly bothered people." (M. Midgley, *Beast and Man*, p. 268).

consciousness "Consciousness operates in the same way as medicine in its sampling of the events and processes of the body and of what goes on in the total mind. It is organized in terms of purpose. It is a short-cut device to enable you to get quickly at what you want; not to act with maximum wisdom in order to live, but to follow the shortest logical causal path to get what you next want, which may be dinner; it may be a Beethoven sonata; it may be sex. Above all, it may be money or power." (Gregory Bateson, *Steps to an Ecology of Mind*, p. 433).

"cross-quarter days" Robert Graves defines "cross-quarter days" as Candlemas, May Day, Lamas Day and Halloween. ("Witches in 1964." *Virginia Quarterly Review*, v. XL, #4 (1964), pp. 550-559). If we consider that the four main earth festivals—solstices and equinoxes divide the year into four quarters—we could call them quarter days. Graves' term, "cross-quarter days" fits the festivals, between each of the main festival days. Others have picked up this term since Graves' originally proposed it.

Cultigen man-made plants (C. Sauer, *Agricultural Origins and Dispersions*, p.25).

devolution The *Oxford English Dictionary* states that it was first used in print in 1623 by Cockeram "*Deuolution*, [sic] a rolling downe." In 1695 Woodward wrote about the "devolution of Earth down upon the Valleys, from the Hills..." The famous English jurist Sir William Blackstone in 1765: "This devolution of power, to the people at large, includes in it a dissolution of the whole form of government established by that people." Devolving is neither revolutionary nor evolutionary—merely going back to our roots in the land itself. The First International Assembly of the Fourth World was held in London in 1980 with 400 representatives from minority nations and small communities—all devolving. (See *Coevolution Quarterly # 38*, winter 1981.) Earlier in 1980 Planet Drum published Michael Zwerin's *Devolutionary Notes*, concerning the growing movement in Europe. The bioregional movement in this country is another aspect. Essentially it means paying attention to your own place on earth. Gary Snyder says that it will take us 3000 years to learn how to do it right, again. The most famous statements of the Taoist theory of regressive devolution occur in books of the 2nd century B.C.—the *Huai Nan Tzu* and the 1st century Confucian *Li Chi* (Record of Rites).

dolmen "A free-standing megalithic chamber (which may once have been buried in a mound) with a roof formed of a massive capstone." (Mackie, *Megalith Builders*).

dosojin In the Japanese language it is not necessary to distinguish the singular from the plural. "Godhood, kami, is/are not carefully defined. *Dosojin*—earth/ancestral god(s)—is/are worshipped..." (G. De Vos, "Foreword", in Czaja, p. 14) In the glossary, Czaja defines *dosojin* as "Earth Ancestor Deity or Road Ancestor Deity...phallic deity, helping to insure abundance" in all aspects of life. (M. Czaja, *Gods of Myth and Stone*, p. 265).

dreamtime This Australian aboriginal term has many meanings. "As a noun: 1) The Eternal Dream Time. The dreaming of a sacred heroic time long ago when man and nature came to be, a kind of narrative of things that once happened. 2) A kind of charter of things that still happen. 3) A kind of logos or principle or order transcending everything significant. As a verb: 1) The act of dreaming, as reality and symbol, by which the artist is inspired to produce a new song. 2) The act by which the mind makes contact with whatever mystery it is that connects the Dreaming and the Here-and-Now." All the above is based on Jerome Rothenberg's adaptations from W.E.H. Stanner, "Religion, Totemism and Symbolism" in Berndt (ed) *Aboriginal Man in Australia*. Sydney: Angus & Robertson, 1951. Also from Stanner is the sarcastic verse: "White man got no dreaming/Him go 'nother way/White man, him go different/Him got road bilong himself." H. Duerr: "The concept of 'dreamtime' does not refer to any time in the distant *past* to which the Australians supposedly think they can return, which can be 'called up,' 'repeated'...etc. The 'dreamtime' is not past, present or future time: it has no 'location' whatever on the continuum of time...The 'dreamtime' then, represents a perspective for seeing what we see without considering whether it once was or will some day be." (H. Duerr, *Dreamtime*, pp. 119 and 121).

Easter The Germanic word *Ostern*, came from the ancient Aryan word for both east and dawn. Eostre was the dawn goddess. From that came the word for Easter.

ecology The most succinct, yet inclusive definition that I've found is this: "The science of the interrelation between living organisms and their environment, including both the physical and the biotic environments, and emphasizing interspecies as well as intraspecies relations." (Allee et al. 1949). Quoted in A. Vayda and R. Rappaport, "Ecology, Cultural and Noncultural." In J. Clifton, (ed), *Introduction to Cultural Anthropology*. Vayda and Rappaport continue: "[E]cology has generally been regarded as a biological science, and, indeed, terms such as 'relations physiology' have been applied to it. Others, emphasizing the interaction among organisms rather than the effects of the interactions, have regarded ecology as behavioral science." The word, "ecology" was first used in print by Haeckel in 1870.

economics "It isn't that economics does not describe the way people behave in non-monetized societies; it is that economics does not, except in a very specialized sense, describe the way people act in any society, and is not meant to…institutions—which can be thought of as both social, economic, and political function to organize work, to socialize and discipline persons into positions in the economic order, and to distribute claims on consumption." (summary of Frank Knight, 1940, "Anthrop. and Economics." *Journal of Political Economy*. 49:247-268).

ecosystem "The dynamic whole formed by the habitat and the association of living beings that occupy it." P. Dansereau, *Biogeography*, New York: Ronald Press, 1957, p. 323.

ego In Greek, the word *ego*, is the first person of the verb "to have."

enchantment "Enchantment is defined as a 'state of being under a spell' or 'a state of being highly delighted'. The derivation of the word is from the Latin 'cantare', to sing. The prefix 'en' means 'wrap up in', or 'make into'. A state of being wrapped up in or 'in-chanted'." (L. Simms, "The Lamplighter, the Storyteller in the Modern World." *National Storytelling Journal*, winter 1984).

enculturation In his "Introduction," J. Wilbert quotes from Herskovits (1960:39): "The aspects of learning experience which mark off man from other creatures, and by means of which, initially, and in later life, he achieves competence in his culture, may be called *enculturation*." Wilbert continues: "[E]nculturation is the process by which the individual through informal and nonformal modes of cultural transmission learns the language, the technological, socioeconomic, ideational, as well as the cognitive and emotional patterns of culture. It is a life-long learning process that lasts from an individual's infancy to adulthood and 'which can be said to end only with his death'." Further, Wilbert states: "If anything crystallizes in this anthology it is the transcendental ideal of enculturation: to preserve the people's way of life by providing the individual with purpose and meaning." (J. Wilbert, ed., *Enculturation in Latin America: an Anthology*. Los Angeles: UCLA Latin American Center Publication, 1976, p. 40). Enculturation is really what we are trying to do now, in "reinhabitation" and the "old ways." Education as such, developed out of the study of the classics and its essential purpose was to train the elite. This book has consequences for us far beyond what its title might infer.

energy Etymologically, energy means "to be in work" or "at work," deriving from the Greek. Bateson tells us that Thomas Young (1773-1829) "adopted *energy* into physics as a technical term: 'the product (now half the product) of the mass or weight of a body into the square of the number expressing its velocity'." (Bateson, *Angels Fear*, p. 36). Thus the scientists co-opted the ancient Greek, *energy*, and having co-opted it forbade all the rest of us to use it. Nothing makes some scientists more furious than for an ordinary mortal to use the term, energy. You can see the stupidity of this attitude; the word was around long before there was such a thing as science.

entrainment Entrainment refers to the process by which biological rhythms are synchronized by environmental stimuli. Chapple (1970:27) notes that "three major synchronizers of circadian rhythms are light, temperature, and interaction…rituals entrain biological rhythms, synchronizing these to respond to environmental exigencies." (see d'Aquili (ed) *Biogenetic Structure of Ritual*, p. 120). The book referred to here is E. Chapple, *Culture and Biological Man*, 1970.

epistemology "A branch of science combined with a branch of philosophy. As science, epistemology is the study of how particular organisms or aggregates of organisms, 'know,' 'think', and 'decide'. As philosophy, epistemology is the study of the necessary limits and other characteristics of the processes of knowing, thinking and deciding." (Gregory Bateson, *Angels Fear*, p. 208) More simply, epistemology means ways of knowing.

Eranos In the 1920s Frau Olga Froebe-Kapteyn built a hall on the grounds of her estate at the north end of Lago Maggiore near Ascona in Switzerland for the purpose of creating a discussion between eastern and western philosophy. In the search for a title for the discussions, Rudolf Otto suggested the Greek word, *eranos* meaning, "a meal to which everyone contributes." The name thus evokes "the convivial spirit of an unsystematic interchange." (V. Brome, *Jung*, p. 214.)

ethics See ethos.

ethology "The comparative study of behavior…Ethology developed out of zoology, especially through the work of K. Lorenz and N. Tinbergen and is based on the discovery of phylogenetic adaptations in behavior." (I. Eibl-Eibesfeldt, *Ethology: The Biology of Behavior*, pp. vii and 4.) "Lorenz called ethology, 'the comparative study of behavior.' He believes the word, 'comparative' is important here because 'the similarities and dissimilarities of different species are investigated in the hope of discovering how the process of evolution has made each what it is'. " (A. Nisbett, *Konrad Lorenz*, p. 8.) Leyhausen, speaking as an ethologist: "Nowadays critical observers sometimes aver that ethology is preparing to swallow human psychology in its entirety along with social psychology, psychiatry, cultural anthropology…All that we are doing is to add a new, or at least totally neglected, dimension to these disciplines—the dimension of one or two billion years of evolution…It is now a *compelling obligation* for every single science which has in any way to do with human behavior for take this dimension into account also." (P. Leyhausen, *Motivation*). Also, see ethos.

ethos The Greek root of ethics, meaning behavior. Ethology comes from the same root. According to Havelock Ellis the original word, *ethea* may have signified "lair" or "haunt" of an animal. Hesiod used the word. In later Greek, it developed into the meaning of a personal behavior pattern or even personal character and so, in Aristotle, supplied the basis for the term, "ethics." (H. Ellis, *Preface to Plato*, p. 63).

Eurocentric This is a new, but very much needed, word. It describes the narrow point of view that European/American culture is the only real culture—all others are either primitive or backwards. I first heard the word from John Davis, editor of *Earth First*. Later, I found it used on p. 85 of D. Farrelly, *The Book of Bamboo*.

feng-shui Literal trans. "wind and water." This is the "most colloquial Chinese name for the theory and practice of siting attuned to the elements, the name which is most consistently used in classical Chinese sources is *ti li*, 'land patterns'… Wheatley in his *Pivot of the Four Quarters* considered feng-shui to be an 'astro-biological mode of thought,' reflecting the Chinese idea that life (in all its forms) interacts with heaven and is modified and conditioned by the cycle of the five elements." (S. Skinner, *The Living Earth Manual*). It is pronounced somewhat like "foong-shway."

festival Festival, referring originally "to the ritual meal eaten in common at topocosmic crises, came in time to acquire the meaning of an essentially joyous celebration and ultimately to serve as the most appropriate designation of the seasonal ceremonies as a whole." (Gaster, *Thespis*, p. 48).

freedom "Freedom, that most general of negative words, looms over us. It no longer means just the absence of a few specified evils…It no longer means freedom *from* or to *do anything*. It has spread itself to cover the isolation of the individual from all connection with others, therefore from most of what gives life meaning: tradition, influence, affection, personal and local ties, natural roots and sympathies." (M. Midgley, *Beast and Man*, p. 288).

geomancy Geomancy "is really a misnomer for the Chinese practice of feng-shui, as the word as more properly relates to an Arab form of divination which spread north into Europe and south into Africa at the end of the first millennium. The word 'geomancy' was, however, adopted by writers of the mid-nineteenth century (c. 1870) to translate feng-shui." (S. Skinner, *The Living Earth Manual*, p. xi). The Chinese feng-shui deals directly with the earth itself while the Arabic "geomancy" does not.

gnosis Plato's word for knowledge. The "objects" of this knowledge are the "ideas"—the beautiful, the just, the great, etc. Ellis goes on from here, concerning Plato: "But after defining them…and even adds by implication [others] to his list of examples of objects which have to be abstracted and isolated from their application. These are the specific objects of knowledge. (gnosis)." (H. Ellis, *Preface to Plato*, p. 225). Later on "gnosis," "gnostics" and related words came to be considered as relating to special knowledge or understanding, usually "spiritual," and therefore more important than ordinary knowledge. Even to this day gnostic has this connotation; when actually, it's merely another level of abstraction.

heaven "In Chinese heaven, *(tien)* is not the heaven we know, but the mysterious government of the blue sky at noon...a world of pure intensity." (R. Payne, *The White Pony*, p. 24). Later, "Hsün Tzu (313-238 B.C.) clearly equated it with Nature, and Neo-Confucianists identified it with li." (Chan, "Syntheses in Chinese Metaphysics" In C. Moore, (ed) *The Chinese Mind*).

henge "A monument or temple used for religious rites...a roughly circular area of ground, bounded by a ditch with a bank outside it, often enclosing a stone or wooden circle or circles...The earthwork was broken by entrance gaps." (G. Palmer, *Archaeology A-Z*, p. 109).

homologous "Homologous refers to organs and systems of organs which demonstrably have the same phylogenetic origin, such as the skeletal elements in the arm and hand of a man, in the foreleg of a horse, and in the wing of a bird...in short, in all forelimbs of all vertebrates...Analogous refers to organs and systems of organs which have a similar function but different phylogenetic origins, such as the compound eye of an insect and the camera-type eye of a vertebrate...these concepts were originally developed in comparative anatomy." (P. Leyhausen, *Motivation*, p. 277).

Indian There is considerable confusion about which term one should use; therefore I quote Russell Means in his speech, given at the Black Hills Survival Conference: "You notice I use the term American Indian rather than Native indigenous people or Amerindian when referring to my people. There has been some controversy about such terms and, frankly, at this point, I find it absurd. Primarily it seems that American Indian is being rejected as European in origin—which is true. But all the terms in question are European in origin: the only non-European way to speak here is of Lakota—or more precisely, of Oglala, Brule etc...Anyway, when I need to use a European term in order to communicate a sense of all the tribal peoples of this hemisphere put together, I use the terms most widely used by the elders. And that term is American Indian." Also, see primitive.

individuation Beginning with Jung's progressive differentiation of the archetypes—shadow, anima and animus, Old Wise Man and Magna Mater etc., Brome continues: "All these steps contributed to the realization of the transcendent function, which was the progressive synthesis of conscious and unconscious 'material' leading to the process known as individuation. Put very briefly, individuation meant the harmonious unification of many differing aspects in the human personality. Individuation frequently began through the emergence of archetypal images of the self, among them possibly, the quaternity, the mandala and the divine child...However, individuation was not a matter of progression but of deepening introversion towards the unconscious." (B. Brome, *Jung*, p. 282). Jung felt that the drive toward individuation is similar to the biological drive toward completion found throughout nature.

"Industrial Growth Society (IGS)" This phrase comes out of the Norwegian Ecophilosophy group. Sigmund Kvaloy states that there are two basically different sorts of social organization: "The first one, [the IGS] being based on steady or accelerated growth in the production of industrial articles and the use of industrial methods. The second one [Life Necessities Society] is based on producing life necessities and always giving priority to that. There is only one historical example of the first kind of society, our own, which is tending to become global. Most other human societies have been of the second kind. IGS is an abnormal kind of society, which can exist only for a historical second." See Kvaloy's "Complexity and Time" in the "Back-of-the-Book" Section.

"Industrial Revolution" "The name that Engels was apparently the first to give as far back as 1844, though it was later 'sanctified' by A. Toynbee." (J.D. Bernal, *Science in History*, MIT Press, p. 520).

initiation The word initiation in English comes "from a special use of the Latin word, '*inire*' (enter) to signify 'ritual entry into the earth'." Knight continues: "Caves were entrances to the earth conceived as universal mother. To assist the process of fertilization from the sky, magically, double axes, which are the almost universal symbol of the imaginary thunderbolt and therefore of the real lightning stroke, were thrown into the caves. They are found inside Cretan caves in great numbers. Axes of course 'split' like lightning

and meteorites." (W. Knight, *Cumaean Gates*).

inscape The word, "inscape," comes from a poem by Gerard Manley Hopkins. Essentially, landscape and inscape are the same—referring to the fact that both nature, deep within the human, and nature, outside the human, are the same nature.

instinct Tinbergen defines instinct as "a hierarchically organized nervous mechanism which is susceptible to certain priming, releasing and directing impulses of internal as well as of external origin, and which responds by these impulses by coordinated movements that contribute to the maintenance of the individual and the species." (no further bibl. ref.)

landscape "Henry Peacham's text on the art of drawing in 1606 noted that '*landskip*' was a Dutch word involving 'hills, woods, castles, seas, ruins, valleys, hanging rocks, cities, towns...'." (P. Shepard, *Man in the Landscape*, p. 123).

labyrinth Labyrinth means "a place of stone." *La*, meaning "stone" is the root word. Laverna was a goddess of a cleft in the rock on the Aventine in ancient Roman times. Any names of goddesses with *La* at the beginning refer to earth goddesses of the pre-Indo-European time. The word "labrys" means a stone axe. (W.F.J. Knight, *Vergil*, p.149). According to Matthews, the name, labyrinth, in ancient times "is now believed to connote galleries of stone, and it is reasonable on the literary evidence to locate the most famous of all labyrinths in Crete...naturally twisting corridors of a cave, like the Paleolithic...Such maze-like dancing grounds have remained in use all over Europe down to modern Times." (W. Matthews, *Mazes and Labyrinths*, pub. in 1922). In spite of all the supposed "spiritual" and "occult" aspects of ancient labyrinths; in actual fact they concern the rock itself of this earth of ours.

libido "Freud, watching Charcot's Parisian clinic 'girls in their trance postures,' returned to Vienna germinating his erotic theory of the neuroses. The word he chose for the soul's movement and energy, 'libido' comes from the Dionysiac-Aphroditic vocabulary referring originally to *lips*, the downpouring of sexual liquids." (J. Hillman, *Re-Visioning Psychology*, p. 185. He is quoting from R. Onians, *The Origins of European Thought*, p. 472-76).

"Life Necessities Society" See "Industrial Growth Society."

liminal Turner states: "*Limen* signified threshold in Latin...Liminal entities are neither here nor there; they are betwixt and between the positions assigned and arrayed by law, custom, convention, and ceremonial." (V. Turner, *The Ritual Process*, p. 203).

liturgy Comes from the Greek word, *leitourgia*, which derives from *leitos*, public or voluntary and *argon*, work.

"loneliness" and **"solitude"** "Loneliness is the condition of feeling abandoned amid an alien world, cut off from communications. Solitude is the condition of being alone in the presence of a living, familiar world, willing to listen to it, to see and to understand it...sharing its feel and meaning." (E. Kohak, *The Embers and the Stars*, p. 39).

magic See religion.

maze In Knight's time, maze dances to exclude evil influences were still found in Crete. He explains that the Trojan game was a mounted ceremonial performed by young members of the Roman nobility, a maze like thing done on horses. The maze movement of the Truia "were meant to enact magically the exclusion of the undesired being or influences from a grave, and at the same time to admit those who were authorized to visit it." Mazes have been found in Egyptian structures, Megalithic monuments and Christian churches. The earliest Christian church maze is at Orleansville in Algeria (4th century A.D.). Morris dances are maze dances. (Knight, *Cumean Gates*).

meaning "There is no satisfactory operational definition of meaning. Meaning is not empirically verifiable; only subjectively confirmable." (D. Hoy, "Numinous Experiences, Frequent or Rare?" *Jour. of Anal. Psych.*, v. 28, pp. 17-32).

megalith "A large stone used as part of, or as, a structure or monument. Megalithic describes a building made partly or entirely of such massive stones or boulders, without any cement or mortar. Generally these megaliths were built by Neolithic and Chalcolithic (Copper Age) peoples of the western Mediterranean and Atlantic Europe who lived between about 4500 and 1500 B.C." (E. MacKie, *The Megalith Builders*).

menhir A single standing stone.

metaphysics "Metaphysics or the attempt to conceive the world as a whole by means of thought." (B. Russell, *Mysticism and Logic*, p. 1).

myth "The myth is not constructed cortically [in the intellect alone] it wells up from the depths of the individual subconscious rooted in the Collective Unconscious...Myths reveal the positive and negative forces at work in the process of natural selection of our world-wide understanding of life not as man against man but as man working with nature." (*Fields within Fields,* #13 Fall 1974, pp. 31-35). Succinct definitions: "Myths are something that never really happened but always are." (Geri McAndrews, quoting Sallust) and "Myths treat of origins but derive from transitions." (N. Girardot, *Myth and Meaning,* p. 7).

nature "Nature is thus *the* value beyond all joy and sorrow, all good and evil...For 'nature' can mean two things, the one related to the other. First, it means one's own nature, the natal, the innately primitive, the genetically endowed. Second, it means nature in general, the nature of the 'ten thousand things,' the universe as a whole...to be at home in one's nature is to be at home in nature, that self-government is the true form of world-government because nature in one sense is ultimately nature in another, and nature in both senses is the supreme authority (in its natural, non-authoritarian manner) of true sociality." (Wu, *Chuang Tzu,* p. 116).

neophyte (lit. "newly emplanted") In initiation rituals, those being initiated are commonly called neophytes. When being admitted to the mysteries in ancient cults, such as the "mysteries of Attis, the candidate was looked upon as 'one about to die'; when he had performed the required rites he emerged to new life." (Gaster, *Thespis,* p. 43).

numinous The word was coined by Rudolf Otto in 1917 in his book, *The Idea of the Holy,* based on the Latin, *numen.* Otto writes: "The reader is invited to direct his mind to a moment of deeply-felt religious experience... Whoever cannot do this, whoever knows no such moment in his experience, is requested to read no further." (p. 8) Jung's definition of the numinous experience is "...a dynamic agency or effect, not caused by an arbitrary act of the will. On the contrary, it seizes and controls the human subject, who is always rather its victim than its creator. The *numinosum*—whatever its cause may be—is an experience of the subject independent of his will." (Jung, *Coll. Works.* V. 14, par. 6).

omphalos World's navel.

ontogeny The best definition I've found is Leyhausen's: "As most readers will be aware, every single organism has two histories: a very ancient one which it shares with all other organisms of the same species (phylogeny) and a very brief one purely its own, which begins the moment its zygote is formed and ends with its death (ontogeny)...Applied to the phenomena of expression this means that what an organism is at all capable of expressing and how it does so has on the whole already been laid down by the phylogeny of the species, and individual modifications are possible only within the given range of modifiability." (P. Leyhausen, *Motivation,* p. 276).

"Operational environment" See "cognized environment."

orientation Orientation and origin come from the Latin, "oriri," meaning to rise, an awakening relating to the rising sun as the origin of each day.

origin See orientation.

pagan The best understanding of this word comes from the work of John Holland Smith. He begins by pointing out that to the pagan, "paganism" never existed. "It was a figment of the Christian imagination. 'Paganism' was a loose mixture of cults, blended in different proportions at different times and places. It is not far from the truth to say that before Christianity invented it, there was no Roman religion, but only worship, expressed in a hundred-and-one different ways, all the different cults establishing a relationship between the citizen and the divine powers above and below, the universe in which he lived and the state which he served." Latin speaking Christians had long been "calling non-Christians *pagani,* applying the soldier's word for cowards and stay-at-homes to those who would not fight in the army of Christ, the word now doubled its vituperative force; the pagan was henceforward not only a contemptible non-combatant but also—in the other traditional meaning of the word—a rustic, unsophisticated, boorish peasant, to be laughed at for his obstinacy in clinging to old ways his grandfather would have done well to have abandoned." (J. Smith, *The Death of Classical Paganism,* pp. 6 and 81).

pantheist "Pantheists are persons to whom religion is seen as a system of reverent behavior toward the earth rather than subscription to any particular creed or belief." (As defined by the modern, Universal Pantheist Society, P.O. Box 265, Big Pine, CA 93513.) They put out a small seasonal publication.

perceive "The information in ambient light, along with sound, odor, touches, and natural chemicals, is inexhaustible. A perceiver can keep on noticing facts about the world she lives in to the end of her life without ever reaching a limit. There is no threshold for information comparable to a stimulus threshold. Information is not lost to the environment when gained by the individual, it is not conserved like energy." (Gibson, *The Ecological Approach to Visual Perception,* p. 243). Also, see concepts.

percepts See concepts.

"perennial philosophy" Phrase used by Huxley (1970). It was current during Leibnitz' day and he used it to refer to the synthesis of the true. The concept of perennial philosophy has its ancient roots in Neoplatonism and in Plato.

phylogeny See ontogony.

primitive There are many other words used in the same sense as primitive such as archaic societies, primal peoples, aboriginals, indigenous etc. and many discussions as to who or which group to be included; as well as whether "primitive" and similar words are pejorative or not. All this is unnecessary intellectual exercise. To clarify the matter I quote from two authorities. The first is Sylvia Wynter, from Jamaica, in a paper given at the first Ethnopoetics Symposium: "...underlying many of the activities of the past few days, has been the pervasive feeling that we have come here on a quest for the 'primitive',... [we] find that the quest of the primitive is a misnomer for the quest of *human being* now reified into a commodity...Because of this the difference between Western and non-Western cultures is not the difference between civilized and primitive. That is an ideological reading. *The difference is that between the first commodity-culture in the history of human existence and all other cultures. A mutation has occurred."* Essentially humans have become just another object—to be bought and sold. "Humanism has ended in its negation." (*Alcheringa: Ethnopoetics,* 1976) The other authority is Jay Vest. In his unpublished paper, "Algonquian Metaphysics and Wildness: Ontological and Ethical Reflections," he goes into the difference between the primal world view and ethos and the secondary or Western tradition. "By secondary, I mean that this tradition of the West no longer experiences reality in a concrete, living manner, but is ontologically impoverished by abstract rationalization. Conversely the Primal world view is primarily involved, ensconced in reality, in the robust living of life."

productivity "Basic or primary productivity of an ecological community is defined as the rate at which energy is stored by photosynthetic and chemosynthetic organisms (chiefly green plants) in the form of organic substances which can be used as food materials." (R. Rappaport, *Ecology, Meaning and Religion,* p. 19). It has nothing to do with how much 'junk' man produces.

"psychic" and **"psyche"** Psychic means physical and mental. Jung says: "It is characteristic of Western man that he has split apart the physical and the spiritual sides of life for the purpose of gaining knowledge, but these opposites exist together in the psyche, and psychology must recognize the fact. 'Psychic' means physical and mental." (Jung, *Secret of the Golden Flower,* p. 131). Another def. by Jung: "The psyche is a self-regulating system that maintains itself in equilibrium as the body does. Every process that goes too far immediately and inevitably calls forth a compensatory activity. Without such adjustments a normal metabolism would not exist, nor would the normal psyche." (Jung, in Jacobi (ed.) *Psychological Reflections,* p. 51).

religion "Magic may be defined as the imposition of non-physical power to attain a specified end. Religion is the maintenance of abiding relationship." (G. Levy, *Gate of Horn*). Gregory Bateson states that it has been "orthodox in anthropology since the days of Sir James Frazer...to believe that religion is an evolutionary development of magic. Magic is regarded as more primitive and religion as its flowering. In contrast, I view sympathetic...magic as a product of decadence from religion; I regard religion on the whole as the earlier condition." (Bateson, *Angels Fear,* p.56). I go along with Levy and Bateson on this.

Samhain In archaic English, *sam* meant "to bring together or join in marriage, friendship, and to assemble a number of people." (Dawes, *Avebury,* p. 127).

savage Derived from the Latin, *silvaticus,* meaning "of the forest" or "wild." (H. Duerr, *Dreamtime,* p. 67).

self "The kernel of the whole model, the most fundamental of the Archetypes was the Self much better conveyed by the German word *Selbst,* 'the itself—a psychic totality resulting from the merging of many levels of the conscious and unconscious." (V. Brome, Jung, p. 280). *Jung:* "[T]he 'self' thus making a sharp distinction between the ego, which as is well-known, extends only as far as the conscious mind, and the *whole* of the personality, which includes the unconscious as well as the conscious component...The indefinite extent of the unconscious component makes a comprehensive description of the human personality impossible. Accordingly the unconscious supplements the picture with living figures ranging from the animal to the divine..." (Jung, *Coll. Works,* v. 9).

shamanism The most succinct definition that I've found: "Primary shamanism originated in paleolithic times in Central Asia (and perhaps in southwest Europe), and spread throughout Eurasia, across the bridge to Alaska, and down into all of both New World continents. Shamanism is also found in Africa, Australia, New Guinea—everywhere. Probably it arose independently in several places. The techniques of shamanism are singing, dancing, chanting, costuming, story telling. The shaman goes on a journey, or is transformed into other beings, or represents the struggle among beings. In any case, multiple realities are superimposed." (R. Shechner, *Ritual, Play and Performance,* p. 123).

solitude See loneliness.

soul Brief account of how the concept of the soul developed: "Only after Ficino's death (1499) did Florentine philosophical psychology capture Rome. At the Lateran Council of 1513 the Roman Catholic Church promulgated the dogma of the soul's immortality. This dogma, one of the essential fantasies of Renaissance Neoplatonism and subject of Ficino's main writing, by granting the soul eternality affirms the psyche as the equivalent of a God." (J. Hillman, *Re-Visioning Psychology,* p. 255).

spirit Jung: "[We must] reconcile ourselves to the mysterious truth that the spirit is the life of the body seen from within, and the body the outward manifestation of the life of the spirit—the two being really one..."(Jung, *Coll. Works,* v. 10, par. 94).

symbol "[S]ince the symbol derives as much from the conscious as from the unconscious, it is able to unite them both, reconciling their conceptual polarity through its form and their emotional polarity through its numinosity." (Jung, *Coll. Works,* v. 9, pt. ii, par. 280). "[T]he symbol is in fact a part of a whole, a component of a field which also contains the so-called *thing,* as well as the process of symbolizing, and the apprehending individual. In this view, the concept of the symbol is close to the original meaning of the word in Greek. The *symbol,* the broken off part of the coin given to the parting friend, is not a separate element, but carries with it wherever it goes the whole content in which it has participated, as well as the situation of the hospitality during which the coin was broken in half; and when it is finally matched with the remaining half, the whole has value because the symbol has conveyed— not created or applied or evoked—this value." (D. Lee, *Freedom and Culture,* p.79). K. Lorenz: "In the field of human culture, as in that of phylogeny, ritualization can be regarded basically as the development of a system of communication in which the formation of symbols represents a decisive step. The phylogenetically evolved signals...cannot, however, be equated with symbols in the cultural sense...Yet despite these differences the phylogenetically evolved signal and the culturally evolved symbol do have one thing in common: they both originate in the emergence of a creature's ability to 'understand' those behaviour patterns which allow it to predict how a fellow creature is going to react...In phylogenetic ritualization this 'understanding' derives from inherited functions in the receiver, and the behaviour patterns 'understood' in this way are fixed motor patterns. In the cultural context, on the other hand,

sending and receiving signals both depend on learning and the inheritance of acquired characteristics." (K. Lorenz, *Behind the Mirror,* p. 214).

temple "Temple has its roots in the ancient Greek word, *temnos,* to cut off a sacred area, as well as in the Latin *templum* (space), which has survived in the modern 'template' and tempus (time)." (K. Critchlow, *Time Stands Still,* p. 22).

tradition The process by which individually acquired knowledge is passed on from individual to individual through long periods of time is called "tradition."

"transcendent function" "[T]he harmonizing of conscious and unconscious data...an irrational life-process which expresses itself in definite symbols...it is in them [symbols] that the union of conscious and unconscious contents is consummated. I have therefore called the union of opposites the 'transcendent function'...rounding out of the personality into a whole may well be the goal of any psychotherapy." (Jung, *Coll. Works,* v. 9, par. 524)." The aim of Jungian psychotherapy is...to reduce the left hemisphere's inhibition of the right hemisphere and to promote increased communication in both directions across the corpus callosum...The therapeutic objective of achieving great integration between the activities of both hemispheres would then correspond, as Rossi (1977) suggests, to what Jung called the *transcendent function.* The transcendent function resides in the mutual influence of conscious and unconscious, ego and Self." (A. Stevens, *Archetypes,* p. 272).

tribal The word, *tribe* derives from the Latin *tri,* meaning three. A *tribus* was one of three groups of the early Romans. At that time, it meant coming from common ancestors. In general it's been used as a sort of derogatory term for uncivilized societies. More recently the word has been reclaimed and is being used by people trying to find their way to the "old ways." See primitive.

truth "For truth is neither a label nor something to match. Truth is something we *make* with all our senses in a conscious process of remaking the world, as *that* world remakes us." (B. Nevitt, "Via Media with Marshall McLuhan"). "Truth as revelation is not located in the mind, as responding to an object or as that to which an object responds, but in the world itself. Since the world is the interrelation of earth, sky, gods and mortals, this interrelation, the mirror-play, is the primary revelation, the primary truth." (V. Vycinas, *Earth and Gods,* p. 235, writing on Heidegger's concept of the "fourfold:"—earth, sky, gods and mortals).

"Turtle Island" Mostly due to Gary Snyder, this term is being used for the North American continent in place of the usual Eurocentric term. In the Delaware Indians' origin myth everything is water. Then the Great Turtle gradually rose above water level. The mud on its back dried and the Great Tree grew out of it. As the tree grew up to the sky it became a man. When it bent down, a sprout became a woman and these were the first humans. Other Eastern woodland tribes, such as the Iroquois also had the belief that the earth rests on the back of a turtle. The shell of the Box Turtle was used during major Delaware ceremonies. This information comes from a letter by Jay Miller, printed in the Royal Anthropological Journal, *Man.* I do not have the date of the issue. His references are Newcomb 1950: 72 and Hewitt, 1928. In today's symbolizing of the continent, the turtle's left front paw is Alaska, the right paw, Eastern Canada, separated off by Hudson Bay. The right rear paw is Florida. The left paw and the tail are Baja California and Mexico.

Permissions and Acknowledgments (continued from p. 4)

of the author; *Two Cybernetic Frontiers* by Stewart Brand. Copyright © 1974. Permission by Random House Inc.; "The New Song Ceremonial Sun Dance Ritual-1983 and 1984," doctoral dissertation by Sarah Dubin-Vaughn. By permission of the author; "Borne-Native in the San Francisco Bay Region," by Peter Berg. In *Living Here* by the Frisco Bay Mussel Group. Reprinted in *Reinhabiting a Separate Country*, ed. by Peter Berg. Copyright © 1978 Planet Drum Foundation. By Permission of the author; "Totem Salmon," by Freeman House. In the *North Pacific Rim Alive* bundle of Planet Drum. Copyright © 1974. By permission of the author and Peter Berg. "The Perceptual Implications of Gaia," by David Abram, Copyright © 1985. *The Ecologist*, 15:3 (1985). By permission of the author; *Lime Creek Odyssey* by Steven J. Meyers. Copyright © 1986. (In press). By permission of the author; "Renewal of the Dreaming, Spring Equinox." *The Deep Ecologist* (Australia) January 1986. By permission of the editor, John Martin; "The Principle of Extended Identity," by Silas Goldean. By permission of the author; two poems, "Nass River" and "Death as a Helix of Drunken Owls," by Robert MacLean. Copyright © 1970, 1977 and 1985 Robert MacLean.

Grateful acknowledgment is also made for permission to reprint the following selections in the **Back-of-the-Book** section: "Will-of-the-Land: Wilderness Among Early Indo-Europeans," Copyright © 1983 Jay H. Vest. In *Wilderness The Way Ahead* ed. by Vance Martin and Mary Inglis. By permission of the author; "Dreaming Big Wilderness," by Dave Foreman. *Earth First* August 1, 1986, By permission of the author; "Thami Valley, Eastern Nepal," Copyright © 1983 David Abram. By permission of the author; "Hoedads Inc.," by Hal Hartzell. In *Working the Woods Working the Sea* ed. by Finn Wilcox and Jeremiah Gorsline. Copyright © 1986. By permission of Empty Bowl Press. "Land Earth Soil Dirt: Some Notes from the Ground," by Tom Jay. *Upriver Downriver* 8. By permission of the author and editor, Jerry Martien. "One Circle in the Night" by Daniel Menkin. *Wingspan: Journal of the Male Spirit* (spring 1987) Address: 405 Main St. Wakefield, Ma 01880. By permission; "Complexity and Time: Breaking the Pyramid's Reign," by Sigmund Kvaloy. *Resurgence* #106 (1984). By permission of the author.

While I located my Way of the Mountain Learning Center here in this high mountain town, specifically, to have access to the learnings from wild nature in the mountains, such a location presents problems when it comes to documenting such learnings. First, I do not have access to the staff, automatically provided by a university; secondly, I am an eight hour drive from the nearest university library. Verifying and checking sources on materials accumulated over the past thirty years has been complicated, and if any required acknowledgments have been omitted or any rights overlooked, it is unintentional and forgiveness is requested.

Illustration and Photographic Acknowledgments

Julien Puzey: photos on front and back covers and on pp, 99, 210 and 211; illustrations on pp. 20, 52, 67, 114,and 190. Michael A. Darr: illustrations on pp. 79, 119, 206, 229 and borders on pp. 6 & 7, 112 & 113 as well as the decorative lines throughout the book. David LaChapelle: illustrations on pp. 86 and 193 as well as the reproductions of posters on p. 27 and 129 (available from Finn Hill Arts). Text on P. 27, from "Preface" by Gary Snyder to *Turtle Bear and Wolf: Poems* by Peter Blue Cloud. Copyright © 1976 Gary Snyder. Reprinted by permission of Gary Snyder. Text on p. 129 from "Tracking Down the Natural Man," by Colin Kowal first printed in *The Western Slopes Connection* and Reprinted in *The Real Work: Interviews & Talks 1964-1979*. Copyright © Gary Snyder. New Directions Publishing Corp. By permission of Gary Snyder and New Directions; the illustration on p. 24 is from p. 239 of *Chinese Characters* by L. Wieger. Dover Reprint, 1965; Sigmund Kvaloy: illustrations on pp. 165 and 259. These drawings appeared on pp. 221 and 41 of *Friluftsliv Fra Fridtjof Nansen til vare dager*, ed. by G. Breivik, H. Lovmo, M Tegninger, and S. Kvaloy. Copyright © 1978. Universitetsforlaget (Norway). By permission of Sigmund Kvaloy. Fred Adams: illustration on p. 202. By permission of the artist. Planet Drum: illustration on pp. 226 and 227. "Rocky Mountain Lifetime" from the bundle: "Backbone—the Rockies" copyright © 1982 Planet Drum. By permission of Peter Berg. The small design used on the cover and throughout this work is adapted from an early 4th century version of Taoist Cloud Script writing, as found in *Cheng-t'ung Tao-tsang* published in 1436 and printed in L. Wieger, *Taoisme* (2 vol.) 1911-1913. Cloud Script was used to emphasize the unity of yin (clouds, mist) and yang (heaven). I've used this particular form because it is identical with lenticular clouds that I see here in Silverton, forming over Sultan Mountain, before breaking apart to sail out over Molas Pass. For me, the connotation also refers to heaven, earth and man having the same Li.

DATE DUE

MAR 18 2015	
FEB 12 2019	
12/12/23	